CANADA

MINNESOTA
Duluth
Fargo

Lake Superior

MICHIGAN

Lake Huron

WISCONSIN
St. Paul
Minneapolis
Wisconsin R.
Mississippi R.
Milwaukee
Madison
Lansing
Lake Michigan
Detroit

IOWA
Sioux Falls
Des Moines
Chicago
Gary

NEBRASKA
Omaha
Lincoln

Illinois R.
ILLINOIS
Springfield
INDIANA
Indianapolis
Wabash R.
Toledo
OHIO
Columbus
Cleveland
Wheeling
Pittsburgh

Lake Erie

Lake Ontario

NEW YORK
Buffalo
Albany
Hudson R.

MAINE
Augusta
Burlington
Montpelier
VT.
N.H.
Concord
Portland
Manchester
Boston
MASS.
Providence
Hartford
RHODE ISLAND
CONNECTICUT

Newark
New York
Trenton
PENNSYLVANIA
Harrisburg
Philadelphia
NEW JERSEY
Dover
DELAWARE
Baltimore
Annapolis
MD.
Washington, D.C.
Potomac R.
Allegheny R.

MISSOURI
Missouri R.
Topeka
Kansas City
Jefferson City
Wichita
St. Louis

Ohio R.
Cincinnati
Louisville
Frankfort
KENTUCKY
WEST VIRGINIA
Charleston
VIRGINIA
Richmond
Norfolk
Roanoke R.

Cumberland R.
Knoxville
Nashville
TENNESSEE
NORTH CAROLINA
Raleigh
Charlotte
Cape Fear R.

OKLAHOMA
Tulsa
Oklahoma City
ARKANSAS
Arkansas R.
Memphis
Little Rock
Tennessee R.

SOUTH CAROLINA
Columbia
Charleston

ATLANTIC OCEAN

Birmingham
ALABAMA
Montgomery
MISSISSIPPI
Jackson
Mobile
Alabama R.
Chattahoochee R.
Atlanta
GEORGIA
Savannah
Altamaha R.
Santee R.

LOUISIANA
Trinity R.
Sabine R.
Red R.
Mississippi R.
TEXAS
Fort Worth
Dallas
Austin
Houston
Baton Rouge
New Orleans

Tallahassee
Jacksonville
FLORIDA
Tampa
Miami

Gulf of Mexico

APPALACHIAN MOUNTAINS

BAHAMAS

CUBA

Elevation
Feet	Meters
9,843	3,000
6,562	2,000
3,281	1,000
1,640	500
656	200
0	0
Below sea level	Below sea level

67°W   66°W
ATLANTIC OCEAN
San Juan
PUERTO RICO
Ponce
18°N
Caribbean Sea
0   25   50 miles
0   25   50 kilometers

0   200   400 miles
0   200   400 kilometers

95°W   90°W   85°W   80°W

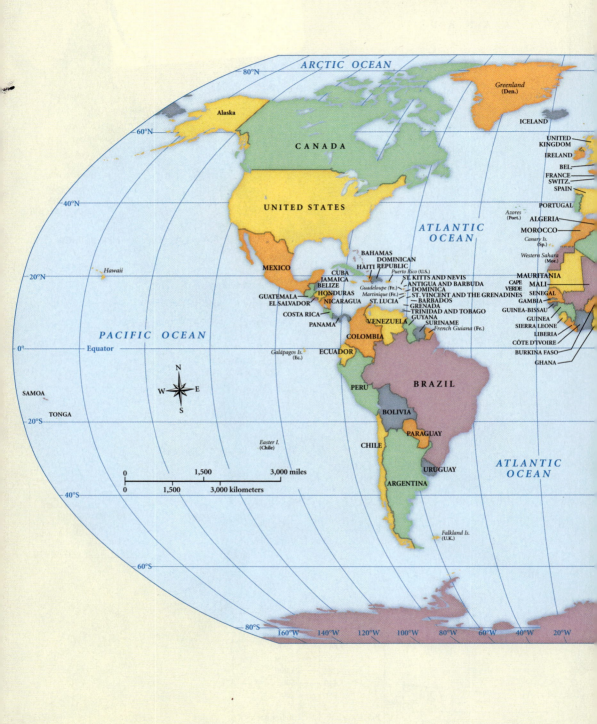

ARCTIC OCEAN

80°N

Greenland (Den.)

ICELAND

Alaska

60°N

CANADA

UNITED KINGDOM
IRELAND
BEL.
FRANCE
SWITZ.
SPAIN

40°N

UNITED STATES

ATLANTIC OCEAN

PORTUGAL

Azores (Port.)
ALGERIA
MOROCCO

Canary Is. (Sp.)

Western Sahara (Mor.)

Hawaii

20°N

MEXICO

BAHAMAS
DOMINICAN
HAITI REPUBLIC
CUBA
JAMAICA
BELIZE
HONDURAS
GUATEMALA
EL SALVADOR
NICARAGUA
COSTA RICA
PANAMA

Puerto Rico (U.S.)
ST. KITTS AND NEVIS
ANTIGUA AND BARBUDA
Guadeloupe (Fr.)
DOMINICA
Martinique (Fr.)
ST. VINCENT AND THE GRENADINES
ST. LUCIA
BARBADOS
GRENADA
TRINIDAD AND TOBAGO
GUYANA
SURINAME
French Guiana (Fr.)

MAURITANIA
CAPE VERDE
MALI
SENEGAL
GAMBIA
GUINEA-BISSAU
GUINEA
SIERRA LEONE
LIBERIA
CÔTE D'IVOIRE
BURKINA FASO
GHANA

VENEZUELA

COLOMBIA

PACIFIC OCEAN

0° Equator

Galápagos Is. (Ec.)

ECUADOR

BRAZIL

PERU

N
W   E
S

SAMOA

BOLIVIA

20°S

TONGA

PARAGUAY

Easter I. (Chile)

CHILE

URUGUAY

ATLANTIC OCEAN

0   1,500   3,000 miles
0   1,500   3,000 kilometers

ARGENTINA

40°S

Falkland Is. (U.K.)

60°S

80°S   160°W   140°W   120°W   100°W   80°W   60°W   40°W   20°W

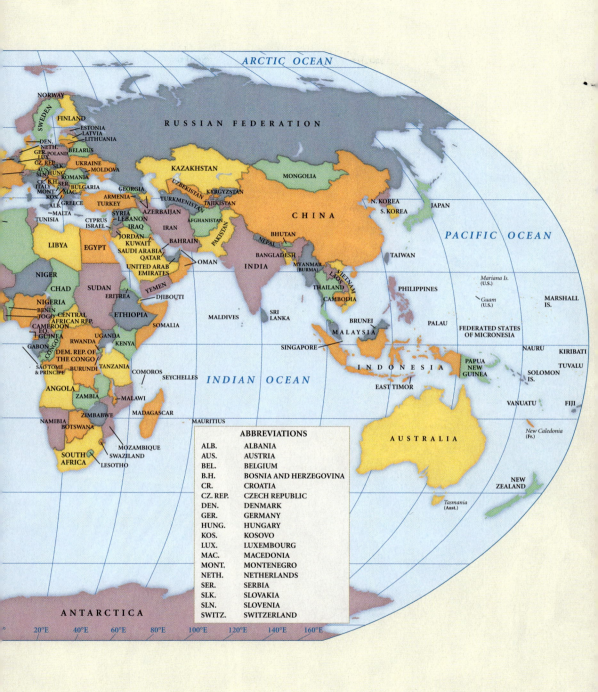

ARCTIC OCEAN

RUSSIAN FEDERATION

NORWAY
SWEDEN
FINLAND
ESTONIA
LATVIA
LITHUANIA
DEN.
NETH.
GER. POLAND
LUX.
BELARUS
CZ. REP.
SLK.
AUS. UKRAINE
SLN.HUNG. MOLDOVA
CR. ROMANIA
ITALY B.H.SER. BULGARIA
MONT. MAC. GEORGIA
KOS. GREECE
ALB.
MALTA
TUNISIA
CYPRUS
ISRAEL
LIBYA
EGYPT

KAZAKHSTAN
MONGOLIA

UZBEKISTAN KYRGYZSTAN
TURKMENISTAN TAJIKISTAN
ARMENIA
TURKEY
AZERBAIJAN
SYRIA LEBANON
JORDAN
IRAN
AFGHANISTAN
PAKISTAN

CHINA

N. KOREA
S. KOREA
JAPAN

PACIFIC OCEAN

IRAQ
KUWAIT
BAHRAIN
SAUDI ARABIA
QATAR
UNITED ARAB
EMIRATES
OMAN
YEMEN
DJIBOUTI

BHUTAN
NEPAL
BANGLADESH
INDIA
MYANMAR
(BURMA)
THAILAND
CAMBODIA

VIETNAM
LAOS

TAIWAN

PHILIPPINES

Mariana Is.
(U.S.)
Guam
(U.S.)

MARSHALL
IS.

NIGER
CHAD SUDAN
NIGERIA
BENIN
TOGO CENTRAL
AFRICAN REP.
CAMEROON
EQ.
GUINEA
GABON
CONGO DEM. REP. OF
THE CONGO
SÃO TOMÉ
& PRÍNCIPE BURUNDI
ERITREA
ETHIOPIA
SOMALIA
UGANDA
RWANDA
KENYA
TANZANIA

MALDIVES
SRI
LANKA

BRUNEI
MALAYSIA
SINGAPORE
INDONESIA

PALAU

FEDERATED STATES
OF MICRONESIA

NAURU KIRIBATI

TUVALU
PAPUA
NEW
GUINEA
SOLOMON
IS.

COMOROS
SEYCHELLES
INDIAN OCEAN
EAST TIMOR
VANUATU FIJI

ANGOLA
ZAMBIA
MALAWI
NAMIBIA
ZIMBABWE
BOTSWANA
MADAGASCAR
MAURITIUS

MOZAMBIQUE
SOUTH
AFRICA SWAZILAND
LESOTHO

AUSTRALIA

New Caledonia
(Fr.)

NEW
ZEALAND

Tasmania
(Aust.)

ANTARCTICA

20°E   40°E   60°E   80°E   100°E   120°E   140°E   160°E

ABBREVIATIONS	
ALB.	ALBANIA
AUS.	AUSTRIA
BEL.	BELGIUM
B.H.	BOSNIA AND HERZEGOVINA
CR.	CROATIA
CZ. REP.	CZECH REPUBLIC
DEN.	DENMARK
GER.	GERMANY
HUNG.	HUNGARY
KOS.	KOSOVO
LUX.	LUXEMBOURG
MAC.	MACEDONIA
MONT.	MONTENEGRO
NETH.	NETHERLANDS
SER.	SERBIA
SLK.	SLOVAKIA
SLN.	SLOVENIA
SWITZ.	SWITZERLAND

FOURTH
EDITION

America
A Concise History

James A. Henretta
University of Maryland

David Brody
University of California, Davis

973.07
H 518
2009

Bedford / St. Martin's
Boston • *New York*

For Bedford / St. Martin's

Publisher for History: Mary Dougherty
Executive Editor for History: William J. Lombardo
Director of Development for History: Jane Knetzger
Developmental Editor: Danielle Slevens
Senior Production Editor: Lori Chong Roncka
Production Supervisor: Jennifer L. Peterson
Executive Marketing Manager: Jenna Bookin Barry
Editorial Assistants: Katherine Flynn and Robin Soule
Production Assistants: Lidia MacDonald-Carr and David Ayers
Text Design: Lisa Buckley
Copy Editor: Barbara Willette
Indexer: Leoni Z. McVey & Associates, Inc.
Photo Research: Pembroke Herbert and Sandi Rygiel / Picture Research Consultants & Archives
Cartography: Mapping Specialists, Ltd.
Cover Design: Billy Boardman
Cover Art: Construction crew with wood-burning balloon-stack locomotive at a crossing of the Green River, West Slope of the Cascades, 1885. Private collection, Peter Newark American Pictures / The Bridgeman Art Library International.
Composition: Aptara
Printing and Binding: RR Donnelley and Sons

President: Joan E. Feinberg
Editorial Director: Denise B. Wydra
Director of Marketing: Karen R. Soeltz
Director of Editing, Design, and Production: Marcia Cohen
Assistant Director of Editing, Design, and Production: Elise S. Kaiser
Managing Editor: Elizabeth M. Schaaf

Library of Congress Control Number: 2008925878

Manufactured in the United States of America.

4   3   2   1   0   9
f   e   d   c   b   a

For information, write: Bedford / St. Martin's, 75 Arlington Street, Boston, MA 02116 (617-399-4000)

ISBN-10: 0–312–48541–7 ISBN-13: 978–0–312–48541–2 (Combined Volume)
ISBN-10: 0–312–48542–5 ISBN-13: 978–0–312–48542–9 (Volume 1: To 1877)
ISBN-10: 0–312–48543–3 ISBN-13: 978–0–312–48543–6 (Volume 2: Since 1865)

Preface

We live in troubled times. Since 2001, in the aftermath of Al Qaeda's attack on the Twin Towers and the Pentagon, the nation has spent years at war in far-away lands. At home, the collapse of a massive housing bubble has ignited a major financial crisis and threatened the security of millions of families. College students—even those who don't think much about America's past—have to ponder these events. How and why did they happen? Such questions are at the heart of historical inquiry. In *America: A Concise History,* we aspire to develop students' abilities to think historically and to explore the relationship between the past and the present. We try to ask the right questions—the big ones and the not-so-big ones—and then write history that illuminates the answers.

One of the intellectual pleasures of textbook writing is the opportunity, with each edition, to revisit our historical narrative and make it better. This time, we have embraced that task again with a particularly ambitious goal. We want to bring *America: A Concise History* into the twenty-first century. On the intellectual side, this goal has led us to give greater attention to cultural history, the subject of much exciting scholarship, and to rethink and recast our post-1945 chapters. On the pedagogical side, it has led us to a back-to-basics approach, by providing an array of learning tools that will engage and instruct today's students. But we have not departed from the core idea of previous editions: to write a concise narrative that retains the comprehensiveness and explanatory power of its parent textbook, *America's History,* and is immediately accessible to every student who enrolls in the U.S. survey course. The story, we hope, tells not only what happened, but also *how* and *why.*

In composing our narrative, we focus not only on the marvelous diversity of peoples who became American but also on the institutions—political, economic, cultural, and social—that forged a common national identity. And we present these experiences in an integrated way, using each historical perspective to make better sense of the others. In our discussion of government and politics, diplomacy and war, we show how they affected—and were affected by—ethnic groups and economic conditions, intellectual beliefs and social changes, and the religious and moral values of the times. Just as important, we place the American experience in a global context. We trace aspects of American society to their origins in European, African, and Asian cultures; consider American industrial and technological development within the framework of the world economy; and plot the foreign relations of the United States as part of an ever-shifting international system of imperial expansion, financial exchange, and diplomatic alliances. In emphasizing the global context, we want to remind students that other nations experienced developments similar to our own and that by a comparative analysis, students can discern what was distinctive and particular to the American experience.

Structure

To give shape and meaning to America's history, we have long divided our narrative into six parts, corresponding to what we understood to be the major phases of American development. Part Six, which carried the story from 1945 to the present, was distinctive in that it was, by definition, unfinished. However, as we move into the twenty-first century, it has become increasingly clear that we have entered a new phase of American history, and that the era that began in 1945 has ended. So now we include a fully realized Part Six, which we call "The Age of Cold War Liberalism, 1945–1980," and a new—an open-ended—Part Seven, which describes the advent of a conservative America in a post–Cold War world. Students who have grown up in this new age will find the times of their parents and grandparents treated as coherent narrative history in Part Six. In Part Seven, "A Divided Nation in a Disordered World, 1980–2008," they will discover an account of an era that is truly their own, carried to the present with a full chapter on the years since 2000.

Given the importance of the part structure in our account, we have taken pains to assist students to benefit fully from this organization. Each part begins with a four-page overview. First, a **thematic timeline** highlights the key developments in politics, the economy, society, culture, and foreign affairs that characterize the entire period; then we flesh out these themes in a corresponding **part essay**. Each part essay focuses on a crucial engine of historical change—primarily economic or cultural in some eras, political or diplomatic in others—that created new conditions of life and transformed social relations.

Within each chapter, we have appended *NEW* **focus questions** to each main section. And where students might stumble over unfamiliar or difficult terms, we provide a **glossary** that defines key concepts, which appear in bold type at their first mention. At the end of the chapter, we remind students of important events in a **chapter timeline** and reiterate the main themes in an **analytical summary**. We have also added a *NEW* feature, **Connections**, that enables students to take a longer view, to see how the chapter relates to prior and forthcoming chapters. Each chapter concludes with **For Further Exploration**, a brief bibliographical essay designed to encourage further reading in historical works and to use the World Wide Web to the best advantage. To assist instructors and advanced students, a **full bibliography** is available on the Web at **bedfordstmartins.com/henrettaconcise**.

Features: Back to Basics

We want to encourage students to experience the past through the words and perspective of those who lived it and, equally important, to learn how to extract meaning from historical evidence. Thus, each chapter contains two page-long primary sources—excerpts from letters, diaries, autobiographies, and public testimony—offering a firsthand view of an event or theme discussed in the chapter. Instructors will find these **American Voices** and **Voices from Abroad** to be a major resource for inducting beginning students into the processes of historical analysis. Each chapter now contains one American Voices and one Voices from Abroad, ensuring that students will understand how events were viewed both nationally and in a global context.

To enliven students' understanding of history, we have peppered the text with more than 150 **illustrations**, most of them in full-color and many new to this edition. We have also provided **informative captions** that set the illustrations in context. Keenly aware that today's students lack geographic literacy, we have included dozens of **maps** and cross-referenced them in the narrative text. Taken together, these documents, maps, and illustrations provide instructors with a trove of teaching materials and students with a chance to enter the life of the past.

Textual Changes

Of all the reasons for a new edition, of course, the most compelling is to improve the text itself. Good narrative history is primarily a product of good sentences and good paragraphs. So our labors have been mostly in the trenches, so to speak, in a line-by-line striving for the vividness and human presence that are the hallmarks of narrative history. We are also partisans of economical writing, believing that brevity is the best antidote to imprecise language and murky argument.

To enhance the narrative flow of our chapters, we have been especially attentive to chronology. That concern led us to reorder a significant amount of material. In Part Two (1776–1820), Chapters 6 and 7 now provide a continuous political narrative from the Declaration of Independence to the Era of Good Feelings. In Part Three (1820–1877), we have followed the suggestion of instructors and now discuss the pre–Civil War South in a single, integrated chapter. In Part Four (1877–1914), our chapter on Gilded Age politics has a better chronological flow and, because it now follows the chapter on the city, provides students with a seamless transition to the Progressive era.

Changes that are even more extensive appear in our treatment of the twentieth century. In Part Five (1914–1945), the three chapters on the 1920s, the Great Depression, and the New Deal have been melded into two crisper, more integrated chapters. All of the chapters in Part Six (1945–1980) and the new Part Seven (1980–2008) have been thoroughly reworked as part of our rethinking of the post-1945 era. In Chapters 26 and 27, we now offer thematic treatments of the 1950s, while Chapters 28 and 29 provide a coherent narrative account of liberalism's triumph under Kennedy and Johnson and its dramatic decline after 1968. Part Seven represents much-expanded coverage of the post-1980 years, with new chapters devoted to social and economic developments and America since 2000. Altogether, these organizational changes represent the biggest shake-up of *America: A Concise History* since its inception.

The revising process also affords us a welcome opportunity to incorporate fresh scholarship. In Part One, we have added new material on African life, the slave trade, and African American ethnicity and have boosted our discussion of the Scots-Irish and the Germans. In Chapter 11, we have added a new section on urban popular culture (masculinity, sexuality, minstrel shows, and racism) drawing on recent advances in cultural history. Inventive scholarship in cultural history also informs Chapter 18 (on the late-nineteenth-century city) and several twentieth-century chapters, including, in Chapter 27, our treatment of consumer culture in the 1950s. Chapter 16 contains fresh information about the impact of farming on the ecosystem of the Great Plains. Chapter 20 incorporates recent insights into the middle-class impulse behind progressivism and underlines the industrial strife that reoriented progressivism toward issues of labor relations. Of the many revisions in the post-1945 chapters, perhaps the most notable derive from the opening of Soviet archives, which allowed us to see the Cold War from the other side of the Iron Curtain and to amend our assessment of the impact of Communism on American life. In addition, Part Six contains fresh material on the civil rights movement, the Vietnam War, and the revival of American conservatism. Even richer are the additions to Part Seven, especially in the treatment of social movements and the information technology revolution in Chapter 31 and, in Chapter 32, an up-to-date and stimulating discussion of events since 2000.

Supplements

Readers of *America: A Concise History* often cite its ancillary package as a key to the book's success in the classroom. These ancillaries provide a flexible yet targeted collection of resources for instructors and a helpful set of study tools for students.

FOR STUDENTS
Print Resources

Documents to Accompany* America's History, *Sixth Edition. Edited by Melvin Yazawa (University of New Mexico) and Kevin Fernlund (University of Missouri, St. Louis) and easily assigned with the concise edition, this primary-source reader offers a chorus of voices from the past to enrich the study of U.S. history. Both celebrated figures and ordinary people, from Frederick Douglass to mill workers, demonstrate the diversity of America's history while putting a human face on historical experience. A wealth of speeches, petitions, advertisements, and posters paint a vivid picture of the social and political life of the time, lending depth and breadth to the textbook discussion. Brief introductions set each document in context, while questions for analysis help link the individual source to larger historical themes. Available free when packaged with the text and now available as an e-book (see next page).

Maps in Context: A Workbook for American History. Written by historical cartography expert Gerald A. Danzer (University of Illinois, Chicago), this skill-building workbook helps students comprehend essential connections between geographic literacy and historical understanding. Organized to correspond to the typical U.S. history survey course, *Maps in Context* presents a wealth of map-centered projects and convenient pop quizzes that give students hands-on experience working with maps. Available free when packaged with the text.

NEW Trade Books. Titles published by sister companies Farrar, Straus and Giroux; Henry Holt and Company; Hill and Wang; Picador; St. Martin's Press; and Palgrave Macmillan are available at a 50 percent discount when packaged with Bedford/St. Martin's textbooks. For more information, visit **bedfordstmartins.com/tradeup**.

NEW *The Bedford Glossary for U.S. History.* This handy supplement for the survey course gives students clear, concise definitions of the political, economic, social, and cultural terms used by historians and contemporary media alike. The terms are historically contextualized to aid comprehension. Available free when packaged with the text.

***U.S. History Matters: A Student Guide to U.S. History Online,* Second Edition.** This resource, written by Alan Gevinson, Kelly Schrum, and Roy Rosenzweig (all of George Mason University), provides an illustrated and annotated guide to 250 of the most useful Web sites for student research in U.S. history as well as advice on evaluating and using Internet sources. This essential guide is based on the acclaimed "History Matters" Web site developed by the American Social History Project and the Center for History and New Media. Available free when packaged with the text.

Bedford Series in History and Culture. Over 100 titles in this highly praised series combine first-rate scholarship, historical narrative, and important primary documents for undergraduate courses. Each book is brief, inexpensive, and focused on a specific topic or period. Package discounts are available.

Historians at Work Series. Brief enough for a single assignment yet meaty enough to provoke thoughtful discussion, each volume in this series examines a single historical question by combining unabridged selections by distinguished historians, each with a different perspective on the issue, with helpful learning aids. Package discounts are available.

NEW *Rand McNally Atlas of American History.* This collection of over 80 full-color maps illustrates key events and eras, from early exploration and settlement, expansion and immigration, to U.S. involvement in wars abroad and on American soil. Introductory pages for each section include brief overviews, timelines, graphs, and photos to quickly establish a historical context. Available for $3 when packaged with the text.

New Media Resources

NEW *America: A Concise History e-Book.* This easy-to-use, dynamic, highly searchable e-book integrates the narrative, maps, and images from *America: A Concise History* with resources from the Online Study Guide, making it the ideal study tool. Instructors can easily add documents, images, and other materials to customize the text, making this e-book perfect for instructors who wish to use electronic texts and documents or build dynamic online courses. Can be packaged *FREE* with the print text or purchased as a stand-alone item at a discount.

NEW *E-Documents to Accompany* America's History, *Sixth Edition*. The most robust gathering of primary sources to accompany any U.S. history survey text is now available online. *E-Documents to Accompany* America's History, *Sixth Edition*, is easily assigned with the concise text and allows instructors to add an electronic dimension to their classes or integrate electronic documents into their online courses.

Online Study Guide at bedfordstmartins.com/henrettaconcise. The popular Online Study Guide for *America: A Concise History* is a free learning tool to help students master the themes and information presented in the textbook and improve their critical thinking skills. Assessment quizzes help students to evaluate their comprehension, and a wide range of further quizzing, map, and primary document analysis activities provide them with the opportunity for further study. Instructors can monitor students' progress through the online Quiz Gradebook or receive e-mail updates.

NEW Audio Reviews for *America: A Concise History,* Fourth Edition, at bedfordstmartins.com/henrettaconcise. Audio Reviews are a new tool that fits easily into students' lifestyles and provides a practical new way for them to study on the move. These 25- to 30-minute summaries of each chapter in *America: A Concise History* highlight the major themes of the text and help reinforce student learning.

Online Bibliography at bedfordstmartins.com/henrettaconcise. Organized by book chapter and topic, the online bibliography provides an authoritative and comprehensive list of references to jump-start student research.

Jules R. Benjamin's A Student's Online Guide to History Reference Sources at bedfordstmartins.com/henrettaconcise. This Web site provides links to history-related databases, indexes, and journals, plus contact information for state, provincial, local, and professional history organizations.

The Bedford Bibliographer at bedfordstmartins.com/henrettaconcise. *The Bedford Bibliographer,* a simple but powerful Web-based tool, assists students with the process of collecting sources and generates bibliographies in four commonly used documentation styles.

The Bedford Research Room at bedfordstmartins.com/henrettaconcise. The Research Room, drawn from Mike Palmquist's *The Bedford Researcher,* offers a wealth of resources—including interactive tutorials, research activities, student writing samples, and links to hundreds of other places online—to support students in courses across the disciplines. The site also offers instructors a library of helpful instructional tools.

Diana Hacker's Research and Documentation Online at bedfordstmartins.com/henrettaconcise. This Web site provides clear advice on how to integrate primary and secondary sources into research papers, how to cite sources correctly, and how to format in MLA, APA, *Chicago,* or CBE style.

The St. Martin's Tutorial on Avoiding Plagiarism at bedfordstmartins.com/ henrettaconcise. This online tutorial reviews the consequences of plagiarism and explains what sources to acknowledge, how to keep good notes, how to organize research, and how to integrate sources appropriately. The tutorial includes exercises to help students practice integrating sources and recognize acceptable summaries.

Critical Thinking Modules at bedfordstmartins.com/henrettaconcise. This Web site offers over two dozen online modules for interpreting maps, audio, visual, and textual sources, centered on events covered in the U.S. history survey.

FOR INSTRUCTORS
Print Resources

Instructor's Resource Manual. Written by Jason Newman (Cosumnes River College, Los Rios Community College District), this popular manual provides both first-time and experienced instructors with valuable teaching tools—annotated chapter outlines, lecture strategies, in-class activities, discussion questions, suggested writing assignments, and related readings and media—to structure and customize their American history course. The new edition includes new Classroom Activities and Oral History Exercises, lists of key terms, and model answers to both the questions in the book and the Chapter Writing Assignments. The manual also offers a convenient, chapter-by-chapter guide to the wealth of supplementary materials available to instructors teaching with *America: A Concise History.* Available on the Book Companion Site at **bedfordstmartins.com/herettaconcise.**

Transparencies. This set of full-color acetate transparencies includes all full-size maps and many other images from the parent textbook, *America's History,* to help instructors present lectures and teach students vital map-reading skills. A guide correlating all of the maps and art to the concise edition is available on the book companion site.

New Media Resources

NEW HistoryClass. Bedford/St. Martin's online learning space for history gives you the right tools and the rich content to create your course, your way. An interactive e-book and e-reader enable you to easily assign relevant textbook sections and primary documents. Additional primary sources supplement the textbook and reader selections and provide more options for class discussion and assignments. Other resources include guidelines for analyzing primary materials, avoiding plagiarism, and citing sources. Access to the acclaimed content library, Make History, provides unlimited access to thousands of maps, images, documents, and Web links. The tried-and-true content of the Online Study Guide offers a range of activities to help students access their progress, study more effectively, and improve their critical thinking skills. Customize provided content and mix in your own with ease—everything in History-Class is integrated to work together in the same space.

Instructor's Resource CD-ROM. This disc provides instructors with ready-made and customizable PowerPoint multimedia presentations built around chapter outlines, maps, figures, and selected images from the textbook plus jpeg versions of all maps, figures, and selected images. Also included are chapter questions formatted in Power-Point for use with i>clicker, a classroom response system.

Computerized Test Bank. A fully updated test bank CD-ROM offers over 80 exercises for each chapter, allowing instructors to pick and choose from a collection of multiple-choice, fill-in, map, and short and long essay questions. Every question includes a textbook page number for easy reference. Correct answers and model essay responses are included for easy grading and the creation of answer keys. Both questions and answers can be easily edited by the instructor for maximum customizability.

Book Companion Site at bedfordstmartins.com/henrettaconcise. This companion Web site gathers all the electronic resources for the text, including the Online Study Guide and related Quiz Gradebook, at a single Web address. Convenient links to lecture, assignment, and research materials, such as PowerPoint chapter outlines and the digital libraries at Make History, are also available from this site.

NEW Make History at bedfordstmartins.com/henrettaconcise. Comprising the content of our five acclaimed online libraries—Map Central, the Bedford History Image Library, DocLinks, HistoryLinks, and PlaceLinks—Make History provides one-stop access to relevant digital content including maps, images, documents, and Web links. Students and instructors alike can search this free, easy-to-use database by key word, topic, date, or specific chapter of *America: A Concise History* and can download the content they find. Instructors can also create entire collections of content and store them online for later use or post their collections to the Web to share with students.

Content for Course Management Systems. A variety of student and instructor resources developed for this textbook are ready for use in course management systems such as WebCT, Blackboard, and other platforms. This e-content includes nearly all of the offerings from the book's Online Study Guide as well as the book's test bank.

Videos and Multimedia. A wide assortment of videos and multimedia CD-ROMs on various topics in American history is available to qualified adopters.

Acknowledgments

We are very grateful to the following scholars and teachers who reported on their thoughts about and experiences with the Third Edition. Their comments often challenged us to rethink or justify our interpretations and always provided a check on accuracy down to the smallest detail. Thanks are due to: Rod Andrew Jr., Clemson University; Miles L. Bradbury, University of Maryland; Paul Buelow, Indiana University–Purdue University Indianapolis; B. R. Burg, Arizona State University; James Carroll, Iona College; Sharon A. Roger Hepburn, Radford University; Pamela Hronek, Arkansas State University; Kara L. Lawson, Hillsborough Community College; Scott Lingenfelter, Roosevelt University; Delores McBroome, Humboldt State University;

Marianne F. McKnight, Salt Lake Community College; David M. Parker, California State University, Northridge; Jon E. Purmont, Southern Connecticut State University; David Rayson, Normandale Community College; Stephen Russell, Northern Essex Community College; Robert M. Sandow, Lock Haven University of Pennsylvania; Shawn Selby, Ohio University; Michael David Tegeder, Santa Fe Community College.

As the authors of *America: A Concise History*, we know better than anyone how much this Fourth Edition is the work of other hands and minds. In that regard, we are grateful to Lynn Dumenil, our fellow author through the first three editions, for laying the foundation for our treatment of the twentieth century. We also want to thank Mary Dougherty, William Lombardo, and Jane Knetzger, who oversaw the Fourth Edition, and Danielle Slevens, who used her critical skills to improve our text. As usual, Joan E. Feinberg has been generous in providing the resources needed to produce a handsome volume. Lori Chong Roncka expertly guided our book through the production process; Donna Dennison, Billy Boardman, and Rose Corbett Gordon provided the research and design for our covers; and Karen Soeltz and Jenna Bookin Barry used their superb marketing skills to help this book reach the classroom. We also thank the rest of our editorial and production team for their dedicated efforts: Katherine Flynn, Alix Roy, Adrianne Hiltz, Lidia MacDonald-Carr, and David Ayers; Pembroke Herbert and Sandi Rygiel at Picture Research Consultants and Archives; and Sandy Schechter. Finally, we want to express our appreciation for the invaluable assistance of Patricia Deveneau, whose work contributed in many ways to the intellectual vitality of this new edition of *America: A Concise History*.

James A. Henretta
David Brody

Brief Contents

Contents

CHAPTER 4
Growth and Crisis in Colonial Society, 1720–1765   96

PART TWO

The New Republic, 1763–1820   128

CHAPTER 5

Toward Independence: Years of Decision, 1763–1776   132

CHAPTER 8
Creating a Republican Culture, 1790–1820   225

CHAPTER 11
Religion and Reform, 1820–1860 319

CHAPTER 14
Two Societies at War, 1861–1865   407

CHAPTER 19
Politics in the Age of Enterprise, 1877–1896   551

CHAPTER 28
The Liberal Consensus: Flaming Out, 1960–1968   823

CHAPTER 31

A Dynamic Economy, A Divided People, 1980–2000   916

List of Maps

About the Authors

JAMES A. HENRETTA is Priscilla Alden Burke Professor of American History at the University of Maryland, College Park. Among other books, he has published *Evolution and Revolution: American Society, 1600–1820*; *The Origins of American Capitalism*; and an edited volume, *Republicanism and Liberalism in America and the German States, 1750–1850*. His most recent publications include "Charles Evans Hughes and the Strange Death of Liberal America" (*Law and History Review*, 2006), derived from his ongoing research on the liberal state in New York, 1820–1975, and "Magistrates, Lawyers, Legislators: The Three Legal Systems of Early America," in the *Cambridge History of American Law* (2008).

DAVID BRODY is Professor Emeritus of History at the University of California, Davis. He is the author, among other books, of *Steelworkers in America*; *Workers in Industrial America: Essays on the 20th Century Struggle*; *In Labor's Cause: Main Themes on the History of the American Worker*; and, most recently, *Labor Embattled: History, Power, Rights*. His current research is on labor law and workplace regimes during the Great Depression.

America

A Concise History

PART ONE

The Creation of American Society

1450–1763

ECONOMY	SOCIETY	GOVERNMENT
From staple crops to internal growth	**Ethnic, racial, and class divisions**	**From monarchy to republic**
1450 ▸ Native American subsistence economy ▸ Europeans fish off North American coast	▸ Sporadic warfare among Indian peoples ▸ Spanish conquest of Mexico and Peru (1519–1535)	▸ Rise of monarchical nation-states in Europe
1600 ▸ First staple export crops: furs and tobacco	▸ English-Indian wars ▸ African servitude begins in Virginia (1619)	▸ James I claims divine right to rule England ▸ Virginia House of Burgesses (1619)
1640 ▸ South Atlantic System emerges: ▸ Mercantilist regulation: first Navigation Act (1651)	▸ White indentured servitude shapes Chesapeake society ▸ Indians retreat inland; Africans lose rights (1670s)	▸ English Puritan Revolution ▸ Stuart restoration (1660) ▸ Bacon's Rebellion in Virginia (1675)
1680 ▸ Tobacco trade stagnates ▸ Rice cultivation expands in South Carolina after 1700	▸ Indian slavery expands in the Carolinas ▸ Ethnic Dutch rebellion in New York (1689)	▸ Dominion of New England (1686–1689) ▸ Glorious Revolution ousts James II (1688–1689)
1720 ▸ Mature yeoman farm economy in North ▸ 1740s: Imports from Britain increase	▸ Major Scots-Irish and German migration ▸ Growing inequality in rural and urban areas	▸ Rise of the colonial representative assemblies ▸ Era of salutary neglect in colonial administration
1760 ▸ End of British military aid sparks postwar recession	▸ Uprisings by tenants and backcountry farmers	▸ Britain vanquishes France in "Great War for Empire" (1756–1763)

RELIGION	CULTURE
From hierarchy to pluralism	**The creation of American identity**
▶ Protestant Reformation begins (1517) and sparks century of religious warfare	▶ Diverse Native American cultures in eastern woodlands
▶ Persecuted English Puritans and Catholics migrate to America	▶ Puritans implant Calvinism, education, and freehold ideal
▶ Puritans in Massachusetts Bay quash "heresy" ▶ Religious liberty in Rhode Island	▶ Aristocratic aspirations in Chesapeake region
▶ Rise of tolerance among colonial Protestants ▶ Wars with Catholic France in Europe and America	▶ Emergence of African American language and culture
▶ German and Scots-Irish Pietists in Middle Atlantic region ▶ Great Awakening (1740s)	▶ Expansion of colleges, newspapers, and magazines ▶ Franklin and the American Enlightenment
▶ Rise of Evangelical Baptists in Virginia	▶ First signs of a distinct American identity within the Atlantic world

Historians know that societies evolve through decades, even centuries, of human endeavor and experience. Historians also know that the first Americans were hunters and gatherers who migrated to the Western Hemisphere from Asia. Over many generations, these migrants—the Native Americans—came to live in many different environments and cultures. In much of North America, they developed kinship-based societies that relied on farming and hunting. But in the lower Mississippi River Valley around A.D. 900, Native Americans fashioned a hierarchical social order similar to those of the great civilizations of the Aztecs, Mayas, and Incas.

In Part One, we describe how Europeans, with their steel weapons, attractive trade goods, and diseases, shredded the fabric of most Native American cultures. Throughout the Western Hemisphere, men and women of European origin—the Spanish in Mesoamerica and South America, the French in Canada, the English along the Atlantic coast—gradually achieved domination over the native peoples.

Our story focuses on the Europeans who settled in the English mainland colonies.

They expected to transplant their traditional societies, cultures, and religious beliefs in the soil of the New World. But things did not work out exactly as planned. In learning to live in the new land, English, Germans, and Scots-Irish created societies that differed from those of their homelands in their economies, social character, political systems, religions, and cultures. Here, in brief, is the story of that transformation as we explain it in Part One.

ECONOMY

Many European settlements were great economic successes. Europe at the time consisted of poor, overcrowded, and unequal societies that periodically suffered devastating famines. But with few people and a bountiful natural environment, the settlers in North America created a bustling economy. In the northern mainland colonies, communities of independent farm families in rural areas and merchants and artisans in port towns and cities prospered in what British and German migrants called "the best poor man's country."

SOCIETY

Simultaneously, some European settlements became places of oppressive captivity for Africans, with profound consequences for America's social development. As the supply of white indentured servants from Europe dwindled after 1680, planters in the Chesapeake region imported enslaved African workers to grow tobacco. Wealthy British and French planters in the West Indies bought hundreds of thousands of slaves from African traders and rulers and forced them to labor on sugar plantations. Slowly and with great effort, the slaves and their descendants created a variety of African American cultures within the European-dominated societies in which they lived.

GOVERNMENT

The first English migrants transplanted authoritarian institutions to America, and the home government intervened frequently in their affairs. But after the Glorious Revolution of 1688, white settlers in the English mainland colonies devised an increasingly free and competitive political system. Thereafter, local governments and representative assemblies became more powerful and created a tradition of self-rule that would spark demands for political independence from Britain after the Great War for Empire ended in 1763.

RELIGION

The American experience profoundly changed religious institutions and values. Many migrants fled from Europe because of conflicts among rival Christian churches and persecution by government officials. For the most part, they practiced their religions in America without interference. Religion became more prominent in colonial life after the evangelical revivals of the 1740s, and the churches became less dogmatic. Americans increasingly rejected the harshest tenets of Calvinism (a strict version of Protestantism), and a significant minority of educated colonists embraced the rationalism of the European Enlightenment. As a result, American Protestant Christianity became increasingly tolerant, democratic, and optimistic.

CULTURE

New forms of family and community life arose in the new American society. The first English settlers lived in patriarchal families ruled by dominant fathers and in communities controlled by men of high status. However, by 1750, many American fathers no longer strictly managed their children's lives, and because of widespread property ownership, many men and some women enjoyed personal independence. American society was increasingly pluralistic, composed of migrants from many European ethnic groups — English, Scots, Scots-Irish, Dutch, and Germans — as well as enslaved Africans and Native American peoples. Distinct regional cultures developed in New England, the Middle Atlantic colonies, the Chesapeake, and the Carolinas. Consequently, an overarching American identity based on the English language, English legal and political institutions, and shared experiences emerged very slowly.

The story of the colonial experience is both depressing and uplifting. Europeans and their diseases destroyed many Native American peoples, and European planters held tens of thousands of Africans in bondage. However, white migrants enjoyed unprecedented opportunities for economic security, political freedom, and spiritual fulfillment. This dual experience — of black bondage and white freedom — would continue far into the American future.

The Emergence of an Atlantic World: Europe, Africa, and America

1450–1620

Soon there will come from the rising sun a different kind of man from any you have yet seen. . . . [After that,] the world will fall to pieces.

— A Spokane Indian prophet

"Before the French came among us," an elder of the Natchez people of Mississippi explained, "we were men . . . and we walked with boldness every road, but now we walk like slaves, which we shall soon be, since the French already treat us . . . as they do their black slaves." Before the 1490s, the Natchez and the other native peoples of the Western Hemisphere knew nothing about the light-skinned inhabitants of Europe and the dark-complexioned peoples of Africa. But when Christopher Columbus, a European searching for a sea route to Asia, encountered the peoples of the Western Hemisphere in 1492, the destinies of four continents quickly became intertwined. On his second voyage, Columbus carried a cargo of enslaved Africans, initiating the centuries-long trade that would produce an African diaspora and many triracial societies in the Americas.

As the Natchez elder knew well, the resulting assemblage of peoples was based on exploitation, not equality. By the time he urged resistance against the alien intruders, the French were too numerous and strong. With the help of Indian allies, they savagely killed hundreds of Natchez and sold the survivors into slavery on the sugar plantations of the West Indies. The fate of the Natchez was not unique. In the three centuries following Columbus's voyage, many Native American peoples came under the domination of the Spanish, Portuguese, French, English, and Dutch, who seized their lands and often worked them with enslaved Africans.

How did this happen? How did Europeans become leaders in world trade and create an economically integrated Atlantic World? What made Native Americans vulnerable to conquest by European adventurers? And what led to the transatlantic trade in African slaves? In the answers to these questions lie the origins of the United States.

Native American Societies

When the Europeans arrived, most Native Americans—about forty million—lived in Mesoamerica (present-day Mexico and Guatemala) and along the western coast of South America (present-day Peru); another seven million resided in lands to the north, in what is now the United States and Canada. Native peoples in the north mostly lived in simple hunter-gatherer or agricultural communities governed by kin ties. But those in Mesoamerica and Peru resided in societies ruled by warrior-kings and priests, creating civilizations whose art, religion, society, and economy were as complex as those of Europe and the Mediterranean.

The First Americans

According to the Navajos, history began when their ancestors emerged from under the earth. For the Iroquois, the story of their Five Nations started when people fell from the sky. Most twenty-first-century anthropologists and historians believe that the first inhabitants of the Western Hemisphere were migrants from Asia. Strong archeological and genetic evidence suggests that in the last Ice Age, which began about 20,000 years ago, small bands of tribal hunters followed herds of game across a 100-mile-wide land bridge between Siberia and Alaska. An oral history of the Tuscarora Indians, who settled in present-day North Carolina, tells of a famine in the old world and a journey over ice toward where "the sun rises," a trek that brought their ancestors to a lush forest with abundant food and game.

Most anthropologists believe that the main migratory stream from Asia lasted from about 15,000 to 9,000 years ago. Then the glaciers melted, and the rising ocean waters submerged the land bridge and created the Bering Strait (Map 1.1). Around 8,000 years ago, a second movement of peoples, now traveling by water across the narrow strait, brought the ancestors of the Navajos and the Apaches to North America. The forebears of the Aleut and Inuit peoples, the "Eskimos," came in a third migration around 5,000 years ago. Then, for 300 generations, the peoples of the Western Hemisphere were largely cut off from the rest of the world.

For centuries, the first Americans lived as hunter-gatherers, subsisting on the abundant wildlife and vegetation. As the larger species of animals—mammoths, giant beavers, and horses—died out because of overhunting and climate change, hunters became adept at killing more elusive game: rabbits, deer, and elk. By about 6000 B.C., some Native American peoples in present-day Mexico and Peru were raising domesticated crops. They gradually bred maize into an extremely nutritious plant that had a higher yield per acre than did wheat, barley, or rye, the staple cereals of Europe. They also learned to plant beans and squash with the maize, a mix of crops that provided a nourishing diet and kept the soil fertile. The resulting agricultural surplus encouraged population growth and eventually laid the economic foundation for wealthy, urban societies in Mexico, Peru, and the Mississippi River Valley.

The Mayas and the Aztecs

The flowering of civilization in Mesoamerica began around 700 B.C. among the Olmec people, who lived along the Gulf of Mexico. Subsequently, the Mayas of the Yucatán Peninsula of Mexico and the neighboring rain forests of Guatemala built large urban

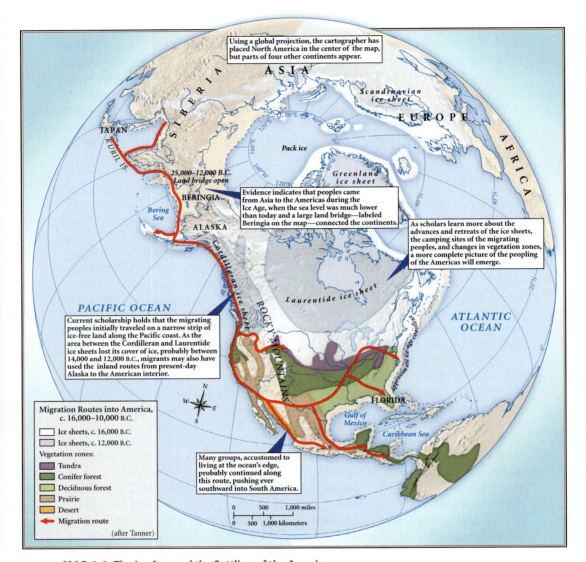

MAP 1.1 The Ice Age and the Settling of the Americas

Some 16,000 years ago, a sheet of ice covered much of Europe and North America. Using a broad bridge of land connecting Siberia and Alaska, hunting peoples from Asia migrated to North America in search of woolly mammoths and other large game animals and ice-free habitats. By 10,000 B.C., the descendants of these migrant peoples had moved south to present-day Florida and central Mexico. In time, these peoples would settle the entire vast continents of South and North America.

centers that relied on elaborate systems of water storage and irrigation. By A.D. 300, more than 20,000 people were living in the Mayan city of Tikal [*TEE-kall*]. Most were farmers, whose labor built the city's huge stone temples. An elite class claiming descent from the gods ruled Mayan society and lived in splendor on goods and taxes extracted from peasant families. Drawing on the religious and artistic traditions of the Olmecs,

Mayan artisans decorated temples and palaces with depictions of jaguars, warrior-gods, and religious images. Mayan astronomers created a calendar that recorded historical events and accurately predicted eclipses of the sun and the moon. Mayan scholars developed hieroglyphic writing to record royal lineages and wars. These skills in calculation and writing enhanced the authority of the ruling class of warriors and priests and provided the Mayans with a sense of history and identity. By facilitating the movement of goods and ideas, they also increased the prosperity of Mayan society and the complexity of its culture.

Beginning around 800, Mayan civilization went into decline. Evidence suggests that a two-century-long drought led to an economic crisis and prompted overtaxed peasants to desert the temple cities and retreat to the countryside. By 900, many religious centers had been abandoned. The few intact Mayan city-states would vigorously resist the Spanish invaders in the 1520s.

A second major Mesoamerican civilization developed in the highlands of Mexico around the city of Teotihuacán [*tee-o-ti-hue-KON*], with its magnificent Pyramid of the Sun. At its zenith, about A.D. 500, Teotihuacán had more than one hundred temples, some 4,000 apartment buildings, and a population of at least 100,000. By 800, the city was in decline, the victim of long-term drought and recurrent invasions by seminomadic warrior peoples. Eventually, one of these invading peoples, the Aztecs, established an even more extensive empire.

The Aztecs settled on an island in Lake Texcoco in the great central valley of Mexico. There, in 1325, they began to build a new city, Tenochtitlán [*ten-och-tit-LAN*], Mexico City today. The Aztecs mastered the complex irrigation systems and written language of the resident peoples and established an elaborate culture with a hierarchical social order. Priests and warrior-nobles ruled over twenty **clans** of free Aztec commoners who farmed communal land. The nobles also used huge numbers of non-Aztec slaves and serfs to labor on their private estates.

An aggressive people, the Aztecs soon subjugated most of central Mexico. Their rulers demanded both economic and human tribute from scores of subject peoples, and their priests brutally sacrificed untold thousands of men and women to ensure fertile fields and the daily return of the sun.

Aztec merchants forged trading routes that crisscrossed the empire and imported furs, gold, textiles, food, and obsidian from as far north as the Rio Grande and as far south as present-day Panama. By 1500, Tenochtitlán was a metropolis, with magnificent palaces and temples and more than 200,000 inhabitants—making it far larger than most European cities. The splendor of the city and its elaborate crafts dazzled Spanish soldiers. "These great towns and pyramids and buildings arising from the water, all made of stone, seemed like an enchanted vision," marveled one Spaniard. The Aztecs' strong institutions, military power, and wealth posed a formidable challenge to any adversary, at home or from afar.

The Indians of the North

The Indian societies north of the Rio Grande were less complex and less coercive than those to the south. They lacked occupational diversity, social hierarchy, and strong state institutions. Most northern peoples lived in self-governing tribes made up of clans, groups of related families that traced their lineage to a real or legendary common ancestor. These tribal communities were self-centered; anyone outside the narrow boundaries of kin was alien. Tellingly, their names for themselves — Innu, Lenape, and dozens of others — mean "human beings" or "real people." Clan elders and village chiefs set war policy, conducted ceremonies, and resolved personal feuds. They also enforced customs such as a ban on marriage between clan members. But elders and chiefs did not form a distinct and powerful ruling class; instead, they used personal authority within the kinship system to win acceptance of their policies.

The culture of these lineage-based societies did not encourage the accumulation of material goods. Individual ownership of land was virtually unknown. As a French missionary among the Iroquois noted, they "possess hardly anything except in common." The elders would urge members to share food and other scarce goods, fostering an ethic of reciprocity rather than one of accumulation. "You are covetous, and neither generous nor kind," the Micmac Indians of Nova Scotia told acquisitive French fur traders in the late 1600s. "As for us, if we have a morsel of bread, we share it with our neighbor."

Over the centuries, some Indian peoples became adept in trade or conquest. By A.D. 100, the vigorous Hopewell people of present-day Ohio had increased their food supply by domesticating plants, organized themselves in large villages, and set up a trading network that stretched from present-day Louisiana to Wisconsin. They imported obsidian from the Yellowstone region of the Rocky Mountains, copper from the Great Lakes, and pottery and marine shells from the Gulf of Mexico. The Hopewells built large burial mounds with extensive earthworks that still survive, and skilled Hopewell artisans fashioned striking ornaments to bury with the dead. For unknown reasons, the Hopewells' elaborate trading network collapsed around 400.

Another complex culture developed among the Pueblo peoples of the Southwest: the Hohokams, Mogollons, and Anasazis. By A.D. 600, Hohokam [*ho-HO-kam*] people in the high country of present-day Arizona and New Mexico were using irrigation to grow two crops a year, fashioning fine pottery with red-on-buff designs, and worshipping their gods on platform mounds; by 1000, they were living in elaborate multiroom stone or mud-brick structures called **pueblos**. To the east, in the Mimbres Valley of present-day New Mexico, the Mogollon [*mo-gee-YON*] people developed a distinctive black-on-white pottery. And by A.D. 900, to the north, the Anasazi people had become master architects. They built residential-ceremonial villages in steep cliffs, a pueblo in Chaco Canyon that housed 1,000 people, and 400 miles of straight roads. But the culture of the Pueblo peoples gradually collapsed after 1150 as soil exhaustion and extended droughts disrupted maize production, and they abandoned Chaco Canyon and other communities. The descendants of these peoples — including the Acomas, Zunis, and Hopis — later built strong but smaller village societies better suited to the dry and unpredictable climate of the American Southwest.

The last large-scale culture to emerge north of the Rio Grande was the Mississippian. By about A.D. 800, the farming technology of Mesoamerica had reached the

Mississippi River Valley, perhaps carried by Mayan refugees from the war-torn Yucatán Peninsula. By planting new strains of maize and beans, the Mississippian peoples produced an agricultural surplus. They then built small, fortified temple cities, where a robust culture developed. By 1150, the largest city, Cahokia [*ka-HO-kee-ah*], near present-day St. Louis, boasted a population of 15,000 to 20,000 and more than one hundred temple mounds, one of them as large as the great Egyptian pyramids. As in Mesoamerica, the tribute paid by peasant farmers supported a privileged class of nobles and priests who waged war against neighboring chiefdoms, patronized artisans, and claimed descent from the Sun God.

By 1350, the Mississippian civilization was in rapid decline. The large population had overburdened the environment, depleting nearby forests and herds of deer. The Indians died from tuberculosis and other urban diseases. Still, Mississippian institutions and practices endured for centuries. When Spanish conquistador Hernán de Soto invaded the region in the 1540s, he found the Apalachee [*ap-a-LA-chee*] and Timucua [*TEE-moo-KOO-wa*] Indians living in permanent settlements under the command of powerful chiefs. "If you desire to see me, come where I am," a chief told de Soto, "neither for you, nor for any man, will I set back one foot." A century and a half later, French traders and priests found the Natchez people rigidly divided among hereditary chiefs, nobles and honored people, and a bottom class of peasants. "Their chiefs possess all authority and distribute their favors and presents at will," a Frenchman noted. Undoubtedly influenced by Mesoamerican rituals, the Natchez marked the death of a chief by sacrificing his wives and burying their remains in a ceremonial mound (see Voices from Abroad, p. 13).

The cultures of the native peoples of eastern North America were diverse. Like the Natchez, the Creeks, Choctaws, and Chickasaws who lived in present-day Alabama and Mississippi had once been organized in powerful chiefdoms. However, the European epidemic diseases introduced by de Soto's expedition in the 1540s killed thousands of Indians and destroyed their traditional institutions. The survivors of the various chiefdoms intermarried and settled in smaller, less powerful agricultural communities.

In these Muskogean-speaking societies—and among the Algonquian-speaking and Iroquoian peoples who lived to the north and east—farming became the work of women. While the men hunted and fished, the women used flint hoes and raised corn, squash, and beans. Because of the importance of farming, a **matrilineal** system of kinship and inheritance developed among some eastern Indian peoples, including the Five Nations of the Iroquois, who resided in present-day New York State. Women cultivated the fields around semipermanent villages and passed the use rights to these fields to their daughters. In these matrilineal societies, the father stood outside the main lines of descent and authority; the principal responsibility for child rearing fell on the mother and her brothers, and men often lived with their sisters rather than with their wives. Among these peoples, religious rituals centered on the agricultural cycle. The Iroquois, for example, celebrated green corn and strawberry festivals. Although the eastern Indian peoples of 1500 enjoyed an adequate diet, their lives were hard and their populations grew slowly.

When Europeans intruded into North America, the strong Indian city-states that had once flourished in the Southwest and in the Mississippi River Valley had vanished.

Iroquois Women at Work, 1724

As this European engraving suggests, Iroquois women took responsibility for growing food crops. Several of the women at the top are hoeing the soil into small hillocks, while others are planting corn and beans. The lower section shows other women tapping sugar maples and boiling the sap to make maple syrup. The woman at the left is probably grinding corn into flour; later she would add water to make flat patties for baking. Newberry Library, Chicago.

The Customs of the Natchez, 1730 FATHER LE PETITE

The beliefs and institutions of the Mississippian culture (A.D. 1000–1450) survived for centuries among the Natchez people, who lived in present-day Mississippi. Around 1730, Father Le Petite, one of the hundreds of French Jesuit priests who lived among the Indians, wrote a fine description of Natchez society in a letter to his religious superiors in France. However, he misunderstood the reasons why the chief is succeeded by his sister's son: In a matrilineal society, lines of descent and inheritance pass through women, not men.

MY REVEREND FATHER, *The peace of Our Lord.*

This Nation of Savages inhabits one of the most beautiful and fertile countries in the World, and is the only one on this continent which appears to have any regular worship. Their Religion in certain points is very similar to that of the ancient Romans. They have a Temple filled with Idols, which are different figures of men and of animals, and for which they have the most profound veneration. Their Temple in shape resembles an earthen oven, a hundred feet in circumference. They enter it by a little door about four feet high, and not more than three in breadth. Above on the outside are three figures of eagles made of wood, and painted red, yellow, and white. Before the door is a kind of shed with folding-doors, where the Guardian of the Temple is lodged. . . .

The Sun is the principal object of veneration to these people; as they cannot conceive of anything which can be above this heavenly body, nothing else appears to them more worthy of their homage. It is for the same reason that the great Chief of this Nation, who knows nothing on the earth more dignified than himself, takes the title of brother of the Sun, and the credulity of the people maintains him in the despotic authority which he claims. To enable them better to converse together, they raise a mound of artificial soil, on which they build his cabin, which is of the same construction as the Temple. When a great Chief dies, his many wives are killed and are buried with him and personal goods in a great ceremonial mound. . . .

. . . [O]ne of their principles is . . . the immortality of the soul, and when they leave this world they go, they say, to live in another, there to be recompensed or punished.

In former times the Nation of the *Natchez* was very large. It counted sixty Villages and eight hundred Suns or Princes; now it is reduced to six little Villages and eleven Suns. [Its] Government is hereditary; it is not, however, the son of the reigning Chief who succeeds his father, but the son of his sister, or the first Princess of the blood. This policy is founded on the knowledge they have of the licentiousness of their women. They are not sure, they say, that the children of the chief's wife may be of the blood Royal, whereas the son of the sister of the great Chief must be, at least on the side of the mother.

SOURCE: Reuben Gold Thwaites, ed., *The Jesuit Relations and Allied Documents* (Cleveland: Murrow Brothers, 1900), 68: 121–135.

There were no great Indian empires or religious centers, as there were in Mesoamerica, that could sustain a campaign of military and spiritual resistance to European invaders. "When you command, all the French obey and go to war," the Chippewa chief Chigabe [*chi-GAH-bee*] remarked to a French general, but "I shall not be heeded and obeyed by my nation." Because households and lineages were the basis of his society, Chigabe explained, "I cannot answer except for myself and for those immediately allied to me."

> ▶ What were the main characteristics of the Indian civilizations of Mesoamerica?
>
> ▶ How were eastern woodland Indian societies organized and governed?

Europe Encounters Africa and the Americas, 1450–1550

In 1400, few observers would have predicted that Europeans would become overlords of the Western Hemisphere and dominate trade in Africa. A thousand years after the fall of the Roman empire, Europe remained a mosaic of small and relatively weak kingdoms. Moreover, around 1350, a vicious plague from the subcontinent of India — the Black Death — had killed one-third of Europe's population. Peoples in other regions had stronger economies and governments. China and India together accounted for more than half of world manufacturing output and had the potential to seize control of world commerce. Indian and Arab merchants already controlled most of Europe's trade with southern Asia. And between 1411 and 1422, large Chinese fleets militarily subdued competitors as they traded around the Indian Ocean and along the eastern coast of Africa.

European Agricultural Society

In 1450, there were just a few large cities in Western Europe: Only Paris, London, and Naples had as many as 100,000 residents. Most Europeans were **peasants** who lived in small agricultural communities. Peasant families usually owned or leased a small dwelling in the village center and had the right to farm the surrounding fields. The fields were open, not divided by fences or hedges, so cooperative farming was a necessity. The community decided which crops to grow, and every family followed its dictates. Because output was limited and there were few good roads, most trade was local. Neighboring families exchanged surplus grain and meat and bartered their farm products for the services of local millers, weavers, and blacksmiths. Most peasants yearned to be **yeomen**, to own enough land to support their family in comfort, but relatively few achieved that goal.

For European peasants, as for Native Americans, the rhythm of life followed the seasons. The agricultural year began in late March, when the ground thawed and dried and the villagers began the exhausting work of spring plowing and then planting wheat, rye, and oats. During these busy months, men sheared the thick winter wool of their sheep, which the women washed and spun into yarn. In June, peasants cut the first crop of hay and stored it as winter fodder for their livestock. During the summer, life was more relaxed, and families had the time to repair their houses and barns. Fall brought the strenuous harvest, followed by solemn feasts of thanksgiving and riotous

Artisan Family
Workers made goods by hand in the preindustrial world, and output was slow, so economic survival required the labor of the entire family. Here, a fifteenth-century French woodworker planes a panel of wood while his wife twists flax fibers into linen yarn for the family's clothes and their young son cleans up wood shavings from the workshop floor. Giraudon/Art Resource, New York.

bouts of merrymaking. As winter approached, peasants slaughtered excess livestock and salted or smoked the meat. During the cold months, they threshed grain and wove textiles, visited friends and relatives, and celebrated the winter solstice or the birth of Christ. Just before the farming cycle began again in the spring, they held carnivals, celebrating with drink and dance the end of the long winter night. Even births and deaths followed the seasons: More successful conceptions took place in early summer than at any other time of the year. And many rural people died either in January and February, victims of viral diseases, or in August and September in epidemics of fly-borne dysentery.

For most peasants, survival meant constant labor, breaking the soil with primitive wooden plows and harvesting hay and grain with small hand sickles. In the absence of today's high-quality seeds, chemical fertilizers, and pesticides, output was pitifully small—less than one-tenth of present-day yields. The margin of existence was small, and that corroded family relationships. Malnourished mothers fed their babies sparingly, calling them "greedy and gluttonous," and many newborn girls were "helped to die" so that their older brothers would have enough to eat. Disease killed about half of all peasant children before the age of twenty-one. Assault, murder, and rape were woven into the fabric of daily life, and hunger was a constant companion. "I have seen the latest epoch of misery," a French doctor reported as famine struck. "The inhabitants . . . lie down in a meadow to eat grass, and share the food of wild beasts." Often destitute, usually exploited by landlords and nobles, many peasants drew on strong religious beliefs and an inclination to "count blessings" and accepted their harsh existence.

Others hoped for a better life for themselves and their children. It was the peasants of Spain, Germany, and Britain who would supply the majority of white migrants to the Western Hemisphere.

Hierarchy and Authority

In traditional hierarchical societies—Mesoamerican or European—authority came from above. In Europe, kings and princes owned vast tracts of land, forcibly conscripted men for military service, and lived in splendor off the peasantry's labor. Yet monarchs were far from supreme: Local nobles also owned large estates and controlled hundreds of peasant families. Collectively, these nobles challenged royal authority with both their military power and their legislative institutions, such as the French *parlements* and the English House of Lords.

Just as kings and nobles ruled society, so men governed families. Rich or poor, the man was the head of the house, his power justified by the teachings of the Christian church. As one English clergyman put it: "The woman is a weak creature not embued with like strength and constancy of mind"; consequently, law and custom "subjected her to the power of man." Once she married, an Englishwoman assumed her husband's surname and had to submit to his orders and physical "correction," which was completely legal. Moreover, a wife surrendered to her husband the legal right to all her property. Her sole protection: When he died, she received a **dower**, usually the use during her lifetime of one-third of the family's land and goods.

Men also controlled the lives of their children, who usually worked for their father into their middle or late twenties. Then landowning peasants would give land to their sons and dowries to their daughters and choose marriage partners of appropriate wealth and status. In many regions, fathers bestowed all their land on their eldest son, a practice known as **primogeniture**, forcing many younger children to join the ranks of the roaming poor. In this kind of society, few men—and even fewer women—had much personal freedom or individual identity.

Hierarchy and authority prevailed in traditional European society both because of the power of established institutions—family, church, and village—and because, in a violent and unpredictable world, they offered ordinary people a measure of security. Carried by migrants to America, these security-conscious institutions would shape the character of family and society well into the eighteenth century.

The Power of Religion

For centuries, the Roman Catholic Church was the great unifying institution in Western Europe. The pope in Rome stood at the head of a vast religious hierarchy of cardinals, bishops, and priests. Catholic tracts and theologians preserved Latin, the great language of classical scholarship, and Christian dogma provided a common understanding of God, the world, and human history. Every village had a church, and the holy shrines that dotted the byways of Europe were reminders of the Church's teachings and authority.

Christian doctrine penetrated deeply into the everyday lives of peasants. Originally, most Europeans were **pagans**. Like the Indians of North America, they were animists who believed that elemental forces, such as the sun, rain, and wind, governed the natural world and that these spiritual forces had to be heeded and honored. However, Christian priests taught the peasants that spiritual power came from outside nature, from a supernatural God who had sent his divine son, Jesus Christ, into the world to save humanity from its sins. The Church devised a religious calendar that transformed pagan agricultural festivals into Christian holy days. The winter solstice, which for pagans marked the return of the sun, became the feast of Christmas, to celebrate the birth of Christ. To avert famine and plague, Christianized peasants no longer made ritual offerings to nature; instead, they offered prayers to Christ.

The Church also taught that Satan, a lesser and wicked supernatural being, was constantly challenging God by tempting people to sin. If a devout Christian fell mysteriously ill, the cause might be an evil spell cast by a witch in league with Satan. Prophets who spread **heresies**—doctrines that were inconsistent with the teachings of the Church—were seen as the tools of Satan. Suppressing false doctrines became an obligation of Christian rulers. So did combating Islam, a religion that, like Christianity, proclaimed a single god. Following the death in A.D. 632 of the prophet Muhammad, the founder of Islam, the newly converted Arab peoples of the Mediterranean used force and persuasion to spread the Muslim faith into sub-Saharan Africa, India, Indonesia, and deep into Spain and the Balkan regions of Europe. Between 1096 and 1291, Christian armies undertook a series of Crusades to halt this Muslim advance and win back the holy lands where Christ had lived.

The crusaders had some military successes, but their most profound impact was on European society. Religious warfare intensified Europe's Christian identity and prompted the persecution of Jews and their expulsion from many European countries. The Crusades also broadened the economic horizons of the merchants of Western Europe, who set out to capture the trade routes that stretched from Constantinople to China and from the Mediterranean Sea to the Indian Ocean.

The Renaissance Changes Europe, 1300–1500

The Crusades exposed educated Europeans to Byzantine and Arab learning and reacquainted them with the achievements of classical antiquity. Arabs had access to the silks and spices of the East and had acquired magnetic compasses, water-powered mills, and mechanical clocks, mostly from the Chinese. Moreover, Arab scholars carried on the legacy of Byzantine civilization, which had preserved the great achievements of the Greeks and Romans in medicine, philosophy, mathematics, astronomy, and geography. Stimulated by this knowledge, first Italy and then the countries of northern Europe experienced a rebirth of cultural life and economic energy.

The Renaissance had the most profound impact on the upper classes. Merchants from the Italian city-states of Venice, Genoa, Florence, and Pisa dispatched ships to Alexandria, Beirut, and other eastern Mediterranean ports, where they purchased goods from China, India, Persia, and Arabia to be sold throughout Europe. The enormously profitable commerce created wealthy merchants, bankers, and textile manufacturers who conducted trade, lent vast sums of money, and spurred technological innovation in silk and wool production. These Italian moneyed elites ruled their city-states as **republics**, with no prince or king. They celebrated **civic humanism**, an **ideology** that praised public virtue and service to the state and in time profoundly influenced European and American conceptions of government.

Perhaps no other age in European history has produced such a flowering of artistic genius. Michelangelo, Andrea Palladio, and Filippo Brunelleschi designed and built great architectural masterpieces. Leonardo da Vinci, Jacopo Bellini, and Raphael produced magnificent religious paintings, setting styles and standards that have endured into the modern era.

This creative energy inspired Renaissance rulers. In *The Prince* (1513), Niccolò Machiavelli offered unsentimental advice on how monarchs could increase their political power. The kings of Western Europe followed his advice, creating royal law courts and bureaucracies to reduce the power of the landed nobility and forging alliances with merchants and urban artisans. Monarchs allowed merchants to trade throughout their realms, granted privileges to the artisan organizations called **guilds**, and safeguarded commercial transactions in royal law courts, thereby encouraging domestic manufacturing and foreign trade. In return, kings and princes extracted taxes from towns and loans from merchants to support their armies and officials. This mutually enriching alliance of monarchs and merchants propelled Europe into its first age of overseas expansion.

Under the direction of Prince Henry (1394–1460), Portugal led a surge of maritime expansion. In 1415, as a young soldier of the Crusading Order of Christ, Henry

Astronomers at Istanbul (Constantinople), 1581
Arab and Turkish scholars transmitted ancient texts and learning to Europeans during the Renaissance and provided much of the geographical and astronomical knowledge that European explorers used during the sixteenth century, the great Age of Discovery. Ergun Cagatay, Istanbul.

learned of Arab merchants' rich trade in gold and slaves across the Sahara Desert. Seeking a maritime route to this trade's source in West Africa, Henry drew on the work of Renaissance thinkers and Arab and Italian geographers. In 1420, he founded a center for oceanic navigation and astronomical observation in the south of Portugal. He urged his captains to find a way around Cape Bojador in North Africa, a region of fierce winds and treacherous currents, and to explore the feared "Sea of Darkness" to the south. Eventually, Henry's mariners sailed far into the Atlantic, where they discovered and colonized the Madeira and Azore islands; from there, they sailed to the sub-Saharan African coast. By 1435, Portuguese sea captains had reached Sierra Leone, where they exchanged salt, wine, and fish for African ivory and gold. By the 1440s, the Portuguese were trading in humans as well, the first Europeans to engage in the long-established African trade in slaves. Henry's mission of enhancing Portugal's wealth through trade with West Africa had succeeded.

West African Society and Slavery

Vast and diverse, West Africa stretches along the coast from present-day Senegal to the Democratic Republic of Congo. In the 1400s, tropical rain forest covered much of the coast, but a series of great rivers—the Senegal, Gambia, Volta, Niger, and Congo—provided relatively easy access to the woodlands and savannas of the interior, where most people lived. There were few coastal cities because there was little seaborne trade (Map 1.2).

Most West Africans lived in extended families in small villages and farmed modest plots. Normally, the men cleared the land and the women planted and harvested the crops. On the plains, farmers grew millet and cotton and set their livestock out to graze; the forest peoples planted yams and harvested oil-rich palm nuts. Forest dwellers exchanged palm oil and kola nuts, a highly-valued stimulant, for the textiles and leather goods that savanna dwellers produced. Similarly, merchants collected valuable salt, which was produced along the coast and mined in great deposits in the Sahara, and traded it for iron, gold, and manufactures along the Niger and other rivers.

West Africans lived in diverse ethnic groups and spoke four basic languages, each with many dialects. Among West Atlantic–speakers, the Fulani and Wolof peoples were most numerous. Mande-speakers in the upper Niger region included the Malinke and Bambara peoples; the Yorubas and the Ibos of southern Nigeria spoke varieties of the Kwa language. Finally, the Mossis and other Voltaic-speakers inhabited the area along the upper Volta River. Most of these peoples lived in societies that were similar to those of the Mayans and Aztecs: socially stratified states ruled by kings and princes. Some lived in city-states that produced high-quality metal, leather, textiles, and pottery. Other West African societies were stateless, organized by household and lineage, much like those of the eastern woodland Indians.

Spiritual beliefs varied greatly. West Africans who lived immediately south of the Sahara—the Fulanis in Senegal, Mande-speakers in Mali, and Hausas in northern Nigeria—learned about Islam from Arab merchants and missionaries. Although some West Africans worshipped only the Muslim god, Allah, most recognized other gods as well as spirits that lived in the earth, in animals, and in plants. Many Africans also believed that their kings had divine attributes and could contact the spirit world. They

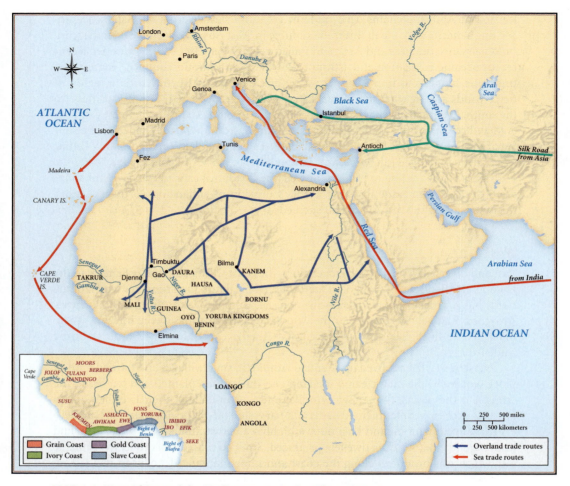

MAP 1.2 West Africa and the Mediterranean in the Fifteenth Century
Trade routes across the Sahara Desert had long connected West Africa with the Mediterranean. Gold, ivory, and slaves moved north and east; fine textiles, spices, and the Muslim faith traveled south and west. Beginning in the 1430s, the Portuguese opened up maritime trade with the coastal regions of West Africa, which were home to many peoples and dozens of large and small states. Within a decade, they would join in the slave trade there.

treated their ancestors with great respect, partly because they believed that the dead resided in a nearby spiritual realm and could intercede in their lives. Most West African peoples had secret societies, such as the Poro for men and the Sande for women, that united people from different lineages and clans. These societies educated their members in sexual practices, conducted adult initiation ceremonies, and used public humiliation to enforce codes of conduct and morality.

Early European traders had a positive impact on West Africa by introducing new plants and animals. Portuguese merchants brought coconuts from East Africa; oranges and lemons from the Mediterranean; pigs from Western Europe; and, after 1492, maize, manioc, and tomatoes from the Americas. They also expanded existing African trade networks. From small, fortified trading posts on the coast, merchants shipped metal products, manufactures, and slaves along the coast and to inland regions and took gold, ivory, and pepper in return. For much of the inland trade, the Portuguese relied on Africans, since Portuguese ships could travel no more than 150 miles up the slow-flowing Gambia and lesser distances on the other rivers. Yellow fever, malaria, and dysentery quickly struck down Europeans who spent time in the interior of West Africa, often killing as many as half of them each year.

Portuguese adventurers continued their quest for an ocean route to Asia. In 1488, Bartholomeu Dias rounded the Cape of Good Hope, the southern tip of Africa; ten years later, Vasco da Gama reached India. Although the Arab, Indian, and Jewish merchants along India's Malabar Coast tried to exclude him from trading there, da Gama acquired a highly profitable cargo of cinnamon and pepper, which were used to flavor and preserve meat. To acquire more spices and Indian textiles, da Gama returned to India in 1502 with twenty-one fighting vessels, which outmaneuvered and outgunned the Arab fleets. That expedition netted 1,700 tons of spices, as much as flowed through Venice in an entire year. Soon the Portuguese government set up fortified trading posts for its merchants at key points around the Indian Ocean, in Indonesia, and along the coast of China. In a transition that began the momentous growth of European wealth and power, the Portuguese replaced the Arabs as the leaders in world commerce.

Portuguese traders joined African states and Arab merchants in the slave trade. Bonded labor — slavery, serfdom, or indentured servitude — was the norm in most premodern societies, and in Africa it took the form of slavery. Some people were held in bondage as security for debts; others were sold into servitude by their kin, often in exchange for food in times of famine; many others were captured in wars. Most slaves worked as agricultural laborers or served in slave armies. And most were treated as property. Sometimes their descendants became low-status members of society, but many others endured hereditary bondage. Sonni Ali, the ruler from 1464 to 1492 of the powerful upper Niger Islamic kingdom of Songhay, personally owned twelve "tribes" of hereditary agricultural slaves, many of them seized in raids against stateless peoples.

A significant number of West Africans became **trade slaves**, sold as agricultural workers from one kingdom to another or carried overland in caravans by Arab traders to the Mediterranean region. When the renowned Tunisian traveler Ibn Battua trekked northward across the Sahara from the Kingdom of Mali around 1350, he traveled with a caravan of 600 female slaves, who were destined for domestic service or concubinage in North Africa, Egypt, and the Ottoman Empire. The first Portuguese in Senegambia found that the Wolof king, who commanded a horse-mounted warrior aristocracy, "supports himself by raids which result in many slaves. . . . He employs these slaves in cultivating the land allotted to him; but he also sells many to the [Arab] merchants in return for horses and other goods."

To exploit this trade in slaves, Portuguese merchants established forts at small port cities — first at Elmina in 1482 and later at Gorée, Mpinda, and Loango — where they bought gold and slaves from African princes and warlords. Initially, they carried a few thousand Africans each year to work on sugar plantations in the Cape Verde

Islands, the Azores, and the Madeira Islands; they also sold slaves in Lisbon, which soon had an African population of 9,000. After 1550, the maritime slave trade—the vast forced diaspora of African peoples—expanded enormously as Europeans set up sugar plantations in the lands of Brazil and the West Indies.

Europeans Explore America

Explorers financed by the Spanish monarchs, King Ferdinand of Aragon and Queen Isabel of Castile, discovered the Western Hemisphere for Europeans. As Renaissance rulers, Ferdinand and Isabel saw national unity and foreign commerce as the keys to power and prosperity. Married in an arranged match to combine their Christian kingdoms, the young rulers (r. 1474–1516) completed the centuries-long *reconquista.* In 1492, their armies captured Granada, the last Islamic state in Western Europe. Using Catholicism to build a sense of "Spanishness," they launched the brutal Inquisition against suspected Christian heretics and expelled or forcibly converted thousands of Jews and Muslims.

Simultaneously, Ferdinand and Isabel sought trade and empire by enlisting the services of Christopher Columbus, a mariner from Genoa. Misinterpreting the findings of Italian geographers, Columbus believed that the Atlantic Ocean, long feared by Arab merchants as a 10,000-mile-wide "green sea of darkness," was a much narrower channel of water separating Europe from Asia. Although dubious about Columbus's theory, Ferdinand and Isabel arranged financial backing from Spanish merchants and dispatched him to find a western route to Asia.

Columbus set sail in three small ships in August 1492. Six weeks later, after a perilous voyage of 3,000 miles, he disembarked on an island in the present-day Bahamas. Believing that he had reached Asia—"the Indies" in fifteenth-century parlance—Columbus called the native inhabitants *Indians* and the islands *the West Indies.* Surprised by the rude living conditions of the native people, Columbus expected them to "easily be made Christians." With ceremony and solemnity, he symbolically claimed the islands for Spain and for Christendom by giving them the names of the Spanish royal family and Catholic holy days. Columbus then explored the neighboring Caribbean islands and demanded tribute from the local Taino [*TIE-no*], Arawak [*air-a-WAK*], and Carib peoples. Buoyed by the natives' stories of rivers of gold lying "to the west," Columbus left forty men on the island of Hispaniola (present-day Haiti and the Dominican Republic) and returned triumphantly to Spain.

Although Columbus brought back no gold, the Spanish monarchs supported three more voyages. During those expeditions, Columbus began the colonization of the West Indies, transporting more than a thousand Spanish settlers—all men—and hundreds of domestic animals. He also began the transatlantic trade in slaves, carrying Indians to bondage in Europe and Africans to work as artisans and farmers in the new Spanish settlements. But Columbus failed to find either golden treasures or great kingdoms, and his death in 1506 went virtually unnoticed.

A German geographer soon labeled the continents "America" in honor of a Genoese explorer, Amerigo Vespucci. Vespucci, who had explored the new-found region around 1500, denied that it was part of Asia. He called it a *nuevo mundo,* a "new world."

For its part, the Spanish crown called the continents *Las Indias* ("the Indies") and wanted to make them a new Spanish world.

The Spanish Conquest

Spanish adventurers ruled the peoples of the Caribbean with an iron hand. After subduing the Arawaks and Tainos on Hispaniola, the Spanish probed the mainland for gold and slaves. In 1513, Juan Ponce de León explored the coast of Florida and gave that peninsula its name. In the same year, Vasco Núñez de Balboa crossed the Isthmus of Darien (Panama) and became the first European to see the Pacific Ocean. Rumors of rich Indian kingdoms in the interior encouraged other Spaniards, including hardened veterans of the *reconquista,* to launch an invasion. They had the support of the Spanish monarchs, who offered successful conquistadors (conquerors) titles, vast estates, and Indian laborers to farm them.

Hernán Cortés (1485–1547) conquered an empire and destroyed a civilization. Cortés came from a family of minor gentry in Spain and, seeking military adventure and material gain, sailed to Santo Domingo in 1506. Ambitious and charismatic, he distinguished himself in battle, putting down a revolt and serving in the conquest of Cuba. These exploits and marriage to a well-connected Spanish woman won Cortés an extensive Cuban estate and a series of administrative appointments.

Eager to increase his fortune, Cortés jumped at a chance in 1519 to lead an expedition to the mainland. He landed with 600 men near the Mayan settlement of Potonchan, which he quickly overpowered. Then Cortés got lucky. The defeated Mayans presented him with slave women to serve as servants and concubines. Among them was Malinali, a young woman of noble birth and, a Spanish soldier noted, "of pleasing appearance and sharp-witted and outward-going." Malinali also spoke Nahuatl, the

Malinche and Cortés

This Aztec pictograph (c. 1540) shows Cortés with Malinche (Mariana in Spanish), his Nahuatl-speaking interpreter, advisor, and mistress. Signifying her dual identity as an Indian and a European, Malinche wears native clothes but holds a rosary. Bibliothèque Nationale de France, Paris.

For more help analyzing this image, see the Online Study Guide at **bedfordstmartins .com/henrettaconcise**.

Aztecs' language. Cortés took her as his mistress and interpreter, and soon she became his guide. When the Spanish leader learned from Malinali the extent of the Aztec empire, his goal became power rather than plunder. He would depose its king, Moctezuma [*mok-tah-ZOO-mah*], and take over his realm.

Of Malinali's motives for helping Cortés, there is no record. Like his Spanish followers, she may have been dazzled by his powerful personality. She may have calculated that Cortés was her best hope for escaping slavery and reclaiming her noble status. Whatever her reasons, Malinali's loyalty was complete. As the Spanish marched on the Aztec capital of Tenochtitlán, she risked her life by warning Cortés of a surprise attack in the city of Cholula, and she helped him to negotiate his way into the Aztec capital. "Without her," concluded Bernal Díaz del Castillo, the Spanish chronicler of the conquest, the Spaniards would "have been unable to surmount many difficulties."

Awed by the military prowess of the Spanish invaders, Moctezuma received Cortés with great ceremony, only to become his captive. When the emperor's supporters tried to expel the invaders, they faced superior European military technology. The sight of the Spaniards in full metal armor, with guns that shook the heavens and inflicted devastating wounds, made a deep impression on the Aztecs, who knew how to purify gold but not how to produce iron tools or weapons. Moreover, the Aztecs had no wheeled carts or cavalry, and their warriors, fighting on foot with flint- or obsidian-tipped spears and arrows, were no match for mounted Spanish conquistadors wielding steel swords and aided by vicious attack dogs. Although heavily outnumbered and suffering great losses, Cortés and his men were able to fight their way out of the Aztec capital.

Winning a battle was one thing; conquering an empire was another. Had Moctezuma ruled a united empire, he could have overwhelmed the 600 well-armed Spanish invaders. But many Indian peoples hated the Aztecs, and Cortés deftly exploited their anger. With the help of Malinali, now known by the honorific Nahuatl name Malinche, he formed military alliances with the subject peoples whose wealth had been seized by Aztec nobles and whose people had been sacrificed to the Aztec sun god. The Aztec empire collapsed, the victim not of superior military technology but of a vast internal rebellion instigated by the wily Cortés (see American Voices, p. 25).

The Spanish also had a silent ally: disease. Separated from the Eurasian land mass for thousands of years, the inhabitants of the Americas had no immunities to common European diseases. A massive smallpox epidemic lasting seventy days ravaged Tenochtitlán after the Spanish exodus, "striking everywhere in the city," according to an Aztec source, and killing Moctezuma's brother and thousands more. "They could not move, they could not stir. . . . Covered, mantled with pustules, very many people died of them." Subsequent outbreaks of smallpox, influenza, and measles killed hundreds of thousands of Indians and sapped the survivors' morale. Exploiting this demographic weakness, Cortés quickly extended Spanish rule over the Aztec empire. His lieutenants then moved against the Mayan city-states of the Yucatán Peninsula, eventually conquering them as well.

In 1524, Francisco Pizarro led a Spanish military expedition toward Peru, home of the rich and powerful Inca empire, which stretched 2,000 miles along the Pacific coast of South America. To govern this far-flung empire, the Inca rulers had laid 24,000 miles of roads and built dozens of administrative centers, carefully constructed of

Cortés and Moctezuma Meet BERNAL DÍAZ DEL CASTILLO

Bernal Díaz was an unlikely chronicler of great events. Born poor, he went to America as a common soldier in 1514 and served under conquistadors in Panama and Cuba. In 1519, he joined Cortés's expedition and received an estate in present-day Guatemala, where he lived out his life. In his old age, Díaz wrote *The True History of the Conquest of New Spain,* a compelling memoir written from a soldier's perspective.

When we arrived near to Mexico, . . . the Great Moctezuma got down from his litter, and those great Caciques [aristocrats] supported him with their arms beneath a marvelously rich canopy of green coloured feathers with much gold and silver embroidery . . . which was wonderful to look at. The Great Moctezuma was richly attired according to his usage, and he was shod with sandals, the soles were of gold and the upper part adorned with precious stones. . . .

Many other Lords walked before the Great Moctezuma, sweeping the ground where he would tread and spreading cloths on it, so that he should not tread on the earth. Not one of these chieftains dared even to think of looking him in the face, but kept their eyes lowered with great reverence. . . .

When Cortés was told that the Great Moctezuma was approaching, and he saw him coming, he dismounted from his horse, and when he was near Moctezuma, they simultaneously paid great reverence to one another. Moctezuma bade him welcome and our Cortés replied through Doña Marina [Malinche, Cortés's Indian mistress and interpreter] wishing him very good health. . . . And then Cortés brought out a necklace which he had ready at hand, made of glass stones, . . . which have within them many patterns of diverse colours, these were strung on a cord of gold and with musk so that it should have a sweet scent, and he placed it round the neck of the Great Moctezuma. . . .

Then Cortés through the mouth of Doña Marina told him that now his heart rejoiced having seen such a great Prince, and that he took it as a great honour that he had come in person to meet him. . . .

Thus space was made for us to enter the streets of Mexico, without being so much crowded. But who could now count the multitude of men and women and boys who were in the streets and in canoes on the canals, who had come out to see us. It was indeed wonderful. . . .

They took us to lodge in some large houses, where there were apartments for all of us. . . .

Cortés thanked Moctezuma through our interpreters, and Moctezuma replied, "Malinche, you and your brethren are in your own house, rest awhile," and then he went to his palaces, which were not far away, and we divided our lodgings by companies, and placed the artillery pointing in a convenient direction, and [we were ordered] . . . to be much on the alert, both the cavalry and all of us soldiers. A sumptuous dinner was provided for us according to their use and custom, and we ate it at once. So this was our lucky and daring entry into the great city of Tenochtitlán Mexico on the 8th day of November the year of our Saviour Jesus Christ, 1519.

SOURCE: Bernal Díaz del Castillo, *The True History of the Conquest of New Spain,* trans. A. P. Maudslay (1632; London: Routledge, 1928), 272–275.

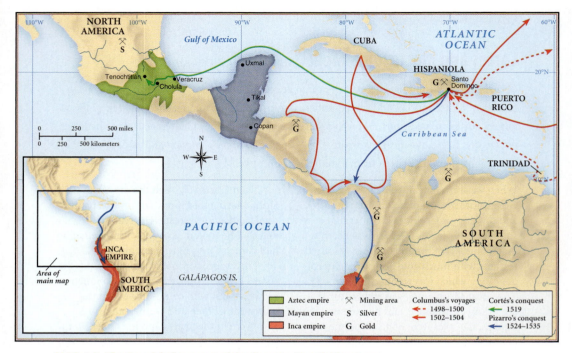

MAP 1.3 The Spanish Conquest of the Great Indian Civilizations

The Spanish first invaded and settled the islands of the Caribbean. Rumors of a golden civilization led to Cortés's invasion of the Aztec empire in central Mexico in 1519. By 1535, other Spanish conquistadors had conquered the Mayan temple cities of the Yucatán Peninsula and the Inca empire in Peru, completing one of the great conquests in world history.

For more help analyzing this map, see the Online Study Guide at **bedfordstmartins.com/henrettaconcise.**

finely crafted stone. An Inca king, claiming divine status, ruled the empire with the help of a bureaucracy staffed by noblemen. By the time Pizarro and his small force of 168 men and 67 horses finally reached Peru in 1532, half of the Inca population had died from European diseases spread by Indian traders. Weakened militarily and fighting over succession to the throne, the Inca nobility was easy prey for Pizarro's army. In only thirteen years, Spain had become the master of the wealthiest and most populous regions of the Western Hemisphere (Map 1.3).

The Spanish invasion changed life forever in the Americas. Disease and warfare wiped out virtually all of the Indians of Hispaniola — at least 300,000 people. In Peru, the population plummeted from nine million in 1530 to fewer than 500,000 a century later. Mesoamerica suffered the greatest losses: In one of the great demographic disasters in world history, its population of thirty million Native Americans in 1500 had dwindled to just three million in 1650.

Once the conquistadors had triumphed, the Spanish monarchs quickly created an elaborate bureaucratic empire. From its headquarters in Madrid, the Council of the Indies issued laws and decrees to viceroys, governors, judges, and other Spanish officials in America. But the conquistadors and their descendants remained powerful because they secured judgeships and other bureaucratic positions for family members and held *encomiendas*, royal grants that gave them legal control of the labor of the native population. They ruthlessly exploited the surviving Native Americans, forcing them to raise crops and cattle both for local consumption and for export to Europe. The Spaniards also permanently altered the natural environment: The livestock (horses, cattle, sheep, and goats), grain crops (wheat, barley, and rice), and human diseases (smallpox, measles, chickenpox, influenza, malaria, and yellow fever) of Africa and Eurasia became part of life in the Americas.

The Spanish conquest had a significant ecological impact on Europe and Africa as well. In a process that historians call the **Columbian Exchange**, the food products of the Western Hemisphere — especially maize, potatoes, manioc, sweet potatoes, and tomatoes — were transferred to other continents, where they significantly increased agricultural yields and population growth. Thus, in the century after these crops reached China (around 1700), the population doubled. A less welcome transfer was the virulent strain of syphilis Columbus's crew members took back to Europe with them. Nor was that all. The gold and silver that had formerly honored Aztec gods now gilded the Catholic churches of Europe and flowed into the countinghouses of Spain. From there, vast amounts of silver flowed to China, home to 125 million people in 1650, where it was in great demand for use as money. In exchange, Spain received valuable silks, spices, and ceramics. As Spain's American wealth flowed around the globe between 1540 and 1640, it made that nation the richest and most powerful in Europe. Indeed, Spain now claimed a "lordship of all the world."

Meanwhile, the once magnificent civilizations of Mexico and Peru lay in ruins. "Of all these wonders" — the great city of Tenochtitlán, the bountiful irrigated fields, the rich orchards, the overflowing markets — "all is overthrown and lost, nothing left standing," recalled Bernal Díaz, who had been a young soldier in Cortés's army. The surviving Indian peoples lost a vital part of their cultural identity when Spanish priests suppressed many traditional religious ceremonies and gave Catholic identities to Indian gods. As early as 1531, an Indian convert reported a vision of a dark-skinned Virgin Mary, later known as the Virgin of Guadalupe, a Christian version of the "corn mother" who traditionally protected the maize crop.

A new society took shape on the lands emptied by disease and exploitation. Between 1500 and 1650, at least 350,000 Spaniards migrated to Mesoamerica and western South America. More than 75 percent were men — at first poor, unmarried, and unskilled refugees from Andalusia and later a broader mix of Castilians — and many of them took Indian women as wives or mistresses. Consequently, a substantial mixed-race population, called **mestizos**, quickly appeared, along with an elaborate race-based **caste system**. Around 1800, near the end of the colonial era, Spanish America stretched from the tip of South America to the northern border of present-day California. It contained about 17 million people: a dominant caste of 3.2 million Spaniards; 5.5 million people of mixed Indian and European genetic

▶ Compare and contrast the main characteristics of traditional European society, West African society, and the Native American societies of the eastern woodlands.

▶ Why and how did Portugal and Spain pursue overseas commerce and conquest?

and cultural heritage; 1.0 million enslaved Africans; and 7.5 million Indians, who lived mostly on marginal lands. The sudden and harsh collision among the peoples of three old worlds—European, African, Native American—transformed them all as it integrated them into a single Atlantic world.

The Protestant Reformation and the Rise of England, 1500–1620

Even as Catholic fervor prompted the forced conversion of Indians in America and Muslims and Jews in Spain, Christianity ceased to be a unifying force in European society. During the 1520s, religious doctrines preached by Martin Luther and other reformers divided Europe between Catholic and Protestant states and plunged the continent into a century-long series of religious wars. During these conflicts, France replaced Spain as the most powerful European state, and Holland and England emerged as Protestant nations determined to colonize the Western Hemisphere.

The Protestant Movement

Over the centuries, the Catholic Church had become a large and wealthy institution. Renaissance popes and cardinals used the Church's wealth to patronize the arts and enrich themselves. Pope Leo X (r. 1513–1521) received half a million ducats (about $20 million in 2008 dollars) a year from the sale of religious offices. Such corruption encouraged ordinary priests and monks to seek economic or sexual favors. One English reformer denounced the clergy as a "gang of scoundrels" who should be "rid of their vices or stripped of their authority," but he was ignored. Other critics of the Church, such as Jan Hus of Bohemia, were executed as heretics.

In 1517, Martin Luther, a German monk and professor at the university in Wittenberg, took up the cause of reform. Luther viewed the world as the site of a primordial combat between God and the devil. His *Ninety-five Theses* condemned the Church for encouraging practices that condoned human depravity, such as the granting of **indulgences**, certificates that allegedly pardoned sinners from punishment in the afterlife. Outraged by Luther's charges, the pope dismissed him from the Church, and the Holy Roman Emperor, King Charles I of Spain (r. 1516–1556), threatened Luther with punishment. However, the princes of northern Germany, who were resisting the emperor's authority for political reasons, protected Luther from arrest, thus allowing the protest movement to survive.

Luther took issue with Roman Catholic doctrine in three major respects. First, he rejected the belief that Christians could secure salvation through good deeds or the purchase of indulgences; instead, Luther argued that people could be saved only by grace, which came as a "free gift" from God. Second, he downplayed the role of the clergy as mediators between God and the people and proclaimed a much more democratic outlook. "Our baptism consecrates us all without exception and makes us all priests." Third, he said that believers must look to the Bible—not to Church officials or doctrine—as the ultimate authority in matters of faith. So that every literate German could read the Bible, for centuries available only in Latin, Luther translated it into German.

Peasants as well as princes heeded Luther's attack on authority and, to his dismay, mounted social protests of their own. In 1524, many German peasants rebelled against their manorial lords. Fearing social revolution, Luther urged obedience to established political institutions and condemned the teachings of the Anabaptists (who rejected the baptism of infants) and other groups of religious dissidents. Assured of Luther's social conservatism, most princes in northern Germany embraced his teachings and broke from Rome, thereby gaining the power to appoint bishops and control the Church's property within their domains. To restore Catholic doctrine and his own political authority, the Holy Roman Emperor dispatched armies to Germany, setting off a generation of warfare. Eventually, the Peace of Augsburg (1555) divided Germany into Lutheran states in the north and Catholic principalities in the south.

John Calvin, a French theologian in Geneva, Switzerland, established the most rigorous Protestant regime. Even more than Luther, Calvin stressed human weakness and God's omnipotence. His *Institutes of the Christian Religion* (1536) depicted God as an awesome and absolute sovereign who governed the "wills of men so as to move precisely to that end directed by him." Calvin preached the doctrine of **predestination**, the idea that God chooses certain people for salvation before they are born and condemns the rest to eternal damnation. In Geneva, he set up a model Christian community, eliminating bishops and placing spiritual power in the hands of ministers chosen by their congregations. Ministers and pious laymen ruled the city, prohibiting frivolity and luxury. "We know," wrote Calvin, "that man is of so perverse and crooked a nature, that everyone would scratch out his neighbor's eyes if there were no bridle to hold them in." Calvin's authoritarian doctrine won converts all over Europe; it became the theology of the Huguenots in France, the Reformed churches in Belgium and Holland, and the Presbyterians and Puritans in Scotland and England.

In England, King Henry VIII (r. 1509–1547) initially opposed Protestantism. However, in 1534, when the pope refused to annul his marriage to the Spanish princess Catherine of Aragon, Henry broke with Rome and placed himself at the head of a national church, the Church of England, which promptly granted the king an annulment. Henry made few changes in Catholic doctrine, organization, and ritual, but he allowed the spread of Protestant teachings. Faced with popular pressure for greater reform, Henry's daughter and successor, Queen Elizabeth I (r. 1558–1603), approved a Protestant confession of faith that incorporated both the Lutheran doctrine of salvation by grace and the Calvinist belief in predestination. To satisfy traditionalists, Elizabeth retained the Catholic ritual of Holy Communion—now conducted in English rather than Latin—as well as the hierarchy of bishops and archbishops.

Elizabeth's compromises angered radical Protestants, who condemned the power of bishops as "proude, pontificall and tyrannous" as well as "anti-Christian and devilish and contrary to the Scriptures." These reformers took inspiration from the presbyterian system pioneered in Calvin's Geneva and developed by John Knox for the Church of Scotland. In Scotland, congregations elected lay elders (presbyters) who helped ministers and participated in the synods (councils) that decided Church doctrine. By 1600, five hundred Church of England clergy demanded the elimination of bishops and a republican-like presbyterian form of church government.

Other radical English Protestants called themselves "unspotted lambs of the Lord" or Puritans. These extraordinarily devout Calvinists wanted to "purify" the church of all Catholic teachings and magical or idolatrous practices. Puritans refused to burn incense or to pray to dead saints; a carefully argued sermon was the focus of their religious service. They placed special emphasis on the "conversion experience," the felt infusion of God's grace, and the "calling," the duty to serve God in one's ordinary life and work. To ensure that all men and women had direct access to God's commands in the Bible, Puritans encouraged literacy and Bible study. Finally, most Puritans wanted authority over spiritual and financial matters to rest primarily with local congregations. Eventually, thousands of Puritans and Presbyterian migrants would establish churches in North America based on these radical Protestant doctrines.

The Dutch and English Challenge Spain

Luther's challenge to Catholicism in 1517 came just two years before Cortés began his conquest of the Aztec empire, and the two events became linked. Gold and silver from Mexico and Peru made Spain the wealthiest nation in Europe and King Philip II (r. 1556–1598) its most powerful ruler. In addition to Spanish America, Philip presided over wealthy states in Italy; the commercial and manufacturing provinces of the Spanish Netherlands (present-day Holland and Belgium); and, after 1580, Portugal and all its possessions in America, Africa, and the East Indies. "If the Romans were able to rule the world simply by ruling the Mediterranean," boasted a Spanish priest, "what of the man who rules the Atlantic and Pacific oceans, since they surround the world?"

An ardent Catholic, Philip tried to root out Islam in North Africa and Protestantism in the Netherlands and England. He failed to do either. A massive Spanish fleet defeated a Turkish armada at Lepanto in the eastern Mediterranean in 1571, freeing 15,000 Christian galley slaves, but Muslims continued to rule all of North Africa. Moreover, the Spanish-controlled Netherlands remained a hotbed of Calvinism. These Dutch- and Flemish-speaking provinces had grown wealthy from trade with the Portuguese empire and from weaving wool and linen. To protect their Calvinist faith and political liberties, they revolted against Spanish rule in 1566. After fifteen years of war, the seven northern provinces declared their independence, becoming the Dutch Republic (or Holland) in 1581.

Elizabeth I of England had aided the Dutch cause by dispatching 6,000 troops to Holland. She also supported military expeditions to extend direct English rule over Gaelic-speaking Catholic regions of Ireland. Calling the Irish "wild savages" who were "more barbarous and more brutish in their customs . . . than in any other part of the world," English troops brutally massacred thousands, prefiguring the treatment of Indians in North America. In 1588, to meet Elizabeth's challenge, Philip sent a Spanish Armada — 130 ships and 30,000 men — against England. Philip intended to restore Catholicism to England and Ireland and then to wipe out Calvinism in Holland. But he failed utterly when English ships and a fierce storm destroyed the Spanish fleet.

Nevertheless, Philip continued to spend his American gold and silver on religious wars. This ill-advised militaristic policy diverted resources from industrial investment in Spain. Oppressed by high taxes on agriculture and fearful of military service, more than 200,000 residents of Castile, the richest region of Spain, migrated to America. By the time of Philip's death in 1598, Spain was in serious economic decline.

Elizabeth I (r. 1558–1603)

Dressed in richly decorated clothes that symbolize her power, Queen Elizabeth I relishes the destruction of the Spanish Armada, which appears in the background. The queen's hand rests on a globe, asserting England's claims in the Western Hemisphere and its imperial ambitions. Woburn Abbey Collection, by permission of the Marquess of Tavistock and the Trustees of the Bedford Estates.

As mighty Spain faltered, tiny Holland prospered—the economic miracle of the seventeenth century. Amsterdam emerged as the financial capital of northern Europe, and the Dutch Republic replaced Portugal as the dominant trader in Indonesia and West Africa. Dutch merchants also looked across the Atlantic: They created the West India Company (1621), which invested in sugar plantations in Brazil and established the fur-trading colony of New Netherland along the Hudson River.

England also emerged as a European power in the sixteenth century, its economy stimulated, as colonial advocate Richard Hakluyt noted, by a "wounderful increase of our people." As England's population soared from three million in 1500 to five million in 1630, its monarchs supported the expansion of commerce and manufacturing. English merchants had long supplied European weavers with high-quality wool; around 1500, they created their own **outwork** textile industry. Merchants bought wool from the owners of great estates and then sent it "out" to landless peasants to spin and weave into cloth in their small cottages. The government aided textile entrepreneurs by setting low rates for wages, and it helped merchants by awarding monopoly privileges in foreign markets. Queen Elizabeth granted monopolies to the Levant Company (to trade tin for silk and spices in Turkey) in 1581, the Guinea Company (to exchange manufactures for slaves in Africa) in 1588, and the East India Company (to import cotton cloth and spices from India) in 1600.

This system of state-assisted manufacturing and trade became known as **mercantilism**. By encouraging textile production, Elizabeth hoped to reduce imports and increase exports, giving England a favorable balance of trade. The queen and her advisors wanted gold and silver to flow into the country in payment for English goods, enriching the merchant community and stimulating further economic expansion. Increased trade also boosted import duties, which swelled the royal treasury and the monarch's power. By 1600, Elizabeth's mercantile policies had laid the foundations for overseas colonization. Now the English, as well as the Dutch, had the merchant fleets and wealth needed to challenge Spain's domination of the Western Hemisphere.

The Social Causes of English Colonization

England sent more than merchant fleets and manufactures to America. The rapid growth of the English population provided a large body of settlers, many of them fleeing economic hardship caused by an upheaval known today as the **Price Revolution**. The massive influx of American gold and silver had doubled the money supply of Europe and sparked a major inflation.

The landed nobility in England was the first casualty of the Price Revolution. Aristocrats customarily rented out their estates on long leases for fixed rents, which provided a secure income and plenty of leisure. As one English nobleman put it, "We eat and drink and rise up to play and this is to live like a gentleman." Then inflation struck. In less than two generations, the price of goods tripled while the nobility's income from rents barely increased. As the purchasing power of the aristocracy fell, that of the **gentry** and the yeomen rose. The gentry, who were nonnoble landholders with substantial estates, kept pace with inflation by renting land on short leases at higher rates. Yeomen, described by a European traveler as "middle people of a condition between gentlemen and peasants," owned small farms that they worked with family labor. As wheat prices tripled, yeomen used the profits to build larger houses and provide their children with land.

Economics influenced politics. As nobles lost wealth, the influence of their branch of Parliament, the House of Lords, weakened. Simultaneously, members of the rising gentry entered the House of Commons, the political voice of the propertied classes, and demanded that the Commons have power over taxation and other policies. Thus the Price Revolution encouraged the rise of representative institutions in which rich commoners and property-owning yeomen had a voice. This development had profound consequences for English — and American — political history.

The Price Revolution likewise transformed the lives of peasants, who made up three-fourths of the English population. The economic stimulus of Spanish gold spurred the expansion of the textile industry. To increase the supply of wool, profit-minded landlords and wool merchants persuaded Parliament to pass **enclosure acts**, laws that allowed owners to kick peasants off their lands, fence in their fields, and put sheep to graze there. The dispossessed peasant families lived on the brink of poverty, spinning and weaving wool or working as agricultural wage laborers. Wealthy men had "taken farms into their hands," an observer noted in 1600, "whereby the peasantry of England is decayed and become servants to gentlemen."

The coming of "The Little Ice Age," a century-long series of remarkably long and cold winters that began about 1600, magnified the impact of these social changes. As crop yields diminished, grain prices soared and social unrest increased. "Thieves and rogues do swarm the highways," warned one justice of the peace, "and bastards be multiplied in parishes." Seeking work, thousands of young men and women migrated to America as **indentured** servants; in exchange for their passage across the Atlantic, they sold their labor (and freedom) for four or five years. Dispossessed peasants and weavers threatened by a recession in the cloth trade were likewise ready to try their luck elsewhere. Thousands of yeomen families were also on the move, looking for affordable land on which to settle their children. By 1640, over 100,000 English and Scots had migrated to Ulster in Ireland, and 50,000 more had moved to North America and the Caribbean Islands. As Puritans looked for religious freedom and peasants for economic security, they formed a powerful migratory movement.

▶ How did Protestant religious doctrine differ from that of Roman Catholicism?

▶ What factors prompted the large-scale migration of English men and women to America?

▶ What was the impact of the Columbian Exchange in food, people, diseases, and gold on the Americas, Europe, and Africa?

SUMMARY

In this chapter, we have seen that the first human inhabitants of the Western Hemisphere were hunter-gatherers from Asia. Their descendants would form many cultures and speak many languages. In Mesoamerica, the Mayan and Aztec peoples developed populous agricultural societies and highly sophisticated religious and political systems; so, too, did the Incas along the western coast of South America. The Hopewell, Pueblo, and Mississippian peoples of North America likewise created complex societies and cultures; but in 1500, most Indians north of the Rio Grande lived in small self-governing communities of foragers, hunters, and farmers.

We have also traced the maritime expansion that brought Europeans to the Americas. The Spanish crown, eager to share in Portugal's mercantile success, financed expeditions to find new trade routes to Asia. When Christopher Columbus revealed a "new world" to Europeans in 1492, Spanish adventurers undertook to conquer it. By 1535, conquistadors had destroyed the civilizations of Mesoamerica and Peru and inadvertently introduced diseases that would kill millions of Native Americans. Through the Columbian Exchange of crops, animals, plants, and diseases, there was a significant alteration in the ecology of much of the world.

Population growth, religious warfare, and American gold and silver transformed European society in the sixteenth century. As the cost of religious warfare sapped Spain's strength, the rise of strong governments in Holland, France, and England, along with a class of increasingly powerful merchants, enhanced the economies of those countries and whetted their appetite for overseas expansion.

Connections: Society

In the essay that opens Part One, we noted that "Europeans, with their steel weapons, attractive trade goods, and diseases, shredded the fabric of most Native American cultures." In this chapter, you have read the first part of that story: the Spanish invasion of Mesoamerica and South America. In Chapter 2, we compare the interaction of Native Americans with various European peoples: the Spanish in New Mexico and Florida, the French in Louisiana, and the Dutch and English in New York and New England. Chapter 2 concludes with an analysis of Native Americans in the English colonies as of 1700. Later chapters explain how Native Americans continued to shape the history of the eastern seaboard, even as their numbers and strength underwent a sharp decline. Part One concludes with the Great War for Empire (1756–1763). That war was known in the British colonies as the French and Indian War and rightly so: It was yet another effort by Native Americans to defend their lands from Anglo-American settlers.

TIMELINE

13,000–3000 B.C.	▸ Asian migrants reach North America	**1513**	▸ Juan Ponce de León explores Florida
3000 B.C.	▸ Farming begins in Mesoamerica	**1517**	▸ Martin Luther sparks Protestant Reformation
A.D. 100–400	▸ Flourishing of Hopewell culture	**1519–1521**	▸ Hernán Cortés conquers Aztec empire
300	▸ Rise of Mayan civilization	**1520–1650**	▸ Price Revolution
500	▸ Zenith of Teotihuacán civilization	**1532–1535**	▸ Francisco Pizarro vanquishes Incas
600	▸ Pueblo cultures emerge	**1534**	▸ Henry VIII establishes Church of England
632–1100	▸ Arab people adopt Islam and spread its influence	**1536**	▸ John Calvin publishes *Institutes of the Christian Religion*
800–1350	▸ Development of Mississippian culture	**1550–1630**	▸ English crown supports mercantilism
1096–1291	▸ Crusades link Europe with Arab learning		▸ Parliament passes enclosure acts
1300–1450	▸ Italian Renaissance		
1325	▸ Aztecs establish capital at Tenochtitlán	**1556–1598**	▸ Reign of Philip II, king of Spain
1430 on	▸ Portugal trades along West and Central African coasts	**1558–1603**	▸ Reign of Elizabeth I, queen of England
		1560–1620	▸ Growth of English Puritan movement
1492	▸ Christopher Columbus makes first voyage to America	**1588**	▸ Storms and English ships destroy Spanish Armada
1498	▸ Portugal's Vasco da Gama reaches India		

The coming of those settlers to the Chesapeake region and New England between 1600 and 1675 will be a major theme of Chapter 2.

FOR FURTHER EXPLORATION

Kenneth Pomeranz, *The Great Divergence: Europe, China, and the Making of the Modern World Economy* (2000), examines the impact of the Americas on world history. Brian M. Fagan, *The Great Journey: The People of Ancient America* (1987), and Alvin M. Josephy Jr., ed., *America in 1492: The World of the Indian Peoples Before the Arrival of Columbus* (1991) are reliable and vividly written studies. For the European background of colonization, consult George Huppert's highly readable study, *After the Black Death* (2nd ed., 1998); see also the engaging biography by William D. Phillips, with Carla Rahn Phillips, *The Worlds of Christopher Columbus* (1992). Two Public Broadcasting Service (PBS) videos examine the ancient civilizations of Mesoamerica: *Odyssey: Maya Lords of the Jungle* (1 hour) and *Odyssey: The Incas* (1 hour). Also, log onto "1492: An Ongoing Voyage" (**www.loc.gov/exhibits/1492/intro.html**) for images and analysis of the native cultures of the Western Hemisphere.

Peter Laslett, *The World We Have Lost* (3rd ed., 1984), paints a vivid portrait of seventeenth-century English society; see also Andrew McRae, *God Speed the Plough* (2002), and Ethan Shagan, *Popular Politics and the English Reformation* (2003). "Martin Luther" (**www.luther.de/e/index.html**) offers biographies and striking images of the era of the Protestant Reformation. Giles Milton, *Nathaniel's Nutmeg* (1999), tells the rousing tale of European competition for the spice trade and, subsequently, the New World.

TEST YOUR KNOWLEDGE

To assess your mastery of the material in this chapter and for Web sites, images, and documents related to this chapter, visit **bedfordstmartins.com/henrettaconcise**.

The Invasion and Settlement of North America

1550–1700

> Indians are the rock,
> European peoples are the
> sea, and history seems a
> constant storm.
>
> — Richard White,
> *The Middle Ground* (1991)

Establishing colonies in North America was not for the faint of heart. First came a long voyage over stormy, dangerous waters; shipwrecks, spoiled food, and disease claimed many lives along the way. Of three hundred migrants to New France in 1663, for example, seventy died en route. Those who survived had to build shelters and plant crops, and many faced hostile Indian peoples. "We neither fear them nor trust them," declared Puritan settler Francis Higginson, but rely on "our musketeers." Still, despite great risks and uncertain rewards, English, French, and Spanish migrants by the tens of thousands crossed the Atlantic during the seventeenth century. They were either driven by poverty and religious persecution at home or drawn by the promise of land, gold, or — according to one pious migrant — promoting "the Christian religion to such People as yet live in Darkness."

For Native Americans, the European invasion was a catastrophe. Whether they came as settlers, fur traders, or missionaries, the white-skinned people and their African slaves brought new diseases and religions that threatened the Indians' lives and cultures. "Our fathers had plenty of deer and skins, . . . and our coves were full of fish and fowl," Narragansett chief Miantonomi reminded the Montauk people in 1642, "but these English having gotten our land . . . their cows and horses eat the grass, and their hogs spoil our clam banks, and we shall all be starved." Miantonomi called for united resistance: "We [are] all Indians [and must] say brother to one another, . . . otherwise we shall all be gone shortly." The chief's unsuccessful plea foretold the course of North American history: The European invaders would advance, enslaved Africans would endure, and Indian peoples would decline.

The Rival Imperial Models of Spain, France, and Holland

In Mesoamerica, the Spanish seized the Indians' lands, converted many to Catholicism, and made them dig for gold and farm large estates. In the sparsely populated eastern regions of North America, French and Dutch merchants created fur-trading colonies, and the native peoples retained their lands and political autonomy. Whatever the Europeans' goals, Indian peoples diminished in numbers and soon rebelled.

New Spain: Colonization and Conversion

In their ceaseless quest for gold, Spanish explorers penetrated deep into the present-day United States. In the 1540s, Francisco Vásquez de Coronado searched in vain for the fabled seven golden cities of Cíbola; what he discovered instead were the southern reaches of the Grand Canyon, the Pueblo peoples of the Southwest, and the grasslands of Kansas. Meanwhile, Hernán de Soto and a force of 600 Spaniards were cutting a bloody swath across the Southeast, battling the Apalachees in northern Florida and the Coosas in northern Alabama but finding no gold (Map 2.1).

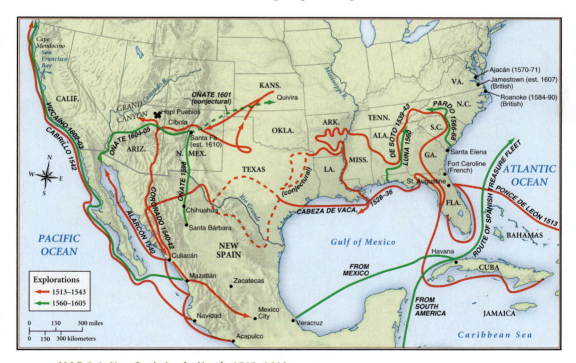

MAP 2.1 New Spain Looks North, 1513–1610

The search for gold drew Spanish explorers first to Florida and then deep into the present-day United States. When the wide-ranging expeditions of Hernán de Soto and Francisco Vásquez de Coronado failed to find gold or flourishing Indian civilizations, authorities in New Spain limited northern settlements to St. Augustine in Florida (to protect the treasure fleet) and Santa Fe in the upper Rio Grande Valley.

For more help analyzing this map, see the Online Study Guide at **bedfordstmartins.com/henrettaconcise**.

By the 1560s, Spanish officials had given up the search for gold and were focusing on the defense of their empire. Roving English "sea dogs" were plundering Spanish treasure ships, and French Protestants were settling in Spanish-claimed Florida. Following King Philip II's order to cast out the Frenchmen "by the best means," Spanish troops massacred 300 members of the "evil Lutheran sect" near the St. John River. To safeguard the route of the treasure fleet, Spain established a fort at St. Augustine in 1565, making it the first permanent European settlement in the future United States. However, raids by the Calusas and Timucuas wiped out a dozen other Spanish military outposts in Florida, and Algonquins destroyed Jesuit religious missions along the Atlantic coast, including one near the Chesapeake Bay.

These military setbacks and the urgings of Franciscan friars prompted Spanish leaders to adopt a new policy: They would conquer the Indian peoples by Christianizing them. The Comprehensive Orders for New Discoveries (1573) placed responsibility for pacification primarily in the hands of missionaries, not conquistadors. Over the next century, scores of Franciscan friars set up missions among the Apalachees in Florida and the Pueblo peoples in the lands the Spanish named Nuevo México. The friars often learned Indian languages, but they also systematically attacked the natives' culture. And their methods were anything but peaceful. Protected by Spanish soldiers, missionaries whipped Indians who continued to practice **polygamy**, smashed the Indians' religious idols, and punished anyone who worshipped traditional gods. On one occasion, forty-seven "sorcerers" in Nuevo México were whipped and sold into slavery.

La V.M. María de Jesús de Agreda, Predicando a los Chichimecos del Nuebo-méxico.

Conversion in New Mexico

Franciscan friars, aided by nuns of various religious orders, introduced Catholicism to the Indian peoples north of the Rio Grande. This 1631 engraving shows nun María de Jesús de Agreda preaching to nomadic peoples (the Chichimecos) in New Mexico. Nettie Lee Benson Latin American Collection, University of Texas at Austin.

Religious conversion, cultural assimilation, and forced labor went hand in hand. The Franciscans encouraged the Indians to talk, cook, dress, and walk like Spaniards. They ignored laws that protected the native peoples and allowed privileged Spanish landowners (*encomenderos*) to extract goods and forced labor from the native population. The missions themselves depended on Indian workers to grow crops and carry them to market.

Native Americans initially tolerated the Franciscans because they feared military reprisals and hoped to learn the friars' spiritual secrets. But when Christian prayers failed to protect their communities from European diseases, droughts, and raids by nomadic Apaches and Pawnees, many Pueblo people returned to their ancestral gods. The people of Hawikuh refused to become "wet-heads" (as the Indians called baptized Christians) "because with the water of baptism they would have to die."

In 1598, the tense relations between Indians and Spaniards in New Mexico exploded into open warfare. An expedition of 500 Spanish soldiers and settlers led by Juan de Oñate seized corn and clothing from the Pueblo peoples and murdered or raped those who resisted. When Indians of the Acoma pueblo retaliated by killing 11 soldiers, the Spanish troops destroyed the pueblo and murdered 800 men, women, and children. Faced with bitterly hostile native peoples, most settlers left New Mexico. In 1610, the Spanish returned, founded the town of Santa Fe, and reestablished the system of missions and forced labor. Over the next two generations, European diseases, forced tribute, and raids by nomadic plains Indians reduced the population of Pueblo peoples from 60,000 to just 17,000.

In 1680, in a carefully coordinated rebellion, the Indian shaman Popé and his followers killed more than 400 Spaniards and forced 1,500 colonists (and 500 Pueblo and Apache slaves) to flee 300 miles to El Paso. The Pueblo peoples burned "the seeds which the Spaniards sowed" and planted "only maize and beans, which were the crops of their ancestors." Repudiating Christianity, they desecrated churches and rebuilt the sacred kivas, the round stone structures in which they had long worshiped. Like many later Native American rebels, Popé marched forward while looking backward, hoping to restore the traditional way of life.

It was not to be. A decade later, Spain reasserted control over most of the Pueblo peoples. The oppressed natives rebelled again in 1696 and were again subdued. Exhausted by a generation of warfare, the Pueblos agreed to a compromise that allowed them to practice their own religion and avoid forced labor. In return, they accepted a dependent position in New Mexico and helped the Spanish defend their settlements and farms against nomadic Apaches and Comanches.

Spain had maintained its northern empire, but it failed to assimilate the Indian peoples. Some Pueblo Indians had married Spaniards, and their offspring formed a bicultural mestizo population, but most continued to practice the old ways. As a Franciscan friar admitted, "They are still drawn more by their idolatry and infidelity than by the Christian doctrine."

Spanish officials experienced a similar disappointment in Florida. In the early 1700s, English raids from Carolina destroyed most of the Spanish missions and killed or enslaved most Catholic converts. These setbacks persuaded Spanish officials to halt the settlement of the distant northern province of California. Santa Fe and St. Augustine stood alone as the northern outposts of Spain's American empire.

New France: Furs and Warfare

Far to the northeast, the French were also confronting native peoples. In the 1530s, Jacques Cartier had claimed the lands bordering the Gulf of St. Lawrence for France. The first permanent settlement came in 1608, when Samuel de Champlain founded the fur-trading post of Quebec. But the colony languished until 1662, when King Louis XIV (r. 1643–1714) turned New France into a royal colony and subsidized the migration of indentured servants. Servants served a term of thirty-six months, received a yearly salary, and could eventually lease a farm—terms far more generous than those for indentured servants in the English colonies.

Nonetheless, few people moved to New France, in part because it was a cold and forbidding country "at the end of the world." In addition, state policies and laws discouraged migration. To expand France's boundaries in Europe, Louis XIV drafted tens of thousands of men into military service. The Catholic monarch also barred Huguenots (French Calvinist Protestants) from migrating to New France. Moreover, the legal system gave peasants strong rights to their village lands in France, and migrants to New France found an oppressive, aristocratic- and church-dominated feudal system. In the village of Saint Ours in Quebec's fertile Richelieu Valley, for example, peasants paid 45 percent of their wheat crop to nobles and the Catholic Church. In 1698, the European population of the colony was only 15,200, compared to 100,000 residents in the English settlements.

Lacking settlers, New France became a vast enterprise for acquiring furs, which were in great demand in Europe to make felt hats and fur garments. To secure plush beaver pelts from the Huron Indians, who controlled trade north of the Great Lakes, Champlain provided the Huron with manufactured goods. Selling pelts, an Indian told a French priest, "makes kettles, hatchets, swords, knives, bread." It also made guns, which Champlain sold to the Huron to fight the expansionist-minded Five Iroquois Nations of New York, who wanted to run the fur trade. Searching for more furs, explorer Jacques Marquette reached the Mississippi River in present-day Wisconsin in 1673 and traveled as far south as Arkansas. Then, in 1681, Robert de La Salle traveled down the majestic river to the Gulf of Mexico, trading as he went. As a French priest noted with disgust, La Salle and his associates hoped "to buy all the Furs and Skins of the remotest Savages, who, as they thought, did not know their Value; and so enrich themselves in one single voyage." To honor Louis XIV, La Salle named the region Louisiana, where the port of New Orleans on the Gulf of Mexico was established in 1718.

Despite their small numbers, the French had a disastrous impact. By unwittingly introducing European diseases, they triggered epidemics that killed from 25 to 90 percent of many Indian peoples. Moreover, by bartering guns for furs, the French (and the Dutch) sparked a series of deadly wars. The Five Iroquois Nations were the prime aggressors. From their strategic geographical location in central New York, the Iroquois could obtain guns and goods from Dutch merchants at Albany and quickly attack other Indian peoples. Iroquois warriors moved to the east along the Mohawk River as far as New England and south along the Delaware and Susquehanna rivers as far as the Carolinas. They traveled north via Lake Champlain and the Richelieu River to Quebec. And they journeyed west via the Great Lakes to exploit the rich fur-bearing lands of the upper Mississippi River Valley.

The rise of the Iroquois was breathtakingly rapid. In 1600, the Iroquois numbered about 30,000 and lived in large towns of 500 to 2,000 inhabitants. Over the next two decades, they organized themselves in a confederation of Five Nations: Senecas, Cayugas, Onondagas, Oneidas, and Mohawks. Partly in response to a virulent smallpox epidemic in 1633, which cut their number by one-third, the Iroquois waged a series of devastating wars against the Hurons (1649), Neutrals (1651), Eries (1657), and Susquehannocks (1660)—all Iroquoian-speaking peoples. They razed the villages and killed most of the men, cooking and eating their flesh to gain access to their spiritual powers. They took thousands of women and children as captives and ritually adopted them into Iroquois lineages. The conquered Hurons met a more dire fate: They simply ceased to exist as a distinct people; survivors trekked westward and joined other remnant peoples to form a new tribe, the Wyandots.

Between 1625 and 1763, hundreds of French priests lived among the Iroquois and other peoples of the Great Lakes region. Most were members of the Society of Jesus (or Jesuits), a Catholic religious order founded to combat the Protestant Reformation. These priests—unlike the Spanish Franciscan monks—came to understand and respect the Indians' values. One Jesuit noted the Huron belief that "our souls have desires which are inborn and concealed, yet are made known by means of dreams." For their part, many Indian peoples initially welcomed the French "Black Robes" as powerful spiritual beings with magical secrets, including the ability to forge iron. But when prayers to the Christian god did not protect them from disease, the Indians grew skeptical. A Peoria chief charged that a priest's "fables are good only in his own country; we have our own [religious beliefs], which do not make us die as his do." When a drought struck, Indians lashed out at the missionaries. "If you cannot make rain, they speak of nothing less than making away with you," lamented one Jesuit.

Whatever the limits of their spiritual powers, the French Jesuits did not exploit Indian labor. Moreover, they tried to keep brandy, which wreaked havoc among the natives, from becoming a bargaining chip in the French fur trade. And the Jesuits won converts by adapting Christian beliefs to the Indians' needs. In the 1690s, for example, the Jesuits introduced the cult of the Virgin Mary to the young women of the Illinois people. Its emphasis on chastity reinforced existing beliefs among the Illinois that unmarried women were "masters of their own body."

Despite the Jesuits' efforts, the French fur-trading system brought cultural devastation. Epidemics killed tens of thousands of Indians, and Iroquois warriors murdered thousands more. Nor did the Iroquois escape unscathed. In 1666 and again in the 1690s, French armies invaded their lands, burned villages and cornfields, and killed many warriors. "Everywhere there was peril and everywhere mourning," recalled an oral Iroquois legend.

New Netherland: Commerce and Conquest

By 1600, Holland had emerged as the financial and commercial hub of northern Europe. Exploiting the country's strategic location at the mouth of the great Rhine River and near the Baltic sea, enterprising Dutch merchants controlled the trade of northwestern Europe. Dutch entrepreneurs dominated the European banking, insurance, and textile industries; Dutch merchants owned more tons of shipping and employed more sailors than did the combined fleets of England, France, and Spain. Indeed, the Dutch managed much of the world's commerce. During their struggle for independence from Spain (and its Portuguese dependency), the Dutch seized Portuguese forts in Africa, Brazil, and Indonesia, gaining control of the Atlantic trade in slaves and the Indian Ocean commerce in East Indian spices and Chinese silks and ceramics.

In 1609, Dutch merchants dispatched an Englishman, Henry Hudson, to locate a western route to the riches of the East Indies. After Hudson explored the North American river that bears his name, the merchants built Fort Orange (Albany) in 1614 to trade for furs with the Munsee and Lenape Indians. In 1621, the Dutch government chartered the West India Company and gave it a monopoly over the trade in American furs and West African slaves. Three years later, the company founded the town of New Amsterdam on Manhattan Island and made it the capital of the colony of New Netherland.

The new colony did not thrive. The population of the Dutch Republic was small—just 1.5 million people, compared to 5 million in Britain and 20 million in France—and relatively prosperous. Consequently, few Dutch settlers moved to the fur-trading posts, making them vulnerable to rival European nations. To encourage migration, the West India Company granted huge estates along the Hudson River to wealthy Dutchmen and smaller land grants to English and Dutch settlers. But in 1664, New Netherland had just 5,000 residents, and fewer than half of them were Dutch.

Nonetheless, New Netherland flourished as a fur-trading enterprise. Dutch traders at Fort Orange cultivated good relations with the powerful Iroquois who controlled the fur trade; in 1633, the traders exported 30,000 beaver and otter pelts. Dutch settlers near New Amsterdam were less respectful of their Algonquian-speaking neighbors. They seized prime farming land from the Indians and took over their trading network, in which corn and wampum from Long Island were exchanged for furs from Maine. In response, the Algonquins launched a war that nearly destroyed the colony. "Almost every place is abandoned," the settlers lamented, "whilst the Indians daily threaten to overwhelm us." To defeat the Algonquins, the Dutch waged vicious warfare—maiming, burning, and killing hundreds—and formed an alliance with the Mohawks, who were no less brutal. Thereafter, the Mohawks controlled Indian access to Albany, and their dialect became the language of business in the small fur-trading outpost.

After the crippling Indian war, the West India Company largely ignored New Netherland, focusing instead on the profitable trade in African slaves and Brazilian sugar. In New Amsterdam, Governor Peter Stuyvesant ruled in an authoritarian fashion. He rejected demands of English Puritans on Long Island for a representative system of government and alienated the colony's increasingly diverse population of Dutch, English, and Swedish migrants. Consequently, the residents of New Amsterdam offered little resistance when England invaded the colony in 1664.

The Duke of York, the overlord of the new English colony of New York, initially ruled with a mild hand: He allowed the Dutch residents to retain their property, legal system, and religious institutions. That policy changed after the Dutch briefly recaptured the colony in 1673. The duke's governor, Edmund Andros, shut down the Dutch courts, imposed English law, and demanded an oath of allegiance. Dutch residents responded by avoiding the English courts and resisting cultural assimilation: They spoke Dutch, married among themselves, and worshipped at the Dutch Reformed Church. Once dominant over the Algonquins, the Dutch had themselves become a subject people. As a group of Anglicans noted in 1699, New York "seemed rather like a conquered Foreign Province held by the terror of a Garrison, than an English colony."

▶ What were the colonial goals of the Spanish, French, and Dutch? How successful were they in achieving these goals?

▶ What happened to the Five Nations of the Iroquois between 1600 and 1700? Were the Iroquois better off at the beginning of the period or at the end? Why?

The English Arrive: The Chesapeake Experience

Unlike their European rivals, the English founded settler-colonies in North America. But that was not the plan of the London investors who financed an expedition to Virginia in 1607. They expected to establish a trade factory, like those recently set up in India, Sierra Leone, and Morocco, to buy goods from the native peoples—gold, if possible, or fruits, dyes, olives, and sugar. Not finding such goods, migrants settled in the Chesapeake Bay region and created a tobacco-growing society. Prominent families ruthlessly pursued their dreams of wealth by exploiting the labor of indentured English servants and enslaved Africans.

Settling the Tobacco Colonies

The first English settlements in North America were organized privately, first by minor nobles and later by merchants and religious dissidents. Although the English monarch and ministry approved these ventures, they did not control them. This policy meant that the English settlements, unlike the state-supervised Spanish and French colonies, enjoyed considerable autonomy and developed in astonishingly different ways.

The private ventures organized by the nobles were abject failures. In the 1580s, Sir Humphrey Gilbert's settlement in Newfoundland collapsed for lack of financing, and Sir Ferdinando Gorges's colony along the coast of Maine floundered in the harsh climate. Sir Walter Raleigh's three expeditions to North Carolina likewise ended in disaster when 117 settlers on Roanoke Island vanished without a trace. (Roanoke is still known as the "lost colony.")

Merchants then took charge of English expansion. In 1606, King James I (r. 1603–1625) granted to the Virginia Company of London all the lands stretching from present-day North Carolina to southern New York. To honor the memory of Elizabeth I, the never-married "Virgin Queen," the company's directors named the region Virginia. For the Virginia Company, as for the French and Dutch, trade with the native population was the primary goal. The first expedition, in 1607, was limited to male traders—no women, farmers, or ministers—who were the employees or "servants" of the company. They were to procure their own food and to ship gold, exotic crops, and Indian goods to England. Some employees were young gentlemen with personal ties to the company's shareholders: a bunch of "unruly Sparks, packed off by their Friends to escape worse

The Tobacco Economy

Most farmers in Virginia — poor and rich — raised tobacco. Wealthy planters used indentured servants and slaves, like those pictured here, to grow and process the crop. The workers cured the tobacco stalks by hanging them for several months in a well-ventilated shed; then they stripped the leaves and packed them tightly into large plantation-made barrels, or hogsheads, for shipment to Europe. Library of Congress.

For more help analyzing this image, see the Online Study Guide at **bedfordstmartins.com/ henrettaconcise.**

Destinies at home." Others were cynical men looking for a quick profit: All they wanted, one of them said, was to "dig gold, refine gold, load gold."

But there was no gold, and the traders were poorly equipped to deal with the new environment. Arriving in Virginia after an exhausting four-month voyage, they settled on a swampy, unhealthy peninsula, which they named Jamestown to honor the king. Because the adventurers lacked access to fresh water and refused to plant crops, they quickly died off; only 38 of the 120 men were alive nine months later. Death rates remained high. By 1611, the Virginia Company had dispatched 1,200 settlers to Jamestown, but fewer than half had survived. "Our men were destroyed with cruell diseases, as Swellings, Fluxes, Burning Fevers, and by warres," reported one of the settlement's leaders, "but for the most part they died of meere famine."

The local Indians were initially suspicious of the new arrivals. However, Powhatan, the chief of the thirty tribes living between the James and Potomac rivers, treated the English traders as potential allies and a source of valuable goods. A "grave majestical man," according to explorer John Smith, Powhatan allowed his 14,000 Algonquian-speaking followers to exchange their corn for English cloth and iron hatchets. To integrate the English traders into his domain of Tsenacommacah, Powhatan arranged a marriage between his daughter Pocahontas and John Rolfe, an English colonist. This tactic failed because Rolfe had imported tobacco seed from the West Indies and produced a crop of "pleasant, sweet, and strong Tobacco," which fetched a high price in England. Eager to become rich by planting tobacco, thousands of English settlers embarked for Virginia. Now Powhatan accused the English of coming "not to trade but to invade my people and possess my country."

To foster the flow of migrants, the Virginia Company allowed individual settlers to own land, granting 100 acres to every freeman and more to those who imported servants. The company also issued a "greate Charter" that created a system of representative government. The House of Burgesses, which first convened in 1619, could make laws and levy taxes, although the governor and the company council in England could veto its acts. By 1622, land ownership, self-government, and a judicial system based on "the lawes of the realme of England" had attracted some 4,500 new recruits. To encourage Virginia's transition to a settler colony, the company recruited dozens of "Maides young and uncorrupt to make wifes to the Inhabitants."

The influx of land-hungry English migrants and conversion-minded ministers sparked an all-out revolt by the Indian peoples. The uprising was led by a mysterious chief named Opechancanough [O-pee-chan-KA-no], who was Powhatan's younger brother and successor. Some evidence suggests that early Spanish explorers had taken Opechancanough to Spain in the 1570s and that when he returned as part of a Jesuit mission, he killed the missionaries. There is no doubt that in 1609, Opechancanough personally confronted the English invaders, captured Captain John Smith, and then spared his life. Subsequently, the Indian chief "stood aloof" from the English settlers and "would not be drawn to any Treaty." In particular, he resisted English proposals to place Indian children in schools where they would be "brought upp in Christianytie." After Opechancanough became the main chief in 1621, he told the chief of the Potomacks: "Before the end of two moons, there should not be an Englishman in all their Countries."

Opechancanough almost succeeded. In 1622, he coordinated a surprise attack by twelve Indian tribes that killed 347 English settlers, nearly one-third of the white population. The English fought back by seizing the fields and food of those they now saw as "naked, tanned, deformed Savages." To secure the safety of their colony, the European invaders declared "a perpetual war without peace or truce" that lasted for a decade. They sold captured warriors into slavery, "destroy[ing] them who sought to destroy us," and took control of "their cultivated places . . . possessing the fruits of others' labour."

Shocked by the Indian uprising, James I revoked the charter of the Virginia Company and, in 1624, made Virginia a royal colony. Now the king and his ministers appointed the governor and a small advisory council. James retained the House of Burgesses but stipulated that his Privy Council, a committee of leading ministers, must ratify all legislation. The king also decreed the legal establishment of the Church of England, which meant that residents had to pay taxes to support its clergy. These institutions—a royal governor, an elected assembly, a formal legal system, and an established Anglican church—became the model for royal colonies throughout English America.

A second tobacco-growing colony, with a very different set of institutions, developed in neighboring Maryland. King Charles I (r. 1625–1649), James's successor, was secretly sympathetic toward Catholicism. In 1632, he granted the lands bordering the vast Chesapeake Bay to Cecilius Calvert, a Catholic aristocrat who carried the title Lord Baltimore. As the territorial lord (or proprietor) of Maryland, Baltimore could sell, lease, or give away the land as he pleased. He also had the authority to appoint public officials and to found churches.

Lord Baltimore wanted Maryland to become a refuge for Catholics, who were subject to persecution in England. In 1634, twenty gentlemen, mostly Catholics, and 200 artisans and laborers, mostly Protestants, established St. Mary's City, which overlooked the mouth of the Potomac River. To minimize religious confrontations, the proprietor instructed the governor (his brother, Leonard Calvert) to allow "no scandall nor offence to be given to any of the Protestants" and to "cause All Acts of Romane Catholicque Religion to be done as privately as may be."

Maryland's population grew quickly because the Calverts imported scores of artisans and offered ample lands to wealthy migrants. But political conflict constantly threatened the colony's stability. Disputing Lord Baltimore's lordly powers, settlers demanded that he govern in accordance with the "Advice, Assent, and Approbation" of the freemen. They elected a representative assembly and insisted on the right to initiate legislation, which Baltimore grudgingly granted. Anti-Catholic agitation by Protestant settlers also threatened the Calverts' religious goals. To protect his coreligionists, who remained a minority, Lord Baltimore persuaded the assembly to enact the Toleration Act (1649), which granted all Christians the right to follow their beliefs and hold church services.

In Maryland, as in Virginia, tobacco quickly became the main crop. Indians had long used tobacco as a medicine and a stimulant, and the English came to crave the nicotine it contained. By the 1620s, they were smoking, chewing, and snorting tobacco with abandon. James I initially condemned tobacco as a "vile Weed" whose "black stinking fumes" were "baleful to the nose, harmful to the brain, and dangerous to the lungs." But the king's attitude changed as taxes on imported tobacco bolstered the royal treasury.

European demand for tobacco set off a forty-year economic boom in the Chesapeake region. "All our riches for the present do consist in tobacco," a planter remarked in 1630. Exports rose from three million pounds in 1640 to ten million pounds in 1660. Initially, most plantations were small, farmed by families or male partners. But after 1650, migrants from gentry or noble families established large estates along the coastal rivers. Coming primarily from southern England, where tenants and wage laborers farmed large manors, they recreated that hierarchical system by buying indentured servants to work their lands (see Voices from Abroad, p. 47).

For rich and poor alike, life in the Chesapeake colonies was harsh. The scarcity of towns deprived settlers of community (Map 2.2). Families were equally scarce because there were few women, and marriages often ended with the death of a young spouse. Pregnant women were especially vulnerable to malaria, which was spread by the mosquitoes that flourished in the warm climate. Many mothers died after bearing a first or second child, so orphaned children (along with unmarried young men) formed a large segment of the society. Sixty percent of the children born in Middlesex County, Virginia, before 1680 lost one or both of their parents before they were thirteen. Death was a constant presence. Some 15,000 English migrants arrived in Virginia between 1622 and 1640, but the population rose only from 2,000 to 8,000.

Magisterial Justice in Maryland

Tens of thousands of English indentured servants came to Maryland and Virginia in the seventeenth century, hoping for a better life. Many found only oppressive masters and unforgiving magistrates. When two indentured servants in Lower Norfolk County in Virginia stole some food, the justices of the county court ordered the sheriff to lash them 100 times on their bare backs. English servants who shirked from work and demanded adequate food faced a similar fate at the hands of Maryland magistrates—in this case the governor and council of the colony—who themselves held bound laborers and were determined to enforce strict discipline.

To the honorable the Governor and Council of Maryland:

The humble petition of Richard Preston showeth:

That your petitioner's servants did, upon the 5th day of the last week, called Thursday, peremptorily and positively refuse to go and do their ordinary labor upon the account (as they then alleged) that if they had not flesh [meat], they could not work. Your suppliant's answer then was to them, that if they would not go to work unless they had flesh, I could not help it; for I had not flesh then to give them (. . . And at night returning home, found that his said servants had not been at work upon the account of not having that day some meat, although until that time they have not wanted for the most part, since the crop of tobacco was in, to have meat three times in the week and at least twice . . . And they continuing still in that obstinate rebellious condition, although I have instead of flesh for the present provided sugar, fish, oil, and vinegar for them, am constrained to address myself to this court, that according to equity and their demerits they may receive such censure as shall be judged equal for such perverse servants. . . .

To the honorable the Governor and Council:

The humble Petition of John Smith, Richard Gibbs, Samuel Coplen, Samuel Styles, etc., servants to Mr. Richard Preston, showeth:

That Mr. Preston doth not allow your petitioners sufficient provisions for the enablement to our work, but straitens us so far that we are brought so weak we are not able to perform the employments he puts us upon. We desire but so much as is sufficient, but he will allow us nothing but beans and bread. . . .

Upon these petitions of Mr. Richard Preston and his servants, and upon examination of the said servants present in court: the court, taking the same into serious consideration, ordered that these servants now petitioning . . . be forthwith whipped with 30 lashes each. . . .

And thereupon the said servants, kneeling on their knees, asking and craving forgiveness of their master and the court for their former misdemeanor and promising all compliance and obedience hereafter, their penalty is remitted or suspended at present. But they are to be of good behavior towards their said master ever hereafter.

SOURCE: John Demos, ed., *Remarkable Providences, Readings in Early American History* (Boston: Northeastern University Press, 1972): 135–137.

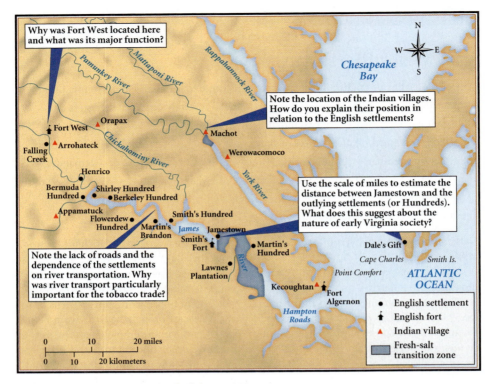

MAP 2.2 River Plantations in Virginia, c. 1640
The first migrants settled in widely dispersed plantations along the James River. The growth of the tobacco economy promoted this pattern: Wealthy planter-merchants would trade with English ship captains from their riverfront plantations. Consequently, few substantial towns or trading centers developed in the Chesapeake region.

Masters, Servants, and Slaves

Still, the prospect of owning land continued to lure settlers. By 1700, more than 100,000 English migrants had come to Virginia and Maryland, mostly as indentured servants. Shipping registers from the English port of Bristol reveal the backgrounds of 5,000 embarking servants. Three-quarters were young men, many of them displaced by the enclosure of their village lands (see Chapter 1). They came to Bristol searching for work; once there, merchants persuaded them to sign contracts to labor in America. The indenture contracts bound the men—and a much smaller number of women—to work for a master for four or five years, after which they would be free to marry and work for themselves.

For merchants, servants were valuable cargo: Their contracts fetched high prices from Chesapeake (and West Indian) planters. For the plantation owners, indentured servants were an incredible bargain. During the tobacco boom, a male servant could produce five times his purchase price in a single year. To maximize their gains, most masters ruthlessly exploited their servants, forcing them to work long hours, beating them without cause, and withholding permission to marry. If servants ran away or became pregnant, masters went to court to increase the term of their service. Female servants were especially vulnerable to abuse. As a Virginia law of 1692 stated, "dissolute masters have gotten their maids with child; and yet claim the benefit of their service." Planters got rid of uncooperative servants by selling their contracts. As one Englishman remarked in disgust, in Virginia, "servants were sold up and down like horses."

Most indentured servants in the Chesapeake colonies did not escape from poverty. Half the men died before completing the term of their contract, and another quarter remained landless. Only one-quarter achieved their quest for property and respectability. Female servants generally fared better. Men had grown "very sensible of the Misfortune of Wanting Wives," so many propertied planters married female servants. By migrating to the Chesapeake, these few—and very fortunate—men and women escaped a life of landless poverty.

Fate was equally mixed for the first African workers. In 1619, John Rolfe noted that "a Dutch man of warre . . . sold us twenty Negars"—slaves shipped from the Portuguese port of Luanda in Angola. For a generation, the number of Africans remained small. About 400 Africans lived in the Chesapeake colonies in 1649, just 2 percent of the population; in 1670, only 5 percent of the population was black. Though some of these early African workers served their English masters for life, they were not legally enslaved. English **common law** did not acknowledge **chattel slavery**, the ownership of a human being as property. Moreover, many of these Africans came from the Kingdom of Kongo, where Portuguese missionaries had converted the king and some of the people to Christianity. Knowing the ways of Europeans, these workers found means to escape their bondage. Some ambitious African freemen even purchased slaves, bought the labor contracts of white servants, or married Englishwomen.

Mobility for Africans ended in the 1660s with the collapse of the tobacco boom. Tobacco had once sold for 24 pence a pound; now it fetched just one-tenth of that. The "low price of Tobacco requires it should bee made as cheap as possible," declared Virginia planter Nicholas Spencer, and "blacks can make it cheaper than whites." As the English-born elite imported fewer English servants and more African slaves, Chesapeake legislators grew more race-conscious and enacted laws that undercut the status of blacks. By 1671, the Virginia House of Burgesses had forbidden Africans to own guns or join the militia. It also barred them—"tho baptized and enjoying their own Freedom"—from owning white servants and from claiming freedom by becoming Christians. Being black was increasingly a mark of inferior legal status, and slavery was becoming a permanent and hereditary condition. As an English clergyman observed, "These two words, Negro and Slave had by custom grown Homogeneous and convertible."

The Seeds of Social Revolt

As the tobacco boom went bust, long-standing social conflicts flared into political turmoil. Falling tobacco prices signaled an imbalance in the market: Exports doubled between 1670 and 1700, outstripping European demand. But it also reflected Parliament's passage of Acts of Trade and Navigation in 1651, 1660, and 1663. The Navigation Acts allowed only English or colonial-owned ships to enter American ports, thereby excluding Dutch merchants, who paid the highest prices for tobacco, sold the best goods, and provided the cheapest shipping services. The legislation also required the colonists to ship tobacco, sugar, and other "enumerated articles" only to England, where monarchs continually raised import duties, stifling market demand. By the 1670s, tobacco planters were getting just a penny a pound for their crop; one Virginian grumbled that the planters had become mere "beneficial Slaves" to England's merchants and monarch.

Despite low prices, Virginians continued to plant tobacco because there was no other cash crop. To preserve soil fertility without costly manuring, yeomen families adopted a long-fallow system (rotating fields over a twenty-year cycle) and pocketed just enough income to scrape by. Worse off were newly freed indentured servants, who could not earn enough to buy tools and seed or to pay the fees required to claim their right to fifty acres of land. Many ex-servants had to sell their labor again, either signing new indentures or becoming wage workers or tenant farmers.

Consequently, after 1670, an elite of planter-merchants dominated the Chesapeake colonies. Like the English gentry, they prospered from the ownership of large estates that they leased to the growing population of former servants. Many well-to-do planters also became commercial middlemen and moneylenders. They set up retail stores and charged commissions for shipping the tobacco produced by smallholding farmers. This elite accumulated nearly half the land in Virginia by securing grants from royal governors. In Maryland, well-connected Catholic planters were equally powerful; by 1720, one of those planters, Charles Carroll, owned 47,000 acres of land, farmed by scores of tenants, indentured servants, and slaves.

Bacon's Rebellion

As these aggressive planter-entrepreneurs confronted a multitude of free, young, and landless laborers, armed political conflict rocked Virginia during the 1670s. This violent struggle left a mixed legacy: a decrease in class conflict among whites and increasing racial divisions because of massive imports of enslaved Africans.

William Berkeley, who first served as governor of Virginia between 1642 and 1652, suppressed a major Indian uprising in 1644. Appointed governor again in 1660, Berkeley bestowed large land grants on members of his council. The councilors promptly exempted their own lands from taxation and appointed their friends as local justices of the peace and county judges. To win the cooperation of the House of Burgesses, Berkeley bought off legislators with land grants and lucrative appointments as sheriffs and tax collectors. But social unrest surfaced when the corrupt Burgesses changed the voting system to exclude landless freemen, who by now constituted half the adult white men. Property-holding yeomen retained the vote, but they were angered by falling tobacco prices, political corruption, and "grievous taxations" that threatened the "utter ruin of us the poor commonalty." Berkeley and his gentry allies were living on borrowed time.

An Indian conflict lit the flame of social rebellion. When the English intruded into Virginia in 1607, there were 30,000 Native Americans living there; by 1675, the number had dwindled to only 3,500. By comparison, the number of Europeans had multiplied to 38,000 and the number of Africans to about 2,500. Most Indians lived on treaty-guaranteed territory along the frontier. Now poor **freeholders** and landless former servants demanded that the natives be expelled or exterminated. Opposition to western expansion came from wealthy river-valley planters, who wanted a ready supply of tenant farmers and wage laborers, and from Berkeley and the planter-merchants, who traded with the Indians for furs.

Fighting broke out late in 1675, when a vigilante band of Virginia militiamen murdered thirty Indians. Defying Berkeley's orders, a larger force of 1,000 militiamen then surrounded a fortified Susquehannock village and killed five chiefs who came out to negotiate. The Susquehannocks, who had recently migrated from the north, retaliated by killing 300 whites on outlying plantations. To avoid an Indian war, Berkeley proposed a defensive military strategy: a series of frontier forts to deter Indian intrusions. The settlers dismissed this scheme as a useless plot by planters and merchants to impose high taxes and take "all our tobacco into their own hands."

Nathaniel Bacon emerged as the leader of the rebels. A young, well-connected migrant from England, Bacon held a position on the governor's council. But residing on a frontier estate, he differed with Berkeley on Indian policy. When the governor refused Bacon a military commission to attack nearby Indians, he used his commanding personal presence to mobilize his neighbors and attack the peaceful Doeg Indians.

Nathaniel Bacon

Condemned as a rebel and a traitor in his own time, Nathaniel Bacon emerged in the late nineteenth century as an American hero, a harbinger of the Patriots of 1776. Famed jeweler and glassmaker Tiffany & Co. of New York probably designed and fabricated this stained-glass window. Installed in a Virginia church, it endowed Bacon with semisacred status.
The Association for the Preservation of Virginia Antiquities.

Condemning the frontiersmen as "rebels and mutineers," Berkeley expelled Bacon from the council and had him arrested. But Bacon's armed men forced the governor to release their leader and to hold legislative elections. The newly elected House of Burgesses enacted far-reaching political reforms that curbed the powers of the governor and the council and restored voting rights to landless freemen.

These much-needed reforms came too late. Bacon remained bitter toward Berkeley, and poor farmers and indentured servants resented years of exploitation by wealthy planters, arrogant justices of the peace, and "wicked & pernicious Counsellors." As one yeoman rebel complained, "A poor man who has only his labour to maintain himself and his family pays as much [in taxes] as a man who has 20,000 acres." Backed by 400 armed men, Bacon issued a "Manifesto and Declaration of the People" that demanded the death or removal of the Indians and an end to the rule of wealthy "parasites." "All the power and sway is got into the hands of the rich," Bacon proclaimed as his army burned Jamestown to the ground and plundered the plantations of Berkeley's allies. When Bacon died suddenly of dysentery in October 1676, the governor took revenge, dispersing the rebel army, seizing the estates of well-to-do rebels, and hanging twenty-three men.

Bacon's Rebellion was a pivotal event in the history of the Chesapeake colonies. Thereafter, landed planters retained their dominance by curbing corruption and appointing ambitious yeomen to public office. They appeased yeomen and tenants by cutting taxes and supporting expansion onto Indian lands. Most important, planters sought to forestall another rebellion by poor whites by cutting the use of indentured servants. Instead, planters imported thousands of African laborers, and in 1705, the Burgesses explicitly legalized chattel slavery. Those fateful decisions committed subsequent generations of Americans to a social system based on racial exploitation.

► What were the various systems of bound labor that took hold in the Chesapeake colonies? What accounts for the appearance of these systems?

► Compare the Indian uprising in Virginia in 1622 with Bacon's Rebellion in 1675. What were the consequences of each for Virginia's development?

Puritan New England

As the scramble for wealth escalated in the Chesapeake, Puritan settlers created colonies in New England that had strong ethical and spiritual goals. Between 1620 and 1640, thousands of Puritans fled to America seeking land and religious freedom. By distributing land broadly, the Puritans built a society of independent farm families. And by establishing a "holy commonwealth," they tried to preserve a "pure" Christian faith. Their "errand into the wilderness" gave a moral dimension to American history that survives today.

The Puritan Migration

New England differed from other European colonies in America. Unruly male adventurers founded New Spain and Jamestown, and male traders dominated life in New France and New Netherland. By contrast, the leaders of the Plymouth and Massachusetts Bay colonies were pious Protestants, and the settlers there included women and children as well as men.

The Pilgrims who settled in Plymouth were religious separatists — Puritans who had left the Church of England. When King James I threatened to drive Puritans "out of the land, or else do worse," some Puritans left England to live among Dutch Calvinists in Holland. Subsequently, thirty-five of these exiles resolved to migrate to America to maintain their English identity. Led by William Bradford and joined by sixty-seven migrants from England, they sailed to America in 1620 aboard the *Mayflower* and settled near Cape Cod in southeastern Massachusetts. Lacking a royal charter, they "combine[d] ourselves together into a civill body politick." The Mayflower Compact, the first American constitution, used the Puritans' self-governing religious congregation as the model for its political structure.

The first winter in Plymouth tested the Pilgrims. Of the 102 migrants who arrived in November, only half survived until spring. But then Plymouth became a healthy and thriving community. The cold climate inhibited the spread of mosquito-borne diseases, and the Pilgrims' religious discipline maintained a strong work ethic. Moreover, a smallpox epidemic in 1618 had killed most of the local Wampanoag people, so the migrants faced few external threats. The Pilgrims built solid houses and planted ample crops, and their number grew rapidly. By 1640, there were 3,000 settlers in Plymouth. To ensure political stability, they issued a written legal code that provided for representative self-government, broad political rights, property ownership, and religious freedom of conscience.

Meanwhile, England plunged deeper into religious turmoil. King Charles I repudiated certain Protestant doctrines, including the role of grace in salvation. English Puritans, now powerful in Parliament, accused the king of "popery" — of holding Catholic beliefs. In 1629, Charles dissolved Parliament, claimed the authority to rule by "divine right," and raised money through royal edicts and the sale of monopolies. When Archbishop William Laud, whom Charles chose to head the Church of England, dismissed hundreds of Puritan ministers, thousands of Puritan families fled to America.

That exodus began in 1630 with the departure of 900 Puritans led by John Winthrop, a well-educated country squire who became the first governor of the Massachusetts Bay Colony. Calling England morally corrupt and "overburdened with people," Winthrop sought land for his children and a place in Christian history for his people. "We must consider that we shall be as a City upon a Hill," Winthrop told the migrants. "The eyes of all people are upon us." Like the Pilgrims, the Puritans envisioned a reformed Christian society with "authority in magistrates, liberty in people, purity in the church," as minister John Cotton put it. By creating a genuinely "New" England, they hoped to inspire religious reform throughout Christendom.

Winthrop and his associates governed the Massachusetts Bay Colony from the town of Boston. They transformed their **joint-stock corporation**, the General Court of shareholders, into a representative political system with a governor, council, and assembly. To ensure rule by the godly, the Puritans limited the right to vote and hold office to men who were church members. Rejecting the Plymouth Colony's policy of religious tolerance, the Massachusetts Bay Colony established Puritanism as the state-supported religion, barred other faiths from conducting services, and used the Bible as a legal guide. "Where there is no Law," they said, magistrates should rule "as near the law of God as they can." Over the next decade, about 10,000 Puritans migrated to the colony, along with 10,000 others fleeing hard times in England.

The New England Puritans emulated the simplicity of the first Christians. They eliminated bishops, censuring them as "traitours unto God," and placed power in the hands of the ordinary members of the congregation—hence the name Congregationalist for their churches. Following the teachings of John Calvin, many Puritans embraced predestination, the doctrine that God had chosen (before their birth) only a few saints for salvation. Many church members lived in great anxiety, uncertain that God had chosen them as members of the "elect." Some hoped for a conversion experience, the intense spiritual sensation of receiving God's grace and being "born again." Other Puritans relied on "preparation," the confidence in salvation that came from spiritual guidance by their ministers. Still others believed that God considered them his chosen people, the new Israelites, who would be saved if they obeyed his laws.

To maintain God's favor, the Massachusetts Bay magistrates purged their society of religious dissidents. One target was Roger Williams, the Puritan minister in Salem, a coastal town north of Boston. Williams opposed the decision to establish Congregationalism as the state religion and praised the Pilgrims' separation of church and state. He advocated toleration, arguing that political magistrates had authority over only the "bodies, goods, and outward estates of men," not their spiritual lives. Moreover, Williams questioned the Puritans' seizure of Indian lands. The magistrates banished him from the colony in 1636.

Williams and his followers settled fifty miles south of Boston, founding the town of Providence on land purchased from the Narragansett Indians. Other religious dissidents settled nearby at Portsmouth and Newport. In 1644, these settlers obtained a corporate charter from Parliament for a new colony—Rhode Island—with full authority to rule themselves. In Rhode Island, as in Plymouth, there was no legally established church, and individuals could worship God as they pleased.

The Massachusetts Bay magistrates sensed a second threat to their authority in Anne Hutchinson. The wife of a merchant and a mother of seven, Hutchinson held weekly prayer meetings for women in her house and accused various Boston clergymen of placing too much emphasis on good behavior. Like Martin Luther, Hutchinson denied that salvation could be earned through good deeds: There was no "covenant of works"; God bestowed salvation only through the "covenant of grace." Moreover, Hutchinson declared that God "revealed" divine truth directly to individual believers, a controversial doctrine that the Puritan magistrates denounced as heretical.

The magistrates also resented Hutchinson because of her sex. Like other Christians, Puritans believed that both men and women could be saved. But gender equality stopped there. Women were inferior to men in earthly affairs, said leading Puritan divines, who instructed married women: "Thy desires shall bee subject to thy husband, and he shall rule over thee." The same was true in church affairs. According to Pilgrim minister John Robinson, women "are debarred by their sex from ordinary prophesying, and from any other dealing in the church wherein they take authority over the man." Puritan women could not be ministers or lay preachers, and they had no vote in the congregation. In 1637, the magistrates put Hutchinson on trial for teaching that inward grace freed an individual from the rules of the church and found her guilty of holding heretical views. Banished, she followed Roger Williams into exile in Rhode Island.

These coercive policies and a desire for better farm land prompted some Puritans to migrate to the Connecticut River Valley. In 1636, pastor Thomas Hooker and his congregation established the town of Hartford, and other Puritans settled along the river at Wethersfield and Windsor. In 1660, they secured a charter from King Charles II (r. 1660–1685) for the self-governing colony of Connecticut. Like Massachusetts Bay, Connecticut had a legally established church and an elected governor and assembly; however, it granted voting rights to most property-owning men, not just church members as in the original Puritan colony.

Meanwhile, England had fallen into a religious war. When Archbishop Laud imposed a Church of England prayer book on Presbyterian Scotland in 1642, a Scottish army invaded England. Thousands of English Puritans (and hundreds of American Puritans) joined the Scots, demanding religious reform and Parliamentary power. After years of civil war, the parliamentary forces led by Oliver Cromwell emerged victorious. In 1649, Parliament executed King Charles I, proclaimed a republican commonwealth, and banished bishops and elaborate rituals from the Church of England.

The Puritan triumph in England was short-lived. Popular support for the Commonwealth ebbed, especially after 1653, when Cromwell took dictatorial control. After his death in 1658, moderate Protestants and a resurgent aristocracy restored the monarchy and the hierarchy of bishops. For many Puritans, Charles II's accession to the throne in 1660 represented the victory of the Antichrist, the false prophet described in the final book of the New Testament.

For the Puritans in America, the restoration of the monarchy began a new phase of their "errand into the wilderness." They had come to New England to preserve the "pure" Christian church, expecting to return to Europe in triumph. When the failure of the English Revolution dashed that sacred mission, ministers exhorted their congregations to create a godly republican society in America. The Puritan colonies now stood as outposts of Calvinism and the Atlantic republican tradition.

Puritanism and Witchcraft

Like Native Americans, Puritans believed that the physical world was full of supernatural forces. Devout Christians saw signs of God's (or Satan's) power in blazing stars, birth defects, and other unusual events. Noting that the houses of many ministers "had been smitten with Lightning," Cotton Mather, a prominent Puritan theologian, wondered "what the meaning of God should be in it."

This belief in "forces" and "spirits" stemmed in part from Christian teachings—the Catholic belief in miracles, for example, and the Protestant faith in grace. It also reflected a pagan influence. When Samuel Sewall, a well-educated Puritan merchant and judge, moved into a new house, he fended off evil spirits by driving a metal pin into the floor. Thousands of ordinary Puritan farmers followed the pagan astrological charts printed in almanacs to determine the best times to plant crops, marry, and make other important decisions.

Zealous ministers attacked these practices as "superstition" and condemned the "cunning" individuals who claimed powers as healers or prophets. Indeed, many Christians believed such conjurers were Satan's "wizards" or "witches." People in the town of Andover "were much addicted to sorcery," claimed one observer, and "there

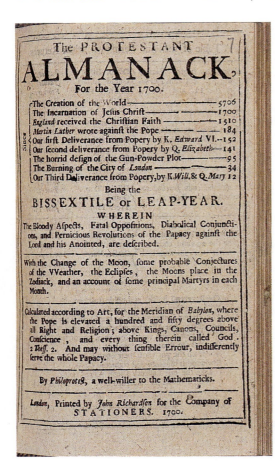

The Creation of the World —————— 5706
The Incarnation of Jefus Chrift————1700
England received the Chriftian Faith ——1510
Martin Luther wrote againft the Pope ———184
Our firft Deliverance from Popery by K. *Edward* VI.--152
Our fecond deliverance from Popery by Q. *Elizabeth*—141
The horrid defign of the Gun-Powder Plot————95
The Burning of the City of *London* ——————34
Our Third Deliverance from Popery,by K.*Will.*& Q.*Mary* 12

The Protestant Almanack, 1700
The conflict between Protestants and Catholics took many forms. To reinforce the religious identity of English Protestants, the Company of Stationers published a yearly almanac that charted not only the passage of the seasons but also the "Pernicious Revolutions of the Papacy against the Lord and his Anointed." By permission of the Syndics of Cambridge University Library.

were forty men in it that could raise the Devil as well as any astrologer." Between 1647 and 1662, civil authorities in New England hanged fourteen people for witchcraft, mostly older women accused of being "double-tongued" or of having "an unruly spirit."

The most dramatic episode of witch-hunting occurred in Salem in 1692. Several young girls experienced strange seizures and then accused various neighbors of bewitching them. When judges at the trials of the accused witches allowed the use of "spectral" evidence—visions seen only by the girls—the accusations spun out of control. Eventually, Massachusetts Bay authorities arrested and tried 175 people for the crime of witchcraft and executed nineteen of them. The causes of this mass hysteria were complex and are still debated. Some historians point to group rivalries: Many of the accusers were the daughters or servants of poor farmers, whereas many of the alleged witches were wealthier church members or their friends. Because eighteen of those put to death were women, other historians claim the trials were part of a broader Puritan effort to subordinate women. Still other scholars focus on political instability in Massachusetts Bay in the early 1690s (see Chapter 3) and on fears raised by recent Indian attacks in nearby Maine, which had killed the parents of some of the young accusers.

Whatever the cause, the Salem episode marked a turning point in the handling of witchcraft accusations. Shaken by the executions, government officials now discouraged legal prosecutions for witchcraft. Equally important was the impact of the European Enlightenment, a major intellectual movement that began around 1675 and promoted a rational, scientific view of the world. Increasingly, educated people explained accidents and sudden deaths by reference to "natural causes," not witchcraft. Thus, unlike Cotton Mather (1663–1728), who believed that lightning was a supernatural sign, Benjamin Franklin (1706–1790) and other well-read men of his generation would conceive of lightning as a natural phenomenon.

A Yeoman Society, 1630–1700

In building their communities, New England Puritans consciously rejected the feudal practices of English society. Many Puritans came from middling families in East Anglia, a region of pasture lands and few manors. They had no desire to live as tenants of wealthy aristocrats or submit to oppressive taxation by a distant government. They had "escaped out of the pollutions of the world," the settlers of Watertown in Massachusetts Bay declared, and vowed "to sit down . . . close togither" in self-governing communities. Accordingly, the General Courts of Massachusetts Bay and Connecticut bestowed the title to each township on a group of settlers, or **proprietors**, who then distributed the land among the male heads of families.

Widespread ownership of land did not mean equality of wealth or status. "God had Ordained different degrees and orders of men," proclaimed Boston merchant John Saffin, "some to be Masters and Commanders, others to be Subjects, and to be commanded." Town proprietors normally awarded the largest plots to men of high social status, who often became selectmen and justices of the peace. However, all families received some land, and most adult men had a vote in the **town meeting**, the main institution of local government (Map 2.3).

In this society of independent households and self-governing communities, ordinary farmers had much more political power than Chesapeake yeomen and European peasants did. Although Nathaniel Fish was one of the poorest men in the town of Barnstable — he owned just a two-room cottage, eight acres of land, an ox, and a cow — he was a voting member of the town meeting. Each year, Fish and other Barnstable farmers levied taxes; enacted ordinances governing fencing, road building, and the use of common fields; and chose the selectmen who managed town affairs. The farmers also selected the town's representatives to the General Court, which gradually displaced the governor as the center of political authority. For Fish and thousands of other ordinary settlers, New England had proved to be a new world of opportunity.

▶ Why did the Puritans of Massachusetts Bay create an established church and persecute dissenters when they had fled England to escape those things?

▶ What were the main characteristics of the social and political structure of the New England colonies? Why did they develop in that fashion?

▶ Why were there were no major witchcraft scares in the Chesapeake colonies and no uprising in New England like Bacon's Rebellion?

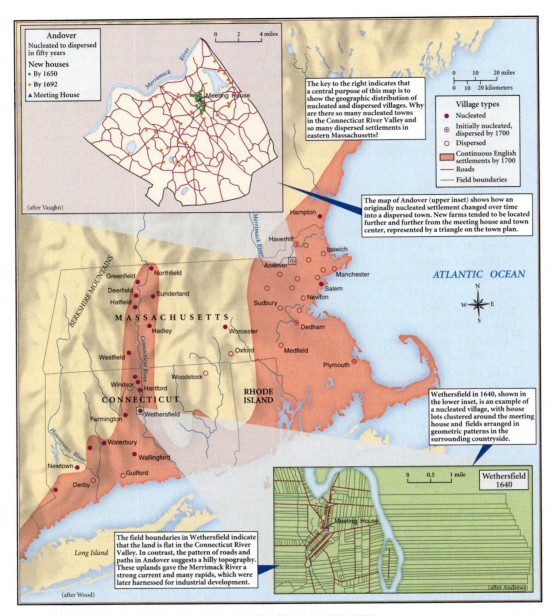

The key to the right indicates that a central purpose of this map is to show the geographic distribution of nucleated and dispersed villages. Why are there so many nucleated towns in the Connecticut River Valley and so many dispersed settlements in eastern Massachusetts?

The map of Andover (upper inset) shows how an originally nucleated settlement changed over time into a dispersed town. New farms tended to be located further and further from the meeting house and town center, represented by a triangle on the town plan.

Wethersfield in 1640, shown in the lower inset, is an example of a nucleated village, with house lots clustered around the meeting house and fields arranged in geometric patterns in the surrounding countryside.

The field boundaries in Wethersfield indicate that the land is flat in the Connecticut River Valley. In contrast, the pattern of roads and paths in Andover suggests a hilly topography. These uplands gave the Merrimack River a strong current and many rapids, which were later harnessed for industrial development.

Andover
Nucleated to dispersed in fifty years
New houses
• By 1650
• By 1692
▲ Meeting House
(after Vaughn)

Village types
• Nucleated
◉ Initially nucleated, dispersed by 1700
○ Dispersed
▢ Continuous English settlements by 1700
— Roads
— Field boundaries

Wethersfield 1640
(after Andrews)

(after Wood)

MAP 2.3 Settlement Patterns in New England Towns, 1630–1700

Initially, most Puritan towns were compact. Regardless of the topography — hills or plains — families lived close to one another in the village center and traveled daily to work in the surrounding fields. This pattern is clear in the 1640 map of Wethersfield, which is situated on the broad plains of the Connecticut River Valley. The first settlers in Andover, Massachusetts, also chose to live in the village center. However, the rugged topography of eastern Massachusetts encouraged the townspeople to disperse; by 1692, many Andover residents were living on their own farms.

The Eastern Indians' New World

Native Americans along the Atlantic coast also lived in a new world, but for them, it was a bleak and dangerous place. Epidemics of smallpox struck with devastating results. In New England, so many Indians were stricken, an observer reported, they were "not able to help one another, no not to make a fire nor fetch a little water to drink, nor any to bury the dead." The European invaders took over the depopulated areas and ejected other Indian peoples from their ancestral lands. A few Indian peoples, most prominently the Iroquois, used European guns and manufactures to resist white intrusion and to dominate other tribes. Still other native peoples retreated into the mountains or moved westward to preserve their traditional cultures.

Puritans and Pequots

As the Puritans embarked for New England, they pondered the morality of intruding on Native American lands. "By what right or warrant can we enter into the land of the Savages?" they asked themselves. Responding to such concerns, John Winthrop detected God's hand in a recent smallpox epidemic: "If God were not pleased with our inheriting these parts," he asked, "why doth he still make roome for us by diminishing them as we increase?" Citing the Book of Genesis, the Massachusetts Bay magistrates declared that the Indians had not "subdued" their land and therefore had no "just right" to it.

Believing they were God's chosen people, the Puritans often treated Native Americans with a brutality equal to that of the Spanish conquistadors and Nathaniel Bacon's frontiersmen. When Pequot warriors attacked English farmers who had intruded onto their Connecticut River Valley lands in 1636, a Puritan militia attacked a Pequot village and massacred some 500 men, women, and children. "God laughed at the Enemies of his People," one soldier boasted, "filling the Place with Dead Bodies."

Like most Europeans, English Puritans saw the Indians as culturally inferior "savages." But the Puritans were not *racists* as the term is understood today. To their minds, Europeans and Native Americans were genetically the same. The Indians were white people with sun-darkened skin and "sin," not race, accounted for their degeneracy. "Probably the devil" delivered these "miserable savages" to America, Cotton Mather suggested, "in hopes that the gospel of the Lord Jesus Christ would never come here." This interpretation of the Indians' history inspired Puritan minister John Eliot to translate the Bible into Algonquian and to convert Indians to Christianity. Because of the rigorous admissions standards, only a few Native Americans became full members of Puritan congregations; nevertheless, Eliot and his colleagues turned fourteen Indian villages, such as Natick (Massachusetts) and Maanexit (Connecticut), into **praying towns**. Like the Franciscan missions in New Mexico, these towns were intended as intensely Christian communities. By 1670, more than 1,000 Indians lived in these settlements, having forsaken much of their independence and traditional culture.

Metacom's Rebellion

By the 1670s, New England whites outnumbered Indians by three to one. The English population had grown to some 55,000, while the number of native peoples had plummeted—from an estimated 120,000 in 1570 to 70,000 in 1620, to barely 16,000.

To Metacom (King Philip), leader of the Wampanoags, the future looked grim. When his people copied English ways by raising hogs and selling pork in Boston, Puritan officials accused them of selling at "an under rate" and placed restrictions on their trade. When Indians killed wandering livestock that damaged their cornfields, authorities denounced them for violating English property rights.

Like Opechancanough in Virginia and Popé in New Mexico, Metacom concluded that the Europeans had to be ousted from Indian lands. In 1675, the Wampanoags' leader forged a military alliance with the Narragansetts and Nipmucks and attacked white settlements throughout New England. They went to war, a group of Indians told Roger Williams, because the English "had forced them to it." Almost every day, settler William Harris fearfully reported, he heard new reports of the Indians' "burneing houses, takeing cattell, killing men & women & Children: & carrying others captive." Bitter fighting continued into 1676 and ended only when the Indian warriors ran short of gunpowder and when the Massachusetts Bay government hired Mohegan and Mohawk warriors, who ambushed and killed Metacom.

The rebellion was a deadly affair. Indians destroyed 20 percent of the English towns in Massachusetts and Rhode Island and killed 1,000 settlers, nearly 5 percent of the adult population. The very future of the Puritan experiment hung in the balance. Had "the Indeans not been divided," remarked one settler, "they might have forced us [to evacuate] to Som Islands: & there to have planted a little Corne, & fished for our liveings." But the natives' own losses—from famine and disease, death in battle, and sale into slavery—were much larger: About 4,500 Indians died, one-quarter of an already-diminished population. Many of the surviving Wampanoag, Narragansett, and Nipmuck peoples migrated farther into the New England backcountry, where they intermarried with Algonquin tribes allied to the French. Over the next century, these displaced Indian peoples would take their revenge, joining with French Catholics to attack their Puritan enemies (see American Voices, p. 61).

The Human and Environmental Impact of the Fur Trade

As English towns filled the river valleys along the Atlantic coast, the Indians who lived in the great forested areas beyond the Appalachian Mountains remained independent. Yet the distant Indian peoples—the Iroquois, Ottawas, Crees, Illinois, and many more—also felt the European presence through the fur trade. As they bargained for woolen blankets, iron cookware, knives, and guns, Indians learned to avoid the French at Montreal, who demanded two beaver skins for a woolen blanket. Instead, they dealt with the Dutch and English merchants at Albany, who asked for only one pelt and who could be played off against one another. "They are marvailous subtle in their bargains to save a penny," an English trader noted with displeasure. "They will beate all markets and try all places . . . to save six pence." Still, because the Indians had no way of knowing the value of their pelts in Europe, they rarely secured the highest possible price.

Nor could they control the European impact on their societies. European diseases, guns, and rum sapped the vitality of many Indian peoples. In South Carolina, a smallpox epidemic killed nearly half of the Catawbas, and "strong spirits" took a toll among the survivors: "Many of our people has Lately Died by the Effects of that Strong Drink."

A Captivity Narrative   MARY ROWLANDSON

Mary Rowlandson, a minister's wife in Lancaster, Massachusetts, was one of many settlers taken captive by the Indians during Metacom's war. Mrs. Rowlandson spent twelve weeks in captivity before being ransomed by her family for the considerable sum of £20. Her account of this ordeal, *The Sovereignty and Goodness of God* (1682), was written in part to assert her moral purity (that she had not been sexually exploited), so that she could again live as a respectable Puritan woman. But Mrs. Rowlandson's dramatic and literary skills made it one of the most popular prose works of its time.

On the tenth of February 1675, came the Indians with great numbers upon Lancaster: their first coming was about sunrising; hearing the noise of some guns, we looked out; several houses were burning, and the smoke ascending to heaven. . . . [T]he Indians laid hold of us, pulling me one way, and the children another, and said, "Come go along with us"; I told them they would kill me: they answered, if I were willing to go along with them, they would not hurt me. . . .

The first week of my being among them I hardly ate any thing; the second week I found my stomach grow very faint for want of something; and yet it was very hard to get down their filthy trash; but the third week . . . they were sweet and savory to my taste. I was at this time knitting a pair of white cotton stockings for my [Indian] mistress; and had not yet wrought upon a sabbath day. When the sabbath came they bade me go to work. I told them it was the sabbath-day, and desired them to let me rest, and told them I would do as much more tomorrow; to which they answered me they would break my face. . . .

During my abode in this place, Philip [Metacom] spake to me to make a shirt for his boy, which I did, for which he gave me a shilling. I offered the money to my master, but he bade me keep it; and with it I bought a piece of horse flesh. Afterwards he asked me to make a cap for his boy, for which he invited me to dinner. I went, and he gave me a pancake, about as big as two fingers. It was made of parched wheat, beaten, and fried in bear's grease, but I thought I never tasted pleasanter meat in my life. . . .

My master had three squaws, living sometimes with one, and sometimes with another one. . . . [It] was Weetamoo with whom I had lived and served all this while. A severe and proud dame she was, bestowing every day in dressing herself near as much time as any of the gentry of the land: powdering her hair, and painting her face, going with necklaces, with jewels in her ears, and bracelets upon her hands. When she had dressed herself, her work was to make girdles of wampom and beads. . . .

On Tuesday morning they called their general court (as they call it) to consult and determine, whether I should go home or no. And they all as one man did seemingly consent to it, that I should go home. . . .

SOURCE: C. H. Lincoln, ed., *Original Narratives of Early American History: Narratives of Indian Wars,* 1675–1699 (New York: Barnes and Noble, 1952), 14: 139–41.

Most native societies also lost their economic independence. As they exchanged furs for European-made iron utensils and woolen blankets, Indians neglected their traditional artisan skills, making fewer flint hoes, clay pots, and skin garments. "Every necessity of life we must have from the white people," a Cherokee chief complained. Religious autonomy vanished as well. When French missionaries won converts among the Hurons, Iroquois, and Illinois, they divided Indian communities into hostile religious factions.

Likewise, constant warfare for furs altered the dynamics of tribal politics by shifting power from cautious elders to headstrong young warriors. The sachems (chiefs), a group of young Seneca warriors said scornfully, "were a parcell of Old People who say much but who Mean or Act very little." The position and status of Indian women changed in especially complex ways. Traditionally, eastern woodland women had a voice in political councils because they were the chief providers of food and handcrafted goods. As a French Jesuit noted of the Iroquois, "The women are always the first to deliberate . . . on private or community matters. They hold their councils apart and . . . advise the chiefs . . . , so that the latter may deliberate on them in their turn." The disruption of farming by warfare and the influx of European goods undermined the economic basis of women's power. Yet, paradoxically, among victorious warring tribes such as the Iroquois, the influence of women probably increased in other respects; for example, women were responsible for the cultural assimilation of hundreds of captives.

There is no doubt that the sheer extent of the fur industry—the slaughter of hundreds of thousands of beaver, deer, otter, and other animals—profoundly altered the environment. As early as the 1630s, a French Jesuit worried that the Montagnais people, who lived north of the St. Lawrence, were killing so many beaver that they

Ætatis suæ 21. Aº 1616.

An English View of Pocahontas
By depicting the Indian princess Pocahontas as a well-dressed European woman, the artist casts her as a symbol of peaceful assimilation into English culture. In actuality, marriages between white men (often fur traders) and Indian women usually resulted in bilingual families that absorbed elements from both cultures.
National Portrait Gallery, Smithsonian Institution/ Art Resource, New York.

would "exterminate the species in this Region, as has happened among the Hurons." As the animal populations died off, streams ran faster (there were fewer beaver dams) and the underbrush grew denser (there were fewer deer to trim the vegetation). The native environment, as well as its animals and peoples, were now part of a new American world of relentless exploitation and little civility.

▶ Compare the causes of the uprisings led by Popé in New Mexico and Metacom in New England. Which was more successful? Why?

▶ What were the major social and environmental developments that made America a new world for both Europeans and Indians?

SUMMARY

We have seen that Spain created a permanent settlement in North America in 1565 and that England, France, and the Dutch Republic did likewise between 1607 and 1614. All of these European incursions spread devastating diseases among the native peoples. All reduced some Indians to subject peoples. And except for the Dutch, all involved efforts to spread Christianity. There were important differences as well. The French and the Dutch established fur-trading colonies, while the Spanish and the English created settler colonies. However, Spanish settlers intermarried with the Indians, but the English did not.

We also saw major differences and similarities between England's Chesapeake colonies, in which bound laborers raised tobacco for export to Europe, and those in New England, where pious Puritan yeoman lived in self-governing farming communities. But both regions boasted representative political institutions. Both experienced Indian wars in the first decades of settlement (in Virginia in 1622 and in New England in 1636) and again in 1675–1676. Indeed, the simultaneous eruption of Bacon's Rebellion and Metacom's War suggests that the histories of the two English regions had begun to converge.

Connections: Religion

In the essay that opens Part One, we stated that

> The American experience profoundly changed religious institutions and values. . . . American Protestant Christianity became increasingly tolerant, democratic, and optimistic.

In Chapter 2, we began our discussion of religion by discussing the migration of Anglicans to Virginia, Catholics to Maryland, and Puritans to New England. We saw how religious diversity and ideological principles thwarted attempts to enforce spiritual conformity in Massachusetts Bay and to create strong established churches in Maryland, Plymouth Colony, and Rhode Island. We will revisit issues of religious uniformity and tolerance in Chapter 3, in a discussion of Quakers in Pennsylvania and West New Jersey in the 1680s, and in Chapter 4, with an analysis of the migration to British North America between 1720 and 1760 of Scots-Irish Presbyterians, German Lutherans, and other European Protestants.

TIMELINE

1539–1543 ▸	Coronado and de Soto lead gold-seeking expeditions	**1630** ▸	Puritans found Massachusetts Bay Colony
1565 ▸	Spain establishes a fort at St. Augustine	**1634** ▸	Maryland settled as Catholic refuge
1598 ▸	Acomas rebel in New Mexico	**1636** ▸	Puritan-Pequot War
1603–1625 ▸	Reign of James I, advocate of "divine right" of kings	**1636** ▸	Roger Williams founds Providence, Rhode Island
1607 ▸	English traders settle Jamestown	**1637** ▸	Anne Hutchinson banished from Massachusetts Bay
1608 ▸	Samuel de Champlain founds Quebec	**1640s** ▸	Iroquois initiate wars over fur trade
1614 ▸	Dutch set up fur-trading post at Fort Orange (Albany)	**1642–1659** ▸	Puritan Revolution in England
1619 ▸	First Africans arrive in the Chesapeake region	**1651** ▸	First Navigation Act
▸	House of Burgesses convenes in Virginia	**1660** ▸	Restoration of English monarchy
1620 ▸	Pilgrims found Plymouth Colony	▸	Tobacco prices fall and remain low
1620–1660 ▸	Chesapeake colonies experience tobacco boom	**1664** ▸	English conquer New Netherland
1621 ▸	Dutch West India Company granted charter	**1675** ▸	Bacon's Rebellion
		1675–1676 ▸	Metacom's uprising
1622 ▸	Opechancanough's uprising	**1680** ▸	Popé's rebellion in New Mexico
1624 ▸	Virginia becomes a royal colony	**1692** ▸	Salem witchcraft trials
1625–1649 ▸	Charles I reigns and is executed	**1705** ▸	Virginia enacts law defining slavery

The forced migration of hundreds of thousands of Africans, one of the central themes of Chapter 3, will add complexity to our story of colonial religion. Some African slaves were Muslims; many more relied for spiritual substance and moral guidance on African gods and the powers they saw in nature. As we will see in Chapter 4, the Great Awakening, a far-reaching Christian revival during the 1740s and 1750s, brought only a few Africans into Christian churches but significantly increased the diversity of religious institutions and beliefs among Europeans. As the timeline for Part One suggests, key themes of the American experience include religious liberty, pluralism, and tolerance.

FOR FURTHER EXPLORATION

For an insightful narrative of Spain's northern adventures, consult David Weber, *The Spanish Frontier in North America* (1992). Bernard Bailyn, *The Peopling of British North America* (1986), presents a brief, vivid history of English settlement. In *American Slavery, American Freedom* (1975), Edmund Morgan offers a compelling portrait of life in early Virginia. John Demos, *The Unredeemed Captive: A Family Story from Early America* (1994), relates the gripping tale of Eunice Williams, a Puritan girl who was captured by and lived her life among the Mohawks. Two other fine studies of Native American life are James Merrell, *The Indians' New World: Catawbas and Their Neighbors* (1989), and Colin Calloway, *New Worlds for All: Indians, Europeans, and the Remaking of Early America* (1997).

Two fine Web sites are "Caleb Johnson's Mayflower History" (**www.mayflowerhistory .com/**) and "The Plymouth Colony Archive Project" (**etext.lib.virginia.edu/users/deetz/**). For insight into life in colonial New England, see the Web site for *Colonial House* (**www.pbs.org/wnet/colonialhouse/about.html**) and the Web site for the "Salem Witchcraft Trials" (**etext.lib.virginia.edu/salem/witchcraft/**). "Colonial Williamsburg" (**www.colonialwilliamsburg.org/history/**) offers an extensive collection of documents, illustrations, and secondary texts about colonial life. A two-hour-long PBS video, *Surviving Columbus*, traces the history of the Pueblo Indians over 450 years. "First Nations Histories" (**www.tolatsga.org/Compacts.html**) offers information on many North American Indian peoples.

TEST YOUR KNOWLEDGE

To assess your mastery of the material in this chapter and for Web sites, images, and documents related to this chapter, visit **bedfordstmartins.com/henrettaconcise**.

Creating a British Empire in America

1660–1750

These two words, Negro and Slave, [have become] Homogeneous and Convertible; even as Negro and Christian, Englishman and Heathen, are [now] made opposites.

— The Reverend Morgan Godwyn, 1680

When Charles II came to the throne in 1660, England was a second-class commercial power, its merchants picking up the crumbs left by the worldwide maritime empire of the Dutch. "What we want is more of the trade the Dutch now have," declared the Duke of Albemarle, a trusted minister of the king and a proprietor of Carolina. To get it, the English government embarked on a century-long quest for trade and empire. It passed a series of Navigation Acts, designed to exclude Dutch ships from its colonies, and it went to war to destroy Holland's maritime dominance. By the 1720s, Great Britain (the recently unified kingdoms of England and Scotland) had seized control of the transatlantic trade in American sugar and African slaves. The emerging British Empire, boasted the ardent imperialist Malachy Postlethwayt, "was a magnificent superstructure of American commerce and naval power on an African foundation."

That was only the half of it. British commerce increasingly spanned the world. It exported woolen goods to Europe, America, and Africa. Its merchants bought cotton textiles in India to trade for slaves in West Africa and carried silver to China to exchange for tea, ceramics, and silks. To protect the empire's valuable sugar colonies and trade routes, British ministers repeatedly went to war, first against the Dutch and then against the French. The goal—to preserve a mercantile system in British America and win "free entry" into the commerce of other empires—was increasingly successful. Boasted one English pamphleteer: "We are, of any nation, the best situated for trade, . . . capable of giving maritime laws to the world."

That dictum included Britain's North American colonies. When imperial official Edward Randolph reported from New England in the early 1670s that "there is no notice taken of the act of navigation," the home government undertook to impose its political will on the American settlements.

The Politics of Empire, 1660–1713

Before 1660, England governed its New England and Chesapeake colonies haphazardly. Taking advantage of that laxness and the English civil war, local "big men" (oligarchies of Puritan magistrates and tobacco planters) ran their societies as they wished. After the monarchy was restored in 1660, royal bureaucrats tried to impose order on the unruly settlements and, enlisting the aid of Indian allies, warred with rival European powers.

The Great Aristocratic Land Grab

When Charles II (r. 1660–1685) ascended the English throne, he quickly established new settlements: the Restoration Colonies, as historians call them. In 1663, Charles paid off a monetary and political debt to eight loyal noblemen with the gift of Carolina, an area long claimed by Spain and populated by thousands of Indians. He bestowed an equally huge grant on his brother James, the Duke of York, who received New Jersey and the just-conquered Dutch colony of New Netherland (now renamed New York). James quickly conveyed the ownership of New Jersey to two of the Carolina proprietors.

In one of the great land grabs in history, a handful of English nobles had taken title to vast provinces. Like Lord Baltimore's Maryland, their new colonies were proprietorships: The aristocrats owned all the land and could rule as they wished, provided their laws conformed broadly to those of England. Most proprietors envisioned a traditional European society presided over by a landed gentry and the Church of England. The Fundamental Constitutions of Carolina (1669), for example, prescribed a **manorial system**, with a mass of serfs governed by a handful of powerful nobles.

The manorial system proved to be a fantasy. The first settlers in North Carolina were primarily poor families and runaway servants from Virginia and English Quakers, an equality-minded radical Protestant sect (also known as the Society of Friends). Quakers "think there is no difference between a Gentleman and a labourer," complained one Anglican clergyman. Refusing to work on large manors, the settlers raised corn, hogs, and tobacco on modest family farms. In 1677, inspired by Bacon's Rebellion in Virginia, the residents of Albemarle County staged their own uprising. Angered by taxes on tobacco exports to support the Anglican Church, they rebelled again in 1708. The residents were "stubborn and disobedient," a wealthy Anglican landowner charged, and by deposing a series of governors, they forced the proprietors to abandon their dreams of a feudal society.

In South Carolina, the colonists also refused to accept the Fundamental Constitutions. Many of the white settlers there were migrants from the overcrowded sugar-producing island of Barbados, and they wanted to create a hierarchical society based on slavery. They used enslaved workers—both Africans and Native Americans—to raise cattle and food crops for export to the West Indies. Carolina merchants also opened a lucrative trade in deerskins with neighboring Indian peoples. In exchange for rum and guns, the Carolinians' Indian trading partners also provided slaves—captives from other Native American peoples. By 1708,

William Penn's Treaty with the Indians, 1683

In 1771, Benjamin West executed this famous picture of William Penn's meeting with the Lenni-Lanapes, who called themselves "the Common People." As a Quaker, Penn refused to seize Indian lands; instead, he negotiated their purchase. Penn was favorably impressed by the Lenni-Lanapes: "For their persons they are generally tall, straight, well built, and of singular proportion," he wrote in 1683. "They tread strong and clever, and mostly walk with a lofty chin." Pennsylvania Academy of the Fine Arts, Philadelphia.

For more help analyzing this image, see the Online Study Guide at **bedfordstmartins.com/henrettaconcise**.

white Carolinians were working their coastal plantations with 1,400 Indian and 2,900 African slaves, and brutal Indian warfare continued in the backcountry. South Carolina would remain a violent frontier settlement until the 1720s.

In dramatic contrast to the Carolinians, the 15,000 migrants who settled in Pennsylvania in the late seventeenth century pursued a pacifistic policy toward Native Americans and quickly became prosperous. In 1681, Charles II bestowed Pennsylvania (which included present-day Delaware) on William Penn in payment for a large debt owed to Penn's father. The younger Penn was born to wealth, owned substantial estates in Ireland and England, and lived lavishly — with a country mansion, fine clothes, and eight servants. Destined by birth for courtly pursuits, Penn instead joined the Quakers, who condemned extravagance. Penn designed Pennsylvania as a refuge for his fellow Quakers, who were persecuted in England because they refused to serve in the military or pay taxes to support the Church of England. Penn himself spent more than two years in jail for preaching his beliefs.

Like the Puritans, the Quakers wanted to restore Christianity to its early simple spirituality. But they rejected the Puritans' pessimistic Calvinist doctrines, which restricted salvation to a small elect. The Quakers followed the teachings of two English visionaries, George Fox and Margaret Fell, who argued that God had imbued all men — and women — with an "inner light" of grace or understanding. Reflecting this emphasis on gender equality, 350 Quaker women would serve as ministers in the colonies.

Penn's Frame of Government (1681) applied the Quakers' radical beliefs to politics. It ensured religious freedom by prohibiting a legally established church, and it promoted political equality by allowing all property-owning men to vote and hold office. Cheered by these provisions, thousands of Quakers—mostly yeomen families from the northwest Midland region of England—flocked to Pennsylvania. Initially, they settled along the Delaware River near the city of Philadelphia, which Penn himself laid out in a grid with wide main streets and many parks. To attract European Protestants, Penn published pamphlets in Dutch and German promising cheap land and religious toleration. In 1683, migrants from Saxony founded Germantown (just outside Philadelphia), and thousands of other Germans soon followed. Ethnic diversity, pacifism, and freedom of conscience made Pennsylvania the most open and democratic of the Restoration Colonies.

From Mercantilism to Imperial Dominion

As Charles II gave away his American lands, his ministers devised policies to keep colonial trade in English hands. Since the 1560s, the English crown had used government subsidies and charters to stimulate English manufacturing and foreign trade. Now it extended these mercantilist policies to the American settlements through the Navigation Acts.

According to mercantilist theory, the colonies would produce agricultural goods and raw materials, which English merchants would carry to England. Certain goods would be exported immediately to Europe in return for **specie** (gold or silver coin) or goods; other goods would be manufactured into finished products and then exported. The Navigation Act of 1651 kept this trade in English hands. It excluded Dutch merchants from the English colonies and required that goods be carried on ships owned by English or colonial merchants. New parliamentary acts in 1660 and 1663 strengthened the ban on foreign traders, required the colonists to ship sugar and tobacco only to England, and mandated that colonists import European goods only through England. To pay the customs officials who enforced these mercantilist laws, the Revenue Act of 1673 imposed a "plantation duty" on American exports of sugar and tobacco.

The English government backed these policies with military force. In three commercial wars between 1652 and 1674, the English navy drove the Dutch from New Netherland, seized control of commerce in the North Atlantic, and contested Holland's control of the Atlantic slave trade by attacking Dutch forts and ships along the West African coast. Meanwhile, English merchants expanded their fleets, which increased in capacity from 150,000 tons in 1640 to 340,000 tons in 1690.

Many colonists ignored the mercantilist laws and continued to trade with Dutch merchants and to import sugar and molasses from the French West Indies. The Massachusetts Bay assembly boldly declared: "The laws of England are bounded within the seas [surrounding it] and do not reach America." Outraged by this insolence, an English customs official called for troops to "reduce Massachusetts to obedience." Instead, the Lords of Trade—the administrative body charged with colonial affairs—opted for a punitive legal strategy. In 1679, it denied the claim of Massachusetts Bay to New Hampshire and eventually established a completely separate royal colony there. Then, in 1684, the Lords of Trade persuaded an English court to annul the charter of Massachusetts Bay because the Puritan government had violated the Navigation Acts and virtually outlawed the Church of England.

The Puritans' troubles had only begun, thanks to the accession of King James II (r. 1685–1688). The new monarch was an aggressive and inflexible ruler. During the reign of Oliver Cromwell, James had grown up in exile in France, and he admired its authoritarian king, Louis XIV. Believing that monarchs had a "divine right" to rule, James instructed the Lords of Trade to impose strict royal control on the American colonies. In 1686, the Lords revoked the corporate charters of Connecticut and Rhode Island and merged them with the Massachusetts Bay and Plymouth colonies to form a new royal province, the Dominion of New England. As governor of the Dominion, James II appointed Sir Edmund Andros, a hard-edged former military officer. Two years later, James II added New York and New Jersey to the Dominion, creating a vast colony that stretched from Maine to Pennsylvania.

The Target of the Glorious Revolution: James II

In Godfrey Kneller's portrait of James II (r. 1685–1688), the king's stance and facial expression suggest his forceful, arrogant personality. James set out to consolidate England's North American empire, but his arbitrary measures and Catholic sympathies prompted rebellions that cost him the throne. National Portrait Gallery, London.

The Dominion extended to America the authoritarian model of colonial rule the English government had imposed on Catholic Ireland. When England had recaptured New York from the Dutch in 1674, James II refused to allow an elective assembly and ruled by decree. Now he imposed absolutist rule on the entire Dominion by ordering Governor Andros to abolish the existing legislative assemblies. In Massachusetts, Andros immediately banned town meetings, angering villagers who prized local self-rule, and advocated public worship in the Church of England, offending Puritan Congregationalists. Even worse, from the colonists' perspective, the governor challenged all land titles granted under the original Massachusetts Bay charter. Andros offered to provide new deeds, but only if the colonists would agree to pay an annual fee.

The Glorious Revolution in England and America

Fortunately for the colonists, James II angered English political leaders as much as Andros alienated American settlers. The king revoked the charters of English towns, rejected the advice of Parliament, and aroused popular opposition by openly practicing Roman Catholicism. Then, in 1688, James's Spanish Catholic wife gave birth to a son, raising the prospect of a Catholic heir to the throne. To forestall that outcome, Protestant bishops and parliamentary leaders in the Whig Party led a quick and bloodless coup known as the Glorious Revolution. Backed by the populace and the military, they forced James into exile and in 1689 enthroned Mary, his Protestant daughter by his first wife, and her Dutch Protestant husband, William of Orange. The Whigs were not democrats: They wanted political power, especially the power to levy taxes, in the hands of the gentry, merchants, and other substantial property owners. Whig politicians forced King William and Queen Mary to accept a Declaration of Rights, which created a constitutional monarchy that enhanced the powers of the House of Commons at the expense of the crown.

To justify their coup, the members of Parliament relied on political philosopher John Locke. In his *Two Treatises on Government* (1690), Locke rejected the divine right monarchy celebrated by James II; instead, he argued that the legitimacy of government rests on the consent of the governed and that individuals have inalienable natural rights to life, liberty, and property. Locke's celebration of individual rights and representative government had a lasting influence in America, where many political leaders wanted to expand the powers of the colonial assemblies.

The Glorious Revolution sparked rebellions by Protestant colonists in Massachusetts, Maryland, and New York. When news of the coup reached Boston in April 1689, Puritan leaders, supported by 2,000 militiamen, seized Governor Andros, accused him of Catholic sympathies, and shipped him back to England. Heeding American complaints of authoritarian rule, the new monarchs broke up the Dominion of New England. However, they refused to restore the old Puritan-dominated government of Massachusetts Bay; instead, in 1692, they created a new royal colony (which included Plymouth and Maine). The new charter empowered the king to appoint the governor and customs officials; it gave the vote to all male property owners, not just Puritan church members; and it eliminated Puritan restrictions on the Church of England.

The uprising in Maryland had economic as well as religious causes. Since 1660, falling tobacco prices had hurt smallholders, tenant farmers, and former indentured servants. These poorer farmers were overwhelmingly Protestants, and they resented the rising taxes and the high fees imposed by wealthy proprietary officials, who were mostly Catholics. When Parliament ousted James II, a Protestant association mustered 700 men and forcibly removed the Catholic governor. The Lords of Trade supported this Protestant initiative: They suspended Lord Baltimore's proprietorship, imposed royal government, and made the Church of England the legal religion in the colony. This arrangement lasted until 1715, when Benedict Calvert, the fourth Lord Baltimore, converted to the Anglican faith and the king restored the proprietorship to the Calvert family.

In New York, Jacob Leisler led the rebellion against the Dominion of New England. Leisler was a German soldier who had worked for the Dutch West India Company, become a merchant, and married into a prominent Dutch family in New York. He was also a militant Calvinist, rigid and hot tempered. When New England settlers on Long Island, angered by James's prohibition of representative institutions, learned of the king's ouster, they repudiated the Dominion. The rebels quickly won the support of Dutch Protestant artisans in New York City, who welcomed the succession of Queen Mary and her Dutch husband. Led by Leisler, the Dutch militia ousted Lieutenant Governor Nicholson, an Andros appointee and an alleged Catholic sympathizer.

Initially, all classes and ethnic groups rallied behind Leisler, who headed a temporary government. However, Leisler's denunciations of political rivals as "popish dogs" and "Roages, Rascalls, and Devills" soon alienated many English-speaking New Yorkers. When Leisler imprisoned forty of his political opponents, imposed new taxes, and championed the artisans' cause, the prominent Dutch merchants who had traditionally controlled the city's government condemned his rule. In 1691, the merchants found an ally in Colonel Henry Sloughter, the newly appointed governor, who had Leisler indicted for treason. Convicted by an English jury, Leisler was hanged and then decapitated, an act of ethnic vengeance that corrupted New York politics for a generation.

The Glorious Revolution of 1688–1689 began a new, nonauthoritarian political era in both England and America. In England, William and Mary ruled as constitutional monarchs and promoted an empire based on commerce. Because the new Protestant monarchs wanted colonial support for a war against Catholic France, they accepted the overthrow of the Dominion of New England and allowed the restoration of self-government in Massachusetts and New York. Parliament created a Board of Trade in 1696 to supervise the American settlements, but it had limited success. Settlers and proprietors resisted the board's attempt to install royal governments, as did many English political leaders, who feared an increase in monarchical power. The result was another period of lax political administration during which the home government imposed only a few laws and taxes on the mainland settlements. It allowed local elites to rule the American colonies and encouraged English merchants to develop them as sources of trade.

Imperial Wars and Native Peoples

In a world of commercial competition, Britain's success depended on both mercantile skills and military power. Between 1689 and 1815, Britain fought a series of increasingly intense wars with France. To win wars in Western Europe and the Caribbean,

British leaders created a powerful central state that spent three-quarters of its revenue on military and naval expenses. As the wars spread to the North American mainland, they involved colonists and Native Americans, both of whom tried to turn the fighting to their own advantage.

The first significant battles in North America occurred during the War of the Spanish Succession (1702–1713), which pitted Britain against France and Spain. English settlers in the Carolinas armed the Creeks, whose 15,000 members farmed the fertile lands along the present-day border of Georgia and Alabama. A joint English-Creek expedition attacked Spanish Florida, burning the town of St. Augustine but failing to capture the nearby fort. To protect Havana in nearby Cuba, the Spanish reinforced St. Augustine and unsuccessfully attacked Charleston, South Carolina.

The Creeks had their own agenda: To become the dominant tribe in the region, they needed to vanquish their longtime enemies, the pro-French Choctaws to the west and the Spanish-allied Apalachees to the south. Beginning in 1704, a force of Creek and Yamasee warriors destroyed the remaining Franciscan missions in northern Florida, attacked the Spanish settlement at Pensacola, and captured 1,000 Apalachees, whom they sold to South Carolinian slave traders for use in the West Indies. Simultaneously, a Carolina-supplied Creek expedition attacked the Iroquois-speaking Tuscarora people of North Carolina, killing hundreds, executing 160 male captives, and sending 400 women and children into slavery. The surviving Tuscaroras migrated to the north and joined the Iroquois in New York (who now became the Six Iroquois Nations). The Carolinians, having used Indians to kill Spaniards, now died at the hands of their former allies. When English traders demanded the payment of trade debts in 1715, the Creeks and Yamasees revolted. They killed 400 colonists before being overwhelmed by the Carolinians and their new Indian allies, the Cherokees.

Native Americans also joined in the warfare between French Catholics in Canada and English Protestants in New England. With French aid, Catholic Mohawk and Abenaki warriors took revenge on their Puritan enemies. They destroyed English settlements in Maine, and in 1704, they attacked the western Massachusetts town of Deerfield, where they killed 48 residents and carried 112 into captivity. In response, New England militia attacked French settlements and, in 1710, joined with British naval forces to seize Port Royal in French Acadia (Nova Scotia). However, a major British–New England expedition against the French stronghold at Quebec failed miserably.

The New York frontier remained quiet. French and English merchants did not want to disrupt the lucrative fur trade, and the Iroquois, tired of war, had adopted a policy of "aggressive neutrality." In 1701, the Iroquois concluded a peace treaty with France and its Indian allies. Simultaneously, the Iroquois renewed the Covenant Chain, a series of military alliances with the English government in New York and its Indian friends (see Chapter 2). For the next half century, the Iroquois exploited their strategic location between the English and the French colonies by trading with both but refusing to fight for either. The Iroquois's strategy, according to their Delaware ally Teedyuscung, was "to defend our land against both."

Stalemated militarily in America, Britain won major territorial and commercial concessions through its victories in Europe. In the Treaty of Utrecht (1713), Britain obtained Newfoundland, Acadia, and the Hudson Bay region of northern Canada from France, as well as access through Albany to the western Indian trade. From Spain,

▶ What was the role of the colonies in the British mercantilist system?

▶ Explain the causes and the results of the Glorious Revolutions in England and America.

Britain acquired the strategic fortress of Gibraltar at the entrance to the Mediterranean and a thirty-year contract to supply slaves to Spanish America. These gains advanced Britain's quest for commercial supremacy, preserved its Protestant monarchy, and brought peace to eastern North America for a generation.

The Imperial Slave Economy

Britain's focus on America reflected the growth of a new agricultural and commercial order—the South Atlantic System—which produced sugar, tobacco, rice, and other subtropical products for an international market. At its center stood plantation societies ruled by European planter-merchants and worked by hundreds of thousands of enslaved Africans.

The South Atlantic System

The South Atlantic System had its center in Brazil and the West Indies, and sugar was its primary product. Before 1500, the world's people enjoyed few sweeteners—mostly honey and fruit juices. Then European planters developed sugarcane plantations in Brazil and the islands of the Caribbean Sea. The craving for the potent new sweetener was so intense that by 1900, sugar accounted for an astonishing 20 percent of the calories consumed by the world's people.

European merchants, investors, and planters garnered the profits of the South Atlantic System. Following mercantilist principles, they provided the plantations with tools and equipment to grow and process the sugarcane and ships to carry it to Europe. But it was the Atlantic slave trade that made the system run. Between 1520 and 1650, Portuguese traders accounted for 95 percent of the 820,000 Africans carried across the Atlantic—about 4,000 slaves each year before 1600 and 10,000 annually thereafter. Over the next half century, the Dutch dominated the Atlantic slave trade; then, between 1700 and 1800, the British became the prime carriers, transporting about 2.5 million of the total of 6.1 million Africans sent to the Americas. To secure this vast number of workers, European merchants relied on African-run slave-catching systems. These systems extended far into Africa's interior and funneled captives to Elmina, Calabar, Luanda, and other slave ports.

The cultivation of sugar—and, after 1750, coffee—drove the slave trade. In the 1620s, the English colonized a number of small West Indian islands: St. Christopher, Nevis, Montserrat, and especially Barbados, which had an extensive amount of arable land. Until the 1650s, most settlers were English, smallholders and indentured servants, who exported tobacco and livestock hides. In fact, there were more English residents in the West Indies (some 44,000) than in the Chesapeake (12,000) and New England (23,000) colonies combined.

Sugar transformed Barbados and the other islands into slave-based plantation societies. To provide raw sugar for refineries in Amsterdam, Dutch merchants provided English planters with money to buy land, sugar-processing equipment, and

A Sugar Mill in the French West Indies, 1655
Sugar powered the South Atlantic System. Its production demanded hard labor and considerable expertise. As this romanticized view shows, field slaves did the hard work, cutting the sugarcane and carrying or carting it to the oxen- (or wind-) powered mill, where it was pressed to yield the juice. Then skilled slave artisans took over. They carefully heated the juice and, at the proper moment, added ingredients to produce granulated sugar. The remaining liquid was molasses, a bitter-tasting sweetener that could be distilled into rum. The Granger Collection, New York.

slaves. By 1680, an elite group of 175 planters dominated Barbados's economy; they owned more than half the land and half the slaves, who numbered more than 50,000. In 1692, exploited Irish servants and island-born African slaves staged a major uprising, which was brutally suppressed. As social inequality and racial conflict increased, hundreds of English farmers fled to South Carolina and the large island of Jamaica, which England had seized from Spain in 1655. But the days of Caribbean smallholders were numbered. English sugar merchants soon invested heavily in Jamaica; by 1750, it had 700 large sugar plantations worked by more than 105,000 slaves and had become the wealthiest British colony.

Sugar was a rich man's crop because it could be produced most efficiently on large plantations. Scores of slaves planted and cut the sugarcane, which was then processed by expensive equipment—crushing mills, boiling houses, distilling apparatus—into raw sugar, molasses, and rum. The affluent planter-merchants who controlled the sugar industry drew annual profits of more than 10 percent on their investment. As Scottish economist Adam Smith noted in his famous treatise *The Wealth of Nations* (1776), sugar was the most profitable crop in Europe and America.

The South Atlantic System brought wealth to the entire British—and European—economy. Most British West Indian plantations belonged to absentee landlords who lived in England, where they spent their profits and formed a powerful "sugar lobby." Moreover, the Navigation Acts kept the trade in British sugar in the hands of British merchants, who exported it to foreign markets. By 1750, British reshipments of American sugar and tobacco to Europe accounted for half the nation's exports. Enormous profits also flowed into Britain from the slave trade. The value of the guns, iron, rum, cloth, and other European products used to buy slaves was relatively small—only about one-tenth (in the 1680s) to one-third (by the 1780s) of the value of the crops those slaves produced in America. This substantial differential allowed the Royal African Company and other English traders to sell slaves in the West Indies for three to five times what they paid for them in Africa.

These massive profits drove the expansion of the slave trade. At its height in the 1790s, Britain annually exported 300,000 guns to Africa, and a British ship carrying 300 to 350 slaves left an African port every other day. This commerce stimulated the entire British economy. English and Scottish shipyards built hundreds of vessels, and thousands of people worked in trade-related industries: building port facilities and warehouses, refining sugar and tobacco, distilling rum from molasses, and manufacturing textiles and iron products for the growing markets in Africa and America. Over 1,000 British merchant ships plied the Atlantic by 1750, providing a supply of experienced sailors and laying the foundation for the supremacy of the Royal Navy.

Africa, Africans, and the Slave Trade

As the South Atlantic System enhanced European prosperity, it imposed enormous costs on West and Central Africa. Between 1550 and 1870, the Atlantic slave trade uprooted almost eleven million Africans, draining many lands south of the Sahara of people and wealth. Equally important, the slave trade changed African society. By directing commerce away from the savannas and the Islamic world across the Sahara, the Atlantic slave trade diminished the economic and cultural vitality of many interior states and peoples. It also prompted the growth of militaristic centralized states in the coastal areas and the use of European manufactures and Indian textiles throughout the continent (Map 3.1).

Warfare and slaving had been an integral part of African life for centuries, driven by conflicts among numerous states and ethnic groups. But the South Atlantic System dramatically increased the demand for African labor, and slaving wars became a favorite tactic of ambitious kings and plundering warlords. "Whenever the King of Barsally wants Goods or Brandy," an observer noted, "the King goes and ransacks some of his enemies' towns, seizing the people and selling them." Supplying the Atlantic trade became a way of life in

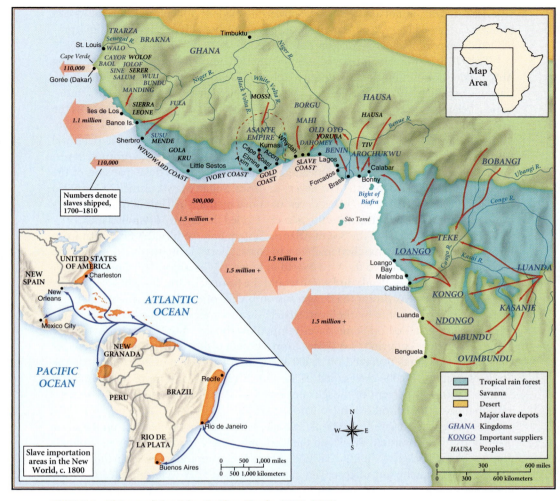

MAP 3.1 Africa and the Atlantic Slave Trade, 1700–1810

The tropical rain forest of West Africa was home to scores of peoples and dozens of kingdoms. Some kingdoms became aggressive slavers. Dahomey's army, for example, seized tens of thousands of captives in wars with neighboring peoples and sold them to European traders. About 15 percent of the captives died during the grueling Middle Passage, the transatlantic voyage between Africa and the Americas. Most of the survivors labored on sugar plantations in Brazil and the British and French West Indies.

the West African state of Dahomey, where the royal house monopolized the sale of slaves and used European guns to create a military despotism. Dahomey's army, which included a contingent of 5,000 women, systematically raided the interior for captives; between 1680 and 1730, Dahomey annually exported 20,000 slaves exported from the ports of Allada and Whydah. The Asante kings along the Gold Coast also used European firearms and slave trading to expand their political dominion during the 1720s. Conquering neighboring states along the coast and Muslim kingdoms in the savanna, they created a prosperous empire of three million to five million people. Yet participation in Atlantic trade remained a choice for Africans, not a necessity. The powerful kingdom of Benin, famous for its cast bronzes and carved ivory, kept its many male slaves for labor at home and, for a time, prohibited the export of all slaves, male and female.

The trade in humans produced untold misery. Hundreds of thousands of young Africans died, and millions more endured a brutal life in the Americas. In Africa itself, class divisions hardened as people of noble birth enslaved and sold those of lesser status. Gender relations shifted as well. Men constituted two-thirds of the slaves sent across the Atlantic because European planters paid more for "men and stout men boys" and because Africans sold women captives in local or Saharan slave markets as agricultural workers, house servants, and concubines. The resulting sexual imbalance prompted men to take several wives, changing the meaning of marriage. Finally, the expansion of the Atlantic trade increased the extent of slavery in Africa. Sultan Mawlay Ismail of Morocco (r. 1672–1727) owned 150,000 black slaves, obtained by trade in Timbuktu and by wars in Senegal. In Africa, as in the Americas, slavery eroded the dignity of human life.

The Africans sold into the South Atlantic System had the bleakest fate. Torn from their villages, they were marched in chains to coastal ports. From there, they made the perilous **Middle Passage** to the New World in hideously overcrowded ships. The captives had little to eat or drink, and some would die from dehydration. The feces, urine, and vomit below deck prompted dangerous outbreaks of dysentery, which took more lives. "I was so overcome by the heat, stench, and foul air that I nearly fainted," reported a European doctor. Some slaves jumped overboard, choosing to drown rather than endure more suffering (see Voices from Abroad, p. 80). Others staged violent revolts. Slave uprisings occurred on 2,000 voyages, roughly one of every ten Atlantic passages. Nearly 100,000 slaves died in these insurrections, and more than a million others — about 15 percent of those transported — died of diseases such as dysentery and smallpox on the month-long journey.

For those who survived the Middle Passage, things only got worse. Life on the sugar plantations of northwestern Brazil and the West Indies was a lesson in relentless exploitation. The slaves worked ten hours a day under the hot semitropical sun; slept in flimsy huts; and lived on a starchy diet of corn, yams, and dried fish. They were subjected to brutal discipline: "The fear of punishment is the principle [we use] . . . to keep them in awe and order," one planter declared. With sugar prices high and the cost of slaves low, many planters simply worked their slaves to death and then bought more. Between 1708 and 1735, British planters on Barbados imported about 85,000 Africans; however, the island's black population increased by only 4,000 (from 42,000 to 46,000). The constant influx of new slaves kept the black population thoroughly "African" in its languages, religions, and culture. "Here," wrote a Jamaican observer, "each different nation of Africa meet and dance after the manner of their own country . . . [and] retain most of their native customs."

Slavery in the Chesapeake and South Carolina

Following Bacon's Rebellion, planters in Virginia and Maryland presided over a "tobacco revolution." They now grew tobacco on large plantations rather than smallholdings and, taking advantage of the British slave trade, staffed them with enslaved Africans rather than white indentured servants. By 1720, Africans made up 20 percent of the Chesapeake population, and slavery had become a core institution, not just one of several forms of unfree

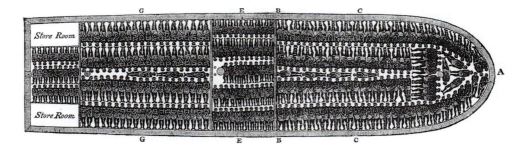

Two Views of the Middle Passage

The 1846 watercolor shows the cargo hold of a slave ship on a voyage to Brazil, which imported large numbers of Africans until the 1860s. Painted by a ship's officer, the picture minimizes the brutality of the Middle Passage—none of the slaves are in chains—and captures the Africans' humanity and dignity. A naval architect's drawing of packed-in slaves in a ship's hold better captures the actual conditions on most slave ships. Peabody and Essex Museum/Bridgeman Art Library.

The Brutal "Middle Passage"   OLAUDAH EQUIANO

Olaudah Equiano claimed to have been born in Igboland (in present-day southern Nigeria). But two scholars, one African and one Euro-American, writing independently, have recently argued that Equiano was born into slavery in South Carolina and drew on conversations with African-born slaves to write a fictitious history of an idyllic West African childhood, his enslavement at the age of eleven, and a traumatic passage across the Atlantic. It now appears that Equiano was a plantation slave who was purchased by an English sea captain. He bought his freedom in 1766, settled in London, became an antislavery activist, and, in 1789, published the memoir containing these selections.

My father, besides many slaves, had a numerous family of which seven lived to grow up, including myself and a sister who was the only daughter. . . . One day, when all our people were gone out to their works as usual and only I and my dear sister were left to mind the house, two men and a woman got over our walls, and in a moment seized us both. . . .

At length, after many days' travelling, during which I had often changed masters, I got into the hands of a chieftain in a very pleasant country. This man had two wives and some children, and they all used me extremely well and did all they could to comfort me, particularly the first wife, who was something like my mother. . . . I was again sold and carried through a number of places till . . . at the end of six or seven months after I had been kidnapped I arrived at the sea coast.

The first object which saluted my eyes when I arrived on the coast was the sea, and a slave ship which was then riding at anchor and waiting for its cargo. I now saw myself deprived of all chance of returning to my native country. . . . I was soon put down under the decks, and there I received such a salutation in my nostrils as I had never experienced in my life; so that with the loathsomeness of the stench and crying together, I became so sick and low that I was not able to eat, nor had I the least desire to taste any thing. I now wished for the last friend, death, to relieve me; but soon, to my grief, two of the white men offered me eatables, and on my refusing to eat, one of them held me fast by the hands and laid me across I think the windlass, and tied my feet while the other flogged me severely. . . . One day, when we had a smooth sea and moderate wind, two of my wearied country-men who were chained together (I was near them at the time), preferring death to such a life of misery, somehow made it through the nettings and jumped into the sea.

At last we came in sight of the island of Barbados; the white people got some old slaves from the land to pacify us. They told us we were not to be eaten but to work, and were soon to go on land where we should see many of our country people. This report eased us much; and sure enough soon after we were landed there came to us Africans of all languages.

SOURCE: *The Interesting Narrative of the Life of Olaudah Equiano, or Gustavus Vassa, the African, Written by Himself* (London, 1789), 15, 22–23, 28–29.

labor. Equally important, slavery was now defined in racial terms. Virginia legislators prohibited sexual intercourse between English and Africans in 1692; in 1705, they defined virtually all resident Africans as slaves: "All servants imported or brought into this country by sea or land who were not Christians in their native country shall be accounted and be slaves."

Still, conditions for slaves in Virginia and Maryland were much less severe than those in the West Indies, and slaves in the Chesapeake lived relatively long lives. Unlike sugar and rice, which were "killer crops" that demanded strenuous labor, tobacco cultivation required only steady, careful, physically undemanding labor. Slaves planted the young tobacco seedlings in the spring, hoed and weeded the crop during the summer, and in the fall picked and hung the leaves to cure over the winter. Moreover, diseases did not spread easily among Chesapeake slaves, because plantation quarters were less crowded and more dispersed than those in the West Indies. Finally, because tobacco profits were low, planters avoided the purchase of new slaves and treated their workers less harshly than West Indian planters did.

Some tobacco planters tried to increase their workforce by buying female slaves and encouraging them to have children. In 1720, women made up more than one-third of the Africans in Maryland, and the black population had begun to increase naturally. One absentee owner instructed his plantation agent "to be kind and indulgent to the breeding wenches, and not to force them when with child upon any service or hardship that will be injurious to them." By midcentury, slaves made up one-third of the Chesapeake population, and more than three-quarters of them were American born.

Slaves in South Carolina labored under much more oppressive conditions. The colony grew slowly until 1700, when planters began to plant and export rice to southern Europe, where it was in great demand. To expand production, planters imported thousands of Africans — some of them from rice-growing societies. By 1705, Africans formed a majority of the total population and 80 percent of those in rice-growing areas.

Most rice plantations lay in inland swamps, and the work was dangerous and exhausting. Slaves planted, weeded, and harvested the rice in ankle-deep mud. Pools of putrid water bred mosquitoes, which transmitted diseases that claimed hundreds of African lives. Other slaves, forced to move tons of dirt to build irrigation works, died from exhaustion. "The labour required [for growing rice] is only fit for slaves," a Scottish traveler remarked, "and I think the hardest work I have seen them engaged in." In South Carolina, as in the West Indies and Brazil, there were many slave deaths and few births, and the importation of new slaves constantly "re-Africanized" the black population.

The Emergence of an African American Community

Slaves came from many different states and peoples in West Africa and the Central African regions of Kongo and Angola. White planters welcomed ethnic diversity to deter slave revolts. "The safety of the Plantations," declared a widely read English pamphlet, "depends upon having Negroes from all parts of Guiny, who do not understand each other's languages and Customs and cannot agree to Rebel." By accident or design, most plantations drew laborers of many languages, including Kwa, Mande, and Kikongo. Of the slaves imported after 1730 into the Upper James River region of Virginia, 41 percent came from various ethnic groups in present-day Nigeria, and another 25 percent came from West-Central Africa. The rest hailed from the Windward and Gold coasts, Senegambia, and

Sierra Leone. In South Carolina, many plantation owners preferred laborers from the Gold Coast and Gambia, who had a reputation as hardworking farmers. But as African sources of slaves shifted southward after 1730, more than 30 percent of the colony's workers came from Kongo and Angola.

Initially, the slaves did not think of themselves as Africans or blacks but as members of a specific family, clan, or people — Wolof, Hausa, Ibo, Yoruba, Teke, Ngola — and they associated with others who shared their language and customs. In the Upper James River region, Ibo men and women arrived in equal numbers, married each other, and maintained their Ibo culture.

Over time, the slaves made friendships and married across ethnic lines. In the process, Africans created new languages. One was the Gullah dialect of the South Carolina lowlands, which combined English and African words in an African grammatical structure. "They have a language peculiar to themselves," a missionary reported, "a wild confused medley of Negro and corrupt English." In the Chesapeake region, where there were more American-born slaves, most people of African descent gradually lost their native tongues. In the 1760s, a European visitor to Virginia reported with surprise that "all the blacks spoke very good English."

A common language — Gullah or English or French (in Louisiana and the French West Indies) — was one key to the emergence of an African American community. A nearly equal number of men and women — which encouraged marriage, stable families, and continuity between generations — was another. In South Carolina, the high death rate among slaves undermined ties of family and kinship; but after 1725, Chesapeake-area blacks created strong nuclear families and extended kin relationships. Thus, all but 30 of the 128 slaves on one of Charles Carroll's estates in Maryland were members of two extended families. These African American kin groups passed on family names, traditions, and knowledge to the next generation, and gradually, a distinct culture developed. As one observer suggested, blacks had created a separate world, "a Nation within a Nation."

As the slaves forged a new identity, they carried on certain African practices but let others go. Many Africans arrived in America with ritual scars that white planters called "country markings"; these signs of ethnic identity fell into disuse on culturally diverse plantations. But the slaves' African heritage took tangible forms in hairstyles, the motifs used in wood carvings and pottery, the large wooden mortars and pestles used to hull rice, and the design of houses, in which rooms were arranged from front to back in a distinctive "I" pattern, not side by side as was common in English dwellings.

African values also persisted. Some slaves passed on Muslim beliefs, and many more told their children of the spiritual powers of conjurers, known as obeah or ifa, who knew the ways of the African gods. Thus, enslaved Yorubas consulted Orunmila, the god of fate, and other Africans (a Jamaican planter noted) relied on obeah "to revenge injuries and insults, discover and punish thieves and adulterers; [and] to predict the future."

Resistance and Accommodation

There were drastic limits on creativity among African Americans. Most slaves were denied education, the chance to accumulate material possessions, or the opportunity to create associations. Slaves who challenged these boundaries did so at their peril.

"Virginian Luxuries"
This painting by an unknown artist (c. 1810) depicts the physical and sexual exploitation inherent in a slave society. On the right, an owner chastises a male slave by beating him with a cane; on the left, ignoring the cultural and legal rules prohibiting sexual intercourse between whites and blacks, a white master prepares to bed his black mistress. Abby Aldrich Rockefeller Folk Art Collection, Colonial Williamsburg Foundation.

Planters whipped slaves who refused to work; some turned to greater cruelties. Declaring the chronic runaway Ballazore an "incorrigible rogue," a Virginia planter ordered all his toes cut off: "Nothing less than dismembering will reclaim him." Thomas Jefferson, who witnessed such punishments on his father's Virginia plantation, noted that each generation of whites was "nursed, educated, and daily exercised in tyranny": The relationship "between master and slave is a perpetual exercise of the most unremitting despotism on the one part, and degrading submission on the other." A fellow Virginian, planter George Mason, agreed: "Every Master is born a petty tyrant."

The extent of white violence depended on the size and density of the slave population. As Virginia planter William Byrd II complained in 1736, "Numbers make them insolent." In the northern colonies, where there were few slaves, white violence was sporadic. But plantation owners and overseers in the sugar- and rice-growing areas, where Africans outnumbered Europeans eight to one, routinely whipped assertive slaves. They prohibited their workers from leaving the plantation without special passes and called on their poor white neighbors to patrol the countryside at night, a duty that (authorities regularly reported) was "almost totally neglected."

Slaves dealt with their plight in several ways. Some newly arrived Africans fled to the frontier, where they established traditional villages or married into Indian tribes. American-born blacks who were fluent in English fled to towns, where they tried to pass as free men and women. The African Americans who remained enslaved bargained continually with their masters over the terms of their bondage. Some blacks bartered extra work for better food and clothes; others seized a small privilege and dared the master to revoke it. In that way, Sundays gradually became a day of rest—asserted as a right, rather than granted as a privilege. When bargaining failed, slaves protested silently by working slowly or stealing. Others, provoked beyond endurance, killed their owners or overseers. In the 1760s, in Amherst County, Virginia, a slave killed four whites; in Elizabeth City County, eight slaves strangled their master in bed. A few blacks even plotted rebellion, despite white superiority in guns and, in many regions, in numbers as well.

Predictably, South Carolina witnessed the largest slave uprising: the Stono Rebellion of 1739. The Catholic governor of the Spanish colony of Florida instigated the revolt by promising freedom to fugitive slaves. By February 1739, at least sixty-nine slaves had escaped to St. Augustine, and rumors circulated "that a Conspiracy was formed by Negroes in Carolina to rise and make their way out of the province." When war between England and Spain broke out in September (see p. 92), seventy-five Africans rose in revolt and killed a number of whites near the Stono River. According to one account, some of the rebels were Portuguese-speaking Catholics from the Kingdom of Kongo attracted by the prospect of life in Catholic Florida. Displaying their skills as soldiers—decades of brutal slave raiding in Kongo had militarized the society there—the rebels marched toward Florida "with Colours displayed and two Drums beating." White militia killed many of the Stono rebels, preventing a general uprising; after this, frightened whites cut slave imports and tightened plantation discipline.

William Byrd and the Rise of the Southern Gentry

As the southern colonies became full-fledged slave societies, life changed for whites as well as for blacks. Consider the career of William Byrd II (1674–1744). Byrd's father, a successful planter-merchant in Virginia, hoped to marry his children into the English gentry. To smooth his son's entry into landed society, Byrd sent him to England for his education. But his status-conscious classmates at the Felsted School shunned young Byrd, calling him a "colonial," a first bitter taste of the gradations of rank in English society.

Other rejections followed. Lacking aristocratic connections, Byrd was denied a post with the Board of Trade, passed over three times for the royal governorship of Virginia, and rejected in his efforts to marry a rich Englishwoman. In 1726, at age fifty-two, Byrd finally gave up and moved back to Virginia, where he sometimes felt he was "being buried alive." Accepting his lesser destiny as a member of the colony's elite, Byrd built an elegant brick mansion on the family's estate at Westover, sat in "the best pew in the church," and won an appointment to the governor's council.

William Byrd II's experience mirrored that of many planter-merchants, trapped in Virginia and South Carolina by the curse of their inferior colonial status. They used their wealth to rule over white yeomen families and tenant farmers and resorted to violence to exploit enslaved blacks, the American equivalent of the oppressed peasants of Europe. The planters used Africans to grow food as well as tobacco; to build houses, wagons, and tobacco casks; and to make shoes and clothes. By making their plantations self-sufficient, the Chesapeake elite survived the depressed tobacco market between 1670 and 1720.

To prevent another uprising like Bacon's Rebellion, the Chesapeake gentry addressed the concerns of middling and poor whites (see Chapter 2). They gradually lowered taxes: In Virginia, the annual head tax (on each adult man) fell from forty-five pounds of tobacco in 1675 to just five pounds in 1750. The gentry encouraged smallholders to improve their economic lot by investing in slaves, and many did so. By 1770, 60 percent of the English families in the Chesapeake colonies owned at least one slave. On the political front, planters now allowed poor yeomen and some tenants to vote. The strategy of the leading families—the Carters, Lees, Randolphs, and Robinsons—was to curry favor with these voters by bribing them with rum, money, and the promise of minor offices in county governments. In return, they expected the yeomen and tenants to elect them to office and defer to their rule. This horse-trading solidified the social position of the planter elite, which used its control of the House of Burgesses to limit the power of the royal governor. Hundreds of yeomen farmers benefited as well, tasting political power and garnering substantial fees and salaries as deputy sheriffs, road surveyors, estate appraisers, and grand jurymen.

Even as wealthy Chesapeake gentlemen formed political ties with smallholders, they consciously set themselves apart culturally. As late as the 1720s, many leading planters were boisterous, aggressive men who enjoyed the amusements of common folk—from hunting, hard drinking, and gambling on horse races to demonstrating their manly prowess by forcing themselves on female servants and slaves. As time passed, the planters began—like William Byrd II—to model themselves on the English aristocracy, remaining sexual predators but learning from advice books how to act like gentlemen in other regards: "I must not sit in others' places; Nor sneeze, nor cough in people's faces. Nor with my fingers pick my nose, Nor wipe my hands upon my clothes." Cultivating **gentility**—a refined but elaborate lifestyle—they replaced their modest wooden houses with mansions of brick and mortar. Robert "King" Carter, who owned hundreds of slaves, built a house that was seventy-five feet long, forty-four feet wide, and forty feet high; he filled it with fine furniture and rugs. Planters sent their sons to London to be educated as lawyers and gentlemen. But unlike Byrd's father, they expected their sons to return to America, marry local heiresses, and assume their fathers' roles: managing plantations, socializing with fellow gentry, and running the political system.

Wealthy Chesapeake and South Carolina women likewise emulated the English elite. They read English newspapers and fashionable magazines, wore the finest English clothes, and dined in the English fashion, with an elaborate afternoon tea. To improve their daughters' marriage prospects, parents hired English tutors to teach them proper etiquette. Once married, planter women deferred to their husbands, reared pious children, and maintained elaborate social networks, in time creating a new ideal: the southern gentlewoman. Using the profits generated by enslaved Africans in the South Atlantic System of commerce, wealthy planters formed an increasingly well educated, refined, and stable ruling class.

The Northern Maritime Economy

The South Atlantic System had a broad geographical reach. As early as the 1640s, New England farmers supplied the sugar islands with bread, lumber, fish, and meat. As a West Indian explained, planters "had rather buy foode at very deare rates than produce it by labour, soe infinite is the profitt of sugar works." By 1700, the economies of the West Indies and New England were closely interwoven. Soon farmers and merchants in New York, New Jersey, and Pennsylvania were also shipping wheat, corn, and bread to the Caribbean. By the 1750s, about two-thirds of New England's exports and half of those from the Middle Colonies went to the British and French sugar islands.

The sugar economy linked Britain's entire Atlantic empire. In return for the sugar they sent to England, West Indian planters received credit—in the form of **bills of exchange**—from London merchants. The planters used these bills to buy slaves from Africa and to pay North American farmers and merchants for their provisions and shipping services. The mainland colonists then exchanged the bills for British manufactures, primarily textiles and iron goods.

The West Indian trade created the first American merchant fortunes and the first urban industries (Map 3.2). Merchants in Boston, Newport, Providence, Philadelphia, and New York invested their profits in new ships; some set up manufacturing enterprises, including twenty-six refineries that processed raw sugar into finished loaves. Mainland distilleries turned West Indian molasses into rum—more than two and a half million gallons in Massachusetts alone by the 1770s. Merchants in Salem, Marblehead, and smaller New England ports built a major fishing industry by selling salted mackerel and cod to the sugar islands and to southern Europe. Baltimore merchants transformed their town into a major port by developing a bustling export business in wheat, while traders in Charleston shipped deerskins, indigo, and rice to European markets.

As transatlantic commerce expanded—from 500 voyages a year in the 1680s to 1,500 annually in the 1730s—American port cities grew in size and complexity. Seeking jobs and excitement, British and German migrants and young people from the countryside (servant girls, male laborers, and apprentice artisans) flocked to urban areas. By 1750, the populations of Newport and Charleston were nearly 10,000; Boston had 15,000 residents; and New York had almost 18,000. The largest port was Philadelphia, whose population by 1776 had reached 30,000, the size of a large European provincial city. Smaller coastal towns emerged as centers of the lumber and shipbuilding industries. Seventy sawmills dotted the Piscataqua River in New Hampshire, providing low-cost wood for homes, warehouses, and especially shipbuilding. Taking advantage of the Navigation Acts, which allowed colonists to build and own trading vessels, hundreds of shipwrights turned out oceangoing vessels, while other artisans made ropes, sails, and metal fittings for the new fleet. By the 1770s, colonial-built ships made up one-third of the British merchant fleet.

The South Atlantic System extended far into the interior. A fleet of small vessels sailed back and forth on the Hudson and Delaware rivers, delivering cargoes of European manufactures and picking up barrels of flour and wheat to carry to New York and Philadelphia for export to the West Indies and Europe. By the 1750s, hundreds of professional teamsters in Maryland were transporting 370,000 bushels of wheat and corn and 16,000 barrels of flour to urban markets each year—more than 10,000 wagon trips.

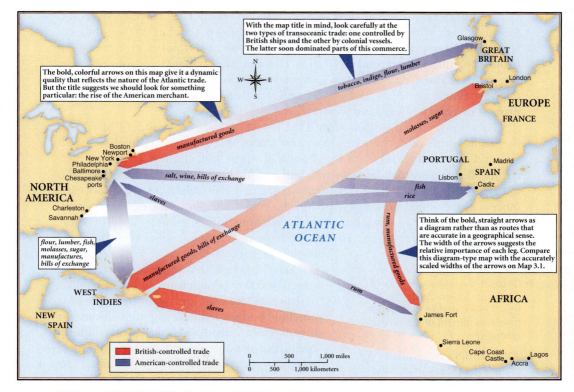

The bold, colorful arrows on this map give it a dynamic quality that reflects the nature of the Atlantic trade. But the title suggests we should look for something particular: the rise of the American merchant.

With the map title in mind, look carefully at the two types of transoceanic trade: one controlled by British ships and the other by colonial vessels. The latter soon dominated parts of this commerce.

Think of the bold, straight arrows as a diagram rather than as routes that are accurate in a geographical sense. The width of the arrows suggests the relative importance of each leg. Compare this diagram-type map with the accurately scaled widths of the arrows on Map 3.1.

■ British-controlled trade
■ American-controlled trade

MAP 3.2 The Rise of the American Merchant, 1750

Throughout the colonial era, British merchant houses dominated the transatlantic trade in manufactures, sugar, tobacco, and slaves. However, by 1750, American-born merchants in Boston, New York, and Philadelphia had seized control of the commerce between the mainland and the West Indies. Newport traders played a small role in the slave trade from Africa, and Boston and Charleston merchants grew rich carrying fish and rice to southern Europe.

For more help analyzing this map, see the Online Study Guide at **bedfordstmartins.com/henrettaconcise**.

To service this traffic, entrepreneurs and artisans set up taverns, horse stables, and barrel-making shops in towns along the wagon roads. Lancaster, in a prosperous wheat-growing area of Pennsylvania, boasted more than 200 German and English artisans and a dozen merchants.

Prosperous merchants dominated seaport cities. In 1750, about forty merchants controlled over 50 percent of Philadelphia's trade; they had taxable assets averaging £10,000, a huge sum at the time. Like the Chesapeake gentry, urban merchants modeled themselves after the British upper classes, importing design books from England and building Georgian-style mansions to display their wealth. Their wives created a genteel culture by decorating their houses with fine furniture and entertaining guests at elegant dinners.

Artisan and shopkeeper families, the middle ranks of seaport society, made up nearly half the population. Innkeepers, butchers, seamstresses, shoemakers, weavers, bakers, carpenters, masons, and dozens of other skilled workers toiled to gain a competency — an income sufficient to maintain their families in modest comfort and dignity. Wives and husbands often worked as a team, teaching the "mysteries of the craft" to their children. Some artisans aspired to wealth and status, an entrepreneurial ethic that prompted them to hire apprentices and expand production. However, most artisans were not well-to-do. During his working life, a tailor was lucky to accumulate £30 worth of property, far less than the £2,000 owned at death by an ordinary merchant or the £300 listed in the **probate inventory** of a successful blacksmith.

Laboring men and women formed the lowest ranks of urban society. Merchants needed hundreds of dockworkers to unload manufactured goods and molasses from inbound ships and reload them with barrels of wheat, fish, and rice. Often, the merchants filled these demanding jobs with enslaved blacks and indentured servants, who until the 1750s made up 30 percent of the workforce in Philadelphia and New York City; otherwise, they hired unskilled wageworkers. Poor white and black women—single, married, or widowed—eked out a living by washing clothes, spinning wool, or working as servants or prostitutes. To make ends meet, laboring families sent their children out to work.

Periods of stagnant commerce threatened the financial security of merchants and artisans alike. For laborers, seamen, and seamstresses, whose household budgets left no margin for sickness or unemployment, depressed trade meant hunger, dependence on public charity, and—for the most desperate—petty thievery or prostitution. The sugar- and slave-based South Atlantic System brought economic uncertainty as well as opportunity to the people of the northern colonies.

> ► Describe the major elements of the South Atlantic System and how it worked. How did it shape the development of the various colonies?
>
> ► What role did Africans play in the expansion of the Atlantic slave trade? What role did Europeans play?

The New Politics of Empire, 1713–1750

The South Atlantic System changed the politics of empire. British ministers, pleased with the wealth produced by the trade in staple crops, ruled the colonies with a gentle hand. The colonists took advantage of that leniency to strengthen their political institutions and eventually challenged the rules of the mercantilist system.

The Rise of Colonial Assemblies

After the Glorious Revolution of 1688–1689, representative assemblies in America followed the example of the English Whigs by limiting the powers of crown officials. In Massachusetts during the 1720s, the assembly repeatedly ignored the king's instructions to provide the royal governor with a permanent salary, and legislatures in North Carolina, New Jersey, and Pennsylvania did the same. Using such tactics, the colonial legislatures gradually took control of taxation and appointments, which angered imperial bureaucrats and absentee proprietors. "The people in power in America," complained William Penn during a struggle with the Pennsylvania assembly, "think nothing taller than themselves but the Trees."

Leading the increasingly powerful assemblies were members of the colonial elite. Although most property-owning white men had the right to vote, only men of wealth and status stood for election. In New Jersey in 1750, 90 percent of assemblymen came from influential political families. In the same decade in Virginia, seven members of the wealthy Lee family sat in the House of Burgesses and, along with other powerful families, dominated its major committees. In New England, affluent descendants of the original Puritans formed a core of political leaders. "Go into every village in New England," John Adams wrote in 1765, "and you will find that the office of justice of the peace, and even the place of representative, have generally descended from generation to generation, in three or four families at most."

However, neither elitist assemblies nor wealthy property owners could impose unpopular edicts on the people. Purposeful crowd actions were a fact of colonial life. An uprising of ordinary citizens overthrew the Dominion of New England in 1689. In New York, mobs closed houses of prostitution; in Salem (Massachusetts), they ran people with infectious diseases out of town; and in New Jersey in the 1730s and 1740s, mobs of farmers battled with proprietors who were forcing tenants off disputed lands. When officials in Boston restricted the sale of farm produce to a single public market, a crowd destroyed the building, and its members defied the authorities to arrest them. "If you touch One you shall touch All," an anonymous letter warned the sheriff, "and we will show you a Hundred Men where you can show one." These expressions of popular discontent, combined with the growing authority of the assemblies, created a political system that was broadly responsive to popular pressure and increasingly resistant to British control.

Salutary Neglect

British colonial policy during the reigns of George I (r. 1714–1727) and George II (r. 1727–1760) allowed the rise of American self-government. Royal bureaucrats, pleased by growing trade and import duties, relaxed their supervision of internal colonial affairs. In 1775, British political philosopher Edmund Burke would praise this strategy as salutary neglect.

Salutary neglect was a by-product of the political system developed by Sir Robert Walpole, the Whig leader in the House of Commons from 1720 to 1742. By providing supporters with appointments and pensions, Walpole won parliamentary approval for his policies. However, his patronage appointments filled the British government, including the Board of Trade and the colonial bureaucracy, with political hacks. When Governor Gabriel Johnson arrived in North Carolina in the 1730s, he vowed to curb the powers of the assembly and "make a mighty change in the face of affairs." Receiving little support from the Board of Trade, Johnson renounced reform and decided "to do nothing which can be reasonably blamed, and leave the rest to time, and a new set of inhabitants."

Walpole's tactics also weakened the empire by undermining the legitimacy of the political system. **Radical Whigs** protested that Walpole had betrayed the Glorious Revolution by using patronage and bribery to create a strong Court (or Kingly) Party. The Country Party — its members were landed gentlemen — likewise warned that Walpole's policies of high taxes and a bloated royal bureaucracy threatened British

Sir Robert Walpole, the King's Minister
All eyes are on Sir Robert Walpole (left) as he offers advice to the Speaker of the House of Commons. A brilliant politician, the treasury secretary held the confidence of George I and George II, the German-speaking monarchs from the duchy of Hanover, and used patronage to command a majority in the Commons. Walpole's personal motto, "Let sleeping dogs lie," helps explain his colonial policy of salutary neglect. © National Trust Photographic Library/John Hammond.

liberties. Heeding these arguments, colonial legislators complained that royal governors abused their patronage powers. To preserve American liberty, the colonists strengthened the powers of the representative assemblies, unintentionally laying the foundation for the American independence movement (see American Voices, p. 91).

Protecting the Mercantile System

Apart from patronage, Walpole's American policy focused on protecting British commercial interests. Initially, Walpole pursued a cautious foreign policy to allow Britain to recover from a generation of war (1689–1713) against Louis XIV of France. But in 1732, he provided a parliamentary subsidy for the new colony of Georgia, situated in a region long claimed by Spain. Georgia's reform-minded trustees envisioned the colony as a refuge for Britain's poor. To create a society of independent family farmers, the trustees limited most land grants to five hundred acres and outlawed slavery.

Walpole had little interest in social reform; he subsidized Georgia to protect the valuable rice-growing colony of South Carolina. It did exactly the opposite. Britain's expansion into Georgia outraged Spanish officials, who were already angry over British intrusions into the trade with New Spain. British merchants had silently taken over the Andalusian firms that held a monopoly on Spanish-American trade, and now—in a massive illegal commerce—provided many of the slaves and manufactures imported by the Spanish colonies. To counter Britain's commercial imperialism, Spanish naval

Confronting the House of Burgesses   ALEXANDER SPOTSWOOD

During the eighteenth century, the American representative assemblies expanded their popular appeal and political power. Many assemblies used their newfound authority to resist imperial governors, who often viewed them with contempt. Alexander Spotswood, who became governor of Virginia in 1710, remarked that the colony's voters had chosen "a set of representatives whom heaven has not generally endowed with the ordinary qualifications requisite to legislators." Spotswood's efforts to reduce the powers of the Burgesses made him few friends; in 1722, his enemies used their influence in London to have him removed from office.

To ye Council of Trade,
October 15, 1712
MY LORDS:

. . . [T]he Mob of this Country, having tried their Strength in the late Election and finding themselves able to carry whom they please, have generally chosen representatives of their own Class, who as their principal Recommendation have declared their resolution to raise no Tax on the people. . . . This is owing to a defect in the Constitution, which allows to every one, tho' but just out of the Condition of a Servant, and that can but purchase half an acre of Land, an equal Vote with the Man of the best Estate in the Country. . . .

December the 17ᵗʰ 1714

. . . The Council declare that they cannot advise the Governor to move for any alteration in the present method of Electing of Burgesses, some being of opinion that this is not a proper time, & others that the present manner of electing of Burgesses & the qualifications of the elected is sufficiently provided for by the Laws now in force. . . .

To Mr. Secretary James Stanhope,
July 15, 1715

I cannot forbear regretting that I must always have to do with ye Representatives of ye Vulgar People, and mostly with such members as are of their Stamp and Understanding, for so long as half an Acre of Land, . . . qualifys a man to be an Elector, the meaner sort of People will ever carry ye Elections, and the humour generally runs to choose such men as are their most familiar Companions, who very eagerly seek to be Burgesses merely for the lucre of the Salary, and who, for fear of not being chosen again, dare in Assembly do nothing that may be disrelished out of the House by ye Common People. Hence it often happens that what appears prudent and feasible to his Majesty's Governors and Council here will not pass with the House of Burgesses. . . .

To the Lords Commissioners of Trade,
May 23, 1716

. . . The behaviour of [Philip Ludwell Jr., the colony's auditor] in constantly opposing whatever I have offered for ye due collecting the Quitt rents . . . [and] his stirring up ye humours of the people before the last election of Burgesses . . . would have made me . . . suspend him from ye Council, but I find by the late Instructions I have received from his Majesty that Power is taken from ye Governor and transferred upon the majority of that Board, and while there are no less than seven of his Relations there, it is impossible to get a Majority to consent to the Suspension of him. . . .

SOURCE: R. A. Brock, ed., *The Official Letters of Alexander Spotswood* (Richmond: Virginia Historical Society, 1885), 2: 1–2, 124, 154–155.

forces had stepped up their seizure of illegal traders, including mutilation of an English sea captain, Robert Jenkins.

Yielding to Parliamentary pressure, Walpole declared war on Spain in 1739. The so-called War of Jenkins's Ear (1739–1741) was a largely unsuccessful attack on Spain's empire in North America. In 1740, British regulars failed to capture St. Augustine because South Carolina whites, still shaken by the Stono Rebellion, refused to commit militia units to the expedition. A year later, a major British and American assault on the prosperous Spanish seaport of Cartagena (in present-day Colombia) also failed. Instead of enriching themselves with Spanish booty, hundreds of troops from the mainland colonies died in the attack, mostly from tropical diseases.

The War of Jenkins's Ear quickly became part of a general European conflict, the War of the Austrian Succession (1740–1748). Massive French armies battled British-subsidized German forces in Europe, and French naval forces roamed the West Indies, vainly trying to conquer a British sugar island. There was little fighting in North America until 1745, when 3,000 New England militiamen, supported by a British naval squadron, captured Louisbourg, a French fortress at the entrance to the St. Lawrence River. To the dismay of New England Puritans, who feared invasion from Catholic Quebec, the Treaty of Aix-la-Chapelle (1748) returned Louisbourg to France. The treaty made it clear to colonial leaders that England would act in its own interests, not theirs.

The American Economic Challenge

The Walpole ministry had its own complaints about American economic activities. The Navigation Acts stipulated that the colonies were to produce staple crops and to consume British manufactured goods. To enforce the British monopoly on manufacturing, Parliament prohibited Americans from selling colonial-made textiles (Woolen Act, 1699), hats (Hat Act, 1732), and iron products such as plows, axes, and skillets (Iron Act, 1750).

However, the Navigation Acts had a major loophole: They allowed Americans to own ships and transport goods. Colonial merchants exploited those provisions to take control of 75 percent of the transatlantic trade in manufactures and 95 percent of the commerce between the mainland and the British West Indies. In fact, by the 1720s, the British sugar islands could not absorb all the flour, fish, and meat produced by mainland settlers. So, ignoring Britain's intense rivalry with France, colonial merchants sold their produce to its sugar islands, the wealth-producing epicenter of its American empire. Soon French planters were producing low-cost sugar that drove British products off the European market. When American rum distillers began to buy cheap molasses from the French islands, the West Indian "sugar lobby" intervened. It persuaded Parliament to enact the Molasses Act of 1733. The act allowed the mainland colonies to export fish and farm products to the French islands but — to give a price advantage to British sugar planters — placed a high tariff on French molasses. American merchants and legislators protested that the Molasses Act would cut off molasses imports, which would cripple the distilling industry, cut farm exports, and, by slashing colonial income, reduce the mainland's purchases of British goods. When Parliament ignored these arguments, American merchants smuggled in French molasses by bribing customs officials. Luckily for the Americans, British sugar prices rose sharply in the late 1730s, so the act was not rigorously enforced.

The lack of currency in the colonies prompted another conflict with British officials. To pay for manufactured goods, American merchants gave British merchants the bills of exchange and the gold and silver coins earned in the West Indian trade. These payments drained the colonial economy of money, which made it difficult for Americans to borrow funds or to buy and sell goods among themselves. To remedy the problem, ten colonial assemblies established public **land banks** that lent paper money to farmers, who pledged their land as collateral for the loans. Farmers used the currency to buy tools or livestock or to pay their creditors, thereby stimulating trade. However, some assemblies, particularly the legislature in Rhode Island, issued huge quantities of paper money (which consequently fell in value) and required merchants to accept it as legal tender. English merchants and other creditors rightly complained that they were being forced to accept devalued money. So in 1751, Parliament passed the Currency Act, which barred the New England colonies from establishing new land banks and prohibited the use of publicly issued paper money to pay private debts.

These conflicts over trade and paper money angered a new generation of English political leaders. In 1749, Charles Townshend of the Board of Trade charged that the American assemblies had assumed many of the "ancient and established prerogatives wisely preserved in the Crown"; he vowed to replace salutary neglect with more rigorous imperial control.

The wheel of empire had come full circle. In the 1650s, England had set out to create a centrally managed Atlantic empire and, over the course of a century, achieved the military and economic aspects of that goal. Mercantilist legislation, maritime warfare, commercial expansion, and the forced labor of a million African slaves brought prosperity to Britain. However, internal unrest (the Glorious Revolution) and a policy of salutary neglect had weakened Britain's political authority over its American colonies. Recognizing the threat self-government posed to the empire, British officials in the late 1740s vowed to reassert their power in America—an initiative that would have disastrous results.

▶ How did the ideas and policies of the English Whigs affect British and colonial politics between 1700 and 1760?

▶ What was the British policy of salutary neglect? Why did the British follow this policy? What consequences did it have for the British colonies in North America?

▶ Describe the connection in the eighteenth century between the South Atlantic System and the politics of empire.

SUMMARY

In this chapter, we examined two processes of change: one in politics and one in society and economy. The political story began in the 1660s with Britain's attempt to centralize control over its American possessions. Parliament passed the Acts of Trade and Navigation to keep colonial products and trade in English hands. Then King James II abolished representative institutions in the northern colonies and created the authoritarian Dominion of New England. The Glorious Revolution of 1688–1689 reversed these policies, restoring American self-government and ushering in the era of salutary neglect.

The social and economic story centers on the development of the South Atlantic System of production and trade. It involved an enormous expansion in African slave raiding; the Atlantic slave trade; and the cultivation of sugar, rice, and tobacco in America. This complex story includes the creation of an exploited African American labor force in the southern mainland and West Indian colonies and of prosperous communities of European American farmers, merchants, and artisans on the North American mainland. How would the two stories turn out? In 1750, slavery and the South Atlantic System seemed firmly in place; however, the days of salutary neglect appeared to be numbered.

Connections: Economy **and** Government

In the essay opening Part One, we noted that

> some European settlements became places of oppressive captivity for Africans. . . . [P]lanters in the Chesapeake region imported enslaved African workers to grow tobacco. Wealthy British and French planters in the West Indies bought hundreds of thousands of slaves . . . and forced them to labor on sugar plantations.

The expansion of the South Atlantic System of slavery and staple-crop production dramatically changed the British colonies. In 1675, the three major English settlements—in the Chesapeake, New England, and Barbados—were small in numbers and reeling from Indian attacks and social revolts. By 1750, British settlements in North America and the Caribbean had more than 2 million residents; produced vast amounts of sugar, rice, tobacco, wheat, and corn; and were no longer in danger of being destroyed by Indian attacks. The South Atlantic System had brought wealth and opportunity to the white inhabitants not only in the sugar islands but also on the North American mainland.

If expansion solved some problems, it created others. As we have seen in Chapter 3, imperial officials imposed mercantilist laws regulating the increasingly valuable colonies and repeatedly went to war to safeguard them. This story of expanding imperial authority and warfare continues in Chapter 4, with Britain's "Great War for Empire," a vast military conflict intended to expand British commercial power throughout the world and to establish Britain as the dominant nation in Europe.

FOR FURTHER EXPLORATION

On England's empire, see Michael Kammen, *Empire and Interest: The American Colonies and the Politics of Mercantilism* (1970), and Linda Colley, *Britons: Forging the Nation, 1707–1837* (1992). For multicultural tensions in early New York, read Joyce Goodfriend, *Before the Melting Pot: Society and Culture in Colonial New York City, 1664–1730* (1992). Richard Bushman, *King and People in Provincial Massachusetts* (1985), explores eighteenth-century imperial politics.

Betty Wood, *Origins of American Slavery* (1998), David Eltis, *The Rise of African Slavery in the Americas* (2000), and Ira Berlin, *Many Thousands Gone: The First Two Centuries of Slavery in North America* (1999), are fine studies. See also Philip D. Morgan,

TIMELINE

1651 ▶ First Navigation Act	**1720–1742** ▶ Sir Robert Walpole leads Parliament
1660–1685 ▶ Reign of King Charles II	**1720–1750** ▶ African American community forms
1663 ▶ Charles II grants Carolina proprietorship	▶ Rice exports from South Carolina soar
1664 ▶ English capture New Netherland, rename it New York	▶ Chesapeake planter aristocracy emerges
1681 ▶ William Penn founds Pennsylvania	▶ Seaport cities expand
1685–1688 ▶ Reign of King James II	**1732** ▶ Parliament charters Georgia, challenging Spain
1686–1689 ▶ Dominion of New England	▶ Hat Act
1688–1689 ▶ Glorious Revolution in England and America	**1733** ▶ Molasses Act
1689 ▶ William and Mary ascend throne in England	**1739** ▶ Stono Rebellion in South Carolina
▶ Revolts in Massachusetts, Maryland, and New York	**1739–1748** ▶ War in Europe
1689–1713 ▶ England, France, and Spain at war	▶ Sporadic warfare against Spain in the Caribbean and France in Canada
1696 ▶ Parliament creates Board of Trade	**1750** ▶ Iron Act restricts colonial iron manufactures
1705 ▶ Virginia enacts slavery legislation	**1751** ▶ Currency Act prohibits land banks in New England and use of paper money as legal tender
1714–1750 ▶ British policy of salutary neglect allows American assemblies to gain power	

Slave Counterpoint: Black Culture in the Eighteenth-Century Chesapeake and Low Country (1998). A good primary source is Olaudah Equiano, *The Interesting Narrative of the Life of Olaudah Equiano* (1789, 1995). On Africa, begin with Paul Bohannan and Philip Curtin, *Africa and the Africans* (3rd ed., 1988).

The PBS video *Africans in America* has a good Web site (**www.pbs.org/wgbh/aia/part1/title.html**). Writings by enslaved and free African Americans are at "Digital History" (**www.digitalhistory.uh.edu/black_voices/black_voices.cfm**). For a "Visual Record" of "The Atlantic Slave Trade and Slave Life in the Americas," go to (**hitchcock.itc.virginia.edu/Slavery/**). Also see the Library of Congress exhibit "African-American Odyssey" at (**lcweb2.loc.gov/ammem/aaohtml/**).

TEST YOUR KNOWLEDGE

To assess your mastery of the material in this chapter and for Web sites, images, and documents related to this chapter, visit **bedfordstmartins.com/henrettaconcise**.

Growth and Crisis in Colonial Society
1720–1765

> To lie low before God, as in the dust, that I might be nothing, and that God might be all.
>
> —Jonathan Edwards

In 1736, Alexander MacAllister left the Highlands of Scotland for the back-country of North Carolina, where his wife and three sisters soon joined him. Over the years, MacAllister prospered as a landowner and mill proprietor and had only praise for his new home. Carolina was "the best poor man's country I have heard in this age," he wrote to his brother Hector, urging him to "advise all poor people . . . to take courage and come." In North Carolina, there were no landlords to keep "the face of the poor . . . to the grinding stone," and so many Highlanders were arriving that "it will soon be a new Scotland." Here, on the far margins of the British empire, people could "breathe the air of liberty, and not want the necessarys of life." Some 300,000 European migrants—primarily Highland Scots, Scots-Irish, and Germans—heeded MacAllister's advice and helped to swell the population of Britain's North American settlements from 400,000 in 1720 to almost two million by 1765.

The rapid increase in white settlers and the arrival of nearly 300,000 enslaved Africans transformed life in every region of British America. Long-settled towns in New England became overcrowded; antagonistic ethnic and religious communities in the Middle Atlantic colonies jostled uneasily with one another; and the influx of the MacAllisters and thousands of other Celtic and German migrants altered the social landscape of the southern backcountry. Everywhere, two European cultural movements—the Enlightenment and Pietism—changed the tone of intellectual and spiritual life. Most important, as the migrants and the landless children of long-settled families moved inland, they sparked wars with the native peoples and with France and Spain, which were also vying for empire in North America. A generation of dynamic growth produced a decade of deadly warfare that would set the stage for a new era in American history.

Freehold Society in New England

In the 1630s, the Puritans left a country in which a small elite of nobles and gentry owned 75 percent of the arable land and farmed it with **leaseholding** tenants and propertyless workers. In New England, the Puritans set out to create a yeoman society of relatively equal landowning farm families. They succeeded all too well. By 1750, the migrants' descendants had parceled out all of the best farmland, threatening the future of the freehold ideal.

Farm Families: Women and the Rural Household Economy

The Puritans' vision of social equality did not extend to women. Puritan ideology placed the husband firmly at the head of the household, with almost complete control over his dependents. The Reverend Benjamin Wadsworth of Boston advised women in *The Well-Ordered Family* (1712) that being richer, more intelligent, or of higher social status than their husbands mattered little: "Since he is thy Husband, God has made him the head and set him above thee." It was a wife's duty "to love and reverence" her husband.

Women learned their subordinate role throughout their lives. Small girls watched their mothers defer to their fathers. As young women, they saw the courts prosecute many women and very few men for the crime of fornication (having sexual intercourse outside of marriage). And they learned that their marriage portions would be inferior in kind and size to those of their brothers. Thus, Ebenezer Chittendon of Guilford (Connecticut) left all his land to his sons, decreeing that "Each Daughter [shall] have half so much as Each Son, one half in money and the other half in Cattle." Because English law had eliminated many customary restrictions on inheritances, fathers could divide their property as they pleased.

In rural New England — and throughout the colonies — women assumed the role of dutiful helpmeets (helpmates) to their husbands. Farmwives tended gardens that provided fresh vegetables and herbs. They spun thread and yarn from flax or wool and then wove it into cloth for shirts and gowns. They knitted sweaters and stockings, made candles and soap, churned milk into butter and pressed curds into cheese, fermented malt for beer, preserved meats, and mastered dozens of other household tasks. "Notable women," the most accomplished practitioners of these domestic arts, won praise and high status in rural communities.

Bearing and rearing children were equally important tasks. Most women in New England married in their early twenties and by their early forties had given birth to six or seven children, usually delivered with the help of a neighbor or a midwife. Such large families sapped the physical and emotional strength of most mothers for twenty or more of their most active years. One Massachusetts woman confessed that she had little time for religious activities because "the care of my Babes takes up so large a portion of my time and attention." Yet most full members of Puritan congregations were women: "In a Church of between *Three* and *Four* Hundred *Communicants*," the eminent minister Cotton Mather noted, "there are but few more than *One* Hundred *Men;* all the Rest are Women." Many women became full members, revivalist Jonathan Edwards suggested, because they feared the dangers of childbirth and because that status meant that "their children may be baptized."

As the size of farms shrank in long-settled communities, many couples chose to have fewer children. After 1750, women in Andover, a typical farm village in Massachusetts, bore an average of only four children and had time and energy to pursue other tasks. Farm women now made yarn, cloth, or cheese to exchange with neighbors or sell to shopkeepers, which raised their families' standard of living. Or, like Susan Huntington of Boston, the wife of a prosperous merchant, they spent more time in "the care & culture of children, and the perusal of necessary books, including the scriptures."

Still, women's lives remained tightly bound by a web of legal and cultural restrictions. Ministers praised women's piety but excluded them from an equal role in the church. When Hannah Heaton, a farmwife in Connecticut, grew dissatisfied with her Congregationalist minister, thinking him unconverted and a "blind guide," she sought out Quaker and evangelist Baptist churches that welcomed questioning women. However, by the 1760s, many evangelical congregations had reinstituted traditional gender roles. "The government of Church and State must be . . . family government" controlled by its "king," declared the Danbury (Connecticut) Baptist Association. Willingly or not, most colonial women abided by the custom that, as essayist Timothy Dwight put it, they should be "employed only in and about the house and in the proper business of the sex."

Farm Property: Inheritance

By contrast, European men who migrated to the colonies escaped many traditional constraints, including the curse of landlessness. "The hope of having land of their own & becoming independent of Landlords is what chiefly induces people into America," an official noted in the 1730s. Owning property gave formerly dependent peasants a new social identity.

Property ownership and family authority were closely related. Most migrating Europeans wanted sizable farms that would provide sustenance for themselves and ample land for their children. Parents who could not provide some of their offspring with land placed them as indentured servants in more prosperous households. When the indentures ended at age eighteen or twenty-one, propertyless sons faced a decades-long climb up the agricultural ladder, from laborer to tenant and finally to freeholder.

Sons and daughters in well-to-do farm families were luckier: They received a marriage portion when they reached the age of twenty-three to twenty-five. That portion — land, livestock, or farm equipment — repaid children for their past labor and allowed parents to choose their children's partners, which they did not hesitate to do. Parents' security during old age depended on a wise choice of son- or daughter-in-law. Although the youths could refuse an unacceptable match, they did not have the luxury of falling in love with and marrying whomever they pleased.

Marriage under eighteenth-century English common law was not a contract between equals. A bride relinquished to her husband the legal ownership of all her property. After his death, she received a dower right — the right to use, but not sell, one-third of the family's property; on the widow's death or remarriage, her portion was divided among the children. The widow's property rights were subordinate to those of the family line, which stretched across the generations.

A father's duty was to provide inheritances for his children, and men who did not do so lost status in the community. Some fathers willed the family farm to a single son, providing their other children with money, an apprenticeship, or uncleared frontier tracts or requiring the inheriting son to do so. Other yeomen moved their families to the frontier, where life was hard but land was cheap and abundant. "The Squire's House stands on the Bank of the Susquehannah," traveler Philip Fithian reported from the Pennsylvania backcountry in the early 1760s. "He tells me that he will be able to settle all his sons and his fair Daughter Betsy on the Fat of the Earth."

These farmers' historic achievement was the creation of whole communities of independent property owners. A French visitor noted the sense of personal dignity in this rural world, which contrasted sharply with that of European peasants. Throughout the northern colonies, he found "men and women whose features are not marked by poverty . . . or by a feeling that they are insignificant subjects and subservient members of society."

The Crisis of Freehold Society

How long would this happy circumstance last? Because of high rates of natural increase, New England's population doubled with each generation. The Puritan colonies had about 100,000 people in 1700, nearly 200,000 in 1725, and almost 400,000 in 1750. In long-settled areas, farms had been divided and then subdivided; now many were so small — fifty acres or less — that parents could provide only one child with an adequate inheritance. In the 1740s, the Reverend Samuel Chandler of Andover was "much distressed for land for his children," seven of whom were young boys. A decade later, in nearby Concord, about 60 percent of the farmers owned less land than their fathers had.

Because parents had less to give their sons and daughters, they had less control over their children's lives. The traditional system of arranged marriages broke down as young people engaged in premarital sex and used the urgency of pregnancy to win permission to marry. Throughout New England, the number of premarital conceptions rose dramatically, from about 10 percent of firstborn children in the 1710s to more than 30 percent in the 1740s. Given another chance, young people "would do the same again," an Anglican minister observed, "because otherwise they could not obtain their parents' consent to marry."

Even as family dynamics changed, New England families maintained the freeholder ideal. Some parents chose to have smaller families and used birth control: abstention, coitus interruptus, or primitive condoms. Other families petitioned the provincial government for frontier land grants and hacked new farms out of the forests of central Massachusetts, western Connecticut, and, eventually, New Hampshire and Vermont. Still others improved their farms' productivity by replacing the traditional English crops of wheat and barley with high-yielding potatoes and maize, known as Indian corn. Corn was an especially wise choice: It yielded a hearty food for people, and its leaves furnished feed for cattle and pigs, which provided farm families with milk and meat. Gradually, New England changed from a grain economy to a livestock economy and became a major exporter of salted meat to the plantations of the West Indies.

Finally, New England farmers adapted their agriculture by developing the full potential of what one historian has called the "household mode of production." In this system of community exchange, families swapped labor and goods with one another. Women and children worked in groups to spin yarn, sew quilts, and shuck corn. Men

► In what ways were the lives of women and men in New England similar? In what ways were they different?

► What was the threat to the freehold ideal in midcentury New England, and what new strategies did farming families use to preserve it?

loaned one another tools, draft animals, and grazing land. Farmers plowed fields owned by artisans and shopkeepers, who repaid them with shoes, furniture, or store credit. In part because currency was in short supply, no cash changed hands. Instead, farmers, artisans, and shopkeepers recorded their debits and credits and "balanced" the books every few years by transferring small amounts of cash. This system allowed households—and the region's economy—to maximize output and so preserve the freehold ideal.

The Middle Atlantic: Toward a New Society, 1720–1765

The Middle Atlantic colonies—New York, New Jersey, and Pennsylvania—became home to peoples of differing origins, languages, and religions. Scots-Irish Presbyterians, English and Welsh Quakers, German Lutherans and Moravians, and Dutch Reformed Protestants formed ethnic and religious communities that coexisted uneasily with one another.

Economic Growth and Social Inequality

Ample fertile land attracted migrants to the Middle Atlantic colonies, and grain exports to Europe and the West Indies financed their rapid settlement. Between 1720 and 1770, a growing demand for food doubled the price of wheat. By increasing their exports of wheat, corn, flour, and bread, Middle Atlantic farmers brought prosperity to the region. The population of the area surged from 120,000 in 1720 to 450,000 in 1765.

Many migrants refused to settle in New York's fertile Hudson River Valley—and with good reason. There, wealthy Dutch and English families—Van Rensselaers, Philipses, Livingstons, and Clarks—presided over huge manors created by the Dutch West India Company and English governors (Map 4.1). Like Chesapeake planters, the New York landlords aspired to live like European gentry, but few migrants wanted to labor as poor, dependent peasants. To attract tenants, the manorial lords had to grant them long leases and the right to sell their improvements—their houses and barns, for example—to the next tenant. Still, the number of tenant families rose slowly; the vast 100,000-acre Van Rensselaer estate had only 82 tenants in 1714 and 345 in 1752 but jumped to 700 by 1765.

Most tenant families hoped that with hard work, they could sell enough wheat to buy their own farmsteads. But preindustrial technology during the crucial harvest season limited their output. As the wheat ripened, it had to be harvested before it sprouted and became useless. Yet a worker with a hand sickle could reap only half an acre of wheat, rye, or oats a day. The cradle scythe, a tool introduced during the 1750s, doubled or tripled the amount of grain a worker could cut. Even so, a family with two adult workers could reap only about twelve acres of grain—perhaps 150 to 180 bushels of

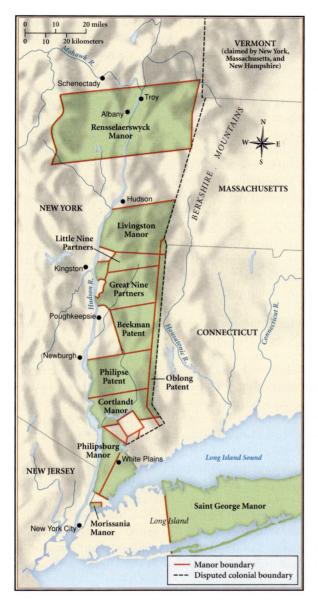

MAP 4.1 The Hudson River Manors

Dutch and English manorial lords owned much of the fertile eastern shore of the Hudson River, where they leased farms on perpetual contracts to German tenants and refused to sell land to freehold-seeking migrants from overcrowded New England. This powerful landholding elite produced Patriot leaders, such as Gouverneur Morris and Robert Livingston, and prominent American families, such as the Roosevelts.

wheat. After reserving enough grain for food and seed, the remainder might be worth £15, enough to buy salt and sugar, tools, and cloth, but little else. The road to land ownership was not an easy one.

In rural Pennsylvania and New Jersey, wealth was initially distributed more evenly. The first Quakers arrived with few resources and lived simply in small houses with one or two rooms, a sleeping loft, a few benches or stools, and some wooden platters and cups. Only the wealthiest families ate off pewter or ceramic plates imported from England or Holland.

However, the expanding trade in wheat and an influx of poor settlers sharpened social divisions. By the 1760s, eastern Pennsylvania landowners with large farms were using the labor of slaves and poor migrants to grow wheat. Other ambitious men were buying up land and dividing it into small tenancies, which they let out on profitable leases. Still others were making money by providing new settlers with farming equipment, sugar and rum from the West Indies, and financial services. These large-scale farmers, rural landlords, speculators, storekeepers, and gristmill operators formed a distinct class of agricultural capitalists. They displayed their wealth by building large stone houses, furnishing them with expensive mahogany tables and four-poster beds, and laying their tables with elegant linen and handsomely decorated Dutch dinnerware.

In sharp contrast, one-half of Middle Atlantic's white men owned no land and little personal property. Some propertyless men were the sons of farmers and would eventually inherit part of the family estate. But many more were Scots-Irish "inmates"—single men or families, explained a tax assessor, "such as live in small cottages and have no taxable property, except a cow." In the predominantly German settlement of Lancaster, Pennsylvania, a merchant noted an "abundance of Poor people" who "maintain their Families with great difficulty by day Labour." Although these Scots-Irish and German settlers hoped eventually to become landowners, sharply rising land prices prevented many from realizing their dreams.

Some hard-pressed migrants turned to crime, which rose sharply after 1720. Previously, merchant Isaac Norris recalled, "we could Safely go to bed with our doors open but now Robberies, housebreaking, Rapes, & other crimes are become Common." In 1732, the Philadelphia Society of Friends publicly identified the perpetrators as "the vicious and scandalous Refuse of other Countries," a charge confirmed by recent scholarship. Pennsylvania's religious peoples—Quakers, Mennonites, Amish, Moravians, and Dunkards—broke relatively few laws; most crimes were committed by people who were propertyless or indentured servants or Scots-Irish (and often all three).

Merchants and artisans took advantage of the ample labor supply to set up an outwork system. They bought wool or flax from farmers and paid propertyless workers and land-poor farm families to spin it into yarn or weave it into cloth. In the 1760s, an English traveler reported that hundreds of Pennsylvanians had turned "to manufacture, and live upon a small farm, as in many parts of England." In both the Middle Atlantic and New England, many communities were now as crowded and socially divided as those in rural England, and many families feared a return to the lowly status of the European peasant.

Cultural Diversity

The middle colonies were not a melting pot. Most European migrants held tightly to their traditions, creating a patchwork of ethnically and religiously diverse communities. In 1748, a traveler counted no fewer than twelve religious denominations in Philadelphia, including Anglicans, Baptists, Quakers, Swedish and German Lutherans, Mennonites, Scots-Irish Presbyterians, and Roman Catholics.

Migrants preserved their cultural identity by marrying within their ethnic groups and maintaining their Old World customs (see Voices from Abroad, p. 103). A major

What, Then, Is the American, This New Man? J. HECTOR ST. JOHN DE CRÈVECOEUR

A Frenchman by birth, Crèvecoeur (1735–1813) came to America during the French and Indian War, married a merchant's daughter, and settled in Orange County, New York, where he lived as a "gentleman farmer." In 1782, he published *Letters from an American Farmer,* a justly famous book of essays that offered a European perspective on the new land and its people.

[The people here] are a mixture of English, Scotch, Irish, French, Dutch, Germans, and Swedes. From this promiscuous breed, that race now called Americans have arisen. The eastern provinces [New England] must indeed be excepted as being the unmixed descendants of Englishmen. I have heard many wish that they had been more intermixed also; I for my part, . . . I respect them for what they have done; for the accuracy and wisdom with which they have settled their territory; for the decency of their manners; for their early love of letters; their ancient college [Harvard], . . . for their industry. . . .

In this great American asylum, the poor of Europe have . . . become men: in Europe they were as so many useless plants, wanting vegetative mould and refreshing showers; they withered, and were mowed down by want, hunger, and war; but now, by the power of transplantation, like all other plants they have taken root and flourished! Formerly they were not numbered in any civil lists of their country, except in those of the poor; here they rank as citizens. . . .

What, then, is the American, this new man? He is either an European or the descendant of an European; hence that strange mixture of blood, which you will find in no other country. I could point out to you a family whose grandfather was an Englishman, whose wife was Dutch, whose son married a French woman, and whose present four sons have now four wives of different nations. *He* is an American, who, leaving behind him all his ancient prejudices and manners, receives new ones from the new mode of life he has embraced, the new government he obeys, and the new rank he holds. . . .

How much wiser, in general, the honest Germans than almost all other Europeans; . . . and [by] the most persevering industry, they commonly succeed. . . . The Scotch and the Irish [are different]. . . . out of twelve families of emigrants of each country, generally seven Scotch will succeed, nine German, and four Irish. The Scotch are frugal and laborious, but their wives cannot work so hard as German women, who on the contrary vie with their husbands, and often share with them the most severe toils of the field. . . . The Irish do not . . . prosper so well; they love to drink and to quarrel; they are litigious and soon take to the gun, which is the ruin of everything; they seem beside to labour under a greater degree of ignorance in husbandry than the others. . . . [In Ireland,] their potatoes, which are easily raised, were perhaps an inducement to laziness . . . and their whisky [there was] too cheap.

SOURCE: J. Hector St. John de Crèvecoeur, *Letters from an American Farmer,* ed. Albert E. Stone (New York: Penguin, 1981) 68–71, 85.

exception were the Huguenots, Calvinists expelled from Catholic France in the 1680s who resettled in Holland, England, and the British colonies. Huguenots in American port cities—Boston, New York, and Charleston—soon lost their French identity by intermarrying with other Protestants. More typical were the Welsh Quakers. Seventy percent of the children of the original Welsh migrants to Chester County, Pennsylvania, married other Welsh Quakers, as did 60 percent of the third generation.

In Pennsylvania and western New Jersey, Quakers shaped the culture, at first because of their numbers and later because of their wealth and social cohesion. Most Quakers came from pastoral farming regions of England and carried with them traditions of local village governance, popular participation in politics, and social equality. Quakers were also pacifists, so Pennsylvania officials negotiated treaties with Native Americans and bought their lands rather than seizing them. However, in 1737, Governor Thomas Penn used sharp tactics to oust the Lenni-Lenape (or Delaware) Indians from a vast area, creating bitterness that would lead to war in the 1750s. By that time, Quakers had extended their religious values of equality and justice to African Americans. Many Quaker meetings (congregations) condemned the institution of slavery, and some expelled members who continued to keep slaves.

The Quaker vision of a "peaceable kingdom" attracted 100,000 German migrants who were fleeing their homelands because of military conscription, religious persecution, and high taxes. First to arrive, in 1683, were the Mennonites, religious dissenters drawn by the promise of religious freedom. In the 1720s, a larger wave of German migrants arrived from southwestern Germany and Switzerland, refugees from religious upheaval and overcrowded villages. "Wages were far better" in Pennsylvania, Heinrich Schneebeli reported to his friends in Zurich, and "one also enjoyed there a free unhindered exercise of religion." A third wave of Germans and Swiss—nearly 40,000 strong—landed in Philadelphia between 1749 and 1756. Some were redemptioners, indentured servants who migrated as individuals or families; but many more were propertied farmers and artisans in search of better opportunities for their children.

Germans soon dominated many districts of eastern Pennsylvania, and thousands more moved down the Shenandoah Valley into the western parts of Maryland, Virginia, and the Carolinas. The migrants carefully guarded their cultural heritage. A minister in North Carolina admonished young people "not to contract any marriages with the English or Irish," emphasizing that "we owe it to our native country to do our part that German blood and the German language be preserved in America." Well beyond 1800, these settlers spoke German, read German-language newspapers, attended church services in German, and preserved German farming practices, which sent women into the fields to plow and reap.

As Germans and Protestants, these settlers readily accepted life as subjects of Britain's German-born and German-speaking Protestant monarchs, George I (1714–1727) and George II (1727–1760). They generally avoided politics except to protect their cultural practices; for example, they insisted that married women should have the right to hold property and write wills, as they did in Germany.

Migrants from Ireland formed the largest group of incoming Europeans, about 115,000 in number. Although some were Irish and Catholic, most were Scots and Presbyterian, the descendants of the Calvinist Protestants sent to Ireland during the seventeenth century to solidify English rule. Once in Ireland, the Scots faced hostility from

German Farm in Western Maryland
Beginning in the 1730s, wheat became a major export crop in Maryland and Virginia. The farm in this engraving is probably owned by Germans because the harvesters are using oxen, not horses, and women are working in the field alongside the men. Using "a new method of reaping," possibly of German origin, the harvesters cut only the grain-bearing tip of the plants, leaving the wheat stalks in the fields to be eaten by livestock. Library of Congress.
For more help analyzing this image, see the Online Study Guide at **bedfordstmartins.com/henrettaconcise**.

both Irish Catholics and English officials and landlords. The Irish Test Act of 1704 restricted voting and office holding to members of the Church of England. English mercantilist regulations placed heavy import duties on the linens made by Scots-Irish weavers, and Scots-Irish farmers paid heavy taxes. "Read this letter, Rev. Baptist Boyd," a migrant to New York wrote back to his minister, "and tell all the poor folk of ye place that God has opened a door for their deliverance . . . all that a man works for is his own; there are no revenue hounds to take it from us here."

Lured by such reports, thousands of Scots-Irish families sailed for the colonies. The first of these migrants landed in Boston in the 1710s and settled primarily in New Hampshire. By 1720, most were sailing to Philadelphia, attracted by the religious tolerance there. Seeking cheap land, they moved to central Pennsylvania and the fertile Shenandoah Valley, which stretched along the backcountry from Maryland to North Carolina. Governor William Gooch of Virginia welcomed the Scots-Irish presence to secure "the Country against the Indians"; but an Anglican planter thought them as dangerous as "the Goths and Vandals of old" had been to the Roman Empire. Like the Germans, the Scots-Irish retained their culture, living in ethnic communities and holding firm to the Presbyterian Church.

Religious Identity and Political Conflict

In Western Europe, the leaders of church and state condemned religious diversity (Map 4.2). "To tolerate all [religions] without controul is the way to have none at all," declared an Anglican clergyman. Both English and German ministers carried such

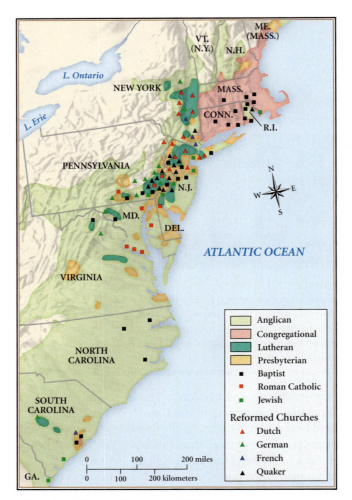

MAP 4.2 Religious Diversity in 1750

By 1750, religious diversity was on the rise, not only in the multiethnic middle colonies but also through-out British North America. Baptists had increased their numbers in New England, long the stronghold of Congregationalists, and would soon become important in Virginia. Already there were good-sized pockets of Presbyterians, Lutherans, and German Reformed in the South, where Anglicanism was the established religion.

For more help analyzing this map, see the Online Study Guide at **bedfordstmartins.com/henrettaconcise.**

sentiments to Pennsylvania. "The preachers do not have the power to punish anyone, or to force anyone to go to church," complained Gottlieb Mittelberger, an influential German minister. As a result, "Sunday is very badly kept. Many people plough, reap, thresh, hew or split wood and the like." He concluded: "Liberty in Pennsylvania does more harm than good to many people, both in soul and body."

Mittelberger was mistaken. Although ministers in Pennsylvania could not invoke government authority to uphold religious values, the result was not social anarchy.

Instead, religious sects enforced moral behavior through communal self-discipline. Quaker families and institutions were tight-knit. Families attended a weekly meeting for worship and a monthly meeting for business. Every three months, a committee from the monthly meeting reminded parents to provide their children with proper religious instruction. Parents took the committee's words to heart. "If thou refuse to be obedient to God's teachings," Walter Faucit of Chester County admonished his son, "thou will be a fool and a vagabond." The committee also supervised adult behavior: A Chester County meeting, for example, disciplined one of its members "to reclaim him from drinking to excess and keeping vain company." Significantly, Quaker meetings allowed couples to marry only if they had land and livestock sufficient to support a family. As a result, the children of well-to-do Friends usually married within the sect, while poor Quakers remained unmarried, wed later in life, or married without permission — in which case they were often ousted from the meeting. These marriage rules helped build a self-contained and prosperous Quaker community.

In the 1740s, Quaker dominance in Pennsylvania came under attack. The flood of German and Scots-Irish migrants reduced Quakers to a mere 30 percent of the residents. Moreover, the Scots-Irish in central Pennsylvania were demanding an aggressive Indian policy, challenging the pacifism of the Quaker-dominated assembly. Quaker politicians sought allies among German settlers, many of whom embraced the Quakers' policies of pacifism and voluntary (not compulsory) militia service. In return, German leaders demanded fair representation in the assembly and legislation that respected their inheritance customs.

By the 1750s, politics throughout the Middle Atlantic had become a steaming cauldron of ethnic-based conflicts. In New York, a Dutchman declared that he "Valued English Law no more than a Turd," while in Pennsylvania, Benjamin Franklin disparaged the "boorish" character and "swarthy complexion" of German migrants. The attempts of Scots-Irish Presbyterians, German Baptists, and German Lutherans to form "a general confederacy" against the Pennsylvania Quakers were likely to fail, a European visitor predicted, because of "a mutual jealousy, for religious zeal is secretly burning." The region's experiment in social diversity prefigured the bitter ethnic conflicts that would characterize much of American society in the centuries to come.

▶ Who were the new migrants to the middle colonies? Why did they leave Europe? What were their goals in British North America?

▶ What were the main issues that divided the ethnic and religious groups of the middle colonies?

The Enlightenment and the Great Awakening, 1720–1765

Two great European cultural movements reached America between the 1720s and the 1760s: the Enlightenment and Pietism. The Enlightenment, which emphasized the power of human reason to understand and shape the world, appealed especially to urban artisans and well-educated men and women from merchant or planter families. Pietism, an evangelical Christian movement that stressed the individual's personal relationship with God, attracted many more adherents, primarily farmers and urban laborers. To-gether, the two movements transformed American intellectual and cultural life.

The Enlightenment in America

To explain the workings of the natural world, some settlers relied on folk wisdom. Swedish settlers in Pennsylvania, for example, attributed magical powers to the great white mullein, a common wildflower, and treated fevers by tying the plant's leaves around their feet and arms. Others relied on religion. Most Christians believed the earth stood at the center of the universe and that God (and Satan) intervened directly and continuously in human affairs.

The scientific revolution of the sixteenth and seventeenth centuries challenged both folk and traditional Christian worldviews. In the 1530s, the astronomer Copernicus observed that the earth traveled around the sun, not vice versa. Copernicus's discovery suggested that humans occupied a more modest place in the universe than Christian theology assumed. Eventually, Sir Isaac Newton, in his *Principia Mathematica* (1687), used the sciences of mathematics and physics to explain the movement of the planets around the sun. Newton's laws of motion and gravity described how the universe could operate by means of natural forces. This explanation, which did not require the constant intervention of a supernatural being to guide the planets, undermined the traditional Christian understanding of the cosmos.

In the century between the publication of *Principia Mathematica* and the French Revolution of 1789, the philosophers of the European Enlightenment used empirical research and scientific reasoning to study all aspects of life, including social institu-tions and human behavior. Enlightenment thinkers advanced four fundamental prin-ciples: the lawlike order of the natural world, the power of human reason, the "natural rights" of individuals (including the right to self-government), and the progressive improvement of society.

English philosopher John Locke was a major contributor to the Enlightenment. In his *Essay Concerning Human Understanding* (1690), Locke discussed the impact of environment and experience on human behavior and beliefs. He argued that the char-acter of individuals and societies was not fixed but could be changed through educa-tion, rational thought, and purposeful action. Locke's *Two Treatises of Government* (1690) advanced the revolutionary theory that political authority was not given by God to monarchs, as James II had insisted (see Chapter 3). Instead, it derived from social compacts that people made to preserve their "natural rights" to life, liberty, and property. In Locke's view, the people should have the power to change government policies — or even their form of government.

Locke's ideas and those of other Enlightenment thinkers came to America by way of books, travelers, and educated migrants. Some clergymen responded to these ideas by devising a rational form of Christianity. Rejecting supernatural interventions and a vengeful Calvinist God, Congregationalist minister Andrew Eliot maintained that "there is nothing in Christianity that is contrary to reason." The Reverend John Wise of Ipswich, Massachusetts, used Locke's political principles to defend the Puritans' practice of vesting power in ordinary church members. Just as the social compact formed the basis of political society, Wise argued, so the religious covenant among the lay members of the congregation made them — not the bishops of the Church of

England or even ministers like himself—the proper interpreters of religious truth. The Enlightenment influenced Puritan minister Cotton Mather as well. When a measles epidemic ravaged Boston in the 1710s, he thought that only God could end it. A decade later, when smallpox struck the town, Mather turned to a scientific remedy by joining with physician Nicholas Boyleston to advocate the new technique of inoculation.

Benjamin Franklin was the exemplar of the American Enlightenment. Born in Boston in 1706 to a devout Calvinist family and apprenticed as a youth to a printer, Franklin was a self-taught man. While working as a printer and journalist in Philadelphia, he formed "a club of mutual improvement" that met weekly to discuss "Morals, Politics, or Natural Philosophy." These discussions and Enlightenment literature, rather than the Bible, shaped Franklin's mind. As Franklin explained in his *Autobiography* (1771), "From the different books I read, I began to doubt of Revelation [God-revealed truth]."

Like many urban artisans, wealthy Virginia planters, and affluent seaport merchants, Franklin became a **deist**. Deism was a way of thinking, not a church. "My own mind is my own church," said deist Thomas Paine. "I am of a sect by myself," added Thomas Jefferson. Influenced by Enlightenment science, deists believed that a Supreme Being (or Grand Architect) had created the world, allowed it to operate through the laws of nature, and did not intervene directly in history or in people's lives. Rejecting the divinity of Christ and the authority of the Bible, deists relied on people's "natural reason," their innate moral sense, to define right and wrong. Thus, Franklin, a onetime slave owner, came to question the morality of racial bondage and repudiated it as he contested the colonists' political bondage to the British.

Franklin popularized the practical outlook of the Enlightenment in *Poor Richard's Almanack* (1732–1757), an annual publication read by thousands, and in the American Philosophical Society (1743–present), an institution devoted to "the promotion of useful knowledge." Taking this message to heart, Franklin invented bifocal lenses for eyeglasses, the Franklin stove, and the lightning rod. His book on electricity, published in England in 1751, won praise as the greatest contribution to science since Newton's discoveries. Inspired by Franklin, ambitious printers in America's seaport cities published newspapers and gentlemen's magazines, the first significant nonreligious publications to appear in the colonies. The European Enlightenment, then, added a secular dimension to colonial cultural life, foreshadowing the great contributions to republican political theory by the American intellectuals of the revolutionary era: John Adams, James Madison, and Thomas Jefferson.

American Pietism and the Great Awakening

As many educated Americans turned to deism, thousands of other colonists embraced Pietism. This Christian movement had its origins in Germany around 1700 and emphasized "pious" behavior (hence the name). In its emphasis on a mystical union with God and in its emotional services, Pietism appealed to the hearts of individuals rather than to their minds. In the 1720s, German migrants carried Pietism to America and sparked a religious **revival**. In Pennsylvania and New Jersey, Dutch minister Theodore Jacob Frelinghuysen moved from church to church, preaching rousing emotional sermons to German settlers and encouraging church members to spread the message of spiritual urgency. A decade later, William Tennent and his son Gilbert copied Frelinghuysen's approach and led revivals among Scots-Irish Presbyterians throughout the Middle Atlantic region.

Simultaneously, an American-born Pietist movement appeared in Puritan New England. The original Puritans were intensely pious Christians, but over the decades, their spiritual zeal had faded. In the 1730s, Jonathan Edwards restored that zeal to Congregational churches in the Connecticut River Valley. Edwards was born in 1703, the fifth child and only son among the eleven children of Timothy and Esther Stoddard Edwards. Jonathan's father was a poorly paid rural minister, but his mother was the daughter of Solomon Stoddard, a famous preacher who taught that God was compassionate and that sainthood was not limited to a select few.

As a young man, Edwards rejected Stoddard's thinking. Inspired by the harsh theology of John Calvin, he preached that men and women were helpless and completely dependent on God. In his most famous sermon, "Sinners in the Hands of an Angry God" (1741), Edwards declared: "There is Hell's wide gaping mouth open; and you have nothing to stand upon, nor any thing to take hold of: there is nothing between you and Hell but the air; 'tis only the power and mere pleasure of God that holds you up." According to one observer, the response was electric: "There was a great moaning and crying through the whole house. What shall I do to be saved—oh, I am going to Hell."

Surprisingly, Edwards's writings contributed to Enlightenment thought. The New England minister accepted Locke's argument in the *Essay Concerning Human Understanding* (1690) that ideas are the product of experience as conveyed by the senses; but Edwards argued that people's ideas also depended on their passions. Edwards used his theory of knowledge to justify his preaching, suggesting that vivid words would "fright persons away from Hell" and promote conversions. News of Edwards's success stimulated religious fervor up and down the Connecticut River Valley.

George Whitefield transformed the local revivals of Edwards and the Tennents into a Great Awakening that spanned the British colonies. Whitefield had his awakening after reading German Pietists, and he became a follower of John Wesley, the founder of English Methodism. In 1739, Whitefield carried Wesley's fervent message to America, where he attracted huge crowds of "enthusiasts" from Georgia to Massachusetts. "Religion is become the Subject of most Conversations," the *Pennsylvania Gazette* reported. "No books are in Request but those of Piety and Devotion." Whitefield's preaching so impressed Benjamin Franklin that when the revivalist asked for contributions, Franklin emptied the coins in his pockets "wholly into the collector's dish, gold and all." By the time Whitefield reached Boston, the Reverend Benjamin Colman reported, the people were "ready to receive him as an angel of God" (see American Voices, p. 111).

Whitefield owed his appeal to his compelling presence. "He looked almost angelical; a young, slim, slender youth . . . cloathed with authority from the Great God," wrote a Connecticut farmer. Like most evangelical preachers, Whitefield did not read his sermons but spoke from memory. He gestured eloquently, raised his voice for dramatic effect, and at times assumed a female persona—a woman in labor struggling to deliver the word of God. When the young preacher told his spellbound listeners that they had all sinned and must seek salvation, hundreds of men and women suddenly felt a "new light" within them. As "the power of god come down,"

A Quest for Assurance SARAH OSBORNE

Born in London in 1714, Sarah Osborne came to the colonies in 1722 with her parents, who settled in Newport, Rhode Island, in 1729. Throughout her youth, Osborne struggled with deep feelings of emotional distress and guilt, which were largely relieved by her conversion experience during the Great Awakening.

I was married to Mr. Samuel Wheaten, being in my eighteenth year, October 21, 1731, and went with my husband, the next winter, to see his friends in the country. . . . After I came home, I met with much affliction in many respects. It seemed to me that the whole world were in arms against me. I thought I was the most despised creature living upon earth. I used to pray to God in secret to relieve me; but did not, as I ought, see his hand in permitting it so to be, as a just punishment for my vile sins: And therefore was not humbled under it as I ought; but let nature rise, and acted very imprudently, in many respects. I was then with child, and often lamented that I was to bring a child into such a world of sorrow. . . .

My child was born on Oct. 27, 1732. The next spring, my husband returned home; but went to sea again, and died abroad in November, 1733.

In Sept. 1740, God in mercy sent his dear servant [George] Whitefield here, which in some measure stirred me up. But when Mr. [Gilbert] Tennent came soon after, it pleased God to bless his preaching so to me, that it roused me. But I was all the winter after exercised with dreadful doubts and fears about my state. I questioned the truth of all I had experienced, and feared I had never yet passed through the pangs of the new birth, or ever had one spark of grace. . . .

I continued thus till March, 1741. and then it pleased God to return Mr. Tennent

to us again. . . . But while he was here, I was more than ever distressed. I had lost the sensible manifestations of Christ's love. . . . And [Mr. Tennent] struck directly at those things, for which I had so foolishly and wickedly pleaded Christian example, such as singing songs, dancing and foolish jesting. . . . He said, he would not say there was no such thing as a dancing Christian, but he had a very mean opinion of such as could bear to spend their time so, when it is so short, and the work for eternity so great. Then, and not till then, was I fully convinced what prodigal wasters of precious time such things were. And, through grace, I have abhorred them all ever since. . . .

About this time I had the offer of a second marriage, with one who appeared to be a real Christian (and I could not think of being unequally yoked with one who was not such). . . . I concluded it was the will of God that I should accept of the offer, and accordingly was married to Mr. Henry Osborn, on the fifth day of May, 1742. . . . Soon after this, we fell into disagreeable and difficult worldly circumstances, with respect to living and paying the debts we owed. . . . [But] God ordered things so that our creditors were paid to their satisfaction.

SOURCE: Samuel Hopkins, ed., *Memoirs of the Life of Mrs. Sarah Osborn* (Worcester, MA: Leonard Worcester, 1799), 39–55.

George Whitefield, Evangelist
No painting could capture Whitefield's magical appeal, although this image conveys his open demeanor, religious intensity, and appeal to listeners. When Whitefield spoke to a crowd near Philadelphia, an observer noted, his words were "sharper than a two-edged sword. . . . Some of the people were pale as death; others were wringing their hands . . . and most lifting their eyes to heaven and crying to God for mercy." Courtesy, Trustees of the Boston Public Library.

Hannah Heaton recalled, "my knees smote together . . . it seemed to me I was a sinking down into hell . . . but then I resigned my distress and was perfectly easy quiet and calm . . . it seemed as if I had a new soul & body both." Strengthened and self-confident, these "New Lights" were eager to spread Whitefield's message.

Religious Upheaval in the North

Like all cultural explosions, the Great Awakening was controversial. Conservative ministers—"Old Lights"—condemned the "cryings out, faintings and convulsions" in revivalist meetings and the New Lights' claims of "working Miracles or speaking with Tongues." Charles Chauncy, a minister in Boston, also attacked the New Lights for allowing women to speak in public: It was "a plain breach of that commandment of the LORD, where it is said, Let your WOMEN keep silence in the churches." In Connecticut, Old Lights persuaded the legislature to prohibit evangelists from speaking to congregations without their ministers' permission. Although Whitefield insisted, "I am no *Enthusiast*," he found many pulpits closed to him when he returned to Connecticut in 1744. But the New Lights refused to be silenced. Dozens of farmers, women, and artisans roamed the countryside, condemning the Old Lights as "unconverted" sinners and willingly accepting imprisonment: "I shall bring glory to God in my bonds," a dissident preacher wrote from jail.

The Awakening undermined support for legally established churches and their tax-supported ministers. In New England, New Lights left the Congregational Church and founded 125 "separatist" churches that supported their ministers through voluntary contributions. Other religious dissidents joined Baptist congregations, which also condemned government support of churches. "God never allowed any civil state upon earth to impose religious taxes," declared Baptist preacher Isaac Backus. In New York and New Jersey, the Dutch Reformed Church split in two because New Lights refused to accept the doctrines decreed by conservative church authorities in Holland.

Indeed, the Great Awakening challenged the authority of all ministers, whose status had long rested on respect for their education and knowledge of the Bible. In an influential pamphlet, *The Dangers of an Unconverted Ministry* (1740), Gilbert Tennent asserted that ministers' authority should come not from theological training but from the conversion experience. Reaffirming Martin Luther's belief in the priesthood of all Christians, Tennent suggested that anyone who had experienced the redeeming grace of God could speak with ministerial authority. Isaac Backus also celebrated a spiritual democracy, noting with approval that "the common people now claim as good a right to judge and act in matters of religion as civil rulers or the learned clergy." When challenged by her minister, Sarah Harrah Osborne, a New Light "exhorter" in Rhode Island, refused "to shut up my mouth . . . and creep into obscurity."

In many rural villages, revivalism reinforced communal values by challenging the moneygrubbing practices of merchants and land speculators. Jonathan Edwards spoke for many rural farm families when he charged that a miserly spirit was more suitable "for wolves and other beasts of prey, than for human beings."

As religious enthusiasm spread, churches founded new colleges to educate their young men and train ministers. New Light Presbyterians established the College of New Jersey (Princeton) in 1746, and New York Anglicans founded King's College (Columbia) in 1754. Baptists set up the College of Rhode Island (Brown) in 1764; two years later, the Dutch Reformed Church subsidized Queen's College (Rutgers) in New Jersey. However, the main intellectual legacy of the Great Awakening was not education for the privileged few but a new sense of authority among the many. A European visitor to Philadelphia remarked in surprise, "The poorest day-laborer . . . holds it his right to advance his opinion, in religious as well as political matters, with as much freedom as the gentleman."

Social and Religious Conflict in the South

In the southern colonies, where the Church of England was legally established, religious enthusiasm triggered social conflict. Anglican ministers generally ignored the spiritual needs of African Americans (about 40 percent of the population), and landless whites (another 20 percent) attended church irregularly. Middling white freeholders (35 percent of the residents) formed the core of most Church of England congregations. Prominent planters and their families (just 5 percent) held the real power, and they used their control of parish finances to discipline their ministers. One clergyman complained that dismissal awaited any minister who "had the courage to preach against any Vices taken into favor by the leading Men of his Parish."

Consequently, the Great Awakening challenged the dominance of both the Anglican Church and the planter elite. In 1743, bricklayer Samuel Morris, inspired by reading George Whitefield's sermons, led a group of Virginia Anglicans out of the church. Seeking a deeper religious experience, Morris invited New Light Presbyterian ministers to lead their prayer meetings. Soon Presbyterian revivals erupted among the English residents in the Tidewater region, where they threatened the social authority of the Virginia gentry. Traditionally, planters and their well-dressed families arrived at Anglican services in fancy carriages drawn by well-bred horses, and the men flaunted their power by marching in a body to their front-pew seats. Such ritual displays of the gentry's superiority would be meaningless if freeholders attended Presbyterian churches. Moreover, religious pluralism threatened the tax-supported status of the Anglican Church.

To halt the spread of New Light ideas, Virginia's governor William Gooch denounced them as "false teachings," and Anglican justices of the peace closed down Presbyterian meetinghouses. This harassment kept most white yeomen and poor tenants families in the Church of England; so did the fact that many well-educated Presbyterian ministers did not preach in the "enthusiastic" style preferred by illiterate farmers.

New Light Baptist ministers did not hesitate to reach out to ordinary folk. During the 1760s, their vigorous preaching and democratic message converted thousands of white farm families. The Baptists were radical Protestants whose central ritual was adult (rather than infant) baptism. Once men and women had experienced the infusion of grace—had been "born again"—they were baptized in an emotional public ceremony, often involving complete immersion in water.

Even slaves were welcome at Baptist revivals. During the 1740s, George Whitefield had urged Carolina planters to bring their slaves into the Christian fold, but white hostility and the commitment of Africans to their ancestral religions kept the number of converts low. The first significant Christian conversions came in Virginia in the 1760s, as native-born African Americans responded to the Baptists' message that all people were equal in God's eyes. Sensing a threat to the system of racial slavery, the House of Burgesses imposed heavy fines on Baptists who preached to slaves without their owners' permission.

The Baptists' insurgency posed other threats to gentry authority. Their preachers repudiated the social hierarchy, urging followers to call one another "brother" and "sister," and attacked the planters' rakish lifestyle. As planter Landon Carter complained, the Baptists were "destroying pleasure in the Country; for they encourage ardent Prayer; strong & constant faith, & an intire Banishment of *Gaming, Dancing,* & Sabbath-Day Diversions." The gentry responded with violence. Hearing Baptist Dutton Lane condemn "the vileness and danger" of drunkenness and whoring, planter John Giles took the charge personally: "I know who you mean! and by God I'll demolish you." In Caroline County, an Anglican posse attacked Brother John Waller at a prayer meeting. Waller "was violently jerked off the stage; they caught him by the back part of his neck, beat his head against the ground, and a gentleman gave him twenty lashes with his horsewhip."

Despite these attacks, Baptist congregations multiplied. By 1775, about 15 percent of Virginia's whites and hundreds of black slaves had joined Baptist churches. To signify their state of grace, some Baptist men "cut off their hair, like Cromwell's round-headed chaplains." Others forged a new evangelical masculinity—"crying, weeping, lifting up the eyes, groaning" when touched by the Holy Spirit but defending themselves with vigor. "Not able to bear the insults" of a heckler, a group of Baptists "took [him] by the neck and heels and threw him out of doors," setting off a bloody brawl.

The Baptist revival in the Chesapeake challenged traditional authority but did not overturn it. Rejecting the requests of evangelical women, Baptist men kept church authority in the hands of "free born male members"; and Anglican slaveholders retained control of the political system. Still, the Baptist insurgency infused the lives of poor tenant families with spiritual meaning and empowered yeomen to defend their economic interests. Moreover, as Baptist ministers spread Christianity among slaves, the cultural gulf between blacks and whites shrank, undermining one justification for slavery and giving some blacks a new religious identity. Within a generation, African Americans would develop distinctive versions of Protestant Christianity.

▶ In what ways did the Enlightenment and the Great Awakening prompt Americans to challenge traditional sources of authority?

▶ How did the Baptist insurgency in Virginia challenge conventional assumptions about race, gender, and class?

The Midcentury Challenge: War, Trade, and Social Conflict, 1750–1765

Between 1750 and 1765, a series of events transformed colonial life. First, Britain embarked on a war against the French in America, which became a worldwide conflict: the Great War for Empire. Second, a surge in trade boosted colonial consumption and placed Americans deeply in debt to British creditors. Third, westward migration sparked new conflicts with Indian peoples, armed disputes between settlers and speculators, and backcountry rebellions against eastern-controlled governments.

The French and Indian War Becomes a War for Empire

By 1754, France and Britain had laid claim to much of the land west of the Appalachians, but few Europeans had moved into that vast area (Map 4.3). The mountainous terrain discouraged access from the British colonies, and the Indian peoples that inhabited the region firmly opposed white settlement.

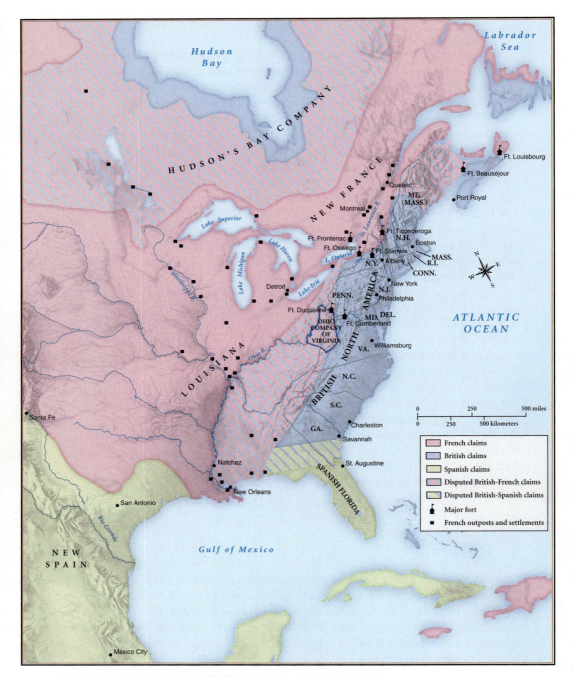

MAP 4.3 European Spheres of Influence in North America, 1754

France and Spain laid claim to vast areas of North America and relied on their Indian allies to combat the numerical superiority of British settlers. For their part, Native Americans played off one European power against another. As a British official observed, "To preserve the Ballance between us and the French is the great ruling Principle of Modern Indian Politics." By expelling the French from North America, the Great War for Empire destroyed this balance and left the Indian peoples on their own to resist encroaching Anglo-American settlers.

For decades, Iroquois and other native peoples had used their control of the fur trade to obtain guns and subsidies from French and British officials. By the 1740s, however, this strategy of playing off the French against the British was breaking down. The Europeans resented the rising cost of "gifts"; equally important, the alliances between the Indians and the British were crumbling as Anglo-American demands for western lands escalated. In the late 1740s, the Mohawks rebuffed attempts by Sir William Johnson, an Indian agent and land speculator, to settle Scottish migrants west of Albany. The Iroquois also responded angrily when Virginia Governor Robert Dinwiddie, along with Virginia land speculators and London merchants, formed the Ohio Company in 1749. The company's royal grant of 200,000 acres lay in the upper Ohio River Valley, an area the Iroquois controlled through alliances with the Delaware and Shawnee peoples. "We don't know what you Christians, English and French intend," the outraged Iroquois complained; "we are so hemmed in by both, that we have hardly a hunting place left."

To repair ties with the Iroquois, the British Board of Trade called a meeting at Albany in June 1754. At the Albany Congress, delegates from Britain's mainland colonies denied any designs on Iroquois lands and asked the Indians for help against New France. Though small in numbers, the French colony had a broad reach. In the 1750s, the 15,000 French farm families who lived along the St. Lawrence River provided food and supplies to the fur-trading settlements of Montreal and Quebec and the hundreds of fur traders, missionaries, and soldiers who lived among the western Indian peoples. To counter French expansion, Benjamin Franklin proposed a Plan of Union. Franklin's plan included a continental assembly that would manage trade, Indian policy, and defense in the West. But neither Franklin's plan nor a proposal by the Board of Trade for a political "union between ye Royal, Proprietary, & Charter Governments" was in the cards. British ministers worried that a union would spark American demands for independence, and provincial leaders feared that a consolidated government would undermine the authority of their assemblies.

Meanwhile, the Ohio Company's land grant alarmed French authorities. To stop British settlers from pouring into the Ohio River Valley, they constructed a series of forts. One, Fort Duquesne, stood at the point where the Monongahela and Allegheny rivers join to form the Ohio River (present-day Pittsburgh). In response, Governor Dinwiddie dispatched a military expedition led by Colonel George Washington, a young Virginia planter and Ohio Company stockholder. In July 1754, French troops seized Washington and his men, prompting Virginian and British expansionists to demand war. Henry Pelham, the British prime minister, urged calm: "There is such a load of debt, and such heavy taxes already laid upon the people, that nothing but an absolute necessity can justifie our engaging in a new War."

Pelham could not control the march of events. In Parliament, William Pitt, a rising British statesman, and Lord Halifax, the new head of the Board of Trade, were strong advocates for expansion. They persuaded Pelham to dispatch military forces to America to attack the French forts. In June 1755, British and New England troops captured Fort Beauséjour in Nova Scotia (Acadia). Soldiers from Puritan Massachusetts then seized nearly 10,000 French Acadians and deported them to France, the West Indies, and Louisiana (where they became known as Cajuns). English and Scottish Protestants took over the farms the French Catholics left behind.

These Anglo-American successes were quickly offset by a stunning defeat. In July 1755, 2,000 British regulars and Virginia militiamen advancing on Fort Duquesne marched into a deadly ambush. A much smaller force of French soldiers and Delaware and Shawnee warriors rained fire on the British force, taking the life of the British commander, General Edward Braddock, and killing or wounding half of his troops. "We have been beaten, most shamefully beaten, by a handfull of Men," Washington complained bitterly as he led the militiamen back to Virginia.

The Great War for Empire

By 1756, the conflict in America had spread to Europe, where it was known as the Seven Years' War. There, it pitted Britain and Prussia against France, Spain, and Austria. When Britain mounted major offensives in India and West Africa as well as in North America, the conflict became a Great War for Empire. Since 1700, Britain had reaped unprecedented profits from its overseas trading empire; now it vowed to crush France, the main obstacle to further expansion.

William Pitt emerged as the architect of the British war effort. Pitt, the grandson of the East Indies merchant "Diamond" Pitt, was a committed expansionist with a touch of arrogance. "I know that I can save this country and that I alone can," he boasted. In fact, Pitt was a master of strategy, both commercial and military, and planned to cripple France by seizing its colonies. In designing the critical campaign against New France, Pitt exploited a demographic advantage: On the North American mainland, King George II's two million subjects outnumbered the French by fourteen to one. To mobilize the colonists, Pitt paid half the cost of their troops and supplied them with arms and equipment, at a cost of £1 million a year. He also committed a fleet of British ships and 30,000 British soldiers to the American conflict.

Beginning in 1758, the powerful Anglo-American forces moved from one triumph to the next. They forced the French to abandon Fort Duquesne (which they renamed Fort Pitt); then they captured Fort Louisbourg, a French stronghold at the mouth of the St. Lawrence. In 1759, a force led by British General James Wolfe sailed down the St. Lawrence and took Quebec, the heart of France's American empire. The Royal Navy prevented French reinforcements from crossing the Atlantic, allowing British forces to complete the conquest of Canada in 1760 by capturing Montreal.

Elsewhere, the British also went from success to success. Fulfilling Pitt's dream, the East India Company ousted French traders from India; and British forces seized French Senegal in West Africa and the sugar islands Martinique and Guadeloupe in the French West Indies. From Spain, the British won Cuba and the Philippine Islands. The Treaty of Paris of 1763 confirmed Britain's triumph. It granted the British sovereignty over half the continent of North America, including French Canada, all French territory east of the Mississippi River, and Spanish Florida. The French empire in North America had shrunk to a handful of sugar islands in the West Indies, and Britain had forged a commercial and colonial empire that was nearly worldwide.

Britain's territorial acquisitions alarmed Indian peoples from New York to Michigan, who rightly feared an influx of British troops and Anglo-American settlers. To encourage the French to return, the Ottawa chief Pontiac declared, "I am French, and I want to die French." Neolin, a Delaware prophet, went further. He taught that the

Pipe of Peace

In 1760, the Ottawa chief Pontiac welcomed British troops to his territory. Here, he is shown offering a pipe of peace to their commander, Major Robert Rogers. Three years later, as British troops built forts in Indian lands and Anglo-American settlers moved west, Pontiac led a coordinated Indian uprising against the new European intruders. Library of Congress.

Indians' decline stemmed from their dependence on European goods, guns, and rum. He called for the expulsion of the white-skinned invaders: "If you suffer the English among you, you are dead men. Sickness, smallpox, and their poison [rum] will destroy you entirely." In 1763, inspired by Neolin's vision, Pontiac led a group of loosely confederated tribes (stretching geographically from the New York Senecas to the Minnesota Chippewas) in a major uprising. In Pontiac's Rebellion, Indian forces seized nearly every British military garrison west of Fort Niagara, besieged the fort at Detroit, and killed or captured more than 2,000 settlers. But the Indian alliance gradually weakened, and British military expeditions defeated the Delawares near Fort Pitt and broke the siege of Detroit. In the peace settlement, Pontiac and his allies accepted the British as their new political "fathers." In return, the British issued the Proclamation of 1763, which prohibited white settlements west of the Appalachians. It was an edict the colonists would ignore.

British Industrial Growth and the Consumer Revolution

Britain owed its military and diplomatic success to its unprecedented economic resources. Since 1700, when it had wrested control of many oceanic trade routes from the Dutch, Britain had become the dominant commercial power in the Atlantic and Indian oceans. By 1750, it had also become the first country to use new manufacturing technology and work discipline to expand output. This combination of commerce and industry would soon make Britain the most powerful nation in the world.

Mechanical power was key to Britain's Industrial Revolution. British artisans designed and built water mills and steam engines that efficiently powered a wide array of machines: lathes for shaping wood, jennies and looms for spinning and weaving textiles, and hammers for forging iron. The new power-driven machinery produced woolen and linen textiles, iron tools, furniture, and chinaware in greater quantities than traditional manufacturing methods—and at lower cost. Moreover, the entrepreneurs who ran the new workshops drove their employees hard, forcing them to work long hours and to keep pace with the machines. To market the abundant factory-produced goods, English and Scottish merchants extended a full year's credit to colonial shopkeepers instead of the traditional six months'. Americans soon were purchasing 30 percent of all British exports.

To pay for British manufactures, the colonists increased their exports of tobacco, rice, indigo, and wheat. In Virginia, farmers moved into the Piedmont, a region of plains and rolling hills inland from the Tidewater counties. Using credit advanced by Scottish merchants, planters bought land, slaves, and equipment and grew tobacco, which they exported to expanding markets in France and central Europe. In South Carolina, rice planters increased their wealth and luxurious lifestyles by using British government subsidies to develop indigo plantations. By the 1760s, they were exporting the deep blue dye to English textile factories and 65 million pounds of rice a year to Holland and southern Europe. Simultaneously, New York, Pennsylvania, Maryland, and Virginia became the breadbasket of the Atlantic world, supplying Europe's exploding population with wheat. In Philadelphia, export prices for wheat jumped almost 50 percent between 1740 and 1765.

Americans used their profits from agricultural exports to buy English manufactures. Although this "consumer revolution" raised living standards, it landed many consumers—and the colonies as a whole—in debt. Even during the booming wartime economy of the 1750s, exports paid for only 80 percent of imported British goods. The remaining 20 percent—the Americans' trade deficit—was financed by Britain through the extension of credit and Pitt's military expenditures. When the military subsidies ended in 1763, the colonies fell into an economic recession. Merchants looked anxiously at their overstocked warehouses and feared bankruptcy. "I think we have a gloomy prospect before us," a Philadelphia trader noted in 1765, "as there are of late some Persons failed, who were in no way suspected." The increase in transatlantic trade had made Americans more dependent on overseas credit and markets.

The Struggle for Land in the East

In good times and bad, the colonial population continued to grow, intensifying the demand for arable land. Consider the experience of Kent, Connecticut. The settlers who founded the town in 1738 were descended from the original Puritan migrants. Like earlier generations, they had moved inland to establish new farms, but Kent stood at the colony's western boundary. To provide for the next generation, many

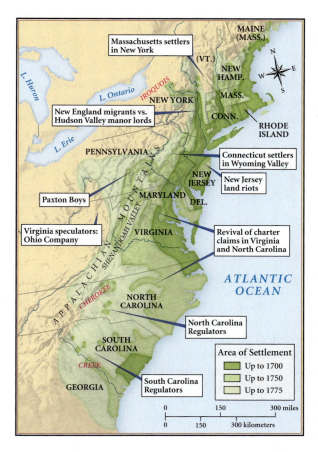

MAP 4.4 Westward Expansion and Land Conflicts, 1750–1775
Between 1750 and 1775, the mainland population more than doubled — from 1.2 million to 2.5 million — triggering both migration westward and legal battles over land, which had become increasingly valuable. Violence broke out in eastern areas, where tenant farmers and small-holders contested landlords' titles, and in the backcountry, where migrating settlers fought with Indians, rival claimants, and the officials of eastern-dominated governments.

Kent families joined the Susquehanna Company (1749), which speculated in lands in the Wyoming Valley along the upper Susquehanna River in present-day northeastern Pennsylvania. As settlers took up farmsteads there, the company urged the Connecticut legislature to claim the region on the basis of Connecticut's "sea-to-sea" royal charter of 1662. However, King Charles II had also granted the Wyoming Valley region to William Penn, and the Penn family had sold farms there to Pennsylvania residents. By the late 1750s, settlers from Connecticut and Pennsylvania were at war, burning down their rivals' houses and barns.

Simultaneously, three distinct but related land disputes broke out in the Hudson River Valley (Map 4.4). Dutch tenant farmers, Wappinger Indians, and migrants from Massachusetts asserted ownership rights to lands long claimed by the Van Rensselaer, Livingston, and other manorial families. When the manorial lords turned to the legal system to uphold their claims, Dutch and English farmers in Westchester, Dutchess, and Albany counties rioted to close the courts. In response, New York's royal governor ordered British General Thomas Gage and two regiments of troops to assist local sheriffs and manorial bailiffs to put down the mobs. They suppressed the tenant uprisings, intimidated the Wappingers, and evicted the Massachusetts squatters.

Other land disputes erupted in New Jersey and the southern colonies, as landlords and English aristocrats successfully asserted legal claims based on long-dormant seventeenth-century charters. One court decision upheld the right of Lord Granville, an heir of an original Carolina proprietor, to collect an annual tax on land in North Carolina; another decision awarded ownership of the entire northern neck of Virginia (along the Potomac River) to Lord Fairfax.

The revival of proprietary claims by manorial lords and English nobles testified to the rising value of land along the Atlantic coastal plain. It also reflected the maturity of the colonial courts, which now had enough authority to uphold property rights. And it underscored the increasing similarities between rural societies in Europe and America. To avoid being reduced to the status of European peasants, native-born yeomen and tenant families joined the stream of European migrants searching for cheap land near the Appalachian Mountains.

Western Uprisings and Regulator Movements

As would-be landowners moved westward, they sparked conflicts over Indian policy, political representation, and debts. During the war with France, Delaware and Shawnee warriors had exacted revenge for Thomas Penn's land swindle of 1737 by destroying frontier farms in Pennsylvania and killing hundreds of residents. Scots-Irish settlers demanded the expulsion of all Indians, but Quaker leaders refused. So in 1763, a group of Scots-Irish frontiersmen called the Paxton Boys took matters into their own hands and massacred twenty members of the peaceful Conestoga tribe. When Governor John Penn tried to bring the murderers to justice, 250 armed Scots-Irish advanced on Philadelphia. Benjamin Franklin intercepted the angry mob at Lancaster and arranged a truce, averting a battle with the militia. Prosecution of the Paxton Boys failed for lack of witnesses, and the Scots-Irish dropped their demands that the Indians be expelled; but the episode left a legacy of racial hatred and political resentment.

Violence also broke out in the backcountry of South Carolina, where land-hungry Scottish and Anglo-American settlers clashed repeatedly with Cherokees during the war with France. When the war ended in 1763, a group of landowning vigilantes, the Regulators, tried to suppress outlaw bands of whites that were stealing cattle. The Regulators also had political goals: They demanded that the eastern-controlled government provide western districts with more courts, fairer taxation, and greater representation in the assembly. Fearing slave revolts, the lowland rice planters who ran the South Carolina assembly compromised with the Regulators rather than fighting them. In 1767, the assembly created courts in the western counties and reduced the fees for legal documents; but it refused to reapportion the legislature or lower western taxes. Like the Paxton Boys in Pennsylvania, the South Carolina Regulators won attention to western needs but failed to wrest power from the eastern elite.

In 1766, a more radical Regulator movement arose in the backcountry of North Carolina. The economic recession of the early 1760s brought a sharp fall in tobacco prices, and many farmers could not pay their debts. When creditors sued, judges directed sheriffs to seize the debtors' property and sell it to pay debts and court costs.

Governor Tryon and the Regulators Meet at Hillsborough, 1768
Orange County, North Carolina, was home to the Sandy Creek Association, a group of Quakers led by Herman Husband, a powerful advocate of social justice and a leader of the Regulator movement. In September 1768, Royal Governor William Tryon and the low-country militia confronted a group of Regulators near Hillsborough. As this engraving suggests, the potential for violence was high and only narrowly averted. In 1771, Tryon engaged the Regulators in a battle near the Alamance River, twenty miles west of Hillsborough. Courtesy, North Carolina State Archives.

Backcountry farmers—including many German and Scots-Irish migrants—denounced the merchants' lawsuits, both because they generated high fees for lawyers and court officials and because they violated rural custom, which allowed loans to remain unpaid in hard times.

To save their farms from grasping creditors and tax-hungry officials, North Carolina's debtors defied the government's authority. Disciplined mobs of farmers intimidated judges, closed courts, and freed their comrades from jail. Significantly, the Regulators proposed a coherent set of reforms. They proposed legislation to lower legal fees and allow tax payments in the "produce of the country" rather than in cash. They demanded greater representation in the assembly and a new revenue system, which would tax each person "in proportion to the profits arising from his estate." All to no avail. In May 1771, Royal Governor William Tryon decided to suppress the Regulators. Mobilizing British troops and the eastern militia, Tryon defeated a large Regulator force at the Alamance River. When the fighting ended, thirty men lay dead, and Tryon summarily executed seven insurgent leaders. Not since Bacon's Rebellion in Virginia in 1675 (see Chapter 2) had a domestic political conflict caused so much bloodshed.

▶ What impact did the Industrial Revolution in England have on the American colonies?

▶ What were the causes of unrest in the American backcountry in the mid-eighteenth century?

▶ In what ways were the various regions in British North America — New England, Middle Atlantic, the South (see Chapter 3), the backcountry — becoming increasingly similar between 1720 and 1750? In what ways were they becoming different?

In 1771, as in 1675, colonial conflicts became linked with imperial politics. In Connecticut, the Reverend Ezra Stiles defended the North Carolina Regulators. "What shall an injured & oppressed people do," he asked, when faced with "Oppression and tyranny?" Stiles's remarks reflected growing resistance to recently imposed British policies of taxation and control. In 1771, as in 1686 when James II imposed the Dominion of New England, the American colonies still depended on Britain for their trade and military defense. However, by the 1760s, the mainland settlements had evolved into a complex society with the potential to exist independently. British policies would determine the direction the maturing colonies would take.

SUMMARY

In this chapter, we observed the dramatic transformation of British North America between 1720 and 1765. There was an astonishing surge in population — from 400,000 to almost two million — the combined result of natural increase, European migration, and the trade in African slaves. Three other transatlantic developments brought equally great changes: The European Enlightenment, European Pietism, and substantial imports of consumer goods from England altered the cultural landscape.

We noted that the colonists confronted three major regional challenges. In New England, crowded towns and ever-smaller farms threatened the yeoman ideal of independent farming, prompting families to limit births, move to the frontier, or participate in an "exchange" economy. In the Middle Atlantic colonies, Dutch, English, German, and Scots-Irish residents maintained their religious and cultural identities, which led to bruising ethnic conflicts. Finally, westward migration into the backcountry and the Ohio River Valley set off conflicts with Indian peoples, civil unrest among white settlers, and, ultimately, the Great War for Empire. In the aftermath of the war, Britain stood triumphant in Europe and America.

Connections: Culture

In the essay opening Part One, we provided an outline of cultural changes in America between 1600 and 1765:

> New forms of family and community life arose in the new American society . . . [, which was] increasingly pluralistic, composed of migrants from many European ethnic groups . . . as well as enslaved Africans and Native American peoples. Distinct regional cultures developed in New England, the Middle Atlantic colonies, the Chesapeake, and the Carolinas.

In tracking the trajectory of Britain's North American colonies, we can see a crucial turning point around 1700. Until then, most settlers came from England, bringing with them traditional English social and political structures: Fathers ruled families, and authoritarian leaders dominated politics. Then came a massive wave of migrants: enslaved Africans, Germans, Scots-Irish, and Scots. By 1765, these migrants and their descendants formed a majority of the population. As British North America became more diverse, life became less repressive and more open to innovation.

A second phase of change began around 1740. More farmers sold goods in distant markets; a responsive system of government prompted more men to seek office; declining parental power gave young people greater marriage choices; and an outburst

TIMELINE

1710s–1730s ▶ Enlightenment ideas spread to America

▶ Germans and Scots-Irish settle in Middle Atlantic region

▶ Theodore Jacob Frelinghuysen conducts Pietist revivals

1730s ▶ William and Gilbert Tennent lead Presbyterian revivals

▶ Jonathan Edwards mobilizes piety in New England

1739 ▶ George Whitefield sparks Great Awakening

1740s–1760s ▶ Old Light–New Light conflicts

▶ Small farms in New England threaten freehold ideal

▶ Ethnic and religious conflict in Middle Atlantic region

▶ Religious denominations establish colleges

1743 ▶ Benjamin Franklin founds American Philosophical Society

▶ Samuel Morris starts Presbyterian revivals in Virginia

1749 ▶ Virginia speculators organize Ohio Company; Connecticut farmers form Susquehanna Company

1750s ▶ American consumer imports increase debts to English merchants

1754 ▶ French and Indian War begins

▶ Albany Congress of colonial delegates and Iroquois

1756 ▶ Britain begins Great War for Empire

1759–1760 ▶ Britain completes conquest of Canada

1760s ▶ Land conflicts along New York and New England border

▶ Baptists win converts in Virginia

1763 ▶ Pontiac's Rebellion leads to Proclamation of 1763

▶ Treaty of Paris ends Great War for Empire

▶ Scots-Irish Paxton Boys massacre Indians in Pennsylvania

1771 ▶ Royal governor puts down Regulator revolt in North Carolina of pietistic enthusiasm shook established churches and advanced religious toleration. Together, these developments provided white colonists in British North America (as we stated in the opening essay) with "unprecedented opportunities for economic security, political freedom, and spiritual fulfillment."

FOR FURTHER EXPLORATION

Stories of individuals bring alive the social history of eighteenth-century America. In *Good Wives* (1982) and *A Midwife's Tale* (1990), Laurel Thatcher Ulrich paints a vivid picture of women's experiences. For additional materials on Ballard, see **www .pbs.org/amex/midwife** and **www.DoHistory.org**. Benjamin Franklin's *Autobiography* (1771) shows his Enlightenment sensibility and his pursuit of wealth and fame. See also "Benjamin Franklin . . . in His Own Words" (**www.loc.gov/exhibits/treasures/ franklin-home.html**) and "The Electric Franklin" (**www.ushistory.org/franklin/ index.htm**).

Harry S. Stout's *The Divine Dramatist: George Whitefield and the Rise of Modern Evangelicalism* (1991) evokes the charismatic preacher's flair for theatrics "Jonathan Edwards On-Line" (**www.JonathanEdwards.com/**) presents the writings of the great philosopher and preacher.

"Colonial Currency and Colonial Coin" (**www.coins.nd.edu/ColCurrency/index .html**) suggests the dimensions of daily economic life, and "Bethlehem Digital History Project" (**bdhp.moravian.edu/**) documents the experiences of migrant German religious sectarians. On settler-Indian relations, see Jane T. Merritt, *At the Crossroads: Indians and Empires on a Mid-Atlantic Frontier, 1700–1763* (2003), and Gregory Evans Dowd, *War Under Heaven: Pontiac, the Indian Nations, and the British Empire* (2002). For the French and Indian War, see the PBS series "The War That Made America" and its Web site (**www.thewarthatmadeamerica.com/**).

TEST YOUR KNOWLEDGE

To assess your mastery of the material in this chapter and for Web sites, images, and documents related to this chapter, visit **bedfordstmartins.com/henrettaconcise**.

PART TWO

The New Republic
1 7 6 3 – 1 8 2 0

GOVERNMENT	DIPLOMACY	ECONOMY
Creating republican institutions	European entanglements	Expanding commerce and manufacturing
1763 ▶ Stamp Act Congress (1765) ▶ Committees of correspondence ▶ First Continental Congress (1774)	▶ Treaty of Paris (1763) gives Britain control of Canada and Florida	▶ Merchants defy Sugar and Stamp Acts ▶ Boycotts spur domestic manufacturing
1775 ▶ Second Continental Congress (1775) ▶ States institute republican constitutions	▶ Independence declared (1776) ▶ Treaty of Alliance with France (1778)	▶ Manufacturing expands during war ▶ Curtailed trade and severe inflation threaten economy
1780 ▶ Articles of Confederation ratified (1781) ▶ Legislatures emerge as supreme in states ▶ Philadelphia convention drafts U.S. Constitution (1787)	▶ Treaty of Paris (1783) ▶ Britain restricts U.S. trade with West Indies ▶ U.S. government signs treaties with Indian peoples	▶ Bank of North America founded (1781) ▶ Commercial recession (1783–1789) ▶ Land speculation continues in West
1790 ▶ Conflict over Alexander Hamilton's economic policies ▶ First national parties: Federalists and Republicans	▶ Wars between France and Britain ▶ Jay's Treaty and Pinckney's Treaty (both 1795) ▶ Undeclared war with France (1798)	▶ First Bank of the United States (1792–1811) ▶ States charter business corporations ▶ Outwork system grows
1800 ▶ Jefferson's "Revolution of 1800" reduces activism of national government ▶ Chief Justice Marshall asserts judicial powers	▶ Napoleonic Wars (1802–1815) ▶ Louisiana Purchase (1803) ▶ Embargo Act (1807)	▶ Cotton output expands ▶ Farm productivity improves ▶ Embargo encourages U.S. manufacturing
1810 ▶ Triumph of Republican Party and end of Federalist Party ▶ State constitutions democratized	▶ War of 1812 (1812–1815) ▶ John Quincy Adams makes border treaties ▶ Monroe Doctrine (1823)	▶ Second Bank of the United States chartered (1816–1836) ▶ Supreme Court guards property ▶ Emergence of a national economy

SOCIETY	CULTURE
Defining liberty and equality	**Pluralism and national identity**
▸ Artisans seek influence ▸ Quebec Act (1774) allows Catholicism	▸ Patriots call for American unity ▸ Concept of "popular sovereignty" takes hold
▸ Judith Sargent Murray writes *On the Equality of the Sexes* (1779) ▸ Emancipation begins in the North	▸ Thomas Paine's *Common Sense* (1776) calls for a republic ▸ Influx of migrants from Europe slows
▸ Virginia enacts religious freedom legislation (1786) ▸ Politicians and ministers praise "republican motherhood"	▸ Noah Webster defines American English ▸ State cessions and land ordinances create national domain in West ▸ German settlers keep own language
▸ Bill of Rights ratified (1791) ▸ Creation of French Republic (1793) sparks ideological debate ▸ Sedition Act limits freedom of press (1798)	▸ Indians form Western Confederacy (1790) ▸ Second Great Awakening (1790–1860) ▸ Divisions emerge between South and North
▸ New Jersey denies suffrage to propertied women (1807) ▸ Atlantic slave trade legally ends (1808)	▸ Tenskwatawa and Tecumseh revive Western Confederacy ▸ Percentage of native-born citizens increases
▸ Suffrage for white men expands ▸ American Colonization Society (1817) ▸ Missouri Compromise (1819–1821)	▸ War of 1812 tests national unity ▸ Religious benevolence produces social reform

"The American war is over," Philadelphia Patriot Benjamin Rush declared in 1787, "but this is far from being the case with the American Revolution. On the contrary, nothing but the first act of the great drama is closed. It remains yet to establish and perfect our new forms of government." As we will suggest in Part Two, the job was even greater than Rush imagined. The republican revolution that began with the Patriot resistance movement of 1765 and took shape with the Declaration of Independence in 1776 reached far beyond politics. It challenged many of the values and institutions of the colonial social order and forced Americans to consider fundamental changes in their economic, religious, and cultural practices. Here, in summary, are the main themes of our discussion of America's new political and social order.

GOVERNMENT

Once Americans had repudiated their allegiance to Britain and its monarch, they faced the task of creating a new system of government. In 1776, no one knew how the states should go about setting up republican institutions. Nor did Patriot leaders know whether there should be a permanent central authority along the lines of the Continental Congress. It would take experimentation stretching over an entire generation to find out. It would take even longer to assimilate a new institution—the political party—into the workings of government. However, by 1820, years of difficult political compromise and constitutional revision had resulted in republican national and state governments that commanded the allegiance of their citizens.

DIPLOMACY

To create and preserve their new republic, Americans of European descent fought two wars against Great Britain, an undeclared war against France, and many battles with Indian peoples. The wars against Britain divided the country into bitter factions—Patriots against Loyalists in the War of Independence and pro-war Republicans versus antiwar Federalists in the War of 1812—and expended much blood and treasure. The extension of American sovereignty and settlements into the trans-Appalachian west was a cultural disaster for Indian peoples, who were brutally displaced from their lands. Despite these wars, by 1820, the United States had emerged as a strong independent state. Freed from a half-century of entanglement in European wars and diplomacy, its people began to exploit the riches of the continent.

ECONOMY

By the 1760s, the expansion of production and commerce had established the foundation for a vigorous national economy. Beginning in the 1780s, northern merchants financed a banking system and organized a rural system of manufacturing. Simultaneously, state governments used charters and other privileges to assist businesses and to improve roads, bridges, and waterways. Meanwhile, southern planters continued to use enslaved African Americans and exported a new staple crop—cotton—to markets in the North and in Europe. Many yeomen farm families migrated westward to grow grain. Those in the East turned out raw materials such as leather and wool for burgeoning manufacturing enterprises and made shoes, textiles, tinware, and other handicrafts for market sale. By 1820, the young American republic was on the verge of achieving economic as well as political independence.

SOCIETY

As Americans confronted the challenges of creating a republican society, they found themselves divided by gender, race, religion, and class. They disagreed over fundamental issues such as legal equality for women, the status of slavery, the meaning of free speech and religious liberty, and the extent of public responsibility for social inequality. As we shall see, political leaders managed to resolve some of these disputes. Legislatures abolished slavery in the North, broadened religious liberty by allowing freedom of conscience, and, except in New England, ended the system of legally established churches. However, Americans continued to argue over social equality, in part because their republican creed placed authority in the family and society in the hands of men of property. This arrangement denied power and status not only to slaves but also to free blacks, women, and poor white men.

CULTURE

The British colonies in North America contained a diversity of peoples and ways of life. This complexity jeopardized the effort to define an American culture and identity. Native Americans still lived in their own clans and nations; and black Americans, one-fifth of the enumerated population, were developing a new, African American culture. White Americans were also enmeshed in vigorous regional cultures — New England, Middle Atlantic, and Southern — and in strong ethnic communities: English, Scottish, Scots-Irish, German, and Dutch. However, over time, the political institutions began to unite Americans of diverse backgrounds, as did their increasing participation in the market economy and in evangelical Protestant churches. By 1820, to be an American meant, for many members of the dominant white population, to be a republican, a Protestant, and an enterprising individual in a capitalist-run market system.

Toward Independence: Years of Decision
1763–1776

The said [Stamp]
act is contrary to the
rights of mankind and
subversive of the English
Constitution.

— Town meeting of Leicester,
Massachusetts, 1765

As the Great War for Empire ended in 1763, Massachusetts soldier Seth Metcalf and other American colonists celebrated the triumph of British arms. Metcalf thanked "the Great Goodness of God" for the "General Peace" that was so "perculary Advantageous to the English Nation." Just two years later, Metcalf was less certain of God's favor. "God is angry with us of this land," the pious Calvinist wrote in his journal, "and is now Smiting [us] with his Rod Especially by the hands of our Rulers."

The rapid disintegration of the bonds uniting Britain and America — an event that Metcalf ascribed to Divine Providence — mystified many Americans. How had it happened, the president of King's College in New York asked in 1775, that such a "happily situated" people were ready to "hazard their Fortunes, their Lives, and their Souls, in a Rebellion"? Unlike other colonial peoples, white Americans lived in a prosperous, self-governing society. They had little to gain and much to lose by rebelling.

Or so it seemed in 1763, before the British government began to reform the imperial system. "This year Came an act from England Called the Stamp Act . . . which is thought will be very oppressive," Metcalf reflected. The British effort to transform a loose empire into more of a transatlantic nation-state prompted violent resistance and a downward spiral of ideological and political conflict that ended in a war for American independence. Could careful statecraft and political compromise have saved the empire? The likely answer is yes. But neither statecraft nor compromise was in evidence. Instead, the inflexibility of British ministers and the passionate determination of Patriot leaders destroyed the British empire in North America.

Imperial Reform, 1763–1765

The Great War for Empire left a mixed legacy. Britain's armies had driven the French out of Canada and the Spanish out of Florida, and Britain now dominated eastern North America (Map 5.1). But the war had been costly, and to reduce the

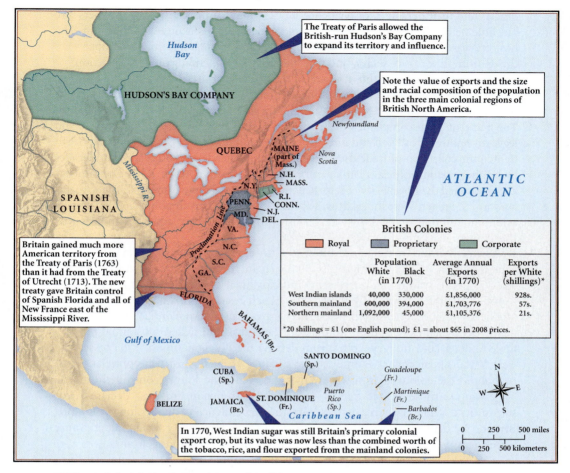

The Treaty of Paris allowed the British-run Hudson's Bay Company to expand its territory and influence.

Note the value of exports and the size and racial composition of the population in the three main colonial regions of British North America.

Britain gained much more American territory from the Treaty of Paris (1763) than it had from the Treaty of Utrecht (1713). The new treaty gave Britain control of Spanish Florida and all of New France east of the Mississippi River.

British Colonies

	Royal		Proprietary		Corporate

	Population White (in 1770)	Population Black (in 1770)	Average Annual Exports (in 1770)	Exports per White (shillings)*
West Indian islands	40,000	330,000	£1,856,000	928s.
Southern mainland	600,000	394,000	£1,703,776	57s.
Northern mainland	1,092,000	45,000	£1,105,376	21s.

*20 shillings = £1 (one English pound); £1 = about $65 in 2008 prices.

In 1770, West Indian sugar was still Britain's primary colonial export crop, but its value was now less than the combined worth of the tobacco, rice, and flour exported from the mainland colonies.

MAP 5.1 Britain's North American and Caribbean Empire in 1763
The Treaty of Paris gave Britain control of the eastern half of North America and strengthened its position in the West Indies. To protect the empire's new territories on the continent, British ministers dispatched troops to Florida and Quebec. They also instructed the troops to uphold the terms of the Proclamation of 1763, which prohibited Anglo-American settlement west of the Appalachian Mountains.

enormous war debt, the British ministry imposed new taxes on the American possessions. More fundamentally, the war spurred Parliament to redefine the empire: Salutary neglect, with its flexible emphasis on trade and colonial self-government, gave way to rigid regulations, imperial administrators, and direct rule by Parliament.

The Legacy of War

The war strained the relationship between Britain and its North American colonies. British generals and American leaders disagreed sharply on military strategy, and the presence of 25,000 British troops revealed sharp cultural differences. The arrogance of British officers and their demands for deference shocked many Americans: British soldiers "are but little better than slaves to their officers," declared a Massachusetts militiaman. The hostility was mutual. British general James Wolfe complained that colonial troops were drawn from the dregs of society and that "there was no depending on them in action."

The war also exposed the weakness of the royal governors. In theory, the governors had extensive political powers, including command of the provincial militia; in reality, they shared power with the colonial assemblies, a situation that outraged British officials. The Board of Trade complained that in Massachusetts "almost every act of executive and legislative power is ordered and directed by votes and resolves of the General Court." To tighten the collection of trade duties, which colonial merchants had evaded for decades by bribing customs officials, Parliament passed the Revenue Act of 1762. The ministry also instructed the Royal Navy to seize American vessels carrying supplies from the mainland to the French West Indies. It was absurd, declared a British politician, that French armies attempting "to Destroy one English province . . . are actually supported by Bread raised in another."

Britain's military victory resulted in a fundamental shift in policy: the peacetime deployment of an army of 10,000 men in North America. King George III (r. 1760–1820) wanted military commands for his friends, and the king's ministers feared a possible rebellion by the 60,000 French residents of Canada, Britain's new northern province. The Native Americans were also a concern. Pontiac's Rebellion had nearly overwhelmed Britain's frontier forts, and it would take a substantial military force to deter land-hungry whites from defying the Proclamation of 1763 by settling west of the Appalachian Mountains (see Chapter 4). Finally, British politicians worried about the colonists' loyalty now that the French no longer controlled Canada. "The main purpose of Stationing a large Body of Troops in America," declared treasury official William Knox, "is to secure the Dependence of the Colonys on Great Britain." By deploying an army in America, the British ministry was prepared to use force against conquered Frenchmen, unruly Indians, or rebellious colonists.

But troops cost money, which was in short supply. Britain's national debt had soared from £75 million in 1756 to £133 million in 1763. Indeed, the interest on the war debt was consuming 60 percent of the national budget. To restore fiscal stability, prime minister Lord Bute decided to raise taxes. The Treasury Department opposed increasing the land tax, which was paid primarily by the gentry and aristocracy, who wielded great influence in Parliament. So Bute taxed the people who had little political power—the poor and middling classes—by imposing higher import duties on tobacco and sugar, thus raising their cost to consumers. Parliament also increased excise levies—essentially sales taxes—on salt, beer, and distilled spirits, once again passing on the cost of the war to the king's ordinary subjects. Left unresolved was the question of taxing the American colonists, who, like Britain's poor, had little influence in Parliament.

To collect the taxes—old and new—the government doubled the size of the tax bureaucracy. Scores of customs agents patrolled the coasts of southern Britain, arresting smugglers and seizing tons of French wines and Flemish textiles. Convicted smugglers faced heavy penalties, including death or forced "transportation" to America. Despite protests by the colonial assemblies, nearly 50,000 English criminals had already been banished to America as indentured servants.

The price of empire abroad had turned out to be higher taxes and government scrutiny at home. These developments confirmed the worst fears of the British opposition parties, the Radical Whigs and Country Party. They complained that the huge war debt placed the treasury at the mercy of the "monied interest," the banks and financiers who reaped millions of pounds in interest from government bonds. They charged that the tax bureaucracy now contained thousands of patronage positions filled with "worthless pensioners and placemen." To reverse the growth of government power — and the consequent threats to personal liberty and property rights — reformers in Britain demanded a more representative Parliament. The Radical Whig John Wilkes called for an end to **rotten boroughs**, tiny electoral districts whose voters were controlled by wealthy aristocrats and merchants. In domestic affairs, as in colonial policy, the war had transformed British political life.

George Grenville: Imperial Reformer

A member of Parliament since 1741, George Grenville was widely conceded to be one of the ablest men in Great Britain. But he faced difficult financial issues. When he became prime minister in 1763, the nation was mired in debt, and British taxpayers were paying nearly five times as much in taxes as free Americans were. Grenville decided that new revenue would have to come from America.

Grenville set out to reform the imperial system. He began by winning passage of the Currency Act of 1764, which banned all the American colonies (not just New

George Grenville, Architect of the Stamp Act

This portrait, painted in 1763, suggests Grenville's energy and ambition. As prime minister, he was determined to reform the imperial system and ensure that the colonists shared the cost of the empire. The Earl of Halifax, Garrowby, Yorkshire.

England) from using paper money as legal tender. Now American shopkeepers, planters, and farmers would have to pay their debts to British merchants in gold or silver coin, which was always in short supply.

Grenville also won parliamentary approval of the Sugar Act of 1764 to replace the widely ignored Molasses Act of 1733 (see Chapter 3). The prime minister and his subordinates understood the pattern of colonial trade: They knew that mainland settlers had to sell at least some of their wheat, fish, and lumber in the French sugar islands to accumulate funds to buy British manufactures. So Grenville resisted demands from British sugar planters, who wanted to cut off all mainland trade with the French islands by levying a duty of 6 pence per gallon on French molasses; instead, he settled on a duty of 3 pence per gallon.

This carefully crafted policy garnered little support in America. New England merchants—among them John Hancock of Boston—had made their fortunes smuggling French molasses. In 1754, Boston merchants paid customs duties on a mere 400 hogsheads of molasses even as they imported the 40,000 hogsheads that were used by sixty-three Massachusetts distilleries. Merchants claimed publicly that the Sugar Act would wipe out trade with the French islands and ruin the distilling industry; privately, they vowed to evade the duty by smuggling or by bribing officials.

More important, the merchants' political allies raised constitutional objections to the Sugar Act. The Speaker of the Massachusetts House of Representatives argued that the new legislation was "contrary to a fundamental Principall of our Constitution: That all Taxes ought to originate with the people." "They who are taxed at pleasure by others cannot possibly have any property, and they who have no property, can have no freedom," warned governor Stephen Hopkins of Rhode Island. The Sugar Act raised other constitutional issues as well. Merchants prosecuted under the act would be tried by a **vice-admiralty court**, a maritime tribunal run by a British-appointed judge. American assemblies had long opposed the vice-admiralty courts and had found ways to have merchants who were accused of violating the Navigation Acts tried by local common-law courts, where they often were acquitted by friendly juries. The Sugar Act closed this legal loophole by extending the jurisdiction of the vice-admiralty courts to all customs offenses.

The new taxes and courts imposed by the Sugar Act revived old American fears of British control. The influential Virginia planter Richard Bland admitted that the colonies were subject to the Navigation Acts, which restricted their manufactures and commerce. But, he protested, the American settlers "were not sent out to be the Slaves but to be the Equals of those that remained behind." John Adams, a young Massachusetts lawyer who was defending John Hancock on a charge of smuggling, claimed that the vice-admiralty courts "degrade every American . . . below the rank of an Englishman."

While the logic of the Americans' arguments appeared compelling, some of their facts were wrong. The Navigation Acts certainly favored British merchants and manufacturers. However, trying accused smugglers in vice-admiralty courts was not discriminatory because similar rules had long been in force in Britain. The real issue was the growing administrative power of the British state. Americans had lived for decades under a policy of salutary neglect and an "unwritten constitution" that encouraged political compromise between the king's officials and his subjects. They understood that the new policies would deprive them "of some of their most essential Rights as British subjects," as a committee of the Massachusetts House of Representatives put it.

For their part, British officials insisted on the supremacy of parliamentary laws and denied that colonists should enjoy the traditional legal rights of Englishmen. When royal governor Francis Bernard of Massachusetts heard that the Massachusetts House had objected to the Sugar Act, claiming that there should be no taxation without representation, he asserted that Americans did not have that constitutional right: "The rule that a British subject shall not be bound by laws or liable to taxes, but what he has consented to by his representatives must be confined to the inhabitants of Great Britain only." To Bernard, Grenville, and other imperial reformers, Americans were second-class subjects of the king, their rights limited by the Navigation Acts, parliamentary laws, and British interests.

An Open Challenge: The Stamp Act

Another new tax, the Stamp Act of 1765, sparked the first great imperial crisis. The new levy would cover part of the cost of keeping British troops in America — some £200,000 a year (about $50 million today). The tax would require stamps on all court documents, land titles, contracts, playing cards, newspapers, and other printed items. A similar stamp tax in England was yielding £290,000 a year; Grenville hoped that the American levy would raise £60,000. The prime minister knew that some Americans opposed the tax on constitutional grounds, so he raised the issue explicitly in the House of Commons: Did any member doubt "the power and sovereignty of Parliament over every part of the British dominions, for the purpose of raising or collecting any tax?" No one rose to object.

Confident of Parliament's support, Grenville threatened to impose a stamp tax unless the colonists paid for their own defense. The London merchants who served as agents for the colonial legislatures immediately protested that Americans lacked a continent-wide body that could raise such funds. Colonial officials had met together officially only once, at the Albany Congress of 1754, and not a single assembly had accepted that body's proposals for a continental union (see Chapter 4). Benjamin Franklin, who was in Britain as the agent of the Pennsylvania assembly, proposed another solution to Grenville's challenge: American representation in Parliament. "If you chuse to tax us," he suggested, "give us Members in your Legislature, and let us be one People."

With the exception of William Pitt, British politicians rejected Franklin's idea as too radical. They maintained that the colonists already had **virtual representation** in Parliament because a number of its members were transatlantic merchants and West Indian sugar planters. Colonial leaders were equally skeptical of Franklin's plan. Americans were "situate at a great Distance from their Mother Country," the Connecticut assembly declared, and therefore "cannot participate in the general Legislature of the Nation."

As Grenville moved forward with the Stamp Act, his goal was not only to raise revenue but also to assert a constitutional principle: "the Right of Parliament to lay an internal Tax upon the Colonies." The House of Commons ignored American petitions and passed the new legislation by an overwhelming vote of 205 to 49. At the request of General Thomas Gage, the British military commander in America, Parliament also passed the Quartering Act, which required colonial governments to provide barracks and food for British troops stationed within their borders. Finally, Parliament approved Grenville's proposal that violations of the Stamp Act be tried in vice-admiralty courts.

The design for reform was complete. Using the doctrine of parliamentary supremacy, Grenville had begun to fashion a centralized imperial system in America much like the one already in place in Ireland: British officials would govern the colonies with little regard for the local assemblies. Consequently, Grenville's plan provoked a constitutional confrontation on both the specific issues of taxation, jury trials, and military quartering and the general question of representative self-government.

▶ What were the goals of British imperial reformers?

▶ Why did the colonists object to the new taxes in 1764 and again in 1765? What arguments did they use? How did these conflicts turn into a constitutional crisis?

The Dynamics of Rebellion, 1765–1770

In the name of reform, Grenville had thrown down the gauntlet to the Americans. The colonists had often resisted unpopular laws and arbitrary governors, but they had faced an all-out attack on their institutions only once—in 1686, when James II had unilaterally imposed the Dominion of New England. The danger now was even greater because both the king and Parliament backed the reforms. But the Patriots, as the defenders of American rights came to be called, met the challenge posed by Grenville and his successor, Charles Townshend. They organized protests, both peaceful and violent, and fashioned a compelling ideology of resistance.

Politicians Protest, and the Crowd Rebels

Virginians took the lead. In May 1765, Patrick Henry, a hotheaded young member of the Virginia House of Burgesses, condemned Grenville's legislation and attacked George III for supporting it. In comparing the king to Charles I, whose tyranny had led to his overthrow in the 1640s, Henry seemed to be calling for a new republican revolution. Although the assembly members were shaken by Henry's remarks, which bordered on treason, they condemned the Stamp Act as "a manifest Tendency to Destroy American freedom." In Massachusetts, James Otis, another republican-minded firebrand, persuaded the House of Representatives to call an all-colony congress "to implore Relief" from the act.

Nine colonial assemblies sent delegates to the Stamp Act Congress, which met in New York City in October 1765. The Congress issued a set of resolutions protesting the loss of American "rights and liberties," especially the right to trial by jury. The Stamp Act Resolves also challenged the constitutionality of the Stamp and Sugar Acts by declaring that only the colonists' own elected representatives could tax them. Still, the moderate-minded delegates wanted compromise, not confrontation. They assured Parliament that Americans "glory in being subjects of the best of Kings" and humbly petitioned for repeal of the Stamp Act. But other influential Americans, favoring peaceful resistance, organized a boycott of British goods.

However, popular opposition took a violent form. When the Stamp Act went into effect on November 1, 1765, disciplined mobs demanded the resignation of stamp-tax collectors, most of whom were American-born. In Boston, the **Sons of Liberty** beheaded and burned an effigy of collector Andrew Oliver and then destroyed Oliver's new brick warehouse. Two weeks later, Bostonians attacked the house of Lieutenant Governor

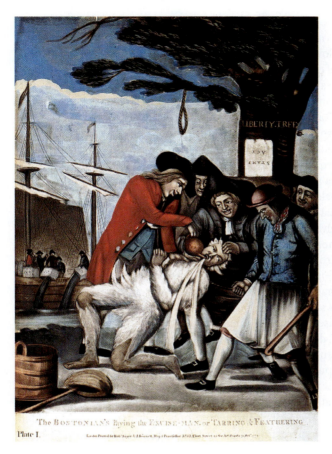

The BOSTONIAN'S Paying the EXCISE-MAN, or TARRING & FEATHERING.

Plate I.   London Printed for Rob.t Sayer & J.Bennett, Map & Printseller, N.º 53 Fleet Street, as the Act directs 31 Oct.r 1774

A British View of American Mobs

This satiric etching of the Sons of Liberty, published in a British magazine, depicts their brutal treatment of John Malcom, a commissioner of customs in Boston. The mob threatened to kill Malcom — notice the noose hanging from the "liberty tree" — but instead tarred and feathered him and forced him to drink huge quantities of tea. In showing this violence and (in the background) the men pouring tea into Boston Harbor, the artist seems to be asking, "Does liberty mean anarchy?" Courtesy, John Carter Brown Library at Brown University.

Thomas Hutchinson, long known as a defender of social privilege and imperial authority; the attackers smashed his furniture, looted his wine cellar, and set fire to his library.

Wealthy merchants such as John Hancock and Patriot lawyers such as John Adams encouraged the mobs, which were usually led by middling artisans and minor merchants. "Spent the evening with the Sons of Liberty," Adams wrote in his diary, "John Smith, the brazier [metalworker], Thomas Crafts, the painter, Edes, the printer, Stephen Cleverly, the brazier; Chase, the distiller; [and] Joseph Field, Master of a vessel." These men knew one another through their work or were drinking buddies at the taverns that became centers of Patriot agitation.

In New York City, nearly 3,000 shopkeepers, artisans, laborers, and seamen marched through the streets breaking streetlamps and windows and crying, "Liberty!" Resistance to the Stamp Act spread far beyond the port cities. In nearly every colony, crowds of angry people — the "rabble," their detractors called them — intimidated royal officials. Near Wethersfield, Connecticut, 500 farmers seized a tax collector, Jared Ingersoll, and forced him to resign his office in "the Cause of the People."

Such crowd actions were common in both Britain and America. Every November 5, Protestant mobs on both sides of the Atlantic burned effigies of the pope to celebrate the failure of a Catholic plot to blow up the Houses of Parliament. Colonial crowds regularly destroyed brothels and rioted against the impressment (forced service) of merchant seamen by the Royal Navy. Governments tolerated the mobs because they usually did little damage and because, short of calling out the militia, there was no means of stopping them.

If rioting was traditional, its political goals were new. In New York City, for example, the leaders of the Sons of Liberty were two minor merchants, Isaac Sears and Alexander McDougall. As Radical Whigs, Sears and McDougall were afraid that imperial reform would undermine political liberty. But many artisans and their journeymen joined the protests because low-priced imports of British shoes and other manufactures (like low-priced Chinese imports today) threatened their livelihood. Some rioters feared new taxes and a parasitic British governing elite. Unlike "the Common people of England," a well-traveled colonist observed, "the people of America . . . never would submitt to be taxed that a few may be loaded with palaces and Pensions . . . while they cannot support themselves and their needy offspring with Bread."

Religion motivated other protesters. Roused by the Great Awakening, evangelical Protestants resented the arrogance of British military officers and the corruption of royal bureaucrats. In New England, where people and memories had long lives, rioters looked back to the antimonarchy sentiments of their great-grandparents. A letter to a Boston newspaper that was signed "Oliver Cromwell," the English republican revolutionary of the 1650s, promised to save "all the Freeborn Sons of America." Finally, the mobs included apprentices, day laborers, and unemployed sailors — young men looking for excitement and, when fortified by drink, eager to resort to violence.

Nearly everywhere, popular resistance nullified the Stamp Act. Fearing a massive assault on Fort George, New York lieutenant governor Cadwallader Colden called on General Gage to use his small military force to protect the stamps. Gage refused. "Fire from the Fort might disperse the Mob, but it would not quell them," he told Colden, and the result would be "an Insurrection, the Commencement of Civil War." Frightened collectors gave up their stamps, and angry Americans forced officials to accept legal documents without them. This popular insurrection gave a democratic cast to the emerging American Patriot movement. "Nothing is wanting but your own Resolution," declared a New York rioter, "for great is the Authority and Power of the People."

Because communication across the Atlantic was slow, the British response to the Stamp Act Congress and the Sons of Liberty would not be known until the spring of 1766. However, royal officials in America already knew that they had lost the popular support that had sustained the empire for three generations. A customs collector in Philadelphia lamented: "What can a Governor do without the assistance of the Governed?"

The Ideological Roots of Resistance

The American resistance movement began in the seaports because British policies directly affected the economic lives of their residents. The Sugar Act raised the cost of molasses to urban distillers; the Stamp Act taxed the newspapers sold by printers and the contracts and other legal documents prepared by lawyers and merchants; and the flood of British manufactures threatened the jobs of seaport artisans. According to one pamphleteer, Americans were being compelled to give the British "our money, as oft and in what quantity they please to demand it."

But some Americans couched their resistance in broader constitutional terms. Many of these men were lawyers drawn into conflict by their economic ties to merchants, who hired them to protect their goods from seizure by customs officials, and by professional motives. As practitioners of English common law, colonial lawyers believed in the importance of trial by jury and generally opposed the extension of judge-run vice-admiralty courts. Composing pamphlets of remarkable political sophistication, Patriot lawyers gave the resistance movement its rationale, its political agenda, and its leaders.

Patriot writers drew on three intellectual traditions. The first was English common law, the centuries-old body of legal rules and procedures that protected the lives and property of the monarch's subjects. In the famous *Writs of Assistance* case of 1761, Boston lawyer James Otis invoked English legal precedents to dispute a general search warrant that allowed customs officials to conduct wide-ranging inspections. And in demanding a jury trial for John Hancock, John Adams appealed to provision in the "29th Chap. of Magna Charta," an ancient document (1215) that "has for many Centuries been esteemed by Englishmen, as one of the . . . firmest Bulwarks of their Liberties." Other lawyers protested that new British measures violated specific "liberties and privileges" embodied in colonial charters as well as Britain's "ancient constitution." They objected as well when the ministry declared that colonial judges served "at the pleasure" of the royal governors, claiming that this would undermine the independence of the judiciary.

A second major intellectual resource was the rationalist thought of the Enlightenment. Virginia planter Thomas Jefferson invoked David Hume and Francis Hutcheson, Enlightenment philosophers who applied reason in their critiques of traditional political practices and in their proposals to correct social ills. Jefferson and other Patriot writers also drew on John Locke, who argued that all individuals possessed certain "natural rights"—among them life, liberty, and property—and that governments must protect those rights (see Chapter 4). And they turned to French philosopher Montesquieu, who argued that a separation of powers among government departments prevented arbitrary rule.

The republican and Whig strands of the English political tradition provided a third ideological source for American Patriots. Puritan New England had long venerated the Commonwealth era, the brief period between 1649 and 1660 when England was a republic (see Chapter 2). After the Glorious Revolution of 1688–1689, many colonists praised the English Whigs for preventing the monarch from imposing taxes and for limiting other monarchical powers. Bostonian Samuel Adams and other Patriot leaders also applauded Britain's Radical Whigs for denouncing political corruption among royal officials and questioning their motives. Joseph Warren, a physician and a Radical Whig Patriot, suggested that the Stamp Act was part of a ministerial plot "to force the colonies into rebellion" and justify the use of "military power to reduce them to servitude" (see American Voices, p. 142).

These arguments—publicized in newspapers and pamphlets—gave intellectual substance to the Patriot movement and turned a series of impromptu riots and tax protests into a formidable political force. The Patriots organized a highly successful boycott of British manufactures to force a repeal of the new imperial measures.

Parliament Compromises, 1766

When news of the Stamp Act riots and the boycott reached Britain, Parliament was already in turmoil. Disputes over domestic policy had led George III to dismiss Grenville as the prime minister, but Grenville's followers demanded that imperial reform

An American View of the Stamp Act SAMUEL ADAMS

Thanks to his education at Harvard College, distiller Samuel Adams had impressive intellectual and literary skills. In this private letter to an English friend, Adams undertakes, in reasoned prose, to refute the arguments used by British ministers to defend the new measures of imperial taxation and control.

To John Smith
December 19, 1765

Your acquaintance with this country . . . makes you an able advocate on her behalf, at a time when her friends have everything to fear for her. . . . The [British] nation, it seems, groaning under the pressure of a very heavy debt, has thought it reasonable & just that the colonies should bear a part; and over & above the tribute which they have been continually pouring into her lap, in the course of their trade, she now demands an internal tax. The colonists complain that this is both burdensome & unconstitutional. They allege, that while the nation has been contracting this debt solely for her own interest, they have [been] subduing & settling an uncultivated wilderness, & thereby increasing her power & wealth at their own expense. . . .

But it is said that this tax is to discharge the colonies' proportion of expense in carrying on the [recent] war in America, which was for their defense. To this it is said, that it does by no means appear that the war in America was carried on solely for the defense of the colonies; . . . there was evidently a view of making conquests, [thereby] . . . advancing her dominion & glory. . . .

There are other things which perhaps were not considered when the nation determined this to be a proportionate tax upon the colonies. . . . The [British] nation constantly regulates their trade, & lays it under what restrictions she pleases. The duties upon the goods imported from her & consumed here . . . amount to a very great sum. . . .

There is another consideration which makes the Stamp Act obnoxious to the people here, & that is, that it totally annihilates, as they apprehend, their essential rights as Englishmen. The first settlers . . . solemnly recognized their allegiance to their sovereign in England, & the Crown graciously acknowledged them, granted them charter privileges, & declared them & their heirs forever entitled to all the liberties & immunities of free & natural born subjects of the realm. . . .

The question then is, what the rights of free subjects of Britain are? . . . It is sufficient for the present purpose to say, that the main pillars of the British Constitution are the right of representation & trial by juries, both of which the Colonists lose by this act. Their property may be tried . . . in a court of Admiralty, where there is no jury. [As for representation], if the colonists are free subjects of Britain, which no one denies, it should seem that the Parliament cannot tax them consistent with the Constitution, because they are not represented. . . .

SOURCE: Harry Alonzo Cushing, ed., *The Writings of Samuel Adams* (New York: G. P. Putnam, 1904).

continue—if necessary, at the point of a gun. The issue for them was the constitutional supremacy of Parliament and its status as one of the few powerful representative bodies in eighteenth-century Europe. "The British legislature," declared Chief Justice Sir James Mansfield, "has authority to bind every part and every subject, whether such subjects have a right to vote or not."

Three other parliamentary factions pushed for repeal of the Stamp Act. The Old Whigs, now led by Lord Rockingham, who had succeeded Grenville as prime minister, had long maintained that America was more important for its "flourishing and increasing trade" than for its tax revenues. A second group, representing British merchants and manufacturers, worried that the American trade boycott was cutting deeply into British exports. A committee of "London Merchants trading to America" had joined with traders in Liverpool, Bristol, and Glasgow to demand repeal. "The Avenues of Trade are all shut up," a Bristol merchant told Parliament. "We have no Remittances and are at our Witts End for want of Money to fulfill our Engagements with our Tradesmen." Finally, former prime minister William Pitt and his allies in Parliament argued that the Stamp Act was a mistake and insisted that it "be repealed absolutely, totally, and immediately." Pitt tried to draw a subtle distinction between taxation and legislation: Parliament lacked the authority to tax the colonies, he said, but its power over America was "sovereign and supreme, in every circumstance of government and legislation whatsoever." As Pitt's ambiguous formula suggested, the Stamp Act raised the difficult constitutional question of Parliament's sovereign powers.

Rockingham was a young and inexperienced minister facing complex issues. He decided on compromise. To mollify the colonists and help British merchants, he repealed the Stamp Act and reduced the duty on molasses imposed by the Sugar Act to a penny a gallon. Then he pacified imperial reformers and hard-liners with the Declaratory Act of 1766, which explicitly reaffirmed Parliament's "full power and authority to make laws and statutes . . . to bind the colonies and people of America . . . in all cases whatsoever." By ending the Stamp Act crisis swiftly, Rockingham hoped that it would be forgotten just as quickly.

Charles Townshend Steps In

Often, the course of history is changed by a small event—an illness, a personal grudge, a chance remark. That was the case in 1767, when Rockingham's government collapsed over domestic issues and George III named William Pitt to head a new government. Pitt was chronically ill with gout, a painful disease of the joints, and often missed parliamentary debates, leaving chancellor of the exchequer Charles Townshend in command. Pitt was sympathetic toward America; Townshend was not. As a member of the Board of Trade, Townshend had demanded restrictions on the colonial assemblies, and he strongly supported the Stamp Act. So in 1767, when Grenville demanded in Parliament that the colonists pay for the British troops in America, Townshend made an unplanned and fateful decision. He promised to find a new source of revenue in America.

The new tax legislation, the Townshend Act of 1767, had both fiscal and political goals. The statute imposed duties on colonial imports of paper, paint, glass, and tea and would raise about £40,000 a year. Townshend allocated some of this revenue for American military expenses but earmarked most of the money to fund a colonial civil list—paying the salaries of royal governors, judges, and other imperial officials. By freeing royal officials from financial dependence on the American assemblies, the ministry would assist them to enforce parliamentary laws and the king's instructions. To strengthen imperial power further, Townshend devised the Revenue Act of 1767. This legislation created a board of customs commissioners in Boston and vice-admiralty courts in Halifax, Boston, Philadelphia, and Charleston. Through taxes imposed by Parliament to finance imperial administration, Townshend intended to undermine the power of American political institutions.

The full implications of Townshend's policies became clear when the New York assembly refused to comply with the Quartering Act of 1765. Fearing an unlimited drain on its treasury, the New York legislature first denied General Gage's requests for barracks and supplies and then offered limited assistance. Townshend demanded full compliance, and to raise the funds, Parliament considered a special duty on New York's imports and exports. The Earl of Shelburne, the new secretary of state, went even further: He proposed the appointment of a military governor with the authority to seize funds from New York's treasury and "to act with Force or Gentleness as circumstances might make necessary." Townshend decided on a less provocative but equally coercive measure: the Restraining Act of 1767, which suspended the New York assembly. Faced with the loss of self-government, New Yorkers reluctantly appropriated funds to quarter the troops.

The Restraining Act raised the stakes for the colonists. Previously, the British Privy Council had invalidated about 5 percent of colonial laws, such as those establishing land banks. Townshend's Restraining Act went much further, declaring that the very existence of American representative assemblies depended on the will of Parliament.

America Debates and Resists Again

The Townshend duties revived the constitutional debate over taxation. During the Stamp Act crisis, some Americans, including Benjamin Franklin, distinguished between external and internal taxes. They suggested that external duties on trade, such as those long mandated by the Navigation Acts, were acceptable to Americans but that direct, or internal, taxes were not. Townshend thought that this distinction was "perfect nonsense," but he indulged the Americans and laid duties only on trade.

Even so, most colonial leaders rejected the legitimacy of Townshend's measures. They agreed with lawyer John Dickinson, author of *Letters from a Farmer in Pennsylvania* (1768), that the real issue was the *intent* of the legislation. Because the Townshend duties were designed to raise revenue (not to regulate trade), they were taxes imposed without consent. In February 1768, the Massachusetts House of Representatives circulated a letter condemning the Townshend Act, and Boston and New York merchants began a new boycott of British goods. Throughout Puritan New England, ministers and public officials discouraged the purchase of "foreign superfluities" and promoted the domestic manufacture of cloth and other necessities.

American women, ordinarily excluded from public affairs, became crucial to the nonimportation movement through their production of **homespun** cloth. During the Stamp Act boycott of 1765, the wives and daughters of Patriot leaders had made more yarn and cloth, but the Townshend boycott mobilized many more patriotic women. Pious farmwives spun yarn at the homes of their ministers. In Berwick, Maine, "true Daughters of Liberty" celebrated American products by "drinking rye coffee and dining on bear venison." Other women's groups supported the boycott by spinning flax and wool to donate to the needy. Just as Patriot men followed tradition by joining crowd actions, so women's protests reflected their customary concern for the well-being of the community.

Newspapers celebrated the exploits of Daughters of Liberty. One Massachusetts town proudly claimed an annual output of 30,000 yards of cloth; East Hartford, Connecticut, reported 17,000 yards. This surge in domestic production hardly replaced British imports, which annually averaged about 10 million yards of cloth, but it brought thousands of women into the public arena.

The boycott mobilized many American men as well. In the seaport cities, the Sons of Liberty published the names of merchants who imported British goods and harassed their employees and customers. By March 1769, the nonimportation movement had spread to Philadelphia; two months later, the members of the Virginia House of Burgesses vowed not to buy duties articles, luxury goods, or slaves imported by British merchants. Reflecting colonial self-confidence, Benjamin Franklin called for a return to the pre-1763 mercantilist system: "Repeal the laws, renounce the right, recall the troops, refund the money, and return to the old method of requisition."

American resistance only increased British determination. When the Massachusetts House's letter opposing the Townshend duties reached London, Lord Hillsborough,

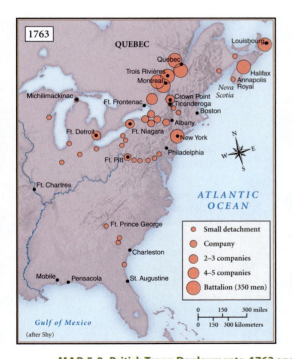
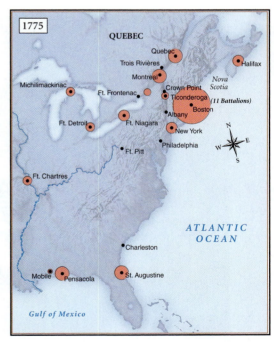

MAP 5.2 British Troop Deployments, 1763 and 1775

As the imperial crisis deepened, British military priorities changed. In 1763, most British battalions were stationed in Canada to deter Indian uprisings and French Canadian revolts. After the Stamp Act riots of 1765, the British established large garrisons in New York and Philadelphia. By 1775, eleven battalions of British regulars occupied Boston, the center of the Patriot movement.

the secretary of state for American affairs, branded it "unjustifiable opposition to the constitutional authority of Parliament." To strengthen the "Hand of Government" in Massachusetts, Hillsborough dispatched General Thomas Gage and 4,000 British troops to Boston. Gage accused Massachusetts leaders of "Treasonable and desperate Resolves" and advised the ministry to "Quash this Spirit at a Blow." Hillsborough proposed isolating Massachusetts from the other colonies and then using the army to bring the rebellious New Englanders to their knees (Map 5.2). In 1765, American resistance had provoked a parliamentary debate; in 1768, it produced a plan for military coercion.

Lord North Compromises, 1770

At this critical moment, the ministry's resolve faltered. A series of harsh winters and dry summers in Great Britain had cut grain output and raised food prices. In Scotland and northern England, thousands of tenants deserted their farms and boarded ships for America; food riots spread across the English countryside. There were also riots in Ireland over the growing military budget there.

Adding to the ministry's difficulties was Radical Whig John Wilkes. Supported by associations of merchants and artisans, Wilkes attacked government corruption and won election to Parliament. Overjoyed, American Patriots drank toasts to Wilkes and

John Wilkes, British Radical

Wilkes won fame on both sides of the Atlantic as the author of *North Briton, Number 45* (depicted on the left), which called for reform of the British political system. At a dinner in Boston, Radical Whigs raised their wineglasses to Wilkes, toasting him forty-five times! But Wilkes had many enemies, including this artist, who depicts him as a cunning demagogue, brandishing the cap of Liberty to curry favor with the mob. Miriam and Ira D. Wallach Division of Art, Prints and Photographs, The New York Public Library. Astor, Lenox and Tilden Foundations.

For more help analyzing this image, see the Online Study Guide at **bedfordstmartins. com/henrettaconcise**.

bought thousands of teapots and mugs emblazoned with his picture. When Wilkes was imprisoned for libel against Parliament, an angry crowd protested his arrest, and troops killed seven protesters in the highly publicized Massacre of Saint George's Field.

The American trade boycott also had a major impact on the British economy. In 1768, the colonies had cut their imports and reduced their trade deficit from £500,000 to £230,000. By 1769, the boycott of British goods and increases in the colonies' exports of goods and shipping services had yielded an American balance-of-payments surplus of £816,000. To end the boycott, British merchants and manufacturers petitioned Parliament for repeal of the Townshend duties. By late 1769, some ministers felt that the Townshend duties were a mistake, and the king no longer supported Hillsborough's plan to use military force against Massachusetts.

Early in 1770, Lord North became prime minister. A witty man and a skillful politician, North set out to save the empire by designing a new compromise. He argued that it was foolish to tax British exports to America (thereby raising their price and decreasing consumption) and persuaded Parliament to repeal most of the Townshend duties. However, North retained the tax on tea as a symbol of Parliament's supremacy. Mollified by the partial repeal, colonial merchants called off the boycott.

Even an outbreak of violence did not destroy North's compromise. During the boycott, New York artisans and workers had taunted British troops, mostly with words but occasionally with stones and fists. In retaliation, the soldiers tore down a Liberty Pole (a Patriot flagpole), setting off a week of street fighting. In Boston, friction over constitutional principles and competition between residents and off-duty British soldiers for jobs triggered a violent conflict. In March 1770, a group of soldiers fired into a crowd of rowdy demonstrators, killing five men. Convinced of a ministerial conspiracy against liberty, Radical Whigs labeled the incident a "massacre" and filled the popular press with accusations that the British had planned the killings.

Although most Americans remained loyal to the empire, five years of conflict over taxes and constitutional principles had taken their toll. In 1765, American leaders had accepted Parliament's authority; the Stamp Act Resolves had opposed only certain "unconstitutional" legislation. By 1770, the most outspoken Patriots— Benjamin Franklin in Pennsylvania, Patrick Henry in Virginia, and Samuel Adams in Massachusetts—had concluded that the British ruling elite was self-interested and indifferent to its colonial responsibilities. So they repudiated parliamentary supremacy and claimed equality for the American assemblies within the empire. Perhaps thinking of various European "composite monarchies," in which kings ruled far-distant provinces acquired by inheritance or conquest, Franklin suggested that the colonies were now "distinct and separate states" with the "the same Head, or Sovereign, the King."

Franklin's suggestion outraged Thomas Hutchinson, the American-born royal governor of Massachusetts. Hutchinson emphatically rejected the idea of "two independent legislatures in one and the same state"; in his mind, the British empire was a whole, its sovereignty indivisible. "I know of no line," he told the Massachusetts assembly, "that can be drawn between the supreme authority of Parliament and the total independence of the colonies."

▶ If Grenville's and Townshend's initiatives had succeeded, how would the character of the British imperial system have changed?

▶ Weigh the relative importance of economic and ideological motives in promoting the colonial resistance movement. Which was more important? Why?

There the matter rested. The British had twice imposed revenue acts on the colonies, and American Patriots had twice forced a retreat. If Parliament insisted on a policy of constitutional absolutism by imposing taxes a third time, some Americans were prepared to resist by force. Nor did they flinch when reminded that George III condemned their agitation. As the Massachusetts House told Hutchinson, "There is more reason to dread the consequences of absolute uncontrolled supreme power, whether of a nation or a monarch, than those of total independence." Fearful of civil war, Lord North's government hesitated to force the issue.

The Road to Independence, 1771–1776

Repeal of the Townshend duties in 1770 restored harmony to the British empire, but strong passions and mutual distrust lay just below the surface. In 1773, those emotions erupted, destroying any hope of compromise. Within two years, the Americans and the British clashed in armed conflict, and Patriot legislators created provisional governments and military forces, the two essentials for independence.

A Compromise Ignored

Once aroused, political passions are not easily quieted. In Boston, Samuel Adams and other radical Patriots continued to warn Americans of imperial domination and, late in 1772, persuaded the town meeting to set up a committee of correspondence "to state the Rights of the Colonists of this Province." Soon, eighty Massachusetts towns had similar committees. When the British government threatened to prosecute Americans in British courts following the burning of the *Gaspée*, a customs vessel, the Virginia House of Burgesses set up its own committee of correspondence. By mid-1773, committees had appeared in Connecticut, New Hampshire, and South Carolina.

These committees sprang into action when Lord North and Parliament enacted the Tea Act in May 1773. The act provided financial relief for the East India Company, which was deeply in debt because of military expeditions to extend Britain's influence in India. The Tea Act gave the company a government loan and canceled the English import duty on its tea. The act offended many Americans. Since 1768, when Townshend had placed a duty of 3 pence a pound on tea, most colonists had drunk smuggled Dutch tea. By relieving the East India Company of English duties, the Tea Act made its tea cheaper than that sold by Dutch merchants.

Radical Patriots accused the British government of bribing Americans to give up their principled opposition to the tea tax. As an anonymous woman wrote to the *Massachusetts Spy*, "The use of [British] tea is considered not as a private but as a public evil . . . a handle to introduce a variety of . . . oppressions amongst us." Merchants joined the protest because the East India Company planned to distribute its tea directly to shopkeepers, excluding American vendors from the profits of the trade. "The fear of an Introduction of a Monopoly in this Country," British general Frederick Haldimand reported from New York, "has induced the mercantile part of the Inhabitants to be very industrious in opposing this Step and added Strength to a Spirit of Independence already too prevalent."

The committees of correspondence organized resistance to the Tea Act. They sponsored public bonfires and persuaded their fellow townspeople—sometimes gently, sometimes not—to consign British tea to the flames. When the Sons of Liberty prevented East India Company ships from delivering more tea, Royal Governor Hutchinson hatched a scheme to land the tea and collect the tax. As soon as a shipment of tea arrived in Boston Harbor on the *Dartmouth*, Hutchinson passed the ship through customs. Hutchinson intended to order British troops to unload the tea and supervise its sale by auction. To foil the governor's plan, a group of artisans and laborers disguised as Indians boarded the *Dartmouth* on December 16, 1773; broke open 342 chests of tea (valued at about £10,000, or nearly $900,000 today); and threw them into the harbor. "This destruction of the Tea is so bold and it must have so important Consequences," John Adams wrote in his diary, "that I cannot but consider it as an Epoch in History."

The British Privy Council was furious, as was the king. "Concessions have made matters worse," George III declared. "The time has come for compulsion." Early in 1774, Parliament decisively rejected a proposal to repeal the duty on American tea; instead, it enacted four Coercive Acts to force Massachusetts to pay for the tea and to submit to imperial authority. A Port Bill closed Boston Harbor; a Government Act annulled the Massachusetts charter and prohibited most local town meetings; a new Quartering Act required the colony to build barracks for British troops; and a Justice Act allowed trials for capital crimes to be transferred to other colonies or to Britain.

Patriot leaders branded the measures "Intolerable" and rallied support for Massachusetts. In far-off Georgia, a Patriot warned the "Freemen of the Province" that "every privilege you at present claim as a birthright, may be wrested from you by the same authority that blockades the town of Boston." "The cause of Boston," George Washington declared in Virginia, "now is and ever will be considered as the cause of America." The committees of correspondence had created a firm sense of unity among Patriots.

In 1774, Parliament also passed the Quebec Act, which allowed the practice of Roman Catholicism in Quebec. This concession to Quebec's predominantly Catholic population reignited religious passions in New England, where Protestants associated Catholicism with arbitrary royal government and popish superstition. Because the act extended the boundaries of Quebec into the Ohio River Valley, it likewise angered influential land speculators and politicians in Virginia (Map 5.3). Although the ministry did not intend the Quebec Act as a coercive measure, many colonial leaders saw it as proof of Parliament's intention to control American domestic affairs.

The Continental Congress Responds

In response to the Coercive Acts, Patriot leaders convened a new continent-wide body, the Continental Congress. Twelve mainland colonies sent representatives. Four recently acquired colonies—Florida, Quebec, Nova Scotia, and Newfoundland—refused to participate, as did Georgia, where the royal governor controlled the legislature.

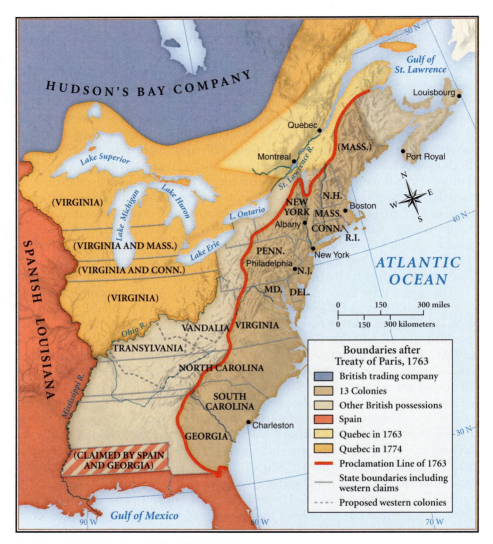

MAP 5.3 British Western Policy, 1763–1774

Despite the Proclamation of 1763, Anglo-American settlers and land speculators proposed two new western colonies: Vandalia and Transylvania. But the Quebec Act of 1774 ruled out the creation of new settlements in the west by reserving most trans-Appalachian lands for Native peoples and by vastly enlarging the boundaries of Quebec, which eliminated the sea-to-sea land claims of many seaboard colonies.

For more help analyzing this map, see the Online Study Guide at **bedfordstmartins.com/henrettaconcise**.

The assemblies of Barbados, Jamaica, and the other British sugar islands, fearful of revolts by their predominately African populations, reaffirmed their allegiance to the crown.

The delegates who met in Philadelphia in September 1774 had distinct agendas. Southern representatives, fearing a British plot "to overturn the constitution and introduce a system of arbitrary government," advocated a new economic boycott.

Independence-minded representatives from New England demanded political union and defensive military preparations. Many delegates from the Middle Atlantic colonies favored a political compromise.

Led by Joseph Galloway of Pennsylvania, these men of "loyal principles" proposed a new political system similar to the plan that Benjamin Franklin had proposed in Albany two decades earlier: Each colony would retain its assembly to legislate on local matters, and a new continent-wide body would handle general American affairs. The king would appoint a president-general to preside over a legislative council selected by the colonial assemblies. Although Galloway's plan gave the council veto power over parliamentary legislation that affected America, the delegates refused to endorse it. With British troops occupying Boston, most thought it was too conciliatory.

Instead, a majority of the delegates passed a Declaration of Rights and Grievances, which demanded the repeal of the Coercive Acts. They repudiated the Declaratory Act of 1766, which had proclaimed Parliament's supremacy over the colonies, and they stipulated that British control be limited to matters of trade. Finally, the Congress approved a program of economic retaliation: Americans would stop importing British goods in December 1774. If Parliament did not repeal the Intolerable Acts by September 1775, the Congress vowed to cut off virtually all colonial exports to Britain, Ireland, and the British West Indies. Ten years of constitutional conflict had culminated in the threat of all-out commercial warfare.

A few British leaders still hoped for compromise. In January 1775, William Pitt, now sitting in the House of Lords as the Earl of Chatham, asked Parliament to renounce its power to tax the colonies and to recognize the Continental Congress as a lawful body. In return for these concessions, he suggested, the Congress should acknowledge parliamentary supremacy and grant a permanent revenue to help defray the British national debt.

The British ministry rejected Chatham's plan. Twice it had backed down in the face of colonial resistance; a third retreat was unthinkable. Branding the Continental Congress an illegal assembly, the ministry rejected Lord Dartmouth's proposal to send commissioners to negotiate a settlement. Instead, Lord North set stringent terms: Americans must pay for their own defense and administration and acknowledge Parliament's authority to tax them. To put teeth in these demands, North imposed a naval blockade on American trade with foreign nations and ordered General Gage to suppress dissent in Massachusetts. "Now the case seemed desperate," the prime minister told Thomas Hutchinson, whom the Patriots had forced into exile in London. "Parliament would not—could not—concede. For aught he could see it must come to violence."

The Countryside Rises Up

Ultimately, the fate of the urban-led Patriot movement would depend on the large rural population. Most farmers had little interest in imperial affairs. Their lives were deeply rooted in the soil, and their prime allegiance was to family and community. But imperial policies had increasingly intruded into the lives of farm families by recruiting their sons for the army and raising their taxes. In 1754, farmers on Long Island, New York, had paid an average of 10 shillings a year in taxes; by 1756, thanks to the Great War for Empire, their taxes had jumped to 30 shillings. Peace brought little relief: The British-imposed Quartering Act kept taxes high, an average of 20 shillings a year, angering farmers in New York and elsewhere.

The urban-led Patriot boycotts of 1765 and 1768 also raised the political consciousness of rural Americans. When the First Continental Congress called for a new boycott of British goods in 1774, it easily established a rural network of committees of safety and inspection to enforce it. In Concord, Massachusetts, 80 percent of the male heads of families and a number of single women signed a "Solemn League and Covenant" supporting nonimportation. In other farm towns, men blacked their faces, disguised themselves in blankets "like Indians," and threatened violence against shopkeepers who traded "in rum, molasses, & Sugar, &c." in violation of the boycott.

Patriots likewise warned that British measures threatened the yeoman tradition of landownership. In Petersham, Massachusetts, the town meeting worried that new British taxes would drain "this People of the Fruits of their Toil." Arable land was now scarce and expensive in older communities, and merchants in new settlements were seizing farmsteads for delinquent debts. By the 1770s, many northern yeomen felt personally threatened by British imperial policies, which, a Patriot pamphlet warned, were "paving the way for reducing the country to lordships."

Despite their higher standard of living, southern slave owners had similar fears. Many Virginia Patriots—including Patrick Henry, George Washington, and Thomas Jefferson—speculated in western lands, and they reacted angrily when first the Proclamation of 1763 and then the Quebec Act of 1774 restricted the land claims of existing colonies. Thanks to their extravagant lifestyle, many Chesapeake planters were deeply in debt to British merchants. Even as planters faced financial disaster, George Washington noted, they lived "genteely and hospitably" and were "ashamed" to adopt frugal ways. Accustomed to being absolute masters on their slave-labor plantations, they resented their financial dependence on British creditors and dreaded the prospect of political subservience to British officials.

That danger now seemed real. If Parliament used the Coercive Acts to subdue Massachusetts, it might turn next to Virginia, dissolving the colony's representative assembly and judicial institutions and assisting British merchants to seize their debt-burdened properties. Consequently, the Virginia gentry supported demands by indebted yeomen farmers to close the law courts so that they could bargain with merchants over debts without the threat of legal action. "The spark of liberty is not yet extinct among our people," declared one planter, "and if properly fanned by the Gentlemen of influence will, I make no doubt, burst out again into a flame."

Loyalist Americans

Other "Gentlemen of influence" worried that resistance to Britain would undermine all political institutions and end in mob rule. Their fears increased when the Sons of Liberty used intimidation and violence to uphold the boycotts. One well-to-do New Yorker complained, "No man can be in a more abject state of bondage than he whose Reputation, Property and Life are exposed to the discretionary violence . . . of the community." As the crisis deepened, such men became Loyalists—so called because they remained loyal to the British crown.

Less affluent Americans also refused to endorse the Patriot cause. In New Jersey and Pennsylvania, thousands of pacifist Quakers and Germans tried to remain neutral. In areas where wealthy landowners became Patriots—the Hudson River Valley of New York, for example—many tenant farmers supported the king because they hated their landlords. Similar social conflicts prompted some Regulators in the North Carolina backcountry and many farmers in eastern Maryland to oppose the Patriots there. Enslaved blacks had little reason to support the cause of their Patriot masters. In November 1774, James Madison reported that some Virginia slaves were planning to escape "when the English troops should arrive."

Prominent Loyalists — royal officials, merchants with military contracts, clergy of the Church of England, and well-established lawyers — tried to mobilize support for the king. Relying on their high status and rhetorical skills, they denounced the Patriot leaders as troublemakers and accused them of working toward independence. But Loyalist leaders found relatively few active followers. A Tory association started by Governor Benning Wentworth of New Hampshire enrolled just fifty-nine members, fourteen of whom were his relatives. At this crucial juncture, Americans who supported resistance to British rule commanded the allegiance — or at least the acquiescence — of the majority of white Americans.

Compromise Fails

When the Continental Congress met in September 1774, Massachusetts was already defying British authority. In August, 150 delegates to an extralegal Middlesex County Congress had advised Patriots to close the existing royal court and to transfer their political allegiance to the popularly elected House of Representatives. After the Middlesex Congress, armed crowds harassed Loyalists and ensured Patriot rule in most of New England.

General Thomas Gage, now the military governor of Massachusetts, tried desperately to maintain imperial power. In September, he ordered British troops in Boston to seize Patriot armories and storehouses in nearby Charlestown and Cambridge. Following that raid, 20,000 colonial militiamen mobilized to safeguard other military supply depots. The Concord town meeting raised a defensive force, the famous **Minutemen**, to "Stand at a minutes warning in Case of alarm." Increasingly, Gage's authority was limited to Boston, where it rested primarily on the bayonets of his 3,500 troops. Meanwhile, the Patriot-controlled Massachusetts House met in defiance of Parliament, collected taxes, bolstered the militia, and assumed the responsibilities of government.

In London, the colonial secretary, Lord Dartmouth, proclaimed Massachusetts to be in "open rebellion" and ordered Gage to march against the "rude rabble." On the night of April 18, 1775, Gage dispatched 700 soldiers to capture colonial leaders and supplies at Concord. Paul Revere and two other Bostonians warned the Patriots; at dawn, local militiamen confronted the British troops first at Lexington and then at Concord. Those skirmishes took a handful of lives. But as the British retreated to Boston, militiamen from neighboring towns repeatedly ambushed them. By the end of the day, 73 British soldiers were dead, 174 had been wounded, and 26 were missing. British fire had killed 49 Massachusetts militiamen and wounded 39 (see Voices from Abroad, p. 154). Too much blood had been spilled to allow another compromise. Twelve years of economic conflict and constitutional debate had culminated in civil violence.

The Second Continental Congress Organizes for War

A month later, in May 1775, Patriot leaders gathered in Philadelphia for the Second Continental Congress. As the Congress opened, 3,000 British troops attacked American fortifications on Breed's Hill and Bunker Hill overlooking Boston. After three assaults

A British View of Lexington and Concord LIEUTENANT COLONEL FRANCIS SMITH

The past vanishes as soon as it occurs and must be reconstructed by historians from documentary evidence. On April 26, 1775, a week after British troops marched on Lexington and Concord, the Patriot-controlled Massachusetts Provincial Congress issued what it called a "true, and authentic account" of the hostilities. The Congress alleged that at Lexington "the regulars rushed on with great violence and first began the hostilities" and that in the retreat of the British troops from Concord, "houses on the road were plundered, . . . women in child-bed were driven by soldiery naked in the streets, [and] old men peaceably in their houses were shot dead." Four days earlier, in his official report to General Gage, British lieutenant colonel Francis Smith offered an account that presented British actions in a much different light. Which version should the historian find more "true, and authentic"?

Sir,—In obedience to your Excellency's commands, I marched on the evening of the 18th inst. with the corps of grenadiers and light infantry for Concord, . . . to destroy all ammunition, artillery, tents &c. . . . Notwithstanding we marched with the utmost expedition and secrecy, we found the country had intelligence or strong suspicion of our coming. . . .

At Lexington . . . [we] found on a green close to the road a body of the country people drawn up in military order, with arms and accoutrements, and, as appeared afterward, loaded. . . . Our troops advanced towards them, without any intention of injuring them . . . ; but they in confusion went off, principally to the left, only one of them fired before he went off, and three or four more jumped over a wall and fired from behind it among the soldiers; on which the troops returned it, and killed several of them. They likewise fired on the soldiers from the Meeting[house] and dwelling-houses. . . .

While at Concord we saw vast numbers assembling in many parts; at one of the bridges they marched down, with a very considerable body, on the light infantry posted there. On their coming pretty near, one of our men fired on them, which they returned; on which an action ensued and some few were killed and wounded. In this affair, it appears that, after the bridge was quitted, they scalped and otherwise ill treated one or two of [our] men who were either killed or severely wounded. . . .

On our leaving Concord to return to Boston they began to fire on us from behind walls, ditches, trees, &c., which, as we marched, increased to a very great degree, and continued . . . for, I believe, upwards of eighteen miles; so that I can't think but it must have been a preconcerted scheme in them, to attack the King's troops the first favorable opportunity that offered; otherwise, I think they could not, in such a short a time from our marching out, have raised such a numerous body. . . .

SOURCE: Massachusetts Historical Society, *Proceedings, 1876* (Boston, 1876), 350ff.

and 1,000 casualties, the British finally dislodged the Patriot militia. Inspired by his countrymen's valor, John Adams exhorted the Congress to rise to the "defense of American liberty" by creating a continental army. He nominated George Washington to lead it. After bitter debate, the Congress approved the proposals, though, Adams lamented, only "by bare majorities."

Despite the bloodshed in Massachusetts, a majority in the Congress still hoped for reconciliation. Led by John Dickinson of Pennsylvania, these moderates won approval of a petition expressing loyalty to George III and asking for repeal of oppressive parliamentary legislation. But Samuel Adams, Patrick Henry, and other zealous Patriots drummed up support for a Declaration of the Causes and Necessities of Taking Up Arms. Americans dreaded the "calamities of civil war," the declaration asserted, but were "resolved to die Freemen rather than to live [as] slaves." George III failed to exploit the divisions among the Patriots; instead, in August 1775, he issued a Proclamation for Suppressing Rebellion and Sedition.

Before the king's proclamation reached America, the radicals in the Congress had won support for an invasion of Canada. They hoped to unleash an uprising among the French inhabitants and add a fourteenth colony to the rebellion. Patriot forces easily defeated the British forces at Montreal; but in December 1775, they failed to capture Quebec City. Meanwhile, American merchants waged the financial warfare promised at the First Continental Congress by cutting off all exports to Britain and its West Indian sugar islands. Parliament retaliated with the Prohibitory Act, which outlawed all trade with the rebellious colonies.

Skirmishes between Patriot and Loyalist forces now broke out. In Virginia, the Patriot-dominated House of Burgesses forced the royal governor, Lord Dunmore, to take refuge on a British warship in Chesapeake Bay. Branding the Patriots "traitors," the governor organized two military forces—one white, the Queen's Own Loyal Virginians, and one black, the Ethiopian Regiment, which enlisted 1,000 slaves who had fled their Patriot owners. In November 1775, Dunmore issued a controversial proclamation promising freedom to black slaves and white indentured servants who joined the Loyalist cause. White planters denounced this "Diabolical scheme," claiming that it "point[ed] a dagger to their Throats." A new rising of the black and white underclasses, as in Bacon's Rebellion in the 1680s, seemed a possibility. In Fincastle County in southwestern Virginia, Loyalist planter John Hiell tried to rouse workers to support the king, telling "a Servant man" that in about a month, "he and all the negroes would get their freedom." Frightened by Dunmore's aggressive tactics, Patriot yeoman and tenant farmers called for a final break with Britain.

In North Carolina, too, military clashes prompted demands for independence. Early in 1776, Josiah Martin, the colony's royal governor, raised a Loyalist force of 1,500 Scottish Highlanders in the backcountry. In response, Patriots mobilized the low-country militia and, in February, defeated Martin's army at the Battle of Moore's Creek Bridge, capturing more than 800 Highlanders. Following this victory, radical Patriots in the North Carolina assembly instructed its delegates in Philadelphia "to concur with the Delegates of other Colonies in declaring Independence, and forming foreign alliances." In May, the Virginia gentry followed suit: Led by James Madison, Edmund Pendleton, and Patrick Henry, the Patriots met in convention and resolved unanimously to support independence.

Thomas Paine's *Common Sense*

As radical Patriots edged toward independence, many colonists retained an affection for the king. Joyous crowds had toasted the health of George III when he ascended the throne in 1760 and again in 1766 when his ministers repealed the Stamp Act. Their loyalty stemmed in part from the character of authority in a patriarchal society. Every father was "a king, and governor in his family," as one group of Baptists put it. Just as people followed the dictates of elders in town meetings and ministers in churches, so they should obey the king, their imperial "father." To deny the king's legitimacy would disrupt the social order.

But by late 1775, many Americans were turning against the monarch. As military conflicts escalated, they accused George III of supporting oppressive legislation and ordering armed retaliation. Surprisingly, agitation became especially intense in Quaker-dominated Philadelphia. Many Philadelphia merchants harbored Loyalist sympathies and refused to join the boycott against the Townshend duties. Consequently, artisans, who made up about half of Philadelphia's workers, became the most powerful force in Philadelphia's Patriot movement. Worried that British imports threatened their small-scale manufacturing enterprises, they organized a Mechanics Association to protect America's "just Rights and Privileges." By February 1776, forty artisans sat with forty-seven merchants on the Philadelphia Committee of Resistance.

Scots-Irish artisans and laborers became Patriots for cultural and religious reasons. They came from Presbyterian families that had fled economic and religious discrimination in British-controlled Ireland, and many of them had embraced the egalitarian message preached by Gilbert Tennent and other New Light ministers (see Chapter 4). As pastor of Philadelphia's Second Presbyterian Church, Tennent had told his congregation that all men and women were equal before God. Applying that idea to politics, New Light Presbyterians shouted in street demonstrations that they had "no king but King Jesus." Republican ideas derived from the European Enlightenment also circulated freely among Pennsylvania artisans. So Patriot leaders Benjamin Franklin and Dr. Benjamin Rush found a receptive audience when they questioned not just the wisdom of George III but the very idea of monarchy.

With popular sentiment in flux, a single pamphlet tipped the balance. In January 1776, Thomas Paine published *Common Sense*, a rousing call for independence and a republican form of government. Paine had served as a minor bureaucrat in the customs service in England and was fired for protesting low wages. In 1774, Paine migrated to Philadelphia, where he met Rush and other Patriots who shared his republican sentiments.

In *Common Sense*, Paine launched an assault on the traditional monarchical order in language that stirred popular emotions. "Monarchy and hereditary succession have laid the world in blood and ashes," Paine proclaimed, leveling a personal attack at George III, "the hard hearted sullen Pharaoh of England." Mixing insults with biblical quotations, Paine blasted the British system of "mixed government" among the three estates of king, lords, and commoners. Paine granted that the system "was noble for the dark and slavish times in which it was created," but now it yielded only "monarchical tyranny in the person of the king" and "aristocratical tyranny in the persons of the peers."

George III and the Royal Family

George III strikes a regal pose, surrounded by his queen and numerous offspring, all brilliantly attired. Patriots repudiated not only monarchy but also the fancy dress and aristocratic manners of the old regime. In its place, they championed a society of republican simplicity. *Family of George III*, by John Zoffany, late eighteenth–early nineteenth century. Royal Collection, St. James's Palace. © H.M. Queen Elizabeth II.

Paine made a compelling case for American independence by turning the traditional metaphor of patriarchal authority on its head: "Is it the interest of a man to be a boy all his life?" he asked. Within six months, *Common Sense* had gone through twenty-five editions and had reached hundreds of thousands of people throughout the colonies. "There is great talk of independence," a worried New York Loyalist noted, "the unthinking multitude are mad for it. . . . A pamphlet called Common Sense has carried off . . . thousands." Paine called on Americans to create independent republican states. "A government of our own is our natural right, 'TIS TIME TO PART."

Independence Declared

Inspired by Paine's arguments and beset by armed Loyalists, Patriot conventions throughout the colonies urged a break from Britain. In June 1776, Richard Henry Lee presented Virginia's resolution to the Continental Congress: "That these United Colonies are, and of right ought to be, free and independent states." Faced with certain defeat, staunch Loyalists and anti-independence moderates withdrew from the Congress, leaving committed Patriots to take the fateful step. On July 4, 1776, the Congress approved the Declaration of Independence (see Documents, p. D-1).

The main author of the Declaration was Thomas Jefferson, a young planter from Virginia. As a Virginia Burgess, Jefferson had mobilized resistance to the Coercive Acts with the pamphlet *A Summary View of the Rights of British America* (1774). Now, to justify independence and republicanism to Americans and the world, Jefferson vilified George III: "He has plundered our seas, ravaged our coasts, burned our towns, and destroyed the lives of our people. . . . A prince, whose character is thus marked by every act which may define a tyrant," Jefferson concluded, conveniently ignoring his own status as a slave owner, "is unfit to be the ruler of a free people."

Employing the ideas of the European Enlightenment, Jefferson proclaimed a series of "self-evident" truths: "that all men are created equal"; that they possess the "unalienable rights" of "Life, Liberty, and the pursuit of Happiness"; that government derives its "just powers from the consent of the governed" and can rightly be overthrown if it "becomes destructive of these ends." By linking these doctrines of individual liberty, **popular sovereignty**, and republican government with American independence, Jefferson established them as the defining political values of the new nation. For Jefferson, as for Paine, the pen proved mightier than the sword. In rural hamlets and seaport cities, crowds celebrated the Declaration by burning effigies of George III and toppling statues of the king. On July 8, 1776, in Easton, Pennsylvania, a "great number of spectators" heard a reading of the Declaration, "gave their hearty assent with three loud huzzahs, and cried out, 'May God long preserve and unite the Free and Independent States of America.'"

► Why did the Patriot movement wane in the early 1770s? Why did the Tea Act reignite colonial resistance?

► The narrative suggests that the British empire could have been saved. Do you agree? Why or why not? At what point during the imperial crisis did peaceful compromise cease to be possible?

SUMMARY

In this chapter, we have focused on a short span of time—a mere decade and a half—and have laid out the plot of a political drama in three acts. In Act I, the Great War for Empire prompts British political leaders to implement a program of imperial reform and taxation. Act II is full of dramatic action, as colonial mobs riot, Patriot writers articulate ideologies of resistance, and British ministers search for compromise between claims of parliamentary sovereignty and assertions of colonial autonomy. Act III takes the form of tragedy: The once-proud British empire dissolves into civil war, an imminent nightmare of death and destruction.

Why did this happen? More than two centuries later, the answers still are not clear. Certainly, the lack of astute leadership in Britain was a major factor. But British leaders faced circumstances that limited their actions: a huge national debt and a deep commitment to the absolute authority of Parliament. Moreover, in America, decades

TIMELINE

1756–1763	▶ War doubles British national debt
1760	▶ George III becomes king
1762	▶ Revenue Act reforms customs service
1763	▶ Treaty of Paris ends Great War for Empire
	▶ Proclamation Line restricts western settlement
	▶ George Grenville becomes prime minister
1764	▶ Parliament passes Sugar Act and Currency Act
	▶ Colonists oppose vice-admiralty courts
1765	▶ Stamp Act imposes direct tax
	▶ Quartering Act requires aid to British troops
	▶ Sons of Liberty riot
	▶ Stamp Act Congress meets in New York City
	▶ First American boycott of British goods
1766	▶ First compromise: Parliament repeals Stamp Act, passes Declaratory Act
1767	▶ Townshend duties on colonial imports
	▶ Restraining Act suspends New York assembly
1768	▶ Second American boycott of British goods

	▶ Daughters of Liberty make "homespun" cloth
1770	▶ Second compromise: Parliament repeals Townshend Act, retains tax on tea
	▶ Boston Massacre
1773	▶ Tea Act aids East India Company; Boston Tea Party
1774	▶ Coercive Acts and Quebec Act anger Patriots
	▶ First Continental Congress meets in Philadelphia
	▶ Third American boycott of British goods
1775	▶ Skirmishes at Lexington and Concord
	▶ Second Continental Congress creates Continental army
	▶ Lord Dunmore promises freedom to Loyalist slaves
	▶ Patriots invade Canada, skirmish with Loyalists in South
1776	▶ Thomas Paine issues *Common Sense*
	▶ Declaration of Independence

of salutary neglect strengthened Patriots' demands for political autonomy, as did the fears and aspirations of artisans and farmers. The trajectory of their histories placed Britain and its American possessions on course for a disastrous—and fatal—collision.

Connections: Government

It is impossible to understand the Patriot resistance movement without understanding political developments during the colonial era. As we noted in the essay opening Part One after 1689, white settlers in the English mainland colonies devised an increasingly free and competitive political system. Thereafter, local governments and representative assemblies became more powerful and created a tradition of self-rule that would spark demands for political independence from Britain.

As we have seen in Chapter 5 and will see again in Chapters 6 and 7, the traditions of localism and self-rule retained their vitality. During the War of Independence, local communities governed themselves through existing institutions or new Committees of Safety. The states assumed the status of sovereign entities, and their legislatures devised new republican constitutions.

The tradition of local and state rule was so strong that it was only with great difficulty that nationalist-minded politicians secured ratification of the Constitution of 1787, which restored a measure of political centralization to American life. Even then, most citizens looked first to their local and state governments. Having resisted and fought a distant British regime, they were not eager to place their affairs in the hands of a remote national government. When Alexander Hamilton and the Federalist Party increased national authority in the 1790s, voters turned them out of office in favor of Thomas Jefferson and his Republican followers, who wanted political power to reside primarily in local and state governments.

FOR FURTHER EXPLORATION

In *Angel in the Whirlwind: The Triumph of the American Revolution* (1997), Benson Bobrick narrates a grand epic that stretches from the French and Indian War to Washington's inauguration. For more complex accounts, read John Ferling, *A Leap in the Dark: The Struggle to Create the American Republic* (2003) and *Almost a Miracle: The American Victory in the War of Independence* (2007). Gary B. Nash, *The Unknown American Revolution: The Unruly Birth of Democracy* (2005), and Woody Holton, *Forced Founders: Indians, Debtors, Slaves, & the Making of the American Revolution in Virginia* (1999), show how ordinary citizens shaped events.

Edmund Morgan and Helen Morgan tell the story of *The Stamp Act Crisis* (1953), and Philip Lawson offers a sympathetic portrait of *George Grenville* (1984). Benjamin Labaree's *The Boston Tea Party* (1979) suggests how a "small" event can alter the course of history; and David Hackett Fischer explains the rise of the radical Patriots in *Paul Revere's Ride* (1994).

Liberty! The American Revolution, a PBS video, has a fine Web site (**www.pbs .org/ktca/liberty/**). For a British perspective, see "The Sceptered Isle: Empire" (**www .bbc.co.uk/radio4/history/empire/regions/americas.shtml**). For fine collections of pamphlets and images, consult **odur.let.rug.nl/~usa/D/index.htm** and **www.research .umbc.edu/~bouton/Revolution.links.htm**. The Web site of the National Gallery of Art (**www.nga.gov**) shows American paintings of the colonial and Revolutionary periods.

TEST YOUR KNOWLEDGE

To assess your mastery of the material in this chapter and for Web sites, images, and documents related to this chapter, visit **bedfordstmartins.com/henrettaconcise**.

Making War and Republican Governments
1776–1789

[Societies] and governments are republican only in proportion as they embody the will of their people.

—Thomas Jefferson, 1813

When the Patriots of Frederick County, Maryland, demanded allegiance to the American cause in 1776, Robert Gassaway would have none of it. "It was better for the poor people to lay down their arms and pay the duties and taxes laid upon them by King and Parliament than to be brought into slavery and commanded and ordered about [by you]," he told the local Patriots. The story was much the same in Farmington, Connecticut, where Patriot officials imprisoned Nathaniel Jones and seventeen other men for "remaining neutral." Throughout the colonies, the events of 1776 forced families to choose the Loyalist or the Patriot side.

The Patriots' control of most local governments gave them an edge in that battle. Patriot leaders organized their neighbors into militia units and recruited volunteers for the Continental army, a ragtag force that held its own on the battlefield. "I admire the American troops tremendously!" exclaimed a French officer. "It is incredible that soldiers composed of every age, even children of fifteen, of whites and blacks, almost naked, unpaid, and rather poorly fed, can march so well and withstand fire so steadfastly."

Military mobilization created political commitment—and vice versa. To encourage Americans to support the war—as soldiers, taxpayers, and republican citizens—Patriot leaders encouraged them to take an active role in government. As the common people exerted their influence, the character of politics changed. "From subjects to citizens the difference is immense," remarked South Carolina Patriot David Ramsay. By raising a democratic army and repudiating monarchical rule, the Patriots launched the age of republican revolution that would throw European nations into turmoil and sweep through Spain's American colonies.

The Trials of War, 1776–1778

The Declaration of Independence coincided with a full-scale British military assault. For two years, British forces manhandled the Continental army. A few inspiring American victories kept the rebellion alive, but during the winters of 1776 and 1777, the Patriot cause hung in the balance.

War in the North

Once the British resorted to military force, few European observers gave the rebels a chance. Great Britain had 11 million people compared to the colonies' 2.5 million, 20 percent of whom were enslaved Africans. Britain also possessed the immense wealth generated by the South Atlantic System and the emerging Industrial Revolution. Its financial resources paid for the most powerful navy in the world, a standing army of 48,000 Britons, and thousands of German (Hessian) soldiers. In addition, Britain had an experienced officer corps and the support of thousands of American Loyalists and many Indian tribes: The Cherokees in the Carolinas, were firmly committed to the British, as were four of the six Iroquois Nations of New York.

By contrast, the Americans were economically and militarily weak. They lacked a strong central government and a source of revenue, and their new Continental army, commanded by General George Washington, consisted of about 18,000 poorly trained recruits. The Patriot militia would not march to distant battles, and American officers had never faced a disciplined European army.

To demonstrate its military superiority, Britain's prime minister, Lord North, ordered General William Howe to capture New York City. His goal was to seize control

Joseph Brant
Mohawk chief Thayendanegea, known as Joseph Brant, was a devout Anglican who helped translate the Bible into the Iroquois language. Brant persuaded four of the six Iroquois Nations to support Britain in the war. In 1778 and 1779, he led Iroquois warriors and Tory rangers in devastating attacks on American settlements in the Wyoming Valley of Pennsylvania and Cherry Valley in New York. In this painting from 1797, Charles Willson Peale provided Brant with European features. Independence National Historic Park, Philadelphia.

For more help analyzing this image, see the Online Study Guide at **bedfordstmartins .com/henrettaconcise**.

of the Hudson River, thereby isolating the radical Patriots in New England from the colonies to the south. As the Second Continental Congress declared independence in Philadelphia in July 1776, Howe landed 32,000 troops — British regulars and German mercenaries — outside New York City. In August 1776, Howe defeated the Americans in the Battle of Long Island and forced their retreat to Manhattan Island. There, Howe outflanked Washington's troops and nearly trapped them. Outgunned and outmaneuvered, the Continental army again retreated, eventually crossing the Hudson River to New Jersey. By December, the British army had pushed the rebels across New Jersey and over the Delaware River into Pennsylvania.

From the Patriots' perspective, winter came just in time. Following eighteenth-century military custom, the British halted their campaign for the cold months, allowing the Americans to catch them off guard. On Christmas night 1776, Washington crossed the Delaware River and staged a surprise attack on Trenton, New Jersey, where he forced the surrender of 1,000 German soldiers. In early January 1777, the Continental army won a small victory at nearby Princeton (Map 6.1). Bright stars in a dark sky, these minor triumphs could not mask British military superiority. "These are the times," wrote Tom Paine, that "try men's souls."

Armies and Strategies

Thanks in part to General Howe, the Continental army remained intact, and the rebellion survived. Howe had opposed the Coercive Acts of 1774, and he still hoped for a political compromise. So he did not try to destroy the American army; he wanted simply to show its weakness and thereby persuade the Continental Congress to give up the struggle. Howe's restrained tactics were understandable, but they cost Britain the opportunity to nip the rebellion in the bud. For his part, Washington acted cautiously so as to avoid a major defeat; he told Congress, "On our Side the War should be defensive." His strategy was to draw the British away from the seacoast, extend their lines of supply, and sap their morale.

Congress had promised Washington a regular force of 75,000 men, but the Continental army never reached even a third of that number. Yeomen refused to be "Haras'd with callouts" that took them away from their families and farms; they insisted on serving in local militias. When the Virginia gentry tried to impose a military draft and three years of service on propertyless men — the "Lazy fellows who lurk about and are pests to Society" — they resisted so fiercely that the legislature had to pay them substantial bounties for short terms of service. The Continental soldiers recruited in Maryland by General William Smallwood were either poor American-born youths or older foreign-born men, often British ex-convicts and former indentured servants. Most enlisted for the bonus of $20 in cash (about $2,000 today) and the promise of 100 acres of land. Molding such recruits into a fighting force was difficult. Even brave men panicked in the face of a British artillery bombardment or flank attack; hundreds deserted, unwilling to submit to the discipline of military life.

The soldiers who stayed resented the contempt their officers had for the "camp followers," the women who fed and cared for the troops. These women made do with little because the Continental army was poorly supplied and faintly praised. Radical

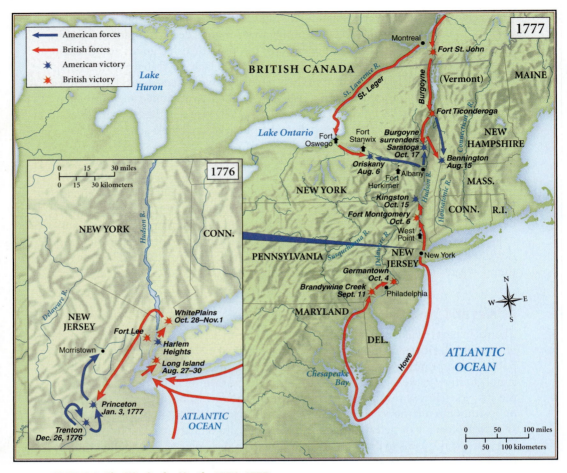

MAP 6.1 The War in the North, 1776–1777

In 1776, the British army drove Washington's forces across New Jersey into Pennsylvania. The Americans counterattacked successfully at Trenton and Princeton and then set up winter headquarters in Morristown. In 1777, British forces stayed on the offensive. General Howe attacked the Patriot capital, Philadelphia, from the south and captured it in early October. Meanwhile, General Burgoyne and Colonel St. Leger launched simultaneous invasions from Canada. With the help of thousands of New England militiamen, American troops commanded by General Horatio Gates defeated Burgoyne in August at Bennington, Vermont, and, in October 1777, at Saratoga, New York, the military turning point in the war.

Whig Patriots believed that a standing army was a threat to liberty; even in wartime, they preferred militias to a professional force. General Philip Schuyler of New York complained that his troops were "weak in numbers, dispirited, naked, destitute of provisions, without camp equipage, with little ammunition, and not a single piece of cannon." Given these handicaps, Washington was fortunate to have escaped an overwhelming defeat.

Victory at Saratoga

Howe's failure to achieve an overwhelming victory dismayed Lord North and his colonial secretary, Lord George Germain. So they launched another major military campaign in 1777. Isolating New England remained the primary goal. To achieve it, Germain planned a three-pronged attack converging on Albany, New York. General John Burgoyne would lead a large contingent of British regulars south from Quebec to Albany. Colonel Barry St. Leger and a force of Iroquois warriors would attack from the west, and General Howe would lead a force northward from New York City.

Howe had a different plan, and it led to a disastrous result. He decided to attack Philadelphia, the home of the Continental Congress, hoping to end the rebellion with a single decisive victory. But instead of marching quickly through New Jersey, Howe loaded his troops onto boats, which sailed along the coast and up the Chesapeake Bay to attack Philadelphia from the south. The strategy worked brilliantly. Howe's troops easily outflanked the American positions along Brandywine Creek in Delaware and, in late September, marched triumphantly into Philadelphia. Howe expected that the capture of the rebels' capital would end the uprising, but the Continental Congress, determined to continue the struggle, fled into the interior.

Howe's slow attack against Philadelphia contributed directly to the defeat of Burgoyne's army. Burgoyne's troops had advanced quickly from Quebec, crossing Lake Champlain, overwhelming the American defenses at Fort Ticonderoga in early July, and driving toward the Hudson River. Then they stalled. Burgoyne — "Gentleman Johnny" — fought with style, stopping early each day to pitch comfortable tents and eat elaborate dinners. The American troops led by General Horatio Gates also slowed Burgoyne's progress by felling huge trees and raiding his supply lines to Canada.

At summer's end, Burgoyne's army of 6,000 British and German troops and 600 Loyalists and Indians was stuck near Saratoga, New York. Desperate for food and horses, the British raided nearby Bennington, Vermont, but were beaten back by 2,000 American militiamen. Patriot forces in the Mohawk Valley also forced St. Leger and the Iroquois to retreat. Making matters worse, the British commander in New York City recalled 4,000 troops he had sent toward Albany and sent them to Philadelphia to bolster Howe's force. While Burgoyne waited in vain for help, thousands of Patriot militiamen from Massachusetts, New Hampshire, and New York joined Gates's forces. They "swarmed around the army like birds of prey," reported an English sergeant, and in October 1777, they forced Burgoyne to surrender (see Voices from Abroad, p. 166).

The battle at Saratoga was the turning point of the war. The Patriots captured more than 5,000 British troops, and their victory ensured the success of American diplomats in Paris, who were seeking a military alliance with France.

Social and Financial Perils

The Patriots' triumph at Saratoga was tempered by wartime difficulties. A British naval blockade had cut supplies of European manufactures and disrupted the New England fishing industry; and the British occupation of Boston, New York, and Philadelphia had reduced domestic trade and manufacturing. As unemployed shipwrights, masons,

The Surrender of Burgoyne, 1777   BARONESS VON RIEDESEL

Frederika Charlotte Louise, Baroness Von Riedesel, was the wife of the commander of the Hessian soldiers in Burgoyne's army. An intrepid woman, the baroness was an eyewitness to the Saratoga campaign and a forthright critic of "Gentleman Johnny" Burgoyne. After Saratoga, she, her husband, and their three children (ages six, three, and one) were held as prisoners of war.

We were halted at six o'clock in the morning [of October 9, 1777], to our general amazement. General Burgoyne ordered the artillery to be drawn up in a line, and to have it counted. This gave much dissatisfaction. . . . At length we recommenced our march; but scarcely an hour had elapsed, before the army was again halted, because the enemy was in sight. They were but two hundred in number, who came to reconnoitre, and who might easily have been taken, had not general Burgoyne lost all his presence of mind. . . .

We reached Saratoga about dark, which was but half an hour's march from the place where we had spent the day. I was quite wet, and was obliged to remain in that condition, for want of a place to change my apparel. I seated myself near the fire, and undressed the children, and we then laid ourselves upon some straw. — I asked general Phillips, who came to see how I was, why we did not continue our retreat, my husband having pledged himself to cover the movement, and to bring off the army in safety. "My poor lady," said he, "you astonish me. Though quite wet, you have so much courage as to wish to go farther in this weather. What a pity it is that you are not our commanding general! He complains of fatigue, and has determined upon spending the night here, and giving us a supper."

It is very true, that General Burgoyne liked to make himself easy, and that he spent half his nights in singing and drinking, and diverting himself. . . .

I refreshed myself at 7 o'clock, the next morning, (the 10th of October,) with a cup of tea, and we all expected that we should soon continue our march. About 2 o'clock [the next day] we heard again a report of muskets and cannon, and there was much alarm and bustle among our troops. My husband sent me word, that I should immediately retire into a house which was not far off. Soon after our arrival, a terrible cannonade began, and the fire was principally directed against the house, where we had hoped to find a refuge, probably because the enemy inferred, from the great number of people who went towards it, that this was the headquarters of the generals, while, in reality, none were there except women and crippled soldiers. We were at last obliged to descend into the cellar, where I laid myself in a corner near the door. My children put their heads upon my knees. An abominable smell, the cries of the children, and my own anguish of mind, did not permit me to close my eyes, during the whole night. . . .

On the 17th of October, the capitulation was carried into effect. The generals waited upon the American general Gates, and the troops surrendered themselves prisoners of war and laid down their arms.

SOURCE: Madame de Riedesel, *Letters and Memoirs Relating to the War of American Independence, and the Capture of the German Troops at Saratoga* (New York, 1827), 173–183.

and laborers moved to the countryside, New York City's population declined from 21,000 to 10,000. In the Chesapeake, the British blockade cut tobacco exports, so planters grew grain to sell to the contending armies. All across the land, farmers and artisans adapted to a war economy.

With goods in short supply, governments requisitioned military supplies directly from the people. In 1776, Connecticut officials asked the citizens of Hartford to provide 1,000 coats and 1,600 shirts, and they assessed smaller towns proportionately. After losing all his shirts "except the one on my back" in the Battle of Long Island, Captain Edward Rogers told his wife that "the making of Cloath . . . must go on." In response, Patriot women in Elizabeth, New Jersey, promised "upwards of 100,000 yards of linnen and woolen cloth." Other women assumed the burdens of farm work while their men were away at war and acquired a taste for decision making. "We have sow'd our oats as you desired," Sarah Cobb Paine wrote to her absent husband. "Had I been master I should have planted it to Corn." Their self-esteem boosted by their wartime activities, some women expected greater legal rights in the new republican society.

Still, goods remained scarce and pricey. Hard-pressed consumers assailed shopkeepers as "enemies, extortioners, and monopolizers" and called for government regulation. But when the New England states imposed price ceilings in 1777, many farmers and artisans refused to sell their goods. Ultimately, a government official admitted, consumers had to pay the higher market prices "or submit to starving."

Even more frightening, the fighting exposed tens of thousands of civilians to deprivation and death. "An army, even a friendly one, are a dreadful scourge to any people," a Connecticut soldier wrote from Pennsylvania. "You cannot imagine what devastation and distress mark their steps." British and American armies marched back and forth across New Jersey, forcing Patriot and Loyalist families to flee their homes to escape arrest—or worse. Soldiers and partisans looted farms, and disorderly troops harassed and raped women and girls.

The war divided many communities. Patriots formed committees of safety to collect taxes and seized property from those who refused to pay. In New England, mobs of Patriot farmers beat suspected Tories and destroyed their property. "Every Body submitted to our Sovereign Lord the Mob," a Loyalist preacher lamented. In parts of Maryland, the number of "nonassociators"—those who refused to join either side—was so large that they successfully defied Patriot organizers. "Stand off you dammed rebel sons of bitches," Robert Davis of Anne Arundel County shouted, "I will shoot you if you come any nearer."

Such defiance exposed the financial weakness of Patriot governments. Most states were afraid to raise taxes, so officials borrowed gold or silver currency from wealthy individuals. When those funds ran out, individual states printed so much paper money—some $260 million all told—that it lost worth, and most people refused to accept it at face value. In North Carolina, even tax collectors eventually rejected the state's currency.

The finances of the Continental Congress collapsed too, despite the efforts of Philadelphia merchant Robert Morris, the government's chief treasury official. Because Congress lacked the authority to impose taxes, Morris relied on funds requisitioned from the states, but they paid late or not at all. So Morris secured loans from

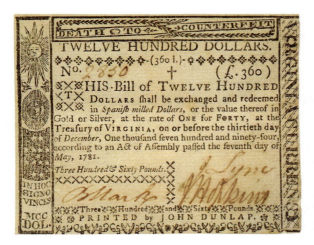

Paper Currency
Symbolizing their independent status, the new state governments printed their own currency. Rejecting the English system of pounds and shillings, Virginia based its currency on the Spanish gold dollar, though it showed the equivalent in English pounds. Initially, $1,200 was equal to £360—a ratio of 3.3 to 1. By 1781, Virginia had printed so much paper money to pay its soldiers and wartime expenses that its currency's value had depreciated to a ratio of 40 to 1.
American Numismatic Society, New York City.

France and Holland and sold Continental bonds to wealthy Americans. Then it issued paper money—some $200 million between 1776 and 1779—that quickly fell in value. In 1778, a family needed $7 in Continental bills to buy goods worth $1 in gold or silver. As the rate of exchange deteriorated—to 42 to 1 in 1779, 100 to 1 in 1780, and 146 to 1 in 1781—it sparked social upheaval. In Boston, a mob of women accosted merchant Thomas Boyleston, "seazd him by his Neck," and forced him to sell his wares at traditional prices. In rural Ulster County, New York, women told the committee of safety to lower food prices or "their husbands and sons shall fight no more." As morale crumbled, some Patriot leaders doubted that the rebellion could succeed.

Fears reached their peak during the winter of 1777. While Howe's army lived comfortably in Philadelphia, Washington's army retreated 20 miles to Valley Forge, where 12,000 soldiers and hundreds of camp followers suffered horribly. "The army. . . . now begins to grow sickly," a surgeon confided to his diary. "Poor food—hard lodging—cold weather—fatigue—nasty clothes—nasty cookery. . . . Why are we sent here to starve and freeze?" Nearby farmers refused to help. Some were pacifists, Quakers and German sectarians unwilling to support either side. Others looked out for their own families, selling grain for the gold offered by British quartermasters but refusing depreciated Continental currency. "Such a dearth of public spirit, and want of public virtue," Washington lamented. By spring, 1,000 hungry soldiers had deserted, and another 3,000 had died from malnutrition and disease. One winter at Valley Forge took as many American lives as had two years of fighting.

► What accounted for British military superiority in the first years of the war? How did the Americans sustain their military effort between 1776 and 1778?

► Who was to blame for Britain's failure to win a quick victory over the American rebels: General Howe, General Burgoyne, or the ministers in London? Explain your answer.

In this dark hour, Baron von Steuben raised the readiness of the American army. A former Prussian military officer, von Steuben was one of a handful of republican-minded foreign aristocrats who helped the American cause. He instituted a strict system of drill and encouraged officers to become more professional. Thanks to von Steuben, the smaller Continental army that emerged from Valley Forge in the spring of 1778 was a much tougher and better-disciplined force.

The Path to Victory, 1778–1783

Wars are often won by astute diplomacy, and so it was with the War of Independence. The Patriots' prospects improved dramatically in 1778, when the Continental Congress concluded a military alliance with France, the most powerful nation in Europe. The alliance gave the Americans desperately needed money, supplies, and, eventually, troops. And it confronted Britain with an international war that challenged its domination of the Atlantic world.

The French Alliance

France and America were unlikely partners. France was Catholic and a monarchy; the United States was Protestant and a federation of republics. From 1689 to 1763, the two peoples had been enemies: New Englanders had brutally uprooted the French population from Acadia (Nova Scotia), and the French and their Indian allies had raided British settlements. But the Comte de Vergennes, the French foreign minister, was determined to avenge the loss of Canada during the Great War for Empire and persuaded King Louis XVI to provide the rebellious colonies with a secret loan and much-needed gunpowder. When news of the rebel victory at Saratoga reached Paris in December 1777, Vergennes sought a formal alliance.

Benjamin Franklin and other American diplomats craftily exploited France's rivalry with Britain to win an explicit commitment to American independence. The Treaty of Alliance of February 1778 specified that once France entered the war, neither partner would sign a separate peace without the "liberty, sovereignty, and independence" of the United States. In return, the Continental Congress agreed to recognize any French conquests in the West Indies.

The alliance gave new life to the Patriots' cause. "There has been a great change in this state since the news from France," a Patriot soldier reported from Pennsylvania. Farmers—"mercenary wretches," he called them—"were as eager for Continental Money now as they were a few weeks ago for British gold." Its confidence bolstered, the Continental Congress addressed the financial demands of the officer corps. Most officers were gentlemen who equipped themselves and often served without pay; in return, they insisted on lifetime military pensions at half pay. John Adams condemned the officers for "scrambling for rank and pay like apes for nuts," but General Washington urged Congress to grant the pensions: "The salvation of the cause depends upon it." Congress reluctantly granted the officers half pay but only for seven years.

Meanwhile, the war had become unpopular in Britain. Radical Whig politicians and republican-minded artisans supported American demands for autonomy and demanded a more representative system of government. The gentry protested increases in the land tax, and merchants condemned new levies on carriages, wine, and imported goods. "It seemed we were to be taxed and stamped ourselves instead of inflicting taxes and stamps on others," a British politician complained.

At first, George III was determined to crush the rebellion. If America won independence, he warned Lord North, "the West Indies must follow them. Ireland would soon follow the same plan and be a separate state, then this island would be reduced to itself, and soon would be a poor island indeed." Stunned by the defeat at Saratoga, the king changed his mind. To thwart an American alliance with France, he authorized North to seek a negotiated settlement. In February 1778, North persuaded Parliament to repeal the Tea and Prohibitory acts and, amazingly, to renounce its power to tax the colonies. But the Patriots, now allied with France and committed to independence, rejected North's overture.

War in the South

The French alliance did not bring a rapid end to the war. When France entered the conflict in June 1778, it tried to capture Barbados or another rich sugar island. Spain, which joined the war against Britain in 1779, wanted to regain Florida and the fortress of Gibraltar at the entrance to the Mediterranean Sea.

For its part, the British government revised its military strategy in America and now focused on the rich tobacco- and rice-growing colonies: Virginia, the Carolinas, and Georgia. The British planned to conquer these colonies and use the Scottish Highlanders in the Carolinas and other Loyalists to hold them. They also hoped to mobilize the Cherokees against the land-hungry Americans and to take advantage of planters' fears of slave uprisings. As a South Carolina delegate explained to the Continental Congress, his state could not contribute recruits to the war "by reason of the great proportion of citizens necessary to remain at home to prevent insurrection among the Negroes."

Implementing Britain's southern strategy became the responsibility of Sir Henry Clinton. Clinton based the main British army in New York City and launched a seaborne attack on Savannah, Georgia; troops commanded by Colonel Archibald Campbell captured the town in December 1778. Mobilizing hundreds of blacks to transport supplies, Campbell moved inland and captured Augusta early in 1779. By year's end, Clinton's forces and local Loyalists controlled coastal Georgia, and 10,000 troops were poised for an assault on South Carolina.

During most of 1780, British forces marched from victory to victory (Map 6.2). In May, Clinton forced the surrender of Charleston, South Carolina, and its American garrison of 5,000 troops. Then Lord Charles Cornwallis assumed control of the British forces and, at Camden, defeated an American force commanded by General Horatio Gates, the hero of Saratoga. Only 1,200 Patriot militiamen joined Gates at Camden—a fifth of the number at Saratoga—and many of them panicked. As Cornwallis took control of South Carolina, hundreds of African Americans fled to freedom behind British lines.

Then the tide of battle turned. Thanks to the Marquis de Lafayette, France finally dispatched troops to the American mainland. A republican-minded aristocrat who had long supported the American cause, Lafayette persuaded Louis XVI to send General Comte de Rochambeau and 5,500 men to Newport, Rhode Island. There, they threatened British forces in New York City.

Meanwhile, Washington dispatched General Nathanael Greene to recapture the Carolinas, where he found "a country that has been ravaged and plundered by both

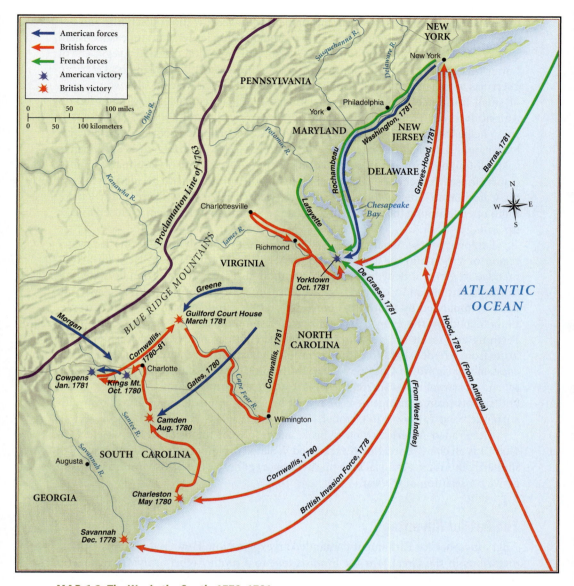

MAP 6.2 The War in the South, 1778–1781

Britain's southern strategy started well. British forces captured Savannah in December 1778, took control of Georgia during 1779, and vanquished Charleston in May 1780. Over the next eighteen months, brutal warfare between British and Loyalist units and the American army and militia raged in the interior of the Carolinas, ending in a stalemate. Hoping to break the deadlock, British general Charles Cornwallis carried the battle into Virginia in 1781. A Franco-American army led by Washington and Lafayette, with the help of the French fleet under Admiral de Grasse, surrounded Cornwallis's forces on the Yorktown Peninsula and forced their surrender.

For more help analyzing this map, see the Online Study Guide at **bedfordstmartins.com/henrettaconcise**.

friends and enemies." To use local militiamen, who were "without discipline and addicted to plundering," Greene placed them under strong leaders and unleashed them on less-mobile British forces. In October 1780, Patriot militia defeated a regiment of Loyalists at King's Mountain, South Carolina, taking about 1,000 prisoners. American guerrillas commanded by the "Swamp Fox," General Francis Marion, also won a series of small but fierce battles. Then, in January 1781, General Daniel Morgan led an American force to a bloody victory at Cowpens, South Carolina. But Loyalist garrisons, helped by the well-organized Cherokees, remained powerful. "We fight, get beaten, and fight again," General Greene declared doggedly. In March 1781, Greene's soldiers fought Cornwallis's seasoned army to a draw at North Carolina's Guilford Court House. Weakened by this **war of attrition**, the British general decided to concede the Carolinas to Greene and seek a decisive victory in Virginia. There, many Patriot militiamen, claiming that "the Rich wanted the Poor to fight for them," refused to take up arms.

Exploiting these social divisions, Cornwallis moved easily through the Tidewater region of Virginia in the early summer of 1781. British forces from New York commanded by General Benedict Arnold, the infamous Patriot traitor, soon bolstered his ranks. As Arnold and Cornwallis sparred near the York Peninsula with an American force commanded by Lafayette, France sent its West Indian fleet to North America. Emboldened by the French naval forces, Washington devised an audacious plan. Feigning an assault on New York City, he secretly marched General Rochambeau's army from Rhode Island to Virginia. Simultaneously, the French fleet massed off the coast, taking control of Chesapeake Bay. By the time the British discovered Washington's scheme, Cornwallis was surrounded, his 9,500-man army outnumbered 2 to 1 on land and cut off from reinforcement or retreat by sea. In a hopeless position, Cornwallis surrendered at Yorktown in October 1781.

The Franco-American victory broke the resolve of the British government. "Oh God! It is all over!" Lord North exclaimed. Isolated diplomatically in Europe, stymied militarily in America, and lacking public support at home, the British ministry gave up active prosecution of the war.

The Patriot Advantage

Angry members of Parliament demanded an explanation. How could mighty Britain, victorious in the Great War for Empire, lose to a motley rebel army? The ministry blamed the military leadership, pointing to a series of blunders. Why had Howe not ruthlessly pursued Washington's army in 1776? Why had Howe and Burgoyne failed to coordinate their attacks in 1777? Why had Cornwallis marched deep into the Patriot-dominated state of Virginia in 1781?

Historians acknowledge British blunders, but they also attribute the rebels' victory to French aid and the support of the American population. About one-third of the white colonists were zealous Patriots, and another third supported the rebellion by paying taxes and joining the militia. Moreover, George Washington played a crucial role as an inspired military leader and an astute politician. By deferring to the civil authorities, he won the support of the Continental Congress and the state governments. Confident of his military abilities, he maintained the support of his officers and

the morale of his men through five long years of war. Finally, Washington had a greater margin for error than the British generals did. Because the Patriots controlled local governments, the American general could mobilize local militias to reinforce the Continental army. Militiamen provided the margin of victory at Saratoga in 1777 and forced Cornwallis from the Carolinas in 1781.

In the end, it was the American people who decided the outcome. Preferring Patriot rule, tens of thousands of farmers and artisans accepted Continental bills in payment for supplies, and thousands of soldiers took them as pay — even as the currency literally depreciated in their pockets. Rampant inflation meant that every paper dollar held for a week lost value, imposing a hidden "currency tax" on those who accepted the paper currency. Each individual tax was small — a few pennies on each dollar. But as millions of dollars changed hands multiple times, these currency taxes paid the huge cost of the American military victory.

Diplomatic Triumph

After Yorktown, diplomats took two years to conclude a peace treaty. Talks began in Paris in April 1782, but the French and Spanish, still hoping for a territorial conquest, stalled for time. Their tactics infuriated the American diplomats: Benjamin Franklin, John Adams, and John Jay. So the Patriot diplomats negotiated secretly with the British, prepared if necessary to ignore the Treaty of Alliance and sign a separate peace. British ministers were eager for a quick settlement because Parliament no longer supported the war, and they feared the loss of a rich sugar island.

Consequently, the American diplomats secured a favorable peace. In the Treaty of Paris, signed in September 1783, Great Britain formally recognized the American independence. Britain retained Canada but relinquished its claims to lands south of the Great Lakes and east of the Mississippi River. The British negotiators did not insist on a separate Indian territory. "In endeavouring to assist you," a Wea Indian complained to a British general, "it seems we have wrought our own ruin."

The treaty also granted Americans fishing rights off Newfoundland and Nova Scotia, prohibited the British from "carrying away any negroes or other property," and guaranteed freedom of navigation on the Mississippi to American citizens "forever." In return, the American government allowed British merchants to pursue legal claims for prewar debts and encouraged the state legislatures to return confiscated property to Loyalists and grant them citizenship.

In the Treaty of Versailles, signed simultaneously, Britain made peace with France and Spain. Neither American ally gained very much. Spain reclaimed Florida from Britain but failed to win back the strategic fortress at Gibraltar. France won control of the Caribbean island of Tobago, small consolation for a war that had sharply raised taxes and quadrupled France's national debt. Just six years later, cries for tax relief and political liberty would spark the French Revolution. Only Americans profited handsomely from the treaties, which gave them independence and access to the trans-Appalachian west.

▶ Why did Britain switch to a southern military strategy? Why did that strategy ultimately fail?

▶ Without the French alliance, would the American rebellion have succeeded? Why or why not?

Creating Republican Institutions, 1776–1787

When the Patriots declared independence, they raised the issue of political power. "Which of us shall be the rulers?" asked a Philadelphia newspaper. The question was multifaceted. Where would power reside: in the national government or the states? Who would control the new republican institutions: traditional elites or average citizens? Would women have greater political and legal rights? What would be the status of the slaves in the new republic?

The State Constitutions: How Much Democracy?

In May 1776, the Second Continental Congress urged Americans to reject royal authority and establish republican governments. Most states quickly complied. "Constitutions employ every pen," an observer noted. Within six months, Virginia, Maryland, North Carolina, New Jersey, Delaware, and Pennsylvania had ratified new constitutions, and Connecticut and Rhode Island had revised their colonial charters by deleting references to the king.

Republicanism meant more than ousting the king. The Declaration of Independence had stated the principle of popular sovereignty: Governments derive "their just powers from the consent of the governed." In the heat of revolution, many Patriots gave this clause a democratic twist. In North Carolina, the backcountry farmers of Mecklenburg County instructed their delegates to the state's constitutional convention to "oppose everything that leans to aristocracy or power in the hands of the rich." In Virginia, voters elected a new assembly that, an eyewitness remarked, "was composed of men not quite so well dressed, nor so politely educated, nor so highly born" as colonial-era legislatures.

This democratic impulse flowered in Pennsylvania, thanks to a coalition of Scots-Irish farmers, Philadelphia artisans, and Enlightenment-influenced intellectuals. In 1776, these insurgents ousted every officeholder of the proprietary government, abolished property ownership as a test of citizenship, and granted all taxpaying men the right to vote and hold office. The Pennsylvania constitution of 1776 also created a unicameral (one-house) legislature with complete power; there was no governor to exercise a veto. Other provisions mandated an extensive system of elementary education and protected citizens from imprisonment for debt.

Pennsylvania's democratic constitution alarmed many leading Patriots. From Boston, John Adams denounced the unicameral legislature as "so democratical that it must produce confusion and every evil work." Along with other conservative Patriots, Adams wanted to restrict office holding to "men of learning, leisure and easy circumstances" and warned of oppression under majority rule: "If you give [ordinary citizens] the command or preponderance in the . . . legislature, they will vote all property out of the hands of you aristocrats."

To counter the appeal of the Pennsylvania Constitution, Adams published *Thoughts on Government* (1776). In that treatise, he adapted the British Whig theory of mixed government (a sharing of power among the monarch, the Houses of Lords, and the Commons) to a republican society. To disperse authority and preserve liberty, he assigned lawmaking, administering, and judging to separate institutions. Legislatures would make laws, the executive would administer them, and the judiciary would

enforce them. Adams also called for a bicameral (two-house) legislature with an upper house of substantial property owners to offset the popular majorities in the lower one. As further curbs on democracy, he proposed an elected governor with veto power and an appointed—not elected—judiciary.

Conservative Patriots endorsed Adams's plea for appointed judges, a bicameral legislature, and property qualifications for voting. The property clauses in the New York Constitution of 1777 excluded 20 percent of white men from voting for members of the assembly and 60 percent from casting ballots for the governor and the upper house. In South Carolina, elite planters used property rules to rule out office holding for about 90 percent of white men. The 1778 constitution required candidates for governor to have a debt-free estate of £10,000 (about $700,000 today), senators to be worth £2,000, and assemblymen to own property valued at £1,000.

The political legacy of the Revolution was complex. Only in Pennsylvania and Vermont were radical Patriots able to create truly democratic institutions. Yet everywhere, representative legislatures had acquired more power, and the politics of electioneering and interest-group bargaining had become more responsive to average citizens.

Women Seek a Public Voice

The extraordinary excitement of the Revolutionary era tested the dictum that only men could engage in politics. Men controlled all public institutions—legislatures, juries, government offices—but upper-class women engaged in political debate and, defying men's scorn, filled their letters, diaries, and conversations with opinions on public issues. "The men say we have no business [with politics]," Eliza Wilkinson of South Carolina complained in 1783. "They won't even allow us liberty of thought, and that is all I want."

These American women did not insist on civic equality with men but only on the end of restrictive customs and laws. Abigail Adams, for example, demanded equal legal rights for married women, who under common law could not own property, enter into contracts, or initiate lawsuits. "Men would be tyrants" if they continued to hold such power over women, Adams declared to her husband John, criticizing him and other Patriots for "emancipating all nations" from monarchical despotism while "retaining absolute power over Wives."

Most politicians ignored women's requests, and most husbands remained patriarchs who dominated their households. Even young men who embraced the republican ideal of "companionate marriage" (see Chapter 8) did not support legal equality or a public role for their wives and daughters. Except in New Jersey, which until 1807 allowed unmarried and widowed female property holders to vote, women remained disfranchised.

The republican belief in an educated citizenry created opportunities for some American women. In her 1779 essay "On the Equality of the Sexes," Judith Sargent Murray argued that men and women had an equal capacity for memory and that women had a superior imagination. She conceded that most women were inferior to men in judgment and reasoning, but only because they had not been trained: "We can only reason from what we know," she argued, and most women had been denied "the opportunity of acquiring knowledge." That situation changed in the 1790s, when the attorney general of Massachusetts declared that girls had an equal right to schooling

Judith Sargent (Murray), Age Nineteen
The well-educated daughter of a wealthy Massachusetts merchant, Judith Sargent enjoyed a privileged childhood. As an adult, however, she endured a difficult seventeen-year marriage to John Stevens, who ultimately went bankrupt, fled from his creditors, and died in the West Indies. In 1788, she married John Murray, a minister who became a leading American Universalist. Her portrait, painted around 1771 by John Singleton Copley, captures the young woman's skepticism, which enabled her to question customary gender roles. Terra Museum of American Art, Chicago, Illinois. Daniel J. Terra Collection.

under the state constitution. By 1850, the literacy rates of women and men in the northeastern states were equal, and educated women again challenged their subordinate legal and political status.

The Loyalist Exodus

The success of republican institutions was facilitated by the departure of 100,000 monarchists, many of whom suffered severe financial losses. John Tabor Kempe, the last royal attorney general of New York, sought compensation of £65,000 sterling (about $4.5 million today) from the British government for Patriot land seizures but received a mere £5,000. Refugees often suffered psychologically too. Loyalists who fled to England complained of "their uneasy abode in this country of aliens." The great number of Loyalist evacuees who settled in Canada or the West Indies likewise lamented their loss. An exiled woman in Nova Scotia confessed: "[I had] such a feeling of loneliness . . . I sat down on the damp moss with my baby on my lap and cried bitterly."

Some Patriots demanded revolutionary justice: the seizure of all Loyalist property and its distribution to needy Americans. While every state seized some Loyalists' property, American leaders worried that wholesale confiscation would impair the nation's commercial credit and violate republican principles. In Massachusetts, officials cited the state's constitution of 1780, which protected every citizen "in the enjoyment of his

life, liberty, and property, according to the standing laws." When state governments did seize the property of flagrant Loyalists, they often auctioned it to the highest bidders, who were usually wealthy Patriots rather than ambitious yeomen farmers or property-less foot soldiers. In a few cases, confiscation did produce a democratic result: In North Carolina, about half the new owners of Loyalist lands were small-scale farmers; in New York, the state government sold farmsteads on the Philipse manor to longtime tenants. When Frederick Philipse III tried to reclaim his estate, the former tenants told him they had "purchased it with the price of their best blood" and "will never become your vassals again." In general, though, the Revolution did not drastically alter the structure of rural society.

Social turmoil was greater in the cities, where Patriot merchants replaced Tories at the top of the economic ladder. In Massachusetts, the Lowell, Higginson, Jackson, and Cabot families moved their trading enterprises to Boston to fill the vacuum created by the departure of the Loyalist Hutchinson and Apthorp clans. In Philadelphia, small-scale Patriot traders stepped into the void left by the collapse of Anglican and Quaker mercantile firms. The War of Independence replaced a traditional economic elite—who invested profits from trade in real estate—with a group of republican entrepreneurs who promoted new trading ventures and domestic manufacturing. This shift advanced America's economic development in the years to come.

The Articles of Confederation

As Patriots embraced independence in 1776, they envisioned a central government with limited powers. Carter Braxton of Virginia thought the Continental Congress should "regulate the affairs of trade, war, peace, alliances, &c." but "should by no means have authority to interfere with the internal police [governance] or domestic concerns of any Colony."

That thinking—of a limited central government—informed the Articles of Confederation, which were approved by the Continental Congress in November 1777. The Articles provided for a loose confederation in which "each state retains its sovereignty, freedom, and independence." As a union of equals, each state had one vote regardless of its population or wealth. Important laws needed the approval of at least nine of the thirteen states, and changes in the Articles required the consent of all states. In the Confederation government, there was neither an executive nor a judiciary. Still, the Confederation government enjoyed considerable authority: The Confederation Congress could declare war, make treaties with foreign nations, adjudicate disputes between the states, borrow and print money, and requisition funds from the states "for the common defense or general welfare."

Although Congress exercised de facto constitutional authority—raising the Continental army, negotiating foreign treaties, and financing the war—disputes over western lands delayed ratification of the Articles until 1781. Many states, particularly Virginia, Massachusetts, and Connecticut, used their royal charters to claim boundaries stretching to the Pacific Ocean. States without western claims—Maryland and Pennsylvania—refused to accept the Articles until the land-rich states relinquished their claims. Threatened by Cornwallis's army in 1781, Virginia gave up its claims, and Maryland, the last holdout, finally ratified the Articles (Map 6.3).

MAP 6.3 The Confederation and Western Land Claims, 1781–1802

The Confederation Congress faced the conflicting state claims to western lands on the basis of their royal charters. For example, notice the huge—and overlapping—territories claimed by New York and Virginia. Between 1781 and 1802, Congress persuaded all of the states to cede their claims, creating a "national domain" open to all citizens. In the ordinances for the domain north of the Ohio River, Congress divided the area into territories, provided for its survey, prohibited slavery, and set up democratic procedures for territories to join the Union. South of the Ohio River, Congress allowed the existing southern states to play a substantial role in the settling of the ceded lands.

The Confederation had a major weakness: It lacked the authority to tax either the states or the people. By 1780, the central government was nearly bankrupt, and General Washington called urgently for a national tax system, warning Congress that otherwise, "our cause is lost." Led by Robert Morris, who became superintendent of finance in 1781, nationalist-minded Patriots tried to expand the Confederation's authority. They persuaded Congress to charter the Bank of North America, a private institution

in Philadelphia, arguing that its notes would stabilize the inflated Continental currency. Morris also created a central bureaucracy that paid army expenses, apportioned war costs among the states, and assumed responsibility for the Confederation's debts. He hoped that the existence of a "national" debt would prompt Congress to enact an import duty to pay it off. However, Rhode Island and New York rejected Morris's proposal for a tax of 5 percent on imports. His state had opposed British duties, New York's representative declared, and it would not accept them from Congress. To raise revenue, Congress looked to the sale of western lands. In 1783, it asserted that the recently signed Treaty of Paris had extinguished the Indians' land rights and made them the property of the United States.

Settlers had already moved to the frontier. In 1784, the residents in what is now eastern Tennessee organized a new state, called it "Franklin," and sought admission to the Confederation. To preserve its authority over the West, Congress refused to recognize Franklin and gave Virginia control over the region. Subsequently, Congress created the Southwest Territory, the future states of Alabama and Mississippi, on lands ceded by North Carolina and Georgia. Because these cessions carried the stipulation that "no regulation . . . shall tend to emancipate slaves," the states that eventually formed in the Southwest Territory (and the entire region south of the Ohio River) allowed slavery.

However, the Confederation Congress banned slavery north of the Ohio River. Between 1784 and 1787, it issued three important ordinances organizing the "Old Northwest." The Ordinance of 1784, written by Thomas Jefferson, divided the region into territories that could become states as their population grew. The Land Ordinance of 1785 promoted settlement by mandating a quick rectangular-grid system of surveying and by encouraging large-scale land purchases. The ordinance specified a minimum price of $1 an acre and required that half of the townships be sold in single blocks of 23,040 acres each, which only large-scale speculators could afford, and the rest in parcels of 640 acres each, which restricted their sale to well-to-do farmers (Map 6.4).

Finally, the Northwest Ordinance of 1787 created the territories that would eventually become the states of Ohio, Indiana, Illinois, Michigan, and Wisconsin. The ordinance prohibited slavery and earmarked funds from land sales for the support of schools. It also specified that Congress would appoint a governor and judges to administer each new territory until the population reached 5,000 free adult men, when the citizens could elect a territorial legislature. When the population reached 60,000, the legislature could devise a republican constitution and apply to join the Confederation.

The land ordinances of the 1780s were a great and enduring achievement of the Confederation Congress. They provided for orderly settlement and the admission of new states on the basis of equality; there would be no dependent "colonies" in the West. But they also perpetuated and extended the geographical division between slave and free areas that would haunt the nation in the coming decades.

Shays's Rebellion

If the future of the West was bright, postwar conditions in the East were grim. The war had crippled the American merchant marine and disrupted the export of tobacco, rice, and wheat. The British Navigation Acts, which had nurtured colonial commerce, now

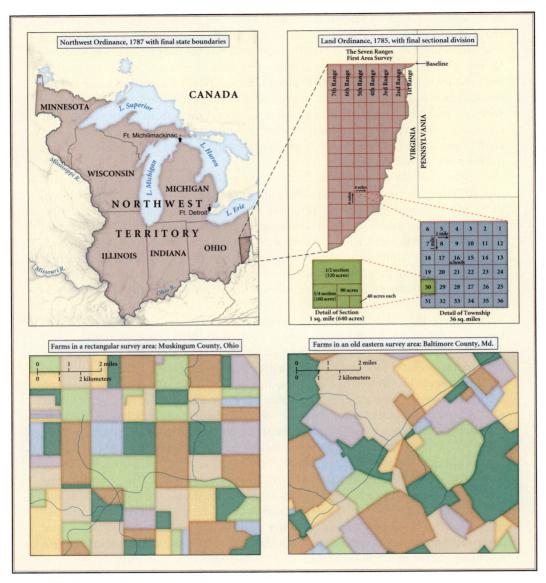

MAP 6.4 Land Division in the Northwest Territory

Throughout the Northwest Territory, government surveyors imposed a rectangular grid on the landscape, regardless of the local topography, so that farmers bought neatly defined tracts of land. The right-angled property lines in Muskingum County, Ohio (lower left), contrasted sharply with those in Baltimore County, Maryland (lower right), where — as in most of the eastern and southern states — boundaries followed the contours of the land.

barred Americans from legal trade with the British West Indies. Moreover, low-priced British manufactures were flooding American markets, driving urban artisans and wartime textile firms out of business.

The fiscal condition of the state governments was equally fragile, primarily because of political conflicts over war debts. On one side were wealthy merchants and landowners who had invested in state bonds or speculated in debt certificates by buying them from farmers and soldiers for less than their face value. These men demanded that the state governments redeem the bonds quickly and at full value, a policy that would require high taxes. On the other side were the elected state legislators. Because the new state constitutions apportioned seats on the basis of population, many legislators now represented western communities and were men of "middling circumstances." By the mid-1780s, such middling farmers and artisans controlled the lower houses of most northern legislatures and formed a sizable minority in southern assemblies. When their constituents demanded tax relief, these representatives usually reduced levies and refused to redeem war bonds. State legislatures also printed paper currency and enacted laws allowing debtors to pay their private creditors in installments. Although wealthy men deplored these measures, claiming that they destroyed "the just rights of creditors," the measures probably prevented social upheaval.

A case in point was Massachusetts, where lawmakers refused to enact debtor-relief legislation, imposed high taxes to pay off the state's war debt, and cut the supply of paper currency. When cash-strapped farmers could not pay their debts, creditors threatened lawsuits. Debtor Ephraim Wetmore heard that merchant Stephan Salisbury "would have my Body Dead or Alive in case I did not pay." To protect their livelihoods, farmers called extralegal conventions that protested the tax increases and property seizures. Then mobs of angry farmers—including men of high status—closed the courts by force. "[I] had no Intensions to Destroy the Publick Government," declared Captain Adam Wheeler, a former town selectman; his goal was simply to prevent "Valuable and Industrious members of Society [being] dragged from their families to prison" because of their debts. These crowd actions grew into a full-scale revolt led by Captain Daniel Shays, a former officer in the Continental army.

As a struggle against taxes imposed by a distant government, Shays's Rebellion resembled colonial resistance to the British Stamp Act. "The people have turned against their teachers the doctrines which were inculcated to effect the late revolution," complained Fisher Ames, a conservative Massachusetts lawmaker. To link themselves to the Patriot movement, Shays's men placed pine twigs in their hats, just as Continental troops had done. But some of the radical Patriots of 1776 condemned the Shaysites: "Those Men, who . . . would lessen the Weight of Government lawfully exercised must be Enemies to our happy Revolution and Common Liberty," charged Samuel Adams. To put down the rebellion, the Massachusetts legislature passed a Riot Act, and Governor James Bowdoin equipped a formidable fighting force, which dispersed Shays's ragtag army during the winter of 1786–1787.

Shays's Rebellion failed, but it suggested that the costs of war and the fruits of independence were not being evenly shared. Middling Patriot families felt they had exchanged British tyrants for American oppressors. Massachusetts voters turned Governor Bowdoin out of office, and debt-ridden farmers in New York, northern Pennsylvania, Connecticut, and New Hampshire closed courthouses and demanded economic relief. British officials in Canada predicted the imminent demise of the United States, and some Americans

▶ What were the main differences between conservative state constitutions, such as that of Massachusetts, and more democratic constitutions, such as Pennsylvania's?

▶ What were the causes of Shays's Rebellion, and what does it tell us about postwar America?

feared for the future of their republican experiment. Events in Massachusetts, declared nationalist Henry Knox, formed "the strongest arguments possible" for the creation of "a strong general government."

The Constitution of 1787

From its creation, the U.S. Constitution was a controversial document, praised as a solution to the nation's woes and condemned as a perversion of its republican principles. Critics charged that republican institutions worked only in small political units — the states. Advocates answered that the Constitution extended republicanism by adding another level of government elected by the people. In this composite political system, the new national government would exercise limited, delegated powers, and the existing state governments would retain authority over all other matters.

The Rise of a Nationalist Faction

Money questions — debts, taxes, and tariffs — dominated the postwar political agenda. Americans who had served the Confederation as military officers, officials, and diplomats viewed these issues from a national perspective and advocated a stronger central government. George Washington, Robert Morris, Benjamin Franklin, John Jay, and John Adams wanted Congress to control foreign commerce and tariff policy. However, lawmakers in Massachusetts, New York, and Pennsylvania, states with strong commercial traditions, insisted on controlling their own tariffs, either to protect their artisans from low-cost imports or to assist their merchants in expanding trade. Most southern states opposed tariffs because planters wanted to import British textiles and ironware at the lowest possible prices.

Nonetheless, some southern leaders became nationalists because of the economic policies of their state legislatures. During the hard times of the 1780s, lawmakers in Virginia and elsewhere had lowered taxes and delayed the redemption of state war bonds. Such actions, lamented Charles Lee of Virginia, a wealthy bondholder, led taxpayers to believe they would "never be compelled to pay" the public debt. Creditors also complained about state laws that "stayed" (delayed) the payment of mortgages and other private debts. "While men are madly accumulating enormous debts, their legislators are making provisions for their nonpayment," complained a South Carolina merchant. To cut the power of the democratic majorities in the state legislatures, creditors favored a stronger central government.

In 1786, James Madison and other nationalists persuaded the Virginia legislature to call a convention to discuss tariff and taxation policies. Only five state governments sent delegates to the meeting in Annapolis, Maryland. Ignoring their small numbers, the delegates called for another convention in Philadelphia. Spurred on by Shays's Rebellion, nationalists in Congress secured a resolution calling for a revision of the Articles of Confederation. "Nothing but the adoption of some efficient plan from the Convention," a fellow nationalist wrote to James Madison, "can prevent anarchy first & civil convulsions afterwards."

The Philadelphia Convention

In May 1787, fifty-five delegates arrived in Philadelphia. They came from every state except Rhode Island, where the legislature opposed increasing central authority. The delegates were men of property: merchants, slaveholding planters, or "monied men." There were no artisans, backcountry settlers, or tenants, and there was only a single yeoman farmer.

Some delegates, such as Benjamin Franklin, had been early advocates of independence. Others, including George Washington and Robert Morris, had risen to prominence during the war. Some influential Patriots missed the convention. John Adams and Thomas Jefferson were serving as American ministers to Britain and France, respectively. The Massachusetts General Court rejected Sam Adams as a delegate because he opposed a stronger national government, and his fellow firebrand from Virginia, Patrick Henry, refused to attend because he "smelt a rat."

The absence of these experienced leaders allowed capable younger nationalists to set the agenda. Declaring that the convention would "decide for ever the fate of Republican Government," James Madison insisted on increased national authority. Alexander Hamilton of New York likewise demanded a strong central government to protect the republic from "the imprudence of democracy."

The delegates elected Washington as their presiding officer and, to prevent popular interference, met in secret. Rather than revising the Articles of Confederation, they considered a scheme for a powerful national government—the so-called Virginia Plan—devised by James Madison. Just thirty-six years old, Madison had arrived in Philadelphia determined to fashion new political institutions run by men of high character. A graduate of Princeton, he had read classical and modern political theory and served in both the Confederation Congress and the Virginia assembly. Once an optimistic Patriot, Madison had become discouraged by the "narrow ambition" and outlook of many state legislators.

Madison's Virginia Plan differed from the Articles of Confederation in three crucial respects. First, the plan rejected state sovereignty in favor of the "supremacy of national authority," including the power to overturn state laws. Second, the national government would be established by the people (not the states), and national laws would operate directly on citizens of the various states. Third, the plan proposed a three-tier election system. Ordinary voters would elect only the lower house of the national legislature, which would name the members of the upper house; then both houses would choose the executive and judiciary.

From a political perspective, Madison's plan had two fatal flaws. First, the provision allowing the national government to veto state laws was unacceptable to most state politicians and citizens. Second, the plan gave the most power to the populous states, because representation in the lower house depended on population. As a Delaware delegate put it, Madison's scheme would allow the populous states to "crush the small ones whenever they stand in the way of their ambitious or interested views."

So small-state delegates rallied behind a plan devised by William Paterson of New Jersey. The New Jersey Plan gave the Confederation the power to raise revenue, control commerce, and make binding requisitions on the states. But it preserved the states' control of their own laws and guaranteed their equality: Each state would have one vote in a unicameral legislature, as in the Confederation Congress. Delegates from the populous states vigorously opposed this provision. After debating the two plans for a month, a bare majority of the states agreed to use Madison's Virginia Plan as the basis of discussion.

This decision raised the odds that the delegates would create a more powerful national government. Outraged by this prospect, two New York representatives accused the delegates of exceeding their mandate to revise the Articles and left the convention. The remaining delegates met six days a week during the hot summer of 1787, debating high principles and discussing practical details. Experienced politicians, they looked for a plan that would be acceptable to most citizens and existing political interests. Pierce Butler of South Carolina invoked a classical Greek precedent: "We must follow the example of Solon, who gave the Athenians not the best government he could devise but the best they would receive."

Representation of large and small states remained the central problem. The Connecticut delegates suggested that the upper chamber, the Senate, have two members from each state, while seats in the lower chamber, the House of Representatives, be apportioned by population (determined every ten years by a national census). After bitter debate, delegates from the populous states reluctantly accepted this "Great Compromise."

Other state-related issues were quickly settled by restricting (or leaving ambiguous) the extent of central authority. Some delegates opposed a national system of courts, warning that "the states will revolt at such encroachments" on their judicial authority. So the convention defined the judicial power of the United States in broad terms, vesting it "in one supreme Court" and leaving the new national legislature to decide whether to establish lower courts within the states. The convention also refused to set a national property requirement for voting in national elections. "Eight or nine states have extended the right of suffrage beyond the freeholders," George Mason of Virginia pointed out. "What will people there say if they should be disfranchised?" Finally, the convention placed the selection of the president in an electoral college chosen on a state-by-state basis and specified that state legislatures would elect members of the U.S. Senate. By giving state legislatures important roles in the new constitutional system, the delegates hoped their citizens would accept a reduction in state sovereignty.

The shadow of slavery hovered over many debates, and Gouverneur Morris of New York brought it into view. Born into the New York aristocracy, Morris initially opposed independence because he feared the "domination of a riotous mob." Having become a Patriot and a nationalist, he came to the Philadelphia convention convinced that the protection of "property was the sole or primary object of Government & Society." To safeguard property rights, Morris demanded life terms for senators, a property qualification for voting in national elections, and a strong president with veto power. Nonetheless, Morris rejected the legitimacy of two traditional types of property: the feudal dues claimed by aristocratic landowners and the ownership of slaves. An advocate of **free markets** and personal liberty, he condemned slavery as "a nefarious institution."

In response, Southern delegates joined together to defend slavery but split over the Atlantic slave trade. George Mason and other Chesapeake planters, who already owned many slaves, wanted to end the trade. Rice planters from South Carolina and Georgia demanded that slave imports continue; otherwise, their states "shall not be parties to the Union." At their insistence, the delegates denied Congress the power to regulate immigration—and so the slave trade—until 1808 (see American Voices, p. 186).

Gouverneur Morris, Federalist Statesman
When the war with Britain broke out, Morris thought about joining the Loyalist cause: He was a snob who liked privilege and feared the common people. ("The mob begins to think and reason," he once noted with disdain.) Morris later became a Federalist for the same reason. He helped write the Philadelphia constitution and, after 1793, strongly supported the Federalist Party.
National Portrait Gallery, Smithsonian Institution/Art Resource, New York.

To preserve national unity, the delegates devised other compromises on other slavery-related issues. To mollify southern planters, they devised a "fugitive" clause that allowed masters to reclaim enslaved blacks (or white indentured servants) who fled to other states. But acknowledging the antislavery sentiments of Morris and other northerners, the delegates did not use the words "slavery" or "slave" in the Constitution; it spoke of citizens and "all other Persons." Because slaves lacked the vote, antislavery delegates wanted to exclude them in apportioning seats in Congress; southerners demanded that they be counted the same as full citizens. Ultimately, the delegates agreed to count each slave as three-fifths of a free person for purposes of representation and taxation, a compromise that helped southern planters to dominate the national government until 1860.

Having addressed the concerns of small states and slave states, the delegates created a powerful procreditor national government. The Constitution and all national legislation would be the "supreme" law of the land. The national government would have broad powers over taxation, military defense, and external commerce and the authority to make all laws "necessary and proper" to implement those and other provisions. To protect creditors and establish the new government's fiscal integrity, the Constitution required the United States to honor the existing national debt. To prevent state governments from aiding debtors, it prohibited the states from issuing paper money or enacting "any Law impairing the Obligation of Contracts."

The proposed constitution was not a "perfect production," Benjamin Franklin admitted on September 17, 1787, as he urged the delegates to sign it. But the great statesman confessed his astonishment at finding "this system approaching so near to perfection." His colleagues apparently agreed; all but three signed the document.

The Constitution and Slavery   MASSACHUSETTS RATIFYING CONVENTION

In Philadelphia, the Framers of the Constitution agreed on a compromise: They gave Congress the power to tax or prohibit slave imports but withheld that power for twenty years. In the Massachusetts convention, the delegates split on this issue and on many others. They eventually ratified the Constitution by a narrow margin: 187 to 168.

Mr. Neal (from Kittery) [an Antifederalist] went over the ground of objection to . . . the idea that slave trade was allowed to be continued for 20 years. His profession, he said, obliged him to bear witness against any thing that should favor the making merchandize of the bodies of men, and unless his objection was removed, he could not put his hand to the constitution. Other gentlemen said, in addition to this idea, that there was not even a proposition that the negroes ever shall be free: and Gen. Thompson exclaimed—"Mr. President, shall it be said, that after we have established our own independence and freedom, we make slaves of others? Oh! Washington . . . he has immortalized himself! but he holds those in slavery who have a good right to be free as he is. . . ."

On the other side, gentlemen said, that the step taken in this article, towards the abolition of slavery, was one of the beauties of the constitution. They observed, that in the confederation there was no provision whatever for its ever being abolished; but this constitution provides, that Congress may after twenty years, totally annihilate the slave trade. . . .

Mr. Heath (Federalist): . . . I apprehend that it is not in our power to do any thing for or against those who are in slavery in the southern states. No gentleman within these walls detests every idea of slavery more than I do: it is generally detested by the people of this commonwealth, and I ardently hope that the time will soon come, when our brethren in the southern states will view it as we do, and put a stop to it; but to this we have no right to compel them.

Two questions naturally arise: if we ratify the Constitution, shall we do any thing by our act to hold the blacks in slavery or shall we become the partakers of other men's sins? I think neither of them: each state is sovereign and independent to a certain degree, and they have a right, and will regulate their own internal affairs, as to themselves appears proper. . . . We are not in this case partakers of other men's sins, for nothing we do voluntarily encourage the slavery of our fellow men. . . .

The federal convention went as far as they could; the migration or immigration &c. is confined to the states, now existing only, new states cannot claim it. Congress, by their ordnance for erecting new states, some time since, declared that there shall be no slavery in them. But whether those in slavery in the southern states, will be emancipated after the year 1808, I do not pretend to determine: I rather doubt it.

SOURCE: Jonathan Elliot, ed., *The Debates . . . on the Adoption of the Federal Constitution* (Philadelphia: J. B. Lippincott, 1863), 1: 103–105, 107, 112, 117.

The People Debate Ratification

The procedure for ratifying the new constitution was as controversial as its contents. The delegates did not submit the Constitution to the state legislatures for their unanimous consent, as required by the Articles of Confederation, because they knew that Rhode Island (and perhaps other states) would reject it. So they arbitrarily specified that it would take effect when ratified by conventions in nine of the thirteen states. Because of its nationalist sympathies, the Confederation Congress winked at this extralegal procedure; surprisingly, most state legislatures also winked and called ratification conventions.

As the constitutional debate began in early 1788, the nationalists seized the initiative with two bold moves. First, they called themselves **Federalists**, suggesting that they supported a federal union—a loose, decentralized system—and obscuring their commitment to a strong national authority. Second, they launched a coordinated campaign in pamphlets and newspapers to explain and justify the Philadelphia constitution.

The opponents of the Constitution, the Antifederalists, had diverse backgrounds and motives. Some, like Governor George Clinton of New York, feared that state governments would lose power. Rural democrats protested that the proposed constitution, unlike most state constitutions, lacked a declaration of individual rights; they also feared that the central government would be run by wealthy men. "Lawyers and men of learning and monied men expect to be managers of this Constitution," worried a Massachusetts farmer, "they will swallow up all of us little folks . . . just as the whale swallowed up Jonah." Giving political substance to these fears, Melancton Smith of New York argued that the large electoral districts prescribed by the Constitution would restrict office holding to wealthy men, whereas the smaller districts used in state elections usually produced legislatures "composed principally of respectable yeomanry."

Smith spoke for many Americans who held traditional republican values. To keep government "close to the people," they wanted the nation of small sovereign republics tied together only for trade and defense—not the "United States" but the "States United." Citing French political philosopher Montesquieu, Antifederalists argued that republican institutions were best suited to cities or small states, a localist perspective that shaped American political thinking well into the twentieth century. "No extensive empire can be governed on republican principles," declared James Winthrop of Massachusetts. Patrick Henry predicted the Constitution would recreate the worst features of British rule: high taxes, an oppressive bureaucracy, a standing army, and a "great and mighty President . . . supported in extravagant munificence."

In New York, where ratification was hotly contested, James Madison, John Jay, and Alexander Hamilton defended the proposed constitution in a series of eighty-five essays collectively called *The Federalist*. *The Federalist* influenced political leaders throughout the country and was subsequently recognized as an important treatise of practical republicanism. Its authors denied that a centralized government would lead to domestic tyranny. Drawing on Montesquieu's theories and John Adams's *Thoughts on Government*, Madison, Jay, and Hamilton pointed out that authority would be divided among the president, a bicameral legislature, and a judiciary. Each branch of government would "check and balance" the others and so preserve liberty.

In "Federalist No. 10," Madison challenged the traditional belief that republican governments were suited only to small political units; rather, a large state would better protect republican liberty. It was "sown in the nature of man," Madison wrote, for individuals to seek power and form factions. Indeed, "a landed interest, a manufacturing interest, a mercantile interest, a moneyed interest, with many lesser interests, grow up of necessity in civilized nations." A free society should welcome such interests but keep any of them from becoming dominant—an end best achieved in a large republic. "Extend the sphere," Madison concluded, "and you take in a greater variety of parties and interests; you make it less probable that a majority of the whole will have a common motive to invade the rights of other citizens."

The delegates who debated these issues in the state ratification conventions included untutored farmers and middling artisans as well as educated gentlemen. Generally, backcountry delegates were Antifederalists, while those from the coast were Federalists. In Pennsylvania, Philadelphia merchants and artisans joined with commercial farmers to ratify the Constitution. Other early Federalist successes came in four less-populous states—Delaware, New Jersey, Georgia, and Connecticut—where delegates hoped a strong national government would offset the power of large neighboring states (Map 6.5).

The Constitution's first real test came in January 1788 in Massachusetts, a hotbed of Antifederalist sentiment. Influential Patriots, including Samuel Adams and Governor John Hancock, opposed the new constitution, as did many followers of Daniel Shays. But Boston artisans, who wanted tariff protection from British imports, supported ratification. To win over other delegates, Federalist leaders assured the convention that they would enact a national bill of rights. By a close vote of 187 to 168, the Federalists carried the day.

Spring brought Federalist victories in Maryland and South Carolina. When New Hampshire narrowly ratified the Constitution in June, the required nine states had approved it. But it took the powerful arguments advanced in *The Federalist* and more promises of a bill of rights to secure the Constitution's adoption in the essential states of Virginia and New York. The votes were close: 89 to 79 in Virginia and 30 to 27 in New York.

Testifying to their respect for popular sovereignty and majority rule, most Americans accepted the verdict of the ratifying conventions. "A decided majority" of the New Hampshire assembly had opposed the "new system," reported Joshua Atherton, but now they said, "It is adopted, let us try it." In Virginia, Patrick Henry vowed to "submit as a quiet citizen" and fight for amendments "in a constitutional way."

Working against great odds, the Federalists had created a national republic and partly restored an elitist system of political authority. They celebrated their triumph by forming great processions in the seaport cities. By marching in an orderly fashion —in conscious contrast to the riotous Revolutionary mobs—and carrying a copy of the Constitution on an "altar of liberty," Federalist-minded citizens affirmed their allegiance to a self-governing republican community and a **civil religion**.

▶ According to the nationalists, what were the central problems of the Articles of Confederation? How did the delegates to the Philadelphia convention address them?

▶ How did the Philadelphia convention resolve three controversial issues: the representation of large and small states, state power, and slavery?

▶ Who were the Antifederalists and why did they oppose the Constitution?

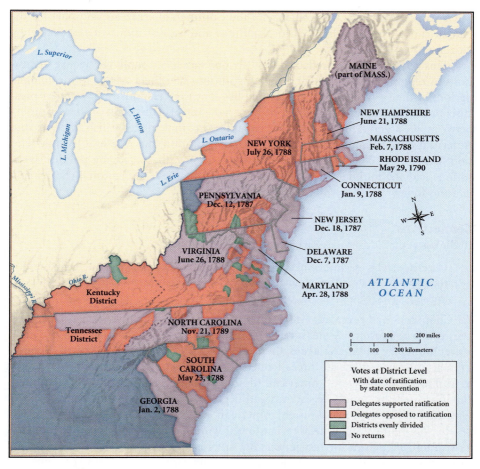

MAP 6.5 Ratifying the Constitution of 1787

In 1907, geographer Owen Libby mapped the votes of members of the state conventions that ratified the Constitution. His map showed that most delegates from seaboard or commercial farming districts, which sent many delegates to the conventions, supported the Constitution, while those from sparsely represented backcountry areas opposed it. Subsequent research has confirmed Libby's socioeconomic interpretation of the voting patterns in North and South Carolina and in Massachusetts. However, other factors influenced delegates elsewhere. For example, in Georgia, delegates from all regions voted for ratification.

SUMMARY

In this chapter, we examined the unfolding of two related sets of events. The first was the war between Britain and its rebellious colonies that began in 1776 and ended in 1783. Two great battles determined the outcome of that conflict: Saratoga in 1777 and Yorktown in 1781. Surprisingly, given the military might of the British empire, both were American victories. These triumphs testify to the determination of George Washington, the resilience of the Continental army, and support for the Patriot cause from hundreds of local militias and tens of thousands of taxpaying citizens.

This popular support reflected the Patriots' success in building effective institutions of republican government. These institutions had their origins in the colonial period, in the town meetings and assemblies that were responsive to popular pressure and increasingly independent of imperial control. They took on new meaning between 1776 and 1781 in the state constitutions that made British subjects into American citizens and in the first national constitution, the Articles of Confederation. Despite the challenges of the postwar economy, these fledging political institutions laid the foundation for the Constitution of 1787, the national charter that endures today.

Connections: Diplomacy

In the essay that introduces Part Two, we pointed out that

> [t]o create and preserve their new republic, Americans of European descent fought two wars against Great Britain, an undeclared war against France, and many battles with Indian peoples.

As Chapter 6 has revealed, American success in the War of Independence was the result, in substantial measure, of French assistance. The French first provided secret monetary and material aid; then, after 1778 and the formal Treaty of Alliance, French military and naval forces helped the Patriots to secure their great victory at Yorktown. It was astute American diplomacy by Benjamin Franklin and others that obtained this French assistance and negotiated a favorable peace treaty. As we will see in Chapter 7, subsequent American diplomatic efforts produced mixed results: The United States nearly went to war with France in 1798, failed to force the British and French to lift restrictions on American merchant vessels in 1807, and precipitated a second, nearly disastrous, war with Great Britain in 1812. Only the purchase of Louisiana from France in 1803 stands out as an unblemished American diplomatic triumph.

Still, the number of these diplomatic initiatives points out the crucial importance of relationships with foreign nations and Native American peoples in the first decades of the United States. Indian warfare and European entanglements—diplomatic, military, commercial, and ideological—stood at the center of American history and are a major focus of our discussion in Chapter 7.

FOR FURTHER EXPLORATION

For vivid accounts of the war, see John C. Dann, ed., *The Revolution Remembered: Eyewitness Accounts of the War for Independence* (1980). "The Virtual Marching Tour" at **www.ushistory.org/brandywine/index.html** offers a multimedia view of Howe's attack on Philadelphia.

Colin G. Calloway, *The American Revolution in Indian Country* (1995), traces the Revolution's impact on native peoples. "Africans in America: Revolution" (**www.pbs .org/wgbh/aia/part2/title.html**) explores the black wartime experience. For blacks who

TIMELINE

1776
- ▶ Second Continental Congress declares independence
- ▶ Howe forces Washington to retreat from New York and New Jersey
- ▶ Pennsylvania approves a democratic state constitution
- ▶ John Adams publishes *Thoughts on Government*

1777
- ▶ Articles of Confederation devised
- ▶ Patriot women contribute to war economy
- ▶ Howe occupies Philadelphia (September)
- ▶ Gates defeats Burgoyne at Saratoga (October)
- ▶ Severe inflation of paper currency begins

1778
- ▶ Franco-American alliance (February)
- ▶ Lord North seeks political settlement; Congress rejects negotiations
- ▶ British adopt southern strategy, capture Savannah (December)

1779
- ▶ British and American forces battle in Georgia

1780
- ▶ Sir Henry Clinton seizes Charleston (May)

- ▶ Guerrilla warfare in Carolinas
- ▶ French troops land in Rhode Island

1781
- ▶ Lord Cornwallis invades Virginia (April), surrenders at Yorktown (October)
- ▶ States ratify Articles of Confederation
- ▶ Large-scale Loyalist emigration

1783
- ▶ Treaty of Paris (September 3) ends war

1784–1785
- ▶ Congress enacts ordinances for new states

1786
- ▶ Nationalists hold convention in Annapolis, Maryland
- ▶ Shays's Rebellion roils Massachusetts

1787
- ▶ Congress passes Northwest Ordinance
- ▶ Constitutional Convention in Philadelphia

1787–1788
- ▶ Jay, Madison, and Hamilton write *The Federalist*
- ▶ Eleven states ratify U.S. Constitution

emigrated to Canada, see **http://epe.lac-bac.gc.ca/100/205/301/ic/cdc/blackloyalists/index.htm** and **http://museum.gov.ns.ca/blackloyalists/index.htm**.

Two important studies of women are Mary Beth Norton, *Liberty's Daughters: The Revolutionary Experience of American Women, 1750–1800* (1980), and Carol Berkin, *Revolutionary Mothers: Women in the Struggle for America's Independence* (2005). For a woman who went to war, see "Masquerade: Deborah Sampson, Continental Soldier" (**forum.wgbh.org/wgbh/forum.php?lecture_id=1654**).

For a dramatic retelling of the Constitutional Convention, see Catherine Drinker Bowen's *Miracle at Philadelphia* (1966). Jack Rakove's *Original Meanings: Politics and Ideas in the Making of the Constitution* (1996) offers a more complex analysis. Michael Kammen, *A Machine That Would Go by Itself* (1986), surveys the changing reputation of the Constitution. David Waldstreicher, *In the Midst of Perpetual Fetes: The Making of American Nationalism, 1776–1820* (1997), probes the meaning of public celebrations.

TEST YOUR KNOWLEDGE

To assess your mastery of the material in this chapter and for Web sites, images, and documents related to this chapter, visit **bedfordstmartins.com/henrettaconcise**.

Politics and Society in the New Republic
1787–1820

The power of the people,
if uncontroverted, is
licentious and mobbish.

— Fisher Ames, Massachusetts
Federalist, 1794

Like an earthquake, the American Revolution shook the European monarchical order, and its aftershocks reverberated for decades. By "creating a new republic based on the rights of the individual, the North Americans introduced a new force into the world," the eminent German historian Leopold von Ranke warned the king of Bavaria in 1854, a force that might cost the monarch his throne. Before 1776, "a king who ruled by the grace of God had been the center around which everything turned. Now the idea emerged that power should come from below [from the people]."

Other republican-inspired upheavals—England's Puritan Revolution of the 1640s and the French Revolution of 1789—had ended in political chaos and military rule. Similar fates befell many Latin American republics that won independence from Spain in the early nineteenth century. But the American states somehow escaped social anarchy and military dictatorship. When the War of Independence ended in 1783, General George Washington left public life to manage his plantation, astonishing European observers. "'Tis a Conduct so novel," American painter John Trumbull reported from London, that it is "inconceivable to People [here]." Washington's voluntary retirement bolstered the authority of elected Patriot leaders, who were fashioning representative republican governments.

This great task absorbed the energy and intellect of an entire generation. As Americans wrote constitutions and enacted new laws, political leaders worried that the measures were too democratic and self-interested. When a bill came before a state legislature, Connecticut conservative Ezra Stiles grumbled, every elected official "instantly thinks how it will affect his constituents" rather than how it would affect the general welfare. What Stiles criticized as the irresponsible pursuit of personal and group advantage, most Americans welcomed. The concerns of ordinary citizens had taken center stage in the halls of government, and the monarchs of Europe trembled.

The Political Crisis of the 1790s

The final decade of the eighteenth century brought fresh challenges for American politics. The Federalists split into two irreconcilable factions over financial policy and the French Revolution. Their leaders, Alexander Hamilton and Thomas Jefferson, offered contrasting visions of the future. Would the United States remain, as Jefferson hoped, an agricultural nation governed by local and state officials? Or would Hamilton's vision of a strong national government and an economy based on manufacturing become reality?

The Federalists Implement the Constitution

The Constitution expanded the dimensions of political life: Previously, voters had elected local and state officials; now they chose national leaders as well. The Federalists swept the election of 1788, winning forty-four seats in the first House of Representatives; only eight Antifederalists won election. As expected, members of the Electoral College chose George Washington as president. John Adams received the second highest number of electoral votes and became vice president.

Once the military savior of his country, Washington now became its political father. At age fifty-seven, the first president was a man of great personal dignity. Knowing he would be setting precedents, Washington proceeded cautiously. He adopted many of the administrative practices of the Confederation and asked Congress to reestablish the existing executive departments: Foreign Affairs (State), Finance (Treasury), and War. He initiated one important practice: The Constitution required the Senate's approval for the appointment of major officials, but Washington insisted that the president had sole authority to remove them, thus ensuring the executive's control over the bureaucracy. To head the Department of State, Washington chose Thomas Jefferson, a fellow Virginian and an experienced diplomat. For secretary of the treasury, he turned to Alexander Hamilton, a lawyer and Washington's military aide during the war. The president designated Jefferson, Hamilton, and Secretary of War Henry Knox as his cabinet, or advisory body.

The Constitution mandated a supreme court, but the Philadelphia convention left to Congress the task of creating other national courts. The Federalists in Congress wanted strong national institutions, and the Judiciary Act of 1789 reflected their vision. The act established a federal district court in each state and three circuit courts to hear appeals from the districts, with the Supreme Court having the final say. The Judiciary Act also allowed cases involving federal laws and powers that were decided in state courts to be appealed to the Supreme Court. This provision ensured that federal judges would have the final say on the meaning of the Constitution.

The Federalists kept their promise to add a declaration of rights to the Constitution. James Madison, now a member of the House of Representatives, submitted nineteen amendments to the First Congress; by 1791, ten had been approved by Congress and ratified by the states. These ten amendments, known as the Bill of Rights, safeguard fundamental personal rights, including freedom of speech and religion, and mandate trial by jury and other legal procedures that protect individual citizens. By easing Antifederalists' concerns about an oppressive national government, the amendments secured the legitimacy of the Constitution. They also addressed, but did not resolve, the issue of federalism: the proper balance between national and state power. That question was extremely controversial until the Civil War and remains important today.

Hamilton's Financial Program

George Washington's most important decision was his choice of Alexander Hamilton as secretary of the treasury. An ambitious self-made man of great charm and intelligence, Hamilton had married into the Schuyler family, influential Hudson River Valley landowners, and had become a prominent lawyer in New York City. At the Philadelphia convention, he took a strongly conservative stance, condemning the "democratic spirit" and calling for an authoritarian government and a president with near-monarchical powers.

As treasury secretary, Hamilton devised bold policies to enhance national authority and to favor financiers and merchants. He outlined his plans in three path-breaking reports to Congress: on public credit (January 1790), on a national bank (December 1790), and on manufactures (December 1791). These reports outlined a coherent program of national mercantilism—in other words, government-assisted economic development.

The financial and social implications of Hamilton's "Report on the Public Credit" made it instantly controversial. Hamilton asked Congress to redeem at face value the $55 million in securities issued by the Confederation that were held by foreign and domestic investors and speculators. He reasoned that as an underdeveloped nation, the United States was heavily dependent on loans from Dutch and British financiers and needed good credit. However, his redemption plan would give enormous profits to speculators, who had bought up depreciated securities. For example, a Massachusetts merchant firm, Burrell & Burrell, had paid $600 for Confederation notes with a face value of $2,500; it stood to reap a profit of $1,900. Such windfall gains offended a majority of Americans, who worked hard for their living and rejected the speculative practices of capitalist financiers. Equally controversial was Hamilton's proposal to pay the Burrells and other Confederation note holders with new interest-bearing securities, thereby creating a permanent **national debt**.

Hamilton's plan for a national debt owned mostly by wealthy families reawakened the fears of Radical Whigs and "Old Republicans." Speaking for the Virginia House of Burgesses, Patrick Henry condemned this plan "to erect, and concentrate, and perpetuate a large monied interest" and warned that it would prove "fatal to the existence of American liberty." James Madison challenged the morality of Hamilton's redemption proposal. Madison demanded that Congress consider the original owners of Confederation securities: the thousands of shopkeepers, farmers, and soldiers who had bought or accepted the securities during the dark days of the war and later sold them to speculators. However, it would have been difficult to trace the original owners, and nearly half the members of the House of Representatives owned Confederation securities and would profit personally from Hamilton's plan. Melding practicality with self-interest, the House rejected Madison's suggestion.

Hamilton then proposed that the national government enhance the public credit by assuming the war debts of the states, some $22 million, a plan that would also favor wealthy creditors. Knowing Hamilton's intentions in advance, Assistant Secretary of the

Treasury William Duer and his associates secretly bought up the war bonds of southern states at cheap rates. Congressional critics of Hamilton's assumption plan condemned Duer's speculation. They also pointed out that some states had already paid off their war debts; in response, Hamilton promised to reimburse those states. Representatives from Virginia and Maryland worried that assumption would enhance the already excessive financial sway of the national government. To quiet their fears, the treasury chief agreed to locate the permanent national capital along the banks of the Potomac, where suspicious southerners could easily watch its operations. Such astute bargaining gave Hamilton the votes he needed to enact both his redemption and assumption plans.

In December 1790, Hamilton issued a second report asking Congress to charter the Bank of the United States, to be jointly owned by private stockholders and the national government. Hamilton argued that the bank would provide financial stability to the specie-starved American economy by making loans to merchants, handling government funds, and issuing bills of credit. These potential benefits persuaded Congress to grant Hamilton's bank a twenty-year charter and send the legislation to the president for his approval.

At this critical juncture, Secretary of State Thomas Jefferson joined with James Madison to oppose Hamilton's financial initiatives. Jefferson had already condemned Duer and the "corrupt squadron of paper dealers" who speculated in southern war bonds. Now he charged that Hamilton's national bank was unconstitutional. "The incorporation of a Bank," Jefferson told President Washington, was not a power expressly "delegated to the United States by the Constitution." Jefferson's argument rested on a *strict* interpretation of the national charter. Hamilton preferred a *loose* interpretation; he told Washington that Article 1, Section 8, empowered Congress to make "all Laws which shall be necessary and proper" to carry out the provisions of the Constitution. Agreeing with Hamilton, the president signed the legislation.

Hamilton now undertook to raise the revenue to pay the annual interest on the national debt. At his insistence, Congress imposed domestic excise taxes, including a duty on whiskey distilled in the United States. These taxes would yield $1 million a year. To raise another $4 million to $5 million, the treasury secretary proposed higher tariffs on foreign imports. Although Hamilton's "Report on Manufactures" (1791) urged the nation to become self-sufficient in manufacturing, he did not support high **protective tariffs** that would exclude foreign products. Rather, he advocated moderate **revenue tariffs** that would pay the interest on the debt and defray the expenses of the national government.

Hamilton's scheme worked brilliantly. As American trade increased, customs revenue rose steadily and defrayed the annual interest on the national debt. Ample tariff revenues also had the unexpected effect of encouraging rapid settlement of the West. Because import duties covered federal government expenses, Congress sold lands in the national domain at ever-lower prices, a policy outcome opposed by Hamilton and favored by his Jeffersonian opponents. In any event, the treasury secretary had devised a strikingly modern fiscal system that provided the new national government with financial stability.

Jefferson's Agrarian Vision

Hamilton paid a high political price for his success. Even before Washington began his second four-year term in 1793, Hamilton's financial measures had split the Federalists into two irreconcilable factions. Most northern Federalists adhered to Hamilton's faction, while most southern Federalists joined a rival group headed by Madison and Jefferson. By the elections of 1794, the two factions had acquired names. Hamilton's supporters remained Federalists; Madison and Jefferson's allies called themselves Democratic Republicans or simply Republicans.

Thomas Jefferson spoke for southern planters and western farmers. Well-read in architecture, natural history, agricultural science, and political theory, Jefferson embraced the optimism of the Enlightenment. He believed in the "improvability of the human race" and deplored the corruption and social divisions that threatened its progress. Having seen the poverty of laborers in British factories, Jefferson doubted that wageworkers had the economic and political independence needed to sustain a republican polity.

Jefferson therefore set his democratic vision of America in an agricultural society of yeomen farm families. "Those who labor in the earth are the chosen people of God," he wrote in *Notes on the State of Virginia* (1785). The grain and meat from their farms would feed European nations, which "would manufacture and send us in exchange our clothes and other comforts." Jefferson's notion of an international division of labor resembled that proposed by Scottish economist Adam Smith in *The Wealth of Nations* (1776).

Turmoil in Europe brought Jefferson's vision closer to reality. The French Revolution began in 1789; four years later, France's new republican government went to war against a British-led coalition of monarchies. As fighting disrupted European farming, wheat prices leaped from 5 to 8 shillings a bushel and remained high for twenty years, bringing substantial profits to Chesapeake and Middle Atlantic farmers. "Our farmers have never experienced such prosperity," remarked one observer. Simultaneously, a boom in the export of raw cotton, fueled by the invention of the cotton gin and the mechanization of cloth production in Britain (see Chapter 9), boosted the economies of Georgia and South Carolina. As Jefferson had hoped, European markets brought prosperity to American agriculturalists.

The French Revolution Divides Americans

American merchants profited even more handsomely from the European war. In 1793, President Washington issued a Proclamation of Neutrality, allowing U.S. citizens to trade with all belligerents. As neutral carriers, American merchant ships were initially allowed to pass through the British naval blockade of French ports, and Americans quickly took over the lucrative sugar trade between France and its West Indian islands. Commercial earnings rose spectacularly, averaging $20 million annually in the 1790s — twice the value of cotton and tobacco exports. As the American merchant fleet increased from 355,000 tons in 1790 to 1.1 million tons in 1808, northern shipbuilders and merchants provided work for thousands of shipwrights, sailmakers, laborers, and seamen. Carpenters, masons, and cabinetmakers in Boston, New York, and Philadelphia found work building warehouses and fashionable "Federal-style" town houses for newly affluent merchants. In Philadelphia, a European visitor reported, "a great number of private houses have marble steps to the street door, and in other respects are finished in a style of elegance."

Federalist Gentry

A prominent New England Federalist, Oliver Ellsworth served as chief justice of the United States from 1796 to 1800. His wife, Abigail Wolcott Ellsworth, was the daughter of a Connecticut governor. In 1792, portraitist Ralph Earl captured the Ellsworths' aspirations by depicting the couple as landed gentry and prominently displaying their mansion (in the window). Like other Federalists who tried to reconcile their wealth and social authority with republican values, Ellsworth dressed with restraint, and his manners, remarked Timothy Dwight, were "wholly destitute of haughtiness and arrogance." Wadsworth Atheneum, Hartford.

Even as Americans profited from the European struggle, they argued passionately over its ideologies. Most Americans had welcomed the French Revolution of 1789 because it abolished feudalism and established a constitutional monarchy. The creation of the First French Republic in 1792 was more controversial. Some Americans applauded the downfall of the monarchy. Urban artisans embraced the egalitarian ideology of the Jacobins, a radical French group, and followed their example by addressing one another as "citizen" and starting democratic political clubs. However, Americans with strong religious beliefs condemned the new French government for rejecting Christianity, closing churches, and promoting a rational religion based on "natural morality." Fearing social revolution at home, wealthy Americans condemned Robespierre and his radical republican followers for executing King Louis XVI and 3,000 aristocrats (see Voices from Abroad, p. 199).

Their fears were well founded. Ideological conflicts and discontent over Hamilton's economic policies sparked a domestic insurgency. In 1794, western Pennsylvania farmers, already angered by the state's conservative fiscal policies, mounted the so-called

Peter Porcupine Attacks Pro-French Americans   WILLIAM COBBETT

The Democratic Republican followers of Thomas Jefferson declared that "he who is an enemy to the French Revolution, cannot be a firm republican." William Cobbett, a British journalist who settled in Philadelphia and wrote under the pen name "Peter Porcupine," rejected that proposition. A strong supporter of the Federalist Party, Cobbett attacked its opponents in caustic and widely read pamphlets and newspaper articles like this one of 1796.

France is a republic, and the decrees of the Legislators were necessary to maintain it a republic. This word outweighs, in the estimation of some persons (I wish I could say they were few in number), all the horrors that have been and that can be committed in that country. One of these modern republicans will tell you that he does not deny that hundreds of thousands of innocent persons have been murdered in France; . . . that its commerce, its manufactures, its sciences, its arts, and its honour, are no more; but at the end of all this, he will tell you that it must be happy, because it is a republic. I have heard more than one of these republican zealots declare, that he would sooner see the last of the French exterminated, than see them adopt any other form of government. Such a sentiment is characteristic of a mind locked up in a savage ignorance.

Shall we say that these things never can take place among us? . . . We are not what we were before the French revolution. Political projectors from every corner of Europe, troublers of society of every description, from the whining philosophical hypocrite to the daring rebel, and more daring blasphemer, have taken shelter in these States.

We have seen the guillotine toasted to three times three cheers. . . . And what would the reader say, were I to tell him of a Member of Congress, who wished to see one of these murderous machines employed for lopping off the heads of the French, permanent in the State-house yard of the city of Philadelphia?

If these men of blood had succeeded in plunging us into a war; if they had once got the sword into their hands, they would have mowed us down like stubble. The word Aristocrat would have been employed to as good account here, as ever it had been in France. We might, ere this, have seen our places of worship turned into stables; we might have seen the banks of the Delaware, like those of the Loire, covered with human carcasses, and its waters tinged with blood: ere this we might have seen our parents butchered, and even the head of our admired and beloved President rolling on a scaffold.

I know the reader will start back with horror. His heart will tell him that it is impossible. But, once more, let him look at the example before us. The attacks on the character and conduct of the aged Washington, have been as bold, if not bolder, than those which led to the downfall of the unfortunate French Monarch [Louis XVI, executed in 1793]. Can it then be imagined, that, had they possessed the power, they wanted the will to dip their hands in his blood?

SOURCE: William Cobbett, *Peter Porcupine in America*, ed. David A. Wilson (Ithaca: Cornell University Press, 1994), 150–154.

Whiskey Rebellion to protest Hamilton's excise tax on spirits. The tax had cut the demand for the corn whiskey the farmers brewed and bartered for eastern manufactures. Like the Sons of Liberty in 1765 and the Shaysites in 1786, the Whiskey Rebels assailed the tax collectors who sent the farmers' hard-earned money to a distant government. But the protesters also waved banners proclaiming the French revolutionary slogan "Liberty, Equality, and Fraternity!" To deter popular rebellion and uphold national authority, President Washington raised an army of 12,000 troops and dispersed the Whiskey Rebels.

Britain's maritime strategy increased political divisions in America. Beginning in late 1793, the British navy stopped American ships carrying French sugar and other goods, eventually seizing 250 vessels. Hoping to protect merchant property through diplomacy, Washington dispatched John Jay to Britain. But Jay returned with a controversial treaty. It ignored the merchants' argument that "free ships make free goods" and accepted Britain's right to remove French property from neutral ships. The treaty also required the U.S. government to make "full and complete compensation" to British merchants for pre–Revolutionary War debts owed by American citizens. In return, the agreement allowed American merchants to submit claims for illegal seizures and required the British to remove their troops and Indian agents from the Northwest Territory. Republicans attacked Jay's Treaty for being too conciliatory, but in 1795, the Senate ratified it by the bare two-thirds majority required by the Constitution. As long as Hamilton and the Federalists were in power, the United States would have a pro-British foreign policy.

The Rise of Political Parties

The appearance of Federalists and Republicans marked a new stage in American politics — what historians call the First Party System. Although colonial legislatures had often divided into factions based on family, ethnicity, or region, they did not have organized political parties. Nor did the new state and national constitutions make any provision for political societies. In fact, most Americans thought parties were dangerous because they were self-interested. Following classical republican principles, political leaders asserted that voters and legislators should act independently and for the public interest. Thus, Senator Pierce Butler of South Carolina criticized his congressional colleagues as "men scrambling for partial advantage, State interests, and in short, a train of narrow, impolitic measures."

But classical republican principles collapsed in the face of sharp conflicts over Hamilton's fiscal policies. Most merchants, creditors, and urban artisans supported the Federalist party and its policies, as did wheat-exporting slaveholders in the Tidewater districts of the Chesapeake. The emerging Republican coalition was more diverse. It included not only southern tobacco and rice planters and debt-conscious western farmers but also Germans and Scots-Irish in the southern backcountry and subsistence farmers in the Northeast.

Party identity crystallized in 1796. To prepare for the presidential election, Federalist and Republican leaders called caucuses in Congress and conventions in the states. They also mobilized popular support by organizing public festivals and processions: The Federalists held banquets to celebrate Washington's birthday in February, and the

Republicans marched through the streets to honor the Declaration of Independence on July fourth.

In the election, voters favored Federalist candidates, giving them a majority in Congress and electing John Adams to the presidency. Adams continued Hamilton's pro-British foreign policy and reacted sharply to seizures of American merchant ships by the French navy. When the French foreign minister Talleyrand solicited a loan and a bribe from American diplomats to stop the seizures, Adams charged that Talleyrand's agents, whom he dubbed X, Y, and Z, had insulted America's honor. In response to the XYZ Affair, the Federalist-controlled Congress cut off trade with France in 1798 and authorized American privateers to seize French ships. The United States and France were waging an undeclared maritime war.

Constitutional Crisis, 1798–1800

Ominously, the controversial foreign policy of the Federalists prompted domestic protest and governmental repression. Republican-minded immigrants from Ireland vehemently attacked Adams's pro-British foreign policy. A Federalist pamphleteer in Philadelphia responded in kind: "Were I president, I would hang them for otherwise they would murder me." To silence its critics, the Federalist-controlled Congress enacted three coercive laws that limited individual rights and threatened the fledgling party system. The Naturalization Act lengthened the residency requirement for American citizenship from five to fourteen years; the Alien Act authorized the deportation of foreigners; and the Sedition Act prohibited the publication of insults or malicious attacks on the president or members of Congress. "He that is not for us is against us," thundered the Federalist *Gazette of the United States*. Using the Sedition Act, Federalist prosecutors arrested more than twenty Republican newspaper editors and politicians, accused them of sedition, and convicted and jailed a number of them.

What followed was a constitutional crisis. With justification, Republicans charged that the Sedition Act violated the First Amendment's prohibition against "abridging the freedom of speech, or of the press." However, they did not appeal to the Supreme Court because the Court's power to review congressional legislation was uncertain and because most of the justices were Federalists. Instead, Madison and Jefferson looked to the state legislatures. At their urging, the Kentucky and Virginia legislatures issued resolutions in 1798 declaring the Alien and Sedition Acts to be "unauthoritative, void, and of no force." The resolutions set forth a **states' rights** interpretation of the Constitution, asserting that the states had a "right to judge" the legitimacy of national laws.

The conflict over the Sedition Act set the stage for the presidential election of 1800. Jefferson, once opposed on principle to political parties, now saw them as a valuable way "to watch and relate to the people" the activities of an oppressive government. With opposition to the French conflict growing and Jefferson preparing for a presidential bid, John Adams reevaluated his foreign policy. Adams was a complicated man: He was easily offended but had great integrity and a strong will. Rejecting Hamilton's advice to declare war against France (and benefit from an upsurge in patriotism), Adams put country ahead of party and entered into diplomatic negotiations that ended the fighting.

Despite Adams's statesmanship, the campaign of 1800 degenerated into name-calling. The Federalists attacked Jefferson's beliefs, branding him an irresponsible pro-French radical and, because he opposed state support of religion in Virginia, "the arch-apostle of irreligion and free thought." Both parties changed state election laws to favor their candidates. In fact, tensions ran so high that rumors circulated of a Federalist plot to stage a military coup.

The election did not end these worries. Thanks to a low Federalist turnout in Virginia and Pennsylvania and the three-fifths rule (which boosted electoral votes in the southern states), Jefferson won a narrow 73 to 65 victory over Adams in the Electoral College. However, the Republican electors also gave 73 votes to Aaron Burr of New York, who was Jefferson's vice presidential running mate. The Constitution specified that in the case of a tie vote, the House of Representatives would choose between the candidates. For thirty-five rounds of balloting, Federalists in the House blocked Jefferson's election, prompting a rumor that Virginia was raising a military force to put Jefferson into office.

Ironically, arch-Federalist Alexander Hamilton ushered in a more democratic era by supporting Jefferson. Calling Burr an "embryo Caesar" and the "most unfit man in the United States for the office of president," Hamilton persuaded key Federalists to allow Jefferson's election. The Federalists' concern for political stability also played a role. As Senator James Bayard of Delaware explained, "It was admitted on all hands that we must risk the Constitution and a Civil War or take Mr. Jefferson."

► What was Hamilton's vision of the future? What policies did he implement to achieve it? How was Jefferson's vision different?

► What were the consequences of the French Revolution in America? How did it affect the development of American politics?

Jefferson called the election the "Revolution of 1800," and so it was. The bloodless transfer of power showed that governments elected by the people could be changed in an orderly way, even in times of bitter partisan conflict. In his inaugural address in 1801, Jefferson praised this achievement, declaring, "We are all Republicans, we are all Federalists." Defying the predictions of European conservatives, the American republican experiment of 1776 had survived a quarter century of economic and political turmoil.

The Westward Movement and the Jeffersonian Revolution

The United States "is a country in flux," a visiting French aristocrat observed in 1799, and "that which is true today as regards its population, its establishments, its prices, its commerce will not be true six months from now." Indeed, the American republic was beginning a period of dynamic westward expansion; between 1790 and 1810, farm families settled as much land as they had during the entire colonial period. George Washington, himself a western land speculator, noted approvingly that ordinary men—the Sons of Liberty—were quickly becoming "the lords and proprietors of a vast tract of continent." Unfortunately for Washington's Federalist Party, most western farmers supported Thomas Jefferson's Republicans.

The Expanding Republic and Native American Resistance

In the Treaty of Paris of 1783, Great Britain relinquished its claims to the trans-Appalachian region and, as one British diplomat put it, left the Indian nations "to the care of their [American] neighbours." *Care* was hardly the right term: Many white Americans wanted to destroy native communities and even the native peoples themselves. "Cut up every Indian Cornfield and burn every Indian town," proclaimed William Henry Drayton, a congressman from South Carolina, so that their "nation be extirpated and the lands become the property of the public." Other leaders, including Henry Knox, Washington's first secretary of war, favored assimilating native peoples into Euro-American society. Tribal lands held in common would be divided among individual Indian families, who would become citizens of the various states. This debate among whites over Indian policy would have an important place on the nation's agenda until 1900, and it continues even today.

Not surprisingly, the major struggle between native peoples and whites centered on land. Invoking the Treaty of Paris and regarding Britain's Indian allies as conquered peoples, the U.S. government asserted its ownership of the trans-Appalachian West. Indian nations rejected that claim, insisting that they had not been conquered and had not signed the Paris treaty. Brushing aside those objections, U.S. commissioners threatened military action to force the pro-British Iroquois peoples—Mohawks, Onondagas, Cayugas, and Senecas—to cede huge tracts in New York and Pennsylvania in the Treaty of Fort Stanwix (1784). New York officials and land speculators used liquor and bribes to take title to millions of additional acres, confining the once powerful Iroquois to reservations.

American negotiators used similar tactics to grab western lands. In 1785, they persuaded the Chippewas, Delawares, Ottawas, and Wyandots to sign away most of the future state of Ohio. The tribes quickly repudiated the agreements, justifiably claiming they were made under duress. To defend their lands, they joined with the Shawnee, Miami, and Potawatomi peoples in the Western Confederacy. Led by Miami chief Little Turtle, confederacy warriors crushed American expeditionary forces sent by President Washington in 1790 and 1791.

Fearing an alliance between the Western Confederacy and the British in Canada, Washington doubled the size of the U.S. Army and ordered General "Mad Anthony" Wayne to lead a new expedition. In August 1794, Wayne defeated the Indians in the Battle of Fallen Timbers (near present-day Toledo, Ohio), but the resistance continued. In the Treaty of Greenville (1795), American negotiators acknowledged Indian ownership of the land. But the Western Confederacy ceded most of Ohio and various strategic sites along the Great Lakes; they also agreed to place themselves "under the protection of the United States, and no other Power whatever." Faced with these American advances, Britain reduced its trade with trans-Appalachian Indian peoples and, following Jay's Treaty (1795), slowly removed its military garrisons (Map 7.1).

The Greenville Treaty sparked a wave of white migration. By 1805, Ohio, a state for just two years, had more than 100,000 residents. Thousands more farm families moved into the future states of Indiana and Illinois, sparking new conflicts with native peoples over land and hunting rights. Declared one Delaware Indian: "The Elks are our horses, the buffaloes are our cows, the deer are our sheep, & the whites shan't have them."

Treaty Negotiations at Greenville, 1795

In 1785, a number of Indian tribes formed the Western Confederacy to prevent white settlement north of the Ohio River. The American victory at the Battle of Fallen Timbers (1794) and the subsequent Treaty of Greenville (1795) opened up the region for white farmers. But the treaty acknowledged many Indian rights because of their near equality in military power. The artist suggests this equality: Notice the height and stately bearing of the Indian leaders and their placement slightly in front of the American officers. Unknown, *Treaty of Greenville*, n.d., Chicago Historical Society.

For more help analyzing this image, see the Online Study Guide at **bedfordstmartins.com/henrettaconcise**.

To alleviate such conflicts, the U.S. government encouraged Native Americans to assimilate into white society. The goal, as one Kentucky Protestant minister put it, was to make the Indian "a farmer, a citizen of the United States, and a Christian." But most Indians rejected assimilation. Even those who embraced Christian teachings retained many of their ancestral values. To think of themselves as individuals or members of a nuclear family, as white Americans were demanding, meant repudiating the clan, the very essence of Indian life. To preserve their traditional cultures, many Indian communities expelled white missionaries and forced Christianized Indians to participate in tribal rites. As a Munsee prophet declared, "There are two ways to God, one for the whites and one for the Indians."

A few Indian leaders sought a middle path. Among the Senecas, the prophet Handsome Lake encouraged traditional animistic ceremonies that gave thanks to the sun, the earth, water, plants, and animals. But he included Christian elements in his teachings — the concepts of heaven and hell, for example — to deter his followers from alcohol, gambling, and witchcraft. Handsome Lake's doctrines divided

MAP 7.1 Indian Cessions and State Formation, 1776–1840

By virtue of the Treaty of Paris with Britain (1783), the United States claimed sovereignty over the entire trans-Appalachian West. The Western Confederacy contested this claim, but the U.S. government upheld it with military force. By 1840, armed diplomacy had forced most Native American peoples to move west of the Mississippi River. White settlers occupied their lands, formed territorial governments, and eventually entered the Union as members of separate — and equal — states.

the Senecas into hostile factions. A conservative group, led by Chief Red Jacket, condemned Indians who accepted white ways and demanded a return to ancestral customs.

Most Indians also rejected the efforts of American missionaries to turn warriors into farmers and women into domestic helpmates. Among eastern woodland peoples, women grew corn, beans, and squash — the mainstays of the Indians' diet — and land cultivation rights passed through the female line. Consequently, women exercised considerable political influence, which they were eager to retain. Nor were Indian men interested in becoming farmers. When war raiding and hunting were no longer possible, they turned to grazing cattle and sheep.

Migration and the Changing Farm Economy

Native American resistance slowed the advance of white settlers but did not stop it. In the years between 1790 and 1820, two great streams of migrants moved out of the southern states. One stream, composed primarily of white tenant farmers and struggling yeomen families, flocked through the Cumberland Gap into Kentucky and Tennessee. "Boundless settlements open a door for our citizens to run off and leave us," a worried eastern landlord lamented in the *Maryland Gazette*, "depreciating all our landed property and disabling us from paying taxes." Many migrants were, in fact, fleeing from this planter-controlled society. They wanted more freedom and hoped to prosper by growing cotton and hemp, which were in great demand.

But many settlers in Kentucky and Tennessee lacked ready cash to buy land. Like the North Carolina Regulators in the 1770s, some poor migrants claimed a customary right to occupy "back waste vacant Lands" sufficient "to provide a subsistence for themselves and their posterity." Virginia legislators, who administered the Kentucky Territory, had a more elitist vision. Although they allowed poor settlers to purchase up to 1,400 acres of land at reduced prices, they sold or granted huge estates of 20,000 to 200,000 acres to scores of wealthy men. When Kentucky became a state in 1792, a handful of land speculators owned one-fourth of the state, while half the white men owned no land and lived as squatters or tenant farmers.

Widespread landlessness—and opposition to slavery—prompted a new migration across the Ohio River into the future states of Ohio, Indiana, and Illinois. In a free community, thought Peter Cartwright, a Methodist lay preacher from southwestern Kentucky who moved to Illinois, "I would be entirely clear of the evil of slavery . . . [and] could raise my children to work where work was not thought a degradation."

Meanwhile, a second stream of southern migrants, made up of slave-owning planters and enslaved African Americans from the Carolinas, moved along the coastal plain toward the Gulf of Mexico. The migrants set up new plantations in the interior of Georgia and South Carolina. Then they moved into the Old Southwest, the future states of Alabama, Mississippi, and Louisiana. "The Alabama Feaver rages here with great violence," a North Carolina planter remarked, "and has carried off vast numbers of our Citizens."

Cotton was key to this migratory surge. Beginning around 1750, the demand for raw wool and cotton increased dramatically as water-powered spinning jennies, weaving mules, and other technological innovations boosted textile production in Europe. South Carolina and Georgia planters began growing cotton, and American inventors—including Connecticut-born Eli Whitney—built machines (called gins) that efficiently extracted seeds from strands of cotton. To grow cotton, the planters imported about 115,000 Africans between 1776 and 1808, when Congress cut off the Atlantic slave trade. The cotton boom financed the rapid settlement of Mississippi and Alabama—in a single year, a government land office in Huntsville, Alabama, sold $7 million of uncleared land—and the two states entered the Union in 1817 and 1819, respectively.

As southern whites and blacks moved across the Appalachians and along the Gulf Coast, a third stream of migrants flowed out of the overcrowded communities of New England. Previous generations of Massachusetts and Connecticut farm families had moved north and east, settling New Hampshire, Vermont, and Maine. Now farmers throughout New England were moving west. Seeking land for their children, thousands of parents packed their wagons with tools and household goods and migrated to New York. By 1820, almost 800,000 New England migrants lived in a string of settlements that stretched from Albany to Buffalo, and many others had moved on to Ohio and Indiana. This vast migration was organized by the settlers, who often moved in large family or religious groups. One traveler reported from central New York: "The town of Herkimer is entirely populated by families come from Connecticut. We stayed at Mr. Snow's who came from New London with about ten male and female cousins." Throughout the Northwest Territory, many new communities were fragments of New England communities that had moved inland.

In New York, as in Kentucky, well-connected speculators snapped up much of the best land. In the 1780s, financier Robert Morris acquired 1.3 million acres in the Genesee region of central New York. The Wadsworth family bought thousands of

Hop Picking, **1801**
Farm labor was nothing new for rural women and children, who had always worked on the farm. What was different after 1800 was the growing number of outworkers: landless or poor families who labored as wageworkers for shopkeepers and manufacturers. In this romanticized watercolor by Lucy Sheldon, a schoolgirl at the Litchfield Female Academy in Connecticut, a young couple and their children pick hops, which they will deliver to a storekeeper or local brewer to be made into beer. Litchfield Historical Society.

acres, seeking to reproduce the manorial system of the Hudson River Valley. To attract tenants, the Wadsworths leased farms rent-free for the first seven years, after which they charged rents. Many New England families chose to buy farms. They signed contracts with the Holland Land Company, a Dutch-owned syndicate of speculators, which allowed settlers to pay for their farms as they worked them.

The new farm economy in the trans-Appalachian West forced major changes in eastern agriculture. Unable to compete with lower-priced New York grains, farmers in New England switched to potatoes, which were high yielding and nutritious. To compensate for the labor of sons and daughters who had moved inland, Middle Atlantic farmers bought more efficient farm equipment. They replaced metal-tipped wooden plows with cast-iron models that dug deeper and required a single yoke of oxen instead of two. Such changes in crop mix and technology kept production high even with fewer workers.

Easterners also used the progressive farming methods touted by British agricultural reformers. "Improvers" in Pennsylvania doubled their average yield per acre by rotating their crops and planting nitrogen-rich clover to offset nutrient-hungry wheat and corn. Yeomen farmers diversified production by raising sheep and selling the wool to textile manufacturers. Many farmers adopted a year-round planting cycle, sowing corn in the spring for animal fodder and then planting winter wheat in September for market sale. Women and girls milked the family cows and made butter and cheese to sell in the growing towns and cities.

White families now worked harder and longer, but their efforts were rewarded with higher output and a better standard of living. Whether hacking fields out of western forests or carting manure to replenish eastern soils, farmers increased their productivity. Westward migration had boosted the farming economy throughout the country.

The Jeffersonian Presidency

From 1801 to 1825, three Republicans from Virginia—Thomas Jefferson, James Madison, and James Monroe—each served two terms as president. Supported by farmers in the South and West and strong Republican majorities in Congress, this "Virginia Dynasty" completed what Jefferson had called the Revolution of 1800. It reversed many Federalist policies and actively supported westward expansion.

When Jefferson took office in 1801, he became the first chief executive to live in the White House in the District of Columbia, the new national capital. His administration began with an international conflict inherited from the Federalists. Beginning in the 1780s, the Barbary States of North Africa had raided merchant ships in the Mediterranean, and like many European nations, the United States had paid an annual bribe to protect its vessels. Jefferson refused to pay this "tribute" and ordered the U.S. Navy to attack the pirates' home ports. But the president did not want all-out war, which would have increased taxes and the national debt, so he eventually negotiated a settlement that restored the tribute at a lower rate.

At home, Jefferson inherited a national judiciary filled with Federalist appointees, including the formidable John Marshall of Virginia, the new chief justice of the Supreme Court. To add more Federalist judges, the outgoing Federalist Congress had passed the Judiciary Act of 1801. The act created sixteen new judgeships and six additional circuit courts, which President Adams filled at the last moment with "midnight appointees." The Federalists "have retired into the judiciary as a stronghold," Jefferson complained, "and from that battery all the works of Republicanism are to be beaten down and destroyed."

Jefferson's fears were soon realized. When Republican legislatures in Kentucky and Virginia repudiated the Alien and Sedition Acts and claimed the authority to determine the constitutionality of national laws, Federalist John Marshall quickly responded. The Constitution stated that "the judicial Power shall extend to all Cases . . . arising under this Constitution [and] the Laws of the United States," which implied that the Supreme Court held the power of constitutional review. The Court claimed this authority when James Madison, the new secretary of state, refused to deliver the commission of William Marbury, one of Adams's midnight appointees. Marbury petitioned the Supreme Court to compel delivery under the terms of the Judiciary Act of 1789. In *Marbury v. Madison* (1803), Marshall asserted that Marbury had the right to the appointment but that the Court did not have the constitutional power to enforce it. In defining the Court's powers, Marshall voided a section of the Judiciary Act of 1789, in effect asserting the Court's authority to review congressional legislation and interpret the constitution. "It is emphatically the province and duty of the judicial department to say what the law is," the chief justice declared, directly challenging the Republican view that the state legislatures had that power.

Ignoring this setback, Jefferson and the Republicans reversed other Federalist policies. When the Alien and Sedition acts expired in 1801, Congress branded them political and unconstitutional and refused to reenact them. It also amended the Naturalization Act to allow resident aliens to become citizens after five years, the original waiting period. Charging the Federalists with grossly expanding the national government's size and power, Jefferson had the Republican Congress shrink it. He abolished all internal taxes, including the excise tax that had sparked the Whiskey Rebellion of 1794. To quiet "Old Republican" fears of a military coup, Jefferson reduced the size of the permanent army. He also secured repeal of the Judiciary Act of 1801, thereby ousting forty of Adams's midnight appointees. But the Republican president retained competent Federalist officeholders, removing only 69 of 433 properly appointed Federalists during his eight years as president.

Jefferson also governed tactfully in fiscal affairs. He tolerated the economically important Bank of the United States, which he had once condemned as unconstitutional. But he chose as his secretary of the treasury Albert Gallatin, a fiscal conservative who believed that the national debt was "an evil of the first magnitude." By limiting expenditures and using customs revenue to redeem government bonds, Gallatin reduced the debt from $83 million in 1801 to $45 million in 1812. With Jefferson and Gallatin at the helm, the nation was no longer run in the interests of northeastern creditors and merchants.

Jefferson and the West

Jefferson had long championed settlement of the West. He celebrated the yeoman farmer in *Notes on the State of Virginia*, wrote one of the Confederation's western land ordinances, and supported Pinckney's Treaty of 1795 with Spain, which allowed settlers to export crops via the Mississippi River and the Spanish-held port of New Orleans.

As president, Jefferson pursued policies that made it easier for farm families to acquire land. In 1796, a Federalist-dominated Congress had set the price of land in the national domain to $2 per acre; by 1820, Republican Congresses had cut that to $1.25 an acre. Inspired by Jeffersonian policies, subsequent Congresses reduced the price still further and, in the Homestead Act of 1862, gave farmsteads to settlers for free.

But international events challenged Jefferson's vision of westward expansion. In 1799, Napoleon Bonaparte seized power in France and sought to reestablish a French empire in America. In 1801, he coerced Spain into signing a secret treaty that returned Louisiana to France and restricted American access to New Orleans, violating Pinckney's Treaty. Napoleon also launched an invasion to restore French rule in Haiti (then called Saint-Domingue), once the richest sugar colony in the Americas. Beginning in 1791, a massive slave revolt had convulsed the island. After years of civil war and Spanish and British invasions, black Haitians led by Toussaint L'Ouverture seized control of the sugar-rich country in 1798. Now Napoleon wanted it back.

Napoleon's actions in Haiti and Louisiana prompted Jefferson to question his party's pro-French foreign policy. "The day that France takes possession of New Orleans," the president warned, "we must marry ourselves to the British fleet and nation." Jefferson feared that France might close the Mississippi River to western farmers, so he instructed Robert Livingston, the American minister in Paris, to negotiate the purchase of New Orleans. Simultaneously, Jefferson sent James Monroe to Britain to negotiate an alliance in case of war with France.

Toussaint L'Ouverture, Haitian Revolutionary and Statesman
The American Revolution represented a victory for republicanism; the Haitian revolt represented a triumph of liberty and a demand for racial equality. After leading the black army that ousted French sugar planters and expelled British forces from Haiti, Toussaint formed a constitutional government in 1801. A year later, he negotiated a treaty with French invaders, who were seeking to recapture the island; the treaty halted Haitian resistance in exchange for a promise that the French would not reinstate slavery. Subsequently, the French seized Toussaint and sent him to France, where he died in a prison in 1803. Snark/Art Resource, New York.

Jefferson's diplomacy yielded a magnificent prize: the entire territory of Louisiana. By 1802, the French invasion of Haiti was faltering in the face of disease and determined black resistance, a new war threatened in Europe, and Napoleon feared an American takeover of Louisiana. Acting with characteristic decisiveness, the French ruler offered to sell not just New Orleans but the entire territory of Louisiana for $15 million (about $500 million today). "We have lived long," Livingston remarked to Monroe as they concluded the Louisiana Purchase in 1803, "but this is the noblest work of our lives."

The Louisiana Purchase forced Jefferson to reconsider his strict interpretation of the Constitution. He had long believed that the national government possessed only the powers expressly delegated to it in the Constitution, but there was no constitutional provision for adding new territory. So Jefferson became a pragmatist. Accepting a loose interpretation, he used the treaty-making powers in the Constitution to complete the deal with France.

A scientist as well as a statesman, Jefferson wanted detailed information about the physical features of the new territory, its plant and animal life, and its native peoples. In 1804, he sent his personal secretary, Meriwether Lewis, to explore the region with William Clark, an army officer. Aided by Indian guides, Lewis and Clark and their party of American soldiers and frontiersmen traveled up the Missouri River, across the Rocky Mountains, and—venturing beyond the bounds of the Louisiana Purchase—down the Columbia River to the Pacific Ocean. After two years, they returned with the first maps of the immense wilderness and vivid accounts of its natural resources and inhabitants (Map 7.2).

A stunning accomplishment, the Louisiana Purchase created new problems. Some New England Federalists, fearing that western expansion would hurt their region and party, talked openly of leaving the Union. When Alexander Hamilton rejected their scheme for a northern confederacy, the secessionists recruited Aaron Burr, the ambitious vice president. Hamilton accused Burr of planning to destroy the Union, and the two men fought an illegal pistol duel that ended in Hamilton's death.

This tragedy propelled Burr into another secessionist scheme. When his term as vice president ended in 1805, Burr moved west to avoid prosecution for dueling. There, he conspired with General James Wilkinson, the military governor of the Louisiana Territory, either to seize territory in New Spain or to launch a rebellion to establish Louisiana as a separate nation. But Wilkinson betrayed Burr, arresting the former vice president as he led an armed force down the Ohio River. In a highly politicized trial presided over by Chief Justice John Marshall, the jury acquitted Burr of treason.

The Louisiana Purchase had increased party conflict and generated secessionist schemes in both New England and the Southwest. Such regional differences would continue, challenging Madison's argument in "Federalist No. 10" that a large and diverse republic was more stable than a small one.

▶ Was there anything the Western Indian Confederacy could have done to limit white expansion and preserve Indian lands? Explain your position.

▶ Why did Jefferson support expansion to the West? Why did eastern farm families leave their communities to go west? Were their reasons the same as Jefferson's?

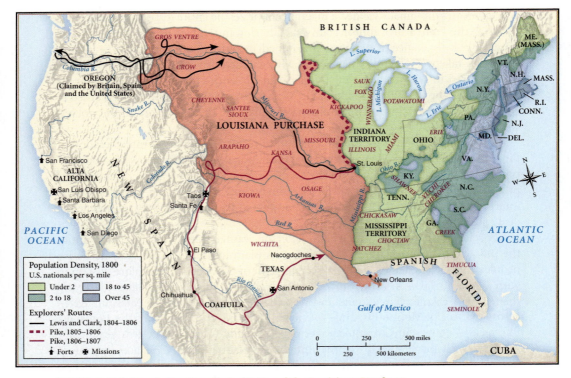

MAP 7.2 U.S. Population Density in 1803 and the Louisiana Purchase

When the United States purchased Louisiana from France in 1803, much of the land between the Appalachian Mountains and the Mississippi River remained in Indian hands: The vast lands west of the Mississippi were virtually unknown, even after the epic explorations of Meriwether Lewis and William Clark and of Zebulon Pike. Still, President Jefferson predicted quite accurately that the vast Mississippi River Valley "from its fertility . . . will ere long yield half of our whole produce, and contain half of our whole population."

The War of 1812 and the Transformation of Politics

Trouble was also brewing in Europe, where war had broken out again in 1802. For the next decade, American politicians tried to safeguard national interests while avoiding war. When this effort finally failed, it sparked dramatic political changes that destroyed the Federalist Party and split the Republicans into National and Jeffersonian factions.

Conflict in the Atlantic and the West

The Napoleonic Wars that ravaged Europe between 1802 and 1815 disrupted American commerce. As Napoleon conquered European countries, he cut off their trade with Britain and seized neutral merchant ships that had stopped there. The British ministry responded with a naval blockade that seized American vessels carrying sugar and molasses from the French West Indies. The British navy also searched American merchant ships for British deserters and used these raids to replenish its crews, a practice known as impressment. Between 1802 and 1811, British naval officers impressed nearly 8,000 sailors, including many American citizens. In 1807, American anger over these seizures turned to outrage when a British warship attacked the U.S. Navy vessel *Chesapeake*, killing three, wounding eighteen, and seizing four alleged deserters. "Never since the battle of Lexington have I seen this country in such a state of exasperation as at present," Jefferson declared.

To protect American interests while avoiding war, Jefferson pursued a policy of peaceful coercion. Working closely with Secretary of State James Madison, he devised the Embargo Act of 1807, which prohibited American ships from leaving their home ports until Britain and France stopped restricting U.S. trade. The embargo was a creative diplomatic measure, probably inspired by the boycotts of the 1760s and 1770s. But it overestimated the reliance of Britain and France on American shipping, and it underestimated the resistance of New England merchants, who feared it would ruin them.

In fact, the embargo weakened the American economy by cutting the gross national product (GNP) by 5 percent. Exports plunged from $108 million in 1806 to $22 million in 1808, hurting farmers as well as merchants. "Would to God," exclaimed one Federalist, "that the Embargo had done as little evil to ourselves as it has done to foreign nations."

Despite popular discontent over the embargo, voters elected Republican James Madison to the presidency in 1808. A powerful advocate for the Constitution, the architect of the Bill of Rights, and a prominent congressman and party leader, Madison had served the nation well. But John Beckley, a loyal Republican, worried that Madison would be "too timid and indecisive as a statesman," and events proved him right. Acknowledging the embargo's failure, Madison replaced it with a series of new economic restrictions, which also failed to persuade Britain or France to respect American interests. "The Devil himself could not tell which government, England or France, is the most wicked," an exasperated congressman declared.

Republican congressmen from the West had no doubt that Britain was the primary offender. They pointed to its continued assistance to the Indians in the Ohio River Valley, a violation of the Treaty of Paris and Jay's Treaty. Bolstered by British guns and supplies, in 1809 the Shawnee war chief Tecumseh [*ta-KUM-sa*] revived the Western Confederacy. His brother, the prophet Tenskwatawa [*tens-QUA-ta-wa*], provided it with a powerful ideology: He urged native peoples to shun Americans, "the children of the Evil Spirit . . . who have taken away your lands"; renounce alcohol; and return to traditional ways. Warriors and wise men from the Kickapoo, Potawatomi, Winnebago, Ottawa, and Chippewa peoples flocked to Tenskwatawa's holy village, Prophetstown, near the juncture of the Tippecanoe and Wabash rivers in the Indiana Territory.

Inspired by the prophet's teachings, Tecumseh mobilized the western Indian peoples for war. William Henry Harrison, the governor of the Indiana territory, decided on a preemptive strike. Taking advantage of Tecumseh's absence in the South (seeking an alliance with the Chickasaws, Choctaws, and Creeks), Harrison mobilized 1,000 troops and militiamen. After trading heavy casualties with the confederacy's warriors at the Battle of Tippecanoe in November 1811, Harrison destroyed Prophetstown.

With Britain assisting Indians in the West and attacking American ships in the Atlantic, Henry Clay of Kentucky, the new Speaker of the House of Representatives, and John C. Calhoun, a rising young congressman from South Carolina, pushed Madison

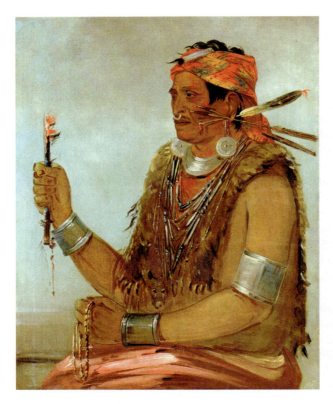

Tenskwatawa, "The Prophet," 1836
Tenskwatawa added a spiritual dimension to Native American resistance by urging a holy war against the invading whites and by calling for a return to sacred ancestral ways. His dress reflects his teachings: Note the animal skin shirt and the heavily ornamented ears. Tenskwatawa's religious message transcended the cultural differences among Indian peoples and helped his brother, Tecumseh, to create a formidable political and military alliance. Smithsonian American Art Museum, Washington, D.C./Art Resource.

toward war. Like other Republican "war hawks" from the West and South, they wanted to seize territory in British Canada and Spanish Florida. With national elections approaching, Madison issued an ultimatum to Britain. When Britain made no quick response, the president asked Congress for a declaration of war. In June 1812, a sharply divided Senate voted 19 to 13 for war, and the House of Representatives concurred, 79 to 49.

The causes of the War of 1812 have been much debated. Officially, the United States went to war because Britain had violated its neutral rights by seizing merchant ships and sailors. But the Federalists in Congress who represented the merchants voted against the war; and in the election of 1812, New England and the Middle Atlantic states cast their 89 electoral votes for the Federalist presidential candidate, De Witt Clinton of New York. Madison amassed most of his 128 electoral votes in the South and West, where voters and their representatives in Congress strongly supported the war. Many historians therefore argue that the conflict was actually "a western war with eastern labels" (see American Voices, p. 215).

The War of 1812

The War of 1812 was a near disaster for the United States, both militarily and politically. An invasion of British Canada in 1812 quickly ended in a retreat to Detroit. But Americans stayed on the offensive in the West. In 1813, American raiders burned the

Federalists and Republicans Debate "Mr. Madison's War"

The decisions of Lyndon B. Johnson and George W. Bush to pursue wars in Vietnam and Iraq stirred sharp political debates and protests. So too did President James Madison's action in 1812 in leading the nation into war. In 1812, Josiah Quincy and other antiwar Federalist congressmen challenged Madison's justification for the war and the Republicans' proposed military strategy. As the war ended in 1815, Hezekiah Niles, the Republican editor of *Niles's Weekly Register*, came to Madison's defense and blamed New England Federalists for American military reverses.

THE FEDERALIST MANIFESTO: How will war upon the land [an invasion of British Canada] protect commerce upon the ocean? . . .

But it is said that war is demanded by honor. . . . If honor demands a war with England, what opiate lulls that honor to sleep over the wrongs done us by France? On land, robberies, seizures, imprisonments, by French authority; at sea, pillage, sinkings, burnings, under French orders. These are notorious. Are they unfelt because they are French? . . .

There is . . . a headlong rushing into difficulties, with little calculation about the means, and little concern about the consequences. With a navy comparatively [small], we are about to enter into the lists against the greatest marine [power] on the globe. With a commerce unprotected and spread over every ocean, we propose to make a profit by privateering, and for this endanger the wealth of which we are honest proprietors. . . .

What are the United States to gain by this war? . . . Let us not be deceived. A war of invasion [of Canada] may invite a retort of invasion. When we visit the peaceable, and as to us innocent, colonies of Great Britain with the horrors of war, can we be assured that our own coast will not be visited with like horrors?

HEZEKIAH NILES'S REJOINDER: It is universally known that the causes for which we declared war are no obstruction to peace. The practice of blockade and impressment having ceased by the general pacification of Europe, our government is content to leave the principle as it was. . . .

We have no further business in hostility, than such as is purely defensive; while that of Great Britain is to humble or subdue us. . . .

I did think that in a defensive war—a struggle for all that is valuable—that all parties would have united. But it is not so—every measure calculated to replenish the treasury or raise men is opposed as though it were determined to strike the "star spangled banner" and exalt the bloody cross. Look at the votes and proceedings of congress—and mark the late spirit [to secede from the Union] . . . that existed in Massachusetts, and see with what unity of action every thing has been done [by New England Federalists] to harass and embarrass the government. Our loans have failed; and our soldiers have wanted their pay, because those [New England merchants] who had the greater part of the monied capital covenanted with each other to refuse its aid to the country. . . . History will shock posterity by detailing the length to which they went to bankrupt the republic.

SOURCES: *Annals of Congress*, 12th Cong., 1st sess., vol. 2, cols. 2219–2221; *Niles Weekly Register*, January 28, 1815.

Canadian capital of York (present-day Toronto), Commodore Oliver Hazard Perry defeated a small British flotilla on Lake Erie, and General William Henry Harrison led a new expedition into Canada. There, he defeated a British and Indian force at the Battle of the Thames, taking the life of Tecumseh, now a British general.

Political divisions prevented a major invasion of Canada in the East. New England Federalists opposed the war and prohibited their states' militias from attacking Canada. Boston merchants and banks refused to lend money to the federal government, making the war difficult to finance. In Congress, Daniel Webster, a dynamic young politician from New Hampshire, led Federalist opposition to higher tariffs and to the national conscription of state militiamen.

Gradually, the tide of battle turned in Britain's favor. When the war began, American privateers had quickly captured scores of British merchant vessels, but the Royal Navy soon seized the initiative. By 1813, a flotilla of British warships was harassing American ships and threatening seaports along the Atlantic coast. In 1814, a British fleet sailed up the Chesapeake Bay, and troops stormed ashore and marched north to attack Washington City. In retaliation for the destruction of York, the British burned the U.S. Capitol and government buildings. After two years of fighting, the United States was stalemated along the Canadian frontier and on the defensive in the Atlantic, and its new capital city lay in ruins. The only positive news came from the Southwest. There, a rugged slave-owning planter named Andrew Jackson and a force of Tennessee militiamen defeated the British- and Spanish-supported Creek Indians in the Battle of Horseshoe Bend (1814) and forced the Indians to cede 23 million acres of land (Map 7.3).

American military setbacks strengthened opposition to the war in New England. In 1814, Massachusetts Federalists called for a convention "to lay the foundation for a radical reform in the National Compact." When New England Federalists met in Hartford, Connecticut, some delegates proposed secession, but most wanted to revise the Constitution. To end Virginia's domination of the presidency, the Hartford Convention proposed a constitutional amendment limiting the office to a single four-year term and rotating it among citizens from different states. The convention also suggested amendments restricting commercial embargoes to sixty days and requiring a two-thirds majority in Congress to declare war, prohibit trade, or admit a new state to the Union.

As a minority party in Congress and the nation, the Federalists could prevail only if the war continued to go badly—a very real prospect. Albert Gallatin warned Henry Clay in May 1814 that Britain's triumph over Napoleon in Europe meant that a "well organized and large army is [now] . . . ready together with a super abundant naval force, to act immediately against us." When the British attacked from Canada in the late summer of 1814, only an American naval victory on Lake Champlain averted a British march down the Hudson River Valley. A few months later, thousands of seasoned British troops landed outside New Orleans, threatening American control of the Mississippi River. With the nation politically divided and under military attack from north and south, Gallatin feared that "a continuance of the war might prove vitally fatal to the United States."

Fortunately for the young American republic, by 1815 Britain wanted peace. The twenty-year war with France had sapped its wealth and energy, so it entered into negotiations with the United States in Ghent, Belgium. At first, the American commissioners—John Quincy Adams, Gallatin, and Clay—demanded territory in

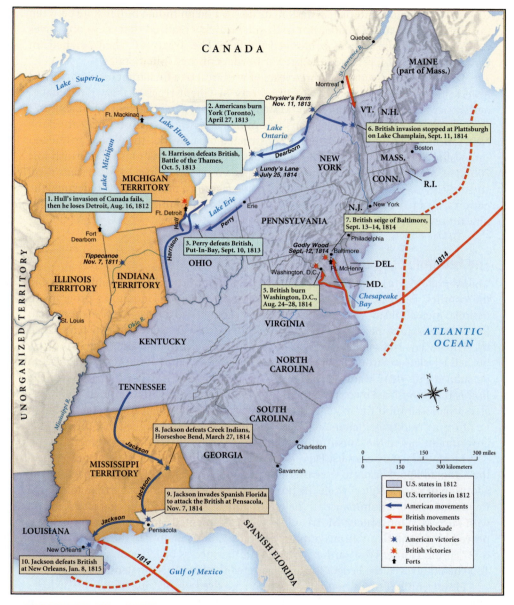

Map labels:

CANADA

Quebec

MAINE
(part of Mass.)

Lake Superior

Montreal

Ft. Mackinac

Lake Huron

2. Americans burn York (Toronto), April 27, 1813

Chrysler's Farm Nov. 11, 1813

VT. N.H.

6. British invasion stopped at Plattsburgh on Lake Champlain, Sept. 11, 1814

Lake Michigan

4. Harrison defeats British, Battle of the Thames, Oct. 5, 1813

Lake Ontario

Dearborn

NEW YORK

MASS.

Boston

MICHIGAN TERRITORY

Lundy's Lane July 25, 1814

CONN.

R.I.

1. Hull's invasion of Canada fails, then he loses Detroit, Aug. 16, 1812

Ft. Detroit

Lake Erie

Perry

Erie

N.J.

New York

PENNSYLVANIA

7. British siege of Baltimore, Sept. 13–14, 1814

Fort Dearborn

Harrison

3. Perry defeats British, Put-In-Bay, Sept. 10, 1813

OHIO

Godly Wood Sept. 12, 1814

Philadelphia

Baltimore

DEL.

1814

Tippecanoe Nov. 7, 1811

Washington, D.C.

Ft. McHenry

ILLINOIS TERRITORY

INDIANA TERRITORY

5. British burn Washington, D.C., Aug. 24–28, 1814

MD.

Chesapeake Bay

St. Louis

Ohio R.

VIRGINIA

ATLANTIC OCEAN

UNORGANIZED TERRITORY

KENTUCKY

Mississippi R.

TENNESSEE

NORTH CAROLINA

SOUTH CAROLINA

8. Jackson defeats Creek Indians, Horseshoe Bend, March 27, 1814

Charleston

0   150   300 miles

0   150   300 kilometers

Jackson

GEORGIA

Savannah

MISSISSIPPI TERRITORY

Jackson

9. Jackson invades Spanish Florida to attack the British at Pensacola, Nov. 7, 1814

☐ U.S. states in 1812
☐ U.S. territories in 1812
→ American movements
→ British movements
--- British blockade
✷ American victories
✷ British victories
⚓ Forts

Jackson

LOUISIANA

Pensacola

SPANISH FLORIDA

New Orleans

10. Jackson defeats British at New Orleans, Jan. 8, 1815

1814

Gulf of Mexico

MAP 7.3 The War of 1812

Unlike the War of Independence, the War of 1812 had few large-scale military campaigns. In 1812 and 1813, most of the fighting took place along the Canadian border, as American armies and naval forces attacked British targets with mixed success (#1–4). The British took the offensive in 1814, launching a successful raid on Washington, but their attack on Baltimore failed, and they suffered heavy losses when they invaded the United States along Lake Champlain (#5–7). Near the Gulf of Mexico, American forces moved from one success to another: General Andrew Jackson defeated the pro-British Creek Indians at the Battle of Horseshoe Bend, won a victory in Pensacola, and, in the single major battle of the war, routed an invading British army at New Orleans (#8–10).

Canada and Florida, and British diplomats insisted on an Indian buffer state between the United States and Canada. But both sides quickly realized that these objectives were not worth the cost of prolonged warfare. The Treaty of Ghent, signed on Christmas Eve 1814, retained the prewar borders of the United States.

That result hardly justified three years of warfare, but a final military victory lifted Americans' morale. Before news of the Treaty of Ghent reached the United States, newspaper headlines proclaimed an "ALMOST INCREDIBLE VICTORY!! GLORIOUS NEWS": On January 8, 1815, General Jackson's troops had crushed the British forces attacking New Orleans. Fighting from carefully constructed breastworks, the Americans rained "grapeshot and cannister bombs" on the massed British formations. The British lost 700 men, and 2,000 more were wounded or taken prisoner; just 13 Americans died, and only 58 suffered wounds. The victory made Jackson a national hero, redeemed the nation's battered pride, and undercut the Hartford convention's demands for a significant revision of the Constitution.

The Federalist Legacy

The War of 1812 ushered in a new phase of the Republican political revolution. Before the conflict, Federalists had strongly supported Alexander Hamilton's program of national mercantilism — a funded debt, a central bank, and tariffs — while Jeffersonian Republicans had opposed it. After the war, the Republicans split into two camps. Led by Henry Clay, National Republicans pursued Federalist-like policies. In 1816, Clay pushed legislation through Congress creating a Second Bank of the United States and persuaded President Madison to sign it. The following year, Clay won passage of the Bonus Bill, sponsored by congressman John C. Calhoun of South Carolina, which created a national fund for roads and other internal improvements. Madison vetoed it. Reaffirming traditional Jeffersonian Republican principles, he argued that the national government lacked the constitutional authority to fund internal improvements.

Meanwhile, the Federalist Party was in severe decline. As one Federalist explained, the National Republicans in the eastern states had "destroyed the Federalist party by the adoption of its principles" while the profarmer policies of Jeffersonians maintained the Republican Party's dominance in the South and West. "No Federal character can run with success," Gouverneur Morris of New York lamented, and the election of 1818 proved him right: Republicans outnumbered Federalists 37 to 7 in the Senate and 156 to 27 in the House. Westward expansion and the success of Jefferson's Revolution of 1800 had destroyed the Federalists and shattered the First Party System.

However, the Federalists' nationalist policies lived on because of John Marshall's long tenure on the Supreme Court. Appointed chief justice by President John Adams in January 1801, Marshall had a personality and intellect that allowed him to dominate the Court until 1822 and strongly influence its decisions until his death in 1835. By winning the support of Joseph Story and other National Republican justices, Marshall shaped the evolution of the Constitution.

Three principles informed Marshall's jurisprudence: judicial authority, the supremacy of national laws, and traditional property rights. Marshall claimed the right of judicial review for the Court in *Marbury v. Madison* (1803), but the Supreme Court did not void another law enacted by Congress until the *Dred Scott* decision in 1857 (see Chapter 13). However, the Marshall Court did frequently use the power of review to overturn state laws that, in its judgment, violated the national constitution.

The important case of *McCulloch v. Maryland* (1819) involved one such law. When Congress created the Second Bank of the United States in 1816, it allowed the bank to set up branches in the states, where it competed with state-chartered banks. To enhance the competitiveness of Maryland banks, the state's legislature imposed a tax on notes issued by the Baltimore branch of the Second Bank. The Second Bank claimed that the tax infringed on national powers and was therefore unconstitutional. Lawyers for the state of Maryland replied, using Jefferson's argument, that Congress lacked the constitutional authority to charter a national bank. Even if a national bank was legitimate, the lawyers argued, Maryland could tax its activities within the state.

Marshall and the National Republicans on the Court firmly rejected both arguments. The Second Bank was constitutional, said the chief justice, because it was "necessary and proper," given the national government's control over currency and credit. Like Alexander Hamilton, Marshall was a loose constructionist: If the goal of a law is "within the scope of the Constitution," then "all means which are appropriate" to secure that goal are also constitutional. The chief justice pointed out that "the power to tax involves the power to destroy" and suggested that Maryland's bank tax would render the national government "dependent on the states," an outcome that Marshall claimed was "not intended by the American people" who ratified the Constitution.

The Marshall Court again asserted the dominance of national over state statutes in *Gibbons v. Ogden* (1824). The decision struck down a New York law granting a monopoly to Aaron Ogden for steamboat passenger service across the Hudson River to New Jersey. Asserting that the Constitution gave the federal government authority over interstate commerce, the chief justice sided with Thomas Gibbons, who held a federal license to run steamboats between the two states.

Finally, Marshall used the Constitution to uphold Federalist notions of property rights. During the 1790s, Jefferson Republicans had celebrated "the will of THE PEOPLE," prompting Federalists to worry that popular sovereignty would result in a "tyranny of the majority." Concerned that state legislatures would enact statutes that infringed on the property rights of wealthy citizens, Federalist judges vowed to void such statutes.

Marshall was no exception. Determined to protect individual property rights, he invoked the contract clause of the Constitution to do it. The contract clause (in Article I, Section 10) prohibits the states from passing any law "impairing the obligation of contracts." Economic conservatives at the Philadelphia convention had inserted the clause to prevent states from passing "stay" laws that kept creditors from seizing the lands and goods of debtors. In *Fletcher v. Peck* (1810), Marshall greatly expanded its scope. The Georgia legislature had granted a huge tract of land to the Yazoo Land Company. When a new legislature canceled the grant, alleging fraud and bribery, speculators who had purchased Yazoo lands appealed to the Supreme Court to uphold their titles. Marshall did so by ruling that the legislative grant was a contract that could not be revoked. His decision was controversial and far-reaching. It limited state power, bolstered vested property rights, and, by protecting out-of-state investors, promoted the development of a national capitalist economy.

The Court extended its defense of vested property rights in *Dartmouth College v. Woodward* (1819). Dartmouth College was a private institution established by a royal charter granted by King George III. In 1816, New Hampshire's Republican legislature enacted a statute converting the school into a public university. The Dartmouth trustees opposed the legislation and hired Daniel Webster to plead their case. A renowned constitutional lawyer and a leading Federalist, Webster used the Court's decision in *Fletcher v. Peck* to argue that the royal charter constituted an unalterable contract. The Marshall Court agreed and upheld the claims of the college.

Even as John Marshall incorporated Federalist principles of judicial review, national supremacy, and vested property rights into the American legal system, voting citizens and political leaders embraced the outlook of the Republican Party. The career of John Quincy Adams was a case in point. Although he was the son of Federalist President John Adams, John Quincy Adams joined the Republican Party before the War of 1812. He won national attention negotiating the Treaty of Ghent, which ended the war.

Adams then served brilliantly as secretary of state for two terms under President James Monroe (1817–1825). In 1817, Adams negotiated the Rush-Bagot Treaty, which limited American and British naval forces on the Great Lakes. In 1818, he concluded another agreement with Britain that set the forty-ninth parallel as the border between Canada and the lands of the Louisiana Purchase. Then, in the Adams-Onís Treaty of 1819, Adams persuaded Spain to cede Florida to the United States (Map 7.4). In return, the American government accepted Spain's claim to Texas and agreed on a boundary between New Spain and the state of Louisiana, which had entered the Union in 1812.

Finally, Adams persuaded President Monroe to declare American national policy with respect to the Western Hemisphere. At Adams's behest, Monroe warned Spain and other European powers in 1823 to keep their hands off the newly independent republican nations in Latin America. The American continents were not "subject for further colonization," the president declared—a policy that thirty years later became known as the Monroe Doctrine. In return, Monroe pledged that the United States would not "interfere in the internal concerns" of European nations. Thanks to Adams, the United States had asserted diplomatic leadership of the Western Hemisphere and won international acceptance of its northern and western boundaries.

The appearance of a national consensus after two decades of bitter party politics prompted observers to dub James Monroe's presidency the "Era of Good Feeling." This political harmony was real but transitory. The Republican Party was increasingly split between the National faction, led by Clay and Adams, and the Jeffersonian faction, soon to be led by Martin Van Buren and Andrew Jackson. The two groups differed sharply over federal support for roads and canals and many other issues. As the aging Jefferson complained about the National Republicans, "You see so many of these new republicans maintaining in Congress the rankest doctrines of the old federalists." This division in the ranks of the Republican Party would soon produce a Second Party System, in which national-minded Whigs and

► Was the War of 1812 "necessary"? If so, why? If not, why did it occur?

► How did the decisions of the Supreme Court between 1801 and 1820 alter the Constitution? How did they change American society?

► Explain the rise and fall of the Federalist Party. Why was the Republican triumph so complete?

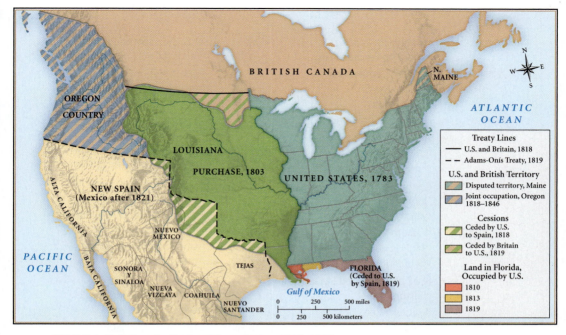

MAP 7.4 Defining the National Boundaries, 1800–1820

After the War of 1812, John Quincy Adams and other American diplomats negotiated treaties with Great Britain and Spain that defined the boundaries between the Louisiana Purchase and British Canada to the north and New Spain (which in 1821 became the independent nation of Mexico) to the south and west. These treaties eliminated the threat of border wars with0 neighboring states, giving the United States a much-needed period of peace and security.

For more help analyzing this map, see the Online Study Guide at **bedfordstmartins.com/henrettaconcise**.

state-focused Democrats would face off against each other (see Chapter 10). By the early 1820s, one cycle of American politics and economic debate had ended, and another was about to begin.

SUMMARY

In this chapter, we have traced three interrelated themes: public policy, westward expansion, and party politics. We began by examining the contrasting public policies advocated by Alexander Hamilton and Thomas Jefferson. A Federalist, Hamilton supported a strong national government and created a fiscal infrastructure (the national debt, tariffs, and a national bank) to spur trade and manufacturing. By contrast, Jefferson wanted to preserve the authority of state governments, and he envisioned an America enriched by farming rather than industry.

The westward movement promoted by Jefferson and his Republican Party sparked new conflicts with the Indian peoples and transformed the agricultural economy by

TIMELINE

1783	► Treaty of Paris opens trans-Appalachian West
1784	► Iroquois peoples cede lands in New York and Pennsylvania
1787	► Northwest Ordinance
1789	► Judiciary Act sets up federal courts
	► French Revolution begins
1790	► Congress approves Hamilton public credit system
1790–1791	► Western Confederacy defeats American armies
1791	► Bill of Rights ratified
	► Bank of the United States chartered
1792	► Kentucky joins Union; Tennessee follows (1796)
	► French Republic founded
1793	► King Louis XVI executed
	► Madison and Jefferson create Republican Party
	► Washington proclaims neutrality in war between Britain and France
1794	► Whiskey Rebellion in western Pennsylvania
	► Battle of Fallen Timbers
1795	► Jay's Treaty with Great Britain debated
	► Pinckney's Treaty with Spain allows U.S. use of Mississippi River
	► Treaty of Greenville aids settlement

1798	► XYZ Affair sparks conflict with France
	► Alien, Sedition, and Naturalization Acts
	► Kentucky and Virginia resolutions contest national authority
1800	► Jefferson elected president in "Revolution of 1800"
1801	► John Marshall becomes chief justice of Supreme Court
1801–1807	► Treasury Secretary Gallatin reduces national debt
1802–1807	► France and Britain seize American ships
1803	► Louisiana Purchase
	► Marshall asserts judicial review in *Marbury v. Madison*
1804–1806	► Lewis and Clark explore West
1807	► Embargo Act cripples American shipping
1809	► Tecumseh and Tenskwatawa revive Western Confederacy
1812–1815	► War of 1812
1817–1825	► Era of Good Feeling
1819	► Adams-Onís Treaty annexes Florida and defines Texas boundary
	► *McCulloch v. Maryland* increases power of national government
	► *Dartmouth College v. Woodward* protects property rights

dramatically increasing the market sale of farm produce. Expansion westward also shaped American diplomatic and military policy, as in the Louisiana Purchase, the War of 1812, and the treaties negotiated by John Quincy Adams.

Finally, there was the unexpected rise of the First Party System. As Hamilton's policies split the political elite, the French Revolution divided Americans into hostile ideological groups. The result was two decades of bitterness over controversial measures: the Federalists' Sedition Act, the Republicans' Embargo Act, and Madison's decision to go to war with Britain. Although the Federalist Party faded away, it left as its enduring legacy Hamilton's financial innovations and John Marshall's constitutional jurisprudence.

Connections: Economy and Society

Before the American Revolution, the northern and southern colonies had distinctly different farming economies: In the North, yeomen families raised grain and livestock; in the South, large scale planters used enslaved laborers to grow tobacco and rice for export. After the Revolution, the northern economy began to diverge in other ways from that of the South. As we noted in the Part Two opening essay:

> Beginning in the 1780s, northern merchants financed a banking system and organized a rural system of manufacturing. . . . Many yeomen farm families . . . turned out raw materials such as leather and wool for burgeoning manufacturing enterprises and made shoes, textiles, tinware, and other handicrafts for market sale.

In Chapter 8, we will explore the creation of a capitalist commonwealth—an increasingly urban, commercial society—in the North. We will show how that society fostered a democratic republican culture that encouraged social mobility for men and new marriage rules and child-rearing practices. In Chapter 8, we also will examine the aristocratic republican culture that remained central to the slave-based society of the South, and we will examine the Missouri crisis of 1819–1821, the first major conflict between these two increasingly distinct societies.

In the part opening, we also noted that many farm families "migrated westward to grow grain." As we will see in Chapter 8, these families were particularly affected by the Second Great Awakening, a religious revival that fundamentally changed American culture.

FOR FURTHER EXPLORATION

James Roger Sharp, *American Politics in the Early Republic* (1993), and Thomas P. Slaughter, *The Whiskey Rebellion* (1986), address the difficulties of the 1790s. Linda Kerber, *No Constitutional Right to Be Ladies: Women and the Obligations of Citizenship* (1999) evaluates the impact of republicanism on women's lives.

Washington's strong leadership is stressed in William Martin's fictionalized biography, *Citizen Washington* (1999). For Washington's correspondence, see **www.virginia.edu/gwpapers/**; for Jefferson's most important writings, go to **http://www.pbs.org/jefferson/frame5.htm**; and for the impact of the French Revolution, try **chnm.gmu.edu/revolution/**. David McCullough's highly readable biography *John Adams* (2001) draws on the Adams Family Papers (**www.masshist.org/digitaladams/aea/**). For more on Alexander Hamilton, see Ron Chernow's *Alexander Hamilton* (2004) and **www.alexanderhamiltonexhibition.org/**. On the tumultuous election of 1800, read John Ferling, *Adams vs. Jefferson* (2004).

For the explorations of Lewis and Clark, visit **www.pbs.org/lewisandclark** and **www.americanjourneys.org/**. For native peoples' lives in this era, consult Gregory Evans Dowd, *A Spirited Resistance: The North American Indian Struggle for Unity,*

1745–1815 (1992) and Theda Perdue, *Cherokee Women: Gender and Culture Change, 1700–1835* (1998).

Ralph Louis Ketcham's *Presidents Above Party: The First American Presidency, 1789–1829* (1984) probes political ideology, while Donald R. Hickey, *The War of 1812: A Forgotten Conflict* (1989), considers its economic and diplomatic context. Also see "The War of 1812" (**members.tripod.com/~war1812/**).

TEST YOUR KNOWLEDGE

To assess your mastery of the material in this chapter and for Web sites, images, and documents related to this chapter, visit **bedfordstmartins.com/henrettaconcise**.

Creating a Republican Culture
1790–1820

> The women, in every free country, have an absolute control of manners: and it is confessed, that in a republic, manners are of equal importance with laws.
>
> — Delaware physician James Tilton, 1790

By the 1820s, a sense of optimism pervaded white American society. "The temperate zone of North America already exhibits many signs that it is the promised land of civil liberty, and of institutions designed to liberate and exalt the human race," declared a Kentucky judge in a Fourth of July speech. White Americans had good reason to feel fortunate. They lived under a representative republican government, free from arbitrary taxation and from domination by an established church.

Inspired by their political freedom, these Americans sought to extend republican principles throughout their society. But what *were* those principles? For entrepreneurial-minded merchants, farmers, and political leaders, republicanism meant the advance of **capitalism**: They wanted to use governmental authority to solidify capitalist cultural values and create a dynamic market economy. Using their influence in state legislatures, they secured mercantilist policies that assisted private businesses and, they claimed, enhanced the "common-wealth." Other citizens celebrated republican social values. In the North, they championed democratic republicanism: equality in family and social relationships. In the South, where class and race sharply divided society, politicians and pamphleteers devised an aristocratic republicanism that stressed liberty for whites rather than equality for all. Yet another vision of American republicanism emerged during the massive religious revival that swept the nation between 1790 and 1850. For the many Americans who embraced the Second Great Awakening, the United States was both a great experiment in republican government and an emergent Christian civilization that would redeem the world—a moral mission that, for better or worse, would inform American diplomacy in the centuries to come.

The Capitalist Commonwealth

"If movement and the quick succession of sensations and ideas constitute life," observed a French visitor to the United States, "here one lives a hundred fold more than elsewhere; here, all is circulation, motion, and boiling agitation." Boiling agitation was especially evident in the Northeast, where republican state legislatures actively promoted banking and commerce. "Experiment follows experiment; enterprise follows enterprise," a European traveler noted, and "riches and poverty follow." Of the two, riches were readily apparent. Beginning around 1800, the average per capita income of Americans increased by more than 1 percent a year — more than 30 percent in a single generation.

Banks, Manufacturing, and Markets

America was "a Nation of Merchants," a British visitor reported from Philadelphia in 1798, "keen in the pursuit of wealth in all the various modes of acquiring it." And acquire it they did, making spectacular profits as the wars triggered by the French Revolution (1793–1815) crippled European merchant firms. Fur trader John Jacob Astor and merchant Robert Oliver became the nation's first millionaires. Oliver first worked for an Irish-owned linen firm in Baltimore and then achieved affluence by trading West Indian coffee and sugar. Astor, who migrated from Germany to New York in 1784, became wealthy carrying furs from the Pacific Northwest to markets in China.

To finance such mercantile ventures, Americans needed a banking system. Before the Revolution, farmers relied on government-sponsored land banks for loans, while merchants arranged partnerships or obtained credit from British suppliers. When the War for Independence cut off British credit, Philadelphia merchants persuaded the Confederation Congress to charter the Bank of North America in 1781, and traders in Boston and New York soon founded similar lending institutions. "Our monied capital has so much increased from the Introduction of Banks, & the Circulation of the Funds," Philadelphia merchant William Bingham boasted in 1791, "that the Necessity of Soliciting Credits from England will no longer exist."

That same year, Federalists in Congress chartered the First Bank of the United States to issue notes and make commercial loans. The Bank's profits averaged a handsome 8 percent annually; by 1805, it had branches in eight major cities. However, Jeffersonians claimed the Bank was unconstitutional and oppressive because it created "a consolidated, energetic government supported by public creditors, speculators, and other insidious men lacking in public spirit of any kind." When the bank's twenty-year charter expired in 1811, Jeffersonian Republicans in Congress refused to renew it. To provide credit, merchants, artisans, and farmers persuaded their state legislatures to charter banks. By 1816, when Congress (now run by National Republicans) chartered the Second Bank of the United States, there were 246 state-chartered banks with tens of thousands of stockholders and $68 million in banknotes in circulation. But many of these state banks were shady operations that issued notes without adequate specie reserves and made ill-advised loans to insiders.

Dubious banking policies helped to bring on the financial Panic of 1819. But the most important cause was an abrupt 30 percent drop in world agricultural prices after

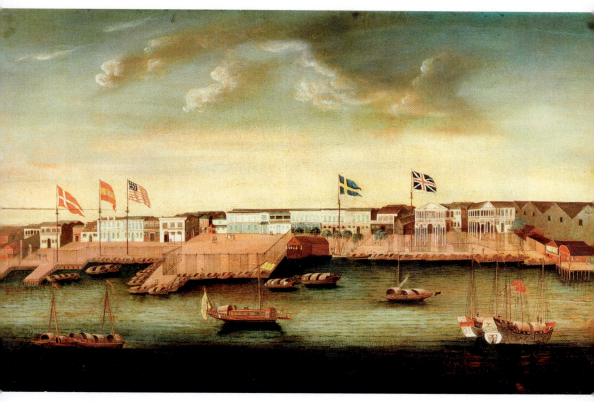

The China Trade
After the Revolution, New England merchants took an active role in the long-standing European trade with China. In this painting by George Chinnery (1774–1852), the American flag flies prominently in front of the warehouse district in Canton. There, merchants exchanged bundles of American furs for cargoes of Chinese silks and porcelain plates, cups, and serving dishes. Bridgeman Art Library Ltd.

the Napoleonic Wars. In Charleston, South Carolina, between 1818 and 1819, the sale price for a pound of cotton fell from 34 cents to 15 cents. As their income plummeted, planters and farmers could not pay their debts to storekeepers, wholesale merchants, and banks, sending those businesses into bankruptcy. Many state banks went bust; those that were still solvent in 1821 had just $45 million in circulation. The panic gave Americans their first taste of a **business cycle**, the periodic expansion and contraction of production and employment inherent in an unregulated market economy.

The Panic of 1819 revealed that artisans and yeomen as well as merchants now depended for their prosperity on the market economy. Before 1800, many New England artisans worked part time and sold their handicrafts locally. In central Massachusetts, a French traveler found many houses "inhabited by men who are both cultivators and artisans." In the Middle Atlantic region, artisans bartered products with neighbors. Clockmaker John Hoff of Lancaster, Pennsylvania, exchanged his fine, wooden-cased instruments for a dining table, a bedstead, and labor on his small farm. By 1820, many artisans—shipbuilders in seacoast towns, ironworkers in Pennsylvania and

The Yankee Peddler, c. 1830

Even in 1830, most Americans lived too far from a market town to go there regularly to buy goods. Instead, they purchased tinware, clocks, textiles, and other manufactured goods from peddlers, often from New England, who traveled far and wide in small horse-drawn vans like the one pictured in the doorway. Courtesy, IBM Corporation, Armonk, New York.

For more help analyzing this image, see the Online Study Guide at **bedfordstmartins.com/henrettaconcise**.

Maryland, and shoemakers in Massachusetts—had expanded their output and were selling their products throughout the nation.

American entrepreneurs encouraged this expansion by developing rural manufacturing networks like those in Europe (see Chapter 1). Enterprising merchants bought raw materials, hired workers in farm families to process them, and sold the finished manufactures in regional or national markets. "Straw hats and Bonnets are manufactured by many families," an official in Maine noted in the 1810s. Merchants shipped these products—shoes, brooms, and palm-leaf hats as well as cups, baking pans, and other tin utensils—to seaport cities. New England peddlers carried them to the rural South, where the peddlers earned the dubious reputation of being hard-bargaining "Yankees."

This business expansion stemmed primarily from innovations in organizing production and in marketing; new technology played only a minor role. During the 1780s, New England and Middle Atlantic merchants had built small mills to power machines that combed wool—and later cotton—into long strands. But until the 1820s, they used the household-based outwork system for the next steps in the textile manufacturing process: Farm women and children spun the strands into thread and yarn on foot-driven spinning wheels, and men in other households used foot-powered looms to weave the yarn into cloth. In 1820, more than 12,000 household workers labored full-time weaving woolen cloth, which was then pounded flat and given a smooth finish in water-powered fulling mills. This mixed system of mill and outwork production soon gave way to fully mechanized factories; the number of water-driven cotton spindles soared from 8,000 in 1809 to 333,000 in 1817.

The expansion of manufacturing offered new opportunities—and new risks—to farmers. Ambitious farm families switched from growing crops for subsistence to raising livestock for sale. They sold meat, butter, and cheese to city markets and cattle hides to the booming shoe industry. "Along the whole road from Boston, we saw women engaged in making cheese," a Polish traveler reported from central Massachusetts. Other farm families raised sheep and sold raw wool to textile manufacturers. Processing these raw materials invigorated many farming towns. In 1792, Concord, Massachusetts, had one slaughterhouse and five small tanneries; a decade later, the town boasted eleven slaughterhouses and six large tanneries.

As the rural economy churned out more goods, it significantly altered the environment. Foul odors from stockyards and tanning pits wafted over Concord and many other leather-producing towns. To secure hemlock bark to process stiff hides into pliable leather, tanners cut down thousands of acres of trees each year. Huge herds of livestock—dairy cows, cattle, and especially sheep—brought the destruction of even more trees, felled to create vast pastures and meadows. By 1850, most of the forests in southern New England and eastern New York were gone: "The hills had been stripped of their timber," New York's *Catskill Messenger* reported, "so as to present their huge, rocky projections." Scores of textile milldams dotted New England's rivers, altering their flow and preventing fish from reaching upriver spawning grounds. Even as the income of many farmers rose, the quality of their natural environment deteriorated.

In the new capitalist-run market economy rural parents and their children worked longer and harder. They made yarn, hats, and brooms during the winter and then turned to their regular farming chores during the warmer seasons. More important, these farm families now depended on the income from wage labor and market sales to purchase the textiles, shoes, and hats they had once made for themselves. The new productive system made families and communities more efficient and prosperous—and more dependent on a market they could not control.

Transportation Bottlenecks and Government Initiatives

America's very size threatened to limit its economic growth. Water transport was the quickest and cheapest way to get goods to market, but many new settlements were not near navigable streams. Consequently, improved overland trade became a high priority. Between 1793 and 1812, the Massachusetts legislature granted charters to more than one hundred private turnpike companies. These charters gave the companies special legal status and often included monopoly rights to a transportation route. Pennsylvania issued fifty-five charters, including one to the Lancaster Turnpike Company. The company quickly built a graded gravel road between Lancaster and Philadelphia, a distance of 65 miles. This venture was expensive and yielded only modest profits but gave an enormous boost to the regional economy. Although turnpike investors received about "three percent annually," Henry Clay estimated, society as a whole "actually reap[ed] fifteen or twenty per cent." A farm woman knew what Clay meant: "The turnpike is finished and we can now go to town at all times and in all weather." A boom in turnpike construction soon connected dozens of inland market centers to seaport cities.

Meanwhile, state governments and private entrepreneurs improved water transport. They dredged shallow rivers to make them navigable and constructed canals to bypass waterfalls or rapids. But settlers in the rapidly growing states of Kentucky and Tennessee and in the southern regions of Ohio, Indiana, and Illinois relied on the great Ohio and Mississippi rivers and their tributaries to market their goods. These settlers paid premium prices for farmland near the rivers, and speculators bought up property in the cities along their banks: Cincinnati, Louisville, Chattanooga, and St. Louis. Farmers and merchants built barges to carry cotton, surplus grain, and meat downstream to New Orleans, which by 1815 was handling about $5 million in agricultural products yearly.

Public Policy: The Commonwealth System

Legislative support for road and canal companies reflected the ideology of mercantilism: government-assisted economic development. Just as the British Parliament had used the Navigation Acts to spur prosperity, so American state legislatures passed measures that their members thought would be "of great public utility" and increase the "common wealth." These laws generally took the form of special charters that bestowed valuable legal privileges. For example, most transportation charters included the valuable power of eminent domain, which allowed turnpike, bridge, and canal corporations to force the sale of privately owned land along their routes. State legislatures aided capitalist flour millers and textile manufacturers, who flooded adjacent farmland when they constructed dams to power their water-driven machinery. In Massachusetts, the Mill Dam Act of 1795, deprived farmers of their traditional right under common law to stop the flooding and forced the farmers to accept "fair compensation" for their lost acreage.

Critics condemned these grants to private enterprises as "Scheme[s] of an evident antirepublican tendency," as some "freeholder citizens" in Putney, Vermont, put it. The award of "peculiar privileges" to corporations, they argued, not only violated the "equal rights" of all citizens but also infringed on the sovereignty of the people. As a Pennsylvanian explained, "Whatever power is given to a corporation, is just so much power taken from the State" and its citizens. Nonetheless, judges in state courts, following the lead of John Marshall's Supreme Court (see Chapter 7), consistently upheld corporate charters and grants of eminent domain to private transportation companies. "The opening of good and easy internal communications is one of the highest duties of government," declared a New Jersey judge.

State mercantilism soon encompassed much more than transportation. Following Jefferson's embargo of 1807, which cut off goods and credit from Europe, the New England states awarded charters to two hundred iron-mining, textile-manufacturing, and banking companies, and Pennsylvania granted more than eleven hundred. By 1820, innovative state governments had created a republican political economy: a Commonwealth

▶ How did promoters of mercantilism (the Commonwealth System) use state and national governments to promote economic growth?

▶ Why did many Americans believe that the grant of special privileges and charters to private businesses violated republican principles?

System that funneled state aid to private businesses whose projects would improve the general welfare.

Toward a Democratic Republican Culture

After independence, many Americans in the northern states embraced a democratic republicanism that celebrated political equality and social mobility. These citizens, primarily members of the emerging **middle class**, redefined the nature of the family and of education by seeking more egalitarian marriages and more affectionate ways of rearing their children.

Social and Political Equality — for White Men

Between 1780 and 1820, hundreds of well-educated Europeans visitors agreed, almost unanimously, that the American republic embodied a genuinely new social order. In his famous *Letters from an American Farmer* (1782), French-born essayist J. Hector St. Jean de Crèvecoeur wrote that European society was composed "of great lords who possess everything, and of a herd of people who have nothing." The United States, by contrast, had "no aristocratical families, no courts, no kings, no bishops."

The absence of a hereditary aristocracy encouraged Americans to condemn inherited social privilege and to extol legal equality for all free men. "The law is the same for everyone" here, noted one European traveler. Yet Americans willingly accepted social divisions that reflected personal achievement. As individuals used their "talents, integrity, and virtue" to amass wealth, their social standing rose — a phenomenon that astounded many Europeans. "In Europe to say of someone that he rose from nothing is a disgrace and a reproach," remarked an aristocratic Polish visitor. "It is the opposite here. To be the architect of your own fortune is honorable. It is the highest recommendation."

Some Americans from long-distinguished families felt threatened by the nouveau riche and their ideology of wealth-driven social mobility. "Man is estimated by dollars," complained Nathaniel Booth, whose family had once dominated the small Hudson River port town of Kingston, New York, "what he is worth determines his character and his position." However, for most white men, such a merit-based system meant the opportunity to better themselves (Map 8.1).

Old cultural rules — and new laws — denied that opportunity to most women and African American men. When women and free blacks invoked the republican doctrine of equality and asked for voting rights, male legislators wrote explicit race and gender restrictions into the law. In 1802, Ohio disfranchised African Americans, and the New York constitution of 1821 imposed a property-holding requirement on black voters. A striking case of sexual discrimination occurred in New Jersey, where the state constitution of 1776 had granted **suffrage** to all property holders. After 1800, as Federalists and Republicans competed for power, they ignored customary gender rules and encouraged property-owning single women and widows to vote. Sensing a threat to the male-dominated political world, in 1807 the New Jersey legislature limited voting rights to white men only. To justify the exclusion of women, legislators invoked both biology and custom: "Women, generally, are neither by nature, nor habit, nor

MAP 8.1 The Expansion of Voting Rights for White Men, 1800 and 1830
Between 1800 and 1830, the United States moved steadily toward political equality for white men. Many existing states revised their constitutions and replaced a property qualification for voting with a less-restrictive criterion (the voter must pay taxes or have served in the militia). Some new states in the West extended the suffrage to all adult white men. As parties sought votes from a broader electorate, the tone of politics became more open and competitive, swayed by the interests and values of ordinary people.

education, nor by their necessary condition in society fitted to perform this duty with credit to themselves or advantage to the public."

Toward a Republican System of Marriage

The controversy over women's political rights mirrored a debate over authority within the household. British and American husbands had long claimed patriarchal power and had firm legal control of the family's property. But as John Adams lamented in 1776, the republican doctrine of political equality had "spread where it was not intended," encouraging some white women to speak out on politics and to demand legal and financial rights. These women insisted that their subordinate social position violated the republican principle of equal natural rights. Patriarchy was not a "natural" rule but a social contrivance, argued Patriot author and historian Mercy Otis Warren, and could be justified only "for the sake of order in families."

Economic and cultural changes also eroded customary paternal authority. In colonial America, most property-owning parents had arranged their children's marriages to protect welfare of the entire family. They looked for a son- or daughter-in-law with proper moral values and sufficient financial resources; the physical attraction and emotional compatibility between the young people were secondary considerations.

The Wedding, **1805**
Bride and groom stare intently into each other's eyes as they exchange vows, suggesting that their union was a love match, not a marriage based on economic calculation. Given the plain costumes of the guests and the sparse furnishings of the room, the unknown artist may have provided a picture of a rural Quaker wedding. Philadelphia Museum of the Fine Arts.

However, as land holdings shrank in long-settled rural communities, many yeomen fathers lacked farms to leave to their children and lost control over the choice of the children's spouses. Young men and women chose their own partners, influenced by a new cultural attitude: **sentimentalism**.

Sentimentalism originated in Europe as part of the Romantic movement and, after 1800, spread quickly through all classes of American society. Rejecting the Enlightenment's emphasis on rational thought, sentimentalism celebrated the importance of "feeling"—a physical, sensuous appreciation of God, nature, and other human beings. This new sensibility soon permeated the pages of German and English literary works, fell from the lips of actors in popular theatrical melodramas, and infused the emotional rhetoric of revivalist preachers.

As the hot sentimental passions of the heart overwhelmed the cool rational logic of the mind, a new marriage system appeared. Magazines praised marriages "contracted from motives of affection, rather than of interest," and many young people looked for a spouse who was, as Eliza Southgate of Maine put it, "calculated to promote my happiness." As young people "fell in love" and married, many fathers saw their roles change from authoritarian patriarchs to watchful paternalists, from dictating their children's behavior to protecting the children from the consequences of their own actions. To guard against a free-spending son-in-law, a wealthy father often placed his daughter's inheritance in a legal trust, where her husband could not get at it. Wrote one Virginia planter to his lawyer: "I rely on you to see the property settlement properly drawn before the marriage, for I by no means consent that Polly shall be left to the Vicissitudes of Life."

As voluntary agreements between individuals, love marriages conformed more closely to republican principles than did arranged matches. In theory, such **companionate marriages** gave wives "true equality, both of rank and fortune" with their husbands, as one Boston man suggested. In practice, though, husbands continued to dominate most marriages, both because male authority was deeply ingrained in cultural mores and because under American common law, husbands controlled the family's property. Moreover, the new love-based marriage system discouraged parents from protecting the interests of young wives, and governments refused to prevent domestic tyranny. As one lawyer noted, women who would rather "starve than submit" to the orders of their husbands were left to their fate. The marriage contract "is so much more important in its consequences to females than to males," a young man at the Litchfield Law School in Connecticut astutely observed in 1820, "for besides leaving everything else to unite themselves to one man, they subject themselves to his authority. He is their all — their only relative — their only hope" (see American Voices, p. 235).

Young adults who chose partners unwisely were severely disappointed when their spouses failed as providers or faithful companions. Before 1800, little could be done; officials granted divorces only in cases of neglect, abandonment, or adultery — serious offenses against the moral order of society. After 1800, most divorce petitions cited emotional, not moral, grounds. One woman complained that her husband had "ceased to cherish her," while a man grieved that his wife had "almost broke his heart." Responding to changing cultural values, several states expanded the legal grounds for divorce to include drunkenness and personal cruelty.

Republican Motherhood

Traditionally, American women spent most of their active adult years bearing and nurturing children. But by the 1790s, the birthrate in the northern seaboard states was dropping dramatically. In the farming village of Sturbridge in central Massachusetts, women who had married before 1750 usually had eight or nine children; in contrast, women who married around 1810 had an average of six children. In the growing seaport cities, native-born white women bore an average of only four children.

The United States was among the first countries in the world to experience this sharp decline in the birthrate — what historians call the demographic transition. There were several causes. Beginning in the 1790s, thousands of young men migrated to the trans-Appalachian West, which increased the number of never-married women in the East and delayed marriage for many more. Women who married later had fewer children. In addition, thousands of white couples in the urban middle classes deliberately limited the size of their families. Fathers favored smaller families so that they could leave their children an adequate inheritance; mothers, influenced by new ideas of individualism and self-achievement, did not want to spend their entire adulthood rearing children. After having four or five children, these couples used birth control or abstained from sexual intercourse.

Women's lives also changed because of new currents in Christian social thought. Traditionally, many religious writers had suggested that women were morally inferior

Female Submission in Marriage CAROLINE HOWARD GILMAN

The ideal American marriage of the early nineteenth century was republican (a contract between equals) and romantic (a match in which mutual love was foremost). Were these ideals attainable, given the social authority of men and the volatility of human passions? In the following excerpt from *Recollections of a Southern Matron* (1838), novelist Caroline Howard Gilman ponders such issues of domestic life. Caroline Howard was born in Boston in 1794 and moved to Charleston, South Carolina, with her husband, Samuel Gilman, a Unitarian minister.

The planter's bride, who leaves a numerous and cheerful family in her paternal home, little imagines the change which awaits her in her own retired residence. She dreams of an independent sway over her household, devoted love and unbroken intercourse with her husband, and indeed longs to be released from the eyes of others, that she may dwell only beneath the sunbeam of his. And so it was with me. After our bustling wedding and protracted journey, I looked forward to the retirement at Bellevue as a quiet port in which I should rest with Arthur. . . . The romance of our love was still in its glow, as might be inferred by the infallible sign of his springing to pick up my pocket-handkerchief whenever it fell. . . .

There we were together, asking for nothing but each other's presence and love. At length it was necessary for him to tear himself away to superintend his interests. . . . But the period of absence was gradually protracted; then a friend some-times came home with him, and their talk was of crops and politics, draining the fields and draining the revenue. . . . A growing discomfort began to work upon my mind. I had undefined forebodings; I mused about past days . . . my physical powers enfee-bled; a nervous excitement followed: I nursed a moody discontent, and ceased a while to reason clearly.

Woe to me had I yielded to this irritable temperament! . . . [Instead,] I was careful to consult my husband in those points which interested him, without annoying him with mere trifles. If the reign of romance was really waning, I resolved not to chill his noble confidence, but to make a steadier light rise on his affections. . . .

This task of self-government was not easy. To repress a harsh answer, to confess a fault and to stop (right or wrong) in the midst of self-defence, in gentle submission, sometimes requires a struggle like life and death; but these *three* efforts are the golden threads with which domestic happiness is woven. . . .

Men are not often unreasonable; their difficulties lie in not understanding the moral and physical structure of our sex. They often wound through ignorance, and are surprised at having offended. How clear is it, then, that woman loses by petulance and recrimination! Her first study must be self-control, almost to hypocrisy. A good wife must smile amid a thousand perplexities. . . .

Nor in these remarks would I chill the romance of some young dreamer, who is reposing her heart on another. Let her dream on . . . but let her be careful.

SOURCE: Anya Jabour, ed., *Major Problems in the History of American Families and Children* (Boston: Houghton Mifflin, 2005), 109–110.

to men and that many women were sexual temptresses. But by 1800, Protestant ministers were blaming men for sexual and social misconduct and claiming that modesty and purity were part of women's nature. Soon political leaders echoed that thinking. In his *Thoughts on Female Education* (1787), Philadelphia physician Benjamin Rush argued that a young woman should receive intellectual training so that she would be "an agreeable companion for a sensible man" and ensure her husband's "perseverance in the paths of rectitude." Rush also called for loyal "republican mothers" who would instruct "their sons in the principles of liberty and government."

Christian ministers readily embraced the idea of **republican motherhood**. "Preserving virtue and instructing the young are not the fancied, but the real 'Rights of Women,'" Reverend Thomas Bernard told the Female Charitable Society of Salem, Massachusetts. He urged his audience to dismiss the public roles for women, such as voting or serving on juries, that English feminist Mary Wollstonecraft had advocated in *A Vindication of the Rights of Woman* (1792). Instead, women should care for their children, a responsibility that gave them "an extensive power over the fortunes of man in every generation."

Raising and Educating Republican Children

Republican values also changed assumptions about inheritance and child rearing. Under English common law, when a father died without a will, his property passed to his eldest son, a practice known as primogeniture (see Chapter 1). After the Revolution, most state legislatures enacted statutes that required that such estates be divided equally among all the offspring. Most American parents applauded these statutes because they already treated their children equally and respectfully.

Indeed, many European visitors believed that republican parents gave their children too much respect and freedom. Because of the "general ideas of Liberty and Equality engraved on their hearts," a Polish aristocrat suggested around 1800, American children had "scant respect" for their parents. Several decades later, a British traveler stood dumbfounded as an American father excused his son's "resolute disobedience" with a smile and the remark "A sturdy republican, sir." The traveler guessed that American parents encouraged such independence to help the young people "go their own way" in the world.

Permissive child rearing was not universal. Foreign visitors interacted primarily with well-to-do Americans, who were mostly members of Episcopal or Presbyterian churches. Such parents often followed the teachings of rationalist religious writers influenced by John Locke and other Enlightenment thinkers. According to these authors, children were "rational creatures" who should be encouraged to act appropriately by means of advice and praise. The parents' role was to develop their child's conscience and self-discipline so that the child would act responsibly. This rationalist method of child rearing was widely adopted by families in the rapidly expanding middle class.

By contrast, many yeomen and tenant farmers, influenced by the Second Great Awakening, raised their children with authoritarian methods. Evangelical Baptist and Methodist writers insisted that children were "full of the stains and pollution of sin" and needed strict rules and harsh discipline. Fear was a "useful and necessary principle in family government," John Abbott, a minister, advised parents; a child "should submit to your authority, not to your arguments or persuasions." Abbott told parents to instill humility in children and to teach them to subordinate their personal desires to God's will.

The values transmitted within families were crucial because most education still took place within the household. In the 1790s, Bostonian Caleb Bingham, an influential textbook author, called for "an equal distribution of knowledge to make us emphatically a 'republic of letters.'" Both Thomas Jefferson and Benjamin Rush proposed ambitious schemes for a comprehensive system of primary and secondary schooling, followed by college for bright young men. They also envisioned a university in which distinguished scholars would lecture on law, medicine, theology, and political economy.

To ordinary citizens, whose teenage children had to work, talk of secondary and college education smacked of elitism. Farmers, artisans, and laborers wanted elementary schools that would instruct their children in the "three Rs": reading, 'riting, and 'rithmetic. In New England, locally funded public schools offered most boys and some girls such basic instruction in reading and writing. However, in other regions, there were few publicly funded schools, and only 25 percent of the boys and perhaps 10 percent of the girls attended private institutions or had personal tutors. Even in New England, only a small percentage of young men and almost no young women went on to grammar school (high school), and fewer than 1 percent of men attended college. "Let anybody show what advantage the poor man receives from colleges," an anonymous "Old Soldier" wrote to the *Maryland Gazette*. "Why should they support them, unless it is to serve those who are in affluent circumstances, whose children can be spared from labor, and receive the benefits?"

Although many state constitutions encouraged support for education, few legislatures acted on this issue until the 1820s. Then a new generation of reformers, primarily merchants and manufacturers, successfully campaigned to raise educational standards by certifying qualified teachers and appointing statewide superintendents of schools. To encourage self-discipline and individual enterprise in students, the reformers chose textbooks such as *The Life of George Washington* (c. 1800). Its author, Parson Mason Weems, used Washington's life to praise honesty and hard work and to condemn gambling, drinking, and laziness. Believing that patriotic instruction would foster shared cultural ideals, reformers required the study of American history. Thomas Low recalled his days as a New Hampshire schoolboy: "We were taught every day and in every way that ours was the freest, the happiest, and soon to be the greatest and most powerful country of the world."

Like Caleb Bingham, writer Noah Webster believed that education should raise the intellectual skills of his fellow citizens. Asserting that "America must be as independent in *literature* as she is in politics," he called on his fellow citizens to free themselves "from the dependence on foreign opinions and manners, which is fatal to the efforts of genius in this country." Webster's *Dissertation on the English Language* (1789) helpfully defined words according to American usage. With less success, it proposed that words be spelled as they were pronounced, that *labour* (British spelling), for example, be spelled *labur*. Still, Webster's famous "blue-back speller," a compact textbook first published in 1783, sold 60 million copies over the next half-century and served the needs of Americans of all backgrounds. "None of us was 'lowed to see a book," an enslaved African American recalled, "but we gits hold of that Webster's old blue-back speller and we . . . studies [it]."

Despite Webster's efforts, a republican literary culture was slow to develop. Ironically, the most accomplished and successful writer in the new republic was Washington Irving, an elitist-minded Federalist. His essays and histories, including *Salmagundi* (1807) and *Dietrich Knickerbocker's History of New York* (1809), which told the tales of "Rip Van Winkle" and "The Legend of Sleepy Hollow," sold well in America and won praise abroad. Impatient with the slow pace of American literary development, Irving lived for seventeen years in Europe, reveling in its aristocratic culture and intense intellectual life.

Apart from Irving, no American author was well known in Europe or, indeed, in the United States. "Literature is not yet a distinct profession with us," Thomas Jefferson told an English friend. "Now and then a strong mind arises, and at its intervals from business emits a flash of light. But the first object of young societies is bread and covering." Not until the 1830s and 1840s would American authors achieve a professional identity and, in the works of Ralph Waldo Emerson and novelists of the **American Renaissance**, make a significant contribution to Western literature (see Chapter 11).

▶ Did American culture become more democratic — for men, women, and African Americans — in the early nineteenth century? If so, how? If not, why not?

▶ How did republican ideas shape parent-child and marriage relationships and expectations?

Aristocratic Republicanism and Slavery

Republicanism in the South differed significantly from that in the North. Enslaved Africans constituted one-third of the South's population and exposed an enormous contradiction in white Americans' ideology of freedom and equality. "How is it that we hear the loudest yelps for liberty among the drivers of Negroes?" British author Samuel Johnson had chided the American rebels in 1775, a point some Patriots took to heart. "I wish most sincerely there was not a Slave in the province," Abigail Adams confessed to her husband, John. "It always appeared a most iniquitous Scheme to me — to fight ourselves for what we are daily robbing and plundering from those who have as good a right to freedom as we have."

The Revolution and Slavery, 1776–1800

In fact, the whites' struggle for independence raised the prospect of freedom for blacks. As the war began, a black preacher in Georgia told his fellow slaves that King George III "came up with the Book [the Bible], and was about to alter the World, and set the Negroes free." Similar rumors, probably prompted by Governor Dunmore's proclamation of 1775 (see Chapter 5), circulated among slaves in Virginia and the Carolinas, prompting thousands of African Americans to flee behind British lines. Two neighbors of Richard Henry Lee, a Virginia Patriot, lost "every slave they had in the world," as did many other planters. In 1781, when the British army evacuated Charleston, more than 6,000 former slaves went with them; another 4,000 left from Savannah. All told, 30,000

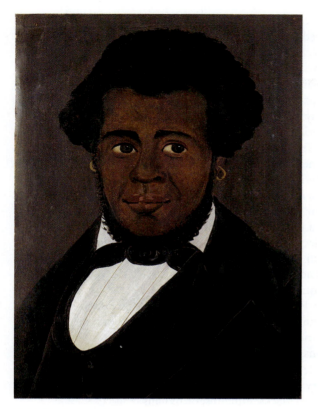

Captain Absalom Boston
Absalom Boston was born in 1785 on the island of Nantucket, Massachusetts, the heart of America's whaling industry. A member of a community of free African American whalers who had been manumitted by their Quaker owners, Boston went to sea at age fifteen. By the age of thirty, he had used his earnings to become the proprietor of a public inn. In 1822, Boston became the first black master with an all-black crew to undertake a whaling voyage from Nantucket. Later, he served as a trustee of the island's African School. Nantucket Historical Association.

blacks may have fled their owners. Hundreds of freed black Loyalists settled permanently in Canada. More than 1,000 others, poorly treated by British officials in Nova Scotia, sought a better life in Sierra Leone, West Africa, a settlement established by English antislavery organizations.

Yet thousands of African Americans supported the Patriot cause. Eager to raise their social status, free blacks in New England volunteered for military service in the First Rhode Island Company and the Massachusetts "Bucks." In Maryland, a significant number of slaves took up arms for the rebels in return for the promise of freedom. Enslaved Virginians struck informal bargains with their Patriot owners, trading loyalty in wartime for the hope of liberty. In 1782, the Virginia assembly passed a **manumission** act, which allowed individual owners to free their slaves; within a decade, planters had released 10,000 slaves.

Quakers took the lead in condemning slavery. Beginning in the 1750s, Quaker evangelist John Woolman urged Friends to free their slaves, and many did so. Rapidly growing evangelical Christian churches, notably the Methodists and the Baptists, initially advocated emancipation and admitted both enslaved and free blacks to their congregations. In 1784, a conference of Virginia Methodists declared that slavery was "contrary to the Golden Law of God on which hang all the Law and Prophets."

Enlightenment philosophy challenged the widespread belief among whites that Africans were inherently inferior to Europeans. John Locke had argued that ideas were not innate but stemmed from a person's experiences in the world. Accordingly, Enlightenment-influenced Americans suggested that the debased condition of blacks reflected their oppressive captivity: "A state of slavery has a mighty tendency to shrink and contract the minds of men." Defying popular opinion, Quaker philanthropist Anthony Benezet declared that African Americans were "as capable of improvement as White People" and funded a Philadelphia school for their education.

These religious and intellectual currents encouraged legal change. In 1784, judicial rulings abolished slavery in Massachusetts; over the next twenty years, every state north of Delaware enacted gradual emancipation legislation. These laws recognized white property rights by requiring slaves to buy their freedom by years — even decades — of additional labor. For example, the New York Emancipation Act of 1799 allowed slavery to continue until 1828 and freed slave children only at the age of twenty-five. As late as 1810, almost 30,000 blacks in the northern states — nearly one-fourth of the African Americans living there — were still enslaved. White opposition to black freedom and equality reflected fears of job competition and racial melding. Even as Massachusetts ended slavery in the state, the legislature reenacted an old law that prohibited whites from marrying blacks, mulattos, or Indians.

The tension in American republican ideology between liberty and property rights was greatest in the South, where enslaved African Americans represented a huge financial investment. Some Chesapeake tobacco planters, moved by religious principles or an oversupply of workers, allowed blacks to buy their freedom through paid work as artisans or laborers. Manumission and self-purchase gradually brought freedom to one-third of the African American residents of Maryland. The Virginia legislature, which had opened the door to manumission in 1782, shut it a decade later. Following the lead of Thomas Jefferson, who owned more than one hundred slaves, the legislators now argued that slavery was a "necessary evil" required to maintain white supremacy and the luxurious planter lifestyle. Resistance to black freedom was even greater in North Carolina, where the legislature condemned Quaker manumissions as "highly criminal and reprehensible." The slave-hungry rice- and cotton-growing states of South Carolina and Georgia totally rejected emancipation. Between 1790 and 1808, merchants and planters in the Lower South imported about 115,000 Africans — nearly half the number introduced into Britain's mainland settlements during the entire colonial period.

The debate over emancipation among Chesapeake whites ended in 1800, when Virginia authorities thwarted an uprising planned by Gabriel Prosser, an enslaved artisan, and hanged him and thirty of his followers. "Liberty and equality have brought the evil upon us," a letter to the *Virginia Herald* proclaimed, denouncing such doctrines as "dangerous and extremely wicked." To preserve their privileged social position, southern whites redefined republicanism: Its principles of individual liberty and legal equality applied only to members of the "master race," creating what historians call a *herrenvolk* (master people) republic.

The North and South Grow Apart

European visitors to the United States agreed that the South formed a distinct society, and many questioned its character. New England was home to religious "fanaticism," according to a British observer, but "the lower orders of citizens" there had "a better education, are more intelligent, and better informed" than those he met in the South. "The state of poverty in which a great number of white people live in Virginia" surprised the Marquis de Chastellux. Other visitors to the South commented on the rude manners, heavy drinking, and weak work ethic of its residents. White tenants and smallholding farmers seemed only to have a "passion for gaming at the billiard table, a cock-fight or cards," and many planters squandered their wealth on extravagant lifestyles while their slaves endured bitter poverty.

Some southerners worried that human bondage corrupted their society by encouraging ignorance and poverty among whites as well as blacks. A South Carolina merchant observed, "Where there are Negroes a White Man despises to work, saying what, will you have me a Slave and work like a Negroe?" Meanwhile, wealthy planters wanted a compliant labor force that was content with the drudgery of agricultural work. Consequently, they trained many of their slaves as field hands, allowing only a few to learn the arts of the blacksmith, carpenter, or bricklayer. Able to hire tutors for their own children, planters did little to provide ordinary whites with elementary schooling. In 1800, the political leaders of Essex County, Virginia, spent about 25 cents per person for local government, including schools, while their counterparts in Acton, Massachusetts, allocated about $1 per person. This difference in support for education mattered: By the 1820s, nearly all native-born men and women in New England could read and write; more than one-third of white southerners lacked these basic skills.

As the northern states ended human bondage, the South's commitment to slavery became a political issue. At the Philadelphia convention in 1787, northern delegates had accepted clauses allowing slave imports for twenty years and guaranteeing the return of fugitive slaves (see Chapter 6). Seeking additional protection for their "peculiar institution," southerners in the new national legislature won approval of James Madison's resolution that "Congress have no authority to interfere in the emancipation of slaves, or in the treatment of them within any of the States."

Nonetheless, slavery remained a contested issue. The black revolt in Haiti brought 6,000 white and mulatto refugees to the United States in 1793, and their stories of atrocities struck fear into the hearts of American slave owners. Simultaneously, northern politicians assailed the British impressment of American sailors as just "as oppressive and tyrannical as the slave trade" and demanded the end of both. When Congress outlawed American participation in the Atlantic slave trade in 1808, some northern representatives called for an end to the interstate trade in slaves. In response, southern leaders mounted a defense of their labor system. "A large majority of people in the Southern states do not consider slavery as even an evil," declared one congressman. The South's political clout—its domination of the presidency and the Senate—ensured that the national government would continue to protect slavery. During the War of 1812, American diplomats vigorously demanded compensation for slaves freed by British troops. Subsequently, Congress enacted legislation upholding the property rights of slave owners in the District of Columbia.

Political conflict increased as the South expanded its slave-based agricultural economy into the lower Mississippi Valley. Antislavery advocates had hoped that slavery would die out naturally as the Atlantic slave trade ended and the tobacco economy declined. Their hopes quickly faded as the cotton boom increased the demand for slaves, and Louisiana (1812), Mississippi (1817), and Alabama (1819) joined the Union with state constitutions that permitted slavery.

These events prompted a group of influential Americans to found the American Colonization Society, which proposed a new solution to the issues of slavery and race. According to Henry Clay—a Society member, Speaker of the House of Representatives, and slave owner—racial bondage had placed his state of Kentucky "in the rear of our neighbors . . . in the state of agriculture, the progress of manufactures, the advance of improvement, and the general prosperity of society." Slaves had to be freed, Clay and other colonizationists argued, and then sent back to Africa. Clay predicted that emancipation without removal would lead to "a civil war that would end in the extermination or subjugation of the one race or the other." To prevent racial chaos, the Colonization Society encouraged planters to emancipate their slaves, who now numbered almost 1.5 million people. But few planters responded to the Society's plea, and in the end, it resettled only about 6,000 African Americans in Liberia, a colony that the Society established on the west coast of Africa.

Most free blacks strongly opposed this and other colonization schemes. As Bishop Richard Allen of the African Methodist Episcopal Church put it, "this land which we have watered with our tears and our blood is now our mother country." Allen spoke from experience. Born into slavery in Philadelphia in 1760 and sold to a farmer in Delaware, Allen had grown up in bondage. In 1777, Freeborn Garretson, an itinerant preacher, converted Allen to Methodism and convinced Allen's owner that on Judgment Day, slaveholders would be "weighted in the balance, and . . . found wanting." Allowed to buy his freedom, Allen paid off his owner and then enlisted in the Methodist cause, becoming a "licensed exhorter" and then a regular minister in Philadelphia. In 1795, Allen formed a separate black congregation, the Bethel Church; in 1816, he became the first bishop of a new denomination: the African Methodist Episcopal Church. Two years later, 3,000 African Americans met in Allen's church to condemn colonization and to claim citizenship. Sounding the principles of democratic republicanism, they vowed to defy racial prejudice and advance in American society using "those opportunities . . . which the Constitution and the laws allow to all."

The Missouri Crisis, 1819–1821

The failure of colonization set the stage for a major battle over slavery. In 1818, Congressman Nathaniel Macon of North Carolina warned slave owners that radical members of the "bible and peace societies" hoped to use the national government to raise "the question of emancipation." And so they did. When Missouri applied for admission to the Union in 1819 with a constitution that allowed slavery, Congressman James Tallmadge of New York proposed an amendment: He would accept Missouri's constitution only if it banned the entry of new slaves and provided for the emancipation of existing slaves. Missouri whites rejected Tallmadge's proposals, and the northern majority in the House of Representatives blocked the territory's admission.

White southerners were horrified. "It is believed by some, & feared by others," Alabama senator John Walker reported from Washington, that Tallmadge's amendment was "merely the entering wedge and that it points already to a total emancipation of the blacks." Mississippi congressman Christopher Rankin warned his northern colleagues, "You conduct us to an awful precipice, and hold us over it." To underline their commitment to slavery, southerners used their power in the Senate—where they held half the seats—to withhold statehood from Maine, which was seeking to separate itself from Massachusetts.

In the ensuing debate over slavery, southerners advanced three constitutional arguments. First, invoking the principle of "equal rights," they argued that Congress could not impose conditions on Missouri that it had not imposed on other territories seeking statehood. Second, they maintained that the Constitution guaranteed a state's sovereignty with respect to its internal affairs and domestic institutions, such as slavery and marriage. Finally, they insisted that Congress had no authority to infringe on the property rights of individual slaveholders. Going beyond these constitutional arguments, southern leaders reaffirmed their commitment to human bondage. Abandoning the argument that slavery was a "necessary evil," they now invoked religion to champion it as a "positive good." "Christ himself gave a sanction to slavery," declared Senator William Smith of South Carolina. "If it be offensive and sinful to own slaves," a prominent Mississippi Methodist added, "I wish someone would just put his finger on the place in Holy Writ."

Controversy raged in Congress and in newspapers for two years before Henry Clay put together a series of political agreements known collectively as the Missouri Compromise. Faced with unwavering southern opposition to Tallmadge's amendment, a group of northern congressmen deserted the antislavery coalition. They accepted a deal that allowed Maine to enter the Union as a free state in 1820 and Missouri to follow as a slave state in 1821. This agreement preserved a balance in the Senate between North and South and set a precedent for future admissions to the Union. For their part, southern senators accepted the prohibition of slavery in the vast northern section of the Louisiana Purchase, the lands north of latitude 36°30′ (the southern boundary of Missouri) (Map 8.2).

As they had in the Constitutional Convention of 1787, white politicians had preserved the Union by compromising over slavery. But the task had become more difficult. The delegates in Philadelphia had resolved their sectional differences in two months; it took Congress two years to work out the Missouri Compromise, and their agreement did not command universal support. "If we

▶ How did the aristocratic republicanism of the South differ from the democratic republicanism of the North?

▶ What compromises over slavery did the members of Congress make to settle the Missouri crisis? Who benefited most from the agreement?

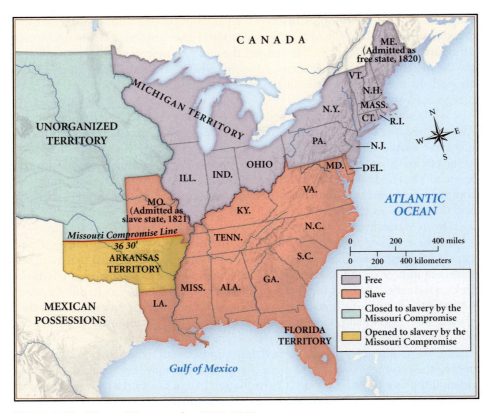

MAP 8.2 The Missouri Compromise, 1820–1821

The Missouri Compromise resolved for a generation the issue of slavery in the lands of the Louisiana Purchase. The agreement prohibited slavery north of the Missouri Compromise line (36°30′ north latitude), with the exception of the state of Missouri. To maintain an equal number of senators from free and slave states in the U.S. Congress, the compromise provided for the nearly simultaneous admission to the Union of Maine and Missouri.

For more help analyzing this map, see the Online Study Guide at **bedfordstmartins.com/henrettaconcise**.

yield now, beware," the *Richmond Enquirer* warned as southern congressmen agreed to exclude slavery from most of the Louisiana Purchase. "What is a *territorial* restriction to-day becomes a *state* restriction tomorrow." The fate of the western lands, enslaved blacks, and the Union itself were now inextricably intertwined, raising the specter of civil war and the end of the American republican experiment. As the aging Thomas Jefferson exclaimed during the Missouri crisis, "This momentous question, like a fire-bell in the night, awakened and filled me with terror."

Protestant Christianity as a Social Force

Throughout the colonial era, religion played a significant role in American life but not an overwhelming one. Then, beginning in 1790, a series of religious revivals planted the values of Protestant Christianity deep in the national character, giving a spiritual definition to American republicanism. These revivals especially changed the lives of blacks and of women. Thousands of African Americans absorbed the faith of white Baptists and Methodists and created a distinctive and powerful institution: the black Christian church. Evangelical Christianity also created new public roles for women, especially in the North, and set in motion a long-lasting movement for social reform.

A Republican Religious Order

The demand for greater liberty unleashed by the republican revolution of 1776 forced American lawmakers to devise new relationships between church and state. Previously, only the Quaker- and Baptist-controlled governments of Pennsylvania and Rhode Island had rejected a legally **established church** and compulsory religious taxes. Then, a convergence of factors—Enlightenment principles, wartime needs, and Baptist ideology—created a new religious regime of toleration and liberty.

Events in Virginia revealed the dynamics of change. In 1776, James Madison and George Mason used Enlightenment ideas of religious toleration to persuade the state's constitutional convention to guarantee all Christians the "free exercise of religion." No longer would the Anglican Church hold a privileged legal status. Virginia's Anglican political elite needed the support of Presbyterians and Baptists in the independence struggle, so it accepted the legitimacy of their churches. Baptists used their growing numbers to oppose the use of taxes to support religion. They convinced lawmakers to reject a bill, supported by George Washington and Patrick Henry, that would have imposed a tax to fund all Christian churches. Instead, in 1786, the Virginia legislature enacted Thomas Jefferson's Bill for Establishing Religious Freedom, which made all churches equal in the eyes of the law and granted direct financial support to none.

Elsewhere, the old order of a single established church crumbled away. In New York and New Jersey, the sheer number of denominations—Episcopalian, Presbyterian, Dutch Reformed, Lutheran, and Quaker, among others—prevented lawmakers from agreeing on an established church or compulsory religious taxes. Congregationalism remained the official state church in New England until the 1830s, but members of other denominations could now pay taxes to their own churches.

The separation of church and state was not complete because many influential Americans believed that religious institutions promoted morality and respect for governmental authority. "Pure religion and civil liberty are inseparable companions," a group of North Carolinians advised their minister. "It is your particular duty to enlighten mankind with the unerring principles of truth and justice, the main props of all civil government." Accepting this premise, most state governments indirectly supported churches by exempting their property and ministers from taxation.

Freedom of conscience also came with sharp cultural limits. In Virginia, Jefferson's Bill for Establishing Religious Freedom prohibited religious requirements for holding public office, but other states discriminated against anyone who dissented from the doctrines of Protestant Christianity. The North Carolina Constitution of 1776 disqualified from public employment any citizen "who shall deny the being of God, or the Truth of the Protestant Religion, or the Divine Authority of the Old or New Testament." No Catholics or Jews need apply. New Hampshire's constitution contained a similar provision until 1868.

Americans influenced by Enlightenment deism and by Evangelical Protestantism condemned these religious restrictions. Jefferson, Franklin, and other American intellectuals maintained that God had given humans the power of reason so that they could determine moral truths for themselves. To protect society from "ecclesiastical tyranny," they demanded complete freedom of conscience. Many evangelical Protestants also demanded religious liberty; their goal was to protect their churches from an oppressive government. Isaac Backus, a New England minister, warned Baptists not to incorporate their churches or accept public funds because that might lead to state control. In Connecticut, a devout Congregationalist welcomed "voluntarism," the uncoerced funding of churches by their members, because it allowed the laity to control the clergy, thereby furthering self-government and "the principles of republicanism."

The Second Great Awakening

Overshadowing such debates, a decades-long series of religious revivals — the Second Great Awakening — made the United States a genuinely Christian society. The churches that prospered during the revivals were primarily those that preached spiritual equality and governed themselves democratically. Because bishops and priests dominated the Roman Catholic Church, it attracted few Protestants, who preferred Luther's doctrine of the priesthood of all believers. Nor did the Catholic Church appeal to the unchurched — the great number of Americans who ignored or repudiated all religious institutions. Likewise, few Americans joined the Protestant Episcopal Church, the successor to the Church of England, because it also had a clerical hierarchy of bishops and was dominated by its wealthiest lay members. The Presbyterian Church attracted more adherents, in part because its churches elected laymen to the synods, the congresses that determined doctrine and practice. Evangelical Methodist and Baptist churches were by far the most popular. The Baptists boasted a republican church organization, with self-governing congregations. Both Baptists and Methodists developed an egalitarian religious culture marked by communal singing and emotional services.

Baptists and Methodists assumed a prominent role in the revivalist movement that began in the 1790s, as they evangelized the cities and the backcountry of New England. A new sect of Universalists, who repudiated the Calvinist doctrine of predestination and preached universal salvation, gained tens of thousands of converts, especially in Massachusetts and northern New England. After 1800, enthusiastic camp meetings swept the frontier regions of South Carolina, Tennessee, Ohio, and Kentucky. The largest gathering, at Cane Ridge in Kentucky in 1801, lasted for nine electrifying days and nights and attracted almost 20,000 people (Map 8.3). With these revivals, Baptist and Methodist preachers reshaped the spiritual landscape throughout the South. Offering a powerful emotional message and the promise of religious fellowship, revivalists attracted both unchurched individuals and pious families searching for social ties in their new frontier communities (see Voices from Abroad, p. 248).

The Second Great Awakening changed the denominational makeup of American religion. The most important churches of the colonial period — the Congregationalists, Episcopalians, and Quakers — grew slowly from the natural increase of their members. But Methodist and Baptist churches expanded spectacularly by winning converts, and soon they were the largest denominations. In the urbanized Northeast,

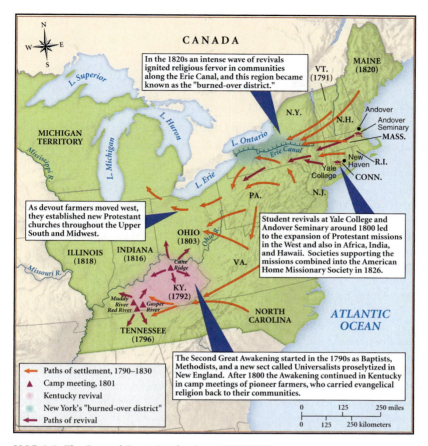

In the 1820s an intense wave of revivals ignited religious fervor in communities along the Erie Canal, and this region became known as the "burned-over district."

As devout farmers moved west, they established new Protestant churches throughout the Upper South and Midwest.

Student revivals at Yale College and Andover Seminary around 1800 led to the expansion of Protestant missions in the West and also in Africa, India, and Hawaii. Societies supporting the missions combined into the American Home Missionary Society in 1826.

The Second Great Awakening started in the 1790s as Baptists, Methodists, and a new sect called Universalists proselytized in New England. After 1800 the Awakening continued in Kentucky in camp meetings of pioneer farmers, who carried evangelical religion back to their communities.

- ← Paths of settlement, 1790–1830
- ▲ Camp meeting, 1801
- Kentucky revival
- New York's "burned-over district"
- ← Paths of revival

MAP 8.3 The Second Great Awakening, 1790–1860

The awakening lasted for decades and invigorated churches in every part of the nation. The revivals in Kentucky and New York State were particularly influential. As thousands of farm families migrated to the West, they carried with them the fervor generated by the Cane Ridge revival in Kentucky in 1801. Between 1825 and 1835, the area along the Erie Canal in New York witnessed so many revivals that it came to be known as the Burned-over District.

pious women aided their ministers by holding prayer meetings and providing material aid to members and potential converts. In the rural South and West, Methodist preachers followed a circuit, "riding a hardy pony or horse" with their "Bible, hymn-book, and Discipline" to visit existing congregations on a regular schedule. These preachers established new churches by searching out devout families, bringing them together for worship, and then appointing lay elders to lead the congregation and enforce moral discipline.

Evangelical ministers copied the "practical preaching" techniques of George Whitefield and other eighteenth-century revivalists (see Chapter 4). To attract converts, preachers spoke from memory in plain language but with a flamboyant style and theatrical gestures. "Preach without papers" and emphasize piety rather than theology, advised one minister, "seem earnest & serious; & you will be listened to with Patience, & Wonder."

A Camp Meeting in Indiana   FRANCES TROLLOPE

Frances Trollope, the mother of British novelist Anthony Trollope, lived for a time in Cincinnati, where she owned a store that sold imported European goods. Her critical and at times acerbic *Domestic Manners of the Americans* (1832) was a best-seller in Europe and the United States. Here, she provides a vivid description of a revivalist meeting in Indiana around 1830.

We reached the ground about an hour before midnight, and the approach to it was highly picturesque. The spot chosen was the verge of an unbroken forest, where a space of about twenty acres appeared to have been partially cleared for the purpose. . . . Four high frames, constructed in the form of altars, were placed at the four corners of the inclosure; . . . a rude platform was erected to accommodate the preachers, fifteen of whom attended this meeting, and . . . preached in rotation, day and night, from Tuesday to Saturday.

When we arrived, the preachers were silent; but we heard issuing from nearly every tent mingled sounds of praying, preaching, singing, and lamentation. . . . The floor [of one of the tents] was covered with straw, which round the sides was heaped in masses, that might serve as seats, but which at that moment were used to support the heads and arms of the close-packed circle of men and women who knelt on the floor.

Out of about thirty persons thus placed, perhaps half a dozen were men. One of these [was] a handsome-looking youth of eighteen or twenty. . . . His arm was encircling the neck of a young girl who knelt beside him, with her hair hanging dishevelled upon her shoulders, and her features working with the most violent agitation; soon after they both fell forward on the straw, as if unable to endure in any other attitude the burning eloquence of a tall grim figure in black, who, standing erect in the center, was uttering with incredible vehemence an oration that seemed to hover between praying and preaching. . . .

One tent was occupied exclusively by Negroes. They were all full-dressed, and looked exactly as if they were performing a scene on a stage. . . . One or two [women] had splendid turbans; and all wore a profusion of ornaments. The men were in snow white pantaloons, with gay colored linen jackets. One of these, a youth of coal-black comeliness, was preaching with the most violent gesticulations. . . .

At midnight, a horn sounded through the camp, which, we were told, was to call the people from private to public worship. . . . There were about two thousand persons assembled.

One of the preachers began in a low nasal tone, and, like all other Methodist preachers, assured us of the enormous depravity of man. . . . Above a hundred persons, nearly all females, came forward, uttering howlings and groans so terrible that I shall never cease to shudder when I recall them. They appeared to drag each other forward, and on the word being given, "let us pray," they fell on their knees . . . and they were soon all lying on the ground in an indescribable confusion of heads and legs.

SOURCE: Frances Trollope, *Domestic Manners of the Americans* (London: Whittaker, Treacher, 1832), 139–142.

Women in the Awakening
The Second Great Awakening was a pivotal moment in the history of American women. In this detail from *Religious Camp Meeting*, painted by J. Maze Burbank in 1839, all the preachers are men, but women fill the audience and form the majority of those visibly "awakened." By transforming millions of women into devout Christians, the Awakening provided Protestant churches with dedicated workers, teachers, and morality-minded mothers. When tens of thousands of these women also joined movements for temperance, abolition, and women's rights, they spurred a great wave of social reform. Old Dartmouth Historical Society/New Bedford Whaling Museum, New Bedford, Massachusetts.

In the South, evangelical religion was initially a disruptive force because many ministers spoke of spiritual equality and criticized slavery. Husbands and planters grew angry when their wives became more assertive and when blacks joined their congregations. To retain white men in their churches, Methodist and Baptist preachers gradually adapted their religious message to justify the authority of yeomen patriarchs and slave-owning planters. A Baptist minister declared that a man was naturally at "the head of the woman," and a Methodist conference proclaimed "that a Christian slave must be submissive, faithful, and obedient."

Other evangelists persuaded planters to spread Protestant Christianity among their African Americans slaves. During the eighteenth century, most blacks had maintained the religious practices of their African homelands, giving homage to African gods and spirits or practicing Islam. "At the time I first went to Carolina," remembered Charles Ball, a former slave, "there were a great many African slaves in the country. . . . Many of them believed there were several gods [and] I knew several . . . Mohamedans [Muslims]." Then, in the mid-1780s, Protestant evangelists converted hundreds of African Americans along the James River in Virginia and throughout the Chesapeake region.

Subsequently, black Christians adapted Protestant teachings to their own needs. They generally ignored the doctrines of original sin and Calvinist predestination as well as biblical passages that encouraged unthinking obedience to authority. Some African American converts envisioned the Christian God as a warrior who had liberated the Jews. Their own "cause was similar to the Israelites," preacher Martin Prosser told his fellow slaves as they plotted rebellion in Virginia in 1800. "I have read in my Bible where God says, if we worship him, . . . five of you shall conquer a hundred and a hundred of you a hundred thousand of our enemies." Confident of a special relationship with God, Christian slaves prepared themselves spiritually for emancipation, the first step in their journey to the Promised Land.

Influenced by republican ideology, many whites also rejected the Calvinists' emphasis on human depravity and weakness; instead, they celebrated human reason and free will. In New England, many educated Congregationalists discarded the mysterious concept of the Trinity—Father, Son, and Holy Spirit—and, taking the name Unitarians, worshipped a "united" God. "The ultimate reliance of a human being is, and must be, on his own mind," argued William Ellery Channing, a famous Unitarian minister. A children's catechism conveyed the denomination's optimistic message: "If I am good, God will love me, and make me happy."

Other New England Congregationalists softened traditional Calvinist doctrines. Lyman Beecher, the preeminent Congregationalist clergyman of the early nineteenth century, preached the traditional Christian belief that people had a natural tendency to sin; but, rejecting predestination, he affirmed the capacity of all men and women to choose God. In accepting the doctrine of free will, Beecher testified to the growing belief that people could shape their destiny. "Free Will" Baptists held similar views.

Reflecting this optimism, Reverend Samuel Hopkins linked individual salvation to religious benevolence—the practice of disinterested virtue. As the Presbyterian minister John Rodgers explained, fortunate individuals who had received God's grace had a duty "to dole out charity to their poorer brothers and sisters." Heeding this message, pious merchants in New York City founded the Humane Society and other charitable organizations. By the 1820s, so many devout Protestant men and women had embraced benevolent reform that conservative church leaders warned them not to neglect spiritual matters. Still, improving society emerged as a key element of the new religious sensibility. Said Lydia Maria Child, a devout Christian social reformer: "The only true church organization [is] when heads and hearts unite in working for the welfare of the human-race."

By the 1820s, Protestant Christians were well positioned to undertake that task. Unlike the First Great Awakening, which split churches into warring factions, the Second Great Awakening fostered cooperation among denominations. Religious leaders founded five interdenominational societies: the American Education Society (1815), the Bible Society (1816), the Sunday School Union (1824), the Tract Society (1825), and the Home Missionary Society (1826). Although based in eastern cities—New York, Boston, and Philadelphia—these societies ministered to the nation, dispatching hundreds of missionaries to western regions and distributing tens of thousands of religious pamphlets.

Increasingly, Protestant ministers and laypeople saw themselves as part of a united religious movement that could change the course of history. "I want to see our state evangelized," declared a pious churchgoer near the Erie Canal (where the fires of revivalism were so hot that the region was known as the "Burned-over District"): "Suppose the great State of New York in all its physical, political, moral, commercial, and pecuniary resources should come over to the Lord's side. Why it would turn the scale and could convert the world. I shall have no rest until it is done."

Because the Second Great Awakening aroused such enthusiasm, religion became an important force in political life. On July 4, 1827, the Reverend Ezra Stiles Ely called on the members of the Seventh Presbyterian Church in Philadelphia to begin a "Christian party in politics." Ely's sermon, "The Duty of Christian Freemen to Elect Christian Rulers," proclaimed a religious goal for the American republic—an objective that Thomas Jefferson and John Adams would have found strange and troubling. The two founders had both died precisely a year before, on July 4, 1826, the fiftieth anniversary of the Declaration of Independence, and had gone to their graves believing that America's mission was to spread political republicanism. In contrast, Ely urged the United States to become an evangelical Christian nation dedicated to religious conversion at home and abroad: "All our rulers ought in their official capacity to serve the Lord Jesus Christ." Similar calls for a union of church and state would arise again during the Third (1880–1900) and Fourth (1970–present) Great Awakenings among American Christians.

Women's New Religious Roles

The upsurge in religious enthusiasm prompted women to demonstrate their piety and even to found new sects. Mother Ann Lee organized the Shakers in Britain and then, in 1774, migrated to America, where she attracted numerous recruits; by the 1820s, Shaker communities dotted the American countryside from New Hampshire to Indiana (see Chapter 11). Jemima Wilkinson, a young Quaker woman in Rhode Island, founded a more controversial sect. Stirred by reading George Whitefield's sermons, Wilkinson had a vision that she had died and been reincarnated as Christ. Wilkinson declared herself the "Publick Universal Friend," dressed in masculine attire, and preached a new gospel. Her teachings blended the Calvinist warning of "a lost and guilty, gossiping, dying World" with Quaker-inspired plain dress, pacifism, and abolitionism. Wilkinson's charisma initially won scores of converts, but her radical lifestyle and ambiguous gender aroused hostility, and her sect dwindled away.

These female-led sects were less significant than the activities of thousands of women in mainstream churches. For example, women in New Hampshire managed more than fifty local "cent" societies that raised funds for the Society for Promoting Christian Knowledge, New York City women founded the Society for the Relief of

Poor Widows, and young Quaker women in Philadelphia ran the Society for the Free Instruction of African Females.

Women took charge of religious and charitable enterprises both because they were excluded from other public roles and because of their numbers. After 1800, more than 70 percent of the members of New England Congregational churches were women. This shift in membership prompted Congregational ministers to end traditional gender-segregated prayer meetings, and evangelical Methodist and Baptist preachers encouraged mixed-sex praying. "Our prayer meetings have been one of the greatest means of the conversion of souls," a minister in central New York reported in the 1820s, "especially those in which brothers and sisters have prayed together."

Far from leading to sexual promiscuity, as critics feared, mixing the men and women promoted greater self-discipline. Believing in female virtue, many young women and the men who courted them now postponed sexual intercourse until after marriage — previously a much rarer form of self-restraint. In Hingham, Massachusetts, and many other New England towns, more than 30 percent of the women who married between 1750 and 1800 bore a child within eight months of their wedding day; by the 1820s, the rate had dropped to 15 percent.

As women claimed new spiritual authority, men tried to curb their power. In the North as in the South, evangelical Baptist churches that had once advocated spiritual equality now prevented women from voting on church matters or offering testimonies of faith before the congregation. Those activities, one layman declared, were "directly opposite to the apostolic command in [Corinthians] xiv, 34, 35, 'Let your women learn to keep silence in the churches.'" "Women have a different *calling*," claimed another man. "That they *be chaste, keepers at home* is the Apostle's direction." But such injunctions merely changed the locale of women's activism. Embracing the concepts of republican and Christian motherhood, mothers throughout the United States founded maternal associations to encourage proper child rearing. By the 1820s, *Mother's Magazine* and other newsletters, widely read in hundreds of small towns and villages, were giving women a sense of shared purpose and identity.

Religious activism advanced female education. Churches established academies where girls from the middling classes received intellectual and moral instruction. Emma Willard, the first American advocate of higher education for women, opened the Middlebury Female Seminary in Vermont in 1814 and later founded girls' academies in Waterford and Troy, New York. Beginning in the 1820s, women educated in these seminaries and academies displaced men as public-school teachers, in part because women accepted lower pay than men would. Female schoolteachers earned from $12 to $14 a month with room and board — less than a farm laborer. But as schoolteachers, women had an acknowledged place in public life, a goal that previously had been beyond their reach.

▶ Which American churches were the most republican in their institutions and ideology?

▶ Why did Protestant Christianity and Protestant women emerge as forces for social change?

Just as the ideology of democratic republicanism had expanded voting rights and the political influence of ordinary men in the North, so the values of Christian republicanism had bolstered the public authority of middling women. The Second

Great Awakening made Americans a fervently Protestant people. Along with the values of republicanism and capitalism, this religious impulse formed the core of an emerging national identity.

SUMMARY

Like all important ideologies, republicanism has many facets. We have explored three of them in this chapter. We saw how state legislatures created capitalist common-wealths in which governments actively supported private businesses that contributed to the public welfare. This republican-inspired policy of state mercantilism remained dominant until the 1840s, when it was replaced by classical liberal doctrines (see Chapter 10).

We also saw how republicanism gradually changed social and family values. The principle of legal equality encouraged social mobility among white men and prompted men and women to seek companionate marriages. Republicanism likewise encouraged parents to provide their children with equal inheritances and to allow them to choose their marriage partners. In the South, republican doctrines of liberty and equality co-existed uneasily with slavery and ultimately were restricted to the white population.

Finally, we observed the complex interaction of republicanism and religion. Stirred by republican principles, many citizens joined democratic and egalitarian denomina-tions, particularly Methodist and Baptist churches. Inspired by "benevolent" ideas and the enthusiastic preachers of the Second Great Awakening, many women devoted their energies to religious purposes and social reform organizations. The result of all these initiatives—in economic policy, social relations, and religious institutions—was the creation of a distinctive American republican culture.

Connections: Culture

Between the 1760s and the 1820s, Americans began to create a common culture, a sense of American nationality that would flower in the nineteenth century. As we sug-gested in the essay that opened Part Two,

> [b]y 1820, to be an American meant, for many members of the dominant white popula-tion, to be a republican, a Protestant, and an enterprising individual in a capitalist-run market system.

The creation of a national culture took place in stages. As we saw in Chapter 5, the Patriot movement generated a sense of American identity—in contrast to a Virginian or New York identity—and the republican revolution of 1776 gave it ideological con-tent. In Chapters 6 and 7, we noted how the creation of a national government, first in the Confederation and then under the Constitution of 1787, augmented that political identity even as it generated conflicts between Federalists and Republicans. Simultane-ously, the intense focus on financial gain by tens of thousands of entrepreneurial farm-ers, planters, artisans, and merchants shaped a culture that placed a high value on hard work and economic achievement. Finally, in this chapter, we saw how the Revolution increased religious liberty and set in motion the revivalism and reformism that added Christian and benevolent components to the emergent American identity.

TIMELINE

1782	▶ St. Jean de Crèvecoeur publishes *Letters from an American Farmer*	**1795**	▶ Massachusetts Mill Dam Act assists textile industry
	▶ Virginia allows manumission (reversed in 1792)	**1800**	▶ Gabriel Prosser plots slave uprising in Virginia
1783	▶ Noah Webster issues his "blue-back" speller	**1800s**	▶ Rise of sentimentalism and of companionate marriages
1784	▶ Massachusetts abolishes slavery; other northern states provide for gradual emancipation		▶ Women's religious activism; founding of female academies
			▶ Religious benevolence sparks social reform
1787	▶ Benjamin Rush writes *Thoughts on Female Education*	**1801**	▶ Cane Ridge revival in Kentucky
1790s	▶ States grant charters to corporations	**1807**	▶ New Jersey excludes propertied women from suffrage
	▶ Private companies build toll roads and canals		
	▶ Merchants develop rural outwork system	**1816**	▶ Congress charters Second Bank of the United States
	▶ Chesapeake blacks become Protestants	**1817**	▶ American Colonization Society founded
	▶ Parents limit family size as farms shrink	**1819**	▶ Sharp decline in farm prices sets off panic
	▶ Second Great Awakening expands church membership	**1819–1821**	▶ Missouri Compromise devised
1791	▶ Congress charters First Bank of the United States	**1820s**	▶ States enhance public education
1792	▶ Mary Wollstonecraft's *A Vindication of the Rights of Woman* is published		▶ Women become schoolteachers

FOR FURTHER EXPLORATION

R. Kent Newmyer, *The Supreme Court Under Marshall and Taney* (1968), concisely analyzes constitutional development. Jeffrey L. Pasley, Andrew W. Robertson, and David Waldstreicher, eds., *Beyond the Founders: New Approaches to the Political History of the Early American Republic* (2004), shows how ordinary citizens promoted a democratic polity. Jack Larkin, *The Reshaping of Everyday Life, 1790–1840* (1997), explores the changing texture of daily life, as does the Web site **memorialhall.mass.edu/collection/index.html**.

For changing marriage rules, consult Nancy Cott, *Public Vows: A History of Marriage and the Nation* (2000); for an intimate portrayal of family life in Maine, read Laurel Thatcher Ulrich, *A Midwife's Tale: The Life of Martha Ballard* (1990), and consult the Web sites **www.pbs.org/amex/midwife** and **www.DoHistory.org**.

Jan Lewis's *The Pursuit of Happiness* (1983) explores the lives of the paternalistic slave-owning gentry of the Upper South, while James David Miller, *South by Southwest: Planter Emigration and Identity in the Slave South* (2002), discusses their migration to the Mississippi Valley. For discussions of slavery, see Douglas R. Egerton, *Gabriel's Rebellion: The Virginia Slave Conspiracies of 1800 and 1802* (1995) and the references in Chapter 12.

In *The Democratization of American Christianity* (1987), Nathan Hatch traces the impact of Evangelical Protestantism. Other fine overviews of American religion are Mark A. Noll, *America's God: From Jonathan Edwards to Abraham Lincoln* (2003), and Bernard Weisberger, *They Gathered at the River* (1958).

TEST YOUR KNOWLEDGE

To assess your mastery of the material in this chapter and for Web sites, images, and documents related to this chapter, visit **bedfordstmartins.com/henrettaconcise**.

PART THREE

Economic Revolution and Sectional Strife

1820–1877

ECONOMY	SOCIETY	GOVERNMENT
The economic revolution occurs	**A new class structure emerges**	**Creating a democratic polity**
1820 ▸ Waltham textile factory opens (1814) ▸ Erie Canal completed (1825) ▸ Market economy expands nationwide ▸ Cotton belt emerges in South	▸ Business class emerges ▸ Rural women and girls recruited as factory workers ▸ Mechanics form craft unions ▸ Waged work increases	▸ Spread of universal white male suffrage ▸ Rise of Andrew Jackson and Democratic Party ▸ Anti-Masonic Party rises and declines
1830 ▸ Protective tariffs (1828, 1832) trigger nullification crisis ▸ Panic of 1837 ▸ U.S. textiles compete with British	▸ Depression (1837–1843) shatters labor movement ▸ New urban popular culture appears	▸ Whig Party forms (1834) ▸ Second Party System emerges ▸ Jackson expands presidential power
1840 ▸ Irish immigrants join labor force ▸ *Commonwealth v. Hunt* (1842) assists unions; but workers remain "servants"	▸ Working-class districts emerge in cities ▸ Irish and German inflow sparks nativist movement	▸ Log cabin campaign (1840) mobilizes voters ▸ Antislavery parties: Liberty (1840) and Free-Soil (1848)
1850 ▸ Surge of cotton output in South and of railroads in North and Midwest ▸ Manufacturing expands	▸ Expansion of farm society into Midwest and Far West ▸ Free-labor ideology justifies inequality	▸ Whig Party disintegrates ▸ Republican Party founded (1854) ▸ Rise of southern secessionists
1860 ▸ Republicans enact Whigs' policy agenda: Homestead Act (1862), railroad aid, high tariffs, and national banking	▸ Emancipation Proclamation (1863) ▸ Free blacks in the South struggle for control of land	▸ Thirteenth Amendment (1865) ends slavery ▸ Fourteenth Amendment (1868) extends legal and political rights
1870 ▸ Panic of 1873	▸ Rise of sharecropping in the South	▸ Fifteenth Amendment (1870) extends vote to black men

CULTURE	SECTIONALISM
Reforming people and institutions	**From compromise to Civil War and Reconstruction**
▸ American Colonization Society (1817) ▸ Benevolent reform movements ▸ Revivalist Charles Finney ▸ Emerson and Transcendentalism	▸ Missouri crisis and compromise (1819–1821) ▸ David Walker's *Appeal . . . to the Colored Citizens of the World* (1829) ▸ Domestic slave trade moves African Americans west
▸ Joseph Smith founds Mormonism ▸ Temperance crusade expands ▸ Female Moral Reform Society (1834)	▸ Ordinance of Nullification (1832) and Force Bill (1833) ▸ W. L. Garrison forms American Anti-Slavery Society (1833)
▸ Fourierist and other communal settlements founded ▸ Seneca Falls women's convention (1848)	▸ Texas annexation (1845), Mexican War (1846–1848), and Wilmot Proviso (1846) increase sectional conflict
▸ Harriet Beecher Stowe's *Uncle Tom's Cabin* (1852) ▸ Anti-immigrant movement grows; Know-Nothing Party	▸ Compromise of 1850 ▸ Kansas-Nebraska Act (1854) and "Bleeding Kansas" ▸ *Dred Scott* decision (1857)
▸ U.S. Sanitary Commission founded (1861) ▸ Freedman's Bureau assists ex-slaves	▸ South Carolina leads secession movement ▸ Confederate States of America (1861–1865)
▸ Freed African Americans create schools and churches	▸ Compromise of 1877 ends Reconstruction

"The procession was nearly a mile long . . . [and] the democrats marched in good order to the glare of torches," a French visitor remarked in amazement during the election of 1832. "These scenes belong to history . . . the wondrous epic of the coming of democracy." As we will see in Part Three, history was being made in many ways between 1820 and 1877. A series of overlapping revolutions were transforming American society. One was political: the creation of a genuinely democratic polity. The second was economic: In 1820, the United States was predominately an agricultural nation; by 1877, the nation boasted one of the world's most powerful industrial economies. Third, there was far-reaching social and cultural change, including the Second Great Awakening, great movements of social reform, and the advent of a complex intellectual culture. These transformations affected every aspect of life in the North and Midwest and brought important changes in the South as well. Here, in brief, is an outline of that story.

ECONOMY

Impressive advances in industrial production, transportation, and trade transformed the nation's economy. Factory owners used high-speed machines and a new system of labor discipline to boost the output of goods dramatically. Manufacturers produced 5 percent of the country's wealth in 1820 but more than 30 percent in 1877. And thanks to enterprising merchants and entrepreneurs, who developed a network of canals and railroads and an integrated system of markets, they now sold their products throughout the nation.

SOCIETY

The new economy created a class-based society in the North and Midwest. A wealthy elite of merchants, manufacturers, bankers, and entrepreneurs rose to the top of the social order. To maintain social stability, they adopted a paternalistic program of benevolent reform. But an expanding urban middle class created a distinct material and religious culture and lent support to movements for radical social reform. A mass of propertyless workers, impoverished immigrants from Germany and Ireland, joined enslaved African Americans at the bottom of the social order. Meanwhile, slavery expanded in numbers and scope as planters created new plantations as far south and west as Texas.

GOVERNMENT

The rapid growth of political parties sparked the creation of a competitive and responsive democratic polity. Farmers, workers, and entrepreneurs persuaded governments to improve transportation, shorten workdays, and award valuable corporate charters. Catholic immigrants from Ireland and Germany entered politics to protect their cultures from restrictive legislation advocated by Protestant nativists and reformers.

With Andrew Jackson at its head, the Democratic Party led a political and constitutional revolution that cut government aid to financiers, merchants, and corporations. To contend with the Democrats, the Whig Party (and, in the 1850s, the Republican Party) devised a competing program that stressed economic development, moral reform, and individual social mobility. This party competition engaged the energies of the electorate and helped to unify a fragmented social order.

CULTURE

Between 1820 and 1860, a series of reform movements, many with religious roots and goals, swept across America. Dedicated men and women preached the gospel of temperance, Sunday observance, prison reform, and many other causes. A few Americans pursued their social dreams in utopian communities, but most reformers worked within the existing society. Abolitionists and women's rights activists demanded radical changes: the overthrow of the patriarchal legal order throughout the nation and the immediate end of slavery in the South. As southerners defended slavery as a "positive good," antislavery advocates demanded free soil in the West and an end to the "slave power."

SECTIONALISM

The economic revolution and social reform sharpened sectional divisions: The North developed into an urban industrial society based on free labor, whereas the South remained a rural agricultural society dependent on slavery. Following the Mexican War (1846–1848), northern and southern politicians struggled bitterly over the introduction of slavery in the vast territories seized from Mexico and the unsettled lands of the Louisiana Purchase. The election of Republican Abraham Lincoln in 1860 prompted the secession of the South from the Union and the Civil War. The conflict became a total war, a struggle between two societies, not just between two armies. Because of new military technology, disease, and huge armies, the two sides endured unprecedented casualties and costs.

The fruits of victory for the North were substantial. The Republican Party ended slavery and imposed its economic policies and constitutional doctrines on the South. But in the face of massive resistance from white southerners during the era of Reconstruction, northerners abandoned the effort to secure full political and civil rights for African Americans. These decades, which began with impressive economic, political, and social achievements, thus ended on the bitter notes of a costly war, an acrimonious peace, and half-won freedoms.

Economic Transformation
1820–1860

> The truth was [the American farmer and artisan] believed in Work first of all, so that every human being should stand in his own shoes, indebted only to his own efforts for his living and his place in the world.
>
> — Francis Henry Underwood, *Quabbin*, 1893

In 1804, life turned grim for eleven-year-old Chauncey Jerome of Connecticut. His father died suddenly, and Jerome faced indentured servitude on a nearby farm. Knowing that few farmers "would treat a poor boy like a human being," Jerome bought out his indenture by making dials for clocks and became a journeyman clockmaker for Eli Terry. A manufacturing wizard, Terry had designed an enormously popular desk clock with brass parts; his business turned Litchfield, Connecticut, into the clock-making center of the United States. In 1816, Jerome set up his own clock factory. By organizing work more efficiently and using new machines that made interchangeable metal parts, he drove down the price of a simple clock from $20 to $5 and then to less than $2. By the 1840s, he was selling his clocks in England, the hub of the Industrial Revolution; two decades later, his workers were turning out 200,000 clocks a year, clear testimony to American industrial enterprise. By 1860, the United States was not only the world's leading exporter of cotton and wheat but also the third-ranked manufacturing nation behind Britain and France.

"Business is the very soul of an American: the fountain of all human felicity," Francis Grund observed shortly after arriving from Europe. "It is as if all America were but one gigantic workshop, over the entrance of which there is the blazing inscription, 'No admission here, except on business.'" As the editor of *Niles' Weekly Register* in Baltimore put it, there was an "almost universal ambition to get forward." Stimulated by the entrepreneurial culture of early-nineteenth-century America, thousands of artisan-inventors like Eli Terry and Chauncey Jerome and thousands of merchants and traders propelled the country into a new economic era. Two great changes defined that era: the **Industrial Revolution**—the growth and mechanization of industry—and the **Market Revolution**—the expansion and integration of markets.

Not all Americans embraced the new ethic of enterprise, and many did not share in the new prosperity. The spread of industry and commerce created a class-divided society that challenged the founders' vision of an agricultural republic with few distinctions of wealth. As the philosopher Ralph Waldo Emerson warned in 1839: "The invasion of Nature by Trade with its Money, its Credit, its Steam, [and] its Railroad threatens to . . . establish a new, universal Monarchy."

The American Industrial Revolution

Industrialization came to the United States between 1790 and 1820, as merchants and manufacturers reorganized work routines and built factories. Thanks to **mass production**, goods that once had been luxury items became part of everyday life. The rapid construction of turnpikes, canals, and railroads by state governments and private entrepreneurs, working together in the Commonwealth System (see Chapter 8), allowed manufactures to be sold throughout the land.

The Division of Labor and the Factory

Rising rates of production stemmed initially from changes in the organization of work. Consider the shoe industry. Traditionally, New England shoemakers turned leather hides into finished shoes and boots in small wooden shacks called "ten-footers," where they determined the pace of work. During the 1820s and 1830s, the merchants and manufacturers of Lynn, Massachusetts, gradually displaced these independent artisans by introducing an outwork system and a **division of labor**. The employers hired semi-skilled journeymen and set them up in large shops cutting leather into soles and uppers. They sent out the upper sections to dozens of rural Massachusetts towns, where women binders sewed in fabric linings. The manufacturers then had other journeymen attach the uppers to the soles and return the shoes to the central shop for inspection, packing, and sale. The new system turned employers into powerful "shoe bosses" and eroded workers' wages and independence. But the division of labor dramatically increased the output of shoes and cut their price.

For products not suited to the outwork system, manufacturers created the modern **factory**, which concentrated production under one roof. For example, in the 1830s, Cincinnati merchants built large slaughterhouses that processed thousands of hogs every month. The technology remained simple: A system of overhead rails moved the hog carcasses past workers; the division of labor made the difference. One worker split the animals, another removed the organs, and others trimmed the carcasses into pieces. Packers then stuffed the cuts of pork into barrels and pickled them to prevent spoilage. The Cincinnati system was so efficient and quick—processing sixty hogs an hour—that by the 1840s, the city was known as "Porkopolis." By 1850, factories were slaughtering hogs at an enormous volume: 334,000 a year. Reported Frederick Law Olmsted:

> We entered an immense low-ceiling room and followed a vista of dead swine, upon their backs, their paws stretching mutely toward heaven. Walking down to the vanishing point, we found there a sort of human chopping-machine where the hogs were converted into commercial pork. . . . Plump falls the hog upon the table, chop, chop; chop, chop; chop,

Pork Packing in Cincinnati
The only modern technology in this Cincinnati pork-packing plant was the overhead pulley that carried hog carcasses past the workers. The plant's efficiency came from its organization, a division of labor in which each worker performed a specific task. Plants like this pioneered the design of the moving assembly line, which would reach a high level of sophistication in the early twentieth century in Henry Ford's automobile factories. Cincinnati Historical Society.

For more help analyzing this image, see the Online Study Guide at **bedfordstmartins.com/henrettaconcise**.

chop, fall the cleavers. . . . We took out our watches and counted thirty-five seconds, from the moment when one hog touched the table until the next occupied its place.

Some factories boasted impressive new technology. In the 1780s, Oliver Evans, a prolific Delaware inventor, built a highly automated flour mill driven by waterpower. His machinery lifted the wheat to the top of the mill, cleaned the grain as it fell into hoppers, ground it into flour, and then cooled the flour as it was poured into barrels. Evans's factory, remarked one observer, "was as full of machinery as the case of a watch." It needed only six men to mill 100,000 bushels of wheat a year — perhaps ten times as much as they could grind in a traditional mill.

By the 1830s, factory owners were using newly improved stationary steam engines to manufacture a wide array of products. Previously, most factories processed agricultural goods: pork, leather, wool, and cotton; by the 1840s, they were fabricating metal goods. Cyrus McCormick of Chicago used power-driven machines to make parts for reaping machines, which workers assembled on a power-driven conveyor belt. In Hartford, Connecticut, Samuel Colt built an assembly line to produce his invention, the six-shooter revolver. These advances in technology and factory organization alarmed British observers: "The contriving and making of machinery has become so common in this country . . . [that] it is to be feared that American manufacturers will become exporters not only to foreign countries, but even to England."

The Textile Industry and British Competition

British textile manufacturers were particularly worried about American competition. They persuaded the British government to prohibit the export of textile machinery and the emigration of **mechanics** who knew how to build it. Lured by high wages, though, thousands of British mechanics disguised themselves as ordinary laborers and sailed to the United States. By 1812, there were at least three hundred British mechanics at work in the Philadelphia area alone.

Samuel Slater was the most important of them. Slater came to America in 1789 after working for Richard Arkwright, who invented the most advanced British machinery for spinning cotton. Slater reproduced Arkwright's innovations in merchant Moses Brown's cotton mill in Providence, Rhode Island; its opening in 1790 symbolized the start of the Industrial Revolution in America.

In competing with British mills, American manufacturers had the advantage of an abundance of natural resources. The nation's farmers produced an abundance of cotton and wool, and the fast-flowing rivers cascading down from the Appalachian foothills to the Atlantic coastal plain provided a cheap source of energy. From Massachusetts to Delaware, these waterways were soon dotted with industrial villages and large textile mills, some as large as 150 feet long, 40 feet wide, and four stories high.

Still, British textile producers easily undersold their American competitors. Thanks to cheap transatlantic shipping and low interest rates in Britain, they could import raw cotton from the United States, manufacture it into cloth, and sell it in America at a bargain price. Moreover, thriving British companies could slash prices to drive fledgling American firms out of business. The most important British advantage was cheap labor: Britain had a larger population—about 12.6 million in 1810 compared to 7.3 million Americans—and thousands of landless laborers who were willing to take low-paying factory jobs. To offset these advantages, American entrepreneurs won help from the federal government. In 1816, 1824, and 1828, Congress passed tariff bills that protected textile manufacturers from imports of cotton and woolen cloth. But in 1833, under pressure from southern planters, western farmers, and urban consumers—who wanted inexpensive imports—Congress began to reduce the tariffs (see Chapter 10), cutting the profits of American firms.

American producers used two other strategies to compete with their British rivals. First, they improved on British technology. In 1811, Francis Cabot Lowell, a wealthy Boston merchant, toured British textile mills, secretly making detailed drawings of their power machinery. Paul Moody, an experienced American mechanic, then copied the machines and improved their design. In 1814, Lowell joined with merchants Nathan Appleton and Patrick Tracy Jackson to form the Boston Manufacturing Company. Having raised the staggering sum of $400,000, they built a textile plant in Waltham, Massachusetts—the first factory in America to perform all the operations of cloth making under one roof. Thanks to Moody's improvements, Waltham's power looms operated at higher speeds than British looms and needed fewer workers.

The second strategy was to tap a new and cheaper source of labor. In the 1820s, the Boston Manufacturing Company recruited thousands of young women from farm families. To appeal to the women, it provided them with rooms in boardinghouses and with evening lectures and other cultural activities. To reassure parents about their daughters' moral welfare, the mill owners enforced strict curfews, prohibited alcoholic beverages, and required regular church attendance. At Lowell (1822), Chicopee (1823), and other sites in Massachusetts and New Hampshire, the company built new cotton factories that used this labor system, known as the Waltham Plan.

Mill Girl, c. 1850
This fine daguerreotype (an early photograph) shows a neatly dressed textile worker about twelve years of age. The harsh working conditions in the mill have taken a toll on her spirit and body: The girl's eyes and mouth show little joy or life, and her hands are rough and swollen. She probably worked either as a knotter, tying broken threads on spinning jennies, or as a warper, straightening out the strands of cotton or wool as they entered the loom. Jack Naylor Collection.

By the early 1830s, more than 40,000 New England women were working in textile mills. As an observer noted, the wages were "more than could be obtained by the hitherto ordinary occupation of housework," the living conditions were better than those in crowded farmhouses, and the women had greater independence. Lucy Larcom became a textile operative at age eleven so that she could support herself and not be "a trouble or burden or expense" to her widowed mother. Other women operatives used their wages to pay off their father's farm mortgages, send their brothers to school, or accumulate a marriage dowry for themselves.

A few operatives just had a good time. Susan Brown, a Lowell weaver, spent half of her earnings on food and lodging and the rest on plays, concerts, lectures, and a two-day excursion to Boston. Like most textile workers, Brown soon tired of the rigor of factory work and the never-ceasing clatter of the machinery, which ran twelve hours a day, six days a week. After eight months, she quit, lived at home for a time, and then moved to another mill. Whatever the hardships, waged work gave young women a sense of freedom and autonomy. "Don't I feel independent!" a woman mill worker wrote to her sister. "The thought that I am living on no one is a happy one indeed to me" (see American Voices, p. 265).

The owners of the Boston Manufacturing Company were even happier. By combining tariff protection with improved technology and cheap female labor, they could undersell their British rivals. Their textiles were also cheaper than those made in New York and Pennsylvania, where farmworkers were better paid than in New England and

Early Days at Lowell   LUCY LARCOM

Lucy Larcom (1824–1893) went to work in a textile mill in Lowell, Massachusetts, when she was eleven years old and remained there for a decade. She then migrated to Illinois with her sisters and a great tide of other New Englanders. In later life, Larcom became a teacher and a writer. In her autobiography, she described the contradictory impact of industrial labor— confining and yet liberating—on the lives of young women from farms and rural villages.

I never cared much for machinery. The buzzing and hissing and whizzing of pulleys and rollers and spindles and flyers around me often grew tiresome. I could not see into their complications, or feel interested in them. But in a room below us we were sometimes allowed to peer in through a sort of blind door at the great waterwheel that carried the works of the whole mill. It was so huge we could only watch a few of its spokes at a time, and part of its dripping rim, moving with a slow, measured strength through the darkness that shut it in. It impressed me with something of the awe which comes to us in thinking of the great Power which keeps the mechanism of the universe in motion. . . .

We did not call ourselves ladies. We did not forget that we were working girls, wearing coarse aprons suitable to our work, and that there was some danger of our becoming drudges. I know that sometimes the confinement of the mill became very wearisome to me. In the sweet June weather I would lean far out of the window, and try not to hear the unceasing clash of sound inside. Looking away to the hills, my whole stifled being would cry out

Oh, that I had wings!

Still I was there from choice, and

The prison unto which we doom ourselves,
No prison is.

I regard it as one of the privileges of my youth that I was permitted to grow up among these active, interesting girls, whose lives were not mere echoes of other lives, but had principle and purpose distinctly their own. Their vigor of character was a natural development. The New Hampshire girls who came to Lowell were descendants of the sturdy backwoodsmen who settled that State scarcely a hundred years before. Their grandmothers had suffered the hardships of frontier life. . . . Those young women did justice to their inheritance. They were earnest and capable; ready to under-take anything that was worth doing. My dreamy, indolent nature was shamed into activity among them. They gave me a larger, firmer ideal of womanhood. . . .

Country girls were naturally indepen-dent, and the feeling that at this new work the few hours they had of every-day leisure were entirely their own was a satisfaction to them. They preferred it to going out as "hired help." It was like a young man's pleasure in entering upon business for himself. Girls had never tried that experi-ment before, and they liked it. It brought out in them a dormant strength of character which the world did not previously see.

SOURCE: Lucy Larcom, *A New England Girl-hood* (Boston: Houghton Mifflin, 1889), 153–155, 181–183, 196–200.

textile wages consequently were higher. Manufacturers in those states garnered profits by using advanced technology to produce higher-quality cloth. Even Thomas Jefferson, the great champion of yeoman farming, was impressed. "Our manufacturers are now very nearly on a footing with those of England," he boasted in 1825.

American Mechanics and Technological Innovation

By the 1820s, American-born artisans had replaced British immigrants at the cutting edge of technological innovation. Few of these mechanics had a formal education, but they commanded respect as "men professing an ingenious art." In the Philadelphia region, the remarkable Sellars family produced the most important inventors. Samuel Sellars Jr. invented a machine for twisting worsted woolen yarn to give it an especially smooth surface. His son John improved the efficiency of the waterwheels powering the family's sawmills and built a machine to weave wire sieves. John's sons and grandsons ran machine shops that turned out riveted leather fire hoses, papermaking equipment, and eventually locomotives. In 1824, the Sellars family and other mechanics founded the Franklin Institute in Philadelphia. Named after Benjamin Franklin, whom the mechanics admired for his work ethic and scientific accomplishments, the Institute published a journal; provided high-school-level instruction in mechanics, chemistry, mathematics, and mechanical design; and organized exhibits of new products. Crafts-men in Ohio and other states established similar institutes to disseminate technical knowledge and encourage innovation. Around 1820, the U.S. Patent Office issued about two hundred patents for new inventions each year, mostly to gentlemen and merchants. By 1860, the office was awarding four thousand patents annually, mostly to mechanics from modest backgrounds.

American craftsmen pioneered in the development of **machine tools** — machines that made parts for other machines. A key innovator was Eli Whitney (1765–1825), the son of a middling New England farm family. At the age of fourteen, Whitney began manufacturing nails and knife blades; later, he made women's hatpins. Aspiring to wealth and status, Whitney won admission to Yale College and subsequently worked as a tutor on a Georgia cotton plantation. Using his expertise in making hatpins, he built a simple machine that separated cotton seeds from the delicate fibers. Although Whitney patented his cotton "engine" (or "gin," as it became known), other manufac-turers improved on his design and captured the market.

Still seeking his fortune, Whitney decided in 1798 to manufacture military weap-ons. He eventually designed and built machine tools that could rapidly produce inter-changeable musket parts, bringing him the wealth and fame that he had long craved. After Whitney's death, his partner John H. Hall built an array of machine tools to work metal: turret lathes, milling machines, and precision grinders.

Technological innovation now swept through American manufacturing. Mechanics in the textile industry invented lathes, planers, and boring machines that turned out standardized parts for new spinning jennies and weaving looms. Despite being mass-produced, these jennies and looms were precisely made and operated at higher speeds than British equipment. The leading inventor was Richard Garsed: He nearly doubled the speed of the power looms in his father's Delaware factory and patented a cam and harness device that allowed machines to weave damask and other fabrics with elaborate designs. Meanwhile, the mechanics employed by Samuel W. Collins built a machine for pressing and hammering hot metal into dies, or cutting forms. Using this machine, one of Collins's workers could make 300 ax heads a day—compared to twelve using traditional methods. In Richmond, Virginia, Welsh- and American-born mechanics at the Tredegar Iron Works were producing parts for complicated manufacturing equipment at low cost and in great quantities. As a group of British observers noted admiringly, many American products were made "with machinery applied to almost every process . . . all reduced to an almost perfect system of manufacture."

As mass production spread, the American Industrial Revolution came of age. The sheer volume of output elevated some products—such as Remington rifles, Singer sewing machines, and Yale locks—into household names in the United States and abroad. After winning praise at the Crystal Palace Exhibition in London in 1851, the first major international display of industrial goods, Remington, Singer, and other American firms became multinational businesses, building factories in Great Britain and dominating some European markets.

Wageworkers and the Labor Movement

As the Industrial Revolution gathered momentum, it changed the nature of work and of workers' lives. In the early nineteenth century, many American **craft workers** espoused an "artisan-republican" ideology based on the principles of liberty and equality. They saw themselves as a group of small-scale producers, equal to one another and free to work for themselves. The poet Walt Whitman summed up their outlook: "Men must be masters, under themselves."

However, as the outwork and factory systems spread, more and more workers became wage earners. They no longer labored "under themselves" but under the direction of an employer. Unlike young women, who embraced factory work because it freed them from parental control and domestic service, men bridled at their status as coerced wageworkers. To assert their personal independence, male wageworkers repudiated the traditional terms of "master" and "servant"; instead, they used the Dutch word *boss* to refer to their employer. Still, as hired hands, they received meager wages and had little job security. The artisan-republican ideal, a by-product of the American Revolution, was giving way to the harsh reality of waged work—labor as a commodity—in an industrializing capitalist society.

Some wageworkers labored as journeymen carpenters, stonecutters, masons, and cabinetmakers, traditional crafts that required specialized skills and generated a strong sense of identity. This trade-consciousness enabled these workers to form unions and bargain with their master-artisan employers over wages and the increasing length of the workday, which kept them from their families and from educational opportunities. Before 1800, the building trades' workday was twelve hours—6:00 A.M. to 6:00 P.M.—with an hour each for breakfast and lunch. By the 1820s, masters were demanding a longer day during the summer, when it stayed light longer, while paying journeymen the old daily rate. In response, 600 carpenters in Boston went on strike in 1825. The Boston protest failed, but by the mid-1830s, building-trades workers had won a ten-hour day from many employers and from the federal government at the Philadelphia navy yard.

Artisans in other occupations were less successful in preserving their living standards. As aggressive entrepreneurs and machine technology changed the nature of production, shoemakers, hatters, printers, furniture makers, and weavers faced falling income, unemployment, and loss of status. To avoid the regimentation of factory work, some artisans in these trades moved to small towns or set up specialized shops. In New York City, 800 highly skilled cabinetmakers owned small shops that made fashionable or custom-made furniture. In status and income, they outranked a much larger group of 3,200 semitrained workers—disparagingly called "botches"—who labored for wages in factories making cheaper mass-produced tables and chairs. The new industrial system had divided the traditional artisan class into self-employed craftsmen and wage-earning workers.

When wage earners banded together to form unions, they faced a legal hurdle: Under English and American common law, such "combinations" were illegal. As a Philadelphia judge put it, unions were "a government unto themselves" and unlawfully interfered with a "master's" authority over his "servant." Between 1806 and 1847, there were at least twenty-three legal cases accusing unions of "conspiring" to raise wages and thereby injure employers. Despite the legal obstacles, unions bargained over wages and working conditions. In 1830, journeymen shoemakers founded a mutual benefit society in Lynn, Massachusetts, and similar organizations soon appeared in other shoemaking centers. "The division of society into the producing and non-producing classes," the journeymen explained, had made workers like themselves into a mere "commodity" whose labor was bought and sold. As another group of workers put it, "The capitalist has no other interest in us, than to get as much labor out of us as possible. We are hired men, and hired men, like hired horses, have no souls." Indeed, we are "slaves in the strictest sense of the word," declared Lynn shoemakers and Lowell textile workers. But one Lowell worker pointed out, "We are not a quarter as bad off as the slaves of the south. . . . They can't vote nor complain and we can." To exert more pressure on their capitalist employers, in 1834, local unions from Boston to Philadelphia formed the National Trades Union, the first regional union of different trades.

Union leaders criticized the new industrial order by expanding **artisan republicanism** to include waged laborers. Arguing that wage earners were becoming "slaves to a monied aristocracy," they condemned the new outwork and factory systems in which "capital and labor stand opposed." To create a just society in which artisans and waged workers could "live as comfortably as others," they advanced a **labor theory of value**. Under this theory, the price of a good should reflect the labor required to make it, and most of the price should go to those individuals who produced it, not to factory owners, middlemen, or storekeepers. Appealing to the spirit of the American Revolution, which had destroyed the aristocracy of birth, union publicists called for a new revolution to destroy the aristocracy of capital. Armed with this artisan-republican ideology, union men organized nearly fifty strikes for higher wages in 1836.

Women textile operatives were equally active. Competition in the woolen and cotton textile industries was fierce because the mechanization of production caused output to grow faster than demand. As prices fell, manufacturers' revenues declined. To maintain their profits, employers reduced workers' wages and imposed more stringent work rules. In 1828, women mill workers in Dover, New Hampshire, struck against new rules and won some relief; six years later, more than 800 Dover women walked out to protest wage cuts. In Lowell, 2,000 women operatives backed a strike by withdrawing their savings from an employer-owned bank. "One of the leaders mounted a pump," the *Boston Transcript* reported, "and made a flaming . . . speech on the rights of women and the iniquities of the 'monied aristocracy.'" When conditions did not improve, young women in New England refused to enter the mills. Impoverished Irish (and later French Canadian) immigrants took their places.

By the 1850s, workers in many mechanized industries faced unemployment as the supply of manufactures exceeded the demand for them. In 1857, industrial overproduction coincided with a financial panic sparked by the bankruptcies of several railroads. As the economy went into a recession, unemployment rose to 10 percent and reminded Americans of the social costs of the new — and otherwise very successful — system of industrial production.

▶ How did American textile manufacturers compete with British manufacturers? How successful were they?

▶ In what ways did the emerging industrial economy conflict with artisan republicanism? How did wage laborers respond to the new economy?

The Market Revolution

As American factories and farms turned out more goods, businessmen and legislators created faster and cheaper ways to get those products to consumers. Beginning in the late 1810s, they constructed a massive system of canals and roads that linked the states along the Atlantic coast with one another and with the new states in the trans-Appalachian west. This transportation system set in motion both a crucial market revolution and a great migration of people. By 1860, nearly one-third of the nation's citizens lived in the Midwest (the five states carved out of the Northwest Territory — Ohio, Indiana, Illinois, Michigan, and Wisconsin — along with Missouri, Iowa, and Minnesota), where they created a complex society and economy that increasingly resembled those of the Northeast.

The Transportation Revolution Forges Regional Ties

With the Indian peoples in retreat, slave-owning planters from the Lower South settled in Missouri (admitted to the Union in 1821) and pushed on to Arkansas (admitted in 1836). Simultaneously, yeomen farm families from the Upper South joined migrants from New England and New York in farming the fertile lands of the Great Lakes basin. Once Indiana and Illinois were settled, land-hungry farmers poured into Michigan (1837), Iowa (1846), and Wisconsin (1848) (see Voices from Abroad, p. 270). To meet the demand for cheap farmsteads, Congress in 1820 had reduced the price of federal land from $2.00 an acre to $1.25 — just enough to cover the cost of the survey and sale. For $100, a farmer could buy 80 acres, the minimum required under federal law. By the 1840s, this generous land distribution policy had enticed about five million people to states and territories west of the Appalachians (Map 9.1).

To link settler-communities to one another, state governments chartered private companies to build toll roads, or turnpikes. In 1806, Congress approved funds for a

German Immigrants in the Midwest ERNST STILLE

Among the thousands of Germans who flooded into the Midwest between 1830 and 1860 were twenty-three members of the interrelated Stille and Krumme families from the Prussian province of Westphalia in northwestern Germany. Most were younger sons and daughters, who could not hope to inherit farms if they stayed in Westphalia. The letters of Ernst Stille reveal the economic opportunities—and the hardships—they found in America.

Cincinäti, May 20th 1847
Dearest friends and relatives,

We went from Bremen to Neu Orleans in 2 months. . . . The trip from Neu Orleans to Cincinäti took 12 days. When I got here . . . I was lucky enough to get a job with Fr. Lutterbeck from Ladbergen [a village near his home in Prussia]. . . . In April all the brickmakers started to work again, many Germans work this trade and earn a good wage and I set to work at this too and earn a dollar a day, of that I have to pay 7 dollars a month for board and washing. . . . We make 8,500 bricks a day and it's hard work but when we start at 4 o'clock in the morning we can be finished by 3 o'clock, if I can stay healthy I will keep working here since if you're healthy and can stand the work, it pays the best.

The only people who are really happy here are those who were used to work in Germany and with toil and great pains could hardly earn their daily bread. . . . But a lot of people come over here who were well off in Germany but were enticed to leave their fatherland by boastful and imprudent letters from their friends or children and thought they could become rich in America, this deceives a lot of people, since what can they do here, if they stay in the city they can only earn their bread at hard and unaccustomed labor? . . .

Cincinäti, July 10th 1848

At the beginning of April, I started working for Ernst Lots in the brickyard. . . . In the winter no one can work at this trade because of the snow and ice, then there's a huge number of idle people. The main work in the winter is with fat livestock, brought in from the country in large herds, on the outer edge of the city there are large buildings where about 1000 a day are slaughtered and cleaned, then they're brought into the city where they are cut up and salted and put in barrels that's how they're sent from here to other countries. This is a pretty hard and dirty job, that's why most people would rather do nothing for $1/4$ year than do this, but if you want to put up with this you can earn 1 to $1\frac{1}{2}$ dollars a day. . . .

My plan is if I stay in good health for the next couple of years to buy a piece of land and live there, since from my childhood I've been used to farming, I'd rather do that than stay in the city all my life, you can't start very well unless you have 300 dollars.

SOURCE: Walter D. Kamphoefner, Wolfgang Helbid, and Ulrike Sommer, eds., *News from the Land of Freedom: German Immigrants Write Home*, trans. Susan Carter Vogel (Ithaca, NY: Cornell University Press, 1991), 83–87.

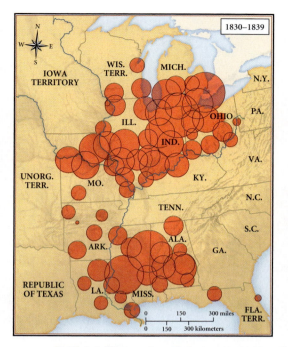

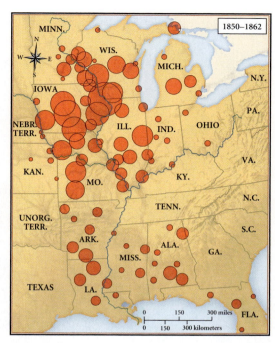

MAP 9.1 Western Land Sales, 1830–1839 and 1850–1862

The federal government set up land offices to sell farmsteads to settlers. During the 1830s, they sold huge amounts of land in the corn and wheat belt of the Old Northwest (Ohio, Indiana, Illinois, and Michigan) and the cotton belt of the Old Southwest (especially Alabama and Mississippi). By the 1850s, most sales of government land were in the upper Mississippi River Valley (particularly Iowa and Wisconsin). Each circle indicates the relative amount of land sold at the land office at its center.

National Road, constructed of compacted gravel, to tie the Midwest to the seaboard states. The project began in Cumberland in western Maryland in 1811; reached Wheeling, Virginia (now West Virginia), on the Ohio River in 1818; and ended in Vandalia, Illinois, in 1839. The National Road and other interregional highways carried migrants and their heavily loaded wagons westward; along the way, they passed herds of livestock destined for eastern markets.

Even on well-built gravel roads, travel over land was slow and expensive. To carry people, crops, and manufactures to and from the Midwest, public money and private businesses developed a water-borne transportation system of unprecedented size, complexity, and cost. The key event was the New York legislature's decision in 1817 to build the Erie Canal, a 364-mile waterway connecting the Hudson River to Lake Erie. At the time, the longest artificial waterway in the United States was just 28 miles long—a reflection of the huge capital cost of canals and the lack of American engineering expertise. But New York's ambitious project had three things in its favor: the vigorous support of New York City's merchants, who wanted access to western markets; the backing of New York's governor, De Witt Clinton, who persuaded the legislature to finance the waterway from tax revenues, tolls, and bond sales to foreign investors; and the relative gentleness of the terrain west of Albany. Even so,

The Erie Canal

This pastoral scene along the Erie Canal near Lockport, New York, only hints at the canal's profound impact on American life. Without the canal, the town in the background would not exist and farmers, such as the man in the foreground, would only have local markets for their cattle and grain. By 1860, the success of the Erie Canal had prompted the construction of a vast system of canals, an infrastructure that was as important to the nation as the railroad network of the late nineteenth century, and the interstate highway and airport transportation systems of the late twentieth century. I. N. Phelps Stokes Collection, Miriam and Ira D. Wallach Division of Art, Prints and Photographs. The New York Public Library. Astor, Lenox and Tilden Foundations.

the task was enormous. Workers — many of them Irish immigrants — had to dig out millions of cubic yards of soil, quarry thousands of tons of rock to build the huge locks that raised and lowered the boats, and construct vast reservoirs to ensure a steady supply of water.

The first great engineering project in American history, the Erie Canal altered the ecology of an entire region. As farming communities and market towns sprang up along the waterway, settlers cut down millions of trees to provide wood for building and heating and land for growing crops and grazing animals. Cows and sheep foraged on pastures that had recently been forests occupied by deer and bears, and spring rains caused massive erosion of the denuded landscape.

Whatever its ecological consequences, the Erie Canal was an instant economic success. The first section, a stretch of 75 miles, opened in 1819 and immediately generated enough revenue to repay its cost. When the canal was completed in 1825, a 40-foot-wide ribbon of water stretched from Buffalo, on the eastern shore of Lake Erie, to Albany, where it joined the Hudson River for a 150-mile trip to New York City. The canal's water "must be the most fertilizing of all fluids," suggested novelist Nathaniel Hawthorne, "for it causes towns with their masses of brick and stone, their churches and theaters, their business and hubbub, their luxury and refinement, their gay dames and polished citizens, to spring up."

The Erie Canal brought prosperity to the farmers of central and western New York and the entire Great Lakes basin. Northeastern manufacturers shipped clothing, boots, and agricultural equipment to farm families; in return, farmers sent grain, cattle, and hogs as well as raw materials (leather, wool, and hemp, for example) to eastern cities and foreign markets. One-hundred-ton freight barges, each pulled by two horses, moved along the canal at a steady 30 miles a day, cutting transportation costs and accelerating the flow of goods. In 1818, the mills in Rochester, New York had processed 26,000 barrels of flour for export to the East; ten years later, their output had soared to 200,000 barrels; and by 1840, it was at 500,000 barrels.

The spectacular benefits of the Erie Canal prompted a national canal boom (Map 9.2). Civic and business leaders in Philadelphia and Baltimore proposed waterways to link their cities to the Midwest. Copying New York's fiscal innovations, they persuaded their state governments to invest in canal companies or to force state-chartered banks to do so. They won state guarantees for canal bonds to encourage British and Dutch investors to buy them. In fact, foreign investors provided almost three-quarters of the $400 million invested in canals by 1840. Soon, a series of waterways connected the farms and towns of the Great Lakes region with the great port cities of New York, Philadelphia, and Baltimore (via the Erie, Pennsylvania, and Chesapeake and Ohio canals) and with New Orleans (via the Ohio and Mississippi Rivers). In 1848, the completion of the Michigan and Illinois Canal, which linked Chicago to the Mississippi River, completed an inland all-water route from New York City to New Orleans.

The steamboat, another product of the industrial age, ensured the economic success of the Midwest's river-borne transportation system. In 1807, engineer-inventor Robert Fulton built the first American steamboat, the *Clermont*, which he piloted up the Hudson River. To navigate shallow western rivers, engineers broadened the steamboats' hulls to reduce their draft and enlarge their cargo capacity. These improved vessels halved the cost of upstream river transport and, along with the canals, dramatically increased the flow of goods, people, and news. In 1830, a traveler or a letter from New York could go by water to Buffalo or Pittsburgh in less than a week and to Detroit or St. Louis in two weeks. Thirty years earlier, the same journeys had taken twice as long.

The states and the national government played key roles in the development of this interregional system of transportation and communication. State legislatures subsidized canals, while the national government created a vast postal system, the first network for the exchange of information. Thanks to the Post Office Act of 1792, the mail system grew rapidly—to more than 8,000 post offices by 1830—and safely carried thousands of letters and millions of dollars of banknotes. The U.S. Supreme Court, headed by John Marshall, likewise encouraged interstate trade by striking down state restrictions on commerce. In *Gibbons v. Ogden* (1824), the Court voided

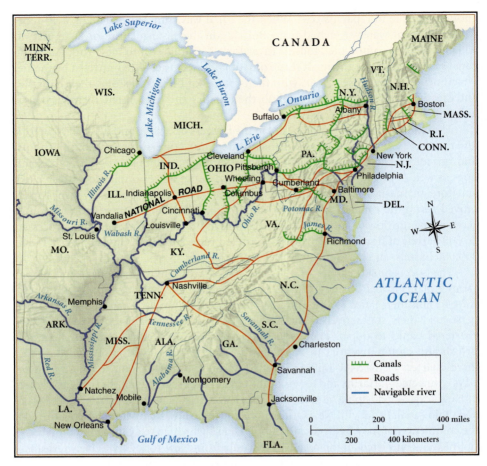

MAP 9.2 The Transportation Revolution: Roads and Canals, 1820–1850

By 1850, the United States had an effective transportation system with three distinct parts. One system, composed of short canals and navigable rivers running into the Atlantic Ocean, carried cotton, tobacco, and other products from the southern countryside to Northern and European markets. The second system, centered on the Erie, Chesapeake and Ohio, and Pennsylvania Mainline canals, linked the major seaport cities of the Northeast to the vast trans-Appalachian region. Finally, a set of regional canals in the Old Northwest connected much of the Great Lakes region to the Ohio and Mississippi rivers and the port of New Orleans.

For more help analyzing this map, see the Online Study Guide at **bedfordstmartins.com/henrettaconcise**.

a New York law that created a monopoly on steamboat travel into New York City and established federal authority over interstate commerce (see Chapter 7). That decision meant that no local or state monopolies—or tariffs—would impede the flow of goods, services, and news across the nation.

By the 1850s, another product of industrial technology—the railroad—was on its way to replacing canals as the center of the national transportation system (Map 9.3). In 1852, canals carried twice the tonnage transported by railroads. Then capitalists in

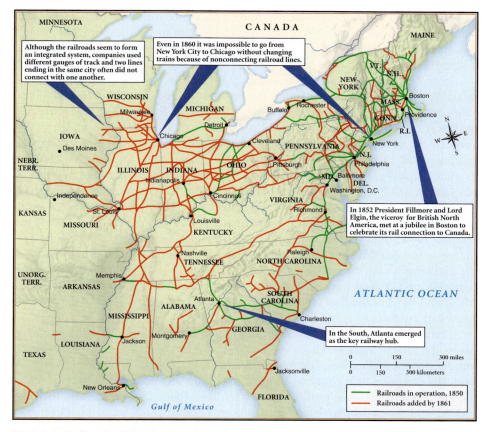

Although the railroads seem to form an integrated system, companies used different gauges of track and two lines ending in the same city often did not connect with one another.

Even in 1860 it was impossible to go from New York City to Chicago without changing trains because of nonconnecting railroad lines.

In 1852 President Fillmore and Lord Elgin, the viceroy for British North America, met at a jubilee in Boston to celebrate its rail connection to Canada.

In the South, Atlanta emerged as the key railway hub.

| | Railroads in operation, 1850 |
| | Railroads added by 1861 |

MAP 9.3 Railroads of the North and South, 1850 and 1861
In the decade before the Civil War, capitalists in the Northeast financed the construction of thousands of miles of new railroad lines in that region and the Midwest, creating an extensive and dense transportation system that stimulated economic development. The South built a more limited system of railroads. In all regions, different railroad companies used different track gauges, which hindered the efficient flow of traffic.

Boston and New York invested heavily in railroad routes; by 1860, railroads were the main carriers of wheat and freight from the Midwest to the Northeast. Serviced by a vast network of locomotive and freight-car repair shops, the Erie Railroad, the Pennsylvania Railroad, the New York Central Railroad, and the Baltimore and Ohio Railroad connected the Atlantic ports—New York, Philadelphia, and Baltimore—with the rapidly expanding Great Lakes cities of Cleveland and Chicago.

The railroad boom of the 1850s expanded commerce in a vast territory around Chicago. Trains carried huge quantities of lumber from Michigan to the treeless prairies of Indiana, Illinois, Iowa, and Missouri, where settlers built 250,000 new farms (covering 19 million acres) and hundreds of small towns. The rail lines moved millions of bushels of wheat to Chicago for transport by boat or rail to eastern markets. Increasingly, they also carried hogs and cattle to Chicago's growing stockyards. In

Jacksonville, Illinois, a farmer decided to feed his entire corn crop of 1,500 bushels "to hogs & cattle, as we think it is more profitable than to sell the corn." "In ancient times," boasted a Chicago newspaper, "all roads led to Rome; in modern times all roads lead to Chicago."

Initially, midwestern settlers relied on manufactured goods made in Britain or in the Northeast. They bought high-quality shovels and spades fabricated at the Delaware Iron Works and the Oliver Ames Company in Easton, Massachusetts; axes forged in Connecticut factories; and steel horseshoes manufactured in Troy, New York. By the 1840s, midwestern entrepreneurs were producing such manufactures: machine tools, hardware, furniture, and especially agricultural implements. Working as a blacksmith in Grand Detour, Illinois, John Deere made his first steel plow out of old saws in 1837; ten years later, he opened a factory in Moline, Illinois, that mass produced the plows. Stronger than the existing cast-iron models built in New York, Deere's steel plows allowed midwestern farmers to cut through the thick sod of the prairies. Other midwestern companies—McCormick and Hussey, for example— mass-produced self-raking reapers that enabled farmers to harvest 12 acres of grain a day (rather than the 2 acres that could be cut by hand). With the harvest bottleneck removed, midwestern farmers planted more acres and shipped vast quantities of wheat and flour to the East and Europe. Flour soon accounted for 10 percent of all American exports.

Extraregional trade also linked southern cotton planters to northeastern textile plants and foreign markets. This commerce in cotton bolstered the wealth of the South but did not transform the economic and social order there as it did in the Midwest. With the exception of Richmond, Virginia, and a few other places, southern planters did not invest their cotton profits in manufacturing. Rather, they continued to invest in land and slaves, which yielded high profits. Lacking cities, factories, and highly trained workers, the South remained tied to agriculture. Although its economy produced more than two-thirds of the world's cotton and accounted for almost two-thirds of American exports (see Chapter 12), the South provided a high standard of living only to the 25 percent of the white population that owned plantations and slaves. In 1860, the annual per capita income in the South was $103, while that of the Northeast was $141. By facilitating the transport of the staple crops of wheat, corn, cotton, and tobacco, the national system of commerce deepened the South's commitment to agriculture and slavery, even as it promoted diversified economies in the Northeast and Midwest.

The Growth of Cities and Towns

The expansion of industry and trade dramatically increased America's urban population. In 1820, there were only 58 towns with more than 2,500 inhabitants in the United States; by 1840, there were 126 urban centers, located mostly in the Northeast and Midwest. During those two decades, the total number of city dwellers grew more than fourfold, from 443,000 to 1,844,000.

The fastest growth occurred in the new industrial towns that sprouted along the "fall line," where rivers began their rapid descent from the Appalachian Mountains to the coastal plain. In 1822, the Boston Manufacturing Company expanded north from its base in Waltham and built a complex of mills in a sleepy Merrimack River village, which was quickly transformed into the bustling textile factory town of Lowell, Massachusetts. The towns of Hartford, Connecticut; Trenton, New Jersey; and Wilmington, Delaware, also became urban centers as mill owners exploited the waterpower of their rivers and recruited workers from the countryside.

Western commercial cities such as Pittsburgh, Cincinnati, and New Orleans grew almost as rapidly. These cities expanded because of their location at points where goods were transferred from one mode of transport to another—from farmers' rafts and wagons, for example, to steamboats or sailing vessels. As the midwestern population grew during the 1830s and 1840s, St. Louis, Detroit, and especially Buffalo and Chicago emerged as dynamic centers of commerce. "There can be no two places in the world," journalist Margaret Fuller wrote from Chicago in 1843, "more completely thoroughfares than this place and Buffalo. . . . the life-blood [of commerce] rushes from east to west, and back again from west to east." To a German visitor, Chicago seemed "for the most part to consist of shops . . . [as if] people came here merely to trade, to make money, and not to live." Chicago's merchants and bankers developed the marketing, provisioning, and financial services that were essential to farmers and small-town merchants in the surrounding countryside. "There can be no better [market] any where in the Union," declared a farmer in Paw Paw, Illinois.

These midwestern commercial hubs quickly became manufacturing centers as well. Capitalizing on the cities' locations as key junctions for railroad lines and steamboats, entrepreneurs built docks, warehouses, flour mills, and packing plants, creating work for hundreds of artisans and factory laborers. In 1846, Cyrus McCormick moved his reaper factory from western Virginia to Chicago to be closer to his midwestern customers. By 1860, St. Louis and Chicago had become the nation's third and fourth largest cities, respectively, after New York and Philadelphia.

The old Atlantic seaports—Boston, Philadelphia, Baltimore, Charleston, and especially New York City—remained important for their foreign commerce and, increasingly, as centers of finance and manufacturing. New York City and nearby Brooklyn grew at a phenomenal rate: Between 1820 and 1860, their combined populations increased nearly tenfold to one million people as tens of thousands of German and Irish immigrants poured into the two cities. Drawing on this abundant supply of labor, New York became a center of small-scale manufacturing and the ready-made clothing industry, which relied on thousands of low-paid seamstresses. "The wholesale clothing establishments are . . . absorbing the business of the country," a "Country Tailor" complained to the *New York Tribune*, "casting many an honest and hardworking man out of employment [and allowing] . . . the large cities to swallow up the small towns."

New York's growth stemmed primarily from its dominant position in foreign and domestic trade. It had the best harbor in the United States and, thanks to the Erie Canal, was the best gateway to the Midwest for immigrants and manufactures and the best outlet for shipments of western grain. Exploiting the city's prime location, in 1818 four Quaker merchants founded the Black Ball Line, a shipping company whose fleet carried cargo, people, and mail between New York and the European ports of Liverpool, London, and Le Havre. It was the first transatlantic service to run on a regular

▶ What roles did state and national government play in the development of America's transportation networks?

▶ Describe the different types of cities that emerged in the United States in the first half of the nineteenth century. How do you explain the differences in their development?

schedule. New York merchants likewise dominated trade with the newly independent South American nations of Brazil, Peru, and Venezuela. New York–based traders took over the cotton trade by offering finance, insurance, and shipping to export merchants in southern ports. By 1840, the port of New York handled almost two-thirds of foreign imports into the United States, almost half of all foreign trade, and much of the immigrant traffic.

Changes in the Social Structure

The Industrial Revolution and the Market Revolution improved the material lives of many Americans by enabling them to live in larger houses, cook on iron stoves, and wear better-made clothes. But especially in the cities, the new economic order spawned distinct social classes: a small but wealthy industrial and commercial elite, a substantial middle class, and a mass of propertyless wage earners. By creating a class-divided society, industrialization posed a momentous challenge to America's republican ideals.

The Business Elite

Before industrialization, white Americans thought of their society in terms of rank: "Notable" families had higher status than families of the "lower orders." Yet in many rural areas, people of different ranks shared a common culture. Gentlemen farmers talked easily with yeomen about crop yields, while their wives conversed about the art of quilting. In the South, humble tenants and aristocratic slave owners enjoyed the same amusements: gambling, cockfighting, and horse racing. Rich and poor attended the same Quaker meetinghouse or Presbyterian church. "Almost everyone eats, drinks, and dresses in the same way," a European visitor to Hartford, Connecticut, reported in 1798, "and one can see the most obvious inequality only in the dwellings."

The Industrial Revolution shattered this agrarian social order, creating a fragmented society composed of distinct classes and cultures. The new economic system pulled many Americans into large cities, thereby accentuating the differences between rural and urban life. Moreover, it made a few city residents — the merchants, manufacturers, bankers, and landlords who made up the business elite — very rich. In 1800, the top 10 percent of the nation's families owned about 40 percent of the wealth; by 1860, the richest 10 percent held nearly 70 percent of the wealth. In large cities such as New York, Chicago, Baltimore, and New Orleans, the superrich — the top 1 percent — owned more than 40 percent of all tangible property (land and buildings, for example) and an even higher share of intangible property (stocks and bonds).

Government tax policies facilitated the accumulation of wealth. In an era before federal taxes on individual and corporate income, the U.S. Treasury raised most of its revenue from tariffs — regressive taxes on textiles and other imported goods that were purchased mostly by ordinary citizens. State and local governments also favored the wealthier classes. They taxed real estate (farms, city lots, and buildings) and tangible personal property (furniture, tools, and machinery) but almost never taxed the stocks and bonds owned by the rich or the inheritances that they passed on to their children.

Consequently, cities that were once socially homogeneous took on an increasingly fragmented character. The wealthiest families consciously set themselves apart. They dressed in well-tailored clothes, rode in fancy carriages, and lived in expensively furnished houses tended by butlers, cooks, and other servants. The women no longer socialized with those of lesser wealth, and the men no longer labored side by side with their journeymen. Instead, they became managers and directors and relied on trusted subordinates to issue orders to hundreds of factory operatives. Increasingly, merchants, manufacturers, and bankers placed a premium on privacy and lived in separate neighborhoods, often at the edge of the city. The geographic isolation of privileged families and the massive flow of immigrants into other districts divided cities spatially along lines of class, race, and ethnicity.

The Middle Class

Standing between wealthy owners and propertyless wage earners was a growing middle class — the social product of the economic revolution. The bulk of the "middling class," a Boston printer explained, was made up of "the farmers, the mechanics, the manufacturers, the traders, who carry on professionally the ordinary operations of buying, selling, and exchanging merchandize." Other members of the middle class came from various professional groups — building contractors, lawyers, and surveyors — who suddenly found their services in great demand and financially profitable. Middle-class business owners, white-collar employees, and professionals were most numerous in the Northeast, where in the 1840s they numbered about 30 percent of the population. But they also could be found in the agrarian South. In 1854, Oglethorpe, Georgia (population: 2,500), a cotton boomtown, had eighty "business houses" and eight hotels.

The growing size, wealth, and cultural influence of the middle class reflected a dramatic rise in urban prosperity. Between 1830 and 1857, the per capita income of Americans increased by about 2.5 percent a year, a remarkable rate never since matched. This surge in income, along with the availability of inexpensive mass-produced goods, fostered a distinct middle-class urban culture. Middle-class husbands earned enough to save about 15 percent of their income, which they used to buy a well-built house in a "respectable part of town." They purchased handsome clothes and drove to work and play in smart carriages. Relieved of much household labor, middle-class wives became purveyors of genteel culture, buying books, pianos, lithographs, and commodious furniture for their front parlors. Affluent middle-class families hired Irish or African American domestic servants, while less prosperous ones relied on the new industrial technology. The middle class outfitted their residences with furnaces that heated water for bathing and for radiators that warmed entire rooms; they bought cooking stoves with ovens and treadle-operated sewing machines. Prosperous urban families now kept their perishable food in iceboxes, which ice-company wagons filled periodically, and bought many varieties of packaged goods. As early as 1825, the Underwood Company of Boston was marketing well-preserved Atlantic salmon in jars.

If material comfort was one distinguishing mark of the middle class, moral and mental discipline was another. Middle-class writers denounced carnivals and festivals as a "chaos of sin and folly, of misery and fun" and, by the 1830s, had managed to suppress them. Ambitious parents were equally concerned with their children's moral and intellectual development. To help their offspring succeed in life, middle-class parents often provided them with a high school education (in an era when most white children received only five years of schooling), and stressed the importance of discipline and hard work. American Protestants had long believed that diligent work in an earthly "calling" was a duty owed to God. Now the business elite and the middle class gave this idea a secular twist by celebrating work as the key to individual social mobility and national prosperity.

Benjamin Franklin gave classical expression to the secular work ethic in his *Autobiography*, which was published in full in 1818 (thirty years after his death) and immediately found a huge audience. Heeding Franklin's suggestion that an industrious man would become a rich one, tens of thousands of young American men saved their money, adopted temperate habits, and aimed to rise in the world. Warner Myers, a Philadelphia housepainter, raised funds from family, friends, and loans and became a builder, constructing sixty houses and garnering ample profits. Countless magazines, children's books, self-help manuals, and novels recounted the stories of similar individuals. The **self-made man** became a central theme of American popular culture and inspired many men (and a few women) to seek wealth. Just as the rural-producer ethic had united the social ranks in pre-1800 America, personal achievement linked the upper and middle classes of the new industrializing society.

Urban Workers and the Poor

As thoughtful business leaders surveyed their industrializing society, they concluded that the yeoman farmer and artisan-republican ideal—a society composed of independent producers—was no longer possible. "Entire independence ought not to be wished for," Ithamar A. Beard, the paymaster of the Hamilton Manufacturing Company, told a mechanics' association in 1827. "In large manufacturing towns, many more must fill subordinate stations and must be under the immediate direction and control of a master or superintendent, than in the farming towns."

Beard had a point. In 1840, all of the nation's slaves and about half of its white workers were laboring for others. The bottom 10 percent of wage earners consisted of casual workers, who were hired on a short-term basis for the most arduous jobs. Poor women washed clothes; their husbands and sons carried lumber and bricks for construction projects, loaded ships, and dug out dirt and stones to build canals. When they could find jobs, these men earned "their dollar per diem," a longtime resident told readers of the *Baltimore American*, but he cautioned that such workers could never save enough "to pay rent, buy fire wood and eatables" when the harbor froze up and they had no work. During business depressions, casual laborers bore the brunt of unemployment; even in good times, their jobs were temporary and dangerous.

Other laborers had greater security of employment, but few were prospering. In Massachusetts in 1825, an unskilled worker earned about two-thirds as much as a mechanic did; two decades later, it was less than half as much. A journeyman carpenter in

Philadelphia reported that he was about "even with the World" after several years of work but that many of his coworkers were in debt. The 18,000 women who made men's clothing in New York City in the 1850s earned just a few pennies a day, less than $80 a year. Such meager wages barely paid for food and rent, so few wage earners could take advantage of the rapidly falling prices of manufactured goods. Only the most fortunate working-class families could afford to educate their children, buy apprenticeships for their sons, or accumulate small dowries for their daughters. Most families sent their ten-year-old children out to work, and the death of a parent often threw the survivors into dire poverty. As a charity worker noted, "What can a bereaved widow do, with 5 or 6 little children, destitute of every means of support but what her own hands can furnish (which in a general way does not amount to more than 25 cents a day)."

Impoverished urban workers gradually congregated in dilapidated housing in bad neighborhoods. Single men and women lived in crowded boardinghouses, while families jammed themselves into tiny apartments in the basements and attics of small houses. As immigrants poured into the nation after 1840, urban populations soared, and developers squeezed more and more dwellings and foul-smelling outhouses onto a single lot. Venturing into the slums of New York City in the 1850s, shocked state legislators found gaunt, shivering people with "wild ghastly faces" living amid "hideous squalor and deadly effluvia, the dim, undrained courts oozing with pollution, the dark, narrow stairways, decayed with age, reeking with filth, overrun with vermin."

Many wage earners sought solace in alcohol. Beer and rum had long been standard fare in many American rituals: patriotic ceremonies, work breaks, barn raisings, and games. But during the 1820s and 1830s, the consumption of intoxicating beverages reached new heights, and alcoholism killed Daniel Tomkins, vice president under James Monroe, and undermined Henry Clay's bid for the presidency. Heavy drinking had an especially devastating impact on urban wage earners, who could ill afford its cost. Although Methodist artisans and ambitious craft workers swore off liquor to protect their work skills, health, and finances, other workers drank heavily on the job—and not just during the traditional 11 A.M. and 4 P.M. "refreshers." A baker recalled how "one man was stationed at the window to watch, while the rest drank." Long before the arrival of spirit-drinking Irish and beer-drinking German immigrants, grogshops dotted almost every block in working-class districts and were focal points of disorder. Unrestrained drinking by young men led to fistfights, brawls, and robberies. The urban police, mostly low-paid watchmen and untrained constables, were unable to contain the lawlessness.

The Benevolent Empire

The disorder among urban wage earners alarmed members of the rising middle class, who wanted safe cities and a disciplined workforce. To improve the world around them, many upwardly mobile men and women embraced religious benevolence. Led by Congregational and Presbyterian ministers, they created organizations of conservative social reform that historians call the **Benevolent Empire**. The ultimate purpose of the reforms was to restore "the moral government of God," explained Presbyterian minister Lyman Beecher, by reducing intemperance and poverty. Reform-minded individuals first regulated their own behavior and then tried to impose discipline into the lives of working people. They would regulate popular behavior—by persuasion if possible, by law if necessary.

The Benevolent Empire targeted age-old evils such as drunkenness, adultery, prostitution, and crime, but its methods were new. Instead of relying on church sermons and the suasion of community leaders, the reformers set out to institutionalize charity and systematically combat evil. They established large-scale organizations: the Prison Discipline Society and the American Society for the Promotion of Temperance, among many others. Each organization had a managing staff, a network of hundreds of chapters, thousands of volunteer members, and a newspaper.

Often acting in concert, these benevolent groups worked to improve society. First, they encouraged people to lead well-disciplined lives by drinking less alcohol and acquiring "regular habits." They persuaded local governments to ban carnivals of drink and dancing, such as Negro Election Day (festivities in which African Americans symbolically took over the government), which had been enjoyed by whites as well as blacks. Second, they devised new institutions to help the needy and to control the unruly. Reformers provided homes of refuge for abandoned children and asylums for the insane, who previously had been confined by their families in attics and cellars. They campaigned to end corporal punishment and to rehabilitate criminals in new, specially designed penitentiaries.

Women formed a crucial part of the Benevolent Empire. Since the 1790s, upper-class women had sponsored charitable organizations such as the Society for the Relief of Poor Widows with Small Children, which was founded in 1797 in New York by Isabella Graham, a devout Presbyterian widow. Her daughter Joanna Bethune set up other charitable institutions, including the Orphan Asylum Society and the Society for the Promotion of Industry, which found jobs for hundreds of poor women as spinners and seamstresses.

Some reformers argued that the decline of the traditional Sabbath was the greatest threat to the "moral government of God." As the market revolution spread, merchants and storekeepers conducted business on Sundays, and urban saloons provided drink and entertainment. To halt these activities, Lyman Beecher and other ministers founded a General Union for Promoting the Observance of the Christian Sabbath in 1828. General Union chapters, replete with women's auxiliaries, sprang up from Maine to Cincinnati and beyond. To rally Christians, the General Union demanded repeal of a law Congress had enacted in 1810 allowing mail to be transported—though not delivered—on Sundays. The Union's members boycotted shipping companies that did business on the Sabbath and campaigned for municipal laws forbidding games and festivals on the Lord's day.

The Benevolent Empire's efforts to impose its Sabbatarian beliefs aroused opposition from workers and freethinkers. Men who labored twelve or fourteen hours a day for six days a week wanted the freedom to spend their one day of leisure as they wished. Shipping company managers wanted to keep goods moving and demanded that the Erie Canal provide lockkeepers on Sundays. They argued that using laws to enforce a particular set of moral beliefs was "contrary to the free spirit of our institutions." When some evangelical reformers proposed teaching Christianity to slaves, they aroused hostility among white southerners. This popular resistance by workers and planters limited the success of the Benevolent Empire.

Charles Grandison Finney: Revivalism and Reform

Presbyterian minister Charles Grandison Finney found a new way to propagate religious values. Finney was not part of the traditional religious elite. Born into a poor farming family in Connecticut, he had planned to become a lawyer and rise into the middle class. But in 1823, Finney underwent an intense conversion experience and chose the ministry as his career. Beginning in towns along the Erie Canal, the young minister conducted emotional revival meetings that stressed conversion rather than doctrine and discipline. Repudiating traditional Calvinist beliefs, he maintained that God would welcome any sinner who submitted to the Holy Spirit. Finney's ministry drew on — and greatly accelerated — the Second Great Awakening, the wave of Protestant revivalism that had begun after the Revolution (see Chapter 8).

Finney's central message was that "God has made man a moral free agent" who could choose salvation. This doctrine of free will was particularly attractive to members of the new middle class, who had already chosen to improve their material lives. But Finney also had great success in converting people at the ends of the social spectrum: the haughty rich, who had placed themselves above God, and the abject poor, who seemed lost to drink and sloth. Finney celebrated their common fellowship in Christ and identified them spiritually with pious middle-class respectability.

Charles Grandison Finney, Evangelist (1792–1875)
When an unknown artist painted this flattering portrait in 1834, Finney was forty-two years old and at the height of his career as an evangelist. Handsome and charismatic, Finney had just led a series of enormously successful revivals in Rochester, New York, and other cities along the Erie Canal. In 1835, he established a theology department at newly founded Oberlin College in Ohio, where he trained a generation of ministers and served as president from 1851 to 1866. Oberlin College Archives.

Finney's most spectacular triumph came in 1830, when he moved his revivals from small towns to Rochester, New York, now a major milling and commercial city on the Erie Canal. Preaching every day for six months and promoting group prayer meetings in family homes, Finney won over the influential merchants and manufacturers of Rochester, who pledged to reform their lives and those of their workers. They promised to attend church, give up intoxicating beverages, and work hard. To encourage their employees to do the same, wealthy businessmen founded a Free Presbyterian church — "free" because members did not have to pay for pew space. Other Evangelical Protestants founded churches to serve transient canal laborers, and pious businessmen set up a savings bank to encourage thrift among the working classes. Meanwhile, Finney's wife Lydia and other pious middle-class women carried the Christian message to the wives of the unconverted, set up Sunday schools for poor children, and formed the Female Charitable Society to assist the unemployed.

Finney's efforts to create a harmonious community of morally disciplined Christians were not completely successful. Skilled workers who belonged to strong craft organizations — boot makers, carpenters, stonemasons, and boatbuilders — protested that they needed higher wages and better schools more urgently than sermons and prayers. Poor people ignored Finney's revival, as did the Irish Catholic immigrants who had recently begun arriving in Rochester and other northeastern cities, bringing with them a hatred of Protestants as religious heretics and political oppressors.

Ignoring this resistance, revivalists from New England to the Midwest copied Finney's evangelical message and techniques. In New York City, wealthy silk merchants Arthur and Lewis Tappan founded a magazine, *The Christian Evangelist*, which promoted Finney's ideas. The revivals swept through Pennsylvania, North Carolina, Tennessee, and Indiana, where, a convert reported, "you could not go upon the street and hear any conversation, except upon religion." The success of the revivals "has been so general and thorough," concluded a Presbyterian general assembly, "that the whole customs of society have changed."

The **temperance movement** proved to be the most successful evangelical social reform. Evangelicals took over the American Temperance Society in 1832; soon the society boasted 2,000 chapters and more than 200,000 members. The society employed the methods of the revivals — group confession and prayer, a focus on the family and the spiritual role of women, and sudden emotional conversion — and took them to northern towns and southern villages. On one day in New York City in 1841, more than 4,000 people took the temperance "pledge." Throughout America, the annual consumption of spirits fell dramatically, from an average of five gallons per person in 1830 to two gallons in 1845.

Evangelical reformers celebrated religion as the key to temperate behavior and moral improvement. Laziness and drinking could not be cured by self-discipline, as Benjamin Franklin had argued; rather, people had to experience a profound change of heart through religious conversion. This evangelical message of individual enterprise and moral discipline appealed to both middle-class Americans and wage-earning citizens. Religion and the ideology of social mobility served as a powerful cement, bonding people to one another in face of economic divisions created by industrialization, market expansion, and increasing cultural diversity.

Immigration and Cultural Conflict

Cultural diversity was the result of vast wave of immigrants. Between 1840 and 1860, about 2 million Irish, 1.5 million Germans, and 750,000 Britons poured into the United States. The British migrants were primarily Protestant and relatively prosperous; their ranks included trained professionals, propertied farmers, and skilled workers. Many German immigrants also came from property-owning farming and artisan families and had sufficient resources to move to the midwestern states of Wisconsin, Iowa, and Missouri. Other Germans and most of the Irish settled in the Northeast, where by 1860, they accounted for nearly one-third of white adults. Most immigrants avoided the South because they opposed slavery or feared competition from enslaved workers.

The poorest migrants were Irish peasants and laborers, who were fleeing a famine caused by severe overpopulation and a devastating blight that destroyed the potato crop. Arriving in dire poverty, the Irish settled mostly in the cities of New England and New York. The men took low-paying jobs as factory hands, construction workers, and canal diggers, while the women became washerwomen and domestic servants. Irish families crowded into cheap tenement buildings with primitive sanitation systems and were the first to die when disease struck. In the summer of 1849, a cholera epidemic took the lives of thousands of poor immigrants in St. Louis and New York City.

In times of hardship and sorrow, immigrants turned to their churches. Many Germans and virtually all the Irish were Catholics, and they fueled the growth of the American Catholic Church. In 1840, there were sixteen Catholic dioceses and 700 churches; by 1860, there were forty-five dioceses and 2,500 churches. Under the guidance of their priests and bishops, Catholics built an impressive network of institutions—charitable societies, orphanages, militia companies, parochial schools, and political organizations—that helped them to maintain both their religion and their German or Irish identity.

The Protestant fervor stirred up by the Second Great Awakening meant that a barrage of anti-Catholic publications greeted the immigrants. One of the most militant critics of Catholicism was artist and inventor Samuel F. B. Morse. In 1834, Morse published *Foreign Conspiracy Against the Liberties of the United States*, which warned of a Catholic threat to American republican institutions. Morse believed that Catholic immigrants would obey the dictates of Pope Gregory XVI, who in an official papal declaration (encyclical) in 1832 had condemned liberty of conscience, freedom of publication, and the separation of church and state. Gregory instructed Catholics to repudiate republicanism and acknowledge the "submission due to princes." Republican-minded Protestants of many denominations shared Morse's fears, and *Foreign Conspiracy* became their handbook.

The social tensions stemming from industrialization intensified anti-Catholic sentiment. During business recessions, unemployed Protestant mechanics and factory workers joined mobs that attacked Catholics, accusing them of taking jobs and driving down wages. These cultural conflicts inhibited the creation of unions, because many Protestant wage earners felt that they had more in common with their Protestant employers than with their Catholic coworkers. Other Protestants formed clubs limited to

Lith. & Pub. by J. Baillie 118 Nassau St N.Y.   and by J. Soule New Bedford Mass.

RIOT IN PHILADELPHIA
JULY 7ᵗʰ 1844.

Anti-Catholic Riots

When riots against Irish Catholics broke out in Philadelphia in July 1844, the governor of Pennsylvania called out the militia to protect Catholic churches and residential neighborhoods. In the foreground, Protestant rioters, depicted by the artist as well-dressed gentlemen, do battle with the militia. The riots resulted in fifteen deaths and dozens of serious injuries. Historical Society of Pennsylvania.

native-born citizens and called for a halt to immigration. Benevolent-minded Protestants supported the anti-Catholic movement for reasons of public policy. As crusaders for public education, they opposed the diversion of tax resources to Catholic schools; as advocates of a civilized society, they condemned the rowdyism of drunken Irish men.

In many northeastern cities, religious and cultural tensions led to violence. In 1834, in Charlestown, Massachusetts, a quarrel between Catholic laborers repairing a convent owned by the Ursuline order of nuns and Protestant workers in a neighboring brickyard turned into a full-scale riot and led to the destruction of the convent. In 1844, in Philadelphia, riots erupted when the Catholic bishop persuaded public-school officials to use both Catholic and Protestant versions of the Bible. Anti-Irish violence incited by

▶ What were the social classes created by the economic revolution? Describe their defining characteristics.

▶ What were the main goals of the Benevolent Empire? To what extent were they achieved?

▶ Weigh the relative importance of the Industrial and Market Revolutions in changing the American economy.

the city's nativist clubs lasted for two months and escalated into open warfare between Protestants and the Pennsylvania militia. Even as the economic revolution brought prosperity to many Americans and attracted millions of immigrants, it divided society along lines of class, ethnicity, and religion.

SUMMARY

In this chapter, we examined the causes of the economic transformation of the first half of the nineteenth century. That transformation had two facets: the increase in production known as the Industrial Revolution and the expansion of commerce known as the Market Revolution. Water and steam were crucial ingredients in both revolutions—driving factory machinery, carrying goods to market on canals and rivers, and propelling steamboats and railroad engines.

We also explored the consequences of that transformation: the rise of an urban society, the increasing similarity between the Northeast and Midwest and their growing difference from the South, and the creation of a class-divided society. Seeking to shape the emerging society, benevolent reformers and evangelical revivalists worked to instill moral discipline and Christian values. But artisan republicans, unionized workers, Irish and German immigrants had their own economic or cultural goals. The result was a fragmented society. Differences of class and culture now split the North just as race and class had long divided the South. As the next chapter suggests, Americans looked to the political system, which was becoming increasingly democratic, to address these divisions. In fact, the tensions among economic inequality, cultural diversity, and political democracy became a troubling—and enduring—part of American life.

Connections: Economy and Society

In 1820, most Americans lived in a rural, agricultural society much like the world of their grandparents. Then, as we noted in the opening essay for Part Three, came dramatic changes that "affected every aspect of life in the North and Midwest and brought important changes in the South as well." In this chapter, we have described the role of industry and commerce in creating a new economy and a new society in the Northeast and the Midwest. Our in-depth analysis of changes in the South appears in Chapter 12, where we describe the enormous expansion in plantation agriculture and cotton production between 1820 and 1860 and the devastating impact of the domestic slave trade on millions of African Americans.

In the opening essay, we also noted that

> The new economy created a class-based society in the North and Midwest. A wealthy elite of merchants, manufacturers, bankers, and entrepreneurs rose to the top of the social order. To maintain social stability, they adopted a paternalistic program of benevolent reform.

The discussion of social reform begun in this chapter continues in Chapter 11, which describes how advocates of temperance, religious utopianism, abolitionism, and women's rights took the reform movement in new directions. The radical outlooks and activities of these new reformers were the result, in part, of the overthrow of the traditional political system and the rise of Jacksonian democracy, the subjects of Chapter 10.

TIMELINE

1782	► Oliver Evans builds automated flour mill	**1820s**	► New England women head to textile factories
1790	► Samuel Slater opens spinning mill in Rhode Island		► Benevolent Empire leads conservative social reform
1792	► Congress passes Post Office Act	**1824**	► *Gibbons v. Ogden* promotes interstate trade
1793	► Eli Whitney manufactures cotton gins	**1830s**	► Emergence of western commercial cities
1800–1830	► Entrepreneurs in shoe industry impose division of labor		► Labor movement gains strength
			► Cities segregate by class
1807	► Robert Fulton's *Clermont*, the first American steamboat		► Middle-class culture emerges
1814	► Boston Manufacturing Company opens cotton mill in Waltham, Massachusetts		► Growth of temperance movement
			► Charles Grandison Finney's revivalist crusade
1816–1828	► Congress places protective tariffs on textiles and other imports	**1840s**	► Irish and German immigration sparks ethnic riots
1817	► Erie Canal begun (completed in 1825)		► Rise of machine-tool industry
1820	► Minimum federal land price reduced to $1.25 per acre	**1850s**	► Expansion of railroads in Northeast and Midwest
1820–1840	► Fourfold increase in city residents in Northeast and Midwest	**1857**	► Overproduction and speculation trigger a financial panic

FOR FURTHER EXPLORATION

Charles G. Sellers, *The Market Revolution: Jacksonian America, 1815–1846* (1991), focuses on the social impact of economic change. Scott A. Sandage, *Born Losers: A History of Failure in America* (2005), explores the fate of the unsuccessful. David Freeman Hawke, *Nuts and Bolts of the Past: A History of American Technology, 1776–1860* (1988), offers an entertaining account, as does "The Eli Whitney Museum & Workshop" (**www.eliwhitney.org/**).

Stephen Aron, *How the West Was Lost: The Transformation of Kentucky from Daniel Boone to Henry Clay* (1996), and Peter Way, *Common Labor: Workers and the Digging of North American Canals, 1780–1860* (1993), assess the underside of westward expansion. For first-person accounts, see "Pioneering the Upper Midwest" (**memory.loc.gov/ammem/umhtml/umhome.html**).

Stuart M. Blumin's *The Emergence of the Middle Class* (1989), discusses urban class formation. Stephen P. Rice, *Minding the Machine: Languages of Class in Early Industrial America* (2004), and David Grimsted, *American Mobbing* (1998), examine the culture wars of the nineteenth century. In *Home and Work* (1990), Jeanne Boydston critically examines changes in women's lives. For the story of a woman in the mills, log onto **www.fordham.edu/halsall/mod/robinson-lowell.html**.

For Evangelical Protestantism, consult Mark A. Noll, *America's God: From Jonathan Edwards to Abraham Lincoln* (2003), Bernard Weisberger's classic study *They Gathered at the River* (1958), and William R. Hutchison, *Religious Pluralism in America: The Contentious History of a Founding Ideal* (2003).

TEST YOUR KNOWLEDGE

To assess your mastery of the material in this chapter and for Web sites, images, and documents related to this chapter, visit **bedfordstmartins.com/henrettaconcise**.

CHAPTER

10

A Democratic Revolution

1820–1844

No free country can exist
without political parties.

— Martin Van Buren (1856)

European visitors to the United States in the 1830s generally praised its republican society but not its political parties and politicians. "The gentlemen spit, talk of elections and the price of produce, and spit again," Frances Trollope reported in *Domestic Manners of the Americans* (1832). In her view, American politics was the sport of self-serving party politicians who reeked of "whiskey and onions." Other Europeans lamented the low intellectual level of American political debate. The "clap-trap of praise and pathos" voiced by a Massachusetts politician "deeply disgusted" Harriet Martineau. Basil Hall was astonished by the shallow arguments and the "conclusions in which nothing was concluded" advanced by the inept "farmers, shopkeepers, and country lawyers" who sat in the New York assembly.

The verdict was unanimous and negative. "The most able men in the United States are very rarely placed at the head of affairs," French aristocrat Alexis de Tocqueville observed in *Democracy in America* (1835). The reason, Tocqueville suggested, lay in the character of democracy itself. Most citizens simply ignored important political issues, refused out of jealousy to elect their intellectual superiors, and listened in awe to "the clamor of a mountebank [a charismatic fraud] who knows the secret of stimulating their tastes."

The European visitors were witnessing the unfolding of the American Democratic Revolution. Before 1815, men of great ability had sat in the seats of government, and the prevailing ideology had been republicanism, rule by "men of TALENTS and VIRTUE," as a newspaper put it. By the 1820s and 1830s, the watchword was *democracy*, which in practice meant rule by popularly elected party politicians. "That the majority should govern was a fundamental maxim in all free governments," declared Martin Van Buren, the most talented of the middle-class professional politicians. The new party politicians often pursued selfish goals, but by encouraging ordinary Americans to burn with "election fever" and support party principles, they provided a sense of identity and purpose amid a fragmented social order.

The Rise of Popular Politics, 1820–1829

Expansion of the **franchise** dramatically symbolized the Democratic Revolution. By the 1830s, most states had opened the franchise to most white men. Nowhere else in the world did ordinary farmers and wage earners exercise such political influence. In England, for example, the Reform Bill of 1832 extended the vote to only 600,000 out of 6 million English men—a mere 10 percent.

The Decline of the Notables and the Rise of Parties

The American Revolution weakened the deferential society of the colonial era but did not overthrow it. Only two state constitutions—those of Pennsylvania and Vermont—allowed all male taxpayers to vote; even in those states, families of low rank continued to accept the leadership of their social "betters." Consequently, wealthy notables—northern landlords, slave-owning planters, and seaport merchants—dominated the political system in the new republic. And rightly so, thought John Jay, the first chief justice of the Supreme Court. As Jay put it in 1810: "Those who own the country are the most fit persons to participate in the government of it." Jay and other notables managed local elections by building up an "interest": lending money to small farmers, giving business to storekeepers, and treating their tenants to rum at election time. An outlay of $20 for refreshments, remarked one poll watcher, "may produce about 100 votes." This gentry-dominated system kept men who lacked wealth and powerful family connections from running for office.

The struggle to expand the suffrage began in the 1810s. Reformers in Maryland invoked the egalitarian language of republicanism: Property qualifications were a "tyranny" because they endowed "one class of men with privileges which are denied to another." To defuse this criticism and deter migration to the West, legislators in Maryland and other seaboard states grudgingly accepted a broader franchise. But the new voters quickly changed the tone of politics, rejecting politicians who flaunted their high social status by wearing "top boots, breeches, and shoe buckles," their hair in "powder and queues." Instead, they elected men who dressed simply and endorsed democracy, even if those politicians favored policies that benefited the wealthy.

Smallholding farmers and ambitious laborers in the Midwest and Southwest likewise challenged the old hierarchical order. In Ohio, a traveler reported, "no white man or woman will bear being called a servant." The constitutions of the new states of Indiana (1816), Illinois (1818), and Alabama (1819) prescribed a broad male franchise, and voters usually elected middling men to local and state offices. A well-to-do migrant in Illinois was surprised to learn that the man who plowed his fields "was a colonel of militia, and a member of the legislature." Once in public office, men from modest backgrounds enacted laws that restricted imprisonment for debt, kept taxes low, and allowed farmers to claim squatters' rights to unoccupied land.

By the mid-1820s, many states had instituted universal white male suffrage or had given the vote to all white men who paid taxes or served in the militia. Only a few—North Carolina, Virginia, and Rhode Island—still required the ownership of freehold property for voting. Moreover, between 1818 and 1821, Connecticut, Massachusetts, and New York wrote more democratic constitutions that reapportioned legislative districts on the basis of population and mandated the popular election (rather than the appointment) of judges and justices of the peace.

Democratic politics was contentious and, because it was run by men on the make, often corrupt. Powerful entrepreneurs and speculators—both notables and self-made men—demanded government assistance for their business enterprises and paid bribes to get it. Speculators won land grants by paying off the members of key committees, and bankers distributed shares of stock to key legislators. When the Seventh Ward Bank of New York City received a charter in 1833, the supervising commissioners set aside one-third of the bank's 3,700 shares of stock for themselves and their friends and almost two-thirds for state legislators and officials, leaving just 40 shares for public sale.

More contention broke out when religious reformers turned to political action to advance the cultural agenda of the Benevolent Empire. In Utica, New York, evangelical Presbyterians called for a town ordinance restricting Sunday entertainment. In response, a local Universalist—a member of a freethinking Protestant denomination—denounced the measure as coercive and called for "Religious Liberty."

The appearance of political parties encouraged such debates over government policy. Revolutionary-era Americans had condemned political "factions" as antirepublican and did not even mention political parties in the national and state constitutions. But as the power of notables waned, political parties came to the fore. By the 1820s, a number of states had disciplined parties managed by professional politicians, often middle-class lawyers and journalists. One observer compared the new organizations to a well-designed textile loom, calling them "machines" that wove the interests of diverse social and economic groups into a coherent legislative program.

Martin Van Buren of New York was the chief architect of the emerging system of party government, at both the state and national levels. The son of a Jeffersonian tavern keeper, Van Buren grew up in the landlord-dominated society of the Hudson River Valley. To get his training as a lawyer, he relied on the powerful Van Ness clan; then, determined not to become a dependent "tool" of a notable family, he repudiated their tutelage. His goal was to create a political order based on party, not family. To justify party government, Van Buren rejected the traditional republican belief that political parties were dangerous; instead, he claimed that the opposite was true: "All men of sense know that political parties are inseparable from free government," because they check a government's inherent "disposition to abuse power."

Between 1817 and 1821, Van Buren turned his "Bucktail" supporters (so called because they wore a deer's tail on their hats) into the first statewide **political machine**. He purchased a newspaper, the *Albany Argus*, and used its pages to promote his policies and get out the vote. **Patronage** was an even more important tool. When Van Buren's Bucktails won control of the New York legislature in 1821, they acquired a political "interest" much greater than that of the notables: the power to appoint some six thousand of their followers to positions in New York's legal bureaucracy of judges, justices of the peace, sheriffs, deed commissioners, and coroners. This **spoils system** was fair, Van Buren suggested, because it "would operate sometimes in favour of one party, and sometimes of another." And party government was thoroughly republican, he added, based as it was on majority rule. To enact important legislation, Van Buren insisted on disciplined voting as determined by a **party caucus**. On one crucial occasion, the "Little Magician"—a nickname referring to Van Buren's height and political dexterity—held an elaborate banquet to praise seventeen New York legislators for sacrificing "individual preferences for the general good."

The Election of 1824

The advance of political democracy and party government in the states undermined the old notable-dominated system of national politics. After the War of 1812, the aristocratic Federalist Party virtually disappeared, and the Republican Party splintered into competing factions (see Chapter 7). As the election of 1824 approached, no fewer than five Republican candidates campaigned for the presidency. Three were veterans of President James Monroe's cabinet: Secretary of State John Quincy Adams, the son of former president John Adams; Secretary of War John C. Calhoun; and Secretary of the Treasury William H. Crawford. The fourth candidate was Henry Clay of Kentucky, the dynamic Speaker of the House of Representatives; the fifth was General Andrew Jackson, now a senator from Tennessee.

When a caucus of Republicans in Congress selected Crawford as the party's official nominee, the other candidates refused to withdraw and sought popular support. Because of democratic reforms, eighteen of the twenty-four states required popular elections (rather than a vote of the state legislature) to choose their representatives to the Electoral College. Each candidate had strengths. Thanks to his diplomatic successes as Secretary of State (see Chapter 7), John Quincy Adams enjoyed national recognition; and his Massachusetts origins gave him the electoral votes of New England. Henry Clay based his candidacy on his **American System**, an integrated program of national economic development similar to the Commonwealth policies pursued by state governments. Clay wanted to enhance the powers of the Second Bank of the United States and to use tariff revenues to build roads and canals. His nationalistic program won praise in the West, which needed transportation improvements, but elicited sharp criticism in the South, which relied on rivers to market its cotton and had few manufacturing industries to protect. William Crawford of Georgia, an ideological heir of Thomas Jefferson, denounced Clay's American System as a scheme that would "consolidate" political power in Washington. Recognizing Crawford's appeal in the South, John C. Calhoun of South Carolina withdrew from the presidential race and endorsed Andrew Jackson.

As the hero of the Battle of New Orleans, Jackson benefited from the wave of patriotism that flowed from the War of 1812. Born in the Carolina backcountry, Jackson had settled in Nashville, Tennessee, where he formed ties to influential families through marriage and his career as an attorney and slave-owning cotton planter. His rise from common origins symbolized the new democratic age, and his reputation as a "plain solid republican" attracted voters in all regions.

Still, Jackson's strong showing in the election surprised most political leaders. The Tennessee senator received 99 of the 261 votes cast by members of the Electoral College; Adams garnered 84 votes; Crawford, who had suffered a stroke during the campaign, won 41; and Clay finished with 37 (Map 10.1). Because no candidate received an absolute majority, the Twelfth Amendment to the Constitution (ratified in 1804) specified that the House of Representatives would choose the president from among the three highest vote-getters. This procedure worked against Jackson because many congressmen

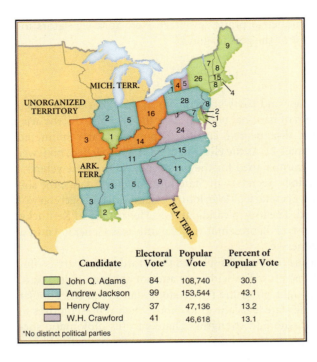

Candidate	Electoral Vote*	Popular Vote	Percent of Popular Vote
John Q. Adams	84	108,740	30.5
Andrew Jackson	99	153,544	43.1
Henry Clay	37	47,136	13.2
W.H. Crawford	41	46,618	13.1

*No distinct political parties

MAP 10.1 The Presidential Election of 1824

Regional voting dominated the presidential election of 1824. John Quincy Adams captured every electoral vote in New England and most of those in New York. Henry Clay carried Ohio and Kentucky, the most populous trans-Appalachian states; and William Crawford took the southern states of Virginia and Georgia. Only Andrew Jackson claimed a national constituency, winning Pennsylvania and New Jersey in the East, Indiana and most of Illinois in the Midwest, and much of the South. Only 356,000 Americans voted, about 27 percent of the eligible electorate.

feared that the rough-hewn "military chieftain" might become a tyrant. Out of the race himself, Henry Clay used his influence as Speaker to thwart Jackson's election. Clay assembled a coalition of congressmen from New England and the Ohio River Valley that voted Adams into the presidency. Adams showed his gratitude by appointing Clay his secretary of state, which was the traditional steppingstone to the presidency.

Clay's appointment was a politically fatal mistake for both men. Jackson supporters accused Clay and Adams of making a secret deal. Condemning what Calhoun labeled a "corrupt bargain" that thwarted the popular will, they vowed that Clay would never become president.

The Last Notable President: John Quincy Adams

As president, Adams called for bold national leadership. "The moral purpose of the Creator," he told Congress, was to use the president and all public officials to "improve the conditions of himself and his fellow men." Adams called for the establishment of a national university in Washington, extensive scientific explorations in the Far West, and a uniform standard of weights and measures. Most important, he endorsed Henry Clay's American System of national economic development and its three key elements: protective tariffs to stimulate manufacturing, federally subsidized roads and canals to facilitate commerce, and a national bank to control credit and provide a uniform currency.

Manufacturers, entrepreneurs, and farmers in the Northeast and Midwest welcomed Adams's proposals. But those policies won little support in the South, where planters opposed protective tariffs, which raised the price of manufactures, and smallholders feared powerful banks that could force them into bankruptcy. From his deathbed,

John Quincy Adams
This famous daguerreotype of the former president, taken about 1843 by Philip Haas, conveys his rigid personality and high moral standards. Although these personal attributes contributed to Adams's success as an antislavery congressman from Massachusetts in the 1830s and 1840s, they hindered his effectiveness as the nation's chief executive. Metropolitan Museum of Art, New York. Gift of I. N. Phelps Stokes, Edward S. Hawes, Alice Mary Hawes, Marion Augusta Hawes.

Thomas Jefferson condemned Adams for promoting "a single and splendid government of aristocracy [of money] . . . riding and ruling over the plundered ploughman and beggared yeomanry."

Other politicians objected to the American System on constitutional grounds. In 1817, President Madison had vetoed the Bonus Bill, which would have used the national government's income from the Second Bank of the United States to fund improvement projects in the states. Such projects, Madison had argued, were the sole responsibility of the states, a sentiment widely shared among Old Republicans. After a trip to Monticello to meet Thomas Jefferson, Martin Van Buren declared his allegiance to the constitutional "doctrines of the Jefferson School." Now a member of the U.S. Senate, Van Buren joined the Old Republicans in defeating most of Adams's proposals for national subsidies for roads and canals.

The farthest-reaching battle of the Adams administration came over tariffs. The Tariff of 1816 placed relatively high duties on imports of cheap English cotton cloth, allowing New England textile producers to dominate that market. In 1824, Adams and Clay secured a new tariff that protected manufacturers in New England and Pennsylvania against imports of iron goods and more expensive English woolen and cotton textiles. Without these tariffs, the U.S. producers might have faced the fate of the once world-dominant textile industry in India, which was destroyed in the early nineteenth century by the free trade policies imposed by the British imperial regime.

Recognizing the appeal of tariffs, Van Buren and his Jacksonian allies hopped on the bandwagon. By placing higher tariffs on wool, hemp, and other imported raw materials, they hoped to win the support of the wool- and hemp-producing farmers in New York, Ohio, and Kentucky for Jackson's presidential candidacy in 1828. The tariff had become a prisoner of politics. "I fear this tariff thing," remarked Thomas Cooper, the president of the College of South Carolina and an advocate of free trade, which has become "by some strange mechanical contrivance . . . a machine for manufacturing Presidents, instead of broadcloths, and bed blankets." Disregarding southern protests, northern Jacksonians joined with supporters of Adams and Clay to enact the Tariff of 1828, which significantly raised duties on raw materials, textiles, and iron goods.

The new tariff enraged the South. As the world's cheapest producer of raw cotton, the South did not need a tariff to protect its main industry. Moreover, by raising the price of manufactures, the tariff cost southern planters about $100 million a year. Planters had to buy either higher-cost American textiles and iron goods, thus enriching northeastern businesses and workers, or highly dutied British imports, thus paying the expenses of the national government. The new tariff was "little less than legalized pillage," an Alabama legislator declared, calling it a "Tariff of Abominations."

Ignoring the Jacksonians' support for the Tariff of 1828, most southerners blamed President Adams for the new act. They also criticized Adams's Indian policy. A deeply moral man, the president supported the land rights of Native Americans against expansionist whites. In 1825, U.S. commissioners had secured a treaty from one Creek faction to cede Creek lands in Georgia to the United States for eventual sale to the citizens of Georgia. When the Creek National Council repudiated the treaty, claiming that it was fraudulent, Adams called for new negotiations. Eager to acquire the Creeks' land, Georgia governor George M. Troup attacked the president as a "public enemy . . . the unblushing ally of the savages." Joining with Georgia's representatives in Congress, Troup persuaded Congress to extinguish the Creeks' land titles, forcing most Creeks to leave the state.

Elsewhere in the nation, Adams's primary weakness was his out-of-date political style. The last notable to serve in the White House, he acted the part: aloof, moralistic, and paternalistic. When Congress rejected his activist economic policies, Adams questioned the wisdom of the people and advised elected officials not to be "palsied [enfeebled] by the will of our constituents." Ignoring his waning popularity, the president did not use patronage to reward his supporters and allowed hostile federal officials to remain in office. Rather than "run" for reelection in 1828, Adams "stood" for it, telling supporters, "If my country wants my services, she must ask for them."

"The Democracy" and the Election of 1828

Martin Van Buren and the professional politicians handling Andrew Jackson's campaign had no reservations about running for office. The Little Magician's goal was to recreate the national political coalition that Thomas Jefferson had formed; he therefore championed policies that appealed both to northern farmers and artisans (the "plain Republicans of the North") and to southern slave owners and smallholding planters. John C. Calhoun, Jackson's vice-presidential running mate, brought his South

Carolina allies into Van Buren's party, and Jackson's close friends in Tennessee rallied voters there and throughout the Old Southwest. By forming a national political party, Jackson's friends hoped to reconcile the diverse economic and social "interests" that, as James Madison had predicted in "Federalist No. 10," would inevitability exist in a large republic.

At Van Buren's direction, the Jacksonians orchestrated a massive publicity campaign. In New York, fifty newspapers declared their support for Jackson on the same day. Elsewhere, Jacksonians organized mass meetings, torchlight parades, and barbecues to celebrate their candidate's frontier origin and rise to fame. With the cry of "Jackson for ever!," they praised "Old Hickory" as a "natural" aristocrat, a self-made man.

The Jacksonians called themselves Democrats or "the Democracy," names that conveyed their egalitarian message. As Thomas Morris told the Ohio legislature, he and other Democrats believed that the republic had been corrupted by legislative charters that gave "a few individuals rights and privileges not enjoyed by the citizens at large." The Democracy would destroy such "artificial distinction in society," Morris promised. Jackson himself declared that "equality among the people in the rights conferred by government" was the "great radical principle of freedom."

Jackson's message of equal rights and popular rule appealed to many social groups. His hostility to business corporations and to Clay's American System won support from northeastern artisans and workers who felt threatened by industrialization. Jackson also captured the votes of Pennsylvania ironworkers and New York farmers who had been enriched by the controversial Tariff of Abominations. Yet by astutely declaring his preference for a "judicious" tariff that would balance regional interests, Jackson remained popular in the South as well. In the Southeast and the Midwest, Old Hickory garnered votes because his well-known hostility toward Native Americans reassured white farmers who favored Indian removal.

The Democrats' celebration of popular rule carried Jackson into office. In 1824, about one-quarter of the eligible electorate had voted; in 1828, more than one-half went to the polls, and 56 percent of voters cast their ballots for the senator from Tennessee (Figure 10.1). Jackson received 178 of 261 electoral votes and became the first president from a trans-Appalachian state. As the president-elect traveled to Washington, he cut a dignified figure. According to an English observer, he "wore his hair carelessly but not ungracefully arranged, and in spite of his harsh, gaunt features looked like a gentleman and a soldier." Still, Jackson's popularity frightened men of wealth. Senator Daniel Webster of Massachusetts, a former Federalist and now a corporate lawyer, warned his clients that the new president would "bring a breeze with him. Which way it will blow, I cannot tell [but] . . . my fear is stronger than my hope." Supreme Court Justice Joseph Story shared Webster's apprehensions. Watching an unruly Inauguration Day crowd climb over the elegant furniture in the White House to congratulate Jackson, Story lamented: "the reign of King 'Mob' seemed triumphant."

▶ Was there a necessary connection between the growth of democracy and the emergence of disciplined political parties, or was it just a coincidence? Explain your answer.

▶ How do you explain John Quincy Adams's great success as secretary of state (see Chapter 7) and his relative lack of success as president?

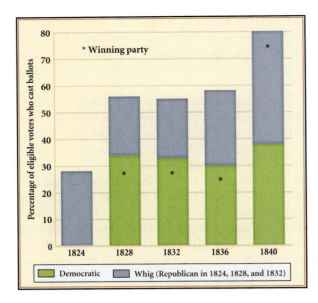

FIGURE 10.1 Changes in Voting Patterns, 1824–1840
Voter participation soared in 1828 and again in 1840 as competition heated up between Democrats and Whigs, who advocated different policies and philosophies of government.

The Jacksonian Presidency, 1829–1837

American-style political democracy—a broad franchise, a disciplined political party, and policies favoring specific groups of voters—ushered Andrew Jackson into office. Jackson used his popular mandate to transform the presidency and the policies of the national government. During his two terms in the White House, he enhanced presidential authority, destroyed the nationalistic American System, and implemented a new ideology of government. An Ohio supporter summarized Jackson's vision: "the Sovereignty of the People, the Rights of the States, and a Light and Simple Government."

Jackson's Agenda: Rotation and Decentralization

Although Jackson had a formal cabinet, for policymaking he relied primarily on an informal group of advisors: his "Kitchen Cabinet." Its most influential members were Kentuckians Francis Preston Blair, who edited the *Washington Globe*, and Amos Kendall, who wrote Jackson's speeches; Roger B. Taney of Maryland, who became attorney general, treasury secretary, and then chief justice of the Supreme Court; and, most important, Secretary of State Martin Van Buren.

Following Van Buren's practice in New York, Jackson used patronage to create a disciplined national party. He insisted on replacing "property in office" (a view that officials held office just as individuals held land) with rotation of officeholders: When an administration was voted out, its bureaucratic appointees would have to leave government service. Rotation would not lessen expertise, Jackson insisted, because public duties were "so plain and simple that men of intelligence may readily qualify themselves for their performance." William L. Marcy, a New York Jacksonian, put it more bluntly: Government jobs were like the spoils of war, and "to the victor belong the

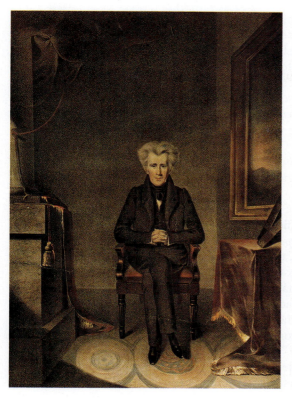

President Andrew Jackson, 1830
The new president came to Washington with a well-deserved reputation as an aggressive Indian fighter and dangerous military leader. But in this official portrait, he looks "presidential": His dress and posture, and the artist's composition, created the image of a calm, deliberate statesman. Subsequent events would show that Jackson had not lost his hard-edged authoritarian personality. Library of Congress.

spoils of the enemy." Using the spoils system, Jackson dispensed government jobs to reward friends and win backing for his policies.

Jackson's priority was to destroy the American System and all national plans for economic development. As Henry Clay noted apprehensively, the new president wanted "to cry down old constructions of the Constitution . . . to make all Jefferson's opinions the articles of faith of the new Church." Declaring that the "voice of the people" called for "economy in the expenditures of the Government," Jackson rejected national subsidies for transportation projects, which he also opposed on constitutional grounds. In 1830, he vetoed four internal improvement bills, including an extension of the National Road, arguing that they infringed "the reserved powers of states." These vetoes also represented an indirect attack on the protective tariffs, another controversial part of the American System, because Clay proposed to use them to fund canals and roads. As Senator William Smith of South Carolina noted, "destroy internal improvements and you leave no motive for the tariff."

The Tariff and Nullification

The Tariff of 1828 had helped Jackson to win the presidency, but it saddled him with a major political crisis. There was fierce opposition to high tariffs throughout the South, especially in South Carolina. South Carolina was the only state with an African American majority—56 percent of the population in 1830—and its slave owners, like the white sugar planters in the West Indies, feared a black rebellion. They also worried about the legal abolition of slavery. The British Parliament was on track to end slavery in the West Indies in 1833; South Carolina planters, remembering attempts to limit slavery in Missouri (see Chapter 8), worried that the U.S. Congress might do the same. So they attacked the tariff, both to lower rates and to discourage other uses of federal power.

The crisis began in 1832, when high-tariff congressmen ignored southern warnings that they were "endangering the Union" and reenacted the Tariff of Abominations. In response, leading South Carolinians called a state convention in November, which boldly adopted an Ordinance of Nullification. The ordinance declared the tariffs of 1828 and 1832 to be null and void; prohibited the collection of those duties in South Carolina after February 1, 1833; and threatened secession if federal officials tried to collect them.

South Carolina's act of **nullification** rested on the constitutional arguments developed in *The South Carolina Exposition and Protest* (1828). Written anonymously by Vice President John C. Calhoun, the *Exposition* gave a localist interpretation to the federal union. Because each geographic region had distinct interests, localists argued, protective tariffs and other national legislation that operated unequally on the various states lacked fairness and legitimacy—in fact, they were unconstitutional. An obsessive defender of the interests of the white South, Calhoun exaggerated the frequency of such legislation, declaring, "Constitutional government and the government of a majority are utterly incompatible."

Advancing an alternative interpretation of the Constitution, Calhoun used the arguments first advanced by Jefferson and Madison in the Kentucky and Virginia resolutions of 1798. Because the U.S. Constitution had been ratified by conventions in the various states, the resolutions suggested, sovereignty lay in the states, not in the people. Beginning from this premise, Calhoun developed a states' rights interpretation of the Constitution, arguing that a state convention could declare a congressional law to be unconstitutional and therefore void within the state's borders. Replying to this argument, which had no support in the text of the Constitution, Senator Daniel Webster of Massachusetts presented a nationalist interpretation that celebrated popular sovereignty and congressional legislation securing the "general welfare."

Jackson hoped to find a middle path between Webster's strident nationalism and Calhoun's radical doctrine of localist federalism. The Constitution clearly gave the federal government the authority to establish tariffs, and, Jackson would enforce that power, whatever the cost. The president declared that South Carolina's Ordinance of Nullification not only violated the letter of the Constitution but also was "unauthorized by its spirit . . . and destructive of the great object for which it was formed." "Disunion by armed force is treason," he warned. At Jackson's request, Congress passed a Force Bill early in 1833; it authorized the president to use military means to compel South Carolina's obedience to national laws. Simultaneously, Jackson addressed the South's objections to high import duties by winning passage of an act that, by 1842, reduced tariff rates to the modest levels of 1816. They remained low because western wheat farmers joined southern planters in advocating cheap imports and abundant exports. "Illinois wants a market for her agricultural products," declared Senator Sidney Breese in 1846, "she wants the market of the world."

Having won the *political* battle by securing a reduction in duties, the South Carolina convention gave up its *constitutional* quest and rescinded its nullification of the tariff. Jackson was satisfied. He had addressed the economic demands of the South while upholding the constitutional principle that no state could nullify a law of the United States—a principle that Abraham Lincoln would embrace to defend the Union during the secession crisis of 1861.

The Bank War

In the middle of the tariff crisis, Jackson faced a major challenge from the political supporters of the Second Bank of the United States. Founded in Philadelphia in 1816 (see Chapter 7), the bank was a privately managed institution that operated under a twenty-year charter from the federal government, which owned 20 percent of its stock. The Second Bank's most important role was to stabilize the nation's money supply, which consisted primarily of notes and bills of credit—in effect, paper money—issued by state-chartered banks. Those banks promised to redeem the notes on demand with "hard" money—that is, gold or silver coins (also known as specie). By collecting those notes and regularly demanding specie, the Second Bank kept the state banks from issuing too much paper money and depreciating its value.

This cautious monetary policy pleased creditors—the bankers and entrepreneurs in Boston, New York, and Philadelphia, whose capital investments were underwriting economic development. However, ordinary Americans were afraid that the Second Bank would force the closure of state banks, leaving people holding worthless paper notes. Some politicians opposed the Second Bank because of the arrogance of its president, Nicholas Biddle. "As to mere power," Biddle boasted, "I have been for years in the daily exercise of more personal authority than any President habitually enjoys." Fearing Biddle's influence, bankers in New York and other states wanted the specie owned by the federal government deposited in their own institutions rather than in the Second Bank. Other expansion-minded bankers, including friends of Jackson's in Nashville, wanted to escape supervision by any central bank.

Although the Bank had many enemies, a political miscalculation by its friends brought its downfall. In 1832, Henry Clay and Daniel Webster persuaded Biddle to seek an early extension of the bank's charter (which still had four years to run). They had the votes in Congress to enact the required legislation and hoped to lure Jackson into a veto that would split the Democrats just before the 1832 elections.

Jackson turned the tables on Clay and Webster. He vetoed the rechartering bill and issued a masterful veto message that blended constitutional arguments with class rhetoric and patriotic fervor. Adopting Thomas Jefferson's position, Jackson declared that Congress had no constitutional authority to charter a national bank, which was "subversive of the rights of the States." He also attacked the Second Bank as "dangerous to the liberties of the people." Employing the populist republican rhetoric of the American Revolution, Jackson condemned the Bank as a nest of special privilege and monopoly power that promoted "the advancement of the few at the expense of . . . farmers, mechanics, and laborers." Finally, the president evoked patriotic sentiment by pointing out that British aristocrats owned much of the bank's stock. Such a powerful institution should be "purely American," Jackson declared.

Jackson's attack on the bank carried him and Martin Van Buren, his long-time ally and new running mate, to victory in 1832. Old Hickory and "Little Van" overwhelmed Henry Clay, who headed the National Republican ticket, by 219 to 49 electoral votes. Jackson's most fervent supporters were eastern workers and western farmers, who blamed the Second Bank for urban price increases and stagnant farm prices. "All the flourishing cities of the West are mortgaged to this money power," charged Senator Thomas Hart Benton, a Jacksonian from Missouri. "They may be devoured by it at any moment." But many of Jackson's supporters had prospered during a decade of strong economic growth. Along with thousands of middle-class Americans — lawyers, clerks, shopkeepers, and artisans — they wanted an equal opportunity to rise in the world and cheered Jackson's attack on privileged corporations.

Early in 1833, Jackson called on Roger B. Taney to weaken the Second Bank, which still had four years left on its charter. A strong opponent of corporate privilege, Taney assumed control of the Treasury Department and promptly withdrew the government's gold and silver from the Second Bank. He deposited the specie in various state banks, which critics called Jackson's "pet banks." To justify this abrupt (and probably illegal) transfer, Jackson declared that his reelection represented "the decision of the people against the bank" and gave him a mandate to destroy it. This sweeping claim of presidential power was new and radical. Never before had a president claimed that victory at the polls allowed him to pursue a controversial policy or to act independently of Congress.

The "bank war" escalated into an all-out political battle. In March 1834, Jackson's opponents in the Senate passed a resolution written by Henry Clay that censured the president and warned of executive tyranny: "We are in the midst of a revolution, hitherto bloodless, but rapidly descending towards a total change of the pure republican character of the Government, and the concentration of all power in the hands of one man." Jackson was not deterred by Clay's charges or Congress's censure. "The Bank is trying to kill me but I will kill it," he vowed to Van Buren. And so he did. When the Second Bank's national charter expired in 1836, Jackson prevented its renewal.

Jackson had destroyed both national banking — the creation of Alexander Hamilton — and the American System of protective tariffs and internal improvements that Henry Clay and John Quincy Adams had instituted. The result was a profound reduction in economic activism and creative policymaking by the national government. "All is gone," observed a Washington newspaper correspondent. "All is gone, which the General Government was instituted to create and preserve."

Indian Removal

The status of Native American peoples posed an equally complex political problem. By the late 1820s, white voices throughout the South and Midwest were calling for the Indian peoples to be resettled west of the Mississippi River. Many easterners who were sympathetic to Native Americans also favored resettlement. Removal to the West seemed the only way to protect Indian peoples from alcoholic devastation and financial exploitation and to preserve the Indians' culture.

However, most Indians did not want to leave their ancestral lands. The Old Southwest was home to the Cherokees and Creeks in Georgia, Tennessee, and Alabama; the

Chickasaws and Choctaws in Mississippi and Alabama; and the Seminoles in Florida. During the War of 1812, Andrew Jackson had forced the Creeks to relinquish millions of acres of land, but Indian peoples still controlled vast tracts. Moreover, the mixed-blood offspring of white traders and Indian women had assumed the leadership of many peoples. Growing up in a bicultural world, mixed-bloods knew the political ways of whites. Most of them strongly resisted removal, and some favored assimilation into white society.

A number of mixed-blood Indians had already adopted the institutions and the lifestyle of southern planters. James Vann, a Georgia Cherokee, owned more than twenty black slaves, two trading posts, and a gristmill. Forty other mixed-blood Cherokee families each owned twenty or more African American slaves. To protect their property and the lands of their people, the mixed-bloods promoted a strong Indian identity. Sequoyah perfected a system of writing for the Cherokee language in 1821; six years later, he and other mixed-bloods devised a new charter of Cherokee government modeled directly on the U.S. Constitution. Full-blood Cherokees, who made up 90 percent of the population, resisted many of these cultural and political innovations but were equally determined to retain their ancestral lands. "We would not receive money for land in which our fathers and friends are buried," one full-blood chief declared. "We love our land; it is our mother."

What the Cherokees wanted carried no weight with the Georgia legislature. In 1802, Georgia had given up its western land claims in return for a federal promise to extinguish Indian landholdings in the state. Now it demanded fulfillment of that pledge. Having spent his military career fighting Indians and seizing their lands, Andrew Jackson gave full support to Georgia. On assuming the presidency, he withdrew the federal troops that had protected Indian enclaves there and in Alabama and Mississippi. The states, he declared, were sovereign within their borders.

Jackson then pushed the Indian Removal Act of 1830 through Congress. The act granted money and land in present-day Oklahoma and Kansas to Native American peoples who would give up their ancestral holdings (see American Voices, p. 304). To persuade Indians to move, government officials promised that they could live on the new lands, "they and all their children, as long as grass grows and water runs." When Chief Black Hawk and his Sauk and Fox followers refused to move from rich farmland in western Illinois in 1832, Jackson sent troops to expel them. Rejecting Black Hawk's offer to surrender, the American army pursued him into the Wisconsin Territory and, in the brutal eight-hour Bad Axe Massacre, killed 850 of Black Hawk's 1,000 warriors. Over the next five years, American diplomatic pressure and military power forced seventy Indian peoples to sign treaties and move west of the Mississippi (Map 10.2).

In the meantime, the Cherokees had carried their case to the Supreme Court, where they claimed the status of a "foreign nation." In *Cherokee Nation v. Georgia* (1831), Chief Justice John Marshall denied the Cherokees' claim of independence and declared that Indian peoples were "domestic dependent nations." However, in *Worcester v. Georgia* (1832), Marshall and the court sided with the Cherokees against Georgia. Voiding Georgia's extension of state law over the Cherokees, the court held that Indian nations were "distinct political communities, having territorial boundaries, within which their authority is exclusive [and this is] guaranteed by the United States."

A Sacred Reverence for Our Lands   BLACK HAWK

Black Hawk (1767–1838), or Makataimeshekiakiak in the language of his people, was a chief of the Sauk and Fox. In 1833, he dictated his life story to a government interpreter, and a young newspaper editor published it. Here, Black Hawk describes the coming of white settlers to his village, near present-day Rock Island, Illinois, and his decision to resist removal to lands west of the Mississippi River.

We had about eight hundred acres in cultivation. The land around our village . . . was covered with bluegrass, which made excellent pasture for our horses. . . . The rapids of Rock river furnished us with an abundance of excellent fish, and the land, being good, never failed to produce good crops of corn, beans, pumpkins, and squashes. We always had plenty—our children never cried with hunger, nor our people were never in want. Here our village had stood for more than a hundred years.

[In 1828] Nothing was now talked of but leaving our village. Ke-o-kuck [the principal chief] had been persuaded to consent to . . . remove to the west side of the Mississippi. . . . [I] raised the standard of opposition to Ke-o-kuck, with full determination not to leave my village. . . . I was of the opinion that the white people had plenty of land and would never take our village from us. . . .

During the [following] winter, I received information that three families of whites had arrived at our village and destroyed some of our lodges, and were making fences and dividing our corn-fields for their own use. . . . I requested them [to leave, but some weeks later] we came up to our village, and found that the whites had not left it—but that others had come, and that the greater part of our corn-fields had been enclosed. . . . Some of the whites permitted us to plant small patches in the fields they had fenced, keeping all the best ground for themselves. . . . The white people brought whiskey into our village, made people drunk, and cheated them out of their homes, guns, and [beaver] traps!

That fall [1829] I paid a visit to the agent, before we started to our hunting grounds. . . . He said that the land on which our village stood was now ordered to be sold to individuals; and that, when sold, our right to remain, by treaty, would be at an end, and that if we returned next spring, we would be forced to remove! I refused . . . to quit my village. It was here, that I was born—and here lie the bones of many friends and relatives. For this spot I felt a sacred reverence, and never could consent to leave it, without being forced therefrom.

[In the spring of 1831] I directed my village crier to proclaim, that my orders were, in the event of the [Indian] war chief coming to our village to remove us [to honor the treaty], that not a gun should be fired, nor any resistance offered. That if he determined to fight, for them to remain quietly in their lodges, and let them kill them if he chose.

SOURCE: David Jackson, ed., *Black Hawk: An Autobiography* (Urbana: University of Illinois Press, 1964), 88–90, 95–97, 111–113.

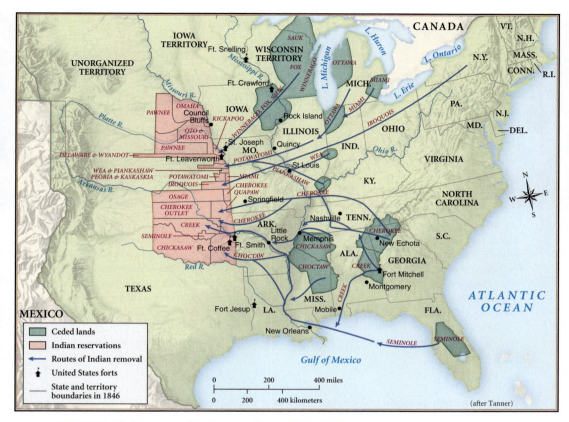

MAP 10.2 The Removal of Native Americans, 1820–1846

Beginning in the 1820s, the U.S. government forced scores of Native American peoples to sign treaties that exchanged Indian land in the East for money and designated reservation land west of the Mississippi River. In the 1830s, the government used military force to expel the Cherokees, Chickasaws, Choctaws, Creeks, and many Seminoles from their ancestral homes in the Old Southeast and to resettle them in the Indian Territory, in the present-day states of Oklahoma and Kansas.

For more help analyzing this map, see the Online Study Guide at **bedfordstmartins.com/henrettaconcise**.

Instead of guaranteeing the Cherokees' territory, the U.S. government took it from them. In 1835, American officials negotiated the Treaty of New Echota with a minority Cherokee faction and insisted that all Cherokees abide by it and move to the new Indian Territory. When only 2,000 of 17,000 Cherokees had moved by the deadline of May 1838, President Martin Van Buren ordered General Winfield Scott to enforce the treaty. Scott's army rounded up some 14,000 Cherokees and forcibly marched them 1,200 miles to the Indian Territory, an arduous journey that they described as the Trail of Tears. Along the way, 3,000 Indians died of starvation and exposure.

After the Creeks, Chickasaws, and Choctaws moved west of the Mississippi, the Seminoles were the only numerically significant Indian people remaining in the Old Southwest. With the aid of runaway slaves who had married into the tribe, the Seminoles fought a successful guerrilla war against the U.S. Army during the 1840s

Raising Public Opinion Against the Seminoles

During the eighteenth century, hundreds of enslaved blacks fled South Carolina and Georgia and found refuge in Spanish Florida, where they lived among and intermarried with the Seminole people. This color engraving from the 1830s, showing red and black Seminoles butchering respectable white families, was intended to bolster political support for the forced removal of the Seminoles to the Indian Territory. By the mid-1840s, after a decade of warfare, the U.S. Army had forced 2,500 Seminoles to migrate to Oklahoma. However, another 2,500 Seminoles continued their armed resistance and eventually won a new treaty allowing them to live in Florida. Granger Collection.

For more help analyzing this image, see the Online Study Guide at **bedfordstmartins.com/henrettaconcise**.

and retained their lands in Florida, which was still a sparsely settled frontier region. The Seminoles were an exception. The Jacksonians had forced the removal of most eastern Indian peoples.

The Jacksonian Impact

Jackson's legacy, like that of every great president, is complex and rich. On the institutional level, he permanently expanded the authority of the nation's chief executive by identifying it with the voice of the people. As Jackson put it, "The President is the direct representative of the American people." Assuming that role during the nullification crisis, he upheld national authority by threatening the use of military force, laying the foundation for Lincoln's defense of the Union a generation later. At the same time (and somewhat contradictorily), Jackson curbed the reach of the national government. By undermining Henry Clay's American System of national banking, protective tariffs, and internal improvements, Jackson reinvigorated the Jeffersonian tradition of a limited and frugal central government.

Jackson also undermined the constitutional jurisprudence of John Marshall by appointing Roger B. Taney as Marshall's successor. During his long tenure as chief justice from 1835 to 1864, Taney partially reversed the nationalist and vested-property-rights decisions of the Marshall Court and gave constitutional legitimacy to Jackson's policies of states' rights and free enterprise. In the landmark case *Charles River Bridge Co. v. Warren Bridge Co.* (1837), Taney declared that a legislative charter—in this case, to build and operate a toll bridge—did not necessarily bestow a monopoly and that a legislature could charter a competing bridge to promote the general welfare: "While the rights of private property are sacredly guarded, we must not forget that the community also has rights." This decision directly challenged Marshall's interpretation of the contract clause of the Constitution in *Dartmouth College v. Woodward* (1819), which had stressed the binding nature of public charters (see Chapter 7). By limiting the property and monopoly claims of existing canal and turnpike companies, the decision allowed legislatures to charter competing railroads that would provide cheaper and more efficient transportation.

Other decisions by the Taney Court limited Marshall's nationalistic interpretation of the commerce clause by enhancing the regulatory role of state governments. For example, in *Mayor of New York v. Miln* (1837), the Taney Court ruled that New York State could use its "police power" to inspect the health of arriving immigrants. The Court also restored to the states some of the economic powers they had exercised before 1787. In *Briscoe v. Bank of Kentucky* (1837), for example, the justices allowed a bank owned by the state of Kentucky to issue currency, despite the wording of the U.S. Constitution (Article I, Section 10) that prohibits states from issuing "bills of credit."

Inspired by Jackson and Taney's example, Democrats in the various states mounted their own constitutional revolutions. Between 1830 and 1860, twenty states called conventions to write new constitutions to extend democracy. Most of these constitutions gave the vote to all white men and reapportioned state legislatures on the basis of population. They also brought government "near to the people" by mandating the election, rather than the appointment, of most public officials, including sheriffs, justices of the peace, and judges.

The new constitutions also embodied the principles of **classical liberalism**, or **laissez-faire**, by limiting the government's role in the economy. (Twentieth-century social-welfare liberalism endorses the opposite principle: that government should intervene in economic and social life. See Chapter 24.) As president, Jackson had destroyed the American System; his disciples in the states now attacked the Commonwealth philosophy: the use of chartered corporations and state funds to promote economic development. Most Jackson-era constitutions prohibited states from granting special charters to corporations or extending loans and credit guarantees to private businesses. "If there is any danger to be feared in . . . government," declared a New Jersey Democrat, "it is the danger of associated wealth, with special privileges." The revised constitutions also protected taxpayers by setting strict limits on state debt and encouraging judges to enforce them. Said one New York reformer, "We will not trust the legislature with the power of creating indefinite mortgages on the people's property."

"The world is governed too much," the Jacksonians proclaimed as they embraced a small-government, laissez-faire outlook. The first American populists, they celebrated the power of ordinary people to make decisions in the marketplace and the voting booth.

▶ What were Andrew Jackson's policies on banking and tariffs? Did they help or hurt the American economy? Why?

▶ Why did Jackson support Indian removal? Did removal help to preserve or to destroy Native American cultures? Explain your answer.

▶ How did the constitutional interpretations of the Taney Court and the new Jacksonian state constitutions alter the American legal and constitutional system?

Class, Culture, and the Second Party System

The rise of the Democracy and Jackson's tumultuous presidency sparked the creation in the mid-1830s of a second national party: the **Whigs**. For the next two decades, Whigs and Democrats competed fiercely for votes and won support from different cultural groups. Many Evangelical Protestants became Whigs, while most Catholic immigrants and traditional Protestants joined the Democrats. By debating issues of economic policy, class power, and moral reform, party politicians offered Americans a choice between competing programs and political leaders. "Of the two great parties," remarked philosopher and essayist Ralph Waldo Emerson, the Democracy "has the best cause . . . for free trade, for wide suffrage." The Whig party, he said, "has the best men."

The Whig Worldview

The Whig Party arose in 1834, when a group of congressmen banded together to oppose Andrew Jackson's policies and his high-handed, "kinglike" conduct. They took the name *Whigs* to identify themselves with the pre-Revolutionary American and British parties — also called Whigs — that had opposed the arbitrary actions of British monarchs. The Whigs accused "King Andrew I" of violating the Constitution by creating a spoils system and increasing presidential authority. Jackson's "executive usurpation," they charged, undermined government by elected legislators, who were the true representatives of the sovereign people.

Initially, the Whigs were a diverse group drawn from various political factions. However, under the leadership of Senators Webster of Massachusetts, Clay of Kentucky, and Calhoun of South Carolina, the Whigs gradually articulated a distinct vision. Their goal, like that of the Federalists of the 1790s, was a political world dominated by men of ability and wealth; unlike the Federalists, though, the Whig elite would be chosen by talent, not birth.

The Whigs celebrated the entrepreneur and the enterprising individual: "This is a country of self-made men," they boasted, pointing to the relative absence of permanent distinctions of class and status among white citizens. Embracing the Industrial Revolution, northern Whigs welcomed the investments of "moneyed capitalists," which provided workers with jobs and so "bread, clothing and homes." Whig Congressman Edward Everett told a Fourth of July crowd in Lowell, Massachusetts, that there should be a "holy alliance" among laborers, owners, and governments. Many workers agreed, especially those who labored in the New England textile factories and Pennsylvania iron mills that benefited from protective tariffs. To ensure prosperity, Everett and other northern Whigs called for a return to the American System.

Support for the Whigs in the South rested on the appeal of specific policies and politicians, not the Whigs' social vision. Some southern Whigs were wealthy planters who invested in railroads and banks or sold their cotton to New York merchants. The majority were yeomen whites who resented the grip over state politics held by low-country planters, most of whom were Democrats. In addition, some Virginia and South Carolina Democrats became Whigs because, like John C. Calhoun, they favored states' rights and condemned Andrew Jackson's crusade against nullification.

Like Calhoun, most southern Whigs rejected the Whig Party's enthusiasm for high tariffs and social mobility. Calhoun was extremely conscious of class divisions in society. He believed that the northern Whig ideal of equal opportunity was contradicted not only by slavery, which he considered a fundamental American institution, but also by the wage-labor system of industrial capitalism. "There is and always has been in an advanced state of wealth and civilization a conflict between labor and capital," Calhoun declared in 1837. He urged slave owners and factory owners to unite against their common foe: a working class composed of enslaved blacks and property-less whites.

Most northern Whigs rejected Calhoun's class-conscious social ideology. "A clear and well-defined line between capital and labor" might fit the slave South or class-ridden European societies, Daniel Webster conceded, but in the North, "this distinction grows less and less definite as commerce advances." Ignoring the ever-increasing mass of propertyless immigrants, Webster focused on the growing size of the northern middle class, whose members generally supported Whig candidates. In the election of 1834, the Whigs won a majority in the House of Representatives by appealing to Evangelical Protestants and upwardly mobile families—prosperous farmers, small-town merchants, and skilled industrial workers in New England, New York, and the new communities along the Great Lakes.

Many of these Whig voters had previously supported the Anti-Masonic Party, a powerful but short-lived political party that formed in the late 1820s. As their name implies, Anti-Masons opposed the Order of Freemasonry, a republican organization that arose in eighteenth-century Europe. The order was a secret society of men whose rituals were closely guarded. Freemasonry spread rapidly in America and attracted political leaders—including George Washington, Henry Clay, and Andrew Jackson—and ambitious businessmen. By the mid-1820s, there were 20,000 Masons in New York State, organized into 450 local lodges. Following the kidnapping and murder in 1826 of William Morgan, a New York Mason who had threatened to reveal the order's secrets, the Freemasons fell into disrepute. Thurlow Weed, a Rochester newspaper editor, spearheaded the Anti-Masonic Party, which condemned the order as a secret aristocratic fraternity and ousted its members from local and state offices.

The Whigs recruited Anti-Masons to their party by endorsing the Anti-Masons' support for temperance, equality of opportunity, and evangelical morality. Throughout the Northeast and Midwest, Whig politicians advocated legal curbs on the sale of alcohol and local ordinances that preserved Sunday as a day of worship. The Whigs also won congressional seats in the Ohio and Mississippi valleys, where farmers, bankers, and shopkeepers favored Henry Clay's American System. For these citizens of the growing Midwest, the Whigs' program of government subsidies for roads, canals, and bridges was as important as their moral agenda.

In the election of 1836, the Whig Party faced Martin Van Buren, the architect of the Democratic Party and Jackson's handpicked successor. Van Buren denounced the American System and warned that its revival would create an oppressive system of "consolidated government." Positioning himself as a defender of individual rights, Van Buren opposed the efforts of Whigs and moral reformers to use state laws to impose temperance and national laws to abolish slavery. "The government is best which governs least" became his motto in economic, cultural, and racial matters.

Celebrating a Political Triumph, 1836
To commemorate Martin Van Buren's election in 1836 and to reward his supporters, the Democrat Party distributed thousands of snuffboxes inscribed with the new president's portrait. By using gifts and other innovative measures to enlist the loyalty of voters, Van Buren and his allies transformed American politics from an upper-class avocation to a democratic contest for votes and power. Collection of Janice L. and David J. Frent.

To oppose Van Buren, the Whigs ran four candidates, each with a strong regional reputation. Their plan was to garner enough electoral votes to throw the contest into the House of Representatives. However, the Whig tally — 73 electoral votes collected by William Henry Harrison of Ohio, 26 by Hugh L. White of Tennessee, 14 by Daniel Webster of Massachusetts, and 11 by W. P. Magnum of Georgia — fell far short of Van Buren's 170 votes. Still, the four Whig candidates won 49 percent of the popular vote, showing that the party's message of economic and moral improvement had a broad appeal (see Voices from Abroad, p. 311).

Labor Politics and the Depression of 1837–1843

As the Democrats struggled with Whigs on the national level, they faced a challenge from urban artisans and workers. In 1827, artisans and workers in Philadelphia organized the Mechanics' Union of Trade Associations, a group of fifty unions with 10,000 members. The following year, they founded a Working Men's Party to secure "a just balance of power . . . between all the various classes." The new party campaigned for the abolition of banks, fair taxation, and universal public education and blazed the trail for similar organizations: By 1833, laborers had established Working Men's Parties in fifteen states.

The new parties had a clear agenda. The Industrial Revolution and the Market Revolution had brought prosperity to bankers and entrepreneurs, but rising prices and stagnant wages had cut the living standards of many urban artisans and wage earners. Seeing "the glaring inequality of society," workers organized for political action. "Past experience teaches us that we have nothing to hope from the aristocratic orders of society," declared the New York Working Men's Party. It vowed "to send men of our own description, if we can, to the Legislature at Albany" to secure laws that would abolish private banks, chartered monopolies, and debtors' prisons. In Philadelphia, the Working Men's Party demanded higher taxes on the wealthy and, in 1834, persuaded the Pennsylvania legislature to authorize tax-supported schools so that workers' children could rise in the world.

The goal of the workingmen's parties was a society without dependent wage earners. In this republic of artisans, said labor intellectual Orestes Brownson, "All men will be

Parties in the United States ALEXIS DE TOCQUEVILLE

In *Democracy in America* (1835), Alexis de Tocqueville presented both a philosophical analysis of American society and an astute description of its political institutions. Here, the republican-minded French aristocrat explains the role of lawyers in American politics, why there are no "great political parties," and how regional and class interests threaten the political system.

We perceive that the authority they have entrusted to the members of the legal profession, and the influence that these individuals exercise in the government, are the most powerful existing security against the excesses of democracy. . . . Men who have made a special study of the laws derive from [that] occupation certain habits of order, a taste for formalities, . . . which naturally render them very hostile to the revolutionary spirit and the unreflecting passions of the multitude. . . . Lawyers belong to the people by birth and interest, and to the aristocracy by habit and taste; they may be looked upon as the connecting link between the two great classes of society. . . .

The political parties that I style great are those which cling to principles rather than to their consequences. . . . Great political parties . . . are not to be met with in the United States at the present time. Parties, indeed, may be found which threaten the future of the Union; but there is none which seems to contest the present form of government or the present course of society. The parties by which the Union is menaced do not rest upon principles, but upon material interests. These interests constitute, in the different provinces of so vast an empire, rival nations rather than parties. Thus, upon a recent occasion [the Tariff of 1832 and the nullification crisis] the North contended for the system of commercial prohibition, and the South took up arms in favor of free trade, simply because the North is a manufacturing and the South an agricultural community; and the restrictive system that was profitable to the one was prejudicial to the other. . . .

The deeper we penetrate into the inmost thought of these parties, the more we perceive that the object of the one [the Whigs] is to limit and that of the other [the Democrats] to extend the authority of the people. . . .

To quote a recent example, when President Jackson attacked the Bank of the United States, the country was excited, and parties were formed; the well-informed classes rallied round the bank, the common people round the President. But it must not be imagined that the people had formed a rational opinion upon a question which offers so many difficulties to the most experienced statesmen. By no means. The bank is a great establishment, which has an independent existence; and the people . . . are startled to meet with this obstacle to their authority [and are] led to attack it, in order to see whether it can be shaken, like everything else.

SOURCE: Alexis de Tocqueville, *Democracy in America* (1835; New York: Random House, 1981), 1: 94–99.

independent proprietors, working on their own capitals, on their own farms, or in their own shops." Like Jacksonian Democrats, artisan republicans demanded equal rights and attacked chartered corporations. "The only safeguard against oppression," argued William Leggett, a leading member of the New York Loco-Foco (Equal Rights) Party, "is a system of legislation which leaves to all the free exercise of their talents and industry." Working Men's candidates won office in many cities, but divisions over policy and the parties' weakness in statewide contests soon took a toll. By the mid-1830s, most politically active workers had joined the Democratic Party and were urging it to eliminate protective tariffs and tax the stocks and bonds of wealthy capitalists.

When equality-conscious workers formed unions to bargain for higher wages for themselves, employers attacked the union movement. In 1836, clothing manufacturers in New York City agreed to dismiss workers who belonged to the Society of Journeymen Tailors and circulated a list—a so-called **blacklist**—of the society's members. The employers also brought lawsuits to overturn **closed-shop agreements** that required them to hire only union members. They argued that these contracts violated both the common law and legislative statutes that prohibited "conspiracies" in restraint of trade.

Judges usually sided with the employers. In 1835, the New York Supreme Court found that a shoemakers' union in Geneva had illegally caused "an industrious man" to be "driven out of employment" because he would not join the union. "It is important to the best interests of society that the price of labor be left to regulate itself," the court declared. When a court in New York City upheld a conspiracy verdict against a tailors' union, a crowd of 27,000 people denounced the decision in a mass meeting, and tailors circulated handbills warning that the "Freemen of the North are now on a level with the slaves of the South." Workers found allies among jurors. In 1836, local juries hearing conspiracy cases acquitted shoemakers in Hudson, New York; carpet makers in Thompsonville, Connecticut; and plasterers in Philadelphia.

At this juncture, the Panic of 1837 threw the American economy—and the union movement—into disarray. The panic began when the Bank of England, hoping to boost the faltering British economy, sharply curtailed the flow of money and credit to the United States. Since 1822, British manufacturers had extended credit to southern planters to expand cotton production, and British investors had purchased millions of dollars of the canal bonds issued by northern states. Suddenly deprived of British funds, American planters, merchants, and canal corporations had to withdraw specie from domestic banks to pay their commercial debts and interest on their foreign loans. When British textile mills drastically reduced their purchases of raw cotton from the South, cotton prices plummeted from 20 cents a pound to 10 cents or less.

The drain of specie to Britain and falling cotton prices set off a financial panic. On May 8, the Dry Dock Bank of New York City closed its doors, and worried depositors began to withdraw gold and silver coins from other banks. Within two weeks, every bank in the United States stopped trading specie and curtailed credit, turning a financial panic into an economic crisis. "This sudden overthrow of the commercial credit" had a "stunning effect," observed Henry Fox, the British minister in Washington. "The conquest of the land by a foreign power could hardly have produced a more general sense of humiliation and grief."

A second, longer-lasting downturn began in 1839. To revive the economy after the Panic of 1837, state governments had increased their investments in canals and railroads. As they issued more and more bonds to finance these ventures, bond prices fell sharply in Europe, sparking a four-year-long financial crisis. The international crisis engulfed state governments in America, which were unable to meet the substantial interest payments on their bonds. Nine states defaulted on their obligations, prompting foreign creditors to cut the flow of new capital to the United States. Bumper crops drove down cotton prices even further, bringing more bankruptcies.

The American economy fell into a deep depression. By 1843, canal construction had dropped by 90 percent, and prices had fallen by nearly 50 percent. Unemployment reached almost 20 percent of the workforce in seaports and industrial centers. Minister Henry Ward Beecher described a land "filled with lamentation . . . its inhabitants wandering like bereaved citizens among the ruins of an earthquake, mourning for children, for houses crushed, and property buried forever."

By creating a surplus of unemployed workers, the depression devastated the labor movement. In 1837, 6,000 masons, carpenters, and other building-trades workers lost their jobs in New York City, depleting unions' rosters and destroying their bargaining power. By 1843, most local unions and all the national labor organizations had disappeared, along with their newspapers.

The subsequent decades brought few gains for workers or their unions. In *Commonwealth v. Hunt* (1842), Chief Justice Lemuel Shaw of the Massachusetts Supreme Judicial Court upheld the rights of workers to form unions. Shaw's decision overturned common-law precedents by ruling that a union was not an inherently illegal organization and could strike to enforce a closed-shop agreement. But courts found other ways to deter unions, such as issuing **injunctions** that prohibited workers from picketing or striking. Moreover, judges continued to apply the traditional common-law principles to the workplace; this meant, as one legal treatise put it, that "all who are in the employ of another" were "servants" and hence subject to their master-employer. Still, workers won some political victories. Continuing Jackson's effort to recruit laboring men and women to the Democratic Party, President Van Buren signed an executive order in 1840 setting a ten-hour day for federal employees. Increasingly, workers' struggles—like conflicts over tariffs, banks, and internal improvements—were fought out in the political arena.

"Tippecanoe and Tyler Too!"

Many Americans blamed the Democrats for the depression of 1837–1843. In particular, they criticized Jackson for destroying the Second Bank and for issuing the Specie Circular of 1836, which required western settlers to use gold and silver coins to pay for farms in the national domain.

The public turned its anger on Van Buren, who took office just as the panic struck. Ignoring the pleas of influential bankers, the new president refused to revoke the Specie Circular or take other actions that might have reversed the downturn. Holding to his philosophy of limited government, Van Buren advised Congress that "the less government interferes with private pursuits the better for the general prosperity."

As the depression deepened in 1839, this laissez-faire policy commanded less and less political support. Worse, Van Buren's major piece of economic legislation, the Independent Treasury Act of 1840, actually delayed recovery. The act pulled federal specie out of Jackson's pet banks (which had used it to back loans) and placed it in government vaults, where it did no economic good at all.

Determined to exploit Van Buren's weakness, the Whigs organized their first national convention in 1840 and nominated William Henry Harrison of Ohio for president and John Tyler of Virginia for vice president. A military hero of the Battle of Tippecanoe and the War of 1812, Harrison was well advanced in age (sixty-eight) and had little political experience. But the Whig leaders in Congress, Clay and Webster, wanted a president who would rubber-stamp their program for protective tariffs and a national bank. An unpretentious, amiable man, Harrison told voters that Whig policies were "the only means, under Heaven, by which a poor industrious man may become a rich man without bowing to colossal wealth."

Panic and depression stacked the political cards against Van Buren, but the election turned as much on style as on substance. It became the great "log cabin campaign"—the first time two well-organized parties competed for the loyalties of a mass electorate through a new style of campaigning. Whig songfests, parades, and well-orchestrated mass meetings drew new voters into politics. Whig speakers assailed "Martin Van Ruin" as a manipulative politician with aristocratic tastes—a devotee of fancy wines and elegant clothes, as indeed he was. Less truthfully, they portrayed Harrison as a self-made man who was happy living in a log cabin and quaffing hard cider, a drink of the common people. In fact, Harrison's father was a wealthy Virginia planter who had signed the Declaration of Independence, and Harrison himself lived in a series of elegant mansions.

The Whigs boosted their electoral hopes by welcoming women to campaign festivities. Previously, women had been excluded not only from voting but also from marching in political parades. Jacksonian Democrats were particularly committed to politics as a "manly" affair and insinuated that politically minded females were akin to "public" women, the prostitutes who plied their trade in theaters and other public places. But the Whigs recognized that Christian women from Yankee families, a key Whig constituency, had already entered American public life through the temperance movement and other benevolent activities. In October 1840, Daniel Webster addressed a meeting of 1,200 Whig women, praised their efforts for moral reform, and urged them to back Whig candidates. "This way of making politicians of their women is something new under the sun," noted one Democrat, worried that it would bring more Whig men to the polls. And it did: More than 80 percent of the eligible male voters cast ballots in 1840, up from fewer than 60 percent in 1832 and 1836. Heeding the Whig campaign slogan "Tippecanoe and Tyler Too," they voted Harrison into the White House with 53 percent of the popular vote and gave the Whigs a majority in Congress.

Led by Clay and Webster, the Whigs in Congress were poised to reverse the Jacksonian revolution. But their hopes were short-lived; barely a month after his inauguration, Harrison died of pneumonia, and the nation got "Tyler Too." But in what capacity: as acting president or as president? The Constitution was vague on the issue.

The Log Cabin Campaign, 1840

During the Second Party System, politics became more responsive to the popular will as ordinary people voted for candidates who shared their values and lifestyles. The barrels of hard cider framing this homemade campaign banner evoke the drink of the common man, while the central image falsely portrays William Henry Harrison as a poor and simple frontier farmer. New-York Historical Society, New York City.

Ignoring his Whig associates in Congress, who feared a strong president like Jackson, Tyler took the presidential oath of office and declared his intention to govern as he pleased. As it turned out, that would not be like a Whig.

Tyler had served in the House and the Senate as a Jeffersonian Democrat, firmly committed to slavery and states' rights. He had joined the Whigs only to protest Jackson's stance against nullification. On economic issues, Tyler shared Jackson's hostility to the Second Bank and the American System. So the new president vetoed Whig bills that would have raised tariffs and created a new national bank. Disgusted, most of Tyler's cabinet resigned in 1842, and the Whigs expelled Tyler from their party. "His Accidency," as he was called by his critics, was now a president without a party.

The split between Tyler and the Whigs allowed the Democrats to regroup. The party vigorously recruited supporters among subsistence farmers in the North, smallholding planters in the South, and former members of the Working Men's parties in the cities. It also won support among Irish and German Catholic immigrants—whose numbers had increased during the 1830s—by backing their demands for religious and cultural freedom. This pattern of **ethnocultural politics**, as historians refer to the practice of voting along ethnic and religious lines, now became a prominent feature of American life. Thanks to these urban and rural recruits, the Democrats remained the majority party in most parts of the nation. Their program of equal rights, states' rights, and cultural liberty was more attractive than the Whig platform of economic nationalism, moral reform, and individual mobility.

> ► How did the ideology of the Whigs differ from that of the Jacksonian Democrats?
>
> ► Chapter 10 argues that a democratic revolution swept America in the decades after 1820. What evidence does the text present to support this argument? How persuasive is it?

SUMMARY

In this chapter, we have examined the causes and the consequences of the democratic political revolution that accompanied the economic transformation of the early nineteenth century. We saw that the expansion of the franchise weakened the political system run by notables of high status. In its place emerged a system managed by professional politicians, men like Martin Van Buren, who were mostly of middle-class origin.

We also witnessed a revolution in government policy, as Andrew Jackson and his Democratic party dismantled the political foundation of the mercantilist system. On the national level, Jackson destroyed Henry Clay's American System; on the state level, Democrats wrote new constitutions that ended the Commonwealth System of government charters and subsidies to private businesses.

Finally, we watched the emergence of the Second Party System. Following the splits in the Republican Party during the election of 1824, two new parties—the Democrats and the Whigs—developed on the national level and eventually absorbed the members of the Anti-Masonic and Working Men's parties. The new party system established universal suffrage for white men and a mode of representative government that was responsive to ordinary citizens. In their scope and significance, these political innovations matched the economic advances of the Industrial and Market Revolutions.

Connections: Government

In this chapter, we witnessed the process that transformed the elite-dominated republican polity described in Chapters 7 and 8 into a democratic political culture and the Second Party System of Whigs and Democrats. As we observed in the essay that opened Part Three:

> The rapid growth of political parties sparked the creation of a competitive and responsive democratic polity. . . . This party competition engaged the energies of the electorate and helped to unify a fragmented social order.

TIMELINE

1810s	▶ State constitutions expand voting rights for white men
	▶ Martin Van Buren creates a disciplined party in New York
1825	▶ John Quincy Adams elected president, adopts Henry Clay's American System
1828	▶ Artisans in Philadelphia organize Working Men's Party
	▶ Tariff imposes high duties on imported goods
	▶ Andrew Jackson elected president
	▶ John C. Calhoun's *The South Carolina Exposition and Protest*
1830	▶ President Jackson vetoes extension of National Road
	▶ Congress enacts Jackson's Indian Removal Act
1831	▶ *Cherokee Nation v. Georgia* denies Indians' claim of national sovereignty
1832	▶ President Jackson vetoes renewal of Second Bank's charter
	▶ South Carolina adopts Ordinance of Nullification
	▶ *Worcester v. Georgia* upholds political autonomy of Indian peoples

1833	▶ Congress passes Force Bill and compromise tariff
1834	▶ Whig Party formed by Henry Clay, John C. Calhoun, and Daniel Webster
1835	▶ Roger Taney named Supreme Court chief justice
1836	▶ Martin Van Buren elected president
1837	▶ *Charles River Bridge Co. v. Warren Bridge Co.* weakens chartered monopolies
	▶ Panic of 1837 derails labor movement
1838	▶ Thousands of Cherokees die on Trail of Tears
1839–1843	▶ International financial crisis; American economic depression
1840	▶ Whigs triumph in log cabin campaign
1841	▶ John Tyler succeeds William Henry Harrison as president
1842	▶ *Commonwealth v. Hunt* legitimizes trade unions

We will continue the story of America's political development in Chapter 13, which covers the years between 1844 and 1860. There, we will watch the disintegration of the Second Party System over the issue of slavery. Such slavery-related political crises were not new; as the discussion in Chapter 8 showed, the North and the South quarreled bitterly between 1819 and 1821 over the extension of slavery into Missouri. At that time, notable politicians raised in the old republican culture resolved the issue through compromise. Would democratic politicians be equally adept at fashioning a compromise over slavery in the territories seized from Mexico in 1848? Even more important, would their constituents accept that compromise? By 1848, the United States had become a more complex and contentious society, a change that reflected the appearance of new cultural movements and radical reform organizations, which are the subject of Chapter 11.

FOR FURTHER EXPLORATION

George Dangerfield, *The Era of Good Feelings* (1952), remains the classic study, but see Sean Wilentz, *The Rise of American Democracy: Jefferson to Lincoln* (2005). For a concise survey, read Harry L. Watson, *Liberty and Power: The Politics of Jacksonian America* (1990). The Internet Public Library (**www.ipl.org/div/potus/jqadams.html**) covers the election of 1824 and the Adams administration. For the Whigs, consult Merrill D. Peterson, *The Great Triumvirate: Webster, Clay, and Calhoun* (1987).

Robert V. Remini, *The Life of Andrew Jackson* (1988), highlights Jackson's triumphs and shortcomings. Robert J. Conley, *Mountain Windsong: A Novel of the Trail of Tears* (1992), evokes the impact of Jackson's Indian policy, as does Sean Michael O'Brien, *In Bitterness and in Tears: Andrew Jackson's Destruction of the Creeks and Seminoles* (2003). For material on the Cherokees, see **cherokeehistory.com/**.

Alexis de Tocqueville's classic, *Democracy in America* (1835), incisively views American society and political institutions and is available online at **xroads.virginia .edu/~hyper/detoc/home.html**. For political cartoons, go to "American Political Prints, 1766–1876" at **loc.harpweek.com/**.

TEST YOUR KNOWLEDGE

To assess your mastery of the material in this chapter and for Web sites, images, and documents related to this chapter, visit **bedfordstmartins.com/henrettaconcise**.

CHAPTER

11 Religion and Reform
1820–1860

> Slavery must fall because it stands in direct hostility to all the grand movements, principles, and reforms of our age, because it stands in the way of an advancing world.
>
> — Unitarian minister William Ellery Channing (1848)

"The spirit of reform is in every place," the children of legal reformer David Dudley Field wrote in their handwritten monthly *Gazette* in 1842:

> The labourer with a family says "reform the common schools"; the merchant and the planter say, "reform the tariff," the lawyer "reform the laws," the politician "reform the government," the abolitionist "reform the slave laws," the moralist "reform intemperance," . . . the ladies wish their legal privileges extended, and in short, the whole country is wanting reform.

Like many Americans, the young Field children sensed that the political whirlwind of the 1830s had transformed the way people thought about themselves and about society. Suddenly, thousands of men and women, inspired by the economic progress and democratic spirit of the age and by the religious optimism of the Second Great Awakening, believed that they could improve both their personal lives and society as a whole. Some dedicated themselves to the cause of reform. William Lloyd Garrison began as an antislavery advocate and then went on to embrace women's rights, pacifism, and the abolition of prisons. Such obsessive individuals, warned Unitarian minister Henry W. Bellows, were pursuing "an object, which in its very nature is unattainable — the perpetual improvement of the outward condition."

Reform was complex and contradictory. Some reformers wanted to improve society by promoting morality and preventing certain types of behavior. The first wave of American reformers, the benevolent religious improvers of the 1820s, championed regular church attendance, temperance, and a strict moral code. Their righteousness prompted one critic to protest, "A peaceable man can hardly venture to eat or

319

drink, . . . to correct his child or kiss his wife, without obtaining the permission . . . of some moral or other reform society."

A second wave of reformers, which emerged during the 1830s and 1840s, was more intent on liberating people from archaic customs and encouraging new lifestyles. These reformers were mostly middle-class northerners and midwesterners who promoted a bewildering assortment of radical ideals: extreme individualism, common ownership of property, the immediate emancipation of slaves, and sexual equality. Although their numbers were small, these reformers challenged the legitimacy of well-established cultural practices and belief, winning the attention—and often the horrified opposition—of the majority of Americans. As one fearful southerner saw it, radical reformers favored a chaotic world in which there would be "No-Marriage, No-Religion, No-Private Property, No-Law and No-Government."

Individualism: The Ethic of the Middle Class

Those fears were not exaggerated. Rapid economic development and geographical expansion had weakened many traditional institutions and social rules, forcing individuals to fend for themselves. In 1835, Alexis de Tocqueville coined a new word, *individualism*, to describe the social relations in the United States. Native-born white Americans were "no longer attached to each other by any tie of caste, class, association, or family," the French aristocrat lamented, and so lived in social isolation. Unlike Tocqueville who mourned the breakdown of social ties, the New England transcendentalist Ralph Waldo Emerson (1803–1882) celebrated the liberation of the individual from traditional constraints. Emerson's vision influenced thousands of ordinary Americans and a generation of important artists.

Ralph Waldo Emerson and Transcendentalism

Emerson was the leading voice of **transcendentalism**, an intellectual movement rooted in the religious soil of New England. Its first advocates were Unitarian ministers from well-to-do New England families, who questioned the constraints of their Puritan heritage (see Chapter 8). For inspiration, they turned to European romanticism, a new conception of self and society. Romantic thinkers, such as German philosopher Immanuel Kant and English poet Samuel Taylor Coleridge, rejected the ordered, rational world of the eighteenth-century Enlightenment. They searched for the passionate aspects of the human spirit and sought deeper insight into the mysteries of existence. By tapping their intuitive powers, the young Unitarians believed, people could come to know the infinite and the eternal.

As a Unitarian, Emerson already stood outside the mainstream of American Protestantism. Unlike most Christians, Unitarians believed that God was a single being, not a trinity of Father, Son, and Holy Spirit. In 1832, Emerson took a more radical step by resigning his Boston pulpit and rejecting all organized religion. He moved to Concord, Massachusetts, and gradually worked out his transcendentalist beliefs. In influential essays, Emerson explored what he called "the infinitude of the private man," the idea of the radically free individual.

The Founder of Transcendentalism
As this painting of Ralph Waldo Emerson by an unknown artist indicates, the young philosopher was an attractive man, his face brimming with confidence and optimism. With his radiant personality and incisive intellect, Emerson deeply influenced dozens of influential writers, artists, and scholars and enjoyed great success as a lecturer to the emerging middle class. The Metropolitan Museum of Art, bequest of Chester Dale, 1962 [64.97.4].

The young philosopher argued that people were trapped by inherited customs and institutions. They wore the ideas of earlier times—the tenets of New England Calvinism, for example—as a kind of "faded masquerade," and they needed to shed those values. "What is a man born for but to be a Reformer, a Remaker of what man has made?" Emerson asked. In his view, an individual could be remade only by discovering his or her "original relation with Nature" and entering into a mystical union with the "currents of Universal Being." The ideal setting for this transcendent discovery was under an open sky, in solitary communion with nature.

Emerson's genius lay in his ability to translate such abstract ideas into examples that made sense to middle-class Americans. His essays suggested that nature was saturated with the presence of God, a pantheistic outlook that departed from traditional Christian doctrine. Emerson also warned that the new market society was diverting the nation's emotional energy—that the focus on work, profits, and consumption was debasing Americans' spiritual lives. "Things are in the saddle," he wrote, "and ride mankind."

The transcendentalist message of self-realization reached hundreds of thousands of people, primarily through Emerson's writings and lectures. Public lectures had become a spectacularly successful way of spreading information and fostering discussion among the middle classes. Beginning in 1826, the Lyceum movement promoted "the general diffusion of knowledge" through lecture tours by hundreds of poets, preachers, scientists, and reformers. The movement took its name and inspiration from the public hall where the ancient Greek philosopher Aristotle taught. The Lyceum became an important cultural institution in the North and Midwest—but not in the South, where the middle class was smaller and popular education was a lower priority. In 1839, nearly 150 lyceums in Massachusetts invited lecturers to address more than 33,000 subscribers. Emerson was the most popular speaker, delivering 1,500 lectures in more than 300 towns in twenty states.

Emerson celebrated individuals who rejected tradition and exhibited both self-discipline and civic responsibility. His words spoke directly to the personal experience of many middle-class Americans, who had left family farms to make their way in the urban world. The great revivalist Charles Grandison Finney described his own religious conversion in Emersonian terms: as taking place in the woods, alone, the mystical union of an individual with God. Like Emerson, Finney told his listeners to transcend old doctrines and constraints. "God has made man a moral free agent," Finney declared, endowing individuals with the ability—and the responsibility—to determine their spiritual fate.

Emerson's Literary Influence

Emerson took as one of his tasks the remaking of American literature. In an address entitled "The American Scholar" (1837), the philosopher issued a literary declaration of independence. He urged American writers to free themselves from the "courtly muse" of Old Europe; instead, they should celebrate democracy and individual freedom and should find inspiration in the experiences of ordinary Americans: "the ballad in the street; the news of the boat; the glance of the eye; the form and gait of the body."

One young New England intellectual, Henry David Thoreau (1817–1862), heeded Emerson's call and sought inspiration from the natural world. In 1845, depressed by his beloved brother's death, Thoreau built a cabin near Walden Pond in Concord, Massachusetts, and lived alone there for two years. In 1854, he published *Walden, or Life in the Woods,* an account of his search for meaning beyond the artificiality of "civilized" society:

> I went to the woods because I wished to live deliberately, to front only the essential facts of life, and see if I could not learn what it had to teach, and not, when I came to die, discover that I had not lived.

Thoreau's book had little impact during his lifetime but has become an essential text of American literature. *Walden*'s most famous metaphor provides an enduring justification for independent thinking: "If a man does not keep pace with his companions, perhaps it is because he hears a different drummer." Beginning from this premise, Thoreau advocated social nonconformity and civil disobedience against unjust laws.

As Thoreau was seeking independence and self-realization for men, Margaret Fuller (1810–1850) was exploring the possibilities of freedom for women. Born into a wealthy Boston family, Fuller mastered six languages, read broadly in classic works of literature, and educated her four siblings. Becoming interested in Emerson's ideas, she started a transcendental "conversation," or discussion group, for educated Boston women in 1839. Soon Fuller was editing the leading transcendentalist journal, *The Dial*. In 1844, she published *Woman in the Nineteenth Century*, which proclaimed that a "new era" was changing the relationships between men and women.

Fuller's philosophy began with the transcendental belief that women, like men, could develop a mystical relationship with God that gave them identity and dignity. Every woman therefore deserved psychological and social independence — the ability "to grow, as an intellect to discern, as a soul to live freely and unimpeded." "We would have every arbitrary barrier thrown down," she wrote, and "every path laid open to Woman as freely as to Man." Embracing that vision, Fuller became the literary critic of the *New York Tribune* and traveled to Italy to report on the Revolution of 1848. Her adventurous life led to an early death; in 1850, she drowned in a shipwreck while returning to the United States. But Fuller's life and writings inspired a rising generation of women writers and reformers.

Another writer who responded to Emerson's call was the poet Walt Whitman (1819–1892). When Whitman first met Emerson, he said, he had been "simmering, simmering"; then Emerson "brought me to a boil." Whitman worked as a printer, a teacher, a journalist, an editor of the *Brooklyn Eagle*, and an influential publicist for the Democratic Party. But poetry was the "direction of his dreams." In *Leaves of Grass*, a collection of wild, exuberant poems first published in 1855 and constantly revised and expanded, Whitman recorded in verse his efforts to transcend various "invisible boundaries": between solitude and community, between prose and poetry, even between the living and the dead. At the center of *Leaves of Grass* is the individual — the figure of the poet — "I, Walt." He begins alone: "I celebrate myself, and sing myself." But because he has an Emersonian "original relation" with nature, Whitman claims perfect communion with others: "For every atom belonging to me as good belongs to you." Whitman celebrates democracy as well as himself by seeking an intimate, mystical relationship with a mass audience. For Emerson, Thoreau, and Fuller, the individual had a divine spark; for Whitman, the individual had expanded to become divine, and democracy assumed a sacred character.

The transcendentalists were optimistic but not naive. Whitman wrote about human suffering with passion, and Emerson laced his accounts of transcendence with twinges of anxiety. "I am glad," he once said, "to the brink of fear." Thoreau was gloomy about everyday life: "The mass of men lead lives of quiet desperation." Still, dark murmurings remain muted in their work, overshadowed by assertions that nothing was impossible for the individual who could break free from tradition.

Emerson's writings also influenced two great novelists, Nathaniel Hawthorne and Herman Melville, who had more pessimistic worldviews. Both sounded powerful warnings that unfettered egoism could destroy individuals and those around them. Hawthorne brilliantly explored the theme of excessive individualism in his novel *The Scarlet Letter* (1850). The two main characters, Hester Prynne and Arthur Dimmesdale, challenge their seventeenth-century New England community in the most blatant way: by committing adultery and producing a child. Their decision to ignore social restraints results not in liberation but in degradation: a profound sense of guilt and the condemnation of the community.

Herman Melville explored the limits of individualism in even more extreme and tragic terms and emerged as a scathing critic of transcendentalism. His most powerful statement was *Moby Dick* (1851), the story of Captain Ahab's obsessive hunt for a mysterious white whale that ends in death for Ahab and all but one member of his crew. Here, the quest for spiritual meaning in nature brings death, not transcendence, because Ahab, the liberated individual, lacks inner discipline and self-restraint.

Moby Dick was a commercial failure. The middle-class audience that read American fiction refused to follow Melville into the dark, dangerous realm of individualism gone mad. Readers also lacked enthusiasm for Thoreau's advocacy of civil disobedience during the U.S. war with Mexico (see Chapter 13) and for Whitman's boundless claims of a mystical union between the man of genius and the democratic masses. What middle-class readers emphatically preferred were the more modest examples of individualism offered by Emerson and Finney: personal improvement through spiritual awareness and self-discipline.

Brook Farm

To escape the constraints of America's emerging market society, transcendentalists and other reformers created ideal communities, or utopias. They hoped these planned societies, which organized life in new ways, would allow people to realize their spiritual potential. The most important transcendentalist communal experiment was Brook Farm, founded just outside Boston in 1841. Intellectual life at Brook Farm was electric. Hawthorne lived there for a time and later used the setting for his novel *The Blithedale Romance* (1852); Emerson, Thoreau, and Fuller were residents or frequent visitors. A former member recalled that they "inspired the young with a passion for study, and the middle-aged with deference and admiration, while we all breathed the intellectual grace that pervaded the atmosphere."

Whatever its spiritual rewards, Brook Farm was an economic failure. The residents hoped to escape the ups and downs of the market economy by becoming self-sufficient in food and exchanging their surplus milk, vegetables, and hay for manufactures. However, most members were ministers, teachers, writers, and students who had few farming skills; only the cash of affluent residents kept the enterprise afloat. After a devastating fire in 1846, the organizers disbanded the community and sold the farm.

► What were the main beliefs of transcendentalism, and how did American writers incorporate them into their work?

► What is the relationship between transcendentalism and individualism? Between transcendentalism and social reform? Between transcendentalism and the middle class?

With the failure of Brook Farm, the Emersonians abandoned their quest for a new social system. They accepted the brute reality of the emergent industrial order and tried to reform it, especially through the education of workers and the movement to abolish slavery.

Rural Communalism and Urban Popular Culture

Even as Brook Farm collapsed, thousands of Americans were joining communal settlements in rural areas of the Northeast and Midwest (Map 11.1). Many communalists were farmers and artisans seeking refuge during the economic depression that began

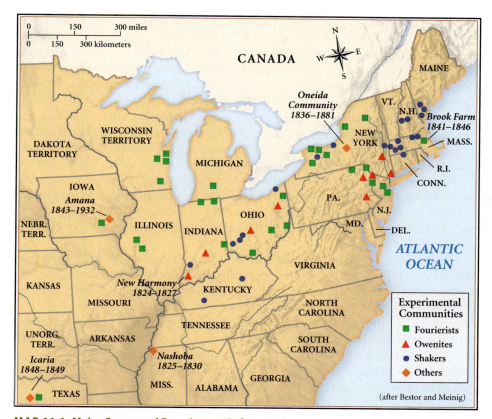

MAP 11.1 Major Communal Experiments Before 1860

Some experimental communities settled along the frontier, but the vast majority chose relatively secluded areas in well-settled regions of the North and Midwest. Because of their opposition to slavery, communalists usually avoided the South. Most secular experiments failed within a few decades, as the founders lost their reformist enthusiasm or died off; religious communities, such as those of the Shakers and the Mormons, were longer-lived.

with the Panic of 1837 and lasted seven years. However, these rural utopias were also symbols of social protest and experimentation. By advocating the common ownership of property and unconventional forms of marriage and family life, the communalists challenged capitalist values and traditional gender roles.

Simultaneously, tens of thousands of rural Americans and European immigrants poured into the larger cities of the United States. There, they created a popular culture that repudiated customary sexual norms, reinforced traditional racist feelings, and encouraged new styles of dress and behavior.

Mother Ann Lee and the Shakers

The Shakers were the first successful American communal movement. In 1770, Ann Lee Stanley (Mother Ann), a young cook in Manchester, England, had a vision that she was an incarnation of Christ and that sexual lust had caused Adam and Eve to be banished from the Garden of Eden. Four years later, she led a few followers to America, where they established a church near Albany, New York. Because of the ecstatic dances that were part of their worship, the sect became known as the Shakers (see Voices from Abroad, p. 327). After Mother Ann's death in 1784, the Shakers honored her as the Second Coming of Christ, withdrew from the profane world, and formed disciplined religious communities. Members embraced the common ownership of property; accepted strict oversight by church leaders; and pledged to abstain from alcohol, tobacco, politics, and war. Shakers also repudiated sexual pleasure and marriage. Their commitment to celibacy followed Mother Ann's testimony against "the lustful gratifications of the flesh as the source and foundation of human corruption."

The Shakers' theology was as radical as their social thought. They held that God was "a dual person, male and female" and that Mother Ann represented God's female component. This doctrine prompted Shakers to repudiate male leadership and to place community governance in the hands of both women and men — the Eldresses and the Elders.

Beginning in 1787, Shakers founded twenty communities, mostly in New England, New York, and Ohio. Their agriculture and crafts, especially furniture making, acquired a reputation for quality that made most Shaker communities self-sustaining and even comfortable. Because the Shakers did not engage in sexual intercourse, they relied on conversions and the adoption of thousands of young orphans to increase their numbers. During the 1830s, 3,000 adults joined the Shakers, attracted by their communal intimacy and sexual equality. Women converts outnumbered men more than two to one, and converts included blacks as well as whites. To Rebecca Cox Jackson, an African American seamstress from Philadelphia, the Shakers seemed to be "loving to live forever." As the supply of orphans dried up during the 1840s and 1850s (with the increase in public and private orphanages), Shaker communities stopped growing and eventually began to decline. By 1900, the Shakers had virtually disappeared, leaving as their material legacy a distinctive plain but elegant style of wood furniture.

Arthur Brisbane and Fourierism

As the Shakers' growth slowed during the 1840s, the American Fourierist movement mushroomed. Charles Fourier (1777–1837) was a French reformer who devised an eight-stage theory of social evolution that predicted the imminent decline of individualism and capitalism. According to Arthur Brisbane, Fourier's leading disciple in America, Fourierism would free workers from the "menial and slavish system of Hired Labor or Labor for Wages," just as republicanism had freed Americans from the slavish monarchical system of government. In a Fourierist society, men and women would not work for themselves or employers but for the community, in cooperative groups called phalanxes. The members of a phalanx would be its shareholders; they would own its property in common, including stores and a bank, a school, and a library.

Fourier and Brisbane saw the phalanx as a humane **socialistic** system that would liberate women as well as men. "In society as it is now constituted," Brisbane wrote, individual freedom was possible only for men, while "woman is subjected to unremitting and slavish domestic duties." In the "new Social Order . . . based upon Associated households," men would share women's domestic labor and thereby increase sexual equality.

The Mystical World of the Shakers

Foreigners were both attracted to and distressed by the strange religious practices that they observed in the United States. In a passage written in the early 1840s, an anonymous British visitor describes a Shaker dance and the sect's intimate contact with spiritual worlds inaccessible to those without faith.

At half past seven P.M. on the dancing days, all the members . . . assemble in the large hall. . . . The chief Elder stepped into the center of the space, and gave an exhortation for about five minutes, concluding with an invitation to them all to "go forth, old men, young men and maidens, and worship God with all [your] might in the dance." . . .

First they formed a procession and marched around the room in double-quick time, while four brothers and sisters stood in the center singing for them. . . . They commenced dancing, and continued it until they were pretty well tired. During the dance the sisters kept on one side, and the brothers on the other, and not a word was spoken by any one of them. . . . [Then] each one took his or her place in an oblong circle formed around the room, and all waited to see if anyone had received a "gift," that is, an inspiration to do something odd. Then two of the sisters would commence whirling round like a top, with their eyes shut; and continued this motion for about fifteen minutes. . . .

On some occasions when a sister had stopped whirling, she would say, "I have a communication to make." . . . The first message I heard was as follows[:] "Mother Ann has sent two angels to inform us that a tribe of Indians has been round here two days, and want the brothers and sisters to take them in. They are outside the building there, looking in at the windows." I shall never forget how I looked round at the windows, expecting to see the yellow faces, when this announcement was made; but I believe some of the old folks who eyed me, bit their lips and smiled. . . .

The next dancing night we again assembled in the same manner as before. . . . The elder then urged upon the members the duty of "taking them in." Whereupon eight or nine sisters became possessed of the spirits of Indian squaws, and about six of the brethren became Indians. Then ensued a regular pow-wow, with whooping and yelling and strange antics, such as would require a Dickens to describe. . . . These performances continued till about ten o'clock: then the chief Elder requested the Indians to go away, telling them they would find someone waiting to conduct them to the Shakers in the heavenly world. . . .

At one of the meetings . . . two or three sisters commenced whirling . . . and revealed to us that Mother Ann was present at the meeting, and that she had brought a dozen baskets of spiritual fruit for her children; upon which the Elder invited all to go forth to the baskets in the center of the floor, and help themselves. Accordingly they all stepped forth and went through the various motions of taking fruit and eating it. You will wonder if I helped myself to the fruit, like the rest. No; I had not faith enough to see the baskets or the fruit.

SOURCE: Noel Rae, ed., *Witnessing America* (New York: Penguin Press, 1966), 372–373.

Brisbane skillfully promoted Fourier's ideas in his influential book *The Social Destiny of Man* (1840), a regular column in Horace Greeley's *New York Tribune*, and hundreds of lectures, many of them in towns along the Erie Canal. Fourierist ideas found a receptive audience among educated farmers and craftsmen, who yearned for economic stability and communal solidarity in the wake of the Panic of 1837. During the 1840s, Fourierists started nearly one hundred cooperative communities, mostly in western New York and the Midwest. However, most of these communities collapsed within a decade because of disputes over work responsibilities and social policies. The decline of Fourierism revealed the difficulty of establishing a utopian community in the absence of a charismatic leader or a compelling religious vision.

John Humphrey Noyes and the Oneida Community

John Humphrey Noyes (1811–1886) was both charismatic and deeply religious. He ascribed the Fourierists' failure to their secular outlook and took as his model the pious Shakers, the true "pioneers of modern Socialism." The Shakers' marriageless society also appealed to Noyes and inspired him to create a community that defined sexuality and gender roles in radically new ways.

Noyes was a well-to-do graduate of Dartmouth College who became a minister after hearing a sermon by Charles Grandison Finney. Dismissed as the pastor of a Congregational church for holding unorthodox beliefs, Noyes turned to perfectionism. Perfectionism was an Evangelical Protestant movement of the 1830s that attracted thousands of New Englanders who had moved to New York and Ohio. Perfectionists believed that Christ had already returned to earth (the Second Coming); consequently, as the Bible suggested, people could aspire to sinless perfection in their earthly lives. Unlike most perfectionists, who lived conventional personal lives, Noyes rejected marriage, seeing it as the major barrier to perfection. "Exclusiveness, jealousy, quarreling have no place at the marriage supper of the Lamb," Noyes wrote. Like the Shakers, Noyes wanted to liberate individuals from sin by reforming sexual relationships. But instead of the Shakers' celibacy, Noyes and his followers embraced "complex marriage," in which all the members of the community were married to one another.

Noyes's marriage system highlighted the growing debate over the legal and cultural constraints on women. One reason for his rejection of monogamy was to free women from their status as the property of their husbands, as they were by custom and by common law. To give women the time and energy to participate fully in the community, Noyes urged them to avoid multiple pregnancies. He asked men to assist in this effort by avoiding orgasm during intercourse. To raise the children of the community, Noyes set up nurseries run by both men and women. Symbolizing their quest for equality, Noyes's women followers cut their hair short and wore pantaloons under calf-length skirts.

In 1839, Noyes established a perfectionist community near his hometown of Putney, Vermont. When he introduced the practice of complex marriage in the mid-1840s, local outrage forced Noyes to relocate the community to an isolated area near Oneida, New York. By the mid-1850s, the Oneida settlement had 200 residents; it became financially self-sustaining when the inventor of a highly successful steel animal trap joined the community. With the profits from trap making, the Oneidians diversified

into the production of silverware. When Noyes fled to Canada in 1879 to avoid prosecution for adultery, the community abandoned complex marriage but retained its
cooperative spirit. Its members founded Oneida Community, Ltd., a jointly owned
silverware-manufacturing company that maintained some of its communal features
until the middle of the twentieth century.

The historical significance of the Oneidians, Shakers, and Fourierists does not lie in
their numbers, which were small, or in their fine crafts. Rather, their importance stems
from their radical repudiation of traditional sexual norms and of the capitalist principles and class divisions of the emerging market society. Their utopian communities
stood as countercultural blueprints for a more egalitarian social and economic order.

Joseph Smith and the Mormon Experience

The Shakers and the Oneidians were radical utopians because they rejected traditional
definitions of marriage and family. But because their communities remained small,
they aroused relatively little hostility. The Mormons, members of the Church of Jesus
Christ of Latter-day Saints, were utopians with a conservative social agenda: to perpetuate the traditional patriarchal family. But because of their cohesive organization
and substantial numbers, the Mormons provoked more animosity than the radical
utopians did.

Like many social movements of the era, Mormonism emerged from the religious
ferment among families of Puritan descent who lived along the Erie Canal. The founder
of the Mormon Church was Joseph Smith Jr. (1805–1844). Smith was born in Vermont
to a poor farming and shop-keeping family, who migrated to Palmyra in central New
York. In a series of religious experiences that began in 1820, Smith came to believe that
God had singled him out to receive a special revelation of divine truth. In 1830, he published *The Book of Mormon*, which he claimed to have translated from ancient hiero-
glyphics on gold plates that an angel named Moroni had shown to him. *The Book of
Mormon* told the story of ancient civilizations from the Middle East that had migrated
to the Western Hemisphere and of the visit of Jesus Christ, soon after the Resurrection,
to one of them. Smith's account explained the presence of native peoples in the Americas
and integrated them into the Judeo-Christian tradition.

Smith proceeded to organize the Church of Jesus Christ of Latter-day Saints. Seeing himself as a prophet in a sinful, excessively individualistic society, Smith revived
traditional social doctrines, among them patriarchal authority within the family. Like
many Protestant ministers, he encouraged practices that were central to individual
success in the age of capitalist markets and factories: frugality, hard work, and enterprise. But Smith also placed great emphasis on communal discipline that would safeguard the Mormon "New Jerusalem" from individualism and rival religious doctrines.
His goal was a church-directed society that would ensure moral perfection.

Smith struggled for years to establish a secure home for his new religion. Constantly harassed by hostile anti-Mormons, Smith and his growing congregation trekked
west and eventually settled in Nauvoo, Illinois, a town they founded on the Mississippi
River (Map 11.2). By the early 1840s, Nauvoo had become the largest utopian community in the United States, with 30,000 inhabitants. The rigid discipline and secret rituals
of the Mormons — along with their prosperity, hostility toward other sects, and bloc

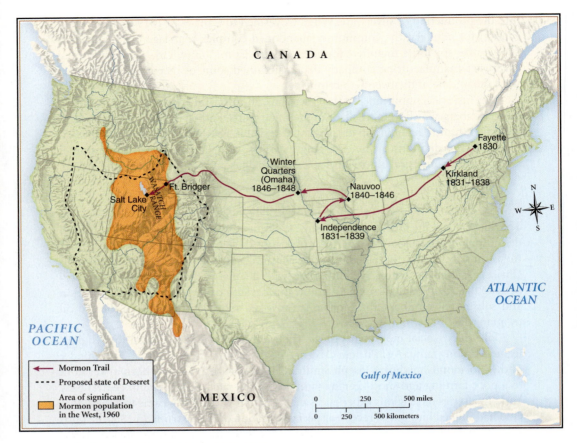

MAP 11.2 The Mormon Trek, 1830–1848

Because of their unorthodox religious views and communal solidarity, Mormons faced hostility first in New York and then in Missouri and Illinois. After founder Joseph Smith Jr. was murdered, Brigham Young led the polygamist faction of Mormons into lands thinly populated by Native American peoples. From Omaha, the migrants followed the path of the Oregon Trail to Fort Bridger and then struck off to the southwest. In 1847, they settled along the Wasatch Mountains in the basin of the Great Salt Lake, on Indian lands that were then part of Mexico and are now in Utah.

voting in Illinois elections—fueled resentment among their neighbors. Resentment turned to overt hostility when Smith refused to abide by any Illinois law of which he disapproved, asked Congress to turn Nauvoo into a separate federal territory, and declared himself a candidate for president of the United States.

Moreover, Smith claimed to have received a new revelation that justified polygamy, the practice of a man having multiple wives. When leading Mormon men took several wives, they sparked a contentious debate within the Mormon community and enraged Christians in neighboring towns. In 1844, Illinois officials arrested Smith and charged him with treason for allegedly conspiring to create a Mormon colony in Mexican territory. An anti-Mormon mob stormed the jail in Carthage, Illinois, where Smith and his brother were being held and murdered them.

A Mormon Man and His Wives
The practice of polygamy split the Mormon community and, because it deviated from traditional religious principles, enraged other Christian denominations. This Mormon household, pictured in the late 1840s, was unusually prosperous, partly because of the labor of the husband's multiple wives. Although the cabin provides cramped quarters for such a large family, it boasts a brick chimney and—a luxury for any pioneer home—a glass window. Library of Congress.

Led by Brigham Young, Smith's leading disciple and an energetic missionary, about 10,000 Mormons fled the United States. Beginning in 1847, they crossed the Great Plains into Mexican territory and settled in the Great Salt Lake Valley in present-day Utah. Using cooperative labor and an elaborate irrigation system based on communal water rights, the Mormon pioneers quickly spread planned agricultural communities along the base of the Wasatch mountain range. Many Mormons who rejected polygamy remained in the United States. Under the leadership of Smith's son, Joseph Smith III, they formed the Reorganized Church of Jesus Christ of Latter-day Saints and settled throughout the Midwest.

When the United States acquired title to Mexico's northern territories in 1848 (see Chapter 13), the Salt Lake Mormons petitioned Congress to create a vast new state, Deseret, which would stretch from present-day Utah to the Pacific coast. Instead, Congress set up the much smaller Utah Territory in 1850 and named Brigham Young its governor. In 1858, President James Buchanan responded to pressure from Protestants to eliminate polygamy by removing Young from the governorship and sending a small army to Salt Lake City. However, the "Mormon War" proved bloodless. Fearing that the forced abolition of polygamy would serve as a precedent for ending slavery, the pro-South Buchanan withdrew the troops. (To enable Utah to win admission to the Union in 1896, its citizens ratified a constitution that "forever" banned the practice of polygamy. But the state government has never strictly enforced that ban.)

Mormons had succeeded even as other social experiments had failed. By endorsing private property and individual enterprise, Mormons became prosperous contributors to the new market society. However, their leaders resolutely used strict religious controls to create patriarchal families and disciplined communities, reaffirming traditional values. This blend of economic innovation, social conservatism, and hierarchical leadership, in combination with a strong missionary impulse, created a wealthy and expansive church that now claims a worldwide membership of about twelve million people.

Urban Popular Culture

As utopian reformers organized communities in the countryside, rural migrants and foreign immigrants created a new urban culture. In 1800, American cities were overgrown towns with rising death rates: New York had only 60,000 residents, and Philadelphia had 41,000; and life expectancy at birth was a mere twenty-five years. Then urban growth accelerated as a huge in-migration outweighed the high death rates. By 1840, New York's population had ballooned to 312,000; Philadelphia and its suburbs had 150,000 residents; and three other cities — New Orleans, Boston, and Baltimore — each had about 100,000. By 1860, New York had become a metropolis with more than a million residents: 813,000 in Manhattan and another 266,000 in the adjacent community of Brooklyn.

These new cities, particularly New York, generated a new urban culture. Thousands of young men and women from rural areas had flocked to the city searching for adventure and fortune, but many found only a hard life. Young men labored for meager wages in the construction crews that erected thousands of new buildings each year. Others worked as low-paid clerks or operatives in hundreds of mercantile and manufacturing firms. The young women had an even harder time. Thousands toiled as live-in domestic servants, ordered about by the mistress of the household and often sexually exploited by their masters. Thousands more scraped out a bare living as needlewomen in New York's booming clothes manufacturing industry. Unwilling to accept the humiliations of domestic service or the subsistence wages of the needlewoman, many of these and other young girls turned to prostitution. In the 1850s, Dr. William Sanger's careful survey found 6,000 women engaged in commercial sex. Three-fifths of them were native-born whites, and the rest were foreign immigrants; most were between fifteen and twenty years old. Half were or had been domestic servants, half had children, and half were infected with syphilis.

Commercialized sex — and sex in general — formed one facet of the new urban culture. "Sporting men" engaged freely in sexual conquests; otherwise respectable married men kept mistresses in handy apartments; and working men frequented bawdy houses. New York City had some two hundred brothels in the 1820s and five hundred by the 1850s. Prostitutes openly advertised their wares on Broadway, the city's most fashionable thoroughfare, and welcomed clients on the infamous "Third Tier" of the theaters. Many men considered access to illicit sex to be a right. "Man is endowed by nature with passions that must be gratified," declared the *Sporting Whip*, a working-class magazine. Reverend William Berrian, pastor of the ultra-respectable Trinity Episcopal Church, did not disagree; he remarked from the pulpit that he had resorted to "a house of ill-fame" a mere ten times.

Promiscuity formed only the tip of the urban sexual iceberg. Freed from family oversight, young working men and women in the city pursued romantic adventure. Many moved from partner to partner until they chanced on an ideal mate. To enhance their attractiveness, they strolled along Broadway in the latest fashions: elaborate bonnets and silk dresses for young women; flowing capes, leather boots, and silver-plated walking sticks for young men. Rivaling the elegance on Broadway was the colorful dress on the Bowery, the broad avenue that ran up the east side of lower Manhattan. By day, the "Bowery Boy" worked as an apprentice or journeyman; by night, he prowled the streets as a "consummate dandy," his hair cropped at the back of his head "as close as scissors could cut," with long front locks "matted by a lavish application of *bear's grease*, the ends tucked under so as to form a roll and brushed until they shone like glass bottles." The "B'hoy," as he was called, cut a dashing figure as he walked along with a "Bowery Gal" in a striking dress and shawl: "a light pink contrasting with a deep blue" or "a bright yellow with a brighter red."

Popular entertainment was a third facet of the new urban culture in New York. Workingmen could partake of traditional rural blood sports — rat and terrier fights — at Sportsmen Hall, or they could crowd into the pit of the Bowery Theatre to see the "Mad Tragedian," Junius Brutus Booth, deliver a stirring performance of Shakespeare's *Richard III*. Middle-class couples looked forward to an evening at the huge Broadway Tabernacle, where they could hear an abolitionist lecture and see the renowned Hutchinson Family Singers of New Hampshire lead the audience in a roof-raising rendition of their antislavery anthem, "Get Off the Track." Or they could visit the museum of oddities (and hoaxes) created by P. T. Barnum, the great cultural entrepreneur and founder of the Barnum & Bailey Circus.

The most popular theatrical entertainments were the minstrel shows. Performed by white actors in blackface, minstrel shows were a complex blend of racist caricature and social criticism. Minstrelsy began around 1830, when a few individual actors put on blackface and performed comic song-and-dance routines. The most famous was John Dartmouth Rice, whose "Jim Crow" blended a weird shuffle-dance-and-jump with unintelligible lyrics delivered in "Negro dialect." By the 1840s, there were hundreds of minstrel troupes, whose members sang rambling improvised songs. The actor-singers poked racist fun at the African Americans they caricatured, portraying them as lazy, sensual, and irresponsible while simultaneously using them to criticize white society. The minstrels ridiculed the drinking habits of Irish immigrants, parodied the speech of recent German arrivals, denounced women's demands for political rights, and mocked the arrogance of upper-class men.

Still, by performing in blackface, the minstrels declared the importance of being white. In particular, their racism encouraged Irish and German immigrants to identify with the dominant culture of native-born whites and eased their entry into New York society. Foreign-born migrants piled into New York beginning in the 1830s; by 1855, 200,000 Irish men and women lived there, along with 110,000 Germans. German-language shop signs dominated entire sections, and German foods (sausages, hamburgers, sauerkraut) and food customs (such as drinking beer in family *biergärten*) became part of the city's culture. The mass of impoverished Irish migrants found allies in the American Catholic Church, which soon became an Irish-dominated institution, and the Democratic Party, which gave them a foothold in the political process.

Rampant Racism
Minstrel shows and music were immensely popular among whites and hugely damaging to the status and self-respect of blacks. Still, minstrelsy had so much appeal that a group of black entertainers, Gavitt's Original Ethiopian Serenaders, joined the circuit. Black abolitionist Frederick Douglass was not impressed. "It is something gained when the colored man in any form can appear before a white audience," he remarked after watching the group perform, "but they must represent the colored man rather as he is, than as Ethiopian Minstrels usually represent him to be. They will *then* command the respect of both races; whereas *now* they only shock the taste of the one, and provoke the disgust of the other." Courtesy, The Library Company of Philadelphia.

For more help analyzing this image, see the Online Study Guide at **bedfordstmartins.com/henrettaconcise**.

Many native-born New Yorkers took alarm as hordes of ethnically diverse migrants altered the city's traditional culture. They organized a nativist movement—a final aspect of the new urban world. Beginning in the mid-1830s, nativists called for a halt to immigration and mounted a cultural and political assault on foreign-born residents (see Chapter 9). Gangs of B'hoys assaulted Irish youths in the streets, employers restricted Irish workers to the most menial jobs, and temperance reformers denounced the German fondness for beer. In 1844, the American Republican Party, with the endorsement of the Whigs, swept the city elections by highlighting the emotional issues of temperance, anti-Catholicism, and nativism.

▶ What accounts for the proliferation of rural utopian communities in nineteenth-century America?

▶ In what respects were the new cultures of the mid-nineteenth century—those of utopian communalists and of urban residents—different from the mainstream culture described in Chapters 8 and 9? How were they alike?

In the city, as in the countryside, new values were challenging old beliefs. The sexual freedom that Noyes advocated at Oneida had its counterpart in the commercialized sex and male promiscuity in New York City. Similarly, the disciplined rejection of tobacco and alcohol by the Shakers and the Mormons found a parallel in the Washington Temperance Society and other urban reform organizations. American society was in ferment, and the outcome was far from clear.

Abolitionism

Like other reform movements, abolitionism drew on the religious enthusiasm of the Second Great Awakening. Around 1800, reformers had argued that human bondage was contrary to republicanism and liberty. By the 1830s, abolitionists were condemning slavery as a sin that it was their moral duty to end. Their demands for an immediate end to slavery led to fierce political debates, urban riots, and sectional conflicts.

Black Social Thought: Uplift, Race Equality, and Rebellion

Beginning in the 1790s, leading African Americans in the North advocated a strategy of social uplift. They encouraged free blacks to "elevate" themselves through education, temperance, and hard work. By securing "respectability," they argued, blacks could assume a position of equality with whites. To promote that goal, black leaders—men such as James Forten, a Philadelphia sailmaker; Prince Hall, a Boston barber; and ministers Hosea Easton and Richard Allen (see Chapter 8)—founded an array of churches, schools, and self-help associations. Capping this effort in 1827, John Russwurm and Samuel D. Cornish of New York published the first African American newspaper, *Freedom's Journal*.

The black quest for respectability elicited a violent response from whites in Boston, Pittsburgh, and other northern cities, who refused to accept African Americans as their social equals. "I am Mr. _____'s *help*," a white maid informed a British visitor, "I am no *sarvant*; none but *negers* are *sarvants*." Such racial contempt prompted white mobs to terrorize black communities. The attacks in Cincinnati were so violent and destructive that several hundred African Americans fled to Canada for safety.

Responding to the attacks, David Walker published a stirring pamphlet: *An Appeal . . . to the Colored Citizens of the World* (1829). Walker was a free black from North Carolina who had moved to Boston, where he sold secondhand clothes and *Freedom's Journal*. A self-educated man, Walker used history and morality to attack racial slavery. His *Appeal* ridiculed the religious pretensions of slaveholders, justified slave rebellion, and in Christian Biblical language warned of a slave revolt if justice were delayed. "We must and shall be free," he told white Americans. "And woe, woe, will be it to you if we have to obtain our freedom by fighting. . . . Your DESTRUCTION is at hand, and will be speedily consummated unless you REPENT." Walker's pamphlet quickly went through three printings and, carried by black merchant seamen, reached free African Americans in the South.

In 1830, Walker and other African American activists called a national convention in Philadelphia. The delegates refused to endorse Walker's radical call for a slave revolt, but they were not any happier with the program of uplift among free blacks. Instead, this new generation of activists demanded freedom and "race-equality" for all those of African descent. They urged free blacks to use every legal means, including petitions and other forms of political protest, to break "the shackles of slavery."

As Walker threatened violence in Boston, Nat Turner, a slave in Southampton County, Virginia, staged a bloody revolt—a chronological coincidence that had far-reaching consequences. As a child, Turner had taught himself to read and had hoped for emancipation, but a new master forced him into the fields, and another new owner separated him from his wife. Becoming deeply spiritual, Turner had a religious vision in which "the Spirit" explained that "Christ had laid down the yoke he had borne for the sins of men, and that I should take it on and fight against the Serpent, for the time was fast approaching when the first should be last and the last should be first." Taking an eclipse of the sun in August 1831 as an omen, Turner and a handful of relatives and friends rose in rebellion and killed at least fifty-five white men, women, and children. Turner hoped that hundreds of slaves would rally to his cause, but he mustered only sixty men. The white militia quickly dispersed his poorly armed force and took their revenge. One company of cavalry killed forty blacks in two days and put the heads of fifteen of them on poles to warn "all those who should undertake a similar plot." Turner died by hanging, still identifying his mission with that of his Savior. "Was not Christ crucified?" he asked.

Deeply shaken by Turner's Rebellion, the Virginia assembly debated a law providing for gradual emancipation and colonization abroad. When the assembly rejected the bill by a vote of 73 to 58, the possibility that southern planters would voluntarily end slavery was gone forever. Instead, the southern states toughened their slave codes, limited black movement, and prohibited anyone from teaching slaves to read. They would meet Walker's radical *Appeal* with radical measures of their own.

Evangelical Abolitionism

Concurrently with Walker's and Turner's religiously suffused attacks on slavery, a cadre of northern Evangelical Christians launched a moral crusade to abolish the institution immediately. If planters did not allow slaves their God-given status as free moral agents, these radical Christians warned, they faced revolution in this world and damnation in the next.

The most determined abolitionist was William Lloyd Garrison (1805–1879). A Massachusetts-born printer, Garrison had worked in Baltimore during the 1820s helping to publish the *Genius of Universal Emancipation*, an antislavery newspaper. In 1830, Garrison went to jail, convicted of libeling a New England merchant engaged in the domestic slave trade. The following year, Garrison moved to Boston, where he started his own weekly, *The Liberator*, and founded the New England Anti-Slavery Society.

From the outset, *The Liberator* demanded the immediate abolition of slavery without compensation to slaveholders. His goal was absolute, Garrison declared: "I will not retreat a single inch—AND I WILL BE HEARD." Garrison accused the American Colonization Society (see Chapter 8) of perpetuating slavery because of its voluntary approach, and assailed the U.S. Constitution as "a covenant with death and an agreement with Hell" because it implicitly accepted racial bondage.

In 1833, Garrison met with Theodore Weld and sixty other abolitionists, black and white, and established the American Anti-Slavery Society. The society received financial support from Arthur and Lewis Tappan, wealthy silk merchants in New York City. Women abolitionists established separate organizations, including the Philadelphia Female Anti-Slavery Society, founded by Lucretia Mott in 1833, and the Anti-Slavery Conventions of American Women, formed by a network of local societies in the late 1830s. The women raised money for *The Liberator* and carried the movement to the farm villages of the Midwest, where they distributed abolitionist literature and collected thousands of signatures on antislavery petitions.

Abolitionist leaders developed a three-pronged plan of attack. They began by appealing to religious Americans. In 1837, Weld published *The Bible Against Slavery*, which used passages from Christianity's holiest book to discredit slavery. Two years later, Weld teamed up with the Grimké sisters—Angelina, whom he married, and Sarah. The Grimkés had left their father's plantation in South Carolina, converted to Quakerism, and taken up the abolitionist cause in Philadelphia. In *American Slavery as It Is: Testimony of a Thousand Witnesses* (1839), Weld and the Grimkés addressed a simple question: "What is the actual condition of the slaves in the United States?" Using reports from southern newspapers and firsthand testimony, they presented a mass of incriminating evidence. Angelina Grimké told of a treadmill that South Carolina slave owners used for punishment:

> One poor girl, [who was] sent there to be flogged, and who was accordingly stripped naked and whipped, showed me the deep gashes on her back— I might have laid my whole finger in them—large pieces of flesh had actually been cut out by the torturing lash.

The book sold more than 100,000 copies in a single year.

To distribute their message, the abolitionists used the latest techniques of mass communication. With the help of new steam-powered printing presses, the American Anti-Slavery Society distributed thousands of pieces of literature in 1834. In 1835, the society launched a "great postal campaign" to flood the nation, including the South, with a million pamphlets.

The abolitionists' second tactic was to aid African Americans who had fled from slavery. They provided lodging and jobs for escaped blacks in free states and created the Underground Railroad, an informal network of whites and free blacks in Richmond, Charleston, and other southern towns that assisted fugitives from the Lower South. In Baltimore, a free African American sailor loaned his identification papers to future abolitionist Frederick Douglass, who used them to escape to New York. Harriet Tubman and other runaway slaves risked reenslavement or death by returning repeatedly to the South to help others escape. "I should fight for . . . liberty as long as my strength lasted," Tubman explained, "and when the time came for me to go, the Lord would let them take me." Thanks to the Railroad, about 1,000 African Americans reached freedom in the North each year.

There, they faced an uncertain future, because most whites did not favor civic equality for African Americans. Voters in six northern and midwestern states adopted constitutional amendments that denied or limited the franchise for free blacks. "We want no masters," declared a New York artisan, "and least of all no negro masters."

Moreover, the Fugitive Slave Law (1793) allowed owners and their hired slave catchers to seize suspected runaways and carry them back to bondage. To thwart these efforts, white abolitionists and free blacks in northern cities formed mobs that attacked slave catchers and released their captives.

A political campaign was the final element of the abolitionists' program. In 1835, the American Anti-Slavery Society bombarded Congress with petitions demanding the abolition of slavery in the District of Columbia, an end to the interstate slave trade, and a ban on admission of new slave states. By 1838, petitions with close to 500,000 signatures had arrived in Washington.

Such activities drew support from thousands of deeply religious farmers and small-town proprietors. The number of local abolitionist societies grew from 200 in 1835 to 2,000 by 1840, with nearly 200,000 members, including many leading transcendentalists. Emerson condemned Americans for supporting slavery, and Thoreau, claiming that the Mexican War was an attempt to extend slavery, refused to pay taxes and submitted to arrest. In 1848, he published "Resistance to Civil Government," an essay urging individuals to follow a higher moral law.

Opposition and Internal Conflict

Still, abolitionists remained a small minority. Perhaps 10 percent of northerners and midwesterners strongly supported the movement, and another 20 percent were sympathetic to its goals. The opponents of abolition were more numerous and equally aggressive. The abolitionists' agitation, they warned, risked "embroiling neighborhoods and families — setting friend against friend, overthrowing churches and institutions of learning, embittering one portion of the land against the other." Wealthy men feared that the attack on slaves as property might become a general assault on all property rights; conservative clergymen condemned the public roles that abolitionist women assumed; and northern merchants and textile manufacturers supported the southern planters who supplied them with cotton. Northern wage earners feared that freed blacks would work for lower wages and take their jobs. Finally, whites almost universally opposed "amalgamation," the racial mixing and intermarriage that Garrison seemed to support by holding meetings of black and white abolitionists of both sexes.

Racial fears and hatreds led to violent mob actions. White workers in northern towns laid waste to places where blacks and whites mixed, such as taverns and brothels; and they attacked "respectable" African American institutions such as churches, temperance halls, and orphanages. In 1833, a mob of 1,500 New Yorkers stormed a church in search of Garrison and Arthur Tappan. Another white mob swept through Philadelphia's African American neighborhoods, clubbing and stoning residents and destroying homes and churches. Fearing change, "gentlemen of property and standing" — lawyers, merchants, and bankers — broke up an abolitionist convention in Utica, New York, in 1835. Two years later, a mob in Alton, Illinois, shot and killed Elijah P. Lovejoy, editor of the abolitionist *Alton Observer*. By pressing for emancipation and equality, the abolitionists revealed the extent of racial prejudice and the impossibility of integrating "respectable" blacks into the white middle class. In fact, the abolitionist crusade had heightened race consciousness, which prompted whites — and blacks — to identify across class lines with members of their own race.

Racial solidarity was especially strong in the South, where whites banned abolitionists and demanded that northern states do the same. The Georgia legislature offered a $5,000 reward to anyone who would kidnap Garrison and bring him south to be tried for inciting rebellion. In Nashville, vigilantes whipped a northern college student for distributing abolitionist pamphlets; in Charleston, a mob attacked the post office and destroyed sacks of abolitionist mail. After 1835, southern postmasters simply refused to deliver mail suspected to be of abolitionist origin.

Politicians joined the fray. President Andrew Jackson, a longtime slave owner, asked Congress in 1835 to restrict the use of the mails by abolitionist groups. Congress refused, but in 1836, the House of Representatives adopted the so-called gag rule. Under this informal rule, which remained in force until 1844, antislavery petitions to the House were automatically tabled and not discussed, keeping the explosive issue of slavery off the congressional stage.

Assailed by racists from the outside, abolitionists fought among themselves over policy and gender issues. Many antislavery clergymen opposed an activist role for women and condemned the Grimké sisters for lecturing to mixed-sex audiences. But Garrison had broadened his reform agenda to include pacifism, the abolition of prisons, and women's rights: "Our object is universal emancipation, to redeem women as well as men from a servile to an equal condition." In 1840, Garrison's demand that the American Anti-Slavery Society support women's rights helped to split the abolitionist movement. Abby Kelley, Lucretia Mott, Elizabeth Cady Stanton, and other women's rights advocates remained with Garrison in the American Anti-Slavery Society and assailed both the institutions that bound blacks and the customs that constrained free women.

Garrison's opponents founded a new organization, the American and Foreign Anti-Slavery Society, which focused its energies on ending slavery through political means. Its members mobilized their churches to oppose racial bondage and established the Liberty Party, the first antislavery political party. In 1840, the new party nominated James G. Birney, a former Alabama slave owner, for president. Birney and the Liberty Party argued that the Constitution did not recognize slavery and, consequently, that slaves automatically became free when they entered areas of federal authority, including the District of Columbia and the national territories. However, Birney won few votes, and the future of political abolitionism appeared dim.

Popular violence in the North, government suppression in the South, and internal schisms stunned the abolitionist movement. By melding the energies and ideas of Evangelical Protestants, moral reformers, and transcendentalists, it had raised the banner of antislavery to new heights, only to face a hostile and widespread backlash. "When we first unfurled the banner of *The Liberator*," Garrison admitted, "it did not occur to us that nearly every religious sect, and every political party would side with the oppressor."

▶ How did black social thought change over the first half of the nineteenth century? What role did black activists play in the abolitionist movement?

▶ How did the abolitionists' proposals and methods differ from those of earlier antislavery movements (see Chapter 8)? Why did those proposals and methods arouse such hostility in the South and in the North?

The Women's Rights Movement

The prominence of women among the abolitionists reflected a broad shift in American culture. By joining religious revivals and reform movements such as the temperance crusade and the abolitionist movement, women entered public life. Their activism caused issues of gender—sexual behavior, marriage, family authority—to become subjects of debate. The debate entered a new phase in 1848, when some reformers focused on women's rights and demanded complete equality with men.

Origins of the Women's Movement

"Don't be afraid, not afraid, fight Satan; stand up for Christ; don't be afraid." So spoke Mary Walker Ostram on her deathbed in 1859. Her religious convictions were as firm at the age of fifty-eight as they had been in 1816, when she helped to found the first Sunday school in Utica, New York. Married to a lawyer-politician but childless, Ostram had devoted her life to Evangelical Presbyterianism and its program of benevolent social reform. In his eulogy after her death, her minister, Philemon Fowler, celebrated Ostram as a "living fountain" of faith, an exemplar of "Women's Sphere of Influence" in the world.

Even as the Reverend Fowler heaped praise on Ostram, he rejected a public presence for women. Like men of the Revolutionary era, Fowler believed that women should limit their political role to that of "republican mother," instructing "their sons in the principles of liberty and government." Women inhabited a "separate sphere" and had no place in "the markets of trade, the scenes of politics and popular agitation, the courts of justice and the halls of legislation." "Home is her peculiar sphere and members of her family her peculiar care," Fowler concluded.

But Ostram and many other middle-class women had already transcended these roles by participating in the Second Great Awakening. Their spiritual activism bolstered their authority within the household and allowed them to influence many areas of family life, including the timing of pregnancies. Publications like *Godey's Lady's Book*, a popular monthly periodical, and Catherine Beecher's *Treatise on Domestic Economy* (1841) taught women how to make their homes examples of middle-class efficiency and domesticity. Women in propertied farm families were equally vigilant. To protect their homes and husbands from alcoholic excess, they joined the Independent Order of Good Templars, a family-oriented temperance organization that granted them full membership.

Some women used their religious activities to enhance other women's lives. In 1834, a group of middle-class women in New York City founded the Female Moral Reform Society and elected Lydia Finney, the wife of revivalist Charles Grandison Finney, as its president. The society sought to curb prostitution in New York City and to protect single women from moral corruption. Rejecting the sexual double standard, its members demanded chastity for men as well as for women. By 1840, the Female Moral Reform Society had grown into a national association, with 555 chapters and 40,000 members throughout the North and Midwest. Employing only women as agents, the society provided moral guidance for young women who were living away from their families and working as factory operatives, seamstresses, or servants. Society members visited brothels, where they sang hymns, offered prayers, searched for runaway girls, and noted the names of clients. They also founded homes of refuge for prostitutes and won the passage of laws in Massachusetts and New York that made seduction a crime.

Other women set out to improve public institutions, and Dorothea Dix (1801–1887) was their model. Dix's paternal grandparents were prominent Bostonians, but her father, a Methodist minister, ended up an impoverished alcoholic. Poor and emotionally abused as a child, Dix grew into a compassionate young woman with a strong sense of moral purpose. She used her grandparents' resources to set up charity schools to "rescue some of America's miserable children from vice" and became a successful author. By 1832, she had published seven books, including *Conversations on Common Things* (1824), an enormously successful treatise on natural science and moral improvement.

In 1841, Dix took up a new cause. Discovering that insane women were jailed alongside male criminals, she persuaded Massachusetts lawmakers to enlarge the state hospital to accommodate indigent mental patients. Exhilarated by that success, Dix began a national movement to establish separate state hospitals for those with mental illness. By 1854, she had traveled more than 30,000 miles and had visited eighteen state penitentiaries, 300 county jails, and more than 500 almshouses in addition to innumerable hospitals. Issuing dozens of reports, Dix prompted many states to expand their public hospitals and improve their prisons.

Both as reformers and as teachers, other northern women transformed public education. From Maine to Wisconsin, women vigorously supported the movement led by Horace Mann to increase the number of elementary schools and improve the quality of instruction. As secretary of the Massachusetts Board of Education from 1837 to 1848, Mann lengthened the school year; established teaching standards in reading, writing, and arithmetic; and improved instruction by recruiting well-educated women as teachers. The intellectual leader of the new women educators was Catherine Beecher, who founded academies for young women in Hartford and Cincinnati. In widely read publications, Beecher argued that "energetic and benevolent women" were better qualified than men were to impart moral and intellectual instruction to the young. By the 1850s, most teachers were women, both because local school boards heeded Beecher's arguments and because the boards could hire women at a lower salary than men. As teachers as well as reformers, women were now part of public life.

Abolitionist Women

Women were central to the antislavery movement. One of the first abolitionists recruited by William Lloyd Garrison was Maria W. Stewart, an African American, who spoke to mixed audiences of men and women in Boston in the early 1830s. As abolitionism blossomed, scores of white women delivered lectures condemning slavery, and thousands more made home "visitations" to win converts to their cause (Map 11.3).

Women abolitionists were particularly aware of the special horrors of slavery for their sex. In her autobiography, *Incidents in the Life of a Slave Girl*, black abolitionist Harriet Jacobs described being forced to have sexual relations with her white owner: "I cannot tell how much I suffered in the presence of these wrongs." According to Jacobs and the other female slaves, such sexual assaults were compounded by the cruel treatment they suffered at the hands of their owners' wives, who were enraged by their husbands' promiscuity. In her best-selling novel, *Uncle Tom's Cabin* (1852), Harriet

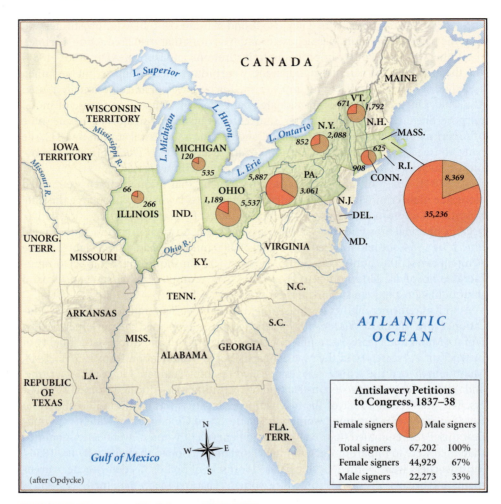

MAP 11.3 Women and Antislavery, 1837–1838

Beginning in the 1830s, antislavery advocates dispatched dozens of petitions to Congress demanding an end to human bondage. Women accounted for two-thirds of the 67,000 signatures on the petitions submitted in 1837–1838, suggesting the importance of women in the antislavery movement and the extent of female organizations and social networks. Lawmakers, eager to avoid sectional conflict, had devised the so-called gag rule, an informal agreement to table the petitions without discussion.

For more help analyzing this map, see the Online Study Guide at **bedfordstmartins.com/henrettaconcise**.

Beecher Stowe charged that one of the greatest moral failings of slavery was the degradation of slave women.

When men challenged their public activism, white abolitionist women grew increasingly conscious of their own degraded social and legal status. In 1836, Congregationalist clergymen in New England assailed Angelina and Sarah Grimké for addressing mixed male and female audiences. For justification, Sarah Grimké turned to the Bible: "The Lord Jesus defines the duties of his followers in his Sermon on the Mount . . .

Sojourner Truth

Few women had as interesting a life as Sojourner Truth. Born "Isabella" in Dutch-speaking rural New York about 1797, she labored as a slave until 1827. Following a religious vision, Isabella moved to New York City, learned English, and worked for deeply religious — and ultimately fanatical — Christian merchants. In 1843, in search of further spiritual enlightenment, she took the name "Sojourner Truth" and left New York. After briefly joining the Millerites (who believed the world would end in 1844), Truth became famous as a forceful speaker on behalf of abolitionism and women's rights. This illustration, showing Truth addressing an antislavery meeting, suggests her powerful personal presence. Miriam and Ira D. Wallach Division of Art, Prints and Photographs. The New York Public Library.

without any reference to sex or condition," she wrote. "Men and women are CREATED EQUAL! They are both moral and accountable beings and whatever is right for man to do is right for woman." In a pamphlet debate with Catherine Beecher (who believed that women should exercise power primarily as wives, mothers, and schoolteachers), Angelina Grimké pushed the argument beyond religion, invoking Enlightenment principles to claim equal civic rights for women:

> It is a woman's right to have a voice in all the laws and regulations by which she is governed, whether in Church or State. . . . The present arrangements of society on these points are a violation of human rights, a rank usurpation of power, a violent seizure and confiscation of what is sacredly and inalienably hers.

By 1840, female abolitionists were asserting that traditional gender roles amounted to the "domestic slavery" of women. "How can we endure our present marriage relations," asked Elizabeth Cady Stanton, since they gave a woman "no charter of rights, no individuality of her own?" Said another female reformer: "The radical difficulty . . . is that women are considered as *belonging* to men" (see American Voices, p. 344). Having acquired a public voice and political skills in the crusade for African American freedom, thousands of northern women now advocated greater rights for themselves.

The Program of Seneca Falls and Beyond

During the 1840s, women's rights activists devised a pragmatic program of reform. They did not challenge the institution of marriage or the conventional division of labor within the family. Instead, they tried to strengthen the legal rights of married women, especially

A Farm Woman Defends the Grimké Sisters   KEZIAH KENDALL

The Grimké sisters' abolitionist lecture tour of New England sparked an enormous outcry from ministers and social conservatives, who questioned the propriety of women assuming public roles and demanding civic equality. In a Lyceum lecture in 1839, titled "The Legal Rights of Women," Simon Greenleaf, Royall Professor of Law at Harvard College, defended legal and customary restrictions on women's lives. Replying to Greenleaf, Keziah Kendall—possibly a fictional person created by a women's rights advocate—sent him the following letter, which two historians recently found among his papers.

My name is Keziah Kendall. I live not many miles from Cambridge, on a farm with two sisters, one older, one younger than myself. I am thirty two. Our parents and only brother are dead—we have a good estate—comfortable house—nice barn, garden, orchard &c and money in the bank besides. . . . Under these circumstances the whole responsibility of our property, not less than twenty five thousand dollars rest upon me. . . .

Well—our milkman brought word when he came from market that you were a going to lecture on the legal rights of women, and so I thought I would go and learn. Now I hope you wont think me bold when I say, I did not like that lecture much . . . [because] there was nothing in it but what every body knows. . . .

What I wanted to know, was good reasons for some of those laws that I cant account for. . . . One Lyceum lecture that I heard in C[ambridge] stated that the Americans went to war with the British, because they were taxed without being represented in Parliament. Now we [women] are taxed every year to the full amount of every dollar we possess—town, county, state taxes—taxes for land, for movable [property], for money and all. Now I don't want to [become a legislative] representative [or] . . . a "constable or a sheriff," but I have no voice about public improvements, and I don't see the justice of being taxed any more than the "revolutionary heroes" did.

Nor do I think we are treated as Christian women ought to be, according to the Bible rule of doing to others as you would others should do unto you. I am told (not by you) that if a woman dies a week after she's married that her husband takes all her personal property and the use of [all] her real estate as long as he lives—if a man dies his wife can have her thirds [use of only one-third of the estate]—this does not come up to the Gospel rule. . . .

Another thing . . . women have joined the Antislavery societies, and why? Women are kept for slaves as well as [black] men—it is a common cause, deny the justice of it, who can! To be sure I do not wish to go about lecturing like the Misses Grimkie, but I have not the knowledge they have, and I verily believe that if I had been brought up among slaves as they were . . . and felt a call from humanity to speak, I should run the venture of your displeasure, and that of a good many others like you.

SOURCE: Dianne Avery and Alfred S. Konefsky, "The Daughters of Job: Property Rights and Women's Lives in Mid-Nineteenth-Century Massachusetts," *Law and History Review* 10 (Fall 1992): 323–356.

Crusading Women Reformers
Elizabeth Cady Stanton (1815–1902) and Susan B. Anthony (1820–1906) were a dynamic duo of social reformers. Cady was the well-educated daughter of a New York judge and an early abolitionist. In 1840, she married abolitionist lawyer Henry Stanton, by whom she had seven children. Anthony was raised as a Quaker, taught school for ten years, and then became a temperance activist. Stanton and Anthony became intimate friends and led a successful struggle to expand New York's Married Women's Property Law of 1848. During the Civil War, they set up the Women's Loyal National League, which supported the Union war effort and helped to win passage of the Thirteenth Amendment. In 1866, they were among the founders of the American Equal Rights Association, which demanded the vote for women as well as African American men.
©Bettmann/ Corbis.

with respect to property. This initiative won crucial support from affluent men, who wanted to protect their family's assets in case their businesses went bankrupt in the volatile market economy. By ensuring that their married daughters had property rights, fathers also hoped to protect them (and their inheritances) from financially irresponsible sons-in-law. These considerations prompted legislatures in three states—Mississippi, Maine, and Massachusetts—to enact married women's property acts between 1839 and 1845. Three years later, women activists in New York won a more comprehensive statute that became the model for laws in fourteen other states. This statute of 1848 gave women full legal control over the property they brought to a marriage.

That same year, Elizabeth Cady Stanton and Lucretia Mott organized a gathering of women's right activists in the small New York town of Seneca Falls. Seventy women and thirty men attended the meeting, which issued a rousing manifesto for women's equality. Taking the Declaration of Independence as a model, the attendees extended its republican ideology to women. "All men and women are created equal," the Declaration of Sentiments declared, yet "the history of mankind is a history of repeated injuries and usurpations on the part of man toward woman" and "the establishment of an absolute tyranny over her." To persuade Americans to right this long-standing wrong, the activists resolved to "employ agents, circulate tracts, petition the State and National legislatures, and endeavor to enlist the pulpit and the press on our behalf." By staking out claims for equality for women in public life, the Seneca Falls reformers repudiated both the natural inferiority of women and the ideology of **separate spheres**.

Most men dismissed the Seneca Falls declaration as nonsense, and many women also repudiated the activists and their message. Writing in her diary, one small-town mother and housewife lashed out at the female reformer who "aping mannish manners . . . wears absurd and barbarous attire, who talks of her wrongs in harsh tone, who struts and strides, and thinks that she proves herself superior to the rest of her sex."

Still, the women's rights movement grew in strength and purpose. In 1850, delegates to the first national women's rights convention in Worcester, Massachusetts, hammered out a program of action. The women called on churches to revise notions of female inferiority in their theology. Addressing state legislatures, they proposed laws to guarantee the custody rights of mothers in the event of divorce or a husband's death and to allow married women to institute lawsuits and testify in court. Finally, they began a concerted campaign to win the vote for women. The national women's rights convention of 1851 declared that suffrage was "the corner-stone of this enterprise, since we do not seek to protect woman, but rather to place her in a position to protect herself."

The activists' legislative campaign required talented organizers and lobbyists. The most prominent political operative was Susan B. Anthony (1820–1906). Anthony came from a Quaker family and, as a young woman, participated in the temperance and anti-slavery movements. That experience, Anthony explained, had given her political skills and taught her "the great evil of woman's utter dependence on man." Joining the women's right movement, she worked closely with Elizabeth Cady Stanton. Anthony created a network of political "captains," all women, who relentlessly lobbied state legislatures. In 1860, her efforts secured a New York law granting women the right to control their own wages (which fathers or husbands had previously managed), to own property acquired by "trade, business, labors, or services," and, if widowed, to assume sole guardianship of their children. Genuine individualism for women, the dream of transcendentalist Margaret Fuller, had moved a tiny step closer to reality. Both in such small and much larger ways, the midcentury reform movements had altered the character of American culture.

► Why did religious women such as Mary Walker Ostram and the Grimké sisters become social reformers?

► How do you explain the appearance of the women's rights movement? What were its goals, and why did they arouse intense opposition?

► Did the era of reform increase or decrease the American commitment to, and practice of, liberty? In what ways?

SUMMARY

In this chapter, we examined four major cultural movements of the mid-nineteenth century and analyzed the new popular culture in New York City. Our discussion of the transcendentalists highlighted the influence of Ralph Waldo Emerson on the great literary figures of the era; we also linked transcendentalism to the rise of individualism and the character of middle-class culture.

Our analysis of communal movements probed the efforts of communalists to devise new rules for sexual behavior, gender relationships, and property ownership.

We saw that successful communal experiments—Mormonism, for example—began with a charismatic leader and a religious foundation and endured if they developed strong, authoritarian institutions.

We also traced the personal and ideological factors that linked the abolitionist and women's rights movements. Lucretia Mott, Elizabeth Cady Stanton, and the Grimké sisters began as antislavery advocates; but, denied access to lecture platforms by male abolitionists, they gradually became staunch defenders of women's rights. This transition was a logical one: Both enslaved blacks and married women were "owned" by men, either as property or as their legal dependents. Consequently, the efforts of women's rights advocates to abolish the legal prerogatives of husbands were as controversial as the abolitionists' efforts to end the legal property rights of slave owners. As reformers took aim at these deeply rooted institutions and customs, many Americans feared that such activism would not perfect society but destroy it.

Connections: Culture

Before 1800, the United States contained three distinct regional cultures: those of New England, the Middle Atlantic, and the South. The presence (or absence) of three eighteenth-century migrant cultures—African, German, and Scots-Irish—in a region partially explained its distinct character. As we saw in Chapter 8, between 1790 and 1820, the migrant societies slowly acquired an American identity, and all of the regions integrated republican ideology and Protestant Christianity into their cultural outlook. Then, as we noted in the essay opening Part Three,

> a series of reform movements, many with religious roots and goals, swept across America. Dedicated men and women preached the gospel of temperance, Sunday observance, prison reform, and many other causes.

These reform movements sparked a series of culture wars, as temperance advocates won laws regulating drink, Sabbatarians curtailed Sunday amusements, white mobs rioted against abolitionists, and community hostility forced Mormons westward. The arrival of millions of Catholic migrants from Germany and Ireland sparked more cultural conflicts. Meanwhile, in the South, a vast movement of peoples—white and black—into the lower Mississippi Valley created a new "cotton states" culture, which we discuss in the next chapter.

FOR FURTHER EXPLORATION

Ronald Walters, *American Reformers, 1815–1860* (1978), and Robert H. Abzug, *Cosmos Crumbling* (1994), cover the reform movements and their religious roots. Peter S. Field, *Ralph Waldo Emerson* (2003), Charles Capper, *Margaret Fuller* (1992), and David S. Reynolds, *Walt Whitman's America* (1995), are fine biographies. Good Web sites include **www.vcu.edu/engweb/transcendentalism/** and **religiousmovements.lib.virginia .edu/**. For religious utopianism gone mad, read Paul E. Johnson and Sean Wilentz, *The Kingdom of Matthias* (1995).

On abolitionism, read James B. Stewart, *Holy Warriors: The Abolitionists and American Slavery* (1976); Mark Perry, *Lift Up Thy Voice: The Grimké Family's Journey* (2001); and Catherine Clinton, *Harriet Tubman: The Road to Freedom* (2004). Nat

TIMELINE

1826 ▸	Lyceum movement begins	▸	Commercial sex flourishes in New York City
1829 ▸	David Walker's *Appeal . . . to the Colored Citizens of the World*	**1841** ▸	Transcendentalists found Brook Farm
1830 ▸	Joseph Smith issues *The Book of Mormon*	▸	Dorothea Dix reforms prisons and hospitals
1830s ▸	Ralph Waldo Emerson defines transcendentalism	**1844** ▸	Margaret Fuller publishes *Woman in the Nineteenth Century*
▸	Emergence of minstrelsy shows		
▸	Nativists denounce immigration	**1845** ▸	Henry David Thoreau withdraws to Walden Pond
1831 ▸	William Lloyd Garrison founds *The Liberator* and American Anti-Slavery Society (1833)	**1846** ▸	Mormon followers of Brigham Young reach Salt Lake
▸	Nat Turner's uprising in Virginia	**1848** ▸	John Humphrey Noyes founds Oneida Community
1834 ▸	New York women create Female Moral Reform Society	▸	Seneca Falls convention advocates women's equality
1835 ▸	Abolitionists launch mail campaign; antiabolitionists riot against them	**1850** ▸	Nathaniel Hawthorne publishes *The Scarlet Letter*
1836 ▸	House of Representatives adopts gag rule on antislavery petitions	**1851** ▸	Herman Melville issues *Moby Dick*
▸	Grimké sisters defend public roles for women	**1852** ▸	Harriet Beecher Stowe writes *Uncle Tom's Cabin*
1840 ▸	Liberty Party candidate James G. Birney runs for president	**1855** ▸	Walt Whitman publishes *Leaves of Grass*
1840s ▸	Fourierist communities arise in Midwest	**1858** ▸	"Mormon War" over polygamy

Turner's uprising is the focus of Stephen B. Oates, *The Fires of Jubilee* (1975). For antiabolitionism and minstrelsy, read David Roediger, *The Wages of Whiteness* (1995).

On the women's rights movement, begin with Mary C. Kelley, *Learning to Stand and Speak: Women, Education, and Public Life in America's Republic* (2006); Ellen DuBois, *Feminism and Suffrage* (1978); and Kathleen Barry, *Susan B. Anthony* (1988). See also the Web site for Seneca Falls (**www.nps.gov/wori/home.htm**).

TEST YOUR KNOWLEDGE

To assess your mastery of the material in this chapter and for Web sites, images, and documents related to this chapter, visit **bedfordstmartins.com/henrettaconcise**.

12

The South Expands: Slavery and Society
1820–1860

A prime able-bodied slave is worth three times as much to the cotton or sugar planter as to the Maryland agriculturalist.

— *Frederick [Maryland] Examiner*, 1858

Life in South Carolina had been good to James Lide. A slave-owning planter who lived near the Pee Dee River, Lide and his wife had raised twelve children and lived in relative comfort. Content with his lot, Lide had long resisted the "Alabama Fever" that had prompted thousands of Carolina families to move west. Finally, at age sixty-five, probably seeking land for his many offspring, he moved his slaves and family — including six children and six grandchildren — to a plantation near Montgomery, Alabama. There, the family took up residence in a squalid double log cabin with airholes but no windows. Even as their living conditions improved, the Lides' family life remained unsettled. "Pa is quite in the notion of moving somewhere," his daughter Maria reported a few years later; "his having such a good crop seems to make him more anxious to move." Although James Lide lived out his years in Alabama, many of his children did not. In 1854, at the age of fifty-eight, Eli Lide moved to Texas, telling his father, "Something within me whispers onward and onward."

The story of the Lide family was the story of American society. Between 1800 and 1860, white planters from the South as well as yeomen farmers from the North were moving west. The South's "master class was one of the most mobile in history," notes historian James Oakes. The planters' goal was to make the West into a "slave society" similar to those their fathers and grandfathers had built in Virginia and South Carolina. Using their own muscles and those of thousands of enslaved African Americans, the planters brought millions of acres of land into cultivation. By 1840, the South was at the cutting edge of the American Market Revolution. The region annually produced and exported 1.5 million bales of raw cotton — over two-thirds of the world's supply — and its economy was larger and richer than those of most nations. "Cotton is King," boasted the *Southern Cultivator*, the leading Georgia farm journal, "and wields an astonishing influence over the world's commerce."

No matter how rich they were, few cotton planters in the southwestern states of Alabama, Mississippi, and Texas lived in elegant houses or led cultured lives. The slave owners of the Cotton South largely abandoned the aristocratic gentility of the Chesapeake region and the Carolinas. These agricultural capitalists wanted to make money. "To sell cotton in order to buy negroes—to make more cotton to buy more negroes, 'ad infinitum,' is the aim . . . of the thorough-going cotton planter," a New England traveler reported from Mississippi in 1835. "His whole soul is wrapped up in the pursuit." A generation later, Frederick Law Olmsted found that little had changed: In Mississippi, "the plantations are all large" but their owners do not live well, he observed; "the greater number have but small and mean residences." Plantation women were especially aware of the loss of genteel surroundings and polite society. Raised in North Carolina, where she was "blest with every comfort, & even luxury," a "discontented" Mary Drake found Mississippi and Alabama "a dreary waste."

Tens of thousands of enslaved African Americans in the Lower Mississippi River Valley knew what "dreary waste" really meant: unremitting toil, unrelieved poverty, and profound sadness. Sold south from Maryland, where his family had lived for generations, Charles Ball's father became "gloomy and morose" and, when threatened again with sale, ran off and disappeared. He had good reason: On new cotton plantations, slaves labored from "sunup to sundown" and from one end of the year to the other. As one field hand put it, there was "no time off [between] de change of de seasons. . . . Dey was allus clearin' mo' lan' or sump." Day by day, the forced labor of unwilling black migrants produced the great wealth of the Cotton South. Always wanting more, southern planters and politicians plotted to extend their plantation economy across the continent.

Creating the Cotton South

American slavery took root on the tobacco plantations of the Chesapeake and in the rice fields of the Carolina Low Country. It grew to maturity on the sugar fields of Louisiana, the hemp farms of Kentucky and Tennessee, and especially on the cotton plantations of the states bordering the Gulf of Mexico: Alabama, Mississippi, and Texas (Figure 12.1). The transplantation of slavery to these new lands brought vast changes to the lives of enslaved blacks, slave-owning planters, and white farmers. And it led

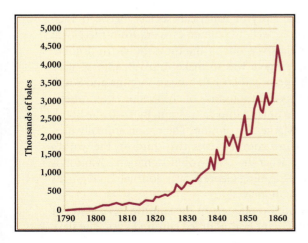

FIGURE 12.1 The Surge in Cotton Production, 1835–1860

Between 1835 and the mid-1840s, southern planters doubled their output of 500-pound bales of cotton from one million per year to two million. Production doubled again in the 1850s, reaching four million bales per year by the end of the decade. Because the price of raw cotton rose slightly (from about 11 cents a pound in the 1830s to 13 cents in the 1850s), planters reaped substantial profits, reinforcing their commitment to the slave system.

SOURCE: Robert William Fogel and Stanley L. Engerman, *Time on the Cross* (Boston: Little, Brown, 1974), fig. 25.

planters to believe that American slavery could keep expanding. "We want land, and have a right to it," declared a Georgia planter on the eve of the Civil War.

The Domestic Slave Trade

In 1817, when the American Colonization Society announced its plan to return freed blacks to Africa (see Chapter 8), the southern plantation system was expanding rapidly, as was the demand for slave labor. In 1790, the western boundary of the plantation system ran through the middle of Georgia; by 1830, it stretched through western Louisiana; by 1860, the slave frontier extended far into Texas (Map 12.1). That advance of 900 miles more than doubled the geographical area cultivated by slave labor and nearly increased the number of slave states from eight in 1800 to fifteen by 1850. The federal government promoted this expansion by buying Louisiana from the French in 1803, removing Native Americans from the southeastern states in the 1830s, and annexing Texas and Mexican lands in the 1840s.

To cultivate this vast area, white planters looked for enslaved laborers first in Africa and then in the Chesapeake region. Between 1776 and 1809, when Congress outlawed the Atlantic slave trade, planters imported about 115,000 Africans. "The Negro business is a great object with us," one slave trader declared, "the Planter will . . . sacrifice every thing to attain Negroes." Despite the influx, the demand for labor far exceeded the supply. Consequently, cotton planters imported new African workers illegally, through the Spanish colony of Florida until 1819 and then through the Mexican province of Texas. Yet these Africans—about 50,000 between 1810 and 1869—did not satisfy the demand for labor.

So planters looked to the Chesapeake region, home in 1800 to nearly half of the nation's black population. Throughout this region, the African American population was growing rapidly from natural increase—an average of 27 percent a decade—and creating a surplus of enslaved laborers. Before the War of 1812, so-called Georgia traders had exploited this surplus; after 1815, the internal trade expanded vastly in scope and size. Between 1818 and 1829, planters in just one Maryland county—Frederick—sold at least 952 slaves to traders or cotton planters. Each decade, about 10 percent of the African Americans in the main exporting states of the Upper South—Maryland and Virginia before 1820, plus the Carolinas by 1830, plus Kentucky by 1840—suffered a similar fate.

The "mania for buying negroes" resulted in a massive forced migration. Seventy-five thousand slaves left Virginia during the 1810s and another 75,000 during the 1820s. The number of unwilling Virginia migrants jumped to nearly 120,000 during the 1830s and then averaged 85,000 during the 1840s and 1850s. In Virginia alone, then, 440,000 African Americans were ripped from communities where their families had lived for three or four generations. By 1860, more than one million slaves had been forced to leave the Upper South.

This movement of African Americans took two forms: transfer and sale. Looking for new opportunities, thousands of Chesapeake and Carolina planters—men like James Lide—sold their plantations and moved to the Southwest with their slaves. Many other planters in the Old South gave slaves to sons and daughters who were moving west. This transfer of entire or partial plantations accounted for about 40 percent of the African American migrants. The rest—about 60 percent of the one million

1790

1830

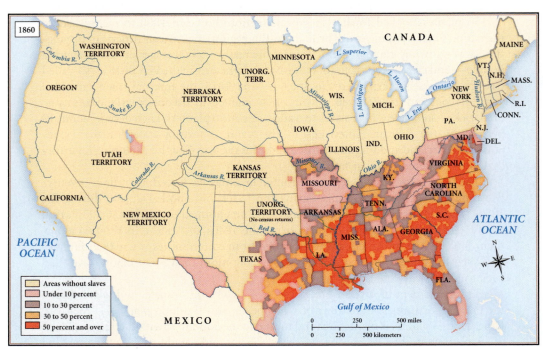

1860

	Areas without slaves
	Under 10 percent
	10 to 30 percent
	30 to 50 percent
	50 percent and over

migrants—were "sold south." By 1860, a majority of African Americans lived and worked in the Deep South, the lands that stretched from Georgia to Texas.

Just as the Atlantic slave trade was a major eighteenth-century business, so the domestic slave trade emerged as a crucial commercial enterprise between 1800 and 1860. The trade took two forms: a coastal system through the Atlantic seaports and inland commerce using rivers and roads. The coastal system sent thousands of slaves to the sugar plantations in Louisiana, the former French territory that entered the Union in 1812. Slave traders scoured the countryside near the port cities of the Chesapeake and the Carolinas—Baltimore, Alexandria, Richmond, and Charleston—searching, as one of them put it, for "likely young men such as I think would suit the New Orleans market." Each year, hundreds of muscular young slaves passed through the auction houses of the port cities bound for the massive trade mart in New Orleans. Because this traffic in laborers was highly visible, it elicited widespread condemnation by northern abolitionists.

Sugar was a "killer" crop, and Louisiana (like the West Indies) soon had a well-deserved reputation among African Americans "as a place of slaughter," where hundreds died each year from disease, overwork, and brutal treatment. A Maryland farmer refused to consent to his daughter's marriage to a Louisiana sugar planter, remarking, "Mit has never been used to seeing negroes flayed alive and it would kill her."

The inland system that sent slaves to the Cotton South was less apparent than the coastal trade but much more extensive. It also relied on professional slave traders, who went from one rural village to another buying "young and likely Negroes." The traders then marched their purchases in coffles—columns of slaves bound to one another—to Alabama, Mississippi, and Missouri in the 1830s and to Arkansas and Texas in the 1850s. One slave described the arduous journey: "Dem Speculators would put the chilluns in a wagon usually pulled by oxens and de older folks was chained or tied together sos dey could not run off." Once a coffle reached its destination, the trader would sell slaves "at every village in the county."

Chesapeake and Carolina planters provided the trade with its human cargo. Some planters sold slaves when poor management or their own extravagances threw them into debt. "Trouble gathers thicker and thicker around me," Thomas B. Chaplin of South Carolina lamented in his diary, "I will be compelled to send about ten prime Negroes to Town on next Monday, to be sold." Many more planters doubled as slave traders, earning substantial profits by traveling south to sell some of their slaves and those of their neighbors. Prices marched in step with those for cotton; during the boom years of the 1850s, said one planter, a slave that "wouldn't bring over $300, seven years ago, will fetch $1000, cash, quick, this year." Exploiting this demand, Thomas Weatherly of South Carolina drove his surplus slaves to Hayneville, Alabama, where he

◀ **MAP 12.1   Distribution of the Slave Population in 1790, 1830, and 1860**

The cotton boom shifted many African Americans to the Old Southwest. In 1790, most slaves lived and worked on the tobacco plantations of the Chesapeake and on the rice and indigo plantations of South Carolina and Georgia. By 1830, hundreds of thousands of enslaved blacks labored on the cotton and sugar lands of the Lower Mississippi Valley. Three decades later, the centers of slavery lay along the Mississippi River and in an arc of fertile cotton land—the "black belt"—sweeping from Mississippi through Georgia.

For more help analyzing this map see the Online Study Guide at **bedfordstmartins.com/henrettaconcise**.

lived "in his tents" and "sold ten negroes last week." Colonel E. S. Irvine, a member of the South Carolina legislature and "a highly respected gentleman" in white circles, likewise traveled frequently "to the west to sell a drove of Negroes."

The domestic slave trade was crucial to the prosperity of the southern economy. It provided thousands of workers to fell the forests and plant cotton in the Gulf states, and it bolstered the economy of the Upper South. By selling their surplus workers, tobacco, rice, and grain planters in the Chesapeake and Carolinas added about 20 percent to their income. The domestic slave trade, remarked a Maryland newspaper, served as "an almost universal resource to raise money."

For African American families, the domestic slave trade was a personal disaster that accentuated their status—and vulnerability—as property. On this issue, blacks and whites agreed. W. C. Pennington, a former slave, reflected, "The being of slavery, its soul and its body, lives and moves in the chattel principle, the property principle, the bill of sale principle." A South Carolina master put it more crudely: The slave's earnings "belong to *me* because I bought him." There was an "immense amount of capital which is invested in slave property," Henry Clay observed. "It is owned by widows and orphans, by the aged and infirm, as well as the sound and vigorous. It is the subject of mortgages, deeds of trust, and family settlements." The Whig politician concluded, "I know that there is a visionary dogma, which holds that negro slaves cannot be the subject of property. I shall not dwell long on this speculative abstraction. That is property which the law declares to be property."

As a slave owner himself, Clay knew that property rights were a key to slave discipline. As one master put it, "I govern them . . . without the whip by stating . . . that I should sell them if they do not conduct themselves as I wish." The threat was effective. "The Negroes here dread nothing on earth so much as this," an observer in Maryland noted. "They regard the south with perfect horror, and to be sent there is considered as the worst punishment that could be inflicted on them."

But such sales were inflicted on thousands of families and destroyed about one in every four slave marriages. "I am Sold to a man by the name of Peterson a trader," lamented a Georgia slave. "My Dear wife for you and my Children my pen cannot Express the griffe I feel to be parted from you all." The trade encompassed children and young people as well as adults; in northern Maryland, boys and girls were sold away at an average age of seventeen years. "Dey sole my sister Kate," Anna Harris remembered decades later, "and I ain't seed or heard of her since." The trade also separated almost one-third of all slave children under the age of fourteen from one or both of their parents. Sarah Grant remembered, "Mamma used to cry when she had to go back to work because she was always scared some of us kids would be sold while she was away." Well might she worry, for slave traders worked quietly and quickly. "One night I lay down on de straw mattress wid my mammy," Vinny Baker recalled, "an' de nex' mo'nin I woke up an' she wuz gone." When their owner sold seven-year-old Laura Clark and ten other children from their plantation in North Carolina, Clark sensed that she would see her mother "no mo' in dis life."

Despite these sales, 75 percent of slave marriages remained unbroken, and the majority of children lived with one or both parents until puberty. Consequently, the sense of family among African Americans remained strong. Sold from Virginia to

BY HEWLETT & RASPILLER,

On Saturday, 14th April, inst.

At 1-2 12 o'clock, at Hewlett's Exchange,
WILL BE SOLD,

24 HEAD OF SLAVES,

Lately belonging to the Estate of Jno. Erwin, of the parish of Iberville. These Slaves have been for more than 10 years in the country, and are all well acclimated, and accustomed to all kinds of work on a Sugar Plantation. There are among them a first rate cooper, a first rate brick maker, and an excellent hostler and coachman. They will be sold chiefly in families.

TERMS-----One year's credit, payable in notes endorsed to the satisfaction of the vendor, and bearing mortgage until final payment. Sales to be passed before Carlisle Pollock, Esq. at the expense of the purchasers.

Fielding,	aged 27 years, field hand,		
Sally,	aged 24 do. field hand and cook,		150
Levi, aged 26 years,	cooper and field hand,		
Aggy, do. 24 do.	house servant and field hand.		
James, do. 6 do.			2100
Emeline, 8 do.			
Stephen, 3 do.			
Priscilly, 1 do.			
Bill, aged 24 years,	field hand,		
Leah, do. 22 do.	field hand,		1600
Rosette, do. 8 do.			
Infant child.			
Alfred, aged 22 years,	brick maker, servant and field hand,		1800
Charlotte, do. 20 years,	house servant and field hand,		
Infant.			
Forrester, aged 41 years,	hostler, house servant and field hand,		1200
Mary, aged 22 years,	field hand and cook.		
Infant.			
Harry, aged 24 years,	field hand,		1400
Charity, aged 24 years,	field hand,		
Polly, aged 22 years,	house servant and seamstress,		800
Sam, aged 2 years.			
Bedford, aged 14 years,	field hand,		700
Mahaly, aged 12 years,	field hand,		500.
			11200

The Business of Slavery

In the 1850s, Virginia slaves were still being "sold South." The painting, *Slave Auction in Richmond, Virginia* (1852), captures the apprehension of the enslaved women and the discontent of the man, none of whom can control their fate. Whites — plantation overseer, slave trader, top-hatted aristocratic planter — lurk in the background, where they are completing the commercial transaction. The illustration to the left, a public notice for a slave auction to be held in Iberville, Louisiana, advertises "24 Head of Slaves" as if they were cattle — a striking statement on the business of slavery. The Granger Collection, New York / Library of Congress.

For more help analyzing this image, see the Online Study Guide at bedfordstmartins.com/henrettaconcise.

Texas in 1843, Hawkins Wilson carried with him a detailed mental picture of his family. Twenty-five years later, a freedman, Wilson set out to find his "dearest relatives" in Virginia. "My sister belonged to Peter Coleman in Caroline County and her name was Jane. . . . She had three children, Robert[,] Charles and Julia, when I left — Sister Martha belonged to Dr. Jefferson. . . . Sister Matilda belonged to Mrs. Botts."

During the quarter century between sale and freedom, Hawkins Wilson and thousands of other African American migrants constructed new lives for themselves in the Mississippi River Valley. Undoubtedly, many of them did so with a sense of foreboding. From personal experience, they knew that their lives could be shaken to the core at any moment. Like Charles Ball, some "longed to die, and escape from the bonds of my tormentors." Even moments of joy were shadowed by the darkness of slavery. Knowing that sales often ended slave marriages, a white minister blessed one couple "for so long as God keeps them together."

Many white planters "saw" only the African American marriages that endured and ignored those they had broken. Consequently, many slave owners considered themselves benevolent masters, committed to the welfare of "my family, black and white." Some masters gave substance to this paternal ideal by treating with kindness various "loyal and worthy" slaves: the drivers who commanded their workers, the mammy who raised their children, and the house servants who catered to their needs. By safeguarding the families of these slaves from sale, planters convinced themselves that they "sold south" only "coarse" troublemakers and uncivilized slaves who had "little sense of family." Other owners were more honest about the human cost of their pursuit of wealth. "Tomorrow the negroes are to get off" to Kentucky, a slave-owning woman in Virginia wrote to a friend, "and I expect there will be great crying and morning, with children Leaving there mothers, mothers there children, and women there husbands."

Whether or not they acknowledged the slaves' pain, few southern whites questioned the morality of the domestic slave trade. As a committee of the Charleston City Council responded to abolitionist criticism, slavery was completely consistent "with moral principle and with the highest order of civilization," as was "the removal of slaves from place to place, and their transfer from master to master, by gift, purchase, or otherwise."

The Dual Cultures of the Planter Elite

Westward movement profoundly affected the small elite of extraordinarily wealthy planter families who stood at the top of southern society. These families — about 3,000 in number — each owned more than 100 slaves and huge tracts of the most fertile lands. Their ranks included many of the richest families in the United States. On the eve of the Civil War, southern planters accounted for nearly two-thirds of all American men with wealth of $100,000 or more.

The plantation elite consisted of two distinct groups. The first group consisted of the traditional aristocrats of the Old South. As tobacco and rice production soared after 1700, a wealthy elite dominated the social and political life of the Tidewater region of the Chesapeake and the low country of South Carolina and Georgia. During the eighteenth century, these planters built impressive mansions and adopted the manners and values of the English landed gentry (see Chapter 3). Their aristocratic culture survived the revolution of 1776 and soon took on a republican character. Classical republican theorists had long

A Louisiana Plantation, 1861
This view of a Louisiana plantation by Marie Adrien Persac, a French-born artist, presents an exquisitely detailed but romanticized vision of the planter lifestyle. Well-dressed slaves stand amid neatly spaced rows of cotton as the women of the household prance by on well-groomed horses. Off to the right, smoke rises from the chimneys of a small mill, probably used to process the sugarcane grown elsewhere on the plantation. Louisiana State University Museum of Art.

identified political tyranny as a major threat to liberty, and southern aristocrats, who feared government interference with their property in slaves, embraced this ideological outlook. To prevent despotic rule by democratic demagogues or radical legislatures, planters demanded that authority rest in the hands of incorruptible men of "virtue."

Affluent planters cast themselves as the embodiment of this ideal—a republican aristocracy (see Chapter 8). "The planters here are essentially what the nobility are in other countries," declared James Henry Hammond of South Carolina. "They stand at the head of society & politics . . . [and form] an aristocracy of talents, of virtue, of generosity and courage." These wealthy planters criticized the increasingly democratic polity and middle-class society that was developing in the Northeast and Midwest. "Inequality is the fundamental law of the universe," declared one aristocratic-minded planter. Others condemned professional politicians as "a set of demagogues" and questioned the legitimacy of universal suffrage. "Times are sadly different now to what they were when I was a boy," lamented South Carolinian David Gavin. Then, the "Sovereign people, alias mob" had little influence; now they vied for power with the elite. How can "I rejoice for a freedom," Gavin demanded to know, "which allows every bankrupt, swindler, thief, and scoundrel, traitor and seller of his vote to be placed on an equality with myself?"

To maintain their privileged identity, aristocratic planters married their sons and daughters to one another and taught them to follow in the parents' footsteps: the men working as planters, merchants, lawyers, newspaper editors, and ministers and the women hosting plantation balls and church bazaars. To confirm their social preeminence, planters lived extravagantly and entertained graciously. James Henry Hammond built a Greek Revival mansion with a center hall spanning 53 feet by 20 feet, its floor embellished with stylish Belgian tiles and expensive Brussels carpets. "Once a year, like a great feudal landlord," a guest recounted, Hammond "gave a fete or grand dinner to all the country people."

Rice planters remained at the apex of the plantation aristocracy. In 1860, the fifteen proprietors of the vast plantations in All Saints Parish in the Georgetown District of South Carolina owned 4,383 slaves, who annually grew and processed fourteen million pounds of rice. As inexpensive Asian rice entered the world market and cut the profit margins of Carolina planters, they sold some slaves and worked the others harder, two strategies that allowed them to sustain their luxurious lifestyle. The "hospitality and elegance" of Charleston and Savannah impressed savvy English traveler John Silk Buckingham. Buckingham likewise found "polished" families among long-established French Catholic planters in New Orleans and along the Mississippi River. There, "the sugar and cotton planters live in splendid edifices, and enjoy all the luxury that wealth can impart" (see Voices from Abroad, p. 359).

In tobacco-growing regions, the lives of the planter aristocracy followed a different trajectory, in part because slave ownership was widely diffused. In the 1770s, about 60 percent of white families in the Chesapeake region owned at least one African American slave. As many wealthy tobacco planters moved their plantations and slaves to the Cotton South, middling planters (who owned between five and twenty slaves) came to dominate the economy. The descendants of the old planter aristocracy remained influential in the Chesapeake, but increasingly as slave-owning grain farmers, lawyers, merchants, industrialists, and politicians. The slaves they didn't need for their businesses, they hired out, sold, or allowed to purchase their freedom.

Although this genteel planter aristocracy flourished primarily around the periphery of the South—in Virginia, South Carolina, and Louisiana—its members took the lead in defending slavery. Ignoring the old Jeffersonian defense of slavery as a "necessary evil" (see Chapter 8), southern apologists now maintained that slavery was a positive good that allowed a civilized lifestyle for whites and provided tutelage for genetically inferior Africans. "As a race, the African is inferior to the white man," declared Alexander Stephens, the future vice president of the Confederacy. "Subordination to the white man, is his normal condition." Stephens and other apologists depicted planters and their wives as aristocratic models of "disinterested benevolence," who provided food and housing for their workers and cared for them in old age. One wealthy Georgian declared that "Plantation government should be eminently patriarchal"; the planter, as

The Racial Complexities of Southern Society
BERNHARD, DUKE OF SAXE-WEIMAR-EISENACH

In 1828, Bernhard, Duke of the German principality of Saxe-Weimar-Eisenach, published an account of his *Travels . . . Through North America*. Subsequently, Bernhard compiled a distinguished military record in the Royal Dutch Army and then ruled his principality from 1853 until his death in 1862. In this selection, Bernhard describes the racial intricacies of New Orleans society.

In New Orleans we were invited to a subscription ball. These affairs are held twice a week, on Tuesdays and Fridays, in the same hall, the French theater. Only good society is invited to these balls. The first to which we came was not very well attended; but most of the ladies were very nice looking and well turned out in the French manner. Their clothing was elegant after the latest Paris fashions. They danced very well and did credit to their French dancing masters. . . .

The native men are far from matching the women in elegance. And they stayed only a short time, preferring to escape to a so-called "Quarterons Ball" which they find more amusing and where they do not have to stand on ceremony.

A "quarteron" (octoroon) is the offspring of a mestizo mother and a white father, just as the mestizo is the child of a mulatto and a white man. The "quarterons" are almost completely white. There would be no way of recognizing them by their complexion, for they are often fairer than the Creoles. Black hair and eyes are generally the signs of their status, although some are quite blond. The ball is attended by the free "quarterons." Yet the deepest prejudice reigns against them on account of their colored origin; the white women particularly feel or affect to feel a strong repugnance to them.

Marriage between colored and white people is forbidden by the laws of the state.

Yet the "quarterons," for their part, look upon the Negroes and mulattoes as inferiors and are unwilling to mix with them. The girls therefore have no other recourse than to become the mistresses of white men. The "quarterons" regard such attachment as the equivalent of marriage. They would not think of entering upon it other than with a formal contract in which the man engages to pay a stipulated sum to the mother or father of the girl. The latter even assumes the name of her lover and regards the affair with more faithfulness than many a woman whose marriage was sealed in a church.

Some of these women have inherited from their fathers and lovers, and possess considerable fortunes. Their status is nevertheless always very depressed. They must not ride in the street in coaches, and their lovers can bring them to the balls in their own conveyances only after nightfall. They must never sit opposite a white lady, nor may they enter a room without express permission. . . . But many of these girls are much more carefully educated than the whites, behave with more polish and more politeness, and make their lovers happier than white wives their husbands.

SOURCE: C. J. Jeronimus, ed., *Travels by His Highness Duke Bernhard of Saxe-Weimar-Eisenach Through North America in the Years 1825 and 1826*, trans. William Jeronimus (Lanham, MD: University Press of America, 2001), 343, 346–347.

"the *pater-familias*, or head of the family, should, in one sense, be the father of the whole concern, negroes and all."

Taking this ideology to heart, many planters tried to influence their slaves' behavior. Some built cabins for their workers and insisted that the buildings be whitewashed regularly. Many others supervised their slaves' religious lives. They built churches on their plantations, welcomed evangelical preachers, and often required their slaves to attend services. A few planters encouraged African Americans who had spiritual "gifts" to serve as exhorters and deacons. The motives of the slaveowners were mixed. Some acted from sincere Christian belief; others wanted to counter abolitionist criticism or to use religious teachings to control their workers.

Indeed, religion served increasingly as a justification for human bondage. Protestant ministers in the South pointed out that the Hebrews, God's chosen people, had owned slaves and that Jesus Christ had never condemned slavery. As Hammond told a British abolitionist in 1845, "What God ordains and Christ sanctifies should surely command the respect and toleration of man." But many aristocratic apologists were absentee owners or delegated authority to overseers and rarely glimpsed the day-to-day brutality of the slave regime. "I was at the plantation last Saturday and the crop was in fine order," an absentee's son wrote to his father, "but the negroes are most brutally scarred & several have run off."

The Inherent Brutality of Slavery
Like all systems of forced labor, American racial slavery relied on physical coercion. Slave owners and overseers routinely whipped slaves who worked slowly or defied the orders of whites. On occasion, the whip was applied with such ferocity that the slave died or was permanently injured. This photograph of a slave named Gordon stands as graphic testimony to the inherent brutality of the system. National Archives.

There was much less hypocrisy and far less elegance among the second group of elite planters: the market-driven entrepreneurs of the Cotton South. "The glare of expensive luxury vanishes" in the black soil regions of Alabama and Mississippi, John Silk Buckingham noted as he traveled through the Cotton South, and aristocratic paternalism vanished as well. A Mississippi planter put it plainly: "Everything has to give way to large crops of cotton, land has to be cultivated wet or dry, negroes [must] work, hot or cold." Angry at being sold south and pressed to hard labor, many slaves grew "mean" and stubborn. Those who would not labor were subject to the lash. "Whiped all the hoe hands," Alabama planter James Torbert wrote matter-of-factly in his journal. Overseers pushed their workers hard because their salaries often depended on the quantity of cotton they were able "to make for the market." "When I wuz so tired I cu'dnt hardly stan'," a Mississippi slave recalled, "I had to spin my cut of cotton befor' I cu'd go to sleep. We had to card, spin, an' reel at nite."

Cotton was a demanding crop because of its long growing season. Slaves plowed the land in March, dropped seeds into the ground in early April, and, once the plants began to grow, continually chopped away the surrounding grasses. In between these tasks, they planted the corn and peas that would provide food for them and the plantation's hogs and chickens. When the cotton bolls ripened in late August, the long four-month picking season began. Slaves in the Cotton South, concluded traveler Frederick Law Olmsted, worked "much harder and more unremittingly" than those in the tobacco regions. Moreover, fewer slaves acquired craft skills. No coopers were needed to make casks for tobacco or sugar; no engineers were required to build the irrigation systems for the rice fields.

To increase output, profit-conscious cotton planters began during the 1820s to use a rigorous **gang-labor system**. Previously, many planters had either supervised their workers sporadically or assigned them jobs and let them work at their own pace. Now masters with twenty or more slaves organized disciplined teams, or "gangs," supervised by black drivers and white overseers. They instructed the supervisors to work the gangs at a steady pace, clearing and plowing land or hoeing and picking cotton. A traveler in Mississippi described two gangs returning from work:

> First came, led by an old driver carrying a whip, forty of the largest and strongest women I ever saw together; they were all in a simple uniform dress of a bluish check stuff, the skirts reaching little below the knee; . . . they carried themselves loftily, each having a hoe over the shoulder, and walking with a free, powerful swing.

Next marched the plow hands with their mules, "the cavalry, thirty strong, mostly men, but a few of them women." Finally, "a lean and vigilant white overseer, on a brisk pony, brought up the rear."

The cotton planters' quest for profits was enormously successful. Cotton monoculture and the failure to rotate crops on a regular basis depleted the nutrients in the soil and gradually reduced the output per acre. Still, because slaves working in gangs finished as much work in thirty-five minutes as white yeomen planters did in an hour, the gang-labor system produced impressive profits and became ever more prevalent. In one Georgia county, the percentage of slaves working in gangs doubled between 1830 and 1850 and increased further during the 1850s. As the price of raw cotton surged after 1846, the wealth of the planter class exploded in size. It was no wonder: Nearly two million enslaved African Americans now labored on the plantations of the Cotton South and annually produced four million bales of the valuable fiber.

Planters, Smallholding Yeomen, and Tenants

Although the South was a "slave society"—that is, the institution of slavery affected all aspects of life there—most white southerners did not own slaves. The absolute number of slave owners increased constantly between 1800 and 1860, but the white population of the South rose even faster. Consequently, the percentage of white families who held blacks in bondage continually decreased: from 36 percent in 1830, to 31 percent in 1850, to about 25 percent a decade later. However, slave ownership varied by region. In some cotton-rich counties, 40 percent or more of the white families owned slaves; in the hill country near the Appalachian Mountains, the proportion dropped to 10 percent.

Among the privileged minority of 395,000 families who owned slaves in 1860, there was a strict hierarchy. The top one-fifth of these families—a planter elite numbering just 5 percent of the South's white population—owned twenty or more slaves. This elite dominated the economy, owning over 50 percent of the entire slave population of four million and growing 50 percent of the South's cotton crop. The average wealth of these planters was $56,000; by contrast, the average southern yeoman or northern farmer owned property worth a mere $3,200.

Substantial proprietors, another fifth of the slave-owning population, held title to six to twenty slaves. These "middle-class" planters played a significant role in the slave society: They owned almost 40 percent of the African American population and produced more than 30 percent of the cotton. Many owners pursued dual careers as skilled artisans or professional men. For example, many of the fifteen slaves owned by Samuel L. Moore worked in his brick factory; the others labored on his Georgia farm. In Macon County, Alabama, James Tolbert owned a plantation that yielded 50 bales of cotton a year, but Tolbert also ran a sawmill, "which pays as well as making Cotton." Dr. Thomas Gale used the income from his medical practice to buy a Mississippi plantation that annually produced 150 bales of cotton. In Alabama, lawyer Benjamin Fitzpatrick used the profits from his legal practice to buy ten slaves.

Many other lawyers joined Fitzpatrick as slave-owning planters, and some became influential politicians. Throughout the Cotton South, lawyers became wealthy by handling the affairs of elite planters, representing merchants and storekeepers in suits for debt, and settling disputes over property. They became well known by helping smallholders and tenants register their deeds and contracts. Standing at the legal crossroads of their small towns and personally known by many residents, lawyers regularly won election to public office. Fewer than 1 percent of the male population, lawyers made up 16 percent of the Alabama legislature in 1828 and an astounding 26 percent in 1849.

The smallholders who made up the majority of slave owners were much less visible than the wealthy grandees and the lawyer-planters. Because they worked the land themselves, they were similar in some respects to yeomen farmers in the North. These slave owners held from one to five black laborers in bondage and claimed title to a few hundred acres of land. Some smallholders were well-connected young men, who would rise to wealth when their father's death blessed them with more land and slaves. Others were poor but ambitious men trying to pull themselves up by their bootstraps, encouraged to do so by elite planters and proslavery advocates. "Ours is a pro-slavery form of Government, and the pro-slavery element should be increased," declared a Georgia newspaper. "We would like to see every white man at the South the owner of a family of negroes."

Taking this advice to heart, aspiring planters saved or borrowed enough to acquire more land and more laborers. Many achieved modest prosperity. One German settler in Alabama reported in 1855 that "nearly all his countrymen" who emigrated with him were now slaveholders. "They were poor on their arrival in the country; but no sooner did they realize a little money than they invested it in slaves," whose labor made them well-to-do.

Influenced by the patriarchal ideology of the planter class, yeomen farmers ruled their smallholdings with a firm hand. According to a South Carolina judge, the male head of the household had authority over all the dependents — wives, children, and slaves — and the legal right on his property "to be as churlish as he pleases." The wives of southern yeomen had very little power; like women in the North, they lost their legal identity when they married. Looking for ways to express their concerns and interests, southern women turned to religion and usually outnumbered male church members by a ratio of two to one. Women welcomed the message of spiritual equality preached in Evangelical Baptist and Methodist churches, and they hoped that the church community would hold their husbands to the same standards of Christian behavior to which they were held. But most churches supported patriarchal rule and told female members to remain in "wifely obedience," whatever the actions of their husbands.

Lords of their own households, most southern yeomen nevertheless lived and died hardscrabble farmers. They worked alongside their slaves in the fields, struggled to make ends meet as their families grew, and moved regularly in search of opportunity. In 1847, James Buckner Barry left North Carolina with his new wife and two slaves to settle in Bosque County, Texas. There, he worked part-time as an Indian fighter while his slaves toiled on a drought-ridden farm that barely kept the family in food. In South Carolina, W. J. Simpson struggled for years as a smallholding cotton planter and then gave up. He hired out one of his two slaves and went to work as an overseer on his father's farm.

Other smallholders fell from the privileged ranks of the slave-owning classes. Having sold their land and slaves to pay off debts, they joined the large group of propertyless tenants who farmed the estates of wealthy landlords. In 1860, in Hancock County, Georgia, there were 56 slave-owning planters and 300 propertyless white farm laborers and factory workers; in nearby Hart County, 25 percent of the white farmers were tenants. Across the South, about 40 percent of the white population worked as tenants or farm laborers; as the *Southern Cultivator* observed, they had "no legal right nor interest in the soil [and] no homes of their own."

Propertyless whites enjoyed few of the benefits of slavery and suffered many of the same ill consequences. Because hard labor was deemed fit only for enslaved blacks, white workers received little respect. Nor could they hope for a better life for their children, because planters refused to pay taxes to fund public schools. Moreover, wealthy planters bid up the price of slaves, depriving white laborers and tenants of easy access to the slave labor required to accumulate wealth. Finally, planter-dominated legislatures forced all white men — whether they owned slaves or not — to serve in the patrols and militias that deterred black uprisings. For their sacrifices, poor whites gained only the psychological satisfaction that they ranked above blacks. As Alfred Iverson, a U.S. senator from Georgia, explained: A white man "walks erect in the dignity of his color and race, and feels that he is a superior being, with the more exalted powers and privileges than others." To reinforce this sense of racial and social superiority, planter James Henry Hammond told his poor white neighbors, "In a slave country every freeman is an aristocrat."

Rejecting that half-truth, many southern whites fled planter-dominated counties and sought farms in the Appalachian hill country and beyond — in western Virginia, Kentucky, Tennessee, Missouri, and the southern regions of Illinois and Indiana. Living as yeomen farmers, they used family labor to grow foodstuffs for sustenance. To obtain cash or store credit to buy agricultural implements, cloth, shoes, salt, and other necessities, yeomen families sold their surplus crops, raised hogs for market sale, and — when the price of cotton rose sharply in the 1850s — grew a few bales. Their goals were modest: On the family level, they wanted to preserve their holdings and buy enough land to set up their children as small-scale farmers. As citizens, smallholders wanted to control their local government and elect men of their own kind to public office. But thoughtful yeomen realized that the cotton revolution had undercut the democratic potential of the Revolutionary era and sentenced family farmers to a subordinate place in the southern social order. They could hope for a life of independence and dignity only by moving north or farther west, where labor was "free" and hard work was respectable.

The Politics of Democracy

Despite their economic and social prominence, the slave-owning elite could not easily control the political life of the Cotton South. Unlike the planter-aristocrats of the eighteenth century, they lived in a republican society with representative institutions. The Alabama Constitution of 1819 granted suffrage to all white men. It also provided for a **secret ballot**; apportionment based on population; and the election of county supervisors, sheriffs, and clerks of court. Given these democratic provisions, political factions in Alabama had to compete with one another for popular favor. When a Whig newspaper sarcastically asked whether the state's policies should "be governed and controlled by the whim and caprice of the majority of the people," Democrats stood forth as champions of the common folk whose hands were callused from hard work. They called on "Farmers, Mechanics, laboring men" to repudiate Whig "aristocrats . . . the soft handed and soft headed gentry."

To curry favor among voters, Alabama Democrats chose candidates and policies that would command popular support, such as low taxes. Their Whig opponents favored higher taxes in order to provide government subsidies for banks, canals, roads, and other internal improvements; but they also turned to candidates who appealed to the common people. Most candidates from both parties were men of substance. In the early 1840s, nearly 90 percent of Alabama's legislators owned slaves, testimony to the power of the slave-owning minority. But relatively few lawmakers—only about 10 percent—were rich planters, a group voters by and large distrusted. "A rich man cannot sympathize with the poor," declared one candidate. Consequently, the majority of elected state officials and most county officials in the Cotton South came from the ranks of middle-class planters and planter-lawyers.

Whatever their social rank, Alabama's legislators usually enacted policies that reflected the interests of the slave-owning population. However, they took care not to anger the mass of yeomen farmers and propertyless whites by favoring too many expensive measures, such as the public works projects that the Whigs favored. "Voting against appropriations is the safe and popular side," one senator declared, and his colleagues agreed; until the 1850s, they rejected most of the bills that would have granted subsidies to railroads, canals, and banks. They also refrained from laying "oppressive" taxes on the people, particularly the poor white majority who owned no slaves. Between 1830 and 1860, the Alabama legislature obtained about 70 percent of the state's revenue from taxes on slaves and land. Another 10 to 15 percent came from levies on carriages, gold watches, and other luxury goods and on the capital invested in banks, transportation companies, and manufacturing enterprises.

If taxes in Alabama had a democratic thrust, those elsewhere in the South did not. In some states, wealthy planters used their political influence to exempt slave property from taxation. And they shifted the burden of land taxes to backcountry yeomen by taxing farms on the basis of acreage rather than value. Planter-legislators also spared themselves the cost of building fences around their crops by enacting laws that required yeomen to fence in their livestock. Moreover, during the 1850s, wealthy legislators throughout the South used public funds to subsidize the canals and railroads in which they had invested.

Seen from one perspective, these government subsidies were desperately needed. Even as the top 10 percent of the white population grew rich from the cotton, rice, tobacco, and sugar produced by their slaves, the economic well-being of ordinary southerners—white and black—did not improve significantly. In fact, the South's standard of living fell behind that of the North. Both in 1840 and in 1860, the per capita wealth of the South was only 80 percent of the national average, while that in the industrializing Northeast was 139 percent of the average.

This comparison between the South and the Northeast tells only part of the story. If the South had been a separate nation in 1860, its economy would have been the fourth most prosperous in the world, with a per capita income higher than that of France and Germany. As a contributor to a Georgia newspaper argued in the 1850s, it was beside the point to complain about "tariffs, and merchants, and manufacturers" because "the most highly prosperous people now on earth, are to be found in these very [slave] States."

The paradox is that this judgment was both right and wrong. Many white southerners did enjoy higher living standards than other peoples of the world, but most African Americans—30 percent of the population—lived in dire and permanent poverty. Perceptive southerners recognized that their plantation-based economy and slave system failed to provide rising incomes for the majority of the population. Pointing to South Carolina's fixation on an "exclusive and exhausting" system of agriculture, textile entrepreneur William Gregg asked, "Who can look forward to the future destiny of our State . . . without dark forebodings?" Other leaders acknowledged the South's predicament but blamed it on outsiders: "Purely agricultural people," intoned planter-politician James Henry Hammond, "have been in all ages the victims of rapacious tyrants grinding them down."

Such thinking discouraged purposeful private or government action that might have created a more diversified economy. Wealthy southerners continued to invest in land and slaves, a strategy that brought substantial short-run profits from the booming cotton market but diverted capital resources and entrepreneurial energies from more productive forms of economic activity. In particular, southerners failed to take advantage of the technological innovations of the nineteenth century—water- and steam-powered factories, machine tools, steel plows, and crushed-gravel roads, for example—that would have raised the region's productivity. Urban growth, the key to prosperity in Europe and the North, occurred mostly in the commercial cities around the periphery of the South: New Orleans, St. Louis, and Baltimore. Factories, often staffed by slave labor, likewise appeared primarily in the Chesapeake region, which had already diversified its economy and had a surplus of bound workers. Within the Cotton South, a few wealthy planters invested in railroads but only to open up new lands for commercial farming; when the Western & Atlantic Railroad reached the Georgia upcountry, the cotton crop quickly doubled. Cotton—and agriculture—remained "King."

Slavery worked in yet another way to deter industrialization. Fearing competition from slave labor, European immigrants refused to settle in the South. Their absence deprived the region of hardworking families and of laborers who could have drained swamps, dug canals, smelted iron, and worked on railroads. When entrepreneurs tried to hire slaves for such tasks, planters said that "a negro's life is too valuable to be risked" at the dangerous work. Other slave owners feared that being hired out would make their slaves too independent. As a planter explained to Frederick Law Olmsted, such workers "had too much liberty . . . and got a habit of roaming about and taking care of themselves."

Despite the enormous expansion in the territory and exports of the South between 1800 and 1860, it remained an economic colony: Great Britain and the North bought its staple crops and provided its manufactures, financial services, and shipping facilities. In 1860, most southerners—some 84 percent—still worked in agriculture, more than double the percentage in the northern states; and southern factories turned out only 10 percent of the nation's manufactured goods. Textile entrepreneur William Gregg lamented that the combination of cotton and slavery had been to the South

▶ How would you explain the large and expanding domestic trade in slaves between 1800 and 1860? What combination of factors produced this result?

▶ By 1860, what different groups made up the South's increasingly complex society? How did these groups interact in the political arena?

what the [gold and silver] mines of Mexico were to Spain. It has produced us such an abundant supply of all the luxuries and elegances of life, with so little exertion on our part, that we have become enervated, unfitted for other and more laborious pursuits.

The African American World

By the 1820s, the cultural life of most slaves consisted of a complex blend of African and American influences. It reflected both the values and customs of their West African ancestors and the language, laws, and religious beliefs of the dominant white society. This mix of cultural values persisted for decades, both because whites discouraged blacks from assimilating into their society and because slaves prized many aspects of their African heritage.

Evangelical Black Protestantism

The appearance of Black Christianity exemplified the synthesis in the United States of African and European cultures. Evangelical Protestantism came to the white South with the Second Great Awakening between 1790 and 1840. Baptist and Methodist preachers converted thousands of white families and hundreds of enslaved blacks (see Chapter 8). Until that time, African-born blacks, often identifiable by their ritual scars, had maintained the religious practices of their homelands: Some practiced Islam, but the majority called on African gods and spirits. As late as 1842, Charles C. Jones, a Presbyterian minister, noted that the blacks on his family's plantation in Georgia believed "in second-sight, in apparitions, charms, witchcraft . . . [and other] superstitions brought from Africa." Fearing "the consequences" for their own souls if they withheld "the means of salvation from them," Jones and other zealous white Protestant preachers and planters set out to save African American souls for Christ.

Other Protestant crusaders came from the ranks of pious black men and women. Converted to Christianity in the Chesapeake and then swept off to the Cotton South by the domestic slave trade, they carried the evangelical message of emotional conversion, ritual baptism, and communal spirituality with them. Equally important, they adapted Protestant doctrines to black needs. Enslaved Christians pointed out that masters and slaves were all "children of God" and should be dealt with according to the Golden Rule: Treat others as you would be treated by them. Moreover, black preachers generally ignored the doctrines of original sin and predestination as well as biblical passages that encouraged unthinking obedience to authority. A white minister in Liberty County, Georgia, reported that when he urged slaves to obey their masters, "one half of my audience deliberately rose up and walked off."

Indeed, many African American converts envisioned the deity as the Old Testament warrior who had liberated the Jews and saw themselves as Chosen People: "de people dat is born of God." Charles Davenport, a Mississippi slave, recalled black preachers' "exhort[ing] us dat us was the chillum o' Israel in de wilderness an' de Lawd done sont us to take dis lan' o' milk an' honey." It was a vision of Christ that impelled Nat Turner to lead a bloody rebellion against slavery in Virginia (see Chapter 11).

As successive generations of slaves worshipped a European Christian god, they continued to express their religiosity in distinctively African ways. The thousands of African Americans who joined the Methodist Church respected its ban on profane dancing but praised the Lord in the African-derived "ring shout." Minister Henry George Spaulding explained the "religious dance of the Negroes" this way:

> Three or four, standing still, clapping their hands and beating time with their feet, commence singing in unison one of the peculiar shout melodies, while the others walk around in a ring, in single file, joining also in the song.

The songs themselves were usually collective creations, devised spontaneously from bits of old hymns and tunes. Recalled an ex-slave:

> We'd all be at the "prayer house" de Lord's day, and de white preacher he'd splain de word and read whar Esekial done say—*Dry bones gwine ter lib ergin.* And, honey, de Lord would come a-shinin' thoo dem pages and revive dis ole nigger's heart, and I'd jump up dar and den and holler and shout and sing and pat, and dey would all cotch de words and I'd sing it to some ole shout song I'd heard 'em sing from Africa, and dey'd all take it up and keep at it, and keep a-addin' to it, and den it would be a spiritual.

By such African-influenced means, black congregations devised a distinctive and joyous brand of Protestant worship to sustain them on the long journey to emancipation and the Promised Land. "O my Lord delivered Daniel," the slaves sang, "O why not deliver me too?"

Forging Families and Creating Culture

Black Protestantism was one facet of an increasingly homogeneous African American culture in the rural South. Even in South Carolina, a major point of entry for imported slaves, only 20 percent of the black residents in 1820 had been born in Africa. The transfer of slaves into the Lower Mississippi Valley encouraged the decline of regional practices and the emergence of a core black culture. A prime example was the fate of the Gullah dialect (see Chapter 3). Long spoken by residents of the Carolina low country, Gullah did not take root on the cotton plantations of Alabama and Mississippi, because there were many more speakers of the black English spoken in the Chesapeake. Black English, like Gullah, used double-negatives and other African grammatical forms but consisted primarily of English words rendered with a West African pronunciation (for example, with "th" spoken as "d," as in "de preacher").

As the black population was becoming more culturally homogeneous, African influences remained important. At least one-third of the slaves who entered the United States between 1776 and 1809 came from the Congo region of West-Central Africa, and they brought their culture with them. As traveler Isaac Holmes reported in 1821, "In Louisiana, and the state of Mississippi, the slaves . . . dance for several hours during Sunday afternoon. The general movement is in what they call the Congo dance." Similar descriptions of blacks who "danced the Congo and sang a purely African song to the accompaniment of . . . a drum" appeared as late as 1890.

African Americans also continued to respect African incest taboos by shunning marriages between cousins. On the Good Hope Plantation on the Santee River in South Carolina, nearly half of the slave children born between 1800 and 1857 were related by blood to one another; yet when they married, only one union (out of forty-one) took place between cousins. This taboo was not learned from their white owners: Among the 440 South Carolina men and women who owned at least one hundred slaves in 1860, cousin marriages were frequent, in part because they kept wealth and political power within an extended family.

Unlike white marriages, slave unions were not recognized by law. Southern legislatures and courts prohibited legal marriages among slaves so that their sale would not break a legal bond. Still, many African Americans had their marriages performed by Christian ministers. Others publicly marked their married state by following the African custom of jumping over a broomstick together. Once married, young couples in the Cotton South who had been seized from their parents in the Chesapeake region often adopted older slaves in their new communities as their "aunts" and "uncles." The slave trade had destroyed their family but not their family values.

The creation of such fictive kinship ties was part of a complex community-building process. Naming children was another. Recently imported slaves frequently

Antebellum Slave Quarters
During the colonial period, owners often housed their slaves in communal barracks by gender. In the nineteenth century, slaves usually lived in family units in separate cabins. The slave huts on this South Carolina plantation were sturdily built but had few windows. Inside, they were sparsely furnished. William Gladstone.

gave their children African names. Males who were born on Friday, for example, were often called Cuffee—the name of that day in several West African languages. Many American-born parents chose names of British origin, but they usually named sons after fathers, uncles, or grandfathers and daughters after grandmothers. Those who were transported to the Cotton South often named their children for relatives they had left behind. Like incest rules and marriage rituals, this intergenerational sharing of names evoked memories of a lost world and solidified kin ties in the present one.

Negotiating Rights

By forming stable families and strong communities, African Americans gradually created a sense of order in the harsh and arbitrary world of slavery. In a few regions, slaves won substantial control over their lives. Blacks in the rice-growing lowlands of South Carolina successfully asserted the right to labor by the "task" rather than to work under constant supervision. Each day, task workers had to complete a precisely defined job—for example, turn over a quarter-acre of land, hoe half an acre, or pound seven mortars of rice. By working hard, many finished their tasks "by one or two o'clock in the afternoon," a Methodist preacher reported, and had "the rest of the day for themselves, which they spend in working their own private fields . . . planting rice, corn, potatoes, tobacco &c. for their own use and profit." Slaves on sugar and cotton plantations were less fortunate. The gang-labor system imposed a regimented work schedule, and many owners prohibited slaves from growing crops on their own. "It gives an excuse for trading," explained one slave owner, and that encouraged roaming and independence.

Planters worried constantly that enslaved African Americans—a majority of the population in most counties of the Cotton South—would rise in rebellion. They knew that, legally speaking, masters had virtually unlimited power over their slaves. Justice Thomas Ruffin of the North Carolina Supreme Court wrote in a decision in 1829: "The power of the master must be absolute to render the submission of the slave perfect." But absolute power required unremitting and brutal coercion, and only the most hardened or most sadistic masters had the stomach for that. Some southern whites wanted no part of such violence. "These poor negroes, receiving none of the fruits of their labor, do not love work," explained one farm woman, "if we had slaves, we should have to . . . beat them to make use of them."

Moreover, passive resistance by African Americans seriously limited the power of their owners. Slaves slowed the pace of work by feigning illness and "losing" or breaking tools. Some blacks insisted that people be sold "in families." One Maryland slave, faced with transport to Mississippi and separation from his wife, "neither yields consent to accompany my people, or to be exchanged or sold," his owner reported. Because of the bonds of community among African Americans in the Chesapeake and Carolinas and the increasing black majorities in the Gulf states, masters ignored slaves' feelings at their peril. A slave (or his relatives) might retaliate by setting fire to the master's house and barns, poisoning the white family's food, or destroying crops or equipment. Fear of resistance, as well as the increasingly critical scrutiny of abolitionists, prompted many masters to reduce their reliance on the lash. Instead, they tried to devise "a wholesome and well regulated system" of work discipline by using positive incentives such as food and special privileges to manage their laborers. As Frederick Law Olmsted noted, "Men of sense have discovered that it was better to offer them rewards than to whip them." Nonetheless, owners always had the option of resorting to violence, and many masters continued to satisfy themselves sexually by raping their female slaves.

Slavery remained an exploitative system grounded in fear and coercion. Over the decades, hundreds of individual slaves responded to this violence by attacking their masters and overseers. Blacks such as Gabriel and Martin Prosser in Virginia (1800) plotted mass uprisings, but only a few—among them, Nat Turner (1831)—mounted revolts that took revenge on their white captors. Most slaves recognized that uprisings would be futile; they lacked the strong institutions—such as the communes of free peasants or serfs in Europe, for example—needed to organize a successful rebellion. Moreover, whites were numerous, well armed, and determined to maintain their position of racial superiority (see American Voices, p. 372).

Escape was equally problematic. Blacks in the Upper South could flee to the North, but that meant leaving their family and kin. Slaves in the Lower South could seek freedom in Spanish Florida until 1819, when the United States annexed that territory. Even then, hundreds of blacks continued to flee to Florida, where they intermarried with the Seminole Indians. Elsewhere in the South, small groups of escaped slaves eked out a meager existence in deserted marshy areas or mountain valleys.

Given these limited options, most slaves chose to build the best possible lives for themselves on the plantations where they lived. To do so, they gradually evolved a positive mode of resistance by demanding—and, in many cases, winning—a greater share of the product of their labor, much as unionized workers in the North were trying to do. Thus, slaves insisted on getting paid for "overwork" and on their right to cultivate a garden and sell its produce. "De menfolks tend to de gardens round dey own house," recalled a Louisiana slave. "Dey raise some cotton and sell it to massa and git li'l money dat way." That money was theirs to do with as they wished. An Alabama slave remembered buying "Sunday clothes with dat money, sech as hats and pants and shoes and dresses." By the 1850s, thousands of African Americans were reaping the rewards of this underground economy. But even as their material circumstances improved, few slaves accepted the legitimacy of their fate. Although he was well fed and never whipped, a former slave explained to an English traveler, he knew he had been oppressed: "I was cruelly treated because I was kept in slavery."

The Free Black Population

Some African Americans managed to escape slavery through flight or manumission. The proportion of free blacks rose from 8 percent of the African American population in 1790 to about 13 percent between 1820 and 1840 and then fell to 11 percent by 1860. Of all free blacks in 1840 (some 386,000) and again in 1860 (488,000), nearly half lived in the North. Many of these African Americans were refugees from the South—either runaway slaves or, more often, free blacks who feared reenslavement.

Few free blacks in the North enjoyed unfettered freedom. Most whites regarded African Americans as their social inferiors and did all they could to confine blacks to low-paying jobs. In rural areas, free blacks worked as farm laborers or tenant farmers; in towns and cities, they toiled as domestic servants, laundresses, or day laborers. Only a small number of free African Americans owned land. "You do not see one out of a

Memories of Slavery   MOLLIE DAWSON

Mollie Dawson was born into slavery in 1852 in Texas, to which her owner had migrated from Tennessee. When Dawson told her story to the Writers' Project of the Work Projects Administration in the 1930s, she was eighty-five years old.

Mah maw was de slave of Nath Newman and dat made me his slave. Mah maw's name was Sarah Benjamin. Mah father's name was Carrol Benjamin, and he belonged ter different white folks. . . .

Mah mother and father was slavery time married darkies. Dat didn't mean nuthin' dem days, but jest raisin' mo' darkies, and every slave darkie woman had ter do dat whether she wanted to or not. Dey would let her pick out a man, or a man pick him out a woman, and dey was married, and if de woman wouldn't have de man dat picks her, dey would take her ter a big stout high husky nigger somewhere and leave her a few days, jest lak dey do stock now'days, and she bettah begin raisin' chilluns, too. . . .

Mah mother and father never did love each other lak dey ought to, so dey separated as soon as dey was free. Mah father married another woman by law. Mah mother married George Baldwin, and dey lives together fer about twelve years. Dey separated den, and she married Alfred Alliridge and dey lives together till she dies. . . .

I was too young ter do much work durin' slavery time, but I picks lots of cotton, and all de pay we got fer it was a place ter stay, water ter drink, wood ter burn, food ter eat, and clothes ter wear, and we made de food and clothes ourselves. We eats corn pones three times a day, 'ceptin' Sunday and Christmas mornings; Maser Newman lets us have flour fer biscuits, den.

In de summah we wore cotton clothes. All of dem was made on de plantation. Some of de women would spin and some would weave and some would make clothes. . . .

Maser Newman was a tall, slender man nearly six foot tall and was blue-eyed. He sho' was good ter all us slaves, but we all knew he means fer us ter work. He never whipped any of us slaves, but he hit one of de men wid a leather line 'bout two times once, 'cause dis slave kinda talked back ter him. . . .

Maser Newman was a slow easy-goin' sort of a man who took everything as it comes, takin' bad and good luck jest alak. . . . Maser Newman was lots older dan his wife. She was a real young woman, and they 'peared ter think quite a bit of each other. . . . Maser and Missus Newman jest had two chilluns and both of dem was little girls. . . . Dey sho' was pretty little gals and dey was smart, too. Dey played wid de little slave chilluns all de time, and course dey was de boss, same as deir mother and father.

Maser Newman was a poor man, compared wid some of de other slave owners. He only had about seven slaves big enough ter work all de year round in de fields. . . . He didn't have no drivah; he would jest start dem all out ter work, and dey kept at it all day. But he generally worked around pretty close ter dem.

SOURCE: James Mellon, ed., *Bullwhip Days* (New York: Weidenfeld & Nicolson, 1988), 421–428.

A Master Bridge Builder
Horace King (1807–1885) was
a self-made man of color, a rare
achievement in the nineteenth-
century South. Born a slave of
mixed European, African, and Native
American (Catawba) ancestry, King
built major bridges in Georgia,
Alabama, and Mississippi during
the early 1840s. After winning his
freedom in 1846, he built and ran a
toll bridge across the Chattahoochee
River in Alabama. During the Civil
War, King worked as a contractor
for the Confederacy; during
Reconstruction, he served two terms
as a Republican in the Alabama
House of Representatives. Collection of
the Columbus Museum, Columbus, Georgia;
Museum Purchase.

hundred . . . that can make a comfortable living, own a cow, or a horse," a traveler in
New Jersey noted. In addition, northern blacks were usually forbidden to vote, attend
public schools, or sit next to whites in churches. Only a few states extended the vote to
free blacks, and blacks could testify against whites in court only in Massachusetts. The
federal government did not allow free African Americans to work for the postal service,
claim public lands, or hold a U.S. passport. As black activist Martin Delaney remarked
in 1852, "We are slaves in the midst of freedom."

Of the few African Americans who were able to make full use of their talents,
several achieved great distinction. Mathematician and surveyor Benjamin Banneker
(1731–1806) published an almanac and helped to lay out the new capital in the District of Columbia; Joshua Johnston (1765–1832) won praise for his portraiture; and
merchant Paul Cuffee (1759–1817) acquired a small fortune from his business enterprises. More impressive and enduring were the community institutions that the
early generations of free African Americans created. Throughout the North, these
largely unknown men and women founded schools, mutual-benefit organizations,
and fellowship groups, often called Free African Societies. Discriminated against by
white Protestants, they formed their own congregations and a new religious denomination: the African Methodist Episcopal Church, headed by Bishop Richard Allen
(see Chapter 8).

These institutions gave free African Americans a sense of cultural autonomy. They
also institutionalized sharp social divisions within the black community. "Respectable"
blacks tried, through their dress, conduct, and attitude, to win the "esteem and patronage" of prominent whites—first Federalists and then Whigs and abolitionists—who

were sympathetic to their cause. Such efforts separated these blacks from their impoverished fellows, who distrusted both whites and blacks who "acted white."

In the slave states the free black population numbered approximately 94,000 in 1810 and 245,000 in 1860. Most of these men and women lived in coastal cities—Mobile, Memphis, New Orleans—and in the Upper South. In Maryland on the eve of the Civil War, half of the black population was free, and many more were "term" slaves, guaranteed their freedom in exchange for a few more years of work. But free blacks faced many dangers. Those accused of crimes were often denied a jury trial, and those charged with vagrancy were sometimes forced back into slavery. To prove their free status, African Americans had to carry manumission documents, which did not protect them from being kidnapped and sold. However, because skilled Europeans generally would not migrate to the South, free blacks formed the backbone of the region's urban artisan workforce. African American carpenters, blacksmiths, barbers, butchers, and shopkeepers played prominent roles in the economies of Baltimore, Richmond, Charleston, and New Orleans.

As a privileged group among African Americans, free blacks had divided loyalties. To advance the welfare of their families, they were tempted to distance themselves from plantation slaves and absorb white culture and values. Some privileged blacks adopted the perspective of the planter class. David Barland, one of twelve children born to a white Mississippi planter and his black slave Elizabeth, owned no fewer than eighteen slaves. In neighboring Louisiana, some free blacks supported secession because they "own slaves and are dearly attached to their native land."

These men were exceptions. Most free African Americans acknowledged their ties to the great mass of slaves, some of whom were their relatives. "We's different [from whites] in color, in talk and in 'ligion and beliefs," said one. White planters reinforced unity among blacks by justifying slavery as a "positive good" and, in the 1840s and 1850s, by calling for the reenslavement of free African Americans. Knowing that their own liberty was not secure as long as slavery existed, free blacks sought liberty for everyone of African ancestry. As a delegate to the National Convention of Colored People in 1848 noted, "Our souls are yet dark under the pall of slavery." In the rigid caste system of American race relations, free blacks stood as symbols of hope to enslaved African Americans and as symbols of danger to most whites.

► Why do certain African practices (the ring shout and incest taboos, for example) persist in the United States, and why have others (such as ritual scarring) disappeared?

► What were the successes of African Americans in building families, creating a culture, and winning rights? In what endeavors did they not succeed?

► Why in 1860 did white southerners remain committed to the institution of slavery and its expansion?

SUMMARY

In this chapter, we have focused on the theme of an expanding South. Beginning about 1800, the plantation system expanded from its traditional home in the Upper South to the Mississippi Valley and beyond. Powered by cotton, this movement westward divided the planter elite into aristocratic paternalists and entrepreneurial capitalists and involved the forced migration of more than one million enslaved African Americans.

We also examined the character of white and black societies in the Cotton South. After 1820, fewer than one-third of white families owned slaves, and another third were yeomen farmers; propertyless tenant farmers and laborers made up the rest. Many whites joined Evangelical Protestant churches, as did blacks, who infused their churches with African modes of expression. Indeed, church and family became core institutions of African American society, providing strength and solace amid the tribulations of slavery.

Connections: Society and Culture

Following the Tobacco and Rice Revolutions around 1700 and the importation of thousands of enslaved Africans, the South became a dual society. People of English and African ancestry shared geographical space but little else. As we discovered in Chapter 3, they spoke different languages, worshipped different gods, and had a different legal status. Coercion — forced work and forced sex — characterized most interactions between the two peoples.

This dual society began to break down during the Revolutionary era (see Chapter 8). By 1780, most slaves had been born in America, and most spoke English; some had become Christians; and thousands would soon become free, the result of gradual emancipation in the North and individual manumissions in the Chesapeake region. Coercion remained a potent force, but as masters and slaves negotiated work rules, the use of physical force became a measure of last resort. Thus, as we noted in the essay that opened Part Three, it was not surprising that "southern planters increasingly defended slavery as a 'positive good'" and considered slaves to be a part of their extended family.

Of course, as we saw in this chapter, the behavior of most planters contradicted their words. They callously sold hundreds of thousands of African Americans and treated black members of their "families" far differently than they did their white kin. Still, the social and cultural differences between the two peoples continued to diminish. By the 1840s, slaves spoke black English, practiced black Protestantism, and were on their way to becoming a black peasantry — a dependent agricultural people similar to the oppressed peasant peoples of Ireland and Central Europe. Indeed, as we shall see in Chapter 15, the abolition of slavery and the events of Reconstruction (1865–1877) would leave most African Americans as poor sharecroppers, a peasantry in fact if not in name.

FOR FURTHER EXPLORATION

Studies of slave owners include Charlene M. Boyer Lewis, *Ladies and Gentlemen on Display: Planter Society at the Virginia Springs, 1790–1860* (2001); William Kauffman Scarborough, *Masters of the Big House* (2003); Jeffrey Robert Young, *Domesticating Slavery: The Master Class in Georgia and South Carolina, 1670–1837* (1999); and James David Miller, *South by Southwest: Planter Emigration and Identity* (2002). On plantation discipline and resistance, see Sally E. Hadden, *Slave Patrols: Law and Violence in Virginia and the Carolinas* (2001), and John Hope Franklin and Loren Sweninger, *Runaway Slaves, Rebels on the Plantation* (1999). Edward Ball discusses his slaveholding ancestors in *Slaves in the Family* (1998). Stephanie McCurry's *Masters of Small Worlds* (1995) offers fine analysis of southern yeomen families.

TIMELINE

1810s ▶ Africans from Congo region influence black culture

▶ Natural increase produces surplus of slaves in Old South

▶ Domestic slave trade expands, disrupting black family life

1812 ▶ Louisiana becomes a state; its sugar production increases

1817 ▶ Mississippi admitted to the Union; Alabama follows (1819)

1820s ▶ Substantial growth in free black population in North and South

▶ Slave-owning aristocrats in Old South adopt paternalistic ideology

▶ Entrepreneurial planters in Cotton South turn to gang labor

▶ Southern Methodists and Baptists become socially conservative

▶ More African Americans adopt Christian beliefs

1830s ▶ Defenders of slavery argue it is a "positive good"

▶ Boom in cotton production

▶ Percentage of slave-owning families falls

▶ Slaves in Deep South develop strong families and core culture

▶ Yeomen farm families in South retreat to hill country

▶ Lawyers become influential in southern politics

1840s ▶ Southern Whigs advocate economic diversification

▶ Gradual emancipation completed in North

1850s ▶ Price of slaves and cotton rises; production expands

▶ Underground black economy grows

▶ Southern states subsidize railroads, but industrialization remains limited

Ira Berlin's *Generations of Captivity* (2003) details the changing character of slavery and African American society. See also "Slavery and the Making of America" at **www.pbs.org/wnet/slavery/about/index.html** and "The Church in the Southern Black Community" at **docsouth.unc.edu/church/index.html**. Marcus Wood, *Blind Memory: Visual Representations of Slavery in England and America, 1780–1865* (2000), and Walter Johnson, *Soul by Soul: Life Inside the Antebellum Slave Market* (1999), are important studies. Two document-rich Web sites are "The African-American Mosaic" at **www.loc.gov/exhibits/african/intro.html** and "Slaves and the Courts, 1740–1860" at **lcweb2.loc.gov/ammem/aaohtml/**.

TEST YOUR KNOWLEDGE

To assess your mastery of the material in this chapter and for Web sites, images, and documents related to this chapter, visit **bedfordstmartins.com/henrettaconcise**.

The Crisis of the Union
1844–1860

> This government was made by our fathers, by white men for the benefit of white men and their posterity forever.
>
> — Illinois Senator Stephen Douglas, 1858

Throughout the nation during the 1850s, crusaders for temperance and abolition battled defenders of personal liberties and property rights. The struggle in South Carolina was especially intense. When temperance activists demanded a "Maine law" to prohibit the sale of intoxicants, Randolph Turner, a candidate for the South Carolina assembly, was outraged: "Legislation upon Liquor would cast a shade on my character which as a Caucassian [sic] and a white man, I am not willing to bear." Indeed, Turner vowed to shoulder his musket and, with "hundreds of men in this district, . . . fight for individual rights, as well as State Rights."

In Washington, South Carolina Congressman Preston Brooks battled for "Southern Rights." In an inflammatory speech in 1856, Senator Charles Sumner of Massachusetts denounced the South and, mixing invective with metaphor, declared that Senator Andrew P. Butler of South Carolina had taken "the harlot slavery" as his mistress. Outraged by Sumner's verbal attack on his uncle, Brooks accosted the Massachusetts legislator in the Senate chamber and beat him unconscious with a walking cane. As the impact of Brooks's attack reverberated throughout Washington and the nation, Axalla Hoole of South Carolina and other proslavery migrants in the Kansas Territory leveled their guns at an armed force of abolitionist settlers. Passion and violence had replaced political compromise as the hallmark of American public life.

The upsurge in political violence in the 1850s had complex roots. The immediate catalyst was the admission of Texas to the Union in 1845 and the acquisition of vast territories from Mexico in 1848. But the fuel for the fire was the increasing friction between the northern and southern states and the South's alarm about the potential consequences of this animosity. As John C. Calhoun told the Senate in 1850, white southerners feared the North's increasing wealth, political power, and moral righteousness, especially its "long-continued agitation of the slavery question."

A population surge in the West added another dimension to this sectional conflict. Inspired by the nation's growing population and wealth, many Americans supported the idea of **Manifest Destiny**, believing that it was their duty to extend republican institutions to the Pacific Ocean. But whose republican institutions: the aristocratic traditions of the slaveholding South or the more democratic customs of the reform-minded North and Midwest? Beginning in 1844, leading politicians in the North, South, and West addressed this question. The task of answering it was much more difficult than they expected or had the political sagacity to resolve. Ultimately, their failures would rip the nation apart.

Manifest Destiny: South and North

The crisis over slavery in Missouri in 1819 (see Chapter 8) threw a fright into the nation's politicians. For the next two decades, the professional politicians who managed the Second Party System avoided policies that would lead to another such regional confrontation. This strategy worked as long as the geographical boundaries of the United States remained unchanged. But during the 1840s, as the ideology of Manifest Destiny led Americans toward the Pacific Ocean, the threat of a new clash loomed large.

The Independence of Texas

By the 1830s, settlers from the Ohio River Valley and the South had carried both yeoman farming and plantation slavery into Arkansas and Missouri. Between those states and the Rocky Mountains stretched the semiarid lands of the Great Plains. An army explorer, Major Stephen H. Long, thought the area "almost wholly unfit for cultivation" and called it the Great American Desert. Settlers looking for land therefore turned south, to the Mexican province of Texas.

Texas was occupied primarily by Indian peoples, but it had long been a zone of European conflict. In the eighteenth century, Spanish authorities in Mexico had installed a military garrison in Texas to deter the French in Louisiana from moving into the region. After the Louisiana Purchase (1803), the Spanish worried that Americans would migrate into Texas. However, the Adams-Onís Treaty of 1819 guaranteed Spanish sovereignty over the region.

After winning independence from Spain in 1821, the Mexican government encouraged the settlement of Texas by offering land grants both to its own citizens and to Americans. One early grantee was Moses Austin, an American land speculator who settled white tenants and smallholding farmers on his vast estate. His son, Stephen F. Austin, acquired even more land from the Mexican government—some 180,000 acres—which he sold to incoming settlers. These American residents resisted assimilation into Mexican society. In 1829, Austin and other grantees requested—and won—an exemption from a law that ended slavery in Mexico. By 1835, about 27,000 white Americans and 3,000 African American slaves were raising cotton and cattle in eastern and central Texas. They far outnumbered the

3,000 Mexican residents, who lived primarily near the western towns of Goliad and San Antonio.

When the Mexican government asserted greater political control over Texas in the 1830s, the Americans split into two groups. Members of the "peace party," led by Stephen Austin and other longtime settlers, accepted Mexican rule but campaigned for greater political autonomy. The "war party," headed mostly by recent migrants from Georgia, demanded independence. Austin won significant concessions from Mexican authorities, but in 1835, Mexico's president, General Antonio López de Santa Anna, nullified them. Santa Anna's goal was to strengthen the authority of the national government throughout Mexico. Fearing that outcome, the war party provoked a rebellion that most of the American settlers ultimately supported. On March 2, 1836, the American rebels proclaimed the independence of Texas and adopted a constitution that legalized slavery.

President Santa Anna vowed to put down the rebellion. On March 6, he led an army that wiped out the rebel garrison defending the Alamo in San Antonio and then

Assault on the Alamo

After a thirteen-day siege, on March 6, 1836, a Mexican army of 4,000 stormed the wall of the small fort — originally a Spanish mission — in San Antonio. "The first to climb were thrown down by bayonets . . . or by pistol fire," reported a Mexican officer. After a half-hour of continuous and costly assaults, the attackers won control of the wall. This contemporary woodcut shows the fierceness of the battle, which took the lives of all 250 Texan defenders; 1,500 Mexicans were killed or wounded in the fighting. Archives Division, Texas State Library.

For more help analyzing this image, see the Online Study Guide at **bedfordstmartins.com/henrettaconcise**.

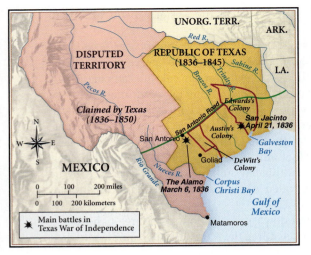

MAP 13.1 American Settlements and the Texas War of Independence

During the 1820s, Mexican officials granted huge tracts of land in Texas to Stephen F. Austin and other land speculators, who encouraged Americans to migrate to Texas and grow cotton. By 1835, the nearly 30,000 American settlers in Texas far outnumbered Mexican residents. To put down the American revolt, General Santa Anna led an army of 6,000 men into Texas in early 1836. Overwhelming the Texans at the Alamo in March, the Mexicans set out in pursuit of the Texas Provisional Government, which had fled to Galveston. But in April, Santa Anna was captured, and his army was defeated at the Battle of San Jacinto by a Texan force commanded by Sam Houston.

took control of Goliad (Map 13.1). Santa Anna thought that he had crushed the rebellion, but New Orleans and New York newspapers romanticized the heroism of the Texans and the deaths at the Alamo of folk heroes Davy Crockett and Jim Bowie. Drawing on anti-Catholic sentiment aroused by Irish immigration, journalists described the Mexicans as tyrannical butchers in the service of the pope. Hundreds of American adventurers, lured by offers of land grants, flocked to Texas to join the rebel army. Led by General Sam Houston, the Texas rebels routed the Mexican army in the Battle of San Jacinto in April 1836, establishing de facto independence. The Mexican government refused to recognize the Texas Republic but abandoned efforts to reconquer it.

The Texans voted by plebiscite (a vote of the people) for annexation by the United States, but President Martin Van Buren refused to bring the issue before Congress. As a Texas diplomat reported, Van Buren and other American politicians feared that annexation would spark a war with Mexico and, beyond that, a "desperate death-struggle . . . between the North and the South; a struggle involving the probability of a dissolution of the Union."

The Push to the Pacific

The annexation of Texas became a pressing issue in the 1840s, as expansionists developed continental ambitions. The term *Manifest Destiny*, coined in 1845 by John L. O'Sullivan, the editor of the *Democratic Review*, captured those dreams. As O'Sullivan put it, "Our manifest destiny is to overspread the continent allotted by Providence for the free development of our yearly multiplying millions." Underlying the rhetoric of Manifest Destiny was a sense of American cultural and racial superiority: The "inferior" peoples who lived in the Far West—Native Americans and Mexicans—were to be brought under American dominion, taught republicanism, and converted to Protestantism.

MAP 13.2 Territorial Boundaries in Oregon, 1819–1846

As nearly 10,000 American settlers arrived in the Oregon Country in the early 1840s, British officials tried to keep them south of the Columbia River. However, the migrants — and fervent midwestern expansionists — asserted that Americans could settle anywhere in the territory, raising the prospect of armed conflict. In 1846, British and American diplomats resolved the dispute by dividing the region at the forty-ninth parallel.

Residents of the Ohio River Valley had already cast their eyes westward to the fertile lands of the Oregon Country. This region, which stretched along the Pacific Coast between Russian-occupied lands in Alaska and the Mexican province of California, was claimed by both Britain and the United States. Since 1818, a British-American agreement had allowed fur traders and settlers from both nations to live there. The British-run Hudson's Bay Company developed a lucrative fur trade north of the Columbia River, while several hundred Americans settled to the south, in the fertile Willamette Valley (see Chapter 16). On the basis of this settlement, the United States claimed sovereignty of the area between California and the Columbia River (Map 13.2).

In 1842, American interest in Oregon increased dramatically. The U.S. Navy published a glowing report of fine harbors in the Puget Sound, which were already being used by New England merchants plying the China trade. In the same year, a party of one hundred farmers journeyed along the Oregon Trail, which fur traders and explorers had blazed through the Great Plains and the Rocky Mountains (Map 13.3). Their letters from Oregon told of a mild climate and fertile soil.

"Oregon fever" suddenly raged. In May 1843, 1,000 men, women, and children — in more than one hundred wagons and with 5,000 oxen and cattle — gathered in Independence, Missouri, for the six-month trek to Oregon. The migrants were mostly yeomen farming families from the southern border states (Missouri, Kentucky, and Tennessee) looking for free land and a new life. These pioneers overcame flooding streams, dust storms, dying livestock, and a few armed encounters with Indians before reaching the Willamette Valley, a journey of 2,000 miles. Over the next two years, another 5,000 settlers reached Oregon, and the numbers continued to grow.

MAP 13.3 Routes to the West, 1835–1860

By the 1840s, a variety of trails spanned the arid zone between the ninety-fifth meridian and the Pacific Coast. From the south, El Camino Real linked Mexico City to the California coast and to Santa Fe. From the east, the Mormon, Oregon, and Santa Fe trails carried more than 250,000 Americans from departure points on the Mississippi and Missouri rivers to Utah communities, the California gold fields, and Oregon farms. By the 1860s, the Pony Express and Butterfield Overland Company were providing reliable communication between the eastern states and California.

By 1860, about 250,000 Americans had braved the Oregon Trail, 65,000 heading for Oregon and the rest to California in the Gold Rush. More than 34,000 of them died in the effort, mostly from disease and exposure; fewer than 500 deaths resulted from Indian attacks. The walking migrants wore three-foot-deep paths, and their wagons carved five-foot-deep ruts across sandstone formations in southern Wyoming—tracks that are visible today. Women found the trail especially difficult because it boosted the authority of their husbands, who directed the enterprise, and added the labor of driving wagons and animals to their usual chores. About 2,500 women endured pregnancy or gave birth during the long journey, and some did not survive. "There was a woman died in this train yesterday," Jane Gould Tortillott noted in her diary. "She left six children, one of them only two day's old."

About 3,000 of the pioneers of the 1840s ended up in the Mexican province of California. They left the Oregon Trail along the Snake River, trudged down the California Trail, and settled in the interior along the Sacramento River. The region had few Native peoples and even fewer Mexicans. California was a remote outpost of Spain's American empire and was settled only in the 1770s, when Spanish authorities built a chain of religious missions and forts (presidios) along the coast. New England merchants struck up trade with the Spanish settlers, buying sea otter pelts and carrying them to China.

Settlement and commerce increased after Mexican independence. To promote California's development, the Mexican government took over the Franciscan-run missions and liberated the 20,000 Indians who had been persuaded to work on them. Some mission Indians rejoined their Native American tribes, but many intermarried with mestizos (Mexicans of mixed Spanish and Indian ancestry) and worked on the large cattle ranches that Mexican entrepreneurs set up in California.

These ranches linked California to the American economy. New England merchants dispatched dozens of agents westward to buy leather and tallow for use in the booming Massachusetts boot and shoe industry. Many of those agents married into the families of the elite Mexican landowners and ranchers — the *Californios* — and adopted their dress, manners, outlook, and Catholic religion (see Chapter 16). A crucial exception was Thomas Oliver Larkin, the most successful merchant in the coastal town of Monterey. Larkin worked closely with Mexican ranchers, but he remained an American in outlook and hoped that California would be peacefully annexed to the United States.

Like Larkin, the American migrants in the Sacramento River Valley did not want to assimilate into Mexican society. Many were squatters or held land grants of dubious legality. Others hoped to emulate the Americans in Texas by colonizing the country and then seeking annexation to the United States. However, in the early 1840s, these settlers numbered only about 700; by contrast, 7,000 Mexicans and 300 American traders lived along the coast.

The Fateful Election of 1844

The election of 1844 determined the American government's policy toward California, Oregon, and Texas. Since 1836, when Texas requested annexation, many southern leaders had advocated territorial expansion to extend slavery. Cautious party politicians and northern abolitionists resisted their efforts. Now there were rumors that Britain wanted the Mexican government to cede California in payment for large debts owed to British investors. Southern leaders also believed that Britain was encouraging Texas to remain independent and had designs on Spanish Cuba, which some southerners wanted to annex. To thwart possible British schemes, southern expansionists demanded the immediate annexation of Texas.

At this crucial juncture, Oregon fever and Manifest Destiny altered the political and diplomatic landscape in the North. In 1843, Americans in the Ohio River Valley and the Great Lakes states organized "Oregon conventions." In July, Democratic and Whig politicians attended a national meeting that demanded that the United States seize Oregon all the way to 54°40' north latitude, the southern border of Russian Alaska. With northern Democrats demanding expansion in Oregon, southern Democrats seized the opportunity to champion the annexation of Texas. The southerners had the strong support of President John Tyler, a proslavery zealot. Disowned by the Whigs because of his opposition to Henry Clay's nationalist economic program, Tyler hoped to win reelection in 1844 as a Democrat. To curry favor among northern expansionists, Tyler proposed to seize all of Oregon.

In April 1844, Tyler and John C. Calhoun, a southern expansionist and the new secretary of state, sent the Senate a treaty to bring Texas into the Union. Two rival presidential candidates, Democrat Martin Van Buren and Whig Henry Clay, quickly declared their opposition. Knowing that annexation would raise the controversial issue of the expansion of slavery, these cautious party politicians persuaded the Senate to reject the treaty.

Expansion into Texas and Oregon became the central issue in the election of 1844. The Democrats passed over Tyler, whom they did not trust, and Van Buren, whom southerners despised for his opposition to annexation. They selected as their candidate Governor James K. Polk of Tennessee, a slave owner who favored the acquisition of Texas. Widely known as "Young Hickory," Polk was a protégé of Andrew Jackson and, like his mentor, a man of iron will and boundless ambition for the nation. Accepting the claim in the Democratic Party platform that both areas already belonged to the United States, Polk campaigned for the "Re-occupation of Oregon and the Re-annexation of Texas." He insisted that the United States claim "the whole of the territory of Oregon" to the Alaskan border. "Fifty-four forty or fight!" became his jingoistic cry.

The Whigs nominated Henry Clay, who again championed his American System of high tariffs, internal improvements, and national banking. Clay initially dodged the issue of Texas but ultimately supported annexation. His position disappointed thousands of antislavery northern Whigs, who cast their ballots for James G. Birney of the Liberty Party (see Chapter 11). Birney garnered less than 3 percent of the national vote but took enough Whig votes in New York to cost Clay that state. By narrowly winning New York's thirty-six electoral votes, Polk captured the presidency; without New York, he would have lost by seven electoral votes.

Following Polk's victory, Democrats in Congress called for the immediate annexation of Texas. However, they lacked the two-thirds majority in the Senate needed to ratify a treaty of annexation with the Republic of Texas. So the Democrats admitted Texas to the Union with a joint resolution of Congress, which required just a majority vote in each house. Following a

► What ideas did the term *Manifest Destiny* reflect? Did it cause historical events, or was it merely a description of events? What were those events?

► Why, after two decades of hesitation, did some politicians support territorial expansion in the 1840s? What was the fate of those who supported and those who opposed expansion?

convention in Austin, which drafted a constitution, Texas citizens again voted for annexation, and Texas became the twenty-eighth state in December 1845. Polk's strategy of linking Texas and Oregon had put him in the White House and Texas in the Union. Shortly, it would make the expansion of the South—and its system of slavery—the central topic of American politics.

War, Expansion, and Slavery, 1846–1850

The acquisition of Texas whetted Polk's appetite. The president now saw the possibility of acquiring all the Mexican lands between Texas and the Pacific Ocean. If necessary, he was ready to go to war to get them. What he and the majority of the Democratic Party consciously ignored was the crisis over slavery that this expansion would unleash. Like other American presidents, Polk learned that war is a dangerous military and political option.

The War with Mexico, 1846–1848

Since gaining independence in 1821, Mexico had not prospered. Its stagnant economy yielded few surpluses and only modest tax revenues, which were quickly devoured by a bloated bureaucracy and interest payments on foreign debts. The distant northern provinces of California and New Mexico contributed little to the national economy and remained sparsely settled, with a Spanish-speaking population of only 75,000 in 1840. Still, Mexican officials vowed to preserve their nation's historic boundaries; so when the Texas constitutional convention voted on July 4, 1845, to enter the American Union, Mexico broke off diplomatic relations with the United States.

Taking advantage of this diplomatic rupture, President Polk set in motion his plans to acquire Mexico's northern provinces. To intimidate the Mexican government, he ordered General Zachary Taylor and an American army of 2,000 soldiers to occupy disputed lands between the Nueces River (the historic southern boundary of Spanish Texas) and the Rio Grande, which the Republic of Texas had claimed as its border with Mexico. Simultaneously, Polk launched a secret diplomatic initiative. He sent John Slidell, a Louisiana congressman, to Mexico in December 1845 and told him to secure the Rio Grande boundary and to buy the Mexican provinces of California and New Mexico for $30 million. But Mexican officials, arguing that the annexation of Texas was illegal, refused to see Slidell. Purchasing New Mexico and California was not an option.

Anticipating Slidell's failure, Polk had already embarked on an alternative plan. He hoped to foment a revolution in California that, like the rebellion in Texas, would lead to a request for annexation. In October 1845, Secretary of State James Buchanan told merchant Thomas Oliver Larkin, now the U.S. consul in the port of Monterey, to encourage influential Mexican residents to seek independence and union with the United States. To add military muscle to this scheme, Polk ordered American naval commanders to seize San Francisco Bay and California's coastal towns in case of war with Mexico. The president also had the War Department dispatch Captain John C. Frémont and an "exploring" party of heavily armed soldiers into Mexican territory. By December 1845, Frémont had reached California's Sacramento River Valley.

Events now moved quickly toward war. Polk ordered General Taylor toward the Rio Grande to incite an armed response by Mexico. "We were sent to provoke a fight," recalled Ulysses S. Grant, then a young officer serving with Taylor, "but it was essential that Mexico should commence it." When the armies clashed near the Rio Grande in May 1846, Polk delivered the war message he had drafted long before. Taking liberties with the truth, the president declared that Mexico "has passed the boundary of the United States, has invaded our territory, and shed American blood upon the American soil." Ignoring Whig pleas for a negotiated settlement, the Democratic majority in Congress voted for war, a decision that was greeted with great popular acclaim. To avoid a simultaneous conflict with Britain, Polk retreated from his demand for "fifty-four forty or fight" and accepted a British proposal to divide the Oregon Country at the forty-ninth parallel.

American forces in Texas quickly established their military superiority. Zachary Taylor's army crossed the Rio Grande, occupied Matamoros, and, after a fierce six-day battle in September 1846, took the interior Mexican town of Monterrey. Two months later, a U.S. naval squadron in the Gulf of Mexico seized Tampico, Mexico's second most important port. By the end of 1846, the United States controlled much of northeastern Mexico (Map 13.4).

Fighting had also broken out in California. In June 1846, naval commander John Sloat landed 250 marines in Monterey and declared that California "henceforward will be a portion of the United States." Almost simultaneously, American settlers in the Sacramento River Valley staged a revolt and, supported by Frémont's forces, captured the town of Sonoma, where they proclaimed an independent "Bear Flag Republic." To cement these victories, Polk ordered army units to capture Santa Fe in New Mexico and then march to California. Despite stiff Mexican resistance, American forces secured control of California early in 1847.

Polk expected these American victories to end the war, but he had underestimated the Mexicans' national pride and the determination of President Santa Anna. Santa Anna attacked Taylor's army in northeastern Mexico and, in the battle of Buena Vista in February 1847, nearly defeated it.

To bring Santa Anna to terms, Polk accepted General Winfield Scott's plan to capture the Mexican capital. In March 1847, Scott captured the port of Veracruz and began a 260-mile march to Mexico City. Leading Scott's 14,000 troops was a cadre of talented West Point officers who would become famous in the Civil War: Robert E. Lee, George Meade, and P. G. T. Beauregard. Scott's troops crushed Santa Anna's forces at Cerro Gordo and at Churubusco, just outside Mexico City, and seized the Mexican capital in September 1847. Those defeats cost Santa Anna his presidency, and a new Mexican government made peace with the United States.

A Divisive Victory

Initially, the war with Mexico ignited an explosion of patriotic support. Politicians and newspaper editors hailed the conflict as a noble struggle to extend American republican institutions. However, the war soon divided the nation. A few Whigs—among them Charles Francis Adams of Massachusetts (the son of President John Quincy Adams) and Joshua Giddings of Ohio—opposed the war from the beginning on moral grounds. Known as **conscience Whigs**, they warned of a southern conspiracy to add

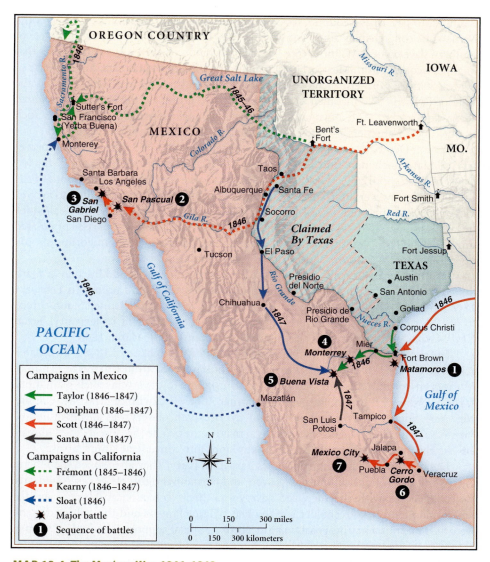

MAP 13.4 The Mexican War, 1846–1848

Departing from Fort Leavenworth in present-day Kansas, American forces commanded by Captain John C. Frémont and General Stephen Kearny defeated Mexican armies in California in 1846 and early 1847. Simultaneously, U.S. troops under General Zachary Taylor and Colonel Alfred A. Doniphan won victories over General Santa Anna's forces far to the south of the Rio Grande. In mid-1847, General Winfield Scott mounted a successful attack on Mexico City, ending the war.

new slave states and ensure permanent control of the federal government by slave-holding Democrats. Antislavery Whigs grew bolder when voters repudiated Polk's war policy in the elections of 1846 and gave their party control of Congress.

Polk's expansionist policies split the Democrats into sectional factions. As early as 1839, Democratic Senator Thomas Morris of Ohio had warned that "the power of slavery is aiming to govern the country, its Constitutions and laws." In 1846, David Wilmot, a Democratic congressman from Pennsylvania, took up that refrain. To check the power of southern slave owners, Wilmot proposed the prohibition of slavery in any territories that might be acquired from Mexico. His plan rallied antislavery northerners. In the House of Representatives, northern Democrats joined forces with antislavery Whigs to pass the Wilmot Proviso. "The madmen of the North . . . ," grumbled the *Richmond Enquirer,* "have, we fear, cast the die and numbered the days of this glorious Union." Fearing just such an outcome, southerners and proslavery Democrats in the Senate killed the proviso.

Fervent Democratic expansionists now became even more aggressive. Polk, Secretary of State Buchanan, and Senators Stephen A. Douglas of Illinois and Jefferson Davis of Mississippi called for the United States to take Mexican territory south of the Rio Grande. However, John C. Calhoun and other southern leaders wanted to avoid a longer war and the need to assimilate a huge number of Mexicans. So they called for the annexation only of New Mexico and California, Mexico's most sparsely populated provinces. "Ours is a government of the white man," Calhoun proclaimed, and should never incorporate "into the Union any but the Caucasian race."

To unify the Democratic Party before the next election, Polk and Buchanan abandoned their hyperexpansionist dreams and accepted Calhoun's policy. In February 1848, Polk signed the Treaty of Guadalupe Hidalgo, in which the United States agreed to pay Mexico $15 million in return for more than one-third of its territory: Texas, New Mexico, and California. The Senate ratified the treaty in March 1848.

The passions that the war had aroused dominated the election of 1848. The Senate's rejection of the Wilmot Proviso prompted antislavery advocates to revive Thomas Morris's charge of a massive "Slave Power" conspiracy. To thwart any such plan, thousands of ordinary northerners, including farmer Abijah Beckwith of Herkimer County, New York, joined the **free-soil movement**. To Beckwith, slavery was an institution of "aristocratic men" and a danger to "the great mass of the people [because it] . . . threatens the general and equal distribution of our lands into convenient family farms."

The free-soilers quickly organized as a political party. They abandoned the Liberty Party's emphasis on the sinfulness of slavery and the natural rights of African Americans. Instead, like Beckwith, they depicted slavery as a threat to republican liberties and the Jeffersonian ideal of a freeholder society. The Wilmot Proviso and the call for free soil were the first antislavery proposals to attract broad popular support. Hundreds of women in the Great Lakes states joined the female free-soil organizations formed by the American and Foreign Anti-Slavery Society. Still, the free-soilers' shift in emphasis—from freeing slaves toward preserving the West for white freehold farming—led abolitionist William Lloyd Garrison to denounce free-soil doctrine as racist "whitemanism."

Nonetheless, Frederick Douglass, the foremost black abolitionist, endorsed the free-soil movement. Born to an enslaved woman on a Maryland plantation in 1818, Douglass grew up as Frederick Bailey. He never knew the identity of his father, though it was undoubtedly his owner, Thomas Auld. Auld had Frederick raised by his brother in Baltimore, where he learned to read and mingled with free blacks. Later, when Frederick faced deportation to the Deep South for attempting to escape from plantation labor, Auld again intervened. In 1835, he returned Frederick to Baltimore, allowed him to hire himself out as a caulker, and promised him freedom in eight years, at the age of twenty-five.

Frederick plunged enthusiastically into the life of Baltimore's free African American community. He courted a free black woman, Anna Murray; joined the East Baltimore Mental Improvement Society; and hatched a plan of escape. In 1838, he borrowed the identification papers of a free African American sailor and sailed to New York City. He took the last name Douglass, married Murray, and settled in New Bedford, Massachusetts. Inspired by Garrison, Douglass lectured for the American Anti-Slavery Society and quickly became a celebrity. His partly African ancestry drew crowds to his lectures, as did his commanding presence, dramatic rhetoric, and forceful intellect.

Gradually, Douglass's views diverged from those of Garrison. To rid America of the sin of slavery, Garrison wanted to expel the southern states from the Union. To Douglass, that policy was madness because it would perpetuate slavery. Rejecting Garrison's moral radicalism, he founded an antislavery newspaper, the *North Star*, and became a political abolitionist, dedicated to using political agitation and government power to overthrow slavery. In 1848, Douglass attended the Buffalo convention that established the Free-Soil Party and endorsed its political strategy of confronting the South.

The conflict over slavery took a toll on Polk and the Democratic Party. Scorned by Whigs and Free-Soilers and exhausted by his rigorous dawn-to-midnight work regime, Polk refused to run for a second term; he would die just three months after leaving office. In his place, the Democrats nominated Senator Lewis Cass of Michigan, an avid expansionist who had advocated buying Cuba, annexing Mexico's Yucatán Peninsula, and taking all of Oregon. To maintain party unity, Cass deliberately took a vague position on the question of slavery in the West. He promoted a new idea—squatter sovereignty—that would allow settlers in each territory to determine its status as free or slave.

Cass's political ingenuity failed to unify the Democracy. Demanding unambiguous opposition to the expansion of slavery, some northern Democrats joined the newly formed Free-Soil Party, which nominated Martin Van Buren for president. Van Buren genuinely supported free soil, but he also wanted to punish southern Democrats for denying him the presidential nomination in 1844. To attract Whig votes, the Free-Soilers chose conscience-Whig Charles Francis Adams as their candidate for vice president.

To keep their party intact, the Whigs nominated General Zachary Taylor for president. Taylor was a Louisiana slave owner, but he had not taken a position on the charged issue of slavery in the territories. Moreover, the general's military exploits had made him a popular hero. Known as "Old Rough and Ready," Taylor had a common touch that won him the affection of his troops. In 1848, as in 1840, running a military hero worked for the Whigs. Taylor took 47 percent of the popular vote to Cass's 42 percent. However, Taylor won a majority in the Electoral College (163 to 127) only because Van Buren and the Free-Soil ticket took the votes of enough Democrats to cause Cass to lose New York's electoral votes. The bitter debate over the Wilmot Proviso had fractured the Democratic Party in the North and changed the dynamics of national politics.

1850: Crisis and Compromise

Even before Taylor took office, events in California triggered a new political crisis over slavery. In January 1848, workmen building a mill for John A. Sutter in the Sierra Nevada foothills in northern California discovered flakes of gold. Sutter was a Swiss

A ROAD SCENE IN CALIFORNIA.

The Gold Rush Creates a Mix of Peoples

This well-composed drawing by German-born artist and California prospector Charles Nahl captures the racial complexity of the gold rush. Displaced from their home by a horde of newcomers, a Native American family trudges away from the gold fields (left). Meanwhile, a contingent of Chinese miners marches toward the diggings (center), and a group of American men struggle to right their overturned wagon. University of California at Berkeley, Bancroft Library.

immigrant who had arrived in California in 1839, became a Mexican citizen, and established an estate in the Sacramento River Valley. He tried to keep the discovery a secret; but by May 1848, Americans from Monterey and San Francisco were pouring into the foothills. When President Polk confirmed the discovery in December, the gold rush was on. By January 1849, 61 crowded ships had left northeastern ports to sail around Cape Horn to San Francisco; by May, 12,000 wagons had crossed the Missouri River bound for the gold fields. By the end of 1849, more than 80,000 people (the "forty-niners") had arrived in California (see Chapter 16).

The rapid settlement of California revived the national debate over free soil. The forty-niners, who lived in crowded, chaotic towns and mining camps, demanded the formation of a territorial government to protect their lives and property. Hoping to prevent a debate over slavery, President Taylor advised the Californians to apply for statehood immediately; in November 1849, they ratified a state constitution that prohibited slavery. Taylor had never believed that the defense of slavery in the South required its expansion into the territories. Now, urged on by William H. Seward, the former Whig governor of New York, Taylor tried to strengthen the Whig Party in the North by appealing to Free-Soilers and northern Democrats.

As part of this political strategy, he urged Congress to admit California as a free state.

The resulting political impasse produced passionate debates in Congress and four distinct positions with respect to slavery in the territories. On the verge of death, John C. Calhoun took his usual extreme stance. Like Senator Albert Gallatin Brown of Mississippi, Calhoun had long resented the "social and sectional degradation" of the South by northern critics. To uphold southern honor, he proposed a constitutional amendment that would permanently balance the political power of the North and the South by creating a dual presidency. Calhoun also advanced the radical position that Congress had no constitutional authority to regulate slavery in the territories. That argument ran counter to a half century of practice. In 1787, Congress had prohibited slavery in the Northwest Territory; and in the Missouri Compromise of 1820, it had extended that ban to most of the Louisiana Purchase.

Calhoun's assertion that the territories were open to slavery won support in the Deep South, but many southerners favored a more moderate proposal to extend the Missouri Compromise line to the Pacific Ocean. This plan won the backing of Pennsylvanian James Buchanan, the former secretary of state, and other influential northern Democrats. Because such an extension would guarantee slave owners access to some western territory, including a separate state in southern California, they saw it as a an easy way to resolve the crisis.

A third alternative was squatter sovereignty — allowing territorial residents to decide the issue. Lewis Cass had advanced this idea in1848, and Democratic Senator Stephen Douglas of Illinois was now its champion. Douglas called his plan *popular sovereignty* to emphasize its roots in republican ideology, and it had considerable appeal. Politicians liked the fact that it would remove the explosive issue of slavery from national politics; local settlers welcomed the power it would put in their hands. However, popular sovereignty was a vague and slippery concept. Could residents accept or ban slavery when a territory was first organized? Or must they delay that decision until a territory had enough people to frame a constitution and apply for statehood?

For their part, antislavery advocates were unwilling to accept any plan for California that might allow the expansion of slavery there or elsewhere. Senator Salmon P. Chase of Ohio, elected by a Democratic–Free-Soil coalition, and Senator William H. Seward, a New York Whig, urged a fourth position: that federal authorities restrict slavery within its existing boundaries and then extinguish it completely. Condemning slavery as "morally unjust, politically unwise, and socially pernicious" and invoking "a higher law than the Constitution," Seward demanded bold action to protect freedom, "the common heritage of mankind."

Standing on the brink of disaster, senior Whig and Democratic politicians worked desperately to preserve the Union. With the help of Millard Fillmore, who became president in 1850 after Zachary Taylor's sudden death, Whig leaders Henry Clay and Daniel Webster and Democrat Stephen A. Douglas secured the passage of five separate laws known collectively as the Compromise of 1850. To mollify the South, the Compromise included a new Fugitive Slave Act that enlisted federal magistrates in the task of returning runaway slaves. To satisfy the North, the legislation admitted California as a free state, resolved a boundary dispute between

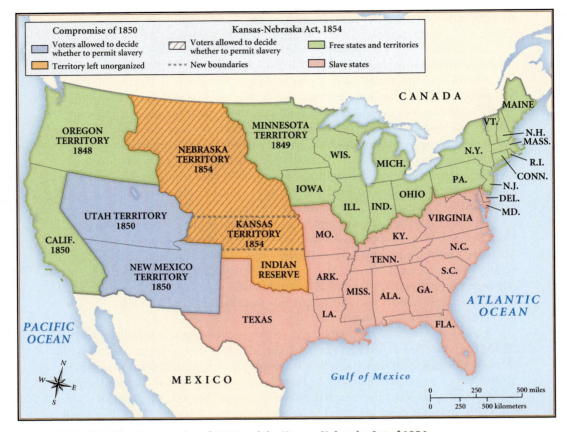

MAP 13.5 The Compromise of 1850 and the Kansas-Nebraska Act of 1854

Vast territories were at stake in the contest over the expansion of slavery. The Compromise of 1850 resolved the status of lands in the Far West: California would be a free state, and the settlers of the Utah and New Mexico territories would vote for or against slavery (the concept of popular sovereignty). The decision in 1854 to void the Missouri Compromise of 1820 and use popular sovereignty to decide the fate of slavery in the Kansas and Nebraska territories sparked a bitter local war and revealed a fatal flaw in the concept.

For more help analyzing this map, see the Online Study Guide at **bedfordstmartins.com/henrettaconcise**.

New Mexico and Texas in favor of New Mexico, and abolished the slave trade (but not slavery) in the District of Columbia. Finally, the Compromise organized the rest of the lands acquired from Mexico into the territories of New Mexico and Utah and left the decision over slavery in those vast areas to popular sovereignty (Map 13.5).

The Compromise averted a secession crisis in 1850, but only barely. During the debate, the governor of South Carolina warned that there was not "the slightest doubt" that his state would leave the Union. He and other militant secessionists (known as "fire-eaters") in Georgia, Mississippi, and Alabama organized special conventions to safeguard "Southern Rights" through secession. In Georgia, U.S. Congressman Alexander H. Stephens called on the delegates to make "the necessary preparations of men and money, arms and munitions, etc. to meet the emergency." However, most convention delegates remained committed to the Union — though now only conditionally. Accepting the principle of secession, they agreed to leave the Union if Congress abolished slavery anywhere or refused to grant statehood to a territory with a proslavery constitution. Political wizardry had solved the immediate crisis, but the underlying issue of slavery remained unresolved.

> ▶ Why did President Polk go to war with Mexico? Why did the war become so divisive in Congress and the country?
>
> ▶ What issues were resolved by the Compromise of 1850? Who benefited more from its terms: the North or the South? Why?

The End of the Second Party System, 1850–1858

The architects of the Compromise of 1850 expected it to last for a generation, as the Missouri Compromise had. Their hopes were quickly dashed. Demanding freedom for fugitive slaves and free soil in the West, antislavery northerners refused to accept the Compromise. For their part, proslavery southerners plotted to extend slavery into the West, the Caribbean, and Central America. The resulting disputes destroyed the Second Party System and deepened the crisis of the Union.

Resistance to the Fugitive Slave Act

The Fugitive Slave Act proved the most controversial element of the Compromise. Under its terms, federal magistrates in the northern states determined the status of alleged runaway slaves. The law denied a jury trial to the accused blacks and even the right to testify. Using its provisions, southern owners reenslaved about 200 fugitives (as well as some free northern blacks).

The plight of the runaways and the appearance of slave catchers in the North and Midwest aroused popular hostility. Ignoring the threat of substantial fines and prison sentences, free blacks and white abolitionists aided fugitive slaves and interfered with their capture. In October 1850, Boston abolitionists helped two slaves to escape and drove a Georgia slave catcher out of town. Rioters in Syracuse, New York, broke into a courthouse to free a fugitive slave. Abandoning his commitment to nonviolence, Frederick Douglass declared, "The only way to make a Fugitive Slave Law a dead letter is to make half a dozen or more dead kidnappers." As if in response, a deadly confrontation took place in the Quaker village of Christiana, Pennsylvania, in September 1851. About twenty African Americans exchanged gunfire with Maryland slave catchers, killing two of them. Federal authorities indicted thirty-six blacks and four whites for treason and other crimes. But a Pennsylvania jury acquitted one defendant, and public opinion in the North forced the government to drop the charges against the rest.

Upping the ante was Harriet Beecher Stowe's abolitionist novel, *Uncle Tom's Cabin* (1852), which boosted northern opposition to the Fugitive Slave Act. By imbedding the moral principles of abolitionism into heartrending personal situations, Stowe's melodramatic book evoked empathy and outrage throughout the North. Legislators in northern states added their opposition to the fugitive act, claiming that it violated state sovereignty by interfering in their legal affairs. In response, they enacted a new set of

personal-liberty laws that increased the legal rights of their residents, including accused fugitives. In 1857, the Wisconsin Supreme Court went even further. In *Ableman v. Booth*, it ruled that the Fugitive Slave Act was void in Wisconsin because it violated state law and the constitutional rights of Wisconsin's citizens. Taking a states' rights stance—a position usually associated with the South—the Wisconsin court denied the authority of federal courts to review its decision. When the case reached the U.S. Supreme Court in 1859, Chief Justice Roger B. Taney led a unanimous Court in affirming the supremacy of federal courts over state courts—a position that has stood the test of time—and upheld the constitutionality of the Fugitive Slave Act. But by then, as Frederick Douglass had hoped, popular opposition had made the act a "dead letter."

The Political System in Decline

The conflict over slavery split both major political parties along sectional lines. The Whigs, weakened by the death of Henry Clay, chose General Winfield Scott, another hero of the war with Mexico, as their presidential candidate in 1852. But many southern Whigs refused to support Scott because northern Whigs opposed slavery. The Democrats were equally divided: Southerners wanted a candidate who accepted Calhoun's constitutional argument that all territories were open to slavery; but northern and midwestern Democrats advocated popular sovereignty, as did the three leading candidates—Lewis Cass of Michigan, Stephen Douglas of Illinois, and James Buchanan of Pennsylvania. Ultimately, the party settled on a compromise nominee, Franklin Pierce of New Hampshire, a congenial man who was sympathetic to the South. Thanks to the Democrats' cautious strategy, they swept the election. Many Free-Soilers voted for Pierce, reuniting the Democratic Party; still split over slavery, the Whig Party fragmented into sectional wings and would never again wage a national campaign.

As president, Pierce pursued an expansionist foreign policy. To assist northern merchants, he sent a mission to Japan to negotiate a commercial treaty. To mollify southern expansionists, he tried to buy Mexican lands south of the Rio Grande. When Mexico rejected his offer, Pierce settled for the purchase of a narrow slice of land that enabled his negotiator, James Gadsden, to build a transcontinental rail line from New Orleans to California.

Pierce's most controversial foreign policy initiatives came in the Caribbean and Central America. American slave traders, financed from New York City, carried about 25,000 slaves to Spanish-owned Cuba annually during the 1850s; southern expansionists were equally active there, funding clandestine military expeditions and encouraging Cuban slave owners to declare independence and join the United States. Beginning in 1853, Pierce covertly supported new military expeditions to Nicaragua and Cuba and threatened war with Spain over the seizure of an American ship. Northern Democrats in Congress denounced this aggressive diplomacy, and Pierce and Secretary of State William L. Marcy backed down. When Marcy's attempt to buy the island from Spain for $130 million also failed, he arranged in 1854 for American diplomats in Europe to issue the so-called Ostend Manifesto, which urged Pierce to seize Cuba. Leaked to newspapers, the Ostend Manifesto revived northern fears of a "Slave Power" conspiracy. Determined resistance by northern politicians scuttled the planters' dreams of an American slave empire in the Caribbean.

The Kansas-Nebraska Act and the Rise of New Parties

The Caribbean was a sideshow. The main stage was the West, where a major controversy in 1854 destroyed the Second Party System and sent the Union spinning toward disaster. The Missouri Compromise prohibited new slave states in the Louisiana Purchase north of 36°30′; consequently, southern senators had long delayed its division into territories. Now residents of the Ohio River Valley and the Upper South demanded its settlement. Senator Stephen A. Douglas of Illinois led the charge, partly because he wanted a transcontinental railroad to run through the area and link Chicago to California. In 1854, Douglas introduced a bill to extinguish Native American rights on the central Great Plains and organize the large free territory of Nebraska.

Douglas's bill conflicted with the plans of southern politicians. They wanted to open up the Louisiana Purchase to slavery and to have a southern city—New Orleans, Memphis, or St. Louis—as the eastern terminus of a transcontinental railroad. To win southern support, Douglas made two major concessions. First, he amended his bill so that it explicitly repealed the Missouri Compromise and organized the region on the basis of popular sovereignty. Second, Douglas agreed to the formation of two territories, Nebraska and Kansas, giving southerners the hope that Kansas would become a slave state. Douglas knew that his bill would "raise a hell of a storm" in the North. To win over northern congressmen, he argued that Kansas was not suited to plantation agriculture and would become a free state. After weeks of bitter debate, the Senate enacted the Kansas-Nebraska Act. To get the act through the House of Representatives, where sixty-six northern Democrats defied party policy and initially opposed it, President Pierce used pressure and patronage to persuade twenty-two members to change their votes, allowing the measure to squeak through.

The Kansas-Nebraska Act was a disaster for the American political system. It finished off the Whig Party and nearly destroyed the Democrats (as 70 percent of the northern Democrats who voted for the act lost their seats in the election of 1854). Denouncing the act as "part of a great scheme for extending and perpetuating supremacy of the slave power," northern Whigs and "anti-Nebraska" Democrats abandoned their old parties. They joined with Free-Soilers and abolitionists in a new Republican Party.

The new party was a coalition of "strange, discordant and even hostile elements," one Republican observed, but its leaders shared an economic philosophy that reflected their bitter opposition to slavery. Republicans condemned slavery because it degraded the dignity of manual labor and drove down the wages and working conditions of free white workers. Like Thomas Jefferson, they praised the morality of a society based on "the middling classes who own the soil and work it with their own hands." Abraham Lincoln, an Illinois Whig who became a Republican, conveyed the party's vision of social justice. "There is no permanent class of hired laborers among us," he declared; consequently, every free man had a chance to become a property owner. Ignoring the increasing class divisions in the industrializing North and Midwest, Lincoln and his fellow Republicans celebrated the values of republican liberty and individual enterprise.

The Republicans faced strong competition from the American, or Know-Nothing, Party. The party had its origins in the anti-immigrant and anti-Catholic movements of the 1840s (see Chapter 9). In 1850, these secret nativist societies banded together as the Order of the Star-Spangled Banner; the following year, they entered politics, forming the American Party. Its secrecy-conscious members often replied, "I know nothing" to outsiders' questions, thus giving the party its nickname. The party's program was far from secret: It wanted to unite all native-born Protestants against the "alien menace" of Irish and German Catholics, prohibit further immigration, and institute literacy tests for voting. In 1854, voters elected dozens of Know-Nothing candidates to the House of Representatives and gave the American Party control of the state governments of Massachusetts and Pennsylvania. The emergence of a major nativist party suddenly became a real possibility.

Meanwhile, thousands of settlers rushed into the Kansas Territory, putting Douglas's theory of popular sovereignty to the test. On the side of slavery, Missouri Senator David R. Atchison encouraged residents of his state to cross temporarily into Kansas to vote in crucial elections there. Opposing Atchison was the abolitionist New England Emigrant Aid Society, which dispatched hundreds of free-soilers to Kansas. In March 1855, the Pierce administration stepped into the fray by accepting the legitimacy of the proslavery territorial legislature meeting in Lecompton, Kansas, which had been elected primarily by border-crossing Missourians. However, the majority of Kansas residents favored free soil and refused allegiance to the Lecompton government.

In May 1856, both sides turned to violence, prompting Horace Greeley of the *New York Tribune* to label the territory as "Bleeding Kansas." A proslavery gang, seven hundred strong, sacked the free-soil town of Lawrence, wrecking two newspaper offices, looting stores, and burning buildings. The attack enraged John Brown, a fifty-six-year-old abolitionist from New York and Ohio, who commanded a volunteer free-state

Armed Abolitionists in Kansas, 1859

The confrontation between North and South in Kansas took many forms. In the spring of 1859, Dr. John Doy (seated) slipped across the border into Missouri and tried to lead thirteen slaves to freedom in Kansas, only to be captured and jailed in St. Joseph, Missouri. The serious-looking men standing behind Doy, well armed with guns and Bowie knives, attacked the jail and carried Doy back to Kansas. The photograph memorialized their successful exploit. Kansas State Historical Society.

militia that had arrived too late to save the town. Brown was a complex man with a long record of failed businesses, but he had an intellectual and moral intensity that won the trust of influential people. Taking vengeance for the sack of Lawrence, Brown and a few followers murdered five proslavery settlers at Pottawatomie. Abolitionists must "fight fire with fire" and "strike terror in the hearts of the proslavery people," Brown declared. The southerners' attack on Lawrence and the Pottawatomie killings started a guerrilla war in Kansas that took nearly two hundred lives (see American Voices, p. 398).

Buchanan's Failed Presidency

The violence in Kansas dominated the presidential election of 1856. The two-year-old Republican Party counted on anger over Bleeding Kansas to boost the party's fortunes. Its platform denounced the Kansas-Nebraska Act and, alleging a Slave Power conspiracy, demanded that the federal government prohibit slavery in all the territories. Republicans called for federal subsidies for transcontinental railroads, reviving an element of the Whig's economic program that was popular among midwestern Democrats. For president, the Republicans nominated Colonel John C. Frémont, a free-soiler who had won fame in the conquest of Mexican California.

The American Party entered the election with equally high hopes, but like the Whigs and Democrats, it split along sectional lines over slavery. The southern faction of the American party nominated former Whig president Millard Fillmore, while the northern contingent endorsed Frémont—thanks to clever maneuvering by Republican political operatives. During the campaign, Frémont and the Republicans won the votes of many Know-Nothing workingmen in the North by demanding a ban on foreign immigrants and high tariffs on foreign manufactures. As a Pennsylvania Republican put it, "Let our motto be, protection to everything American, against everything foreign." In New York, Republicans likewise shaped their policies "to cement into a harmonious mass . . . all of the Anti-Slavery, Anti-Popery and Anti-Whiskey" voters.

The Democrats reaffirmed their support for popular sovereignty and the Kansas-Nebraska Act, and nominated James Buchanan of Pennsylvania. A tall, dignified man, Buchanan was an experienced but unimaginative politician with a prosouthern outlook. Thanks to southern support and the Democrats' organizational strength in the North, Buchanan won the three-way race with 1.8 million votes (45 percent) and 174 electoral votes. Frémont polled 1.3 million votes (33 percent) and 114 electoral votes; but a small shift to Frémont in the popular vote in Illinois and Pennsylvania would have given him those states and the presidency.

The dramatic restructuring of parties was now apparent. With the splintering of the American Party over slavery, the Republicans had replaced the Whigs as the second major party. However, the Republican Party had no support in the South, so it was a sectional rather than a national party; consequently, a Republican triumph in the next presidential election might destroy the Union. A North Carolina newspaper threatened as much during the election of 1856: "If the Republicans should succeed, the result will be a separation of the states. No human power can prevent it." The fate of the republic hinged on President Buchanan's ability to quiet the passions of the past decade.

Events—and his own values and weaknesses—conspired against Buchanan. In 1856, the Supreme Court had heard the case of *Dred Scott v. Sandford*, which raised the controversial issue of Congress's constitutional authority over slavery in the territories.

"Bleeding Kansas": A Southern View   AXALLA JOHN HOOLE

Early in 1856, Axalla John Hoole and his bride left South Carolina to build a new life in the Kansas Territory (K.T.). These letters from Hoole to his family show that things did not go well from the start and gradually got worse; after eighteen months, the Hooles returned to South Carolina. A Confederate militia captain during the Civil War, Axalla Hoole died in the Battle of Chickamauga in September 1863.

Kansas City, Missouri, Apl. 3d., 1856. The Missourians . . . are very sanguine about Kansas being a slave state & I have heard some of them say it shall be . . . but generally speaking, I have not met with the reception which I expected. Everyone seems bent on the Almighty Dollar, and as a general thing that seems to be their only thought. . . . [T]he supper bell has rung and I must close. Give my love to [the family] and all the Negroes. . . .

Lecompton, K.T., Sept. 12, 1856. I have been unwell ever since the 9th of July. . . . I thought of going to work in a few days, when the Abolitionists broke out and I have had to stand guard of nights when I ought to have been in bed, took cold which . . . caused diarrhea. . . . Betsie is well. . . . I am now in Lecompton, almost all of the Proslavery party between this place and Lawrence are here. We brought our families here, as we thought that we would be better able to defend our-selves. . . .

Lane [and a force of abolitionists] came against us last Friday (a week ago to-day). As it happened we had about 400 men with two cannon—we marched out to meet him, though we were under the impression at the time that we had 1,000 men. We came in gunshot of each other, but the regular [U.S. Army] soldiers came and interfered, but not before our party had shot some dozen guns, by which it is reported that five of the Abolitionists had been killed or wounded. We had strict orders . . . not to fire until they made the attack, but some of our boys would not be restrained. I was a rifleman and one of the skirmishers, but did all that I could to restrain our men though I itched all over to shoot myself. . . .

July the 5th., 1857. I fear, Sister, that [our] coming here will do no good at last, as I begin to think that this will be made a Free State at last. 'Tis true we have elected Proslavery men to draft a state constitu-tion, but I feel pretty certain, if it is put to a vote of the people, it will be rejected, as I feel pretty confident that they have a majority here at this time. The South has ceased all efforts, while the North is redoubling her exertions. We nominated a candidate for Congress last Friday—Ex-Gov. Ransom of Michigan. I must confess I have not much faith in him, tho he professes to hate the abolitionists bitterly. . . . If we had nominated a Southern man, he would have been sure to have been beaten. . . .

SOURCE: William Stanley Hoole, ed., "A Southerner's Viewpoint of the Kansas Situation, 1856–1857," *Kansas Historical Quarterly* 3 (1934): 43–65, 149–171, passim.

Dred Scott was an enslaved African American who had lived for a time with his owner, an army surgeon, in the free state of Illinois and in the Wisconsin Territory, where the Northwest Ordinance (1787) prohibited slavery. Seeking freedom for himself and his family, Scott claimed that residence in a free state and a free territory had made him free. Buchanan hoped that the Court would reject Scott's appeal and pressured the two justices from his home state of Pennsylvania to side with their southern colleagues. Then, learning of the justices' vote in advance, the President urged Americans to accept the court's decision as permanently settling the issue of slavery in the territories. In the event, seven of the nine justices issued opinions declaring that Scott was still a slave. But they could not agree on the legal issues, so the case did not result in a binding principle of constitutional law.

Chief Justice Roger B. Taney of Maryland, a slave owner himself, wrote the most influential opinion. He declared that Negroes, whether enslaved or free, could not be citizens of the United States and that Scott therefore had no right to sue in federal court. That argument was controversial enough, given that free blacks were citizens in many states, which presumably gave them access to the federal courts. But then Taney proceeded to make two even more controversial claims. First, he endorsed John C. Calhoun's argument: Relying on the Fifth Amendment, which prohibited "takings" of property without due process of law, Taney ruled that Congress could not prevent southern citizens from taking their slave property into the territories and owning it there. Consequently, the chief justice concluded, the provisions of the Northwest Ordinance and the Missouri Compromise that prohibited slavery had never been constitutional. Second, Taney declared that Congress could not give to territorial governments any powers that it did not possess. Because Congress had no authority to prohibit slavery in a territory, neither did a territorial government. Taney thereby endorsed Calhoun's interpretation of popular sovereignty: Only when settlers wrote a constitution and requested statehood could they prohibit slavery.

In a single stroke, Taney had declared the Republicans' antislavery platform to be unconstitutional. The Republicans could never accept the legitimacy of Taney's broader arguments. Led by Senator Seward of New York, they accused the Chief Justice and President Buchanan of participating in the Slave Power conspiracy.

Buchanan then added fuel to the raging constitutional fire. Ignoring reports that antislavery residents held a clear majority in Kansas, he refused to allow a referendum on the constitution written by the proslavery Lecompton legislature. Instead, early in 1858, the president recommended the admission of Kansas as a slave state. Angered by Buchanan's machinations, Stephen Douglas, the most influential Democratic senator, broke with the president and persuaded Congress to deny statehood to Kansas. (Kansas would enter the Union as a free state in 1861.) Still determined to aid the South, Buchanan informed Congress in December 1858 that he was resuming negotiations to buy Cuba. By pursuing a proslavery agenda — first in *Dred Scott* and then in Kansas and Cuba — Buchanan widened the split in his party and the nation.

▶ Did the Compromise of 1850 fail? Or would it have succeeded if the Kansas-Nebraska Act of 1854 had either not been enacted or contained different provisions?

▶ What were the main constitutional arguments advanced during the debate over slavery in the territories? Which of those arguments influenced Chief Justice Taney's opinion in *Dred Scott*?

Abraham Lincoln and the Republican Triumph, 1858–1860

As the Democratic Party split along sectional lines, the Republicans gained support in the North and Midwest. Abraham Lincoln of Illinois emerged as the pivotal figure in American politics—the only Republican leader whose policies and temperament might have saved the Union. But few southerners trusted Lincoln, and his presidential candidacy revived secessionist agitation in the Deep South.

Lincoln's Political Career

The middle-class world of storekeepers, lawyers, and entrepreneurs in the small towns of the Ohio River Valley shaped Lincoln's early career. He came from a hardscrabble yeoman farm family that was continually on the move—from Kentucky, where Lincoln was born in 1809, to Indiana and then to Illinois. In 1831, Lincoln rejected his father's life as a subsistence farmer and became a store clerk in New Salem, Illinois. Socially ambitious, Lincoln sought entry into the middle class by mastering its literary and professional culture; he joined the New Salem Debating Society, read Shakespeare, and studied law.

Admitted to the bar in 1837, Lincoln moved to Springfield, the new state capital. There, he met Mary Todd, the cultured daughter of a Kentucky banker; they married in 1842. The couple was a picture in contrasts: Her tastes were aristocratic; his were humble. She was volatile; he was easygoing but suffered bouts of depression that tried her patience and tested his character.

Abraham Lincoln, 1859
Lincoln was not a handsome man, and he photographed poorly. In fact, his campaign photographs were often retouched to hide his prominent cheekbones and nose. More important, no photograph ever captured Lincoln's complex personality, verbal wit, and intensity of spirit and intellect. To grasp Lincoln, it is necessary to read his words. Chicago Historical Society.

Lincoln's ambition was "a little engine that knew no rest," his closest associate remarked, and it prompted him to seek fame and fortune in politics. An admirer of Henry Clay, Lincoln joined the Whig Party and won election to four terms in the Illinois legislature, where he promoted education, banks, canals, and railroads. He became a dexterous party politician, adept in the distribution of patronage and the passage of legislation.

In 1846, the rising lawyer-politician won election to a Congress that was bitterly divided over the Wilmot Proviso. Lincoln had long felt that human bondage was unjust but did not believe that the federal government had the constitutional authority to tamper with slavery in the South. With respect to the war with Mexico, he took a middle ground. He supported bills for military appropriations but voted for Wilmot's proposal to prohibit slavery in any acquired territories. And he personally proposed that Congress enact legislation for the gradual (and thus compensated) emancipation of slaves in the District of Columbia. Lincoln argued that a series of measures — firm opposition to the expansion of slavery, gradual emancipation, and the colonization of freed blacks in Africa — was the only practical solution to the problems of slavery and racial diversity. Both abolitionists and proslavery activists heaped scorn on Lincoln's pragmatic policies, and he lost his bid for reelection. Dismayed by the rancor of ideological politics, he withdrew from politics and prospered as a lawyer representing railroads and manufacturers.

Lincoln returned to the political fray after passage of Stephen Douglas's Kansas-Nebraska Act. Shocked by the act's repeal of the Missouri Compromise, Lincoln warned that the American "republican robe is soiled and trailed in the dust" and called on the citizens of Illinois to "repurify it and wash it white in the spirit, if not the blood of the Revolution." Rejecting Stephen Douglas's advocacy of popular sovereignty, Lincoln reaffirmed his position that slavery be allowed to continue in the South but that the national government should exclude it from the territories. Beyond that, Lincoln likened slavery to a cancer that had to be cut out if the nation's republican ideals and moral principles were to endure.

Abandoning the Whig Party in favor of the Republicans, Lincoln quickly emerged as their leader in Illinois. Campaigning for the U.S. Senate against Douglas in 1858, Lincoln alerted his audiences to the threat posed by the Slave Power. He warned that the proslavery Supreme Court might soon declare that the Constitution "does not permit a state to exclude slavery from its limits," just as it had decided in *Dred Scott* that "neither Congress nor the territorial legislature" could ban slavery in the territories. In that event, "we shall awake to the reality . . . that the Supreme Court has made Illinois a slave state." This prospect of slavery spreading into the North informed Lincoln's famous "House Divided" speech. Quoting from the Bible, "A house divided against itself cannot stand," he predicted that American society "cannot endure permanently half slave and half free. . . . It will become all one thing, or all the other."

The Senate race in Illinois attracted national interest because of Douglas's prominence in the Democratic Party and Lincoln's reputation as a formidable speaker. During a series of seven debates, Douglas declared his support for white supremacy: "This government was made by our fathers, by white men for the benefit of white men," he asserted, attacking Lincoln for supporting "negro equality." Put on the defensive by Douglas's racial rhetoric, Lincoln advocated economic opportunity for free blacks but not equal political rights. He asked how Douglas could accept the *Dred Scott* decision (which protected slave owners' property in the territories) yet advocate popular sovereignty (which asserted settlers' power to exclude slavery). Douglas responded with the so-called Freeport Doctrine: that a territory's residents could exclude slavery simply by not adopting laws to protect it. That position pleased neither proslavery advocates nor antislavery activists, but the Democrats won a narrow victory in Illinois, and the state legislature reelected Douglas to the U.S. Senate.

The Union Under Siege

His debates with Douglas gave Lincoln a national reputation, and the election of 1858 established the Republican Party as a formidable political force, as it won control of the House of Representatives and various state legislatures. Shaken by the Republican advance, southern Democrats divided into moderates and fire-eaters. The moderates, who included Senator Jefferson Davis of Mississippi, strongly defended "Southern Rights;" they wanted ironclad political or constitutional protections for slavery. The fire-eaters—men such as Robert Barnwell Rhett of South Carolina and William Lowndes Yancey of Alabama—repudiated the Union and actively promoted the secession of the southern states. Radical antislavery northerners played into their hands. Senator Seward of New York declared that freedom and slavery were locked in "an irrepressible conflict," and militant abolitionist John Brown showed what that might mean. In October 1859, Brown led eighteen heavily armed black and white men in a raid on the federal arsenal at Harpers Ferry, Virginia. Brown hoped to arm local slaves with the arsenal's weapons and lead a black rebellion that would end slavery and establish a new constitutional regime of racial equality.

Republican leaders condemned Brown's unsuccessful raid, but Democrats called his plot "a natural, logical, inevitable result of the doctrines and teachings of the Republican party." The state of Virginia charged Brown with treason, tried him in court, and sentenced him to be hanged. But transcendentalist reformers Henry David Thoreau and Ralph Waldo Emerson called Brown "an angel of light" and a "saint awaiting his martyrdom," and antislavery northerners leaped to Brown's defense. The slaveholding states looked to the future with fear. "The aim of the present black republican organization is the destruction of the social system of the Southern States, without regard to consequences," warned one newspaper. Once Republicans came to power, another southern paper warned, they "would create insurrection and servile war in the South—they would put the torch to our dwellings and the knife to our throats." Brown predicted as much. As he faced the gallows, Brown apocalyptically warned "that the crimes of this guilty land will never be purged away but with blood."

Nor could the South count on the Democratic Party to protect its interests. At the party's convention in April 1860, northern Democrats rejected Jefferson Davis's proposal to protect slavery in the territories, prompting the delegates from eight southern states to quit the meeting. At a second Democratic convention in Baltimore, northern and midwestern delegates nominated Stephen Douglas for president; meeting separately, southern Democrats nominated the sitting vice president, John C. Breckinridge of Kentucky.

A French Banker Analyzes the Election of 1860 and the Threat of Secession SALOMON DE ROTHSCHILD

Salomon de Rothschild, the son of Baron James de Rothschild of Paris, traveled around the United States from 1859 to 1861. In a series of detailed letters to his cousin Nathaniel in London, Rothschild offered an astute and often cynical analysis of the sectional crisis. Although his comments are generally evenhanded, Rothschild feared social revolution and so favored the South.

You know that the . . . United States was made up of two great parties, the Democrats and the Republicans. These two parties were subdivided into groups, only a few, but extremely violent ones. The abolitionists were the extremist Republicans; the "fire-eaters" or secessionists, the extremist Democrats. Fanaticism and the extremist parties always win out, and, exactly as I expressed my forebodings to you a very long time ago, abolitionism on one side and secession on the other dragged along the moderate neutrals despite themselves.

The point of departure was, as you know, the slavery question. Naturally, this institution, on which the wealth of the South was based, was defended to the limit by those who profited from it. Two reasons pushed the people of the North to seek to destroy slavery by any means. The first . . . was a simple humanitarian reason. In a free country like America, there must be no slaves, and complete equality must reign in all ranks of society. . . . But the real sentiment that guided them . . . was the spirit of leveling; everyone must be equal in abjection. They cannot tolerate someone in the South having 200 arms for his use while they have only their own two. This sentiment was the first seed of the social revolution which is at this very moment taking giant strides behind the political revolution.

You doubtless have read in the newspapers about the first effects of Lincoln's election; . . . several Southern states — Florida, Georgia, Alabama, and Mississippi, with South Carolina as their guide — have for all practical purposes seceded from the United States and are going to form a new confederation. . . .

[A compromise to restore the Union is unlikely, Rothschild writes in another letter, because] the South is simply a producer and consumer; the West and the North, and especially the East, are almost entirely manufacturers, but they need strong [tariff] protection. The South could supply itself with all necessary items in Europe, at prices from twenty-five to forty percent lower. . . . Therefore it wants to escape from this tax. . . . [But] a strong reduction in these duties would completely ruin the eastern states of New Jersey and Pennsylvania, which could not compete with the cheap prices attained by England and even by France. Thousands of men would find themselves unemployed and would therefore threaten the well-being and the very existence not only of their employers, but even of the merchants and the producers in those areas, leading to an imminent danger of social revolution, which the North must avoid at all costs. . . .

The future is as black as it can be. . . .

SOURCE: Sigmund Diamond, ed., *A Casual View of America, 1859–1861: The Home Letters of Salomon de Rothschild* (Stanford, CA: Stanford University Press, 1961), 82–83, 118–119.

With the Democrats divided, the Republicans sensed victory in 1860. They courted white voters with a free-soil platform that opposed both slavery and racial equality: "Missouri for white men and white men for Missouri," declared that state's Republican platform. The national Republican convention chose Lincoln as its presidential candidate because his position on slavery was more moderate than that of the best-known Republicans, Senators William Seward of New York and Salmon Chase of Ohio, who demanded abolition. Lincoln also conveyed a compelling egalitarian image that appealed to small-holding farmers and wage earners. And Lincoln's home territory—the rapidly growing Midwest—was crucial in the competition between Democrats and Republicans.

The Republican strategy worked. Although Lincoln received only 40 percent of the popular vote, he won an absolute majority in the Electoral College by carrying every northern and western state except New Jersey. Douglas took 30 percent of the popular ballot but won electoral votes only in Missouri and New Jersey. Breckinridge captured every state in the Deep South as well as Delaware, Maryland, and North Carolina. Finally, John Bell, a former Tennessee Whig nominated by the compromise-seeking Constitutional Union Party, carried the Upper South states of Kentucky, Tennessee, and Virginia (see Voices from Abroad, p. 403).

▶ What was Lincoln's position on slavery during the 1850s? Did it differ from that of Stephen Douglas? Explain your answer.

▶ What was the relationship between the collapse of the Second Party System of Whigs and Democrats and the Republican victory in the election of 1860?

▶ Some historians claim that the mistakes of a "Blundering Generation" of political leaders led, by 1860, to the imminent breakup of the Union. Do you agree? Why or why not?

The Republicans had united voters in the Northeast, the Midwest, and the Pacific Coast behind free soil and had gained national power. A revolution was in the making. Slavery had permeated the American federal republic for so long and so thoroughly that southerners had come to see it as part of the constitutional order—an order that was now under siege. "I am old enough to remember the horrors of St. Domingo [Haiti]," Chief Justice Taney noted, fearful of a massive black uprising. At the very least, warned John Townsend of South Carolina, a Republican administration in Washington might well suppress "the inter-State slave trade" and thereby "*cripple this vital Southern institution*" of slavery." To many southerners, it seemed time to think carefully about Lincoln's statement in 1858 that the Union must "become all one thing, or all the other."

SUMMARY

In this chapter, we examined three related themes: the movement of Americans into Texas and Oregon in the 1830s and 1840s, the causes and consequences of the Mexican war of the late 1840s, and the disintegration of the Second Party System during the 1850s. We saw that the political agendas of Presidents John Tyler and James Polk—their determination to add territory and slave states to the Union—pushed the United States into the Mexican war. The consequences of the war were immense because the acquisition of new territory raised the explosive question of the expansion of slavery.

To resolve the resulting crisis, Henry Clay, Daniel Webster, and Stephen Douglas devised the Compromise of 1850. Their efforts were in vain. Antislavery northerners defied the Fugitive Slave Act, and expansionist-minded southerners sought new slave states in the Caribbean. Ideology (the pursuit of absolutes) replaced politics (the art of compromise) as the ruling principle of American politics.

The Second Party System rapidly disintegrated. The Whig Party vanished, and two issue-oriented parties, the nativist American Party and the antislavery Republican Party, competed for its members. As the Republicans gained strength, the Democratic Party splintered into sectional factions over Bleeding Kansas and other slavery-related issues. The stage was set for Lincoln's victory in the climactic election of 1860.

Connections: Sectionalism

Sectionalism has been an enduring factor in American history. In the seventeenth century, English migrants created distinct societies in the Chesapeake and in New England; after 1700, those regions and that of Middle Atlantic developed along different lines. Then, as we pointed out in the essay that began Part Three, in the early nineteenth century,

> economic revolution and social reform sharpened sectional divisions: The North developed into an urbanizing society based on free labor, whereas the South remained a rural agricultural society dependent on slavery.

As we saw in Chapter 8, the first major conflict between North and South came in 1819–1821 over the admission of Missouri to the Union as a slave state. Then, as we learned in Chapter 10, the conflict over the Tariff of Abominations and Nullification from 1829 to 1832 revived the sectional struggle. Both crises ended with a compromise. As we have just seen, political leaders crafted the Compromise of 1850 to resolve yet another sectional conflict. However, as Chapter 14 will reveal, the crisis sparked by the election of Republican Abraham Lincoln could not be peacefully resolved. Nor did the Union's triumph in the Civil War end sectional strife. As Chapter 15 will demonstrate, Reconstruction created new sectional antagonisms and ended only with the Compromise of 1877 — yet another political bargain struck to paper over divisive social differences and conflicts.

FOR FURTHER EXPLORATION

Patricia Nelson Limerick, *The Legacy of Conquest* (1989), offers a provocative analysis of the West; see also **www.pbs.org/thewest**. For California pioneer stories, log onto **lcweb2.loc.gov/ammem/cbhtml/cbhome.html**. On early Texas history, see **www.tsl.state.tx.us/treasures/**. For a dual American and Mexican perspective on the war with Mexico, consult **www.pbs.org/usmexicanwar**.

David Potter, *The Impending Crisis, 1848–1861* (1976), covers political history. For slavery's impact on the crisis, see **www.pbs.org/wgbh/aia/home.html**. Two recent works — John Patrick Daly, *When Slavery Was Called Freedom* (2002), and Leonard L. Richards, *The Slave Power: The Free North and Southern Domination, 1780–1860* (2000) — offer broad cultural analyses. See also William A. Link, *Roots of Secession: Slavery and Politics in Antebellum Virginia* (2003) and Manisha Sinha, *The Counterrevolution of Slavery* (2000).

TIMELINE

1844 ▶	James Polk is elected president	**1851** ▶	American (Know-Nothing) Party forms
1845 ▶	John Slidell's diplomatic mission fails	**1852** ▶	Harriet Beecher Stowe publishes *Uncle Tom's Cabin*
▶	Texas is admitted into the Union	**1854** ▶	Ostend Manifesto argues for seizure of Cuba
1846 ▶	United States declares war on Mexico	▶	Kansas-Nebraska Act tests popular sovereignty
▶	Treaty with Britain divides Oregon Country	▶	Republican Party forms
▶	Wilmot Proviso is approved by House but not by Senate	**1856** ▶	Turmoil in Kansas undermines popular sovereignty
1847 ▶	American troops capture Mexico City	▶	James Buchanan is elected president
1848 ▶	Gold is discovered in California	**1857** ▶	*Dred Scott v. Sandford* allows slavery in U.S. territories
▶	In Treaty of Guadalupe Hidalgo, Mexico cedes its provinces of California, New Mexico, and Texas to United States	**1858** ▶	President Buchanan backs Lecompton constitution
▶	Free-Soil Party forms	▶	Abraham Lincoln and Stephen Douglas debate in U.S. Senate race
1850 ▶	Compromise of 1850 seeks to preserve the Union	**1859** ▶	John Brown leads armed raid on federal arsenal at Harpers Ferry
▶	Northern abolitionists reject Fugitive Slave Act	**1860** ▶	Abraham Lincoln is elected president in four-way contest
▶	South seeks to acquire Spanish Cuba		

Eric Foner, *Free Soil, Free Labor, Free Men* (1970), probes the ideology of the Republican Party. For an evocative treatment of Lincoln, read Stephen Oates, *With Malice Toward None: A Life of Abraham Lincoln* (1977). The justices' opinions in the *Dred Scott* case are at **odur.let.rug.nl/~usa/D/1851-1875/dredscott/dredxx.htm**; for Lincoln's response, see **www.usconstitution.com/AbrahamLincolnonDredScottDecision.htm**. "*Uncle Tom's Cabin* and American Culture: A Multi-Media Archive" (**jefferson.village .virginia.edu/utc/**) neatly places the novel in its literary and cultural context.

TEST YOUR KNOWLEDGE

To assess your mastery of the material in this chapter and for Web sites, images, and documents related to this chapter, visit **bedfordstmartins.com/henrettaconcise**.

Two Societies at War

1861–1865

No, you dare not make war on cotton. No power on earth dares to make war upon it. Cotton is king.

— South Carolina Senator James H. Hammond (1858)

"What a scene it was," Union soldier Elisha Hunt Rhodes wrote in his diary at Gettysburg in July 1863. "Oh the dead and the dying on this bloody field." Thousands of men had already died, and the slaughter would continue for two more years. "What is this all about?" asked Confederate lieutenant R. M. Collins as another gruesome battle ended. "Why is it that 200,000 men of one blood and tongue . . . [are] seeking one another's lives? We could settle our differences by compromising and all be at home in ten days." But there was no compromise, an outcome that President Lincoln found beyond human comprehension. "God wills this contest, and wills that it shall not yet end," he reflected in 1862; even on the eve of victory in 1865, Lincoln confessed his uncertainty: "The Almighty has His own purposes."

To explain why Southerners seceded and then fought to the bitter end is not simple, but racial slavery is an important part of the answer. For southern politicians, the Republican victory in 1860 presented an immediate danger to the slave-owning republic that had existed since 1776. Lincoln won not a single electoral vote in the South, and his Republican Party had vowed to prevent the extension of slavery.

Moreover, Southerners did not believe Lincoln when he promised not "directly or indirectly, to interfere with the institution of slavery in the States where it exists." To the contrary, a southern newspaper declared: "The mission of the Republican party was to meddle with everything—to meddle with the domestic institutions of other States, and to meddle with family arrangements in their own states—to overthrow Democracy, Catholicism and Slavery." Soon, a southern senator warned, "cohorts of Federal office-holders, Abolitionists, may be sent into [our] midst" to mobilize enslaved blacks. The result would be bloody slave revolts and racial intermixture—by which Southerners meant sexual relations between black men and white women, given that white owners had already fathered untold thousands of children by their black women slaves.

"Better, far better! endure all horrors of civil war," insisted a Confederate recruit from Virginia, "than to see the dusky sons of Ham leading the fair daughters of the South to the altar." To preserve black slavery and the supremacy of white men, radical Southerners chose the dangerous enterprise of secession.

Lincoln and the North would not let them go in peace. Living in a world still ruled by kings and princes, northern leaders believed that the collapse of the American Union might destroy for all time the possibility of a democratic republican government. "We cannot escape history," the new president eloquently declared. "We shall nobly save, or meanly lose, the last best hope of earth." A young Union army recruit from Ohio put the issue simply: "If our institutions prove a failure . . . of what value will be house, family, or friends?"

And so came the Civil War. Called the "War Between the States" by Southerners and the "War of the Rebellion" by Northerners, the struggle continued until the great issues of the Union and slavery had finally been resolved. The cost was incredibly high: more lives lost than the combined total in all the nation's other wars and a century-long legacy of bitterness between the triumphant North and the vanquished South.

Fields of Death

Fought with mass armies and new weapons, the Civil War took a huge toll in human lives, as is evidenced by this grisly photograph of a small section of the battlefield at Antietam, Maryland. At Shiloh, Tennessee, General Ulysses Grant surveyed a field "so covered with dead that it would have been possible to walk . . . in any direction, stepping on dead bodies, without a foot touching the ground." Library of Congress.

For more help analyzing this image, see the Online Study Guide at **bedfordstmartins.com/henrettaconcise**.

Secession and Military Stalemate, 1861–1862

After Lincoln was elected in November 1860, secessionist fervor swept through the Deep South. But the veteran party leaders in Washington, who had run the country for a generation, still hoped to save the Union. In the four months between Lincoln's election and his inauguration on March 4, 1861, they struggled to forge a new compromise.

The Secession Crisis

Secession occurred first in South Carolina, the home of John C. Calhoun, Nullification, and Southern Rights. Robert Barnwell Rhett and other fire-eaters had called for secession since the crisis of 1850, and their goal was now within reach. "Our enemies are about to take possession of the Government," warned a South Carolinian, and will act like a "conqueror over a subjugated and craven people." Frightened by that prospect, a special state convention voted unanimously on December 20 to dissolve "the union now subsisting between South Carolina and other States."

Fire-eaters elsewhere in the Deep South quickly called similar conventions and mobilized vigilantes to suppress local Unionists. In early January, white Mississippians joyously enacted a secession ordinance. Within a month, Florida, Alabama, Georgia, Louisiana, and Texas had also left the Union (Map 14.1). In February, the jubilant secessionists met in Montgomery, Alabama, to proclaim a new nation: the Confederate States of America. Adopting a provisional constitution, the delegates named Jefferson Davis of Mississippi, a former U.S. senator and secretary of war, as the Confederacy's president and Alexander Stephens, a congressman from Georgia, as vice president.

Secessionist fervor was less intense in the four states of the Middle South (Virginia, North Carolina, Tennessee, and Arkansas), where there were fewer slaves. White opinion was also sharply divided in the four border slave states (Maryland, Delaware, Kentucky, and Missouri), where yeomen farmers had greater political power. During the 1850s, journalist Hinton Helper of North Carolina had warned yeomen that "the slaveholders . . . have hoodwinked you." Influenced partly by such sentiments, the legislatures of Virginia and Tennessee refused to join the secessionist movement and urged a compromise.

Meanwhile, the Union government floundered. Addressing Congress in December 1860, President Buchanan declared secession illegal. But the president, timid and indecisive, claimed that the federal government lacked authority to restore the Union by force. Buchanan's weakness prompted South Carolina to demand the surrender of Fort Sumter, a federal garrison in Charleston Harbor. When the South Carolinians would not allow a merchant ship to resupply the fort, Buchanan refused to order the navy to escort it into the harbor.

Instead, the outgoing president urged Congress to find a compromise. The plan proposed by Senator John J. Crittenden of Kentucky received the most support. Crittenden's plan had two parts. The first, which Congress approved, called for a constitutional amendment to protect slavery from federal interference in any state where it already existed. Crittenden's second provision called for the westward extension of the Missouri Compromise line (36°30′ north latitude) to the California border. Slavery would be barred north of the line and protected to the south, including any territories

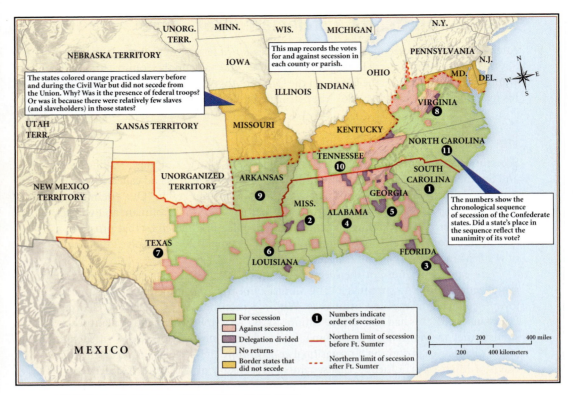

The states colored orange practiced slavery before and during the Civil War but did not secede from the Union. Why? Was it the presence of federal troops? Or was it because there were relatively few slaves (and slaveholders) in those states?

This map records the votes for and against secession in each county or parish.

The numbers show the chronological sequence of secession of the Confederate states. Did a state's place in the sequence reflect the unanimity of its vote?

Legend:
- For secession
- Against secession
- Delegation divided
- No returns
- Border states that did not secede
- ● Numbers indicate order of secession
- — Northern limit of secession before Ft. Sumter
- --- Northern limit of secession after Ft. Sumter

0   200   400 miles
0   200   400 kilometers

MAP 14.1 The Process of Secession, 1860–1861

The states of the Deep South had the highest concentration of slaves, and they led the secessionist movement. After the attack on Fort Sumter in April 1861, the states of the Middle South joined the Confederacy. Yeomen farmers in Tennessee and the backcountry of Alabama, Georgia, and Virginia opposed secession but, except in the region that became West Virginia, rallied to the Confederate cause. Consequently, the South entered the Civil War with its white population relatively united.

"hereafter acquired," thus raising the prospect of expansion into Cuba or Central America. On strict instructions from President-elect Lincoln, congressional Republicans rejected this part of Crittenden's plan. Lincoln was firmly committed to free soil and—with good reason—feared that this provision would allow new imperialist adventures. Senator Albert G. Brown of Mississippi had candidly stated in 1858: "I want Cuba . . . I want Tamaulipas, Potosi, and one or two other Mexican States; and I want them all . . . for the planting or spreading of slavery." In 1787, 1821, and 1850, the North and South had managed to resolve their differences over slavery. In 1861, there would be no compromise.

In his inaugural address in March 1861, Lincoln carefully outlined his views on slavery and the Union. He promised to safeguard slavery where it existed but vowed to prevent its expansion. Beyond that, Lincoln declared that the Union was "perpetual"; consequently, the secession of the Confederate states was illegal. The Republican president declared his intention to "hold, occupy, and possess" federal property in the seceded states and "to collect duties and imposts" there. If military force was necessary to preserve the Union, Lincoln—like Andrew Jackson during the nullification crisis—would use it. The choice was the South's: Return to the Union or face war.

The Upper South Chooses Sides

The South's decision came quickly. The garrison at Fort Sumter urgently needed food and medicine. Upholding his promise to defend federal property, Lincoln dispatched an unarmed ship to supply the fort. However, Jefferson Davis and his Confederate associates wanted a military confrontation, so Davis demanded the surrender of the fort. Major Robert Anderson refused, and the Confederate forces opened fire on April 12. An ardent fire-eater named Edmund Ruffin supposedly shot off the first cannon. Two days later, the Union defenders capitulated. On April 15, Lincoln called 75,000 state militiamen into federal service for ninety days to put down an insurrection "too powerful to be suppressed by the ordinary course of judicial proceedings."

Northerners responded to Lincoln's call to arms with wild enthusiasm. Asked to provide thirteen regiments of volunteers, Republican governor William Dennison of Ohio sent twenty regiments. Many northern Democrats supported the Union. "Every man must be for the United States or against it," Democratic leader Stephen Douglas declared. "There can be no neutrals in this war, only patriots—or traitors." How then might the Democratic Party function as a "loyal opposition," supporting the Union while challenging many of Lincoln's policies? It would not be an easy task.

Whites in the Middle and Border South now had to choose between the Union and the Confederacy, and their decision was crucial. Those eight states accounted for two-thirds of the South's white population, more than three-fourths of its industrial production, and well over half of its food. They were home to many of the nation's best military leaders, including Colonel Robert E. Lee of Virginia, a career officer whom veteran General Winfield Scott recommended to Lincoln to lead the new Union army. These states were also geographically strategic. Kentucky, with its 500-mile border on the Ohio River, was essential to the movement of troops and supplies. Maryland was vital to the Union's security because it bordered the nation's capital on three sides.

The weight of history decided the outcome in Virginia, the original home of American slavery. Three days after the fall of Fort Sumter, a Virginia convention approved secession by a vote of 88 to 55, the dissenters being drawn mainly from the yeomen-dominated northwestern counties. Elsewhere, Virginia whites rallied to the Confederate cause. "The North was the aggressor," declared Richmond lawyer William Poague as he enlisted. "The South resisted her invaders." Refusing Scott's offer of the Union command, Robert E. Lee resigned from the U.S. Army. "Save in defense of my native state," Lee told Scott, "I never desire again to draw my sword." Arkansas, Tennessee, and North Carolina quickly joined Virginia in the Confederacy.

Lincoln moved aggressively to hold the states of the Border South, where relatively few families owned slaves. To secure the railway line connecting Washington to the Ohio River Valley, the president ordered General George B. McClellan to take control of northwestern Virginia. In October 1861, yeomen voters there overwhelmingly approved the creation of a separate breakaway territory, West Virginia, which was admitted to the Union in 1863. Unionists easily carried the day in Delaware but not in Maryland, where slavery was still entrenched. A pro-Confederate mob attacked

Massachusetts troops traveling through Baltimore, causing the war's first combat deaths: four soldiers and twelve civilians. When Maryland secessionists destroyed railroad bridges and telegraph lines, Lincoln ordered Union troops to occupy the state and arrest Confederate sympathizers, including legislators. He released them only in November 1861, after Unionists had secured control of Maryland's government.

Lincoln was equally energetic and resourceful in the Southwest. To win Missouri (and control of the Missouri and upper Mississippi rivers), Lincoln mobilized the German American militia, which strongly opposed slavery; in July, it defeated a force of Confederate sympathizers commanded by the state's governor. Despite continuing raids by Confederate guerrilla bands, the Union retained control of Missouri (see Voices from Abroad, p. 413). In Kentucky, secessionist and Unionist sentiment was evenly balanced, so Lincoln moved cautiously. He allowed Kentucky's thriving trade with the Confederacy to continue until August, when Unionists took over the state government. When the Confederacy responded to the cutoff of trade by invading Kentucky in September, Illinois volunteers commanded by Ulysses S. Grant drove them out. Mixing military force with political persuasion, Lincoln had kept four border states (Delaware, Maryland, Missouri, and Kentucky) and the northwestern portion of Virginia in the Union.

Setting War Objectives and Devising Strategies

In his first speeches as President of the Confederacy, Jefferson Davis identified the Confederates' cause with that of the Americans of 1776: Like their grandfathers, white Southerners were fighting for the "sacred right of self-government." The Confederacy sought "no conquest, no aggrandizement . . . ; all we ask is to be let alone." Davis's implicit renunciation of western expansion was ironic, because it was the slave owners' quest to extend slavery that had sparked Lincoln's election and southern secession. Still, this decision simplified the Confederacy's military strategy; it needed only to defend its boundaries to achieve independence as a slave-owning republic. Ignoring the strong antislavery sentiment among potential European allies, the Confederate constitution explicitly ruled out gradual emancipation or any other law "denying or impairing the right of property in negro slaves." Confederate Vice President Alexander Stephens insisted that his nation's "cornerstone rests upon the great truth that the Negro is not equal to the white man, that slavery—subordination to the superior race—is his natural or normal condition."

Lincoln responded to Davis in a speech to Congress on July 4, 1861. Portraying secession as an attack on popular government, America's great contribution to world history, Lincoln saw the struggle as a test of "whether a constitutional republic . . . [can] maintain its territorial integrity against a domestic foe." Determined to crush the rebellion, Lincoln rejected General Winfield Scott's strategy of peaceful persuasion through economic sanctions and a naval blockade. Instead, the president insisted on an aggressive military campaign and a policy of unconditional surrender.

Lincoln hoped that a quick strike against the Confederate capital of Richmond, Virginia, would end the rebellion. Many Northerners were equally optimistic. "What a picnic," thought one New York volunteer, "to go down South for three months and clean up the whole business." So in July 1861, Lincoln ordered General Irvin McDowell and an army of 30,000 men to attack General P. G. T. Beauregard's force of 20,000 troops at Manassas, a rail junction in Virginia 30 miles southwest of Washington.

German Immigrants and the Civil War Within Missouri ERNEST DUVERGIER DE HAURANNE

Thousands of German immigrants settled in Missouri in the two decades before the Civil War; and as this letter written by Ernest Duvergier de Hauranne indicates, most of them supported the Union cause. Duvergier de Hauranne (1843–1877), a Frenchman, traveled widely, and his letters home offer intelligent commentary on American politics and society.

St. Louis, September 12, 1864

Missouri is to all intents and purposes a rebel state, an occupied territory where the Federal forces are really nothing but a garrison under siege; even today it is not certain what would happen if the troops were withdrawn. Party quarrels here are poisoned by class hatreds. . . . The old Anglo-French families, attached to Southern institutions, harbor a primitive, superstitious prejudice in favor of slavery. Conquered now, but full of repressed rage, they exhibit the implacable anger peculiar to the defenders of lost causes.

The more recent German population is strongly abolitionist. They have brought to the New World the instincts of European democracy, together with its radical attitudes and all-or-nothing doctrines. Ancient precedents and worn-out laws matter little to them. They have not studied history and have no respect for hallowed injustices; but they do have, to the highest degree, that sense of moral principle which is more or less lacking in American democracy. They aren't afraid of revolution: to destroy a barbarous institution they would, if necessary, take an axe to the foundations of society.

Furthermore, their interests coincide with their principles. . . . The immigrant arrives poor and lives by his work. A newcomer, having nothing to lose and caring little for the interests of established property owners, sees that the subjection of free labor to the ruinous competition of slave labor must be ended. At the same time, his pride rebels against the prejudice attached to work in a land of slavery; he wants to reestablish its value. . . .

There is no mistaking the hatred the two parties, not to say the two peoples, have for each other. . . . As passions were coming to a boil, the Federal government sent General [John C.] Frémont here as army commander and dictator. . . . An abolitionist and a self-made man, he put himself firmly at the head of the German party, determined to crush the friends of slavery. . . . He left the abolitionist party in the West organized, disciplined, stronger and more resolute, but he also left the pro-Southern party more exasperated than ever, and society divided, without intermediaries, into two hostile camps . . . .

Bands of guerrillas hold the countryside, where they raid as much as they please; politics serves as a fine pretext for looting. Their leaders are officers from the army of the South who receive their orders from the Confederate government. . . . These "bushwackers," who ordinarily rob indiscriminately, maintain their standing as political raiders by occasionally killing some poor, inoffensive person. . . . You can see what emotions are still boiling in this region that is supposed to be pacified.

SOURCE: Ernest Duvergier de Hauranne, *A Frenchman in Lincoln's America* (Chicago: Lakeside Press, 1974), 1: 305–309.

McDowell launched a strong assault near Manassas Creek (also called Bull Run), but panic swept his troops when the Confederate soldiers counterattacked, shouting the hair-raising rebel yell. "The peculiar corkscrew sensation that it sends down your backbone under these circumstances can never be told," one Union veteran wrote. "You have to feel it." McDowell's troops—along with the many civilians who had come to observe the battle—retreated in disarray to Washington.

The rout at Bull Run made it clear that the rebellion would not be easily crushed. Lincoln replaced McDowell with General McClellan and enlisted an additional million men, who would serve for three years in the newly created Army of the Potomac. A cautious military engineer, McClellan spent the winter of 1861 training the recruits; then, early in 1862, he launched a major offensive. With great logistical skill, the Union general transported 100,000 troops by boat down the Potomac River to the Chesapeake Bay and landed them on the peninsula between the York and James rivers (Map 14.2). Ignoring Lincoln's advice to "strike a blow" quickly, McClellan advanced slowly toward the South's capital, allowing the Confederates to mount a counterstroke. To relieve the pressure on Richmond, a Confederate army under Thomas J. "Stonewall" Jackson marched rapidly northward through the Shenandoah Valley in western Virginia and threatened Washington. Lincoln recalled 30,000 troops from McClellan's army to protect the Union's capital, and Jackson returned quickly to Richmond to bolster the main Confederate army commanded by General Robert E. Lee. Lee launched a ferocious attack that lasted for days (from June 25 to July 1), in which the Confederates suffered 20,000 casualties to the Union's 10,000. When McClellan failed to exploit the Confederates' losses, Lincoln ordered a withdrawal, and Richmond remained secure.

Hoping for victories that would humiliate Lincoln's government, Lee went on the offensive. Joining with Jackson in northern Virginia, he routed Union troops in the Second Battle of Bull Run (August 1862) and then struck north through western Maryland. There, he nearly met with disaster. When Lee divided his force, sending Jackson to capture Harpers Ferry in West Virginia, a copy of Lee's orders fell into McClellan's hands. But the Union general again failed to exploit his advantage. He delayed his attack, allowing Lee's depleted army to occupy a strong defensive position behind Antietam Creek, near Sharpsburg, Maryland. Outnumbered 87,000 to 50,000, Lee desperately fought off McClellan's attacks until Jackson's troops arrived and saved the Confederates from a major defeat. Appalled by the number of Union casualties, McClellan allowed Lee to retreat to Virginia.

The fighting at Antietam was savage. A Wisconsin officer described his men "loading and firing with demoniacal fury and shouting and laughing hysterically." A sunken road—nicknamed Bloody Lane—was filled with Confederate bodies two and three deep, and the advancing Union troops knelt on "this ghastly flooring" to shoot at the retreating Confederates. The battle at Antietam on September 17, 1862, remains the bloodiest single day in U.S. military history. Together, the Confederate and Union dead numbered 4,800 and the wounded 18,500, of whom 3,000 soon died. (By comparison, there were 6,000 American casualties on D-Day, which began the invasion of Nazi-occupied France in World War II.)

In public, Lincoln claimed Antietam as a Union victory; privately, he criticized McClellan for not fighting Lee to the bitter end. A masterful organizer of men and supplies, McClellan lacked the stomach for all-out warfare. Lincoln dismissed McClellan as his chief commander and began what turned out to be a long search for an effective

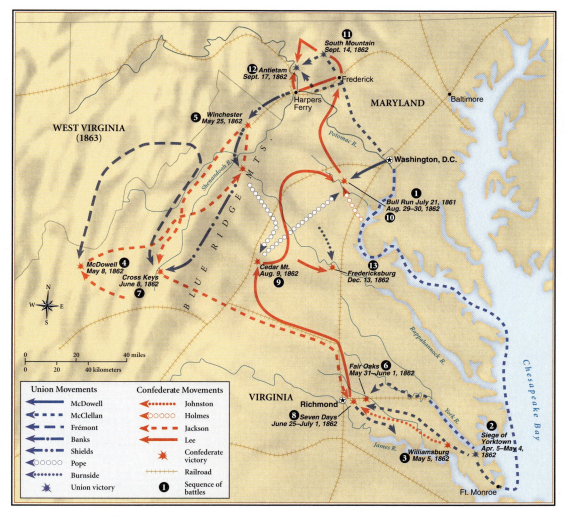

MAP 14.2 The Eastern Campaigns of 1862

Many of the great battles of the Civil War took place in the 125 miles separating the Union capital, Washington, D.C., and the Confederate capital, Richmond, Virginia. During 1862, Confederate generals Thomas J. "Stonewall" Jackson and Robert E. Lee won defensive victories that protected the Confederate capital (3, 6, 8, and 13) and launched offensive strikes against Union forces guarding Washington (1, 4, 5, 7, 9, and 10). They also suffered a defeat — at Antietam (12), in Maryland — that was almost fatal. The victors in these battles were usually either too bloodied or too timid to exploit their advantage.

replacement. His first choice was Ambrose E. Burnside, who proved to be more daring but less competent than McClellan. In December, after heavy losses in futile attacks against well-entrenched Confederate forces at Fredericksburg, Virginia, Burnside resigned his command, and Lincoln replaced him with Joseph "Fighting Joe" Hooker. As 1862 ended, the Confederates were optimistic: They had won a stalemate in the East.

In the West, Union commanders were more successful (Map 14.3). Their goal was to control the Ohio, Mississippi, and Missouri rivers, dividing the Confederacy and reducing

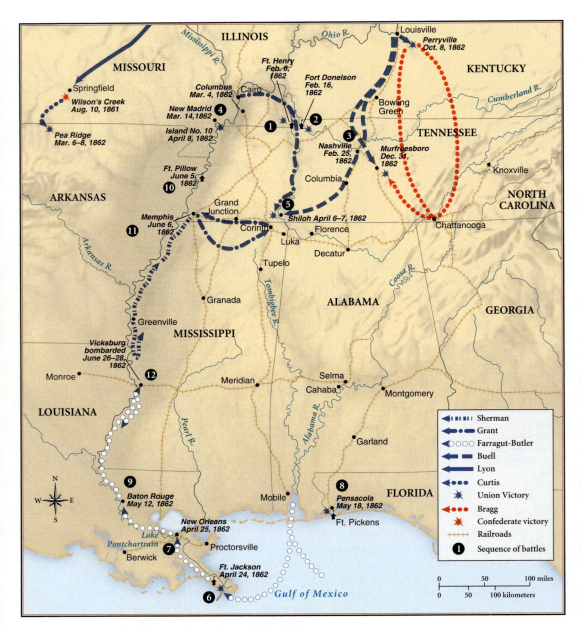

MAP 14.3 The Western Campaigns, 1861–1862

As the Civil War intensified in 1862, Union and Confederate military and naval forces fought to control the great valleys of the Ohio, Tennessee, and Mississippi rivers. From February through April 1862, Union armies moved south through western Tennessee (1–3 and 5). By the end of June, Union naval forces controlled the Mississippi River north of Memphis (4, 10, and 11) and from the Gulf of Mexico to Vicksburg (6, 7, 9, and 12). These military and naval victories gave the Union control of crucial transportation routes, kept Missouri in the Union, and carried the war to the borders of the states of the Deep South.

the mobility of its armies. Because Kentucky did not join the rebellion, the Union already dominated the Ohio River Valley. In 1862, the Union army launched innovative land and water operations to take charge of the Tennessee and Mississippi rivers as well. General Ulysses S. Grant used riverboats clad with iron plates to capture Fort Henry on the Tennessee River and Fort Donelson on the Cumberland River. When Grant moved south to seize critical railroad lines, a Confederate army led by Albert Sidney Johnston and P. G. T. Beauregard caught him by surprise near a small log church named Shiloh. But Grant relentlessly committed troops until he forced a Confederate withdrawal. As the fighting at Shiloh ended on April 7, Grant surveyed a large field "so covered with dead that it would have been possible to walk over the clearing in any direction, stepping on dead bodies, without a foot touching the ground." The cost in lives was high, but Lincoln was pleased: "What I want . . . is generals who will fight battles and win victories."

Three weeks later, Union naval forces commanded by David G. Farragut struck the Confederacy from the Gulf of Mexico. They captured New Orleans and took control of 1,500 plantations and 50,000 slaves in the surrounding region. The Union now held the South's financial center and largest city and had struck a strong blow against slavery. Workers on many plantations looted their owners' mansions and refused to labor unless they were paid wages. Slavery there "is forever destroyed and worthless," declared one Northern reporter. Union victories in the West had significantly undermined Confederate strength in the Mississippi River Valley.

▶ Why was there no new compromise over slavery in 1861? How important was the conflict at Fort Sumter? Would the Confederacy — and the Union — have decided to go to war in any event?

▶ In the first years of the war, what were the political and military strategies of each side? Which side was the more successful? Why?

Toward Total War

The military carnage in 1862 revealed that the war would be long and costly. After Shiloh, Grant later remarked, he "gave up all idea of saving the Union except by complete conquest." The Civil War increasingly resembled the **total wars** that would come in the twentieth century, conflicts that drew on the entire resources of the society and made civilian lives and property legitimate objects of attack. Aided by the Republican Party and a talented cabinet, Lincoln skillfully organized an effective central government and promoted ruthless generals prepared to wage all-out war. Jefferson Davis had less success at harnessing the resources of the South, because the eleven states of the Confederacy remained suspicious of centralized rule and southern yeomen grew increasingly skeptical of the war effort.

Mobilizing Armies and Civilians

Initially, patriotic fervor filled both armies with eager young volunteers. All he heard "was War! War! War!" recalled one Union recruit. Even those of sober minds joined up. "I don't think a young man ever went over all the considerations more carefully than I did," reflected William Saxton of Cincinnatus, New York. "It might mean sickness, wounds, loss of limb, and even life itself. . . . But my country was in danger." The call for volunteers was equally successful in the South, which boasted a strong military tradition, a supply of trained officers, and a culture that stressed duty and honor. "Would you, My Darling, . . . be willing to leave your Children under such a [despotic Union] government?" James B. Griffin of Edgefield, South Carolina, asked his wife. "No—I know you would sacrifice every comfort on earth, rather than submit to it." However, enlistments declined as potential recruits learned the realities of mass warfare: heavy losses to epidemic diseases in the camps and wholesale death on the battlefields. Both governments soon faced the need for conscription.

The Confederacy was the first to act. In April 1862, following the bloodshed at Shiloh, the Confederate Congress imposed the first legally binding draft in American history. Laws extended existing enlistments for the duration of the war and required three years of military service from all men between the ages of eighteen and thirty-five. In September 1862, after the heavy casualties at Antietam, the Confederacy raised the age limit to forty-five. The South's draft had two loopholes, both controversial. First, it exempted one white man—the planter, a son, or an overseer—for each twenty slaves, allowing some whites on large plantations to avoid military service. This provision, Mississippi Senator James Phelan warned Jefferson Davis, "has aroused a sprit of rebellion in some places." Second, draftees could hire substitutes. By the time this loophole was closed in 1864, the price of a substitute had risen to $300 in gold, three times the annual wage of a skilled worker. Laborers and yeomen farmers angrily complained that it was "a rich man's war and a poor man's fight."

Consequently, some Southerners refused to serve. Because the Confederate constitution vested sovereignty in the individual states, the government in Richmond could not compel military service. Strong governors such as Joseph Brown of Georgia and Zebulon Vance of North Carolina simply ignored President Davis's first draft call in early 1862. Elsewhere, state judges issued writs of **habeas corpus**—a legal instrument used to protect people from arbitrary arrest—and ordered the Confederate army to release reluctant draftees. However, the Confederate Congress overrode the judges' authority to free conscripted men, so the government was able to keep substantial armies in the field well into 1864.

The Union government acted more ruthlessly toward reluctant recruits and potential foes. To deter resistance by Confederate sympathizers, Lincoln suspended habeas corpus and, over the course of the war, imprisoned about 15,000 people without trial. The president also placed civilians who discouraged enlistments or resisted the draft under the jurisdiction of military courts, preventing acquittals by sympathetic local juries. But Union governments primarily used incentives to fill the ranks. When the Militia Act of 1862 set local recruitment quotas, many states, counties, and towns avoided conscription by using cash bounties of as much as $600 (about $11,000 today) and signed up nearly one million men. The Union also allowed men to avoid military service by providing a substitute or paying a $300 fee.

When the Enrollment Act of 1863 finally initiated conscription in the North, recent German and Irish immigrants often refused to serve. It was not their war, they said. Northern Democrats used the furor over conscription to bolster support for their party, which took an increasingly critical stance toward Lincoln's policies. Using racist invective, they accused Lincoln of drafting poor whites to free blacks, who would flood the cities and take their jobs. "Slavery is dead," declared a Democratic newspaper in Cincinnati, "the negro is not, there is the misfortune." In July 1863, the immigrants' hostility brought violence to New York City. For five days, Irish and German workers ran rampant, burning draft offices, sacking the homes of influential Republicans, and attacking the police. The rioters lynched and mutilated a dozen African Americans, drove hundreds of black families from their homes, and burned down the Colored Orphan Asylum. Lincoln rushed in Union troops who had just fought at Gettysburg; they killed more than one hundred rioters and suppressed the immigrant mobs.

The Union government won greater support among native-born middle-class citizens. In 1861, prominent New Yorkers established the U.S. Sanitary Commission to provide medical services and prevent the spread of epidemic diseases among the troops. Through its network of 7,000 local auxiliaries, the commission collected clothing and food. "I almost weep," reported a local agent, "when these plain rural people come to send their simple offerings to absent sons and brothers." The Commission also recruited battlefield nurses and doctors for the Union Army Medical Bureau. Despite these efforts, dysentery, typhoid, and malaria spread through the camps, as did mumps and measles, viruses that were dangerous to nonimmune rural recruits. Diseases and infections killed about 250,000 Union soldiers, roughly twice the number who died in combat. Still, thanks to the Sanitary Commission, Union troops had a much lower mortality rate than did the soldiers in nineteenth-century European wars. Confederate armies were less fortunate. Thousands of women volunteered as nurses, but the Confederate health system was poorly organized. Scurvy was a special problem for southern soldiers, who lacked vitamin C in their diets, and they died from camp diseases at a high rate.

War relief had a significant impact on women's lives. More than 200,000 northern women worked as volunteers in the Sanitary Commission and the Freedman's Aid Society, which collected supplies for liberated slaves, and some women took leading roles in wartime agencies. Dorothea Dix (see Chapter 11) served as superintendent of

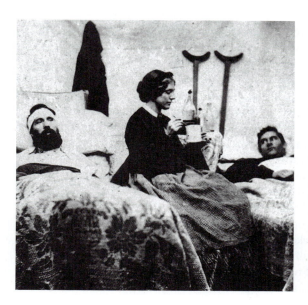

Hospital Nursing
Working as nurses in battlefront hospitals, thousands of Union and Confederate women gained firsthand experience of the horrors of war. A sense of calm prevails in this behind-the-lines Union hospital in Nashville, Tennessee, as nurse Anne Belle tends to the needs of soldiers recovering from their wounds. Most Civil War nurses were volunteers; they spent time cooking and cleaning for their patients as well as tending their injuries. U.S. Army Military History Institute.

female nurses and, by successfully combating the prejudice against women's providing medical treatment to men, opened a new occupation to women. Thousands of educated Union women became clerks in the expanding government bureaucracy, while southern women staffed the efficient Confederate postal service. In both societies, millions of women assumed new economic responsibilities. They took over many farm tasks; filled jobs in schools and offices; and served as operatives in textile, shoe, and food-processing factories. A few women even took on military duties as spies, scouts, and (disguising themselves as men) soldiers. As nurse Clara Barton, who later founded the American Red Cross, recalled, "At the war's end, woman was at least fifty years in advance of the normal position which continued peace would have assigned her."

Mobilizing Resources

Wars are usually won by the side that has greater resources and better economic organization. In this regard, the Union had a distinct advantage. With nearly two-thirds of the nation's population, two-thirds of the railroad mileage, and almost 90 percent of the industrial output, the North's economy was far superior to the South's. The North had a great advantage in the manufacture of cannon and rifles because many of its arms factories were equipped for mass production.

But the Confederate position was far from weak. Virginia, North Carolina, and Tennessee had substantial industrial capacity. Richmond, with its Tredegar Iron Works, was already an important manufacturing center, and in 1861, the city received the gun-making machinery from the U.S. armory at Harpers Ferry. The production at the Richmond armory, the purchase of Enfield rifles from Britain, and the capture of 100,000 Union guns enabled the Confederacy to provide every infantryman with a modern rifle-musket by 1863.

Moreover, with nine million people, the Confederacy could mobilize enormous armies. The one-third of Southerners who were slaves contributed to the war effort by producing food for the army and cotton for export. Confederate leaders counted on **"King Cotton"** to provide the revenue to purchase clothes, boots, blankets, and weapons from abroad. They also intended to use cotton as a diplomatic weapon to persuade Britain and France, whose textile factories needed raw cotton, to grant the Confederacy diplomatic recognition. However, British manufacturers had stockpiled cotton, and they found new sources in Egypt and India. Still, the South's hope was partially fulfilled. Although Britain never recognized the Confederacy as an independent nation, it granted the rebel government the status of a belligerent power — with the right under international law to borrow money and purchase weapons. The odds, then, did not necessarily favor the Union, despite its superior resources.

To mobilize northern resources, the Republican-dominated Congress enacted a program of government-assisted economic development that far surpassed Henry Clay's American System. The Republicans imposed huge tariffs (averaging nearly 40 percent) on various foreign goods, thereby winning the political support of northeastern manufacturers and workers. They also provided northern and midwestern farmers with "free land." The Homestead Act of 1862 gave settlers the title to 160 acres of public land after five years of residence. Secretary of the Treasury Salmon P. Chase created an integrated national banking system (far more powerful than the First and

Second Banks of the United States) by forcing thousands of local banks to accept federal charters and regulations. Finally, the Republican Congress implemented Clay's program for a nationally financed system of internal improvements. In 1862, it chartered the Union Pacific and Central Pacific companies to build a transcontinental railroad line and granted them lavish subsidies. This comprehensive economic program won the Republican Party the allegiance of farmers, workers, and entrepreneurs and bolstered the Union's ability to fight a long war.

New industries sprang up to meet the army's need for guns, clothes, and food. More than 1.5 million men served in the Union army, and they consumed more than half a billion pounds of pork and other packed meats. To meet this demand, Chicago railroads built new lines to carry thousands of hogs and cattle to the city's ever-larger stockyards and slaughtering houses. By 1862, Chicago had passed Cincinnati as the meatpacking capital of the nation, bringing prosperity to thousands of midwestern farmers and great wealth to Philip D. Armour and other meatpacking entrepreneurs.

A similar concentration of capital occurred in many industries. The war, an observer noted, gave a few men "the command of millions of money"; such massed financial power threatened not only the prewar society of small producers but also the future of democracy. Americans "are never again to see the republic in which we were born," lamented abolitionist and social reformer Wendell Phillips.

The Confederate government took longer to develop a coherent economic policy. True to its states' rights philosophy, the Confederacy initially left most economic matters to the state governments. However, as the realities of total war became clear, the Davis administration took some extraordinary measures: It built and operated shipyards, armories, foundries, and textile mills; commandeered food and scarce raw materials such as coal, iron, copper, and lead; requisitioned slaves to work on fortifications; and exercised direct control over foreign trade. Ordinary southern citizens increasingly resented and resisted these measures by the central government in Richmond, forcing Confederate leaders to rely increasingly on white solidarity: President Davis warned that a Union victory would destroy slavery "and reduce the whites to the degraded position of the African race."

For both sides, the cost of fighting a total war was enormous. The annual spending of the Union government shot up from $63 million in 1860 to more than $865 million in 1864. To raise that enormous sum, the Republicans established a powerful modern state that secured funds in three ways. First, the government increased tariffs; placed high excise duties on alcohol and tobacco; and imposed direct taxes on business corporations, large inheritances, and incomes. These levies paid for about 20 percent of the cost. Treasury bonds financed another 65 percent. The National Banking Acts of 1863 and 1864 forced most banks to buy and hold those bonds; and Jay Cooke, a Philadelphia banker working for the Treasury Department, used newspaper ads and 2,500 subagents to persuade nearly one million northern families to buy them.

The Union paid the remaining cost of the war by printing paper money. The Legal Tender Act of 1862 authorized $150 million in paper currency—which soon became known as **greenbacks**—and required the public to accept them as legal tender. Like the Continental currency issued during the Revolution, the greenbacks were not backed by specie; but they were issued in relatively limited amounts and so did not depreciate disastrously in value. By imposing broad-based taxes, borrowing from the middle classes, and creating a national monetary system, the Union government had created a modern fiscal state.

The financial demands on the South were equally great, but it lacked a powerful central government that could tax and borrow. The Confederate Congress fiercely opposed taxes on cotton exports and slaves, the most valuable property held by wealthy planters; and the urban middle class and yeomen farm families refused to bear the entire tax burden. Consequently, the Confederacy covered less than 5 percent of its expenditures through taxation. The government paid for another 35 percent by borrowing, although wealthy planters and foreign bankers grew increasingly wary of investing in Confederate bonds that might never be redeemed.

So the Confederacy had to pay about 60 percent of its expenses by printing paper money. The flood of currency created a spectacular inflation: By 1865, prices had risen to ninety-two times their 1861 level. As the vast supply of money (and a shortage of goods) caused food prices to soar, riots broke out in more than a dozen southern cities and towns. In Richmond, several hundred women broke into bakeries, crying, "Our children are starving while the rich roll in wealth." In Randolph County, Alabama, women confiscated grain from a government warehouse "to prevent starvation of themselves and their families." As inflation increased, Southerners refused to accept Confederate money, sometimes with serious consequences. When South Carolina storekeeper Jim Harris rejected the currency presented by a group of soldiers, they raided his storehouse and "robbed it of about five thousand dollars worth of goods." Army supply officers likewise seized goods from merchants and offered payment in worthless IOUs. Facing a public that feared strong government and high taxation, the Confederacy could sustain the war effort only by seizing its citizens' property.

▶ Which government — the Union or the Confederacy — imposed greater military and economic burdens on its citizens? How successful were their respective strategies?

▶ What were the main economic policies enacted by the Republican-controlled Congress?

The Turning Point: 1863

By 1863, the Lincoln administration had finally created an efficient war machine, an integrated financial system, and a set of strategic priorities. Henry Adams, the grandson of John Quincy Adams and a future novelist and important historian, noted the change from his diplomatic post in London: "Little by little, one began to feel that, behind the chaos in Washington power was taking shape; that it was massed and guided as it had not been before." Slowly but surely, the tide of the struggle shifted toward the Union.

Emancipation

When the war began, antislavery Republicans demanded that their party make abolition — as well as restoration of the Union — a goal of the war. The fighting should continue, declared a Massachusetts abolitionist, "until the Slave power is completely subjugated, and *emancipation made certain*." Because slave-grown crops sustained the Confederacy, activists justified black emancipation on military grounds. As Frederick Douglass put it, "Arrest that hoe in the hands of the Negro, and you smite the rebellion in the very seat of its life."

As abolitionists pressed their case, enslaved African Americans exploited the disorder of wartime to seize freedom for themselves. When three slaves reached the camp of General Benjamin Butler in Virginia in May 1861, he labeled them "contraband of war" (a term for goods that can be legitimately seized, according to international law) and refused to return them. Butler's term stuck, and within a few months, thousands of "contrabands" were camping with Union armies. Near Fredericksburg, Virginia, an average of 200 blacks appeared every day, "with their packs on their backs and handkerchiefs tied over their heads—men, women, little children, and babies." To provide these fugitives with legal status, Congress passed the Confiscation Act in August 1861, authorizing the seizure of all property, including slaves, used to support the rebellion.

Radical Republicans—Treasury Secretary Salmon Chase, Senator Charles Sumner of Massachusetts, and Representative Thaddeus Stevens of Pennsylvania—now saw a way to use wartime legislation to destroy slavery. A longtime member of Congress, Stevens was a masterful politician, skilled at fashioning legislation that could win majority support. In April 1862, Stevens and the Radicals persuaded Congress to end slavery in the District of Columbia by providing compensation for owners. In June, Congress outlawed slavery in the federal territories (finally enacting the Wilmot Proviso of 1846); and in July, it passed a second Confiscation Act. This act overrode the property rights of Confederate planters by declaring "forever free" all fugitive slaves and all slaves captured by the Union army. Emancipation had become an instrument of war.

Initially, Lincoln had rejected emancipation as a war aim, but faced with thousands of contrabands and Radical Republican pressure, he moved cautiously toward that goal. In July 1862, Lincoln drafted a general proclamation of emancipation, and in August, he wrote a public letter to Horace Greeley of the *New York Tribune* linking black freedom to the war effort. "If I could save the Union without freeing any slave, I would do it," the president stated, "and if I could save it by freeing all the slaves, I would do it." By implicitly raising the issues of military necessity and his constitutional authority, Lincoln was laying the foundation for the destruction of slavery.

Now he waited for a Union victory. Considering the Battle of Antietam "an indication of the Divine Will," Lincoln issued the proclamation of emancipation five days later, on September 22, 1862. The president based its legal authority on his responsibility as commander in chief to suppress the rebellion. The proclamation stated that slavery would be legally abolished in all states that remained out of the Union on January 1, 1863. The rebel states could preserve slavery by renouncing secession. None chose to do so.

The proclamation was politically astute. Lincoln wanted to avoid opposition from slave owners in the Union-controlled border states, such as Maryland and Missouri, so the proclamation left slavery intact in those states. It also permitted slavery to continue in areas occupied by Union armies: western and central Tennessee, western Virginia, and southern Louisiana. Consequently, the Emancipation Proclamation did not immediately free a single slave. Yet, as abolitionist Wendell Phillips understood, Lincoln's proclamation had moved slavery to "the edge of Niagara," and it would soon be swept over the brink. Advancing Union troops became the agents of slavery's destruction. "I became free in 1863, in the summer, when the yankees come by and said I could go work for myself," recalled Jackson Daniel of Maysville, Alabama. As Lincoln now saw it, "the old South is to be destroyed and replaced by new propositions and ideas."

Emancipation was extraordinarily controversial. In the Confederacy, Jefferson Davis labeled it the "most execrable measure recorded in the history of guilty man"; in the North, it produced a racist backlash among white voters. During the congressional election of 1862, the Democrats denounced emancipation as unconstitutional, warned of slave uprisings, and claimed that freed blacks would take white jobs. If slaves became free, a nativist New Yorker suggested, "every one" of them should "shoulder an Irishman and leave the Continent." Such sentiments propelled Democrat Horatio Seymour into the governor's office in New York; if abolition was a war goal, Seymour argued, the South should not be conquered. Other Democrats swept to victory in Pennsylvania, Ohio, and Illinois, and the party gained thirty-four seats in Congress. But the Republicans still held a twenty-five-seat majority in the House and had gained five seats in the Senate. Lincoln refused to retreat. On New Year's Day 1863, he signed the Emancipation Proclamation. To reassure Northerners, Lincoln urged slaves to "abstain from all violence" and justified emancipation as an "act of justice." "If my name ever goes into history," he said, "it was for this act."

Vicksburg and Gettysburg

The fate of the proclamation would depend on Republican political success and Union military victories. The outlook was not encouraging on either front. Democrats had gained significantly in the election of 1862, and popular support was growing for a negotiated peace. Two brilliant victories in Virginia by Lee, whose army defeated Hooker's forces at Fredericksburg (December 1862) and Chancellorsville (May 1863), further eroded northern support for the war.

At this critical juncture, General Grant mounted a major offensive in the West to split the Confederacy in two. Grant drove south along the west bank of the Mississippi and then crossed the river near Vicksburg, Mississippi. There, he defeated two Confederate armies and laid siege to the city. After repelling Union assaults for six weeks, the exhausted and starving Vicksburg garrison surrendered on July 4, 1863. Five days later, Union forces took Port Hudson, Louisiana (near Baton Rouge), and seized control of the Mississippi River. Grant had taken 31,000 prisoners; cut off Louisiana, Arkansas, and Texas from the rest of the Confederacy; and prompted thousands of slaves to desert their plantations or demand wages.

As Grant had advanced toward Mississippi in May, Confederate leaders had argued over the best strategic response. President Davis and other politicians wanted to reinforce Vicksburg and send an army to Tennessee to relieve pressure on Mississippi. But General Robert E. Lee, buoyed by his victories over Hooker, favored a new invasion of the North. That strategy, Lee suggested, would either draw Grant's forces to the east or give the Confederacy a major victory that would destroy the North's will to fight.

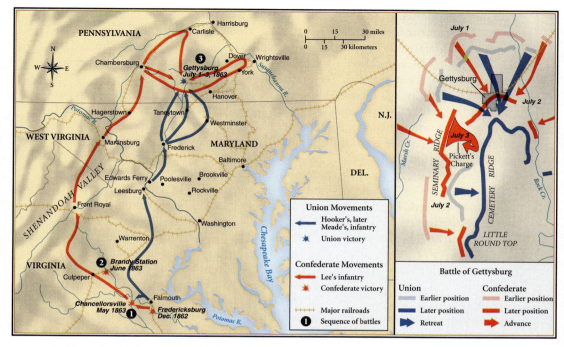

MAP 14.4 Lee Invades the North, 1863

After Lee's victories at Chancellorsville (1) in May and Brandy Station (2) in June, the Confederate forces moved northward, constantly shadowed by the Union army. On July 1, the two armies met accidentally near Gettysburg. In the ensuing battle (3), the Union army, commanded by General George Meade, emerged victorious, primarily because it was much larger than the Confederate force and held well-fortified positions along Cemetery Ridge, which gave its units a major tactical advantage.

Lee won out. In June 1863, he maneuvered his army north through Maryland into Pennsylvania. The Army of the Potomac moved along with him, positioning itself between Lee and Washington, D.C. On July 1, the two great armies met by accident at Gettysburg, Pennsylvania, in what became a decisive confrontation (Map 14.4). On the first day of battle, Lee drove the Union's advance guard to the south of town. General George G. Meade, who had just replaced Hooker as the Union commander, placed his troops in well-defended hilltop positions and called up reinforcements. By the morning of July 2, Meade had 90,000 troops to Lee's 75,000. Aware that he was outnumbered but intent on victory, Lee ordered assaults on Meade's flanks but failed to turn them. General Richard B. Ewell refused to risk his men in an all-out assault on the Union's right flank, and General Longstreet, on the Union's left, failed to dislodge Meade's forces from the hill known as Little Round Top.

On July 3, Lee decided on a dangerous frontal assault against the center of the Union line. After the heaviest artillery barrage of the war, Lee ordered General George E. Pickett and his 14,000 men to take Cemetery Ridge. Anticipating this attack, Meade had reinforced his line with artillery and his best troops. When Pickett's men charged across a mile of open terrain, they were met by deadly fire from artillery and rifle-muskets; thousands were killed, wounded, or captured. As the three-day battle ended, the Confederates had suffered 28,000 casualties, one-third of the Army of Northern Virginia, while 23,000 of Meade's soldiers lay killed or wounded. Shocked by the bloodletting, Meade allowed the Confederate units to escape. Lincoln was furious. "As it is," the president brooded, "the war will be prolonged indefinitely."

Still, Gettysburg was a great Union victory and, together with the simultaneous triumph at Vicksburg, was the major turning point in the war. Southern armies would never again invade the North, and Southern citizens began to criticize the military effort. The Confederate elections of 1863 went sharply against the politicians who supported Jefferson Davis.

Vicksburg and Gettysburg also transformed the political situation in the North and in Europe. In the fall of 1863, Republicans swept state and local elections in Pennsylvania, Ohio, and New York. Equally important, American diplomats finally cut the flow of advanced weapons to the Confederacy. In 1862, British shipbuilders had supplied the Confederacy with an ironclad cruiser, the *Alabama*, which had sunk or captured more than one hundred Union merchant ships; and the delivery of two more ironclad cruisers was imminent. News of the Union victories changed everything. Charles Francis Adams, the American minister, persuaded the British government to impound the ships; the ministry did not want to risk Canada or its merchant ships by provoking the United States. Moreover, Britain had become increasingly dependent on imports of wheat and flour from the American Midwest, and British workers and reformers were strongly opposed to slavery. "King Cotton" diplomacy had failed; "King Wheat" stood triumphant. "Rest not your hopes in foreign nations," President Jefferson Davis now advised his nation, "This war is ours; we must fight it ourselves."

▶ What prompted Lincoln to issue the Emancipation Proclamation: the pressure exerted by antislavery Republican politicians or the pressure exerted by the thousands of "contrabands" who had freed themselves? Explain your answer.

▶ Why were the battles at Gettysburg and Vicksburg significant? How did they change the tide of war strategically? How did they change it diplomatically? How did they change it psychologically?

The Union Victorious, 1864–1865

The Union victories of 1863 meant that the South could not win its independence through a decisive military triumph. However, the Confederacy could still hope for a battlefield stalemate and a negotiated peace. Lincoln faced the daunting task of winning an overwhelming victory, or he would lose the support of northern voters.

Soldiers and Strategy

Two developments allowed the Union to prosecute the war with continued vigor: the enlistment of African American soldiers and the emergence of capable and determined generals. As early as 1861, free African Americans and fugitive slaves had volunteered for the Union army, hoping to end slavery and, as Frederick Douglass put it, win "the right to citizenship in the United States." The prospect of military service for blacks offended many northern whites. "I am as much opposed to slavery as any of them," a New York officer wrote to his local newspaper, "but I am not willing to be put on a level with the negro and fight with them." Moreover, most Union generals doubted that former slaves would make good soldiers. So the Lincoln administration initially refused to enlist African Americans; nonetheless, free and contraband blacks, eager to fight, formed regiments in New England, South Carolina, Louisiana, and Kansas.

The Emancipation Proclamation changed popular thinking and military policy. The proclamation invited former slaves to serve in the Union army, and northern whites, their ranks depleted by thousands of casualties, now accepted that blacks should share in the fighting and dying. The valor exhibited by the first African American regiments to go into combat also influenced northern opinion. In January 1863, Thomas Wentworth Higginson, the white abolitionist commander of the First South Carolina Volunteers, wrote a glowing newspaper account of the black regiment's military prowess. In July, a heroic and costly attack on Fort Wagner, South Carolina, by the Fifty-fourth Massachusetts Infantry convinced many Union officers of the value of black soldiers. The War Department authorized black enlistment, and as white resistance to conscription mounted, the Lincoln administration recruited as many African Americans as it could. Without black soldiers, the president suggested late in 1864, "we would be compelled to abandon the war in three weeks." By the spring of 1865, nearly 200,000 African Americans were serving the Union.

Military service did not end racial discrimination. Initially, black soldiers were paid less than white soldiers ($10 a month versus $13); they won equal pay only by threatening

Black Soldiers in the Union Army
Determined to end racial slavery, 200,000 African Americans volunteered for service in the Union army in 1864 and 1865, boosting the northern war effort at a critical moment. These proud soldiers were members of the 107th Colored Infantry, stationed at Fort Corcoran near Washington, D.C. In January 1865, their regiment participated in the daring capture of Fort Fisher, which protected Wilmington, North Carolina, the last Confederate port open to blockade runners. Library of Congress.

to lay down their arms. Moreover, blacks served under white officers in segregated regiments and were used primarily to build fortifications, garrison forts, and guard supply lines. Despite this treatment, African Americans volunteered for military service in disproportionate numbers because they were fighting for freedom and a new social order. "Hello, Massa," said one black soldier to his former master, who had been taken prisoner. "Bottom rail on top dis time." The worst fears of the secessionists had come true: Through the agency of the Union army, blacks had risen in a great rebellion against slavery.

As African Americans bolstered the army's ranks, Lincoln finally found an efficient and ruthless commanding general. In March 1864, Lincoln placed General Ulysses S. Grant in charge of all Union armies and created a unified structure of command. From then on, the president determined the general strategy, and Grant implemented it. Lincoln favored a simultaneous advance against all the major Confederate armies, a strategy that Grant had long favored, to achieve a decisive victory before the election of 1864.

As the successful western campaign of 1863 showed, Grant knew how to fight a war that relied on industrial technology and targeted an entire society. At Vicksburg, he had besieged the whole city and forced its surrender. Then, in November 1863, he had used railroads to charge to the rescue of an endangered Union army near Chattanooga, Tennessee. Moreover, Grant argued that the efforts of earlier Union commanders "to conserve life" through cautious tactics had merely prolonged the war. He was willing to accept heavy casualties, an aggressive stand that earned him a reputation as a butcher of both enemy armies and his own men.

In May 1864, Grant ordered two major offensives. Personally taking charge of the 115,000-man Army of the Potomac, he set out to destroy Lee's force of 75,000 troops in Virginia. Simultaneously, Grant instructed General William Tecumseh Sherman, who shared his ruthless outlook, to invade Georgia and take Atlanta. "All that has gone before is mere skirmish," Sherman wrote as he prepared for battle. "The war now begins."

Grant advanced toward Richmond, hoping to force Lee to fight in open fields, where the Union's superior manpower and artillery would prevail. Remembering his tactical errors at Gettysburg, Lee remained in strong defensive positions and attacked only when he held an advantage. The Confederate general seized that opportunity twice, winning narrow victories in early May 1864 at the extraordinarily bloody battles of the Wilderness and Spotsylvania Court House. At Spotsylvania, the soldiers fought at point-blank range, often using their bayoneted rifles as spears. Despite heavy losses in these battles and then at Cold Harbor, Grant drove on (Map 14.5). Although his attacks severely eroded Lee's forces, which suffered 31,000 casualties, Union losses were even higher: 55,000 men.

The fighting took a heavy psychological toll. "Many a man has gone crazy since this campaign began from the terrible pressure on mind and body," observed a Union captain. As the morale of the soldiers weakened, many deserted. In June 1864, Grant laid siege to Petersburg, an important railroad center near Richmond. Protracted trench warfare—like that in France in World War I—took a terrible toll. Union and Confederate soldiers built complex networks of trenches, tunnels, and artillery emplacements stretching for forty miles along the eastern edge of Richmond and Petersburg. Invoking the intense imagery of the Bible, an officer described the continuous artillery barrages and sniping as "living night and day within the 'valley of the shadow of death.'" The stress was especially great for the outnumbered Confederate troops, who spent months in the muddy, hellish trenches without rotation to the rear.

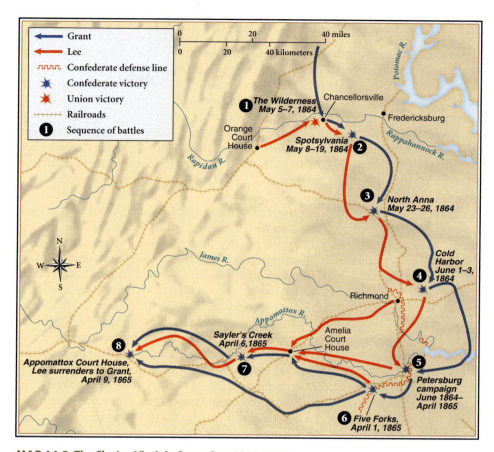

MAP 14.5 The Closing Virginia Campaign, 1864–1865

Beginning in May 1864, General Ulysses S. Grant launched an all-out campaign against Richmond. By threatening General Robert E. Lee's lines of supply from Richmond, Grant tried to lure him into open battle. Lee avoided a major test of strength. Instead, he retreated to defensive positions and inflicted heavy casualties on Union attackers at the Wilderness, Spotsylvania Court House, North Anna, and Cold Harbor (1–4). From June 1864 to April 1865, the two armies faced each other across defensive fortifications outside Richmond and Petersburg (5), a protracted siege that was finally broken by Grant's flanking maneuver at Five Forks (6). Lee's surrender followed shortly.

As time passed, Lincoln and Grant felt pressures of their own. The enormous casualties and continued military stalemate threatened Lincoln with defeat in the November election. The Republican outlook worsened in July, when a raid near Washington by Jubal Early's cavalry forced Grant to divert his best troops from the Petersburg campaign. To punish farmers in the Shenandoah Valley, who had provided aid to Early and Lee, Grant ordered General Philip H. Sheridan to turn the region into "a barren waste." Sheridan's troops conducted a scorched-earth campaign, destroying grain, barns, and gristmills. These terrorist tactics violated the military norms of the day, which treated civilians as noncombatants. Grant's practice of carrying the war to Confederate citizens was changing the definition of conventional warfare.

The Election of 1864 and Sherman's March

As the siege at Petersburg dragged on, Lincoln's hopes for reelection depended on General Sherman in Georgia. Sherman had gradually penetrated to within about thirty miles of Atlanta, a great railway hub at the heart of the Confederacy. Although his army outnumbered that of General Joseph E. Johnston—90,000 men to 60,000 men—Sherman avoided a direct attack and slowly pried the Confederates out of one defensive position after another. Finally, on June 27, at Kennesaw Mountain, Sherman engaged Johnston in a set battle, only to suffer 3,000 casualties—five times the Confederates' losses. By late July 1864, the Union general had advanced to the northern outskirts of Atlanta, but the next month brought little gain. Like Grant, Sherman seemed bogged down in a hopeless campaign.

Meanwhile, the presidential campaign of 1864 was well under way. In June, some delegates to the Republican convention tried to prevent Lincoln's renomination. But the convention endorsed the president's war strategy, demanded the Confederacy's unconditional surrender, and called for a constitutional amendment to abolish slavery. It likewise accepted Lincoln's political strategy. To attract border-state and Democratic voters, the Republicans took a new name, the National Union Party, and chose Andrew Johnson, a Tennessee slave owner and Unionist Democrat, as Lincoln's running mate. The Democratic convention met in late August and nominated General George B. McClellan for president. Lincoln had twice removed McClellan from military commands: first for an excess of caution and then for his opposition to emancipation. Like McClellan, the Democratic delegates rejected freedom for blacks and condemned Lincoln's repression of domestic dissent. However, they split into two camps over the issue of continuing the war until the Union was restored. A substantial contingent of Peace Democrats called for a "cessation of hostilities" and a constitutional convention to restore peace. Although personally a War Democrat, McClellan promised if elected to recommend to Congress an immediate armistice and a peace convention. Hearing this news, Confederate vice president Alexander Stephens celebrated "the first ray of real light I have seen since the war began." He predicted that if Atlanta and Richmond held out, Lincoln could be defeated and McClellan could be persuaded to accept an independent Confederacy.

Stephens's hopes collapsed on September 2, 1864, as Atlanta fell to Sherman's army. In a stunning move, the Union general pulled his troops from the trenches, swept around the city, and destroyed its rail links to the south. Fearing that Sherman would encircle his army, Confederate general John B. Hood abandoned the city. "Atlanta is ours, and fairly won," Sherman telegraphed Lincoln, sparking hundred-gun salutes and wild Republican celebrations in northern cities. "We are *gaining* strength," Lincoln warned Confederate leaders, "and may, if need be, maintain the contest indefinitely."

A deep pessimism settled over the Confederacy. Mary Chesnut, a plantation mistress and general's wife, "felt as if all were dead within me, forever" and foresaw the end of the Confederacy: "We are going to be wiped off the earth," she wrote in her diary. Recognizing the dramatic change in the military situation, McClellan repudiated the Democratic peace platform, and dissident Republicans abandoned efforts to dump Lincoln. The National Union Party went on the offensive, attacking McClellan's inconsistency and attacking Peace Democrats as "copperheads" (poisonous snakes) who were hatching treasonous plots.

Lincoln won a clear-cut victory in November. The president received 55 percent of the popular vote and won 212 of 233 electoral votes. Republicans and National

Unionists captured 145 of the 185 seats in the House of Representatives and increased their Senate majority to 42 of 52 seats. Many Republicans owed their victory to the votes of Union troops, who wanted to crush the rebellion and end slavery.

Legal emancipation was already under way at the edges of the South. In 1864, Maryland and Missouri amended their constitutions to free their slaves, and the three occupied states—Tennessee, Arkansas, and Louisiana—followed suit. Still, abolitionists worried that the Emancipation Proclamation, which was based on the president's wartime powers, would lose its force at the end of the war. Urged on by Lincoln and National Equal Rights League, the Republican Congress approved the Thirteenth Amendment, ending slavery, in January 1865 and sent it to the states for ratification. Slavery was nearly dead.

Thanks to William Tecumseh Sherman, the Confederacy was nearly dead as well. As a young military officer stationed in the South, Sherman had been sympathetic to the outlook of the planter class, and felt that slavery upheld social stability. But Sherman was also a firm supporter of the Union. Secession meant "anarchy," he told his southern friends in early 1861. "If war comes . . . I must fight your people whom I best love." Serving under Ulysses S. Grant, Sherman distinguished himself at Shiloh and Vicksburg. Taking command of a Union army in Tennessee, he developed the philosophy and tactics of "hard war." "When one nation is at war with another, all the people of one are enemies of the other," Sherman declared, turning his troops loose against civilians suspected of helping Confederate guerrillas. After guerrillas fired on a boat with Unionist passengers near Randolph, Tennessee, Sherman sent a regiment to destroy the town, asserting, "We are justified in treating all inhabitants as combatants."

After capturing Atlanta, Sherman decided on a bold hard-war strategy. Instead of pursuing the retreating Confederate army northward into Tennessee, he proposed to move south, live off the land, and "cut a swath through to the sea." To persuade Lincoln and Grant to approve his unconventional plan, Sherman argued that his march would devastate Georgia and be "a demonstration to the world, foreign and domestic, that we have a power [Jefferson] Davis cannot resist." The Union general lived up to his pledge. "We are not only fighting hostile armies," Sherman wrote, "but a hostile people, and must make old and young, rich and poor, feel the hard hand of war." He left Atlanta in flames and, during his 300-mile march to the sea (Map 14.6), his army consumed or demolished everything in its path. A Union veteran wrote, "[We] destroyed all we could not eat, stole their niggers, burned their cotton & gins, spilled their sorghum, burned & twisted their R.Roads and raised Hell generally." The havoc so demoralized Confederate soldiers that many deserted their units and fled home to protect their farms and families (see American Voices, p. 433). When Sherman reached Savannah in mid-December, the city's 10,000 defenders left without a fight.

Georgia's African Americans treated Sherman as a savior. "They flock to me, old and young, they pray and shout and mix up my name with Moses . . . as well as 'Abram Linkom', the Great Messiah of 'Dis Jubilee.'" To provide for the hundreds of blacks now following his army, Sherman issued Special Field Order No. 15, which set aside 400,000 acres of prime rice-growing land for the exclusive use of freedmen. By June 1865, some 40,000 blacks were cultivating "Sherman lands." Many freedmen believed that the lands were to be theirs forever, belated payment for generations of unpaid labor: "All the land belongs to the Yankees now and they gwine divide it out among de coloured people."

In February 1865, Sherman invaded South Carolina, both to link up with Grant at Petersburg and to punish the instigators of nullification and secession. His troops

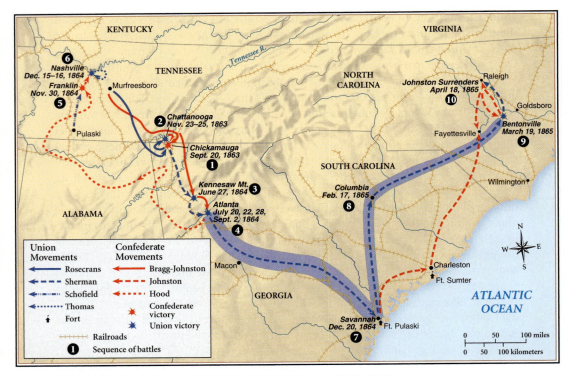

MAP 14.6 Sherman's March Through the Confederacy, 1864–1865

The Union victory in November 1863 at Chattanooga, Tennessee (2), was almost as critical as the victories in July at Gettysburg and Vicksburg because it opened up a route of attack into the heart of the Confederacy. In mid-1864, General Sherman advanced on the railway hub of Atlanta (3 and 4). After finally taking the city in September 1864, Sherman relied on other Union armies to stem General Hood's invasion of Tennessee (5 and 6) while he began a devastating "March to the Sea." By December, Sherman had reached Savannah (7); from there, he cut a swath through the Carolinas (8–10).

For more help analyzing this map, see the Online Study Guide at **bedfordstmartins.com/henrettaconcise**.

ravaged the countryside as they cut a comparatively narrow swath across the state. After capturing South Carolina's capital, Columbia, they burned the business district, most churches, and the wealthiest residential neighborhoods. "This disappointment to me is extremely bitter," lamented Jefferson Davis. By March, Sherman had reached North Carolina and was on the verge of linking up with Grant and crushing Lee's army.

Grant's war of attrition in Virginia had already exposed a weakness in the Confederacy: rising class resentment among poor whites. Angered by slave owners' exemptions from military service and fearing that the Confederacy was doomed, ordinary southern farmers now repudiated the draft. "All they want is to git you . . . to fight for their infurnal negroes," grumbled an Alabama hill farmer. More and more soldiers fled their units. "I am now going to work instead of to the war," vowed David Harris, another backcountry yeoman. By 1865, at least 100,000 men had deserted from Confederate armies, prompting a reluctant Confederate Congress to allow the enlistment of black soldiers and President Davis to issue an executive order granting freedom to blacks who served. But the fighting finished too soon to reveal whether any slaves would have fought for the Confederacy.

Sherman's March Through Georgia   DOLLY SUMNER LUNT

"We must make old and young, rich and poor, feel the hand of war," General William Tecumseh Sherman wrote to General Grant late in 1864, indicating his intention to carry the war to the South's civilian population. Dolly Sumner Lunt of Covington, Georgia, soon found out what Sherman meant. Born in Maine in 1817, Dolly Sumner went south to teach school, married a slave owner, and, after his death, ran the family's plantation, apparently in a benevolent fashion. Her wartime journal describes the plantation's fate at Sherman's hands.

November 19, 1864

Slept in my clothes last night, as I heard that the Yankees went to neighbor Montgomery's on Thursday night at one o'clock, searched his house, drank his wine, and took his money and valuables. As we were not disturbed, I walked after breakfast . . . up to Mr. Joe Perry's, my nearest neighbor, where the Yankees were yesterday. Saw Mrs. Laura [Perry] in the road surrounded by her children . . . looking for her husband. . . . Before we were done talking, up came Joe and Jim Perry from their hiding-place. Jim was very much excited. Happening to turn and look behind, as we stood there, I saw some bluecoats coming down the hill. Jim immediately raised his gun, swearing he should kill them anyhow.

"No, don't" said I, and ran home as fast as I could.

I could hear them cry "Halt! Halt!" and their guns went off in quick succession. Oh God, the time of trial has come. . . .

I hastened back to my frightened servants [slaves] and told them they had better hide, and then went back to the gate to claim protection and a guard. But like demons they [Sherman's troops] rushed in! . . . The thousand pounds of meat in my smokehouse is gone in a twinkling, my flour, my meat, my lard, butter, eggs . . . all gone. My eighteen fat turkeys, hens, chickens . . . are shot down in my yard and hunted as if they were rebels themselves. Utterly powerless I ran out and appealed to the guard.

"I cannot help you, Madam; it is orders."

As I stood there, from my lot I saw driven, first, old Dutch, my dear old buggy horse . . . ; then came old May, my brood mare, . . . with her three-year-old colt. . . . There they go! There go my mules, my sheep, and worse than all, my boys [younger slaves]. . . . Their parents are with me, and how sadly they lament the loss of their boys. Their cabins are rifled of every valuable. . . . Poor Frank's chest was broken open, his money and tobacco taken. He has always been a money-making and saving boy, not infrequently has his crop brought him five hundred dollars and more. . . .

Sherman himself and a greater portion of his army passed my house that day . . . ; they tore down my garden palings, made a road through my back-yard and lot field . . . desolating my home—wantonly doing it when there was no necessity for it. . . .

As night drew its sable curtains around us, the heavens from every point were lit up with flames from burning buildings.

SOURCE: *Eyewitnesses and Others: Readings in American History* (New York: Holt, Rinehart and Winston, 1991), 1: pp. 413–417.

The symbolic end of the war took place in Virginia. In April 1865, Grant finally gained control of the crucial railroad junction at Petersburg and cut off Lee's supplies. Lee abandoned Richmond and retreated toward North Carolina to join up with Confederate forces there. While Lincoln visited the ruins of the Confederate capital and was mobbed by joyful ex-slaves, Grant cut off Lee's escape route. On April 9, almost four years to the day after the attack on Fort Sumter, Lee surrendered at Appomattox Court House, Virginia. By late May, all the Confederate generals had stopped fighting, and the Confederate army and government simply melted away.

The hard and bitter conflict was finally over. Union armies had destroyed slavery and the Confederate armies and governments; the South's factories, warehouses, and railroads were in ruins, as were many of its farms and some of its most important cities. Almost 260,000 Confederate soldiers had paid for secession with their lives. On the other side, more than 360,000 Northerners had died for the Union, and thousands more had been maimed. Was it all worth the price? Delivering his second inaugural address as the fighting entered its final phase, Abraham Lincoln could not justify the hideous carnage and fell back on his religious faith: "so still it must be said 'the judgments of the Lord are true and righteous altogether.'"

But what of the war's results? A New York census taker suggested that the conflict had undermined "autocracy" and had an "equalizing effect" on society. Slavery was gone from the South, he reflected, and in the North, "military men from the so called 'lower classes' now lead society, having been elevated by real merit and valor." However perceptive these remarks, they ignored the wartime emergence of a new financial aristocracy that would soon preside over a "Gilded Age" of wealth and excess. Nor was the sectional struggle yet concluded. As the North began to reconstruct the South and the Union, it found those tasks to be almost as hard and bitter as the war itself.

▶ How did the emancipation edict affect the politics and military affairs of the North?

▶ What were the strengths and weaknesses of Grant's and Sherman's military strategy and tactics? How were their ways of warfare different from traditional military practice?

▶ Why did the North win the Civil War?

SUMMARY

In this chapter, we surveyed the dramatic events of the Civil War. Looking at the South, we watched the fire-eaters declare secession, form a new Confederacy, and attack Fort Sumter. Subsequently, we saw its generals repulse Union attacks against Richmond and go on the offensive. However, as the war continued, the inherent weaknesses of the Confederacy came to the fore. Enslaved workers fled or refused to work, and yeomen farmers refused to fight for an institution that primarily benefited wealthy planters.

Examining the North, we witnessed its initial military failure. Its generals — McClellan and Meade — moved slowly to attack and refused to pursue their weakened foes. But over time, the Union's significant advantages in industrial output, financial resources, and military manpower became manifest. Congress created efficient systems of banking and war finance; Lincoln found efficient and ruthless generals; and the emancipation and recruitment of African Americans provided an abundant supply of soldiers determined to preserve their freedom.

We explored the impact of the war on civilians in both regions: the imposition of conscription and high taxes; the increased workload of farm women; and the constant food shortages and soaring prices. Above all else, there was the omnipresent fact of death—a tragedy that touched nearly every family, North and South.

Connections: Government

Since the beginning of the American republic, political leaders have argued over the scope and powers of the national government. As we learned in Chapter 7, Alexander Hamilton interpreted the Constitution expansively and devised a policy of national mercantilism. In response, Thomas Jefferson and James Madison created the Republican Party, which subsequently reduced the scope of the national government and relied on state governments to promote economic development. In the 1820s, as we discussed in Chapter 10, Henry Clay and John Quincy Adams revived Hamilton's nationalistic program. Their American System proposed a national bank to oversee the financial system, national tariff protection for American manufacturers, and national subsidies for roads, canals, and other internal improvements. As we noted in the essay that opened Part Three, in the Jacksonian revolution of the 1830s and 1840s,

> the Democratic Party led a political and constitutional revolution that cut government aid to financiers, merchants, and corporations.

We saw in this chapter that the Republican administration of Abraham Lincoln reversed those Jacksonian policies by extending aid to farmers, railroads, and corporations. Indeed, as we will see in Chapter 17, these Hamilton-Clay-Lincoln initiatives continued in the late nineteenth century. By enacting and upholding legislation favorable to banks and corporations, Congress and the federal judiciary actively promoted the development of a powerful industrial economy. The Jeffersonian-Jacksonian ideology of small government remained strong in the South but, after the Civil War, it receded as a significant force in national life.

FOR FURTHER EXPLORATION

James M. McPherson, *The Battle Cry of Freedom* (1988), and Charles P. Roland, *An American Iliad* (1991), narrate wartime events. For the outbreak of the war, read Richard Current, *Lincoln and the First Shot* (1963). John Hope Franklin, *The Emancipation Proclamation* (1963), explains that important edict.

Nancy Scott Anderson and Dwight Anderson, *The Generals: Ulysses S. Grant and Robert E. Lee* (1988), provide a vivid popular account. Good scholarly analyses include Mark Grimsley, *The Hard Hand of War* (1995), and Gary W. Gallagher, *The Confederate War* (1997). William W. Freehling, *The South vs. the South* (2001), explores anti-Confederate sentiment.

For firsthand accounts, see James M. McPherson, *For Cause and Comrades* (1997); Ira Berlin et al., eds., *Freedom's Soldiers: The Black Military Experience* (1998); and Earl J. Hess, *The Union Soldier in Battle* (1997). Michael Shaara's *Killer Angels* (1974) is a masterful novel about the Battle of Gettysburg.

TIMELINE

1860
▶ Abraham Lincoln elected president (November 6)
▶ South Carolina votes to secede (December 20)

1861
▶ President Lincoln inaugurated (March 4)
▶ Confederates fire on Fort Sumter (April 12)
▶ Virginia leads Upper South into Confederacy (April 17)
▶ General Butler labels fugitive slaves "contraband of war" (May)
▶ Confederates rout Union at Bull Run (July 21)
▶ First Confiscation Act allows seizure of Confederate property (August)

1862
▶ Legal Tender Act authorizes greenbacks (February)
▶ Battle of Shiloh: Union advances in West (April 6–7)
▶ Confederacy introduces first draft (April)
▶ Congress passes Homestead (free land) Act (May)
▶ Congress provides subsidies to transcontinental railroads (July)
▶ Second Confiscation Act frees contraband slaves (July)
▶ Union halts Confederate offensive at Antietam (September 17)

▶ Lincoln issues preliminary Emancipation Proclamation (September 22)

1863
▶ Lincoln signs Emancipation Proclamation (January 1)
▶ Union wins battles at Gettysburg (July 1–3) and Vicksburg (July 4)
▶ Enrollment Act prompts immigrant riots in New York City (July)

1864
▶ Lincoln gives Ulysses S. Grant command of all Union armies (March)
▶ Grant begins advance on Richmond (May)
▶ William Tecumseh Sherman takes Atlanta (September 2)
▶ President Lincoln is reelected (November 8)
▶ Sherman marches through Georgia (November and December)

1865
▶ Congress passes Thirteenth Amendment, ending slavery (January)
▶ Robert E. Lee surrenders at Appomattox Court House (April 9)
▶ Lincoln assassinated by John Wilkes Booth (April 14)
▶ Thirteenth Amendment ratified by states (December 6)

For women's lives, look at *Mary Chesnut's Civil War*, edited by C. Vann Woodward (1981); Jane E. Schultz, *Women at the Front* (2004); and Laura F. Edwards, *Scarlett Doesn't Live Here Anymore* (2000).

For Civil War photographs, log onto **memory.loc.gov/ammem/ndlpcoop/nhihtml/cwnyhshome.html** and **memory.loc.gov/ammem/cwphtml/cwphome.html**. Edward L. Ayers, *In the Presence of Mine Enemies* (2003), explores wartime life in two communities and has a fine Web site at **jefferson.village.virginia.edu/vshadow2/**. For the black experience, go to **www.history.umd.edu/Freedmen/home.html**.

TEST YOUR KNOWLEDGE

To assess your mastery of the material in this chapter and for Web sites, images, and documents related to this chapter, visit **bedfordstmartins.com/henrettaconcise**.

Reconstruction
1865–1877

I felt like a bird out of a cage. Amen. Amen. Amen. I could hardly ask to feel better than I did on that day.

— Houston H. Holloway, a former slave recalling his emancipation in 1865

In his second inaugural address, President Lincoln spoke of the need to "bind up the nation's wounds." No one knew better than Lincoln how daunting a task that would be. Slavery was finished. That much was certain. But what system of labor should replace plantation slavery? What rights should the freedmen be accorded beyond emancipation? How far should the federal government go to settle these questions? And, most immediately pressing, on what terms should the rebellious states be restored to the Union?

The last speech that Lincoln delivered, on April 11, 1865, demonstrated his command of these issues. Reconstruction, he said, had to be regarded as a practical problem, not a theoretical one. It could be solved only if Republicans remained united, even if that meant compromising on principled differences that divided them, and only if the defeated South gave its consent, even if that came at the price of forgiving the South's transgressions. The speech revealed the middle ground, both magnanimous and open-minded, on which Lincoln hoped to reunite a wounded nation.

What course Reconstruction might have taken had Lincoln lived is one of the unanswerable questions of American history. On April 14, 1865 — five days after Lee's surrender at Appomattox — Lincoln was shot in the head at Ford's Theatre in Washington by John Wilkes Booth, a prominent Shakespearian actor and Confederate sympathizer who had been plotting to abduct Lincoln and rescue the South. After Lee's surrender, Booth became bent on revenge. Without regaining consciousness, Lincoln died on April 15, 1865.

With one stroke, John Wilkes Booth sent Lincoln to martyrdom, hardened many Northerners against the South, and handed the presidency to a man utterly lacking in Lincoln's moral sense and political judgment: Vice President Andrew Johnson.

Presidential Reconstruction

The problem of Reconstruction—how to restore rebellious states to the Union—had not been addressed by the Founding Fathers. The Constitution does not contemplate the possibility of secession. Had the Confederate states, upon seceding, legally left the Union? If so, their reentry surely required legislative action by Congress. If not, if even in defeat they retained their constitutional status, then the terms for restoring them to the Union might be considered an administrative matter best left to the president. In a constitutional system based on the **separation of powers**, the absence of clarity on so fundamental a matter made for explosive politics. The ensuing battle between the White House and Capitol Hill over who was in charge became one of the fault lines in Reconstruction's stormy history.

Lincoln's Way

As wartime president, Lincoln had the elbow room to take the lead, offering in December 1863 a general amnesty to all but high-ranking Confederates. When 10 percent of a rebellious state's voters had taken an oath of loyalty, the state would be restored to the Union, provided that it approved the Thirteenth Amendment abolishing slavery (see Chapter 14). The Confederate states rejected Lincoln's Ten Percent Plan, however, and congressional Republicans proposed a harsher substitute. The Wade-Davis Bill, passed on July 2, 1864, laid down, as conditions, an oath of allegiance to the Union by a majority of each state's adult white men; new governments formed only by those who had never borne arms against the North; and permanent disfranchisement of Confederate leaders. The Wade-Davis Bill served notice that the congressional Republicans were not about to hand over Reconstruction policy to the president.

Lincoln **pocket vetoed** the Wade-Davis Bill by leaving it unsigned when Congress adjourned. At the same time, he initiated informal talks with congressional leaders aimed at a compromise. It was this effort that Lincoln was addressing when he appealed for Republican flexibility in his last speech. Lincoln's successor, however, had no such inclination. Andrew Johnson took the view that Reconstruction was the president's prerogative. By an accident of timing, he was free to act on his convictions. Although the 38th Congress had adjourned in March 1865, under leisurely rules that went back to the early republic the 39th Congress was not scheduled to convene until December 1865.

Johnson Seizes the Initiative

Johnson was a self-made man from the hills of eastern Tennessee. Born in 1808, he was apprenticed as a boy to a tailor. With no formal schooling—his wife was his teacher—Johnson prospered. His tailor shop became a political meeting place, and natural leader that he was, he soon entered local politics with the backing of Greeneville's small farmers and laborers. In 1857, he became a U.S. senator.

Loyal to the Union, Johnson refused to leave the Senate when his state seceded. In this, he was utterly alone; no southern colleague joined him. When federal forces captured Nashville in 1862, Lincoln appointed Johnson Tennessee's military governor.

Andrew Johnson
The president was not an easy man. This photograph of Andrew Johnson (1808–1875) conveys some of the prickly qualities that contributed so centrally to his failure to reach an agreement with Republicans on a moderate Reconstruction program.
Library of Congress.

Tennessee was bitterly divided—Unionist in the east and Rebel in the west. Johnson's assignment was to hold the state together, and he did so, with an iron hand. He was rewarded by being named Lincoln's running mate in 1864. Choosing this war Democrat seemed a smart move, designed to promote wartime unity and court southern Unionists.

In May 1865, just a month after Lincoln's death, Johnson advanced his version of Reconstruction. He offered amnesty to all Southerners who took an oath of allegiance to the Constitution except for high-ranking Confederate officials. Johnson appointed provisional governors for the southern states, requiring as conditions for their restoration only that they revoke their ordinances of secession, repudiate their Confederate debts, and ratify the Thirteenth Amendment. Within months, all the former Confederate states had met Johnson's terms and had functioning elected governments.

At first, Republicans responded favorably. The moderates were sympathetic to Johnson's argument that it was up to the states, not the federal government, to define the rights of the freedmen. Even the Radicals—Republicans who demanded a hard line toward the South—held their fire. The stern treatment of Confederate leaders pleased them, and they awaited signs of good faith such as generous treatment of the freed slaves.

Nothing of the sort happened. The South lay in ruins (see Voices from Abroad, p. 440), but Southerners held fast to the old order. The newly seated legislatures moved to restore slavery in all but name. They enacted laws—known as **Black Codes**— designed to drive the former slaves back to the plantations by imposing severe penalties on vagrancy, placing heavy restrictions on black workers, and legalizing forms of apprenticeship that came close to slavery. The new governments had been formed mostly by southern Unionists, but when it came to racial attitudes, little distinguished these loyalists from the Confederates. Despite his hard words, moreover, Johnson

The Devastated South   DAVID MACRAE

In this excerpt from *The Americans at Home* (1870), an account of his tour of the United States, Scottish clergyman David Macrae describes the war-stricken South as he found it in 1867–1868, at a time when the crisis over Reconstruction was boiling over.

I was struck with a remark made by a Southern gentleman in answer to the assertion that Jefferson Davis [the president of the Confederacy] had culpably continued the war for six months after all hope had been abandoned.

"Sir," he said, "Mr. Davis knew the temper of the South as well as any man in it. He knew if there was to be anything worth calling peace, the South must win; or, if she couldn't win, she wanted to be whipped—well whipped—thoroughly whipped."

The further south I went, the oftener these remarks came back upon me. Evidence was everywhere that the South had maintained the desperate conflict until she was utterly exhausted. . . . Almost every man I met at the South, especially in North Carolina, Georgia, and Virginia, seemed to have been in the army; and it was painful to find many who had returned were mutilated, maimed, or broken in health by exposure. When I remarked this to a young Confederate officer in North Carolina, and said I was glad to see that he had escaped unhurt, he . . . pulled up one leg of his trousers, and showed me that he had an iron rod there to strengthen his limb, and enable him to walk without limping, half of his foot being off. He showed me on the other leg a deep scar made by a fragment of a shell; and these were two of but seven wounds which had left their marks upon his body. When he heard me speak of relics, he said, "Try to find a North Carolina gentleman without a Yankee mark on him."

Nearly three years had passed when I traveled through the country, and yet we have seen what traces the war had left in such cities as Richmond, Petersburg, and Columbia. The same spectacle met me at Charleston. Churches and houses had been battered down by heavy shot and shell hurled into the city from Federal batteries at a distance of five miles. . . . Over the country districts the prostration was equally marked. Along the track of Sherman's army especially, the devastation was fearful—farms laid waste, fences burned, bridges destroyed, houses left in ruins, plantations in many cases turned into wilderness again.

The people had shared in the general wreck, and looked poverty-stricken, careworn, and dejected. Ladies who before the war had lived in affluence, with black servants round them to attend to their every wish, were . . . so utterly destitute that they did not know when they finished one meal where they were to find the next. . . . Men who had held commanding positions . . . were filling humble situations—struggling, many of them, to earn a bare subsistence. . . . I remember dining with three cultured Southern gentlemen . . . all living together in a plain little wooden house, such as they would formerly have provided for their servants. Two of them were engaged in a railway office, the third was seeking a situation, frequently, in his vain search, passing the large blinded house where he had lived in luxurious ease before the war.

SOURCE: Allan Nevins, ed., *America Through British Eyes* (Gloucester, MA: Peter Smith, 1968), 345–347.

forgave ex-Confederate leaders easily, as long as he got the satisfaction of humbling them when they appealed for pardons. Soon the ex-Confederates, emboldened by Johnson's indulgence, were filtering back into the halls of power. Old comrades packed the delegations to the new Congress, including even Alexander Stephens, the former vice president of the Confederacy. This was the last straw for the Republicans.

Under the Constitution, Congress is "the judge of the Elections, Returns and Qualifications of its own Members" (Article 1, Section 5). With this power, the Republican majorities in both houses refused to admit the southern delegations when Congress convened in early December 1865, effectively blocking Johnson's Reconstruction program. The southern states then backed away from the Black Codes, replacing them with regulatory ordinances that were silent on race yet, in practice, applied only to blacks. On top of that, racial violence erupted across the South. In Tennessee, a Nashville newspaper reported that white gangs "are riding about whipping, maiming and killing all negroes who do not obey the orders of their former masters, just as if slavery existed." Congressional Republicans concluded that the South was intent on circumventing the Thirteenth Amendment and that the federal government had to intervene.

Back in March 1865, before adjourning, the 38th Congress had established the Freedmen's Bureau to aid ex-slaves during the transition from war to peace. Now, in early 1866, Congress voted to extend the Freedmen's Bureau's life, gave it direct funding for the first time, and authorized its agents to investigate mistreatment of blacks.

More extraordinary was a civil rights bill, which declared the ex-slaves to be citizens; granted them, along with every other citizen, equal rights of contract, access to the courts, and protection of person and property; and authorized U.S. attorneys to bring enforcement suits in the federal courts. Provoked by an unrepentant South, Republicans demanded that the federal government, not the individual states, assume responsibility for the civil rights of the freedmen.

Acting on Freedom

While Congress debated, emancipated slaves acted on their own ideas about freedom (see American Voices, p. 442). Freedom meant many things—the end of punishment by the lash; the ability to move around; the reuniting of families; and the opportunity to found schools, to form churches and social clubs, and, not least, to engage in politics. Across the South, blacks held mass meetings, paraded, and formed organizations. Topmost among their demands was the right to vote—"an essential and inseparable element of self-government." No less than their former masters, ex-slaves intended to be actors in the savage drama of Reconstruction.

Ownership of land, the ex-slaves believed, was the basis for true freedom. In the chaotic final months of the war, freedmen seized control of plantations where they could. In Georgia and South Carolina, General William T. Sherman had reserved large coastal tracts for liberated slaves and settled them on forty-acre plots. Sherman just did not want to be bothered with the refugees as his army drove across the Lower South, but the freedmen assumed that Sherman's order meant that the land would be theirs. When the war ended, resettlement became the responsibility of the Freedmen's Bureau. Many black families stayed on their old plantations, awaiting redistribution of

Relishing Freedom JOURDON ANDERSON

Folklorists have recorded the sly ways that slaves found, even in bondage, for "puttin' down" their masters. But only in freedom—and beyond reach in a northern state—could Jourdon Anderson's sarcasm be expressed so openly, with the jest that his family might consider returning if they first received the wages due them, calculated to the dollar, for all those years in slavery. Anderson's letter, although probably written or edited by a white friend in Dayton, surely is faithful to what the ex-slave wanted to say.

Dayton, Ohio
August 7, 1865.
To My Old Master, Colonel P. H. Anderson, Big Spring, Tennessee.
Sir:

I got your letter, and was glad to find that you had not forgotten Jourdon. . . . I thought the Yankees would have hung you long before this, for harboring Rebs they found at your house. I suppose they never heard about your going to Colonel Martin's house to kill the union soldier that was left by his company in their stable. Although you shot at me twice before I left you, I did not want to hear of your being hurt, and am glad you are still living. It would do me good to go back to the dear old home again, and see Miss Mary and Miss Martha and Allen, Esther, Green, and Lee. Give my love to them all, and tell them I hope we will meet in the better world, if not in this. . . .

I want to know particularly what the good chance is you propose to give me. I am doing tolerably well here. I get twenty-five dollars a month, with victuals and clothing; have a comfortable home for Mandy,—the folks call her Mrs. Anderson,—and the children—Milly, Jane, and Grundy—go to school and are learning well. . . . We are kindly treated. Sometimes we overhear others saying, "Them colored people were slaves" down in Tennessee. The children feel hurt when they hear such remarks; but I tell them it was no disgrace in Tennessee to belong to Colonel Anderson. Many darkeys would have been proud, as I used to be, to call you master. . . .

Mandy says she would be afraid to go back without some proof that you were disposed to treat us justly and kindly; and we have concluded to test your sincerity by asking you to send us our wages for the time we served you. . . . I served you faithfully for thirty-two years, and Mandy twenty years. At twenty-five dollars a month for me and two dollars a week for Mandy, our earnings would amount to eleven thousand six hundred and eighty dollars. Add to this the interest for the time our wages have been kept back, and deduct what you paid for our clothing, and three doctor's visits to me, and pulling a tooth for Mandy, and the balance will show what we are in justice entitled to. . . .

In answering this letter, please state if there would be any safety for my Milly and Jane, who are now grown up, and both good-looking girls. . . . I would rather stay here and starve—and die, if it come to that—than have my girls brought to shame by the violence and wickedness of their young masters. . . .

Say howdy to George Carter, and thank him for taking the pistol from you when you were shooting at me.

From your old servant,
Jourdon Anderson

SOURCE: Stanley I. Kutler, ed., *Looking for America: The People's History*, 2nd ed., 2 vols. (New York: W. W. Norton, 1979), 2: 4–6, 24–27.

the land. When the South Carolina planter Thomas Pinckney returned home, his freed slaves told him: "We ain't going nowhere. We are going to work right here on the land where we were born and what belongs to us."

Johnson's amnesty plan, entitling pardoned Confederates to recover property seized during the war, blasted these hopes. In October 1865, Johnson ordered General Oliver O. Howard, head of the Freedmen's Bureau, to restore the plantations on the Sea Islands off the South Carolina coast to their white owners. The dispossessed blacks protested: "Why do you take away our lands? You take them from us who have always been true, always true to the Government! You give them to our all-time enemies! That is not right!" On the Sea Islands and elsewhere, former slaves resisted efforts to evict them. Led by black army veterans, they fought pitched battles with plantation owners and bands of ex-Confederate soldiers. Landowners struck back hard. Often aided by federal troops, the local whites generally prevailed in this land war.

In early 1866, as planters prepared for a new growing season, a battle took shape over the labor system that would replace slavery. Convinced that blacks needed supervision, planters wanted to retain the **gang-labor system** of the past, but with wages replacing the food, clothing, and shelter that the slaves had once received. The Freedmen's Bureau, although watchful against exploitative labor contracts, sided with the planters.

Wage Labor of Former Slaves
This photograph, taken in South Carolina shortly after the Civil War, shows former slaves leaving the cotton fields. Ex-slaves were organized into work crews that were probably not very different from earlier slave gangs, although they now labored for wages and their plug-hatted boss bore little resemblance to the slave drivers of the past. New-York Historical Society.

The main thing, its reform-minded founders had always believed, was that dependency not be encouraged "in the guise of guardianship." Rely on your "own efforts and exertions," an agent told a large crowd of freedmen in North Carolina; "make contracts with the planters" and "respect the rights of property."

This was advice given with little regard for the world in which those North Carolina freedmen lived. It was not only their unequal bargaining power they worried about or even that their ex-masters' real desire was to reenslave them under the guise of "free" contracts. In their eyes, the condition of wage labor was, by definition, debasing. The rural South was not like the North, where working for wages had become the norm and qualified a man as independent. In the South, selling one's labor to another — in particular, selling one's labor to work another's land — implied not freedom, but dependency. "I mean to own my own manhood," responded one South Carolina freedman to an offer of wage work. "I'm going to own my own land."

The wage issue cut to the core of the former slaves' struggle for freedom. Nothing had been more horrifying than the condition of slavery, in which their persons had been the property of others. When a master cast his eye on a slave woman, her husband had no recourse, nor, for that matter, was rape of a slave a crime. In a famous oration celebrating the anniversary of emancipation, the Reverend Henry M. Turner spoke bitterly of the time when "our wives were sold and husbands bought, children were begotten and enslaved by their fathers." That was why formalizing marriage was so urgent a matter and why, when planters demanded that freedwomen go back into the fields, blacks resisted so resolutely. "I seen on some plantations," one freedman recounted, "where the white men would . . . tell colored men that their wives and children could not live on their places unless they work in the fields. The colored men [answered that] whenever they wanted their wives to work they would tell them themselves; and if he could not rule his own domestic affairs on that place he would leave it and go someplace else."

The reader will see the irony in this definition of freedom: It assumed the wife's subordinate role and designated her labor the husband's property. But if that was the price of freedom, freedwomen were prepared to pay it. Far better to take a chance with their own men than with their ex-masters.

Many former slaves voted with their feet, abandoning their old plantations and seeking better lives in the towns and cities of the South. Those who remained in the countryside refused to work the cotton fields under the hated gang-labor system. Whatever system of labor finally might emerge, it was clear that the freedmen would never settle for anything resembling the old plantation system.

The efforts of former slaves to control their own lives challenged deeply entrenched white attitudes. "The destiny of the black race," asserted one Texan, could be summarized "in one sentence — subordination to the white race." And when freedmen resisted, white retribution was swift and often terrible. In Pine Bluff, Arkansas, "after some kind of dispute with some freedmen," whites set fire to their cabins and hanged twenty-four of the inhabitants — men, women, and children. The toll of murdered and beaten blacks mounted into untold thousands.

The governments established under Johnson's plan put the stamp of legality on these efforts to enforce white supremacy. Blacks "would be *just as well* off with no law at all or no Government," concluded a Freedmen's Bureau agent, as with the justice they got under the restored white rule.

In this unequal struggle, blacks turned to Washington. "We stood by the government when it wanted help," a black Mississippian wrote President Johnson. "Now . . . will it stand by us?"

Congress Versus President

Andrew Johnson was not the man to ask. In February 1866, he vetoed the Freedmen's Bureau bill. The bureau, Johnson charged, was an "immense patronage," showering benefits on blacks that were never granted to "our own people." Republicans could not muster enough votes to override his veto. A month later, again rebuffing his critics, Johnson vetoed the civil rights bill, arguing that federal protection of black rights constituted "a stride toward centralization." His racism, hitherto muted, now blazed forth: "This is a country for white men, and by God, as long as I am president, it shall be government for white men."

Galvanized by Johnson's attack, the Republicans went into action. In early April, they got the necessary two-thirds majorities in both houses and enacted the Civil Rights Act. Republican resolve was reinforced by news of mounting violence in the South, culminating in three days of rioting in Memphis. Forty-six blacks were left dead, and hundreds of homes, churches, and schools were burned. In July, an angry Congress renewed the Freedmen's Bureau over a second Johnson veto.

Anxious to consolidate their gains, Republicans moved to enshrine black civil rights in an amendment to the Constitution. The heart of the Fourteenth Amendment was Section 1, which declared that "all persons born or naturalized in the United States" were citizens. No state could abridge "the privileges or immunities of citizens of the United States"; deprive "any person of life, liberty, or property, without due process of law"; or deny anyone "the equal protection of the laws." These phrases were intentionally vague, but they established the constitutionality of the Civil Rights Act and, more important, the basis on which the courts and Congress could erect an enforceable standard of equality before the law in the states.

For the moment, however, the Fourteenth Amendment was most important as a factor in partisan politics. With the 1866 congressional elections approaching, Johnson somehow figured he could turn the Fourteenth Amendment to his advantage. He urged the states not to ratify it. Months earlier, Johnson had begun maneuvering against the Republicans. He failed in his attempt at building a coalition of white Southerners, northern Democrats, and conservative Republicans under the banner of a new National Union Party, however, and his campaign against the Fourteenth Amendment became, effectively, a campaign for the Democratic Party.

Republicans responded furiously, unveiling a practice that would become known as "waving the bloody shirt." The Democratic Party was traitorous, charged Indiana governor Oliver Morton, "a common sewer and loathsome receptacle, into which is emptied every element of treason North and South." In late August, Johnson embarked on a disastrous "swing around the circle"—a railroad tour from Washington to Chicago and St. Louis and back—that violated the custom that presidents not campaign personally. Johnson made matters worse by engaging in shouting matches with hecklers and insulting the hostile crowds.

The 1866 elections inflicted a humiliating defeat on Johnson and gave the Republicans a three-to-one majority in Congress. They considered themselves "masters of the situation" and free to proceed "entirely regardless of [Johnson's] opinions or wishes." The Republican Party emerged with a new sense of unity—a unity that coalesced not at the center but at the extreme, around the unbending program of the Radical minority. The Radicals represented the abolitionist strain within the Republican Party. Most of them hailed from New England or from the upper Midwest, an area settled by New Englanders. They were led in the Senate by Charles Sumner of Massachusetts and in the House by Thaddeus Stevens of Pennsylvania. For them, Reconstruction was never primarily about restoring the Union. It was about remaking southern society.

Only a handful of Radicals went as far as Stevens in demanding that the plantations be treated as "forfeited estates of the enemy" and broken up into small farms for the former slaves. About securing the freedmen's civil and political rights, however, there was agreement. In this endeavor, Radicals had no qualms about expanding the powers of the national government. "The power of the great landed aristocracy in those regions, if unrestrained by power from without, would inevitably reassert itself," warned Congressman George W. Julian of Indiana. Radicals regarded the Republican Party as God's instrument for regenerating the South.

▶ Why can the enactment of southern Black Codes in 1865 be considered a turning point in the course of Reconstruction?

▶ Why did ex-slaves, struggling for freedom after emancipation, resist working for wages?

▶ To what extent was President Johnson responsible for the radicalization of the Republican Party in 1866?

At first, in the months after Appomattox, few but the Radicals themselves imagined that so extreme a program had any chance of enactment. Yet as fury mounted against the unrepentant South, Republicans became ever more radicalized until, in the wake of the smashing congressional victory of 1866, they embraced the Radicals' vision of a reconstructed South.

Radical Reconstruction

Afterward, thoughtful Southerners admitted that the South had brought radical Reconstruction on itself. "We had, in 1865, a white man's government in Alabama," remarked Johnson's provisional governor, "but we lost it." The "great blunder" was not to "have at once taken the negro right under the protection of the laws." Remarkably, the South remained defiant even after the 1866 elections. Every state legislature but Tennessee's rejected the Fourteenth Amendment. It was as if they could not imagine that fully functioning governments sanctioned by the president might be swept away. But that, in fact, is just what the Republicans intended to do.

Congress Takes Command

The Reconstruction Act of 1867, enacted in March, treated the South as a conquered land, dividing it into five military districts, each under the command of a Union general (Map 15.1). The price for reentering the Union was granting the vote to the freedmen and disfranchising any of the South's leaders who had participated in the rebellion. Each military commander was ordered to register all eligible adult males, black as well as white; supervise the election of state conventions; and make certain that the new constitutions

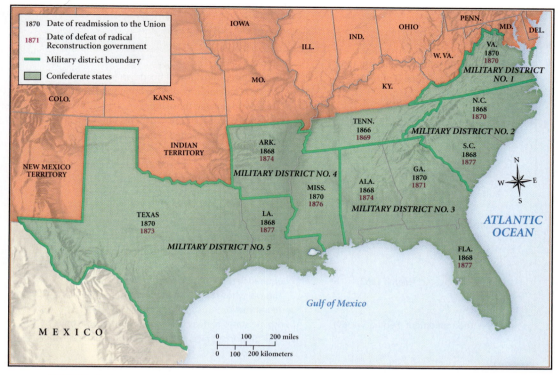

Map legend:
- 1870 — Date of readmission to the Union
- 1871 — Date of defeat of radical Reconstruction government
- ——— Military district boundary
- Confederate states

MAP 15.1 Reconstruction

The federal government organized the Confederate states into five military districts during radical Reconstruction. For each state, the first date indicates when that state was readmitted to the Union; the second date shows when Radical Republicans lost control of the state government. All the ex-Confederate states rejoined the Union from 1868 to 1870, but the periods of radical rule varied widely. Republicans lasted only a few months in Virginia; they held on until the end of Reconstruction in Louisiana, Florida, and South Carolina.

For more help analyzing this map, see the Online Study Guide at **bedfordstmartins.com/henrettaconcise**.

contained guarantees of black **suffrage**. Congress would readmit a state to the Union once these conditions were met and the new state legislature approved the Fourteenth Amendment (thus ensuring the needed ratification by three-fourths of the states). A companion bill, the Tenure of Office Act, restricted the president's authority to dismiss senior officials without senatorial consent (Table 15.1).

Seemingly defeated, Johnson was just biding his time. In August 1867, after Congress adjourned, he "suspended" Secretary of War Edwin M. Stanton, a supporter of radical Reconstruction, and replaced him with the commander of the army, Ulysses S. Grant. Next, Johnson replaced four of the commanding generals. Johnson, however, had misjudged Grant, who publicly objected to the president's machinations. When the Senate reconvened in the fall, it overruled Stanton's suspension. Grant, now an open enemy of Johnson's, resigned so that Stanton could resume his office.

On February 21, 1868, Johnson formally dismissed Stanton. The feisty secretary of war responded by barricading the door of his office. Three days later, for the first

TABLE 15.1	Primary Reconstruction Laws and Constitutional Amendments
Law (Date of Congressional Passage)	**Key Provisions**
Thirteenth Amendment (January 1865*)	Prohibited slavery
Civil Rights Act of 1866 (April 1866)	Defined citizenship rights of freedmen
	Authorized federal authorities to bring suit against those who violated those rights
Fourteenth Amendment (June 1866†)	Established national citizenship for persons born or naturalized in the United States
	Prohibited the states from depriving citizens of their civil rights or equal protection under the law
	Reduced state representation in House of Representatives by the percentage of adult male citizens denied the vote
Reconstruction Act of 1867 (March 1867‡)	Divided the South into five military districts, each under the command of a Union general
	Established requirements for readmission of ex-Confederate states to the Union
Tenure of Office Act (March 1867)	Required Senate consent for removal of any federal official whose appointment had required Senate confirmation
Fifteenth Amendment (February 1869)	Forbade states to deny citizens the right to vote on the grounds of race, color, or "previous condition of servitude"
Ku Klux Klan Act (April 1871)	Authorized the president to use federal prosecutions and military force to suppress conspiracies to deprive citizens of the right to vote and enjoy the equal protection of the law

*Ratified by three-fourths of all states in December 1868.
†Ratified by three-fourths of all states in July 1868.
‡Ratified by three-fourths of all states in March 1870.

time in U.S. history, House Republicans introduced articles of **impeachment** against a sitting president, employing the power granted the House of Representatives by the Constitution to charge high federal officials with "Treason, Bribery, or other high Crimes and Misdemeanors." The House serves, in effect, as the prosecutor in such cases, and the Senate serves as the court. Eleven counts of presidential misconduct were brought against Johnson, nine of them violations of the Tenure of Office Act.

The case went to the Senate, with Chief Justice Salmon P. Chase presiding. After an eleven-week trial, thirty-five senators on May 15 voted for conviction—one vote short of the two-thirds majority required. Seven moderate Republicans voted for acquittal along with twelve Democrats. The dissenting Republicans felt that removing a president for defying Congress was too damaging to the constitutional system of checks and balances, even for the sake of punishing Johnson. And they were wary of the alternative: the Radical Republican Benjamin F. Wade, the president pro tem of the Senate, who, since there was no vice president, stood next in line for the presidency. Despite his acquittal, however, Johnson had been defanged. For the remainder of his term, he was powerless to alter the course of Reconstruction.

The impeachment controversy made Grant, already the North's war hero, a Republican hero as well, and he easily won the party's presidential nomination in 1868. Although he supported radical Reconstruction, Grant also urged reconciliation between the sections. His Democratic opponent, Horatio Seymour, a former governor of New York, almost declined the nomination because he doubted that the Democrats could overcome the stain of disloyalty.

As Seymour feared, the Republicans "waved the bloody shirt," stirring up old wartime emotions against the Democrats to great effect. Grant did about as well in the North (55 percent) as Lincoln had in 1864. Overall, Grant won by a margin of 52.7 percent and received 214 of 294 electoral votes. The Republicans also retained two-thirds majorities in both houses of Congress.

In the wake of their smashing victory, the Republicans produced the last major piece of Reconstruction legislation: the Fifteenth Amendment, which forbade either the federal government or the states to deny citizens the right to vote on the basis of race, color, or "previous condition of servitude." The amendment left room for **poll taxes** and property requirements, a necessary concession to northern and western states that already relied on such provisions to keep immigrants and the "unworthy" poor from the polls. A California senator warned that in his state, with its rabidly anti-Chinese sentiment (see Chapter 16), any restriction on that power would "kill our party as dead as a stone."

Despite grumbling by Radical Republicans, the amendment passed without modification in February 1869. Congress required the states still under federal control—Virginia, Mississippi, Texas, and Georgia—to ratify it as a condition for being readmitted to the Union. A year later, the Fifteenth Amendment became part of the Constitution.

Woman Suffrage Denied

If the Fifteenth Amendment troubled some proponents of black suffrage, this was nothing compared to the outrage felt by women's rights advocates. They had fought the good fight for the abolition of slavery for so many years, only to be abandoned when the chance finally came to get the vote for women. All it would have taken was one more word in the Fifteenth Amendment so that the protected categories for voting would have read "race, color, *sex*, or previous condition."

In a decisive debate in May 1869 at the Equal Rights Association, the black abolitionist Frederick Douglass pleaded for understanding. "When women, because they are women, are hunted down . . . dragged from their homes and hung upon lamp posts . . . when their children are not allowed to enter schools; then they will have an urgency to obtain the ballot equal to our own." Not even all his black sisters agreed. "If colored men get their rights, and not colored women theirs," protested Sojourner Truth, "you see the colored men will be masters over the women, and it will be just as bad as it was before." As for white women in the audience, remarked Frances Harper in support of Douglass, they "all go for sex, letting race occupy a minor position," or worse. In her despair, Elizabeth Cady Stanton lashed out in ugly racist terms against "Patrick and Sambo and Hans and Ung Tung," aliens who were ignorant of the Declaration of Independence and yet entitled to vote while the most accomplished of American women remained voteless. Douglass's resolution in support of the Fifteenth Amendment failed, and the Equal Rights convention broke up in acrimony.

At this searing moment, a rift opened in the women's movement. The majority, led by Lucy Stone and Julia Ward Howe, reconciled themselves to disappointment. Organized into the American Woman Suffrage Association, these moderates remained loyal to the Republican Party in hopes that once Reconstruction had been settled, it would be time for the woman's vote. The group led by Elizabeth Cady Stanton and Susan B. Anthony, however, struck out in a new direction. The embittered Stanton declared that woman "must not put her trust in man." The new organization that she headed, the New York–based National Woman Suffrage Association, accepted only women, focused exclusively on women's rights, and resolutely took up the battle for a federal woman suffrage amendment.

The fracturing of the women's movement obscured the common ground the two sides shared. Both appealed to constituencies beyond the narrow confines of evangelical reform. Both elevated suffrage as the preeminent women's issue. And both were energized for the battles that lay ahead. "If I were to give vent to all my pent-up wrath concerning the subordination of woman," Lydia Maria Child wrote to Republican Senator Charles Sumner in 1872, "I might frighten *you*. . . . Suffice it, therefore, to say, either the theory of our government is *false*, or women have a right to vote." If radical Reconstruction seemed a barren time for women's rights, in fact it had planted the seeds of the modern feminist movement.

Republican Rule in the South

Between 1868 and 1871, all the southern states met the congressional stipulations and rejoined the Union. Protected by federal troops, state Republican organizations set up Reconstruction administrations that remained in power for periods ranging from a few months in Virginia to nine years in South Carolina, Louisiana, and Florida. Their core support came from African Americans, who constituted a majority of registered voters in Alabama, Florida, South Carolina, and Mississippi.

Ex-Confederates called Southern whites who supported Reconstruction **scalawags**— an ancient Scots-Irish term for runty, worthless animals. Northern whites they denounced as **carpetbaggers**—self-seeking interlopers who carried all their property in cheap suitcases called carpetbags. Such labels glossed over the actual diversity of these white Republicans.

Some carpetbaggers, while motivated by personal profit, also brought capital and skills. Others were Union army veterans who found the climate, people, and economic opportunities of the South appealing. And interspersed with the self-seekers were many idealists anxious to advance the cause of emancipation.

The scalawags were even more diverse. Some were former slave owners, ex-Whigs and even ex-Democrats drawn to Republicanism as the best way to attract northern capital to southern railroads, mines, and factories. But most hailed from the backcountry districts and wanted to rid the South of its slaveholding aristocracy. They had generally fought against, or at least refused to support, the Confederacy, believing that slavery had victimized whites as well as blacks. "Now is the time," a Georgia scalawag wrote, "for every man to come out . . . and vote for liberty as we have been in bondage long enough."

Hiram R. Revels

In 1870, Hiram R. Revels (1822–1901) was elected to the U.S. Senate from Mississippi to fill Jefferson Davis's former seat. Revels was a free black man from North Carolina who had migrated to the North and attended Knox College in Illinois. He recruited blacks for the Union army and, as an ordained Methodist minister, served as chaplain of a black regiment in Mississippi, where he settled after the war. Library of Congress.

The Democrats' scorn for black leaders, whom they regarded as ignorant field hands, was just as misguided as stereotypes about white Republicans. The first African American leaders in the South came from an elite of free blacks. They were joined by northern blacks who moved south to join the battle for radical Reconstruction. Like their white allies, many were Union army veterans. Some were employed by the Freedmen's Bureau or northern missionary societies. Others had escaped from slavery and were returning home. One of these ex-slaves was Blanche K. Bruce, who had been tutored on the Virginia plantation of his white father. During the war, Bruce escaped and established a school for ex-slaves in Missouri. In 1869, he moved to Mississippi and became active in politics; in 1874, he became Mississippi's second black U.S. senator.

As the reconstructed Republican governments of 1867 began to function, African American speakers, some financed by the Republican Party, fanned out into the old plantation districts and recruited ex-slaves. Still, few of the new leaders were field hands; most had been preachers or artisans. The literacy of one ex-slave, Thomas Allen, who was a Baptist minister and shoemaker, helped him to win election to the Georgia legislature. "In my county," he recalled, "the colored people came to me for instructions, and I gave them the best instructions I could. I took the *New York Tribune* and other papers, and in that way I found out a great deal, and I told them whatever I thought was right."

Although never proportionate to their numbers in the population, blacks became officeholders across the South. In South Carolina, African Americans constituted a majority in the lower house of the legislature in 1868. Three were elected to Congress; another joined the state supreme court. Over the entire course of Reconstruction, 20 African Americans served in state administrations as governor, lieutenant governor, secretary of state, treasurer, or superintendent of education; more than 600 served as state legislators; and 16 were congressmen.

The Republicans had ambitious plans. They wanted to end the South's dependence on cotton agriculture, build an entrepreneurial economy like the North's, and make a better life for all southerners. Although they fell short, they accomplished more than their critics gave them credit for. The new constitutions expanded the rights of married women, enabling them to hold property and earnings independent of their husbands'—"a wonderful reform," a Georgia woman wrote, for "the cause of Women's Rights." Property qualifications for the vote were eliminated, as were the ordinances restricting the lives of the freedmen. Republican social programs called for the establishment of hospitals, more humane penitentiaries, and asylums for orphans and the insane. Money poured into road-building projects and the region's shattered railroad network.

Freedmen's School, c. 1870

This rare photograph shows the interior of one of the 3,000 freedmen's schools established across the South after the Civil War. Although many of these schools were staffed by white missionaries, a main objective of northern educators was to prepare blacks to take over the classrooms. The teacher shown here is surely one of the first. Library of Congress.

For more help analyzing this image, see the Online Study Guide at **bedfordstmartins.com/henrettaconcise**.

The Reconstruction governments overreached, however. State debts mounted rapidly, and as crushing interest on bonds fell due, public credit collapsed. On top of that, much spending was wasted or ended up in the pockets of public officials. Corruption was ingrained in American politics and rampant everywhere in this era, not least in the Grant administration itself. Still, in the free-spending atmosphere of the southern Republican regimes, corruption was especially luxuriant and damaging to the cause of radical Reconstruction.

Nothing, however, could dim the achievement in public education, where the South had lagged woefully. Republican state governments vowed to make up for lost time, viewing education as the foundation for a democratic order. African Americans of all ages rushed to the newly established schools, even when they had to pay tuition. An elderly man in Mississippi explained his hunger for education: "Ole missus used to read the good book [the Bible] to us . . . on Sunday evenin's, but she mostly read dem places where it says, 'Servants obey your masters.' . . . Now we is free, there's heaps of tings in that old book we is just suffering to learn."

The building of schools was joined by a larger effort to fortify the institutions that had sustained the African Americans in the slave days, most especially Christianity. Now, in freedom, they left the white-dominated congregations, where they had sat in segregated balconies, and built churches of their own. These churches joined together to form African American versions of the Southern Methodist and Baptist denominations,

including, most prominently, the National Baptist Convention and the African Methodist Episcopal Church. Everywhere, the black churches served not only as places of worship but also as schools, social centers, and political meeting halls.

Black clerics were community leaders and often political leaders as well. As Charles
H. Pearce, a Methodist minister in Florida, declared, "A man in this State cannot do his
whole duty as a minister except he looks out for the political interests of his people."
Calling forth the special destiny of the ex-slaves as the new "Children of Israel," black
ministers provided a powerful religious underpinning for the Republican politics of
their congregations.

The Quest for Land

In the meantime, the freedmen were locked in a great economic struggle with their
former owners. In 1869, the Republican government of South Carolina had established a land commission empowered to buy property and resell it on easy terms to the
landless. In this way, about 14,000 black families acquired farms. South Carolina's land
distribution plan showed what was possible, but it was the exception and not the rule.
Despite a lot of rhetoric, Republican regimes elsewhere did little to help the freedmen
fulfill their dreams. Federal efforts proved equally feeble. The Southern Homestead
Act of 1866 offered eighty-acre grants to settlers, limited for the first year to freedmen
and southern Unionists. The advantage was mostly symbolic, however, since only
marginal land was made available, off the beaten track in swampy, infertile parts of the
Lower South.

There was no reversing President Johnson's order restoring confiscated lands to
ex-Confederates. Property rights, it seemed, trumped everything else, even for most
Radical Republicans. The Freedmen's Bureau, which had earlier championed the land
claims of the ex-slaves, now devoted itself to teaching them how to be good agricultural laborers.

While yearning for farms of their own, most freedmen started out with no option
but to work for their former owners. But not, they vowed, under the conditions of
slavery; there would be no gang work, no overseers, no fines or punishments, no regulation of their private lives. In certain parts of the South, wage work became the
norm—for example, on the great sugar plantations of Louisiana financed by northern capital. But cotton planters lacked the money to pay wages, at least until the crop
came in, and sometimes, in lieu of a straight wage, they offered a share of the crop. As
a wage, this was a bad deal for the freedmen, but if they could be paid in shares for
their work, why could they not pay in shares to rent the land they worked?

Planters resisted, believing, as one wrote, that "wages are the only successful system of controlling hands." But in a battle of wills that broke out all across the cotton
South, the planters yielded to "the inveterate prejudices of the freedmen, who desire to
be masters of their own time."

Thus sprang up the distinctive laboring system of cotton agriculture known as
sharecropping, in which the freedmen worked as renters, exchanging their labor for
the use of land, house, implements, and sometimes seed and fertilizer and typically
turning over half of their crops to the landlord (Map 15.2). The sharecropping system
joined laborers and land owners in a common sharing of risks and returns. But it was

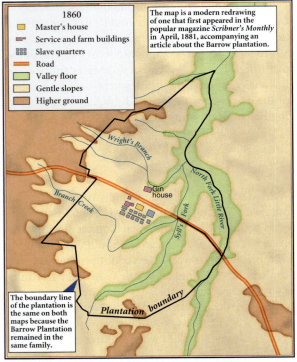

1860

- Master's house
- Service and farm buildings
- Slave quarters
- Road
- Valley floor
- Gentle slopes
- Higher ground

The map is a modern redrawing of one that first appeared in the popular magazine *Scribner's Monthly* in April, 1881, accompanying an article about the Barrow plantation.

Wright's Branch

North Fork Little River

Branch Creek

Gin house

Sylt's Fork

The boundary line of the plantation is the same on both maps because the Barrow Plantation remained in the same family.

Plantation boundary

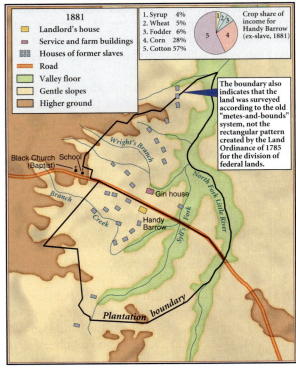

1881

- Landlord's house
- Service and farm buildings
- Houses of former slaves
- Road
- Valley floor
- Gentle slopes
- Higher ground

1. Syrup 4%
2. Wheat 5%
3. Fodder 6%
4. Corn 28%
5. Cotton 57%

Crop share of income for Handy Barrow (ex-slave, 1881)

The boundary also indicates that the land was surveyed according to the old "metes-and-bounds" system, not the rectangular pattern created by the Land Ordinance of 1785 for the division of federal lands.

Black Church School (Baptist)

Wright's Branch

North Fork Little River

Branch Creek

Gin house

Sylt's Fork

Handy Barrow

Plantation boundary

MAP 15.2 The Barrow Plantation, 1860 and 1881

Comparing the 1860 map of this central Georgia plantation with the 1881 map reveals the impact of sharecropping on patterns of black residence. In 1860, the slave quarters were clustered near the planter's house. In contrast, the sharecroppers scattered across the plantation's 2,000 acres, building cabins on the ridges of land between the low-lying streams. The name Barrow was common among the sharecropping families, which almost certainly means that they had been slaves on the Barrow plantation who, years after emancipation, had not moved away. For all the sharecroppers, freedom surely meant not only their individual lots and cabins but also the school and church shown on the map.

a very unequal relationship, given the force of southern law and custom on the white landowner's side and the sharecroppers' dire economic circumstances. Starting out penniless, they had no way of making it through the first growing season without borrowing for food and supplies.

Country storekeepers stepped in. Bankrolled by their northern suppliers, they furnished the sharecropper with provisions and took as collateral a **lien** on the crop, effectively assuming ownership of the cropper's share and leaving him only the proceeds that remained after his debts had been paid. Once indebted at one store, sharecroppers were no longer free to shop around. They became easy targets for exorbitant prices, unfair interest rates, and crooked bookkeeping. As cotton prices declined during the 1870s, more and more sharecroppers failed to settle accounts and fell into permanent debt.

And if the merchant was also the landowner or conspired with the landowner, the debt became a pretext for forced labor, or **peonage**, although evidence now suggests that sharecroppers generally managed to pull up stakes and move on once things became hopeless. Sharecroppers always thought twice about moving, however, because part of their "capital" was being known and well regarded in their home communities. Freedmen who lacked that local standing generally found sharecropping hard going and ended up in the ranks of agricultural laborers.

In the face of so much adversity, black families struggled to better themselves. The saving advantage of sharecropping was that it mobilized husbands and wives in a common enterprise while shielding both from personal subordination to whites. Wives were doubly blessed. Neither field hands for their ex-masters nor dependent housewives, they became partners laboring side by side with their husbands. The trouble with sharecropping, one planter grumbled, was that "it makes the laborer too independent; he becomes a partner, and has to be consulted."

The battle between planters and freedmen was by no means unique to the American South. Whenever slavery ended—in Haiti after the slave revolt of 1791, in the British Caribbean by abolition in 1833, in Cuba and Brazil by gradual emancipation during the 1880s—planters bent on restoring a gang-labor system battled ex-slaves bent on gaining economic autonomy. The outcome depended on the ex-slaves' access to land. Where vacant land existed, as in British Guiana, or where plantations could be seized, as in Haiti, the ex-slaves became subsistence farmers. Where land was beyond reach, as in British Barbados or Antigua, the ex-slaves returned to plantation labor as wageworkers, although often in some combination with customary rights to housing and garden plots. The cotton South fit neither pattern. The freedmen did not get the land, but neither did the planters get field hands. What both got was sharecropping.

There are two ways of explaining this outcome. One is political. In other countries, emancipated slaves rarely got political rights. Even in the British islands, where substantial self-government existed, high property qualifications effectively disfranchised the ex-slaves. In the United States, however, hard on the heels of emancipation came, for a brief era, a real measure of political power for the freedmen. Sharecropping took shape during Reconstruction, and there was no going back afterward.

That there was no going back suggests a second reason why sharecropping prevailed: It was a good fit for cotton agriculture. We can see this in the experience of other countries that became major producers in response to the global cotton famine set off by the Civil War. In all these places — India, Egypt, Brazil, and West Africa — some variant of the sharecropping system emerged.

Most striking was the adoption everywhere of crop-lien laws, at the behest of the international merchants and bankers who put up the capital. Indian and Egyptian villagers got the advances they needed to shift from subsistence agriculture to cotton but at the price of being placed, as in America, permanently under the thumb of the furnishing merchants. Implicit in advancing that money, of course, was the realization that cotton, unlike sugar cane, could be raised efficiently by small farmers (provided they had the lash of indebtedness always on their backs). American planters resisted sharecropping because they started at a different place: not traditional, subsistence economies that had to be converted to cotton but a proven plantation system over which they had been absolute masters.

For America's ex-slaves, sharecropping was not the worst choice; it certainly beat laboring for their former owners. But for southern agriculture, the costs were devastating. Sharecropping committed the South inflexibly to cotton because, as a market crop, it generated the cash required by landlords and furnishing merchants. Neither soil depletion nor low prices ever enabled sharecroppers to shift away from cotton. With farms leased on a year-to-year basis, neither tenant nor owner had much incentive to improve the property. And the crop-lien system lined merchants' pockets with unearned profits that might otherwise have gone into agricultural improvement. The result was a stagnant farm economy, blighting the South's future and condemning it to economic backwardness — a kind of retribution for the fresh injustices being visited on the people it had once enslaved.

▶ Do you think it was predictable in 1865 that five years later, the ex-slaves would receive a constitutional right to vote? Was it predictable that, having gone that far, the nation would deny the vote to women? Why or why not?

▶ Why did the ex-slaves' struggle for land result in the sharecropping system?

The Undoing of Reconstruction

Ex-Confederates were blind to the achievements of radical Reconstruction. Indeed, no amount of success could have persuaded them that it was anything but an abomination, denying them their rightful place in southern society. Led by the planters, ex-Confederates staged a massive counterrevolution designed to "redeem" the South. But the Redeemers could not have succeeded on their own. They needed the complicity of the North. The undoing of Reconstruction is as much about northern acquiescence as about southern resistance.

Counterrevolution

Insofar as they could win at the ballot box, southern Democrats took that route. They got ex-Confederates restored to the voting rolls, they put forward tickets appealing to southern patriotism, and they campaigned against black rule. But force was equally acceptable. Throughout the Deep South, especially where black voters were heavily concentrated, ex-Confederates organized secretly and terrorized blacks and their white allies.

Nathan Bedford Forrest in Uniform, c. 1865
Before he became Grand Wizard of the Ku Klux Klan, Forrest had been a celebrated cavalry general in the Confederate army. This photograph shows him in uniform before he was mustered out. Library of Congress.

No one looms larger in this bloody story than Nathan Bedford Forrest, the Confederacy's most decorated cavalry general. Born in poverty in 1821, he had scrambled up the booming cotton economy and had become a big-time Memphis slave trader and Mississippi plantation owner. A man of fiery temper, he championed secession. When the war broke out, Forrest immediately formed a Tennessee cavalry regiment, fought bravely (and was badly wounded) at the battle of Shiloh, and won fame as a daring cavalry raider. On April 12, 1864, his troopers perpetrated one of the war's worst atrocities, the slaughter of black troops at Fort Pillow, Tennessee, acting on rumors that they had harassed local whites.

Although nominally in control since 1862, Union authorities never managed to subdue Tennessee's irreconcilable Confederate sympathizers. William G. Brownlow, the Republican who was elected governor in 1865, was a tough man, a former prisoner of the Confederates who was not shy about calling his enemies to account. They struck back with a campaign of terror, targeting especially Brownlow's black supporters. Amid this general mayhem, some among their number formed the first den of the Ku Klux Klan in late 1865 or early 1866.

As it proliferated across the state, the Klan turned to General Forrest, who had been trying, unsuccessfully, to rebuild his prewar fortunes. Late in 1866, at a secret meeting in Nashville, Forrest donned the robes of Grand Wizard. His activities are mostly cloaked in mystery, but there is no mystery about why Forrest gravitated to the Klan. For him, the Klan was politics by other means, the instrument by which disfranchised former Confederates like himself might strike a blow against the despised Republicans who ran Tennessee.

In many towns, the Klan became virtually identical to the Democratic Party. In fact, Klan members—including Forrest—dominated Tennessee's delegation to the Democratic national convention of 1868. On the ground, the Klan unleashed a murderous campaign of terror. Although Governor Brownlow responded resolutely, in the end it was the Republicans, not the Klan, who cracked. In March 1869, Brownlow retreated to the U.S. Senate. The Democrats were on their way back to power, and the Klan, having served its purpose, was officially disbanded in Tennessee.

Elsewhere, the Klan raged on, murdering Republican politicians, burning black schools and churches, and attacking Republican Party gatherings. By 1870, the Democrats had seized power in Georgia and North Carolina and were making headway across the South.

Congress responded by passing legislation designed to put down the Ku Klux Klan and enforce the rights of ex-slaves under the Fourteenth and Fifteenth Amendments. These so-called Enforcement Laws authorized federal prosecutions, military intervention, and martial law to suppress terrorist activities. In South Carolina, where the Klan became most deeply entrenched, federal troops occupied nine counties, made hundreds of arrests, and drove as many as 2,000 Klansmen from the state.

The Grant administration's assault on the Klan, while raising the spirits of southern Republicans, also revealed how dependent they were on Washington. The potency of the anti–Ku Klux Klan legislation, a Mississippi Republican wrote, "derived alone from its source" in the federal government. "No such law could be enforced by state authority, the local power being too weak." If they were to prevail over antiblack terrorism, Republicans needed what one carpetbagger described as "steady, unswerving power from without."

But northern Republicans grew weary of Reconstruction and the endless bloodshed it seemed to produce. Prosecuting Klansmen was an uphill battle against all-white juries and unsympathetic federal judges. After 1872, prosecutions began to drop off, and many Klansmen received hasty pardons. Then the constitutional underpinnings of the antiterrorist campaign came into question, culminating in the Supreme Court's decision in *U.S. v. Cruikshank* (1876) that the federal government had exceeded its authority. If the civil rights of the ex-slaves were being violated by individuals or private groups (such as the KKK), that was a state responsibility and beyond the federal jurisdiction.

In a kind of self-fulfilling prophecy, the reluctance of the Grant administration to shore up Reconstruction guaranteed that it would fail. One by one, Republican governments fell victim to the massive resistance of their ex-Confederate enemies: Texas in 1873, Alabama and Arkansas in 1874, Mississippi in 1875.

The Mississippi campaign showed all too clearly what the Republicans were up against. As elections neared in 1875, paramilitary groups such as the Rifle Clubs and Red Shirts operated openly. Mississippi's Republican governor, Adelbert Ames, a Congressional Medal of Honor winner from Maine, appealed to President Grant for federal troops, but Grant refused. Brandishing their guns and stuffing the ballot boxes, the Redeemers swept the 1875 elections and took control of Mississippi. Facing impeachment, Governor Ames resigned his office and returned to the North.

By 1876, Republican governments, backed by token U.S. military units, remained in only three southern states: Louisiana, South Carolina, and Florida. Elsewhere, the former Confederates were back in power.

The Acquiescent North

The faltering of Reconstruction stemmed from more than battle fatigue, however. Sympathy for the freedmen began to wane. The North was flooded with one-sided, often racist reports, such as James M. Pike's *The Prostrate State* (1873), describing South Carolina in the grip of "a mass of black barbarism." The impact of this propaganda could be seen in the fate of the ambitious civil rights bill that Charles Sumner introduced in 1870 to enforce, among other things, the rights of African Americans to equal access to public accommodation, schools, and jury service. By the time the bill passed in 1875, it had been stripped of its key provisions. The Supreme Court finished the demolition job when it declared the remnant Civil Rights Act unconstitutional in 1883.

The political cynicism that overtook Sumner's Civil Rights Act signaled the Republican Party's reversion to politics as usual. In many states, a second generation took over the party—men such as Roscoe Conkling of New York, who had little enthusiasm for Reconstruction except when it benefited the Republican Party. As the party lost headway in the South, they lost interest in the battle for black rights. In Washington, President Grant presided benignly over this transformation of his party, turning a blind eye to corruption even as it began to creep into the White House.

Even the high-minded antislavery Christian reformers turned against Reconstruction. The touchstone for them was "free labor," the idea of America as a land of self-reliant, industrious property owners. They had framed the Civil War as a battle between "free labor" and its antithesis, the plantation society of masters and slaves. Now, with the South defeated, the question became, Would the emancipated slaves embrace "free labor"? No, asserted propaganda such as Pike's *The Prostrate South*. Instead of choosing self-reliance, the freedmen were running riot, demanding patronage, becoming dependents of the corrupt Reconstruction regimes. With this tragic misreading of the former slaves—and of their uphill struggle for land and self-rule—Republican allies drifted away and turned against radical Reconstruction.

These advocates of "free labor," once zealous for black freedom, clambered to the safer ground of civil service reform. Henceforth, it was the evils of corrupt politics that would claim their attention. They repudiated the wartime expansion of federal power and refashioned themselves as **liberals**—believers in free trade, market competition, and limited government. And with unabashed elitism, they denounced universal suffrage, which "can only mean in plain English the government of ignorance and vice."

American reform had arrived at a dispiriting watershed. The grand impulse that had driven the antislavery struggle, insofar as it survived the trauma of Reconstruction, now took the form of pallid efforts at purifying American politics, with Grant as the first target.

As Grant's administration lapsed into cronyism, a revolt took shape inside the Republican Party, led by an influential collection of intellectuals, journalists, and reform-minded businessmen. Unable to deny Grant renomination in 1872, the dissidents broke away and formed a new party under the name Liberal Republican. Their candidate was Horace Greeley, longtime publisher of the *New York Tribune* and veteran of American reform in all its variety, including antislavery. The Democrats, still in disarray, also nominated Greeley, notwithstanding his editorial diatribes against them. A poor campaigner, Greeley was assailed so bitterly that, as he said, "I hardly knew whether I was running for the Presidency or the penitentiary."

Grant won overwhelmingly, capturing 56 percent of the popular vote and every electoral vote. Yet the Liberal Republicans had managed to shift the terms of political debate in the country. The agenda they had established—civil service reform, limited government, reconciliation with the South—was adopted by the Democrats, who were shedding their reputation for disloyalty and reclaiming their status as a legitimate national party.

Charges of Republican corruption, which had been mounting ever since Grant's reelection, came to a head in 1875. The scandal involved the Whiskey Ring, a network of liquor distillers and treasury agents who defrauded the government of millions of dollars of excise taxes on whiskey. The ringleader was a Grant appointee, and Grant's own private secretary, Orville Babcock, had a hand in the thievery. The others went to prison, but Grant stood by Babcock, possibly perjuring himself to save his secretary from jail. The stench of scandal, however, had engulfed the White House.

On top of this, the economy fell into a severe depression, triggered in 1873 by the bankruptcy of the Northern Pacific Railroad. Its main investor, Jay Cooke, had been the chief financier of the Civil War and was well connected in Washington, raising suspicions that Republican financial manipulation had caused the depression. Grant's administration responded ineffectually, rebuffing the pleas of debtors for relief by increasing the money supply (see Chapter 19).

Among the casualties of the bad economy was the Freedman's Savings and Trust Company, which held the small deposits of thousands of ex-slaves. When the bank failed in 1874, Congress refused to compensate the depositors, and many lost their life savings. In denying their pathetic pleas, Congress was signaling also that Reconstruction had lost its moral claim on the country. National politics had moved on. Concerns about the economy and political fraud, not the South, absorbed northern voters as another presidential election approached in 1876.

The Political Crisis of 1877

Abandoning Grant, the Republicans nominated Rutherford B. Hayes, governor of Ohio, a colorless figure but untainted by corruption—in other words, a safe man. His Democratic opponent was Samuel J. Tilden, governor of New York, a Wall Street lawyer with a reform reputation for cleaning up New York City politics. The Democrat Tilden, of course, favored **home rule** for the South; but so, more discreetly, did the Republican Hayes. Reconstruction actually did not figure prominently in the campaign and was mostly subsumed under broader Democratic charges of "corrupt centralism" and "incapacity, waste, and fraud." Little was said about the states still ruled by Reconstruction governments: Florida, South Carolina, and Louisiana.

Once the returns started coming in on election night, however, those three states began to loom very large indeed. Tilden led in the popular vote and seemed headed for victory until sleepless politicians at Republican headquarters realized that the electoral vote stood at 184 to 165, with the 20 votes from Florida, South Carolina, and Louisiana still uncertain. If Hayes took those votes, he would win by a margin of one. Republicans still controlled the election machinery in the three states; citing Democratic fraud and intimidation, they certified Republican victories. Newly elected Democratic officials also sent in electoral votes for Tilden, and when Congress met in early 1877, it faced two sets of electoral votes from those states.

The Constitution does not provide for this contingency. All it says is that the president of the Senate (in 1877, a Republican) opens the electoral certificates before the House (Democratic) and the Senate (Republican) and that "the Votes shall then be counted" (Article 2, Section 1). Suspense gripped the country. There was talk of inside deals, of a new election, even of a violent coup. Just in case, the commander of the army, General William T. Sherman, deployed four artillery companies in Washington. Finally, Congress appointed an electoral commission to settle the question. The commission included seven Republicans, seven Democrats, and, as the deciding member, David Davis, a Supreme Court justice not known to have fixed party loyalties. However Davis disqualified himself by accepting an Illinois seat in the Senate. He was replaced by Republican justice Joseph P. Bradley, and by a vote of 8 to 7, the commission awarded the disputed votes to Hayes.

Outraged Democrats had one more trick up their sleeves. They controlled the House of Representatives, and they stalled a final count of the electoral votes so as to prevent Hayes's inauguration on March 4. But a week before, secret Washington talks had begun between southern Democrats and Ohio Republicans representing Hayes. Exactly what deal was struck will probably never be known, but on March 1, the House Democrats suddenly ended their delaying tactics, the ceremonial counting of votes went forward, and Hayes was inaugurated on schedule. He soon ordered the Union troops back to their barracks, and the last Republican administrations in the South fell. Reconstruction had ended.

In 1877, political leaders on all sides seemed ready to say that what Lincoln had called "the work" was complete. But for the former slaves, the work had only begun. Reconstruction turned out to have been a magnificent aberration, a leap beyond what most white Americans actually felt was due their black fellow citizens. Still, something real had been achieved: three rights-defining amendments to the Constitution, some elbow room to advance economically, and, not least, a stubborn confidence among blacks that by their own efforts, they could lift themselves up. Things would, in fact, get worse before they got better, but the work of Reconstruction was imperishable and could never be erased.

▶ Why did the Redeemers resort to terror in their campaign to regain political control of the South?

▶ What changes in the North explain why the Republicans abandoned the battle for Reconstruction?

▶ Do you believe that the failure of Reconstruction was primarily a failure of leadership? Or, to put it more concretely, do you think that the outcome might have been different had Lincoln lived or had chosen a different vice president or had Andrew Johnson not been followed by Ulysses S. Grant? Explain your answer.

SUMMARY

By any measure—in lives, treasure, or national harmony—the Civil War was the most shattering event in American history. In this chapter, we describe how the nation picked up the pieces. Reconstruction confronted two great tasks: restoring the rebellious states to the Union and incorporating the emancipated slaves into the national citizenry. The two tasks were inseparably part of a single grand struggle.

Reconstruction went through three phases. In the presidential phase, Lincoln's successor Andrew Johnson unilaterally offered the South easy terms for reentering the Union. This might have succeeded had Southerners responded with restraint, but instead, they adopted oppressive Black Codes and welcomed ex-Confederates back into power. Infuriated by southern arrogance, congressional Republicans closed ranks behind the Radicals, embraced the freedmen's demand for full equality, placed the South under military rule in 1867, and inaugurated radical Reconstruction.

In this second phase, the new Republican state governments tried to transform the South's decrepit economic and social structures, while on the plantations, ex-slaves battled for economic independence. No amount of accomplishment, however, could reconcile the ex-Confederates to Republican rule, and they staged a violent counter-revolution in the name of white supremacy and "redemption."

Distracted by Republican scandals and economic problems, the Grant admin-istration had little stomach for a protracted guerrilla war in the South. Left on their own, the Reconstruction governments fell one by one to Redeemer intimidation and violence. In this third phase, as Reconstruction wound down, the concluding event was the contested election of 1876, which the Republicans resolved by trading their last remaining southern strongholds — South Carolina and Louisiana — for retention of the White House. On that unsavory note, Reconstruction ended.

Connections: Sectionalism

In many ways, Reconstruction marked the final stage in a long-developing struggle between sections. As the essay that opened Part Three noted:

> The North developed into an urbanizing society based on free labor, whereas the South remained a rural agricultural society dependent on slavery.

In Chapter 13, we described how the sectional crisis that arose from these differences broke the Union apart in 1861. The Civil War (Chapter 14) tested the war-making capacities of the rival systems. At first, the advantage lay with the military prowess of the agrarian South, but in the end, the superior resources of the industrial North prevailed. Even in defeat, however, the South could not be forced into a national mold. That was the ultimate lesson of Reconstruction. In the aftermath, the South persisted on its own path, as we will see in Chapter 17, which discusses the South's distinctive low-wage labor system, and Chapter 19, which describes its one-party, whites-only politics. The gradual, if partial, dissolution of southern uniqueness in the twentieth century is a theme of later chapters of this book.

FOR FURTHER EXPLORATION

The best book on Reconstruction is Eric Foner's major synthesis, *Reconstruction: America's Unfinished Revolution, 1863–1877* (1988), available also in a shorter version. *Black Reconstruction in America* (1935), by the African American activist and scholar W. E. B. Du Bois, deserves attention as the first book on Reconstruction that stressed the role of blacks in their own emancipation. On the freedmen, Leon F. Litwack, *Been in the Storm So Long: The Aftermath of Slavery* (1979), provides a stirring account.

TIMELINE

1863 ▶ Lincoln announces his Ten Percent Plan

1864 ▶ Wade-Davis Bill passed by Congress
▶ Lincoln pocket vetoes Wade-Davis Bill

1865 ▶ Freedmen's Bureau established
▶ Lincoln assassinated; Andrew Johnson succeeds as president
▶ Johnson implements his restoration plan

1866 ▶ Civil Rights Act passes over Johnson's veto
▶ Memphis riots
▶ Johnson makes disastrous "swing around the circle"; Republicans carry congressional elections

1867 ▶ Reconstruction Act

1868 ▶ Impeachment crisis
▶ Fourteenth Amendment ratified
▶ Ulysses S. Grant elected president

1870 ▶ Ku Klux Klan at peak of power
▶ Fifteenth Amendment ratified

1872 ▶ Grant's reelection

1873 ▶ Panic of 1873 ushers in depression of 1873–1877

1875 ▶ Whiskey Ring scandal undermines Grant administration

1877 ▶ Compromise of 1877; Rutherford B. Hayes becomes president
▶ Reconstruction ends

More recent emancipation studies emphasize slavery as a labor system: Julie Saville, *The Work of Reconstruction: From Slave to Wage Laborer in South Carolina, 1860–1870* (1994), and Amy Dru Stanley, *From Bondage to Contract* (1999), which expands the discussion to show what the onset of wage labor meant for freedwomen. In *Gendered Strife & Confusion: The Political Culture of Reconstruction* (1997), Laura F. Edwards explores via a close-grained local study the impact of "peripheral" people—the ordinary folk of both races—on Reconstruction politics. Eric Foner, *Nothing But Freedom: Emancipation and Its Legacy* (1983), helpfully places emancipation in a comparative context. William S. McFeely, *Grant: A Biography* (1981), deftly explains the politics of Reconstruction. The emergence of the sharecropping system is explored in Gavin Wright, *Old South, New South* (1986), and Edward Royce, *The Origins of Southern Sharecropping* (1993). On the Compromise of 1877, see C. Vann Woodward's classic *Reunion and Reaction* (1956). A helpful Web site on Reconstruction, with documents and illustrations, can be found at **www.pbs.org/wgbh/amex/reconstruction/index .html**, which derives from the PBS documentary in the *American Experience* series.

TEST YOUR KNOWLEDGE

To assess your mastery of the material in this chapter and for Web sites, images, and documents related to this chapter, visit **bedfordstmartins.com/henrettaconcise**.

PART FOUR

A Maturing Industrial Society

1877–1914

SOCIETY	ECONOMY	CULTURE
The West	**The triumph of industrialization**	**The industrial city**
1877 ▸ Nomadic Indian life ends	▸ Andrew Carnegie launches modern steel industry ▸ Knights of Labor becomes national movement (1878)	▸ National League founded (1876) ▸ Dwight L. Moody pioneers urban revivalism
1880 ▸ Chinese Exclusion Act (1882) ▸ Dawes Act divides tribal lands (1887)	▸ Gustavus Swift pioneers vertically integrated firm ▸ American Federation of Labor (1886)	▸ Electrification brightens city life ▸ First Social Register defines high society (1888)
1890 ▸ U.S. Census declares westward movement over ▸ Wounded Knee Massacre; Indian resistance ends ▸ California national parks established	▸ United States surpasses Britain in iron and steel output ▸ Economic depression (1893–1897) ▸ Industrial merger movement begins	▸ Immigration from southeastern Europe rises sharply ▸ William Randolph Hearst's *New York Journal* pioneers yellow journalism
1900 ▸ California farmers rely on Japanese labor ▸ "Gentlemen's Agreement" (1908) excludes Japanese workers	▸ Immigrants dominate factory work ▸ Industrial Workers of the World (1905)	▸ Social progressivism comes to the city ▸ Movies begin to overtake vaudeville
1910 ▸ Women vote in western states ▸ Government approves Hetch Hetchy reservoir	▸ Henry Ford builds first automobile assembly line	▸ Urban liberalism ▸ World War I halts European immigration

POLITICS	DIPLOMACY
From status quo to progressive reform	**An emerging world power**
▶ Election of Rutherford B. Hayes ends Reconstruction	▶ United States becomes net exporter
▶ Ethnocultural issues dominate state and local politics ▶ Civil service reform (1883)	▶ Diplomacy of inaction ▶ Naval buildup begins
▶ Black disfranchisement in South ▶ Populist Party founded (1892) ▶ William McKinley wins presidency; defeats Bryan's free-silver crusade (1896)	▶ Social Darwinism and Anglo-Saxonism promote expansion ▶ Spanish-American War (1898–1899); conquest of the Philippines
▶ McKinley assassinated; Roosevelt inaugurates progressivism in national politics ▶ Hepburn Act regulates railroads (1906)	▶ Panama cedes Canal Zone to United States (1903) ▶ Roosevelt Corollary to Monroe Doctrine (1904)
▶ NAACP (1910) ▶ Woodrow Wilson elected (1912) ▶ New Freedom legislation creates Federal Reserve, FTC	▶ Taft's diplomacy promotes U.S. business ▶ Wilson proclaims U.S. neutrality in World War I

The year 1876 marked the hundredth anniversary of the Declaration of Independence. In celebration, the nation mounted a Centennial Exposition where it had all begun: in Philadelphia. Observing the hectic preparations, the German journalist Ernst Otto Hopp anticipated the impact of this grand world's fair on his European compatriots. They "will be astounded at the vision of American production. . . . The pits of Nevada will display their enormous stores of silver, Michigan its copper, California its gold and quicksilver, Missouri its lead and tin, Pennsylvania its coal and iron. . . . And from a thousand factories will come the evidences of the wonders of American mechanical skill." Herr Hopp got it right. In 1876, the country he described as a "young giant" was on the cusp of becoming, for better or worse, the economic powerhouse of the world. In Part Four, we undertake to explain how that happened and what it meant for American life.

THE WEST

In his catalogue of achievements, Ernst Hopp emphasized the mining pits of Nevada and California's gold and mercury. He might also have mentioned the corn, wheat, and livestock flowing cityward from the Great Plains. For it was the eastern demand for new sources of food and mineral resources that drove the final surge of western settlement and integrated the Great Plains and Far West into the nation's industrializing economy. Defending their way of life, western Indians were ultimately defeated not so much by army rifles as by encroaching railroads, mines, ranches, and farms. These same forces disrupted the old established Hispanic communities of the Southwest but spurred Asian, Mexican, and European migrations that made for a multiethnic western society.

INDUSTRY

As momentous as the final settlement of the West was the fact that for the first time, as the decade of the 1870s passed, farmers no longer constituted a majority of working Americans. Henceforth, America's future would be linked to its development as an industrializing society. In the manufacturing sector, production became increasingly mechanized and increasingly directed at making the capital goods that undergirded economic growth. As the railroad system was completed, big business began to dominate American enterprise. The labor movement became firmly established, and as immigration surged, the foreign-born and their children became America's workers. What had been partial and limited now became general and widespread. America turned into a land of factories, corporate enterprise, and industrial workers.

THE CITY

Industrialization also transformed the nation's urban life. By 1900, one in five Americans lived in cities. That was where the jobs were: as workers in the factories; as clerks and salespeople; as members of a new, salaried middle class of managers, engineers, and professionals; and, at the apex, a wealthy elite of investors and entrepreneurs. The city was more than just a place to make a living, however. It provided a setting for an urban lifestyle unlike anything seen before in America.

POLITICS

The unfettered, booming economy of the Gilded Age at first marginalized political life—or rather, it marginalized state and federal government, which, for most Americans, was very nearly invisible. The major parties remained robust because they exploited a culture of popular participation and embraced the ethnic and religious identities of their constituencies. The depression of the 1890s triggered a major challenge to the political status quo with the rise of the agrarian Populist Party and its radical demand for free silver. The election of 1896 turned back that challenge and established the Republicans as the dominant national party.

Still unresolved was the threat that corporate power posed to the marketplace and democratic politics. How to curb the trusts dominated national debate during the Progressive era. From different angles, political reformers, women progressives, and urban liberals went about the business of cleaning up machine politics and making life better for America's urban masses. African Americans, victimized by disfranchisement and segregation, found allies among white progressives and launched a new drive for racial equality.

DIPLOMACY

Finally, America's dynamic economic development altered the country's foreign relations. In the decades after the Civil War, America had been inward-looking, neglectful of its navy and inactive diplomatically. The business crisis of the 1890s brought home the need for a more aggressive foreign policy aimed at advancing the nation's overseas economic interests. In short order, the United States went to war with Spain, acquired an overseas empire, and became actively engaged in Latin America and Asia. There was no mistaking America's standing as a Great Power and, as World War I approached, no evading the entanglements that came with that status.

The American West

Who are to go there?
The territory consists
of mountains almost
inaccessible, and low
lands . . . where rain
never falls, except during
spring. . . . Why sir, sir,
of what use will this be for
agricultural purposes? I
would not, for that purpose,
give a pinch of snuff for the
whole territory.

— Senator George McDuffie speaking
in Congress about acquiring California
from Mexico, 1843

In the waning decades of the nineteenth century, America seemed like two nations. One was an advanced industrial society—the America of factories and sprawling cities. But another America remained frontier country, with pioneers streaming onto the Great Plains, repeating the old dramas of "settlement" they had been performing ever since Europeans had first set foot on the continent. Indian wars and industrial strikes shared headlines in the daily press. The last tragic episode in the suppression of the Plains Indians, the massacre at Wounded Knee, South Dakota, occurred only eighteen months before the great Homestead steel strike of 1892.

This alignment of events from the distant worlds of factory and frontier was no accident. The final surge of settlement across the Great Plains and the Far West was powered by the same economic forces that were driving American industrialism—thus this remarkable convergence of historic events: The U.S. Census of 1890 declared that a "frontier of settlement" no longer existed; the "unsettled area has been so broken into . . . that there can hardly be said to be a frontier line." That same year, the United States overtook Great Britain as the world's leading steel producer.

The Great Plains

During the 1860s, agricultural settlement reached the western margins of the tall-grass prairie. Beyond, roughly at the ninety-eighth meridian (Map 16.1), stretched a vast, dry country, uninviting to farmers accustomed to woodlands and ample rainfall. They

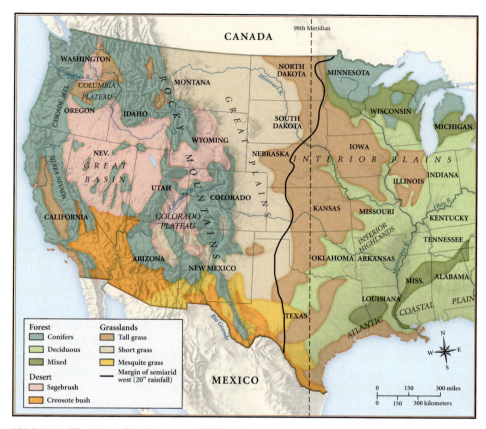

MAP 16.1 The Natural Environment of the West, 1860s

As settlers pushed into the Great Plains and beyond the line of semiaridity, they sensed the overwhelming power of the natural environment. In a landscape without trees for fences and barns and without adequate rainfall, ranchers and farmers had to relearn their businesses. The Native Americans who peopled the plains and mountains had learned to live in this environment, but this knowledge counted for little against the ruthless pressure of the settlers to domesticate the West.

saw it much as did the New York publisher Horace Greeley on his way to California in 1859: "a land of starvation," "a treeless desert," baking in heat in the daytime and "chill and piercing" cold at night.

Greeley was describing the Great Plains. The geologic event that created the Great Plains occurred sixty million years ago when the Rocky Mountains arose out of the ocean covering western North America. With no outlet, the shallow inland sea to the east dried up. Because the moisture-laden winds from the Pacific spent themselves on the western slopes of the Sierras, the climate was dry, interspersing cycles of rainfall and drought. Bunch grasses such as blue grama, the linchpin of this fragile ecosystem, matted the easily blown soil into place and sustained a rich wildlife dominated by grazing antelope and buffalo. What the dry short-grass country had not permanently sustained, until the past few centuries, was human settlement.

Indians of the Great Plains

Probably 100,000 Native Americans lived on the Great Plains at mid-nineteenth century. They were a diverse people, divided into six linguistic families and at least thirty tribal groupings. On the eastern margins, the Mandans, Arikaras, and Pawnees planted corn and beans and lived in permanent villages. Smallpox and measles introduced by Europeans ravaged these settled tribes. Less vulnerable to epidemics because they were dispersed were the hunting tribes on the Great Plains: Kiowas and Comanches in the southwest; Arapahos and Cheyennes on the central plains; and, to the north, Blackfeet, Crows, and the great Sioux nation.

Originally, the Sioux had been eastern prairie people, occupying settlements in the lake country of northern Minnesota. When fish and game dwindled, some tribes drifted westward across the Missouri River. These Sioux, or Lakota (meaning "allies"), became nomadic, living in portable skin tepees and hunting buffalo. From tribes to the southwest, they acquired horses. Once mounted, the Sioux became splendid hunters and formidable fighters, claiming the entire Great Plains north of the Arkansas River as their hunting grounds.

A society that celebrates the heroic virtues of hunting and war—men's work—is likely to define gender roles sharply. But before the Sioux had horses, it took the efforts of both men and women to construct the "pounds" into which, beating the brush side by side, they endeavored to stampede the buffalo herds. Once on horseback, however, the men rode off to the hunt while the women stayed behind to prepare the mounting piles of buffalo skins. Subordination to the men was not how Sioux women understood their unrelenting labor; this was their allotted share in a partnership on which the proud, nomadic life of the Sioux depended.

Dependent on nature's bounty for survival, the Sioux endowed every manifestation of the natural world with sacred meaning. Unlike Europeans, they conceived of God not as a supreme being but, in the words of the pioneering ethnologist Clark Wissler, as a "series of powers pervading the universe": Wi, the sun; Skan, the sky; Maka, the earth; Inyan, the rock. Below these came the moon, the wind, and the buffalo down through a hierarchy embodying the entire natural order.

By prayer and fasting, Sioux prepared themselves to commune with these mysterious powers. Medicine men provided instruction, but the religious experience was personal, open to both sexes. The vision, when a supplicant achieved it, attached itself to some object—a feather, an animal skin, or a shell—that was tied into a sacred bundle and became the person's lifelong talisman. In the Sun Dance, the entire tribe celebrated the rites of coming of age, fertility, the hunt, and combat, followed by fasting and dancing in supplication to Wi, the sun.

The world of the Lakota Sioux was not self-contained. From their earliest days as nomadic hunters, they had exchanged pelts and buffalo robes for the produce of agriculturalist Pawnees and Mandans. When white traders appeared on the upper Missouri River during the eighteenth century, the Sioux began to trade with them. Although the buffalo remained their staff of life, the Sioux came to rely as well on the traders' kettles, blankets, knives, and guns. The trade system they entered was linked to the Euro-American market economy, yet it was also integrated into the Sioux way of life. Everything depended on keeping the Great Plains as the Sioux had found it: wild grassland on which the buffalo ranged free.

Wagon Trains, Railroads, and Ranchers

On first encountering the Great Plains, Euro-Americans thought these unforested lands best left to the Indians. After exploring a drought-stricken stretch in 1820, Major Stephen H. Long declared it "almost wholly unfit for cultivation, and of course uninhabitable by a people depending upon agriculture for their subsistence."

For years thereafter, maps marked the plains as the **Great American Desert**. In 1834, Congress formally designated the Great Plains as permanent Indian country. The army wanted the border forts, stretching from Lake Superior to Fort Worth, Texas, constructed of stone because they would be there forever. Trade with the Indians would continue, but now it would be closely supervised and licensed by the federal government, with the Indian country otherwise off limits to whites.

Events swiftly overtook the nation's solemn commitment as Americans began to eye Oregon and California. Indian country became a bridge to the Pacific. The first wagon train headed west for Oregon from Missouri in 1842. Soon thousands of emigrants traveled the Oregon Trail to the Willamette Valley or cut south beyond Fort Hall into California. Approaching Fort Hall in 1859, Horace Greeley thought "the white coverings of the many emigrant and transport wagons dotting the landscape" gave "the trail the appearance of a river running through great meadows, with many ships sailing on its bosom."

Talk about a railroad to the Pacific soon surfaced in Washington. How else could the Pacific territories acquired from Mexico and Britain in 1848 (see Chapter 13) be linked to the Union? The project languished while North and South argued over the route. Meanwhile, the Indian country was crisscrossed by overland freight lines, and Pony Express riders delivered mail between Missouri and California. In 1861, telegraph lines brought San Francisco into instant communication with the East. The next year, with the South in rebellion, the federal government finally moved forward with the transcontinental rail project.

No private company could be expected to foot the bill by itself. The construction costs were staggering, and not much traffic could be expected along the thinly populated route. So the federal government awarded generous land grants plus millions of dollars in loans to the two companies that undertook the transcontinental project.

The Union Pacific, building westward from Omaha, made little headway until the Civil War ended but then advanced rapidly across Indian country, reaching Cheyenne, Wyoming, in November 1867. It took the Central Pacific nearly that long, moving eastward from Sacramento, California, to cross the Sierra Nevada. Both then worked furiously — since the government subsidy was based on miles of track laid — until, to great fanfare, the tracks met at Promontory, Utah, in 1869. None of the other railroads following westward routes made it as far as the Rockies before the Panic of 1873 brought all construction to an abrupt halt (see Chapter 17).

By then, however, railroad tycoons had changed their minds about the Great Plains. No longer did they see it through the eyes of the Oregon-bound settlers: as a place to be gotten through en route to the Pacific. They realized that railroads were laying the basis for the economic exploitation of the Great Plains. With economic recovery in 1878, construction soared. During the 1880s, 40,000 miles of western track were laid west of the Mississippi, including links from southern California, via the

Southern Pacific to New Orleans and via the Santa Fe to Kansas City, and from the Northwest, via the Northern Pacific to St. Paul, Minnesota.

Grazing buffalo made it easy to imagine the Great Plains as cow country. But first the buffalo had to go. All that it would take were the right commercial incentives. A small market for buffalo robes had existed for years, and hunters made good livings provisioning army posts and leading sporting parties. Then in the early 1870s, as eastern tanneries learned how to cure the hides, the demand for buffalo skins skyrocketed. Parties of professional hunters with high-powered rifles began a systematic slaughter of the buffalo. Already diminished by disease and shrinking pasturage, the great herds almost vanished within ten years. Many people spoke out against this mass killing, but no way existed to stop people bent on making a quick dollar.

In south Texas, about five million head of longhorn cattle already grazed on Anglo ranches, hardly worth bothering about because they could not be profitably marketed. In 1865, however, the Missouri Pacific Railroad reached Sedalia, Missouri, far enough west to be accessible to Texas ranchers. At the Sedalia terminus, a longhorn worth $3 in Texas might command $40. With this incentive Texas ranchers inaugurated the famous Long Drive, hiring cowboys to herd the longhorn cattle hundreds of miles north to the railroads that were pushing west across Kansas.

At Abilene, Ellsworth, and Dodge City, ranchers sold their cattle, and trail-weary cowboys crowded into saloons. These cattle towns captured the nation's imagination as symbols of the Wild West. The reality was much more ordinary. The cowboys, many

Cowboys on the Open Range

In open-range ranching, cattle from different ranches grazed together. At the roundup, cowboys separated the cattle by owner and branded the calves. Cowboys, celebrated in dime novels, were really farmhands on horseback, with the skills to work on the range. An ethnically diverse group, including blacks and Hispanics, they earned $25 a month, plus meals and a bed in the bunkhouse, in return for long hours of grueling, lonesome work. Library of Congress.

of them African American and Hispanic, were in fact farmhands on horseback who worked long hours under harsh conditions for small pay. Colorful though it seemed, the Long Drive was actually a makeshift method of bridging a gap in the developing transportation system. As soon as railroads reached the Texas range country during the 1870s, ranchers abandoned the Long Drive.

The Texas ranchers owned or leased the huge tracts of land they used. North of Texas, where the land was in the public domain, cattlemen simply helped themselves. Hopeful ranchers would spot a likely area along a creek and claim as much land as they could qualify for under federal homesteading laws, plus what might be added by the fraudulent claims taken out by one or two ranch hands. By common usage, ranchers had a "range right" to all the adjacent land rising up to the divide—the point where the land sloped down to the next creek.

News of easy money traveled fast. Rail connections were in place or coming in. The grass was free. The rush was on, drawing from as far away as Europe both hardheaded investors and romantics (such as the recent Harvard graduate Teddy Roosevelt) eager for a taste of the Wild West. By the early 1880s, the plains overflowed with cattle—as many as 7.5 million head ravaging the grass and trampling the water holes.

A cycle of good weather only postponed the inevitable disaster. When it came—a hard winter in 1885, a severe drought the following summer, then record blizzards and bitter cold—cattle died by the hundreds of thousands. An awful scene of rotting carcasses greeted the cowhands as they rode out onto the range the following spring. The boom collapsed, leaving behind a more enduring ecological catastrophe: the destruction of native grasses from overgrazing by the cattle herds.

Abandoning open-range ranching, cattlemen fenced their land and planted hay. Instead of merely exploiting the plains ecosystem, they now shaped it to their own purposes. Ranching entered a more placid, domesticated era. In the meantime, Hispanic shepherds from New Mexico brought sheep in to feed on the mesquite and prickly pear that supplanted the native grasses. Sheep raising, previously scorned by ranchers as unmanly and threatening to cattle, became a major enterprise in the sparser high country.

As the romance faded on the ground, it flowered in the American imagination. The grand perpetrator of a mythic West, William F. Cody, was a barely educated, hard-drinking ex-guerrilla fighter (and occasional horse thief). At loose ends after the Civil War, Cody got a lucky break in 1867 when he was hired to provide buffalo meat for work crews laying railroad track through Indian country in Kansas. Cody's skills as a buffalo hunter soon won him the name "Buffalo Bill." In 1868, Indian war broke out, and Cody got his second claim to fame as an intrepid army scout.

Out of these promising materials, a legendary figure emerged. In July 1869, the dime novelist Ned Bunting came through Kansas, met Cody, and immediately wrote *Buffalo Bill, the King of the Border Men*, the first of some 1,700 potboilers featuring Cody and his exploits. Cody's mythic West became full blown in his traveling Wild West Show, first staged in 1883, which toured the country offering displays of horsemanship, sharpshooting by Little Annie Oakley, and real Indians (in one season, Chief Sitting Bull toured with the company). Long after the authentic world that lay behind the make-believe was gone, Buffalo Bill's Wild West Show kept it alive in legend, where it still remains in the cowboys and Indians that populate our movies and television screens.

Homesteaders

No westerners had less in common with Buffalo Bill's world than the settlers who followed the cattlemen onto the Great Plains. Before coming, of course, they needed to be persuaded that crops would grow in that dry country. Powerful interests worked hard to overcome the popular notion that the plains were the Great American Desert. The railroads, eager to sell off the public land they had been granted, advertised aggressively and offered cut-rate tickets. Land speculators, transatlantic steamship lines, and the western states and territories joined the campaign. So did the federal government, which offered 160 acres of public land to all comers under the Homestead Act (1862).

"Why emigrate to Kansas?" asked a testimonial in *Western Trail*, the Rock Island Railroad's gazette. "Because it is the garden spot of the world. Because it will grow anything that any other country will grow, and with less work. Because it rains here more than any other place, and at just the right time."

As if to confirm the optimists, a wet cycle occurred between 1878 and 1886. Some settlers attributed the increased rainfall to soil cultivation and tree planting. Others credited God. As a settler on the southern plains remarked, "The Lord just knowed we needed more land an' He's gone and changed the climate."

No amount of optimism, however, could dispel the pain of migration. "That last separating word of *Farewell!* sinks deeply into the heart," one pioneer woman recorded in her diary, thinking of family and friends left behind. Then came the treeless plains. "Such an air of desolation," wrote a Nebraska-bound woman; another, from Texas spoke of "such a lonely country."

Some women were liberated by this hard experience. Prescribed gender roles broke down as women became self-reliant in the face of danger and hardship. When husbands died or gave up, wives operated farms on their own. Even with a man around, women contributed crucially to the farm enterprise. Farming might be thought of as a dual economy, in which men's labor brought in the big wage at harvest time while women provisioned the family day by day with their garden plots and saleable eggs and butter. If the crop failed, it was women's labor that carried the family through. No wonder farming placed a high premium on marriage: A mere 2.4 percent of Nebraska women in 1900 had never married.

Male or female, the vision of new land beckoned people onto the plains. By the 1870s, the older agricultural states had filled up, and farmers looked hungrily westward. The same excitement took hold in northern Europe, as Norwegians and Swedes for the first time joined the earlier German migration. At the peak of the "American fever" in 1882, over 105,000 Scandinavians left for the United States. Swedish and Norwegian became the primary languages in parts of Minnesota and the Dakotas.

The motivation for most settlers, American or European, was to better themselves economically. But for some southern blacks, Kansas briefly represented something more precious: the Promised Land of racial freedom. In the spring of 1879, with Reconstruction over, black communities fearful of white vengeance were swept by enthusiasm for Kansas. Within a month or so, some 6,000 blacks left Mississippi and Louisiana, most of them with nothing more than the clothes on their backs and faith in the Lord. They called themselves Exodusters, participants in the exodus to the dry prairie. The 1880 census reported 40,000 blacks in Kansas—by far the largest African American

The Shores Family, Custer County, Nebraska, 1887
Whether the Shores family came west as Exodusters, we do not know. But in 1887, when this photograph was taken, they were well settled on their Nebraska farm, though still living in sod houses. The patriarch of the family, Jerry Shores, an ex-slave, is second from the right. Nebraska State Historical Society.

concentration in the West aside from Texas, whose expanding cotton frontier attracted hundreds of thousands of black migrants during the 1870s and 1880s.

No matter where they came from, homesteaders found the plains an alien place. A cloud of grasshoppers might descend and destroy a crop in a day; a brush fire or hailstorm could do the job in an hour. What forested land had always provided—ample water, lumber for cabins and fencing, firewood—was absent. For shelter, settlers often cut dugouts into hillsides and then, after a season or two, erected houses made of turf cut from the ground.

The absence of trees, on the other hand, made clearing the land easier. New technology helped. Steel plows enabled homesteaders to break the tightly matted ground, and barbed wire provided cheap, effective fencing against roaming cattle. Strains of hard-kernel wheat that tolerated the extreme temperatures of the plains came in from Europe. With good crops, homesteaders began to anticipate the wood-frame house, deep well, and full coal bin that might make life tolerable on the plains.

In the mid-1880s, the dry years came and wrecked those hopeful calculations. "From day to day," reported the budding novelist Stephen Crane from Nebraska, "a wind hot as an oven's fury . . . raged like a pestilence," destroying the crops and leaving farmers "helpless, with no weapon against this terrible and inscrutable wrath of

Buffalo Chips

With no trees around for firewood, settlers on the plains had to make do with dried cow and buffalo droppings. Gathering the "buffalo chips" must have been a regular chore for Ada McColl and her daughter on her homestead near Lakin, Kansas, in 1893. Kansas State Historical Society.

For more help analyzing this image, see the Online Study Guide at **bedfordstmartins.com/henrettaconcise**.

nature." Land that had only recently been settled emptied out as homesteaders fled in defeat — 50,000 of them from the Dakotas between 1885 and 1890.

Other settlers held on. Stripped of the illusion that rain followed the plow, the survivors came to terms with the semiarid climate. One answer lay in dry-farming methods, which involved deep planting to bring subsoil moisture to the roots and quick harrowing after rainfalls to turn over a dry mulch that slowed evaporation. Dry farming developed most fully on the huge corporate farms in the Red River Valley of North Dakota. But even family farms, the norm elsewhere, could not survive on less than 300 acres of grain crops plus machinery for plowing, planting, and harvesting. Dry farming was not for unequipped homesteaders.

In this struggle, settlers regarded themselves as nature's conquerors, striving, as one pioneer remarked, "to get the land subdued and the wilde nature out of it." Much about its "wilde nature" was, of course, hidden to these strangers to the Great Plains. They had no way of knowing that the attack on biodiversity, which was what farming the plains really meant, opened pathways for exotic, destructive pests and weeds or that plowing under the native bunch grasses rendered the soil vulnerable to erosion and sandstorms. Few people counted the environmental costs when money was to be made. By the turn of the century, about half the nation's cattle and sheep, one-third of its cereal crops, and nearly three-fifths of its wheat came from the Great Plains. But it was not a sustainable achievement. In the twentieth century, this celebrated nation's bread basket was revealed to have been, in the words of modern scientists, "the largest, longest-run agricultural and environmental miscalculation in American history."

Farmers' Woes

Taming the Great Plains involved little of the "pioneering" that Americans associated with the westward movement. The railroads came before the settlers, eastern capital financed the ranching bonanza, dry farming depended on sophisticated technology, and western wheat traded on world markets.

American farmers embraced this commercial world. In frontier areas, where newly developed land appreciated rapidly, they anticipated as much profit, if not more, from the rising value of the land as from the crops it produced. In boom times, they rushed into debt to acquire more land and better farm equipment. All these enthusiasms—for cash crops, for land speculation, for borrowed money, for new technology—bore witness to the conviction that farming was, as one agricultural journal remarked, a business "like all other business."

Somehow, however, farmers went unrewarded for their faith in free enterprise. The basic problem was that they remained individual operators in an ever more complex and far-flung economic order. They were, in certain ways, aware of their predicament. They understood, for example, the disadvantages they faced in dealing with the big businesses that supplied them with machinery, arranged their credit, and marketed their products.

One answer was cooperation. In 1867, Oliver H. Kelley, a government clerk, founded the National Grange of the Patrons of Husbandry mainly in hopes of improving the social life of farm families. The Grange soon added cooperative programs, purchasing in bulk from suppliers and setting up its own banks, insurance companies, grain elevators, and, in Iowa, even a manufacturing plant for farm implements. Although most of these programs eventually failed, the cooperative idea was highly resilient and would be embraced by every successive farmers' movement. The power of government might also be enlisted on the farmers' side. In the early 1870s, the Grange encouraged independent political parties that ran on antimonopoly platforms. In a number of prairie states, these agrarian parties enacted so-called Granger laws regulating grain elevators, fixing maximum railroad rates, and prohibiting discriminatory treatment of small and short-haul shippers.

Farmers turned to cooperatives and state regulation out of a deep sense of organizational disadvantage. But what really put them at risk was beyond anyone's control: the movement of farm prices. Especially endangered were farmers exposed to the global commodity markets, most notably wheat farmers. In the 1870s, the major wheat-growing states had been Illinois, Wisconsin, and Minnesota. These states had been at the center of the Granger agitation of that decade. By the 1880s, wheat had moved onto the Great Plains. Among the indebted farmers of Kansas, Nebraska, and the Dakotas, the deflationary economy of the 1880s made for stubbornly hard times. All that was needed to bring on a real crisis was a sharp drop in world prices for wheat.

The Fate of the Indians

What of the Native Americans who inhabited the Great Plains? Basically, their history has been told in the foregoing account of western settlement. "The white children have surrounded me and have left me nothing but an island," lamented the great Sioux chief Red Cloud in 1870, the year after the completion of the transcontinental railroad. "When we first had all this land we were strong; now we are all melting like snow on a hillside, while you are grown like spring grass."

Settlement proceeded in the face of provisions for a permanent Indian country written into federal law and ratified by treaties with various tribes. As incursions increased from the late 1850s onward, the Indians resisted as best they could, striking back all along the frontier: the Apaches in the Southwest, the Cheyenne and Arapahos in Colorado, and the Sioux in the Wyoming and Dakota Territories. The Indians hoped that if they resisted stubbornly enough, the whites would tire of the struggle and leave them in peace. This reasoning seemed not altogether fanciful, given the country's exhaustion after the Civil War. But the federal government did not give up; instead, it formulated a new policy for dealing with the western Indians: the reservation solution.

Few whites questioned the necessity of moving the Native Americans out of the path of settlement and into reservations. That had been the fate of the eastern and southern tribes. Now, however, Indian removal included something new: a strategy for undermining the Indians' tribal way of life. The first step was a peace commission appointed in 1867 to persuade the western Indians to cede their lands and move to reservations. There, under the tutelage of the Office of Indian Affairs, they would be wards of the government until they learned "to walk on the white man's road."

The government set aside two extensive areas, allocating the southwestern quarter of the Dakota Territory—present-day South Dakota west of the Missouri River—to the Lakota Sioux tribes and assigning what is now Oklahoma to the southern Plains Indians along with the major southern tribes—the Choctaw, Cherokee, Chickasaw, Creek, and Seminole—and eastern Indians who had been removed there thirty years before. Scattered reservations went to the Apaches, Navajos, and Utes in the Southwest and to the mountain Indians in the Rockies and beyond.

That the Plains Indians would resist was inevitable. "You might as well expect the rivers to run backward as that any man who was born a free man should be contented when penned up and denied liberty to go where he pleases," said Chief Joseph of the Nez Percé, who led his people in 1877, including women and children, on an epic 1,500-mile march from eastern Oregon to escape confinement in a small reservation. In a series of heroic engagements, the Nez Percé fought off the pursuing army units until, after four months of extraordinary hardship, the remnants of the tribe finally surrendered in Montana near the Canadian border.

The U.S. Army was thinly spread, down after the Civil War to a total force of 27,000. But these were veteran troops, including 2,000 black cavalrymen of the Ninth and Tenth Regiments, whom Indians called, with grim respect, "buffalo soldiers." Technology also favored the army. Telegraph communications and railroads enabled the troops to be quickly concentrated; repeating rifles and Gatling machine guns increased their firepower. Because of tribal rivalries, the army could always find Indian allies. Worst of all, beyond the U.S. Army's advantages or the Indians' disunity, was the overwhelming impact of white settlement.

Resisting the reservation solution, the Indians fought on for years—in Kansas in 1868 and 1869, in the Red River Valley of Texas in 1874, and sporadically among the fierce Apaches, who made life miserable for white settlers in the Southwest until their wily chief Geronimo was finally captured in 1886. On the northern plains, the crisis came in 1875, when the Office of Indian Affairs—despite an 1868 treaty—ordered the Sioux to vacate their Powder River hunting grounds (in what is now northeastern Wyoming) and withdraw to the reservation.

Led by Sitting Bull, Sioux and Cheyenne warriors gathered on the Little Big Horn River west of the Powder River country. In a typical concentrating maneuver, army columns from widely separated forts converged on the Little Big Horn. The Seventh Cavalry, commanded by Civil War hero George A. Custer, came upon the Sioux encampment on June 25, 1876. Disregarding orders, the reckless Custer sought out battle on his own. He attacked from three sides, hoping to capitalize on the element of surprise. But his forces were spread too thin. The other two contingents fell back to defensive positions, but Custer's own force of 256 men was surrounded and annihilated by Crazy Horse's warriors. It was a great victory but not a decisive one. The day of reckoning was merely postponed.

Pursued by the U.S. military, physically exhausted Sioux bands one by one gave up and moved to the reservation. Last to come in were Sitting Bull's followers. They had retreated to Canada, but in 1881, after five hard years, they recrossed the border and surrendered at Fort Buford, Montana.

Not Indian resistance, but white greed wrecked the reservation solution. In the mid-1870s, prospectors began to dig for gold in the Black Hills, land that was sacred to the Sioux and entirely inside their Dakota reservation. Unable to hold back the gold seekers, the government opened up the Black Hills at their own risk. In 1877, after Sioux resistance had crumbled, federal agents forced the tribes to cede the western third of their Dakota reservation.

The Indian Territory of Oklahoma met a similar fate. White homesteaders coveted the two million fertile acres that had not been assigned. The "boomer" movement, stirred up initially by railroads operating in the Indian Territory, agitated for an opening of this so-called Oklahoma District to settlers. In 1889, the government reluctantly placed the Oklahoma District under the Homestead Act. On April 22, 1889, a horde of claimants rushed in and staked out the entire district within a few hours. Two tent cities—Guthrie with 15,000 people and Oklahoma City with 10,000—were in full swing by nightfall.

In the meantime, the campaign to move the Indians onto "the white man's road" went relentlessly forward. During the 1870s, the Office of Indian Affairs developed a program to train Indian children for farm work and prepare them for citizenship. Some attended reservation schools; the less lucky were sent to distant boarding schools. The Mother Hubbard dresses and shirts and trousers they had to wear visibly demonstrated that these bewildered children were being inducted into white society (see American Voices, p. 481).

And not a moment too soon, believed many avowed friends of the Native Americans. The Indians had never lacked sympathizers, especially in the East, where reformers created the Indian Rights Association after the Civil War. The movement got a boost from Helen Hunt Jackson's influential book *A Century of Dishonor* (1881), which told the story of the unjust treatment of the Indians. What would save them, the reformers

Indian School

In this photograph taken at the Riverside Indian School in Anadarko, Oklahoma Territory, the pupils have been shorn of their braids and dressed in laced shoes, Mother Hubbard dresses, and shirts and trousers—one step on the journey into the mainstream of American society. Children as young as five years of age were separated from their families and sent to Indian schools like this one that taught them new skills while encouraging them to abandon traditional Indian ways. University of Oklahoma, Western History Collections.

believed, was assimilation into white society. The reformers also favored efforts by the Office of Indian Affairs to undermine tribal authority. Above all, the reformers esteemed private property as a "civilizing force" and hence advocated **severalty**, land ownership by individuals.

The result was the Dawes Severalty Act (1887), authorizing the president to carve up tribal lands, with each family head receiving an allotment of 160 acres. The land would be held in trust for twenty-five years, and the Indians would be granted U.S. citizenship. Remaining reservation lands would be sold off, the proceeds to be placed in an Indian education fund.

The Sioux were among the first victims of the Dawes Act. The federal government, announcing that it had gained tribal approval, opened the Sioux's "surplus" land to white settlement on February 10, 1890. But no surveys had been made, nor had the Indians yet received their land allotments. On top of these signs of bad faith, drought wiped out the Indians' crops that summer. It seemed beyond endurance. They had lost their ancestral lands. They faced a future as farmers, which was alien to their traditions. And immediately confronting them was a winter of starvation.

But news of salvation had also come. An Indian messiah, a holy man who called himself Wovoka, was preaching a new religion on a Paiute reservation in Nevada. God had appeared in a vision and told him that the whites would disappear, all the Indians

Becoming White ZITKALA-ŠA (GERTRUDE SIMMONS BONNIN)

Zitkala-Ša, known later as the author Gertrude Simmons Bonnin, recalled in 1900 her painful transformation from Sioux child to pupil at a Quaker mission school in Indiana.

The first day . . . a paleface woman, with white hair, came up after us. We were placed in a line of girls who were marching into the dining room. These were Indian girls, in stiff shoes and closely clinging dresses. The small girls wore sleeved aprons and shingled hair. As I walked noiselessly in my soft mocassins, I felt like sinking into the floor, for my blanket had been stripped from my shoulders. . . . Late in the morning, my friend Judewin gave me a terrible warning. Judewin knew a few words of English; and she had overheard the paleface woman talk about cutting our long, heavy hair. Our mothers had taught us that only unskilled warriors who were captured had their hair shingled by the enemy. Among our people, short hair was worn by mourners, and shingled hair by cowards! . . . In spite of myself, I was carried downstairs and tied fast in a chair. I cried aloud, shaking my head all the while until I felt the cold blades of the scissors against my neck, and heard them gnaw off one of my thick black braids. Then I lost my spirit. . . .

Now, as I look back upon the recent past, I see it from a distance, as a whole. I remember how, from morning till evening, many specimens of civilized peoples visited the Indian school. The city folks with canes and eyeglass, the countrymen with sun-burned cheeks and clumsy feet. . . . Both sorts of these Christian palefaces were alike astounded at seeing the children of savage warriors so docile and industrious.

As answers to their shallow inquiries they received the students' sample work to look upon. Examining the neatly figured pages, and gazing upon the Indian girls and boys bending over their books, the white visitors walked out of the schoolhouse well-satisfied: they were educating the children of the red man! . . .

In this fashion many have passed idly through the Indian schools during the last decade, afterward to boast of their charity to the North American Indian. But few there are who have paused to question whether real life or long lasting death lies beneath this semblance of civilization.

SOURCE: Linda K. Kerber and Jane De-Hart Mathews, eds., *Women's America: Refocusing the Past*, 2nd ed. (New York: Oxford University Press, 1987), 254–257.

of past generations would return to Earth, and life on the Great Plains would be as it was before the white man appeared. Wovoka urged Indians to prepare themselves by practicing the Ghost Dance, a day-long ritual that sent the spirits of the dancers rising to heaven. As the frenzy of the Ghost Dance swept through some Sioux encampments in 1890, resident whites became alarmed and called for army intervention.

Wovoka had a fervent following among the Minneconjous, where the medicine man Yellow Bird held sway. But with their chief, Big Foot, desperately ill with pneumonia, the Minneconjous agreed to come in under military escort to Wounded Knee

Creek on December 28. The next morning, when the soldiers attempted to disarm the Indians, a battle exploded in the encampment. Among the U.S. troopers, 25 died; among the Indians, 146 men, women, and children perished, many of them shot down as they fled.

Wounded Knee was the final blow against the Plains Indians but not the end of their story. The division of tribal lands now proceeded without hindrance. The Lakota Sioux fared relatively well, and many of the younger generation settled down as small farmers and stock grazers. The most fortunate tribes, ironically, were probably those occupying infertile land that settlers did not want. The flood of whites into South Dakota and Oklahoma, on the other hand, left the Indians as small minorities in lands that had once been wholly theirs: There were 20,000 Sioux in a South Dakotan population of 400,000 in 1900 and 70,000 of various tribes in a population of a million when Oklahoma became a state in 1907.

▶ What was the role of the railroads in the settlement of the Great West?

▶ How would you characterize the agricultural settlers' relationship to the natural environment of the Great Plains?

▶ What was the new Indian reservation policy, and why was it a failure?

Even so, tribal life survived. All along, Native American cultures had been adaptive, changing in the face of adversity and even absorbing features of white society. This cultural resilience persisted—in religion, in tribal structure, in crafts—but the fostering preconquest world was gone, swept away, as an Oklahoma editor put it in the year of statehood, by "the onward march of empire."

The Far West

On the western edge of the Great Plains, the Rocky Mountains rise up to form a great barrier between the mostly flat eastern two-thirds of the continent and the rugged Far West. Beyond the Rockies, the desertlike Great Basin begins, covering western Utah and all of Nevada. Separating this arid interior from the Pacific Ocean are two great mountain ranges—the Sierra Nevada and, to the north, the Cascades—beyond which lies a coastal region that is cool and rainy in the north but increasingly dry southward, until, in southern California, rainfall becomes almost as sparse as in the interior.

Clearly, the transmountain West could not be occupied in standard American fashion—that is, by a multitude of settlers moving along a broad front and, homestead by homestead, bringing it under cultivation. The wagon trains heading to Oregon's Willamette Valley adopted an entirely different strategy: the planting of an island of settlement in a vast, often barren landscape.

New Spain had pioneered this strategy centuries earlier, when it had sent the first wagon trains 700 miles northward from Mexico into the upper Rio Grande Valley and established Santa Fe. When the United States seized the Mexican Southwest in 1848, 250 years later, the only significant Anglo settlement was around the Great Salt Lake in Utah, where persecuted Mormons had planted a New Zion. Fewer than 100,000 Euro-Americans—roughly 25,000 of them Anglo, the rest Hispanic—lived in the entire Far West when it became U.S. territory.

The Mining Frontier

More emigrants would be coming, certainly, but the Far West seemed unlikely to be a big draw. California was "hilly and mountainous," noted a U.S. naval officer in 1849, too dry for farming and surely not "susceptible of supporting a very large population." He had not taken account of the recent discovery of gold in the Sierra foothills. California would indeed support a very large population, drawn not by arable land but by dreams of gold.

Extraction of mineral wealth became the basis for the Far West's development (Map 16.2). By 1860, when Indians still dominated the Great Plains, California was a booming state with 300,000 residents. In a burst of city building, San Francisco became a bustling metropolis — it had 57,000 residents in 1860 — and was the hub of a mining empire that stretched to the Rockies.

As easy pickings in the California gold country ended, prospectors began to pull out and spread across the West in hopes of striking it rich elsewhere. Gold was discovered on the Nevada side of the Sierra Nevada, in the Colorado Rockies, and along the

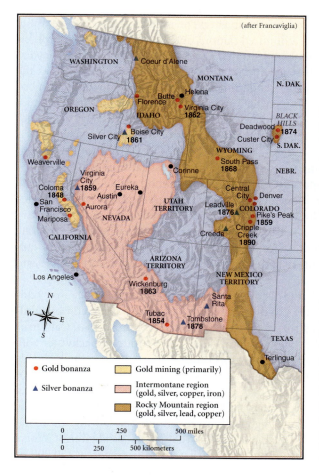

MAP 16.2 The Mining Frontier, 1848–1890

The Far West was America's gold country because of its geological history. Veins of gold and silver form when molten material from the earth's core is forced up into fissures caused by the tectonic movements that create mountain ranges, such as the ones that dominate the far western landscape. It was these veins, the product of mountain-forming activity many thousands of years earlier, that prospectors began to discover after 1848 and furiously exploit. Although widely dispersed across the Far West, the lodes that they found followed the mountain ranges bisecting the region and bypassing the great plateaus not shaped by the ancient tectonic activity.

For more help analyzing this map, see the Online Study Guide at bedfordstmartins.com/henrettaconcise.

Fraser River in British Columbia. New strikes occurred in Montana and Wyoming during the 1860s and a decade later in the Black Hills of South Dakota.

News of gold turned wild, remote areas almost overnight into mob scenes of prospectors, traders, gamblers, prostitutes, and saloon keepers (see Voices from Abroad, p. 485). At least 100,000 fortune seekers flocked to the Pike's Peak area of Colorado in the spring of 1859. Trespassers on government or Indian land, the prospectors made their own law. The mining codes devised at community meetings limited mining claims to what a person could reasonably work. This kind of informal lawmaking also became an instrument for discriminating against Mexicans, Chinese, and African Americans in the gold fields. It turned into hangman's justice for the many outlaws who infested the mining camps.

The heyday of the prospectors was always brief. They were equipped only to skim gold from the surface outcroppings and streambeds. Extracting the metal that was locked in underground lodes required mine shafts and crushing mills — and therefore capital, technology, and business organization. At every gold-rush site, the prospector soon gave way to entrepreneurial development and large-scale mining. Rough mining camps turned into big towns.

Consider Nevada's Virginia City, which started out as a bawdy, ramshackle mining camp but then, with the opening of the Comstock silver lode in 1859, acquired a stock exchange, fancy hotels, even Shakespearean theater. The rough edges were never quite smoothed out, however. In 1870, a hundred saloons operated day and night, brothels lined D Street, and men outnumbered women two to one. In its booming heyday, Virginia City seemed a place that would last forever. In the 1880s, however, as the Comstock lode played out, Virginia City declined and, in a fate all too familiar in bonanza mining, became a ghost town. What remained, likewise entirely familiar, was a ravaged landscape, with mountains of debris, poisoned water sources, and woods denuded by the mines' ravenous need for timbering. Comstock, one critic remarked, was "the tomb of the forests of the Sierras."

In its final stage, the mining frontier entered the industrial world. At some sites, gold and silver proved less important than the more common metals — copper, lead, and zinc — needed by eastern industry. Entrepreneurs raised capital, built rail connections, financed the technology for treating the lower-grade copper deposits, constructed smelting facilities, and recruited a labor force. As elsewhere in corporate America, the western mining industries went through a process of consolidation, culminating by the turn of the century in near-monopoly control of western copper and lead production.

Without its mineral wealth, the history of the Far West would have been very different. Oregon's Willamette Valley, not dry California, had mostly attracted westward-bound settlers before the gold strike at Sutter's Mill in 1848. But for that, California would likely have remained like the Willamette Valley: an agricultural backwater with no markets for its products and a slow-growing population. In 1860, although already a state, Oregon had scarcely 25,000 inhabitants, and its principal city, Portland, was little more than a village.

Booming California and its tributary mining country pulled Oregon from the doldrums by creating a market for Oregon's produce and timber. During the 1880s, Oregon and Washington (which became a state in 1889) grew prodigiously. Where scarcely 100,000 settlers had lived twenty years earlier, there were nearly 750,000 by

A Western Boom Town   BARON JOSEPH ALEXANDER VON HÜBNER

During a leisurely trip around the world in 1871, Baron von Hübner, a distinguished Austrian diplomat, traveled across the United States, taking advantage of the newly completed transcontinental railroad to see the Wild West. After observing Mormon life in Salt Lake City, he went northward to Corinne, Utah, near the juncture where the Central Pacific and Union Pacific railroads met. The baron might have arrived with romantic notions of the Wild West, which were popular among Europeans of his class. That was not, however, how he departed.

Corinne has only existed for four years. Sprung out of the earth as if by enchantment, this town now contains upwards of 2,000 inhabitants, and every day increases in importance. It is a victualing center for the advanced posts of the [miners] in Idaho and Montana. A coach runs twice a week to Virginia City and to Helena, 350 and 500 miles to the north. Despite the serious dangers and the terrible fatigue of the journeys, these diligences are always full of passengers. Various articles of consumption and dry goods of all sorts are sent in wagons. The "high road" is but a rough track in the soil left by the wheels of the previous vehicles.

The streets of Corinne are full of white men armed to the teeth, miserable looking Indians dressed in the ragged shirts and trousers furnished by the federal government, and yellow Chinese with a business-like air and hard, intelligent faces. No town in the Far West gave me so good an idea as this little place of what is meant by "border life," the struggle between civilization and savage men and things. . . .

All commercial business centers in Main Street. The houses on both sides are nothing but boarded huts. I have seen some with only canvas partitions. . . . The lanes alongside of the huts, which are generally the resort of Chinese women of bad character, lead into the desert, which begins at the doors of the last houses. . . .

To have on your conscience a number of man-slaughters committed in full day, under the eyes of your fellow citizens; to have escaped the reach of justice by craft, audacity, or bribery; to have earned a reputation for being "sharp," that is, for knowing how to cheat all the world without being caught—those are the attributes of the true rowdy in the Far West. . . . Endowed as they often are with really fine qualities—courage, energy, and intellectual and physical strength—they might in another sphere and with the moral sense which they now lack, have become valuable members of society. But such as they are, these adventurers have a reason for being, a providential mission to fulfill. The qualities needed to struggle with and conquer savage nature have naturally their corresponding defects. Look back, and you will see the cradles of all civilization surrounded with giants of Herculean strength ready to run every risk and to shrink from neither danger nor crime to attain their ends. It is only by the peculiar temper of the time and place that we can distinguish them from the backwoodsman and rowdy of the United States.

SOURCE: Oscar Handlin, ed., *This Was America* (Cambridge, MA: Harvard University Press, 1949), 313–315.

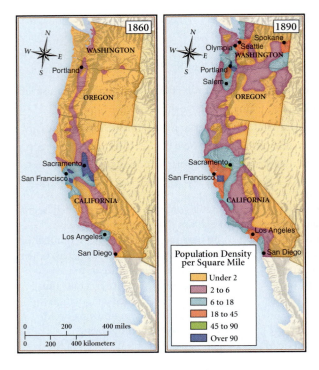

MAP 16.3 The Settlement of the Pacific Slope, 1860–1890
In 1860, the settlement of the Pacific slope was remarkably uneven—fully under way in northern California and scarcely begun anywhere else. By 1890, a new pattern had begun to emerge, with the swift growth of southern California foreshadowed and the settlement of the Pacific Northwest well launched.

1890 (Map 16.3). Portland and Seattle blossomed into important commercial centers, both prospering from a mixed economy of farming, ranching, logging, and fishing.

At a certain point, especially as railroads gave access to eastern markets, this diversified growth became self-sustaining. But what had triggered it—what had provided the first markets and underwritten the economic infrastructure—was the bonanza mining economy, at the hub of which stood San Francisco, the metropolis for the entire Far West.

Hispanics, Chinese, and Anglos

California was the anchor of two distinct far western regions. First, it joined with Oregon and Washington to form the Pacific slope. Second, by climate and Hispanic heritage, California was linked to the Southwest, which today includes Arizona, New Mexico, and Texas.

There, along a 1,500-mile borderland, outposts had been planted over many years by the viceroys of New Spain. Most populous were the settlements along New Mexico's upper Rio Grande Valley. The main town, Santa Fe, contained 4,635 residents in 1860. Farther down the Rio Grande was El Paso, nearly as long-settled but much smaller, and to the west, in present-day Arizona, was Tucson, an old *presidio* (garrison) town. At the western end of this Hispanic crescent, in California, a Spanish-speaking population was scattered in the old presidio towns along the coast and on a patchwork of great ranches.

The economy of this Hispanic crescent consisted primarily of cattle and sheep ranching. In south Texas, there were family-run ranches. Everywhere else, the social order was highly stratified. At the top stood the dons occupying royal land grants, proudly Spanish and devoted to the traditional life of a landed aristocracy. Below them, with little in between, was a laboring class of servants, artisans, *vaqueros* (cowboys), and farm hands. New Mexico also contained a large *mestizo* population: people of mixed Hispanic and Indian blood, Spanish-speaking and Catholic, but still faithful to the village life of their Pueblo heritage.

Pueblo Indians still occupied much of the Rio Grande Valley, living according to the old ways and rendering the New Mexico countryside a patchwork of Hispanic and Pueblo settlements. To the north, a vibrant new tribe, the Navajos, had taken shape, warriors like the Apaches from whom they were descended but also skilled at crafts and sheep raising.

New Mexico was one place where European and Native American cultures managed a successful, if uneasy, coexistence and where the Indian inhabitants were equipped to hold their own against the Anglo challenge. In California, by contrast, the Hispanic occupation had taken a greater toll on the indigenous hunter-gatherer peoples, undermining their tribal structure, reducing them to forced labor, and making them easy prey for the aggressive Anglo miners and settlers, who, in short order, nearly wiped out California's once numerous Indians.

The fate of the Hispanic Southwest after 1848 depended on the rate of Anglo immigration. In New Mexico, which remained isolated even after the railroads arrived in the 1880s, the Santa Fe elite more than held its own, incorporating the Anglo newcomers into Hispanic society through intermarriage and business partnerships. In California, however, expropriation of the great ranches was relentless, even though the 1848 treaty with Mexico had recognized the property rights of the *Californios* and made them U.S. citizens. Around San Francisco, the great ranches disappeared almost in a puff of smoke. Farther south, where Anglos were slower to arrive, the dons held on longer, but by the 1880s, just a handful of the original Hispanic families still retained their Mexican land grants.

The New Mexico peasants found themselves equally embattled. Crucial to their livelihood was the grazing of livestock on communal lands. But these were customary rights that could not withstand legal challenge when Anglo ranchers established title and began putting up fences. The peasants responded as best they could. Their subsistence economy relied on a gendered division of labor. Women tended the small gardens, engaged in village bartering, and maintained the households. With the loss of the communal lands, the men began migrating seasonally to the Colorado mines and sugar beet fields, earning dollars while leaving the village economy in their wives' hands.

Elsewhere, hard-pressed New Mexicans struck back for what they considered rightfully theirs. When Anglo ranchers began to fence communal lands in San Miguel County, *los pobres* (the poor ones) mounted an effective campaign of harassment against the interlopers. After 1900, when Anglo farmers swarmed into south Texas, the displaced *Tejanos* (Hispanic residents of Texas) mounted sporadic but persistent night-riding attacks. Much of the raiding by Mexican "bandits" from across the border in the years before World War I more nearly resembled a civil war by embittered Hispanics who had lived north of the Rio Grande for generations (see Chapter 21).

But they, like the New Mexico villagers who became seasonal wage laborers, could not avoid being driven into the ranks of a Mexican-American working class. The developing Anglo economy also began to attract increasing numbers of immigrants from Mexico itself.

Mexican Miners

When large-scale mining began to develop in Arizona and New Mexico in the late nineteenth century, Mexicans crossed the border to earn Yankee dollars. In this unidentified photograph from the 1890s, the men are wearing traditional clothing, indicating perhaps that they are recent arrivals at the mine. Division of Cultural Resource, Wyoming Department of Commerce.

Railroads were being built, copper mines were opening in Arizona, cotton and vegetable agriculture was spreading in south Texas, and orchards were being planted in southern California. In Texas, the Hispanic population increased from about 20,000 in 1850 to 165,000 in 1900. Some came as contract workers for railway gangs and harvest crews; virtually all were relegated to the lowest-paying and most back-breaking work; and everywhere, they were discriminated against by Anglo employers and workers.

The galloping economic development that drew Mexican migrants also accounted for the exceptionally high rate of European immigration to the West. One-third of California's population was foreign-born, more than twice the level for the country as a whole. Most numerous were the Irish, followed by the Germans and British. But there was another group unique to the West: the Chinese.

Attracted initially by the California gold rush, 200,000 Chinese came to the United States between 1850 and 1880. In those years, they constituted a considerable minority of California's population — around 9 percent — but because virtually all were actively employed, they represented probably a quarter of the state's labor force. Elsewhere in the West, at the crest of mining activity, their numbers could surge remarkably, to over 25 percent of Idaho's population in 1870, for example.

The arrival of the Chinese was part of a worldwide Asian migration that had begun in the mid-nineteenth century. Driven by poverty, the Chinese went to Australia, Hawaii, and Latin America; Indians to Fiji and South Africa; and Javanese to Dutch colonies in the Caribbean. Most of these Asians migrated as **indentured** servants, which in effect made them the property of others. In America, however, indentured servitude was no longer lawful—by the 1820s, state courts were banning it as involuntary servitude—so the Chinese came as free workers, going into debt for their passage money but not surrendering their personal freedom or right to choose their employers.

Once in America, Chinese immigrants normally entered the orbit of the Six Companies, a powerful confederation of Chinese merchants in San Francisco's Chinatown. Most were young men eager to earn a stake and return to their native Cantonese villages. The few Chinese women—the male-female ratio was thirteen to one—worked as servants and prostitutes, victims of the desperate poverty that drove the Chinese to America. Until the early 1860s, when surface mining played out, Chinese men labored mainly in the California gold fields—as prospectors where white miners permitted it and as laborers and cooks where they did not. Then, when construction began on the transcontinental railroad, the Central Pacific hired Chinese workers. Eventually, they constituted four-fifths of the railroad's labor force, doing most of the pick-and-shovel work involved in laying the track across the Sierra Nevada.

When the transcontinental railroad was completed in 1869, the Chinese scattered. Some stayed in railroad construction gangs; others labored in California's Central Valley as agricultural workers or, if they were lucky, became small farmers. The mining districts of Idaho, Montana, and Colorado also attracted large numbers of Chinese, but according to the 1880 census, nearly three-quarters remained in California. "Wherever we put them, we found them good," remarked Charles Crocker, one of the promoters of the Central Pacific. "Their orderly and industrious habits make them a very desirable class of immigrants."

White workers did not share Crocker's enthusiasm. Elsewhere in the country, racism was directed against African Americans; in California, where there were few blacks, it targeted the Chinese. "They practice all the unnameable vices of the East," wrote the young journalist Henry George. "They are utter heathens, treacherous, sensual, cowardly and cruel." Sadly, this vicious racism was intertwined with labor's republican ideals. The Chinese, argued George, would "make nabobs and princes of our capitalists, and crush our working classes into the dust . . . substitut[ing] . . . a population of serfs and their masters for that population of intelligent freemen who are our glory and our strength."

The anti-Chinese frenzy climaxed in San Francisco in the late 1870s when mobs ruled the streets. The fiercest agitator, an Irish teamster named Denis Kearney, quickly became a dominant figure in the California labor movement. Under the slogan "The Chinese Must Go!," Kearney led a Working Men's Party against the state's major parties. Democrats and Republicans jumped on the bandwagon, joining together in 1879 to write a new state constitution replete with anti-Chinese provisions. In 1882, Congress passed the Chinese Exclusion Act, which barred further entry of Chinese laborers into the country.

The injustice of this law—no other nationality was similarly targeted—rankled the Chinese. Why us, protested one woman to a federal agent, and not the Irish, "who were always drunk and fighting?" Merchants and American-born Chinese, who were free to come and go, routinely registered a newly born son after each trip, enabling many an unrelated "paper son" to enter the country. Even so, resourceful as the Chinese were at evading the exclusion law, the flow of immigrants slowed to a trickle.

But the job opportunities that had attracted the Chinese to America did not subside. If anything, the West's agricultural development intensified the demand for cheap labor, especially in California, which was shifting from wheat, the state's first great cash crop, to fruits and vegetables. Such intensive agriculture required lots of workers — stoop labor, meagerly paid, and mostly seasonal. This was not, as one San Francisco journalist put it, "white men's work." That ugly phrase serves as a touchstone for California agricultural labor as it would thereafter develop — a kind of caste labor system, always drawing some downtrodden, footloose whites yet basically defined along color lines.

But if not the Chinese, then who? First, Japanese immigrants, who by the early twentieth century constituted half of the state's agricultural labor force. Then, when anti-Japanese agitation closed off that population flow in 1908, Mexico became the next, essentially permanent, source of migratory workers for California's booming commercial agriculture.

The irony of the state's social evolution is painful to behold. Here was California, a land of limitless opportunity, boastful of its democratic egalitarianism, yet simultaneously, and from its very birth, a racially torn society, at once exploiting and despising the Hispanic and Asian minorities whose hard labor helped to make California the enviable land it was.

Golden California

Life in California contained all that the modern world of 1890 had to offer: cosmopolitan San Francisco, comfortable travel, colleges and universities, even resident painters and writers. Yet California was still remote from the rest of America, a long journey away and, of course, differently and spectacularly endowed by nature. Location, environment, and history all conspired to set California somewhat apart from the American nation.

What Californians yearned for was a cultural tradition of their own. Closest to hand was the bonanza era of the forty-niners, captured on paper by Samuel Clemens. Clemens left his native Missouri for Nevada in 1861. He did a bit of prospecting, worked as a reporter, and adopted the pen name Mark Twain. In 1864, he arrived in San Francisco, where he became a newspaper columnist writing about what he pronounced "the livest, heartiest community on our continent."

Listening to the old miners in Angel's Camp in 1865, Twain jotted down one tale in his notebook, as follows:

> Coleman with his jumping frog — bet stranger $50 — stranger had no frog, and C. got him one: — in the meantime stranger filled C's frog full of shot and he couldn't jump. The stranger's frog won.

In Twain's hands, this fragment was transformed into a tall tale that caught the imagination of the country and made his reputation as a humorist. "The Celebrated Jumping

Frog of Calaveras County" somehow encapsulated the entire world of make-or-break optimism in the mining camps.

In such short stories as "The Luck of Roaring Camp" and "The Outcasts of Poker Flat," Twain's fellow San Franciscan Bret Harte developed this theme and firmly implanted it in California's memory. But this past was too raw, too suggestive of the tattered beginnings of so many of the state's leading citizens—in short, too disreputable—for an up-and-coming society.

Then, in 1884, Helen Hunt Jackson published her novel *Ramona*. In this story of a half-Indian girl caught between two cultures, Jackson intended to advance the cause of the Native Americans, but she placed her tale in the evocative context of early California, and that rang a bell. By then, the missions planted by the Catholic Church had been long abandoned. Now that lost world of "sun, silence and adobe" became all the rage. Sentimental novels and histories appeared in abundance. There was a movement to restore the missions. Many communities began to stage Spanish fiestas, and the mission style of architecture enjoyed a great vogue among developers.

In its Spanish past, California found the cultural traditions it needed. The same kind of discovery was taking place elsewhere in the Southwest, although in the case of Santa Fe and Taos, there really were live Hispanic roots to celebrate.

All this enthusiasm was strongly tinged with commercialism. So was a second distinctive feature of California's development: the exploitation of its climate. While northern California boomed, the southern part of the state remained sparsely populated, too dry for anything but grazing and some chancy wheat growing. What it did have, however, was an abundance of sunshine. At the beginning of the 1880s, amazing news of the charms of southern California burst upon the country: "There is not any malaria, hay fever, loss of appetite, or languor in the air; nor any thunder, lightning, mad dogs . . . or cold snaps." This publicity was mostly the work of the Southern Pacific Railroad, which had reached Los Angeles in 1876 and was eager for traffic.

When the Santa Fe Railroad arrived in 1885, a furious rate war broke out. One-way fares from Chicago or St. Louis to Los Angeles dropped to $25 or less. Thousands of people, mostly midwesterners, poured in. Los Angeles County, which had less than 3 percent of the state's population in 1870, had 12 percent by 1900. By then, southern California was firmly established as the land of sunshine. It had found a way to translate climate into riches.

California wheat farmers made the same discovery when they began to convert to "specialty" crops. Some of these, such as the peaches and pears grown in the Sierra foothills, competed with crops elsewhere in the country, but others—oranges, almonds, and raisins—required California's Mediterranean climate. By 1910, the state had essentially abandoned wheat, its original money crop, and was shipping vast quantities of fruit across the country.

Although heavily dependent on migrant labor—hence its reputation as an "industrial" form of agriculture—California fruit farming was carried on mostly by small operators because it required intensive, hands-on cultivation. Indeed, the vineyards around Fresno, the source of virtually all the nation's raisins, began as a planned community, sold off in 20-acre units. What perhaps came closer to an industrial model were the big cooperatives set up by these modest-sized producers to market and brand their crops. For most Americans, the taste of California came via Sunkist oranges, Sun Maid raisins, and Blue Diamond almonds.

That California was specially favored by nature, some Californians knew even as the great stands of redwoods were being hacked down, the streams polluted, and the hills torn apart by reckless hydraulic mining. Back in 1864, influential Americans who had visited it prevailed on Congress to grant to the state of California "the Cleft, or Gorge in the granite peak of the Sierra Nevada Mountain, known as Yosemite Valley," which would be reserved "for public pleasuring, resort, and recreation." When the young naturalist John Muir arrived in California four years later, he headed straight for Yosemite. Its "grandeur . . . comes as an endless revelation," he wrote.

Muir's environmentalism was at once scientific and romantic. An exacting researcher, he demonstrated for the first time that Yosemite was the product of glacial action. California scientists who accepted Muir's thesis were persuaded also by his concept of wilderness as a laboratory and joined him against "despoiling gain-seekers . . . eagerly trying to make everything immediately and selfishly commercial." Married to Muir's scientific appeal, however, was a powerful dose of romanticism, sanctifying nature as sacred space and elevating its defense into a kind of religious crusade, a battle "between landscape righteousness and the devil."

One result of Muir's zeal was the creation of California's national parks in 1890: Yosemite, Sequoia, and General Grant (later part of King's Canyon). Another was a campaign launched immediately afterward to mandate a system of national forest reserves. A third was the formation in 1892 of the Sierra Club, which became a powerful voice for the defenders of California's wilderness.

They won some and lost some. Developers insisted that California's thirsty cities could not grow without tapping the abundant snow pack of the Sierra Nevada. By the turn of the century, Los Angeles faced a serious water shortage. The answer was a 238-mile aqueduct to the Owens River in the southern Sierra. A bitter controversy blew up over this immense project, driven by the resistance of local residents to the flooding of the beautiful Owens Valley. More painful for John Muir and his preservationist allies was their failure to save the Hetch Hetchy Valley—"one of nature's rarest and most precious mountain temples," in Muir's words—on the northern edge of Yosemite National Park. After years of controversy, the federal government in 1913 approved the damming of Hetch Hetchy's Tuolumne River to serve the water needs of San Francisco.

▶ Why is mining the key to understanding the settlement of the Far West?

▶ Why can we speak of a distinctly California history in the late nineteenth century?

▶ Although frontier history is generally treated as an Anglo-American story, in the Far West it is much more about ethnic diversity. Why?

When the stakes became high enough, nature preservationists such as John Muir generally came out on the short end. Even so, something original and distinctive had been added to California's heritage: the linking of a society's well-being with the protection of its natural environment. This realization, in turn, said something important about the nation's relationship to the West. If the urge to conquer and exploit persisted, at least it was now tempered by a sense that nature's bounty was not limitless. This, more than any announcement by the U.S. Census that a "frontier line" no longer existed, registered the country's acceptance that the age of heedless westward expansion had ended.

SUMMARY

In this chapter, we traced the final stages of the Euro-American occupation of the continental United States, now strongly driven by the nation's industrial development. The trans-Mississippi West provided raw materials for eastern industry and food products for the nation's cities and got in return the implements of industrialism, from railroads to barbed wire, that accelerated settlement. The patterns of settlement, however, differed in the two great ecological regions that make up the trans-Mississippi West.

East of the Rockies, the Great Plains remained in 1860 the ancestral home to nomadic Indian tribes. With the U.S. military leading the way, cattle ranchers and homesteaders in short order displaced the Indians and domesticated the Great Plains. Despite fierce resistance, by 1890 the Indians had been crowded onto reservations and forced to abandon their tribal ways of life.

Beyond the Rockies, where the terrain was arid and largely uninhabitable, occupation took the form of islands of settlement. And while arable land had been the lure for settlers up to that point, what drove settlement in the Far West was the discovery of mineral wealth.

Also distinctive of Far Western development was its dominance by a single state, California, which anchored both the crescent of southwestern Hispanic settlement and the Pacific slope region northward to Canada. The discovery of gold set off a huge migration that overwhelmed the scattered Hispanic population and transformed California into a populous, partly urbanized state. California developed a distinctive culture that capitalized on its rediscovered Hispanic heritage and its climate and natural environment. California also capitalized on the Chinese, Japanese, and Mexicans who provided the state's cheap labor, infusing a dark streak of racism into its otherwise sunny culture.

Connections: The American West

As readers of earlier chapters know, there were many "Wests" in American history. Colonists considered the Appalachians the West; for Jeffersonians, it was the Ohio Valley; for Jacksonians, it was the Mississippi Valley. The land beyond the Mississippi Valley—the Great Plains, the Rockies, and the Pacific slope—constitutes the last American West, the region that remains, even to readers of this text, the country's West. What distinguishes the settlement of this last American West is that it was driven by, and in turn helped drive, America's industrial revolution. Students should bear this in mind as they read Chapter 17, and also note the West's impact on American politics, via the Populist movement in the 1890s (Chapter 19) and progressivism after 1900 (Chapter 20). In the twentieth century, the West becomes increasingly absorbed in the national narrative, but students should be watchful for where its distinctive role pops up, as, for example, Hollywood in the 1920s (Chapter 23), the defense industry during World War II (Chapter 25), and postwar suburbanization (Chapter 27).

TIMELINE

1849 ▸ California gold rush	**1875** ▸ Sioux ordered to vacate Powder River hunting grounds; war breaks out
▸ Chinese migration begins	
1862 ▸ Homestead Act	**1876** ▸ Battle of Little Big Horn
1864 ▸ Yosemite Valley reserved as public park	**1877** ▸ San Francisco anti-Chinese riots
1865 ▸ Long Drive of Texas longhorns begins	**1879** ▸ Exoduster migration to Kansas
	1882 ▸ Chinese Exclusion Act
1867 ▸ Patrons of Husbandry (the Grange) founded	**1884** ▸ Helen Hunt Jackson's novel *Ramona* published
▸ U.S. government adopts reservation policy for Plains Indians	**1886** ▸ Dry cycle begins on the Great Plains
	1887 ▸ Dawes Severalty Act
1868 ▸ Indian treaty confirms Sioux rights to Powder River hunting grounds	**1889** ▸ Oklahoma opened to white settlement
	1890 ▸ Indian massacre at Wounded Knee, South Dakota
1869 ▸ Union Pacific–Central Pacific transcontinental railroad completed	▸ U.S. Census declares end of the frontier

FOR FURTHER EXPLORATION

Western history starts with Frederick Jackson Turner's famous essay "The Significance of the Frontier in American History" (1893), reprinted in Ray A. Billington, ed., *Frontier and Section: Selected Essays of Frederick Jackson Turner* (1961). In recent years, there has been a reaction against Turnerian scholarship for being Eurocentric—that is, seeing western history only through the eyes of frontiersmen and settlers—and for masking the rapacious underside of western settlement. Patricia N. Limerick's skillfully argued *The Legacy of Conquest* (1987) opened the debate. Richard White's *"It's Your Misfortune and None of My Own": A New History of the American West* (1991) provides the fullest synthesis. On women's experiences—another primary concern of the new scholarship—a useful introduction is Susan Armitage and Elizabeth Jameson, eds., *The Women's West* (1987). On the Plains Indians, a lively account is Robert M. Utley, *The Indian Frontier of the American West* (1984). On the integration of the Plains economy with the wider world, an especially rich book is William Cronon, *Nature's Metropolis: Chicago and the Great West* (1991). Sarah Deutsch, *No Separate Refuge* (1987), offers an imaginative treatment of the New Mexican peasantry. On the Asian migration to America, see Ron Takaki, *Strangers from a Different Shore* (1989). Kevin Starr, *California and the American Dream, 1850–1915* (1973), describes the emergence of a distinctive California culture. A comprehensive Web site with many links is **www.americanwest.com**.

TEST YOUR KNOWLEDGE

To assess your mastery of the material in this chapter and for Web sites, images, and documents related to this chapter, visit **bedfordstmartins.com/henrettaconcise**.

Capital and Labor in the Age of Enterprise
1877–1900

An almost total revolution has taken place, and is yet in progress, in every branch and in every relation of the world's industrial and commercial system.

— David A. Wells, *Recent Economic Changes*, 1899

Reconstruction ended in 1877. That year also marked the nation's first great labor crisis. Much like the dot .com bust of our own time, the post–Civil War railroad boom collapsed after the Panic of 1873. Railroad building ground to a halt, workers lost their jobs, and wages fell. On July 16, 1877, railroad workers went on strike to protest a wage cut at the Baltimore and Ohio Railroad. In towns along the B&O tracks, crowds cheered as the strikers attacked company property. The strike rippled across the country. The Pennsylvania Railroad's roundhouse in Pittsburgh went up in flames on July 21, and at many rail centers, rioters and looters roamed freely. Only the arrival of federal troops restored order. On August 15, President Rutherford B. Hayes wrote in his diary, "The strikers have been put down *by force*." The Great Strike of 1877 had been crushed, but only after raising the specter of social revolution.

Then recovery came. Within months, railroad building resumed. In the next fifteen years, the output of manufactured goods increased by over 150 percent. Confidence in the nation's industrial future rebounded. "Upon [material progress] is founded all other progress," asserted a railroad president in 1888. "Can there be any doubt that cheapening the cost of necessaries and conveniences of life is the most powerful agent of civilization and progress?"

That magnate's boast represents the confident face of America's industrial revolution. President Hayes's anxious diary entries suggest a darker side. After 1877, armories— fortresses designed to withstand assault by future strikers and rioters—became part of the urban landscape. The need for armories signified the paradox that an industrial economy celebrated for its dynamism was also an economy brutally indifferent to the many who fell by the wayside and hence an economy that was never secure, never free of social conflict.

Industrial Capitalism Triumphant

Economic historians speak of the late nineteenth century as the age of the Great Deflation, a time when worldwide prices fell steadily. Falling prices normally signal economic stagnation; there is not enough demand for available goods and services. In England, a mature industrial power, the Great Deflation did indeed signal economic decline. In the United States, by contrast, industrial expansion went into high gear during the Great Deflation. Manufacturing efficiencies enabled American firms to earn profits and invest in improved equipment even though prices for their products fell. Real income for Americans increased by nearly 50 percent (from $388 to $573 per capita) between 1877 and 1900. The industrializing economy was a wealth-creating machine beyond anything the world had ever seen (Figure 17.1).

The Age of Steel

By the 1870s, factories were a familiar sight in America. But the consumer goods they produced—textiles, shoes, paper, and furniture—mainly replaced articles made at home or by individual artisans. Gradually, however, a different kind of demand developed as the country's economy surged. Railroads needed locomotives; new factories needed machinery; cities needed trolley lines, sanitation systems, and commercial structures. Railroad equipment, machinery, and construction materials were capital goods, that is, goods that added to the nation's productive capacity.

Central to the capital-goods sector was a technological revolution in steel making. A large iron industry already existed, turning out wrought iron, a malleable metal easily worked by blacksmiths and farmers. But wrought iron was ill suited for industrial uses and did not stand up under heavy railway traffic. In 1856, the British inventor Henry Bessemer designed a refining furnace that turned raw iron into an essentially new product: steel, a metal more durable than wrought iron and, on top of that, much cheaper to produce because the process required virtually no hands-on labor. The Bessemer converter attracted many users, but it was Andrew Carnegie who fully exploited its potential.

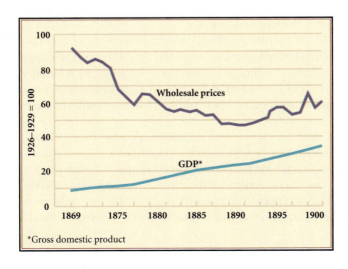

FIGURE 17.1 Business Activity and Wholesale Prices, 1869–1900

This graph shows the key feature of the performance of the late-nineteenth-century economy: While output was booming, the price of goods was falling.

Carnegie's was the great American success story. He arrived impoverished from Scotland in 1848 at the age of twelve, became a telegraph operator, then went to work for the Pennsylvania Railroad and rapidly scaled the managerial ladder. In 1865, Carnegie struck out on his own as an iron manufacturer, selling mainly to his network of friends in the railroad business.

In 1872, Carnegie erected a massive steel mill outside Pittsburgh, with the Bessemer converter as its centerpiece. Ferrous metallurgy involves three steps: Blast furnaces smelt ore into pig iron; the pig iron is refined into usable metal, either wrought iron or steel; and finally, the refined metal is stamped or rolled into desired shapes. The Bessemer converter broke a bottleneck at the refining stage, enabling Carnegie's engineers to construct larger blast furnaces and faster rolling mills. They designed an integrated plant, with iron ore entering at one end and coming out the other end as finished steel rails. Carnegie's new plant became the industry's model, soon displacing the iron mills that had once dotted western Pennsylvania.

The United States was blessed with rich mineral resources for steel making. From the great Mesabi range in northern Minnesota, iron ore came down the Great Lakes by ship in vast quantities. The other key ingredient, coal, arrived from the great Appalachian field that stretched from Pennsylvania to Alabama. A minor enterprise before the Civil War, coal production doubled every decade after 1870, exceeding 400 million tons a year by 1910.

As steam engines became the nation's energy workhorses, prodigious amounts of coal began to be consumed by industries that had previously depended on waterpower. The turbine, utilizing continuous rotation rather than the steam engine's back-and-forth piston motion, marked another major advance during the 1880s. With the coupling of the steam turbine to the electric generator, the nation's energy revolution was completed, and after 1900, America's factories began converting to electric power.

The Railroad Boom

Water transportation met the country's needs before the Civil War. Yet it was love at first sight when locomotives arrived from Britain in the early 1830s. Americans were impatient for the year-round, on-time service not achievable by canal barges and riverboats. By 1860, as a network of tracks crisscrossed the eastern half of the country, the railroad clearly was on the way to becoming industrial America's mode of transportation.

The question was, who would pay for it? Railroads could be state enterprises, like the canals, or they could be financed by private investors. Unlike most European countries, the United States chose free enterprise. Even so, government played a big role. Many states and localities lured railroads with offers of financial aid, mainly by buying railroad bonds. Land grants were the principal means by which the federal government encouraged interregional rail construction.

The most important boost, however, was not money or land but a legal form of organization—the corporation—that enabled private capital to be raised in prodigious amounts. Investors who bought stock in the railroads enjoyed *limited liability*: They risked only the money they had invested; they were not personally liable for the railroad's debts. A corporation could also borrow money by issuing interest-bearing bonds, which was initially how the railroads raised most of the money they needed.

Railroad building generally was assigned to construction companies, which, despite the name, were primarily financial structures. Hiring contractors and suppliers often involved persuading them to accept the railroad's bonds as payment and, when that failed, wheeling and dealing to raise cash by selling or borrowing on the bonds. The construction companies were notoriously corrupt. In the case of the Union Pacific's Credit Mobilier, probably half the construction funds was pocketed by the promoters.

The railroad business was not for the faint of heart. Most successful were promoters who had the best access to capital, such as Cornelius Vanderbilt, who started with the fortune he had made in the steamboat business. Vanderbilt was primarily a consolidator, linking previously independent lines and ultimately, via his New York Central, providing unified railroad service between New York City and Chicago. James J. Hill, who without federal subsidy made the Great Northern into the best of the transcontinental railroads, was certainly the nation's champion railroad builder. In contrast, Jay Gould, who at various times controlled the Erie, Wabash, Union Pacific, and Missouri Pacific railroads, always remained a stock market speculator at heart. But even Gould, though he rigged stock prices and looted his properties, made a positive contribution. By throwing his weak railroads against better-established operators (in hopes of being bought out), he forced down rates and benefited shippers. A gifted strategist, Gould was an early promoter of interregional railroads, the catalyst that prompted Vanderbilt's creation of the New York Central.

Railroad development in the United States was often sordid, fiercely competitive, and subject to boom and bust. Yet promoters raised vast sums of capital and built a network bigger than the rest of the world's combined. By 1900, virtually no corner of the country lacked rail service (Map 17.1).

Along with this prodigious growth came increasing efficiency. The early railroads, built by competing local companies, had been a jumble of disconnected segments. Varying local times made scheduling a nightmare. In 1883, the railroads rebelled and, acting on their own, divided the country into the standard time zones that are still in use. By the end of the 1880s, a standard track gauge (4 feet, 8½ inches) had been adopted nationwide. Fast-freight firms and standard accounting procedures enabled shippers to move goods without breaks in transit, transfers between cars, or the other delays that had once bedeviled them.

At the same time, railroad technology was advancing. Durable steel rails permitted heavier traffic. Locomotives became more powerful. To control the greater mass being hauled, the inventor George Westinghouse perfected the automatic coupler, the air brake, and the friction gear for starting and stopping a long line of cars. Costs per ton-mile fell by 50 percent between 1870 and 1890, resulting in a steady drop in freight rates for shippers.

The railroads fully met the transportation needs of the maturing industrial economy. For investors, however, the costs of freewheeling competition were painfully high. Many railroads were saddled with huge debts from the extravagant construction era. When the economy turned bad, as it did in 1893, one-third of the industry went into bankruptcy.

Out of the rubble came a sweeping railroad reorganization. This was primarily the handiwork of Wall Street investment banks such as J. P. Morgan & Co. and Kuhn Loeb & Co., whose initial role had been to market railroad stocks and bonds. When

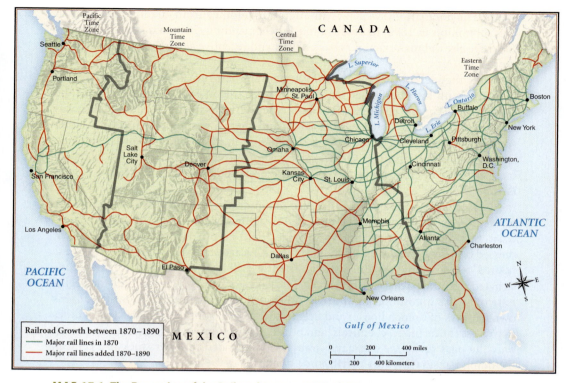

MAP 17.1 The Expansion of the Railroad System, 1870–1890

In 1870, the nation had 53,000 miles of rail track; in 1890, it had 167,000 miles. That burst of construction essentially completed the nation's rail network, although there would be additional expansion for the next two decades. The main areas of growth were in the South and west of the Mississippi. The time zones introduced in 1883 are marked by the thick gray lines.

For more help analyzing this map, see the Online Study Guide at **bedfordstmartins.com/henrettaconcise.**

railroads failed, the investment bankers stepped in to pick up the pieces. They persuaded investors to accept lower interest rates or put up more money. They eased competitive pressures by consolidating rivals. By the early twentieth century, half a dozen great regional systems had emerged, and the nerve center of American railroading had shifted to Wall Street.

Large-Scale Enterprise

Until well into the industrial age, most manufacturers operated on a small scale, producing mainly for nearby markets. Then, after the Civil War, big business arrived. "Combinations of capital on a scale hitherto wholly unprecedented constitute one of the remarkable features of modern business methods," the economist David A. Wells wrote in 1889. He could see "no other way in which the work of production and distribution can be prosecuted." Why did Wells find big business inevitable?

Most of all, it was inevitable because of the American market. Unlike Europe, the United States was not fractured by national borders that impeded the flow of goods. The population, swelled by immigration, jumped from 40 million in 1870 to over 60 million in 1890. Railroads linked the expanding cities to distant producers. Nowhere else did manufacturers have so vast and receptive a market for standardized products.

How they seized that opportunity is perhaps best revealed in the meatpacking industry. With the opening of the Union Stock Yards in 1865, Chicago became the cattle market for the country. Livestock came in by rail from the Great Plains, was auctioned off at the Chicago stockyards, and then was shipped to eastern cities, where, as in the past, the cattle were slaughtered in local "butchertowns." Such an arrangement—a national livestock market but localized processing—adequately met the needs of city people and could have done so indefinitely, as was the case in Europe.

Gustavus F. Swift, a shrewd Chicago cattle dealer from Massachusetts, saw the future differently. He recognized that local slaughterhouses lacked the scale to utilize waste by-products or cut labor costs. If he could keep it fresh in transit, however, dressed beef could be processed in bulk at the Chicago stockyards. Once his engineers figured out a cooling system, Swift invested in a fleet of refrigerator cars and constructed a central packing plant next to Chicago's stockyards. This was only the beginning of Swift's innovations. In the cities that received his chilled meat, Swift built his own network of branch houses and fleets of delivery wagons. He constructed facilities to process the fertilizer, chemicals, and other usable by-products (wasting, it was said, only the pig's squeal). As demand grew, Swift expanded to other stockyard centers, including Kansas City, Fort Worth, and Omaha.

Step by step, Swift created a new kind of enterprise: a vertically integrated firm capable of encompassing within its own structure all the functions of an industry. Several big Chicago pork packers followed Swift's lead. By 1900, five firms, all of them nationally organized and vertically integrated, produced nearly 90 percent of the meat shipped in interstate commerce.

The term that describes this condition is **oligopoly**—market dominance by the few. In meatpacking, that was mostly the result of the vertically integrated firm, which simply outperformed the livestock dealers and small slaughterhouses that populated the earlier industry. But at the consuming end, where competition was stronger, Swift and fellow Chicago packers cut prices and drove independent distributors to the wall. And that brings into focus the second reason for large-scale enterprise: not greater efficiency, but market control. The impulse for market control, although universally felt, was strongest in bonanza industries, where no player started with any particular advantage and the market was especially chaotic, as, for example, in the petroleum industry.

Rural Americans had long noticed pools of petroleum oozing up mysteriously from the bowels of the earth. Snake-oil salesmen sometimes added the black stuff to their concoctions. Farmers used it to grease their wagons. Mostly, it was just a nuisance. Then, in the 1850s, experimenters figured out how to extract kerosene, a clean-burning fuel that was excellent for domestic heating and lighting. All they needed to create an industry was the crude oil. One likely place was Titusville, Pennsylvania, where the air stank from pools of petroleum. In 1859, Edwin L. Drake drilled down and struck oil at 69 feet. Overnight, a forest of derricks and makeshift refineries sprang up around Titusville. However, the refining soon shifted to centers with better trans-shipping facilities. Chief among these, once it got a rail connection to the Pennsylvania fields in 1863, was Cleveland, Ohio.

At that time, John D. Rockefeller was an up-and-coming Cleveland grain dealer, twenty-four years old and doing nicely, thanks to the Civil War (which he, like Carnegie and virtually all the budding tycoons of his time, sat out). Initially skeptical of the wild oil business, Rockefeller soon plunged in. He had a sharp eye for able partners, a genius for finance, and strong nerves. Betting on the industry's future, he borrowed heavily to expand capacity. Within a few years, his firm—Standard Oil of Ohio—was Cleveland's leading refiner, and Rockefeller was casting his eyes on the entire industry.

His natural allies were the railroads, which, like him, hated the boom-and-bust of the oil business. What they wanted was predictable, high-volume traffic, and for a good customer such as Rockefeller, they offered secret rebates that gave him a leg up on competitors. Then, in 1870, hit by another oil bust, the railroads concocted a remarkable scheme. Operating under the cloak of the innocent-sounding South Improvement Company, they invited key refiners, including Rockefeller, to join a conspiracy to take over the industry. The participants would cease competing and instead divide up traffic and production. For the cooperating refiners, there was this delicious bonus: rebates not only on their own shipments, but also on those of their rivals.

With this deal in his pocket, Rockefeller offered his Cleveland competitors a stark choice: Sell out or die. News of the conspiracy leaked out, and the South Improvement Company collapsed under a hail of denunciations, but not before Rockefeller had taken over the Cleveland industry. With his power-play tactics perfected, he was on his way to national dominance. By the early 1880s, Standard Oil controlled 95 percent of the nation's refining capacity.

Rockefeller was not satisfied merely to milk his monopoly advantage in refining. Obsessed from the outset with efficiency, he was quick to see the advantages of vertical integration. In this, Rockefeller was like Gustavus Swift, intent on designing a business structure capable of serving a national (in Rockefeller's case, international) market. Starting with refining, Standard Oil rapidly added a vast distribution network, oil pipelines and tankers, and even, despite Rockefeller's distaste for speculative ventures, a big stake in the oil fields.

In retailing, the lure of a mass market brought comparable changes. For rural consumers, Montgomery Ward and Sears, Roebuck developed huge mail-order enterprises. From Vermont to California, farm families selected identical goods from catalogues and became part of a nationwide consumer market. In the cities, retailers followed different strategies. The department store, pioneered by John Wanamaker in Philadelphia in 1875, soon became a fixture in downtowns across the country. Alternatively, retailers could reach consumers efficiently by opening a chain of stores, which was the strategy of the Great Atlantic and Pacific Tea Company (A&P) and F. W. Woolworth.

Americans were ready consumers of standardized, mass-marketed goods. Geographically mobile, they were not partial to distinctive local products, as Europeans were. Moreover, social class in America, though by no means absent, was blurred at the edges and did not decree, for example, class-specific ways of dressing. Foreign visitors often noted that ready-made clothing made it difficult to tell salesgirls from debutantes on city streets.

Kellogg's Toasted Corn Flakes
Like crackers, sugar, and other nonperishable products, cereal had traditionally been sold in bulk from barrels. In the 1880s, the Quaker Oats Company hit on the idea of selling oatmeal in boxes of standard size and weight. A further wrinkle was to process the cereal so that it could be consumed directly from the box (with milk) for breakfast. Lo and behold: Kellogg's Corn Flakes! This is one of Kellogg's earliest advertisements. Picture Research Consultants & Archives.

For more help analyzing this image, see the Online Study Guide at **bedfordstmartins.com/henrettaconcise**.

Innovative national marketers ran into trouble, however, with shop owners, who put up stiff resistance, sometimes agitating for ordinances to keep Swift and A&P at bay. Nor were standardized goods universally welcomed. Many people were leery, for example, of Swift's Chicago beef. How could it be wholesome weeks later in Boston or Philadelphia? Cheap prices helped, but advertising mattered more.

Modern advertising was born in the late nineteenth century. By 1900, companies were spending over $90 million a year for space in newspapers and magazines. Advertisements urged readers to bathe with Pears's soap, eat Uneeda biscuits, sew on a Singer machine, and snap pictures with a Kodak camera. The active molding of demand became a major challenge for the managers of America's national firms.

So, even more urgently, did the task of controlling such far-flung enterprises. Nothing in the world of small business prepared Swift and his fellow industrialists for this challenge. Fortunately for them, railroaders had already paved the way. On a 50-mile road, remarked the Erie executive Daniel C. McCallum, the superintendent could personally attend to every detail. But 500-mile trunk lines were too big for even the most energetic superintendent. It was in "the want of a system" that lay "the true secret of their failure." Step by step, always under the prod of necessity, the trunk lines separated overall management from day-to-day operations, departmentalized operations by function (maintenance of way, rolling stock, traffic), and defined lines of communication. By the end of the 1870s, the railroads' managerial crisis had been resolved.

Just in time to provide a model for emerging industrial firms such as Swift's. With few exceptions, vertically integrated firms followed a centralized, functionally departmentalized plan, with a main office housing top executives and departments covering specific areas of activity: purchasing, auditing, production, transportation, or sales. These functionally defined departments provided "middle management," something not seen before in American industry. Although factory managers functioned much as they always had, middle managers undertook entirely new tasks, directing the flow of goods and information through the integrated enterprise. They were key innovators, equivalent in matters of business practice to engineers in improving technology.

By the turn of the century, the hundred largest companies controlled roughly one-third of the nation's total productive capacity. The day of small manufacturers had not passed. They still flourished, or at least survived, in many fields. Indeed, places such as Philadelphia were hubs of small-scale, diversified industry that excelled in what economic historians have called "flexible specialization." But the dominant form of industrial organization had become, and would long remain, large-scale enterprise.

▶ What factors account for the rise of the American steel industry in the late nineteenth century?

▶ Why did the railroad network grow so rapidly after the Civil War? What consequences did this have for the country's economic development?

▶ How do you account for the growth of large-scale enterprise in the late nineteenth century?

The World of Work

In a free-enterprise system, profit drives the entrepreneur and produces, at the apex, the multimillionaire Carnegies and Rockefellers. But the industrial order is not populated only by profit makers. It includes — in vastly larger numbers — wage earners. Economic change always affects working people but rarely as drastically as it did in the late nineteenth century.

Labor Recruits

Industrialization invariably set people in motion. Farm folk migrated to cities. Artisans entered factories. An industrial labor force emerged. This happened in the United States as it did in Europe, but with a difference. In the late nineteenth century, rural Americans, although highly mobile and frequently city-bound, mostly rejected factory work. They lacked the industrial skills for the higher-paid jobs as rollers, molders, and machinists, but they did have skills — language, basic literacy, a cultural ease — that made them employable in the multiplying **white-collar** jobs in offices and retail stores.

So the United States could not rely primarily on its own people for a supply of factory workers, except in the South. There, a low-wage industrial sector emerged after Reconstruction as local boosters tried to build a "New South" and catch up with the

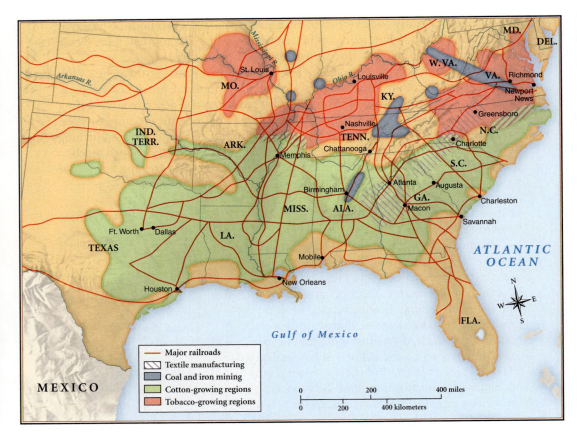

MAP 17.2 The New South, 1900
The economy of the Old South focused on raising staple crops, especially cotton and tobacco. In the New South, staple agriculture continued to dominate, but there was marked industrial development as well. Industrial regions evolved, producing textiles, coal and iron, and wood products. By 1900, the South's industrial pattern was well defined.

North (Map 17.2). The textile mills that sprouted in the Carolinas and Georgia recruited workers from the surrounding hill farms, where people struggled to make ends meet. Paying rock-bottom wages, the new mills had a competitive advantage of as much as 40 percent lower labor costs over the long-established New England industry.

The labor system that evolved was based on hiring whole families. "Papa decided he would come because he didn't have nothing much but girls and they had to get out and work like men," recalled one woman. It was not Papa, in fact, but his girls whom the mills wanted, to work as spinners and loom tenders. Only they could not be recruited individually; no right-thinking parent would have permitted that. Hiring by family, on the other hand, was already familiar; after all, everyone worked on the farm. So the family system of mill labor developed, with a labor force that was half female and very young. In the 1880s, one-quarter of all southern textile workers were under fifteen years of age.

In the mill villages, workers built close-knit, supportive communities, but for whites only. Although blacks sometimes worked as day laborers and janitors, they hardly ever got jobs as operatives in the cotton mills. The same was true of James B. Duke's cigarette factories, where machine-tending was restricted to white women.

In extractive natural-resource industries, the South's other growth sector, employers recruited with little regard for race. Logging in the vast pine forests, for example, was racially integrated, with a labor force evenly divided between blacks and whites. There was a similar racial mix in Alabama's booming iron industry, which by 1890 was producing nearly a million tons of metal annually.

What distinguished the southern labor market was that it was insulated from the rest of the country. Few southerners, black or white, left for the higher-wage North. This was because the South was a place apart, with social and racial mores that discouraged all but the most resourceful from seeking opportunity elsewhere. For blacks, moreover, opportunity was scarce everywhere. Modest numbers of blacks did migrate out of the South — roughly 80,000 between 1870 and 1890 and another 200,000 between 1890 and 1910. Most settled for day labor and service jobs. Industrial work was available, but not for them. Employers turned black applicants away from their one best chance for a fair shake at American opportunity because immigrant workers already supplied companies with as much cheap labor as they needed.

The migration from the Old World had started in the 1840s, when over one million Irish fled the potato famine. In the following years, as European agriculture became increasingly commercialized, the peasant economies began to fail, first in Germany and Scandinavia and then, later in the nineteenth century, across Austria-Hungary, Russia, Italy, and the Balkans. This upheaval set off a mass movement of Europeans, some of them going to Europe's own mines and factories, others heading for South America and Australia, but most coming to the United States. Along with the peasantry came many seasoned workers, some of them — like hand-loom weavers — displaced by new technologies, others lured by higher American wages.

Ethnic origin largely determined the work that immigrants took in America. Seeking to use skills they already had, the Welsh labored as tin-plate workers, the English as miners, the Germans as machinists and traditional artisans (for example, bakers and carpenters), the Belgians as glass workers, and the Scandinavians as seamen on Great Lakes boats. For common labor, employers had long counted on the brawn of Irish rural immigrants.

As mechanization advanced, the demand for ordinary labor skyrocketed, and increasing numbers of people from southern and eastern Europe began to arrive (Figure 17.2). Heavy, low-paid labor became their domain (see Voices from Abroad, p. 507). An investigator trying to get a job in the mills was told that the blast furnaces were "Hunky work," not suitable for him or any other American. The derogatory term *Hunky,* although referring to Hungarian workers, was applied indiscriminately to Poles, Slovaks, and other ethnic Slavs arriving in America's industrial districts and, for all these groups, was tinged with racism. In the steel districts, it was commonly said that Hunky work was not for "white" men, that is, old-stock Americans.

The newcomers moved within well-defined networks, following relatives or fellow villagers already in America and relying on them to help land a job. A high degree of ethnic clustering resulted, even within a single factory. At the Jones and Laughlin

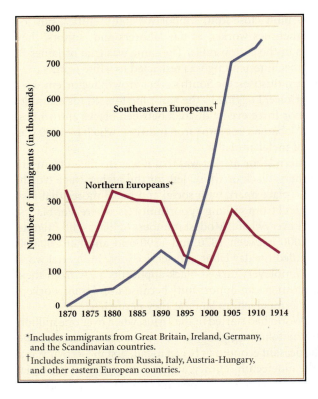

*Includes immigrants from Great Britain, Ireland, Germany, and the Scandinavian countries.

†Includes immigrants from Russia, Italy, Austria-Hungary, and other eastern European countries.

FIGURE 17.2 American Immigration, 1870–1914
This graph shows the surge of European immigration in the late nineteenth century. Northern Europe continued to send substantial numbers, but they were overshadowed after 1895 by southern Europeans pouring into America to work in mines and factories.

steel works in Pittsburgh, for example, the carpentry shop was German, the hammer shop Polish, and the blooming mill Serbian. Immigrants also had different job preferences. Men from Italy, for instance, favored outdoor work, often laboring in gangs under a *padrone* (boss), much as they had in Italy.

The immigrants who entered heavy industry were farmers, displaced by the breakdown of traditional peasant economies. Many had lost their land and fallen into the class of dependent servants. They could reverse that bitter fate only by finding the money to buy property. In Europe, job-seeking peasants commonly tried seasonal agricultural labor or temporary work in nearby cities. America represented merely a larger leap, made possible by cheap and speedy steamships across the Atlantic. The peasant immigrants, most of them young and male, regarded their stay in America as temporary, although, once there, many changed their minds. About half did return, departing in great numbers during depression years. No one knows how many left because they had saved enough and how many left for lack of work. For their American employers, it scarcely mattered. What did matter was that the immigrants took the worst jobs and were always available when they were wanted. For the new industrial order, they made an ideal labor supply.

Over four million women, a quarter of the nonfarm labor force, worked for wages in 1900. The opportunities they found were shaped by gender — by the fact that they were women. Traditionally, wives were not supposed to work outside the home; in fact,

Pittsburgh Inferno   COUNT VAY DE VAYA UND LUSKOD

Count Vay de Vaya und Luskod, a Hungarian nobleman and high functionary in the Catholic Church, crossed the United States several times between 1903 and 1906 en route to his post as the Vatican's representative to Asia. In a book about his travels, he expresses his distress at the plight of his countrymen laboring in the mills of the Pittsburgh steel district.

The bells are tolling for a funeral. The modest train of mourners is just setting out for the little churchyard on the hill. Everything is shrouded in gloom, even the coffin lying upon the bier and the people who stand on each side in threadbare clothes and with heads bent. Such is my sad reception at the Hungarian workingmen's colony at McKeesport. Everyone who has been in the United States has heard of this famous town, and of Pittsburgh, its close neighbor. . . .

Fourteen-thousand tall chimneys are silhouetted against the sky . . . discharg[ing] their burning sparks and smok[ing] incessantly. The realms of Vulcan could not be more somber or filthy than this valley of the Monongahela. On every hand are burning fires and spurting flames. Nothing is visible save the forging of iron and the smelting of metal. . . .

And this fearful place affects us very closely, for thousands of immigrants wander here from year to year. Here they fondly seek the realization of their cherished hopes, and here they suffer till they are swallowed up by the inferno. He whom we are now burying is the latest victim. Yesterday he was in full vigor and at work at the foundry, toiling, struggling, hoping — a chain broke, and he was killed. . . .

This is scarcely work for mankind. Americans will hardly take anything of the sort; only [the immigrant] rendered desperate by circumstances . . . and thus he is at the mercy of the tyrannous Trust, which gathers him into its clutches and transforms him into a regular slave.

This is one of the saddest features of the Hungarian emigration. In making a tour of these prisons, wherever the heat is most insupportable, the flames most scorching, the smoke and soot most choking, there we are certain to find compatriots bent and wasted with toil. Their thin, wrinkled, wan faces seem to show that in America the newcomers are of no use except to help fill the moneybags of the insatiable millionaires. . . . In this realm of Mammon and Moloch everything has a value — except human life. . . . Why? Because human life is a commodity the supply of which exceeds the demand. There are always fresh recruits to supply the place of those who have fallen in battle; and the steamships are constantly arriving at the neighboring ports, discharging their living human cargo still further to swell the phalanx of the instruments of cupidity.

SOURCE: Oscar Handlin, ed., *This Was America* (Cambridge, MA: Harvard University Press, 1949), 407–410.

fewer than 5 percent did so in 1890. Only among African Americans did many wives—above 30 percent—work for wages. Among whites, the typical working woman was under twenty-four and single; upon marrying, she quit her job and became a homemaker. When married women worked, remarked one observer, it "was usually a sign that something had gone wrong"—their husbands had died, deserted them, or lost their jobs.

Since women were held to be inherently different from men, it followed that they not be permitted to do "men's work." Nor, regardless of her skills, could a woman be paid a man's wage because, as one investigator reported, "it is expected that she has men to support her." The ideal at the time was not equal pay for equal work, but a "family wage" for men that would enable wives to stay home. The occupation that served as the baseline for women's jobs was domestic service, which was always poorly paid or, in a woman's own home, not paid at all.

At the turn of the century, women's work fell into three categories. A third worked as domestic servants. Another third held "female" white-collar jobs in teaching, nursing, sales, and office work. The remaining third worked in industry, mostly in the garment trades and textile mills but also in other industries in "light" jobs as inspectors, packers, and assemblers. Few worked as supervisors, fewer in the skilled crafts, and nearly none as day laborers.

Although invariably defined as male or female, the allocation of jobs was anything but fixed. Telephone operators and store clerks, originally male occupations, became female over a period of decades. Once women dominated an occupation, people attached feminine attributes to it, even though very similar or even identical work elsewhere was done by men. Jobs identified as women's work became unsuitable for men. There were no male telephone operators by 1900. And wherever they worked, women earned less than the lowest-paid males. In industry, women's wages came to roughly $7 a week, $3 less than that of unskilled men.

Opposition to the employment of wives, although expressed in sentimental and moral terms, was based on solid necessity. Cooking, cleaning, and tending the children were not income-producing or reckoned in terms of money. But everyone knew that the family household could not function without the wife's contribution. Therefore, her place was in the home.

Working-class families, however, found the going hard on a single income. Talk of a "family wage" was mostly just that—the talk of speech makers. Only among highly skilled workers, wrote one investigator, "was it possible for the husband unaided to support his family." That meant that, as the children grew old enough, they went to work. One of every five children under sixteen worked outside the home in 1900. "When the people own houses," remarked a printer from Fall River, Massachusetts, "you will generally find that it is a large family all working together."

Autonomous Labor

No one supervised the coal miner (see American Voices, p. 509). He was a tonnage worker, paid for the amount of coal he produced. He provided his own tools, worked at his own pace, and knocked off early when he chose. Such autonomous craft workers—almost all of them men—flourished in many branches of nineteenth-century industry.

A Miner's Son JOHN BROPHY

John Brophy (1883–1963), an important mine union official, recalls in an oral history what mining was like in his boyhood, a time when mining was still pick-and-shovel work and machinery had not yet eroded the prized skills of the miner.

I got a thrill at the thought of having an opportunity to go and work in the mine . . . alongside my father. . . . I was conscious of the fact that my father was a good workman; that he took pride in his calling . . . with everything kept in shape, and the timbering done well — all of these things: the rib side, the roadway, the timbering, the fact that you kept the loose coal clean rather than cluttered all over the workplace, the skill with which you undercut the vein, the judgment in drilling the coal after it had been undercut and placing the exact amount of explosive so that it would do an effective job of breaking the coal from the solid. . . .

Under the older conditions of mining under which I went to work with my father, the miner exercised considerable freedom in his working place in determining the pace of his work and the selection of the order of time in the different job operations. Judgment was everywhere along the line, and there was also necessary skill. It was the feel of all this. You know that another workman in another place was a good miner, a passable miner, or an indifferent one. . . . I think that was one of the great satisfactions a miner had — that he was his own boss within the workplace. . . .

The miner is always aware of danger, that he lives under dangerous conditions in the workplace, because he's constantly uncovering new conditions as he advances in the workingplace, exposing new areas of roof, discovering some weakened condition or break which may bring some special danger. There is also the danger that comes from a piece of coal slipping off the fast and falling on the worker as he lays prone on the bottom doing his cutting. . . .

Then there is the further fact that the miners by and large lived in purely mining communities which were often isolated. They developed a group loyalty . . . because involved in it was not only earning a living, but a matter of health and safety, life and death were involved in every way. You find time and again miners, in an effort to rescue their fellow workers, taking chances which quite often meant death for themselves. . . .

Along with that is a sense of justice. There was the very fact the miner was a tonnage worker and that he could be short weighed and cheated in various ways and . . . it was important to have a [union] representative of the miners to see that the weighing was properly done and properly credited to the individual miner. . . . At least on one side of my family there are at least four generations of [British] miners, and I say this with a sense of pride; very much so. I'm very proud of the fact that there is this long tradition of miners who have struggled with the elements.

SOURCE: Jerold S. Auerbach, ed., *American Labor: The Twentieth Century* (Indianapolis: Bobbs-Merrill, 1966), 44–48.

Breaker Boys

In the anthracite districts of eastern Pennsylvania, giant machines called "breakers" processed the coal as it came out of the mines, crushing it and sorting it by size for sale as domestic fuel. The boys shown in this photograph had the job of picking out the stones as the processed coal came down the chutes, working long hours in a constant cloud of coal dust for less than a dollar a day. Breaker boy was the first job, often begun before the age of ten, in a lifetime in the mines. The photograph does not show any old men, but sick and disabled miners often ended their careers as breaker boys — hence the saying among coal diggers, "Twice a boy and once a man is the poor miner's life." Library of Congress.

They were mule spinners in cotton mills; puddlers and rollers in iron works; molders in stove-making; and machinists, glass blowers, and skilled workers in many other industries.

In the shop, they abided by the *stint*, a self-imposed limit on how much they would produce each day. This informal system of restricting output infuriated efficiency-minded engineers. But to the worker, it signified "unselfish brotherhood" with fellow employees. The male craft worker took pride in a "manly" bearing, toward both his fellows and the boss. One day, a shop in Lowell, Massachusetts, posted regulations requiring all employees to be at their posts in work clothes at the opening bell and to remain, with the shop door locked, until the dismissal bell. A machinist promptly packed his tools, declaring that he had not "been brought up under such a system of slavery."

Underlying this ethical code was a keen sense of the craft, each with its own history and customs. Hat finishers—masters of the art of applying fur felting to top hats and bowlers—had a language of their own. When a hatter was hired, he was "shopped"; if fired, he was "bagged"; when he quit work, he "cried off"; and when he took an apprentice, the boy was "under teach." The hatters, mostly in Danbury, Connecticut, and Orange, New Jersey, formed a distinctive, self-contained community.

Working women found much the same kind of social meaning in their jobs. Department-store clerks, for example, developed a work culture just as robust as that of any male craft group. The most important fact about wage-earning women, however, was their youth. For many, their first job was a chance to be independent, to form friendships, and to experience, however briefly, a fun-loving time of nice clothes, dancing, and other "cheap amusements." Young male workers, by contrast, underwent a process of job socialization presided over by seasoned, older workers. Being young mattered to male workers, certainly, but did not define work experience as it did for young women.

To some degree, their youthful preoccupations made it easier for working women to accept low pay and taxing labor. But this did not mean that they lacked a sense of solidarity or self-respect. A pretty dress, while it might appear frivolous to the casual observer, conveyed the message that the working girl considered herself as good as anyone. Rebellious youth culture sometimes united with job grievances to produce astonishing strike movements, as was demonstrated, for example, after the turn of the century by the Jewish garment workers of New York and the Irish American telephone operators of Boston.

Rarely, however, did women workers wield the kind of craft power that the skilled male worker commonly enjoyed. He hired his own helpers, supervised their work, and paid them from his earnings. In the late nineteenth century, when increasingly sophisticated production called for closer shop-floor supervision, many factory managers shifted this responsibility to craft workers. In a system of inside contracting used by metal-fabricating firms, skilled employees bid for each production run, taking full responsibility for the operation, paying their crew, and pocketing the profits.

Dispersal of authority was characteristic of nineteenth-century industry. The aristocracy of the workers—the craftsmen, inside contractors, and foremen—enjoyed a high degree of autonomy. But their subordinates often paid dearly for that independence. Any worker who paid his helpers from his own pocket might be tempted to exploit them. In Pittsburgh, foremen were known as "pushers," notorious for driving their gangs mercilessly. On the other hand, industrial labor was on a human scale. People dealt with each other face to face, often developing cohesive ties within the shop. Striking craft workers commonly received the support of helpers and laborers, and labor gangs sometimes walked out on behalf of a popular foreman.

Systems of Control

As technology advanced, a de-skilling process cut into the proud independence that was characteristic of nineteenth-century craft work. One cause was a new system of manufacture—Henry Ford named it "**mass production**"—that lent itself to mechanization. Agricultural implements, typewriters, bicycles, and, after 1900, automobiles were assembled from standardized parts. The **machine tools** that cut, drilled, and ground these metal parts were originally operated by skilled machinists. But because they produced long runs of a single item, these machine tools became more specialized; thus, they became *dedicated* machines—machines set up to do the same job over and over without the need for skilled operatives.

In the manufacture of sewing machines, one machinist complained in 1883, "the trade is so subdivided that a man is not considered a machinist at all. One man may make just a particular part of a machine and may not know anything whatever about another part of the same machine." Such a worker, noted one observer, "cannot be master of a craft, but only master of a fragment."

Mechanization made it easier to control workers, but that was only an incidental benefit; employers favored automatic machinery because it increased output. Gradually, however, the idea took hold that focusing on workers—getting them to work harder or more efficiently—might itself be a way to reduce the cost of production.

The pioneer in this field was Frederick W. Taylor. An expert on metal-cutting methods, Taylor believed that the engineer's approach might be applied to managing workers, hence the name for his method: **scientific management**. To extract the maximum from the individual worker, Taylor suggested two basic reforms. First, eliminate the brain work from manual labor. Managers would assume "the burden of gathering together all of the traditional knowledge which in the past has been possessed by the workmen and then of classifying, tabulating, and reducing this knowledge to rules, laws, and formulae." Second, withdraw the authority that workers had exercised on the shop floor. They would now "do what they are told promptly and without asking questions or making suggestions. . . . The duty of enforcing . . . rests with the management alone."

Once managers had the knowledge and the power, they would be able to put labor on a "scientific" basis. This meant subjecting each task to a time-and-motion study by an engineer timing the job with a stopwatch. Workers would be paid at a differential rate—that is, a certain amount if they met the stopwatch standard and a higher rate for additional output. Taylor's assumption was that only money mattered to workers and that they would respond automatically to the lure of higher earnings.

Scientific management was not, in practice, a great success. Implementing it proved to be very expensive, and workers stubbornly resisted the job-analysis method. "It looks to me like slavery to have a man stand over you with a stopwatch," complained one iron molder. A union leader insisted that "this system is wrong, because we want our heads left on us." Far from solving the labor problem, as Taylor claimed it would, scientific management poisoned relations on the shop floor.

Yet Taylor achieved something of fundamental importance. He was a brilliant publicist, and his teachings spread throughout American industry. Taylor's disciples moved beyond his simplistic economic psychology, creating the new fields of personnel work and industrial psychology, whose practitioners purported to know how to extract more and better labor from workers. A threshold had been crossed into the modern era of labor management.

► Why were ethnicity and gender key determinants in how jobs were allocated in late-nineteenth-century industry?

► What accounts for the high degree of autonomy that many workers enjoyed in the early phases of industrialization? Why did that autonomy steadily erode as industrialization advanced?

So the circle closed on American workers. With each advance, the quest for efficiency eroded their cherished autonomy, diminishing them and cutting them down to fit the industrial system. The process occurred unevenly. For textile workers, the loss had come early. Miners and ironworkers felt it much more slowly. Others, such as construction workers, escaped almost entirely. But increasing numbers of workers found themselves in an environment that crushed any sense of mastery or even understanding.

The Labor Movement

Wherever it took hold, industrialization spurred workers to form labor unions. The movements they built, however, varied from one country to another. In the United States, workers were especially torn about how to proceed, and only in the 1880s did they settle on a labor movement that was distinctively American, like no other. While European movements embraced some variant of politically engaged socialism, American unionists rejected politics and emphasized **collective bargaining** with employers.

Reformers and Unionists

Thomas B. McGuire, a New York wagon driver, was ambitious. He had saved $300 from his wages "so that I might become something of a capitalist eventually." But his venture as a cab driver in the early 1880s soon failed:

> Corporations usually take that business themselves. They can manage to get men, at starvation wages, and put them on a hack, and put a livery on them with a gold band and brass buttons, to show that they are slaves — I beg pardon; I did not intend to use the word slaves; there are no slaves in this country now — to show that they are merely servants.

Slave or liveried servant, the symbolic meaning was the same to McGuire. He was speaking of the crushed aspirations of the independent American worker.

What would satisfy the Thomas McGuires of the nineteenth century? Only the establishment of an egalitarian society that enabled every citizen to be economically independent. This republican goal resembled Jefferson's yeoman society, but labor reformers had no interest in returning to an agrarian past. They accepted industrialism but not the accompanying distinction between capitalists and workers. In the future, all would be "producers," laboring together in what labor reformers commonly called the "cooperative commonwealth." This was the ideal that inspired the Noble and Holy Order of the Knights of Labor.

Founded in 1869 as a secret society of garment workers in Philadelphia, the Knights of Labor spread to other cities and, by 1878, had emerged as a national movement. The Knights boasted an elaborate ritual that appealed to the fraternal spirit of nineteenth-century workers. The local assemblies engendered a comradely spirit, very much like the Masons or Odd Fellows. For the Knights, however, fraternalism was harnessed to labor reform. The goal was to "give voice to that grand undercurrent of mighty thought, which is today [1880] crystallizing in the hearts of men, and urging them on to perfect organization through which to gain the power to make labor emancipation possible."

But how was "emancipation" to be achieved? Through cooperation, the Knights argued. They intended to set up factories and shops that would be owned by the employees. As these cooperatives flourished, American society would be transformed into a cooperative commonwealth. But little was actually done. Instead, the Knights devoted themselves to "education." Their leader, Grand Master Workman Terence V. Powderly, regarded the organization as a vast labor college open to all but lawyers and saloonkeepers. The cooperative commonwealth would arrive in some mysterious way as lectures, discussions, and

"BY INDUSTRY WE THRIVE."

The Knights of Labor
The caption on this union card—"By Industry We Thrive"—expresses the core principle of the Knights of Labor that everything of value is the product of honest labor. The two figures are ideal representations of that "producerist" belief—handsome workers, respectably attired, doing productive labor. A picture of the Grand Master Workman, Terence V. Powderly, hangs on the wall, benignly watching them. Picture Research Consultants & Archives.

publications spread the group's message. Social evil would not end in a day but "must await the gradual development of educational enlightenment."

The labor reformers, exemplified by the Knights, expressed the grander aspirations of American workers. Another kind of organization—the trade union—tended to their everyday needs. Apprenticeship rules regulated entry into a trade, and the **closed shop**—reserving all jobs for union members—kept out lower-wage and incompetent workers. Union rules specified the terms of work, sometimes in minute detail. Above all, trade unionism defended the craft worker's traditional skills and rights.

The trade union also expressed the craft's social identity. Hatters took pride in their alcohol consumption, an on-the-job privilege that was jealously guarded. Other craft unions had an uplifting character. A Birmingham ironworker claimed that his union's "main object was to educate mechanics up to a standard of morality and temperance, and good workmanship." Some unions emphasized mutual aid. Because operating trains was a high-risk occupation, the railroad brotherhoods provided accident and death benefits. On and off the job, the unions played a big part in the lives of craft workers.

The earliest unions were local bodies, sometimes limited to a single ethnic group, especially among German workers. As expanding markets intruded, breaking down their ability to control local conditions, unions formed national organizations, beginning with the International Typographical Union in 1852. By the 1870s, molders, ironworkers, bricklayers, and about thirty other trades had done likewise. The national union, uniting local unions of the same trade, was becoming the dominant organizational form in America.

The practical job interests of trade unionists might have seemed a far cry from the idealism of the Knights of Labor. But both kinds of motives arose from a single workers' culture. Seeing no conflict, many workers carried membership cards in both the Knights and a trade union. And because the Knights tended to become politically active and to field independent slates of candidates, that too became a magnet attracting trade unionists interested in local politics.

Trade unions generally barred women, and so did the Knights until 1881, when women shoe workers in Philadelphia struck in support of their male coworkers and won the right to form their own local assembly. By 1886, probably 50,000 women belonged to the Knights of Labor. Their courage on the picket line prompted the rueful remark that women "are the best men in the Order." For a handful of women, the Knights provided a rare chance to take up leadership roles as organizers and officials.

Similarly, the Knights of Labor grudgingly opened the door for black workers, in deference to the Order's egalitarian principles. The Knights could rightly boast that their "great work has been to organize labor which was previously unorganized."

The Emergence of the AFL

In the early 1880s, the Knights began to act more like a trade union, negotiating over wages and hours and going on strike to win demands. They made especially effective use of boycotts against "unfair" employers. And with the economy booming, the Knights began to win strikes, including a major victory against Jay Gould's Southwestern railway system in 1885. Workers flocked to the organization, and its membership jumped from 100,000 to perhaps 700,000.

Frightened by the rapid growth of the Knights, the national trade unions pressed for a clear separation of roles, with the Knights confined to labor reform activities. This was partly a battle over turf, but it also reflected a divergence of labor philosophies.

On the union side, the key figure was Samuel Gompers, a Dutch-Jewish cigar maker whose family had emigrated to New York in 1863. Gompers was a worker-intellectual, a familiar type in the craft trades, little educated but widely read and engaged by ideas. Gompers always contended that what he missed at school (he had gone to work at age ten) he more than made up for in the shop, where cigar makers commonly paid one of their number to read to them while they worked.

Worker-intellectuals such as Gompers gravitated to New York's radical circles, hotbeds of debate during the 1870s about revolutionary action. Partly out of these debates, partly from his own experience in the Cigar Makers Union, Gompers hammered out a doctrine that he called "pure-and-simple unionism." "Pure" referred to membership: strictly limited to workers, organized by craft and occupation, with no participation by middle-class reformers. "Simple" referred to goals: only what immediately benefited workers—wages, hours, and working conditions. Pure-and-simple unionism focused on the workplace and distrusted politics. Its aim was collective bargaining with employers.

For Gompers, the key word was *power*. "No matter how just," he said, "unless the cause is backed up with power to enforce it, it is going to be crushed and annihilated." At the crux of the dispute with the Knights was Gompers's conviction that with their grand schemes, they did not understand American power realities, and on top of that, by mucking around on union turf, they undercut power-building unions.

In December 1886, prompted by the challenge from the Knights, the national trade unions formed the American Federation of Labor (AFL), with Gompers as president. The AFL in effect locked into place the trade union structure as it had evolved by the 1880s. Underlying this structure was the belief that workers had to take the world as it was, not as they dreamed it might be.

The issue that provoked the rupture between the rival movements was the eight-hour workday. Nothing, the trade unions believed, would do more to improve the everyday lives of American workers. The Knights leaders, although sympathetic, regarded shorter hours as a distraction from higher goals. When the trade unions set May 1, 1886, as the deadline for achieving the eight-hour workday, the Knights demurred. But many Knights, ignoring the leadership, responded enthusiastically, and as the deadline approached, a wave of strikes broke out across the country.

At one such eight-hour-day strike, at the McCormick reaper works in Chicago, a battle erupted on May 3, leaving four strikers dead. Chicago was a hotbed of **anarchism** — the revolutionary advocacy of a stateless society — and local anarchists, most of them German immigrants, called a protest meeting the next evening at Haymarket Square. When police began to disperse the crowd, someone threw a bomb that killed or wounded several of the police, who responded with wild gunfire. Most of the casualties came from police bullets. Despite the lack of evidence, the anarchists were found guilty of murder and criminal conspiracy. Four were executed, one committed suicide, and the others received long prison sentences — victims of one of the great miscarriages of American justice.

Seizing on the antiunion hysteria set off by the Haymarket affair, employers took the offensive. They broke strikes violently, compiled blacklists of strikers, and forced workers to sign **yellow-dog contracts**, in which, as a condition of employment, workers pledged not to join labor organizations. If trade unionists needed any confirmation of the tough world in which they lived, they found it in Haymarket and its aftermath.

The Knights of Labor, hard-hit despite its official opposition to the eight-hour strikes, never recovered from Haymarket. In the meantime, the more resilient AFL took firm root, justifying Gompers's confidence that he had found the correct formula for an American labor movement. What he overlooked was the inclusiveness of the Knights of Labor. The AFL was far less welcoming to women and blacks, confining them, where they were admitted, to separate, second-class organizations. It was a flaw that would come back to haunt the labor movement.

Industrial War

Radical as its intellectual origins were, pure-and-simple unionism was conservative in effect. American trade unions did not challenge the economic order. All they wanted was a larger share for working people. But it was precisely that claim against company profits that made American employers so opposed to collective bargaining. In the 1890s, they unleashed a fierce counterattack on the trade union movement.

The skilled workers of Homestead, Pennsylvania, the site of one of Carnegie's steel mills, imagined themselves safe from that threat. They earned good wages, lived comfortably, and generally owned their own homes. The mayor of the town was one of their own. And they had faith in Andrew Carnegie—for had not Good Old Andy said in a famous magazine article that workers had as sacred a right to combine as did capitalists?

Espousing high-toned principles made Carnegie feel good, but a healthy profit made him feel even better. He decided that collective bargaining had become too expensive, and he was confident that newly installed machinery had given him the upper hand over his skilled workers. Carnegie fled to a remote estate in Scotland, leaving behind a second-in-command well qualified to do the dirty work. This was Henry Clay Frick, a former coal baron and a veteran union fighter.

After a brief pretense at bargaining, Frick announced that effective July 1, 1892, the company would no longer deal with the Amalgamated Association of Iron and Steel Workers. If the employees wanted to work, they would have to come back on an individual basis. The mill had already been fortified so that strikebreakers could be brought in. At stake for Carnegie's employees now were not just wages but a way of life.

At dawn on July 6, barges were seen approaching Homestead up the Monongahela River. On board were armed guards hired by the Pinkerton Detective Agency to take possession of the steel works. The strikers opened fire, and a bloody battle ensued. When the Pinkertons surrendered, they were pummeled by the enraged women of Homestead as they retreated to the railway station. Frick appealed to the governor of Pennsylvania, who called out the state militia. The great steel works was opened to strikebreakers, while union leaders and town officials were arrested on charges of riot, murder, and treason.

The defeat at Homestead ended any lingering illusions about the sanctity of workers' communities such as Homestead. "Men talk like anarchists or lunatics when they insist that the workmen of Homestead have done right," asserted one conservative journal. Nothing could be permitted to interfere with Carnegie's property rights or threaten law and order.

The Homestead strike ushered in a decade of industrial war, pitting working people against corporate industry and, even more formidably, against their own government. Workers learned that lesson at a place that seemed even less likely a site for class warfare than Homestead.

Pullman, Illinois, was a model factory town, famous for its spacious city plan. The town's sole employer was George M. Pullman, inventor of the sleeping car that had brought comfort and luxury to railway travel. When business fell off during the economic depression in 1893, Pullman cut wages but not the rents for company housing. Confronted by a workers' committee in May 1894, Pullman denied any connection between his roles as employer and landlord. He then fired the workers' committee.

The strike that ensued would have warranted only a footnote in American history but for the fact that the Pullman workers belonged to the American Railway Union (ARU), a rapidly growing new union of railroad workers. Its leader, Eugene V. Debs, directed ARU members not to handle Pullman sleeping cars, which, though operated by the railroads, were owned and serviced by the Pullman Company. This was a **secondary labor boycott**: Force was applied on a second party (the railroads) to bring pressure on the primary target (Pullman). Since the railroads insisted on running the Pullman cars, a strike soon spread across the country, threatening the entire economy.

The railroads deftly drew the federal government into the dispute. Their hook was the U.S. mail cars, which the railroads attached to every train hauling Pullman cars. When strikers stopped these trains, the railroads appealed to President Cleveland to protect the U.S. mail. Cleveland's attorney general Richard Olney, a former railroad lawyer, unabashedly sided with his former employers. When federal troops failed to get the trains running, Olney obtained court injunctions prohibiting the ARU leaders from conducting the strike. Debs and his associates refused, were declared in contempt of court, and were jailed. Leaderless, the strike disintegrated.

No one could doubt why the great Pullman boycott had failed: It had been crushed by the naked use of government power on behalf of the railroad companies.

American Radicalism in the Making

While not every victim of oppression is radicalized, some are. And when social injustice is most painfully felt, when the power realities stand openly revealed, the process of radicalization speeds up. Such was the case during the 1890s. Out of the industrial strife of that decade emerged the main forces of twentieth-century American radicalism.

Very little in Eugene Debs's background would have suggested that he would one day become the nation's leading Socialist. A native of Terre Haute, Indiana, a prosperous railroad town, Debs grew up believing in the essential goodness of American society. A popular young man-about-town, Debs considered a career in politics or business but instead got involved in the local labor movement. In 1880, at the age of twenty-five, he was elected national secretary-treasurer of the Brotherhood of Locomotive Firemen, one of the craft unions that represented the skilled operating trades on the railroads. Troubled by his union's indifference to the low-paid track and yard laborers, Debs left his comfortable post for the American Railway Union, which was an **industrial union**, that is, a union open to all railroad workers, regardless of skill. That was why the Pullman workers were eligible for ARU membership.

The Pullman strike visibly changed Debs. Sentenced to six months in a federal prison, he emerged an avowed radical. Initially, Debs identified himself as a Populist (see Chapter 19), but he quickly gravitated to the Socialist camp.

German refugees had brought the ideas of Karl Marx, the radical German theorist, to America after the failed European revolutions of 1848. Marx postulated a class struggle between capitalists and workers, ending in a revolution that would abolish private ownership of the means of production and bring about a classless society. Little noticed by most Americans, Marxist socialism had a following in the German American communities of Chicago and New York. With the formation of the Socialist Labor Party in 1877, Marxist socialism established a permanent, if narrowly based, presence in American politics.

When Eugene Debs appeared in their midst in 1897, the Socialists were in disarray. Despite the recent crisis of American capitalism, their party had made little headway. Many blamed the party head, Daniel De Leon, who valued ideological purity above winning elections. Debs joined the revolt against the dogmatic De Leon and helped launch the rival Socialist Party of America in 1901.

Industrial Violence

Strikes in the western mining districts were generally bloody affairs. On management's side, the mayhem was often perpetrated by the forces of law and order. This photograph shows a line of mounted troopers during the 1894 strike at Cripple Creek, Colorado, viewed from the rear. From the front, the sight was more fearsome because the formation of the troopers suggests that they might be about to charge and begin breaking heads. Denver Public Library, Western History Division.

A spellbinding campaigner, Debs talked socialism in an American idiom, making Marxism persuasive to many ordinary citizens. Under him, the new party began to break out of its immigrant base and attract American-born voters. In Texas, Oklahoma, and Minnesota, socialism exerted a powerful appeal among distressed farmers. The party was also successful at attracting women activists. Inside of a decade, with a national network of branches and state organizations, the Socialist Party had become a force to be reckoned with in American politics.

Farther west a different brand of American radicalism was taking shape. After many years of mostly friendly relations, things turned ugly in the western mining camps during the 1890s. New corporate owners wanted to be rid of the miners' union, the Western Federation of Miners (WFM). Moreover, silver and copper prices began to drop, bringing pressure on miners' wages. When strikes resulted, they took an especially violent turn.

In 1892, striking miners at Coeur d'Alene, a silver-mining district in northern Idaho, engaged in gun battles with company guards, sent a car of explosive powder careering into the Frisco mine, and threatened to blow up the smelters. Martial law was declared, the strikers were imprisoned in stockades, and the strike was broken. In subsequent miners' strikes, government intervention was equally naked and unrestrained. By 1897, the WFM president, Ed Boyce, was calling on all union members to arm themselves, and his rhetoric—he called the wage system "slavery in its worst form"—developed a hard edge.

Led by the fiery Boyce and "Big Bill" Haywood, the WFM joined in 1905 with left-wing Socialists to create a new movement, the Industrial Workers of the World (IWW). The Wobblies, as IWW members were called, fervently supported the Marxist class struggle—but at the workplace rather than in politics. They believed that by resisting at the point of production and ultimately by launching a **general strike**, the workers would bring about a revolution. A new society would emerge, run directly by the workers. The term **syndicalism** describes this brand of workers' radicalism.

▶ How would you distinguish between labor reform and trade unionism?

▶ Why did the AFL prevail over the Knights of Labor?

▶ Why were the 1890s the critical period in the rise of American radicalism?

In both its major forms—politically-oriented Socialism and the syndicalist IWW—American radicalism flourished after the 1890s, but only on a limited basis and never with the possibility of seizing national power. Nevertheless, Socialists and Wobblies served a real purpose. American radicalism, by its sheer vitality, bore witness to what was exploitative and unjust in the new industrial order.

SUMMARY

In this chapter, we traced the emergence of modern American industrialism, which involved an unrivaled capacity for supplying the capital goods and energy to the nation's factories and cities and, on the demand side, an efficient railway network that gave producers easy access to national markets. We showed how entrepreneurs such as Swift and Rockefeller, eager to exploit this opportunity, built vertically integrated firms capable of managing far-flung, complex business activities. Also new—and troubling—was the market power that was suddenly in the hands of great firms such as Rockefeller's Standard Oil.

On the labor side, the biggest challenge was finding enough workers for America's burgeoning industries. The South recruited local populations of both races, while the industrial North relied on European immigrants. Race, ethnicity, and gender became defining features of the American working class. Mass production—the high-volume output of standardized products—accelerated the productivity of industry but also de-skilled workers and mechanized their jobs, as did the systematizing methods of Frederick W. Taylor's scientific management.

In these years, after much trial and error, the American labor movement took shape. The Knights of Labor enjoyed one final surge in the mid-1880s and succumbed to the AFL. The AFL's emphasis on securing a larger share for workers evoked fierce opposition from employers. The resulting industrial warfare of the 1890s stirred new radical impulses, leading both to the political socialism of Eugene V. Debs and to the industrial radicalism of the IWW.

Connections: The Economy

The economic developments described in this chapter originated far back in the nineteenth century, when the factory system first emerged and roads, canals, and the early railroads launched a market revolution (Chapter 9). The industrial power that resulted gave the North the upper hand in the Civil War, while in turn the war effort further stimulated the North's industrial development (Chapter 14). Only afterward, however, in the years covered by this chapter, was that development fully consolidated, and as we observed in the essay opening Part Four, "what had been partial and limited now became general and widespread." Virtually every aspect of America's subsequent history has been shaped by its industrial power, from the nation's foray into imperial politics in the 1890s (Chapter 21) to the dramatic rise in living standards in the 1920s (Chapter 23), when mass-produced automobiles and other consumer durables began to flow to ordinary Americans, to the social upheaval that led to the New Deal (Chapter 24) when the industrial economy broke down. Because it is so central a fact of our modern history, students should be attentive to the impact of American industrialism as they read beyond Chapter 17.

TIMELINE

1869 ▶ Knights of Labor founded in Philadelphia

1872 ▶ Andrew Carnegie starts construction of Edgar Thomson steelworks near Pittsburgh

1873 ▶ Panic of 1873 ushers in economic depression

1875 ▶ John Wanamaker establishes first department store in Philadelphia

1877 ▶ Baltimore and Ohio workers initiate nationwide railroad strike

1878 ▶ Gustavus Swift introduces refrigerator car

1879 ▶ Jay Gould begins to build Missouri Pacific railway system

1883 ▶ Railroads establish national time zones

1886 ▶ Haymarket Square bombing in Chicago

▶ American Federation of Labor (AFL) founded

1892 ▶ Homestead steel strike crushed

▶ Wave of western miners' strikes begins

1893 ▶ Panic of 1893 leads to national depression

▶ Surge of railroad bankruptcies; reorganization by investment bankers begins

1894 ▶ President Cleveland sends troops to break Pullman boycott

1895 ▶ Southeastern European immigration exceeds northern European immigration for first time

▶ Frederick W. Taylor formulates scientific management

1901 ▶ Eugene V. Debs helps found Socialist Party of America

1905 ▶ Industrial Workers of the World (IWW) launched

FOR FURTHER EXPLORATION

For students new to economic history, biography offers an accessible entry point. The biographical literature is especially rich because of an ongoing debate about what contribution the great magnates made to America's industrial success. The initiating book was Matthew Josephson's classic *The Robber Barons* (1934), which, as the title implies, argued that America's great fortunes were built on the wealth that others had created. The contrary view was taken by Julius Grodinsky, whose *Jay Gould: His Business Career, 1867–1892* (1957) explained masterfully how this railroad buccaneer helped shape the transportation system. Since then, there have been superb, mostly sympathetic, business biographies, including Joseph F. Wall, *Andrew Carnegie* (1970); Ron Chernow, *Titan: The Life of John D. Rockefeller* (1998); and Jean Strause, *Morgan: American Financier* (1999). On labor's side, the biographical literature is nearly as rich. The founder of the AFL is the subject of a lively brief biography by Harold Livesay, *Samuel Gompers and Organized Labor in America* (1978). His main critic is treated with great insight in Nick Salvatore, *Eugene V. Debs: Citizen and Socialist* (1982). The IWW leader William D. Haywood is the subject of Peter Carlson's, *Roughneck* (1982). Biography tends to overlook the foot soldiers of history, but social historians have tried in recent years to tell their stories, as Paul Krause does in *The Battle for Homestead, 1880–1892* (1992). There is an excellent Web site on Andrew Carnegie at **http:// andrewcarnegie.tripod.com.**

TEST YOUR KNOWLEDGE

To assess your mastery of the material in this chapter and for Web sites, images, and documents related to this chapter, visit **bedfordstmartins.com/henrettaconcise**.

The Industrial City: Building It, Living in It

These vast aggregations of humanity, where he who seeks isolation may find it more truly than in a desert; where wealth and poverty touch and jostle; where one revels and another starves within a few feet of each other — they are the centers and types of our civilization.

— Henry George, 1883

Visiting his fiancée's Missouri homestead in 1894, Theodore Dreiser was struck by "the spirit of rural America, its idealism, its dreams." But this was an "American tradition in which I, alas, could not share," Dreiser wrote. "I had seen Pittsburgh. I had seen Lithuanians and Hungarians in their [alleys] and hovels. I had seen the girls of the city — walking the streets at night." Only twenty-three years old at the time, Dreiser would go on to write one of the great American urban novels, *Sister Carrie* (1900), about one young woman in the army of small-town Americans flocking to the Big City. But Dreiser, part of that army, already knew that between rural America and Pittsburgh, an unbridgeable chasm had opened up.

In 1820, after two hundred years of settlement, the vast majority of Americans lived in rural areas. After that, decade by decade, the urban population swelled until, by 1900, one of every five Americans was a city dweller. Nearly 6.5 million people inhabited just three great cities: New York, Chicago, and Philadelphia (Table 18.1).

The city was where the factories went up and where the new immigrants settled, constituting one-third of all big-city residents in 1900. Here, too, lived the millionaires, and a growing white-collar class. For all these people, the city was more than a place to make a living. It provided the setting for an urban culture unlike anything seen before in the United States. City people, although differing vastly among themselves, became distinctively and recognizably urban.

TABLE 18.1	Ten Largest Cities by Population, 1870 and 1900		
1870		**1900**	
City	**Population**	**City**	**Population**
1. New York	942,292	New York	3,437,202
2. Philadelphia	674,022	Chicago	1,698,575
3. Brooklyn*	419,921	Philadelphia	1,293,697
4. St. Louis	310,864	St. Louis	575,238
5. Chicago	298,977	Boston	560,892
6. Baltimore	267,354	Baltimore	508,957
7. Boston	250,526	Cleveland	381,768
8. Cincinnati	216,239	Buffalo	352,387
9. New Orleans	191,418	San Francisco	342,782
10. San Francisco	149,473	Cincinnati	325,902

*Brooklyn was consolidated with New York in 1898.
SOURCE: U.S. Census data.

Urbanization

"The greater part of our population must live in cities," declared the Congregational minister Josiah Strong. And from another writer, "There was no resisting the trend." Why this sense of inevitability? Because of another inevitability of American life: industrialism.

Until the Civil War, cities were the places where goods were bought and sold for distribution into the interior or out to world markets. Early industry, by contrast, sprang up mostly in the countryside, where factories had access to water power, nearby fuel and raw materials, and workers recruited from farms and villages.

As industrialization proceeded, city and factory began to merge. Once steam engines came along, mill operators no longer depended on water-driven power. Railroads enabled factory builders to locate at the places best situated in relation to suppliers and markets. Iron makers gravitated to Pittsburgh because of its superior access to coal and ore fields. Chicago, midway between western livestock suppliers and eastern markets, became a great meatpacking center. Geographic concentration of industry meant urban growth. So did the rising scale of production. A plant that employed thousands of workers instantly created a small city in its vicinity, sometimes in the form of a company town like Aliquippa, Pennsylvania, which became, body and soul, the property of the Jones and Laughlin Steel Company. Other firms built big plants at the edges of large cities, close to an ample labor force and transportation facilities. The boundaries between industrial towns sometimes blurred, and, as in northern New Jersey or along Lake Michigan south of Chicago, extended urban-industrial areas emerged.

Older commercial cities meanwhile industrialized. Warehouse districts could readily be converted to small-scale manufacturing; a distribution network was right at hand. In addition, as gateways for immigrants, port cities offered abundant cheap labor. Boston, Philadelphia, Baltimore, and San Francisco became hives of small-scale, labor-intensive industry. New York, with its enormous pool of immigrant workers, became a magnet for the garment trades, cigar making, and diversified light industry. Preeminent as a city of trade and finance, New York also ranked as the nation's largest manufacturing center.

City Innovation

As cities expanded, so did their growing problems. How would so many people move around, communicate, and have their physical needs met? No less than industry, the city demanded innovation and, in the end, compiled just as impressive a record of technological achievement.

The older commercial cities had been compact, densely settled around harbors or riverfronts. As late as 1850, when it had 565,000 people, Philadelphia covered only ten square miles. From the foot of Chestnut Street on the Delaware River, a person could walk almost anywhere in the city within forty-five minutes. Thereafter, as it developed, Philadelphia spilled out and, like American cities everywhere, engulfed the surrounding countryside.

"The only trouble about this town," wrote Mark Twain on arriving in New York in 1867, "is that it is too large. You cannot accomplish anything in the way of business, you cannot even pay a friendly call without devoting a whole day to it. . . . [The] distances are too great." Moving nearly a million New Yorkers around was not as hopeless as Twain thought, but it did challenge the ingenuity of city builders.

The first innovation, dating back to the 1820s, was the omnibus, an elongated version of the horse-drawn carriage. Putting the car on iron tracks then enabled the horses to pull more passengers at a faster clip through crowded city streets. The protruding rails, the chief objection to the horsecar, were overcome by a modest but crucial refinement in 1852: a grooved rail that was flush with the pavement. Next came the electric trolley car, the brainchild primarily of Frank J. Sprague, an engineer once employed by the great inventor Thomas A. Edison. In 1887, Sprague designed an electricity-driven system for Richmond, Virginia: A "trolley" carriage running along an overhead power line was attached by cable to streetcars equipped with an electric motor — hence the name "trolley car." After Sprague's success, the trolley swiftly displaced the horsecar.

In America's great metropolises, however, the streetcar itself was no solution. Congestion led to demands that transit lines be moved off the streets. In 1879, the first elevated railroads went into operation on Sixth and Ninth Avenues in New York City. Powered at first by steam engines, the "els" were converted to electricity following Sprague's success with the trolley. Chicago developed elevated transit most fully. Other cities looked below ground. Boston opened a short underground line in 1897, but it was the completion in 1904 of a subway running the length of Manhattan that demonstrated the full potential of the high-speed underground train. Mass transit had become *rapid* transit.

Equally remarkable was the architectural revolution sweeping metropolitan centers. With steel girders, durable plate glass, and the passenger elevator available by the 1880s, a wholly new way of construction opened up. A steel skeleton supported the building, while the walls, previously weight bearing, served as curtains enclosing the structure. The sky, so to speak, became the limit.

The Chicago Elevated, 1900
This is Wabash Avenue, looking north from Adams Street. For Americans from farms and small towns, this photograph by William Henry Jackson captured something of the peculiarity of the urban scene. What could be stranger than a railroad suspended above the streets in the midst of people's lives? KEA Publishing Services, Ltd.

The first "skyscraper" to be built on this principle was William Le Baron Jenney's ten-story Home Insurance Building (1885) in Chicago. Although unremarkable in appearance — it looked just like the other downtown buildings — Jenney's steel-girdered structure liberated American architecture. A Chicago school arose, dedicated to the design of buildings whose form expressed, rather than masked, their structure and function. The presiding genius was the architect Louis Sullivan, who developed a "vertical aesthetic" of set-back windows and strong columns that gave skyscrapers a "proud and soaring" presence. Chicago pioneered skyscraper construction, but New York, with its unrelenting demand for prime downtown space, took the lead after the mid-1890s. The fifty-five-story Woolworth Building, completed in 1913, marked the beginning of the modern Manhattan skyline.

For ordinary citizens, the electric light was the best evidence that times had changed. Gaslight — illuminated gas produced from coal — had been in use since the early nineteenth century, but at 12 candlepower, the lamps were too dim to brighten the city's downtown streets and public spaces. The first use of electricity, once generating technology made it commercially feasible in the 1870s, was for better city lighting. Charles F. Brush's electric arc lamps, installed in Wanamaker's department store in Philadelphia in 1878, threw a brilliant light and soon replaced gaslight on city streets.

Electric lighting then entered the American home, thanks to Thomas Edison's invention of a serviceable incandescent bulb in 1879. Edison's motto—"Let there be light!"—truly described modern city life.

Before it had any significant effect on industry, electricity gave the city its quickening tempo, lifting elevators, powering streetcars and subway trains, turning night into day. Meanwhile, Alexander Graham Bell's telephone (1876) sped communication beyond anything imagined previously. Twain's complaint of 1867, that it was impossible to carry on business in New York, had been answered: All he needed to do was pick up the phone.

Private City, Public City

City building was mostly an exercise in private enterprise. The profit motive spurred the great innovations—the trolley car, electric lighting, the skyscraper, the elevator, the telephone—and drove urban real estate development. The investment opportunities looked so tempting that new cities sprang up almost overnight from the ruins of the Chicago fire of 1871 and the San Francisco earthquake of 1906. Real estate interests, eager to develop subdivisions, lobbied for streetcar lines pushing outward from the central districts. The subway, predicted the *New York Times,* would open the outer suburbs to "a population of ten millions . . . housed comfortably, healthfully and relatively cheaply"—a gold mine for developers.

America gave birth to what one urban historian has called the "private city," shaped primarily by many individuals, all pursuing their own goals and bent on making money. The prevailing belief was that the sum of such private activity would far exceed what the community might accomplish through public effort.

Yet constitutionally, it was up to municipal governments to draw the line between public and private. New York City was legally entitled to operate a municipally owned subway, the State Supreme Court ruled in 1897. Even private property was subject to whatever regulations the city might impose. Moreover, city governance improved impressively in the late nineteenth century. Though by no means corruption-free, municipal agencies became more professionalized and more expansive in the functions they undertook. Nowhere in the world were there bigger public projects: aqueducts, sewage systems, bridges, and spacious parks.

In the space between public and private, however, was an environmental no-man's land. City streets were often filthy and poorly maintained. "Three or four days of warm spring weather," remarked a New York journalist, would turn Manhattan's garbage-strewn, snow-clogged streets into "veritable mud rivers." Air quality likewise suffered. A visitor to Pittsburgh noted "the heavy pall of smoke which constantly overhangs her . . . until the very sun looks coppery through the sooty haze." As for the lovely hills rising from the rivers, "They have been leveled down, cut into, sliced off, and ruthlessly marred and mutilated."

In earlier times, the urban poor had lived mainly in makeshift wooden structures in alleys and back streets and then, as more prosperous families moved away, in the subdivided homes left behind. As land values climbed after the Civil War, speculators began to erect buildings specifically designed for the urban masses. In New York City, the dreadful result was five- or six-story tenements, structures housing twenty or more families in cramped, airless apartments.

Reformers recognized the problem but seemed unable to solve it. Some favored model tenements financed by public-spirited citizens. But private philanthropy was no answer to escalating land values in downtown areas. The landlords of the poor expected a return on their investment, and that meant high-density, cheaply built housing. This economic fact defied nineteenth-century solutions.

It was not that America lacked an urban vision. On the contrary, an abiding **rural ideal** exerted a powerful influence on city planners. Frederick Law Olmsted, who designed New York City's Central Park, wanted cities that exposed people to the beauties of nature. One of Olmsted's projects, the Chicago Columbian Exposition of 1893, gave rise to the "City Beautiful" movement, which fostered larger park systems, broad boulevards and parkways, and, after the turn of the century, zoning laws and planned suburbs.

But usually it was too little and too late. "Fifteen or twenty years ago a plan might have been adopted that would have made this one of the most beautiful cities in the world," Kansas City's park commissioners reported in 1893. At that time, however, "such a policy could not be fully appreciated." Nor, even if Kansas City had foreseen its future, would it have shouldered the "heavy burden" of trying to shape its development. The American city had placed its faith in the dynamics of the marketplace, not the restraints of a planned future. The pluses and minuses are perhaps best revealed by the following comparison.

Chicago, Illinois, and Berlin, Germany, had virtually equal populations in 1900. But they had very different histories. Seventy years earlier, when Chicago had been a muddy frontier outpost, Berlin was already a city of 250,000 and the royal seat of the Hohenzollerns of Prussia.

With German unification in 1871, the imperial authorities rebuilt Berlin on a grander scale. "A capital city is essential for the state, to act as a pivot for its culture," proclaimed the Prussian historian Heinrich von Treitschke. Berlin served that national purpose—"a center where Germany's political, intellectual, and material life is concentrated, and its people can feel united." Chicago had no such pretensions. It was strictly a place of business, made great by virtue of its strategic grip on the commerce of America's heartland. Nothing in Chicago approached the grandeur of Berlin's monumental palaces and public buildings, nor were Chicagoans witness to the pomp and ceremony of the imperial parades up Berlin's Unter den Linden to the national cathedral.

Yet as a functioning city, Chicago was in many ways superior to Berlin. Chicago's waterworks pumped 500 million gallons of water a day, or 139 gallons of water per person, while Berliners had to make do with 18 gallons. Flush toilets, a rarity in Berlin in 1900, could be found in 60 percent of Chicago's homes. Chicago's streets were lit by electricity, while Berlin still relied mostly on gaslight. Chicago had a much bigger streetcar system, more spacious parks, and a public library that contained many more volumes. And Chicago had just completed an amazing sanitation project that reversed the course of the Chicago River so that its waters—and the city's sewage—would flow away from Lake Michigan.

Giant sanitation projects were one thing; an inspiring urban environment was something else. For well-traveled Americans admiring of things European, the sense of inferiority was palpable. "We are enormously rich," admitted the journalist Edwin

L. Godkin, "but . . . what have we got to show? Almost nothing. Ugliness from an artistic point of view is the mark of all our cities." Thus, the urban balance sheet: a utilitarian infrastructure that was superb by nineteenth-century standards but "no municipal splendors of any description, nothing but population and hotels."

Upper Class/Middle Class

In the early republic, class distinctions had been embedded in the way men and women dressed and demonstrated by the deference they demanded from or granted others. As the industrial city grew, these marks of class weakened. In the anonymity of a big city, recognition and deference no longer served as mechanisms for conferring status. Instead, people began to rely on conspicuous display of wealth, membership in exclusive clubs, and, above all, residence in exclusive neighborhoods.

▶ Why can we say that technological innovation was just as significant in building American cities as it was in driving American industrialization?

▶ Why was the American city not capable of doing a better job of protecting the environment and providing adequate housing for the poor?

▶ If we count the degraded environment and poor housing as failures, why does Chicago come off so well in comparison to Berlin?

The Urban Elite

As early as the 1840s, Boston merchants had taken advantage of the new railway service to escape the congested city. Fine rural estates appeared in Milton, Newton, and other outlying towns. By 1848, roughly 20 percent of Boston's businessmen were making the trip downtown by train. Ferries that plied the harbor between Manhattan and Brooklyn served the same purpose for well-to-do New Yorkers.

As commercial development engulfed the downtown, the exodus by the elite quickened. In Cincinnati, wealthy families settled on the scenic hills rimming the crowded, humid tableland that ran down to the Ohio River. On those hillsides, a traveler noted in 1883, "The homes of Cincinnati's merchant princes and millionaires are found . . . elegant cottages, tasteful villas, and substantial mansions, surrounded by a paradise of grass, gardens, lawns, and tree-shaded roads." Residents of the area, called Hilltop, founded country clubs, downtown gentlemen's clubs, and a round of social activities for the pleasure of Cincinnati's elite.

Despite the attractions of country life, many of the very richest people preferred the heart of the city. Chicago boasted its Gold Coast; San Francisco, Nob Hill; and Denver, Quality Hill. New York novelist Edith Wharton recalled how the comfortable midcentury brownstones gave way to the "'new' millionaire houses," which spread northward on Fifth Avenue along Central Park. Great mansions, emulating the aristocratic houses of Europe, lined Fifth Avenue at the turn of the century.

But great wealth did not automatically confer social standing. An established elite dominated the social heights, even in such relatively raw cities as San Francisco and Denver. It had taken only a generation—sometimes less—for money made in commerce or real estate to shed its tarnish and become "old" and genteel. In long-settled

Boston, wealth passed intact through several generations, creating a closely knit tribe of "Brahmin" families that kept moneyed newcomers at bay. Elsewhere, urban elites tended to be more open, but only to the socially ambitious who were prepared to make visible and energetic use of their money.

In Theodore Dreiser's novel *The Titan* (1914), the tycoon Frank Cowperwood reassures his unhappy wife that if Chicago society will not accept them, "there are other cities. Money will arrange matters in New York—that I know. We can build a real place there, and go in on equal terms, if we have money enough." New York thus came to be a magnet for millionaires. The city attracted them not only as the nation's preeminent financial center but also for the opportunities it offered for display and social recognition.

This infusion of wealth shattered New York's older social elite. Seeking to be assimilated into the upper class, the flood of moneyed newcomers simply overwhelmed it. There followed a curious process of reconstruction, a deliberate effort to define the rules of conduct and identify those who properly "belonged" in New York society.

The key figure was Ward McAllister, a southern-born lawyer who had made a quick fortune in gold-rush San Francisco and then taken up a second career as the arbiter of New York society. In 1888, McAllister compiled the first *Social Register,* "comprising an accurate and careful list" of all those deemed eligible for New York society. McAllister instructed the socially ambitious on how to select guests, set a proper table, arrange a party, and launch a young lady into society. He presided over a round of assemblies, balls, and dinners that defined the boundaries of an elite society. At the apex stood "The Four Hundred"—the cream of New York society. McAllister's list corresponded to those invited to Mrs. William Astor's gala ball of February 1, 1892.

From Manhattan, an extravagant life radiated out to such favored resorts as Saratoga Springs, New York, and Palm Beach, Florida. In Rhode Island, Newport featured a grand array of summer "cottages," crowned by the Vanderbilts' Marble House and The Breakers. Visitors arrived via private railway car or aboard yachts and amused themselves at the races and gambling casinos. In New York City, the rich dined extravagantly at Delmonico's, on one famous occasion while mounted on horseback. The underside to this excess—scandalous affairs, rowdy feasts that ended in police court, the notoriously opulent costume ball thrown at the Waldorf-Astoria by the Bradley Martins at the peak of economic depression in 1897—was avidly followed in the press and awarded the celebrity we now accord to rock musicians and Hollywood stars.

Americans were adept at making money, complained the journalist Edwin L. Godkin in 1896, but they lacked the European aristocratic traditions for spending it: "Great wealth has not yet entered our manners." In their struggle to find the way, the moneyed elite made an indelible mark on urban life. If there was magnificence in the American city, that was mainly their handiwork. And if there was conspicuous waste and display, that too was their doing.

The Suburban World

The middle class left a smaller imprint on the city. Many of its members, unlike the rich, preferred privacy, retreating into a suburban world that insulated them from the hurly-burly of urban life.

Since colonial times, self-employed lawyers, doctors, merchants, and proprietors had been the backbone of a robust American middle class. While independent careers remained important, industrialism spawned a new middle class of salaried employees. Corporate organizations required managers, accountants, and clerks. Industrial technology called for engineers, chemists, and designers, while the distribution system needed salesmen, advertising executives, and store managers. These salaried ranks increased sevenfold between 1870 and 1910—much faster than any other occupational group. Nearly nine million people held white-collar jobs in 1910, more than one-fourth of all employed Americans.

Some members of this white-collar class lived in the row houses of Baltimore and Boston or the comfortable apartment buildings of New York City. More preferred to escape the clamor and congestion of the city. They were attracted by a persisting rural ideal, agreeing with the landscape architect Andrew Jackson Downing that "nature and domestic life are better than the society and manners of town." As trolley service pushed out from the city center, middle-class Americans followed the wealthy into the countryside. All sought what one Chicago developer promised for his North Shore subdivision in 1875: "qualities of which the city is in a large degree bereft, namely, its pure air, peacefulness, quietude, and natural scenery."

The geography of the suburbs was truly a map of class structure; where a family lived told where it ranked socially. As one proceeded out from the city center, the houses became finer, the lots larger, the inhabitants wealthier. Affluent businessmen and professionals had the time for a long commute into town. Closer in, lower-income households generally had more than one wage earner, less secure employment, and jobs requiring movement around the city. It was better for them to be closer to the city center because cross-town transportation lines afforded the commuting flexibility they needed.

Suburban boundaries shifted constantly as working-class city residents who wanted better lives moved to the cheapest suburbs, prompting an exodus of older residents, who in turn pushed the next higher group farther out in search of space and greenery. **Suburbanization** was the sum of countless individual decisions. Each family's move represented an advance in living standards—not only more light, air, and quiet but also better accommodation than the city afforded. Suburban houses were typically larger for the same money and equipped with flush toilets, hot water, central heating, and, by the turn of the century, electricity.

The suburbs also restored an opportunity that city-bound Americans thought they had lost. In the suburbs, home ownership again became the norm. "A man is not really a true man until he owns his own home," propounded the Reverend Russell H. Conwell in "Acres of Diamonds," his famous sermon on the virtues of moneymaking.

Rural America had fostered community life. Not so the suburbs. The grid street pattern, while efficient for laying out lots, offered no natural focus for community; nor did the shops and services that lay scattered along the trolley-car streets. Suburban development conformed to the economics of real estate and transportation, and so did the thinking of middle-class home seekers entering the suburbs. They wanted a house that gave them good value and convenience to the trolley line.

The need for community had lost some of its force for middle-class Americans. Two other attachments assumed greater importance: work and family.

Middle-Class Families

In the pre-industrial economy, work and family life were intertwined. Farmers, merchants, and artisans generally worked at home. The household encompassed not just blood relatives, but everyone living and working there. As industrialism progressed, family life and economic activity parted company. The father departed every morning for the office, and children spent more years in school. Clothing was bought ready-made; increasingly, food came in cans and packages. Middle-class families became smaller, excluding all but nuclear members, and consisting typically by 1900 of husband, wife, and three children.

Within this family circle, relationships became intense and affectionate. "Home was the most expressive experience in life," recalled the literary critic Henry Seidel Canby of his growing up in the 1890s. "Though the family might quarrel and nag, the home held them all, protecting them against the outside world." For such middle-class families, the quiet, tree-lined streets created a domestic space insulated from the harshness of commerce and enterprise.

The burdens of domesticity fell on the wife. It was nearly unheard of for her to seek an outside career — that was her husband's role. Her job was to manage the household. "The woman who could not make a home, like the man who could not support one,

Middle-Class Domesticity

For middle-class Americans, the home was a place of nurture, a refuge from the world of competitive commerce. Perhaps that explains why their residences were so heavily draped and cluttered with bric-a-brac. All of it emphasized privacy and pride of possession. Culver Pictures.

was condemned," Canby remembered. As the physical burdens of household work eased, higher-quality homemaking became the new ideal—a message propagated by Catherine Beecher's best-selling book *The American Woman's Home* (1869) and by such magazines as the *Ladies' Home Journal* and *Good Housekeeping,* which first appeared during the 1880s. This advice literature instructed wives that, in addition to their domestic duties, they had the responsibility for bringing sensibility, beauty, and love to the household. "We owe to women the charm and beauty of life," wrote one educator. "For the love that rests, strengthens and inspires, we look to women."

Womanly virtue, even if much glorified, by no means put wives on equal terms with their husbands. Although the legal status of married women—their right to own property, control separate earnings, make contracts, and get a divorce—improved markedly during the nineteenth century, law and custom still dictated that a wife be submissive to her husband. She relied on his ability as the breadwinner, and despite her superior virtues and graces, she was thought to be below him in vigor and intellect. Her mind could be employed "but little and in trivial matters," wrote one prominent physician, and her proper place was as "the companion or ornamental appendage to man." Middle-class women faced a painful family dilemma. They wanted fewer children but, other than abstinence, were often at a loss about what to do about it. Contraceptive devices, although heavily marketed, were either unreliable or, as in the case of condoms, stigmatized by association with prostitution. Many doctors disapproved of contraception, fearing that uncoupling sex from procreation would release the sexual appetites of men, to the detriment of their health.

On top of that, advocates of birth control had to contend with Anthony Comstock, secretary of the Society for the Suppression of Vice. In that capacity, he campaigned relentlessly to uplift the nation's morals. The vehicle that he chose was a federal law passed at his behest in 1873 prohibiting the sending of obscene materials through the U.S. mails. Comstock's definition of obscenity included any information about birth control or, for that matter, any open discussion of sex. So powerful was Comstock's influence that the suppression of vice became a national obsession during the 1870s.

It is this official writing that has given us the notion of a Victorian age of sexual repression. Letters and diaries suggest that in the privacy of their homes, husbands and wives acted otherwise. Yet they must have done so in constant fear of unwanted pregnancies. A fulfilling sexual relationship was not easily squared with birth control.

Not surprisingly, many bright, independent-minded women rebelled against marriage. More than 10 percent of women of marriageable age remained single, and the rate was much higher among college graduates and professionals. Only half the Mount Holyoke College class of 1902 married. "I know that something perhaps, humanly speaking, supremely precious has passed me by," remarked the writer Vida Scudder. "But how much it would have excluded!" Married life "looks to me often as I watch it terribly impoverished, for women."

If fewer women married, so, of course, did fewer men. We can, thanks to the census, trace the tardy progression into marriage of the male cohort born just after the Civil War: In 1890, when they were in their early thirties, two-fifths were unmarried; a decade later, in their early forties, a quarter still had not married; ultimately, a hard-core, over 10 percent, never married. One historian has labeled the late nineteenth century the Age of the Bachelor, a time when being an unattached male lost its social stigma. A bachelor's counterpart to Vida Scudder's dim view of marriage was this ditty that made the rounds in the early 1880s:

> No wife to scold me
> No children to squall
> God bless the happy man
> Who keeps bachelor's hall.

With its residential hotels, restaurants, and abundant personal services, the urban scene afforded bachelors all the comforts of home and, on top of that, a happy array of men's clubs, saloons, and sporting events.

The appeal of the manly life was not confined to confirmed bachelors. American males were supposed to be independent, which meant being one's own boss. But the salaried jobs they increasingly held left them distinctly not their own bosses. Nor, once employment was no longer centered in the household, could they exert the patriarchal hold over family life that had empowered their fathers and grandfathers. A palpable anxiety arose that the American male was becoming, as one magazine editor warned, "weak, effeminate, decaying." There was a telling shift in language. While people had once spoken of *manhood*, which meant leaving *childhood* behind, they now spoke of *masculinity*, the opposite of *femininity*: Being a man meant surmounting the feminizing influences of modern life.

How was this to be accomplished? By engaging in competitive sports such as football, which became hugely popular in this era. By working out and becoming fit because, as the psychologist G. Stanley Hall put it, "you can't have a firm will without firm muscles." By resorting to the great outdoors, engaging in Theodore Roosevelt's "strenuous life." Or vicariously, by reading books such as Owen Wister's best-selling cowboy novel, *The Virginian* (1902). The surging popularity of westerns and adventure novels was surely a marker of urban dwellers' fear that theirs was not a life for real men.

Women perhaps had it easier. Around 1890, the glimmerings of a sexual revolution appeared in the middle-class family. Experts abandoned the notion, put forth by one popular text, that "the majority of women (happily for society) are not very much troubled by sexual feeling of any kind." In succeeding editions of his book *Plain Home Talk on Love, Marriage, and Parentage,* the physician Edward Bliss Foote began to favor a healthy sexuality that gave pleasure to women as well as men.

During the 1890s, the artist Charles Dana Gibson created the image of the "new woman." In his drawings, the Gibson girl was tall, spirited, athletic, and chastely sexual. She rejected bustles, hoop skirts, and tightly laced corsets, preferring natural styles that did not disguise her female form. In the city, women's sphere began to take on a more public character. Among the new urban institutions that catered to women, the most important was the department store, which became a temple for women's emerging role as consumers.

The offspring of the middle class experienced their own revolution. In the past, children had been regarded as an economic asset — added hands for the family farm, shop, or countinghouse. For the urban middle class, this no longer held true. Parents stopped expecting their children to be productive members of the family. In the old days, Ralph Waldo Emerson remarked in 1880, "Children had been repressed and kept in the background; now they are considered, cosseted, and pampered." There was such a thing as "the juvenile mind," lectured Jacob Abbott in his book *Gentle Measures in the Management and Training of the Young* (1871). The family was responsible for providing a nurturing environment in which the young personality could grow and mature.

Preparation for adulthood became increasingly linked to formal education. School enrollment went up 150 percent between 1870 and 1900. As the years before adulthood began to stretch out, a new stage of life—adolescence—emerged. While rooted in longer years of family dependency, adolescence shifted much of the socializing role from parents to peer group.

Most affected were the daughters of the middle class, who, freed from the chores of housework, now devoted themselves to self-development, including going to high school for many. The liberating consequences surely went beyond their parents' expectations. In a revealing shift in terminology, "young lady" gave way to "school girl," and the daughterly submissiveness of earlier times gave way to self-expressive independence. On achieving adulthood, it was not so big a step for the daughters of the middle class to become Gibson's "new women."

▶ Why is Ward McAllister so significant a figure in the annals of the rich?

▶ Why did the suburbs become so prominent a feature of the late-nineteenth-century city?

▶ In the middle-class family of this era, how might the wife's position have been more stressful than that of her husband? Why?

City Life

With its soaring skyscrapers, jostling traffic, and hum of business, the city symbolized energy and enterprise. When the budding writer Hamlin Garland and his brother arrived in Chicago from Iowa in 1881, they knew immediately that they had entered a new world: "Everything interested us. . . . Nothing was commonplace, nothing was ugly." In one way or another, every city-bound migrant, whether fresh from the American countryside or an arrival from a foreign land, experienced something of this sense of wonder.

The city was utterly unlike the countryside, where every person had been known to his or her neighbors. Mark Twain found New York "a splendid desert, where a stranger is lonely in the midst of a million of his race. . . . Every man rushes, rushes, rushes, and never has time to be companionable [or] to fool away on matters which do not involve dollars and duty and business."

Migrants could never recreate in the city what they had left behind. But they found ways of belonging, they built new institutions, and they learned how to function in an impersonal, heterogeneous environment. An urban culture emerged, and through it, there developed a new breed of American entirely at home in the modern city.

Newcomers

The explosive growth of America's big-city population—a jump from about six million in 1880 to fourteen million in 1900—meant that cities were very much a world of newcomers. Many came from the nation's countryside; half of rural families on the

Mulberry Street, New York City, c. 1900
The influx of southern and eastern Europeans created teeming ghettos in the heart of New York City
and other major American cities. The view is of Mulberry Street, with its pushcarts, street peddlers,
and bustling traffic. The inhabitants are mostly Italians, and some of them, noticing the photographer
preparing his camera, have gathered to be in the picture. Library of Congress.
For more help analyzing this photo, see the Online Study Guide at **bedfordstmartins.com/henrettaconcise**.

move in these years were city bound. But it was migrants marked off by ethnicity who
found city life most daunting. At the turn of the century, upwards of 30 percent of the
residents of most big cities were foreign-born. The biggest ethnic group in Boston was
Irish; in Minneapolis, Swedish; in most other northern cities, German. But by 1910,
southern and eastern Europeans flooded in. Poles took the lead in Chicago; in New
York, it was eastern European Jews; in San Francisco, Italians.

The immigrants had little choice about where they lived; they needed to find cheap
housing near their jobs. Some gravitated to the outlying factory districts; others settled
in the congested downtown **ghettos.** In New York, Italians crowded into the Irish neighborhoods west of Broadway, while Russian and Polish Jews pushed the Germans out of
the Lower East Side (Map 18.1). A colony of Hungarians lived around Houston Street,
and Bohemians occupied the poorer stretches between Fiftieth and Seventy-sixth
Streets. Every city with a large immigrant population experienced this kind of ethnic

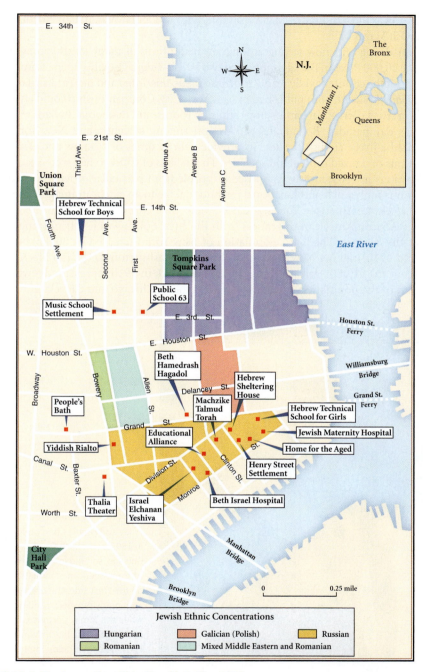

MAP 18.1 The Lower East Side, New York City, 1900

As this map shows, the Jewish immigrants dominating Manhattan's Lower East Side preferred living in neighborhoods populated by those from their home regions of eastern Europe. Their sense of a common identity made for a remarkable flowering of educational, cultural, and social institutions on the Jewish East Side.

For more help analyzing this map, see the Online Study Guide at **bedfordstmartins.com/henrettaconcise**.

sorting out, as did San Francisco, for example, with its Chinatown, Italian North Beach, and Jewish Hayes Valley.

Capitalizing on fellow feeling, immigrant institutions of many kinds sprang up. In 1911, the 20,000 Poles in Buffalo supported two Polish-language daily papers. Immigrants throughout the country avidly read *Il Progresso Italo-Americano* and the Yiddish-language *Jewish Daily Forward*, both published in New York City. Companionship could always be found on street corners, in barbershops and club rooms, and in saloons. Italians marched in saint's day parades, Bohemians gathered in singing societies, and New York Jews patronized a lively Yiddish theater. To provide help in times of sickness and death, the immigrants organized mutual-aid societies. The Italians of Chicago had sixty-six of these organizations in 1903, mostly composed of people from particular provinces or towns. Immigrants built a rich and functional institutional life to an extent unimagined in their native places (see American Voices, p. 539).

The African American migration from the rural South was just beginning at the turn of the century. The black population of New York increased by 30,000 between 1900 and 1910, making New York second only to Washington, D.C., as a black urban center, but the 91,000 African Americans in New York in 1910 represented fewer than 2 percent of the population, and that was also true of Chicago and Cleveland.

The Cherry Family Tree, 1906
Wiley and Fannie Cherry migrated in 1893 from North Carolina to Chicago, settling in the small African American community on the West Side. The Cherrys apparently prospered and by 1906, when this family portrait was taken, had entered the black middle class. When migration intensified after 1900, longer-settled urban blacks such as the Cherrys became uncomfortable with it, and relations with the needy rural newcomers were often tense. Courtesy, Lorraine Heflin/Chicago Historical Society.

Deserted Wives, Wayward Husbands ANONYMOUS

New York's leading Yiddish-language paper, the *Jewish Daily Forward*, carried a famous advice page entitled *Bintel Brief*, which in Yiddish means "bundle of letters." None were more heart-rending than those from abandoned wives, although, as the second letter shows, the husbands could be heard from as well. Nearly unknown in the Old Country, desertion became such a serious problem among Jewish immigrants that the *Daily Forward* ran a regular feature seeking information about wayward husbands.

[1908]
Worthy Editor

Have pity on me and my two small children and print my letter in the *Forward*.

Max! The children and I now say farewell to you. You left us in such a terrible state. You had no compassion for us. For six years I loved you faithfully, took care of you like a loyal servant, never had a happy day with you. Yet I forgive you for everything.

Have you ever asked yourself why you left us? Max, where is your conscience: you used to have sympathy for the forsaken women and used to say their terrible plight was due to the men who left them in dire need. And how did you act? I was a young, educated, decent girl when you took me. You lived with me for six years, during which time I bore you four children. And then you left me.

Of the four children, only two remain, but you have made them living orphans. Who will bring them up? Who will support us? Have you no pity for your own flesh and blood? Consider what you are doing. My tears choke me and I cannot write any more.

Be advised that in several days I am leaving with my two living orphans for Russia. We say farewell to you and beg you to take pity on us and send us enough to live on.

Your Deserted Wife and Children

[1910]
Dear Editor:

This is the voice of thirty-seven miserable men who are buried but not covered over by earth, tied down but not in chains, silent but not mute, whose hearts beat like humans, yet are not like other human beings. . . .

And why are we confined here? For the horrible crime of being poor, not being able to satisfy the mad whims of our wives. That's why we pine away here, stamped with the name "convict." That's why we are despised, robbed of our freedom, and treated like dogs. . . .

The non-support "plague" is the worst plague of all. For the merest nonsense, a man is caught and committed to the workhouse. He doesn't even get a chance to defend himself. Even during the worst times of the Russian reaction people didn't suffer as the men suffer here in America because of their wives. . . . In all the world there isn't such legal injustice as here in the alimony courts.

What do they think, these women! If they believe that the imprisoned husbands, after the six months, will become purified and come out good, sweet and loving, they're making a big mistake. . . .

I appeal to all the women whose husbands are imprisoned for non-support in the workhouse on Blackwell's Island Prison, and I write to them as follows: Their husbands have sworn here that if they, the women, do not have them released in time for *Pesach* [Passover], they will never again return and the women will remain grass widows forever.

SOURCE: Isaac Metzker, ed., *A Bintel Brief: Sixty Years of Letters from the Lower East Side* (New York: Schocken, 1971), 85–86, 110–112.

Urban blacks retreated from the scattered neighborhoods of older times into concentrated ghettos—Chicago's Black Belt on the South Side, for example, or the early outlines of New York's Harlem. Race prejudice cut down on job opportunities. Twenty-six percent of Cleveland's blacks had been skilled workers in 1870; only 12 percent were skilled by 1890. Entire occupations such as barbering (except for a black clientele) became exclusively white. Cleveland's blacks in 1910 worked mainly as domestics and day laborers, with little hope of moving up the job ladder.

In the face of pervasive discrimination, urban blacks built their own communities. They created a flourishing press; fraternal orders; a vast array of women's organizations; and a middle class of doctors, lawyers, and small entrepreneurs. Above all, there were the black churches—twenty-five in Chicago in 1905, mainly Methodist and Baptist. More than any other institution, remarked one scholar in 1913, it was the church "which the Negro may call his own. . . . A new church may be built . . . and . . . all the machinery set in motion without ever consulting any white person. . . . [Religion] more than anything else represents the real life of the race." As in the southern countryside, the church was the central institution for city blacks, and the preacher was the most important local citizen. Manhattan's Union Baptist Church, housed like many others in a storefront, attracted the "very recent residents of this new, disturbing city" and, ringing with spirituals and prayer, made Christianity come "alive Sunday mornings."

Ward Politics

Race and ethnicity divided newcomers. Politics, by contrast, integrated them into the wider urban society. Migrants to American cities automatically became ward residents and acquired a spokesman at city hall. Their alderman got streets paved, water mains extended, or permits granted—so that, for example, in 1888, Vito Fortounescere could "place and keep a stand for the sale of fruit, inside the stoop-line, in front of the northeast corner of Twenty-eighth Street and Fourth Avenue" in Manhattan, or the parishioners of Saint Maria of Mount Carmel could set off fireworks at their Fourth of July picnic.

These favors came via a system of boss control that, although present at every level of party politics, flourished most luxuriantly in the big cities. **Political machines** such as Tammany Hall in New York depended on a grassroots constituency, so they recruited layers of functionaries—precinct captains, ward bosses, aldermen—whose main job was to be accessible and, as best they could, serve the needs of the party faithful.

The machine acted as a rough-and-ready social service agency, providing jobs for the jobless, a helping hand for a bereaved family, and intercession with an unfeeling city bureaucracy. The Tammany ward boss George Washington Plunkitt had a "regular system" when fires broke out in his district. He arranged for housing for burned-out families, "fix[ing] them up till they get things runnin' again. It's philanthropy, but it's politics, too—mighty good politics."

The business community was similarly served. Contractors sought city business, gas companies and streetcar lines wanted licenses, manufacturers needed services and not-too-nosy inspectors, and the liquor trade and numbers rackets relied on a tolerant police force. All of them turned to the machine boss and his lieutenants.

Of course, the machine exacted a price for these services. The tenement dweller gave his vote. The businessman wrote a check. Naturally, some of the money that changed hands leaked into the pockets of machine politicians. This "boodle" could be blatantly corrupt—kickbacks by contractors; protection money from gamblers, saloonkeepers, and prostitutes; payoffs from gas and trolley companies. Boss William Marcy Tweed made *Tammany* a byword for corruption until he was brought down in 1871 by his extravagant graft in the building of a lavish city courthouse. Thereafter, machine corruption became less blatant. The turn-of-the-century Tammanyite George Plunkitt declared that he had no need for kickbacks and bribes. He favored what he called "honest graft," the easy profits that came to savvy insiders. Plunkitt made most of his money building wharves on Manhattan's waterfront. One way or another, legally or otherwise, machine politics rewarded its supporters.

Plunkitt was an Irishman, and so were most of the politicians who controlled Tammany Hall. But by the 1890s, Plunkitt's Fifteenth District was filling up with Italians and Russian Jews. In general, the Irish had no love for these newer immigrants, but Plunkitt played no favorites. On any given day (as recorded in his diary), he might attend an Italian funeral in the afternoon and a Jewish wedding in the evening, and at each, he probably paid his respects with a few Italian words or a choice bit of Yiddish.

In an era when so many forces acted to isolate ghetto communities, politics served an integrating function, cutting across ethnic lines and giving immigrants and blacks a stake in the larger urban order.

Religion in the City

For urban blacks, as we have seen, the church was a mainstay of their lives. So it was for many other city dwellers. But cities were hard on religious practice. All the great faiths—Judaism, Catholicism, and Protestantism—had to scramble to reconcile religious belief with the secular urban world.

About 250,000 Jews, mostly of German origin, already inhabited America when the eastern European Jews began arriving in the 1880s. Well-established and prosperous, the German Jews embraced Reform Judaism, abandoning religious practices—from keeping a kosher kitchen to conducting services in Hebrew—that were "not adapted to the views and habits of modern civilization." This was not the way of the Yiddish-speaking Jews from eastern Europe. Eager to preserve their traditions, they founded their own Orthodox synagogues, often in vacant stores, and practiced Judaism as they had at home.

Insular though it might be, ghetto life in the American city could not recreate the closed village environment on which strict religious observance depended. "The very clothes I wore and the very food I ate had a fatal effect on my religious habits," confessed the hero of Abraham Cahan's novel *The Rise of David Levinsky* (1917). "If you . . . attempt to bend your religion to the spirit of your surroundings, it breaks. It falls to pieces." Levinsky shaved off his beard and plunged into the Manhattan clothing business. Orthodox Judaism survived this shattering of faith but only by reducing its claims on the lives of the faithful.

Catholics faced much the same problem, defined as "Americanism" by the church. To what degree should congregants adapt to American society? Should children attend parochial or public schools? Should they marry non-Catholics? Should the education of clergy be changed? Bishop John Ireland of St. Paul, Minnesota, felt that "the principles of the Church are in harmony with the interests of the Republic." But traditionalists, led by Archbishop Michael A. Corrigan of New York, denied the possibility of such harmony and argued for insulating the church from the pluralistic American environment.

Immigrant Catholics, anxious to preserve what they had known in Europe, generally supported the church's conservative wing. But they also wanted church life to express their ethnic identities. Newly arrived Catholics wanted their own parishes, where they could celebrate their customs, speak their languages, and establish their own parochial schools. When they became numerous enough, they also demanded their own bishops. The Catholic hierarchy, which was dominated by Irish Catholics, felt that the integrity of the church itself was at stake. The demand for ethnic parishes implied local control of church property. And if there were bishops for specific ethnic groups, what would be the effect on the hierarchical structure that unified the church?

With some strain, the Catholic Church managed to satisfy the immigrant faithful. It met the demand for representation by appointing immigrant priests as auxiliary bishops within existing dioceses. Ethnic parishes also flourished. By World War I, there were more than 2,000 foreign-language churches.

For Protestants, the city posed different but not easier challenges. Every major city retained great downtown churches where wealthy Protestants worshipped. Some of these churches, richly endowed, took pride in nationally prominent pastors, such as Henry Ward Beecher of Plymouth Congregational Church in Brooklyn or Phillips Brooks of Trinity Episcopal Church in Boston. But the eminence of these churches, with their fashionable congregations and imposing edifices, could not disguise the growing remoteness of traditional Protestantism from its urban constituency. "Where is the city in which the Sabbath day is not losing ground?" lamented a minister in 1887. The families of businessmen, lawyers, and doctors could be seen in any church on Sunday morning, he noted, "but the workingmen and their families are not there."

The Protestant churches responded by evangelizing among the unchurched and the indifferent. They also began providing reading rooms, day nurseries, clubhouses, vocational classes, and other services. The Salvation Army, which arrived from Great Britain in 1879, spread the gospel of repentance among the urban poor, offering an assistance program that ranged from soup kitchens to shelters for former prostitutes. When all else failed, the down-and-outers of American cities knew they could count on the Salvation Army.

For single people, there were the Young Men's and Women's Christian Associations, which had arrived from Britain before the Civil War. Housing for single women was an especially important mission of the YWCAs. The gymnasiums that made the YMCAs synonymous with "muscular Christianity" were equally important for young men. No other organization so effectively combined activities for young people with an evangelizing appeal through Bible classes, nondenominational worship, and a religious atmosphere.

The social meaning that people sought in religion accounts for the enormous popularity of a book called *In His Steps* (1896). The author, a Congregational minister named Charles M. Sheldon, told the story of a congregation that resolved to live by

Christ's precepts for one year. "If the church members were all doing as Jesus would do," Sheldon asked, "could it remain true that armies of men would walk the streets for jobs, and hundreds of them curse the church, and thousands of them find in the saloon their best friend?"

The most potent form of urban evangelism—revivalism—said little about social uplift. From their eighteenth-century origins, revival movements had steadfastly focused on individual redemption. Earthly problems, revivalists believed, would be solved by converting to Christ. Beginning in the mid-1870s, revival meetings swept through the cities.

The pioneering figure was Dwight L. Moody, a former Chicago shoe salesman and YMCA official. After preaching in Britain for two years, Moody returned to America in 1875 and began staging revival meetings that drew thousands. He preached an optimistic, uncomplicated, nondenominational message. Eternal life could be had for the asking, Moody shouted as he held up his Bible. His listeners needed only "to come forward and take, TAKE!"

Many other preachers followed in Moody's path. The most colorful was Billy Sunday, a once hard-drinking former outfielder for the Chicago White Stockings baseball team who mended his ways and found religion. Like Moody and other city revivalists, Sunday was a farm boy. His ripsnorting attacks on fashionable ministers and the "booze traffic" carried the ring of rustic America. By realizing that many people remained villagers at heart, revivalists found a key for bringing city dwellers back to the church.

City Amusements

City people compartmentalized life's activities, setting the workplace apart from home and working time apart from free time. "Going out" became a necessity, demanded not only as solace for a hard day's work but also as proof that life was better in the New World than in the Old. "He who can enjoy and does not enjoy commits a sin," a Yiddish-language paper told its readers. And enjoyment now meant buying a ticket and being entertained (see Voices from Abroad, p. 544).

Music halls attracted huge audiences. Chicago had six **vaudeville** houses in 1896, twenty-two in 1910. Evolving from tawdry variety and minstrel shows, vaudeville cleaned up its routines, making them suitable for the entire family, and turned into professional entertainment handled by national booking agencies. With its standard program of nine musical, dancing, and comedy acts, vaudeville attained enormous popularity just as the movies arrived. The first primitive films, a minute or so of humor or glimpses of famous people, appeared in 1896 in penny arcades and as filler in vaudeville shows. Within a decade, millions of city people were watching films of increasing length and artistry at nickelodeons (named after the five-cent admission charge) across the country.

For young unmarried workers, the cheap amusements of the city created a new social space. "I want a good time," a New York clothing operator told an investigator. "And there is no . . . way a girl can get it on $8 a week. I guess if anyone wants to take me to a dance he won't have to ask me twice"—hence the widespread ritual among the urban working class of "treating." The girls spent what money they had dressing up;

Coney Island, 1881   JOSÉ MARTÍ

José Martí, a Cuban patriot and revolutionary (see p. 616), was a journalist by profession. In exile from 1880 to 1895, he spent most of his time in New York City, reporting to his Latin American readers on the customs of the Yankees. Martí took special—one might say perverse—pleasure in observing Americans at play.

From all parts of the United States, legions of intrepid ladies and Sunday-best farmers arrive to admire the splendid sights, the unexampled wealth, the dizzying variety, the herculean surge, the striking appearance of Coney Island, the now famous island, four years ago an abandoned sand bank, that today is a spacious amusement area providing relaxation and recreation for hundreds of thousands of New Yorkers who throng to its pleasant beaches every day. . . .

Other nations—ourselves among them—live devoured by a sublime demon within that drives us to the tireless pursuit of an ideal of love or glory. . . . Not so with these tranquil souls, stimulated only by a desire for gain. One scans those shimmering beaches . . . one views the throngs seated in comfortable chairs along the seashore, filling their lungs with the fresh, invigorating air. But it is said that those from our lands who remain here long are overcome with melancholy . . . because this great nation is void of spirit.

But what coming and going! What torrents of money! What facilities for every pleasure! What absolute absence of any outward sadness or poverty! Everything in the open air: the animated groups, the immense dining rooms, the peculiar courtship of North Americans, which is virtually devoid of the elements that compose the shy, tender, elevated love in our lands, the theatre, the photographers' booth, the bathhouses! Some weigh themselves, for North Americans are greatly elated, or really concerned, if they find they have gained or lost a pound. . . .

This spending, this uproar, these crowds, the activity of this amazing ant hill never slackens from June to October, from morning 'til night. . . . Then, like a monster that vomits its contents into the hungry maw of another monster, that colossal crowd, that straining, crushing mass, forces its way onto the trains, which speed across wastes, groaning under their burden, until they surrender it to the tremendous steamers, enlivened by the sound of harps and violins, convey it to the piers, and debouch the weary merrymakers into the thousand trolleys that pursue the thousand tracks that spread through slumbering New York like veins of steel.

SOURCE: Juan de Onís, trans., *The America of José Martí: Selected Writings* (New York: Noonday Press, 1954), 103–110.

their boyfriends paid for the fun. Parental control over courtship broke down, and amid the bright lights and lively music of the dance hall and amusement park, working-class youths forged a more easygoing culture of pleasure-seeking.

The geography of the big city carved out ample space for commercialized sex. Prostitution was not new to urban life, but in the late nineteenth century, it became

The Bowery at Night, 1895
The Bowery (a name dating back to the original Dutch settlement) was a major thoroughfare in downtown Manhattan. This painting by W. Louis Sonntag, Jr. shows the street in all its glory, crowded with shoppers and pleasure seekers. It was during this time that the Bowery gained its raffish reputation. Museum of the City of New York.

more open and more intermingled with other forms of public entertainment. Opium and cocaine were widely available and not yet illegal. In New York, the red-light district was the Tenderloin, running northward from Twenty-third Street between Fifth and Eighth Avenues.

The Tenderloin and the Bowery, farther downtown, were also the sites of a robust gay subculture. The long-held notion that homosexual life was covert, in the closet, in late-nineteenth-century America appears not to be true, at least not in the country's premier city. In certain corners of the city, a gay world flourished, with a full array of saloons, meeting places, and drag balls, which were widely known and patronized by uptown "slummers."

Of all forms of (mostly) male diversion, none was more specific to the city, or so spectacularly successful, as professional baseball. The game's promoters decreed that baseball had been created in 1839 by Abner Doubleday in the village of Cooperstown, New York. Actually, baseball was neither of American origin—stick-and-ball games go far back into the Middle Ages—nor particularly a product of rural life. Under a variety of names, team sports resembling baseball proliferated in early-nineteenth-century America. In an effort to regularize the game, the New Yorker Alexander Cartwright codified the rules in 1845, only to see his Knickerbockers defeated the next year at

Hoboken by the New York Baseball Club in what is regarded as the first modern baseball game. Over the next twenty years, baseball clubs appeared across the country, and intercity competition developed on a scheduled basis. In 1868, the sport became openly professional, following the lead of the Cincinnati Red Stockings in signing players to contracts for the season.

Big-time baseball came into its own with the launching of the National League in 1876. The team owners were profit-minded businessmen who shaped the sport to please the fans. Wooden grandstands gave way to the concrete and steel stadiums of the early twentieth century, such as Fenway Park in Boston, Forbes Field in Pittsburgh, and Shibe Park in Philadelphia. For the urban multitudes, baseball grew into something more than an afternoon at the ballpark. By rooting for the home team, fans found a way of identifying with their city. Amid the diversity and anonymity of urban life, the common experience and language of baseball acted as a bridge among strangers.

Most efficient at this task, however, was the newspaper. James Gordon Bennett, founder of the *New York Herald* in 1835, wanted "to record the facts . . . for the great masses of the community." The news was whatever interested city readers, starting with crime, scandal, and sensational events. After the Civil War, the *New York Sun* added the human-interest story, which made news of ordinary happenings. Newspapers also targeted specific audiences. A women's page offered recipes and fashion news, separate sections covered sports and high society, and the Sunday supplement helped fill the weekend hours. In the competition for readers, the champion newsman was Joseph Pulitzer, the owner of the *St. Louis Post-Dispatch* and, after 1883, the *New York World* (Table 18.2).

Pulitzer was in turn challenged by William Randolph Hearst. Hearst was an unlikely press magnate, the pampered son of a California silver king who, while at Harvard (on the way to being expelled), got interested in Pulitzer's newspaper game. He took over his father's dull *San Francisco Examiner* and rebuilt it into a highly profitable, sensationalist paper. For example, were any grizzly bears left in California? Hearst dispatched a newsman to the Tehachapi Mountains, where, after three months of arduous trapping, he caught a grizzly. The *Examiner* reported all this in exhaustive detail, ending triumphantly with the carnival display of the unfortunate beast. There was much more of the same: rescues, murders, scandals, sob stories, anything that might arouse in readers what an editor called "the gee-whiz emotion." Hearst's brand of sensationalism was dubbed **yellow journalism,** after *The Yellow Kid* (1895), the first comic strip to appear in color.

TABLE 18.2	Newspaper Circulation
Year	**Total Circulation**
1870	2,602,000
1880	3,566,000
1890	8,387,000
1900	15,102,000
1909	24,212,000

SOURCE: *Historical Statistics of the United States*, 2 vols. (Washington, DC: U.S. Bureau of the Census, 1975), 2: 810.

"He who is without a newspaper," said the great showman P. T. Barnum, "is cut off from his species." Barnum was speaking of city people and their hunger for information. Hearst understood this. That's why he made barrels of money.

The Higher Culture

In the midst of this popular ferment, new institutions of higher culture were taking shape in America's cities. A desire for the cultivated life was not, of course, specifically urban. Before the Civil War, the lyceum movement had sent lecturers to the remotest towns, bearing messages of culture and learning. Chautauqua, founded in upstate New York in 1874, carried on this work of cultural dissemination. However, great museums, public libraries, opera companies, and symphony orchestras could flourish only in metropolitan centers.

The nation's first major art museum, the Corcoran Gallery of Art, opened in Washington, D.C., in 1869. New York's Metropolitan Museum of Art started in rented quarters two years later, then moved in 1880 to its permanent site in Central Park and launched an ambitious program of art acquisition. When financier J. Pierpont Morgan became chairman of the board in 1905, the Metropolitan's preeminence was assured. The Boston Museum of Fine Arts was founded in 1876 and Chicago's Art Institute in 1879.

Symphony orchestras also appeared, first in New York under the conductors Theodore Thomas and Leopold Damrosch in the 1870s and then in Boston and Chicago during the next decade. National tours by these leading orchestras planted the seeds for orchestral societies in many other cities. Public libraries grew from modest collections (in 1870, only seven had as many as 50,000 books) into major urban institutions. The greatest library benefactor was Andrew Carnegie, who announced in 1881 that he would build a library in any town or city that was prepared to maintain it. By 1907, Carnegie had spent more than $32.7 million to establish about 1,000 libraries throughout the country.

The late nineteenth century was the great age not only of money making, but also of money giving. Generous with their surplus wealth, new millionaires patronized the arts partly as a civic duty, partly to promote themselves socially, but also out of a sense of national pride.

"In America there is no culture," pronounced the English critic G. Lowes Dickinson in 1909. Science and the practical arts, yes—"every possible application of life to purposes and ends"—but "no life for life's sake." Such condescending remarks received a respectful American hearing out of a sense of cultural inferiority to the Old World. In 1873, Mark Twain and Charles Dudley Warner published a novel, *The Gilded Age*, that satirized America as a land of money-grubbers and speculators. This enormously popular book touched a nerve in the American psyche. Its title has since been appropriated by historians to characterize the late nineteenth century—America's "Gilded Age"—as an era of materialism and cultural shallowness.

Some members of the upper class, such as the novelist Henry James, moved to Europe. But the more common response was to try to raise the nation's cultural level. The newly rich had a hard time of it. They did not have much opportunity to cultivate a taste for art, but they were quick learners. George W. Vanderbilt, grandson of the rough-hewn Cornelius Vanderbilt, championed French Impressionism, and the coal and steel baron Henry Clay Frick built a brilliant art collection that is still housed as a public museum in his mansion in New York City. The enthusiasm of moneyed Americans largely fueled the great cultural institutions that sprang up during the Gilded Age.

A deeply conservative idea of culture sustained this generous patronage. The aim was to embellish life, not to probe or reveal its meaning. "Art," says the hero of the Reverend Henry Ward Beecher's sentimental novel *Norwood* (1867), "attempts to work out its end solely by the use of the beautiful, and the artist is to select out only such things as are beautiful." The idea of culture also took on an elitist cast: Shakespeare, once a staple of popular entertainment (in various bowdlerized versions), was appropriated into the domain of "serious" theater. Simultaneously, the world of culture became feminized. "Husbands or sons rarely share those interests," noted one observer. In American life, remarked the clergyman Horace Bushnell, men represented the "force principle," women the "beauty principle."

The depiction of life, the eminent editor and novelist William Dean Howells wrote, "must be tinged with sufficient idealism to make it all of a truly uplifting character. . . . The finer side of things — the idealistic — is the answer for us." The "genteel tradition," as this literary school came to be known, dominated the nation's purveyors of elite culture — its journals, publishers, and college professors — from the 1860s onward.

But the urban world could not finally be kept at bay. Howells himself resigned in 1881 from the *Atlantic Monthly*, a stronghold of the genteel tradition, and called for a literature that sought "to picture the daily life in the most exact terms possible." In a series of realistic novels — *A Modern Instance* (1882), *The Rise of Silas Lapham* (1885), and *A Hazard of New Fortunes* (1890) — Howells captured the urban middle class. Stephen Crane's *Maggie: Girl of the Streets* (1893), privately printed because no publisher would touch it, unflinchingly described the destruction of a slum girl.

The city had entered the American imagination and become, by the early 1900s, a main theme of American art and literature. And because it challenged so many assumptions of an older, republican America, the city also became an overriding concern of reformers and, after the turn of the century, the main theater in the drama of the Progressive era.

▶ In both politics and religion, established institutions had to find ways of incorporating a flood of newcomers to the city. But the politicians seemed to have an easier time of it. Why?

▶ American cities housed a great many people struggling to get by. Yet they always seemed ready to dig into their pockets for a newspaper or a ticket to the ball game. Why?

▶ Why do we date the arrival of institutions of higher culture with the rise of the industrial city?

SUMMARY

In this chapter, we explored the emergence of a distinctively urban American society. The chapter was concerned, first of all, with how the great nineteenth-century cities came to be built. Urban growth was driven by industrialization — by the geographic concentration of industries, by the increasing scale of production, and by industry's need for city-based financial and administrative services. A burst of innovation brought forth mass transit, skyscrapers, electricity, and much else that made the big city livable. Although not constrained constitutionally, the public sector left city building as much as possible to private initiative and private capital. The result was dramatic growth, with an infrastructure superior to Europe's, but at the price of a degraded environment and squalid living conditions for the poor.

The second concern of this chapter was with an urban class structure defined most visibly by geography. The poor inhabited the inner cities and factory districts, the middle class spread out into the suburbs, and the rich lived insulated in fancy neighborhoods or beyond the suburbs. For the wealthy, an elite society emerged, with an opulent lifestyle and exclusive social organizations. The middle class withdrew into the private world of the family. Intersecting with family were issues of gender identity, with white-collar husbands embracing a cult of masculinity and wives emboldened by the liberating prospects of the "new woman."

Finally, this chapter described the components of a distinctive urban culture. City life was strongly flavored by the ways in which newcomers—European immigrants, southern blacks, small-town whites—adapted to an alien urban environment. In politics and religion, we saw most vividly how American institutions adapted to the newcomers. City life was also distinguished by an explosion of leisure activities, ranging from vaudeville to the yellow press and, at a more elevated level, by the institutions of art, music, and literature that sustain a nation's higher culture.

Connections: Society

Cities always played a disproportionate part in the nation's economic, political, and cultural life. But only in the late nineteenth century, as the United States became an industrial power, did the rural/urban balance shift and the cities develop a distinctly urban culture. The consequences of that development loom large in the battle for reform during the Progressive era (Chapter 20) and in the cultural conflict in the 1920s (Chapter 23). In succeeding decades, we can still distinguish what is distinctively urban in American development, but in truth, urban history and American history increasingly merge as the United States becomes in our own time a nation of urban and suburban dwellers, with farmers the merest fraction of America's population.

FOR FURTHER EXPLORATION

The starting points for modern urban historiography are Sam Bass Warner's pioneering book on Boston, *Streetcar Suburbs, 1870–1900* (1962), and a subsequent work, *The Private City: Philadelphia in Three Periods* (1968), that shows how private decision making shaped the American city. Innovations in urban construction are treated in Carl Condit, *Rise of the New York Skyscraper, 1865–1913* (1996), and Harold L. Platt, *The Electric City: Energy and the Growth of the Chicago Area, 1880–1930* (1991). Aspects of middle-class life are revealed in Howard B. Chudacoff, *The Age of the Bachelor* (1999); Jane Hunter, *How Young Ladies Became Girls: The Victorian Origins of American Girlhood* (2003); Michael Ebner, *Chicago's North Shore: A Suburban History* (1988); and John F. Kasson, *Rudeness and Civility: Manners in Nineteenth-Century America* (1990). On urban life, see especially Gunther Barth, *City People: The Rise of*

TIMELINE

1869 ► Corcoran Gallery of Art, nation's first major art museum, opens in Washington, D.C.

1871 ► Chicago fire

1873 ► Mark Twain and Charles Dudley Warner publish *The Gilded Age*

1875 ► Dwight L. Moody launches urban revivalist movement

1876 ► Alexander Graham Bell patents telephone

► National Baseball League founded

1879 ► Thomas Edison creates practical incandescent light bulb

► Salvation Army, originally formed in Britain, is established in the United States

1881 ► Andrew Carnegie offers to build a library for every American city

1883 ► New York City's Metropolitan Opera founded

► Joseph Pulitzer purchases *New York World*

1885 ► William Jenney builds first steel-framed structure, Chicago's Home Insurance Building

1887 ► First electric trolley line constructed in Richmond, Virginia

1893 ► Chicago World's Fair

► "City Beautiful" movement

1895 ► William Randolph Hearst enters New York journalism

1897 ► Boston builds first American subway

1900 ► Theodore Dreiser publishes *Sister Carrie*

1901 ► New York Tenement House Law

1904 ► New York subway system opens

1906 ► San Francisco earthquake

1913 ► Fifty-five-story Woolworth Building opens in New York City

Modern City Culture (1982); David Block, *Baseball Before We Knew It* (2004); John F. Kasson, *Amusing the Million: Coney Island at the Turn of the Century* (1978); and Kathy Peiss, *Cheap Amusements: Working Women and Leisure in Turn-of-the-Century New York* (1986). The best introduction to Gilded Age intellectual currents is Alan Trachtenberg, *The Incorporation of America: Culture and Society, 1865–1893* (1983). On the Columbian Exposition of 1893, an excellent Web site is "The World's Columbian Exposition: Idea, Experience, Aftermath" at **xroads.virginia.edu/~ma96/WCE/title.html**, including detailed guides to every site at the fair and analysis of its lasting impact.

TEST YOUR KNOWLEDGE

To assess your mastery of the material in this chapter and for Web sites, images, and documents related to this chapter, visit **bedfordstmartins.com/henrettaconcise**.

Politics in the Age of Enterprise
1877–1896

Politics has now become
a gainful profession, like
advocacy, stockbroking,
[or] the dry goods
trade. . . . People go into
it to make a living.

— James Bryce, *American
Commonwealth*, 1888

Ever since the founding of the republic, foreign visitors had been coming to America to observe the political goings-on of a democratic society. The most celebrated of these foreigners was the French aristocrat Alexis de Tocqueville, the author of *Democracy in America* (1832). Fifty years later, an equally distinguished visitor, the Englishman James Bryce, decided that Tocqueville's great book could not be his model, because Tocqueville saw America as "primarily a democracy, the ideal democracy, fraught with lessons for Europe." In his own book, *The American Commonwealth* (1888), Bryce was much less rhapsodic. The robust democracy hailed by Tocqueville had descended into the barren politics of post–Civil War America.

Bryce was anxious, however, not to be misunderstood. Europeans would find in his book "much that is sordid, much that will provoke unfavorable comment." But they needed to be aware of "a reserve of force and patriotism more than sufficient to sweep away all the evils now tolerated, and to make a politics of the country worthy of its material grandeur and of the private virtues of its inhabitants." Bryce was ultimately an optimist: "A hundred times in writing this book have I been disheartened by the facts I was stating; a hundred times has the recollection of the abounding strength and vitality of the nation chased away these tremors."

What was it that Bryce found so disheartening in the practice of American politics? That is this chapter's first subject. The second is the underlying vitality that Bryce sensed and how it reemerged and reinvigorated the nation's politics by the century's end.

Bandanna, 1888 Election
During the late nineteenth century, politics was a vibrant part of America's culture. Party paraphernalia, such as this colorful bandanna depicting the Democratic presidential nominee Grover Cleveland and his running mate, A. G. Thurman, flooded the country. Collection of Janice L. and David J. Frent.

The Politics of the Status Quo, 1877–1893

In times of national ferment, public life becomes magnified. Leaders emerge. Great issues are debated. The powers of government expand. All this had been true of the Civil War and Reconstruction eras, when the nation's political structure had been severely tested, not least by the contested presidential election of 1876. In 1877, with Rutherford B. Hayes safely settled in the White House, the era of sectional strife finally ended.

Political life went on, but it was drained of its drama. The 1880s heralded no Lincolns, no great national debates. Although Union defenders had envisioned a society reshaped by an activist state, now, in the 1880s, political leaders retreated to a more modest conception of national power. An irreducible core of public functions remained, and there was even, as with railroad regulation, grudging acceptance of new federal responsibilities. But the dominant rhetoric celebrated that government which governed least, and as compared to the Civil War and Reconstruction eras, American government did govern less.

The Washington Scene

There were five presidents from 1877 to 1893: Rutherford B. Hayes (Republican, 1877–1881), James A. Garfield (Republican, 1881), Chester A. Arthur (Republican, 1881–1885), Grover Cleveland (Democrat, 1885–1889), and Benjamin Harrison

(Republican, 1889–1893). All were estimable men. Hayes had served effectively as governor of Ohio for three terms, and Garfield had done well as a congressional leader. Arthur, despite his reputation as a hack politician, had shown fine administrative skills as head of the New York customs house. Cleveland enjoyed an enviable reputation as reform mayor of Buffalo and governor of New York. None was a charismatic leader, but circumstances, more than personal qualities, explain why these presidents did not make a larger mark on history.

The president's most demanding task was dispensing **patronage** to the faithful. Under the **spoils system,** government jobs rewarded those who had served the victorious party. In 1881, shortly after taking office, President Garfield was shot and killed. The motives of his assassin, Charles Guiteau, were murky, but civil service reformers blamed a spoils system that left many people disappointed in the scramble for office. The resulting Pendleton Act (1883) established a nonpartisan Civil Service Commission authorized to fill federal jobs by examination. The original list covered only 10 percent of the jobs, however, and the White House still staggered (as Cleveland grumbled) under the "damned, everlasting clatter for office." Executive duties were, in any event, modest. The White House staff consisted of a half dozen assistants plus a few clerks, doorkeepers, and messengers. Budgetary matters were not the president's province but Congress's; federal agencies accordingly paid more heed to the money-dispensing committees on Capitol Hill than to the White House. Of the 100,000 federal employees in 1880, 56 percent worked for the Post Office. Even the important cabinet offices—Treasury, State, War, Navy, and Interior—were sleepy places carrying on largely routine duties. Virtually all federal funding came from customs duties and excise taxes on liquor and tobacco, which produced more money than the government spent.

On matters of national policy, the presidents took a back seat to Congress. This was partly because—unlike the situation in Lincoln's day—they took a modest view of their powers. On the congressional side, party leaders such as Roscoe Conkling, Republican senator from New York, considered themselves the president's equals. Conkling did not hesitate to take on Rutherford B. Hayes over the latter's lenient policy toward the South—hence the name of Conkling's faction, the Stalwarts. James G. Blaine, Conkling's rival and successor as Senate boss—Blaine's faction called itself the Half-Breeds—was equally imperious in dealing with Chester Arthur's administration.

This was the era, in Woodrow Wilson's scathing words, of "congressional government." But Congress was itself ineffective, bogged down by arcane procedures and unruly factions. Nor did either party have a strong agenda. Historically, the Democrats favored states' rights, while the Republicans inherited the Whig enthusiasm for strong government. After Reconstruction, however, the Republicans backed away from state interventionism, and party differences became muddy. On most leading issues of the day—civil service reform, the currency, regulation of the railroads—divisions occurred within the parties, not between them.

Only the **tariff** remained a fighting issue. It was an article of Republican faith, as President Harrison said in 1892, that "the protective system . . . has been a mighty instrument for the development of the national wealth." The tariff was a genuine issue, with real economic consequences, and it stirred strong partisan feelings on both sides. Yet, in practice, the tariff was a negotiable issue like any other. Congressmen voted their constituents' interests regardless of party rhetoric. As a result, tariff bills were generally a patchwork of bargains among special interests.

Late in the decade, after a string of inconclusive revisions, the tariff debate suddenly heated up. An ardent free trader, Cleveland cast off his reluctance and campaigned in 1888 on a platform of thoroughgoing tariff reduction. His narrow defeat emboldened the Republicans, who in 1890 pushed through the McKinley tariff (named for its author, William McKinley), raising average rates to a record 49.5 percent. The issue was by no means laid to rest, however. The McKinley tariff, coinciding with a surge of economic troubles in the country, proved unpopular and threw the Republicans on the defensive as the 1892 elections approached.

Taking a stand on big issues such as the tariff was risky because the parties were so evenly balanced. By the end of Reconstruction, with the South solidly on their side, the Democrats stood on equal terms with the Republicans. Every presidential election from 1876 to 1892 was decided by a thin margin (Map 19.1), and control of Congress regularly changed hands. Under these circumstances, when any false move might tip the scales, caution seemed the best policy.

That did not stop Republican orators from "waving the bloody shirt" against the Democrats. The tactic was not wholly cynical. In various ways, Civil War issues persisted. Pensions for disabled veterans was a perennial question, favored by Republicans as a matter of honor, resisted by Democrats as extravagant and fraud-ridden. In his first term, President Cleveland routinely vetoed pension bills. Cleveland's electoral success—he was the first Democrat in the White House since the 1850s—only hardened the Republican grip on its Civil War legacy. Yet when it came to Reconstruction's real unfinished business—the fate of ex-slaves—the Republicans backed away, never fulfilling their pledge to provide federal funding to combat illiteracy or protect black voters. Nor was there denying the demagogic uses of "waving the bloody shirt" during elections. James Bryce had grounds for criticizing the Republicans for "clinging too long to outworn issues and neglecting the problems . . . which now perplex the country."

Alternatively, campaigns could descend into comedy. In the hard-fought election of 1884, for example, the Democrat Cleveland burst on the scene as a reformer, fresh from his victories over corrupt politicians in New York State. But years earlier, Cleveland, a bachelor, had fathered an illegitimate child, and throughout the campaign, he was dogged by the ditty "Maw, Maw, where's my Paw?" (After his victory, Cleveland's supporters gleefully responded, "He's in the White House, haw-haw-haw.") Cleveland's opponent, James G. Blaine, already on the defensive for his ties to the railroads, was weakened by the unthinking charge of a too ardent Republican clergyman that the Democrats were the party of "Rum, Romanism and Rebellion." In a twinkling, he had insulted Catholic voters and, so some believed, lost the election for Blaine. In the midst of all the mudslinging, the issues got lost.

The triviality of public life in the 1880s derived ultimately from the underlying conviction that little was at stake. Governmental activity was itself considered a bad thing. All the state could do, said Senator Conkling, was "to clear the way of impediments and dangers, and leave every class and every individual free and safe in the exertions and pursuits of life." Conkling was expressing the political corollary to the economic doctrine of **laissez-faire**—the belief, already well-rooted in the Jeffersonian politics of the antebellum era—that the less government interfered, the better.

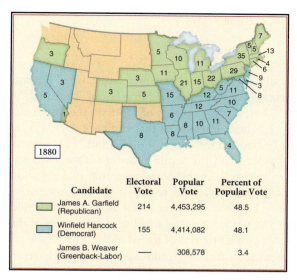

1880

Candidate	Electoral Vote	Popular Vote	Percent of Popular Vote
James A. Garfield (Republican)	214	4,453,295	48.5
Winfield Hancock (Democrat)	155	4,414,082	48.1
James B. Weaver (Greenback-Labor)	—	308,578	3.4

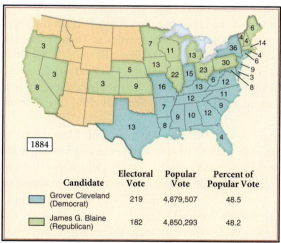

1884

Candidate	Electoral Vote	Popular Vote	Percent of Popular Vote
Grover Cleveland (Democrat)	219	4,879,507	48.5
James G. Blaine (Republican)	182	4,850,293	48.2

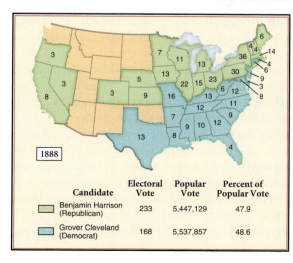

1888

Candidate	Electoral Vote	Popular Vote	Percent of Popular Vote
Benjamin Harrison (Republican)	233	5,447,129	47.9
Grover Cleveland (Democrat)	168	5,537,857	48.6

MAP 19.1 Presidential Elections of 1880, 1884, and 1888

The anatomy of political stalemate is evident in this trio of electoral maps of the 1880s. First, note the equal division of the popular vote between Republicans and Democrats. Second, note the remarkable persistence in the pattern of electoral votes, in which states went overwhelmingly to the same party in all three elections. Finally, we can identify who determined the outcomes: the two "swing" states, New York and Indiana, whose vote shifted every four years, always in favor of the winning candidate.

The Ideology of Individualism

At the peak of the labor troubles of the 1880s, the cotton manufacturer Edward Atkinson gave a talk to the textile workers of Providence, Rhode Island. They had, he told them, no cause for discontent. "There is always plenty of room on the front seats in every profession, every trade. . . . There are men in this audience who will fill some of those seats, but they won't be boosted into them from behind." (There were certainly women in the audience—at least half the textile industry's labor force was female—but, as was the norm for the times, Atkinson assumed that making good mattered only to men.) Atkinson's homely talk went to the roots of conservative American thought: Any man, however humble, could rise as far as his talents would carry him; every person received his just reward, great or small; and the success of the individual, so encouraged, contributed to the progress of the whole.

How persuasive the workers listening to Atkinson found his message, we have no way of knowing. But the confidence with which he presented his case is evidence of the continuing appeal of the **ideology** of individualism in the age of enterprise.

A flood of popular writings trumpeted the creed of individualism, from the rags-to-riches tales of Horatio Alger to success manuals with such titles as *Thoughts for the Young Men of America, or a Few Practical Words of Advice to Those Born in Poverty and Destined to be Reared in Orphanages* (1871). Self-made men such as Andrew Carnegie became cultural heroes. A best seller was Carnegie's *Triumphant Democracy* (1886), which paid homage to a country that enabled a penniless Scottish child to rise from bobbin boy to steel magnate.

From the pulpit, the Episcopal bishop William Lawrence of Massachusetts preached that "godliness is in league with riches." Bishop Lawrence was voicing a familiar theme of American Protestantism: Success in one's earthly calling revealed the promise of eternal salvation. It was all too easy for a conservative ministry to bless the furious acquisitiveness of industrial America. "To secure wealth is an honorable ambition," intoned the Baptist minister Russell H. Conwell.

The celebration of individualism was underscored by social theorizing drawn from the science of biology. Evolution itself—the idea that species are not fixed but ever-changing—went back to the early nineteenth century but lacked any explanatory theory. This was what the British naturalist Charles Darwin provided in *On the Origin of Species* (1859), with his concept of natural selection. In nature, Darwin wrote, all creatures struggle to survive. Individual members of a species are born with random genetic mutations that better fit them for their particular environment—camouflage coloring for a bird or butterfly, for example. These survival characteristics, since they are genetically transmissible, become dominant in future generations, and the species evolves.

Darwin himself disapproved of the term *evolution* (the word does not appear in his book) because it implied an upward progression. In his view, natural selection was blind—there was no intelligent design behind it. Because environments changed randomly, so did the adaptation of species. But Darwin had given evolution the stamp of scientific legitimacy, and other people, less scrupulous than he about drawing larger conclusions, moved confidently to apply evolution to social development.

Foremost was the British philosopher Herbert Spencer, who spun out an elaborate analysis of how human society had advanced through competition and "survival of the fittest." **Social Darwinism,** as Spencer's ideas became known, was championed in America by William Graham Sumner, a sociology professor at Yale. Competition, said Sumner, is a law of nature that "can no more be done away with than gravitation." And who are the fittest? "The millionaires. . . . They may fairly be regarded as the naturally selected agents of society. They get high wages and live in luxury, but the bargain is a good one for society."

Social Darwinists rejected any interference with social processes. "The great stream of time and earthly things will sweep on just the same in spite of us," Sumner wrote in a famous essay, "The Absurd Attempt to Make the World Over" (1894). As for the government, it had "at bottom . . . two chief things . . . with which to deal. They are the property of men and the honor of women. These it has to defend against crime." Beyond that, government should leave people alone.

The Supremacy of the Courts

Suspicion of government not only paralyzed politics; it also shifted power away from the executive and legislative branches. "The task of constitutional government," declared Sumner, "is to devise institutions which shall come into play at critical periods to prevent the abusive control of the powers of a state by the controlling classes in it." Sumner meant the judiciary. From the 1870s onward, the courts increasingly accepted the role that he assigned to them: defending the rights of private property against the tentacles of government.

The main target of the courts was not Washington, but the states. This was because under the federal system, the **residual powers**—those not delegated by the Constitution to the federal government—left the states with primary authority over social welfare and economic regulation. The great question was how to balance the states' police powers to defend the general welfare against the liberty of individuals to pursue their private interests. Most states, caught up in the conservative ethos of the day, were cutting back on expenditures and public services. Even so, there were more than enough state initiatives to alarm vigilant judges. Thus, in the landmark case *In re Jacobs* (1885), the New York State Court of Appeals struck down a law that prohibited cigar manufacturing in tenements on the grounds that such regulation exceeded the police powers of the state.

As the federal courts took up the battle against state activism, they found their strongest weapon in the Fourteenth Amendment (1868), the Reconstruction amendment that prohibited the states from depriving "any person of life, liberty, or property, without due process of law." The due process clause had been introduced to protect the civil rights of the former slaves. But due process protected the property rights and liberty of any "person," and legally, corporations counted as persons. So interpreted, the Fourteenth Amendment became by the turn of the century a powerful restraint on the power of the states to regulate private business.

The Supreme Court similarly hamstrung the federal government. In 1895, the Court ruled that the federal power to regulate interstate commerce did not cover manufacturing and struck down a federal income tax law. And in areas where federal power was undeniable—such as the regulation of railroads—the Supreme Court scrutinized every measure for undue interference with the rights of property.

The preeminent jurist of the day, Stephen J. Field, made no bones about the dangers he saw in the nation's headlong industrial development. "As the inequalities in the conditions of men become more and more marked and . . . angry menaces against order find vent in loud denunciations—it becomes more and more the imperative duty of the court to enforce with a firm hand every guarantee of the Constitution."

▶ A novel published in 1880 speaks derisively of American democracy as being "of the people, by the people, for the benefit of Senators." What was there about the political scene that would have prompted the author to say that?

▶ Why was Darwin's *On the Origin of Species*, which was strictly about biology, important in the development of the ideology of conservatism?

▶ How do you explain the reverence accorded to the judiciary in the late nineteenth century?

Power conferred status. The law, not politics, attracted the ablest people. A Wisconsin judge boasted, "The bench symbolizes on earth the throne of divine justice. . . . Law in its highest sense is the will of God." Judicial supremacy revealed how entrenched the ideology of individualism had become in industrial America and how low American politicians had fallen in the esteem of their countrymen.

Politics and the People

The country might have felt, as Kansas editor William Allen White wrote, "sick with politics" and "nauseated at all politicians," but somehow this did not curb the popular appetite for politics. Proportionately more voters turned out in presidential elections from 1876 to 1892 than at any other time in American history. National conventions attracted huge crowds. "The excitement, the mental and physical strains," remarked an Indiana Republican after the 1888 convention, "are surpassed only by prolonged battle in actual warfare." The convention he described had nominated the colorless Benjamin Harrison on a routine platform. What was all the excitement about?

Cultural Politics: Party, Religion, and Ethnicity

In the late nineteenth century, politics was a vibrant part of the nation's culture. America "is a land of conventions and assemblies," a journalist noted, "where it is the most natural thing in the world for people to get together in meetings, where almost every event is the occasion for speechmaking." During the election season, the party faithful marched in torchlight parades. Party paraphernalia flooded the country: handkerchiefs, mugs, posters, and buttons emblazoned with the Democratic donkey or the Republican elephant, symbols that had been adopted in the 1870s. In an age before movies and radio, politics ranked as one of the great American forms of entertainment.

Party loyalty was a deadly serious matter, however. Long after the killing ended, Civil War emotions ran high. Among family friends in Cleveland, the urban reformer Brand Whitlock recalled, the Republican Party was "a synonym for patriotism, another name for the nation. It was inconceivable that any self-respecting person should be a Democrat"—or, among ex-Confederates in the South, that any self-respecting person could be a Republican.

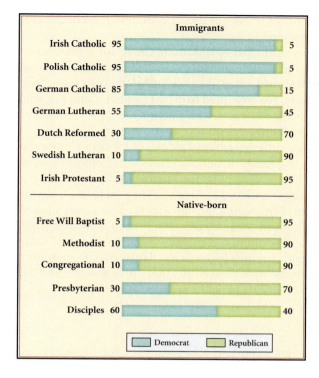

FIGURE 19.1 Ethnocultural Voting Patterns in the Midwest, 1870–1892
These figures demonstrate how voting patterns among midwesterners reflected ethnicity and religion in the late nineteenth century. Especially striking is the overwhelming preference by immigrant Catholics for the Democratic Party. Among Protestants, there was an equally strong preference for the Republican Party by certain groups of immigrants (Swedish Lutherans and Irish Protestants) and the native-born (Free Will Baptists, Methodists, and Congregationalists), but other Protestant groups were more evenly divided in their party preferences.

Beyond these sectional differences, the most important determinants of party loyalty were religion and ethnicity (Figure 19.1). Statistically, northern Democrats tended to be foreign-born and Catholic, while Republicans tended to be native-born and Protestant. Among Protestants, the more *pietistic* a person's faith—that is, the more personal and direct the believer's relationship to God—the more likely he or she was to be a Republican.

During the 1880s, as ethnic tensions built up in many cities, education became an arena of bitter conflict. One issue was whether instruction in the public schools should be in English. In St. Louis, a heavily German city, the long-standing policy of teaching German to all students was overturned after a heated campaign. Religion was an even more explosive issue. Catholics fought a losing battle over public aid for parochial schools, which by 1900 was prohibited by twenty-three states. In Boston, a furious controversy broke out in 1888 over an anti-Catholic history textbook. When the school board withdrew the offending book, angry Protestants elected a new board and returned the text to the curriculum.

Then there was the regulation of public morals. In many states, so-called blue laws restricted activity on Sundays. When Nebraska banned Sunday baseball, the state's courts approved the law as a blow struck in "the contest between Christianity and wrong." But German and Irish Catholics, who saw nothing evil in a bit of fun on Sunday, considered blue laws a violation of their personal freedom. **Ethnocultural** conflict also flared over the liquor question. In many states, evangelical Christians pushed for strict licensing and local-option laws governing the sale of alcohol.

Indiana permitted drinking but only joylessly in rooms containing "no devices for amusement or music . . . of any kind."

Because the hot-button issues of the day—education, the liquor question, and observance of the Sabbath—were also partisan issues, they lent deep significance to party affiliation (see Voices from Abroad, p. 561). Crusading Methodists thought of Republicans as the party of morality. For embattled Irish and German Catholics, who favored "the largest individual liberty consistent with public order," the Democratic Party was the defender of their freedoms.

These divisions might easily have infected national politics as, for example, Senator Blaine showed in 1875 when, angling for the Republican presidential nomination, he proposed a constitutional amendment banning public funding of parochial schools. But Republicans generally held back—and for good reason. They could never be sure that more would be lost than gained by playing the morality card. That was a lesson brought bitterly home to Republicans by the loose talk about "Rum, Romanism, and Rebellion" in the 1884 campaign. The politics of morality is no more potent today than it was in the 1880s, but it functions on a bigger stage. Battles over Demon Rum and the Sabbath played out locally; the equivalent battles today over abortion and gay rights have become national issues and help to define presidential politics.

Organizational Politics

Late-nineteenth-century politics was important also because of the organizational activity it generated. By the 1870s, both major parties had evolved formal, well-organized structures. At the base lay the precinct or ward, where party meetings were open to all members. County, state, and national committees ran the ongoing business of the parties. Conventions determined party rules, adopted platforms, and selected the party's candidates.

Party governance seemed, on its face, highly democratic, since in theory, all power derived from the party members. In practice, however, the parties were run by unofficial internal organizations—political machines—which consisted of insiders willing to do party work in exchange for jobs or the sundry advantages of being connected. Although most evident in city politics (see Chapter 18), the machine system was integral to political life at every level, right up to the national parties. The machines tended toward one-man rule, although the "boss" ruled more by consent than by his own absolute power. Absorbed in the tasks of power brokerage, machine bosses treated public issues as somewhat irrelevant. And the spoils system they managed unquestionably fouled the public realm with the stench of corruption.

Yet the record of machine politics was not wholly negative. In certain ways, the standards of governance got better. Disciplined professionals, veterans of machine politics, proved effective as state legislators and congressmen because they were more experienced in the give-and-take of politics. More important, party machines filled a void in the nation's public life. They did informally much of what the governmental system left undone, especially in the cities.

Even so, machine politics never managed to become respectable. Many of the nation's social elite—intellectuals, well-to-do businessmen, and old-line families—resented a politics that excluded people like themselves, the "best men." There was also

Beer and German American Politics   ERNST BELOW

Ernst Below (1845–1910) toured the United States in the early 1890s, enjoying the hospitality of prosperous German American communities along the way. In this excerpt from his account of his travels, *Bilder aus dem Westen* (1894), the action takes place at a turner festival. *Turner* is the German word for "gymnast." In Germany, the gymnastic movement enjoyed an enormous vogue, helping to weld the spirit of nationalism that had brought about German unification in 1871.

In Kansas City we sat on the veranda, taking coffee with Mr. Held, the attorney. . . . The men spoke of the chances of our host's election to Congress. Our friend, Karl, had the precise news from the battlefield and told of the stratagems used by one party or another in the attempt to make sure of victory. I showed my surprise that an educated, honest, thoughtful man, under such conditions, could bring himself to be concerned with politics.

The next night the great *Turnverein* [Gymnastic Association] hall was brightly lighted. . . . At one end of the hall sat old Kumpf, the former mayor . . . Kumpf was, like most of the old German turners, once a solid Republican. . . . Yet even he was displeased with the flirtation of his party with the temperance and prohibition forces in recent times. [A Democratic city official talking to Kumpf] pointed to . . . Joe Davenport, the Republican candidate for mayor, who was ordering a round of drinks and cigars for everyone.

"Listen to what he says," went on the Democrat. ". . . I know for a fact that he wrote yesterday to the Young Men's Christian Association promising in return for their votes a complete closing of all saloons on Sundays. . . . Go up to the scamp and expose his game!"

. . . Only with difficulty did Old Kumpf succeed in getting the floor and drawing the attention of the crowd. . . . Pointing to Mr. Holmes the rival Democratic candidate who had, unnoticed, come into the hall during the concluding exercises [Kumpf said]: "Although I do not fight for exactly the same principles as this man, still I must acknowledge that he offers a true guarantee against the hypocritical attempts of the prohibitionists. . . . With this in mind, I say, 'long live our next mayor, Mister Holmes!'"

Loud applause arose from all sides; men, women, and children jostled about trying to shake the hand of the future mayor. The band struck up the "Star Spangled Banner" while the whole assemblage rose to its feet and loudly sang the words. . . .

Soon a loud uproar reigned in the refreshment room. One group yelled ridicule against another, as the satellites of Davenport sought to ridicule the sudden change in sentiment. . . .

As I left the hall I was greeted by Rothmann, the director of the German school. He was indignant. . . . "This time at least," he said, "the Germans should have held together to . . . support Held, our [Republican] candidate for Congress. But when it comes to the most vital interest of the Germans in America, they . . . let shortsighted politicians turn their festivals into carnivals, in which a glass of beer can purchase the allegiance of a man."

S O U R C E: Oscar Handlin, ed., *This Was America* (Cambridge, MA: Harvard University Press, 1949), 383–389.

a genuine clash of values. Political reformers called for "disinterestedness" and "independence"—the opposite of the self-serving careerism fostered by the machine system. James Bryce, whose comments opened this chapter, was wined and dined by the political reformers when he came to the United States. His writings were colored by their prejudices, and, like them, he discounted the cultural and organizational contributions of American party politics.

Many of these reformers had earned their spurs as Liberal Republicans who dissented against President Grant's reelection in 1872 (see Chapter 15). In 1884, led by Carl Schurz and Charles Francis Adams Jr., they again left the Republican Party because they could not stomach its tainted candidate, James G. Blaine. Hailing mainly from New York and Massachusetts, these reform Republicans became known as Mugwumps—a derisive bit of contemporary slang, supposedly of Indian origin, referring to pompous persons. The Mugwumps threw their support to Democrat Grover Cleveland and might have ensured his election by giving him the winning margin in New York State.

Denying the machine system's legitimacy, the Mugwumps injected an elitist bias into political opinion. Mark Twain was not alone in proclaiming "an honest and saving loathing for universal suffrage." This democratic triumph of the early republic—a beacon for other nations to follow—now went into reverse as northern states began to impose **literacy tests** and limit the voting rights of immigrants.

The secret ballot, an import from Australia that was widely adopted in the United States around 1890, abetted the Mugwump antidemocratic campaign. Traditionally, voters had submitted party-supplied tickets in public view at the polling place. With the Australian reform, citizens cast their ballots in voting booths, freed from party surveillance, but for the uneducated and foreign-speaking, navigating a lengthy official ballot could be intimidating. So too could new voter registration procedures that registrars commonly used to bar those whom they considered unfit for the suffrage.

The Mugwumps were reformers but not on behalf of social justice. The travails of working people meant little to them, while keeping the state out of the welfare business meant a great deal. Theirs was the brand of "reform" perfectly in keeping with the conservative ethos of the time. In this respect, they and their critics—conservative judges and party leaders who otherwise disdained Mugwumpery—were in agreement.

Women's Political Culture

The young Theodore Roosevelt, an up-and-coming Republican state politician in 1884, spoke contemptuously of the Mugwumps as "man-milliners" (makers of ladies' hats). The sexual slur was not accidental. In attacking organizational politics, the Mugwumps were challenging a bastion of male society. At party meetings, men carried on not only the business of politics but also the rituals of male sociability amid cigar smoke and whiskey. Politics was identified with manliness. It was competitive. It dealt in the commerce of power. Party politics, in short, was no place for a woman.

So, naturally, the idea of women voting met fierce opposition. Acknowledging the uphill battle that lay ahead, suffragists overcame the bitter divisions of the Reconstruction era (see Chapter 15), reuniting in 1890 in the National American Woman Suffrage

Association. In that same spirit of realism, suffragists abandoned efforts to get a constitutional amendment and concentrated on state campaigns. Except out west—in Wyoming, Idaho, Colorado, and Utah—the most they could win was the right to vote for school boards or on tax issues. "Men are ordained to govern in all forceful and material things, because they are men," asserted an antisuffrage resolution, "while women, by the same decree of God and nature, are equally fitted to bear rule in a higher and more spiritual realm, where the strong frame and the weighty brain count for less"—that is to say, not in politics.

Yet this invocation of the doctrine of **separate spheres**—that men and women had different natures and that women's nature fitted them for "a higher and more spiritual realm"—did open a channel for women into public life. "Women's place is Home," acknowledged the journalist Retha Childe Dorr. "But Home is not contained within the four walls of an individual house. Home is the community. The city full of people is the Family. . . . And badly do the Home and Family need their mother." Indeed, since antebellum times, women had engaged in uplifting activities: fighting prostitution, assisting the poor, and agitating for prison reform (see Chapter 9). Because many of these goals required state action, women's organizations of necessity turned to politics, but they had to find a way in (see American Voices, p. 565).

Just before Christmas in 1873, the women of Hillsboro, Ohio, began to hold prayer meetings in front of the town's saloons, appealing to the owners to close their doors and end the misery of families of hard-drinking fathers. Thus began a spontaneous uprising—the "Woman's Crusade"—that spread across the country. From this agitation came the Woman's Christian Temperance Union (WCTU), which, under the guidance of Frances Willard, blossomed into the leading women's organization in the country.

Willard was a suffragist but no admirer of Susan B. Anthony or Lucy Stone. "The clamor for 'rights,'" she felt, was the wrong approach. Better to offer "only prayerful, persistent pleas for the opportunity of duty"—that is, to link the vote to women's concerns as wives and mothers. Willard's political motto was "Home Protection."

The evil of liquor, while genuinely felt by Willard, was not why she abandoned a promising career (she had been the first dean of women at Northwestern University). She regarded the WCTU essentially in political terms, as a vehicle uniquely suited for converting womanly virtue into political power. With men excluded, the WCTU gave the natural leaders among the women space to hone their skills. And for the other members, there was Willard's "Do-Everything" program, an ever-widening array of issues—labor conditions, prostitution, public health, international peace—that introduced these sheltered women to the ills of the world.

Finding a way into men's political realm was not easy, however. Except for the small Prohibition Party, where Willard herself cast her lot, there was no give on granting women the right to vote. But the major parties were actually not as antifemale as their manly facades might have suggested. Understanding all too well that womenfolk influenced their men, both parties in their different ways campaigned for the women's "vote."

In this competition, the Republicans capitalized on their roots in antebellum evangelical reform. Willard's motto, "Home Protection," was not hers alone. Republicans had used the term, or a variant, against slavery, and in Willard's time, they even

OUT OF WORK —
And the reason why.

Wanted, Sober Men

This drawing appeared in a magazine in 1899, twenty-five years after the women of Hillsboro, Ohio, rose in revolt against the town's saloonkeepers and launched the Woman's Christian Temperance Union (WCTU). But the emotion it expresses had not changed: that the saloon was the enemy of the family. Culver Pictures.

For more help analyzing this image, see the Online Study Guide at bedfordstmartins.com/henrettaconcise.

▶ Who were the Mugwumps? Were they important players in post-Reconstruction politics? Why or why not?

▶ What do we mean by *ethno-cultural politics*, and why is it important for an understanding of late-nineteenth-century American politics?

▶ Why was it that women, although they mostly could not vote, nevertheless became important political actors in this era?

used it to defend the tariff: Protection from cheap foreign goods meant higher American wages and hence "protection" for the family. In advancing this profamily line, the Republicans recruited female party operatives and found a pool of them in, of all places, the WCTU.

Not much changed in the short run. The national parties remained against woman suffrage. But the link that the WCTU established between women's social concerns and political participation helped to lay the groundwork for fresh attacks on male electoral politics. In the meantime, even without the vote, the WCTU had demonstrated the potency of women in the public arena.

Race and Politics in the New South

When Reconstruction ended in 1877, so did the hopes of African Americans for equal rights. Southern schools were segregated. Access to jobs, the courts, and social services was racially determined and unequal. Public accommodation was not legally segregated,

The Case for Women's Political Rights HELEN POTTER

In 1883, Helen Potter, a New York educator, testified before the Senate Committee on Education and Labor. She meant to speak about the sanitary conditions of the poor in New York City, but in the course of her testimony, she delivered a powerful indictment of the unequal treatment of women that spoke volumes about the evolving women's political culture of the late nineteenth century.

The Witness: It is really an important question—this of the condition of women in our community. When I was a young girl I had some ambition, and when I heard a good speaker, or when I read something written by a good writer, I had an ambition to do something of that kind myself. I was exceedingly anxious to preach, but the churches would not have me; why, they said that a woman must not be heard. . . .

Question: I suppose you have an idea that women might abolish some of the tricks of the politician's trade?

Answer: Well, sir, it would take them a long time to learn to dare to do those things that men do in the way of politics—to sell and buy votes. . . .

Q: Why do you think that the suffrage is not extended to women by men—what is the true reason, the radical reason, why men do not give up one half their political power to women?

A: Well, it may arise from a false notion of gallantry. I think most men feel like taking care of, and protecting the ladies. . . . It would be all very well, perhaps, if all women . . . had a generous, straightforward honorable man to represent them. But take the case of a good woman who has a drunken husband; how can he represent her? He votes for liquor and for everything he may happen to want, even though it may ruin her and turn her out of doors, and even though it may ruin her children. If the husband is a bad man would it not be better for that woman to represent herself?

Q: What effect do you think the extension of the suffrage to women would have upon their material condition, their wage-earning power and the like?

A: They would get equal pay for equal work of equal value. I do not think a woman ought to be paid the price of an expert, when she is not herself an expert, but I believe there would be a stimulus for a woman to fit herself for the very best work. What stimulus is there for woman to fit herself properly, if she never can attain the highest pay, no matter what sort of work she does? If women had a vote I think larger avenues of livelihood would be opened for them and they would be more respected by the governmental powers.

SOURCE: U.S. Senate Committee on Education and Labor, *Report upon Relations Between Labor and Capital,* II (1885), 627, 629–632.

however, and practices varied across the South. The only exception was on the railroads, where, after 1887, public accommodation became segregated by law.

In politics, the situation was still more fluid. Redemption had not driven blacks out of politics (see Chapter 15). On the contrary, in the post-Reconstruction years, their voter turnout was not far behind that of whites. But blacks did not participate on equal terms. In the black belt areas, where African Americans sometimes outnumbered whites, **gerrymandered** voting districts ensured that while blacks got some offices, political control remained in white hands. Despite widespread intimidation, an impressive majority of black Southerners remained staunchly Republican, refusing, as the last black congressman from Mississippi told his House colleagues in 1882, "to surrender their honest convictions, even upon the altar of their personal necessities."

Whatever hopes blacks entertained for better days, however, faded during the 1880s and then, in the next decade, expired in a terrible burst of racial terrorism.

Biracial Politics

No democratic society can survive if it does not allow competing interests to be heard. In the United States, the two-party system performs that role. The sectional crisis severely tested the two-party system because in both the North and the South, opposing the dominant party came to be seen as treasonable. In the victorious North, despite the best efforts of the Republicans, the Democrats shed their disgrace after the war and reclaimed their status as a major party. In the defeated South, however, the scars of war cut deep, and Reconstruction cut even deeper. The struggle for "home rule" empowered southern Democrats. They had "redeemed" the South from Republican domination — hence the name they adopted: Redeemers. Wrapped in the mantle of the Lost Cause, the Redeemers claimed a monopoly on political legitimacy.

The Republican Party in the South did not fold up, however. On the contrary, it soldiered on, sustained by black loyalty, by a hard core of white support, by Republican patronage, and by a key Democratic vulnerability. This was the gap between the universality that the Democrats claimed as the party of Redemption and domination by a single interest: the South's economic elite.

Class antagonism, though masked by sectional patriotism, was never absent from the South. The Civil War had brought out long-smoldering grievances of hill-country farmers, who felt called on to shed blood for a slaveholding system in which they had no stake. Afterward, class tensions were exacerbated by the spread of farm tenancy and low-wage industrial labor.

Unable to make themselves heard, economically distressed southerners broke with the Democratic Party in the early 1880s. Most notable were the Readjusters, who briefly gained power in Virginia over the issue of Reconstruction debt: They opposed repayment to bond-holding speculators that would have left the state destitute. After subsiding briefly, this agrarian discontent revived mightily in the late 1880s as tenant farmers joined farmers' alliances and helped create the Populist Party (see p. 571).

As this insurgency accelerated, the question of black participation became critical. Racism cut through southern society and, so some thought, especially infected the lowest rungs. "The white laboring classes here," wrote an Alabaman in 1886, "are separated from the Negroes, working all day side by side with them, by an innate consciousness of race superiority." Yet when times got bad enough, hard-pressed whites could also see blacks as fellow victims. "They are in the ditch just like we are," asserted one white Texan. Southern Populists never fully reconciled these contradictory impulses. They did not question the racist conventions of social inequality. Nor were the interests of white farmers and black tenants always in concert.

For their part, black farmers built a political structure of their own. The Colored Farmers' Alliance operated much less openly than its white counterparts — it could be worth a black man's life to make too open a show of his independence — but nevertheless gave black voters a voice at the table with white Populists. The demands of partisan politics, once the break with the Democrats came, clinched the argument for interracial unity. "The accident of color can make no difference in the interest of farmers, croppers, and laborers," argued the Georgian Tom Watson. "You are kept apart that you may be separately fleeced of your earnings." This interracial appeal, even if not always wholehearted, put at risk the foundations of elite southern politics.

One-Party Rule Triumphant

The Democrats struck back with all their might. They played the race card, parading themselves as the "white man's party" while denouncing the Populists for promoting "Negro rule." Yet they shamelessly competed for the black vote. In this, they had many advantages: money, control of the local power structures, and a paternalistic relationship to the black community. When all else failed, mischief at the polls enabled the Democrats to beat back the Populists. Across the South in the 1892 elections, the Democrats snatched victory from defeat by a miraculous vote count, including the votes of many who were long dead or gone.

In the midst of these deadly struggles, the Democrats decided to settle matters once and for all. The movement to disfranchise the blacks, hitherto tentative, swiftly gathered steam (Map 19.2). In 1890, Mississippi adopted a literacy test that effectively drove the state's blacks out of politics. The motives behind it were cynical, but the literacy test could be dressed up as a reform for white Mississippians tired of electoral fraud and violence. Their children and grandchildren, argued one influential figure, should not be left "with shotguns in their hands, a lie in their mouths and perjury on their lips in order to defeat the negroes." Better, a Mississippi journalist wrote, to devise "some legal defensible substitute for the abhorrent and evil methods on which white supremacy rests."

This logic persuaded even some weary Populists. The race question had helped bring them down; now it helped reconcile them to defeat. Embittered whites, ambivalent all along about interracial cooperation, turned their fury on the blacks. Of course, their own vulnerability — their own lack of education — needed to be offset by lenient enforcement of the literacy test. Thus, to take a blatant instance, Louisiana's grandfather clause exempted those entitled to vote on January 1, 1867 (before the Fifteenth Amendment gave freedmen that right), together with their sons and grandsons. But poor whites were not protected from property and poll-tax requirements, and many stopped voting.

Poor whites might have objected more had their spokesmen not been conceded a voice in southern politics. A new brand of demagogic politician came forward to speak for poor whites, appealing not to their economic interests but to their racial prejudices. Tom Watson, the Georgia Populist, rebuilt his political career as a spellbinding race-baiter.

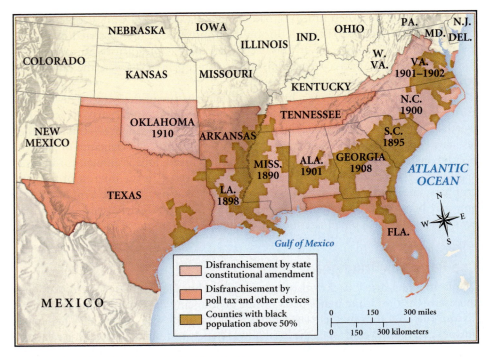

MAP 19.2 Disfranchisement in the New South

In the midst of the Populist challenge to Democratic one-party rule in the South, a movement to deprive blacks of the right to vote spread from Mississippi across the South. By 1910, every state in the region except Tennessee, Arkansas, Texas, and Florida had made constitutional changes designed to prevent blacks from voting, and these four states accomplished much the same result through poll taxes and other exclusionary methods. For the next half century, the political process in the South would be for whites only. For more help analyzing this map, see the Online Study Guide at **bedfordstmartins.com/henrettaconcise**.

In South Carolina, "Pitchfork" Ben Tillman adeptly manipulated images of white manhood. His pitch was that southerners, no matter their class, were bound together by their sturdy independence, their defense of the virtue of white womanhood, and their resistance to outside meddling. A U.S. senator for many years, Tillman was as fiery as Tom Watson in condemning blacks as "an ignorant and debased and debauched race."

A brand of white supremacy emerged that was more virulent than anything blacks had faced since Reconstruction. The color line, hitherto incomplete, became rigid and comprehensive. Segregated seating in trains, first adopted in the late 1880s, provided a precedent for the legal separation of the races. The enforcing legislation, known as **Jim Crow** laws, soon applied to every type of public facility: restaurants, hotels, streetcars, even cemeteries. In the 1890s, the South became a region fully segregated by law for the first time.

The U.S. Supreme Court soon ratified the South's decision. In *Plessy v. Ferguson* (1896), the Court ruled that segregation was not discriminatory—that is, it did not violate the Fourteenth Amendment—provided that blacks had access to accommodations equal to those of whites. The "separate but equal" doctrine ignored the realities of southern life.

Segregated facilities were rarely if ever "equal" in any material sense, and segregation was itself intended to underscore the inferiority of blacks. With a similar disregard for reality, the Supreme Court in *Williams v. Mississippi* (1898) validated the disfranchising devices of the southern states on the grounds that if race was not specified, the rights of blacks to vote under the Fifteenth Amendment were not being violated.

The Case of Grimes County

What this counterrevolution meant is perhaps best captured by the events in Grimes County, a cotton-growing area in east Texas, where African Americans composed more than half of the population. They kept the local Republican Party going after Reconstruction and regularly sent black representatives to the Texas legislature. More remarkably, local white Populists proved immune to Democrats' taunts of "black rule." A Populist-Republican coalition swept the county elections in 1896 and 1898, a surprising remnant of the southern Populist movement.

The next year, defeated Democrats organized the secret White Man's Union. Blacks were forcibly prevented from voting in town elections that year. The two most important black leaders were shot down in cold blood. When the Populist sheriff proved incapable of enforcing the law, the game was up. Reconstituted as the White Man's Party, Democrats emerged in a new guise. They carried Grimes County by an overwhelming vote in 1900. The day after the election, gunmen laid siege to the sheriff's office. They killed his brother and a friend and drove the sheriff, badly wounded, out of the county forever.

The White Man's Party ruled Grimes County for the next fifty years. The whole episode was the handiwork of the county's "best citizens," suggesting how respectable terror had become in the service of white supremacy. Grimes County, said one pillar of the community, intended to "force the African to keep his place." After Populism was crushed in that corner of Texas, blacks could survive only if they stayed out of politics and avoided trouble with whites.

Like the blacks of Grimes County, southern blacks in many other places resisted as best they could. When Georgia adopted the first Jim Crow law applying to streetcars in 1891, Atlanta blacks declared a boycott, and over the next fifteen years, blacks boycotted segregated streetcars in at least twenty-five cities. "Do not trample on our pride by being 'jim crowed,'" the Savannah *Tribune* urged its readers. "Walk!" Ida Wells-Barnett emerged as the most outspoken black crusader against lynching, so enraging the white community in Memphis by the editorials in her newspaper, *Free Speech*, that she was forced in 1892 to leave the city.

Some blacks were drawn to the Back-to-Africa movement, abandoning all hope that they would ever find justice in America. But for most, Africa

▶ The Redeemers imposed a system of one-party rule on the South after Reconstruction. Why was this system initially vulnerable to attack?

▶ How do you explain the disfranchisement of southern blacks during the 1890s? What measures did whites enact to prevent blacks from voting?

▶ What was Jim Crow? Would the answer to the previous question serve also to explain the establishment of Jim Crow in the South?

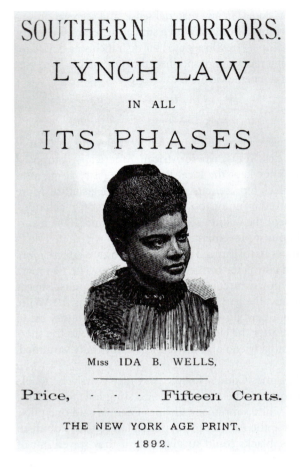

SOUTHERN HORRORS.

LYNCH LAW

IN ALL

ITS PHASES

Miss IDA B. WELLS,

Price,   ·   ·   ·   Fifteen Cents.

THE NEW YORK AGE PRINT,

1892.

Miss Ida B. Wells

In 1887, Ida Wells (Wells-Barnett after she married in 1895) was thrown bodily from a train in Tennessee for refusing to vacate her seat in a section reserved for whites. This experience launched her into a lifelong crusade for racial justice. Her mission was to expose the evil of lynching in the South. This portrait is from the title page of a pamphlet she published in 1892 entitled "Southern Horrors. Lynch Law in All Its Phases." Miriam and Ira D. Wallach Division of Art, Prints and Photographs, The New York Public Library. Astor, Lenox and Tilden Foundations.

was not a real choice. They were Americans, and they had to bend to the raging forces of racism and find a way to survive.

The Crisis of American Politics: The 1890s

Populism was a catalyst for political crisis not just in the South but across the entire nation. But while the result in the South was preservation of one-party rule, in national politics it was a revitalized two-party system.

Ever since Reconstruction, national politics had been stalemated by the even balance between the parties. In the late 1880s, the equilibrium began to break down. Benjamin Harrison's election to the presidency in 1888 was the last close election of the era (Democrat Grover Cleveland actually got a larger popular vote). Thereafter, the tide turned against the Republicans, saddled with the lackluster Harrison administration and Democratic charges that the protectionist McKinley Tariff of 1890 was a giveaway to business. In 1892, Cleveland regained the presidency by the largest margin in twenty years (the only president to be elected to two nonconsecutive terms).

Had everything else remained equal, Cleveland's victory might have initiated an era of Democratic supremacy. But everything else did not remain equal. Farm foreclosures and railroad bankruptcies signaled economic trouble. On May 3, 1893, the stock market crashed. In Chicago, 100,000 jobless workers walked the streets; nationwide, the unemployment rate soared above 20 percent.

As depression set in, which party would prevail—and on what platform—became an open question. The challenge to the status quo arrived from the West and South, where falling grain and cotton prices were devastating farmers.

The Populist Revolt

Farmers were, of necessity, joiners. To overcome their social isolation and provide economic services, they needed organization—hence the appeal of the Granger movement, which had spread across the Midwest after 1867 (see Chapter 16), and, after the Grange's decline, the emergence of farmers' alliances in many rural districts.

From diffuse organizational beginnings, two dominant groups emerged. One was the Farmers' Alliance of the Northwest, which was confined mainly to the midwestern states. More dynamic was the National (or Southern) Farmers' Alliance, which in the mid-1880s spread from Texas to the Great Plains and into the cotton South as "traveling lecturers" extolled the virtues of cooperative activity and reminded farmers of "their obligation to stand as a great conservative body against the encroachments of monopolies and . . . the growing corruption of wealth and power."

The Texas Alliance established a huge cooperative, the Texas Exchange, that marketed the crops of cotton farmers and provided them with cheap loans. When cotton prices fell in 1891, the Texas Exchange failed. The Texas Alliance then proposed a new scheme: a **subtreasury system**, which would enable farmers to store their crops in public warehouses and borrow against the unsold crops from a public fund until the cotton could be profitably sold. The subtreasury plan provided the same credit and marketing facilities as the defunct Texas Exchange but with a crucial difference: The federal government would be the underwriter. When the Democratic Party declared the scheme too radical, the Texas Alliance decided to strike out in politics independently.

These events in Texas revealed, with special clarity, a process of politicization that rippled through the Alliance movement. Rebuffed by the major parties, Alliance men abandoned their Democratic and Republican allegiances, and as state Alliances grew stronger and more impatient, they began to field independent slates of candidates. The confidence gained at the state level led to the formation of the national People's (Populist) Party in 1892. In the elections that year, with the veteran antimonopoly campaigner James B. Weaver as their presidential candidate, the Populists captured a million votes and carried four western states. For the first time, agrarian protest truly challenged the two-party system.

One Populist advantage was the many women in the movement. They had gotten in on the ground floor, when the alliances were just networks of local clubs and the wives had come along with their men. Although prominent as speakers and lecturers, women rarely became top leaders. In deference to the southern wing, the Populist platform was silent on woman suffrage. Still, neither Democrats nor Republicans would have countenanced a spokeswoman such as the fiery Mary Elizabeth Lease, who

MRS. MARY ELIZABETH LEASE AS SHE APPEARED IN 1895 WHEN SHE WAS AT THE HEIGHT OF HER POLITICAL ACTIVITIES IN KANSAS.

Mary Elizabeth Lease
As a political movement, the Populists were short on cash and organization but long on rank-and-file zeal and tub-thumping oratory. No one was more rousing on the stump than Mary Elizabeth Lease, who came from a Kansas homestead and pulled no punches. "What you farmers need to do," she is said to have proclaimed in her speeches, "is to raise less corn and more hell!" Kansas Historical Society.

became famous for calling on farmers "to raise less corn and more hell." The profanity might have been a reporter's invention, but the passion was all hers. Mrs. Lease insisted just as strenuously on Populism's "grand and holy mission . . . to place the mothers of this nation on an equality with the fathers."

"There are but two sides," proclaimed a Populist manifesto. "On the one side are the allied hosts of monopolies, the money power, great trusts and railroad corporations. . . . On the other are the farmers, laborers, merchants and all the people who produce wealth. . . . Between these two there is no middle ground."

By this reasoning, farmers and workers formed a single producer class. The claim was not merely rhetorical. The national platform contained strong labor planks, and party leaders earnestly sought union support. Texas railroad workers and Colorado miners cooperated with the farmers' alliances, got their backing in strikes, and actively participated in forming state Populist parties.

The attraction of Populism, in fact, pulled the labor movement to the left. Inside the American Federation of Labor Samuel Gompers briefly lost control to a faction that advocated a political alliance with the Populists. The center of this agitation was Chicago, where the radical reformer Henry Demarest Lloyd envisioned a farmer-labor party that might actually prevail in America.

In its explicit class appeal — in recognizing that "the irrepressible conflict between capital and labor is upon us" — Populism parted company from the two mainstream parties. Indeed, it had the makings of an American version — a farmer-labor version — of the social democratic parties emerging in Europe at this time. Like the European parties, Populism favored a strong state. In the words of the party's platform: "We believe that the power of government — in other words, of the people — should be expanded as rapidly and as far as the good sense of an intelligent people and the teachings of experience shall justify, to the end that oppression, injustice and poverty should eventually cease in the land."

At the founding Omaha convention in 1892, Populists called for **nationalization** of the railroads and communications; protection of the land, including natural re- sources, from monopoly and foreign ownership; a graduated income tax; and the free and unlimited coinage of silver. From this array of issues, the last — free silver — emerged as the cardinal demand of the Populist Party.

Reeling from rock-bottom prices, embattled farmers gravitated in the early 1890s to the unlimited coinage of silver because they hoped that an increase in the money supply would raise farm prices. In addition, the party's slim resources would be fat- tened by hefty contributions from silver-mining interests. Wealthy mine operators, scornful though they might be of Populist radicalism, yearned for the day when the government would buy at a premium all the silver they could produce.

Free silver triggered a debate for the soul of the Populist Party. Henry Demarest Lloyd voiced labor's objection. He called free silver the "cowbird of reform," stealing in and taking over the nest that others had built. Free silver, if it became the defining party issue, would undercut the broader Populist program and alienate wage earners, who had no enthusiasm for inflationary measures. The bread-and-butter appeal of free silver, however, was simply too great.

But once Populists made that choice, they fatally compromised their party's iden- tity as an independent movement, for free silver was not an issue over which Populists held a monopoly. It was, on the contrary, a question at the very center of mainstream American politics.

Money and Politics

In a rapidly developing economy, the money supply is bound to be hotly contested. Economic growth requires a growing volume of money. How fast the money supply should grow, however, is a divisive question. Having more money in circulation inflates prices and reduces the real cost of borrowing, to the benefit of debtors and commodity producers. The "sound money" people — creditors, individuals on fixed incomes, and established businessmen — have an opposite interest.

Before the Civil War, the main source of the nation's money supply had been state- chartered banks, several thousand of them, all issuing banknotes to borrowers that then circulated as money. The economy's need for money was amply met by the state banks, although the soundness of the banknotes — the ability of the issuing banks to stand behind their notes and redeem them — was always uncertain. There was also massive counterfeiting, since it was virtually impossible to keep track of all the varieties of notes in circulation and distinguish the fake from the real. This freewheeling activity was sharply curtailed by the U.S. Banking Act of 1863, which prohibited state banks from issuing banknotes not backed by U.S. government bonds. However, because the Lincoln administration was printing paper money — greenbacks — to pay for the Civil War, in effect the U.S. Treasury replaced the state banks as the source of easy money.

Once the war ended, the question became: Should the federal government con- tinue in that role? No, argued the sound money interests. Washington had no business printing paper money and should restore the traditional practice of basing the national currency on the amount of specie—gold and silver—held by the U.S. Treasury. In 1875, the sound money interests prevailed, and the circulation of greenbacks as legal tender—that is, backed by nothing more than the good faith of the federal government—came to an end. With state banknotes also in short supply, the country entered an era of chronic **deflation**.

This was the context out of which the silver question emerged. Since the colonial era, both gold and silver had served as specie, but as the supply of silver tightened, it became more valuable as metal than as money, and in 1873 silver was officially dropped as a medium of exchange. Then silver mining in the West surged, and the price of silver suddenly fell. The greenback supporters began agitating for a resumption of the bimetallic policy. If the federal government bought at the fixed ratio prevailing before 1873—16 ounces of silver equaling 1 ounce of gold—silver would flow into the Treasury and greatly expand the volume of money.

With so much at stake for so many people, the currency question became one of the staples of post-Reconstruction politics. Twice the pro-silver coalition in Congress won modest victories. First, the Bland-Allison Act of 1878 required the U.S. Treasury to purchase and coin between $2 million and $4 million worth of silver each month. Then, in the more sweeping Sherman Silver Purchase Act of 1890, an additional 4.5 million ounces of silver bullion was to be purchased monthly, to serve as the basis for new issues of U.S. Treasury notes.

These legislative battles, although hard fought, cut across party lines, in the familiar fashion of post-Reconstruction politics. But in the early 1890s, as hard times set in, silver suddenly became a defining issue between the parties. In particular, it radicalized the Democrats.

Climax: The Election of 1896

As the party in power, the Democrats bore the brunt of responsibility for the economic crisis. Any Democratic president would have been hard pressed, but the man who actually held the job, Grover Cleveland, could hardly have made a bigger hash of it. When jobless marchers—the so-called Coxey's army—arrived in Washington in 1894 to demand federal relief, Cleveland dispersed them forcibly and arrested their leader, Jacob S. Coxey. Cleveland's brutal handling of the Pullman strike (see Chapter 17) further alienated the labor vote.

Most disastrous, however, was Cleveland's stand on the silver question. Cleveland was a committed sound money man. Nothing that happened after the depression set in—not collapsing prices, not the suffering of farmers, not the groundswell of support for free silver within his own party—budged Cleveland. Economic pressures, in fact, soon forced him to abandon a silver-based currency altogether.

With the government's gold reserves dwindling, Cleveland persuaded Congress in 1893 to repeal the Sherman Silver Purchase Act, in effect sacrificing the country's painfully crafted program for a limited bimetallic policy. Then, as his administration's problems deepened, Cleveland turned in 1895 to a syndicate of private bankers led by J. P. Morgan to arrange the gold purchases needed to replenish the Treasury's depleted reserves. The administration's secret negotiations with Wall

Street, once discovered, enraged Democrats and completed Cleveland's isolation from his party.

At their Chicago convention in 1896, the Democrats repudiated Cleveland and turned left. His successor, William Jennings Bryan of Nebraska, was a political phenomenon. Only thirty-six years old, he had already served two terms in Congress and had become a passionate advocate of free silver. Bryan, remarked the journalist Frederic Howe, was "pre-eminently an evangelist" whose zeal sprang from "the Western self-righteous missionary mind." With biblical fervor, Bryan locked up the presidential nomination with a stirring attack on the gold standard: "You shall not press down upon the brow of labor this crown of thorns, you shall not crucify mankind on a cross of gold."

The Democrats had become the party of free silver. No one could be neutral on this defining issue. Gold Democrats went for a splinter Democratic ticket or supported the Republican Party; silver Republicans bolted their party; even the Prohibition Party split into gold and silver wings. The Populists, meeting after the Democratic convention, accepted Bryan as their candidate. The free-silver issue had become so vital that they could not do otherwise. Although they nominated their own vice presidential candidate, Tom Watson of Georgia, the Populists found themselves for all practical purposes absorbed into the Democratic silver campaign.

The Republicans took up the challenge. Their party leader was the wealthy Cleveland iron maker Mark Hanna, a brilliant political manager and an exponent of the new industrial capitalism. Hanna orchestrated an unprecedented money-raising campaign among America's corporate interests. His candidate, William McKinley of Ohio, personified the virtues of Republicanism, standing solidly for high tariffs, sound money, and prosperity. While Bryan broke with tradition and crisscrossed the country by railroad in a furious whistle-stop campaign, the dignified McKinley received delegations at his home in Canton, Ohio. Bryan orated with moral fervor; McKinley talked of economic progress and a full dinner pail.

Not since 1860 had the United States witnessed so hard-fought an election over such high stakes. For the middle class, sound money stood symbolically for the soundness of the social order. With jobless workers tramping the streets and bankrupt farmers up in arms, Bryan's fervent assault on the gold standard struck fear in many hearts. Republicans denounced the Democratic platform as "revolutionary and anarchistic" and Bryan's supporters as "social misfits who have almost nothing in common but opposition to the existing order and institutions."

Though little noticed at the time, ethnocultural influences figured strongly in the campaign. In their bid for electoral dominance in 1892, the Democrats had taken advantage of the Republican reputation as the party of religious intolerance. Now, in 1896, the Republicans beat a strategic retreat from the politics of morality. As a congressman, McKinley had represented an ethnically mixed district of northeastern Ohio. In appealing to his immigrant constituents, he had learned the art of easy tolerance, expressed in his words, "Live and let live." Of the two candidates, the prairie orator Bryan, with his biblical language and moral righteousness, presented the more alien image to traditional Democratic voters in the big cities.

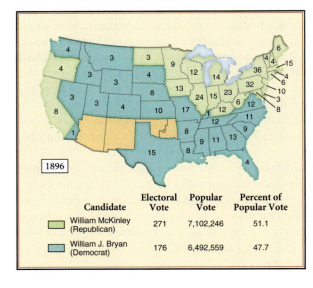

Candidate	Electoral Vote	Popular Vote	Percent of Popular Vote
Grover Cleveland (Democrat)	277	5,555,426	46.1
Benjamin Harrison (Republican)	145	5,182,690	43.0
James B. Weaver (Populist)	22	1,029,846	8.5
Minor parties	—	285,297	2.3

Candidate	Electoral Vote	Popular Vote	Percent of Popular Vote
William McKinley (Republican)	271	7,102,246	51.1
William J. Bryan (Democrat)	176	6,492,559	47.7

MAP 19.3 Presidential Elections of 1892 and 1896

In the 1890s, the age of political stalemate came to an end. In comparing the 1892 map with Map 19.1 (p. 555), note especially Cleveland's breakthrough in the normally Republican states of the upper Midwest. In 1896, the pendulum swung in the opposite direction, McKinley's consolidation of Republican control over the Northeast and Midwest far overbalancing the Democratic advances in the thinly populated western states. The 1896 election marked the beginning of thirty years of Republican dominance in national politics.

McKinley won handily, with 271 electoral votes to Bryan's 176. He kept the ground Republicans had regained in the 1894 midterm elections and pushed into Democratic strongholds, especially in the cities. Boston, New York, Chicago, and Minneapolis, all taken by Cleveland in 1892, went for McKinley in 1896. Bryan ran strongly only in the South, in silver-mining states, and in the Populist West (Map 19.3). But the gains his evangelical style brought him in some Republican rural areas did not compensate for his losses in traditionally Democratic urban districts.

The paralyzing equilibrium in American politics ended in 1896. The Republicans skillfully turned both economic and cultural challenges to their advantage. They persuaded the nation that they were the party of prosperity, and they convinced many traditionally Democratic urban voters that they were sympathetic to ethnic diversity. In so doing, the Republicans became the nation's majority party, notwithstanding the Democratic lock on the South. In 1896, too, electoral politics regained its place as an arena for national debate, setting the stage for the reform politics of the Progressive era.

▶ Farmers, like other Americans, had strong ties to the established parties, yet many of them became Populists anyway. Why?

▶ Grover Cleveland is rated as a fairly good president for his first term and a bad one for his second term. How do you explain that reversal?

▶ It would be hard to imagine American voters today getting excited about the money supply. So why was free silver the hot topic of the 1896 election?

SUMMARY

This chapter was about late-nineteenth-century politics. We started with the period 1877–1892, when the great politics of sectional crisis gave way to an age of political quiescence. Except for the courts, federal institutions were weak, the national parties avoided big issues, and laissez-faire was the prevailing philosophy. Yet while little seemed at stake, politics engendered high levels of popular participation. This was partly because of the entertainment value but, more important, because politics was the arena of ethnic and religious conflict involving parties that were strongly developed and highly active. Finally, while still lacking voting rights, women carved out for themselves, in their role as defenders of the family, a prominent place in politics.

In the South, post-Reconstruction politics followed a different, less settled course because the emergent one-party system was resisted by poor whites and Republican blacks. Biracial southern Populism flared briefly and then failed, triggering a grim reaction that disfranchised African Americans, completed a rigid segregation system, and let loose a terrible cycle of racial violence. Blacks resisted but had to bend to the overwhelming power of white supremacy.

In this chapter's final section, we returned to national politics, which in the 1890s again galvanized the country. Challenged by Populism, the Democratic Party committed itself to free silver, sidetracking the last great third party of the nineteenth century and making the election of 1896 a turning point for the major parties. The Republicans won decisively, ending a paralyzing stalemate and assuring themselves of political dominance for the next thirty years.

Connections: Politics

The immediate antecedents of the political history covered by this chapter are in the sectional crisis of the 1850s (Chapter 13) and the Reconstruction era (Chapter 15), when fundamental questions of Union and slavery were resolved. In the aftermath, politics took a breather and, as we said in the essay opening Part Four, "the major parties remained robust because they exploited a culture of popular participation and embraced the ethnic and religious identities of their constituencies." When the Populist revolt broke out in the early 1890s, southern Democrats took the opportunity to

TIMELINE

1874 ► Woman's Christian Temperance Union founded

1877 ► Rutherford B. Hayes inaugurated as president, marking end of Reconstruction

1881 ► President James A. Garfield assassinated

1883 ► Pendleton Civil Service Act

1884 ► Mugwump reformers leave Republican Party to support Grover Cleveland, first Democrat elected president since 1856

1887 ► Florida adopts first law segregating railroad travel

1888 ► James Bryce's *The American Commonwealth*

1890 ► McKinley Tariff
   ► Democrats sweep congressional elections, inaugurating brief

era of Democratic Party dominance
   ► Mississippi becomes first state to adopt literacy test to disfranchise blacks

1892 ► People's (Populist) Party founded

1893 ► Panic of 1893 leads to national depression
   ► Repeal of Sherman Silver Purchase Act (1890)

1894 ► "Coxey's army" of unemployed fails to win federal relief

1896 ► Election of Republican president William McKinley; free-silver campaign crushed
   ► *Plessy v. Ferguson* upholds constitutionality of "separate but equal" segregation

drive African Americans out of politics and consolidate their own grip on the South, while the Republicans carried the 1896 election and became the dominant national party. It seemed as if politics would then revert to the holding pattern of the 1880s, but instead, as we will see in Chapter 20, the demand for reform took hold, and the two parties—first the Republicans, then the Democrats—embraced progressive politics. Although that impulse seemed exhausted after World War I (Chapter 23), in fact the Progressives had set the stage for the New Deal (Chapter 24).

FOR FURTHER EXPLORATION

Late-nineteenth-century politics is a topic on which historians have had a field day. Mark Wahlgren, *Rum, Romanism & Rebellion: The Making of a President, 1884* (2000), analyzes the first phase of post-Reconstruction national politics. The mass appeal of Gilded Age politics is incisively explored in Michael E. McGerr, *The Decline of Popular Politics: The American North, 1865–1928* (1986). Alexander Keyssar, *The Right to Vote: The Contested History of Democracy in the United States* (2000), is illuminating on the conservative assault on popular politics. Rebecca Edwards, *Angels in the Machinery: Gender in American Party Politics* (1997), reveals women's unexpectedly large role within the main parties. On southern politics, the seminal book is C. Vann Woodward, *Origins of the New South, 1877–1913* (1951). The most far-reaching revision is Edward L. Ayers, *The Promise of the New South* (1992). The process of sectional reconciliation is imaginatively treated in David W. Blight, *Race and Reunion: The Civil War in Memory* (2001). The most recent treatment of disfranchisement is Michael Perman, *Struggle for Mastery: Disfranchisement in the South, 1888–1908* (2001). The key book on Populism is Lawrence Goodwyn, *Democratic Promise: The Populist Moment* (1976), which argues that Populism was a broadly based response to industrial capitalism. Much information on Gilded Age presidents can be found at **americanpresident.org/presidential resources.htm**.

TEST YOUR KNOWLEDGE

To assess your mastery of the material in this chapter and for Web sites, images, and documents related to this chapter, visit **bedfordstmartins.com/henrettaconcise**.

The Progressive Era
1900–1914

Society is looking itself over, in our day, from top to bottom. . . . We are in a temper to reconstruct economic society.

— Woodrow Wilson, 1913

On the face of it, the political tumult of the 1890s ended with William McKinley's election in 1896. After beating back free silver, the victorious Republicans had no stomach for crusades. The main thing, as party chief Mark Hanna said, was to "stand pat and continue Republican prosperity."

Yet beneath the surface, a deep unease had set in. Hard times had unveiled truths not acknowledged in better days—that a frightening chasm, for example, had opened between America's social classes. The great Pullman strike of 1894 had brought the country "to the ragged edge of anarchy," Richard Olney said. It had been his job, as Cleveland's attorney general, to crush the strike (see Chapter 17). But he took little joy from his success. Olney asked himself, rather, how such repressive actions might be avoided in the future. His answer was that the government should regulate labor relations on the railroads and so forestall crippling rail strikes. As a first step, Congress adopted the Erdman Railway Mediation Act in 1898. In such ways did the crisis of the 1890s turn the nation's thinking to reform.

The problems themselves, however, were of older origin. For many decades, Americans had been absorbed in building the industrial economy. Now they paused, looked around, and began to add up the costs: a frightening concentration of corporate power, a rebellious working class, misery in the cities, and the corruption of machine politics.

With the strife-torn 1890s behind them, reform became an absorbing concern of many Americans. It was as if social awareness reached a critical mass around 1900 and set reform activity going as a major, self-sustaining phenomenon. For this reason, the years from 1900 to World War I have come to be known as the Progressive era.

The Course of Reform

Historians sometimes speak of a progressive "movement." But progressivism was not a movement in any meaningful sense. There was no agreed-upon agenda, and there was no unifying organization. Both the Republican and Democratic parties had progressive wings. And different social groups became active at different times and places. The term *progressivism* describes a widespread, many-sided effort after 1900 to build a better society. And yet, if progressivism was many-sided, it did have a center, and that was the urban middle class.

The Middle-Class Impulse

In 1889, Jane Addams and Ellen Gates Starr established Hull House on Chicago's West Side. Flanked by saloons and "horrid little houses" in a neighborhood of mainly Italian immigrants, the dilapidated mansion that they called Hull House was the model for settlement houses that sprang up in the nation's cities, serving as community centers and spark plugs for neighborhood betterment. At the Henry Street Settlement in New York, Lillian Wald made the provision of visiting nurses a major service. Mary McDowell, head of the University of Chicago Settlement, installed a bathhouse, a children's playground, and a citizenship school for immigrants.

The settlement house was a hallmark of social progressivism, and for Jane Addams, it meant a lifetime in ugly surroundings, endlessly battling for garbage removal, playgrounds, better street lighting, and police protection.

Why did she make that choice? Addams was a daughter of the middle class. She might have lived a life of ease, which was what her prosperous parents had intended when they sent her to Rockford College. But Addams came home in 1881 sad and unfulfilled, feeling "simply smothered and sickened by advantages." Hull House became her salvation, enabling her to "begin with however small a group to accomplish and to live."

In retrospect, Addams realized that hers was not an individual crisis but a crisis that afflicted her entire generation. In a famous essay, she spoke of the "subjective necessity" of the settlement house. She meant that it was as much for the young middle-class residents who were so eager to serve as it was for needy slum dwellers.

The generational crisis was also a crisis of faith. Progressives such as Jane Addams characteristically grew up in homes imbued with Christian piety but then found themselves falling away from the faith of their parents. Many went through a religious crisis, ultimately settling on careers in social work, education, or politics. Jane Addams, for one, took up settlement-house work believing that by uplifting the poor, she would herself be uplifted—she would experience "the joy of finding Christ" by acting "in fellowship" with the needy.

The Protestant clergy itself struggled with these issues, translating a long-felt concern for the poor into a theological doctrine: the Social Gospel. The leading exponent was the Baptist cleric Walter Rauschenbusch, whose ideas had been forged by his ministry in the squalid Hell's Kitchen neighborhood of New York City. The churches, said the Reverend Rauschenbusch, should embrace the "social aims of Jesus." The Kingdom of God on Earth would be achieved not by striving for personal salvation but in the cause of social justice.

What gave urgency to these inner callings was the discovery that there was no insulating middle-class Americans from the ills of industrial society. That was a truth borne painfully home to Jane Addams when her eldest sister lay ill in a hospital during the Pullman strike. Held up by the turmoil, her sister's distraught family failed to reach her bedside before she died. Addams feared that such painful episodes, inescapable whenever labor and capital came to blows, would inculcate "lasting bitterness" in middle-class homes. "The present industrial system is in a state of profound disorder," and the middle class had a big stake in "right[ing] it." It was up to reformers like herself, products of the middle class, to take up that task.

Progressive Ideas

Finding solutions, however, was easier said than done. Jane Addams wrote poignantly of her uncertainty, having launched Hull House, about just how to proceed. She "longed for . . . an explanation of the social chaos and the logical steps toward its better ordering." Finding answers depended first of all on the emergence of a new intellectual style that we can call *progressive*.

If the facts could be known, everything else was possible. That was the starting point for progressive thinking. Hence the burst of enthusiasm for scientific investigation: statistical studies; research by privately funded foundations into industrial conditions; and vice commissions in many cities looking into prostitution, gambling, and other moral ills of an urban society. Great faith was also placed in academic expertise. In Wisconsin, the state university became a key resource for Governor Robert La Follette's reform administration—the reason, one supporter boasted, for "the democracy, the thoroughness, and the accuracy of the state in its legislation."

Similarly, progressives were drawn to scientific management, which had originally been intended to rationalize work in factories (see Chapter 17). But its founder, Frederick W. Taylor, argued that his basic approach—the "scientific" analysis of human activity—offered solutions to waste in municipal government, schools, and hospitals and even at home. Scientific management, said Taylor, could solve all the social ills that arise from "such of our acts as are blundering, ill-directed, or inefficient."

Scientific management was an American invention, but progressive intellectuals also felt themselves part of a transatlantic world. Ideas flowed in both directions, with the Americans, in fact, very much on the receiving end. Since the 1870s, Americans had flocked to German universities, absorbing the economics and political science that became key tools of progressive reform. On many fronts, social politics overseas seemed far in advance of the United States. The sense of having fallen behind—that "the tables are turned," as the young progressive Walter Weyl wrote, and that "America no longer teaches democracy to an expectant world, but herself goes to school in Europe and Australia"—was a spur to fresh ideas.

The main thing was to resist ways of thinking that discouraged purposeful action. That was why progressives disdained the Social Darwinists who had so dominated Gilded Age thought (see Chapter 19). "It is folly," pronounced the Harvard philosopher William James, "to speak of the 'laws of history,' as of something inevitable, which science only has to discover, and which anyone can then foretell and observe, but do nothing to alter or avert." Rejecting the pursuit of absolute truths, James advocated instead a philosophy he called **pragmatism**, which judged ideas by their consequences. Philosophy should be concerned with solving problems, James insisted, not with contemplating ultimate ends.

Nowhere were the battle lines more sharply drawn than in the courts, where conservative judges treated the law as if it embodied eternal principles. One such principle was liberty of contract, which the Supreme Court invoked in *Lochner v. New York* (1905) to strike down a state law limiting the hours of bakers. The Court contended that it was protecting the liberty of the bakers. Nonsense, responded the dissenting Justice Oliver Wendell Holmes. If the choice was between working and starving, could it be said that bakers freely chose to work fourteen hours a day?

Legal realism, as Justice Holmes's reasoning came to be known, rested on his conviction that "the life of the law has not been logic; it has been experience." Dean Roscoe Pound of the Harvard Law School called for "the adjustment of principles and doctrines to the human conditions they are to govern rather than assumed first principles." The proper role of the law, added Pound's student Felix Frankfurter, was to be "a vital agency for human betterment."

No practitioner of legal realism took this advice more to heart than the Boston lawyer Louis D. Brandeis, the son of Jewish immigrants from Austria-Hungary. He became known as "the people's lawyer" because, on behalf of the little guy, Brandeis regularly took on the mightiest vested interests in town. Always ready to enlist in a good cause, he embodied progressivism's greatest strength: its capacity for uniting the brainpower of progressive intellectuals with the high-mindedness of social reformers.

The progressive mode of action — idealistic in intent, tough-minded in practice — nurtured a new kind of crusading journalism. During the 1890s, bright new magazines such as *Collier's* and *McClure's*, committed to lively, fact-filled reporting, discovered that their middle-class readers wanted to know about mischief in American life.

In a riveting series in *McClure's*, Lincoln Steffens wrote about "the shame of the cities": the corrupt ties between business and political machines. Ida M. Tarbell attacked the Standard Oil monopoly, and David Graham Phillips told how money controlled the Senate. William Hard exposed industrial accidents in "Making Steel and Killing Men" (1907) and child labor in "De Kid Wot Works at Night" (1908). Hardly a sordid corner of American life escaped the scrutiny of these tireless reporters.

Theodore Roosevelt, among many others, thought that they went too far. In a 1906 speech, he compared them to the man with a muckrake in *Pilgrim's Progress* (by the seventeenth-century English preacher John Bunyan) who was too absorbed with raking the filth on the floor to look up and accept a celestial crown. Thus the term **muckraker** became attached to journalists who exposed the underside of American life. Their efforts were, in fact, health-giving. More than any other group, the muckrakers called the people to arms.

Women Progressives

When she started out, Jane Addams did not regard Hull House as a specifically female enterprise. But, of course, in her personal odyssey, it had mattered that she was a daughter, not a son. And while men were welcome, the settlement houses were overwhelmingly led and staffed by women. Over time, as the reform impulse quickened,

Who Said Muck Rake?
The Smile That Won't Come Off.)

Who Said Muck Rake?

A popular biographer in the 1890s, Ida Tarbell turned her journalistic talents to muckraking. Her first installment of "The History of the Standard Oil Company," which appeared in *McClure's* in November 1902, was a bombshell, with its exposure of John D. Rockefeller's chicanery on the way to fabulous wealth. In this cartoon, Miss Tarbell seems a mild enough lady, but there is her muck rake, and farther in the background, President Roosevelt cowers. That he was paying attention, the cartoon suggests, is apparent in the headline of the newspaper she is reading. Drake Oil Well Museum.

For more help analyzing this image, see the Online Study Guide at **bedfordstmartins.com/henrettaconcise.**

the settlement-house movement became a nodal point for the distinctively feminine cast of social progressivism.

This was in keeping with women's long-established role as the nation's "social housekeepers," those who traditionally shouldered the burden of humanitarian work in American cities. They were the foot soldiers for charity organizations, visiting needy families, assessing their problems, and referring them to relief agencies. After many years of such dedicated labor, Josephine Shaw Lowell of New York City concluded that giving assistance to the poor was not enough. "It is better to save them before they go under, than to spend your life fishing them out afterward." Lowell founded the New York Consumers' League in 1890. Her goal was to improve the wages and working conditions of female clerks in the city's stores by issuing a "White List"—a very short list at first—of cooperating shops.

From these modest beginnings, Lowell's organization spread to other cities and blossomed into the National Consumers' League in 1899. At its head stood a feisty, outspoken woman, Florence Kelley, an early resident of Hull House and then chief factory inspector of Illinois. As she investigated the so-called sweated trades of Chicago, Kelley lost faith in voluntary reform; only factory legislation could rescue exploited workers. When she joined the National Consumers' League, Kelley brought that focus to its work. Under her crusading leadership, the Consumers' League became a powerful advocate for protective legislation for women and children.

Among its achievements, none was more important than the Supreme Court's *Muller v. Oregon* decision in 1908, which upheld an Oregon law limiting the workday for women to ten hours. The Consumers' League recruited Louis Brandeis, whose legal brief devoted a scant two pages to the narrow constitutional issue: whether, under its police powers, Oregon could regulate women's working hours. Instead, Brandeis rested his case on data gathered by the Consumers' League describing the toll that long hours took on women's health and performance of their family duties. The *Muller* decision was a triumph for legal realism and, by approving an expansive welfare role for the states, cleared the way for a lobbying offensive by women's organizations, whose victories included the first law providing public assistance for mothers with dependent children (Illinois, 1911); the first minimum wage law for women (Massachusetts, 1912); more effective child labor laws in many states; and, at the federal level, the Children's and Women's bureaus in the Labor Department.

Women reformers such as Jane Addams and Florence Kelley breathed new life into the suffrage movement. Why, they asked, should a woman who was capable of running a settlement house or lobbying a bill be denied the right to vote? And why should only women like themselves be participating in that fight? By asking that question, they opened the way for working-class women to join the suffrage struggle.

Believing that working women should be encouraged to help themselves, New York reformers in 1903 founded the National Women's Trade Union League. Financed by wealthy supporters, the league organized women workers, helped out in their strikes, and trained working-class leaders. One such leader was Rose Schneiderman, a union organizer among New York's garment workers; another was Agnes Nestor, leader of Illinois glove workers. Although they often resented the patronizing ways of their well-to-do sponsors, such trade union women identified their cause with the broader struggle for women's rights.

Around 1910, suffrage activity began to quicken. In Britain, suffragists had begun to picket Parliament, stage demonstrations, and go on hunger strikes while in jail. Inspired by their example, Alice Paul, a young Quaker who had once lived in Britain, brought those confrontational tactics to the American struggle. Although six western states had granted woman suffrage since 1910, Paul rejected the state-by-state route as too slow (Map 20.1). She advocated a constitutional amendment that would achieve the right to vote in one stroke. In 1916, Paul organized the militant National Woman's Party.

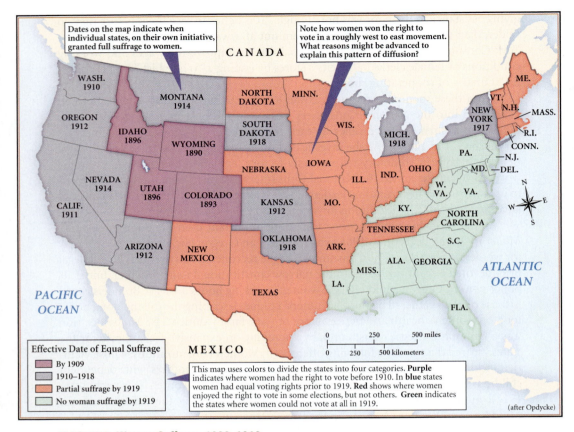

Dates on the map indicate when individual states, on their own initiative, granted full suffrage to women.

Note how women won the right to vote in a roughly west to east movement. What reasons might be advanced to explain this pattern of diffusion?

This map uses colors to divide the states into four categories. **Purple** indicates where women had the right to vote before 1910. In **blue** states women had equal voting rights prior to 1919. **Red** shows where women enjoyed the right to vote in some elections, but not others. **Green** indicates the states where women could not vote at all in 1919.

(after Opdycke)

Effective Date of Equal Suffrage
- By 1909
- 1910–1918
- Partial suffrage by 1919
- No woman suffrage by 1919

MAP 20.1 Woman Suffrage, 1890–1919

By 1909, after more than sixty years of agitation, only four lightly populated western states had granted women full voting rights. A number of other states offered partial suffrage, limited mostly to voting for school boards and such issues as taxes. Between 1910 and 1918, as the effort shifted to the struggle for a constitutional amendment, eleven states joined the list granting full suffrage. The most stubborn resistance was in the South.

For more help analyzing this map, see the Online Study Guide at **bedfordstmartins.com/henrettaconcise**.

The mainstream National American Woman Suffrage Association (NAWSA), from which Paul had split off, was also rejuvenated. Carrie Chapman Catt, a skilled organizer from the New York movement, took over as national leader in 1915. Under her guidance, NAWSA brought a broad-based organization to the campaign for a federal amendment.

In the midst of this ferment, something new began to happen. A younger generation—college-educated, self-supporting—refused to be hemmed in by women's "separate sphere." "Breaking into the Human Race" was the aspiration they proclaimed at a mass meeting in New York in 1914. "We intend simply to be ourselves," declared the chair Marie Jenny Howe, "not just our little female selves, but our whole big human selves."

The women at this meeting called themselves **feminists**, a term just then coming into use. In this, its first incarnation, feminism meant freedom for full personal development. Thus did Charlotte Perkins Gilman, famous for advocating communal kitchens as a solution to home-making drudgery, imagine the new woman: "Here she comes, running, out of prison and off the pedestal; chains off, crown off, halo off, just a live woman."

Feminists were militantly prosuffrage, but unlike their more traditional suffragist sisters, not on the basis that women would uplift American politics. Rather, they demanded the right to vote because they considered themselves just as good as men. Just as it was about to triumph, the suffrage movement was overtaken by a larger revolution that redefined the struggle for women's rights as a battle against all the constraints that prevented women from achieving their potential as human beings.

The feminists also challenged the progressive belief that women were the weaker sex. It was just this argument, at the very heart of Brandeis's brief in the landmark *Muller* case, which rang true with the Supreme Court. "The two sexes differ in structure of body, in the functions to be performed by each, in the amount of physical strength," the Court agreed. "This difference justifies . . . legislation . . . designed to compensate for some of the burdens which rest upon her." But feminists wanted no such compensation. To the surprise of Maryland's progressive governor Charles J. Bonaparte, some feminists objected to his 1914 women's minimum wage bill because it implied that "women need some special care, protection and privilege."

A wedge was growing that would ultimately fracture the women's movement, dividing an older generation of social progressives from feminists who prized gender equality more highly than any welfare benefit.

Urban Liberalism

The evolution of the women's movement — in particular, the recruitment of working-class women to what had been a middle-class struggle — was entirely characteristic of how progressivism evolved more generally.

When the Republican Hiram Johnson ran for California governor in 1910, he was the candidate of the state's middle class. Famous as prosecutor of the corrupt San Francisco boss Abe Ruef, Johnson pledged to purify California politics and curb the Southern Pacific Railroad, the dominating economic power in the state. By his second term, Johnson was championing social and labor legislation and relying on California's working class for support.

Johnson's career reflected a shift in the center of gravity of progressivism. A new strain of progressive reform emerged that historians have labeled *urban liberalism.* To understand this phenomenon, we have to begin with city machine politics.

Thirty minutes before quitting time on Saturday afternoon, March 25, 1911, fire broke out at the Triangle Shirtwaist Company in downtown New York. The flames trapped the workers, who were mostly young immigrant women. Many leaped to their deaths; the rest never reached the windows. The dead, 146 of them, averaged nineteen years of age.

In the wake of the tragedy, the New York State Factory Commission developed a remarkable program of labor reform: fifty-six laws dealing with fire hazards, unsafe machines, industrial homework, and wages and hours for women and children. The chairman of the commission was Robert F. Wagner; the vice chairman was Alfred E. Smith.

The Triangle Tragedy

This drawing, by the artist John Sloan, captures better than any photograph the horror of the Triangle fire. The image of the two women clinging to each other as they fell is accurate. According to observers, a number of young workers, with no other way to escape the flames, chose to fall to their deaths in each other's arms. The fireman who cannot bear to watch is probably a product of Sloan's imagination, but the anguish depicted is true enough, because when the fire trucks arrived, they did not have the equipment to save anyone. The ladders were too short, and the nets the firemen spread too weak. The bodies simply shot right through to the ground. *Harper's Weekly,* May 8, 1915.

Both were Tammany Hall politicians, at the time leaders in the state legislature. They established the commission, participated fully in its work, and marshaled the party regulars to pass the proposals into law—all with the approval of the Tammany bosses.

By its response to the Triangle fire, Tammany was conceding that social problems had outgrown the powers of party machines. Only the state could bar industrial firetraps or alleviate sweatshop work. And if that meant weakening grassroots loyalty to Tammany, so be it. Al Smith and Robert Wagner absorbed the lessons of the Triangle investigation. They formed durable ties with such progressives as the social worker Frances Perkins, who sat on the commission as the representative of the New York Consumers' League, and became urban liberals—advocates of active intervention by the state in uplifting the laboring masses of America's cities.

It was not only altruism that converted politicians such as Smith and Wagner. The city machines faced competition from a new breed of middle-class progressives. One of these was Mayor Brand Whitlock of Toledo, Ohio, whose administration not only attacked city hall corruption but also provided better schools, cleaner streets, and more social services. Whitlock and progressive mayors like him in Cleveland, Jersey City, and elsewhere won over the urban masses and challenged the rule of the machines.

Also confronting the bosses was a challenge from the left. The Socialist Party was making headway in the cities, electing Milwaukee's Victor Berger as the nation's first Socialist congressman in 1910 and winning municipal elections across the country. In the 1912 presidential election, the Socialist candidate Eugene Debs (see Chapter 17) garnered a record 6 percent of the vote. The political universe of the urban machines had changed, and they had to pay closer attention to opinion in the precincts.

Urban liberalism was driven not only by the plight of the downtrodden but also by a felt need to defend them from cultural critics who had long agitated for laws upholding public morality. After 1900, this movement revived, cloaking itself now in the mantle of progressive reform. The Anti-Saloon League—"the Protestant church in action"—became a formidable advocate for prohibition in many states, skillfully attaching Demon Rum to other reform targets. In the League's rhetoric, the saloon made for dirty politics, poverty, and bad labor conditions.

The moral reform agenda expanded to include a new goal: restricting the immigration of southern and eastern Europeans into the United States. Edward A. Ross of the University of Wisconsin denounced "the pigsty mode of life" of Italian and Polish immigrants. The danger, according to respected social scientists, was that America's Anglo-Saxon population would be "mongrelized" and its civilization swamped by "inferior" Mediterranean and Slavic cultures. Feeding on this fear, the Immigration Restriction League spearheaded a campaign to end America's historic open-door policy. Like prohibition, immigration restriction was considered by its proponents to be a progressive reform.

Urban liberals thought otherwise. They denounced prohibition and immigration restriction as attacks on the worthiness of urban immigrants. The Tammany politician Martin McCue accused the Protestant ministry "of seeking to substitute the policeman's nightstick for the Bible."

The trade unions, the other institution that spoke for working people, were slower than the city machines to embrace urban liberalism. In its early years, the American Federation of Labor (AFL) had opposed state interference in labor's affairs. Samuel Gompers preached that workers should not seek from government what they could accomplish by their own economic power and self-help. **Voluntarism**, as trade unionists called this doctrine, did not die out, but it weakened substantially during the progressive years.

The AFL, after all, claimed to speak for the entire working class. When muckrakers exposed exploitation of workers, how could the labor movement fail to respond? In state after state, organized labor joined the battle for progressive legislation and increasingly became its strongest advocate, including most particularly workers' compensation for industrial accidents.

Industrial hazards took an awful toll at the workplace (see American Voices, p. 590). Two thousand coal miners were killed every year, dying from cave-ins and explosions at a rate 50 percent higher than in German mines. Liability rules, based on **common law**, so heavily favored employers that injured workers rarely got more than token compensation. The tide turned quickly once the labor movement got on board;

Tracking Down Lead Poisoning DR. ALICE HAMILTON

Alice Hamilton (1869–1970) studied medicine over the objections of her socially prominent family. When she finally landed a job teaching pathology in Chicago, Dr. Hamilton moved into Jane Addams's Hull House. That experience launched her on a pioneering career in industrial medicine, one of the many paths to social reform that settlement-house work opened up.

When I look back on the Chicago of 1897 I can see why life in a settlement seemed so great an adventure. It was all so new, this exploring of the poor quarters of a big city. . . . To settle down to live in the slums of a great city was a piece of daring as great as trekking across the prairie in a covered wagon. . . .

It was also my experience at Hull House that aroused my interest in industrial diseases. Living in a working-class quarter, coming in contact with laborers and their wives, I could not fail to hear tales of the dangers that working men faced, of cases of carbon-monoxide poisoning in the great steel mills, of painters disabled by lead palsy, of pneumonia and rheumatism among the men in the stockyards. . . .

At the time I am speaking of [1910] Professor Charles Henderson . . . persuaded [the governor] to appoint an Occupational Disease Commission, the first time a state had ever undertaken such a survey. . . . We were staggered by the complexity of the problem we faced and we soon decided to limit our field almost entirely to the occupational poisons . . . lead, arsenic, brass, carbon monoxide, the cyanides, and turpentine. Nowadays [1943], the list involved in a survey of the painters' trade alone is many times as long as that.

But to us it seemed far from a simple task. We could not even discover what were the poisonous occupations in Illinois. . . .

There was nothing to do but begin with trades we knew were dangerous and hoped that as we studied them, we would discover others less well known. My field was to be lead. . . .

One case, of colic and double wrist-drop,* which was discovered in the Alexian Brothers' Hospital, took me on a pretty chase. The man, a Pole, said he had worked in a sanitary-ware factory, putting enamel on bathtubs. . . . The management assured me that no lead was used in the coatings and invited me to inspect the workrooms. . . . Completely puzzled, I made a journey to the Polish quarter to see the palsied man and heard from him I had not even been in the enameling works, only the one for final touching up. The real one was far out on the Northwest Side. I found it and discovered that enameling means sprinkling a finely ground enamel over a red hot tub. . . . The air is thick with enamel dust . . . rich in red oxide of lead. A specimen . . . proved to contain as much as 20 per cent soluble lead—that is, lead that dissolves into solution in the stomach. Thus I nailed down the fact that sanitary-ware enameling is a dangerous lead trade.

*Paralysis of the wrist muscles, causing the hand to droop.

SOURCE: *Exploring the Dangerous Trades: The Autobiography of Alice Hamilton* (Boston: Little, Brown and Co., 1943).

between 1910 and 1917, all the industrial states enacted insurance laws covering on-the-job accidents.

Beyond that, however, the United States did not go. Health insurance and unemployment compensation, although popular in Europe, scarcely made it onto the American political agenda. Old-age pensions, which Britain adopted in 1908, got a serious hearing, only to come up against an odd barrier: The United States already had a pension system of a kind, for Civil War veterans. Easy access — as many as half of all native-born men over age sixty-four or their survivors were collecting veterans' benefits in the early twentieth century — reinforced fears of state-induced dependency. Clarence J. Hicks, an industrial-relations expert, recalled Civil War pensioners idling away the hours around the wood stove in the grocery store in his Wisconsin town. They had decided "that the country owed them a living," lost their initiative, and "retreated from the battle of life."

Not until the Great Depression (see Chapter 23) would the country be ready for a more comprehensive program of social insurance. A secure old age, unemployment insurance, health benefits — these human needs of a modern industrial order were beyond the reach of urban liberals in the Progressive era.

Reforming Politics

Like the Mugwumps of the Gilded Age (see Chapter 19), progressive reformers attacked corrupt party rule, but they did so more adeptly. Indeed, what distinguished political reform after 1900 was that it was no longer an amateurs' project. In the Progressive era, reformers understood politics as well as did the scoundrels they were trying to throw out, and that was why, once the smoke cleared, the political reforms of this era proved enduring. In this, as in other realms, progressivism was a potent mix of idealism and tough-mindedness.

Born in 1855, Robert M. La Follette started as a conventional Wisconsin politician. A Republican congressman, he was a party regular, never doubting that he was in honorable company until, by his own account, a Republican boss offered him a bribe to fix a judge in a railroad case. Awakened by this "awful ordeal," La Follette became a tireless advocate of political reform, which for him meant restoring America's democratic ideals. "Go back to the first principles of democracy; go back to the people," he told his audience when he launched his campaign against the state Republican machine. In 1900, after battling for a decade, La Follette won the Wisconsin governorship on a platform of higher corporate taxes, stricter utility and railroad regulation, and political reform.

The key to lasting reform, La Follette thought, was denying bosses the power to choose the party's candidates. This could be achieved by requiring that nominations be decided not in party conventions but by popular vote. Enacted in 1903, the **direct primary** expressed La Follette's democratic idealism, but it also suited his particular political talents. The party regulars were insiders, more comfortable in the caucus room than out on the stump. But out there was where La Follette excelled. The direct primary gave La Follette a grip on Wisconsin politics that lasted until his death twenty-five years later.

What was true of La Follette was more or less true of all the successful progressive politicians. Like La Follette, Albert B. Cummins of Iowa, William S. U'Ren of Oregon, and Hiram Johnson of California espoused democratic ideals, and all used the direct

Robert M. La Follette

La Follette was transformed into a political reformer when a Wisconsin Republican boss attempted to bribe him in 1891 to influence a judge in a railway case. As La Follette described it in his *Autobiography*, "Out of this awful ordeal came understanding; and out of understanding came resolution. I determined that the power of this corrupt influence . . . should be broken." This photograph captures him at the top of his form, expounding his progressive vision to a rapt audience of Wisconsin citizens at an impromptu street gathering. Library of Congress.

primary as the stepping stone to political power. They practiced a new kind of popular politics, which in a reform age could be a more effective way to power than the back-room techniques of the machine politicians.

Racism and Reform

The direct primary was the flagship of progressive politics — the crucial reform, as La Follette said, for returning politics to "the people." The primary originated not in Wisconsin, however, but in the South, and by the time La Follette got his primary law in 1903, primaries were already operating in seven southern states. In the South, however, the primary was a white primary, the final wrinkle in the campaign to drive African Americans out of politics.

How could this exercise in white supremacy be justified as democratic reform? By the racism that pervaded even the progressive ranks. In a 1902 book on Reconstruction, Professor John W. Burgess of Columbia University pronounced the Fifteenth Amendment "a monstrous thing" for granting blacks the vote. Burgess was southern born, but he was confident that his northern audience saw the "vast differences in political capacity" between blacks and whites. Even the Republican Party offered no rebuttal. Indeed, as president-elect in 1908, William Howard Taft applauded southern disfranchising laws as necessary to "prevent entirely the possibility of domination by . . . an ignorant electorate" and vowed that "the federal government [would have] nothing to do with social

Booker T. Washington

In an age of severe racial oppression, Washington emerged as the acknowledged leader of black people in the United States. He was remarkable both for his ability to act as spokesman to white Americans and for his deep understanding of the aspirations of black Americans. Born a slave, Washington suffered the indignities experienced by all blacks after emancipation. But having been befriended by several whites as he grew to manhood, he also understood what it took to gain white support — and maneuver around white hostility — in the black struggle for equality. Library of Congress.

equality." Taft's successor, Woodrow Wilson, went even further, signaling after he entered the White House in 1913 that he favored segregation of the U.S. civil service.

The dominant black leader of the era was Booker T. Washington, who in a famous speech in Atlanta in 1895 advocated accommodation with the South. Washington considered "the agitation of the question of social equality the extremest folly." The Atlanta Compromise, as his stance became known, avoided a direct assault on white supremacy and urged blacks to start by making themselves productive citizens.

Despite the conciliatory face he put on before white audiences, however, Washington did not concede the struggle. Behind the scenes, he lobbied hard against Jim Crow laws and disfranchisement. In an age of severe racial oppression, no black dealt more skillfully with the elite of white America or wielded greater influence inside the Republican Party. What Washington banked on was black economic progress. When they had grown dependent on black labor and black enterprise, white men of property would recognize the justice of black rights. As Washington put it, "There is little race prejudice in the American dollar."

Black leaders knew Washington as a hard taskmaster, jealous of his authority and not disposed to regard opposition kindly. Even so, opposition surfaced, especially among younger, educated blacks. They thought Washington was conceding too much. He instilled black pride but of a narrowly middle-class and utilitarian kind. What about the special genius of blacks that W. E. B. Du Bois, a Harvard-educated African American sociologist, celebrated in his collection of essays, *The Souls of Black Folk* (1903)? And what of the "talented tenth" of the black population, whose promise could only be stifled by the manual education that Washington advocated?

Moreover, the situation for blacks was deteriorating, even in the North. Over 200,000 blacks migrated from the South between 1900 and 1910, sparking white resentment in northern cities. Attacks on blacks became widespread, capped by a bloody race riot in Springfield, Illinois, in 1908. In the face of all this, many black activists lost patience with Booker T. Washington's silence.

The key critic was William Monroe Trotter, the pugnacious editor of the *Boston Guardian*. "The policy of compromise has failed," Trotter argued. "The policy of resistance and aggression deserves a trial." In 1906, after breaking with Washington, Trotter and Du Bois called a meeting at Niagara Falls—but on the Canadian side because no hotel on the U.S. side would admit blacks. The Niagara Movement that resulted had an impact far beyond the scattering of members it organized. The principles that it affirmed would define the struggle for the rights of African Americans: first, encouragement of black pride; second, an uncompromising demand for full political and civil equality; and finally, the resolute denial "that the Negro-American assents to inferiority, is submissive under oppression and apologetic before insults."

Going against the grain, a handful of white reformers rallied to the African American cause. Among the most devoted was Mary White Ovington, who grew up in an abolitionist family. Like Jane Addams, Ovington became a settlement-house worker but in New York's black ghetto rather than in immigrant Chicago. News of the Springfield race riot of 1908 changed her life.

Convinced that her duty was to fight racism, Ovington called a meeting of sympathetic progressives, which led to the formation of the National Association for the Advancement of Colored People (NAACP) in 1909. Most of the members of the strife-torn Niagara Movement moved over to the NAACP. The organization's national leadership was dominated by whites, with one crucial exception. Du Bois became the editor of the NAACP's journal, *The Crisis*. With an authenticity that only a black voice could provide, Du Bois used that platform to demand equal rights. The NAACP scored its first success in helping to beat back the Wilson administration's effort at segregating the federal civil service.

On social welfare, the National Urban League took the lead, uniting in 1911 the many agencies that served black migrants to northern cities. Like the NAACP, the Urban League was interracial, including both white reformers such as Ovington and black welfare activists such as William Lewis Bulkley, a New York school principal who was the league's main architect.

In the South, welfare work was very much the province of black women who filled, to some extent, the vacuum left by black disfranchisement. Mostly working in the churches and schools, they also utilized the southern branches of the National

Association of Colored Women's Clubs, which had started in 1896. And because their activities seemed unthreatening to white supremacy, black women were able to reach across the color line and find allies among white southern women.

Progressivism was a house of many chambers. Most were infected by the racism of the age, but not all. A saving remnant of white progressives rallied to the cause of racial justice. In alliance with black civil rights advocates, they defined the issues and established the organizations that would spur the struggle for a better life for African Americans over the next half century.

▶ How do you account for the revival of the woman's suffrage movement during the Progressive era?

▶ In what ways did political reformers of the Progressive era (such as Robert La Follette) differ from the Mugwump reformers of the late nineteenth century?

▶ What is the relationship between progressive reform and the struggle for racial equality?

Progressivism and National Politics

Progressivism began at the state and local levels, where problems were immediate and easily seen. But reformers soon realized that many social issues, such as child labor and industrial safety, were best handled by the federal government and that, insofar as these issues concerned the power of big business, there was no place else to turn. Seasoned reformers such as Robert La Follette, angling for a wider stage, migrated to Washington and ultimately formed a progressive bloc on Capitol Hill.

Progressivism burst on the national stage not via Congress, however, but by way of the presidency. This was partly because the White House provided a "bully pulpit"—to use Theodore Roosevelt's phrase. But just as important was the twist of fate that brought Roosevelt to the White House on September 14, 1901.

The Making of a Progressive President

Like many other budding progressives, Theodore Roosevelt was motivated by a high-minded, Christian upbringing. Born in 1858, he always identified himself—loudly—with the cause of righteousness. But Roosevelt did not scorn power and its uses. To the amazement of his socially prominent family, he plunged into Republican politics after graduating from Harvard and maneuvered himself into the New York State legislature. Contemptuous of the gentlemen Mugwumps, he much preferred the company of party professionals. Roosevelt rose in the New York party because he cultivated broad popular support and won over reluctant Republican bosses.

Safely back from the Spanish-American War as the hero of San Juan Hill (see Chapter 21), Roosevelt gained the New York governorship in 1898. He signaled his progressivism by pushing through civil service reform and a tax on corporations and by discharging the corrupt superintendent of insurance over the Republican Party's objections. Most of all, he asserted his confidence in the government's capacity to improve the life of the people.

Hoping to neutralize him, the party chieftains chose Roosevelt in 1900 for what seemed a dead-end job as William McKinley's running mate. Roosevelt accepted reluctantly. But on September 6, 1901, an anarchist named Leon F. Czolgosz shot the president. When McKinley died eight days later, Roosevelt became president, to the dismay of party regulars.

Roosevelt moved cautiously, attending first to politics. Anxious to rein in the conservative bloc in Congress, he adroitly used his patronage powers to gain control of the Republican Party. But Roosevelt was also uncertain about how to proceed. At first, the new president might have been described as a progressive without a cause.

Regulating the Marketplace

Most troubling to Roosevelt was the threat posed by big business to competitive markets. The drift toward large-scale enterprise was itself not new. For many years, companies had been expanding their operations because of the efficiencies that vertical integration offered (see Chapter 17). But the bigger the business, the greater the power over markets. And when, in the aftermath of the depression of the 1890s, promoters scrambled to merge rival firms, the primary motive was not lower costs but the elimination of competition. These mergers—**trusts**, as they were called—greatly concentrated business. By 1910, 1 percent of the nation's manufacturers accounted for 44 percent of the nation's industrial output (see Voices from Abroad, p. 597).

As early as his first annual message, Roosevelt acknowledged the nation's uneasiness with the "real and grave evils" of the trusts. But what weapons could the president use in response?

Under common law, anyone injured by monopoly or illegal restraint of trade could sue for damages. With the passage of the Sherman Antitrust Act of 1890, these common-law rights became enforceable by the federal government when offenses involved interstate commerce. Neither Presidents Cleveland nor McKinley showed much interest, but the Sherman Act was there, waiting to be deployed against abusive economic power.

Roosevelt's opening move was to create a Bureau of Corporations (1903) empowered to investigate business practices and bolster the Justice Department's capacity to mount antitrust suits. The department had already filed such a suit against the Northern Securities Company, a combine of the railroad systems of the Northwest. In a landmark decision, the Supreme Court ordered Northern Securities dissolved in 1904.

That year, Roosevelt handily defeated a weak conservative Democratic candidate, Judge Alton B. Parker. Now president in his own right, Roosevelt stepped up the attack on the trusts. He took on many of the nation's giant firms, including Standard Oil, American Tobacco, and DuPont. His rhetoric rising, Roosevelt became the nation's trust-buster, a crusader against "predatory wealth."

Roosevelt was not antibusiness. He regarded large-scale enterprise as the natural tendency of modern industrialism. Only firms that abused their power deserved punishment. But how to identify those companies? Under the Sherman Act, following common-law practice, the courts decided whether an act in restraint of trade was "unreasonable"—that is, harmful of the public interest—on a case-by-case basis. In the *Trans-Missouri* decision (1897), however, the Supreme Court abandoned this discretionary "rule of reason," holding now that actions that restrained or monopolized trade, regardless of the public impact, automatically violated the Sherman Act.

America in 1905: "Business Is King" JAMES BRYCE

James Bryce, British author of *The American Commonwealth* (1888), visited the United States regularly. In an essay published in 1905, he took stock of the changes of the previous quarter century. What most impressed Bryce, beyond the sheer growth of wealth, was the intensifying concentration of corporate power. In this, he agreed with his old friend Theodore Roosevelt, who, at that very time, was gearing up to do battle with the trusts.

That which most strikes the visitor to America today is its prodigious material development. Industrial growth, swift thirty or forty years ago, advances more swiftly now. . . . The increase of wealth . . . impresses the European more than ever before because the contrast with Europe is greater. The huge fortunes, the fortunes of those whose income reaches or exceeds a million dollars a year, are of course far more numerous than in any other country. . . . With this extraordinary material development it is natural that in the United States, business, that is to say, industry, commerce, and finance, should have more and more come to overshadow and dwarf all other interests, all other occupations. . . . Business is king.

. . . Twenty-two years ago there were no trusts. . . . Even then, however, corporations had covered a larger proportion of the whole field of industry and commerce in America than in Europe, and their structure was more flexible and efficient. Today this is still more the case; while as for trusts, they have become one of the most salient phenomena of the country. . . .

Workingmen follow, though hitherto with unequal steps, the efforts at combination which the lords of production and distribution have been making. The consumer stands, if not with folded hands, yet so far with no clear view of the steps he may make for his own protection. Perhaps his prosperity—for he is prosperous—helps him to be quiescent.

The example of the United States, the land in which individualism has been most conspicuously vigorous, may seem to suggest that the world is passing out of the stage of individualism and returning to that earlier stage in which groups of men formed the units of society. The bond of association was, in those early days, kinship, real or supposed, and a servile or quasi-servile dependence of the weak upon the strong. Now it is the power of wealth which enables the few to combine so as to gain command of the sources of wealth. . . . Is it a paradox to observe that it is because the Americans have been the most individualistic of peoples that they are now the people among whom the art of combination has reached its maximum? The amazing keenness and energy, which were stimulated by the commercial conditions of the country, have evoked and ripened a brilliant talent for organization. This talent has applied new methods to production and distribution and has enabled wealth, gathered into a small number of hands, to dominate even the enormous market of America.

SOURCE: Allan Nevins, ed., *America Through British Eyes* (Gloucester, MA: Peter Smith, 1968), 384–387.

Little noticed at first, *Trans-Missouri* placed Roosevelt in a quandary. He had no desire to hamstring business, but he could not rely on the courts to distinguish between "good" and "bad" trusts. So Roosevelt assumed this task himself, which he could do because as chief executive, he had the power to initiate — or not initiate — antitrust prosecutions by the Justice Department.

In November 1904, with an antitrust suit looming, the United States Steel Corporation approached Roosevelt with a deal: cooperation in exchange for preferential treatment. The company would privately open its books to the Bureau of Corporations and be guided by any finding of wrongdoing. Roosevelt accepted this "gentlemen's agreement" because it suited his interest in accommodating the modern industrial order while maintaining his public image as slayer of the trusts.

The railroads posed a different problem. As quasi-public enterprises, they had never been free of oversight by the states; in 1887, they became subject to federal regulation by the Interstate Commerce Commission (ICC). As with the Sherman Act, this assertion of federal authority was mostly symbolic. Then Roosevelt got started, pushing through in 1903 the Elkins Act, which prohibited discriminatory railway rates that favored preferred or powerful customers — a practice, Ida Tarbell reminded Americans in her muckraking articles, that had enabled Rockefeller to monopolize the oil industry.

With the 1904 election behind him, Roosevelt launched a drive for real railroad regulation. In 1906, after nearly two years of wrangling, Congress passed the Hepburn Railway Act, which empowered the ICC to set maximum shipping rates and prescribe uniform methods of bookkeeping. As a concession to the conservative Republican bloc, however, the courts retained broad powers to review the ICC's rate decisions.

Passage of the Hepburn Act was a triumph of Roosevelt's skills as a political operator. Despite grumbling by Senate progressives, Roosevelt was satisfied. He had achieved a landmark expansion of the government's regulatory powers over business.

Another target was the West's natural resources. Although an ardent outdoorsman, Roosevelt was not a wilderness **preservationist** in the mold of John Muir (see Chapter 16). Having shaken off the illusions of his youthful days as a tenderfoot rancher, Roosevelt accepted the grim reality that the West's abundance, far from being limitless, was a finite and rapidly disappearing resource. Roosevelt was a **conservationist**. He believed in efficient use and sustainability so that "we will hand . . . the water, the wood, the grasses . . . on to our children . . . in better and not worse shape than we got them."

Roosevelt's guiding principle was, as his Public Lands Commission (1903) stated it, "public ownership" — the primacy of federal authority over the public domain for purposes of efficient management. Roosevelt tripled the number of national forests, removed coal lands from private development, and added national parks and (a new category authorized in 1906) many national monuments. Equally important were advances in federal administration, the most important being an expanded Forest Service headed by a professional forester, Gifford Pinchot.

Although mindful of western interests, federal bureaucrats such as Pinchot infuriated ranchers and loggers unaccustomed to interference from Washington. They rebelled against grazing fees and logging restrictions, and their representatives in Washington eventually fought Roosevelt to a draw. Nowhere, in fact, did progressivism face fiercer resistance. Even so, there was no turning back. Roosevelt had reversed a century of heedless exploitation and imprinted conservation on the nation's public agenda.

The protection of consumers, another signature issue for progressives, came mostly thanks to muckraking journalism. What sparked the issue was a riveting series of articles in *Collier's* by Samuel Hopkins Adams exposing the patent-medicine business as "undiluted fraud."

Then, in 1906, Upton Sinclair's novel *The Jungle* appeared. Sinclair thought he was writing about labor exploitation in Chicago meatpacking plants, but what caught the nation's attention were his descriptions of rotten meat and filthy conditions. President Roosevelt, weighing into the legislative battle, authorized a federal investigation of the stockyards. Within months, the Pure Food and Drug Act and the Meat Inspection Act passed, and another administrative agency, the Food and Drug Administration, joined the expanding federal bureaucracy.

During the 1904 presidential campaign, Roosevelt had taken to calling his program the Square Deal. This kind of labeling would become a hallmark of American politics in the twentieth century, emblematic of a political style that dramatized issues, mobilized public opinion, and asserted presidential leadership. But the label meant something of substance as well. After many years of passivity and weakness, the federal government was reclaiming the role it had abandoned after the Civil War.

Roosevelt was well aware that his Square Deal was built on nineteenth-century foundations. In particular, antitrust doctrine seemed inadequate in an age of industrial concentration. It would be better, Roosevelt thought, for the federal government to regulate big business than try to break it up. In his final presidential speeches, Roosevelt dwelled on the need for a reform agenda for the twentieth century. Having chosen to retire after two terms, he bequeathed this task to his chosen successor, William Howard Taft.

Campaigning for the Square Deal
When William McKinley ran for president in 1896, he sat on his front porch in Canton, Ohio, and received delegations of voters. That was not Theodore Roosevelt's way. Roosevelt considered the presidency a "bully pulpit," and he used the office brilliantly to mobilize public opinion and to assert his leadership. The preeminence of the presidency in American public life begins with Roosevelt's administration. Here, at the height of his crusading power, Roosevelt stumps for the Square Deal in the 1904 election. Library of Congress.

The Fracturing of Republican Progressivism

William Howard Taft was an estimable man in many ways. An able jurist and a superb administrator, he had served Roosevelt well as governor-general of the Philippines after the Spanish-American War (see Chapter 21). But he disliked the give-and-take of politics, he distrusted power, and, unlike Roosevelt, he was not one to cut corners. He revered the processes of law and was, in fundamental ways, a conservative.

Taft's Democratic opponent in the 1908 campaign was William Jennings Bryan. This third attempt at the presidency was Bryan's last hurrah, and he made the most of it. Eloquent as ever, Bryan attacked the Republicans as the party of the "plutocrats" and outdid them in urging tougher antitrust legislation, stricter railway regulation, and advanced labor legislation. Almost single-handedly, Bryan moved the Democratic Party into the mainstream of national progressive politics. But his robust campaign was not enough to offset Taft's advantages as Roosevelt's candidate. Taft won comfortably, entering the White House with a mandate to pick up where Roosevelt left off.

By 1909, reform politics had unsettled the Republican Party. On the right, conservatives were girding themselves against further losses. Led by Senator Nelson W. Aldrich of Rhode Island, they were still a force to be reckoned with. On the left, progressive Republicans were rebellious. They thought that Roosevelt had been too easy on business, and with him gone from the White House, they intended to make up for lost time. Reconciling these conflicting forces would have been a daunting task for a master politician. For Taft, it spelled disaster.

First there was the tariff. Progressives considered protective tariffs a major reason why competition had declined. Although Taft had campaigned for tariff reform, he was won over by the conservative Republican bloc and ended up approving the protectionist Payne-Aldrich Tariff Act of 1909, which critics charged sheltered eastern industry from foreign competition.

Next came the Pinchot-Ballinger affair, which pitted Chief Forester Gifford Pinchot against Secretary of the Interior Richard A. Ballinger. Pinchot, a chum of Roosevelt's, accused Ballinger of plotting to transfer resource-rich Alaskan land to a private business group. When Pinchot aired these charges, Taft fired him for insubordination. Despite Taft's strong conservationist credentials, the Pinchot-Ballinger affair marked him as a friend of the "interests" who were bent on plundering the nation's resources.

Taft found himself propelled into the conservative Republican camp, an ally of "Uncle Joe" Cannon, the dictatorial Speaker of the House of Representatives. When a House revolt finally broke Cannon's power in 1910, it was regarded as a defeat for the president as well. Galvanized by Taft's defection, the reformers in the Republican Party became a dissident faction, calling themselves Insurgents.

Home from a year-long safari in Africa, Roosevelt yearned to reenter the political fray. Taft's dispute with the Insurgents gave Roosevelt the cause he needed. But Roosevelt was too astute a politician not to recognize that a party split would benefit the Democrats. He could be spurred into rebellion only by a true clash of principles. On the question of the trusts, just such a clash materialized.

Taft's legalistic mind rebelled at Roosevelt's practice of choosing among trusts when it came to antitrust prosecutions. The Sherman Act was on the books. "We are going to enforce that law or die in the attempt," Taft promised grimly. But he was held back until the Supreme Court reasserted the rule of reason in the *Standard Oil* decision (1911), which meant that, once again, the courts themselves undertook to distinguish between good and bad trusts. With that burden lifted, Taft's attorney general George W. Wickersham stepped up the pace of antitrust actions, immediately targeting the United States Steel Corporation.

One of the charges was that the steel trust had illegally acquired the Tennessee Coal and Iron Company in 1907. Roosevelt had personally approved the transaction, believing that it was necessary—so U.S. Steel representatives had told him—to prevent a financial collapse on Wall Street. Taft's suit against U.S. Steel thus amounted to a personal attack that Roosevelt could not, without dishonor, ignore.

Ever since leaving the White House, Roosevelt had been pondering the trust problem. Between breaking up big business and submitting to corporate rule lay another alternative: The federal government could be empowered to oversee the nation's corporations to make sure they acted in the public interest.

In a speech in Osawatomie, Kansas, in August 1910, Roosevelt made the case for what he called the New Nationalism. The central issue, he argued, was human welfare versus property rights. In modern society, property had to be controlled "to whatever degree the public welfare may require it." The government would become "the steward of the public welfare."

This formulation unleashed Roosevelt. He took up the cause of social justice, adding to his program a federal child labor law, regulation of labor relations, and a national minimum wage for women. Most radical, perhaps, was Roosevelt's attack on the legal system. Insisting that the courts stood in the way of reform, Roosevelt proposed sharp curbs on their powers, even raising the possibility of popular recall of court decisions.

Early in 1912, Roosevelt announced his candidacy for the presidency, immediately sweeping the Insurgent faction into his camp. A bitter party battle ensued. Roosevelt won the states that held primary elections, but Taft controlled the party caucuses elsewhere. Dominated by party regulars, the Republican convention chose Taft. Considering himself cheated out of the nomination, Roosevelt led his followers into a new Progressive Party, soon nicknamed the "Bull Moose Party." In a crusading campaign, Roosevelt offered the New Nationalism to the people.

Woodrow Wilson and the New Freedom

While the Republicans battled among themselves, the Democrats were on the move. The scars caused by the free-silver battle had faded, and William Jennings Bryan's 1908 campaign established the party's progressive credentials. The Democrats made dramatic electoral gains in 1910. And Bryan, after fourteen years as the party's standard-bearer, made way for a new generation of leaders.

The ablest of these was Woodrow Wilson of New Jersey, a noted political scientist who, as its president, had brought Princeton into the front rank of American universities. In 1910, with no political experience, he accepted the Democratic nomination for governor of New Jersey and won. Wilson compiled a sterling reform record, including the direct primary, workers' compensation, and utility regulation, and went on to win the Democratic presidential nomination in 1912.

Wilson possessed—to a fault—the moral certainty that was the hallmark of progressive leaders. The product of a family of Presbyterian clerics, he instinctively assumed the mantle of righteousness. Only gradually, however, did Wilson hammer out, in reaction to Roosevelt's New Nationalism, a coherent reform program, which he called the New Freedom. As he warmed to the debate, Wilson cast his differences with Roosevelt in fundamental terms of slavery and freedom. "This is a struggle for emancipation," he proclaimed in October 1912. "If America is not to have free enterprise, then she can have freedom of no sort whatever." The New Nationalism represented a future of collectivism, Wilson warned, whereas the New Freedom would preserve political and economic liberty.

Wilson actually had much in common with Roosevelt. "The old time of individual competition is probably gone by," Wilson admitted. He even agreed on the need for a strong federal government. He parted company with Roosevelt over means, not ends, confident that the government's existing powers were adequate, with some tinkering, to the task of restraining big business.

Despite all the rhetoric, the 1912 election fell short as a referendum on basic principles. The outcome turned on a more humdrum reality: Wilson won because he kept the Democratic vote, while the Republican vote was split between Roosevelt and Taft. Despite a landslide in the electoral college, Wilson received only 42 percent of the popular vote (Map 20.2).

Yet the 1912 election proved to be a turning point for economic reform. The clash between Roosevelt and Wilson had brought forth, in the New Freedom, a program capable of finally resolving the decade-long crisis over corporate power. Just as important, the election created a rare legislative opportunity. With Congress in Democratic hands, the time was ripe to act on the New Freedom.

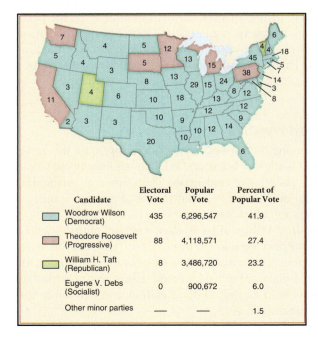

Candidate	Electoral Vote	Popular Vote	Percent of Popular Vote
Woodrow Wilson (Democrat)	435	6,296,547	41.9
Theodore Roosevelt (Progressive)	88	4,118,571	27.4
William H. Taft (Republican)	8	3,486,720	23.2
Eugene V. Debs (Socialist)	0	900,672	6.0
Other minor parties	—	—	1.5

MAP 20.2 Presidential Election of 1912

The 1912 election reveals why the two-party system is so strongly rooted in American politics. The Democrats, though a minority party, won an electoral landslide because the Republicans divided their vote between Roosevelt and Taft. This result indicates what is at stake when major parties splinter. The Socialists, despite a record vote of 900,000, received no electoral votes. To vote Socialist in 1912 meant, in effect, to throw away one's vote.

Long out of power, the Democrats were hungry for tariff reform. The Underwood Tariff Act of 1913 pared rates down to 25 percent, targeting especially the trust-dominated industries. Democrats confidently expected the Underwood Tariff to spur competition and reduce prices for consumers.

Wilson then turned to the nation's banking system, whose key weakness was the absence of a central bank or federal reserve system. The main function of central banks at that time was to back up commercial banks in case they could not meet their obligations to depositors. In the past, this backup role had been assumed by the great New York banks that handled the accounts of outlying banks. If the New York banks weakened, the entire system could collapse. This had nearly happened in 1907, when the Knickerbocker Trust Company failed and panic swept the nation's financial markets.

But if the need for a central bank was clear, the form it should take was hotly disputed. President Wilson, initially no expert, learned quickly and reconciled the reformers and bankers. The resulting Federal Reserve Act of 1913 gave the nation a banking system that was resistant to financial panic. The act delegated operational functions to twelve district reserve banks funded and controlled by their member banks. The Federal Reserve Board imposed public regulation on this regional structure. One crucial new power granted the Federal Reserve was authority to issue currency — federal reserve notes based on assets within the system — that resolved the paralyzing cash shortages during runs on the banks. Another was the Federal Reserve Board's authority to set the discount rate (the interest rate) charged by the district reserve banks to the member banks and thereby regulate the flow of credit to the general public. In one stroke, the act strengthened the banking system and, to a modest degree, reined in Wall Street.

Wilson now turned to the big question of the trusts. He relied heavily on a new advisor: Louis D. Brandeis, the celebrated "people's lawyer." Brandeis denied that bigness meant efficiency. On the contrary, smaller firms that vigorously competed in a free market ran most efficiently. The main thing was to prevent the trusts from unfairly using their power to curb free competition.

Strengthening the Sherman Act, the obvious course, proved hard to do. Was it feasible to say exactly when company practices became illegal? Brandeis decided that it was not, and Wilson assented. In the Clayton Antitrust Act of 1914, amending the Sherman Act, the definition of illegal practices was left flexible, subject to the test of whether an action "substantially lessen[ed] competition or tend[ed] to create a monopoly."

This retreat from a definitive antitrust prescription meant that a federal trade commission would be needed to back up the Sherman and Clayton Acts. Wilson was understandably hesitant, given his opposition during the campaign to Roosevelt's powerful trade commission. At first, Wilson favored an advisory, information-gathering agency. But ultimately, under the 1914 law that established it, the Federal Trade Commission received broad powers to investigate companies and issue "cease and desist" orders against unfair trade practices.

Despite a good deal of commotion, this arduous legislative process was actually an exercise in consensus building. Afterward, Wilson felt that he had brought the long controversy to a successful conclusion; and, in fact, he had. Steering a course between Taft's conservatism and Roosevelt's radical New Nationalism, Wilson carved out a middle way. He brought to bear the powers of government without shattering the constitutional order and curbed corporate abuses without threatening the free-enterprise system.

In the meantime, as one crisis over economic power was being resolved, another boiled up. After midnight on October 1, 1910, an explosion ripped through the *Los Angeles Times* headquarters, killing twenty employees and wrecking the building. It turned out that John J. McNamara, a high official of the AFL's Bridge and Structural Iron Workers Union, was behind the dynamiting and that his brother and another union member had done the deed. Lincoln Steffens gave voice to a question that, in the midst of the national outrage over the bombing, people kept asking: Why would "healthy, good-tempered boys like these McNamara boys . . . believe . . . that the only recourse they have for improving the conditions of the wage earner is to use dynamite against property and life?"

Steffens's question resonated ever more urgently as a wave of violent strikes swept the country: New York garment workers in 1910; railroad workers on the Illinois Central and Harriman lines in 1911; and textile workers, led by the Industrial Workers of the World (see Chapter 17), in Lawrence, Massachusetts, in 1912 and Paterson, New Jersey, in 1913. The IWW presence compounded middle-class fear of class war because the Wobblies did indeed use violent, anticapitalist language. Finally, in a ghastly climactic episode in 1914, state militia torched a tent city at Ludlow during a bitter Colorado coal miners' strike and asphyxiated many strikers' wives and children. Infuriated miners took up arms and plunged Colorado into a civil war that ended only with arrival of the U.S. Army.

The "labor question" was suddenly on the progressive agenda. President Wilson appointed a blue-ribbon U.S. Commission on Industrial Relations, whose job it would be, as the youthful journalist Walter Lippmann wrote, to explain "why America, supposed to become the land of promise, has become the land of disappointment and deep-seated discontent." In its majority report, the Commission took note that workers earning $10 or less a week lived at poverty levels, that they were ground down by repeated spells of unemployment, and that "an almost universal conviction [prevailed] that they, both as individuals and as a class, are denied justice."

The core reason for industrial violence, including the McNamara bombing, was the fierce antiunionism of American employers, which left workers with no voice and no hope for justice in the workplace. In its most important recommendation, the majority report called for federal legislation to protect the right of workers to organize and engage in collective bargaining. If this seemed, in 1915, too radical a proposal, it was in fact the opening shot in a battle for labor rights that would end triumphantly in the New Deal (see Chapter 24).

The immediate effect was to push President Wilson to the left. Having denounced Roosevelt's paternalism, Wilson had at first been unreceptive to what he saw as special-interest demands by organized labor. But now, instructed by the revelations of his Commission on Industrial Relations—and by labor's increasing clout at the polls—Wilson warmed up to the AFL.

As his second presidential campaign drew near, Wilson lost some of his scruples about the paternalism of prolabor legislation. In 1915 and 1916, he championed a host of bills that would be beneficial to American workers: a federal child labor law; the

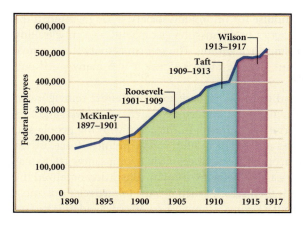

FIGURE 20.1   The Federal Bureaucracy, 1890–1917
The surge in federal employment after 1900 mirrored the surge in government authority under Theodore Roosevelt's progressive leadership. Not even Wilson, though he ran on a platform of limited government, could stem the tide. Numerically, in fact, the federal bureaucracy grew most rapidly during Wilson's first term.

Adamson eight-hour law for railroad workers; and the landmark Seamen's Act, which eliminated age-old abuses of sailors aboard ship. Nor was it lost on observers that, his New Freedom rhetoric notwithstanding, Wilson presided over an ever more active federal government and an ever-expanding federal bureaucracy (Figure 20.1).

Wilson encountered the same dilemma that confronted all successful progressives: the clash of moral principle against the unyielding realities of political life. Progressives were high-minded but not radical. They saw evils in the system, but they did not consider the system itself to be evil. They also prided themselves on being realists. So it stood to reason that Wilson, like other progressives who achieved power, would find his place at the center.

▶ Some observers considered Theodore Roosevelt an anti-business president. Do you agree? Why or why not?

▶ Why did William Howard Taft encounter so much trouble following in the footsteps of Theodore Roosevelt?

▶ Although historians describe the decades following William McKinley's election in 1896 as an age of Republican domination, the Democrat Woodrow Wilson won the presidency in 1912. Why?

But it would be wrong to underestimate their achievement. Progressives made presidential leadership important again, they brought government back into the nation's life, and they laid the foundation for twentieth-century social and economic policy. And, as we shall see, they put an enduring stamp on America's self-definition as a world power.

SUMMARY

In this chapter, we turned to the period between 1900 and World War I, which is distinguishable by the prominence of reform activity—hence its designation as the Progressive era. In these years, America gave its full attention to the problems resulting from industrialization and urban growth. We can discern the common elements of progressivism: a middle-class impulse for improving society, a tough-minded intellectual outlook confident of society's problem-solving capacity, and muckraking journalism that was adept at exposing wrongdoing. The reform activity that ensued, however, cannot be confined within a single mold because it was many-sided and always evolving.

American women took the lead on social welfare, and that effort reinvigorated the struggle for voting rights. Suffragists were divided over tactics, however, and further strains were generated by the rise of feminism. In the cities, working people and immigrants became reform-minded and set in motion a new political force: urban liberalism. Fighting the boss system, once the province of Mugwumps, now fell to seasoned professionals such as Robert La Follette, who simultaneously democratized the political parties and seized power for themselves. When it came to race relations, most progressives were not progressive, but a saving remnant overcame the endemic racism of the age and joined with black activists to forge the major institutions that would fight for black rights in the twentieth century: the NAACP and the Urban League.

At the national level, progressivism arrived via the accidental presidency of Theodore Roosevelt. Accidental or not, Roosevelt used the "bully pulpit" of the presidency against the economic power of corporate business. This overriding problem led to Roosevelt's Square Deal, then to his New Nationalism, and finally to Woodrow Wilson's New Freedom. The role of the federal government expanded dramatically but, despite the rhetoric, in service to a cautious and pragmatic handling of the country's problems.

Connections: Politics

Reform is a recurring theme in American history. The sectional crisis of the 1850s was preceded by reform ferment that sparked both the antislavery and women's rights movements (see Chapter 11). In this chapter, we focused on a second great age of reform, when, as the essay opening Part Four noted, "political reformers, women progressives, and urban liberals went about the business of cleaning up machine politics and making life better for America's urban masses." The Progressive era was cut short by World War I (Chapter 22); and in the aftermath, as the good times of the Roaring Twenties flowed, Americans lost interest in reform (Chapter 23)—but not for long. We will see in Chapter 24 how the Great Depression brought forth the New Deal and an era of sweeping reform that still structures our public life today, despite powerful countercurrents.

FOR FURTHER EXPLORATION

The historical literature on the Progressive era offers an embarrassment of riches. A good entry point is Michael McGerr, *A Fierce Discontent: The Rise and Fall of the Progressive Movement in America, 1870–1920* (2003). The following books are a sampling of the best that has been written about progressivism: John D. Buenker, *Urban Liberalism and Progressive Reform* (1973), on the politics of urban liberalism; Nancy F. Cott, *The Grounding of Modern Feminism* (1987); Robert M. Crunden, *Ministers of Reform, 1889–1920* (1982), on the religious underpinnings; and Naomi Lamoreaux, *The Great Merger Movement in American Business, 1895–1904* (1985). Among stimulating recent

TIMELINE

1889 ▶ Jane Addams and Ellen Gates Starr found Hull House	▶ William Howard Taft elected president
1893 ▶ Panic of 1893 starts depression of the 1890s	**1909** ▶ NAACP formed
1899 ▶ National Consumers' League founded	**1910** ▶ Roosevelt announces the New Nationalism
1900 ▶ Robert M. La Follette elected Wisconsin governor	▶ Woman suffrage movement revives
1901 ▶ President McKinley assassinated; Theodore Roosevelt succeeds him	**1911** ▶ *Standard Oil* decision restores "rule of reason"
1903 ▶ National Women's Trade Union League founded	▶ Triangle Shirtwaist Company fire
1904 ▶ Supreme Court dissolves the Northern Securities Company	**1912** ▶ Progressive Party formed
1906 ▶ Upton Sinclair's *The Jungle* is published	▶ Woodrow Wilson elected president
▶ Hepburn Railway Act	**1913** ▶ Federal Reserve Act
1908 ▶ *Muller v. Oregon* upholds regulation of working hours for women	▶ Underwood Tariff Act
	1914 ▶ Clayton Antitrust Act

books, see Nancy Cohen, *The Reconstruction of American Liberalism* (2002), on the intellectual origins; Julie Greene, *Pure and Simple Politics: The A.F. of L., 1881–1915* (1997), on labor's increasing political involvement; Elizabeth Lasch-Quinn, *Black Neighbors* (1993), on the racial conservatism of settlement-house progressives; Daniel T. Rodgers, *Atlantic Crossings: Social Democracy in a Progressive Age* (1998), a brilliant exploration of progressivism as an international phenomenon; and, as a sparkling narrative, David Von Dreir, *Triangle: The Fire that Changed America* (2003). "Theodore Roosevelt: Icon of the American Century" at **www.npg.si.edu/exh/roosevelt/roocat .htm** presents pictures from the National Portrait Gallery, a biographical narrative, and information on Roosevelt's family and friends.

TEST YOUR KNOWLEDGE

To assess your mastery of the material in this chapter and for Web sites, images, and documents related to this chapter, visit **bedfordstmartins.com/henrettaconcise**.

An Emerging World Power

1877–1914

God has marked the American people as His chosen nation to finally lead in the regeneration of the world. This is the divine mission of America, and it holds for us all the profit, all the glory, all the happiness possible to man.

— Senator Albert J. Beveridge, arguing for U.S. acquisition of the Philippines, 1900

In 1881, Great Britain sent a new envoy to Washington. Sir Lionel Sackville-West was the well-connected son of an earl but otherwise was distinguished only as the lover of a celebrated Spanish dancer. His influential friends wanted to park Sir Lionel somewhere comfortable but out of harm's way. So they made him minister to the United States.

Twenty years later, such an appointment would have been unthinkable. All the European powers staffed their missions in Washington with top-of-the-line ambassadors, and they treated the United States, without question, as a fellow Great Power.

In Sir Lionel's day, the United States scarcely cast a shadow on world affairs. America's navy ranked thirteenth in the world and was a threat mainly to the crews that manned its rickety ships. By 1900, however, the United States was flexing its muscles. It had just made short work of Spain in a brief but decisive war and had acquired an empire stretching from Puerto Rico to the Philippines. America's standing as a rising naval power was manifest, and so was its muscular assertion of national interest in the Caribbean and the Pacific.

Europeans could not be sure of America's future role, since the United States retained its traditional policy against entangling alliances. But foreign offices across the Continent took the United States most seriously and carefully assessed its likely response to every event.

The Roots of Expansion

With a population of fifty million, the United States already ranked with the great European powers in 1880. In industrial production, the nation stood second only to Britain and was rapidly closing the gap. Anyone who doubted the military prowess of Americans needed only to recall the ferocity with which they had fought one another in the Civil War. The great campaigns of Lee, Sherman, and Grant had entered the military textbooks and influenced army strategists everywhere, as was evident in the skirmishing lines and massed charges that the German infantry employed against the French in the Franco-Prussian War of 1870.

And when vital interests were at stake, the United States had shown itself not lacking in diplomatic vigor. The Civil War had put it at odds with both France and Britain. The dispute with France involved Mexico. The French-sponsored regime that had been set up there under Archduke Maximilian in 1863 posed a threat to the security of the American Southwest, whose seizure in 1848 still rankled Mexico. Once the Civil War ended, the United States responded forcefully. In 1867, as American troops under General Philip Sheridan massed on the border, the French military withdrew, abandoning Maximilian to a Mexican firing squad.

With Britain, the thorny issue involved damages to Union shipping by the *Alabama* and other Confederate sea raiders operating from English ports. American hopes of taking Canada as compensation were dashed by Britain's grant of dominion status to Canada in 1867. But four years later, after lengthy negotiations, Britain expressed regret and agreed to the arbitration of the *Alabama* claims, settling to America's satisfaction the last outstanding diplomatic issue of the Civil War.

Diplomacy in the Gilded Age

In the years that followed, the United States lapsed into diplomatic inactivity, not out of weakness but for lack of any clear national purpose in world affairs. The business of building the nation's industrial economy absorbed Americans and turned their attention inward. And while telegraphic cables provided the country with swift overseas communication after the 1860s, wide oceans still kept the world at a distance.

European affairs, which centered on Franco-German rivalry and on bewildering Balkan enmities, hardly registered in the United States. As far as President Cleveland's secretary of state, Thomas F. Bayard, was concerned, "we have not the slightest share or interest [in] the small politics and backstage intrigues of Europe."

In these circumstances, why maintain a big navy? After the Civil War, the fleet gradually deteriorated. Of the 125 ships on the navy's active list, only about 25 were seaworthy at any one time, mainly sailing ships and obsolete ironclads modeled on the *Monitor* of Civil War fame. The administration of Chester A. Arthur (1881–1885) began a modest upgrading program, commissioning new ships, raising the standards for the officer corps, and founding the Naval War College. But the fleet remained small and was deployed mainly for coastal defense.

Diplomacy was likewise of little account. Appointment to the Foreign Service came mostly through the spoils system. American envoys and consular officers were a mixed lot, with many idlers and drunkards among the hardworking and competent. For its part, the State Department tended to be inactive, exerting little control over either policy or its missions abroad. In Asia, Africa, and the Pacific islands, the American presence was likely to be Christian missionaries. Many were women, in a kind of global counterpart to women's role as social uplifters at home. As part of its do-everything program, the Woman's Christian Temperance Union began sending emissaries abroad to proselytize among the natives and convey the message that women's rights were an American cause.

In the Caribbean, the expansionist enthusiasms of the Civil War era subsided. William H. Seward, secretary of state under Lincoln and Andrew Johnson, had imagined an American empire extending from the Caribbean to Hawaii. Nothing came of his grandiose plans or of President Grant's efforts to purchase Santo Domingo (the future Dominican Republic) in 1870. The long-cherished interest in a canal across Central America also faded. Despite its claim to exclusive rights, the United States stood by when a French company headed by the builder of Egypt's Suez Canal, Ferdinand de Lesseps, started to dig across the Panama isthmus in 1880. That project failed, but for lack of funds, not because of American opposition.

Diplomatic activity quickened when the energetic James G. Blaine became secretary of state in 1881. He got involved in a border dispute between Mexico and Guatemala, tried to settle a war Chile was waging against Peru and Bolivia, and called the first Pan-American conference. Blaine's Latin American interventions went badly, however, and his successor canceled the Pan-American conference. This was a characteristic example of Gilded Age diplomacy, driven largely by partisan politics and carried out without any clear sense of national purpose.

Pan-Americanism—the notion of a community of states of the Western Hemisphere—took root, however, and Blaine, returning in 1889 for a second stint at the State Department, approved the plans of the outgoing Cleveland administration for a new Pan-American conference. Little came of it except for an agency in Washington that became the Pan-American Union. Any South American goodwill won by Blaine's efforts was soon blasted by the humiliation that the United States visited on Chile because of a riot against American sailors in Valparaiso in 1891. Threatened with war, Chile apologized and paid an indemnity of $75,000. It was not lost on South Americans that the United States, for all its fine talk about a community of nations, regarded itself as the hemisphere's dominating power and acted accordingly.

In the Pacific, American interest centered on Hawaii, where sugarcane had attracted a horde of American planters. Nominally an independent nation, Hawaii fell under American dominance. An 1875 treaty gave Hawaiian sugar duty-free entry into the American market and warned off other powers. A second treaty in 1887 granted the United States naval rights at Pearl Harbor.

When Hawaii's favored access to the American market was abruptly canceled by the McKinley Tariff of 1890, sugar planters began to plot an American takeover of the islands. They organized a revolt in January 1893 against Queen Liliuokalani and quickly negotiated a treaty of annexation. Before the Senate could approve it, however, Grover Cleveland returned to the presidency and withdrew the treaty. To annex Hawaii, he declared, would violate America's "honor and morality" and an "unbroken tradition" against acquiring territory far from the nation's shores.

Meanwhile, the American presence elsewhere in the Pacific was growing. In 1867, the United States purchased Alaska from Imperial Russia for $7.2 million. This had been at the behest of Moscow, which was anxious to unload an indefensible, treasury-draining

Cutting Sugar Cane, Hawaii.

Sugarcane Plantation, Hawaii

Over 300,000 Asians from China, Japan, Korea, and the Philippines came to work in the Hawaiian cane fields between 1850 and 1920. The hardships they endured are reflected in plantation work songs, such as this one by Japanese laborers:

But when I came what I saw was Hell

The boss was Satan

The lunas [overseers] his helpers.

© Curt Teich Postcard Archives, Lake County Museum.

possession. Secretary of State Seward, ever the expansionist, was happy to oblige, although it took some doing to persuade a dubious Congress. Alaska gave the United States not only a windfall of vast natural resources but also an unlooked-for presence extending across the northern Pacific.

Far to the south, in the Samoan Islands, the United States secured rights in 1878 to a coaling station for its steamships at Pago Pago harbor — a key link on the route to Australia — and established an informal protectorate there. In 1889, after some jostling with Germany and Britain, the rivalry over Samoa ended in a tripartite protectorate, with America retaining its rights in Pago Pago.

American diplomacy in these years has been characterized as a series of incidents, not the pursuit of a foreign policy. Many things happened, but intermittently and without any well-founded conception of national objectives. This was possible because, as the Englishman James Bryce remarked in 1888, America still sailed "upon a summer sea." In the stormier waters that lay ahead, a different kind of diplomacy would be required.

The Economy of Expansionism

"A policy of isolation did well enough when we were an embryo nation," remarked Senator Orville Platt of Connecticut in 1893. "But today things are different. . . . We are 65 million people . . . and regard to our future welfare demands an abandonment of the doctrines of isolation." What especially demanded that Americans look outward was their prodigious economy.

America's gross domestic product — the total value of goods and services — quadrupled between 1870 and 1900. But was American demand big enough to absorb this multiplying output? Over 90 percent of it was consumed at home. Even so, foreign markets mattered. Roughly one-fifth of the nation's agricultural output was exported, and as industry expanded, so did exports of manufactured goods. Between 1880 and 1900, the industrial share of exports jumped from 15 percent to over 30 percent.

American firms began to plant themselves overseas. As early as 1868, the Singer Sewing Machine Company established a factory in Glasgow, Scotland. The giant among American firms doing business abroad was Rockefeller's Standard Oil, with European branches marketing kerosene across the Continent. In Asia, Standard Oil cans, converted into utensils and roofing material, became a visible sign of American market penetration. Brand names such as Kodak (cameras), McCormick (agricultural equipment) and Ford (the Model T) became household words around the world.

Foreign trade was important partly for reasons of international finance. As a developing economy, the United States attracted a lot of foreign capital. The result was a heavy outflow of dollars to pay interest and dividends to foreign investors. To balance this account, the United States needed to export more goods than it imported. In fact, a favorable import-export balance was achieved in 1876 (Figure 21.1). But because of its dependence on foreign capital, America had to be vigilant about its export trade.

Even more important, however, was the relationship that many Americans perceived between foreign markets and social peace at home. Hard times always sparked

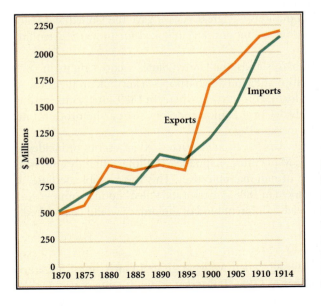

FIGURE 21.1 Balance of U.S. Imports, 1870–1914

By 1876, the United States had become a net exporting nation. The brief reversal after 1888 aroused fears that the United States was losing its foreign markets and helped fuel the expansionist drive of the 1890s.

agrarian unrest and labor strife. The problem, many observers thought, was that the nation's capacity to produce was outrunning its capacity to consume. When the economy slowed, cutbacks in domestic demand drove down farm prices and caused factory layoffs. The answer was to make sure that there would always be enough buyers for America's surplus products, and this meant buyers in foreign markets.

How did these concerns about overseas trade relate to America's foreign policy? The bulk of American exports in the late nineteenth century—over 80 percent—went to Europe and Canada. In these countries, normal diplomatic practice sufficed to protect the nation's economic interests. But if big international players such as Standard Oil needed help, that was available too. Rockefeller was thankful for the "ambassadors and ministers and consuls [who] have aided to push our way into new markets to the utmost corners of the world." In these places—in Asia, Latin America, and other regions that Americans considered "backward"—competition with other industrial powers called for a tougher brand of intervention.

Trade with Asia and Latin America was growing—it was worth $200 million in 1900—and parts of it, such as the Chinese market for American textiles, mattered a great deal to specific industries. The real importance of these non-Western markets, however, was not so much their current value as their future promise. China especially exerted a powerful grip on the American mercantile imagination. Many manufacturers believed that the China trade, although still quite small, would one day be the key to American prosperity. Therefore, China and other beckoning markets must not be closed to the United States.

In the mid-1880s, the pace of European imperialism picked up. After the Berlin Conference of 1884, the European powers rapidly carved Africa up. In a burst of modernizing energy, Japan transformed itself into a major power and challenged China's claims to Korea. In the Sino-Japanese War (1894–1895), Japan's easy victory started a scramble among the Great Powers, including Russia, to divide China into spheres of influence.

On top of all this came the Panic of 1893, setting in motion industrial strikes and agrarian protests that Cleveland's secretary of state, Walter Q. Gresham, like many other Americans, took to be "symptoms of revolution" (see Chapter 17). With the nation's social stability seemingly at risk, securing the markets of Latin America and Asia became an urgent matter.

The Making of a "Large" Foreign Policy

"Whether they will or no, Americans must now begin to look outward. The growing production of the country requires it." So wrote Captain Alfred T. Mahan, voicing an opinion that many others held by 1890. What he added was uniquely his: a strategy of American expansionism. Mahan was a naval officer in an age when the navy was no place for an ambitious young man. Posted to an aging warship cruising Latin America, he spent his spare time reading history. In a library in Lima, Peru, he hit on the idea that great empires—Rome in ancient times, Britain in his own day—had derived their power from control of the seas. This insight became the basis for his *The Influence of Sea Power upon History* (1890), the celebrated book that shaped America's strategic thinking about its role in the world.

The United States should regard the oceans not as barriers, Mahan argued, but as "a great highway . . . over which men pass in all directions." Traversing that highway required a robust merchant marine (America's had fallen on hard times since its heyday in the 1850s), a powerful navy to protect American commerce, and overseas bases. Without coaling stations, Mahan warned, steam-driven warships were "like land birds, unable to fly far from their own shores."

Mahan advocated a canal across Central America enabling the eastern United States to "compete with Europe, on equal terms as to distance, for the markets of East Asia." The canal's approaches would need to be guarded by bases in the Caribbean Sea. Hawaii would have to be annexed to extend American power into the Pacific. What Mahan envisioned was not colonial rule over populations, but control of strategic points in defense of America's trading interests.

Mahan proposed a battleship fleet capable of striking anywhere around the world. In 1890, Congress appropriated funds for three battleships as the first installment on a two-ocean navy. Battleships might be expensive, said Benjamin F. Tracy, Harrison's ambitious secretary of the navy, but they were "the premium paid by the United States for the insurance of its acquired wealth and its growing industries." The battleship took on a special aura for those—like the young Roosevelt—with grand dreams for the United States. "Oh, Lord! If only the people who are ignorant about our Navy could see those great warships in all their majesty and beauty, and could realize how [well fitted they are] to uphold the honor of America!"

The incoming Cleveland administration was less spread-eagled and, by canceling Harrison's scheme for annexing Hawaii, established its antiexpansionist credentials. But after hesitating briefly, Cleveland took up the naval program of his Republican predecessor, pressing Congress just as forcefully for more battleships (five were authorized) and making the same basic argument. The nation's commercial vitality—"free access to all markets," in the words of Cleveland's second secretary of state, Richard Olney—depended on its naval power.

While rejecting the territorial aspects of Mahan's thinking, Cleveland absorbed the underlying strategic arguments. This explains a remarkable crisis that suddenly blew up in 1895 over Venezuela.

For years, a border dispute had simmered between Venezuela and British Guiana. Now the United States demanded that the dispute be resolved. The European powers were carving up Africa and Asia. How could the United States be sure that Europe did not have similar designs on Latin America? Secretary of State Olney made that point in a bristling note to London on July 25, 1895, insisting that Britain accept arbitration or face the consequences. Invoking the Monroe Doctrine, Olney warned that the United States would brook no challenge to its vital interests in the Caribbean. These vital interests were America's, not Venezuela's; Venezuela was not consulted during the entire dispute.

Once the British realized that Cleveland meant business, they backed off and agreed to arbitration of the boundary dispute. Afterward, Olney remarked with satisfaction that, as a great industrial nation, the United States needed "to accept [a] commanding position" and take its place "among the Powers of the earth." Other countries would have to accommodate America's need for access to "more markets and larger markets for the consumption and products of the industry and inventive genius of the American people."

The Ideology of Expansionism

As policymakers hammered out a new foreign policy, a sustaining ideology took shape. One source of expansionist dogma was the Social Darwinist theory that dominated the political thought of this era (see Chapter 19). If, as Charles Darwin had shown, animals and plants evolved through the survival of the fittest, so did nations, according to this theory. "Nothing under the sun is stationary," warned the American social theorist Brooks Adams in *The Law of Civilization and Decay* (1895). "Not to advance is to recede." By this criterion, the United States had no choice; if it wanted to survive, it had to expand.

Linked to Social Darwinism was a belief in the inherent superiority of the Anglo-Saxon "race." In the late nineteenth century, Great Britain basked in the glory of its representative institutions, industrial prosperity, and far-flung empire—all ascribed to the supposed racial superiority of its people and, by extension, of their American cousins. On both sides of the Atlantic, **Anglo-Saxonism** was in vogue. Thus did John Fiske, an American philosopher and historian, lecture the nation on its future responsibilities: "The work which the English race began when it colonized North America is destined to go on until every land on the earth's surface that is not already the seat of an old civilization shall become English in its language, in its religion, in its political habits, and to a predominant extent in the blood of its people."

Fiske entitled his lecture "Manifest Destiny." A half century earlier, this term had expressed the sense of national mission—America's "manifest destiny"—to sweep aside the Native American peoples and occupy the continent. In his widely read book *The Winning of the West* (1896), Theodore Roosevelt drew a parallel between the expansionism of his own time and the assault on the Indians. To Roosevelt, what happened to "backward peoples" mattered little because their conquest was "for the benefit of civilization and in the interests of mankind." More than historical parallels, however, linked the Manifest Destiny of past and present.

In 1890, the U.S. Census reported the end of the continental movement westward: No frontier of unconquered land any longer existed. The psychological impact of that news was profound, spawning, among other things, a new historical interpretation that saw the frontier as the shaper of the nation's character. In a landmark essay setting out this thesis, "The Significance of the Frontier in American History" (1893), the young historian Frederick Jackson Turner suggested a link between the closing of the frontier and overseas expansion. "He would be a rash prophet who should assert that the expansive character of American life has now entirely ceased," Turner wrote. "Movement has been its dominant fact, and, unless this training has no effect upon a people, the American energy will continually demand a wider field for its exercise." As Turner predicted, Manifest Destiny did turn outward.

Thus, a strong current of ideas, deeply rooted in American experience and traditions, justified the new diplomacy of expansionism. The United States was eager to step onto the world stage. All it needed was the right occasion.

▶ What was the relationship between America's economic interests abroad and the expansionist impulse of the late nineteenth century?

▶ Describe Alfred T. Mahan's impact on American strategic thinking in the late nineteenth century.

▶ What were the intellectual currents that encouraged Americans to believe that their country should be an imperial power?

An American Empire

In the early nineteenth century, when its other American colonies broke free, Spain held on to Cuba. Yearning to join their mainland brothers and sisters, Cubans rebelled repeatedly against Spanish rule, most recently in the late 1860s. In February 1895, inspired by the poet José Martí, Cuban patriots rebelled again. Although Martí died in an early skirmish, his followers persisted, mounting a stubborn guerrilla war. The Spanish commander, Valeriano Weyler, responded by forcing entire populations into guarded camps, with devastating results. Out of a population of 1,600,000, as many as 200,000 died of starvation, exposure, or dysentery. *Reconcentration* became a byword for Spanish cruelty.

The Cuban Crisis

By itself, the Cuban cause might not have attracted much interest. Weyler's behavior was no worse than that of any other imperial enforcer; nor were atrocities in short supply elsewhere in the world. Cuban exiles tasked with the job of winning over the Americans, however, arrived in New York at a lucky moment.

William Randolph Hearst had just purchased the *New York Journal*, and he was in a hurry to build readership. Locked in a circulation war with Joseph Pulitzer's *New York World*, Hearst elevated Cuba's agony into flaming front-page headlines. The sporadic fighting took place in the remote interior, beyond the reach of Hearst's correspondents. It did not matter. Rebel claims were good enough for Hearst, and a drumbeat of superheated articles began to appear about mostly nonexistent battles and about Spanish atrocities.

Across the country, powerful sentiments stirred: humanitarian concern for the suffering Cubans, sympathy with their aspirations for freedom, and, as anger against Spain rose, a fiery patriotism that was soon tagged **jingoism**. These sentiments were often entwined with American anxieties over the perceived effeminacy of modern life (see Chapter 18). A gendered language infused the debate, with rebels portrayed as chivalric defenders of Cuban women against the "lustful bondage" of the Spaniards. It would be good for the nation's character, jingoists argued, for Americans to ride to the rescue. The government should not pass up this opportunity, said Senator Albert J. Beveridge, to "manufacture manhood." In this emotion-laden atmosphere, Congress began calling for Cuban independence.

President Cleveland took a cooler view of the situation. His concern was with America's vital interests, which, he told Congress, were "by no means of a wholly sentimental or philanthropic character." The Cuban civil war was disrupting trade and destroying American sugar plantations. Cleveland also was worried that Spain's troubles might draw in other European powers. A chronically unstable Cuba was incompatible with America's strategic interests, particularly the planned interoceanic canal whose Caribbean approaches would have to be safeguarded. If Spain could put down the rebellion, that was fine with Cleveland. But there was a limit, he felt, to how long the United States could tolerate Spain's impotence.

The McKinley administration, on taking office in March 1897, adopted much the same pragmatic line. Like Cleveland, McKinley saw the United States as the dominant Caribbean power, with vital interests at stake. McKinley, however, was inclined to be tougher on the Spaniards. He was upset by their "uncivilized and inhumane conduct," and he had to contend with rising jingoism in the Senate. But the notion, long held by historians, that McKinley was swept along by popular opinion was wrong. McKinley was very much his own man—a skilled politician and a canny, if undramatic, president. In particular, McKinley was sensitive to business fears of any rash action that might disrupt an economy just recovering from depression.

On September 18, 1897, the American minister in Madrid informed the Spanish government that it was time to "put a stop to this destructive war." Either ensure an "early and certain peace," the Spanish were told, or the United States would step in. At first, America's hard line seemed to work. Spain's conservative regime fell, and a liberal government, on taking office in October 1897, recalled General Weyler, backed away from reconcentration, and offered Cuba a limited degree of self-rule. Madrid's incapacity soon became clear, however. In January 1898, Spanish loyalists in Havana rioted against the offer of autonomy. The Cuban rebels, encouraged by the prospect of American intervention, demanded full independence.

On February 9, 1898, Hearst's *New York Journal* published a private letter by Dupuy de Lôme, the Spanish minister to the United States. In it, de Lôme called President McKinley "weak" and "a bidder for the admiration of the crowd." His letter suggested that the Spanish government was not taking the American demands seriously. De Lôme immediately resigned, but the damage had been done.

A week later, the U.S. battle cruiser *Maine* exploded and sank in Havana harbor, with the loss of 260 seamen. "Whole Country Thrills with the War Fever," proclaimed

"Remember the *Maine*!"

In late January 1898, the *Maine* entered Havana harbor on a courtesy call. On the evening of February 15, a mysterious blast sent the U.S. battle cruiser to the bottom. This dramatic lithograph conveys something of the impact of that event on American public opinion. Although no evidence ever linked the Spanish authorities to the explosion, the sinking of the *Maine* fed the emotional fires that prepared the nation for war with Spain. Granger Collection.

For more help analyzing this image, see the Online Study Guide at **bedfordstmartins.com/henrettaconcise**.

the *New York Journal.* From that moment onward, popular passions became a major factor in the march toward war.

McKinley kept his head. He assumed that the sinking had been accidental. A naval board of inquiry, however, issued a damaging report. Disagreeing with a Spanish investigation, the American board improbably blamed a naval mine. (A 1976 naval inquiry disagreed: The more likely cause was faulty ship design that placed explosive munitions too close to coal bunkers prone to spontaneous fires.) No evidence linked the Spanish to the purported mine. But if a mine did sink the ship, then the Spanish were responsible for not protecting an American vessel within their jurisdiction.

President McKinley had no stomach for the martial spirit engulfing the country. He was not swept along by the calls for blood to avenge the *Maine.* But he could not ignore an aroused public opinion. Hesitant business leaders now also became impatient. War was preferable to the unresolved Cuban crisis. On March 27, McKinley cabled to Madrid what was in effect an ultimatum: an immediate armistice for six months and, with the United States as mediator, peace negotiations with the rebels. The Spanish government, although desperate to avoid war, balked at McKinley's added demand that mediation had to result in Cuban independence, which would have meant the Madrid regime's downfall and, indeed, might have jeopardized the Crown itself.

On April 11, McKinley asked Congress for authority to intervene in Cuba. His motives were as he described them: "In the name of humanity, in the name of civilization, in behalf of endangered American interests which give us the right and the duty to speak and to act, the war in Cuba must stop." The War Hawks in Congress—a mixture of empire-minded Republicans such as Henry Cabot Lodge and western Democrats espousing Cuban self-determination—chafed under McKinley's cautious progress. But the president did not lose control, and he defeated their demand for recognition of the rebel government, which would have reduced the administration's freedom of action in dealing with Spain.

The resolutions authorizing intervention in Cuba contained an amendment by Senator Henry M. Teller of Colorado disclaiming any intention by the United States to take possession of Cuba. No European government should say that "when we go out to make battle for the liberty and freedom of Cuban patriots, that we are doing it for the purpose of aggrandizement." This had to be made clear with regard to Cuba, "whatever," Senator Teller added, "we may do as to some other islands."

Did McKinley have in mind "some other islands"? Was this really a war of aggression, secretly aimed at seizing strategic territory from Spain? In a strict sense, it almost certainly was not. It was not because of expansionist ambitions that McKinley forced Spain into a corner. But once war came, McKinley saw it as an opportunity. As he wrote privately after hostilities began, "While we are conducting war and until its conclusion, we must keep all we get; when the war is over we must keep what we want." Precisely what would be forthcoming, of course, depended on the fortunes of battle.

The Spoils of War

Spain declared war on the United States on April 24, 1898. Across the country, regiments began to form. Theodore Roosevelt immediately resigned as assistant secretary of the navy, ordered a fancy uniform, and accepted a commission as lieutenant colonel of a volunteer cavalry regiment that soon became famous as the Rough Riders. Raw recruits poured into makeshift bases around Tampa, Florida. Confusion reigned. Tropical uniforms did not arrive; the food was bad, the sanitation worse; and rifles were in short supply. No provision had been made for getting the troops to Cuba; the government hastily began to collect a miscellaneous fleet of yachts, lake steamers, and commercial boats. Fortunately, the small regular army was a disciplined, highly professional force. Its 28,000 seasoned troops provided a nucleus for the 200,000 civilians who had to be turned into soldiers inside of a few weeks.

The navy was in better shape. Spain had nothing to match America's seven battleships and armored cruisers, and the ships it did have were ill prepared for battle. The Spanish admiral, Pascual Cervera, gloomily expected that his fleet would "like Don Quixote go out to fight windmills and come back with a broken head."

The decisive engagement of the war took place in the western Pacific, not in Cuba. This was the handiwork of Theodore Roosevelt, who, while still in the Navy Department, had gotten the intrepid Commodore George Dewey appointed commander of the Pacific fleet, with instructions that, in the event of war, he was to set sail immediately against the Spanish fleet in the Philippines. When hostilities began, Roosevelt confronted his surprised superior, John Long, and pressured him into validating Dewey's instructions. On May 1, American ships cornered the Spanish fleet in Manila Bay and destroyed it. The victory produced euphoria in the United States. Immediately, part of the army being trained for the Cuban campaign was diverted to the Philippines. Manila, the Philippine capital, fell on August 13, 1898.

With Dewey's naval victory, American strategic thinking clicked into place. "We hold the other side of the Pacific and the value to this country is almost beyond imagination," declared Senator Lodge. "We must on no account let the [Philippine] Islands go." President McKinley agreed, and so did his key advisors. Naval strategists had long coveted an anchor in the western Pacific. At this time, too, the Great Powers were carving up China into spheres of influence. If American merchants wanted a crack at that glittering market, the United States would have to project its power into Asia.

Once the decision for a Philippine base had been made, other decisions followed almost automatically. The question of Hawaii was quickly resolved. After stalling the previous year, annexation of Hawaii went through Congress by joint resolution in July 1898. Hawaii had suddenly acquired a crucial strategic value: It was a halfway station on the way to the Philippines. The navy pressed for a coaling base in the central Pacific; that meant Guam, a Spanish island in the Marianas. There was need also for a strategically located base in the Caribbean; that meant Puerto Rico. By July, before the assault on Cuba, the full scope of McKinley's war aims had crystallized.

In Cuba, the Spanish forces had already been depleted by the long guerrilla war. Tied down by the rebels, they permitted the American landings at Daiquiri to go uncontested. Santiago, where the Spanish fleet was anchored, became the key to the military campaign (Map 21.1). Half-trained and ill-equipped, the American forces might have been checked by a determined opponent. The Spaniards fought to maintain their honor, but they had no stomach for a real war against the Americans.

The main battle, on July 1, occurred near Santiago on the heights commanded by San Juan Hill. Roosevelt's dismounted Rough Riders (there had been no room for horses on the transport ships) seized Kettle Hill. Then the frontal assault against the San Juan

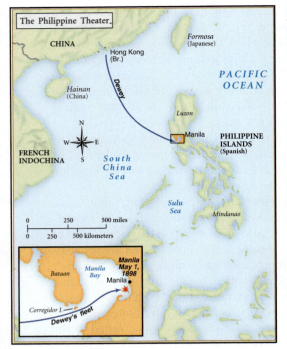

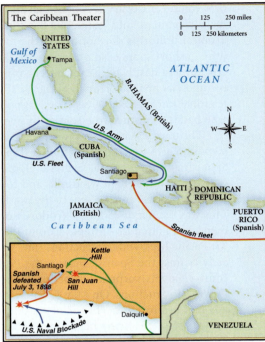

MAP 21.1 The Spanish-American War of 1898

The swift American victory in the Spanish-American War resulted from overwhelming naval superiority. Dewey's destruction of the Spanish fleet in Manila harbor doomed the Spaniards in the Philippines. In Cuba, American ground forces won a hard victory on San Juan Hill, for they were ill equipped and poorly supplied. With the United States in control of the seas, the Spaniards saw no choice but to give up the battle for Cuba.

For more help analyzing this map, see the Online Study Guide at **bedfordstmartins.com/henrettaconcise**.

heights began. Four black regiments bore the brunt of the fighting. White observers grudgingly credited much of the victory to the "superb gallantry" of the black soldiers. In fact, it was not quite a victory. Driven from their forward positions, the Spaniards retreated to a well-fortified second line. The exhausted Americans had suffered heavy casualties; whether they could have mounted a second assault was questionable. They were spared this test, however. On July 3, Cervera's fleet in Santiago harbor made a daylight attempt to run the American blockade and was destroyed. A few days later, convinced that Santiago could not be saved, the Spanish forces surrendered.

The two nations signed an armistice in which Spain agreed to liberate Cuba and cede Puerto Rico and Guam to the United States. American forces occupied Manila pending a peace treaty.

The Imperial Experiment

The big question was the Philippines, an archipelago of 7,000 islands populated—as William R. Day, McKinley's secretary of state, put it in the racist language of that era—by "eight or nine millions of absolutely ignorant and many degraded people."

Emilio Aguinaldo
At the start of the war with Spain, U.S. military leaders brought the Filipino patriot Emilio Aguinaldo back from Singapore because they thought he would stir up a popular uprising that would help defeat the Spaniards. Aguinaldo came because he thought the Americans favored an independent Philippines. These differing intentions — it has remained a matter of dispute what assurances Aguinaldo received — were the root cause of the Filipino insurrection that proved far costlier in American and Filipino lives than the war with Spain that preceded it. © Bettmann/Corbis.

Not even avid American expansionists advocated colonial rule over subject peoples; that was European-style imperialism, not the strategic bases that Mahan and his followers had in mind. Initially, their aim was to keep only Manila. It gradually became clear, however, that Manila was not defensible without the whole of Luzon, the large island on which the city was located.

McKinley surveyed the options. One possibility was to return most of the islands to Spain, but the reputed evils of Spanish rule made that a "cowardly and dishonorable" solution. Another possibility was to partition the Philippines with one or more of the Great Powers. But, as McKinley observed, turning over valuable territory to "our commercial rivals in the Orient—that would have been bad business and discreditable."

Most plausible was Philippine independence. As in Cuba, Spanish rule had already stirred up a rebellion, led by the ardent patriot Emilio Aguinaldo. An arrangement might have been possible like the one being extracted from the Cubans over Guantanamo Bay: the lease of a naval base to the Americans as the price of freedom. But after some hesitation, McKinley concluded that "we could not leave [the Filipinos] to themselves—they were unfit for self-rule—and they would soon have anarchy and misrule over there worse than Spain's was."

As for the Spaniards, they had little choice against what they considered "the immoderate demands of a conqueror." In the Treaty of Paris, they ceded the Philippines to the United States for a payment of $20 million. The treaty encountered harder going at home and was ratified by the Senate (requiring a two-thirds majority) on February 6, 1899, with only a single vote to spare.

Senate opponents of the treaty invoked the country's republican principles. Under the Constitution, argued the conservative Republican George F. Hoar, "no power is given to the Federal Government to acquire territory to be held and governed permanently as colonies" or "to conquer alien people and hold them in subjugation." The alternative — making eight million Filipinos American citizens — was equally unpalatable to the anti-imperialists, who were no more champions of "these savage people" than were the expansionists.

Leading citizens enlisted in the anti-imperialist cause, including the steel king Andrew Carnegie, who offered a check for $20 million to purchase the independence of the Philippines; the labor leader Samuel Gompers, who feared the competition of cheap Filipino labor; and Jane Addams, who believed that women should stand for peace. The key group was a social elite, old-line Mugwumps such as Carl Schurz, Charles Eliot Norton, and Charles Francis Adams. In November 1898, a Boston group formed the first of the Anti-Imperialist Leagues that began to spring up around the country.

Although skillful at publicizing their cause, the anti-imperialists never became a popular movement. They shared little but their anti-imperialism and, within the Mugwump core, lacked the common touch. Moreover, the Democrats, their natural allies, waffled on the issue. Although an outspoken anti-imperialist, William Jennings Bryan, the Democratic standard-bearer, confounded his friends by favoring ratification of the treaty. He hesitated to stake his party's future on opposition to a national policy that he privately believed to be irreversible. Still, if it was an accomplished fact, Philippine annexation came at a higher moral cost than anyone expected.

On February 4, 1899, two days before the Senate ratified the treaty, fighting broke out between American and Filipino patrols on the edge of Manila. Confronted by American annexation, the rebel leader Aguinaldo asserted his nation's independence and turned his guns on the occupying American forces.

The ensuing conflict far exceeded in ferocity the war just concluded with Spain. Fighting tenacious guerrillas, the U.S. Army resorted to the same tactics the Spaniards had employed in Cuba, moving people into towns, carrying out indiscriminate attacks beyond the perimeters, and burning crops and villages. Atrocities became commonplace on both sides. In three years of warfare, 4,200 Americans and many thousands of Filipinos died. The fighting ended in 1902, and William Howard Taft, who had been appointed governor-general of the Philippines, set up a civilian administration. He intended to make the territory a model of American road-building and sanitary engineering.

McKinley's convincing victory over William Jennings Bryan in 1900 suggested popular satisfaction with America's overseas adventure. Yet a strong undercurrent of misgivings was evident as Americans confronted the brutality of the fighting in the Philippines (see American Voices, p. 623). "We are destroying these islanders by the thousands, their villages and cities," protested the philosopher William James. "No life

Making the Philippines Safe for Democracy GENERAL ARTHUR MACARTHUR

General Arthur MacArthur was in on the action in the Philippines almost from the start. He led one of the first units to arrive there in 1898 and in 1900 was reassigned back as commander of the troops. After the insurrection had been put down, MacArthur appeared before a Senate committee to defend America's mission in the Philippines.

At the time I returned to Manila [May 1900] to assume the supreme command it seemed to me that . . . to doubt the wisdom of our [occupation] of the island was simply to doubt the stability of our own institutions. . . . It seemed to me that our conception of right, justice, freedom, and personal liberty was the precious fruit of centuries of strife [and that] we must regard ourselves simply as the custodians of imperishable ideas held in trust for the general benefit of mankind. In other words, I felt that we had attained a moral and intellectual height from which we were bound to proclaim to all as the occasion arose the true message of humanity as embodied in the principles of our own institutions. . . .

To my mind the archipelago is a fertile soil upon which to plant republicanism. . . . We are planting the best traditions, the best characteristics of Americanism in such a way that they can never be removed from that soil. That in itself seems to me a most inspiring thought. . . .

Sen. Thomas Patterson: Do you mean that imperishable idea of which you speak is the right of self-government?

Gen. MacArthur: Precisely so; self-government regulated by law as I understand it in this Republic.

Sen. Patterson: Of course you do not mean self-government regulated by some foreign and superior power?

Gen. MacArthur: Well, that is a matter of evolution, Senator. We are putting these institutions there so they will evolve themselves just as here and everywhere else where freedom has flourished. . . .

Sen. Patterson: Do I understand your claim of right and duty to retain the Philippine Islands is based upon the proposition that they have come to us upon the basis of our morals, honorable dealing, and unassailable international integrity?

Gen. MacArthur: That proposition is not questioned by anybody in the world, excepting a few people in the United States. . . . We will be benefited, and the Filipino people will be benefited, and that is what I meant by the original proposition—

Sen. Patterson: Do you mean the Filipino people that are left alive?

Gen. MacArthur: I do not admit that there has been any unusual destruction of life in the Philippine Islands. . . . I doubt if any war—either international or civil, any war on earth—has been conducted with as much humanity, with as much careful consideration, with as much self-restraint, as have been the American operations in the Philippine Archipelago. . . .

SOURCE: Henry F. Graff, ed., *American Imperialism and the Philippine Insurrection* (Boston: Little, Brown, 1969), 137–139, 144–145.

shall you have, we say, except as a gift from our philanthropy after your unconditional surrender to our will. . . . Could there be any more damning indictment of that whole bloated ideal termed 'modern civilization'?"

There were, moreover, unresolved constitutional issues. The Treaty of Paris, while guaranteeing them freedom of religion, specifically withheld from the inhabitants of the ceded Spanish territories any promise of citizenship. It would be up to Congress to decide their "civil rights and political status." Did this treatment conform to the Constitution? In 1901, the Supreme Court said that it did. The Constitution did not automatically extend citizenship to the acquired territories. Whether the inhabitants would be granted citizenship, or even the constitutional protections available to noncitizens in the United States, was up to Congress.

Overseas expansion was thus distinguished from the nation's continental expansion, marking the new territories as colonies, not future states, and marking the United States irrefutably as a colonial power. In 1916, in accordance with a special commission set up by McKinley, the Jones Act committed the United States to Philippine independence but set no date. (The Philippines achieved independence in 1946.)

▶ Why should a rebellion in Cuba — an internal affair of Spain's — have become a cause for war with the United States?

▶ If America's quarrel with Spain was over Cuba, why was the most important engagement of the Spanish-American War Dewey's naval victory in the Philippines?

▶ If, as Americans repeatedly said, they had fought Spain to help the Cuban people gain independence, how did the United States find itself fighting the Filipino people for just the opposite reason, that is, to prevent them from having independence?

The brutal war in the Philippines rubbed off some of the moralizing gloss but left undeflected America's global aspirations. In a few years, the United States had assembled an overseas empire: Hawaii, Puerto Rico, Guam, the Philippines, and finally, in 1900, several of the Samoan islands that had been jointly administered with Germany and Britain. The United States, remarked the legal scholar John Bassett Moore in 1899, had moved "from a position of comparative freedom from entanglements into a position of what is commonly called a world power."

Onto the World Stage

In Europe, the flexing of America's muscles against Spain caused a certain amount of consternation. The major powers had tried, before war broke out, to intercede on Spain's behalf — but tentatively, because no one was looking for trouble with the Americans. President McKinley had listened politely to their envoys and then proceeded with his war.

The decisive outcome confirmed what the Europeans already suspected. After Dewey's naval victory, the French paper *Le Temps* observed that "what passes before our eyes is the appearance of a new power of the first order." And the *London Times* concluded: "This war must . . . effect a profound change in the whole attitude and policy of the United States. In the future America will play a part in the general affairs of the world such as she has never played before" (see Voices from Abroad, p. 625).

American Goliath   JEAN HESS, ÉMILE ZOLA, AND RUBEN DARIO

Until the 1890s, foreign commentary was mostly about the strange habits of Americans. But once the United States flexed its muscles internationally, the commentary became more anxious, as the following three documents show. What the Goliath did mattered. That is what came from being a Great Power.

JEAN HESS, a Frenchman well traveled in East Asia, questioned American motives for intervening in the Philippines (1899).

Nowhere, in my opinion, better than in the Philippines, has it been shown that modern wars are simply "deals." The American intervention . . . has turned out to be nothing but a speculation of "business men," and not the generous effort of a people . . . procuring for others the liberty that it concedes belongs to all. . . . Back of all these battles, this devastation and mourning, in spite of the newly-born Yankee imperialism, there was only, there is only, what the people of the Bourse [stock market] call a deal.

ÉMILE ZOLA, the great French novelist, feared that America's military adventurism was dealing a blow to the cause of world peace (1900).

Nations which till now seem to have held aloof from the contagion, to have escaped this madness so prevalent in Europe, now appear to be attacked. Thus, since the Spanish war, the United States seems to have become a victim of the war fever. . . . I can detect the generation of vague ideas of future conquest. Until the present time that country wisely occupied itself with its domestic affairs and let Europe severely alone, but now it is donning plumes and epaulets, and will be dreaming of possible campaigns and be carried away with the idea of military glory.

In 1905, a year after the Roosevelt Corollary, the acclaimed Nicaraguan poet RUBEN DARIO issued an impassioned challenge from a small Central American country under the shadow of the Goliath. Dario addressed his poem "To Roosevelt."

The United States is grand and powerful.
. . . .
. . . A wealthy country,
joining the cult of Mammon to the cult of
    Hercules;
while Liberty . . .
. . . raises her torch in New York.
But our own America . . .
. . . .
. . . has lived, since the earliest moments of its
life, in light, in fire, in fragrance, and in love—
the America of Moctezuma and Atahualpa,
. . . .
O men with Saxon eyes and barbarous souls,
our America lives. . . .
. . . Be Careful.
Long live Spanish America!

SOURCES: Philip S. Foner and Robert C. Winchester, eds., *The Anti-Imperialist Reader: A Documentary History of Anti-Imperialism in the United States*, 2 vols. (New York: Holmes and Meier, 1984), 1: 98–99, 417–418; Thomas G. Paterson and Dennis Merrill, eds., *Major Problems in American Foreign Relations*, 2 vols. (Lexington, MA: D. C. Heath, 1995), 1: 508–509; *Selected Poems of Ruben Dario*, trans. Lysander Kemp (Austin: University of Texas Press, 1965).

A Power Among Powers

The politician most ardently agreeing with the *London Times* was the man who, with the assassination of William McKinley, became president on September 14, 1901. Unlike previous presidents, Theodore Roosevelt was an avid student of world affairs, widely traveled and acquainted with many European leaders. He had no doubt about America's role in the world.

It was important, first of all, to uphold the country's honor in the community of nations. The country should never shrink from righteous battle. "All the great masterful races have been fighting races," Roosevelt declared. But when he spoke of war, Roosevelt had in mind actions by the "civilized" nations against "backward peoples." Roosevelt felt "it incumbent on all the civilized and orderly powers to insist on the proper policing of the world." That was why he sympathized with European imperialism and how he justified American dominance in the Caribbean.

As for the "civilized and orderly" policemen of the world, the worst thing that could happen was for them to fall to fighting among themselves. Roosevelt had an acute sense of the fragility of world peace, and he was farsighted about the likelihood—in this, he was truly exceptional among Americans—of a catastrophic world war. He believed in American responsibility for helping to maintain the balance of power.

After the Spanish-American War, the European powers had been uncertain about how to deal with the victor. Only Great Britain, its position in Europe deteriorating in the face of a rising challenge from Germany and soured relations with France and Russia over clashing imperial interests, had a clear view of what it wanted. In its growing isolation, Britain turned to the United States. The Hay-Pauncefote Agreement (1901) gave up Britain's treaty rights to participate in any Central American canal project, clearing the way for a canal under exclusive U.S. control. Two years later, the last of the vexing U.S.-Canadian border disputes—this one involving British Columbia and Alaska—was settled, again to American satisfaction.

No formal alliance was forthcoming, but Anglo-American friendship had become so firm that the British Admiralty designed its war plans on the assumption that America was "a kindred state with whom we shall never have a parricidal war." Roosevelt heartily agreed. "England and United States, beyond any other two powers, should be friendly." In his unflagging efforts to maintain a global balance of power, the cornerstone of Roosevelt's policy was the English relationship.

Among nations, however, what counted was strength, not merely goodwill. Roosevelt wanted "to make all foreign powers understand that when we have adopted a line of policy we have adopted it definitely, and with the intention of backing it up with deeds as well as words." As Roosevelt famously said, "Speak softly and carry a big stick." By a "big stick," he meant, above all, naval power. And that meant a canal across Central America.

Freed by Britain's surrender of its joint canal rights, Roosevelt leased from Colombia a strip of land across Panama, a Colombian province. Furious when the Colombian legislature rejected the proposed treaty, Roosevelt contemplated outright seizure of Panama but settled on a more devious solution. With a Panamanian independence movement brewing, the United States lent covert assistance that brought off a bloodless revolution against Colombia. On November 6, 1903, the United States recognized Panama; two weeks later, it obtained a perpetually renewable lease on a canal zone. Roosevelt never regretted the victimization of Colombia, although the United States paid Colombia $25 million, as a kind of conscience money, in 1922.

Building the canal, one of the heroic engineering feats of the century, involved a vast swamp-clearing project, the construction of a series of great locks, and the excavation of 240 million cubic yards of earth. It took eight years of digging by thousands of hired laborers for the U.S. Army Corps of Engineers to finish the huge project. When the Panama Canal opened in 1914, it gave the United States a commanding position in the Western Hemisphere.

Next came the task of making the Caribbean basin secure. The countries there, said Secretary of State Elihu Root, had been placed "in the front yard of the United States" by the Panama Canal. Therefore, as Roosevelt put it, they had to "behave themselves."

In the case of Cuba, good behavior was readily managed by treaty following the Spanish-American War. Before withdrawing in 1902, the United States reorganized Cuban public finances and concluded a swamp-clearing program that eliminated yellow fever, a disease that had ravaged Cuba for many years. As a condition for gaining independence, Cuba accepted a proviso in its constitution called the Platt Amendment, which gave the United States the right to intervene if Cuban independence was threatened or internal order broke down. Cuba also granted the United States a lease on Guantánamo (which is still in effect), where the U.S. Navy built a large base.

It was a bitter pill for the Cubans, who thought they had made their own revolution, only to find their hard-won independence poisoned at birth. Mutual incomprehension — Americans expected gratitude, while Cubans felt mainly resentment — sowed the seeds of new revolutionary movements and Fidel Castro's future triumph in 1959. Of that, of course, Theodore Roosevelt was oblivious.

Claiming that instability in the Caribbean invited the intervention of European powers, Roosevelt announced in 1904 that the United States would act as "policeman" of the region, stepping in, "however reluctantly, in flagrant cases . . . of wrong-doing or impotence" (Map 21.2). This so-called Roosevelt Corollary to the Monroe Doctrine transformed that Doctrine's broad principle against European interference in Latin America into an unrestricted American right to regulate Caribbean affairs. The Roosevelt Corollary was not a treaty with other states; it was a unilateral declaration sanctioned only by American power and national interest.

Citing the Roosevelt Corollary, the United States intervened regularly in the internal affairs of Caribbean states. In 1905, American personnel took over the customs and debt management of the Dominican Republic and, similarly, the finances of Nicaragua in 1911 and Haiti in 1916. When domestic order broke down, the U.S. Marines occupied Cuba in 1906, Nicaragua in 1909, and Haiti and the Dominican Republic in later years.

The Open Door in Asia

Commercial interest dominated American policy in East Asia, especially the lure of the China market. By the late 1890s, Japan, Russia, Germany, France, and Britain had all carved out spheres of influence in China. Fearful of being frozen out, U.S. Secretary of

MAP 21.2 Policeman of the Caribbean

After the Spanish-American War, the United States vigorously asserted its interest in the affairs of its neighbors to the south. As the record of interventions shows, the United States truly became the "policeman" of the Caribbean.

State John Hay in 1899 sent them an Open Door note claiming the right of equal trade access — an open door — for all nations that wanted to do business in China. Despite its Philippine bases, the United States lacked real leverage in East Asia and elicited only noncommittal responses from the occupying powers. But Hay chose to interpret them as accepting the American open-door position.

When a secret society of Chinese nationalists, the Boxers, rebelled against the foreigners in 1900, the United States sent 5,000 troops and joined the multinational campaign to break the Boxers' siege of the diplomatic missions in Peking (Beijing). America took this opportunity to assert a second principle of the Open Door: that China be preserved as a "territorial and administrative entity." As long as the legal fiction of an independent China survived, so would American claims to equal access to the China market.

In the Caribbean the European powers had acceded to American dominance. But Britain, Germany, France, and Russia were strongly entrenched in East Asia and not inclined to defer to American interests. The United States also confronted a powerful Asian nation — Japan — that had its own vital interests. Although the open-door policy was important to him, Roosevelt recognized higher stakes at risk in the Pacific.

Japan had unveiled its military strength in the Sino-Japanese War of 1894–1895, which had begun the division of China into spheres of influence—not colonies, but regions marked off by the Great Powers over which they asserted informal dominance (Map 21.3). A decade later, provoked by Russian rivalry in Manchuria and Korea, Japan attacked the tsar's fleet at Port Arthur, Russia's leased port in China. In a series of brilliant victories, the Japanese smashed the Russian forces. Anxious to restore a balance of power,

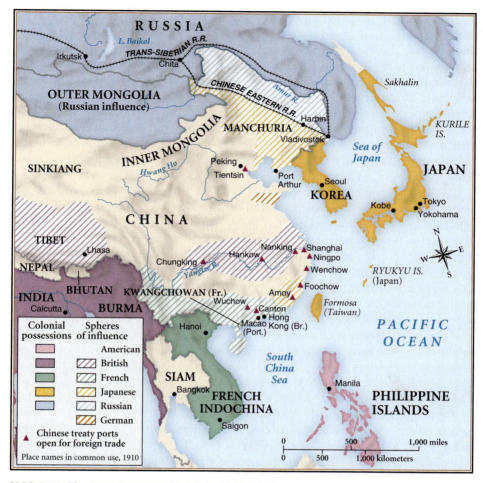

MAP 21.3 The Great Powers in East Asia, 1898–1910

The pattern of foreign dominance over China was via "treaty ports," where the powers based their naval forces, and "spheres of influence" extending from the ports into the hinterland. This map reveals why the United States had a weak hand; it lacked a presence on this colonized terrain. The Boxer Rebellion, by bringing an American expeditionary force to Peking, gave the United States a chance to insert itself onto the Chinese mainland, and American diplomats made the most of the opportunity to defend U.S. commercial interests in China.

Roosevelt mediated a settlement at Portsmouth, New Hampshire, in 1905. Japan emerged as the dominant power in East Asia.

Contemptuous of other Asian nations, Roosevelt respected the Japanese—"a wonderful and civilized people . . . entitled to stand in absolute equality with all the other peoples of the civilized world." He conceded that Japan had "a paramount interest in what surrounds the Yellow Sea, just as the United States has a paramount interest in what surrounds the Caribbean." But American strategic and commercial interests in the Pacific had to be accommodated. The United States approved of Japan's protectorate over Korea in 1905 and then of its declaration of full sovereignty six years later.

However, anti-Asian feeling in California complicated Roosevelt's efforts. In 1906, San Francisco's school board established a segregated school for Asian students, infuriating Japan. The "Gentlemen's Agreement" of 1907, in which Japan agreed to restrict immigration to the United States, smoothed matters over, but periodic racist slights by Americans made for continuing tensions with the Japanese.

Roosevelt meanwhile moved to balance Japan's military power in the Pacific. American battleships visited Japan in 1908 on a global tour that impressively displayed U.S. sea power. Late that year, near the end of his administration, Roosevelt achieved a formal accommodation with Japan. The Root-Takahira Agreement confirmed the status quo in the Pacific as well as the principles of free oceanic commerce and equal trade opportunity in China.

William Howard Taft, however, entered the White House in 1909 convinced that the United States had been short-changed. He pressed for a larger role for American investors, especially in the railroad construction going on in China. An exponent of **dollar diplomacy**—the aggressive coupling of American political and economic interests abroad—Taft hoped that American capital would counterbalance Japanese power and pave the way for increased commercial opportunities. When the Chinese Revolution of 1911 toppled the Manchu dynasty, Taft supported the victorious Chinese Nationalists, who wanted to modernize their country and liberate it from Japanese domination. The United States thus entered a long-term rivalry with Japan that would end in war thirty years later.

The United States had become embroiled in a distant struggle heavy with future liabilities but little by way of the fabulous profits that had lured Americans to Asia.

Wilson and Mexico

On becoming president in 1913, Woodrow Wilson embarked on reforming American foreign policy as well as domestic politics. Wilson did not really differ with Roosevelt or Taft about America's economic interests overseas. He applauded the "tides of commerce" that would arise from the Panama Canal. But he opposed dollar diplomacy, which he believed bullied weaker countries and gave undue advantage to American business. It seemed to Wilson "a very perilous thing to determine the foreign policy of a nation in terms of material interest."

Insisting that the United States conduct its foreign policy in conformity with its democratic principles, Wilson intended to foster "constitutional liberty in the world," especially among the nation's neighbors in Latin America. In a major foreign-policy speech in 1913, Wilson promised that the United States would "never again seek one additional foot of territory by conquest." He was committed to advancing "human rights, national integrity, and opportunity" abroad. To do otherwise would make "ourselves untrue to our own traditions."

Mexico became the primary object of Wilson's ministrations. A cycle of revolution had begun there in 1911. The dictator Porfirio Díaz was overthrown by Francisco Madero, who spoke much as Wilson did about liberty and constitutionalism. But before Madero got very far with his reforms, he was deposed and murdered in February 1913 by one of his generals, Victoriano Huerta. Other powers recognized Huerta's provisional government, but not the United States. Wilson abhorred Huerta, called him a murderer, and pledged "to force him out."

By intervening in this way, Wilson insisted, "we act in the interest of Mexico alone. . . . We are seeking to counsel Mexico for its own good." Wilson meant that he intended to put the Mexican Revolution back on the constitutional path started by Madero. Wilson was not deterred by the fact that American business interests, with big investments in Mexico, favored Huerta.

The emergence of armed opposition in northern Mexico under Venustiano Carranza strengthened Wilson's hand. But Carranza's Constitutionalist movement was ardently nationalist and hated American intervention. Carranza angrily rebuffed Wilson's efforts at bringing about elections by means of a compromise with the Huerta regime. Carranza also vowed to fight any intrusion of U.S. troops in his country. All he wanted from Wilson, Carranza asserted, was recognition of the Constitutionalists' belligerent status so that they could purchase arms in the United States. In exchange for vague promises to respect property rights and "fair" foreign concessions, Carranza finally got his way in 1914. American weapons began to flow to his troops.

When it became clear that Huerta was not about to fall, the United States threw its own forces into the conflict. On the pretext of a minor insult to the U.S. Navy, Wilson ordered the occupation of the port of Veracruz on April 21, 1914, at the cost of 19 American and 126 Mexican lives. At that point, the Huerta regime began to crumble. Carranza nevertheless condemned the United States, and his forces came close to engaging the Americans. When he entered Mexico City in triumph in August 1914, Carranza had some cause to thank the Yankees. But if any sense of gratitude existed, it was overshadowed by the anti-Americanism inspired by Wilson's insensitivity to Mexican pride and revolutionary zeal.

No sooner had the Constitutionalists triumphed than Carranza was challenged by his general, Pancho Villa, with some encouragement by American interests in Mexico. Defeated and driven northward, Villa began to stir up trouble along the border, killing sixteen American civilians taken from a train in January 1916 and raiding the town of Columbus, New Mexico, two months later. Wilson sent 11,000 troops under General John J. Pershing across the border after Villa.

Soon Pershing's force resembled an army of occupation more than a punitive expedition. Mexican public opinion demanded that Pershing withdraw, and armed clashes with Mexican troops began. At the brink of war, the two governments backed off, and U.S. forces began to withdraw in early 1917. Soon after, with a new constitution ratified and elections completed, the Carranza government finally received official recognition from Washington.

The Gathering Storm in Europe

In the meantime, Europe drifted toward war. There were two main sources of tension. One was the rivalry between Germany, the new superpower of Europe, and the European states that felt threatened by its might — above all France, which had been humiliated in the Franco-Prussian War of 1870. The second was the Balkans, where the Ottoman Empire was disintegrating and where, in the midst of explosive ethnic rivalries, Austria-Hungary and Russia were maneuvering for dominance. Out of these conflicts, an alliance system emerged, with Germany, Austria-Hungary, and Italy (the Triple Alliance) on one side and France and Russia (the Dual Alliance) on the other.

Pancho Villa, 1914
This photograph captures General Villa at the height of his powers, at the head of Carranza's northern army in 1914. The next year, he broke with Carranza and, among other desperate tactics, began to attack Americans. Formerly much admired in the United States, Villa became Public Enemy No. 1 overnight. He evaded General Pershing's punitive expedition of 1916, however, demonstrating the difficulties that even modern armies have against a guerrilla foe that knows the terrain and can melt away into a sympathetic population. Brown Brothers.

The tensions in Europe were partially released by European imperial adventures, drawing France into Africa and Russia into Asia. These activities put France and Russia at odds with imperial Britain, effectively excluding Britain from the European alliance system. Fearful of Germany, however, Britain in 1904 resolved its differences with France, and the two countries reached a friendly understanding, or *entente*. When Britain came to a similar understanding with Russia in 1907, the basis was laid for the Triple Entente. A deadly confrontation between two great European power blocs became possible.

In these European quarrels, Americans had no obvious stake or any inclination, in the words of a cautionary Senate resolution, "to depart from the traditional American foreign policy which forbids participation . . . [in] political questions which are entirely European in scope." But on becoming president, Theodore Roosevelt took a lively interest in European affairs and was eager, as the head of a Great Power, to make a contribution to the cause of peace. In 1905, he got his chance.

The Anglo-French entente of the previous year was based partly on a territorial deal in North Africa: The Sudan went to Britain, and Morocco went to France. Then Germany suddenly challenged France over Morocco—a disastrous move that conflicted with Germany's interest in keeping France's attention diverted from Europe. At Kaiser Wilhelm II's behest, Roosevelt arranged an international conference, which was held in January 1906 at Algeciras, Spain. With U.S. diplomats playing a key role, the crisis was defused. Germany got a few token concessions, but France retained its dominance over Morocco.

Algeciras marked an ominous turning point—the first time the power blocs that were fated to come to blows in 1914 squared off against one another. But in 1906, the conference seemed a diplomatic triumph. Roosevelt's secretary of state, Elihu Root, boasted of America's success in "preserv[ing] world peace because of the power of our detachment." Root's words prefigured how the United States would define its role among the Great Powers. It would be the apostle of peace, distinguished by its "detachment," by its lack of selfish interest in European affairs.

Opposing this internationalist impulse, however, was America's traditional suspicion of foreign entanglements. In principle, Americans were all in favor of world peace. Organizations such as the American Peace Society flourished during the Progressive Era. But the country grew nervous when it came to translating principle into practice. Thus, Americans embraced the international movement for the peaceful resolution of disputes among nations. They enthusiastically greeted the Hague Peace Conference of 1899, which established the International Court of Arbitration. Making use of the Court, however, required bilateral treaties with other nations defining the arbitration ground rules. Roosevelt carefully excepted all matters affecting "the vital interests, the independence, or the honor" of the United States. Even so, the Senate shot down Roosevelt's arbitration treaties. Taft's efforts met a similar fate.

When he became Wilson's secretary of state, William Jennings Bryan took a milder route. An apostle of world peace, Bryan devoted himself to negotiating a series of "cooling-off" treaties with other countries—so called because the parties agreed to wait for one year while disputed issues were submitted to a conciliation process. Although admirable, these bilateral agreements had no bearing on the explosive power politics of Europe. As tensions there reached the breaking point in 1914, the United States remained effectively on the sidelines.

Yet at Algeciras, Roosevelt had correctly anticipated what the future would demand of America. So did the French journalist Andre Tardieu, who remarked in 1908:

> The United States is . . . a world power. . . . Its power creates for it . . . a duty—to pronounce upon all those questions that hitherto have been arranged by agreement only among European powers. . . . The United States intervenes thus in the affairs of the universe. . . . It is seated at the table where the great game is played, and it cannot leave it.

▶ What did Roosevelt mean when he said that the United States had to be the policeman of the Caribbean?

▶ Woodrow Wilson believed that the United States should be true to its democratic principles in dealing with Latin America. How would you rate Wilson's approach when he applied it to the Mexican Revolution?

▶ Why in the late nineteenth century did it become untenable for the United States to adhere to its traditional isolation from world affairs?

SUMMARY

In this chapter, we explored America's emergence as a Great Power in the late nineteenth century. By any economic standard, the country already ranked with the major European powers. But America's orientation was inward-looking, with little attention to foreign policy or the military. Economic growth, however, created a need for outlets for its surplus products and forced the country to look outward. By the early 1890s, strategists such as Alfred T. Mahan were calling for a battleship navy, an interoceanic canal, and overseas bases. This expansionist thinking was legitimized by ideas drawn from Social Darwinism, Anglo-Saxon racism, and America's tradition of Manifest Destiny.

The Spanish-American War provided the opportunity for acting on these imperialist inclinations. Swift victory enabled the United States to seize from Spain the key possessions it wanted. In taking the Philippines, however, the United States overstepped an expansionism aimed only at acquiring strategic bases. The result was a Filipino insurrection and resurgent anti-imperialist sentiment at home. Even so, the McKinley administration realized the strategic goals it had set, and the United States entered the twentieth century poised to take its place as a Great Power.

In the Caribbean and Asia, the United States moved aggressively, building the Panama Canal, asserting its dominance over the nearby states, and pressing for the Open Door in China. When Woodrow Wilson became president, he tried to bring the conduct of foreign policy more into conformity with the nation's political ideals, only to have the limitations of that approach revealed by his intervention in the Mexican Revolution. Although world peace was an increasingly popular cause in America, that sentiment did not translate into diplomatic action. The United States stood on the sidelines as a great war engulfed Europe in 1914.

Connections: Diplomacy

For a century after Independence, American diplomacy dealt mostly with the lingering effects of the country's colonial origins (Chapter 8) and its expansionist continental ambitions (Chapter 13). Otherwise, America was content to remain on the diplomatic sidelines until, in the 1890s, it finally burst onto the world stage. As the essay opening Part Four noted:

> In short order, the United States went to war with Spain, acquired an overseas empire, and became actively engaged in Latin America and Asia. There was no mistaking America's standing as a Great Power.

The next chapter describes how the United States handled that challenge in World War I. In Chapter 25, we will see how it learned from its mistakes and tried to do better in World War II. From then on, diplomacy will become a dominant theme in this text, but the question of how America should conduct itself as a Great Power remains as unresolved today as when it first arose in 1900.

FOR FURTHER EXPLORATION

Walter LaFeber, *The American Search for Opportunity, 1865–1913* (1993), is an excellent, up-to-date synthesis. LaFeber emphasizes the need for overseas markets as the source of American expansionism. His immensely influential *The New Empire, 1860–1898* (1963) initiated the scholarly debate on this issue. A robust counterpoint is Fareed

TIMELINE

1875 ▶ Treaty brings Hawaii within U.S. orbit	▶ Guerrilla war in the Philippines
	▶ Open-door policy in China
1876 ▶ United States achieves favorable balance of trade	**1901** ▶ Theodore Roosevelt becomes president; diplomacy of the "big stick"
1881 ▶ Secretary of State James G. Blaine inaugurates Pan-Americanism	**1902** ▶ United States withdraws from Cuba; Platt Amendment gives United States right of intervention
1889 ▶ Conflict with Germany in Samoa	
1890 ▶ Alfred Thayer Mahan's *The Influence of Seapower upon History*	**1903** ▶ United States recognizes Panama and receives grant of Canal Zone
1893 ▶ Annexation of Hawaii fails	**1904** ▶ Roosevelt Corollary to the Monroe Doctrine
▶ Frederick Jackson Turner's "The Significance of the Frontier in American History"	
1894 ▶ Sino-Japanese War begins breakup of China into spheres of influence	**1906** ▶ United States mediates Franco-German crisis over Morocco at Algeciras
1895 ▶ Venezuela crisis	**1907** ▶ Gentlemen's Agreement with Japan
▶ Cuban civil war	
1898 ▶ Spanish-American War	**1908** ▶ Root-Takahira Agreement
▶ Hawaii annexed	**1913** ▶ Intervention in the Mexican Revolution
▶ Anti-imperialist movement launched	**1914** ▶ Panama Canal opens
1899 ▶ Treaty of Paris	▶ World War I begins

Zakaria's *From Wealth to Power* (1998), which asks why the United States was so slow (in comparison to other imperial nations) to translate its economic power into international muscle. Ivan Musicant, *Empire by Default* (1998), offers a full account of the Spanish-American War. The overlooked role of the Cuban rebels is brought to light by Louis S. Perez, *The War of 1898: The United States and Cuba* (1998). One source of the raging jingoism is uncovered in Kristin L. Hoganson, *Fighting for American Manhood: How Gender Provoked the Spanish-American and Philippine-American Wars* (1998). The Mexican Revolution as experienced by the Mexicans is brilliantly depicted in John Womack, *Zapata and the Mexican Revolution* (1968). Michael J. Hogan and Thomas G. Patterson, eds., *Explaining the History of American Foreign Relations*, 2nd ed. (2004), is a useful collection of new essays on historical writings on American diplomacy, much of it pertinent to the period covered by this chapter. The Library of Congress maintains an excellent Web site, "The World of 1898: The Spanish-American War," at **www.loc.gov/rr/hispanic/1898/**, with separate sections on the war in Cuba, the Philippines, Puerto Rico, and Spain.

TEST YOUR KNOWLEDGE

To assess your mastery of the material in this chapter and for Web sites, images, and documents related to this chapter, visit **bedfordstmartins.com/henrettaconcise**.

The Modern State and Society

1914–1945

GOVERNMENT	DIPLOMACY	ECONOMY
The rise of the state	**From isolation to world leadership**	**Prosperity, depression, and war**
1914 ▸ Wartime agencies expand power of federal government ▸ High taxes on the wealthy and corporations to pay for war	▸ United States enters World War I (1917) ▸ Wilson's Fourteen Points (1918)	▸ Shift from debtor to creditor nation ▸ Agricultural prosperity ▸ Postwar business-labor conflicts
1920 ▸ Republican ascendancy ▸ Prohibition (1920–1933) ▸ Business-government partnership ▸ Nineteenth Amendment gives women the vote	▸ Treaty of Versailles rejected by U.S. Senate (1920) ▸ Washington Conference sets naval limits (1922) ▸ Dawes Plan (1924) on reparations	▸ Economic recession (1920–1921) ▸ Booming prosperity (1922–1929) except in agriculture and coal industry ▸ Automobile age begins ▸ Rhetoric of welfare capitalism
1930 ▸ Franklin Roosevelt becomes president (1933) ▸ The New Deal: major government intervention in economy ▸ Social welfare liberalism	▸ Good Neighbor Policy toward Latin America (1933) ▸ Isolationism grows; U.S. neutrality laws ▸ FDR urges intervention	▸ Great Depression (1929–1941) ▸ TVA cuts floods and aids rural development ▸ Rise of CIO and organized labor
1940 ▸ Government mobilizes industry for war output ▸ Massive war budgets and debt ▸ Universal income tax system ▸ GI Bill of Rights	▸ United States enters World War II (1941) ▸ Atomic bombing of Japan (1945) ▸ United Nations created (1945)	▸ War spending ends depression ▸ Business executives join government ▸ Labor unions prosper during war

SOCIETY	CULTURE
Nativism, migration, and social change	**The emergence of a mass national culture**
▶ Southern blacks migrate to factory work in North ▶ Attacks against German Americans ▶ "Red Scare" (1919–1920)	▶ Wartime promotion of national unity ▶ Americanization campaign ▶ Silent screen; Hollywood becomes movie capital of the world
▶ Rise of nativism and revival of Ku Klux Klan ▶ National Origins Act (1924) ▶ Mexican American immigration grows ▶ Harlem Renaissance	▶ Advertising promotes consumer culture ▶ Spread of chain stores ▶ New media — radio, movies — create national popular culture ▶ Image of "Roaring Twenties"
▶ Farming families migrate from dust bowl states to California ▶ Indian New Deal ▶ Reverse migration to Asia and Mexico	▶ Documentary impulse in arts ▶ Works Project Administration assists writers and artists
▶ Internment of Japanese Americans ▶ Segregation in armed forces ▶ Rural whites and blacks migrate to war jobs in cities and West Coast	▶ Movie industry expands and aids war effort ▶ Rationing limits consumer culture ▶ Married women enter workforce in large numbers

In the 1930s, journalist Mark Sullivan described World War I as a "fundamental alteration, from which we would never go back." Sullivan was right: The war was a pivotal point in U.S. history. After 1914, the nation was more organized, more bureaucratic, and more conscious of itself as a distinct society. By 1945, the United States also had a much larger and more powerful national government, which had been created to fight the Great Depression and World War II. The structure of the new political, economic, and social order was largely complete.

GOVERNMENT

An essential feature of modern American society was the steady emergence of a strong national state. American participation in World War I called forth an unprecedented government-directed mobilization of the domestic economy, but in 1919, policymakers dismantled the centralized wartime agencies. During the 1920s, the Harding and Coolidge administrations created a partnership between government and business but relied primarily on corporate capitalism to provide jobs and benefits for the American people. The Great Depression exposed the weakness of that policy and led to Franklin D. Roosevelt's New Deal, which dramatically expanded federal responsibility for the nation's economic and social welfare. America's entry into World War II prompted an even greater expansion in the role played by the national state. Unlike the experience after World War I, the new state apparatus remained in place when the fighting ended.

DIPLOMACY

A second defining feature of modern America was its gradual movement toward a position of world political leadership. Before World War I, European nations dominated world affairs, but from that point on, the United States grew increasingly influential. In 1918, American troops provided the margin of victory for the Allies, and President Wilson shaped the Versailles treaty that ended the war. Although the United States refused to join the League of Nations, its powerful economic position gave it a prime role in international affairs in the 1920s and 1930s. America's global presence accelerated in 1941, when the nation threw all its energies into the war waged against fascist nations in Europe and Asia. Of all the major powers, only the United States emerged physically unscathed from that devastating global conflict. The country was also the only one to possess a powerful and dangerous new weapon: the atomic bomb.

ECONOMY

The dominant international position of the United States was primarily the result of its robust economy. Between 1914 and 1945, the nation boasted the world's most productive economic system, which churned out huge quantities of goods: cars, radios, refrigerators, and many more items — creating a consumer-focused economy and society. The Great Depression hit the United States harder than any other industrialized nation and fueled the dramatic growth of the labor movement in the 1930s. Thanks in part to defense contracts, large-scale corporate businesses assumed an even larger role in the American economy in World War II and afterward, while organized labor declined in significance.

SOCIETY

The character of modern American society reflected two great migrations to urban areas. Between 1880 and 1914, millions of immigrants from central and southern Europe took up residence in American cities, as did millions of native-born Americans from farms and small towns. The growth of metropolitan areas gave the nation an increasingly urban tone. The scale of the European influx alarmed many old-stock white Americans; in 1924, they secured legislation limiting immigration. But immigration from Mexico continued in the West and Southwest, and geographical mobility began to break down regional cultures. African Americans moved north and west to take factory jobs, dust bowl farmers migrated to the Far West, and whites from the Appalachian region took jobs in far-flung World War II defense plants.

CULTURE

Modern America saw the emergence of a mass national culture. By the 1920s, advertising and the new entertainment media—movies, radio, and magazines—were disseminating the new values of consumerism, and the Hollywood movie industry exported this vision of America worldwide. Not even the Great Depression and the goods shortages during World War II diverted citizens from their desire for leisure, self-fulfillment, and consumer goods. The emphasis on consumption and a quest for a rising standard of living remained central to the American experience for the rest of the twentieth century.

22 War and the American State
1914–1920

> It is not the army we must shape and train for war, it is a nation.
>
> —Woodrow Wilson, 1917

In war, as in peace, President Woodrow Wilson and his administration energized the nation with the idealistic rhetoric of Progressivism: "It's Up to You—Protect the Nation's Honor—Enlist Now." "Women! Help America's Sons Win the War: Buy U.S. Government Bonds." "Food Is Ammunition—Don't Waste It." At every turn during the eighteen months of American participation in the Great War—at the movies, in schools and libraries, in shop windows and post offices, at train stations and factories—native-born citizens and recent immigrants encountered dramatic posters urging them to do their share. These posters, now colorful reminders of a bygone era, had the serious goal of unifying the American people in voluntary, self-sacrificing service to the nation.

The posters symbolized the increased presence of the federal government in American life. The new federal bureaucracies that coordinated the war effort began the process that, during the New Deal of the 1930s, would create a national administrative state. These patriotic placards underlined the fact that citizens as well as armies waged modern warfare. The military effort mobilized the energies of the entire population and opened up new jobs for white women and ethnic minorities. The passions of war also sharpened existing social and ideological differences and turned them into crusades of hate, first against those of German origin or descent and then against "Bolsheviks" and socialists. These domestic conflicts—spawned by divisions of class, race, and ethnicity—foreshadowed the social confrontations of the 1920s and 1960s.

The Great War transformed the nation's position in the world. Before the conflict began in 1914, European nations had dominated international politics and trade. Four years of costly and bloody warfare shattered this supremacy. At the war's end, the United States was no longer a regional power; it was now part of the "great game" of international politics and committed, by President Woodrow Wilson, to making the world "safe for democracy." Even as American leaders during the 1920s abandoned this idealistic goal, the nation spread its economic and cultural influence across the globe.

The Great War, 1914–1918

When war erupted in August 1914, most Americans saw no reason to join the struggle among Europe's imperialistic powers. No vital U.S. economic interests were at stake. Indeed, the United States had good commercial relations with the Allied Powers of Great Britain, France, and Russia and the Central Powers of Germany and Austria-Hungary. But a combination of factors—financial commitments, neutrality rights, cultural ties with Britain, and German miscalculations—would finally draw the United States into the war on the Allied side in April 1917.

War in Europe

The Great War had been long in the making. In 1907, France, Russia, and Britain had formed the Triple Entente to counter the Triple Alliance of Germany, Austria-Hungary, and Italy (see Chapter 21). With Europe divided into rival diplomatic and military camps, war became increasingly likely. The spark that ignited the conflict came in Europe's long-standing trouble spot, the Balkans, where Austria-Hungary and Russia were competing for control as the Ottoman Empire slowly disintegrated. Austria's seizure in 1908 of the Ottoman provinces of Bosnia and Herzegovina, with their substantial Slavic populations, had enraged Slavic ideologues in Russia and its ally, the independent Slavic state of Serbia. In response, Serbian terrorists recruited Bosnian Slavs, including university student Gavrilo Princip, to resist Austrian rule. In June 1914, in the town of Sarajevo, Princip assassinated Franz Ferdinand, the heir to the Austro-Hungarian throne, and his wife, the Duchess of Hohenberg.

The complex system of European diplomatic alliances, which for years had maintained a fragile peace, now quickly pulled all the major powers into war. Austria-Hungary blamed Serbia for the assassination and declared war on July 28. Russia, tied by a secret treaty to Serbia, mobilized its armies against Austria-Hungary. Russia's move prompted Germany to declare war on Russia and its ally, France. To attack France, the Germans launched a brutal invasion of the neutral country of Belgium, which caused Great Britain to declare war on Germany. By August 4, nearly all of Europe was at war. The Allied Powers—Great Britain, France, and Russia—confronted the Central Powers of Germany and Austria-Hungary, which were joined by Turkey in November 1914 (Map 22.1).

Two major battle zones emerged in Europe. The British and French (and later the Americans) battled on the Western Front against the Germans. Germany, assisted by Austrians and Hungarians, also fought against the Russians on the Eastern Front. Because most of the warring nations held colonial empires, the conflict spread to the Middle East, Africa, and China, throwing open the future of those areas. Hoping to secure valuable colonies, Italy and Japan soon joined the Allied side, while Bulgaria linked up with the Central Powers.

Because of its worldwide scope and terrible devastation, people soon referred to the conflict as the Great War. New military technology, some of it devised in the United States, made warfare more deadly than ever before. Every soldier carried a long-range, high-velocity rifle that could hit a target at 1,000 yards—a vast technical improvement over the

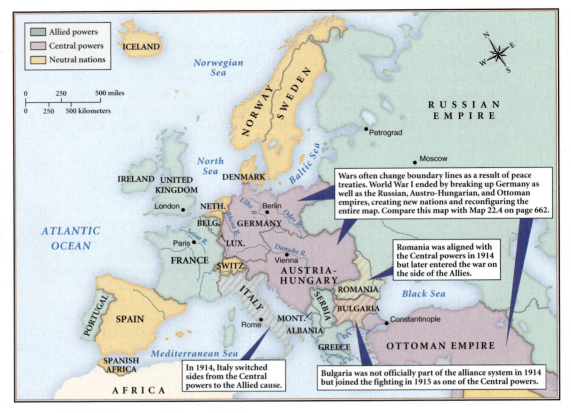

Legend:
- Allied powers
- Central powers
- Neutral nations

Wars often change boundary lines as a result of peace treaties. World War I ended by breaking up Germany as well as the Russian, Austro-Hungarian, and Ottoman empires, creating new nations and reconfiguring the entire map. Compare this map with Map 22.4 on page 662.

Romania was aligned with the Central powers in 1914 but later entered the war on the side of the Allies.

In 1914, Italy switched sides from the Central powers to the Allied cause.

Bulgaria was not officially part of the alliance system in 1914 but joined the fighting in 1915 as one of the Central powers.

MAP 22.1 European Alliances in 1914

In early August 1914, a complex set of interlocking alliances drew all of the major European powers into war. At first, the United States avoided the conflict, which did not directly threaten its national interests. Only in April 1917 did America enter the war on the Allied side.

300-yard range of the rifle-musket used in the American Civil War. The machine gun was an even more deadly technological innovation. Its American-born inventor, Hiram Maxim, had moved to Great Britain in the 1880s to follow a friend's advice: "If you want to make your fortune, invent something which will allow those fool Europeans to kill each other more quickly."

These innovations changed the nature of warfare by giving a tremendous advantage to soldiers in defensive positions. Once the German advance into France ran into fortified positions, it stalled. For four bloody years, millions of soldiers fought from 25,000 miles of heavily fortified trenches that cut across a narrow swath of Belgium and northern France. One side and then the other would mount an attack across "no man's land," only to be caught in a sea of barbed wire or mowed down by machine guns and artillery fire. Trench warfare took an immense psychological toll; thousands of soldiers suffered from shell shock (now known as post-traumatic stress disorder). "I got quite used to carrying shell-shocked patients in the ambulance," British nurse Claire Tisdall recalled. "It was a horrible thing . . . rather like epileptic fits. They became quite unconscious, with violent shivering and shaking."

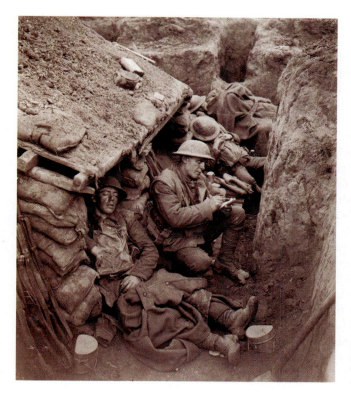

Trench Warfare

Millions of soldiers lived for months at a time in trenches that stretched for hundreds of miles across northern France. This photograph captures a moment of peace, when an exhausted soldier could catch some sleep or scribble a letter to his wife or family. Life in the trenches profoundly scarred many men and created a raft of new psychological ailments: "gas neurosis," "burial-alive neurosis," and "soldier's heart"—all symptoms of shell shock. Imperial War Museum, London.

For more help analyzing this image, see the Online Study Guide at **bedfordstmartins .com/henrettaconcise.**

Trying to break the stalemate, the Germans launched an attack at Ypres in April 1915 that used poison gas, a technological nightmare that amplified the human cost of the war. As the Germans tried to break through the French lines at Verdun between February and December 1916, they suffered 450,000 casualties; the French fared even worse, with 550,000 dead or wounded soldiers. It was all to no avail. From 1914 to 1918, the Western Front barely moved.

The Perils of Neutrality

As the stalemate continued, the United States grappled with its role in the international struggle. Following the outbreak of war, President Wilson called on Americans to be "neutral in fact as well as in name, impartial in thought as well as in action." If he kept America out of the conflict, Wilson reasoned, he could arbitrate—and influence—its ultimate settlement, much as President Theodore Roosevelt had helped to end the Russo-Japanese War of 1905.

The divided loyalties of the American people also prompted Wilson to pursue neutrality. Many Americans, including Wilson himself, felt deep cultural ties to the Allies, especially Britain and France. Yet most Irish Americans deeply resented Britain's centuries-long occupation of their homeland, which still continued. Moreover, ten million Germans had emigrated to the United States, and many of them belonged to German cultural organizations or lived in German-speaking rural communities and urban enclaves. Whatever his personal sympathies, Wilson could not easily have rallied the nation to the Allied side in 1914.

Many politically aware Americans refused to support either side. "It would be folly for the country to sacrifice itself to . . . the clash of ancient hatreds which is urging the Old World to destruction," declared the *New York Sun*. Progressive-minded Republicans, such as Senators Robert La Follette of Wisconsin and George Norris of Nebraska, vehemently opposed American participation in the European conflict. Virtually the entire political left, led principally by Eugene Debs and the Socialist Party, condemned the war as a conflict among greedy capitalist and imperialist nations. A. Philip Randolph and other African American leaders wanted no part of a struggle among white nations. Newly formed pacifist groups, such as the Women's Peace Party, mobilized popular opposition to the war. So did two giants of American industry, Andrew Carnegie and Henry Ford. In December 1915, Ford spent half a million dollars to send one hundred men and women to Europe on a "peace ship" to urge an end to the fighting.

Such sentiments might have kept the nation neutral if the conflict had not spread to the high seas. The United States wished to trade peacefully with all the warring nations, but the combatants would not grant this luxury to anyone. In September 1914, the British imposed a naval blockade on the Central Powers to cut off vital supplies of food, raw materials, and military armaments. The Wilson administration complained strongly at this infringement of the rights of neutral carriers but did not take punitive action. Profit was one reason: A spectacular increase in American trade with the Allies more than made up for the lost commerce with the Central Powers. Trade with Britain and France grew fourfold, from $824 million in 1914 to $3.2 billion in 1916; moreover, by 1917, U.S. banks had lent the Allies $2.5 billion. In contrast, American trade and loans to Germany were minuscule: a mere $56 million by 1917. This provision of goods and credit to the Allies by private corporations undercut the nation's official posture of neutrality.

To cut off this transatlantic trade and challenge the British navy, the Germans launched a devastating new weapon, the U-boat (short for *Unterseeboot*, the "undersea boat," or submarine). In April 1915, the German embassy in Washington issued a warning to civilians that all ships flying the flags of Britain or its allies were liable to destruction. A few weeks later, a German U-boat off the coast of Ireland torpedoed the British luxury liner *Lusitania*, killing 1,198 people, 128 of them Americans. The attack on the unarmed passenger vessel (which was later revealed to have been carrying munitions) incensed Americans; newspapers called it "mass murder" and branded Germans as "Savages drenched with blood." President Wilson sent a series of strongly worded protests to Germany, but tensions subsided in September 1915, when Germany announced that its U-boats would no longer attack passenger ships without warning.

The *Lusitania* crisis prompted Wilson to reconsider his opposition to military preparedness. The president had already tried, and failed, to mediate an end to the European conflict through his aide, Colonel Edward House. With neither side seriously interested in peace negotiations, in the fall of 1915 Wilson endorsed a $1 billion buildup of the American army and the navy.

American public opinion still ran strongly against entering the war, a fact that shaped the election of 1916. The reunited Republican Party passed over the belligerently prowar Theodore Roosevelt in favor of Supreme Court Justice Charles Evans Hughes, a progressive who had served as governor of New York. The Democrats renominated Wilson, who campaigned both on his record as a progressive (see Chapter 20) and as the president who "kept us out of war." Wilson eked out a narrow victory; winning California by a mere 4,000 votes, he secured a slim majority in the Electoral College.

Despite Wilson's campaign slogan, the president found that events pushed him toward war. In January 1917, Germany resumed unrestricted submarine warfare, a decision dictated by the impasse in the land war. In response, Wilson broke off diplomatic relations with Germany in early February. A few weeks later, newspapers published an intercepted dispatch from the German foreign secretary, Arthur Zimmermann, to his minister in Mexico City. Zimmermann urged the Mexican government to join the Central Powers; he promised that if the United States entered the European war, Germany would help Mexico recover "the lost territory of Texas, New Mexico, and Arizona." This threat to lands that the United States had held since the Mexican War of 1846–1848 jolted American opinion. During 1916, civil violence in Mexico had spilled over the border and resulted in the deaths of sixteen U.S. citizens. To halt attacks by Pancho Villa and other insurgents, a U.S. army force commanded by General John J. Pershing occupied parts of northern Mexico (see Chapter 21). As the United States and Mexico edged toward war, American policymakers took the German threat seriously.

Unrestricted submarine warfare and the Zimmermann telegram inflamed anti-German sentiment throughout the nation. German U-boats were now attacking American ships without warning and sank three on March 18 alone. On April 2, 1917, Wilson appeared before a special session of Congress to ask for a declaration of war. He told the legislators that Germany had trampled the nation's rights and imperiled its trade and citizens' lives. But the president did not urge entry into the war on material grounds. Rather, reflecting his Christian zeal and progressive idealism, Wilson justified entry as a moral imperative: "We desire no conquest, no dominion, . . . no material compensation for the sacrifices we shall freely make. We are but one of the champions of the rights of mankind." In a memorable phrase, Wilson suggested that American involvement would make the world "safe for democracy."

Four days later, on April 6, 1917, the United States declared war on Germany. Reflecting the divided feelings of the country, the vote was far from unanimous. Six senators and fifty members of the House voted against entry, including Representative Jeannette Rankin of Montana, the first woman elected to Congress. "You can no more win a war than you can win an earthquake," she said. "I want to stand by my country, but I cannot vote for war."

"Over There"

To native-born Americans, Europe seemed a great distance away—literally "over there," as the lyrics of George M. Cohan's popular song pictured it. Many citizens—and politicians—assumed that the United States would simply provide munitions and economic aid to the Allies. "Good Lord, you're not going to send soldiers over there, are you?" exclaimed Virginia Senator Thomas S. Martin. But when General

John J. Pershing traveled to Europe to find out how the United States could best support the war effort, French general Joseph Joffre put it clearly: "Men, men, and more men."

However, the United States had never maintained a large standing army, and in 1917, the U.S. Army had fewer than 200,000 men. To field a fighting force, Congress enacted a Selective Service Act in May 1917 that instituted a compulsory military draft. In contrast to the Civil War, when resistance was common, conscription went smoothly. One reason was that local, civilian-run draft boards played a central role in the Selective Service System. Still, the process of draft registration demonstrated the bureaucratic potential of the American state and its increasing power over ordinary citizens. On a single day—June 5, 1917—more than 9.5 million men between the ages of twenty-one and thirty registered at their local voting precincts for possible military service. By the end of the war, almost 4 million men, popularly known as "doughboys," plus a few thousand female navy clerks and army nurses, were in uniform. Another 300,000 men (labeled "slackers") evaded the draft, and 4,000 more received classification as conscientious objectors.

President Wilson chose General Pershing to head the American Expeditionary Force (AEF). But before the new army could fight, it had to be trained, outfitted, and carried across the submarine-infested Atlantic. The nation's first significant contribution to the Allied war effort was securing the safety of ocean transport. When the United States entered the war, German U-boats were sinking 900,000 tons of Allied ships each month. By sending merchant and troop ships in armed convoys, the U.S. Navy cut that monthly rate to 400,000 tons by the end of 1917. Surprisingly, no American soldiers were killed on the way to Europe.

Trench warfare on the Western Front continued to take thousands of lives. Allied commanders pleaded for American soldiers fill their depleted units, but Pershing wanted an independent force and waited until the AEF reached full strength. Therefore, until May 1918, the brunt of the fighting fell on the French and British. Their burden increased when the Eastern Front collapsed following the Bolshevik (Communist) Revolution in Russia in November 1917. To consolidate its power at home, the Bolshevik regime, led by Vladimir Ilych Lenin, sought peace with the Central Powers. In the Treaty of Brest-Litovsk in March 1918, the new Russian government surrendered its sovereignty over vast territories in central Europe, including Russian Poland, the Ukraine, and the Baltic provinces. Freed from warfare with Germany, Lenin's Communist government fought a successful three-year civil war against supporters of the ousted tsar, Nicholas II, and other counterrevolutionaries.

When its war with Russia ended, Germany launched a major offensive on the Western Front. By May 1918, the German army had advanced to within 50 miles of Paris. As Allied leaders called desperately for American troops, Pershing committed about 60,000 men to help the French repel the Germans in the battles of Château-Thierry and Belleau Wood (Map 22.2). With American troops arriving in massive numbers, the Allied forces brought the German offensive to a halt in mid-July. By mid-September 1918, American and French troops had forced a German retreat. As September ended, Pershing pitted over one million American soldiers against a vastly outnumbered and exhausted German army holed up in the Argonne forest. By early November, this attack had broken the German defenses protecting the crucial railroad hub at Sedan. The cost was high: 26,000 Americans killed and 95,000 wounded.

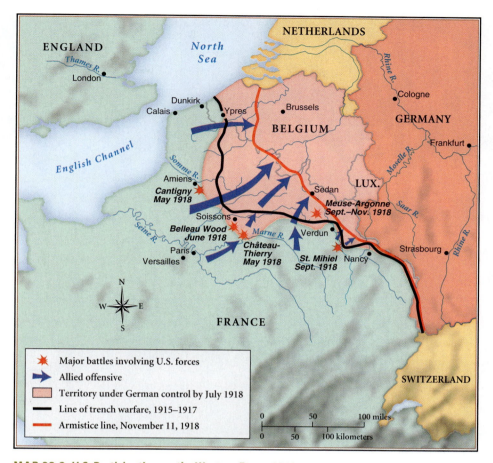

MAP 22.2 U.S. Participation on the Western Front, 1918
When American troops reached the European front in significant numbers in 1918, the Allied and Central Powers had been fighting a deadly war of attrition for almost four years. The influx of American troops and supplies helped to break the stalemate. Successful offensive maneuvers by the American Expeditionary Force included those at Belleau Wood, Château-Thierry, and the Argonne forest.

The flood of American troops and supplies brought the war to a close. Recognizing the inevitability of an Allied victory and facing popular uprisings at home, the German government sued for peace and signed an **armistice** on November 11, 1918. Millions of soldiers and civilians had died, but the Great War was finally over.

The American Fighting Force

About two million American soldiers were in France at the war's end. Two-thirds of the troops had seen some military action, but most Americans escaped the horrors of sustained trench warfare. Still, during the brief period of American participation, 53,000 servicemen died in action, and 203,000 suffered wounds. Another 63,000 died

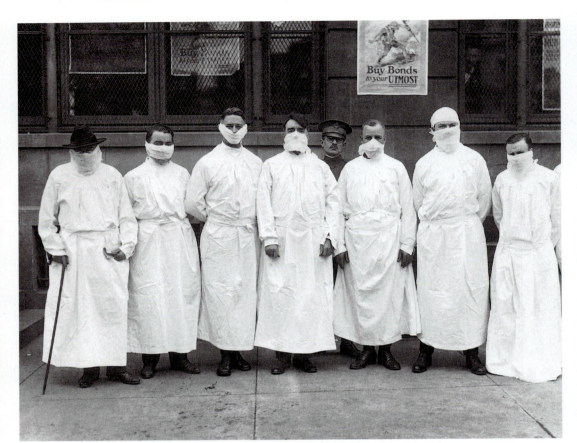

Fighting the Flu

The influenza epidemic of 1918–1919 traversed the globe and killed as many as fifty million people. According to recent research, the flu began as a virus native to wild birds and then mutated into a form that passed easily among humans. In the United States, one-fifth of the population contracted the flu, and more than 500,000 civilians died — ten times the number of American soldiers who died in combat in World War I. The epidemic strained the resources of a public health system already fully mobilized for the war effort. In October 1918 alone, 200,000 Americans died. In this photograph, doctors, army officers, and reporters don surgical masks and gowns before touring a hospital. © Bettmann/Corbis.

from diseases, mainly the devastating influenza pandemic that began in Kansas early in 1918 and, over the next two years, killed at least fifty million people throughout the world. The nation's military deaths were a mere speck compared with the eight million soldiers lost by the Allies and the Central Powers and the 500,000 American civilians who died in the influenza epidemic.

Modern warfare demanded individual bravery from every soldier but produced only a few heroes. The best-known American heroes were Sergeant Alvin York, who single-handedly killed 25 Germans and took 132 prisoners in the battle of Châtel-Chéhéry in the Argonne campaign, and Edward Vernon Rickenbacker, a former professional race car driver. Although of German ancestry, Rickenbacker enlisted immediately once the United States entered the war. Sent to France as a driver, he quickly learned to fly and, in

March 1918, joined the 94th Aero Pursuit Squadron. Eddie dueled in the skies with the German "Flying Circus" led by Manfred von Richthofen, the famous "Red Baron." By the war's end, Rickenbacker had fought in 134 air battles, downed 26 German planes, and become a national hero. His exploits captured the popular imagination and provided a vivid contrast to the monotony of deadly trench warfare.

Heroes or not, most American soldiers were ordinary young men suddenly exposed to the wider world. The army taught them about venereal disease, issued them condoms, and gave them safety razors—changing the sexual outlook and shaving habits of a generation. The recruits reflected the heterogeneity of the nation. The one-fifth of recruits who had been born outside the United States spoke forty-nine different languages, leading some people to call the AEF the American Foreign Legion. Although ethnic diversity worried some observers, most predicted that military service would promote the Americanization of the nation's immigrants.

The "Americanization" of the army remained imperfect at best, with African American soldiers receiving the worst treatment. Over 400,000 black men served in the military, accounting for 13 percent of the armed forces; 92 percent were draftees, a far higher rate than that of whites, who volunteered in greater numbers. Blacks served in segregated units, almost always under the control of white officers, and were assigned the most menial tasks. Despite the policy of segregation, racial conflict disrupted military efficiency and erupted in violence at several camps. The worst incident occurred in August 1917, when black members of the Twenty-fourth Infantry's Third Battalion marched into Houston following a string of racial incidents and killed 15 white civilians and police officers. The army tried 118 soldiers in military courts for mutiny and riot, hanged 19 of them, and sentenced 63 to life in prison (see Voices from Abroad, p. 650).

Unlike African Americans, Native Americans served in integrated combat units. Ironically, racial stereotypes about the natural abilities of Native American men as warriors, adroit tacticians, and camouflage experts enhanced their military reputations; officers gave them hazardous duties as advance scouts, messengers, and snipers. Approximately 13,000, or 25 percent, of the adult male Native American population served during the war, often with distinction. Roughly 5 percent died, compared to 2 percent for the military as a whole.

After the armistice, American troops came home and quickly readjusted to civilian life. Spared the trauma of sustained battle, many members of the AEF had experienced the war "over there" more as tourists than as soldiers. Before joining the army, most recruits had barely traveled beyond their hometowns; for them, the journey to Europe was a once-in-a-lifetime event. Their letters described "old cathedrals, chateaux and ancient towns . . . quite wonderful . . . to eyes so accustomed to the look of the New World."

▶ What were the causes of World War I? What made it a "world" war?

▶ Why did America become involved in the war? How did President Wilson justify his decision to enter the war in 1917? Was the war in the national interest?

In 1919, a group of former AEF officers formed the American Legion "to preserve the memories and incidents of our association in the great war." The word *legion* perfectly captured the romantic memories that many veterans held of their wartime service. Only later did disillusionment cloud their positive memories of the Great War.

German Propaganda and Black Soldiers

During World War I, both sides distributed propaganda tracts, such as this German appeal to "Colored Soldiers." According to Charles Williams, who probed the lives of black recruits, the soldiers' reaction was "We know what they say is true, but don't worry; we're not going over." The memoir of Bruce Wright, an African American volunteer, reveals both the truth of the German claims and the loyalty and hopes of the black soldiers.

To the Colored Soldiers of the U.S. Army,

Hello, boys, what are you doing over there? Fighting the Germans? Why? Have they ever done you any harm? Of course, some white folks and the lying English-American papers told you that the Germans ought to be wiped out for the sake of humanity and democracy. What is democracy? Personal freedom, all citizens enjoying the same rights socially and before the law. Do you enjoy the same rights as the white people do in America, the land of freedom and democracy? Or aren't you rather rated over there as second class citizens? Can you go to a restaurant where white people dine . . . or can you ride in the South in the same street car with white people? And how about the law? Is lynching and the most horrible cruelties connected therewith a lawful proceeding in a democratic country? . . .

Why, then, fight the Germans? . . . Come over to the German lines. You will find friends who will help you along.

I Bruce G. Wright joined Company L. of the sixth regiment Massachusetts National Guard June 15, 1917, at Camp Darling, Framingham Mass. . . . In November we broke camp to leave for the south. Arrived after a two days ride in regular pulman cars at Charlotte N.C. Camp Greene. Were the first colored soldiers seen south of the Mason & Dixon line in full equipment since 1865. The colored people used us fine and everything went well for an *hour* or so. One of the crackers insulted one of our boys and the war began right then for us. We got plenty of practice for the "Boche" by fighting with the dirty crackers. . . . That night there was plenty of disturbance in the town [of] Charlotte and several crackers were bumped off. We lost no men but had some shot up so we had to carry them back to camp. Two days later we were moved out of Charlotte farther north. . . .

The dawn of that first day in the Argonne forest we got our very first look onto "No Mans Land" that we had heard & read so much about. Masses of barbed wire, skeletons of men, tin cans, rotted clothes and an awful smell greeted our eyes & noses. . . . Lived in that living hell until late in August. . . . Twice before had the allies tried to take this sector known as the Champagne but were repulsed in each attack. But now [in September 1918] it was our lot and even though we heard of our own race of people being lynched every day back in the United States. We all wanted to do our best in hope that sooner it would be made easier for those at home. We kept saying to our selves we're fighting for "democracy."

SOURCE: Charles H. Williams, *Sidelights on Negro Soldiers* (Boston: B. J. Brimmer Co., 1923), 70–71; Tracey Lovette Spencer and James E. Spencer Jr., eds., "World War I As I Saw It," *Massachusetts Review* 9 (2007): 141, 144, 156–158.

"Remember Your First Thrill of American Liberty"
U.S. government officials were eager to enlist all Americans in the battle against the Central Powers. They carefully designed patriotic advertising campaigns that urged Americans to buy bonds, conserve food, enlist in the military, and join in the war effort in countless other ways. This poster targeted recent immigrants to the United States, reminding them that "American Liberty" carried with it the "Duty" to buy war bonds. Library of Congress.

War on the Home Front

Fighting World War I required an extraordinary economic effort on the home front. At the height of mobilization, one-fourth of the gross national product went for war production. Although the federal government expanded its power during the emergency, the watchword was voluntarism—and it worked. Business and government proved especially congenial partners, a public-private collaboration long characteristic of American economic life. Similarly, the rapid dismantling of the federal bureaucracy after the war reflected the long-standing preference for limited government. Still, during the war, progressives continued to use governmental policies to shape American society.

Mobilizing Industry and the Economy

Even before the formal declaration of war, the United States had become the arsenal of the Allied Powers. As thousands of tons of American supplies—grain, guns, and manufactured goods—crossed the Atlantic and the Allies paid for them in gold, the United States became a creditor nation. Moreover, as the cost of the war drained British financial reserves, U.S. banks provided capital for investments around the globe. America's shift from debtor to creditor status, which would last until the presidency of Ronald Reagan in the 1980s, guaranteed the nation a major role in international financial affairs and world politics.

Wars are expensive, and World War I was especially so. The Wilson administration spent $33 billion fighting the war—about eight times more than the Union government expended during the Civil War. The disruption of international trade reduced tariff revenues, a major source of federal income, so Treasury Secretary William McAdoo turned for revenue to the income taxes authorized by the Sixteenth Amendment (1913). Working with Democrats in Congress, he secured War Revenue Bills in 1917 and 1918 that embodied progressive principles of economic justice. This legislation did not tax the wages and salaries of working-class and middle-class Americans; rather, it imposed substantial levies on the income of wealthy individuals and the profits of business corporations. Because of this unprecedented state intrusion into the workings of corporate capitalism, by 1918 U.S. businesses were paying over $2.5 billion per year—more than half of all federal taxes.

In all, the federal government raised about one-third of the cost of the war from taxes. Much of the rest came from Liberty Loans, campaigns that persuaded families to support the war by investing in government bonds. "Every person who refuses to subscribe . . . is a friend of Germany," McAdoo asserted. These loans caused the federal debt to soar, from $1 billion in 1915 to $20 billion in 1920.

War mobilization required the coordination of economic production. To the dismay of many progressives who had hoped that the war emergency would increase federal regulation of business, the Wilson administration suspended antitrust laws to encourage output and turned to business executives for economic guidance. Corporate executives flocked to Washington, where they shared power with federal officials on the boards of war-related agencies. The agencies usually sought a middle ground between government direction and corporate autonomy, blunting the reform effort.

The central agency for directing military production was the War Industries Board (WIB), established in July 1917. After a fumbling start that showed the limits of voluntarism, the Wilson administration reorganized the board, placing Bernard Baruch, a Wall Street financier, at its head. Baruch was a superb administrator. Under his direction, the War Industries Board gathered economic data and statistics, allocated scarce resources among industries, ordered factories to convert to war production, set prices, and standardized procedures. Although the WIB had the authority to compel compliance, Baruch preferred to win voluntary cooperation from industry. A man of immense charm, he usually succeeded—helped along by the lucrative military contracts at his disposal. Despite higher taxes, corporate profits soared because of guaranteed income from military production and the economic boom that continued until 1920.

In some instances, the new federal agencies took dramatic, decisive action. When the severe winter of 1917–1918 led to coal shortages in northeastern cities, the Fuel Administration ordered all factories east of the Mississippi River to shut down for four days; then it decreed a high price for coal to increase production. The Railroad War Board, which coordinated the nation's sprawling transportation system, took even more aggressive action in December 1917. To ensure the rapid movement of troops and equipment, it seized control of the railroad industry. To calm holders of the railroads' stock and bonds, the Board guaranteed them a "standard return" and promised to return the carriers to private control at the war's end. Although progressive reformers wanted to aid railroad workers and shippers by continuing federal control, the government fulfilled its pledge.

Perhaps the most successful wartime agency was the Food Administration, created in August 1917 and led by Herbert Hoover, an engineer who had managed major construction and mining projects around the world. Using the slogan "Food will win the war," Hoover convinced farmers to plant grain on 75 million acres of land, up from 45 million acres in 1917. The increased output supplied Americans with food and allowed a threefold rise in food exports to war-torn Europe. Rather than rationing items that were in short supply, the Food Administration mobilized "the spirit of self-denial and self-sacrifice." Hoover sent women volunteers from door to door to persuade housewives to observe "Wheatless" Mondays, "Meatless" Tuesdays, and "Porkless" Thursdays and Saturdays. A Republican in politics, Hoover emerged from the war as one of the nation's most admired public figures.

Following the armistice of November 1918, the government scrambled to dismantle wartime controls. Wilson disbanded the WIB on January 1, 1919, ignoring suggestions that the board was needed to stabilize the economy during demobilization. As a states' rights Democrat, Wilson could tolerate increased federal government authority during an emergency but not as a permanent feature of the economy.

Although the nation's participation in the war lasted just eighteen months, it left an enduring legacy: the modern bureaucratic state. Despite the demise of the WIB, many industries now had close ties to government agencies and executive departments. The Treasury Department had created a modern and progressive system of individual and corporate taxation. Finally, business and government cooperated closely during the war, a process that would continue in the 1920s and afterward.

Mobilizing American Workers

Modern wars are never won solely by armies, business executives, and government leaders. In World War I, farmers, factory workers, and other civilians were key actors in the wartime drama. To reinforce popular patriotism, government propaganda posters exhorted citizens "to do their bit for Uncle Sam."

Workers did their part, and the status of labor unions improved significantly during the war. Samuel Gompers, leader of the American Federation of Labor (AFL), traded his support for the war for a voice on government policy; he sat on the National Defense Advisory Commission. The National War Labor Board (NWLB), formed in April 1918, greatly improved the working lives of laboring men and women. Composed of representatives of labor, management, and the public, the NWLB established an eight-hour day for war workers, with time and a half for overtime, and endorsed equal pay for women workers. In return for a no-strike pledge, the NWLB supported the workers' right to organize unions and required employers to deal with shop committees. When executives at a Smith and Wesson arms factory in Springfield, Massachusetts, discriminated against union employees, the NWLB took over the firm. After years of federal hostility toward labor, the NWLB's new outlook dramatically enhanced the size and power of organized workers. AFL membership grew by almost

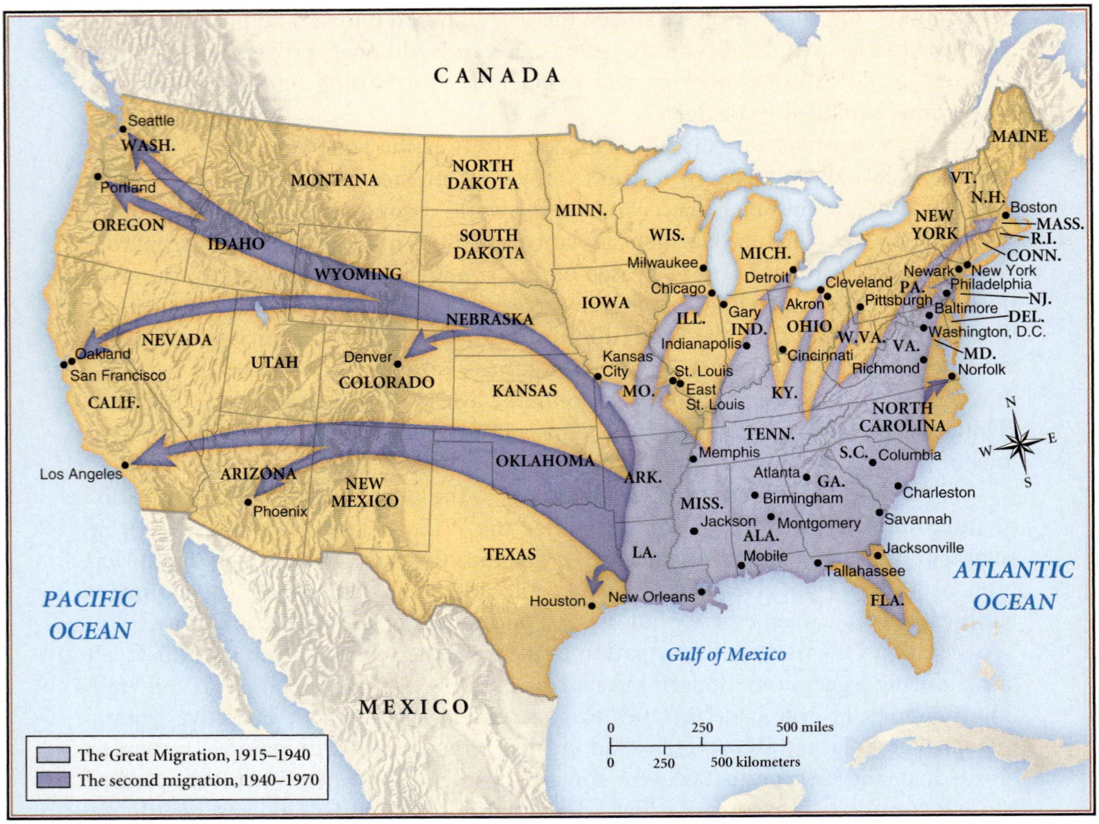

MAP 22.3 The Great Migration and Beyond

Employment opportunities that opened up during World War I and World War II served as catalysts for the Great Migration of African Americans out of the rural South. In the first migration, which began in 1915, blacks headed primarily to industrial cities of the North and Midwest, such as Chicago, New York, and Pittsburgh (see American Voices, p. 656). During World War II, blacks' destinations expanded to include the West, especially Los Angeles, the San Francisco Bay Area, and Seattle. This map simplifies a complex process; individuals and families often moved several times and usually retained close ties with kinfolk in the South.

For more help analyzing this map, see the Online Study Guide at **bedfordstmartins.com/henrettaconcise**.

one million workers, reaching over three million at the end of the war, and the shortage of workers raised wages.

The war emergency also created job opportunities for ethnic and racial minorities. For the first time, northern factories actively recruited African Americans, spawning a "Great Migration" from southern farms to the nation's industrial heartland (Map 22.3). During the war, more than 400,000 African Americans moved northward to St. Louis, Chicago, New York, and Detroit. The rewards were great. Black workers in Henry Ford's Detroit auto works took home $5 day, the same high pay as white workers. Other African Americans looked forward to working in northern meatpacking plants; as one migrant from Mississippi recalled, "You could not rest in your bed at night for thoughts of Chicago." African Americans encountered discrimination in the North—in jobs, housing, and education—but most celebrated their escape from the repressive racism and low pay of the southern agricultural system (see American Voices, p. 656).

Mexican Americans in California, Texas, New Mexico, and Arizona also found new opportunities. Wartime labor shortages prompted them to leave farm labor for industrial jobs in rapidly growing southwestern cities, where they mostly settled in segregated neighborhoods (barrios). Continuing political instability in Mexico combined with a demand for farm workers in the United States encouraged more Mexicans to move across the border. Between 1917 and 1920, at least 100,000 Mexicans entered the United States, and despite discrimination because of their dark skin and Catholic religion, many of them stayed.

Women were the largest group to take advantage of new wartime opportunities. About one million women joined the paid labor force for the first time, and another eight million women gave up low-wage jobs as teachers and domestic servants for higher-paying industrial work. "If the women in the factories stopped work for twenty minutes, the Allies would lose the war," one general declared. Americans soon got used to the sight of female streetcar conductors, train engineers, and defense workers. But most Americans, including many working women, believed that those jobs would return to men after the war.

Wartime Constitutionalism: Woman Suffrage and Prohibition

Activist women used the war effort to push forward women's causes and to campaign for reforms long championed by women. Their efforts helped to secure the passage and ratification of two constitutional amendments: those mandating woman suffrage and Prohibition.

When the war began, the National American Woman Suffrage Association (NAWSA) threw the support of its two million members behind the Wilson administration. Its president, Carrie Chapman Catt, declared that women had to prove their patriotism to advance the cause of the suffrage movement. NAWSA women in thousands of communities promoted food conservation, aided war industry workers, and distributed emergency relief through organizations such as the Red Cross.

Alice Paul and the National Woman's Party (NWP) took a more militant tack to win the vote. Like many other women reformers, Paul was a Quaker. She graduated from Swarthmore College, worked in the settlement house movement, and in 1912 earned a Ph.D. in political science at the University of Pennsylvania. Inspired by the militant British suffragist Christabel Pankhurst, Paul became a congressional lobbyist for NAWSA. But when male politicians refused to support woman suffrage, Paul founded the NWP in 1916. The new party launched an activist campaign of mass meetings and, in July 1917, began picketing the White House. Standing as "Silent Sentinels" and holding woman suffrage banners, Paul and other NWP militants ignored police orders to move on—perhaps the first instance of public nonviolent civil disobedience in American history. Arrested for "obstructing traffic" and sentenced to seven months in jail, Paul and the women protestors went on a hunger strike, which prison authorities met with forced feeding. Public shock at the women's treatment

The Great Migration

The Great Migration of African Americans from the rural South to the urban North was a pivotal moment in black history. Letters written by the migrants offer an evocative view of their lives and aspirations. Recognizing their value, African American historian Emmett J. Scott published a collection of "letters from Negroes of all conditions" in 1919. Given that many migrants spoke "black English," Scott might have edited these letters for grammar and style. What insights do they offer as to the reasons for African American migration?

CHICAGO, ILLINOIS.

My dear Sister:

I am well and thankful to say I am doing well. The weather and everything else was a surprise to me when I came. I got here in time to attend one of the greatest revivals in the history of my life—over 500 people joined the church. We had a Holy Ghost shower. . . . The people are rushing here by the thousands and I know if you come and rent a big house you can get all the roomers you want. You write me exactly when you are coming. I am not keeping house yet I am living with my brother and his wife. My son is in California but will be home soon. He spends his winter in California. I can get a nice place for you to stop until you can look around and see what you want. I am quite busy. I work in Swifts packing Co. in the sausage department. My daughter and I work for the same company—We get $1.50 a day and we pack so many sausages we dont have much time to play but it is a matter of a dollar with me and I feel that God made the path and I am walking therein.

Tell your husband work is plentiful here and he wont have to loaf if he want to work. . . . Well goodbye from your sister in Christ.

SOURCE: *Journal of Negro History* 4, no. 4 (1919): 457, 458–459.

CHICAGO, ILLINOIS, 11/13/17.

Mr. H———

Hattiesburg, Miss.

Dear M———: Yours received sometime ago and found all well and doing well. hope you and family are well.

I got my things alright the other day and they were in good condition. I am all fixed now and living well. I certainly appreciate what you done for us and I will remember you in the near future.

M, old boy, I was promoted on the first of the month I was made first assistant to the head carpenter when he is out of the place I take everything in charge and was raised to $95. a month. You know I know my stuff.

Whats the news generally around H'burg? I should have been here 20 years ago. I just begin to feel like a man. It's a great deal of pleasure in knowing that you have got some privilege My children are going to the same school with the whites and I dont have to umble to no one. I have registered—Will vote the next election and there isnt any "yes sir" and "no sir"—its all yes and no and Sam and Bill.

Florine says hello and would like very much to see you.

All joins me in sending love to you and family. How is times there now? Answer soon, from your friend and bro.

drew renewed attention to the issue of woman suffrage and put new pressure on the Wilson administration.

Impressed by NAWSA's patriotism and worried by the NWP's militancy, President Wilson realized that his campaign to make the world safe for democracy had to begin at home. In January 1918, he urged support for woman suffrage as a "war measure." The constitutional amendment quickly passed the House of Representatives but took eighteen months to get through the Senate and another year to win ratification by the states. On August 26, 1920, Tennessee gave the Nineteenth Amendment the last vote it needed. The goal first declared publicly at the Seneca Falls women's convention in 1848 was finally achieved seventy-two years later.

Other activists also used the war to advance their agendas. Moral reformers concerned with vice and prostitution pestered military officials to keep the army "fit to fight." They encouraged the government to educate soldiers about sexually transmitted diseases and shut down red-light districts near military training camps. Assisted by two Protestant Christian organizations, the Young Men's Christian Association and the Young Women's Christian Association, government officials warned young men and women about the dangers of sexual activity and celebrated "social purity."

Other reformers aided the families of army recruits. Responding to reports of economic hardship among working-class military families, Congress enacted the War Risk Insurance Act in 1917. The act required enlisted men and noncommissioned officers to allot $15 of their monthly pay to their dependents, and the federal government contributed an additional allowance, disbursing almost $570 million to the dependents of servicemen between 1917 and 1921. This wartime program of federal family assistance was unprecedented and, although short-lived, shaped the welfare programs established in the New Deal era (see Chapter 24).

A more dramatic, and often less welcome, intrusion of the federal government into people's private lives resulted from the efforts of prohibitionists. On the eve of World War I, nineteen state legislatures had enacted laws prohibiting the manufacture or sale of alcoholic beverages, and other states allowed local communities to regulate liquor sales. Generally, only industrial states that had large immigrant populations, such as Massachusetts, New York, Rhode Island, Illinois, and California, resisted the movement to impose strict regulations on intoxicating beverages.

Many progressives supported prohibition. Urban reformers, worried about alcoholic husbands, impoverished families, and public morality, considered a ban on drinking to be a benefit to society rather than a repressive denial of individual freedom. Citizens in rural communities equated liquor with the sins of the big cities: prostitution, crime, immigration, machine politics, and public disorder. The churches that had the greatest strength in rural areas, including Methodists, Baptists, and Mormons, also strongly condemned drinking. Rural Protestants dominated the membership of the Anti-Saloon League, which had supplanted the Woman's Christian Temperance Union as the leading prohibition organization.

Temperance advocates knew their enemies. The liquor industry flourished in cities, especially among recent immigrants from Europe and citizens of German and Irish descent. Most saloons served working-class neighborhoods and attracted business by offering free lunches and public toilets. They provided handy gathering places for workers and the loan sharks and machine politicians who wanted their money or votes. Raised in cultures that encouraged social conviviality, many immigrants opposed prohibition. They demanded the freedom to drink what they pleased and resented the attempts of progressive reformers and religious zealots to destroy their ethnic cultures.

The passions of the Great War increased the political momentum of the prohibitionist cause. Intense anti-German hysteria was one spur. Many major breweries — Pabst, Busch, and Schlitz — were owned and run by German Americans, so many native-born citizens now felt that it was unpatriotic to drink beer. Beer consumption also declined because Congress conserved scarce grain supplies by limiting the use of barley, hops, and other grains in breweries and distilleries. The national prohibition campaign culminated in December 1917, when Congress passed the Eighteenth Amendment. Ratified by nearly every state by 1919 and effective on January 16, 1920, the amendment prohibited the "manufacture, sale, or transportation of intoxicating liquors" anywhere in the United States.

The Eighteenth Amendment was the most striking example of a wartime progressive reform. It also stood as yet another example of the widening influence of the national state on matters of economic policy and personal behavior. Unlike woman suffrage, the other constitutional amendment that won wartime passage, Prohibition never gained general public acceptance, and it was repealed by the Twenty-first Amendment in 1933.

Promoting National Unity

John Dewey, a progressive educator and a staunch supporter of American involvement in World War I, argued that wars represented a "plastic juncture" when societies became open to reason and new ideas. Rudolph Bourne, a one-time pupil of Dewey's and an outspoken pacifist, strongly disagreed. "If the war is too strong for you to prevent," Bourne astutely observed, how is it possible to "control and mold [it] to your liberal purposes?" President Wilson shared Bourne's pessimism about wartime passions: "Once lead this people into war, and they'll forget there ever was such a thing as tolerance." But the president knew that he needed to rally support for the war effort. "It is not an army we must shape and train for war," he said, "it is a nation." By backing the campaign to promote "One Hundred Percent Americanism," Wilson undermined the spirit of reform that had elevated him to the highest office in the land.

In April 1917, Wilson formed the Committee on Public Information (CPI). This government propaganda agency, headed by the journalist George Creel, attracted leading progressive reformers and muckraking journalists such as Ida Tarbell and Ray Stannard Baker. Professing lofty goals — educating citizens about democracy, assimilating immigrants, and ending the isolation of rural life — the committee set out to create a national consensus by molding Americans into "one white-hot mass."

The CPI touched the lives of practically every American. It distributed seventy-five million pieces of patriotic literature and reached a huge audience by enlisting thousands of volunteers — "four-minute men" — to deliver short prowar speeches at local movie theaters. Creel called the CPI "the world's greatest adventure in advertising" and hoped that it would "inspire" patriotism without inflaming passions.

However, by 1918, the committee was encouraging its speakers to use inflammatory stories of alleged German atrocities to support the war effort.

As a spirit of conformity pervaded the home front, many Americans became targets of suspicion. Businesses took out newspaper ads instructing citizens to report to the Justice Department "the man who spreads pessimistic stories, cries for peace, or belittles our efforts to win the war." Posters warned Americans to look out for German spies. A quasi-vigilante group, the American Protective League, mobilized about 250,000 self-appointed "agents," furnished them with badges issued by the Justice Department, and told them to spy on neighbors and coworkers. In 1918, the members of the League staged violent raids against draft evaders and opponents of the war.

The Committee on Public Information urged recent immigrants and long-established ethnic groups to become "One Hundred Percent Americans" by giving up their Old World customs and ties. German Americans bore the brunt of this Americanization campaign. Concert halls banned German music and operas, such as Beethoven, Bach, and Wagner, and many school districts prohibited the teaching of the German language. Popular foods such as hamburgers became "liberty sandwiches" or Salisbury steaks; sauerkraut was renamed "liberty cabbage." When the influenza epidemic struck down thousands of Americans, rumors flew that German scientists were spreading germs in the aspirin distributed by Bayer, a German drug company. Although anti-German hysteria dissipated when the war ended, hostility toward "hyphenated Americans"—a new term embracing Irish, Polish, Italian, and Jewish Americans—survived into the 1920s.

During the war, legal authorities tolerated little criticism of established values and institutions. The main legislative tools for curbing dissent were the Espionage Act of 1917 and the Sedition Act of 1918. The Sedition Act prohibited speech, writing, and behavior that might "incite, provoke, or encourage resistance to the United States, or promote the cause of its enemies." The Espionage Act imposed stiff penalties for anti-war activities and allowed the federal government to ban treasonous materials from the mails. The postmaster general revoked the mailing privileges of groups that were considered to be radical, virtually shutting down their publications.

Individuals also felt the long arm of the state. Because the Espionage and Sedition acts defined treason and sedition loosely, they led to the conviction of more than a thousand people. The Justice Department prosecuted Socialists, because they criticized the war and the draft, and the Industrial Workers of the World (IWW), radical workers whose opposition to militarism threatened to disrupt war production in the western lumber and copper industries (see Chapter 17). In September 1917, the Justice Department arrested 113 IWW leaders and charged them with interfering with the war effort. Socialist Party leader Eugene Debs was sentenced to ten years in jail for declaring that the capitalist classes started wars and made the subject classes fight the battles. Victor Berger, a Milwaukee Socialist who had been jailed under the Espionage Act, was twice prevented from taking the seat to which he had been elected in the U.S. House of Representatives.

▶ Did the war effort significantly change the nature of American government or American society? Give examples to justify your argument.

▶ In what ways did the government (and popular opinion) limit civil liberties during the war and with what justification?

The courts rarely resisted these wartime excesses. In *Schenck v. United States* (1919), the Supreme Court upheld the conviction of Charles T. Schenck, the general secretary of the Socialist Party. Schenck had been jailed for mailing pamphlets that urged army draftees to resist induction. Writing for a unanimous court, Justice Oliver Wendell Holmes declared that the freedom of speech guaranteed by the First Amendment did not extend to words that constituted "a clear and present danger to the safety of the country." Such legal restrictions became a permanent feature of American life. Well into the twentieth century, the courts used Holmes's "clear and present danger" test to curb individual freedom in the name of national security.

An Unsettled Peace, 1919–1920

The end of the Great War left a variety of unresolved problems. At home, the Wilson administration had to demobilize the troops and restore military plants to civilian use; abroad, it had to negotiate a peace treaty. President Wilson made peacemaking his highest priority. From December 1918 to June 1919, he bargained and fought with Allied leaders to achieve a new international order. As that mission foundered, ethnic and racial strife erupted in the United States, and fears of domestic radicalism sparked America's first Red Scare.

The Treaty of Versailles

Woodrow Wilson approached the peace negotiations in France with the zeal of a missionary. In January 1917, he had proposed a "peace without victory," arguing that only a "peace among equals" could last. Beyond that, he laid out a plan for a "League of Nations," a permanent organization that would prevent future wars: not a "balance of power, but a community of power; not organized rivalries, but an organized common peace."

To win approval of his new world order, Wilson was ready to appeal to "the peoples of Europe over the heads of their rulers." And well he might. Wildly enthusiastic European crowds greeted the American president as a hero; in Paris, two million people lined the Champs-Élysées to pay tribute to "Wilson the Just." The president scored a diplomatic victory in January 1919 when the Allies accepted his **Fourteen Points** as the basis for the peace negotiations. In this blueprint for the postwar world, the president called for open diplomacy, "absolute freedom of navigation upon the seas," arms reduction, the removal of trade barriers, and **national self-determination** for the peoples of the Austro-Hungarian, Russian, and German empires. Essential to Wilson's vision was the creation of a League of Nations, a multinational organization that would afford "mutual guarantees of political independence and territorial integrity to great and small States alike." The League became Wilson's obsession.

The Fourteen Points embodied the spirit of American progressivism. Widely distributed as propaganda during the final months of the war, Wilson's plan would extend American ideals — democracy, freedom, and peaceful economic expansion — to the rest of the world. The League of Nations, acting as an international regulatory body, would mediate disputes among nations, supervise arms reduction, and — according to the crucial Article X of its covenant — curb aggressor nations through collective military action. Wilson hoped that the presence of the League would ensure that the Great War would be "the war to end all wars." The lofty goals of the American president set the stage for disappointment: His ideals for world reformation proved too far-reaching to be practical or attainable.

Twenty-seven delegations attended the peace conference at Versailles, near Paris. Most came from existing nations; others represented stateless peoples who hoped that the Allied Powers would recognize their claims to national sovereignty. Distrustful of the new Bolshevik regime in Russia, especially given its call for a worker-led revolution against capitalism and imperialism, the Allies deliberately excluded its representatives. That action was hardly surprising; in 1918, the United States, Britain, and Japan had sent thousands of troops to Russia to aid anti-Bolshevik forces. The victorious Allies also barred Germany from the peace conference, choosing instead to work out the details and impose the completed treaty on their defeated foe.

The Big Four—Wilson, Prime Minister David Lloyd George of Great Britain, Premier Georges Clemenceau of France, and Prime Minister Vittorio Orlando of Italy—did most of the negotiating. The three European leaders ignored Wilson's plea for a just peace. They wanted to punish Germany by demanding heavy reparations and treating themselves to the spoils of war. Indeed, Britain, France, and Italy had made secret agreements to divide German colonies in Africa.

Given the Europeans' goals, it is a tribute to Wilson that he influenced the peace settlement as much as he did. The president intervened repeatedly to soften harsh demands for reprisal against Germany. Moreover, he won support for national self-determination, a fundamental principle of the Fourteen Points. In accordance with that precept, the Big Four fashioned the independent states of Austria, Hungary, Poland, Yugoslavia, and Czechoslovakia in central Europe and established four new nations along the Baltic Sea: Finland, Estonia, Lithuania, and Latvia (Map 22.4). This string of states, which stretched from the Baltic to the Mediterranean, embodied the Wilsonian principle of national self-determination and also served as a *cordon sanitaire*—a sanitary zone protecting the peoples of western Europe from direct exposure to the Communist ideology of Soviet Russia.

Wilson had less success in achieving other goals. The diplomats at Versailles dismantled the colonial empires of the Central Powers but did not create independent states; instead, they assigned the colonies to the victorious Allied nations to administer as "mandates." France and England took control of Turkish and German colonies in the Middle East and Africa, and Japan assumed responsibility for the German possessions in East Asia. Moreover, the diplomats ignored representatives of colonized peoples when they sought freedom for their nations; Clemenceau's decision to snub Ho Chi Minh, the future nationalist leader of Vietnam, had grave consequences for France and the United States in the second half of the twentieth century (see Chapter 29). The resistance of European leaders likewise meant that important issues, such as freedom of the seas and free trade, were not discussed. Most important, Wilson was unable to block French and British demands that Germany accept a "war guilt" clause and pay enormous war reparations. In a harsh settlement that left lasting resentment and would lead to a second great war, the Allies forced Germany to give up parts of its territory, coal supplies, merchant ships, valuable patents, and its colonies—and to pay $33 billion in monetary reparations.

	New and reconstituted nations
	Demilitarized or Allied occupation
	British mandates
	French mandates

MAP 22.4 Europe and the Middle East After World War I

World War I and its aftermath dramatically altered the landscape of Europe and the Middle East. In central Europe, the collapse of the German, Russian, and Austro-Hungarian empires brought the reconstitution of Poland and the creation of a string of new states based on the principle of national (ethnic) self-determination. The demise of the Ottoman Empire resulted in the appearance of the quasi-independent territories of Iraq, Syria, Lebanon, and Palestine, whose affairs were supervised by one of the Allied Powers under a mandate from the League of Nations.

Despite such setbacks, Wilson remained cautiously optimistic. He hoped that the League of Nations, which was authorized by the peace treaty, would moderate the terms of the settlement and secure a peaceful resolution of other international disputes. For this to occur, American participation in the League was crucial. So the president set out to persuade the Senate to ratify the Treaty of Versailles. The outlook was not promising. Although major newspapers and important religious denominations supported the treaty, the Republican Party had a majority in the Senate and was openly hostile to the agreement.

Opposition to the treaty and to the League came from several sources. One group, called the "irreconcilables," consisted of western Republican progressives such as William Borah of Idaho, Hiram Johnson of California, and Robert La Follette of Wisconsin. **Isolationist** in outlook, they opposed U.S. involvement in European affairs and membership in the League of Nations. Less dogmatic but more influential was a group of Republicans led by Senator Henry Cabot Lodge of Massachusetts. Lodge and his allies worried that Article X—the provision for collective security—would prevent the United States from pursuing an independent foreign policy. Would Congress and the people, Lodge asked, be "willing to have the youth of America ordered to war" by the League? Wilson refused to accept amendments to the treaty, especially to placate Lodge, a hated political rival. "I shall consent to nothing," he told the French ambassador. "The Senate must take its medicine."

To mobilize popular and political support for the treaty, the president embarked on an extensive and exhausting speaking tour. His impassioned defense of the League of Nations brought large audiences to tears, but the strain proved too much for the sixty-two-year old president. In Pueblo, Colorado, in late September 1919, Wilson collapsed; a week later, back in Washington, he suffered a severe stroke that left him paralyzed on one side of his body. Wilson still refused to compromise and urged Democratic senators to vote against all Republican amendments. When the treaty came up for a vote in November 1919, it failed to win the required two-thirds majority; a second attempt, in March 1920, fell seven votes short.

The treaty was dead, and so was Wilson's leadership of the nation. Although the president slowly recovered from his stroke, he was never the same. During the final eighteen months of the Wilson administration, the federal government drifted as the president's wife, Edith Bolling Galt Wilson, his physician, and the various cabinet heads oversaw its routine administrative activities. The United States never ratified the Versailles treaty or joined the League of Nations, which failed to address the problem of German reparations or the rising colonial demands for self-determination. When Woodrow Wilson died in 1924, his idealistic dream of a just international order lay unfulfilled. The former president himself, remarked David Lloyd George, was "as much a victim of the war as any soldier who died in the trenches."

Racial Strife, Labor Unrest, and the Red Scare

"The World War has accentuated all our differences," a journalist in the popular periodical *World's Work* astutely observed. "It has not created those differences, but it has revealed and emphasized them." In the aftermath of the war, race riots revealed white resistance to the rising expectations of African Americans. Thousands of strikes exposed class tensions, and an obsessive government-led hunt for foreign radicals reflected deep-seated anxieties about social order and the nation's ethnic pluralism.

Many African Americans emerged from the war determined to insist on their rights as American citizens. Thousands of them had fought for their country; millions of others had loyally supported the war effort. But black demands for equal treatment sparked white racism and violence. In the South, the number of lynchings rose from 48 in 1917 to 78 in 1919, including several of African American soldiers in their military uniforms. In the northern states, now home to tens of thousands of southern-born blacks, race riots broke out in more than twenty-five cities. One of the most deadly riots occurred in 1917 in East St. Louis, Illinois; 9 whites and more than 40 blacks died in a conflict prompted by competition over jobs at a defense plant. In Chicago, five days of rioting in July 1919 left 23 blacks and 15 whites dead. By the end of that summer, the death toll from racial violence had reached 120.

The causes of the Chicago riot resembled those in other cities. The wartime influx of 50,000 African Americans had strained the city's social fabric and increased racial tensions. Blacks competed with whites—many of them recent arrivals from central Europe—for scarce housing and jobs. Unionized white workers deeply resented blacks who served as strikebreakers; indeed, in some stockyards and packing plants, white workers considered the words *Negro* and *scab* to be synonymous. In close political elections, black voters often held the balance of power, which allowed their leaders to demand favors and patronage positions.

Ethnic conflicts over jobs and patronage had long been part of the urban scene, but racism turned them into violent confrontations. When gangs of young white men bombed or burned houses in African American neighborhoods or attacked their residents, blacks fought back in self-defense and for their rights as citizens. Wilson's rhetoric about democracy and self-determination had raised their expectations.

Workers also had higher expectations. The economic prosperity and government regulations of the war years had brought them higher pay, shorter hours, and better working conditions. As workers tried to maintain their higher living standards, employers began to cut wages and root out unions. Consumers and native-born Americans generally sided with management. They blamed workers for the rapidly rising cost of living, which jumped nearly 80 percent between 1917 and 1919, and they remained suspicious of unions, which they identified with radicalism and foreigners.

These developments prompted a massive confrontation between employers and workers. In 1919, more than four million wage laborers—one in every five—went on strike, a proportion that has never since been equaled. The year began with a walkout by shipyard workers in Seattle, a strong union town, and spread into a general strike that shut down the city. The strike was nothing less than "an attempted revolution" designed to destroy the government and "duplicate the anarchy of Russia," claimed mayor Ole Hanson. Another major strike disrupted the steel industry, in which 350,000 workers demanded union recognition and an end to twelve-hour shifts. Elbert H. Gary, the head of United States Steel Corporation, refused to negotiate; he hired Mexican and African American strikebreakers, maintained substantial production, and eventually broke the strike.

Public employees fared no better. Late in the year, the Boston police force shocked many Americans by demanding union representation and going on strike to get it. Governor Calvin Coolidge of Massachusetts propelled himself into the political spotlight by declaring, "There is no right to strike against the public safety by anybody, anywhere, any time." Coolidge fired the entire police force, and the strike failed. The public supported the governor's decisive action, and the Republican Party rewarded Coolidge by nominating him in 1920 as its vice presidential candidate.

The impressive gains made by workers and unions during the war swiftly melted away. Inflation cut workers' purchasing power, corporate managers attacked unions, and judges issued coercive injunctions against picketers and strikers. Lacking public support, unions declined throughout the 1920s.

A substantial number of white Americans opposed unions because they feared radicalism. The socialist outlook of many recent immigrants frightened native-born citizens, and the communist ideology of the Russian Bolsheviks terrified them. President Wilson heightened these concerns. As he embarked for Europe in 1919, he warned of "a flood of ultraradicalism, that will swamp the world." When the Bolsheviks founded the Third International (or Comintern) in 1919, an organization that was intended to export communist ideology and foster revolutions throughout the world, Americans began to see radicals everywhere. Hatred of the German "Huns" was quickly replaced by hostility toward the Bolshevik "Reds."

Ironically, as public concern about domestic Bolshevism increased, radical socialists remained few in number and had little political influence. Of the fifty million adults in the United States in 1920, no more than 70,000 belonged to either the fledgling U.S. Communist Party or the Communist Labor Party in 1919. The IWW had been weakened by wartime repression and internal dissent. And Eugene B. Debs, the Socialist candidate for President in 1920, polled only 3.4 percent of the vote, just slightly more than he had in 1904 and 1908. Yet the public and the press continued to blame almost every labor disturbance on alien socialists and radicals. "REDS DIRECTING SEATTLE STRIKE — TO TEST CHANCE FOR REVOLUTION," warned a typical newspaper headline.

Political tensions mounted amid a series of terrorist threats and bombings in the spring of 1919. In April, alert postal workers discovered and defused thirty-four mail bombs addressed to prominent government officials. In June, a bomb detonated outside the Washington townhouse of the recently appointed attorney general, A. Mitchell Palmer. Palmer and his family escaped unharmed, but the bomber was blown to bits. Angling for the presidential nomination, Palmer capitalized on the event by fanning fears of domestic radicalism.

With President Wilson virtually incapacitated, Palmer had a free hand. He set up an antiradicalism division in the Justice Department and appointed J. Edgar Hoover to direct it. Hoover's division shortly became the Federal Bureau of Investigation (FBI). Then the attorney general staged the first of what became known as "Palmer raids." In November 1919, on the second anniversary of the Russian Revolution, Palmer's agents stormed the headquarters of radical organizations. The dragnet pulled in thousands of aliens who had committed no crimes but held anarchist or revolutionary beliefs. Lacking the protection of U.S. citizenship, they could be deported without a formal indictment or trial. In December 1919, the USS *Buford,* nicknamed the "Soviet Ark," sailed to Russia with a cargo of 294 deported radicals, including the famous anarchists Emma Goldman and Alexander Berkman.

The peak of Palmer's power came with his New Year's raids in January 1920. In one night, with the greatest possible publicity, federal agents rounded up 6,000 radicals. The agents invaded private homes, union headquarters, and meeting halls, arresting citizens and aliens alike and denying them access to legal counsel. Palmer was riding high in his ambitions for the presidency, but then he overstepped himself. He predicted that on May Day 1920, a radical conspiracy would attempt to overthrow the U.S. government. State militia units and police went on twenty-four-hour alert to guard the nation against the threat of revolutionary violence, but not a single incident occurred. As the summer of 1920 passed without major labor strikes or renewed bombings, the hysteria of the Red Scare began to abate, and Palmer faded from view.

The wartime legacy of antiradicalism and anti-immigrant sentiment persisted well into the next decade. At the height of the Red Scare in May 1920, police arrested Nicola Sacco, a shoemaker, and Bartolomeo Vanzetti, a fish peddler, for the murder of a paymaster and a security guard during a robbery of a shoe company in South Braintree, Massachusetts. Sacco and Vanzetti were Italian aliens and self-proclaimed anarchists

The Accused Anarchists
Bartolomeo Vanzetti and Nicola Sacco (on the right) sit handcuffed together during their trial for murder. They are well dressed, but to an observer of the time, they would look "foreign," both because of Vanzetti's mustache and because of their "Italian" looks. © Bettmann/Corbis.

who had evaded the draft; both were armed at the time of their arrest. Convicted of the murders, Sacco and Vanzetti sat in jail for six years while supporters appealed their verdicts. In 1927, Judge Webster Thayer denied a motion for a new trial and sentenced them to death. Scholars still debate the question of their guilt, and careful reexamination of the physical evidence has yielded inconclusive results. But many commentators suggested that the immigrants did not receive fair handling by the judicial system because of their ties to radical anarchist groups. As the future Supreme Court justice Felix Frankfurter said at the time, "The District Attorney invoked against them a riot of political passion and patriotic sentiment."

The war—with its nationalistic emphasis on patriotism and traditional cultural values—left

▶ Which nations and peoples attended the Paris Peace Conference? Which nations did not? Which nations and mandates were created at the conference?

▶ What was President Wilson's vision of the postwar world, and how specifically did he propose to achieve it? How did European leaders react to Wilson's ideas? Why did the U.S. Senate refuse to ratify the peace treaty?

▶ What were the main causes and results of postwar social conflicts within the United States?

ugly racial, ethnic, and class tensions in its wake. Still, the United States emerged from World War I a much stronger nation than when it entered. Unlike its European allies and enemies, it had suffered relatively few casualties and no physical destruction to its lands or cities. Indeed, thanks to the war, the United States had become a major international power, both economically and politically.

SUMMARY

In this chapter, we saw that the United States entered the Great War in 1917 because of German violations of American neutral rights at sea, cultural and economic ties to the Allied powers, and Wilson's progressive goal of using American power to create a just world order.

In tracing mobilization on the home front, we explained how the federal government created an army from scratch, boosted agricultural and industrial production, and recruited workers and raw materials for the defense industry. Some reformers—women suffragists, labor organizers, and prohibitionists—successfully used the war emergency to advance their goals. But we also saw how the passions and disruptions of wartime undercut the spirit of progressive reform and increased social tensions. As the fighting in Europe ended, strikes, race riots, and police raids brought violence to American factories and cities.

We explored the challenges facing Wilson as he sought a just and lasting peace. The Versailles treaty embodied only some of the president's Fourteen Points, and his postwar hopes suffered a fatal blow when the Senate refused to ratify the treaty or authorize American participation in the League of Nations. Nonetheless, the United States emerged from the war as a dominant world power, a position that it would retain throughout the twentieth century.

Connections: Diplomacy

During World War I, the United States assumed a powerful role in international affairs. But the nation lacked a strong diplomatic tradition and a respected foreign policy bureaucracy. Moreover, the American public and many members of Congress rejected an active engagement in international politics, prompting the United States to retreat from diplomatic involvement in European and Asian affairs. However, as we noted in the essay that opened Part Five, because the United States had "the world's most productive economic system," its privately owned banks and corporations pulled the nation into the world economy. Our discussion in Chapter 23 will show how American bankers financed the international financial system during the 1920s, assisting Germany to pay war reparations and the Allied Powers to pay their war debts. Chapter 24 will then explain how the collapse of the international economy during the Great Depression prompted Americans to retreat further into political isolationism. Only the threat to democracy posed by fascist governments in Germany, Japan, and Italy by the late 1930s allowed President Franklin Roosevelt to persuade a reluctant nation to prepare for a new war. The story of Roosevelt's initiatives appears in Chapter 25, which also charts the crucial contribution of the United States in the war against the fascist nations. Coming in quick succession, the First and Second World Wars thrust the United States into world affairs. This diplomatic revolution is one of the central themes of Part Five.

TIMELINE

1914	▶ Outbreak of war in Europe
	▶ United States declares neutrality
1915	▶ German submarine sinks *Lusitania*
1915–1940	▶ Great Migration of African Americans to North
1916	▶ Woodrow Wilson reelected president
	▶ Revenue Act of 1916 raises taxes
1917	▶ United States enters World War I
	▶ Selective Service Act initiates draft
	▶ War Industries Board established
	▶ Committee on Public Information established
	▶ Espionage Act
	▶ War Risk Insurance Act protects soldiers' families
	▶ Militants demand woman suffrage
	▶ East St. Louis race riot
	▶ Bolsheviks come to power in Russia
1918	▶ Wilson proposes Fourteen Points peace plan
	▶ Argonne campaign tests U.S. soldiers
	▶ Eugene Debs imprisoned under Sedition Act
	▶ Armistice ends war
	▶ U.S. and Allied troops intervene in Russia
1919	▶ Treaty of Versailles
	▶ Chicago race riot
	▶ Major wave of labor strikes
	▶ Red Scare and Palmer raids
	▶ *Schenck v. United States* limits free speech
	▶ League of Nations defeated in Senate
	▶ Eighteenth Amendment (Prohibition) ratified
	▶ War Industries Board disbanded
1920	▶ Nineteenth Amendment (woman suffrage) ratified
	▶ Sacco and Vanzetti arrested

FOR FURTHER EXPLORATION

For an analysis of the war and its impact, read Hew Strachan, *The First World War* (2004), and log onto **www.pbs.org/greatwar/index.html**, **http://www.bbc.co.uk/history/worldwars/wwone/**, and **www.lib.byu.edu/~rdh/wwi**. Frank Freidel, *Over There* (1990), offers soldiers' vivid firsthand accounts, while Meirion Harries and Susie Harries, *The Last Days of Innocence* (1997), capture the war experience at home and abroad. See also **memory.loc.gov/ammem/collections/rotogravures**. For the war in fiction, read William March, *Company K* (1993), and Ernest Hemingway's *In Our Time* (1925) and *A Farewell to Arms* (1929). For the home front, see *Pale Horse, Pale Rider* (1939) by Katherine Anne Porter.

For studies of "The Deadly Virus: The Influenza Epidemic of 1918," consult **www.archives.gov/exhibits/influenza-epidemic/index.html** and **www.pbs.org/wgbh/amex/**

influenza. On the "Red Scare," go to **newman.baruch.cuny.edu/digital/redscare/ default.htm**. For material on racism, the suffrage movement, and prohibition, log onto **www.authentichistory.com/1900s.html, dl.lib.brown.edu/temperance**, and **www.wpl .lib.oh.us/AntiSaloon/index.html**. William M. Tuttle Jr., *Race Riot: Chicago in the Red Summer of 1919* (1970), places that conflict in a broad context.

To hear "American Leaders Speak: Recordings from World War I and the 1920 Election," go to **memory.loc.gov/ammem/nfhtml**. "The South Texas Border, 1900– 1920" at **memory.loc.gov/ammem/award97/txuhtml/runyhome.html** covers life in the Lower Rio Grande Valley.

TEST YOUR KNOWLEDGE

To assess your mastery of the material in this chapter and for Web sites, images, and documents related to this chapter, visit **bedfordstmartins.com/henrettaconcise**.

Modern Times
1920–1932

[Growing up, I never] thought of myself as an American. I came from Brooklyn, and in Brooklyn there were no Americans; there were Jews and Negroes and Italians and Poles and Irishmen. Americans lived in New England, in the South, in the Midwest: alien people in alien places.

—Norman Podhoretz (b.1930)

The 1920s was a decade filled with sharp contrasts—between Prohibition laws and speakeasy nightclubs, modern science and fundamentalist religion, economic boom and financial bust, popular heroes and social villains. Charles Lindbergh was one of the heroes. In May 1927, Lindbergh flew his small, single-engine plane, *The Spirit of St. Louis*, from New York to Paris, a distance of 3,620 miles. He did it alone and without stopping—a tense journey that stretched over 33 hours. Nobody had ever done this before. Returning home to tickertape parades, Lindbergh became *Time* magazine's first Man of the Year in 1928. The handsome young aviator captivated the nation by combining expertise in modern technology with the traditional virtues of hard work and individual achievement. Amid the grinding routine of modern industrial life, Lindbergh showed that an adventurous individual could make a difference.

Samuel Insull taught Americans the same lesson—with a twist. A financial entrepreneur who was more important than Lindbergh and almost as well known, Insull began the decade as a hero and ended it as a villain. Insull was born in England and came to New York as the personal secretary to the great inventor Thomas Edison. In 1892, he moved to Chicago, where he built a small electrical power company into a giant enterprise. By 1907, Insull's Commonwealth Edison Company was providing electrical power for the entire city; by 1924, his Chicago Rapid Transit Company was offering transportation to many of its residents as well. At the peak of his power in 1929, Insull controlled electric utility companies in 5,000 communities in thirty-two states. To assemble this utility empire, Insull used the tools of modern capitalism: He created a pyramid of holding companies that allowed him to manage companies valued at $500 million with a personal investment of only $27 million. He funded the rest by issuing low-priced stocks and bonds, which nearly one million Americans eagerly snapped up.

Insull's electrical empire, along with Henry Ford's mass production techniques, helped to give Americans the highest standard of living in the world and to create a new consumer culture. Millions of Americans could now enjoy a plethora of assembly-line-produced goods: cars, refrigerators, phonographs, and radios. The values of the nineteenth-century middle classes—the Protestant ethic of hard work, self-denial, and frugality—gave way to an optimistic fascination with consumption, leisure, and self-realization, some of the essential features of modern life.

Then, suddenly and unexpectedly, the collapse of the stock market in 1929 and the coming of the Great Depression threw the nation and its political and business leaders into disarray. By 1932, Insull's pyramid of utility companies had collapsed in bankruptcy, and 600,000 investors had lost their life savings. The Chicago financier fled to Greece and then to Paris, not in triumph—like Lindbergh—but in disgrace. At home, Americans faced silent factories and massive unemployment, putting the optimism of the 1920s to the test.

The Business-Government Partnership of the 1920s

The business-government partnership fostered by World War I expanded throughout the 1920s. As the *Wall Street Journal* enthusiastically proclaimed, "Never before, here or anywhere else, has a government been so completely fused with business."—and, the *Journal* might have added, so successfully fused. The nation's prosperity from 1922 to 1929 seemed to confirm the wisdom of allowing corporate interests to manage economic life. Gone, or at least submerged, was the reform impulse of the Progressive era (see Chapter 20). Middle-class Americans no longer viewed business leaders as greedy robber barons but saw them as respected—even sacred—public figures. President Calvin Coolidge captured the prevailing public mood when he solemnly declared, "The man who builds a factory builds a temple. The man who works there worships there."

Politics in the Republican "New Era"

With the ailing Woodrow Wilson out of the presidential picture in 1920, the Democrats nominated Governor James M. Cox of Ohio for president and Assistant Secretary of the Navy Franklin D. Roosevelt as vice president. The Democratic platform called for U.S. participation in the League of Nations and a continuation of Wilson's progressivism. The Republicans, now led by the conservative, probusiness wing of the party, selected Ohio Senator Warren G. Harding and Massachusetts Governor Calvin Coolidge as their candidates. Sensing the desire of many Americans to put the war and the stresses of 1919 behind them, Harding promised "not heroics but healing, not nostrums but normalcy." On election day, he won in a landslide, beginning a Republican dominance that would last until 1932.

Warren Harding had not been an outstanding state politician in Ohio, and he did not cut an impressive figure in the U.S. Senate. But with victory nearly certain in 1920, Republican Party leaders wanted a pliable candidate. Genial, loyal, and mediocre, "Uncle Warren" fit the bill. Harding knew his limitations and assembled a strong cabinet, composed of progressives as well as conservatives, to guide the government. Charles Evans Hughes, former reform governor, Supreme Court justice, and presidential candidate, took firm control of the State Department. As secretary of agriculture, Henry C. Wallace created new links with farm organizations, while Attorney General Harlan Fiske Stone, a future chief justice, cleaned up the mess at the Department of Justice left by the Palmer raids. Financier Andrew W. Mellon ran the Treasury Department and quickly reduced the high wartime tax rates on corporate and personal income, freeing up money for private investment.

The most active member of the Harding administration was Secretary of Commerce Herbert Hoover, the well-known head of the wartime Food Administration. Under Hoover's direction, the Commerce Department fostered the creation of 2,000 trade associations representing companies in almost every major industry. Government officials worked closely with the associations, providing statistical research, suggesting industry-wide standards, and promoting stable prices and wages. By creating informal governmental ties between government and industry—an "associated state"—Hoover hoped to achieve through voluntary cooperation what Progressive-era reformers had sought through governmental regulation.

Unfortunately, not all government-business cooperation served the interests of the public. The Republican-dominated Federal Trade Commission (FTC) ignored antitrust laws that prohibited collusion among companies to raise prices. Similarly, the Supreme Court, now headed by the former conservative Republican president William Howard Taft, refused to break up the mammoth United States Steel Corporation; as long as there was some competition in the steel industry, the Court ruled, the company's dominant price-setting position was within the law.

If U.S. Steel was law-abiding, many of President Harding's political associates were not. When Harding died suddenly of a heart attack in San Francisco in August 1923, evidence of widespread fraud and corruption in his administration was just coming to light. The worst scandal concerned the secret leasing to private companies of government oil reserves in Teapot Dome, Wyoming, and Elk Hills, California. Secretary of the Interior Albert Fall was eventually convicted of taking $300,000 in bribes and became the first cabinet officer in American history to serve a prison sentence.

Following Harding's death, Vice President Calvin Coolidge moved to the White House. In contrast to Harding's political cronyism and outgoing style, Coolidge personified the austere rectitude of a New England Yankee. Coolidge's reserved personality and unimpeachable morality reassured Republican voters, who were drawn primarily from the native-born Protestants, business owners, and skilled workers but also included propertied farmers and African Americans. To win their backing for his presidential candidacy in 1924, Coolidge called for isolationism in foreign policy, economy in government, tax cuts for business, and limited aid to farmers.

As the Democrats gathered to nominate a candidate, they were sharply divided. Traditionally, the party had drawn its strength from white voters in the Jim Crow South and immigrant-based urban political machines in the North. But in the 1920s,

MAP 23.1 Ku Klux Klan Politics and Violence in the 1920s

Unlike the Reconstruction-era Klan, the Klan of the 1920s had substantial strength in the West and Midwest as well as the South. Although the Klan is often viewed as a rural movement, its strongest "klaverns" were in Los Angeles, Atlanta, Detroit, and other large cities. KKK members operated as moral vigilantes in areas where they were strong; elsewhere, their aggressive tactics triggered riots between Klansmen and their ethnic and religious targets.

these two groups of Democrats disagreed mightily over Prohibition, immigration restriction, and the mounting power of the racist and anti-immigrant Ku Klux Klan (Map 23.1). These cultural conflicts produced a hopeless deadlock between northern supporters of Governor Al Smith of New York and southern and western advocates of former Treasury Secretary William A. McAdoo of California. After 103 ballots, the delegates compromised on John W. Davis, a wealthy and influential Wall Street lawyer who hailed from West Virginia.

The 1924 campaign featured a third-party challenge by Senator Robert M. La Follette of Wisconsin, who ran on the Progressive Party ticket. La Follette's candidacy mobilized reformers and labor leaders as well as disgruntled farmers. His progressive-minded platform called for nationalization of railroads, public ownership of utilities, and a constitutional amendment to allow Congress to overrule the Supreme Court.

The Republicans won an impressive victory: Coolidge received 15.7 million votes to Davis's 8.4 million and La Follette's 4.9 million. Significantly, only 52 percent of the electorate cast ballots in 1924 (and in most subsequent elections), compared to more than 70 percent in presidential elections of the late nineteenth century. A drop in voting by men, rather than apathy among newly enfranchised women voters, caused most of the decline.

After achieving the suffrage in 1920, politically conscious women sought positions in Democratic and Republican party organizations but had little success. African American women were equally unsuccessful as they struggled for voting rights in the South and passage of a federal antilynching law. Women were more influential as lobbyists. The Women's Joint Congressional Committee, a Washington-based coalition of ten white women's organizations, including the newly formed League of Women Voters, lobbied actively for reform legislation. Its major accomplishment was the passage in 1921 of the Sheppard-Towner Federal Maternity and Infancy Act. The first federally funded health-care legislation, the act lowered infant mortality by subsidizing medical clinics, prenatal educational programs, and visiting nurse projects. However, conservatives charged that the Sheppard-Towner Act was part of a Communist plot to socialize American medicine and an attack on the rights of the states, which traditionally handled public health measures. Indeed, many men in Congress supported the act because they feared the voting power of newly enfranchised women. By the late 1920s, when it became clear that women did not vote as a bloc, Congress cut off appropriations for the program.

As support for reform languished on the national level, some state leaders pursued ambitious progressive agendas. In New York, where Al Smith and Robert Wagner were developing a social-welfare liberal agenda (see Chapter 20), new legislation expanded aid to public schools; boosted workers' compensation programs; and created new state forests, scenic parks, and automobile parkways. However, the dominant motif of the 1920s was limited government, which placed responsibility for the nation's well-being in the hands of its corporate business leaders.

Corporate Capitalism

The revolution in business management that began in the 1890s finally triumphed in the 1920s. Large-scale corporate bureaucracies headed by chief executive officers (CEOs) replaced individual- or family-run enterprises as the major form of business organization. Few CEOs owned a significant part of their enterprises, but they—and not the thousands of stockholder owners—controlled daily operations. Moreover, many corporations were so large that they dominated their markets. What the famous eighteenth-century economist Adam Smith had called the "invisible hand" of market forces had given way to the "visible hand" of managers who controlled output, prices, and their own salaries.

Indeed, by 1930, a handful of managers stood at the center of American economic life. Because of a vigorous pattern of consolidation during the 1920s, the two hundred largest businesses controlled almost half the nonbanking corporate wealth in the United States. The largest number of mergers occurred in rapidly growing industries such as chemicals (in which Dupont emerged as the leader), electrical appliances and machinery (Westinghouse and General Electric), and automobiles (General Motors). Rarely did any single corporation monopolize an entire industry; rather, an oligopoly of a few major producers dominated the market.

The nation's financial institutions expanded and consolidated along with its corporations. Total banking assets rose from $48 billion in 1919 to $72 billion in 1929. Mergers between Wall Street banks enhanced the role of New York as the financial center of the United States and, increasingly, the world. In 1929, almost half the nation's banking resources were controlled by 1 percent of American banks, a mere 250 depositories.

Immediately after World War I, the nation experienced a series of economic shocks. As Americans spent their wartime savings, they sparked rampant inflation: Prices jumped by one-third in 1919 alone. Then came a sharp two-year recession that raised unemployment to 10 percent and cut prices more than 20 percent. Finally, the economy began to grow smoothly and many Americans began to benefit from the success of corporate enterprise. Between 1922 and 1929, the gross domestic product grew from $74.1 billion to $103.1 billion, approximately 40 percent, and per capita income rose impressively from $641 to $847 (about $10,000 today, one-third of present per capita income).

An abundance of new consumer products, particularly the automobile, sparked this economic expansion. Manufacturing output expanded 64 percent during the decade, as factories churned out millions of cars, refrigerators, stoves, and radios. To produce these goods, basic industries supplied huge quantities of raw materials: steel, copper, chemicals, natural gas, electrical power, oil, and gasoline. Scientific management, first introduced in 1895 by Frederick W. Taylor (see Chapter 20), was widely implemented in the 1920s. In combination with more efficient machinery and new methods of mass production, it increased productivity by 40 percent, boosting workers' pay and corporate profits.

The economy had some significant weaknesses. Agriculture — which still employed one-fourth of all workers — never fully recovered from the postwar recession. During the war, American farmers had borrowed heavily to expand production, but the revival of European output produced a glut in world markets. The price of wheat quickly dropped by 40 percent, corn by 32 percent, and hogs by 50 percent, and they never completely recovered. Between 1919 and 1929, the farmers' share of the national income plummeted from 16 percent to 8.8 percent. As their income plunged, farmers looked to Congress for help. The McNary-Haugen bills of 1927 and 1928 proposed a system of federal price supports for a slew of agricultural products: wheat, corn, cotton, rice, and tobacco. President Coolidge opposed the bills as "class" (special-interest) legislation and vetoed both of them.

Other "sick industries," particularly coal and textiles, also missed out on the prosperity of the 1920s. Like farmers, these businesses had expanded output during the war and now faced overcapacity and falling prices. This underside of American economic life foreshadowed the Great Depression of the 1930s.

Unlike farmers and miners, industrial workers and white-collar employees shared in the prosperity of the 1920s. Henry Ford and other major corporate employers paid their workers well, thereby increasing their buying power as consumers. Many industries went to a shorter workweek (five full days and a half day on Saturday), giving their employees more leisure time. Profitable firms, such as International Harvester, offered workers two weeks of paid vacation every year.

The 1920s marked the advent of **welfare capitalism**, a system of labor relations that stressed management's responsibility for employees' well-being. At a time when unemployment compensation and government-sponsored pensions did not exist, General Electric, U.S. Steel, and other large corporations offered workers health insurance, old-age pension plans, and the opportunity to buy stock in the company at below-market prices. Other firms subsidized mortgages or contributed to employee savings plans. Their goal was to create a loyal and long-serving workforce, particularly among managers, dedicated office workers, shop supervisors, and skilled machinists. But such welfare plans covered only about 5 percent of the industrial workforce.

Welfare capitalism had a second goal of deterring production-line workers from joining labor unions. Some companies set up employee committees to voice workers' complaints and consult regularly with managers over working conditions. Other corporations accused unions of being un-American because they campaigned for "closed shops" that required workers to become members; employers celebrated the "American Plan" of an open, nonunion shop. Decisions by the conservative-minded Supreme Court undercut union activism and government regulation of the labor market. In *Colorado Coal Company v. United Mine Workers* (1925), the Court ruled that a striking union could be penalized for illegal restraint of trade. The Court also struck down federal legislation regulating child labor, and in *Atkins v. Children's Hospital* (1923), it voided a minimum wage for women workers in the District of Columbia. Such decisions and aggressive antiunion campaigns caused membership in labor unions to fall from 5.1 million in 1920 to 3.6 million in 1929 — only 10 percent of the nonagricultural workforce. Welfare capitalism seemed to represent the wave of the future in industrial relations.

Economic Expansion Abroad

The growing power of U.S. corporations was apparent in the international arena. American manufacturers actively promoted foreign sales of consumer products: radios, telephones, automobiles, and sewing machines. To supply these markets, firms built factories and took over existing businesses in foreign countries. General Electric set up production facilities in Latin America, China, Japan, and Australia; General Motors expanded its sales in Europe by taking over the Vauxhall Motor Company in Britain and Opel in Germany. Other American firms invested abroad in new sources of supply. Seeking lower livestock prices, three major American meatpackers — Swift, Armour, and Wilson — built plants in Argentina. The United Fruit Company developed plantations in Costa Rica, Honduras, and Guatemala; other American companies set up sugar plantations in Cuba and rubber plantations in the Philippines and Malaya. Standard Oil of New Jersey acquired oil reserves in Mexico and Venezuela (a precursor to American oil investments in the Middle East after World War II). During the 1920s, foreign investments by U.S. corporations more than doubled, reaching a total of $15.2 billion.

American banks were equally active in providing funds to European countries to rebuild their war-torn societies and to fulfill their international debt obligations. The

Bananas

... a good mixer
with every fruit that grows

Oranges, apples, grapefruit, pineapples, pears, melons, grapes—all these and many others—blend perfectly with bananas. The distinctive flavor of the banana, when added to a fruit cup, a fruit salad, or any fruit combination, brings out the flavor of the other fruits and makes them taste better.

"Ripe bananas are good for little children."

"EAT plenty of fresh fruits" is now an accepted principle of diet—and the mere sight of mellow, luscious bananas is an invitation to serve many delicious and nourishing fruit combinations.

All year round from the tropics ... Easter, Fourth of July, Thanksgiving, Christmas—every season, every day—bananas are available. Thanks to the nearness and all-year-round productiveness of the tropics, they always can be had at your grocery or fruit store.

Children crave the temptingly flavored banana instinctively. And it is well that they do, for bananas are one of the most important energy-producing foods. Doctors and dietitians consider the banana not only one of the most *valuable* foods, but also one of the most *easily digested* ... as beneficial for grown-ups as for children.

Serve bananas with other fruits, with cereals, with milk or cream ... or serve them plain. But always be sure they are fully ripe (generously flecked with brown spots). If they are not at the proper stage of ripeness when you buy them, let them ripen at room temperature. Never place them in the ice-box.

UNIFRUIT BANANAS
Reg. U. S. Pat. Off.

A United Fruit Company Product

Imported and Distributed by Fruit Dispatch Company
17 Battery Place, New York, N. Y.

American Companies Abroad

United Fruit was one of the many American companies that found opportunities for investment in South America in the 1920s. It then had to "sell" tropical foods to American consumers. To boost sales, the company published elaborate and informative color advertisements. Bananas were sufficiently exotic that the ads explained to consumers how to tell when bananas were ripe and never to put them in the ice-box, the precursor of the electric refrigerator. Duke University Library, Special Collections.

banks loaned money to Germany, enabling it to pay reparations to the Allied Powers. Britain and France then used these funds to pay off their wartime loans from the United States. While American political leaders insisted on payment of these debts ("They hired the money, didn't they?" scoffed President Coolidge), they made repayment very difficult. The Fordney-McCumber Tariff of 1922 followed the long-standing Republican policy of using high tariffs to exclude foreign-made goods.

Unable to sell their goods in the United States, European nations could not easily earn the dollars needed to pay their debts.

In 1924, U.S. diplomats and bankers met with their counterparts from France, Great Britain, and Germany to address the debt situation. The meeting produced the Dawes Plan, named for Charles G. Dawes, the Chicago banker who negotiated the agreement. The plan reduced the reparations that Germany owed to the Allies and provided for substantial American bank loans to assist the Germans in keeping up with the payments. European financial stability now depended on the continuing flow of American capital.

This fragile system of international finance collapsed with the crash of the American stock market in October 1929. The outflow of capital from the United States to Europe slowed and then stopped, undermining the flow of reparation payments. The stock market crisis also increased congressional support for a policy of economic nationalism. The Hawley-Smoot Act of 1930 raised tariffs on imports to an all-time high and made it nearly impossible for the Allied Powers to pay off the remaining $4.3 billion in war loans. Even as American corporations successfully extended their sales and investments to the corners of the earth, American politicians and bankers failed to create a stable structure of international finance.

Foreign Policy in the 1920s

American foreign policy during the 1920s and 1930s was both isolationist and internationalist. By refusing to join the League of Nations and the Court of International Justice (the World Court), the United States declined to play an active role in international politics; in this regard, the nation's stance was clearly isolationist. However, as the Dawes Plan indicates, the United States pursued a vigorous, internationalist economic policy. Officials in the Department of State and the Department of Commerce worked constantly to open up new foreign markets for American manufacturers and bankers and to protect existing American interests in other countries.

These initiatives were particularly important in the Caribbean and Latin America, the site of considerable investments by U.S. companies and considerable military intervention to protect those investments. Both continued during the 1920s. To quell civil unrest and protect American interests, the U.S. government stationed troops in the Dominican Republic from 1916 to 1924. American military forces likewise remained in Nicaragua almost continuously from 1912 to 1933 and in Haiti from 1915 to 1934. Relations with Mexico remained tense, a legacy of U.S. intervention during the Mexican Revolution (see Chapter 21) and of the Mexican government's efforts to **nationalize** its oil and mineral wealth. This Mexican initiative alarmed Standard Oil of New Jersey (owned primarily by the Rockefeller family) and other U.S. petroleum companies with investments in Mexico.

While the United States maintained its dominant position in the Western Hemisphere, it reduced its political and military commitments in East Asia and Europe. The Washington Naval Arms Conference of 1921 revealed American strategy in the Pacific. Secretary of State Charles Evans Hughes won acceptance of a bold plan that placed strict limits on naval expansion. His goals were to avoid huge U.S. naval expenditures and to prevent Japan from expanding its naval forces and becoming the dominant nation in East Asia. The major naval powers agreed to scrap some warships; to halt the construction of large battleships for ten years; and to maintain a fixed ratio of naval tonnage among the fleets of Britain, the United States, Japan, France, and Italy. As one commentator quipped, in a short speech Hughes sank "more ships than all the admirals of the world have sunk in a cycle of centuries."

Seven years later, American Secretary of State Frank Kellogg devised another low-cost diplomatic plan, this time to calm French fears of a new German invasion. To avoid committing the United States to a pact that would guarantee France's territorial integrity, Kellogg persuaded French foreign minister Aristide Briand to support a broader agreement condemning all militarism. Fifteen nations signed the pact in Paris in 1928; forty-eight more approved it later. The signatories agreed to "condemn recourse to war for the solution of international controversies, and renounce it as an instrument of national policy." The U.S. Senate ratified the Kellogg Plan 85 to 1, but critics correctly pointed out that the agreement lacked mechanisms for enforcement and was little more than an "international kiss."

Pious declarations were no cure for the massive economic, political, and territorial problems that World War I had created. U.S. policymakers vacillated, as they would in the 1930s, between assuming a larger role in world events and fearing that treaties would limit their ability to act unilaterally. Their diplomatic efforts would ultimately prove inadequate in the face of the mounting international crises that led to World War II.

> ▶ In what ways did government and business work together during the "new era"? How was it different from the Progressive Era? Why did it change?
>
> ▶ Describe American foreign policy—both political and economic—during the 1920s. Was it isolationist or internationalist?

A New National Culture

The 1920s marked the development of a mass national culture that emphasized leisure, consumption, and amusement. Automobiles, paved roads, the parcel post service, movies, radios, telephones, mass-circulation magazines, brand names, and chain stores suddenly took center stage. Together, they linked Americans—in the mill towns in the southern Piedmont, outposts on the Oklahoma plains, and ethnic enclaves in states along the Atlantic and Pacific coasts—in an expanding web of national experience. In fact, as consumerism spread around the world, American products and culture achieved global influence.

A Consumer Society

In homes across the country during the 1920s, Americans sat down to breakfasts of Kellogg's corn flakes and toast from a General Electric toaster. They got into Ford Model Ts to go to work or to go shopping at Safeway, A&P, or Woolworth's, some of the many chain stores that had sprung up across the country. In the evening, the family gathered to listen to radio programs such as *Great Moments in History*, to catch up on events in the latest issue of *Reader's Digest*, or enjoy the melodramatic tales in *True*

Story; on weekends, they might see the newest Charlie Chaplin film at the local theater. Millions of Americans now shared similar cultural experiences.

Still, many Americans—blacks, immigrants, working-class families, and many farmers—did not participate fully in the new commercial culture or accept its middle-class values. As one historian explains, "Buying an electric vacuum cleaner did not turn Josef Dobrowolski into *True Story*'s Jim Smith." Moreover, the unequal distribution of income limited many consumers' ability to buy the enticing new products. The bottom 40 percent of American families had an average annual income of only $725 (about $8,200 today); after paying for food, housing, and clothing, these families had only $135 to spend on everything else. Many Americans stretched their incomes by taking advantage of newly devised installment plans that allowed people to purchase cars, radios, refrigerators, and sewing machines "on time." "Buy now, Pay later," said the ads, and millions did. By 1927, two-thirds of American cars were financed through monthly payments, and consumer lending grew to $7 billion a year—the tenth-largest business in the United States.

New appliances—electric refrigerators, radios, fans, irons, vacuum cleaners—had a dramatic impact on women's lives. While single women were steadily increasing their participation in the paid workforce, most married women spent their time as house-wives and mothers. Electric appliances made housewives' chores much less arduous but also encouraged middle-class housewives to do their own housework and laundry, replacing human servants with electric ones. The new gadgets also raised standards of cleanliness, encouraging women to spend more time doing household chores. For most women, leisure time remained scarce.

To encourage consumers to view the new products as "necessities" rather than "luxuries," manufacturers were spending no less than $2.6 billion a year on advertising by 1929. A new advertising industry (centered on New York City's Madison Avenue) devised sophisticated ways to spur sales, often aided by experts in the growing academic field of psychology. Some ads for medicine featured white-coated doctors to suggest scientific approval of their products. Other ads appealed to people's social aspirations by depicting elegant men and women who smoked certain brands of cigarettes or drove a Buick, Pierce-Arrow, or other make of car. Ad writers also preyed on people's insecurities, coming up with a variety of socially unacceptable "diseases," such as the dreaded "B.O." (body odor).

Consumers were less the passive victims of manipulative advertising agencies than willing participants in a new culture. For many middle-class Americans, the traditional criteria for judging self-worth—personal character, religious commitment, and social standing—now had a powerful rival: the gratification of personal desires through the acquisition of more and better possessions.

The World of the Automobile

No possession typified the new consumer culture better than the automobile. "Why on earth do you need to study what's changing this country?" a Muncie, Indiana, resident asked sociologists Robert and Helen Lynd. "I can tell you what's happening in just four letters: A-U-T-O!" The showpiece of modern consumer capitalism, the automobile revolutionized American economic and social life.

Mass production of cars stimulated the prosperity of the 1920s. Before the introduction of the moving assembly line in 1913, Ford workers took twelve and a half hours to put together an auto; subsequently, they did the job in only ninety-three minutes. By 1927, Ford was producing a car every twenty-four seconds. Auto sales climbed from 1.5 million in 1921 to 5 million in 1929, a year in which Americans spent $2.58 billion on cars. By the end of the decade, Americans owned 23 million cars—about 80 percent of the world's automobiles—an average of one car for every six people.

The boom in the auto industry rippled through the American economy. It stimulated the steel, petroleum, chemical, rubber, and glass industries and, directly or indirectly, provided jobs for 3.7 million workers. Highway construction became a billion-dollar-a-year enterprise, financed by federal subsidies and state gasoline taxes. Car ownership broke down the isolation of rural life, spurred the growth of suburbs, and, in 1924, spawned the first suburban shopping center: Country Club Plaza outside Kansas City, Missouri.

The auto also changed the way Americans spent their leisure time. Although gasoline was not cheap (about $2.50 a gallon in 2008 prices), Americans took to the roads, becoming a nation of tourists. The American Automobile Association, founded in 1902, estimated that in 1929 about forty-five million people—almost one-third of the population—took vacations by automobile, patronizing the "auto-camps" and tourist cabins that were the forerunners of post–World War II motels. Like the movies, cars changed the dating patterns of young Americans. Contrary to many parents' views, premarital sex was not invented in the backseat of a Ford, but a Model T offered more privacy than did the family living room or the front porch and contributed to increased sexual experimentation among the young.

The Movies and Mass Culture

The new mass media—glossy magazines, radio, and especially movies—formed the centerpiece of a common national culture. American movies had their roots in turn-of-the-century nickelodeons, where for a nickel, working-class audiences viewed one-reel silent films such as *The Great Train Robbery.* By 1910, the moviemaking industry had moved to southern California, which had cheap land, plenty of sunshine, and varied scenery—mountains, deserts, cities, and the Pacific Ocean—within easy reach. By the end of World War I, Hollywood reigned as the movie capital of the world, producing nearly 90 percent of all films.

As directors produced feature films and exhibited them in large, ornate theaters, movies attracted a middle-class audience. Early movie stars, including Buster Keaton, Charlie Chaplin, Mary Pickford, and Douglas Fairbanks, became idols who set national trends in clothing and hairstyles. Then a new cultural icon, the flapper, burst on the scene to represent emancipated womanhood.

Actress Clara Bow was Hollywood's favorite flapper, a bobbed-hair "jazz baby" who won a movie contract at the age of eighteen. Three years later, she was a star—the lead character in *It,* one of the first movies to gross $1 million. Whatever "It" was, Clara had it. With her boyish figure and shock of red hair, she had a strikingly sensual presence; "she could flirt with a grizzly bear," wrote one reviewer. Thousands of young women took Bow as their model. Decked out in short skirts and rolled-down silk stockings, flappers wore makeup, smoked, danced to jazz, and flaunted their liberated lifestyle. Like so many cultural icons, the flappers represented only a tiny minority of women, but thanks to the movies and advertising industry, they became the symbol of women's sexual and social emancipation.

The movies were big business, grossing $1.6 billion in 1926. The large studios — United Artists, Paramount, and Metro-Goldwyn-Mayer — dominated the industry and were run mainly by eastern European Jewish immigrants such as Samuel Goldfish (later Goldwyn). Movies became even more profitable and culturally powerful with the advent of the "talkies." Warner Brothers' *The Jazz Singer* (1927), starring Al Jolson, was the first feature-length film to offer sound. Despite the enormous expense — some $300 million to equip film sets and thousands of theaters with sound equipment — all the major studios quickly made the transition to "talkies." By 1929, the nation's 23,000 movie theaters were selling ninety million tickets a year.

That *The Jazz Singer* was the first talkie was not a coincidence. Jazz music captured the sensibility of the 1920s, especially its creative excitement and sensual character. As a word, *jazz* was originally a vulgar term for the sex act; as music, it was (and is) an improvisational form whose notes are rarely written down. Jazz began in the dance halls and bordellos of turn-of-the century New Orleans and was a thoroughly American — indeed, African American — art form. Most of the early jazz musicians were black, and they carried its rhythms to Chicago, New York, Kansas City, and Los Angeles. The best-known performers were composer-pianist Ferdinand "Jelly Roll" Morton, trumpeter Louis "Satchmo" Armstrong, composer-bandleader Edward "Duke" Ellington, and singer Bessie Smith, "the empress of the Blues."

Phonograph records increased the appeal of jazz and the blues by capturing their spontaneity and transmitting it to a wide audience; jazz, in turn, boosted the infant recording industry. Soon, this uniquely American art form had caught on in Europe, especially in France. Because jazz often expressed black dissent against the straightforward, optimistic rhythms of white music, it became popular among specific types of white Americans — young people, intellectuals, and social outcasts — who felt stifled by middle-class culture. Later in the century, other African American musical forms — notably rhythm-and-blues and hip-hop — would again challenge middle-class values by injecting themes of sex and violence into American popular culture.

Mass-circulation magazines and the radio were also key factors in the creation of a national culture. In 1922, ten magazines each claimed a circulation of at least 2.5 million, including *Time,* the *Saturday Evening Post,* the *Ladies' Home Journal,* and *Good Housekeeping.* Tabloid newspapers, which highlighted crime, sports, comics, and scandals, became part of urban culture, and news services such as the Associated Press (AP) and United Press (UP) appeared on the national scene. Thanks to AP and UP, people across the United States read the same articles.

The newest instrument of mass culture, professional radio broadcasting, was truly a child of the 1920s. In November 1920, station KDKA in Pittsburgh carried the presidential election returns; a mere nine years later, 800 stations, most affiliated with the Columbia Broadcasting System (CBS) or the National Broadcasting Company (NBC), were on the air, and nearly ten million American households (40 percent of the total) owned a radio. Unlike the situation in Europe, where radio was a government monopoly, American radio stations were licensed by the government but privately

CRAZY BLUES
By PERRY BRADFORD

Get this number for your phonograph on Okeh Record No. 4169

PUBLISHED BY
PERRY BRADFORD
MUSIC PUB CO.
1547 BROADWAY, N. Y. C.

All That Jazz

The phonograph machine expanded the popularity of jazz, which now could be heard at home as well as in a city jazz joint. "Crazy Blues" by Mamie Smith and her Jazz Hounds sold a million records in 1920 and convinced record companies that there was a market among African Americans for what were called "race records." By the 1950s, black music had become "American" music. Perry Bradford, the piano player and composer of "Crazy Blues," was also the composer of "Keep A Knockin'," which Little Richard made into a major rock 'n' roll hit in 1957. Division of Political History, Smithsonian Institution, Washington, DC.

owned; they drew their revenue from advertisers and corporate sponsors. One of the most popular radio shows of all time, *Amos 'n' Andy*, which premiered on the NBC network in 1928, featured two white actors playing stereotypical black characters. Stock phrases from the weekly show, such as "Check and double check," quickly became part of everyday speech. So many people "tuned in" (a new phrase of the 1920s, similar to "log on" today) to *Amos 'n' Andy* that other activities came to a halt during the show's airtime.

As the workweek shrank and paid vacations increased, Americans had more time and energy to expend on recreation. Cities and suburbs built baseball diamonds, tennis courts, swimming pools, and golf courses. Sports became a big business as private entrepreneurs built huge football and baseball stadiums and hired professional teams to play in them. Fans could attend games, listen to them on the radio, or catch highlights in the movie newsreels. Star athletes such as boxer Jack Dempsey, golfer Bobby Jones, and baseball slugger Babe Ruth became national celebrities. Excluded from the white teams, outstanding black athletes such as baseball pitcher Satchel Paige played on teams in the Negro National League and the Southern Negro League.

> ▶ How do you explain the rise of a national culture in the 1920s? In what ways did Americans across the nation begin to share common experiences?
>
> ▶ Which had a greater impact on American life: the automobile or the movies? In more specific terms, compare the historical contributions of Henry Ford and Clara Bow.

Redefining American Identity

As movies, radio, advertising, and assembly-line products began to transform the country into a modern, cosmopolitan nation, many Americans welcomed these changes as exciting evidence of progress. Others were uneasy. Flappers dancing to jazz, youthful experimentation in Model Ts, sexually suggestive movies—these harbingers of a new era worried native-born Americans of religious stock. They were also troubled by the powerful presence in American cities of millions of Catholic and Jewish immigrants from Europe and African American migrants from the South. Beneath the clichés of the Jazz Age and the Roaring Twenties were deeply felt tensions that surfaced in conflicts over immigration, religion, Prohibition, and race relations. At stake was the definition of what it meant to be an American.

The Rise of Nativism

Tensions between city dwellers and rural folk escalated sharply during the 1920s. For the first time in the nation's history, more people lived in urban areas—ranging from small towns of 2,500 people to large cities—than in rural areas. There was no mistaking the trend. During the 1920s, about 6 million Americans left farms for the cities. By 1929, ninety-three cities had populations over 100,000. New York City exceeded 7 million; Chicago boasted almost 3 million, and the population of Los Angeles had exploded to 1.2 million. However, because political districts did not reflect this shift in population, rural areas still controlled most state legislatures. As cities demanded more services and tax dollars from state governments, conflict between the two regions was inevitable.

Racial and ethnic pluralism intensified these struggles. When native-born white Protestants—both farmers and city dwellers—looked at their society in 1920, they saw a nation of 105 million people that had changed dramatically in only forty years. During that time, more than 23 million immigrants had come to America, and many of them were Jews or Catholics from southern and eastern Europe. Senator William Bruce of Maryland branded them "indigestible lumps" in the "national stomach," implying that they might never be absorbed into the dominant culture. Such **nativist** sentiments, which recalled the reaction to immigrants from Ireland and Germany in the 1840s and 1850s, were widely shared.

Nativist animosity fueled a new drive against immigration. "America must be kept American," President Coolidge declared in 1924. Congress had banned Chinese immigration in 1882, and Theodore Roosevelt had negotiated a "Gentleman's Agreement" that limited Japanese immigration in 1907 (see Chapter 21). Now nativists charged that there were too many European immigrants and certainly too many who were anarchists, socialists, and radical labor organizers. Responding to these concerns, Congress passed an emergency immigration act in 1921 and a more restrictive measure, the National Origins Act, in 1924. The act cut immigration quotas to 2 percent of each nationality present in the United States in 1890, when the census had listed few people from southeastern Europe and Russia. In 1929, Congress imposed even more restrictive quotas, setting a cap of 150,000 immigrants per year from Europe and continuing to ban most migrants from Asia.

The new laws continued to permit unrestricted immigration from countries in the Western Hemisphere, and Latin Americans arrived in increasing numbers. Over one million Mexicans entered the United States between 1900 and 1930.

Some were fleeing the chaos of the Mexican Revolution of 1910, but many migrated in response to American labor shortages during World War I. Nativists lobbied Congress to cut this flow, and so did the leaders of labor unions, who pointed out that a flood of impoverished migrants would lower wages for all American workers. But Congress heeded the pleas of American employers, especially large-scale farmers in Texas and California, who wanted cheap labor. Only the coming of the Great Depression cut off migration from Mexico.

Another expression of nativism in the 1920s was the revival of the Ku Klux Klan (KKK) (see

Patriotic Protestant Nativism

While the Ku Klux Klan of the 1860s and 1870s stood for the cause of Confederate nationalism and white racism, the new KKK of the 1920s embraced the values of American patriotism and Protestantism. In its view, neither Catholics nor Jews could be real "Americans." This powerful image of a hooded knight on horseback, replete with the symbolism of Flag and Cross, conveys not only the movement's ideology but also its latent violence. Picture Research Consultants & Archives.

The Fight for Americanism   HIRAM WESLEY EVANS

Hiram Wesley Evans was a Texas dentist and the Grand Wizard of the Ku Klux Klan, which boasted a nationwide membership of three million. He published this defense of the Klan in *The North American Review*, a leading journal of opinion. Like fascist movements in Italy and Germany, the Klan focused on racial identity. For the KKK, "real" Americans were those of Nordic (northern European) descent; all others were "aliens," including those of southern or central European ancestry (Italian, Spanish, Polish, Czech, etc.) and those with Jewish or African forebears.

We are a movement of the plain people, very weak in the matter of culture, intellectual support, and trained leadership. We are demanding, and we expect to win, a return of power into the hands of the everyday, not highly cultured, not overly intellectualized, but entirely unspoiled and not de-Americanized, average citizen of the old stock. . . .

This is undoubtedly a weakness. It lays us open to the charge of being hicks and "rubes" and "drivers of second-hand Fords." We admit it. Far worse, it makes it hard for us to state our case and advocate our crusade in the most effective way, for most of us lack skill in language. . . .

To understand the Klan, then, it is necessary to understand the character and present mind of the mass of old-stock Americans. The mass, it must be remembered, as distinguished from the intellectually mongrelized "Liberals."

These are . . . a blend of various peoples of the so-called Nordic race . . . which, with all its faults, has given the world almost the whole of modern civilization. . . . These Nordic Americans for the last generation have found themselves increasingly uncomfortable. . . .

Finally came the moral breakdown that has been going on for two decades. . . . All our traditional moral standards went by the boards or were so disregarded that they ceased to be binding. The sacredness of our Sabbath, of our homes, of chastity, and finally even of our right to teach our own children in our own schools fundamental facts and truths were torn away from us. . . . One more point about the present attitude of the old-stock American: he has revived and increased his long-standing distrust of the Roman Catholic Church. . . . [which is] the chief leader of alienism, and the most dangerous alien power with a foothold inside our boundaries. . . .

The Ku Klux Klan . . . is an organization which gives expression, direction and purpose to the most vital instincts, hopes, and resentments of the old-stock Americans, provides them with leadership, and is enlisting and preparing them for militant, constructive action toward fulfilling their racial and national destiny . . . a definite crusade for Americanism! . . .

There are three of these great racial instincts. . . . These are the instincts of loyalty to the white race, to the traditions of America, and to the spirit of Protestantism, which has been an essential part of Americanism ever since the days of Roanoke and Plymouth Rock. They are condensed into the Klan slogan: "Native, white, Protestant supremacy."

SOURCE: Hiram Wesley Evans, "The Klan's Fight for Americanism," *The North American Review* 223 (March 1926): 37–39.

Chapter 15). Shortly after the premiere in 1915 of *Birth of a Nation*, a popular film that glorified the Reconstruction-era Klan, a group of southerners gathered on Stone Mountain outside Atlanta to revive the racist organization. Taking as its motto "Native, white, Protestant supremacy," the modern Klan recruited thousands of supporters in the Far West, the Southwest, and the Midwest, especially Oregon, Indiana, and Oklahoma. Its largest "klaverns" were in urban areas. The new Klan did not limit its harassment to blacks but targeted Catholics and Jews as well (see American Voices, p. 686). Its tactics remained the same: arson, physical intimidation, and economic boycotts. The KKK also turned to politics, and hundreds of Klansmen won election to local offices and state legislatures. At the height of its power in 1925, the Klan had over three million members — including a strong contingent of women who pursued a political agenda that combined racism, nativism, and equal rights for white Protestant women.

After 1925, the Klan declined rapidly, undermined by internal rivalries, rampant corruption, and the conviction for rape and murder of David Stephenson, the Klan's Grand Dragon in Indiana. In addition, the passage of the National Origins Act in 1924 robbed the Klan of a potent issue. Nonetheless, the Klan remained strong in the Jim Crow South; during the 1930s, some northern Klansmen supported the American Nazi movement, which shared its antiblack and anti-Jewish beliefs.

Legislating Values: Evolution and Prohibition

Other cultural conflicts erupted over religion and alcoholic beverages. The debate between modernist and revivalist Protestants, which had been simmering since the 1890s (see Chapter 18), came to a boil in the 1920s. Modernists, or liberal Protestants, found ways to reconcile their religious beliefs with Charles Darwin's theory of evolution and other scientific principles. Revivalist Protestants, who were strongly rooted in **fundamentalist** Baptist and Methodist churches, insisted on a literal reading of the Bible. So did popular evangelical preachers, such as Billy Sunday and Aimee Semple McPherson, who used storefront churches and open-air revivals to popularize their own brands of charismatic Christian fundamentalism.

Religious controversy entered the political arena when fundamentalists wrote their beliefs into law. In 1925, the Tennessee state legislature made it "unlawful . . . to teach any theory that denies the story of the Divine creation of man as taught in the Bible, and to teach instead that man has descended from a lower order of animals." The American Civil Liberties Union (ACLU), which had been formed during the Red Scare to protect free speech rights, challenged the constitutionality of the law. It intervened in the trial of John T. Scopes, a high school biology teacher, who had taught the principles of evolution to his class and faced a jail sentence for doing so. The case attracted national attention because Clarence Darrow, a famous criminal lawyer, defended Scopes, and William Jennings Bryan, the three-time Democratic presidential candidate and ardent fundamentalist, spoke for the prosecution.

The press dubbed the Scopes trial the "monkey trial." The label referred both to Darwin's argument that human beings and other primates share a common ancestor and to the circus atmosphere at the trial, which was broadcast live over a Chicago radio station. The jury took only eight minutes to deliver its verdict: guilty. Although the

The First Modern Evangelist: Aimee Semple McPherson (1890–1944)
Aimee McPherson founded the Foursquare Gospel Church, which now claims a worldwide membership of over three million. Born as Aimee Kennedy in Ontario, Canada, she married missionary Robert Semple in 1907. After his death in China, she married Harold McPherson and eventually settled in Los Angeles. By 1923, McPherson was preaching to a radio audience and to crowds of 5,000 at her massive Angelus Temple. In 1926, she attracted national attention by disappearing for a month and claiming that she had been kidnapped. Many people suspected that McPherson was at a romantic hideaway with the temple's radio operator, but her preaching career flourished into the 1930s. She died of an overdose of sedatives in 1944. © Bettmann/Corbis.

Tennessee Supreme Court overturned Scopes's conviction, the controversial law remained on the books for more than thirty years. As the 1920s ended, science and religion were locked in a standoff. Beginning in the 1980s, fundamentalists would launch new political attacks against Darwin and modern science (see Chapter 32).

Like the dispute over evolution, Prohibition—the "noble experiment," as it was called—involved the power of the state to enforce social values (see Chapter 22). Americans drank less after the Eighteenth Amendment took effect in January 1920, but those who continued to drink gave the decade its reputation as the Roaring Twenties. Urban ethnic groups—German, Irish, and Italian—had long opposed restrictions on drinking and refused to comply with the new law. Some Americans brewed their own beer or distilled "bathtub gin." Many others patronized illegal saloons and clubs, called speakeasies, which sprang up in every city; there were more than

30,000 speakeasies in New York City alone. Liquor smugglers operated with ease along Canadian and Mexican borders and used speedboats to land cargoes of wine, gin, and liquor along the Atlantic Coast. Organized crime (the "Mob"), already strong among Italians and Jews in major cities, took over the bootleg trade and grew wealthy from its profits. The "noble experiment" turned out to be a dismal failure.

The Americans who favored repeal of the Eighteenth Amendment—the "wets"—slowly built support for their cause in Congress and the state legislatures. The coming of the Great Depression hastened the process as politicians looked for ways to create jobs and raise tax revenues. With the ratification of the Twenty-first Amendment on December 5, 1933, nationwide Prohibition came to an inglorious end.

Intellectual Crosscurrents

As millions of Americans celebrated victory in the Great War and prosperity in peace-time, influential writers and intellectuals rendered bitter dissents. The novelist John Dos Passos railed at the obscenity of "Mr. Wilson's war" in *The Three Soldiers* (1921) and again in *1919* (1932). Ernest Hemingway's novels *In Our Time* (1924), *The Sun Also Rises* (1926), and *A Farewell to Arms* (1929) powerfully portrayed the dehuman-izing consequences and futility of war. In his despairing poem *The Waste Land* (1922), T. S. Eliot portrayed a fragmented civilization in ruins.

Influenced by Eliot's dark vision, writers offered stinging critiques of what they saw as the complacent, moralistic, and anti-intellectual tone of American life. In *Babbitt* (1922), the novelist Sinclair Lewis satirized the stifling conformity of a middle-class businessman. In 1925, Theodore Dreiser wrote his naturalistic masterpiece *An American Tragedy*, and F. Scott Fitzgerald published *The Great Gatsby*, both probing indictments of the mindless pursuit of material goods and wealth.

More affirmative works of art and literature emanated from Harlem, the center of African American life in New York City. During the 1920s, Harlem stood as "the symbol of liberty and the Promised Land to Negroes everywhere," as an influential black minister put it. Talented African American artists and writers flocked to Harlem, where they broke with older genteel traditions of black literature to assert cultural ties to Africa. The poet Langston Hughes drew on the black artistic forms of blues and jazz in *The Weary Blues* (1926), a groundbreaking collection of poems. And he captured the upbeat spirit of the Harlem Renaissance when he asserted, "I am a Negro—and beautiful."

Like Hughes, the leading lights of the Harlem Renaissance championed racial pride. Authors Claude McKay, Jean Toomer, and Jessie Fauset explored the black experience and represented the "New Negro" in fiction. Augusta Savage used sculpture to draw attention to black accomplishments. Zora Neale Hurston spent a decade collecting folklore in the South and the Caribbean and incorporated that material into her short stories and novels. This creative work embodied the ongoing African American struggle to find a way, as the influential black intellectual W. E. B. Du Bois explained, "to be both a Negro and an American."

The vitality of the Harlem Renaissance was short-lived. During the Jazz Age, wealthy white patrons and influential publishers courted its writers. But white interest and black creativity waned as the depression of the 1930s cut incomes and sparked riots in Harlem over jobs and living conditions. However, the writers of the Harlem Renaissance found a new popularity during the civil rights movement of the 1960s, when black intellectuals rediscovered their work.

As black artists championed racial pride, the Universal Negro Improvement Association (UNIA) mobilized African American workers. Led by Jamaican-born Marcus Garvey and based in Harlem, the UNIA championed black separatism. The charismatic Garvey urged blacks to return to Africa, arguing that peoples of African descent would never be treated justly in white-run countries. The UNIA grew rapidly in the early 1920s and soon claimed four million followers, including many recent migrants to northern cities. It published a newspaper, *Negro World*; opened "liberty halls" in northern cities; and solicited funds for the Black Star Line steamship company, to trade with the West Indies and carry American blacks back to Africa.

The UNIA declined as quickly as it had arisen. In 1925, Garvey went to jail for mail fraud because of his solicitations for the Black Star Line; two years later, President Coolidge commuted Garvey's sentence but ordered his deportation to Jamaica. Without Garvey's leadership, his movement quickly collapsed.

Culture Wars: The Election of 1928

Cultural issues — the emotionally charged questions of Prohibition, Protestant fundamentalism, and nativism — set the agenda for the presidential election of 1928. The national Democratic Party, now controlled by its northern urban wing, nominated Governor Alfred E. Smith of New York. Smith was the first presidential candidate to reflect the aspirations of the urban working classes and of European Catholic immigrants. A Catholic and the grandson of Irish peasants, Smith began his political career as a Tammany Hall ward heeler, became a dynamic state legislative leader and reformer, and matured as the effective four-term governor of the nation's most populous state.

But Smith had liabilities. He spoke in a heavy New York accent and sported a brown derby that highlighted his ethnic working-class origins. Middle-class reformers questioned his ties to the political bosses of Tammany Hall; temperance advocates opposed him as a "wet." The governor's greatest handicap was his religion. Although Smith insisted that his beliefs would not affect his duties as president, most Protestants opposed his candidacy. "No Governor can kiss the papal ring and get within gunshot of the White House," declared a Methodist bishop from Buffalo.

The Republican nominee, Secretary of Commerce Herbert Hoover, was also a new breed of candidate. Hoover had never run for any political office and did not run very hard for the presidency, delivering only seven campaign speeches. He rested his candidacy on his outstanding career as an engineer and administrator; for many Americans, he embodied the managerial and technological promise of the Progressive era. Beyond that, Hoover had the benefit of eight years of Republican prosperity and strong support from the business community. He promised voters that his vision of individualism and cooperative endeavor would banish poverty from the United States.

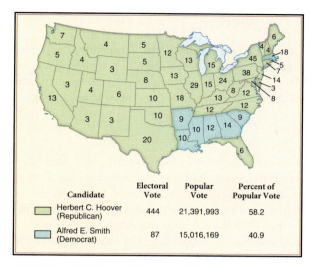

Candidate	Electoral Vote	Popular Vote	Percent of Popular Vote
Herbert C. Hoover (Republican)	444	21,391,993	58.2
Alfred E. Smith (Democrat)	87	15,016,169	40.9

MAP 23.2 Presidential Election of 1928

Historians still debate the extent to which 1928 was a "critical" election, that is, one that produced a significant realignment in voting behavior. Republican Herbert Hoover swept the popular vote and the electoral
vote, but Democrat Alfred E. Smith won majorities not only in the South, his party's traditional stronghold,
but also in Rhode Island, Massachusetts, and (although it is not evident on this map) in all of the large cities
of the North and Midwest. Subsequently, the Democrats won even more votes among African American
and European ethnic groups, making them the nation's dominant political party until the 1980s.

For more help analyzing this map, see the Online Study Guide at **bedfordstmartins.com/henrettaconcise.**

Hoover won a stunning victory. He received 58 percent of the popular vote to
Smith's 41 percent and 444 electoral votes to Smith's 87. Because many southern
Protestants refused to vote for a Catholic, Hoover carried Texas, Virginia, and North
Carolina, breaking the Democratic "Solid South" for the first time since Reconstruction. Equally significant, Smith won the industri-
alized states of Massachusetts and Rhode Island
and carried the nation's twelve largest cities (Map
23.2). The Democrats were on their way to fashioning a new identity as the party of the urban
masses and social welfare liberalism, a reorienta-
tion that the New Deal would push forward in
the 1930s.

Ironically, Herbert Hoover's victory put him
in the unenviable position of leading the United
States when the Great Depression struck in 1929.
Having claimed credit for the prosperity of the
1920s, the Republicans could not escape blame
for the depression.

▶ What changes in American
society prompted the activities
of nativists, the Ku Klux Klan,
and religious fundamentalists?
How did these groups express
their outrage?

▶ What were the similarities and
differences between the Harlem
Renaissance and Marcus Garvey's
UNIA movement?

The Onset of the Great Depression, 1929–1932

Booms and busts are characteristic features of the **business cycle** in capitalist economies, and they were familiar features of the American landscape. Beginning with the Panic of 1819, the United States had experienced a recession or panic about every twenty years. But none was as severe as the Great Depression of the 1930s, and none lasted as long.

Causes and Consequences

The economic downturn began almost imperceptibly in 1927. For five years, Americans had spent money at a faster pace than their incomes had risen. As consumers ran short of cash and credit, spending declined and housing construction slowed. Soon, inventories piled up; in 1928, manufacturers began to cut back production and lay off workers, reinforcing the slowdown. By the summer of 1929, the economy was clearly in recession.

A few commentators noted the slowdown in production, but most celebrated the rapid rise in the stock market. Stock prices surged 40 percent in 1928 and 1929 as investors got caught up in a speculative frenzy. On "Black Thursday," October 24, and again on "Black Tuesday," October 29, the bubble burst. On those two bleak days, millions of shares changed hands in panic trading. Practically overnight, stock values fell from a peak of $87 billion to $55 billion.

The crash exposed long-standing weaknesses in the economy. Agriculture was in the worst shape because farm products had sold at low prices for a decade. In 1929, the yearly income of farmers averaged only $273, compared to $750 for other occupations. Because farmers accounted for one-fourth of the nation's workers, their meager buying power had long been a drag on the economy. Two other major industries—railroads and coal—had also fallen on hard times. As automobile and truck traffic increased, railroad revenues from passenger travel and freight shipments declined, forcing several railroads into bankruptcy. Coal-mining companies experienced similar financial difficulties. Battered by overexpansion, obsolescent machinery, and bitter labor struggles, they faced sharp competition from companies producing other sources of energy: hydroelectric power, fuel oil, and natural gas. A final structural weakness was the unequal distribution of wealth. In 1929, the top 5 percent of American families received 30 percent of the nation's income while the bottom 50 percent received only about 20 percent, most of which was spent on food and housing. Once the depression began, a majority of the population lacked sufficient buying power to revive the economy.

The Great Crash itself had a devastating impact. It wiped out the savings of thousands of individual investors and dealt a severe blow to many banks, which had invested heavily in corporate stocks or lent money to speculators. Hundreds of banks failed, and because bank deposits were uninsured, their depositors lost some or all of their money. Frightened customers withdrew their savings from solvent banks, forcing them to close as well and deepening the crisis.

The American economy now went rapidly downhill. Between 1929 and 1933, the U.S. gross domestic product fell almost by half, from $103.1 billion to $58 billion. Consumption dropped by 18 percent, construction by 78 percent, and private investment by 88 percent. Nearly 9,000 banks closed their doors, and 100,000 businesses failed. The consumer price index declined by 25 percent, and corporate profits fell from $10 billion to $1 billion. Most tellingly, unemployment rose from 3.2 percent to 24.9 percent;

twelve million people were out of work, and many who had jobs took wage cuts. "We didn't go hungry," said one family, "but we lived lean."

The downturn became self-perpetuating. The more the economy contracted, the longer people expected the decline to last; so corporations did not invest in new plants, and consumers refused to buy new cars or appliances. "You could feel the depression deepen," recalled writer Caroline Bird.

President Hoover later blamed the severity of the American depression on the international factors, and his analysis had considerable merit. During the 1920s, the flow of international credit depended on American banks and corporations; their loans and investments in European countries allowed those nations to pay reparations and war debts and to buy U.S. goods. Now U.S. banks and companies reduced their foreign investments, disrupting the European financial system and cutting demand for American exports. The Hawley-Smoot Tariff of 1930 cut trade still further by raising American rates to all-time highs and prompting European governments to impose similar restrictions. When Great Britain also abandoned the "gold standard," which assisted international trade by stabilizing exchange rates among currencies, there was a further contraction of commerce and a fall in demand for American agricultural products.

Soon, the crisis brought on a worldwide depression. In 1929, the United States had produced 40 percent of the world's manufactured goods. As American companies cut back production, they reduced their purchases of Argentine cattle, Brazilian coffee, Chinese silk, Mexican oil, Indonesian rubber, African minerals, and raw materials from many other countries. Thus, the American crash of 1929 undermined fragile economies around the globe.

Herbert Hoover Responds

Campaigning for the presidency in 1928, Herbert Hoover predicted a "final triumph over poverty." Even after the Great Crash, he stubbornly insisted that the downturn was temporary. "The Depression is over," the president told a delegation of business executives in June 1930.

As the slump continued, Hoover adopted a two-pronged strategy. Reflecting his ideology of voluntarism and his longtime reliance on the business community, he turned first to corporate leaders. Hoover asked business executives to maintain wages and production levels and rebuild Americans' confidence in the capitalist economic system.

But the president recognized that voluntarism might not be enough, given the depth of the crisis, and he proposed government action as well. Following the stock market crash, he cut federal taxes in an attempt to boost private spending and corporate investment. Hoover called on state and local governments to provide jobs by investing in public projects; and by 1932, he had secured an unprecedented increase in federal spending for public works to $423 million. Some presidential initiatives were misguided. For instance, the Revenue Act of 1932, which increased taxes to balance the budget, choked both consumption and investment. Similarly, Hoover's refusal to consider direct federal relief for unemployed Americans and to rely on private charity—the "American way," he called it—was a mistake; unemployment during the depression was too massive for private charities and local governments to handle.

Hoover's most innovative program was the Reconstruction Finance Corporation (RFC), which Congress approved in January 1932. The RFC was modeled on the War

Finance Corporation of World War I and, like that agency, stimulated economic activity by providing federal loans to railroads, banks, and other businesses. This strategy of **pump priming**—infusing funds into the major corporate enterprises—was meant to increase production and thereby create new jobs and invigorate consumer spending. This plan might have worked, but the RFC lent money too cautiously; by the end of 1932, it had loaned out only 20 percent of its $1.5 billion in funds.

Compared with previous chief executives—and in contrast to his popular image as a "do-nothing" president—Hoover had responded to the national emergency with government action on an unprecedented scale. But the nation's needs were also unprecedented, and Hoover's programs failed to meet them.

Rising Discontent

As the depression continued, many citizens came to hate Herbert Hoover. The American vocabulary now included "Hoovervilles" (shanty towns where people lived in packing crates) and "Hoover blankets" (newspapers). Rising discontent led

Hoovervilles

By 1930, homeless people had built shantytowns in most of the nation's cities. In New York City, squatters camped out along the Hudson River railroad tracks, built makeshift homes in Central Park, or lived at the city dump. This photograph, taken near the old reservoir in Central Park, looks east toward the fancy apartment buildings of Fifth Avenue and the Metropolitan Museum of Art, at left. © Bettmann/Corbis.

For more help analyzing this image, see the Online Study Guide at **bedfordstmartins.com/henrettaconcise**.

to violence. Bankrupt farmers banded together to resist the bank agents and sheriffs who tried to evict them from their land. To protest low prices for their goods, thousands of farmers joined the Farm Holiday Association, which cut off supplies to urban areas by barricading roads and dumping milk, vegetables, and other foodstuffs onto the roadways. Layoffs and wage cuts led to violent industrial strikes. When coal miners in Harlan County, Kentucky, went on strike over a 10 percent wage cut in 1931, the mine owners called in the state's National Guard, which crushed the union. A confrontation in 1932 between workers and security forces at the Ford Motor Company's giant River Rouge factory left three workers dead and fifty with serious injuries.

Civil disorder erupted in the nation's cities. In 1931 and 1932, unemployed citizens demanded jobs and bread from local authorities, and hard-pressed wage earners staged rent strikes. Some protests were the work of the Communist Party, which hoped to use the depression to overturn the capitalist system. Although the strikes and

The Soup Kitchen

Some of the most vivid images from the depression are of long lines of men standing outside soup kitchens, like the one pictured here, and of well-dressed men on street corners selling apples and offering shoe shines. Most of the people in this line are white men but there are a few blacks. Some of the men wear worker's caps but almost as many wear fedoras, the stylish hat favored by the middle and upper classes. The absence of women is striking; many women chose to endure deprivation rather than violate standards of respectable behavior by soliciting aid in public. © Bettmann/Corbis.

marches received broad support, they won few converts to communism. In the early 1930s, the American Communist Party had only 12,000 members.

Not radicals but veterans staged the most publicized—and most tragic—protest. In the summer of 1932, the "Bonus Army," a ragtag group of about 15,000 unemployed World War I veterans, hitchhiked to Washington to demand immediate payment of their Service Certificates, a pension award that was due to be paid in 1945. "We were heroes in 1917, but we're bums now," one veteran complained bitterly. While their leaders unsuccessfully lobbied Congress, the Bonus Army set up camps near the U.S. Capitol building. Eventually Hoover called out regular army troops under the command of General Douglas MacArthur, who would become a leading figure during World War II and the Korean War. A headstrong commander who habitually exceeded his orders, MacArthur forcefully evicted the marchers and burned their main encampment to the ground. As newsreel footage showing the U.S. Army attacking and injuring its veterans reached movie theaters across the nation, Hoover's popularity plunged.

The 1932 Election

Despite this discontent, the nation was not in a revolutionary mood as the election of 1932 approached. Middle-class Americans had internalized the ideal of the **self-made man** and blamed themselves for their economic hardships. Despair and apathy, not anger, characterized their mood (see Voices from Abroad, p. 697). The Republicans, reluctant to dump an incumbent president, unenthusiastically renominated Hoover. The Democrats turned to Governor Franklin Delano Roosevelt of New York, who had persuaded his state's legislature to run a budget deficit to finance innovative relief and unemployment programs.

Roosevelt, born into a wealthy New York family, was a distant cousin to former president Theodore Roosevelt, whose career he emulated. After attending Harvard College and Columbia University, Roosevelt served as assistant secretary of the navy during World War I (as "T.R." had done before the Spanish-American War). Franklin Roosevelt's service in the Wilson administration, in combination with his famous name and speaking abilities, made him the Democrats' vice presidential nominee in 1920. Then, in 1921, a crippling attack of polio left both of his legs paralyzed for life. Strongly supported by his wife, Eleanor, he slowly returned to public life and campaigned successfully for the governorship of New York in 1928 and again in 1930.

Roosevelt's campaign for the presidency in 1932 pledged vigorous action but gave no indication as to what it might be: "The country needs and, unless I mistake its temper, the country demands bold, persistent experimentation." He won easily, receiving 22.8 million votes to Hoover's 15.7 million. Despite the nation's economic collapse, Americans remained firmly committed to the two-party system. The Socialist Party candidate, Norman Thomas, got fewer than a million votes, and the Communist nominee, party leader William Z. Foster, drew only 100,000 votes.

Elected in November, Roosevelt would not begin his presidency until March 1933. (The Twentieth Amendment, ratified in 1933, set subsequent inaugurations

Breadlines and Beggars MARY AGNES HAMILTON

British writer and Labor Party activist Mary Agnes Hamilton arrived in New York in December 1931. Following a wide-ranging lecture tour, Hamilton wrote a book conveying her impressions of American life. Her observations of conditions in New York City during the grim winter of 1931–1932 suggest the devastation and despair gripping urban America.

One does not need to be long in New York (or for that matter in Chicago, in Cleveland, in Detroit, in Kansas, or in Buffalo) to see that there are plenty of real tragedies, as well as plenty of not-so-real ones. . . . In New York, one has only to pass outside the central island bounded by Lexington and Sixth Avenues to see hardship, misery, and degradation, accentuated by the shoddy grimness of the shabby houses and broken pavements. Look down from the Elevated [railway], and there are long queues of dreary-looking men and women standing in "breadlines" outside the relief offices and the various church and other charitable institutions. Times Square, at any hour of the day and late into the evening, offers an exhibit for the edification of the theater-goer, for it is packed with shabby, utterly dumb and apathetic-looking men, who stand there, waiting for the advent of the coffee wagon run by Mr. W. R. Hearst of the *New York American*. . . . At every street corner, and wherever taxi or car has to pause, men try to sell one apples, oranges, or picture papers. . . . On a fine day, men . . . line every relatively open space, eager to shine one's shoes. It is perhaps because so many people are doing without this "shine," or attempting with unfamiliar hands and a sense of deep indignity to shine their own, that the streets look shabby and the persons on them so much less well-groomed than of yore. The well-shod feet of the States struck me forcibly on my first visit; the ill-cleaned feet of New York struck me as forcibly in January and April 1932. . . . Yes, distress is there; the idle are there. How many, no one really knows. Ten million or more in the country; a million and a half in New York are reported. They are there; as is, admittedly a dark undergrowth of horrid suffering that is certainly more degraded and degrading than anything Britain or Germany knows. Their immense presence makes a grim background to the talk of depression: there is an obscure alarm as to what they may do "if this goes on." . . .

The American people, unfamiliar with suffering, with none of that long history of catastrophe and calamity behind it which makes the experience of European nations, is outraged and baffled by misfortune. . . . The nation now suffers from a despair of any and every kind of leadership. Every institution is assailed; even the sacred foundations of democracy are being undermined. The defeatism that has been so lamentably evidenced in Congress is not peculiar to Congressmen, any more than is the crude individualism of their reactions. It lies like a pall over the spirit of the nation. . . . How to break it nobody knows.

SOURCE: Mary Agnes Hamilton, "In America Today," in *America through British Eyes*, ed. Allan Nevins (Gloucester, MA: Peter Smith, 1968), 443–444.

► What were the domestic and foreign causes of the Great Depression? How did President Hoover respond to the economic emergency?

► In what ways did the state and federal governments intervene in the cultural conflicts and economic crises of 1920s?

► What problems in the economy and society of the United States were exposed by the Great Depression?

for January 20.) As FDR waited, Americans suffered through the worst winter of the depression. Nationwide, the unemployment rate stood at 20 to 25 percent; in three major industrial cities in Ohio, it was staggering: 50 percent in Cleveland, 60 percent in Akron, and 80 percent in Toledo. Public-welfare institutions were totally overwhelmed. Despite dramatic increases in their spending, private charities and public relief agencies reached only a fraction of the needy. The nation's banking system was so close to collapse that many state governors closed banks temporarily to avoid further withdrawals. By March 1933, the nation had hit rock bottom.

SUMMARY

By the 1920s, the United States had become a modern, urban society based on corporate business enterprises and mass consumption. As we have seen, the Republican Party controlled the national government and fostered a close partnership with business interests. At home, Secretary of Commerce Herbert Hoover promoted industry-wide trade associations; abroad, diplomats assisted American businesses while avoiding entangling alliances.

We also explored how movies, radio, and other mass media encouraged the development of a national culture. This emergent culture placed an emphasis on leisure, consumption, and amusement. However, families needed a middle-class income to take full advantage of the goods (such as cars, radios, and vacuum cleaners) and lifestyles promoted by the new advertising industry. Most farmers remained outside the charmed circle of prosperity, as were most African Americans and most working-class immigrants from Europe and Mexico.

Not everyone welcomed the new secular values of the 1920s. Cultural disputes over prohibition, evolution, and immigration led to the creation of the new Ku Klux Klan and further disrupted the already fractured Democratic Party. Republican political ascendancy continued under President Herbert Hoover, who expected to extend the prosperity of the Roaring Twenties.

Instead, Hoover had to deal with the Great Depression. As we have seen, the depression had many causes: speculation in stocks, weaknesses in major industries, and fragile international finances. When Hoover's policies failed, voters turned to Democrat Franklin D. Roosevelt, who entered office facing massive unemployment, a banking crisis, and a despairing citizenry.

Connections: Society

As we noted in the essay that opened Part Five, two central themes of the years between 1914 and 1945 were internal migration within the United States and intolerance toward immigrants and racial minorities. Both were apparent in Chapter 22. There, we described attacks during World War I against German Americans and the postwar riots against newly arrived African Americans in Chicago, East St. Louis, and other cities. As we have just seen in Chapter 23, nativist sentiment reached a peak in the mid-1920s as the "new" Ku Klux Klan harassed Catholics, Jews, and blacks and Congress enacted restrictive immigration legislation. Chapter 24 will continue that story by explaining how the Great Depression of the 1930s prompted a "reverse migration" back to Mexico, Asia, and Europe. It will also discuss the movement to California of 350,000 farmers from the "dust bowl" states of the Great Plains and explain how New Deal agricultural programs forced many African Americans to leave the rural South. Finally, in Chapter 25, we will see that World War II triggered a new round of internal migration

TIMELINE

1920	▶ Eighteenth Amendment imposes Prohibition	**1925**	▶ F. Scott Fitzgerald's *The Great Gatsby* published
	▶ First commercial radio broadcast		▶ Height of Ku Klux Klan's power
	▶ Warren G. Harding elected president		▶ Scopes trial over free speech and the teaching of science
	▶ Census reveals major shift of people from farms to cities	**1927**	▶ First "talkies" in movie industry
1920–1921	▶ Economic recession cuts jobs		▶ Charles Lindbergh's solo flight
1921	▶ Sheppard-Towner Act assists maternal care	**1928**	▶ Herbert Hoover elected president
	▶ Washington Conference leads to naval disarmament		▶ Kellogg-Briand Pact condemning militarism signed
1922–1929	▶ Record economic growth expands consumption	**1929**	▶ Ernest Hemingway's *A Farewell to Arms* published
	▶ Automobile Age begins		▶ Stock market crash
1922	▶ T. S. Eliot's *The Waste Land* published	**1930**	▶ Hawley-Smoot Tariff cuts imports
1923	▶ President Harding dies; succeeded by Calvin Coolidge	**1931**	▶ Miners strike in Harlan County, Kentucky
	▶ *Time* magazine founded	**1932**	▶ Reconstruction Finance Corporation created
1924	▶ Dawes Plan reduces German reparations		▶ Bonus Army rebuffed in Washington
	▶ Teapot Dome scandal		▶ Communist-led hunger marches in cities
	▶ U.S. troops withdrawn from Dominican Republic		▶ Farm Holiday Association dumps produce
	▶ National Origins Act limits immigration		▶ Franklin D. Roosevelt elected president

and race riots and, in an extreme example of racial prejudice, the internment of more than 100,000 Japanese Americans.

FOR FURTHER EXPLORATION

Lynn Dumenil, *The Modern Temper: American Culture and Society in the 1920s* (1995), and Loren Baritz, ed., *The Culture of the Twenties* (1970), provide good overviews. For politics, consult Ellis W. Hawley, *The Great War and the Search for a Modern Order* (1979), and Lee Nash, ed., *Understanding Herbert Hoover* (1987). For fiction, see Sinclair Lewis's classics, *Main Street* (1920) and *Babbitt* (1922). To watch the rise of consumer society, log onto **memory.loc.gov/ammem/coolhtml/coolhome.html**.

On the Harlem Renaissance, read Alain Locke, ed., *The New Negro* (1925), and consult **www.math.buffalo.edu/~sww/circle/harlem-ren-sites.html**. For Marcus Garvey, see **www.pbs.org/wgbh/amex/garvey**. Good studies include Kevin Boyle, *Arc of Justice: A Saga of Race, Civil Rights, and Murder in the Jazz Age* (2004), and David Levering Lewis, *W. E. B. Du Bois* (2000).

"Flapper Station" at **home.earthlink.net/~rbotti** details the new youth culture; on speakeasies and their music, go to **www.authentichistory.com/1920s/music/index .html**. Also see "Jazz Roots" at **www.jass.com** and **www.redhotjazz.com**. On 1920s films, go to **www.filmsite.org/20sintro.html**; for advertisements, see **scriptorium.lib .duke.edu/adaccess**. For America's first media superstar, see **www.charleslindbergh .com**. The Scopes trial is covered at **www.law.umkc.edu/faculty/projects/ftrials/scopes/ scopes.htm**.

For the crash of 1929, see **www.nytimes.com/library/financial/index-1929-crash .html** and **www.pbs.org/wgbh/amex/crash**.

TEST YOUR KNOWLEDGE

To assess your mastery of the material in this chapter and for Web sites, images, and documents related to this chapter, visit **bedfordstmartins.com/henrettaconcise**.

Redefining Liberalism:
The New Deal
1933–1939

the factories are a man killer not venelated or kept up just a bunch of Republickins Grafters. . . . Please help us some way I Pray to God for relief. I am a Christian . . . and a truthful man & have not told you wrong

—Unsigned letter to President Roosevelt from Paris, Texas, 1936

"What is going to become of us?" asked an Arizona man. "I've lost twelve and a half pounds this last month, just thinking. You can't sleep, you know. You wake up at 2 A.M. and you lie and think." Many Americans went sleepless in 1933 as the nation entered the fourth year of the worst economic contraction in its history. Times were hard—very hard—and there was no end in sight.

In his inaugural address in March 1933, President Franklin Delano Roosevelt set out to dispel the gloom and despondency that gripped the nation. "The only thing we have to fear is fear itself," Roosevelt declared. His demeanor grim and purposeful, Roosevelt issued a ringing call "for action, and action now" and promised strong presidential leadership. He would ask Congress for "broad Executive power to wage a war against the emergency, as great as the power that would be given to me if we were in fact invaded by a foreign foe." With these words, Roosevelt launched a program of federal activism—which he called the New Deal—that would change the nature of American government.

The New Deal represented a new form of liberalism, the ideology of individual rights that had long shaped the character of American society and politics. To protect those rights, "classical" nineteenth-century liberals had kept governments small and relatively powerless. Their successors, the "regulatory" liberals of the Progressive era, had safeguarded individual freedom and opportunity by bolstering the authority of the state and federal governments to control large business corporations. New Deal activists went much further—their "social-welfare" liberalism expanded the individual's right to governmental assistance. Beginning in the 1930s and continuing until the 1970s, social welfare liberals increased the scope of national legislation; created a centralized administrative system; and instituted new programs, such as Social Security and Medicare, which increased the responsibility of the national government for the welfare of every American citizen. Their efforts did not go unchallenged. Conservative critics of the New Deal charged that its program of "big government" and "social welfare" was both paternalistic and dangerous—a threat to individual responsibility and personal freedom. During the "Reagan Revolution" of the 1980s, they would seek to undo many of its programs.

The New Deal Takes Over, 1933–1935

The Great Depression destroyed the political reputation of Herbert Hoover and boosted that of Franklin Delano Roosevelt. Ironically, the ideological differences between Hoover and Roosevelt were not vast. Both leaders wished to maintain the nation's economic institutions and social values. Both believed in a balanced government budget and extolled the values of hard work, cooperation, and sacrifice. But Roosevelt's personal charm, political savvy, and willingness to experiment made him immensely popular. Millions of Americans called him by his initials—FDR—which became his nickname. His New Deal programs put people to work and instilled hope for the nation's future.

FDR
Franklin Delano Roosevelt was a successful politician partly because he loved to mix with a crowd. Despite Roosevelt's upper-class status, he had a knack for relating easily to those from all occupations and backgrounds. A well-dressed crowd turned out to greet him in Elm Grove, West Virginia, as he campaigned for the presidency in 1932, but Roosevelt took care to be photographed shaking hands with Italian American coal miner Zeno Santanella. Franklin D. Roosevelt Library.

Roosevelt's Leadership

Roosevelt immediately established a close rapport with the American people. More than 450,000 letters poured into the White House in the week after his inauguration, and they continued to come at a rate of 5,000 a week throughout the 1930s. One person had handled Hoover's public correspondence; Roosevelt needed a staff of fifty. The new president's masterful use of the new medium of radio, especially his "fireside chats," caused many people to consider him a personal friend. Thousands of citizens thanked him, saying, "He gave me a job" or "He saved my home" (see American Voices, p. 704).

Roosevelt's charisma allowed him to bolster the presidential powers that Theodore Roosevelt and Woodrow Wilson had expanded previously. FDR dramatically enlarged the role of the executive branch in setting the budget and initiating legislation. For policy formulation, he relied heavily on financier Bernard Baruch and on a "Brain Trust" of professors from Columbia and Harvard universities: Raymond Moley, Rexford Tugwell, Adolph A. Berle, and Felix Frankfurter. Roosevelt turned as well to his talented cabinet, which included Secretary of the Interior Harold L. Ickes, Frances Perkins at the Labor Department, Henry A. Wallace at Agriculture, and Henry Morgenthau Jr., the Secretary of the Treasury. These talented intellectuals and administrators attracted hundreds of highly qualified recruits to Washington. Young professors and newly trained lawyers streamed out of Ivy League universities into the expanding federal bureaucracy. Inspired by the idealism of the New Deal, many of them would devote their lives to public service and the principles of social-welfare liberalism.

The Hundred Days

Roosevelt promised "action now," and he kept his promise. The first months of his administration produced a whirlwind of activity in Congress, which was now controlled by Democrats. In a legendary legislative session, known as the "Hundred Days," Congress enacted fifteen major bills that focused primarily on four major problems: banking failures, agricultural overproduction, the business slump, and soaring unemployment.

The president and Congress first addressed the banking crisis. Since the stock market crash, bank failures had cut into the savings of nearly nine million families; to prevent more failures, dozens of states had closed their banks. On March 5, the day after his inauguration, FDR declared a national "bank holiday"—a euphemism for closing all the banks—and called Congress into special session. Four days later, Congress passed the Emergency Banking Act—the debate in the House took only thirty-eight minutes—which permitted banks to reopen if a Treasury Department inspection showed that they had sufficient cash reserves.

The act worked because Roosevelt convinced the public that it would. In his first Sunday night fireside chat, to a radio audience estimated at sixty million, the president reassured citizens that federal scrutiny would ensure the safety of their money. When the banking system reopened on March 13, deposits exceeded withdrawals, restoring stability to the nation's basic financial institutions. "Capitalism was saved in eight days," quipped Roosevelt's advisor Raymond Moley. A second banking law of 1933, the Glass-Steagall Act, further restored public confidence by creating the Federal Deposit Insurance Corporation (FDIC), which insured deposits up to $2,500 (and now insures

Ordinary People Respond to the New Deal

Franklin Roosevelt's fireside chats and relief programs prompted thousands of ordinary Americans to write directly to him and his wife Eleanor. Their letters offer a vivid portrait of depression-era America and popular support for (and against) the New Deal. In very different ways, these two letters address the issue of old-age security. R.A. was a sixty-nine-year-old man, an architect and builder in Lincoln, Nebraska; M.A. was a woman who held a low-level, white-collar position in a business corporation.

May 19/ 34
Dear Mrs Roosevelt:
In the Presidents inaugural address delivered from the capitol steps the afternoon of his inauguration he made mention of The Forgotten Man, and I with thousands of others am wondering if the folk who was borned here in America some 60 or 70 years a go are this Forgotten Man, the President had in mind, if we are this Forgotten Man then we are still Forgotten.

We who have tried to be diligent in our support of this most wonderful nation of ours boath social and other wise, we in our younger days tried to do our duty without complaining. . . .

And now a great calamity has come upon us and seemingly no cause of our own it has swept away what little savings we had accumulated and we are left in a condition that is imposible for us to correct, for two very prominent reasons. . . .

First we have grown to what is termed Old Age, this befalls every man.

Second, . . . we are confronted on every hand with the young generation,

them up to $100,000). Four thousand banks had collapsed in the months prior to Roosevelt's inauguration; only sixty-one closed their doors in all of 1934.

The avalanche of legislation continued. Congress created the Home Owners Loan Corporation to refinance home mortgages threatened by foreclosure. It set up the Civilian Conservation Corps (CCC), which mobilized 250,000 young men to do reforestation and conservation work. Two controversial measures were also quickly approved. One set up the Tennessee Valley Authority (TVA), a government-owned entity intended to produce cheap hydroelectric power and encourage economic development in the flood-prone river valley. Conservative critics assailed the TVA as creeping socialism. Moral reformers criticized the second act, which legalized the sale of beer; but full repeal of Prohibition, by constitutional amendment, was already in the works and came in December 1933.

Because farmers formed one-quarter of the workforce, Roosevelt considered effective agricultural legislation "the key to recovery." The national government had long taking our places, this of corse is what we have looked forward to in training our children. But with the extra ordinary crises which left us helpless and placed us in the position that our fathers did not have to contend with. . . .

We have been honorable citizens all along our journey, calamity and old age has forced its self upon us please do not send us to the Poor Farm but instead allow us the small pension of $40.00 per month. . . .

Mrs. Roosevelt I am asking a personal favor of you as it seems to be the only means through which I may be able to reach the President, some evening very soon, as you and Mr. Roosevelt are having dinner together privately will you ask him to read this. And we American citizens will ever remember your kindness.

Yours very truly.

R. A.

Jan. 18, 1937

[Dear Mrs. Roosevelt:]

I . . . was simply astounded to think that anyone could be nitwit enough to wish to be included in the so called social security act if they could possibly avoid it. Call it by any name you wish it, in my opinion, (and that of many people I know) is nothing but downright stealing. . . .

I am not an "economic royalist," just an ordinary white collar worker at $1600 per [year—about $24,000 in 2008]. Please show this to the president and ask him to remember the wishes of the forgotten man, that is, the one who dared to vote against him. We expect to be tramped on but we do wish the stepping would be a little less hard.

Security at the price of freedom is never desired by intelligent people.

M. A.

SOURCE: Robert D. Marcus and David Burner, eds., *America Firsthand,* 7th ed. (Boston: Bedford/St. Martin's, 2007), 180–181, 184.

assisted farmers: through cheap prices for land, the extension services of the Department of Agriculture, and the Federal Farm Loan Act of 1916. But the Agricultural Adjustment Act (AAA) began direct governmental regulation of the farm economy. To solve the problem of overproduction, which resulted in low prices, the AAA set up an allotment system for seven major commodities: wheat, cotton, corn, hogs, rice, tobacco, and dairy products. The act provided cash subsidies to farmers who cut their production; to pay these subsidies, the act imposed a tax on the businesses that processed these commodities, which they in turn passed on to consumers. New Deal policymakers hoped that farm prices would rise as production fell, spurring consumer purchases by farmers and assisting a general economic recovery.

By dumping cash in farmers' hands (a special-interest policy that continues to this day), the AAA stabilized the farm economy. But the act's benefits were not evenly distributed. Subsidies went primarily to the owners of large- and medium-sized farms, who often cut production by reducing the amount of land they rented to tenants and sharecroppers. In the South, where many sharecroppers were black and landowners and government administrators were white, such practices forced 200,000 black families off the land. Some black farmers tried to protect themselves by joining the Southern Tenant Farmers Union (STFU), a biracial organization founded in 1934. "The same chain that holds you hold my people, too," an elderly black farmer reminded his white neighbors. But landowners had such economic power and such support from local sheriffs that the STFU could do little. Denied access to land and government aid, hundreds of thousands of black sharecroppers and white smallholders drifted to the cities.

The New Deal's initial response to the depression in manufacturing was the National Industrial Recovery Act. The act drew on the regulatory practices of Bernard Baruch's War Industries Board during World War I and Herbert Hoover's trade associations of the 1920s. It also reflected European "corporatist" theories of government planning that had been implemented in Italy by Benito Mussolini. A new government agency, the National Recovery Administration (NRA), set up separate self-governing associations in six hundred industries. Each industry—ranging from large corporations producing coal, cotton textiles, and steel to small businesses making pet food and costume jewelry—regulated itself by agreeing on a code of prices and production quotas. When these codes received NRA approval, they had the force of law. The codes outlawed child labor and set minimum wages and maximum hours for adult workers. One of the most far-reaching provisions, Section 7(a), guaranteed workers the right to organize and bargain collectively "through representatives of their own choosing." This right to union representation spurred the initial growth of the labor movement in the 1930s.

In many industries, the trade associations that Commerce Secretary Hoover set up in the 1920s dominated the code-drafting process. Because large companies usually ran these associations, the NRA solidified their power at the expense of smaller enterprises, labor unions, and consumer interests. To sell its regulatory program to skeptical consumers and businesspeople, the NRA launched an extensive public relations campaign, complete with plugs in Hollywood films and "Blue Eagle" stickers with the NRA slogan, "We Do Our Part."

For its part, the Roosevelt administration quickly addressed the intertwined problems of massive unemployment and impoverished working families. By 1933, local governments and private charities had exhausted their resources and looked to Washington for assistance. Although Roosevelt wanted to avoid a budget deficit, he asked Congress to provide relief for millions of unemployed Americans. In May, Congress established the Federal Emergency Relief Administration (FERA). Directed by Harry Hopkins, a hard-driving social work administrator from New York, the FERA provided federal funds to the states for their relief programs. In his first two hours in office, Hopkins distributed $5 million. Over the program's two-year existence, the FERA spent $1 billion.

Roosevelt and Hopkins had strong reservations about the "dole," the nickname for such government welfare payments. As Hopkins put it, "I don't think anybody can go year after year, month after month, accepting relief without affecting his character. . . . It is probably going to undermine the independence of hundreds of thousands of families." To support the traditional values of individualism, the New Deal put people to work. Early in 1933, Congress appropriated $3.3 billion for the Public Works Administration (PWA), a construction program directed by Secretary

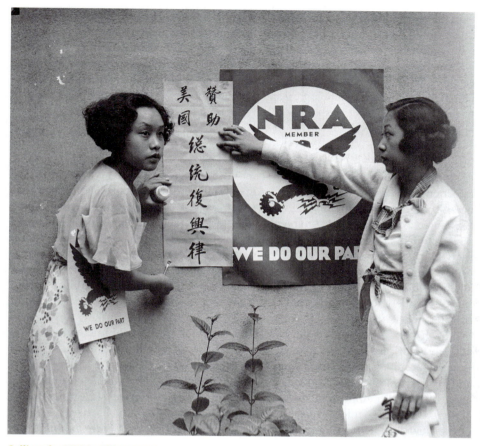

Selling the NRA in Chinatown
To mobilize support for its program, the National Recovery Administration (NRA) distributed millions of posters to businesses and families, urging them to display the "Blue Eagle" in shops, factories, and homes. Here, Constance King and Mae Chinn of the Chinese YMCA affix a poster (and a Chinese translation) to a shop in San Francisco that is complying with the NRA codes. © Bettmann/Corbis.

of the Interior Harold L. Ickes. But Ickes was a careful administrator who approved projects slowly and therefore limited the PWA's effectiveness in providing jobs or spurring recovery. So in November 1933, Roosevelt established the Civil Works Administration (CWA), named Harry Hopkins as its head, and gave it $400 million in PWA funds. Within thirty days, Hopkins had put 2.6 million men and women to work; at its peak in January 1934, the CWA provided jobs for 4 million Americans repairing bridges, building highways, constructing public buildings, and setting up community projects. The CWA, a stopgap measure to get the country through the winter of 1933–1934, lapsed in the spring after spending all its funds.

When an exhausted Congress recessed in June 1933, it had enacted Roosevelt's initial agenda: banking reform, recovery programs for agriculture and industry, unemployment relief and public works, and a host of other measures. Few presidents had won the passage of so many measures in so short a time. (The only future president to do so would be Lyndon Baines Johnson in 1965, as we will see in Chapter 28). A veritable "alphabet soup" of federal agencies—the CCC, CWA, FERA, AAA, and NRA—had suddenly appeared in Washington and began to direct people and projects throughout the nation. Although the vigorous action of the First Hundred Days halted the downward psychological spiral of the Hoover years, it did not break the grip of the depression.

The New Deal Under Attack

As Roosevelt waited anxiously for the economy to revive, he turned his attention to the reform of Wall Street, where insider trading, fraud, and reckless speculation had triggered the financial panic of 1929. In 1934, Congress established the Securities and Exchange Commission (SEC) to regulate the stock market. The commission had broad powers to regulate companies that sold stocks and bonds to the public, to set rules for margin (credit) transactions, and to prevent stock sales by those with inside information on corporate plans. The Banking Act of 1935 authorized the president to appoint a new Board of Governors of the Federal Reserve System, placing control of interest rates and other money-market policies in a federal agency rather than in the hands of private bankers.

Such measures exposed the New Deal to attack from economic conservatives and the political "right." A man of wealth, Roosevelt saw himself as the savior of American capitalism, declaring simply, "To preserve we had to reform." Many bankers and business executives disagreed. To them, FDR became "That Man," a traitor to his class. In 1934, Republican business leaders joined with conservative Democrats in a "Liberty League" that lobbied against the "reckless spending" and "socialist" reforms of the New Deal. Reflecting their outlook, Herbert Hoover condemned the NRA as a "state-controlled or state-directed social or economic system"; that, declared the former president, was "tyranny, not liberalism."

The Supreme Court likewise repudiated many New Deal measures. In May 1935, the Court unanimously ruled that the National Industrial Recovery Act unconstitutionally delegated Congress's power to make laws to a code-writing agency in the executive branch of the government. The case, *Schechter v. United States*, arose when a firm in Brooklyn, New York, sold diseased chickens to local storekeepers in violation of NRA codes. In addition to the delegation issue, the Court declared that the NRA unconstitutionally extended federal authority to intrastate (in contrast to interstate) commerce. Roosevelt publicly protested that the Court's narrow interpretation would return the Constitution "to the horse-and-buggy definition of interstate commerce," but he watched helplessly as the Court struck down more New Deal legislation: the Agricultural Adjustment Act, a Railroad Retirement Act, and the Frazier-Lemke debt relief act.

If business executives and the Supreme Court thought that the New Deal had gone too far, many ordinary Americans believed it had not gone far enough. Francis Townsend, a doctor from Long Beach, California, spoke for the nation's elderly, most of whom had no pensions and feared poverty in their old age. In 1933, Townsend proposed the Old Age Revolving Pension Plan, which would give $200 a month (about

$3,000 today) to citizens over the age of sixty. To receive payments, the elderly would have to retire from their jobs, thus opening their positions to younger workers, and would have to spend the money within a month. Townsend Clubs sprang up across the country, mobilizing mass support for old-age pensions and helping to win passage of the far less ambitious Social Security Act of 1935.

Father Charles Coughlin also challenged Roosevelt's leadership and attracted a large following, especially in the Midwest. A Catholic priest in a Detroit parish, Coughlin had turned to the radio in the mid-1920s to enlarge his pastorate. By 1933, about forty million Americans listened regularly to the Radio Priest's broadcasts. Initially, Coughlin supported the New Deal, but he turned against it when Roosevelt refused to nationalize the banking system and expand the money supply. To promote these programs, proposed earlier by the Populist Party of the 1890s (see Chapter 19), Coughlin organized the National Union for Social Justice.

The most direct political threat to Roosevelt came from Senator Huey Long. As the Democratic governor of Louisiana from 1928 to 1932, the flamboyant Long had achieved stunning popularity. He increased taxes on business corporations; lowered the utility bills of consumers; and built new highways, bridges, hospitals, and schools. Long's accomplishments came at a price: To push through these measures, he had seized almost dictatorial control of the state government. Now a U.S. senator, Long broke with the New Deal in 1934 and, like Townsend and Coughlin, established a national movement. His "Share Our Wealth Society," which boasted over four million members, maintained that the depression stemmed not from overproduction but from underconsumption. Because wealth was so unequally distributed, millions of ordinary families lacked the funds to buy goods and thereby

The Kingfish

Huey Long, the Louisiana governor and senator, called himself "the Kingfish" because, he said, "I'm a small fish here in Washington. But I'm the Kingfish to the folks down in Louisiana." An exceptionally charismatic man and a brilliant campaigner, he attracted a significant following with his "Share Our Wealth" plan, which aimed to redistribute the nation's wealth. Democrats worried that he might run for president in 1936 on a third-party ticket and threaten Franklin Roosevelt's reelection. But in September 1935, Long was killed (perhaps accidentally by shots fired by his bodyguards) during an assassination attempt by a young doctor over a Louisiana political dispute. Long is seen here shaking hands with a Louisiana supporter. Louisiana State Museum.

keep the factories humming. To put money in the hands of consumers, Long's society advocated a tax of 100 percent of all income over $1 million and all inheritances over $5 million. Long hoped that this populist program would carry him into the White House.

Although somewhat simplistic, the economic proposals advanced by Townsend, Coughlin, and Long were no more radical than the NIRA or the AAA. Like the New Deal measures, they were plausible responses to the depression, and some were subsequently endorsed by social-welfare liberals. It was the constitutional views of Coughlin and Long that separated them from the American political mainstream. Neither man had much respect for representative government. "I'm the Constitution around here," Long declared during his governorship, while Coughlin paradoxically suggested that dictatorial rule might be necessary to preserve democracy. Yet many voters did not seem troubled by Long's and Coughlin's authoritarian views and greeted their social policies with increasing enthusiasm. Roosevelt feared that they might join forces with Townsend to form a third party. This prospect encouraged Republicans, who hoped that a split between New Dealers and populist reformers might return their party, and its ideology of small government and free enterprise, to political power.

> ▶ What were the main programs of the New Deal's "Hundred Days"? What were their goals? Evaluate the success of the various programs.
>
> ▶ Explain the criticisms of the New Deal by the political right and the political left. Who were the New Deal's major critics, and what were their alternative programs?

The Second New Deal, 1935–1938

As attacks from the conservative right and the populist left increased, Roosevelt and his advisors fashioned a left-liberal program. Historians have labeled this shift in policy as The Second New Deal. Acknowledging that his policies would not win the support of corporate America, Roosevelt now openly criticized the "money classes," proudly stating, "We have earned the hatred of entrenched greed." He also moved decisively to counter the rising popularity of Townsend, Coughlin, and Long by stealing parts of their programs and, he hoped, much of their thunder. The administration's Revenue Act of 1935 proposed a substantial tax increase on corporate profits and higher income and estate taxes on wealthy citizens. When conservatives attacked this legislation as an attempt to "soak the rich," Congress moderated its tax rates, so it boosted revenue by only $250 million a year. But FDR was satisfied. He had met Huey Long's Share Our Wealth proposal with a wealth plan of his own.

Legislative Accomplishments

The Revenue Act symbolized the administration's new outlook. Unlike the First New Deal, which focused on economic recovery, the Second New Deal emphasized social justice: the use of national legislation to enhance the power of working people and the economic security and welfare of the old, the disabled, and the unemployed.

The first beneficiary of Roosevelt's move to the left was the labor movement. The rising number of strikes in 1934 — about 1,800 job actions involving a total of 1.5 million workers — reflected the dramatic growth of rank-and-file militancy. When the Supreme Court voided the NIRA in 1935, thereby invalidating Section 7(a), labor unions demanded new legislation that would allow workers to organize and bargain collectively. Named for its sponsor, Senator Robert F. Wagner of New York, the Wagner Act (1935) upheld the right of industrial workers to join unions. Because of the opposition of southern Democrats, who looked out for the interests of planters and landlords, the Wagner Act did not apply to farm workers. The act outlawed many practices used by employers to squelch unions, such as firing workers for organizing activities. It established the National Labor Relations Board (NLRB), a federal agency with the authority to protect workers from employer coercion, supervise elections for union representation, and guarantee the process of collective bargaining.

A second initiative, the Social Security Act of 1935, had an even greater impact. Other industrialized societies, such as Germany and Britain, had created national old-age pension systems around 1900, but American Progressives had failed to secure a similar program in the United States. Now millions of citizens had joined the Townsend and Long movements; their demands gave political muscle to pension advocates within the administration, such as Grace Abbott, head of the Children's Bureau, and Secretary of Labor Frances Perkins. They won the president's support for a Social Security Act that provided old-age pensions for most privately employed workers and established a joint federal-state system of compensation for unemployed workers. At the insistence of southern Democrats, Congress excluded farm workers and domestic servants from both programs.

Roosevelt likewise limited the reach of the legislation. Knowing that compulsory pension and unemployment legislation would be controversial, he refused to include a provision for national health insurance because that might doom the entire bill. A firm believer in personal responsibility, the president also insisted that workers bear part of the cost of the new pension and unemployment plans. Consequently, the Social Security System received its funds not from general tax revenues but from mandatory contributions paid by workers and their employers. Decades later, this funding mechanism protected Social Security from the attempt of "new conservatives" to abolish it; having contributed to the pension fund, the American people demanded that they receive its benefits (see Chapter 30).

The Social Security Act was a milestone in the creation of an American **welfare state**. Never before had the federal government assumed such responsibility for the well-being of a substantial majority of the citizenry. In addition to pension and unemployment coverage, the act mandated aid to various categories of Americans: the blind, deaf, and disabled as well as dependent children. These categorical assistance programs to the so-called "deserving poor" grew dramatically after the 1930s. Aid to Dependent Children covered only 700,000 youngsters in 1939; by 1994, its successor, Aid to Families with Dependent Children (AFDC), enrolled 14.1 million Americans, 60 percent of whom were African American or Hispanic. A minor program during the New Deal, AFDC became one of the pillars of the American welfare system and one of the most controversial before it was significantly curtailed in the 1990s (see Chapter 30).

Grand Coulee Dam was constructed at the Columbia River Gorge in central Washington State to generate electric power.

Fort Peck Dam on the Missouri River was designed to control flooding, generate electric power, and improve navigation downstream.

Woodlands reappeared throughout New England after the planting of trees on former pastures.

Kalamazoo erected a new courthouse.

The Wind River area in Wyoming used irrigation projects to reclaim dry lands for agriculture.

Triborough Bridge in New York City improved the flow of traffic.

Los Angeles schools were rebuilt to repair and resist earthquake damage.

Atlanta constructed low-income housing to replace slums.

Navajo capitol was erected in Arizona for tribal meetings and administration.

New levees and dams controlled flooding and promoted navigation on the Mississippi River.

Houston built the Sam Houston Coliseum and Music Hall.

MAP 24.1 Public Works in the New Deal: The PWA in Action, 1933–1939

In 1933 and 1934, the New Deal agencies of the Civilian Conservation Corps (CCC), the Works Progress Administration (WPA), and the Civil Works Administration (CWA) quickly put unemployed people to work, mostly on small-scale projects. The PWA, established in 1933 and directed by Secretary of the Interior Harold Ickes, undertook much larger projects as well. Its goals were to provide jobs, stimulate economic recovery through government spending, and make lasting contributions to the nation's communities. PWA workers built public works that ranged from courthouses to swimming pools, airports to aircraft carriers, the Triborough Bridge to the Grand Coulee Dam, as this map (which shows only a few selected projects) indicates.

Roosevelt was never enthusiastic about public relief programs. But with the election of 1936 on the horizon and ten million Americans still out of work, he won funding for the Works Progress Administration (WPA). Under the energetic direction of Harry Hopkins, the WPA combated the depression by providing jobs rather than relief. Whereas the Federal Emergency Relief Administration of 1933–1934 had supplied grants to state welfare programs, the WPA put workers directly on the federal payroll. Between 1935 and 1943, the WPA spent $10.5 billion and employed 8.5 million Americans. The agency's workers constructed or repaired 651,087 miles of roads; 124,087 bridges; 125,110 public buildings; 8,192 parks; and 853 airports (Map 24.1). Although the WPA was an extravagant operation by the standards of the 1930s, it reached only about one-third of the nation's unemployed and paid low wages. But most WPA workers were thankful for any job that allowed them to eke out a living.

The 1936 Election

As the 1936 election approached, new voters joined the Democratic Party. Many had personally benefited from New Deal programs or knew people who had. One was Jack Reagan, a down-on-his luck shoe salesman (and the father of future President Ronald Reagan), who took a job as a federal relief administrator in Dixon, Illinois, and became a strong supporter of the New Deal. In addition to voters such as Reagan, Roosevelt could count on a potent coalition of organized labor, midwestern farmers, white ethnic groups, northern blacks, and middle-class families concerned about unemployment and old age security. In addition, he commanded the support of Jews, intellectuals, and progressive Republicans. With some difficulty, the Democrats also held onto the votes of their traditional white southern constituency.

The Republicans realized that the New Deal was too popular to oppose directly. So they chose as their candidate the progressive governor of Kansas, Alfred M. Landon. Landon accepted the legitimacy of many New Deal programs but stridently criticized their inefficiency and expense. The Republican candidate also pointed to authoritarian regimes in Italy and Germany, directed by Benito Mussolini and Adolf Hitler, respectively, and hinted that FDR harbored similar dictatorial ambitions.

These charges fell on deaf ears. Roosevelt's victory in 1936 was one of the biggest landslides in American history. The assassination of Huey Long in September 1935 had deflated the threat of a serious third-party challenge; the candidate of the combined Long-Townsend-Coughlin camp, Congressman William Lemke of North Dakota, garnered fewer than 900,000 votes (1.9 percent) for the Union Party ticket. Roosevelt received 60.8 percent of the popular vote and carried every state except Maine and Vermont. The New Deal was at high tide.

Stalemate

"I see one-third of a nation ill-housed, ill-clad, ill-nourished," the president declared in his second inaugural address in January 1937. But any hopes that FDR had for expanding the liberal welfare state were quickly dashed. Within a year, staunch opposition to New Deal initiatives arose in Congress and the South, and a sharp recession undermined confidence in Roosevelt's economic leadership.

Roosevelt's first setback came when he stunned Congress and the nation by asking for fundamental changes in the Supreme Court. In 1935, the Court had struck down a series of New Deal measures and a minimum wage law in New York State by the narrow margin of 5 to 4. With the Wagner Act, the TVA, and Social Security coming up on appeal, the future of the New Deal lay in the hands of a few elderly, conservative-minded judges. To diminish their influence, the president proposed to add a new justice for every member over the age of seventy. Roosevelt's opponents protested that he was trying to "pack" the Court; stunned by this blatant attempt to alter a traditional institution, Congress rejected the proposal after a bitter months-long debate.

If Roosevelt lost the battle, he won the war. Swayed in part by FDR's overwhelming election victory in 1936, the Court upheld a California minimum wage law and the Wagner and Social Security Acts. Moreover, a series of resignations allowed Roosevelt to reshape the Supreme Court; his new appointees, who included Hugo Black, Felix Frankfurter, and William O. Douglas, viewed the Constitution as a "living document" that had to be interpreted in the light of present conditions and generally supported New Deal measures.

Nonetheless, the court-packing fiasco revealed Roosevelt's vulnerability and energized congressional conservatives. Throughout Roosevelt's second term, a conservative coalition composed of southern Democrats and rural Republicans blocked or impeded social legislation. The president did win passage of the National Housing Act of 1937, which mandated the construction of low-cost public housing, and the Fair Labor Standards Act of 1938, which continued the minimum wage, maximum hours, and anti–child labor provisions in the NRA codes. But Congress rejected or modified other administration initiatives, including a far-reaching plan for reorganizing the executive branch of the federal government.

The "Roosevelt recession" of 1937–1938 dealt another blow to the president. From 1933 to 1937, the gross domestic product had grown at a yearly rate of about 10 percent, bringing industrial output and real income back to 1929 levels. Unemployment had declined from 25 percent to 14 percent. "The emergency has passed," asserted Senator James F. Byrnes of South Carolina.

Acting on this assumption, Roosevelt slashed the federal budget, which had been running a modest deficit. Congress cut the WPA's funding in half, causing layoffs of about 1.5 million workers; the Federal Reserve, fearing inflation, raised interest rates. These measures halted recovery; the stock market dropped sharply, and unemployment soared to 19 percent. Quickly reversing course, Roosevelt spent his way out of the recession by boosting funding for the WPA and resuming public works projects.

Although improvised, this spending program accorded with the theories advocated by John Maynard Keynes, a visionary British economist. Keynes transformed economic policymaking in capitalist societies by arguing that government intervention could smooth out the business cycle through **deficit spending** and the manipulation of interest rates. Sharply criticized by Republicans and conservative Democrats in the 1930s, **Keynesian economics** gradually won wider acceptance as defense spending during World War II ended the Great Depression. Today, whatever their rhetoric, all mainstream American politicians accept the legitimacy of such government control of monetary and economic policy.

To restore the vitality of the New Deal, Roosevelt tried to purge the Democratic Party of his most conservative opponents during the primary elections of 1938. His purge failed abysmally, and the Republicans surged forward. Profiting from the "Roosevelt recession" and the court-packing controversy, Republicans picked up eight seats in the Senate, eighty-one seats in the House, and thirteen state governorships.

The New Deal had run out of steam. Roosevelt's political mistakes were partly responsible, but so were his successes. He had met the challenge to American capitalist and democratic institutions posed by the Great Depression. The economy was back on course, and so was normal party politics. Americans had rejected the simplistic programs of demagogic politicians at home and the alluring alternatives offered by fascist and communist regimes

▶ How did the Second New Deal differ from the first? What were FDR's reasons for changing course?

▶ Describe Keynesian economic policies. How important were they to the New Deal?

in Europe. A reformer rather than a revolutionary, Roosevelt had preserved capitalism, democracy, and liberal individualism—even as he transformed them in significant ways. But by 1939, the era of change was over.

The New Deal's Impact on Society

Whatever the limits of the New Deal, it had a tremendous impact on the nation. Its ideology of social-welfare liberalism fundamentally altered Americans' relationship to their government and provided assistance to a wide range of ordinary people: the unemployed, the elderly, white ethnic workers, women, and racial minorities. To serve these diverse constituencies, New Dealers created a sizable federal bureaucracy; the number of civilian federal employees increased by 80 percent between 1929 and 1940 and reached a total of one million. The expenditures—and deficits—of the federal government grew at an even faster rate. In 1930, the Hoover administration spent $3.1 billion and had a surplus of almost $1 billion; in 1939, New Dealers expended $9.4 billion and ran a deficit of nearly $3 billion. But the major increase in government spending came with World War II (and the postwar military buildup), when federal outlays routinely totaled $95 billion and deficits grew to $50 billion. In peace or in war, power was increasingly centered in the nation's capital, not in the states.

The Rise of Labor

Exploiting their dominant position in Congress, Democrats used legislation and tax dollars to win the allegiance of blocs of voters. A prize target was organized labor. Demoralized and shrinking during the 1920s, labor unions increased their numbers and clout during the New Deal. Thanks to Section 7(a) of the National Industrial Recovery Act and the Wagner Act, unions found it easier to organize workers; win recognition from management; and secure higher wages, seniority systems, and grievance procedures. By the end of the decade, the number of unionized workers had tripled to almost nine million, or 23 percent of the nonfarm workforce.

The Congress of Industrial Organizations (CIO) served as the cutting edge of the union movement. It promoted "industrial unionism"; that is, the CIO organized all the workers in an industry, from skilled machinists to broom-pushing janitors, into a single union. John L. Lewis, leader of the United Mine Workers (UMW), was the foremost exponent of industrial unionism. By 1935, he had rejected the philosophy of the American Federation of Labor (AFL), which favored organizing workers on a craft-by-craft basis, and had helped to create the CIO.

The CIO scored its first major victory in the automobile industry. On December 31, 1936, General Motors workers in Flint, Michigan, staged a sit-down strike, vowing to stay at their machines until management agreed to collective bargaining. The workers lived in the factories and machine shops for forty-four days before General Motors recognized their union, the United Automobile Workers (UAW). Shortly thereafter, the CIO won another major victory at the U.S. Steel Corporation, which recognized the Steel Workers union in March 1937. But other steel companies refused to negotiate, sparking a protest at the Republic Steel Corporation in Chicago that took the lives of ten strikers.

The 1930s constituted the most successful period of labor organizing in American history. The sit-down tactic spread rapidly and reached a high point in March 1937, when a total of 167,210 workers staged 170 sit-down strikes. Labor unions called nearly 5,000 strikes that year and won favorable settlements in 80 percent of them. Many middle-class Americans opposed the sit-down tactics, which they considered a violation of private property. In 1939, the Supreme Court accepted this argument and upheld legislation that banned the sit-down tactic.

The leadership of the CIO strongly advocated inclusive unionism. Unlike the AFL, which had long excluded blacks, the CIO actively organized African Americans in the steel and meatpacking industries of the Midwest, often in the face of hostility from white workers. In California, the CIO's organizers set out to win equal pay for Mexican American women in the canning industry. Corporate giants such as Del Monte, McNeill, and Libby paid women around $2.50 a day, while their male counterparts received $3.50 to $4.50. These differentials shrank following the formation in 1939 of the United Cannery, Agricultural, Packing, and Allied Workers, an unusually democratic union in which women played leading roles. Altogether, some 800,000 women workers joined CIO unions.

Labor's new vitality spilled over into political action. The AFL had generally avoided partisan politics, but the CIO quickly allied itself with the Democratic Party and encouraged the nomination of prolabor candidates. The CIO donated $770,000 (equivalent to about $11 million today) to Democratic campaigns in 1936, and its political action committee became a major Democratic contributor during the 1940s.

Nonetheless, the labor movement did not become a dominant force in American life. Roosevelt never gave a high priority to strengthening the labor movement, and unions never enrolled a majority of American wage workers. The Wagner Act proved to be a mixed blessing; while it helped unions win higher wages and better working conditions, it did not redistribute power in American industry. Corporate executives retained authority over most business decisions and fought union demands every step of the way. Moreover, the NLRB, worried about inflation and rising consumer prices, often encouraged unions to lower their wage demands. Despite a decade of gains, organized labor remained a secondary force in American industry.

Women and Blacks in the New Deal

The New Deal did not directly challenge gender inequities, but its programs and policies generally enhanced women's welfare. The Roosevelt administration welcomed women into the higher ranks of government. Frances Perkins, the first woman named to a cabinet post, served as Secretary of Labor throughout Roosevelt's presidency. Molly Dewson, a social reformer turned politician, headed the Women's Division of the Democratic National Committee, where she pushed an issue-oriented program that supported New Deal reforms. Roosevelt's female appointees also included the director of the U.S. Mint, the head of a major WPA division, and a judge on a circuit court of appeals. Often close friends as well as professional colleagues, female appointees worked to open up other opportunities in government for talented women.

Eleanor Roosevelt symbolized the growing prominence of women in public life. In the 1920s, she had worked to expand positions for women in political parties, labor unions, and education. During her years in the White House, Mrs. Roosevelt emerged

A First Lady Without Precedent

Reflecting Eleanor Roosevelt's activism and tendency to turn up in odd places, a famous 1933 *New Yorker* cartoon has one coal miner saying to another, "For gosh sakes, here comes Mrs. Roosevelt." Life soon imitated art. In this photograph from 1935, the first lady emerges from a coal mine in Dellaire, Ohio, still carrying her miner's cap in her left hand and talking to mine supervisor Joseph Bainbridge. Wide World Photos, Inc.

For more help analyzing this image, see the Online Study Guide at **bedfordstmartins .com/henrettaconcise.**

as an independent and influential public figure. She held press conferences for female journalists, wrote a popular syndicated news column called "My Day," and traveled extensively. Descending deep into coal mines to view working conditions, meeting with blacks who were seeking antilynching laws, and talking to people on breadlines, she became the conscience of the New Deal, pushing her husband to do more for the disadvantaged. "I sometimes acted as a spur," Mrs. Roosevelt later reflected, "even though the spurring was not always wanted or welcome." She knew both her value to the president and the limits of her influence: "I was one of those who served his purposes."

Still, without the intervention of Eleanor Roosevelt, Frances Perkins, and other prominent women, New Deal policymakers would have largely ignored the needs of women. Despite their efforts, a fourth of the NRA codes set a lower minimum wage for women than for men performing the same jobs, only 7 percent of the workers hired by the Civil Works Administration were female, and the Civilian Conservation Corps excluded women entirely. Women fared better under the WPA; at its peak, 405,000 women were on the job rolls. Still, most policymakers viewed the depression primarily as a crisis for male breadwinners, and many Americans agreed. When Gallup pollsters in 1936 asked people whether wives should work outside the home when their husbands had jobs, 82 percent said no. Reflecting such sentiments, many state legislatures

Scottsboro Defendants
The 1931 trial in Scottsboro, Alabama, of nine black youths accused of raping two white women became a symbol of the injustices African Americans faced in the South's legal system. Denied access to an attorney, the defendants were found guilty, and eight were sentenced to death. When the U.S. Supreme Court overturned their convictions in 1932, the International Labor Defense organization hired the noted criminal attorney Samuel Leibowitz, who eventually won the acquittal of four defendants and jail sentences for the rest. This photograph, taken in a Decatur jail, shows Leibowitz conferring with Haywood Patterson, in front of the other eight defendants. Brown Brothers.

enacted laws that prohibited married women from taking paid employment. Not until the 1970s would legislators and business executives begin to address women's quest for equal economic rights.

The needs of African Americans likewise received a low priority. Especially in the South, blacks held the lowest-paying jobs and faced harsh social and political discrimination. In a celebrated 1931 case in Scottsboro, Alabama, nine young black men were accused of rape by two white women hitching a ride on a freight train. The women's stories contained many inconsistencies, but within two weeks, a white jury had convicted all nine defendants of rape; eight received the death sentence. After the U.S. Supreme Court overturned the sentences because the defendants had been denied adequate legal counsel, five of the men were again convicted and sentenced to long prison terms. If the Scottsboro case revealed the inequities in the southern legal system, lynching showed southern lawlessness. White mobs lynched twenty blacks in 1930 and twenty-four in 1934.

Such violence and the dispossession of sharecroppers by the AAA prompted a renewal of the "Great Migration" of African Americans to the cities of the North and Midwest. One destination was Harlem, where rents were high because of the black influx during the 1920s, and jobs were scarce. Most white-owned stores in Harlem would not employ African Americans; elsewhere in New York City, hard-pressed whites took over the menial positions traditionally held by blacks—as domestic servants, elevator operators, and garbage collectors. Unemployment in Harlem rose to 50 percent, twice the national rate. In March 1935, discontented blacks went on a rampage. Before order was restored, rioters destroyed millions of dollars in property.

For the majority of white Americans, the events in Scottsboro and Harlem reinforced their belief that blacks were a "dangerous class." Consequently, there was little support for federal intervention to secure the civil rights of African Americans, and New Deal programs reflected prevailing racial attitudes. CCC camps segregated blacks, and most NRA codes did not protect black workers from discrimination. Most tellingly, Franklin Roosevelt repeatedly refused to support legislation making lynching a federal crime, because he needed the votes of white southern Democrats in Congress.

Nevertheless, blacks received significant benefits from New Deal relief programs. Reflecting their poverty, African Americans made up about 18 percent of the WPA's workforce, although they constituted only 10 percent of the population. The Resettlement Administration, established in 1935 to help small farmers and tenants buy land, actively protected the rights of black tenant farmers until angry southerners in Congress drastically cut its appropriations. Such help from New Deal agencies and a belief that the White House—or at least Eleanor Roosevelt—cared about their plight caused a momentous shift in blacks' political allegiance. Since the Civil War, African Americans had staunchly supported the party of Abraham Lincoln, the Great Emancipator; even in the Depression year of 1932, northern blacks overwhelmingly supported Republican candidates. But in 1936, northern blacks gave Roosevelt 71 percent of their votes. In Harlem, where state and federal dollars poured in after the 1935 riot, African American support for the president reached an extraordinary 81 percent. Black voters have remained staunchly Democratic ever since.

African Americans supported the New Deal partly because the Roosevelt administration appointed many blacks to federal office. Among the most important was Mary McLeod Bethune. Born in 1875 in South Carolina, the child of former slaves, Bethune founded the prestigious Bethune-Cookman College. Becoming an educator herself, Bethune served during the 1920s as president of the National Association of Colored Women. Bethune joined the New Deal in 1935, working first as an advisor of the National Youth Administration and then as director of its Division of Negro Affairs. Along with NAACP general secretary Walter White, Bethune had access to the White House and pushed continually for New Deal programs that would directly assist African Americans.

The New Deal also had a powerful impact on Native Americans. Indian peoples had long made up one of the nation's most disadvantaged and powerless minorities. In 1934, their average annual income was only $48, and their unemployment rate was three times the national average. The plight of Native Americans won the attention of Secretary of the Interior Harold Ickes and Commissioner of the Bureau of Indian Affairs John Collier. They pushed for an Indian Section of the Civilian Conservation Corps and earmarked FERA funds and CWA work projects for Indian reservations.

A New Deal for Indians
John Collier, the New Deal's Commissioner for Indian Affairs, was a former social worker who had studied Native American tribal cultures. A critic of the assimilationist policies of the Dawes Act of 1887, Collier led successful efforts to provide Native Americans with communally controlled lands and self-government. Here, Collier(r) speaks with Chief Richard of the Blackfoot Nation, one of the Indian leaders attending the Four Nations celebration at historic Old Fort Niagara, New York, in 1934. © Bettmann/Corbis.

More ambitious was the Indian Reorganization Act of 1934, sometimes called the "Indian New Deal." That law reversed the Dawes Act of 1887 (see Chapter 16) by promoting Indian self-government through formal constitutions and democratically elected tribal councils. A majority of Indian peoples — some 174 tribes — accepted the reorganization policy, but seventy-eight groups refused to participate, primarily because they preferred the traditional way of making decisions by consensus rather than by majority vote. New Deal administrators accepted their refusal. Influenced by academic anthropologists, who celebrated the unique character of native cultures, government officials no longer attempted to assimilate Native Americans into mainstream society. Instead, they embraced a policy of **cultural pluralism** and pledged to preserve Indian languages, arts, and traditions.

Migrants and Minorities in the West

After 1870, the American West — and especially California — grew dramatically in population and wealth (see Chapter 16). By the 1920s, agriculture in California had become a big business — large-scale, intensive, diversified, and oriented toward the national market. Corporate-owned farms produced specialty crops — lettuce, tomatoes, peaches, grapes, and cotton — whose staggered harvests allowed the use of transient laborers. Thousands of workers, initially immigrants from Mexico and Asia and later migrants from the midwestern states, trooped from farm to farm and from crop to crop during the long picking season. Some migrants settled in the rapidly growing cities along the West Coast, especially the sprawling metropolis of Los Angeles. Until the Great Depression, many foreign migrants viewed California as the promised land.

The economic downturn dramatically changed the lives of thousands of Mexican Americans. The 1930 census reported 617,000 Mexican Americans; by 1940, the number had dropped to 377,000. The Hoover administration's policy of deporting illegal immigrants explained part of the decline, but many Mexican farm laborers left voluntarily as the depression deepened. They knew that most local officials would not provide them with relief assistance.

Under the New Deal, the situation of Mexican Americans improved. Those who lived in Los Angeles, El Paso, and other cities qualified for relief more easily, and there was more aid to go around. New Deal initiatives supporting labor unions also assisted the acculturation of Mexicans; for many migrants, membership in the CIO was an important stage in becoming American. Some Mexicans heeded the call of the Democratic Party to join the New Deal coalition. "Franklin D. Roosevelt's name was the spark that started thousands of Spanish-speaking persons to the polls," noted Los Angeles activist Beatrice Griffith.

The farm union organizer César Chávez grew up in such a Spanish-speaking family. In 1934, when Chávez was ten, his father lost his farm near Yuma, Arizona, and the family became part of the migrant workforce in California. They experienced continual discrimination, such as being excluded from restaurants where signs proclaimed "White Trade Only." César's father joined several bitter strikes in the Imperial Valley. All of the strikes failed, including one in the San Joaquin Valley that mobilized 18,000 cotton pickers. But these strikes set the course for the young Chávez; in 1962, he founded the United Farm Workers, a successful union of Mexican American laborers.

Men and women of Asian descent—mostly from China, Japan, and the Philippines—formed a tiny minority of the American population but were a significant presence in some western cities and towns. Immigrants from Japan and China had long faced discrimination; for example, a California law of 1913 prohibited them from owning land. Japanese farmers, who specialized in fruit and vegetable crops, circumvented this restriction by putting land titles in the names of their American-born children. As the depression cut farm prices and racial discrimination excluded young Japanese Americans from nonfarm jobs, about 20 percent of the immigrants returned to Japan.

Chinese Americans were less prosperous than their Japanese counterparts were. Only 3 percent of Chinese Americans worked in professional and technical positions, and discrimination barred them from most industrial jobs. In San Francisco, most Chinese worked in small ethnic businesses: restaurants, laundries, and firms that imported textiles and ceramics. During the depression, they turned for assistance both to traditional Chinese social organizations such as *huiguan* (district associations) and to the city government; in 1931, about one-sixth of San Francisco's Chinese population was receiving public aid. But few Chinese benefited from the New Deal. Until the repeal of the Exclusion Act in 1943, Chinese immigrants were classified as "aliens ineligible for citizenship" and therefore were excluded from most federal programs.

Because Filipino immigrants came from a U.S. territory, they were not affected by the ban on Asian immigration enacted in 1924 (see Chapter 23). During the 1920s, their numbers swelled to about 50,000, many of whom worked as laborers on large corporate-owned farms. As the depression cut wages, Filipino immigration slowed to a trickle, and it was virtually cut off by the Tydings-McDuffie Act of 1934. The act granted independence to the Philippines (which since 1898 had been an American dependency), classified all Filipinos in the United States as aliens, and restricted immigration to fifty people per year.

Even as California lost its dazzle for Mexicans and Asians, it became a destination of hope among farmers fleeing the "dust bowl" of the Great Plains. Between 1930 and 1941, a severe drought afflicted the semiarid states of Oklahoma, Texas, New Mexico, Colorado, Arkansas, and Kansas (see Chapter 16). But the dust bowl was primarily a human creation. Farmers had pushed the agricultural frontier beyond its natural limits, stripping the land of its native vegetation and destroying the delicate ecology of the plains. When the rains ceased and the winds came, nothing remained to hold the soil. Huge clouds of thick dust rolled over the land, turning the day into night.

This ecological disaster prompted a mass exodus. Their crops ruined and their debts unpaid, at least 350,000 "Okies" (so-called whether or not they were from Oklahoma) loaded their meager belongings into beat-up cars and trucks and headed to California. Many were attracted by handbills distributed by commercial farmers that promised good jobs and high pay; instead, they found low wages and terrible living conditions. Before the depression, native-born white workers made up 20 percent of the migratory farm labor force of 175,000; by the late 1930s, Okies accounted for 85 percent of the workers. John Steinbeck's novel *The Grapes of Wrath* (1939) immortalized them and their journey, and New Deal photographer Dorothea Lange's haunting images of California migrant camps gave a personal face to some of the worst suffering of the depression.

A New Deal for the Environment

Concern for the land was a dominant motif of the New Deal, and the shaping of the public landscape was among its most visible legacies. Franklin Roosevelt and Interior Secretary Harold Ickes were avid environmentalists and used public concern over the devastation in the dust bowl to spread the "gospel of conservation." Their national resources policy stressed scientific management of the land and the aggressive use of public authority to care for the natural world.

The most extensive New Deal environmental undertaking was the Tennessee Valley Authority (TVA). Since World War I, experts had recommended the building of dams to control severe flooding and erosion in the Tennessee River Basin, a seven-state area with some of the country's heaviest rainfall (Map 24.2). But when progressive reformers in the 1920s proposed a series of flood-control dams that would also generate cheap electricity, private utility companies blocked the project. As governor of New York, FDR had waged a similar unsuccessful battle to develop public power in the Niagara region. So in 1933, he encouraged Congress to fund the Tennessee project. The TVA was the ultimate watershed demonstration area, integrating flood control, reforestation, electricity generation, and agricultural and industrial development, including the production of chemical fertilizers. The dams and their hydroelectric plants provided cheap electric power for homes and industrial plants and ample recreational opportunities for the valley's residents. The project won praise around the world (see Voices from Abroad, p. 724).

The TVA was an integral part of the Roosevelt administration's effort to keep farmers on the land by enhancing the quality of rural life. The Rural Electrification Administration (REA), established in 1935, was central to that goal. Fewer than one-tenth of the nation's 6.8 million farms had electricity, and private utilities balked at the expense of running lines to individual farms. The REA bypassed this problem by promoting the creation of nonprofit farm cooperatives. For a $5 down payment, local farmers could join the co-op and apply for low-interest federal loans covering the cost of installing power lines. By 1940, 40 percent of the nation's farms had electricity; a decade later, 90 percent did.

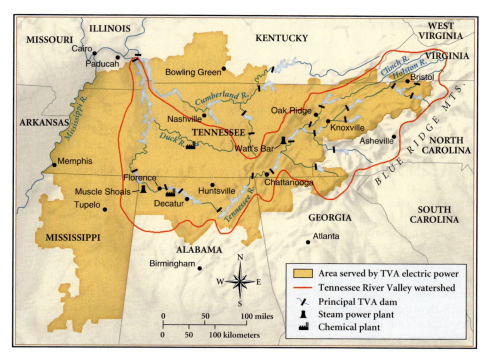

MAP 24.2 The Tennessee Valley Authority, 1933–1952

The Tennessee Valley Authority was the New Deal's farthest-reaching environmental project. Between 1933 and 1952, the TVA built twenty dams and improved five others, taming the flood-prone Tennessee River and its main tributaries. The cheap hydroelectric power generated by the dams brought electricity to hundreds of thousands of area residents, and artificial lakes provided extensive recreational facilities. Widely praised at the time, the TVA came under attack in the 1970s for its practice of strip mining and the pollution caused by its power plants and chemical factories.

For more help analyzing this map, see the Online Study Guide at **bedfordstmartins.com/henrettaconcise**.

Electricity brought relief from the drudgery and isolation of farm life. Electric milking machines and water pumps saved hours of manual labor. Electric irons, vacuum cleaners, and washing machines eased women's burdens, and radios brightened the lives of the entire family. Electric lights extended the time children could read, women could sew, and families could eat their evening meals. One farm woman remembered, "I just turned on the light and kept looking at Paw. It was the first time I'd ever really seen him after dark." Along with the automobile and the movies, electricity broke down the barriers between urban and rural life.

Following the dust bowl disaster, government planners focused on issues of land management and ecological balance. Agents from the Soil Conservation Service taught farmers to prevent soil erosion by tilling hillsides along the contours of the land. Government agronomists persuaded farmers to stop cultivating marginal lands. One of their most widely publicized programs was the Shelterbelts, the planting of 220 million trees running north along the ninety-ninth meridian from Abilene, Texas, to the Canadian border. Planted as a windbreak, the trees also prevented soil erosion.

A Foreigner Looks at the Tennessee Valley Authority   ODETTE KEUN

In 1936, French writer Odette Keun was so impressed by the Tennessee Valley Authority (TVA) that she wrote a book about it. Keun was struck not only by the vast size of the TVA but also by its imaginative scope. By promoting such projects, she argued, democratic governments could ward off popular support for fascist solutions to the Great Depression.

The vital question before democracy is, therefore, not how to bring back an economic freedom which is irretrievably lost, but how to prevent the intellectual freedom, which is still our heritage, from being submerged. It is already threatened. It will be threatened more and more strongly in the years ahead—and the menace, of course, is dictatorship.

Dictatorship springs from two very clear causes. One is the total incapacity of parliamentary government: total, as in Germany in 1933 and in Spain in 1935. To such a breakdown neither the democratic nations of Europe nor America have yet been reduced, although everywhere there are very ominous creaks and cracks, and the authority and prestige of parliamentary institutions have greatly and perilously diminished. The other cause, infinitely closer to us and more dynamic, is the failure of the economic machine to function properly, and by functioning properly I mean ensuring a livelihood for the entire population. No system can survive if it cannot procure food and wages for the people who live under it. . . .

One of the main tenets of liberalism—I reiterate this like a gramophone, but I must get it to sink in—is that all necessary overhauling and adjustment ought to be done in a manner which will minimize the shock to the greatest number, and soften as much as possible the unavoidable human suffering which these changes entail. This opposition to extremes, this practice of a graduated change, we can call "the middle of the road in time and space". . . .

Now I have tried to show that the middle of the road is already being laid down in America. The Tennessee Valley Authority is laying it down. Handicapped and restricted though it is in all sorts of ways, it is the noblest, the most intelligent, and the best attempt made in this country or in any other democratic country to economize, marshal, and integrate the actual assets of a region, plan its development and future, ameliorate its standards of living, [and] establish it in a more enduring security. . . . The economic machine, bad though it is, has not been smashed in the Tennessee Watershed; it is being very gradually, very carefully, very equitably reviewed and amended, and the citizens are being taught and directed, but not bullied, not coerced, not regimented, not frightened, within the constitutional frame the nation itself elected to build. It is not while the Tennessee Valley Authority has the valley in its keeping that despair or disintegration can prepare the ground for a dictatorship and the loss of freedom. The immortal contribution of the TVA to liberalism, not only in America but all over the world, is the blueprint it has drawn, and that it is now transforming into a living reality. . . .

SOURCE: Odette Keun, "A Foreigner Looks at the TVA," in Oscar Handlin, ed., *This Was America* (Cambridge, MA: Harvard University Press, 1949), 547–549.

New Deal projects that enhanced people's enjoyment of the natural environment can be seen today throughout the country. CCC and WPA workers built the famous Blue Ridge Parkway, which connects the Shenandoah National Park in Virginia with the Great Smoky Mountains National Park in North Carolina. In the West, government workers built the San Francisco Zoo, Berkeley's Tilden Park, and the canals of San Antonio. The CCC helped to complete the East Coast's Appalachian Trail and the West Coast's Pacific Crest Trail through the Sierra Nevada. In state parks across the country, cabins, shelters, picnic areas, lodges, and observation towers stand as monuments to the New Deal ethos of recreation coexisting with nature.

The New Deal and the Arts

In response to the Great Depression, many American writers and artists redefined their relationship to society. Some became politically engaged. Never had there been a decade, critic Malcolm Cowley suggested in 1939, "when literary events followed so closely on the flying coat-tails of social events." Because the New Deal funded many arts projects, the link between politics and the arts was both close and controversial.

As the economic downturn dried up private patronage, creative artists, along with other Americans, turned to Washington. A WPA project known as "Federal One" put unemployed artists, actors, and writers to work, but its spirit and purpose extended far beyond relief. New Deal administrators encouraged artists to create projects of interest to the entire community, not just the cultured elite. "Art for the millions" became a popular New Deal slogan and encouraged the painting of murals in hundreds of public buildings.

The Federal Art Project gave work to many young artists who would become the twentieth century's leading painters, muralists, and sculptors. Jackson Pollock, Alice Neel, Willem de Kooning, and Louise Nevelson all received support. The Federal Music Project employed 15,000 musicians, and government-sponsored orchestras toured the country, presenting free concerts of both classical and popular music. Like many New Deal programs, the Music Project emphasized American themes. The composer Aaron Copland wrote his ballets *Billy the Kid* (1938) and *Rodeo* (1942) for the WPA, basing the compositions on western folk motifs. The federal government also employed the musicologist Charles Seeger and his wife, the composer Ruth Crawford Seeger, to catalog hundreds of American folk songs.

The Federal Writers' Project (FWP) provided jobs to 5,000 writers and produced more than 1,000 publications. It collected the oral histories of many Americans, including 2,000 narratives by former slaves, and published a set of popular state guidebooks. Young FWP employees who later achieved fame included Saul Bellow, Ralph Ellison, Tillie Olsen, and John Cheever. The black folklorist and novelist Zora Neale Hurston finished three novels while in the Florida FWP, among them *Their Eyes Were Watching God* (1937). And Richard Wright won the 1938 *Story* magazine prize for the best tale by a WPA writer. Wright used his spare time to complete *Native Son* (1940), a searing novel that took a bitter look at racism.

Of all the New Deal arts programs, the Federal Theatre Project (FTP) was the most ambitious. Under the gifted direction of Hallie Flanagan, the FTP reached an audience of twenty-five to thirty million people in the four years of its existence.

Talented directors, actors, and playwrights, including Orson Welles, John Huston, and Arthur Miller, offered their services. Because many FTP productions took a critical look at American social problems, it came under attack in Congress as sympathetic to communism, and its funding was cut off in 1939.

The WPA arts projects reflected a broad cultural trend called the "documentary impulse." Documentary artists focused on actual events that were relevant to people's lives and presented them in ways that engaged the interest and emotions of the audience. This trend influenced practically every aspect of American culture: literature, photography, art, music, film, dance, theater, and radio. It is evident in John Steinbeck's *The Grapes of Wrath* and in John Dos Passos's *USA* trilogy, which used actual newspaper clippings and headlines in its fictional story. *The March of Time* newsreels, which movie audiences watched before every feature film, presented graphic images of world events for a pretelevision age. New photojournalism magazines, including *Life* and *Look*, carried this documentary approach into millions of living rooms.

The federal government played a leading role in compiling the documentary record of the 1930s. It dispatched journalist Lorena Hickok, writer Martha Gellhorn, and many other investigators to report on the lives of people receiving relief. The Farm Security Administration subsidized the creation of a remarkable set of photographs of the American scene. Under the direction of Roy Stryker, a talented group of photographers—Dorothea Lange, Walker Evans, Ben Shahn, and Margaret Bourke-White—produced haunting images of sharecroppers, dust bowl migrants, and urban homeless that permanently shaped the public image of the Great Depression.

The depression itself left a deep psychic wound, an "invisible scar" in people's minds that lasted for half a century. Labor organizer Larry Van Dusen described it as "a legacy of fear but also a desire for acquisition—property, security." Many Americans who lived through the depression, observed New Dealer Virginia Durr, "reacted by thinking money is the most important thing in the world. Get yours. And get it for your children. Nothing else matters. Not having that stark terror come at you again."

The Legacies of the New Deal

That was the Great Depression: "that stark terror" of losing control over life. The New Deal addressed that deep fear by restoring hope and promising security. FDR's New Deal both extended the regulatory liberalism of the Progressive era and redefined it by creating a powerful national bureaucracy and a social-welfare state. Local and state governments had long been a part of people's everyday lives; now the federal government played a similar role. During the 1930s, millions of people began to pay taxes directly to the Social Security Administration and the Internal Revenue Service, and more than one-third of the population received direct government assistance from new federal programs, including old-age pensions, unemployment compensation, farm loans, relief work, and mortgage guarantees. Furthermore, the government stood ready to intervene in the economy when private enterprise failed to produce economic stability. New legislation regulated the stock market, reformed the Federal Reserve System, and subjected business corporations to federal regulation.

Like all major social transformations, the New Deal was criticized by those who thought it did too much and those who believed it did too little. "Classical" liberals, who gave high priority to small government and individual freedom, correctly pointed out that the New Deal state intruded deeply into the personal and financial lives of the citizenry. For example, the Social Security Act imposed compulsory taxes on workers and forced families to comply with ever more complicated bureaucratic regulations. As one historian has written, the act instigated a "mercantilist regulation of family life not seen since the eighteenth century." Conversely, advocates of social-welfare liberalism complained, also correctly, that the New Deal's safety net had many holes, especially in comparison with the far more extensive welfare systems provided by the governments of western Europe. These critics pointed out that there was no health-care system, that welfare programs excluded domestic workers and farm laborers, and that benefits were minimal in the New Deal programs administered by state governments.

Still, there is no doubt that the New Deal set a pattern of government involvement in social life that would persist for the rest of the twentieth century. In the 1960s, there would be a significant expansion of social-welfare programs during the "Great Society" initiative of President Lyndon Johnson, and most of those programs would remain intact in the wake of the "Reagan Revolution" of the 1980s (see Chapters 28 and 30).

The New Deal also transformed the American political landscape. Since the Civil War — from 1860 to 1932 — the Republican Party had commanded the votes of a majority of Americans. That changed as Franklin Roosevelt's magnetic personality and innovative programs brought millions of voters into the Democratic fold. Democratic recruits included first- or second-generation immigrants from southern and central Europe — Italians, Poles, Slovaks, and Jews — as well as African American migrants to northern cities. Organized labor aligned itself with a Democratic administration that had recognized unions as a legitimate force in modern industrial life. The elderly and the unemployed, assisted by the Social Security Act, likewise supported FDR. This New Deal coalition of ethnic groups, city dwellers, organized labor, blacks, and a cross-section of the middle class formed the nucleus of the northern Democratic Party and supported additional liberal reforms in the decades to come.

From the outset, however, the New Dealers wrestled with a potentially fatal racial issue. Franklin Roosevelt and the national Democratic Party depended heavily on white voters in the South, who were determined to keep African Americans poor and powerless. But many Democrats in the North and West — centers of New Deal liberalism — opposed racial discrimination. As the struggle over civil rights for African Americans became part of the national liberal agenda, it would gradually destroy the Roosevelt coalition. Beginning in the late 1930s, southern Democrats rejected the further expansion of federal power, fearing that it would be used to undermine white rule. This southern Democratic opposition, along with the darkening international scene, caused the New Deal to grind to halt in 1938. As Europe moved toward war and Japan flexed its muscles in the Far East, Roosevelt pushed domestic reform into the background and focused his energies on foreign affairs.

▶ What was the impact of the New Deal on organized labor, women, and racial and ethnic minorities?

▶ When and why did the New Deal end? What was its long-term legacy?

▶ In what ways was the New Deal an evolution of Progressivism? To what extent was it a revolutionary shift in social values and government institutions?

SUMMARY

We have seen how Franklin Delano Roosevelt's First New Deal focused on stimulating recovery, providing relief to the unemployed, and regulating banks and other financial institutions. The Second New Deal was different. Influenced by the persistence of the depression and the popularity of Huey Long's Share the Wealth proposals, FDR promoted social-welfare legislation that provided Americans with economic security.

We also explored the impact of the New Deal on various groups of citizens, especially blacks, women, and unionized workers. Our survey paid particular attention to the lives of the Mexicans, Asians, and Okies who worked in the farms and factories of California. Because New Deal programs assisted such groups, they gravitated toward the Democratic Party. The party's coalition of white southerners, ethnic workers, farmers, and the middle classes gave FDR and other Democrats a landslide victory in 1936.

Finally, we examined the accomplishments of the New Deal. In 1933, it resolved the banking crisis while preserving capitalist institutions and a democratic polity. Subsequently, it expanded the federal government and, through the Social Security system, farm subsidy programs, and public works projects created federal policies that were important to nearly every American. Great dams and electricity projects sponsored by the Tennessee Valley Authority, the Works Project Administration in the West, and the Rural Electrification Administration permanently improved the quality of national life.

Connections: Economy

The performance of the American economy varied widely over the decades. In Chapter 22, we saw how the war in Europe stimulated American industry and agriculture. But as Chapter 23 explained, during the 1920s, the farm economy fell into a two-decade-long crisis. Food surpluses cut farm prices and income, and Presidents Coolidge and Hoover vetoed relief legislation. Chapter 24 described how the New Deal assisted farm owners but forced tenant families off the land. As we will see in Chapter 25, World War II boosted the farm economy, which was increasingly dominated by large-scale producers.

The industrial economy followed a somewhat different pattern. As Chapter 23 explained, a sharp post–World War I recession gave way to an era of prosperity, thanks to the demand for automobiles, radios, and other new consumer goods. However, as the essay that opened Part Five noted, "[t]he Great Depression hit the United States harder than any other industrialized nation," in part because the wages paid to workers were too low to sustain the consumer boom. As this chapter has explained, the New Deal boosted the wages (and consumption) of workers and demonstrated how government intervention could smooth out the business cycle. Chapter 25 will show how massive government military spending during World War II ended the Great Depression and confirmed Keynesian economic theories.

FOR FURTHER EXPLORATION

Robert S. McElvaine, in *The Great Depression* (1984) and *Down and Out in the Great Depression* (1983), analyzes the New Deal and shows its impact on ordinary citizens.

TIMELINE

1931–1937 ▶	Scottsboro case trials and appeals
1933 ▶	FDR's inaugural address and fireside chats
▶	Emergency Banking Act begins the "Hundred Days"
▶	Civilian Conservation Corps (CCC)
▶	Agricultural Adjustment Act (AAA)
▶	National Industrial Recovery Act (NIRA)
▶	Tennessee Valley Authority (TVA)
▶	Townsend Clubs promote Old Age Pension Plan
▶	Twenty-first Amendment repeals Prohibition
1934 ▶	Securities and Exchange Commission (SEC)
▶	Southern Tenant Farmers Union (STFU) founded
▶	Indian Reorganization Act
▶	Senator Huey Long promotes Share Our Wealth Society
▶	Father Charles Coughlin founds National Union for Social Justice

1935 ▶	Harlem riot
▶	Supreme Court voids NRA in *Schechter v. United States*
▶	National Labor Relations (Wagner) Act
▶	Social Security Act creates pension system
▶	Works Progress Administration (WPA)
▶	Huey Long assassinated
▶	Rural Electrification Administration (REA)
▶	Supreme Court voids Agricultural Adjustment Act
▶	Congress of Industrial Organizations (CIO) formed
1936 ▶	Landslide reelection of FDR marks peak of New Deal
▶	General Motors sit-down strike begins
1937 ▶	FDR's Supreme Court plan fails
▶	"Roosevelt recession" raises unemployment
1938 ▶	Fair Labor Standards Act (FLSA)
▶	Conservative southern Democrats oppose New Deal

Katie Loucheim, ed., *The Making of the New Deal: The Insiders Speak* (1983), and Studs Terkel, *Hard Times: An Oral History of the Great Depression* (1970), offer first-person accounts. James Agee and Walker Evans's *Let Us Now Praise Famous Men* (1941) is a compelling portrait of southern poverty. For a memoir of a depression-era childhood, see Russell Baker's *Growing Up* (1982). Classic novels that depict this period are John Steinbeck, *The Grapes of Wrath* (1939); Josephine Herbst, *Pity Is Not Enough* (1933); and Richard Wright, *Native Son* (1940).

For fine collections of 1930s materials, see the "New Deal Network" at **newdeal .feri.org**; "America in the 1930s" at **xroads.virginia.edu/~1930s/home_1.html**; and **www.archives.gov/exhibits/new_deal_for_the_arts/index.html**. For "Voices from the Dust Bowl," go to **memory.loc.gov/ammem/afctshtml/tshome.html**; for photos of the era, go to **lcweb2.loc.gov/ammem/fsowhome.html**. For music, listen to **www.authentichistory.com/1930s.html**. Political cartoons are at **www.nisk.k12.ny.us/fdr**.

The African American experience appears at **memory.loc.gov/ammem/aaohtml/exhibit/aopart8.html**; for the Scottsboro case, log on to **www.law.umkc.edu/faculty/projects/FTrials/scottsboro/scottsb.htm**.

TEST YOUR KNOWLEDGE

To assess your mastery of the material in this chapter and for Web sites, images, and documents related to this chapter, visit **bedfordstmartins.com/henrettaconcise**.

25 The World at War

1939–1945

The Battle of Britain is about to begin. . . . Hitler knows that he will have to break us in this island or lose the war. . . . If we fail, then the whole world, including the United States, including all that we have known and cared for, will sink into the abyss of a new Dark Age.

—British Prime Minister Winston Churchill, 1940

The Second World War was "the largest single event in human history, fought across six of the world's seven continents and all of its oceans. It killed fifty million human beings, left hundreds of millions of others wounded in mind or body and materially devastated much of the heartland of civilization" in both Europe and East Asia. So said the noted military historian John Keegan in a grim judgment that still rings true. The war was so vast and so destructive because it was waged with both technologically advanced weapons and massive armies. The military conflict began in 1939 with a *blitzkrieg* ("lightning war") attack by superbly engineered German tanks across the plains of Poland. It ended in 1945 when American planes dropped two atomic bombs, the product of even more breathtaking scientific breakthroughs, on the Japanese cities of Hiroshima and Nagasaki. In between these demonstrations of technological prowess and devastating power, huge armies confronted and destroyed one another in the fields of France, the forests and steppes of Russia, the river valleys of China, and the sandy deserts of North Africa.

Well might soldiers and civilians dance in the streets around Times Square in New York City in August 1945, celebrating V-J (Victory over Japan) Day. World War II was finally over. Many American lives had been lost and much wealth expended, but the country emerged from the war intact and prosperous. "Those who lost nobody at the front had a pretty good time," one man told journalist Studs Terkel. Like Winston Churchill, many Americans viewed the brutal conflict as the "good war," a successful defense of democratic values from the threat posed by German and Japanese fascism. When the grim reality of the Jewish Holocaust came to light, U.S. participation in the war seemed even more just.

World War II changed the nation's institutions in fundamental ways. The authority of the federal government, which had been increasing since the Progressive era, grew exponentially during the conflict. Equally important, the government remained powerful after the war ended. Federal laws, rules, and practices put in place during the war—universal taxation of incomes, antidiscrimination employment standards, a huge military establishment, and multibillion-dollar budgets, to name but a few—became part of American life. So too did the active participation of the United States in international politics and diplomacy, an engagement intensified by the unresolved issues of the wartime alliance with the Soviet Union. A powerful American state, the product of a long hot war, would remain in place to fight an even longer, more expensive, and more dangerous Cold War.

The Road to War

The Great Depression disrupted economic life around the world and brought the collapse of traditional political institutions. An antidemocratic movement known as fascism, which had developed in Italy during the 1920s, spread to Japan, Germany, and Spain. By the mid-1930s, these nations had instituted authoritarian, militaristic governments led by powerful dictators: Adolf Hitler in Nazi Germany, Benito Mussolini in Italy, Francisco Franco in Spain, and, after 1940, Hideki Tojo in Japan. As early as 1936, President Roosevelt warned Americans that other peoples had "sold their heritage of freedom" and urged them to work for "the survival of democracy" both at home and abroad. Faced with strong isolationist sentiment, FDR began in 1939 to urge Congress and the nation to confront the Fascist powers.

The Rise of Fascism

World War II had its roots in the settlement of World War I (see Chapter 22). Germany deeply resented the harsh terms imposed on it by the Treaty of Versailles, and Japan and Italy revived their dreams of overseas empires. The League of Nations, the collective security system that had been established at Versailles, proved unable to maintain the existing international order.

The first challenge came from Japan. In 1930, that island nation was controlled by a militaristic regime with an expansionist agenda. To become a major industrial power, Japan needed raw materials and overseas markets for its goods. To get them, Japan embarked on a program of military expansion. In 1931, its troops occupied Manchuria, an industrialized province in northern China, and in 1937, it launched a full-scale invasion of China. In both instances, the League of Nations condemned Japan's action but did nothing to stop it.

Japan's defiance of the League encouraged a fascist dictator half a world away: Italy's Benito Mussolini, who had come to power in 1922 and introduced an authoritarian political system. Fascism in Italy and later in Germany rested on an ideology of a powerful state that directed economic and social affairs. It disparaged parliamentary government, independent labor movements, and individual rights. Mussolini described his government as "a dictatorship of the state over many classes cooperating."

The Italian dictator had long denounced the Versailles treaty, which had denied Italy's claim for any of German or Turkish colonies in Africa and the Middle East. So in 1935, he invaded Ethiopia, one of the few independent countries left in Africa. Ethiopian emperor Haile Selassie appealed to the League of Nations, but its verbal condemnation and limited sanctions did not stop Mussolini's forces, which took control of Ethiopia in 1936.

But it was Germany that presented the gravest threat to the existing world order. Huge World War I reparation payments, economic depression, fear of communism, labor unrest, and rising unemployment fueled the ascent of Adolf Hitler and his National Socialist (Nazi) Party. In 1933, Hitler became chancellor of Germany, and the legislature, the *Reichstag*, granted him dictatorial powers to deal with the economic crisis. He soon took the title of *führer* (leader) and outlawed other political parties.

Hitler's goal was nothing short of European domination and world power, as he made clear in his book *Mein Kampf* (*My Struggle*, published in two volumes in 1925 and 1926). His plan was to overturn the territorial settlements of the Versailles treaty, unite Germans living throughout central Europe in a great German fatherland, and annex large areas of eastern Europe. The "inferior races" who lived in these lands — Jews, Gypsies, and Slavs — would be removed or subordinated to the German "master race." A virulent anti-Semite, Hitler had long blamed Jews for Germany's problems. Once in power, he began a sustained and brutal persecution of Jews, which expanded to a campaign of extermination in the early 1940s.

Hitler's strategy for restoring Germany's military power and lost territories was to provoke a series of minor crises, daring Britain and France to go to war to stop him. In 1935, Hitler began to rearm Germany, in violation of the Versailles treaty. No one stopped him. In 1936, he sent troops into the Rhineland, a demilitarized zone under the terms of the treaty; once again, France and Britain took no action. Later that year, Hitler and Mussolini formed a Rome-Berlin Axis, a political and military alliance between the two fascist nations. Also in 1936, Germany signed an Anti-Comintern Pact with Japan, ostensibly to oppose the Comintern, a Soviet-backed organization that spread communist ideology, but in reality to effect a military alliance with Japan.

Isolationists Versus Interventionists

As Hitler's initiatives shook Europe, the Roosevelt administration focused its diplomacy on consolidating American influence in the Western Hemisphere. Secretary of State Cordell Hull implemented a Good Neighbor Policy, under which the United States renounced the use of military force and armed intervention in Latin America. As part of this effort, in 1934 Congress repealed the Platt Amendment, a relic of the Spanish-American War, which asserted the U.S. right to intervene in Cuba's affairs (see Chapter 21). However, the United States kept (and still maintains) a major naval base at Cuba's Guantanamo Bay, and its diplomats continued to intervene in Latin American nations on behalf of American business interests.

Congress and the American public accepted such economic intervention but resisted diplomatic initiatives that might result in political entanglements. In part, this political isolationism reflected disillusion with American participation in World War I. In 1934, Gerald P. Nye, a progressive Republican senator from North Dakota, began a congressional investigation into the profits of munitions makers during World War I. He then tried to determine their influence (and that of the banks that had loaned millions to the Allies) on Wilson's decision to enter the war. Nye's committee concluded that war profiteers, whom it called "merchants of death," had maneuvered the nation into World War I.

Although the Nye committee failed to prove this charge, its factual findings increased isolationist sentiment and prompted a series of legislative acts that prohibited the policies that had allegedly pulled the nation into World War I. Thus, the Neutrality Act of 1935 imposed an embargo on selling arms to warring countries and declared that Americans traveling on the ships of belligerent nations did so at their own risk. In 1936, Congress banned loans to belligerents, and in 1937, it imposed a "cash-and-carry" requirement: If a warring country wanted to purchase nonmilitary goods from the United States, it had to pay cash and carry them in its own ships.

Other Americans, especially writers, intellectuals, and progressive social activists, responded to the rise of fascism in Europe by advocating intervention. Some joined the American Communist Party, which had taken the lead in opposing fascism and was increasing its membership as the depression revealed deep flaws in the capitalist system. Between 1935 and 1938, Communist Party membership peaked at about 100,000, drawn from a wide range of social groups: African American farmers in Alabama, white electrical workers in New York, union organizers, and even a few New Deal administrators. Many intellectuals did not join the party but considered themselves "fellow travelers." They sympathized with the party's objectives, wrote for the *Daily Worker*, the major Communist newspaper, and supported various left-wing groups and causes.

The courting of intellectuals, union members, and liberals reflected a shift in the strategy of the Communist Party. Fearful of German and Japanese aggression, the Soviet leaders instructed Communists in western Europe and the United States to join in a Popular Front with other opponents of fascism. The Popular Front strategy became even more urgent with the outbreak of the Spanish Civil War in 1936. The fascist regimes in Germany and Italy strongly supported an army rebellion led by Generalissimo Francisco Franco against Spain's democratically elected Republican government. The governments of the United States, Great Britain, and France sympathized with the Republican government but remained neutral. Backed only by the Soviet Union and Mexico, the Republican government relied heavily on military volunteers from other countries, including the 3,200-strong American Abraham Lincoln Brigade. But it could not resist the better armed fascist forces. American intellectuals strongly supported the Spanish Republicans but grew increasingly uneasy with the Popular Front because of the rigidity of their Communist associates and the cynical brutality and political repression of dissenters by Soviet leader Joseph Stalin.

Encouraged by the passivity of the Allied Powers during the Spanish Civil War, Hitler expanded his aggression in 1938. He sent troops to annex German-speaking Austria while simultaneously scheming to seize part of Czechoslovakia. Because Czechoslovakia had an alliance with France, war seemed imminent. But at the Munich Conference in September 1938, Britain and France again capitulated, agreeing to let Germany annex the Sudetenland—a German-speaking border area of Czechoslovakia—in return for Hitler's pledge to seek no more territory. The agreement, declared British Prime Minister Neville Chamberlain, guaranteed "peace for our time."

Within six months, however, Hitler's forces had overrun the rest of Czechoslovakia and were threatening to march into Poland. Britain and France, realizing that their policy of appeasement had been disastrous, warned Hitler that further expansion meant war. Then in August 1939, Hitler and Stalin shocked the world by signing a Nonaggression Pact. The pact protected Russia from a German invasion but at a high cost to Soviet prestige; Stalin's tie to Hitler destroyed the Popular Front and severely weakened support for the Communist Party in western Europe and the United States. For Germany, the results of the pact were all positive because it meant that Hitler would not have to wage a two-front war against Britain and France in the west and Russia in the east. On September 1, 1939, Hitler launched a *blitzkrieg* against Poland; two days later, Britain and France declared war on Germany. World War II had begun.

Retreat from Isolationism

Two days after the European war started, the United States officially declared its neutrality. But President Roosevelt made no secret of his sympathies. When war broke out in 1914, Woodrow Wilson had told Americans to be neutral "in thought as well as in action" (p. 643). FDR, by contrast said, "This nation will remain a neutral, but I cannot ask that every American remain neutral in thought as well." The overwhelming majority of Americans—some 84 percent, according to a poll in 1939—supported Britain and France rather than Nazi Germany, but most Americans did not want to be drawn into another war.

At first, the need for American intervention seemed remote. After the German conquest of Poland in September 1939, calm settled over Europe. Then, on April 9, 1940, Nazi tanks overran Denmark. Norway fell next to the Nazi *blitzkrieg*, and the Netherlands, Belgium, and Luxembourg soon followed. Finally, on June 22, 1940, France surrendered. Britain stood alone against Hitler's plans for domination of Europe.

What *Time* magazine would later call America's "thousand-step road to war" had already begun. After a bitter battle in Congress in 1939, Roosevelt won a change in the neutrality laws to allow the Allies to buy arms as well as nonmilitary goods on a cash-and-carry basis. Interventionists, led by journalist William Allen White and his Committee to Defend America by Aiding the Allies, became increasingly vocal. In response, isolationists, including the aviator Charles Lindbergh and Senator Gerald Nye, formed the America First Committee to keep the nation out of the war; they attracted strong support in the Midwest and from conservative newspapers.

Despite the efforts of the America Firsters, in 1940 the United States moved closer to involvement. In May, Roosevelt created the National Defense Advisory Commission and brought two prominent Republicans, Henry Stimson and Frank Knox, into his cabinet as secretaries of war and the navy, respectively. During the summer, the president traded fifty World War I destroyers to Great Britain in exchange for the right to build military bases on British possessions in the Atlantic, circumventing the neutrality laws by using an executive order to complete the deal. In October, a bipartisan vote in Congress approved a large increase in defense spending and instituted the first peacetime draft in American history. "We must be the great arsenal of democracy," FDR declared.

As the war expanded from Europe to its colonial possessions and mandates in North Africa and the oil-rich Middle East, the United States was preparing for the 1940 presidential election. The war had convinced Roosevelt that he should seek an unprecedented third term. Overcoming strong opposition from conservative Democrats, Roosevelt chose the liberal secretary of agriculture, Henry A. Wallace, as his running mate. The Republicans nominated Wendell Willkie of Indiana, a former Democrat who supported many New Deal policies. The two parties' platforms differed only slightly. Both parties pledged aid to the Allies, and both candidates pledged not to send "one American boy into the shambles of another war," as Willkie put it. Willkie's spirited campaign resulted in a closer election than those of 1932 or 1936; nonetheless, Roosevelt won 55 percent of the popular vote.

Roosevelt now undertook to persuade Congress to increase aid to Britain, whose survival he viewed as key to American security. In January 1941, he outlined "four essential freedoms" (freedom of speech and of religion and freedom from want and fear) that he believed it was necessary to protect. Two months later, with Britain no longer able to pay cash for arms, Roosevelt convinced Congress to pass the Lend-Lease Act. The legislation authorized the president to "lease, lend, or otherwise dispose of" arms and other equipment to Britain or any country whose defense was considered vital to the security of the United States. When Hitler abandoned his Nonaggression Pact with Stalin and invaded the Soviet Union in June 1941, the United States promptly extended lend-lease to the Soviets. The implementation of lend-lease marked the unofficial entrance of the United States into the European war.

Roosevelt underlined his support for the Allied cause by meeting in August 1941 with British Prime Minister Winston Churchill. Their joint press release, which became known as the Atlantic Charter, provided the ideological foundation of the Western cause. Like Wilson's Fourteen Points and Roosevelt's Four Freedoms, the charter called for economic collaboration and guarantees of political stability after the war to ensure that people "in all the lands may live out their lives in freedom from fear and want." The charter also supported free trade, national self-determination, and the principle of collective security.

As in World War I, German submarines attacked U.S. and Allied ships that were carrying supplies to Europe. By September 1941, Nazi U-boats and the American navy were attacking each other in the Atlantic, a low-level conflict largely unknown to the American public. With isolationism still a potent force, Roosevelt hesitated to ask Congress for a declaration of war.

The Attack on Pearl Harbor

The crucial provocation came not from Germany but from Japan. Throughout the 1930s, Japanese aggression in China had gradually closed the open-door policy that had allowed European and American trade and investment (see Chapter 21). After Japan's invasion of China in 1937, Roosevelt denounced "the present reign of terror and international lawlessness" and suggested that aggressors be "quarantined" by peace-loving nations. Despite such rhetoric, the United States refused to intervene when Japanese troops sacked the city of Nanking, massacred 300,000 Chinese residents and raped thousands of women, and sank an American gunboat in the Yangtze River.

As Japan pacified coastal areas of China, the imperial ambitions of its military officers expanded. In 1940, General Hideki Tojo became War Minister. Tojo concluded a formal military alliance with Germany and Italy and dispatched Japanese troops to occupy the northern section of the French colony of Indochina (present-day Vietnam). The Imperial Army's goal, supported by Emperor Hirohito, was to create a so-called Greater East Asia Co-Prosperity Sphere, run by Japan and stretching from Indonesia to Korea. The United States responded to the invasion of Indochina by restricting trade with Japan, especially aviation-grade gasoline and scrap metal. Roosevelt hoped that these economic sanctions would deter Japanese aggression. But in July 1941, Japanese troops occupied the rest of Indochina. Roosevelt now froze Japanese assets in the United States and instituted an embargo on all trade with Japan, including vital oil shipments that accounted for almost 80 percent of Japanese consumption.

In October 1941, General Tojo became prime minister and accelerated secret preparations for war against the United States. By November, American military intelligence officials knew that Japan was planning an attack but did not know where it would occur. Early on Sunday morning, December 7, 1941, Japanese bombers attacked Pearl Harbor in Hawaii, killing more than 2,400 Americans. They destroyed or heavily damaged 8 battleships, 3 cruisers, 3 destroyers, and almost 200 airplanes.

Although the assault was devastating, it united the American people (as the Islamic terrorist attack on September 11, 2001, would do some sixty years later). Calling December 7 "a date which will live in infamy," President Roosevelt asked Congress for a declaration of war against Japan. The Senate voted unanimously for war, and the House concurred by a vote of 388 to 1. The lone dissenter was Jeannette Rankin of Montana, who had also opposed American entry into World War I. Three days later, Germany and Italy declared war on the United States, and the United States in turn declared war on those nations.

▶ Compare the impact of the depression on the politics and political institutions of the United States, Italy, and Germany. What are the similarities and differences?

▶ What were the sources of American political isolationism, how was it manifest, and how did FDR deal with it? Did the president maneuver the nation into war?

Organizing for Victory

The task of fighting a global war brought a dramatic increase in the power of the federal government. Coordinating the changeover from civilian to military production, raising an army, and assembling the necessary workforce required a huge expansion in the government bureaucracy. Mobilization on such a scale also demanded cooperation between business executives in major corporations and political leaders in Washington, and this process solidified a partnership that had been growing since World War I. But the most dramatic expansion of authority came in December 1941, when Congress passed the War Powers Act. The legislation gave President Roosevelt unprecedented control over all aspects of the war effort. This act marks the beginning of what historians call the Imperial Presidency: the far-reaching use (and abuse) of executive authority during decades of American world dominance, from 1945 to the present.

Financing the War

Defense mobilization definitively ended the Great Depression. In 1940, the annual gross national product stood at $99.7 billion; in 1945, it reached $211 billion. After-tax profits of American businesses nearly doubled, and farm output grew by one-third. Federal spending of $186 billion on war production powered this advance; by late 1943, two-thirds of the economy was directly involved in the war effort. The government paid for these military expenditures by raising taxes and borrowing money. Astonishingly, the Revenue Act of 1942 expanded the number of people paying income taxes from 3.9 million to 42.6 million. Annual revenue from income taxes jumped to $35.1 billion, facilitated by a payroll deduction system instituted in 1943. Thanks to this revolutionary—and apparently permanent—change in government financing, taxes on personal incomes and business profits paid for half the cost of the war, compared with 30 percent in World War I. The government borrowed the rest, both from wealthy Americans and from ordinary citizens, who invested some of their wartime wages in long-term Treasury bonds. The national debt grew steadily, topping out at $258.6 billion in 1945.

The war brought a significant expansion in the federal bureaucracy. The number of civilians employed by the government increased almost fourfold, to 3.8 million—a far higher rate of growth than that during the New Deal. Leadership of federal agencies changed as the Roosevelt administration relied less on New Deal reformers and more on business executives. Known as "dollar-a-year men" because they accepted only a token government salary, these executives remained on the payrolls of their corporations. Donald Nelson, a former executive at the Sears, Roebuck Company, headed the powerful War Production Board (WPB). The Board awarded defense contracts, allocated scarce resources (such as rubber, copper, and oil) for military uses, and persuaded businesses to convert to military production. For example, it encouraged Ford and General Motors to build tanks rather than cars by granting generous tax write-offs for re-equipping factories and building new ones. In other instances, the board approved "cost-plus" contracts, which guaranteed a profit, and allowed corporations to keep the new steel mills and shipyards after the war.

To secure maximum production, the WPB preferred to deal with major corporations rather than with small businesses. The nation's fifty-six largest corporations received three-fourths of the war contracts; the top ten received one-third. The best-known contractor was Henry J. Kaiser. Already highly successful from building roads in California and the Hoover and Grand Coulee dams, Kaiser became a naval contractor. At his shipyard in Richmond, California, he revolutionized ship construction by applying Henry Ford's techniques of mass production. Previously, most shipbuilding had been done by skilled workers who had served lengthy apprenticeships. To meet wartime production schedules, Kaiser broke the work process down into small, specialized tasks that newly trained workers could do easily. Soon, each of his work crews was building a "Liberty Ship," a large vessel to carry cargo and troops to the war zone, every five days. The press dubbed him the "Miracle Man."

The Kaiser shipyards were also known for their corporate welfare programs, which boosted workers' productivity almost as much as his efficient assembly system did. Kaiser offered his workers day care for their children, financial counseling, subsidized housing, and low-cost health care. The Kaiser Permanente Medical Care Program,

The Miracle Man

Henry Kaiser knew how to run a business with pride and no-nonsense efficiency. He built towns to house his workers, provided them with superior medical care, and organized them to build ships in record time. Here, Kaiser uses an 81-piece, 14-foot-long model to show ship owners and Navy brass how his workers built a 10,400-ton Liberty freighter in the amazing time of four days, fifteen hours, and twenty-six minutes.
© Bettmann/Corbis.

founded in 1942, provided subsidized, prepaid health care for the shipyard workers and their families (and lives on today as one of the nation's largest and most successful health maintenance organizations).

Central to Kaiser's business miracles were his close ties to federal agencies. The government financed the great dams that he built during the depression, and the Reconstruction Finance Corporation lent him $300 million to build shipyards and manufacturing plants during the war. One historian has aptly called Kaiser a "government entrepreneur," one of a new breed of corporate executives that prospered because of government contracts (and continue to do so today). As Secretary of War Henry Stimson explained, in a capitalist country, "you had better let business make money out of the process or business won't work."

Working together, American businesses, their employees, and government agencies produced a prodigious supply of military hardware: 86,000 tanks; 296,000 airplanes; fifteen million rifles and machine guns; 64,000 landing craft; and 6,500 cargo ships and naval vessels. The system of allotting contracts, along with the suspension of the antitrust prosecutions during the war, created huge corporate enterprises. In 1940, the largest 100 American companies produced 30 percent of the industrial output; by 1945, their share had soared to 70 percent. These same corporations formed the core of the nation's military-industrial complex of the Cold War era (see Chapters 26 and 27).

Mobilizing the American Fighting Force

Going to war meant mobilizing human resources, both on the battlefield and the home front. During World War II, the armed forces of the United States enlisted more than fifteen million men and women. The draft boards registered about thirty-one million men between the ages of eighteen and forty-four, but more than half the men failed to meet the physical standards, many because of bad teeth. The military tried to screen out homosexuals but had little success. Indeed, in the services, homosexuals found opportunities to participate in a gay culture more extensive than that in civilian life.

Racial discrimination was also part of military life, directed mainly against the approximately 700,000 blacks in uniform. The National Association for the Advancement of Colored People (NAACP) and other civil rights groups chided the government with reminders such as "A Jim Crow army cannot fight for a free world," but the military continued to segregate African Americans and to assign them menial duties. In contrast, Native Americans and Mexican Americans were never officially segregated; they rubbed elbows (and traded fists) with the sons of European immigrants and native-born soldiers from all regions of the country. "More than half of my platoon is from the South," an Italian American soldier from Brooklyn wrote to his wife from Luxembourg in 1944. "Almost all of them are farmers, many of them are genuine hillbillies, with all that implies."

Approximately 350,000 American women enlisted in the armed services. About 140,000 served as army WACS (Women's Army Corps), and 100,000 joined the naval WAVES (Women Accepted for Volunteer Emergency Service). One-third of the nation's registered nurses, almost 75,000 overall, volunteered for military duty. In addition, about 1,000 WASPs (Women's Airforce Service Pilots) ferried planes and supplies in noncombat areas. The armed forces limited the duties assigned to women, as it did with blacks. Female officers could not command men, and WACS and WAVES were barred from combat duty, although nurses of both sexes served close to the front lines, risking capture or death. Most of the jobs that women did in the military—clerical work, communications, and health care—resembled women's jobs in civilian life.

Workers and the War Effort

As millions of working-age citizens joined the military, the nation faced a critical labor shortage. The defense industries alone provided new jobs for about seven million workers. Substantial numbers of women and blacks joined the industrial workforce; unions, benefiting from the demand for labor, negotiated higher wages and improved conditions for America's workers.

Government officials and corporate recruiters drew on patriotism as they urged women to take jobs in defense industries. "Longing won't bring him back sooner . . . GET A WAR JOB!" one poster urged, while artist Norman Rockwell's famous "Rosie the Riveter" beckoned to women from the cover of the *Saturday Evening Post*. The government directed its publicity at housewives, but many working women gladly abandoned low-paying "women's jobs" as domestic servants or secretaries for higher-paying work in the defense industry. Suddenly, the nation's factories were full of women working as airplane riveters, ship welders, and drill-press operators. Women made up 36 percent of the labor force in 1945, compared with 24 percent at the beginning of the war. Women war workers often faced sexual harassment on the job and usually received lower wages than men did. In shipyards, women with the most seniority and responsibility earned $6.95 a day, whereas the top men made as much as $22 (see American Voices, p. 742).

When the men came home from war, Rosie the Riveter was usually out of a job. But many married women refused to put on aprons and stay home. Women's participation in the paid labor force rebounded by the late 1940s and continued to rise over the rest of the twentieth century, bringing major changes in family life (see Chapter 31).

During the war, workers and unions extended the gains made during the New Deal. By 1945, almost fifteen million workers belonged to a union, up from nine million in 1939. This increase stemmed in part from organized labor's embrace of patriotism. In December 1941, representatives of the major unions made a nonbinding "no-strike" pledge for the duration of the war. Two months later, the Roosevelt administration created the National War Labor Board (NWLB), composed of representatives of labor, management, and the public. The NWLB established wages, hours, and working conditions and had the authority to seize businesses that did not comply.

During its tenure, the NWLB handled 17,650 disputes affecting twelve million workers and seized forty factories. It resolved the controversial issue of mandatory union membership through a compromise: New hires did not have to join a union, but existing members had to keep their union card. Agitation for wage increases caused more serious conflicts. Because managers wanted to keep up production, they were willing to pay higher wages. But government officials tried to restrain pay raises to contain inflation and prevent dramatic rises in prices. Still, workers' incomes rose as much as 70 percent during the war, as many of them took on overtime work which was not covered by wage ceilings.

Despite higher incomes, many union members felt cheated as consumer prices rose and corporate profits soared. Worker dissatisfaction peaked in 1943. John L. Lewis led more than half a million United Mine Workers out on strike, demanding a higher wage increase than that recommended by the NWLB. Lewis's tactics won concessions, but they alienated many Americans and made him one of the most disliked public figures of the 1940s. Congress responded by passing (over Roosevelt's veto) the Smith-Connally Labor Act of 1943, which allowed the president to prohibit strikes in defense industries and forbade political contributions by unions. Congressional hostility would continue to hamper the union movement in the postwar years.

During the war, a new mood of militancy swept through the African American community. "A wind is rising throughout the world of free men everywhere," Eleanor Roosevelt wrote during the war, "and they will not be kept in bondage." Black leaders pointed to parallels between anti-Semitism in Germany and racial discrimination in the United States and waged a "Double V" campaign: victory over Nazism abroad and over racism at home.

Even before Pearl Harbor, black labor activism was on the rise. In 1940, only 240 of the nation's 100,000 aircraft workers were black, and most of them were janitors. African American leaders demanded that the government require defense contractors to hire more blacks. When the government took no action, A. Philip Randolph, head of the Brotherhood of Sleeping Car Porters, the largest black union, announced plans for a march on Washington in the summer of 1941. Roosevelt was not a strong supporter of civil rights, but he wanted to avoid a massive public protest and a disruption of the

Wider Opportunity and Personal Tragedy
PEGGY TERRY AND FANNY CHRISTINA HILL

World War II changed the lives of many Americans. Peggy Terry was born in Oklahoma, grew up in Kentucky, and worked in defense plants in Kentucky and Michigan. Tina Hill grew up in Texas, migrated to California as a domestic servant, and then got a job at North American Aircraft. In the 1980s, the women provided oral histories of their experiences.

Peggy Terry: The first work I had after the Depression was at a shell-loading plant in Viola, Kentucky. . . . They were large shells: anti-aircraft, incendiaries, and tracers. . . . We made the fabulous sum of thirty-two dollars a week [equivalent to about $400 in 2008]. To us it was just an absolute miracle. . . .

You won't believe how incredibly ignorant I was. I knew vaguely that a war had started, but I had no idea what it meant. . . . It didn't occur to us that we were making these shells to kill people. It never entered my head. . . . We were just a bunch of hillbilly women laughin' and talkin'. . . .

Tetryl was one of the ingredients and it turned us orange. Just as orange as an orange. Our hair was streaked orange. Our hands, our face, our neck just turned orange, even our eyeballs. We never questioned. None of us ever asked, What is this? Is this harmful? . . . The only thing we worried about was other women thinking we had dyed our hair. Back then it was a disgrace if you dyed your hair. . . .

My husband was a paratrooper in the war, in the 101st Airborne Division. . . . Until the war he never drank. He never even smoked. When he came back he was an absolute drunkard. And he used to have the most awful nightmares. He'd get up in the middle of the night and start screaming. . . . He started slapping me around and slapped the kids around. He became a brute.

Fanny Christina Hill: I was twenty-four. . . . They had fifteen or twenty departments [at North American Aviation], but all the Negroes went to Department 17 because there was nothing but shooting and bucking rivets. You stood on one side of the panel and your partner stood on this side and he would shoot the rivets with a gun and you'd buck them with the bar. That was about the size of it. I just didn't like it . . . went over to the union and they . . . sent me to another department where you did bench work and I liked that much better. . . .

Some weeks I brought home . . . thirty dollars. . . . I was also getting that fifty dollars a month from my husband [in the army] and that was just saved right away. I was planning on buying a home and a car. . . . [Working at North American] made me live better. It really did. We always say that Lincoln took the bale off of the Negroes. I think there is a statue up there in Washington, D.C., where he's lifting something off the Negro. Well, my sister always said—that's why you can't interview her because she's so radical—"Hitler was the one that got us out of the white folks' kitchen."

SOURCE: Studs Terkel, *"The Good War": An Oral History of World War II* (New York: Pantheon, 1984), 102–111; Sherna B. Gluck, *Rosie the Riveter Revisited* (Boston: G. K. Hall & Co., 1987), 37–42.

Fighting for Freedom at Home and Abroad, 1941

This protester from the Negro Labor Relations League pointedly drew the parallel between blacks serving in the armed forces and winning access to jobs at the Bowman Dairy Company, a Chicago bottler, dried milk producer, and distributor that employed 3,000 workers. Library of Congress.

nation's war preparations. So the President made a deal. Randolph canceled the march, and in June 1941, Roosevelt issued Executive Order 8802. It prohibited "discrimination in the employment of workers in defense industries or government because of race, creed, color, or national origin" and established the Fair Employment Practices Commission (FEPC) to enforce the order. This federal commitment to minority employment rights was unprecedented but limited: It did not affect segregation in the armed forces, and the FEPC could not require compliance with its regulations. Still, the committee successfully resolved about one-third of the more than 8,000 complaints it received.

The League of United Latin American Citizens—the Latino counterpart to the NAACP—likewise challenged long-standing practices of discrimination and exclusion. In Texas, where it was still common to see signs reading "No Dogs or Mexicans Allowed," the organization protested limited job opportunities and the segregation of schools and public facilities. The NAACP itself grew ninefold, to 450,000 members, by 1945, and in

Chicago, James Farmer helped to found the Congress of Racial Equality (CORE), a group that was soon known nationwide for its direct action protests, such as sit-ins. These wartime developments—both federal intervention through the FEPC and African American militancy—laid the groundwork for the civil rights revolution of the 1960s.

Politics in Wartime

During World War II (unlike World War I), there were few attempts to promote progressive social reform. Given the strength of the Axis Powers, the administration focused on the war effort. Moreover, in the 1942 elections, Republicans picked up ten seats in the Senate and forty-seven seats in the House, bolstering the conservative block in Congress. As wartime spending brought full employment, Roosevelt ended various New Deal programs, including the Civilian Conservation Corps and the National Youth Administration.

But Roosevelt raised the prospect of new federal social initiatives. In his State of the Union address in 1944, the president called for a second bill of rights, which would guarantee that Americans had access to education and jobs, adequate food and clothing, and decent housing and medical care. However, Congress created new government benefits only for military veterans, known as GIs (short for "government issue"). The Servicemen's Readjustment Act (1944), popularly known as the "GI Bill of Rights," provided education, job training, medical care, pensions, and mortgage loans for men and women who had served in the armed forces. An extraordinarily influential program, particularly in expanding access to higher education, it distributed almost $4 billion in benefits to nine million veterans between 1944 and 1949; in the 1950s, the GI Bill assisted veterans of the Korean War.

The president's call for social legislation sought to reinvigorate the New Deal political coalition. In the election of 1944, Roosevelt once again headed the Democratic ticket. But party leaders, aware of FDR's health problems and anxious to find a middle-of-the-road successor, dropped Vice President Henry Wallace from the ticket. They feared that Wallace's outspoken support for labor, civil rights, and domestic reform would alienate southern Democrats. In his place they chose Senator Harry S Truman of Missouri. A direct-speaking, no-nonsense politician, Truman was a protégé of Tom Pendergast, the boss of the Democratic machine in Kansas City, and had risen to prominence by heading a Senate investigation into the awarding of wartime defense contracts.

▶ In what ways did World War II contribute to the growth of the federal government? How did it foster what historians now call the military-industrial complex?

▶ What impact did war mobilization have on women, racial minorities, and organized labor? What legislation or government rules affected their lives as workers?

The Republicans nominated Governor Thomas E. Dewey of New York. Only forty-two years old, Dewey had won fame as a U.S. attorney fighting organized crime. Like drug smuggling today, the bootlegging of liquor during Prohibition generated huge profits for highly organized criminal "families." After Prohibition ended, the "mob" ran the "protection" racket, extorting money from businesses by threatening arson or violence. Dewey took on the New York City mobs and, despite his use of controversial "third-degree" (i.e., torture) interrogation tactics, won the admiration of many Americans. Dewey accepted the general principles of welfare state liberalism domestically and internationally in foreign affairs, and so attracted some of Roosevelt's supporters. But a majority of voters preferred political continuity. Roosevelt received 53.5 percent of the nationwide vote and 60 percent in cities of more than 100,000 people, where ethnic minorities and labor unions strongly supported Democratic candidates. The Democratic coalition stood triumphant; the era of Republican political dominance (1896–1932) had come to an end.

Life on the Home Front

The United States escaped the physical devastation that ravaged Europe and East Asia, but the war changed the lives of its citizens, in ways good and bad. Americans welcomed wartime prosperity but shuddered when they saw a Western Union boy on his bicycle, fearing that he carried a War Department telegram reporting the death of someone's son, husband, or father. Citizens also grumbled about annoying wartime regulations and rationing but accepted that their lives would be different "for the duration."

"For the Duration"

Like the soldiers in uniform, people on the home front had wartime responsibilities. They worked on civilian defense committees, recycled old newspapers and scrap material, and served on local rationing and draft boards. About twenty million backyard "victory gardens" produced 40 percent of the nation's vegetables. Various federal agencies encouraged these efforts, especially the Office of War Information (OWI), which disseminated news and promoted patriotism. The OWI urged advertising agencies to link their clients' products to the war effort, arguing that patriotic ads would not only sell goods but also "invigorate, instruct and inspire" the citizenry.

Popular culture, especially the movies, reinforced the connections between the home front and the war effort. Hollywood producers, directors, and actors offered their talents to the War Department. Director Frank Capra created a series of "Why We Fight" documentaries to explain war aims to conscripted soldiers. Movie stars such as John Wayne, Anthony Quinn, and Spencer Tracy portrayed the heroism of American fighting men in many films, such as *Guadalcanal Diary* (1943) and *Thirty Seconds over Tokyo* (1945). Other movies warned of the danger of fascism at home and abroad and showed citizens how they could support the war effort. The Academy Award–winning *Casablanca* (1943), starring Humphrey Bogart, celebrated the quiet patriotism of an ordinary American in German-occupied North Africa, while the box-office hit *Since You Went Away* (1943), starring Claudette Colbert, portrayed a wife who took a defense job while her husband fought.

Average weekly movie attendance soared to over 100 million. Demand was so great that many theaters operated around the clock to accommodate defense workers on the swing and night shifts. In this pretelevision era, newsreels accompanying the feature films kept the public up to date on the war, as did on-the-spot radio broadcasts by Edward R. Murrow and other well-known commentators.

Perhaps the major source of Americans' high morale was wartime prosperity. Defense spending had ended the depression, unemployment had vanished, and per capita income doubled. Midway through the war, 70 percent of Americans reported that they had personally experienced "no real sacrifices." A Red Cross worker put it bluntly: "The war was fun for America. I'm not talking about the poor souls who lost sons and daughters. But for the rest of us, the war was a hell of a good time."

For many Americans, the major inconvenience was the shortage of consumer goods. The Office of Price Administration and other federal agencies subjected almost everything Americans ate, wore, or used during the war years to rationing or regulation. The first major scarcity was rubber. The Japanese conquest of Malaysia and Dutch Indonesia cut off 97 percent of America's imports of natural rubber, an essential raw material. In response, the government created an entirely new synthetic rubber industry, which used natural gas, oil, and various minerals to produce 762,000 tons of rubber a year by late 1944. To conserve rubber supplies for the war effort, the government rationed tires, so many of the nation's thirty million car owners put their cars up on blocks for the duration. As more people walked, they wore out their shoes. In 1944, shoes were rationed to two pairs per person a year, half the prewar usage.

The government also rationed fuel oil, so schools and restaurants shortened their hours, and homeowners lowered their thermostats to 65 degrees. To cut domestic gasoline consumption, the government rationed supplies and imposed a nationwide speed limit of 35 miles per hour, which reduced highway deaths dramatically. By 1943, the government was regulating the amount of meat, butter, sugar, and other foods Americans could buy. Most citizens cooperated with the complicated rationing and coupon system, but at least one-quarter of the population bought items on the black market, especially meat, gasoline, cigarettes, and nylon stockings. Manufacturers of automobiles, refrigerators, and radios, who had been forced to switch to military production, told consumers to save their money and splurge once the war ended.

Migration and Social Conflict

The war often determined where people lived. When husbands entered the armed services, their families often followed them to training bases or points of debarkation. Civilians moved to take high-paying defense jobs. About fifteen million Americans changed residences during the war years, half of them moving to another state. One of them was Peggy Terry, who grew up in Paducah, Kentucky; worked in a shell-loading plant in nearby Viola; and then moved to a defense plant in Michigan. There, she recalled, "I met all those wonderful Polacks [Polish Americans]. They were the first people I'd ever known that were any different from me. A whole new world just opened up."

As the center of defense production for the Pacific war, California bore the brunt and reaped the rewards of wartime migration. The state welcomed nearly three million new residents and grew by 53 percent during the war. "The Second Gold Rush Hits the West," announced the *San Francisco Chronicle* in 1943. One-tenth of all federal dollars flowed into California, and the state's factories turned out one-sixth of all war materials. People went where the defense jobs were: to Los Angeles, San Diego, and cities around San Francisco Bay. Some towns grew practically overnight; within two years of the opening of the huge Kaiser Corporation shipyard in Richmond, California, the town's population had quadrupled.

The growth of war industries prompted the migration of more than one million African Americans from the rural South to California, Illinois, Michigan, Ohio, and

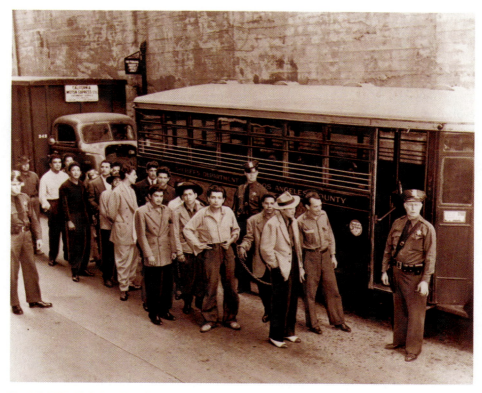

Zoot Suit Youth in Los Angeles

During a four-day riot in June 1943, servicemen in Los Angeles attacked young Latino men wearing distinctive "zoot suits," which were widely viewed as emblems of gang membership and a delinquent youth culture. The police response was to arrest scores of zoot-suiters. Here, a group of handcuffed young Hispanic men is about to board a Los Angeles County Sheriff's bus to make a court appearance. Note the wide-legged pants that taper at the ankle, a feature of the zoot suit. Library of Congress. For more help analyzing this image, see the Online Study Guide at **bedfordstmartins.com/henrettaconcise**.

Pennsylvania—a continuation of the "Great Migration" earlier in the century (see Chapter 22). As migrant blacks and whites competed for jobs and housing, racial conflicts broke out in forty-seven cities during 1943. The worst violence took place in the Detroit area. In June 1943, a riot involving African Americans, southern-born whites, and Polish Americans left thirty-four people dead and hundreds injured.

Racial conflict struck the West as well. In Los Angeles, male Hispanic teenagers formed *pachuco* (youth) gangs. Many dressed in "zoot suits"—broad-brimmed felt hats, pegged trousers, and clunky shoes; they wore their long hair slicked down and carried pocket knives on gold chains. The young women who partied with them favored long coats, huarache sandals, and pompadour hairdos. Some black and working-class white teenagers in Los Angeles and elsewhere took up the zoot-suit style to underline their rejection of middle-class values. To many adults, the zoot suit symbolized juvenile delinquency. When rumors circulated in Los Angeles in July 1943 that a *pachuco* gang had beaten a white sailor, they set off a four-day riot. White servicemen roamed through Mexican American neighborhoods and attacked zoot-suiters, taking special pleasure in slashing their pegged pants. The police, who had their own grudges against the zoot-suiters, did little to stop the violence.

Civil Rights During Wartime

These outbreaks of social violence were severe but limited. Unlike World War I, which evoked widespread harassment of German Americans, the mood on the home front was generally calm in the 1940s. Federal officials interned about 5,000 potentially dangerous German and Italian aliens during the war. But leftists and Communists, prime targets of government repression at the end of World War I, experienced few problems, in part because the Soviet Union and the United States were allies in the fight against right-wing fascist nations.

The internment of Japanese aliens and Japanese American citizens was a glaring exception to this record of tolerance. Immediately after the attack on Pearl Harbor, the West Coast remained calm. Then, as residents began to fear attacks, spies, and sabotage, California's long history of racial animosity toward Asian immigrants came into play (see Chapters 16, 21, and 24). Local politicians and newspapers whipped up sentiment against Japanese Americans, who numbered only about 112,000, had no political power, and lived primarily in ethnic communities in the three Pacific coast states.

Early in 1942, President Roosevelt responded to these fears by issuing Executive Order 9066. The order and a subsequent act of Congress gave the War Department the authority to evacuate Japanese Americans from the West Coast and intern them in relocation camps for the rest of the war. Although there was little if any disloyal or seditious activity among the evacuees, few public leaders opposed the plan. "A Jap's a Jap," snapped General John DeWitt, the officer charged with defense of the West Coast. "It makes no difference whether he is an American citizen or not."

The relocation plan shocked Japanese Americans, more than two-thirds of whom were native-born American citizens. (They were known as the Nisei generation, the children of the immigrant Issei generation.) Army officials gave families only a few days to dispose of their property. Businesses that had taken a lifetime to build were liquidated overnight, and speculators snapped up Japanese Americans' real estate for a fraction of its value. The War Relocation Authority moved the internees to hastily built camps in desolate areas in California, Arizona, Utah, Colorado, Wyoming, Idaho, and Arkansas. Ironically, the Japanese Americans who made up one-third of the population of Hawaii, and presumably posed a greater threat because of their numbers and proximity to Japan, were not interned. They provided much of the unskilled labor in the island territory, and the Hawaiian economy could not function without them.

Cracks soon appeared in the relocation policy. A labor shortage in farming led the government to furlough seasonal agricultural workers from the camps as early as 1942. Authorities also allowed about 4,300 students to attend colleges outside the West Coast military zone. Another route out of the camps was enlistment in the armed services. The 442nd Regimental Combat Team, a unit composed almost entirely of Nisei volunteers, served with distinction in Europe.

Nisei Gordon Hirabayashi was among the few Japanese Americans who actively resisted incarceration. A student at the University of Washington, Hirabayashi was a religious pacifist who had registered with his draft board as a conscientious objector.

He challenged internment by refusing to register for evacuation; instead, he turned himself in to the FBI. "I wanted to uphold the principles of the Constitution," Hirabayashi later stated, "and the curfew and evacuation orders which singled out a group on the basis of ethnicity violated them." Tried and convicted in 1942, he appealed his case to the Supreme Court in *Hirabayashi v. United States* (1943). In that case and in *Korematsu v. United States* (1944), the Court allowed the removal of Japanese Americans from the West Coast on the basis of "military necessity" but avoided ruling on the constitutionality of the internment program. But in *Ex Parte Endo* (1944), the Court held that American citizens of undoubted loyalty could not be confined by government authorities.

The Court's refusal to rule directly on the relocation program underscored the fragility of civil liberties in wartime. Although Congress issued a public apology in 1988 and awarded $20,000 to each of the 80,000 surviving Japanese American internees, it once again gave the government sweeping powers of arrest and detention in the Patriot Act of 2001 (see Chapter 32).

▶ What was the impact of World War II on the everyday life of the majority of Americans?

▶ How do you explain the decision to intern virtually all Americans of Japanese birth or ancestry?

Fighting and Winning the War

World War II was, literally, a war for control of the world. Had the Axis Powers triumphed, Germany would have dominated, either directly or indirectly, all of Europe and much of Africa; Japan would have controlled most of East Asia. To prevent this outcome, which would have crippled democracy in Europe and restricted American power to the Western Hemisphere, the Roosevelt administration took the United States to war. The United States extended aid to Great Britain in the late 1930s, resorted to economic warfare against Germany and Japan in 1940 and 1941, and then fully committed its industrial might and armed forces from 1942 to 1945. Its intervention and that of the Soviet Union decided the outcome of the conflict and shaped the character of the postwar world.

Wartime Aims and Tensions

Great Britain, the United States, and the Soviet Union were the key actors in the Allied coalition. China, France, and other nations played lesser roles. The "Big Three," consisting of President Franklin Roosevelt, Prime Minister Winston Churchill of Great Britain, and Premier Joseph Stalin of the Soviet Union, set military strategy and diplomatic policy. The Atlantic Charter, which Churchill and Roosevelt had drafted in August 1941, set out the Anglo-American vision of the postwar international order. It called for free trade, national self-determination, and collective security. Stalin was not a party to that agreement and disagreed fundamentally with some of its precepts, such as a capitalist-run international trading system. Moreover, he was determined to protect the Soviet Union by setting up a band of Soviet-controlled buffer states along his border with Germany and western Europe.

The first major disagreement among the Allies related to military strategy and timing. The Big Three agreed that defeating Germany (rather than Japan) was the top military priority, but they differed over how best to do it. In 1941, a powerful German army had invaded the Soviet Union and advanced to the outskirts of Leningrad, Moscow, and Stalingrad before being halted in mid-1942 by hard-pressed Russian forces. To relieve pressure on the Soviet army, Stalin wanted the British and Americans to attack Germany by opening a "second front" with a major invasion through France. Roosevelt informally assured Stalin that the Allies would open a second front in 1942, but the British opposed an early invasion, and American war production was not yet sufficient to support it. For eighteen months, Stalin's pleas went unanswered, and the Soviet Union bore the brunt of the fighting. Then, at a conference of the Big Three in Tehran, Iran, in November 1943, Churchill and Roosevelt agreed to attack the German forces in France within six months in return for Stalin's promise to join the fight against Japan. Both sides adhered to this agreement, but the long delay angered Stalin, who became increasingly suspicious about American and British intentions.

The War in Europe

Following the attack on Pearl Harbor, the Allies suffered one defeat after another. German armies pushed deep into Soviet territory in the south; advancing through the wheat fields of the Ukraine and the rich oil fields of the Caucasus, they moved toward the major city of Stalingrad. Simultaneously, the Germans began an offensive in North Africa aimed at seizing the Suez Canal. In the Atlantic, German submarines relentlessly attacked American convoys carrying oil and other vital supplies to Britain and the Soviet Union.

Then, over the winter of 1942–1943, the tide began to turn in favor of the Allies. In the epic Battle of Stalingrad, Soviet forces decisively halted the German advance, killing or capturing 330,000 German soldiers, and slowly began to push westward (Map 25.1). By early 1944, Stalin's troops had driven the German army out of the Soviet Union. Meanwhile, the Allies launched a major offensive in North Africa, Churchill's temporary substitute for a second front in France. Between November 1942 and May 1943, Allied troops under the leadership of General Dwight D. Eisenhower and General George S. Patton defeated Germany's *Afrika Korps*, led by General Erwin Rommel.

From Africa, the Allied command followed Churchill's strategy of attacking the Axis through its "soft underbelly": Sicily and the Italian peninsula. Faced with an Allied invasion, the Italian king ousted Benito Mussolini's Fascist regime in July 1943. But German troops took control of Italy and strenuously resisted the Allied invasion. American and British troops took Rome only in June 1944 and were still fighting German forces in northern Italy when the European war ended in May 1945 (Map 25.2). Churchill's southern strategy proved a time-consuming and costly mistake.

The long-promised invasion of France came on "D-Day," June 6, 1944. That morning, after an agonizing delay caused by bad weather, the largest armada ever assembled moved across the English Channel under the command of General Eisenhower. When American, British, and Canadian soldiers hit the beaches of Normandy, they suffered terrible casualties but secured a beachhead. Over the next few days, more than 1.5 million soldiers and thousands of tons of military supplies and equipment flowed into France. In August, Allied troops liberated Paris; by September, they had driven the Germans out of most of France and Belgium. Meanwhile, long-range Allied bombers had

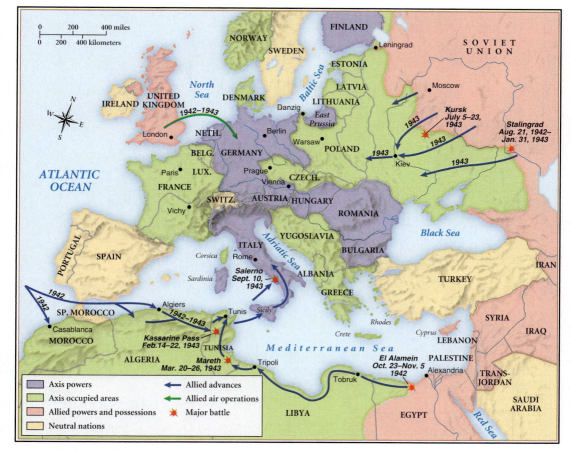

MAP 25.1 World War II in Europe, 1941–1943

Hitler's Germany reached its greatest extent in 1942 when Nazi forces had occupied Norway, France, North Africa, central Europe, and much of western Russia. The tide of battle turned in late 1942 when the Russians halted the German advance at Leningrad and Stalingrad. By early 1943, the Soviet army had launched a massive counterattack at Stalingrad, and Allied forces had driven the Germans from North Africa and invaded Sicily and the Italian mainland.

For more help analyzing this map, see the Online Study Guide at **bedfordstmartins.com/henrettaconcise.**

attacked German cities as well as military and industrial targets. The air campaign killed some 305,000 civilians and soldiers and injured another 780,000.

The Germans were not yet ready to give up, however. In December 1944, they mounted a final offensive in Belgium, the so-called Battle of the Bulge, before being pushed back across the Rhine River into Germany. As American and British troops drove toward Berlin from the west, Soviet troops advanced from the east through Poland. On April 30, 1945, as Russian troops massed outside Berlin, Hitler committed suicide; on May 8, Germany formally surrendered.

As Allied troops advanced into Poland and Germany in the spring of 1945, they came face to face with Adolf Hitler's "final solution of the Jewish question": the extermination camps where six million Jews had been put to death, along with another six million Poles,

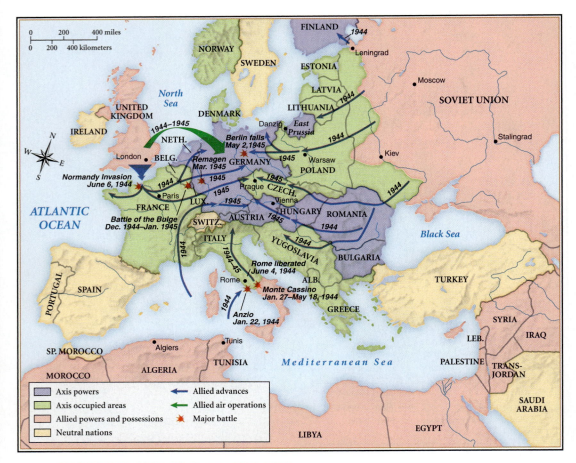

MAP 25.2 World War II in Europe, 1944–1945
By the end of 1943, the Russian army had almost pushed the Germans out of the Soviet Union. By June 1944, when the British and Americans finally invaded France, the Russians had liberated eastern Poland and most of southeastern Europe. By the end of 1944, British and American forces were ready to invade Germany from the west, and the Russians were poised to do the same from the east. Germany surrendered on May 8, 1945.

Slavs, Gypsies, homosexuals, and other "undesirables." Photographs of the Nazi death camps at Buchenwald, Dachau, and Auschwitz showed bodies stacked like cordwood and survivors so emaciated they were barely alive. Quickly published in *Life* and other mass-circulation magazines, the photographs horrified the American public.

The Nazi persecution of German Jews in the 1930s was widely known in the United States. But when Jews began to flee from Germany, the United States refused to relax its strict immigration laws to take them in. American officials, along with those of most other nations, continued this exclusionist policy during World War II as the Nazi regime extended its control over millions of eastern European Jews. Among the various factors that inhibited American action, the most important was widespread anti-Semitism in the State Department, Christian churches, and the public at large. The

The Living Dead

When Allied troops advanced into Germany in the spring of 1945, they came face to face with what had long been rumored: concentration camps, Adolf Hitler's "final solution of the Jewish question." In this picture from Wobbelin concentration camp, which had been liberated by the 82nd Airborne Division of the 9th U.S. Army, emaciated inmates are being taken to a hospital. In the days before the camp was liberated, 1,000 of the 5,000 prisoners had been allowed to starve to death. U.S. Holocaust Memorial Museum.

legacy of the immigration restriction legislation of the 1920s and the isolationist attitudes of the 1930s also discouraged policymakers from assuming responsibility for the fate of the refugees. As later American administrations would learn (as "ethnic cleansing" killed millions in India in the 1940s and Bosnia and Rwanda in the 1990s), political considerations often conflict with humanitarian values. Taking a narrow view of the national interest, the State Department allowed only 21,000 Jewish refugees to enter the United States during the war. But the War Refugee Board, established by President Roosevelt in 1944, following a plea by Secretary of the Treasury Henry Morgenthau, helped to move 200,000 European Jews to safe havens in various countries.

The War in the Pacific

Winning the war against Japan was even more arduous than the campaign against Germany. After crippling the American battle fleet at Pearl Harbor, the Japanese quickly expanded their military presence in the South Pacific, with seaborne invasions of Hong Kong, Wake Island, and Guam. Japanese forces then advanced into Southeast Asia, conquering the Solomon Islands, Burma, and Malaya and threatening Australia and India. By May 1942, they had forced the surrender of American forces in the Philippine Islands and, in the Bataan "death march," callously allowed the deaths of 10,000 American prisoners of war (see Voices from Abroad, p. 754).

At that dire moment, American naval forces scored two crucial victories. In the Battle of the Coral Sea, off southern New Guinea in May 1942, they halted the Japanese offensive against Australia. Then, in June, at the Battle of Midway Island,

Japanese Abuse of Prisoners of War ANTON BILEK

Anton Bilek grew up in a German American family in southern Illinois. In 1939, at age nineteen, he enlisted in the army because jobs were hard to get. Sent to the Philippines in 1940, he was taken prisoner in April 1942. He related his experiences as a POW to Studs Terkel and in his memoir, *No Uncle Sam: The Forgotten of Bataan* (2003).

The next morning, we got orders to get rid of all our arms and wait for the Japanese to come. General King had surrendered Bataan. They came in. First thing they did, they lined us up and started searchin' us. Anybody that had a ring or a wristwatch or a pair of gold-rimmed spectacles, they took 'em. Glasses they'd throw on the floor and break 'em and put the gold rims in their pockets. If you had a ring, you handed it over. If you couldn't get it off, the guy'd put the bayonet right up against your neck. . . .

They moved us about on the road. Here was a big stream of Americans and Filipinos marchin' by. They told us to get in the back of this column. This was the start of the Death March. (A long, deep sigh.) That was a sixty-mile walk. Here we were, three, four months on half-rations, less. The men were already thin, in shock. Undernourished, full of malaria. Dysentery is beginning to spread. . . .

The Japanese emptied out the hospitals. Anybody that could walk, they forced 'em into line. You found all kinda bodies along the road. Some of 'em bloated, some had just been killed. If you fell out to the side, you were either shot by the guards or you were bayoneted and left there. We lost somewhere between six hundred and seven hundred Americans in the four days of the march. The Filipinos lost close to ten thousand.

At San Fernando, we were stuffed into boxcars and taken about thirty-five miles further north. The cars were closed, you couldn't get air. In the hot sun, the temperature got up there. You couldn't fall down because you were held up by the guys stacked around you. You had a lot of guys blow their top, just start screamin'. . . .

[Undernourished and sick] I went blind, momentarily. It scared the hell out of me. I was at the hospital for about two weeks, and the doctor, an American, said, "There's nothing I can do with you. Rest is the only thing. Eat all the rice you can get. That's your only medicine." That's the one thing that pulled me through. He said, "You won't have to go on details." The Japanese were comin' in and they'd take two, three hundred and start 'em repairing a bridge that was blown up. We were losin' a lot of men there. They just couldn't work any more. They were dyin'. . . .

We had 185 men in our squadron when the war started. Three and a half years later, when we were liberated from a prison camp in Japan [where they had to work in a coal mine], we were 39 left. . . . I'm back home. It's all over with. I'd like to forget it. I had nothin' against the Japanese. But I don't drive a Toyota or own a Sony. . . .

SOURCE: Studs Terkel, *"The Good War": An Oral History of World War Two* (New York: Pantheon Books, 1984), 85, 90–91, 95–96.

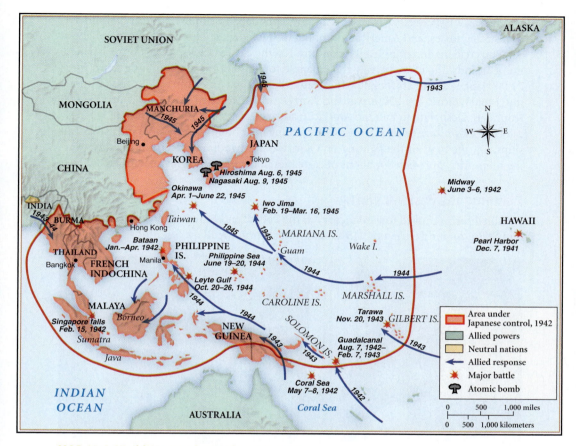

MAP 25.3 World War II in the Pacific, 1941–1945

Following the attack on Pearl Harbor in December 1941, the Japanese rapidly extended their domination in the Pacific. The Japanese flag soon flew as far east as the Marshall and Gilbert Islands and as far south as the Solomon Islands and parts of New Guinea. Japan also controlled the Philippines, much of Southeast Asia, and parts of China. The tide began to turn in mid-1942, when American naval victories at the Coral Sea and Midway stopped Japanese expansion. In 1943 and 1944, Allied forces retook the islands in the central Pacific and they ousted the Japanese from the Philippines early in 1945. The capture of Iwo Jima and Okinawa put American bombers in position to attack Japan itself. As the Soviet army invaded Japanese-occupied Manchuria in August 1945, the United States dropped atomic bombs on Hiroshima and Nagasaki, bringing an end to the war.

the American navy inflicted serious damage on the Japanese fleet. In both battles, dive bombers launched from American aircraft carriers provided the margin of victory.

The American military command, led by General Douglas MacArthur and Admiral Chester W. Nimitz, now took the offensive in the Pacific. For the next eighteen months, American forces advanced slowly toward Japan, taking one island after another in the face of diehard Japanese resistance. In October 1944, MacArthur and Nimitz began the reconquest of the Philippines by winning the Battle of Leyte Gulf, a massive naval encounter in which the Japanese lost practically their entire fleet (Map 25.3).

By early 1945, victory over Japan was in sight. Japanese military forces had suffered devastating losses, and American bombing of the Japanese homeland had killed about 330,000 civilians and crippled its economy. But the closer U.S. forces got to the Japanese home islands, the more fiercely the Japanese fought. On the small island of Iwo Jima, 21,000 Japanese soldiers fought to the death, killing 6,000 American marines and wounding 14,000 more. On Okinawa, the American toll reached 7,600 dead and 32,000 wounded. Desperate to halt the American advance and short of ammunition, Japanese pilots flew *kamikaze* (suicidal) missions, crashing their bomb-laden planes into American ships. On the basis of the fighting on Okinawa and Iwo Jima, American military commanders grimly predicted millions of casualties in the upcoming invasion of Japan.

Planning the Postwar World

As Allied forces moved toward victory in the Pacific and Europe, Roosevelt, Churchill, and Stalin met in February 1945 at Yalta, a resort on the Black Sea. Roosevelt focused

The Big Three at Yalta
With victory in Europe at hand, Roosevelt journeyed in February 1945 to Yalta, on the Black Sea, to meet with Churchill and Stalin. The American president appears visibly ill in this photograph (for comparison, see the photo on p. 702) and would die two months later. The three leaders discussed the controversial issues of the treatment of Germany, the status of Poland and other central European nations, the creation of the United Nations, and Russian entry into the war against Japan. The disputes at Yalta set the stage for the Cold War. Franklin D. Roosevelt Library.

on maintaining Allied unity, which he saw as the key to postwar peace and stability. But two sets of issues, the fates of the British and French colonial empires and of the nations of central and eastern Europe, divided the Big Three. An independence movement in British India, led by Mahatma Gandhi, had gathered strength and caused friction between Roosevelt, who favored Indian independence, and Churchill, who was intent on preserving British rule.

A more serious conflict was Stalin's insistence that Russian national security demanded the creation of pro-Soviet governments in central and eastern Europe. Roosevelt pressed for an agreement that guaranteed self-determination and democratic elections in Poland and neighboring countries. However, given the presence there of Soviet troops, FDR had to accept a pledge from Stalin to hold "free and unfettered elections" at a future time. The three leaders agreed to divide Germany into four administrative zones, each controlled by one of the four powers (the United States, Great Britain, France, and the Soviet Union), and to partition the capital city, Berlin, which lay in the middle of the Soviet zone.

The Big Three also agreed to establish an international body to replace the discredited League of Nations. They decided that the new United Nations organization would have a Security Council composed of the five major Allied powers — the United States, Britain, France, China, and the Soviet Union — and six other nations elected on a rotating basis. They also proposed that the five permanent members of the Security Council should have veto power over decisions of the General Assembly, in which all nations would be represented. Roosevelt, Churchill, and Stalin announced that the United Nations would convene in San Francisco on April 25, 1945.

Roosevelt returned to the United States in February, visibly exhausted by his 14,000-mile trip. The sixty-three-year-old president was a sick man, suffering from heart failure and high blood pressure. On April 12, 1945, during a short visit to his vacation home in Warm Springs, Georgia, Roosevelt suffered a cerebral hemorrhage and died.

When Harry S Truman assumed the presidency, he learned for the first time about the top-secret Manhattan Project and that it was on the verge of testing a new weapon: the atomic bomb. In the first decades of the twentieth century, European physicists, many of them Jewish, had achieved the theoretical breakthroughs that foreshadowed the atomic age. By the 1930s, scientists knew that the tiny nuclei of atoms could be split into yet smaller particles in a process called fission. They also theorized that the fission of highly processed uranium would produce a chain reaction and unleash tremendous amounts of energy. Working at the University of Chicago in December 1942, Enrico Fermi and Leo Szilard, refugees from Fascist Italy and Nazi Germany, produced the first controlled chain reaction. With the aid of German-born refugee Albert Einstein, the greatest theorist of modern physics and a scholar at Princeton, they persuaded Franklin Roosevelt to develop an atomic weapon, warning that German scientists were also working on such nuclear reactions.

The Manhattan Project cost $2 billion (about $24 billion today), employed 120,000 people, and involved the construction of thirty-seven installations in nineteen states — all of this activity hidden from Congress, the American people, and even Vice President Truman. Directed by General Leslie Graves and scientist Robert Oppenheimer, the nation's top physicists assembled the first bomb in Los Alamos,

▶ What was the crucial turning point of the war in Europe? In the Pacific?

▶ Evaluate the relative contributions of the Russians and the Americans to the Allied victory. What were the tensions among the Allies regarding military strategy and post-war territorial issues?

▶ Explain why the United States used atomic weapons against Japan.

New Mexico, and successfully tested it on July 16, 1945. Overwhelmed by its frightening power, Oppenheimer recalled the words from the *Bhagavad Gita*, one of the great texts of Hindu scripture: "I am become Death, Destroyer of Worlds."

Three weeks later, President Truman ordered the dropping of atomic bombs on two Japanese cities: Hiroshima on August 6 and Nagasaki on August 9. Truman was not a reflective man, and he did not question the morality of using such a revolutionary and destructive weapon. Administration officials believed that Japan's military leaders would never surrender unless their country was utterly devastated, and they knew that an American invasion would cost hundreds of thousands of lives. Truman might also have hoped that use of the bomb would intimidate Stalin and ease his objections to American plans for the postwar world. In any event, the atomic bombs achieved the immediate goal. The deaths of 100,000 people at Hiroshima and 60,000 at Nagasaki prompted the Japanese government to surrender on August 10 and to sign a formal agreement on September 2, 1945.

Fascism had been defeated, thanks to a strange alliance between the capitalist nations of the West and the communist government of the Soviet Union. The coming of peace would strain and then destroy the victorious coalition.

SUMMARY

As we have seen, the rise of fascism in Germany, Italy, and Japan led to military expansionism in Europe, Africa, and China. Initially, the American public insisted on noninvolvement. But by 1940, President Roosevelt was mobilizing support for military preparedness and intervention. The Japanese attack on Pearl Harbor in December 1941 brought the nation into World War II.

War mobilization dramatically expanded the federal government. It also boosted geographical and social mobility as women, rural whites, and southern blacks took up work in new defense plants in the Midwest, California, and elsewhere. Government rules assisted both the labor movement and the African American campaign for civil rights. However, religious and racial animosity caused the exclusion of German Jewish refugees and the internment of 112,000 Japanese Americans.

As our account shows, Germany and Japan almost won the war in 1942. By 1943, the Allies had taken the offensive, with advances by the Soviet army in Europe and the American navy in the Pacific; by the end of 1944, Allied victory was all but certain. The United States emerged from the war with an undamaged homeland, sole possession of the atomic bomb, and a set of unresolved diplomatic disputes with the Soviet Union that would soon lead to a four-decade-long Cold War.

Connections: Government

The rise of the state has been a central theme of Part Five. As we stated in the essay that opened Part Five, "World War I called forth an unprecedented government-directed mobilization of the domestic economy," a process that we described in Chapter 22. Chapter 23 explained how that collaboration between government and business corporations continued in the 1920s, as Herbert Hoover promoted the "associated state" and "welfare capitalism." When the Great Depression revealed the flaws in this business-led system, Franklin Roosevelt's New Deal instituted new government programs to spur economic recovery and social welfare. As Chapter 24 made

TIMELINE

1933	▶ Adolf Hitler becomes chancellor of Germany
1935	▶ Italy invades Ethiopia
1935–1937	▶ U.S. Neutrality Acts
1936	▶ Germany reoccupies Rhineland
	▶ Rome-Berlin Axis established
	▶ Japan and Germany sign Anti-Comintern Pact
1937	▶ Japan invades China
1938	▶ Munich agreement between Germany, Britain, and France
1939	▶ Nazi-Soviet Nonaggression Pact
	▶ Germany invades Poland
	▶ Britain and France declare war on Germany
1940	▶ American conscription reinstated
	▶ Germany, Italy, and Japan sign Tri-Partite Pact
1941	▶ Germany invades Soviet Union
	▶ Lend-Lease Act passed
	▶ Fair Employment Practices Commission created
	▶ Atlantic Charter promulgated
	▶ Japanese attack Pearl Harbor

1942	▶ Allies suffer severe defeats in Europe and Asia
	▶ Executive Order 9066 leads to Japanese internment camps
	▶ Battles of Coral Sea and Midway halt Japanese advance
	▶ Women recruited for war industries
1942–1945	▶ Rationing of scarce goods
1943	▶ Race riots in Detroit and Los Angeles
	▶ Fascism falls in Italy
1944	▶ D-Day: Allied landing in France
	▶ GI Bill of Rights enacted
	▶ Supreme Court permits Japanese American internment
1945	▶ Yalta Conference
	▶ Battles of Iwo Jima and Okinawa
	▶ Germany surrenders
	▶ Harry S Truman becomes president after FDR's death
	▶ United Nations convenes
	▶ Atomic bombs dropped on Hiroshima and Nagasaki
	▶ Japan surrenders

clear, the National Recovery Act, the Agricultural Adjustment Act, the Works Project Administration, and other measures made the federal government's codes and policies a part of everyday life. Likewise, the ideology of social welfare liberalism, as manifest in the Social Security Act of 1935, gave the national government major responsibility for the welfare of American citizens. As we saw in Chapter 25, these links between the state and its citizenry grew more pervasive during World War II, with the advent of universal income taxation, passage of the GI Bill of Rights, and the creation of a military-industrial complex. As we noted in the part opening essay, "the new state apparatus remained in place when the fighting ended." In Part Six, which covers the period from 1945 to 1980, we will explain how the federal government remained a dominant force as it fought a Cold War abroad and expanded prosperity at home.

FOR FURTHER EXPLORATION

Henry Steele Commager, *The Story of World War II,* as revised by Donald L. Miller (2001), and Elizabeth Mullener, *War Stories* (2002), cover the military experience. For the home front, read John Morton Blum, *V Was for Victory* (1976), and Lewis A. Erenberg and Susan E. Hirsch, eds., *The War in American Culture* (1996). See also "Cents and Sacrifice" at **www.nauticom.net/www/harts/homefront.html** and "A People at War" at **www.archives.gov/exhibit_hall/index.html**. Powerful war novels include John Hersey, *A Bell for Adano* (1944); James Jones, *From Here to Eternity* (1951); and Norman Mailer, *The Naked and the Dead* (1948).

Two Web sites, **lcweb.loc.gov/exhibits/wcf/wcf0001.html** and **www.loc.gov/rr/print/list/126_rosi.html**, record the contributions of women. See also Sherna B. Gluck, *Rosie the Riveter Revisited* (1988).

Many sites cover the Japanese internment. See **www.lib.washington.edu/exhibits/harmony/default.htm**; **www.densho.org/densho.asp**; and **memory.loc.gov/ammem/aamhtml**. See also "Children of the Camps" at **www.children-of-the-camps.org**.

For oral interviews relating to war combat and civilian life, go to **lcweb2.loc.gov/ammem/afcphhtml/afcphhome.html** and **oralhistory.rutgers.edu**. Truman's decision to drop the atomic bomb remains controversial; log onto **www.lehigh.edu/~ineng/enola**. See also Kai Bird and Martin J. Sherwin, *American Prometheus: The Triumph and Tragedy of J. Robert Oppenheimer* (2005), a masterful biography of the bomb's principal architect.

TEST YOUR KNOWLEDGE

To assess your mastery of the material in this chapter and for Web sites, images, and documents related to this chapter, visit **bedfordstmartins.com/henrettaconcise**.

PART SIX

The Age of Cold War Liberalism

1945–1980

DIPLOMACY	POLITICS	ECONOMY
The Cold War	**Decline of the liberal consensus**	**Ups and downs of U.S. economic dominance**

	DIPLOMACY	POLITICS	ECONOMY
1945	▶ Truman Doctrine (1947) ▶ Marshall Plan (1948) ▶ Berlin blockade ▶ NATO founded (1949)	▶ Truman's Fair Deal liberalism ▶ Taft-Hartley Act (1947) ▶ Truman reelected (1948)	▶ Reconversion from wartime ▶ Strike wave (1946) ▶ Bretton Woods system established: World Bank, IMF
1950	▶ Permanent mobilization: NSC-68 (1950) ▶ Korean War (1950–1953) ▶ U.S replaces France in Vietnam	▶ McCarthyism ▶ Eisenhower's modern Republicanism ▶ Warren Court activism	▶ Rise of military-industrial complex ▶ Industrial economy booms ▶ Labor-management accord
1960	▶ Cuban missile crisis (1962) ▶ Vietnam War escalates (1965) ▶ Tet offensive (1968); peace talks begin	▶ Kennedy's New Frontier ▶ Kennedy assassinated ▶ Great Society, War on Poverty ▶ Nixon's election (1968) ushers in conservative era	▶ Kennedy-Johnson tax cut, military expenditures fuel economic growth
1970	▶ Nixon visits China (1972); SALT initiates détente (1972) ▶ Paris Peace Accords (1973) ▶ Carter brokers Camp David accords between Egypt and Israel (1978) ▶ Iranian revolution; hostage crisis (1979)	▶ Watergate scandal; Nixon resigns (1974) ▶ Weak presidencies of Ford and Carter	▶ Arab oil embargo (1973–1974); inflation surges, while income stagnates ▶ Onset of deindustrialization

SOCIETY	CULTURE
Social movements and demographic diversity	**Consumer culture and its critics**
▶ Migration to cities accelerates ▶ Armed forces desegregated (1948)	▶ End of wartime rationing ▶ Arrival of television ▶ First Levittown (1947)
▶ *Brown v. Board of Education* (1954) ▶ Montgomery bus boycott (1955) ▶ Urban crisis emerges	▶ Growth of suburbia ▶ Sun Belt emerges ▶ Religious revival ▶ Baby boom ▶ Youth culture develops
▶ March on Washington (1963) ▶ Civil rights legislation (1964, 1965) ▶ Student activism ▶ Black Power	▶ Shopping malls spread ▶ Baby boomers swell college enrollment ▶ Hippie counterculture
▶ Revival of feminism ▶ *Roe v. Wade* (1973) ▶ New Right urges conservative agenda	▶ Consumer and environmental protection movements ▶ Deepening social divide over ERA and gay rights

"What Rome was to the ancient world," proclaimed the influential journalist Walter Lippmann in 1945, "what Great Britain has been to the modern world, America is to be to the world of tomorrow." Lippmann's remark captures America's sense of triumphant confidence at the end of World War II. What Lippmann underestimated were the challenges, both global and domestic, confronting the United States. In Part Six, covering the years 1945–1980, we track how the United States fared in its quest to become the Rome of the twentieth century.

DIPLOMACY

Hardly had Lippmann penned his triumphant words in 1945 than the Soviet Union challenged America's plans for postwar Europe. The Truman administration responded by crafting the policies and alliances that came to define the Cold War. That struggle spawned two "hot" wars in Korea and Vietnam and fueled a terrifying nuclear arms race. By the early 1970s, as the bipolar assumptions of the Cold War broke down, the Nixon administration got on better terms with both the Soviet Union and China. The high hopes for détente, however, fell short, and during Carter's tenure, Soviet-U.S. relations lapsed into a state of anxious stalemate. The hostage crisis in Iran revealed that beyond the Cold War, other big challenges, especially from the aggrieved Muslim world, faced the United States.

POLITICS

Lippmann's confidence in America's future stemmed in part from his sense of a nation united on the big domestic questions. Except for a brief postwar reaction, which brought forth the Taft-Hartley Act (1947), the liberal consensus prevailed. And while not much headway was made by Truman's Fair Deal, neither did Republicans under Eisenhower attempt any dismantling of the New Deal. Johnson's ambitious Great Society, however, did provoke a conservative response, and beginning with the debacle of the Democratic convention of 1968, the country moved to the right. The interaction of the domestic and global — the links between liberalism and the Cold War — was especially clear at this juncture because it was Vietnam that, more than anything, undermined the Great Society and the liberal consensus. By the end of the 1970s, with a big assist from the Carter administration, the Democrats had lost the grip they had won under FDR as the nation's dominant party.

ECONOMY

In no realm did America's supremacy seem as secure in the postwar years as in economics. While the war-torn countries of Europe and Asia were picking through the rubble, the American economy boomed, fed both by the military-industrial complex and by a high-spending consumer culture. Real income grew, and collective bargaining became well entrenched. In the 1950s, no country had an economy that was competitive with America's. By the 1970s, however, American industry had been overtaken, and a sad process of dismantling — of deindustrialization — began. At the same time, the inflationary spiral initiated by the Vietnam War speeded up under the impact of the oil embargo of 1973. A decade of "stagflation" set in, and with it, a suspicion that America's vaunted economic powerhouse had seen its best days.

SOCIETY

The victory over Nazism in World War II spurred demands that America make good on its promise of equality for all. In great waves of protests beginning in the 1950s, African Americans—and then women, Latinos, gays, and other minorities—challenged the status quo. Starting with the landmark *Brown v. Board of Education* decision (1954), the country began to outlaw the practices of segregation, discrimination, and disfranchisement that had held minorities down. In the 1970s, however, reaction set in, fueled in part by the growing militancy of blacks and in part by the discovery of a resentful "silent majority" by conservative politicians. Achieving equality, it turned out, was easier said than done.

CULTURE

America's economic power in the postwar years spurred the development of a consumer society that cherished the tract house, the car, and the television set. As millions of Americans moved into suburban subdivisions, the birthrate speeded up, spawning a baby boom generation whose social influence would be felt for the next seventy-five years. Under the surface calm of the 1950s, a mood of cultural rebellion took hold. In the 1960s, it would burst forth in the hippie counterculture and the antiwar movement. Although both subsided in the early 1970s, they left a lasting impact on the country's politics, in particular, as fuel that fed the resurgence of American conservatism.

Walter Lippmann died in 1974. But he had lived long enough to see his high hopes of 1945 blasted by the Cold War, by economic troubles, and by the collapse of the liberal consensus.

Cold War America
1945–1960

> We have been in the
> process of fighting
> monsters without stop for
> a generation and a half,
> looking all that time into
> the nuclear abyss. And
> the abyss has looked back
> into us.
>
> —Daniel Ellsberg, 1971

On May 1, 1950, the residents of Mosinee, Wisconsin, staged a mock Communist takeover of their small mill town. Secret police interrogated citizens. The mayor was carted off to jail. The local paper reappeared as a mini-*Pravda*. Restaurants served only potato soup and black bread. Dreamed up by the American Legion, Mosinee's "Day Under Communism" was a sensational media event with a chilling message: America's way of life was under siege by the Communist menace.

The Mosinee episode captured an irony of life in postwar America. Americans in 1945 had indeed worried about what would follow victory, but not because of the Soviet Union. Weren't we all part of the Grand Alliance? No, what worried Americans was closer to home.

Defense plants were shutting down, war workers were being laid off, and twelve million job-seeking veterans were on the way home. Might the country slide back into the Great Depression? However, such fears soon dissipated. Home building picked up. Cars flowed off the assembly lines. Consumers began to spend like crazy the savings they had piled up during the war. The economy was in fact entering the strongest boom in American history. But instead of being able to settle back and enjoy their prosperity, the good people of Mosinee worried about a Soviet coup in their town. They had exchanged one fear—of economic hard times—for another: the Communist menace.

The conflict between the Soviet Union and the United States, although it did not lead to any direct engagement on the battlefield, inaugurated a long twilight era of international tension—a Cold War—during which either side, armed with nuclear weapons, might have tipped the entire world into oblivion.

At home, the Cold War fostered a climate of suspicion of "subversives" in government, education, and the media. It boosted military expenditures, fueling an arms race between the two superpowers, creating a "military-industrial complex" in the

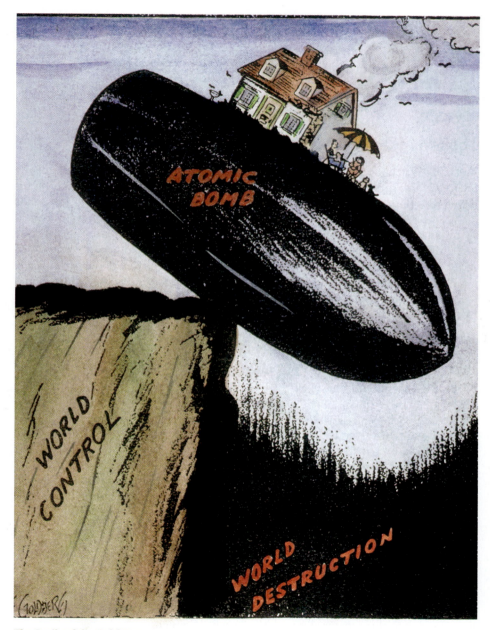

The Perils of the Cold War

In this detail of a 1948 Pulitzer Prize–winning cartoon, Rube Goldberg depicts the perilous nature of America's postwar peace — one that was based largely on atomic supremacy and the threat of nuclear annihilation. University of California at Berkeley, Bancroft Library.

For more help analyzing this image, see the Online Study Guide at **bedfordstmartins.com/henrettaconcise.**

United States, and undergirding an amazing era of economic expansion (see Chapter 27). This prosperity meant that the country could afford to invest more in New Deal programs. But the Cold War also held liberal politics hostage because the ability of the New Deal coalition to advance its domestic agenda depended on its prowess as a Cold Warrior abroad. In all these ways, the line between the international and the domestic blurred. That was an enduring legacy of the Cold War.

The Cold War

The Cold War began in 1946. It ended forty-five years later with the collapse of the Soviet Union. In that intervening period, a vast amount was written by historians about why the Cold War had happened. By no means did all American historians blame the Soviets. Eventually, indeed, the "revisionist" historians—those who held that the United States was primarily at fault—often had the upper hand. The debate was ultimately inconclusive, however, because the scholarly conditions that prevailed really precluded definitive history. For one thing, the Soviet archives were completely closed. More important, perhaps, historians were trying to capture an event that was still unfolding. Only now that it is over can historians look back and gain the perspective needed for understanding why the Cold War occurred.

Descent into Cold War, 1945–1946

World War II itself set the basic conditions for Cold War rivalry. With Germany and Japan defeated and America's British and French allies exhausted, only the two superpowers remained standing in 1945. Even had nothing else divided them, the United States and the Soviet Union would have jostled each other as they moved to fill the vacuum. But, of course, the two countries *were* divided—by ideology, by history, by geography and strategic interest, even by relative power (with the advantage, both militarily and economically, heavily on the American side).

FDR understood that maintaining the U.S.-Soviet alliance was an essential condition for postwar stability. But he also believed that permanent peace depended on the Wilsonian principles of collective security, self-determination, and free trade (see Chapter 22). The challenge was to find a way of reconciling Wilsonian principles with U.S.-Soviet power realities.

This was the challenge that Roosevelt, Churchill, and Stalin faced at the Yalta Conference of February 1945. They agreed there to go forward with the United Nations. The realist side of that grand plan for fostering world peace, demanded by both the U.S. and the Soviet Union, was that permanent seats with veto rights be reserved for them (and their three major allies) on the Security Council.

The paramount problem at Yalta, however, was eastern Europe. Roosevelt and Churchill agreed that Poland and its neighbors would fall under the Soviet "sphere of influence," thus meeting Stalin's demand for secure eastern borders. But the Yalta agreement also called for "free and unfettered" elections, thus upholding the essential principle of democratic self-determination. Implicit in Yalta's details was an expectation—the nub of the deal—that freely elected governments would consent to Soviet domination.

That actually had happened in Finland and, after Yalta, briefly in Czechoslovakia. It could not happen in Poland. For that, Stalin had himself to blame. In 1939, with war impending, he had made his infamous secret pact with Hitler for the partition of Poland. When the Nazis invaded, the Soviet Union seized its apportioned share (and reclaimed much of it when the Nazis retreated in 1944). Then Stalin ordered the execution of the entire Polish officer corps in Katyn Forest, a deed that, when exposed by the Nazis in 1943, caused a rift with the Polish government-in-exile in London. Equally unforgivable was Stalin's betrayal of the Poles of Warsaw late in the war. When they rose against the Germans, the Red Army halted on the outskirts so that any potential anti-Communist opposition could be finished off by the Nazis. Evidently blind to the resentment of his victims, Stalin—American observers reported—was taken aback by the fear and loathing that greeted his approaching armies.

So free elections were out of the question in Poland, a conclusion that Stalin had already arrived at before Yalta. He got the puppet regime he required but never the consent of the Poles or of the Hungarians, Romanians, and other subject peoples of eastern Europe. Stalin's unwillingness—his inability, if he was to fulfill his ambitions—to hold free elections was the precipitating event of the Cold War.

Historians doubt that, had he lived, even the resourceful Roosevelt could have preserved the Grand Alliance. With Harry Truman, no such possibility existed. Truman was inexperienced in foreign affairs. As vice president, he had been kept in the dark about Roosevelt's negotiations. His blunt instinct was to stand up to Stalin. At a meeting held shortly after he took office, the fledgling president berated the Soviet foreign minister, V. M. Molotov, over the Soviets' failure to honor their Yalta agreements. He abruptly halted lend-lease shipments that the Soviets desperately needed and denied their request for $6 billion in credits. Truman used what he called "tough methods" that July at the Potsdam Conference, which had been called to take up postwar planning. After learning of the successful test of America's atomic bomb, Truman "told the Russians just where they got off and generally bossed the whole meeting," recalled Winston Churchill.

Stalin was not taken by surprise. His spy network had kept him informed about the Manhattan Project virtually from its inception in 1942—far earlier than Truman himself knew about it. Nor was Stalin intimidated. His spies assured him that the small American arsenal posed no immediate threat to the Soviet Union. And his own scientists were on a crash course to producing a Soviet bomb, their efforts much eased by atomic bomb blueprints stolen from the Manhattan Project. It was a time, as Stalin said, for strong nerves.

But the atomic issue did enflame tensions, requiring extra displays of toughness by the Soviets, deepening their suspicions of the West, and, on the American side, encouraging a certain swagger. It was unwise, warned Secretary of War Stimson, for the United States to try to negotiate with "this weapon rather ostentatiously on our hip."

In early 1946, the United States tried to head off the impending nuclear race, proposing in the Baruch Plan (named for its sponsor, the financier Bernard Baruch) that all weapons-related development and production be placed under the control of a special U.N. atomic agency. Once international enforcement was fully in place, the United States would dispose of its stockpile of atomic bombs.

Hot on the trail of their own bomb, the Soviets, although they went through the motions of negotiation, rejected the Baruch Plan as an American trick to dominate them. Its failure foreshadowed a frenzied nuclear arms race.

By then, Truman's instinctive toughness was being seconded by his more seasoned advisors, a distinguished group known collectively as the Establishment for their elite pedigrees and high-placed public service. Close students of diplomacy, expert in some cases on Soviet affairs, they concluded that Stalin's actions in eastern Europe were not an aberration but truly reflective of Stalin's despotic regime.

A cogent summary of their views came, ironically, from a former Russian foreign minister, Maxim Litvinoff, who had negotiated America's recognition of the Soviet Union with FDR in 1933. Lamenting the end of wartime cooperation, Litvinoff told a CBS Moscow correspondent that the Soviet Union had returned "to the outmoded concept of security in terms of territory — the more you've got, the safer you are." This was because "the ideological concept prevailing here [is] that conflict between Communist and capitalist worlds is inevitable." The Soviet Union was at that time, in early 1946, expanding its reach, stationing troops in northern Iran, pressing Turkey for access to the Mediterranean, and sponsoring a guerrilla war in Greece. If the current Soviet demands were satisfied, the CBS man asked, what then? "It would lead to the West's being faced, after a more or less short time, with the next set of demands, " replied Litvinoff.

The Containment Strategy

Just how the West should respond was crystallized in February 1946 by George F. Kennan in an 8,000-word cable, dubbed the "Long Telegram," from his post at the U.S. embassy in Moscow. Kennan argued that the Soviet Union was an "Oriental despotism" and Communism just "the fig-leaf" justifying its crimes. For Soviet leaders, hostility to the West provided the essential excuse "for the dictatorship without which they do not know how to rule." The West had no way of altering this perverse internal dynamic. Its only recourse, Kennan wrote in a famous *Foreign Affairs* article a year later, was to meet the Soviets "with unalterable counter-force at every point where they show signs of encroaching upon the interests of a peaceful and stable world." Kennan called for "long-term, patient but firm and vigilant *containment* of Russian expansive tendencies."

Containment, the key word, defined America's evolving strategic stance against the Soviet Union, and Kennan, its author, became one of the most influential advisors in the Truman administration.

On its face, containment seemed a counsel of despair, dooming the United States to a draining, inconclusive struggle without end. In fact, Kennan was more optimistic than that. The Soviet system, he argued with notable foresight, was inherently unstable, and eventually — not in Stalin's time, but eventually — it would collapse. Moreover, the Soviets were not reckless. "If . . . situations can be created in which [conflict] is not to [their] advantage," they would pull back. So it was up to the West to create those situations, avoiding an arms race, picking its fights carefully, exercising patience.

Kennan's attentive readers included Stalin, who had quickly obtained a copy of the classified Long Telegram. To keep things even, Stalin ordered his ambassador in Washington to prepare his own Long Telegram and got back an eerie mirror image of Kennan's analysis, with the United States cast as imperialist aggressor, driven by the crisis of monopoly capitalism, and spending "colossally" on arms and overseas bases.

Like Kennan, the Soviet ambassador was confident of the adversary's instability but, in his case, from a rather shorter-term perspective. America's problem was its British alliance, which was "plagued with great internal contradictions" and bound to explode, probably over differences in the Middle East.

The alliance, in fact, was in difficulty—not out of conflicting interests but because of British exhaustion. In February 1947, London informed Truman that it could no longer afford to support the anti-Communists in Greece, where a bitter guerrilla war was going on. If the Communists won in Greece, Truman worried, that would embolden the Communist parties in France and Italy and, of more immediate concern, lead to Soviet domination of the eastern Mediterranean. In response, the president announced what came to be known as the Truman Doctrine. In a speech on March 12, he asserted an American responsibility "to support free peoples who are resisting attempted subjugation by armed minorities or by outside pressures." To that end, Truman proposed large-scale assistance for Greece and Turkey. "If we falter in our leadership, we may endanger the peace of the world," Truman declared, and "we shall surely endanger the welfare of our own nation." Despite the open-endedness of this military commitment, Congress quickly approved Truman's request for $300 million in aid to Greece and $100 million for Turkey.

In the meantime, Europe was sliding into economic chaos. Devastated by the war, the continent was hit by the worst winter in memory in 1947. People were starving, and European credit was nearing zero. At Secretary of State George C. Marshall's behest, Kennan's small team of advisors came up with a remarkable proposal: a massive infusion of American capital to help get the European economy back on its feet. Speaking at the Harvard commencement in June 1947, Marshall urged the nations of Europe to work out a comprehensive recovery program and then ask the United States for aid, which would be forthcoming.

Truman's pledge of financial aid met significant opposition in Congress. Republicans castigated the Marshall Plan as a huge "international W.P.A." But in the midst of the congressional stalemate, on February 25, 1948, came a Communist takeover in Czechoslovakia. A stark reminder of Soviet ruthlessness, the coup rallied congressional support for the Marshall Plan. In March 1948, Congress voted overwhelmingly to approve funds for the program. Like most other foreign-policy initiatives of the 1940s and 1950s, the Marshall Plan won bipartisan support.

Over the next four years, the United States contributed nearly $13 billion to a highly successful recovery effort. Western European economies revived, industrial production increased 64 percent, and the appeal of the local Communist parties waned. The Marshall Plan was actually a good deal for the United States, providing stronger markets for American goods and fostering the economic interdependence that it wanted to encourage in Europe (see Voices from Abroad, p. 772). Most notably, the Marshall Plan was a strategic masterstroke.

The Soviets had been invited to participate. At first, they did; then Stalin, sensing a trap, ordered his delegation home and, on further reflection, ordered the satellite delegations home as well. It was a clumsy performance, placing the onus for dividing Europe on the Soviets and depriving their threadbare partners of assistance they sorely needed.

The flash point for a hot war, if it existed anywhere, was Germany. This was because the stakes were so high for both sides and because the German situation

Truman's Generous Proposal   JEAN MONNET

Jean Monnet was an eminent French statesman and a tireless promoter of European union. As head of a French postwar planning commission, he helped to oversee the dispersal of Marshall Plan funds, the importance of which he describes in his memoirs.

So we had at last concerted our efforts to halt France's economic decline; but now, once more, everything seemed to be at risk. Two years earlier [1947], we thought that we had plumbed the depths of material poverty. Now we were threatened with the loss of even basic essentials. . . . Our dollar resources were melting away at an alarming rate, because we were having to buy American wheat to replace the crops we had lost during the winter. . . . A further American loan was soon exhausted.

Nor was this grim situation confined to France. Britain too had come to the end of her resources. In February 1947 she had abruptly cancelled her aid to Greece and Turkey, whose burdens she had seemed able to assume in 1945. Overnight, this abrupt abdication gave the United States direct responsibility for part of Europe. Truman did not hesitate for a moment: with the decisiveness that was to mark his actions as President, he at once asked for credits and arms for both Turkey and Greece. . . . [Soon after], he announced the Truman Doctrine of March 12, 1947. Its significance was general: it meant that the United States would prevent Europe from becoming a depressed area at the mercy of Communist advance. On the very same day, the Four-Power Conference began in Moscow. There, for a whole month, George Marshall, Ernest

Bevin, and Georges Bidault argued with Vyacheslav Molotov about all the problems of the peace, and above all about Germany.

When Marshall returned to Washington, he knew that for a long time there would be no further genuine dialogue with Stalin's Russia. The "Cold War," as it was soon to be known, had begun. . . . Information from a number of sources convinced Marshall and his Under-Secretary Dean Acheson that once again, as in 1941, the United States had a great historic duty. And once again there took place what I had witnessed in Washington a few years earlier: a small group of men brought to rapid maturity an idea which, when the Executive gave the word, turned into vigorous action. This time, it was done by five or six people, in total secrecy and at lightning speed. Marshall, Acheson, [William] Clayton, Averell Harriman, and George Kennan worked out a proposal of unprecedented scope and generosity. It took us all by surprise when we read the speech that George Marshall made at Harvard on June 5, 1947. Chance had led him to choose the university's Commencement Day to launch something new in international relations: helping others to help themselves.

SOURCE: Jean Monnet, *Memoirs,* trans. Richard Mayne (New York: Doubleday, 1978), 264–266.

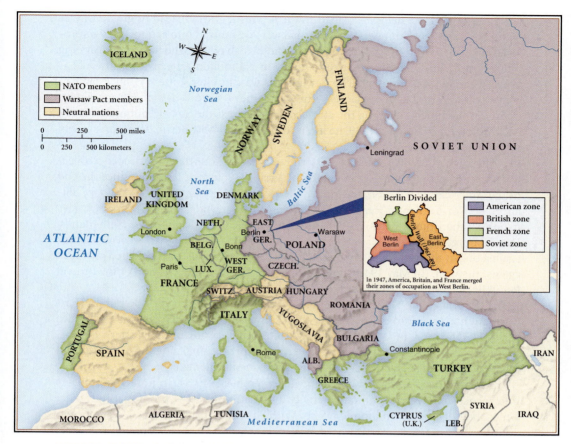

MAP 26.1 Cold War in Europe, 1955

In 1949, the United States sponsored the creation of the North Atlantic Treaty Organization (NATO) — an alliance of ten European nations, the United States, and Canada. West Germany was formally admitted to NATO in May 1955. A few days later, the Soviet Union and seven other Communist nations established a rival alliance, the Warsaw Pact. The divided city of Berlin, with West Berlin located deep in Communist East Germany, was a major flash point in Cold War controversies.

initially was so fluid. At Yalta, Germany's future had been left undecided except that it would be made to pay heavy reparations and be permanently demilitarized. For the time being, a defeated Germany would be divided into four zones of occupation controlled by the Soviet Union, the United States, Britain, and France. A similar arrangement later applied to Berlin (see Map 26.1). When no agreement for a unified state was forthcoming in 1947, the western allies consolidated their zones and prepared to establish an independent federal German republic, supported by an infusion of Marshall Plan money.

Some of that money was slated for West Berlin, in hopes of making it a capitalist showplace deep inside the Soviet zone. On its face, of course, the Allied presence in Berlin was anomalous, an accident of interim wartime arrangements, and was indefensible against the Soviets. That, at any rate, was the way Stalin saw it.

In June 1948, he halted all Allied traffic to West Berlin. Instead of giving way, as Stalin had expected, Truman and the British were galvanized into action. They improvised an airlift. For nearly a year, American and British pilots, who had been dropping bombs on Berlin only four years earlier, flew in 2.5 million tons of food and fuel—nearly a ton for each resident. The Berlin crisis was the closest the two sides came to actual war and probably the closest America came—since it had no other military option at the time—to using the atomic bomb against the Soviet Union. But Stalin backed down. On May 12, 1949, he lifted the blockade. West Berlin became a symbol of resistance to Communism.

The crisis in Berlin persuaded western European nations that they needed a collective security pact with the United States. In April 1949, for the first time since the end of the American Revolution, the United States entered into a peacetime military alliance, the North Atlantic Treaty Organization (NATO). Under the NATO pact, twelve nations—the United States, Canada, Britain, France, Italy, Belgium, the Netherlands, Luxembourg, Denmark, Norway, Portugal, and Iceland—agreed that "an armed attack against one or more of them in Europe or North America shall be considered an attack against them all." In May 1949, those nations also agreed to the creation of the Federal Republic of Germany (West Germany), which joined NATO in 1955.

In response, the Soviet Union set up the German Democratic Republic (East Germany); an economic association, the Council for Mutual Economic Assistance (COMECON); and, in 1955, the Warsaw Pact, a military alliance for eastern Europe. In these parallel steps, the two superpowers were institutionalizing the Cold War and thereby translating tense uncertainty into permanent stalemate.

The final stage in that process came in September 1949, when American military intelligence detected a rise in radioactivity in the atmosphere—proof that the Soviet Union had detonated an atomic bomb. With America's brief tenure as sole nuclear power over, there was a pressing need for a major reassessment of the nation's strategic planning. Truman turned to the National Security Council (NSC), an advisory body established by the National Security Act of 1947 that also created the Department of Defense and the Central Intelligence Agency (CIA).

In April 1950, the NSC delivered its report, known as "NSC-68." Bristling with alarmist rhetoric, the document urged a crash program to maintain America's nuclear edge, including the development of a hydrogen bomb, a thermonuclear device that would be a thousand times more destructive than the atomic bombs that had destroyed Hiroshima and Nagasaki. What American intelligence did not know was that Soviet scientists, unlike their American counterparts, had been working on both tracks all along and were making headway toward a hydrogen bomb. The United States got there first, exploding its first hydrogen bomb in November 1952; the Soviet Union followed in 1953.

Although he accepted the NCS-68 recommendation, Truman had grave misgivings about the furies he was unleashing. This was apparent in his decision to lodge control over nuclear weapons in a civilian agency, not with the military. Truman did not want nuclear weapons incorporated into military planning and treated as a functional part of the nation's arsenal (as they had been at Hiroshima and Nagasaki). Evidence suggests that Stalin had similar misgivings. And with the advent of the hydrogen bomb, the utility of nuclear devices as actual weapons shrank to zero. No political objective could possibly be worth the destructiveness of a thermonuclear exchange.

Testing the Bomb

After World War II, the development of nuclear weapons went on apace, requiring frequent testing to check the capabilities of the more advanced weapons. This photograph shows members of the 11th Airborne Division viewing the mushroom cloud from one such A-bomb test at the Atomic Energy Commission's proving grounds at Yucca Flats in Nevada on November 1, 1951. Finally acknowledging the dangers to the atmosphere (and the people in the vicinity or downwind), the United States and the Soviet Union signed a treaty in 1963 banning above-ground testing. J. R. Eyerman/Time Life Pictures/Getty Images.

A "balance of terror" now prevailed. Paradoxically, that magnified the importance of conventional forces. The United States, having essentially demobilized its wartime army, had treated the atomic bomb as the equalizer against the vast Soviet army. Now, if it wanted a credible deterrent, the only option was a stronger conventional military. To that end, NSC-68 called for increased taxes to finance "a bold and massive program of rebuilding the West's defensive potential to surpass that of the Soviet world." Truman was reluctant to commit to a major defense buildup, fearing that it would overburden the budget. Two months after NSC-68 was completed, events in Asia took that decision out of his hands.

Containment in Asia

Containment was aimed primarily at Soviet expansion in Europe. But as tensions built up in Asia, Cold War doctrines began to influence the American position there as well. At first, America's attention centered on Japan. After dismantling Japan's military, American occupation forces under General Douglas MacArthur drafted a democratic constitution and oversaw the rebuilding of the economy, paving the way for the restoration of Japanese sovereignty in 1951. Considering the scorched-earth war that had just ended, this was a remarkable achievement, thanks partly to the imperious MacArthur but mainly to the Japanese, who put their militaristic past behind them and embraced peace. However, trouble on the mainland then drew America's attention, and the Cold War mentality kicked in.

A civil war had been raging in China since the 1930s as Communist forces led by Mao Zedong (Mao Tse-tung) contended for power with Nationalist forces under Jiang Jieshi (Chiang Kai-shek). Although dissatisfied with the corrupt Jiang regime, American officials did not see Mao as a good alternative, and they resigned themselves to supporting the Nationalists. Between 1945 and 1949, the United States provided more than $2 billion to Jiang's forces, but in August 1949 the Truman administration gave up on the Nationalists and cut off aid. By then, their fate was sealed. The People's Republic of China was formally established under Mao on October 1, 1949, and the remnants of Jiang's forces fled to Taiwan.

Initially, the American response was muted. Both Stalin and Truman expected Mao to take an independent line, as the Communist Tito had just done in Yugoslavia. Mao, however, aligned himself with the Soviet Union, partly out of exaggerated fears that the United States would rearm the Nationalists and send them back to the mainland. As attitudes hardened, many Americans viewed Mao's success as a defeat for the United States. A pro-Nationalist "China lobby" accused Truman's State Department of being responsible for the "loss" of China.

Sensitive to these charges, the Truman administration refused to recognize "Red China" and blocked China's admission to the United Nations. But the United States pointedly refused to guarantee Taiwan's independence, and in fact accepted the outcome on the mainland. Not taken into account, however, was a country that few Americans had ever heard of: Korea, which had been a part of the Japanese empire since 1910.

In Korea, as in Germany, Cold War confrontation grew out of interim arrangements made at the end of the war. The United States and the Soviet Union, both with troops in Korea, had agreed to occupy the nation jointly, dividing their sectors at the thirty-eighth parallel, pending Korea's unification. As tensions rose in Europe, the thirty-eighth parallel hardened into a permanent demarcation line. The Soviets supported a Communist government, led by Kim Il Sung, in North Korea; the United States backed a long-time Korean nationalist, Syngman Rhee, in South Korea.

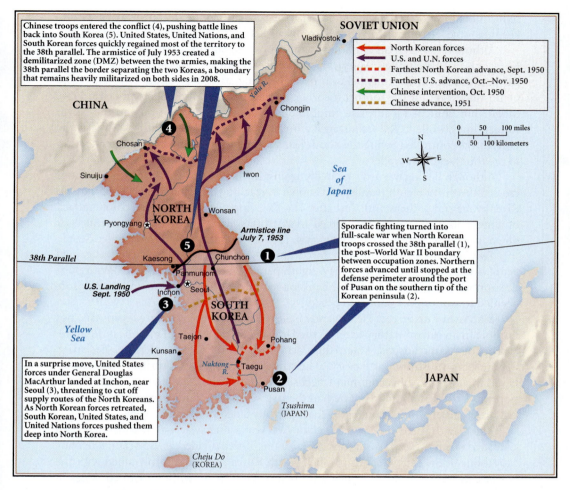

Chinese troops entered the conflict (4), pushing battle lines back into South Korea (5). United States, United Nations, and South Korean forces quickly regained most of the territory to the 38th parallel. The armistice of July 1953 created a demilitarized zone (DMZ) between the two armies, making the 38th parallel the border separating the two Koreas, a boundary that remains heavily militarized on both sides in 2008.

SOVIET UNION

◀──	North Korean forces
◀──	U.S. and U.N. forces
▪▪▪▪	Farthest North Korean advance, Sept. 1950
▪▪▪▪	Farthest U.S. advance, Oct.–Nov. 1950
◀──	Chinese intervention, Oct. 1950
▪▪▪▪	Chinese advance, 1951

Sporadic fighting turned into full-scale war when North Korean troops crossed the 38th parallel (1), the post–World War II boundary between occupation zones. Northern forces advanced until stopped at the defense perimeter around the port of Pusan on the southern tip of the Korean peninsula (2).

In a surprise move, United States forces under General Douglas MacArthur landed at Inchon, near Seoul (3), threatening to cut off supply routes of the North Koreans. As North Korean forces retreated, South Korean, United States, and United Nations forces pushed them deep into North Korea.

MAP 26.2 The Korean War, 1950–1953

The Korean War, which the United Nations officially deemed a "police action," lasted three years and cost the lives of over 36,000 U.S. troops. South and North Korean deaths were estimated at over 900,000. Although hostilities ceased in 1953, the U.S. military and the North Korean army continue to face each other across the demilitarized zone more than fifty years later.

For more help analyzing this map, see the Online Study Guide at **bedfordstmartins.com/henrettaconcise**.

Both leaders were spoiling for a fight, but neither could launch an all-out offensive without the backing of his sponsor. Washington repeatedly said no, and so did Moscow—until Stalin, reading a speech by Secretary of State Dean Acheson declaring South Korea outside America's "defense perimeter," concluded that the United States would not intervene.

On June 25, 1950, the North Koreans launched a surprise attack across the thirty-eighth parallel (Map 26.2). Truman immediately asked the U.N. Security Council to authorize a "police action" against the invaders. The Soviet Union was temporarily boycotting the Security Council to protest China's exclusion from the United Nations, so it could not veto Truman's request. With the Security Council's approval of a "peace-keeping force," Truman ordered U.S. troops to Korea.

Although fourteen other nations sent troops, the rapidly assembled U.N. army in Korea was overwhelmingly American, with General Douglas MacArthur in command. At first, the North Koreans held an overwhelming advantage, occupying the entire peninsula except for the southeast corner around Pusan. But on September 15, 1950, MacArthur launched a surprise amphibious attack at Inchon, far behind the North Korean lines, while U.N. forces staged a breakout from Pusan. Within two weeks, the U.N. forces controlled Seoul, the South Korean capital, and almost all the territory up to the thirty-eighth parallel.

Although Beijing warned repeatedly against further incursions, MacArthur's troops crossed the thirty-eighth parallel on October 9, reaching the Chinese border at the Yalu River by the end of the month. Just after Thanksgiving, a massive Chinese counterattack of almost 300,000 "volunteers" forced MacArthur's forces into headlong retreat back down the Korean peninsula. On January 4, 1951, Communist troops reoccupied Seoul.

Two months later, American forces and their allies counterattacked, regained Seoul, and pushed back to the thirty-eighth parallel. Then stalemate set in. With public support in the United States for a prolonged war waning, Truman and his advisors decided to work for a negotiated peace.

MacArthur disagreed. He fervently believed that America's future lay in Asia, not Europe. In an inflammatory letter to the House minority leader, Republican Joseph J. Martin of Massachusetts, MacArthur denounced the Korean stalemate, declaring, "There is no substitute for victory." The strategy backfired. On April 11, Truman relieved MacArthur of his command, accusing him of insubordination. Truman's decision was highly unpopular, but he had the last word. After failing to win the Republican presidential nomination in 1952, MacArthur faded from public view.

The war dragged on for more than two years after MacArthur's dismissal. An armistice was not signed until July 1953, leaving Korea divided at the original demarcation line at the thirty-eighth parallel. North Korea remained firmly allied with the Soviet Union; South Korea signed a mutual defense treaty with the United States in 1954. The Korean War had lasting consequences. Truman's decision to commit troops without congressional approval set a precedent for future undeclared wars. His refusal to unleash atomic bombs, even when American forces were reeling under a massive Chinese attack, set ground rules for Cold War conflict. The war also expanded American involvement in Asia, transforming containment into a truly global policy.

▶ Why was the United States unable to avoid entering a Cold War with the Soviet Union?

▶ How were the ideas of George F. Kennan reflected in Truman's Cold War policies?

▶ What was the long-term significance of the Korean War?

Finally, Korea ended Truman's resistance to a major military buildup. Overall defense expenditures grew from $13 billion in 1950, roughly one-third of the federal budget, to $50 billion in 1953, nearly two-thirds of the budget. Although military expenditures dropped briefly after the Korean War, defense spending remained at over $35 billion annually throughout the 1950s. American foreign policy had become more global, more militarized, and more expensive. Even in times of peace, the United States now functioned in a state of permanent mobilization.

The Korean War
As a result of Harry Truman's 1948 executive order, the Korean War marked the first time in the nation's history that all troops, such as the men of the Second Infantry Battalion, shown here in Korea in 1950, served in racially integrated combat units. National Archives.

The Truman Era

Harry Truman never intended to be a caretaker president. He had big plans. On September 16, 1945, just fourteen days after Japan surrendered, Truman called for a dramatic expansion of the New Deal, fulfilling the expansive Economic Bill of Rights that Roosevelt had famously proclaimed in his State of the Union Address in 1944 (see Chapter 25). Truman phrased his proposals in just that way, as rights expected by all Americans—the right to a "useful and remunerative" job, good housing, "adequate medical care," "protection from the economic fears of old age," and a "good education." Truman had no way of foreseeing the confounding forces lying in wait. In the end, his high hopes were crushed, and Truman went down in history not, as he had hoped, as FDR's worthy successor, but as a Cold Warrior.

Reconversion

No sooner had Truman finished laying out his domestic program than he was beset by cascading problems over converting the wartime economy to peacetime. Toward the end of the war, left in the dark about the atomic bomb, government planners had assumed that reconversion would be phased in while Japan was being subdued. When the war suddenly ended, no reconversion plan was in place. The hasty dismantling of the vast wartime machine frustrated liberal planners, who had hoped to give small businesses a head start in the peacetime market while the big manufacturers were still bogged down by war production. What worried Truman, however, was runaway inflation. He wanted to keep the wartime Office of Price Administration in place while domestic production caught up with pent-up demand. His efforts at price control were overwhelmed by consumers impatient to spend money and businesses eager to take it from them. The result was that consumer prices soared by 33 percent in the immediate postwar years.

Organized labor was stronger than it had ever been. Union membership swelled to over fourteen million by 1945. Determined to make up for their wartime sacrifices, unionized workers made aggressive demands and mounted crippling strikes in the automobile, steel, and coal industries. General strikes — strikes covering the entire labor force — brought normal life to a halt in half a dozen cities in 1946.

Truman responded erratically. In some cases, he gave way as, for example, when he lifted price controls on steel in early 1946 so that the industry could grant strikers' wage demands. In other instances, Truman tried to show union leaders who was boss. Faced with a devastating railway strike, he threatened to federalize the nation's railroad system and asked Congress for the power to draft striking workers into the army, moves that infuriated union leaders but got the strikers back to work. In November 1946, when coal miners called a strike as winter approached, Truman secured a sweeping court order against the union. Its imperious leader John L. Lewis, having been slapped with a huge fine, tried to negotiate, but Truman turned him away, remarking that he was not going to have "that son of a bitch" in the White House.

Truman's display of toughness against organized labor did little to placate the Republicans, who, having gained control of both houses of Congress in 1946, moved quickly to curb labor's power. In alliance with conservative southern Democrats, they passed the Taft-Hartley Act (1947), a sweeping overhaul of the 1935 National Labor Relations Act. Some of the new provisions aimed at perceived abuses: the secondary boycott, crippling national strikes, and unionization of supervisory employees. Ultimately of greater significance, however, were skillfully crafted changes in procedures and language that, over time, eroded the law's stated purpose of protecting the right of workers to organize and engage in collective bargaining. Unions especially disliked Section 14b, which allowed states to pass "right-to-work" laws prohibiting the **union shop**. Truman issued a ringing veto of the Taft-Hartley bill in June 1947, but Congress overrode the veto.

By 1947, most observers wouldn't have bet a nickel on Truman's future. His popularity ratings had plummeted, and "To err is Truman" became a favorite political jibe. Democrats would have dumped him in 1948 had they found a better candidate. As it was, the party fell into disarray. The left wing split off and formed the Progressive Party, nominating as its candidate Henry A. Wallace, an avid New Dealer whom Truman had fired as secretary of commerce in 1946 because of his vocal opposition to the Cold War. The right-wing challenge came from the South. When northern liberals such as Mayor Hubert H. Humphrey of Minneapolis pushed through a strong civil rights platform at the Democratic convention, the southern delegations bolted and, calling themselves Dixiecrats, nominated Governor J. Strom Thurmond of South Carolina for president. The Republicans meanwhile renominated Thomas E. Dewey, the politically moderate governor of New York who had run a strong campaign against FDR in 1944.

Truman Triumphant

In one of the most famous photographs in American political history, Harry S Truman gloats over an inaccurate headline in the *Chicago Daily Tribune.* Pollsters had predicted a victory for Thomas E. Dewey. However, their primitive polling techniques did not reflect the dramatic surge in support for Truman during the last days of the campaign.
© Bettmann/Corbis.

Truman surprised everyone. He launched a strenuous cross-country speaking tour and hammered away at the Republicans for opposing progressive legislation and, in general, for running a "do-nothing" Congress. By combining these issues with attacks on the Soviet menace abroad, Truman began to salvage his troubled campaign. At his rallies, enthusiastic listeners shouted, "Give 'em hell, Harry!"

Truman won a remarkable victory, receiving 49.6 percent of the vote to Dewey's 45.1 percent. The Democrats also regained control of both houses of Congress. Strom Thurmond carried only four southern states, while Henry Wallace failed to win any electoral votes. Truman retained the support of organized labor, Jewish and Catholic voters in the big cities, and black voters in the North. Most important, he appealed effectively to people like himself from the farms, towns, and small cities in the nation's heartland.

The Fair Deal

In his 1949 State of the Union address, Truman rechristened his program "the Fair Deal." It incorporated the goals he had set out initially—national health insurance, aid to education, a housing program, expansion of Social Security, a higher minimum wage, and a new agricultural program—but also struck out in some new directions. In its attention to civil rights (see Chapter 27), the Fair Deal reflected the growing importance of African Americans to the Democratic Party's urban coalition. And raising the living standards of an ever-greater number of citizens reflected a new liberal vision of the role of the state.

Truman was inspired by the renowned English economist John Maynard Keynes, who had argued that government's **fiscal policy** was capable of preventing economic depressions. In bad times, deficit spending would "prime the pump," reigniting consumer spending and private investment and restoring prosperity. The Employment

Act of 1946, which established a Council of Economic Advisors to assist the president, embodied this Keynesian policy. Truman wanted the Employment Act reinforced by raising its goal to "full" employment and by expanding welfare programs that would undergird consumer purchasing power.

Among the opportunities that came and went, the most notable, in light of the nation's current health-care crisis, was the proposal for national health insurance. This was a popular idea, with strong backing from organized labor, but it was denounced as "socialized medicine" by the American Medical Association, the insurance industry (which had spotted a new profit center), and big corporations, which (to their eventual regret) preferred providing health coverage directly to employees. Lobbying groups were equally effective at defeating Truman's agricultural reforms, which aimed at helping small farmers, and federal aid to education. In the end, the only significant breakthrough, other than improvements in the minimum wage and Social Security, was the National Housing Act of 1949, which authorized the construction of 810,000 low-income units.

Despite Democratic majorities, Congress remained a huge stumbling block. The same conservative coalition that had blocked Roosevelt's initiatives in his second term continued the fight against the Fair Deal. On top of this came the Cold War. The outbreak of fighting in Korea in 1950 was especially damaging, diverting national attention and federal funds from domestic affairs. Another potent diversion was the nation's growing paranoia over internal subversion, the most dramatic effect of the Cold War on American life.

The Great Fear

Was there any significant Soviet penetration of the American government? Historians had mostly debunked the idea, and so, in earlier editions, did this textbook. But we were wrong. Records that have been opened up since 1991 — intelligence files in Moscow and, among U.S. sources, most importantly, the Venona intercepts of Soviet cables — name among American suppliers of information FDR's assistant secretary of the Treasury Department (Harry Dexter White); FDR's administrative aide (Laughlin Currie); a midlevel, strategically placed group in the State Department (including Alger Hiss, who was with FDR at Yalta); and several hundred more, some identified only by code name, working in a range of government departments and agencies.

What are we to make of this? Many of these enlistees in the Soviet cause had been bright young New Dealers in the mid-1930s, when Moscow's Popular Front suggested — to the uninformed, at any rate — that the lines between liberal, progressive, and Communist were blurred and permeable (see Chapter 25). At that time, in the mid-1930s, the United States was not at war and never expected to be. And when war did come, the Soviet Union was an American ally.

The flow of stolen documents speeded up and kept Soviet intelligence privy to all aspects of the American war effort. What most interested Stalin were U.S. intentions about a second front and—an obsessive fear of his—a separate deal with Hitler. Another was, of course, the atomic bomb. Even here, people turned a blind eye to Soviet espionage. Indeed, many Los Alamos scientists thought it a mistake not to tell the Soviets about the bomb. J. Robert Oppenheimer, the director of the Manhattan Project, was inclined to agree. He just didn't like "the idea of having the [secrets] moved out the back door."

Once the Cold War set in, of course, Oppenheimer's indulgent view of Soviet espionage became utterly inadmissible, and the government moved with great fanfare to crack down. In March 1947, President Truman issued an executive order launching a comprehensive loyalty program for federal employees. Of the activities deemed to be "disloyal," the operative one was membership in any of a list of "subversive" organizations compiled by the Attorney General. On that basis, federal loyalty boards mounted witch hunts that wrecked the careers of about 10,000 public servants, not one of whom was ever tried and convicted of espionage.

As for the actual suppliers of information to the Soviets, they seem mostly to have ceased spying once the Cold War began. For one thing, the professional apparatus of Soviet agents who were their controllers was dismantled or disrupted by stepped-up American counterintelligence work. After the war, moreover, most of these well-connected amateur spies moved on to other careers. The State Department official Alger Hiss, for example, was serving as head of the prestigious Carnegie Endowment for International Peace when he was accused in 1948 by Whittaker Chambers, a Communist-turned-informant, of having passed classified documents to him in the 1930s. Skepticism by historians about internal subversion—that it was insignificant—seems justified if we start in 1947, just when the hue-and-cry about internal subversion was blowing up into a second Red Scare (for the first such scare, see Chapter 22).

For this, the Truman administration bore some responsibility. It had legitimized making "disloyalty" the proxy for subversive activity. Others, however, were far more adept at this technique, beginning with the House Un-American Activities Committee (HUAC), which Congressman Martin Dies of Texas and other conservatives had launched back in 1938. After the war, HUAC helped to spark the Great Fear by holding widely publicized hearings on alleged Communist infiltration in the movie industry. A group of writers and directors, soon dubbed the Hollywood Ten, went to jail for contempt of Congress for refusing to testify about their past associations. Hundreds of other actors, directors, and writers whose names had been mentioned in the HUAC investigation were unable to get work, victims of an unacknowledged but very real **blacklist** honored by industry executives (see American Voices, p. 784).

Following Washington's lead, many universities, political organizations, churches, and businesses undertook their own antisubversion campaigns, which often included the requirement that employees take loyalty oaths. In the labor movement, where Communists had served as organizers in the 1930s, charges of Communist domination led to the expulsion of a number of industrial unions by the CIO in 1949. Civil rights organizations such as the NAACP and the National Urban League also expelled Communists or "fellow travelers"—a term used to describe people who were viewed as Communist sympathizers although not members of the Communist Party. Thus, the Great Fear spread from the federal government to the farthest reaches of American associational, cultural, and economic life.

Here, too, however, revelations from the Soviet archives have complicated the picture. Historians have mostly regarded the American Communist Party as a "normal" organization, acting in America's home-grown radical tradition and playing by the rules of the game. Soviet archives clearly show otherwise. The American party was taking money and instructions from Moscow. It was in no way independent, so that when Communists joined other organizations, not only red-baiters found their participation problematic.

Red Hunting on the Quiz Shows MARK GOODSON

Active in the television industry from its earliest days, Mark Goodson was a highly success-ful producer whose game shows included "What's My Line?," "To Tell the Truth," and "Family Feud." In this interview, Goodson recalls his experience in the industry in the early 1950s at the height of the McCarthy period.

I'm not sure when it began, but I believe it was early 1950. At that point I had no connection with the blacklisting that was going on, although I heard about it in the motion picture business and heard rumors about things that had happened on other shows, like "The Aldrich Family". . . .

Soon afterwards, CBS installed a clearance division. There wasn't any discussion. We would just get the word — "drop that person" — and that was supposed to be it. Whenever I booked a guest or a panelist on "What's My Line?" or "I've Got a Secret," one of our assistants would phone up and say, "We're going to use so-and-so." We'd either get the okay, or they'd call back and say, "Not clear," or "Sorry, we can't use them." . . . You were never supposed to tell the person what it was about; you'd just unbook them. They never admitted there was a blacklist. It just wasn't done. . . .

Anna Lee was an English actress on a later show of ours called "It's News to Me." The sponsor was Sanka Coffee, a product of General Foods. The advertising agency was Young & Rubicam. One day, I received a call telling me we had to drop one of our panelists, Anna Lee, immediately. They said she was a radical, that she wrote a column for the *Daily Worker*. They couldn't allow that kind of stuff on the air. They claimed they were getting all kinds of mail. It seemed incongruous to me that this little English girl, someone who seemed very conservative, would be writing for a Communist newspa-per. It just didn't sound right.

I took her out to lunch. After a little social conversation, I asked her about her politics. She told me that she wasn't political, except she voted Conservative in England. Her husband was a Republican from Texas.

I went to the agency and said, "You guys are really off your rocker. Anna Lee is nothing close to a liberal." They told me, "Oh, you're right. We checked on that. It's a different Anna Lee who writes for the *Daily Worker*." I remember being relieved and saying, "Well, that's good. You just made a mistake. Now we can forget this." But that wasn't the case. They told me, "We've still got to get rid of her, because the illusion is just as good as the reality. If our client continues to get the mail, no one is going to believe him when he says there's a second Anna Lee." At that point I lost it. I told them their demand was outrageous. They could cancel the show if they wanted to, but I would not drop somebody whose only crime was sharing a name. When I got back to my office, there was a phone call waiting for me. It was from a friend of mine at the agency. He said, "If I were you, I would not lose my temper like that. If you want to argue, do it quietly. After you left, somebody said, 'Is Goodson a pinko?'"

SOURCE: Griffin Fariello, *Red Scare* (New York: Norton, 1995), 320–324.

Consider the expulsion of the Communist-led industrial unions in 1949. The year before, the CIO had gone all-out for Truman's reelection, in hopes of reversing the hated Taft-Hartley Act. The Communist line was to support Wallace's Progressive Party, and that is what the Communist-led unions did, thereby demonstrating that they were Communists first, trade unionists second—a cardinal sin for the labor movement. The expulsions left in their wake the wrecked lives of many innocent, high-minded trade unionists, and that was true wherever anti-Communism took hold, whether in universities, school boards, or civil rights organizations.

The meteoric rise of Senator Joseph McCarthy of Wisconsin marked the finale of the Great Fear. In February 1950, McCarthy delivered a bombshell during a speech in Wheeling, West Virginia: "I have here in my hand a list of the names of 205 men that were known to the Secretary of State as being members of the Communist Party and who nevertheless are still working and shaping the policy of the State Department." McCarthy later reduced his numbers, and he never released any names or proof, but he had gained the attention he sought. For the next four years, he waged a virulent smear campaign. Critics who disagreed with him exposed themselves to charges of being "soft" on Communism. Truman called McCarthy's charges "slander, lies, character assassination" but could do nothing to curb him. The Republicans, for their part, refrained from publicly challenging their most outspoken senator and, on the whole, were content to reap the political benefits.

In early 1954, McCarthy overreached himself by launching an investigation into subversive activities in the U.S. Army. When lengthy hearings—the first of their kind broadcast on the new medium of television—brought McCarthy's smear tactics into the nation's living rooms, support for him plummeted. In December 1954, the Senate voted 67 to 22 to censure McCarthy for unbecoming conduct. He died from alcohol-related illness three years later at the age of forty-eight, his name forever attached to a period of political repression of which he was only the most flagrant manifestation.

▶ Why did Harry Truman seem to be a failure during his first term in the White House?

▶ How did the Fair Deal differ from the New Deal?

▶ Why have historians revised their views about the significance of espionage in American government? Does this make any difference in terms of how we evaluate McCarthyism?

Modern Republicanism

As Election Day 1952 approached, America seemed ready for change. The question was: How much? With the Republican victory, the country got its answer: Very little. The new president, Dwight D. Eisenhower, set the tone for what his supporters called "modern Republicanism," an updated GOP approach that aimed at moderating, not dismantling, the New Deal state. Eisenhower and his supporters were—despite themselves—successors of FDR, not Herbert Hoover. Foreign policy revealed a similar continuity. Like their precessors, Republicans saw the world in Cold War polarities. They embraced the defense buildup begun during the Korean War and pushed containment to the far reaches of the world.

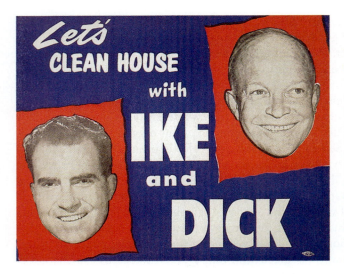

The 1952 Presidential Campaign
The 1952 Republican ticket of Dwight D. Eisenhower and Richard M. Nixon launched an effective attack on the Democratic leadership by stressing the Truman administration's involvement in bribery and influence-peddling scandals and by capitalizing on Truman's failure to end the war in Korea. Collection of Janice L. and David J. Frent.

They Liked Ike

The Republicans' problem was that after twenty years of Democratic rule, they were the minority party. Only one in three registered voters was Republican. The party faithful gave their hearts to Robert A. Taft of Ohio, the Republican leader in the Senate, but their heads told them that only a moderate, less-well-defined candidate was likely to attract the independent vote. General Eisenhower filled the bill. He was an immensely popular figure, widely admired as the architect of D-Day and victory in Europe.

Eisenhower was a man without a political past. Believing that democracy required that the military stand aside, he had never voted. Democrats and Republicans courted him, but it turned out that Eisenhower was a Republican, a believer in balanced budgets and individual responsibility. For regional balance, Eisenhower asked Senator Richard M. Nixon of California to be his running mate. Nixon was youthful, tirelessly partisan, and a strong anti-Communist who had won his spurs by leading HUAC's investigation of Alger Hiss's espionage past.

By 1952, the Truman administration was thoroughly discredited, primarily because of the unpopularity of the Korean War but also because of scandals that Republicans dubbed "the mess in Washington." With a certain relief, the Democrats turned to Governor Adlai E. Stevenson of Illinois, who enjoyed the support of respected liberals, such as Eleanor Roosevelt, and of organized labor. To appease conservative southern voters, the Democrats nominated Senator John A. Sparkman of Alabama for vice president.

Throughout the campaign, Stevenson advocated New Deal–Fair Deal policies with literary eloquence. But Eisenhower's artfully unpretentious speeches were more effective with voters. Eager to attract undecided voters, Eisenhower played down specific questions of policy. Instead, he attacked the Democrats with the "K_1C_2" formula: "Korea, Communism, and Corruption."

That November, Eisenhower won 55 percent of the popular vote, carrying all the northern and western states and four southern states. His triumph did not translate into a new Republican majority, however. Republicans regained control of Congress on his coattails but lost it in 1954 and remained a minority when Eisenhower easily won reelection over Adlai Stevenson in 1956. For most of his tenure, Eisenhower had to work with a Democratic Congress.

The Hidden-Hand Presidency

Although confident as an international leader, Eisenhower started out a novice in domestic affairs. He did his best to set a quieter national mood after the rancorous Truman years. Disliking confrontation, he was reluctant to speak out against Joe McCarthy, and he was not a leader on civil rights. Yet Eisenhower was no stooge as president. Political scientists have characterized his leadership style as the "hidden-hand presidency." Eisenhower manuevered deftly behind the scenes while maintaining a public demeanor of being above the fray. If he sometimes seemed inarticulate and bumbling, that was often a studied effect to mask his real intentions. He in fact ran a tight ship and was always in command.

After 1954, when the Democrats took control over Congress, the Eisenhower administration accepted legislation promoting social welfare. Federal outlays for veterans' benefits, housing, and Social Security increased, and the minimum wage rose from 75 cents an hour to $1. A mark of the government's commitment was the creation in 1953 of the new Department of Health, Education, and Welfare, which consolidated government administration of social programs. Welfare expenditures rose steadily during Eisenhower's tenure, consuming an ever larger share of the federal budget. Like Truman, Eisenhower accepted the government's responsibility for economic performance. Despite his faith in a balanced budget, Eisenhower engaged in deficit spending whenever employment dipped. He intervened even more vigorously when it came to holding in check the inflation sparked by the Korean War.

More striking was the expanded scope of federal activity. In a move that drastically altered America's landscape and driving habits, the National Interstate and Defense Highways Act of 1956 authorized $26 billion over a ten-year period for the construction of a nationally integrated highway system. To link the Great Lakes with the Atlantic Ocean, the United States and Canada co-sponsored in 1959 the construction of the St. Lawrence Seaway. These enormous public works programs surpassed anything undertaken during the New Deal.

And when the Soviet Union launched the first satellite, *Sputnik*, in 1957, the startled United States went into high gear to catch up in this new Cold War space competition. Eisenhower authorized the National Aeronautics and Space Administration (NASA) the following year and, alarmed that the United States was falling behind in science and technology, persuaded Congress to appropriate additional money for college scholarships and university research.

Only in the area of natural resources did the Eisenhower administration actually reduce federal activity, turning over offshore oil to the states and authorizing privately financed hydroelectric dams on the Snake River. In most other ways—New Deal welfare programs, Keynesian intervention in the economy, new departures in public works, scientific research, higher education — the Eisenhower Republicans had become part of a broad **liberal consensus** in American politics. That was the view of a true conservative, Senator Barry Goldwater of Arizona, who remarked sourly that Ike had run a "Dime Store New Deal."

Eisenhower and the Cold War

Every incoming administration likes to proclaim itself a grand departure from its predecessor. Eisenhower's gesture in this direction was his secretary of state, John Foster Dulles, a lawyer highly experienced in world affairs but ill suited by his self-righteous temperament for the craft of diplomacy. Dulles despised "atheistic Communism," and rather than settling for the status quo, he argued for the "liberation" of the "captive countries" of eastern Europe. This was bombast. The power realities that had called forth containment still applied, as was evident in Eisenhower's first important act as president. Redeeming his campaign pledge to resolve the Korean war, Eisenhower stepped up the negotiations that led to an agreement essentially fixing in place the military stalemate at the thirty-eighth parallel.

Stalin's death in March 1953 precipitated an intraparty struggle in the Soviet Union that lasted until 1956, when Nikita S. Khrushchev emerged as Stalin's successor. He soon startled Communists around the world by denouncing Stalin and detailing his crimes and blunders. Khrushchev also surprised Westerners by calling for "peaceful coexistence" and by dealing more flexibly with dissent in the Communist world.

Any hopes of a thaw evaporated when Hungarians rose up in 1956 and demanded that the country leave the Warsaw Pact. Soviet tanks moved into Budapest and crushed the rebellion, an action the United States condemned but could not realistically resist. Some of the blood was on Dulles's hands because he had emboldened the Hungarians with his rhetoric of "rolling back" the Iron Curtain — a pledge that the reality of nuclear weapons made impossible to fulfill.

With no end to the Cold War in sight, Eisenhower turned his attention to containing the cost of containment. Much as had Truman initially done, Eisenhower hoped to economize by relying on a nuclear arsenal and skimping on expensive conventional forces. Nuclear weapons delivered "more bang for the buck," explained Defense Secretary Charles E. Wilson. Under the "New Look" defense policy, the Eisenhower administration stepped up production of the hydrogen bomb, engaged in extensive atmospheric testing, developed the long-range bombing capabilities of the Strategic Air Command, and installed the Distant Early Warning line of radar stations in Alaska and Canada. The Soviets, however, matched the United States weapon for weapon. By 1958, both nations had intercontinental ballistic missiles. When an American nuclear submarine launched an atomic-tipped Polaris missile in 1960, Soviet engineers raced to produce an equivalent weapon.

Eisenhower had second thoughts about the reigning strategic policy — aptly named MAD (Mutually Assured Destruction) — whose premise was that war could be avoided by the certainty that both sides would be annihilated in a nuclear exchange. Eisenhower proposed instead, as a start, an arms-limitation agreement with the Soviet Union. Negotiations were cut short, however, when on May 5, 1960, the Soviets shot down an American U-2 spy plane over their territory. Eisenhower at first denied that the plane was engaged in espionage, but the Soviet Union produced the captured pilot, Francis Gary Powers, and Eisenhower admitted that he had authorized secret flights. In the midst of the dispute, a proposed summit meeting with Khrushchev was canceled, and Eisenhower's last chance for an arms agreement evaporated.

Containment in the Postcolonial World

The containment policy had been devised in response to Soviet threats in Europe, but as intervention in Korea suggested, containment proved to be an expandable concept. New nations were emerging across the Middle East, Africa, and Asia, inspired by powerful anticolonialist movements whose origins went back before World War II. Between 1947 and 1962, the British, French, Dutch, and Belgian empires all but disintegrated. Committed to national self-determination, FDR had favored these developments, often to the fury of his British and French allies. He expected democracies to emerge, new partners in an American-led, free-market world system. But as the Cold War intensified, that confidence began to wane. Both the Truman and Eisenhower administrations often failed to recognize that indigenous nationalist or socialist movements of the **Third World** had their own goals and were not necessarily pawns of the Soviet Union.

Believing that these emerging nations had to choose sides, the United States tried to draw them into collective security agreements, with the NATO alliance in Europe as a model. Secretary of State Dulles orchestrated the creation of the Southeast Asia Treaty Organization (SEATO), which in 1954 linked America and its major European allies with Australia, Pakistan, Thailand, New Zealand, and the Philippines. An extensive system of defense alliances eventually tied the United States to more than forty other countries (Map 26.3). The United States also sponsored a strategically valuable defensive alliance between Iran and Iraq on the southern flank of the Soviet Union.

The Eisenhower administration, less concerned about democracy than stability, tended to support governments, no matter how repressive, that were overtly anti-Communist. Some of America's staunchest allies—the Philippines, Korea, Iran, Cuba, and Nicaragua—were governed by dictatorships or right-wing regimes that lacked broad-based support. Moreover, Dulles often resorted to covert operations against governments that, in his opinion, were too closely aligned with the Soviets.

For such tasks, he used the Central Intelligence Agency (CIA), which had moved beyond its original mandate of intelligence gathering into active, albeit covert, involvement in the internal affairs of foreign countries, even the overthrow of several governments. When Iran's nationalist premier, Muhammad Mossadegh, seized British oil properties in 1953, CIA agents helped to depose him and installed the young Muhammad Reza Pahlavi as Shah of Iran. In 1954, the CIA engineered a coup in Guatemala against the popularly elected Jacobo Arbenz Guzman, who had expropriated land owned by the American-owned United Fruit Company. Eisenhower specifically approved those CIA efforts. "Our traditional ideas of international sportsmanship," he confessed privately, "are scarcely applicable in the morass in which the world now [1955] flounders."

How Eisenhower's confession might entangle America was already unfolding on a distant stage, in a country of no strategic interest and utterly unknown to most Americans. This was Vietnam, part of French Indochina. When the Japanese occupiers

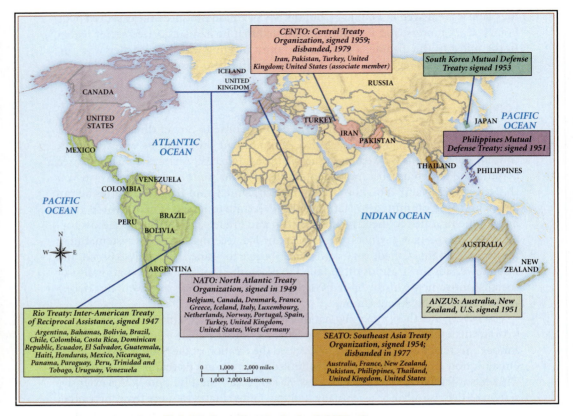

MAP 26.3 American Global Defense Treaties in the Cold War Era

The advent of the Cold War led to a major shift in American foreign policy: the signing of mutual defense treaties. Dating back to George Washington's call "to steer clear of permanent alliances with any portion of the foreign world," the United States had remained officially neutral in conflicts between other nations. As late as 1919, the U.S. Senate had rejected the principle of "collective security," the centerpiece of the League of Nations established by the Treaty of Versailles that ended World War I. In response to fears of Soviet expansion globally, in the late 1940s and 1950s, the United States pledged to defend much of the non-Communist world. As the map illustrates, major treaty organizations to which the United States belonged included NATO, SEATO, CENTO, ANZUS, and the Rio Treaty.

surrendered in August 1945, the Vietminh, the nationalist movement that had led the resistance, seized control with American encouragement. But their leader, Ho Chi Minh, was a Communist, and as the Cold War took hold, his being Communist outweighed America's commitment to self-determination. The next year, when France moved to restore its control over the country, Truman rejected Ho's plea for support in the Vietnamese struggle for independence and sided with France.

Eisenhower picked up where Truman left off. If the French failed, Eisenhower argued, the **domino theory**—a notion that henceforth bedeviled American strategic thinking—would result in the collapse of all non-Communist governments in the region. The United States eventually provided most of the financing, but money was not enough to defeat the tenacious Vietminh. After a fifty-six-day siege in early

1954, the French went down to defeat at the huge fortress of Dienbienphu. The result was the 1954 Geneva Accords, which partitioned Vietnam temporarily at the seventeenth parallel and called for elections within two years that would lead to a unified Vietnam.

The United States rejected the Geneva Accords and immediately set about undermining them. With the help of the CIA, a pro-American government took power in South Vietnam in June 1954. Ngo Dinh Diem, an anti-Communist Catholic who had been residing in the United States, returned to Vietnam as premier. The next year, in a rigged election, Diem became president of an independent South Vietnam. Facing certain defeat by the popular Ho Chi Minh, Diem called off the reunification elections scheduled for 1956.

As the last French soldiers left in March 1956, the United States took over, and South Vietnam became the front line in the American battle to contain Communism in Southeast Asia. To prop him up, the Eisenhower administration sent Diem an average of $200 million a year in aid and a contingent of 675 American military advisors. Few Americans, including probably Eisenhower himself, had any inkling where this might lead.

If Vietnam was still of minor concern, the same could not be said of the Middle East, an area rich in oil and complications. Most volatile was Palestine, populated by Arabs but also historically the ancient land of Israel and coveted by the Zionist movement as the site of a Jewish national home. After World War II, many survivors of the Nazi extermination camps resettled in Palestine, which was still controlled by Britain under a World War I mandate (see Chapter 22). On November 29, 1947, the U.N. General Assembly voted to partition Palestine between Jewish and Arab sectors. When the British mandate ended, Zionist leaders proclaimed the state of Israel. The Arab League nations invaded, but Israel survived. Many Palestinians fled or were driven from their homes during the fighting. The Arab defeat left these people permanently stranded in refugee camps. President Truman quickly recognized the new state, winning crucial support from Jewish voters in the 1948 election but alienating the Arabs.

Two years after gaining independence, Egypt in 1954 came under the rule of Gamal Abdel Nasser, who proclaimed a form of pan-Arab socialism that intended to end the Middle East's dependent, colonial relationship with the West. When the Soviet Union offered Nasser help in building the Aswan Dam on the Nile, Secretary of State Dulles made a counteroffer of American assistance. Angered by Nasser's refusal to distance himself from the Soviets, however, Dulles abruptly withdrew his offer in July 1956.

A week later, Nasser retaliated, nationalizing the Suez Canal, which was the lifeline for western Europe's oil. After several months of fruitless negotiation, Britain and France, in alliance with Israel, attacked Egypt and retook the canal. Taken by surprise and embarrassed because just then he was condemning the Soviet invasion of Hungary, Eisenhower demanded that France and Britain pull back. Egypt reclaimed the Suez Canal and built the Aswan Dam with Soviet support.

In early 1957, concerned that the Soviet Union might step into the vacuum left by Britain's departure from the Middle East, the president announced the Eisenhower Doctrine, which stated that American forces would assist any nation in the region that required aid "against overt armed aggression from any nation controlled by

International Communism." Invoking the doctrine later that year, Eisenhower sent the U.S. Sixth Fleet to the Mediterranean to help King Hussein of Jordan put down a Nasser-backed revolt. A year later, 14,000 troops landed to back up a pro-American government in Lebanon. The Eisenhower Doctrine was further proof of the global reach of containment, in this instance accentuated by the strategic need to protect the West's access to steady supplies of oil.

Eisenhower's Farewell Address

In his final address to the nation, Eisenhower spoke about the power of what he called the **military-industrial complex,** which by then was employing 3.5 million Americans. Its pervasive influence, Eisenhower warned, "is felt in every city, every statehouse, every office of the federal government." Even though his administration had fostered this growing defense establishment, Eisenhower feared its implications for a democratic people: "We must guard against the acquisition of unwarranted influence, whether sought or unsought, by the military-industrial complex," he said. "We must never let the weight of this combination endanger our liberties or democratic processes."

With those words, Dwight Eisenhower showed how well he understood the impact of the Cold War on American life. Only by vigilance could the democratic values of a free people be preserved in an age of unending global struggle.

▶ Why does the text say that Eisenhower was heir to FDR, not Herbert Hoover?

▶ Why was America's deepening involvement in the Third World a phenomenon of the 1950s rather than the 1940s?

▶ In what ways were Truman's and Eisenhower's foreign policies similar? How did they differ?

SUMMARY

We have seen how the Cold War began as a conflict between the United States and the Soviet Union over eastern Europe. Very early in the conflict, the United States adopted a strategy of containment, and although initially intended only for Europe, the strategy quickly expanded to Asia when China was "lost" to Mao's Communists. The first effect of that expansion was the Korean War, after which, under Eisenhower, containment of Communism became America's guiding principle across the Third World. Cold War imperatives meant a major military buildup, a scary nuclear arms race, and unprecedented entanglements across the globe.

We have also seen how, on the domestic front, Truman started out with high hopes for an expanded New Deal, only to be stymied by the problems of reconversion, by resistance from Congress, and by competing spending demands of the Cold War. The greatest Cold War–inspired distraction, however, was a climate of fear over internal subversion by Communists that gave rise to McCarthyism. Truman's successor, Dwight Eisenhower, brought the Republicans back into power. Although personally conservative, Eisenhower proved to be a New Dealer in disguise. He declined to cut back on social welfare programs and broke new ground in federal spending on highways, scientific research, and higher education. When he left office, it seemed that a "liberal consensus" prevailed, with old-fashioned, laissez-faire conservativism mostly marginalized.

Connections: Diplomacy and Politics

In the essay opening Part Six, we started with Walter Lippmann's boast at the close of World War II that "[w]hat Rome was to the ancient world . . . America is to be to the world of tomorrow." Lippmann's confidence in America's future rested in part on his expectation that the Grand Alliance described in Chapter 25 would be durable. Had he gone back farther, to World War I (see Chapter 21), he might not have been so optimistic. Woodrow Wilson's hostile response to the Russian revolution had assumed that the two systems were irreconcilable, a belief that the Soviets fully shared. Once the Cold War began after 1945, it became the dominant event

TIMELINE

1945	▶ Yalta and Potsdam conferences		▶ Soviet Union detonates atomic bomb
	▶ Harry S Truman succeeds Roosevelt		▶ People's Republic of China established
	▶ Senate approves U.S. participation in United Nations	1950–1953	▶ Korean War
		1950	▶ Joseph McCarthy's "list" of Communists in government
1946	▶ George Kennan outlines containment policy		
	▶ Baruch Plan for international control of atomic weapons fails		▶ NSC-68 calls for permanent mobilization
		1952	▶ Eisenhower elected president
1947	▶ Taft-Hartley Act limits union power	1953	▶ Stalin dies
	▶ House Un-American Activities Committee (HUAC) investigates film industry	1955	▶ Geneva Accords partition Vietnam at seventeenth parallel
	▶ Truman Doctrine promises aid to governments resisting Communism	1956	▶ Crises in Hungary and at Suez Canal
			▶ Interstate Highway Act
1948	▶ Marshall Plan aids economic recovery in Europe	1957	▶ Soviet Union launches *Sputnik*
	▶ Communist coup in Czechoslovakia	1958	▶ National Aeronautics and Space Administration (NASA) established
	▶ Truman's executive order desegregating armed forces	1960	▶ U-2 incident leads to cancellation of U.S.-Soviet summit meeting
	▶ Stalin blockades West Berlin; Berlin airlift begins		
1949	▶ North Atlantic Treaty Organization (NATO) founded	1961	▶ Eisenhower warns against military-industrial complex

in American diplomatic history for the next half-century. In the case of the liberal consensus, its roots in the New Deal (Chapter 24) are entirely clear. Between 1945 and 1960, the liberal consensus held sway, even during Eisenhower's presidency; but after peaking in the mid-1960s with Johnson's Great Society (Chapter 28), it went into decline. The New Deal structure itself remained durable, despite the reaction against the War on Poverty, but the Democratic Party's grip on the country began to fail, and by the close of the Carter administration, conservatism and the Republican Party were clearly in the ascendancy (Chapter 29).

FOR FURTHER EXPLORATION

James T. Patterson, *Grand Expectations: The United States, 1945–1974* (1996), offers a detailed, comprehensive account of this period. For a reconsideration of the Cold War from a post–Cold War perspective, see especially John Lewis Gaddis, *We Now Know: Rethinking Cold War History* (1997). On the Fair Deal, the best treatment is Alonzo Hamby, *Beyond the New Deal: Harry S. Truman and American Liberalism* (1973). Jennifer Klein, *For All These Rights* (2003), is a probing analysis of why the United States failed to develop a national health-care system. On McCarthyism, David Oshinsky, *A Conspiracy So Immense: The World of Joe McCarthy* (1983), is excellent. Key books containing documents and analysis of Soviet espionage are John E. Haynes and Harvey Klehr, *The Secret World of American Communism* (1995) and *Venona: Decoding Soviet Espionage in America* (1999). On the 1950s, see J. Ronald Oakley, *God's Country: America in the Fifties* (1986). David Halberstam's *The Fifties* (1993) offers a brief but searing account of CIA covert activities in Iran and Guatemala. For an exceptionally rich Web site on the Cold War, including materials from former Communist-bloc countries, log on to **www.wilsoncenter.org/index.cfm?topic_id=1409&fuseaction=topics.home**. At **www.trumanlibrary.org/whistlestop/student_guide.htm** is a searchable collection from the Harry S Truman Presidential Library, organized into categories such as the Truman Doctrine, the Berlin airlift, the desegregation of the armed forces, and the 1948 presidential campaign.

TEST YOUR KNOWLEDGE

To assess your mastery of the material in this chapter and for Web sites, images, and documents related to this chapter, visit **bedfordstmartins.com/henrettaconcise**.

The Age of Affluence
1945–1960

The nation of the well-off must be able to see through the wall of affluence and recognize the alien citizens on the other side. And there must be vision in the sense of purpose, of aspiration. . . . [T]here must be a passion to end poverty, for nothing less than that will do.

—Michael Harrington, 1962

In 1959, at the height of the Cold War, Vice President Richard Nixon traveled to Moscow to open America's National Exhibit. After sipping Pepsi-Cola, Nixon and Soviet Premier Nikita Khrushchev got into a heated discussion of the relative merits of Soviet and American societies. Standing in the kitchen of a model American home, they talked dishwashers, toasters, and televisions, not rockets, submarines, and missiles. Images of the "kitchen debate" flashed across TV screens around the world.

What was so striking about the Moscow exhibition was the way its American planners enlisted affluence and mass consumption in service to Cold War politics. The suburban lifestyle trumpeted at the exhibition symbolized the superiority of capitalism over Communism.

During the postwar era, Americans did enjoy the world's highest standard of living. But behind the affluence, things were not as they seemed. The suburban calm masked contradictions in women's lives and cultural rebelliousness among young people. Suburban growth often came at the expense of cities, sowing the seeds of inner-city decay and exacerbating racial tensions. Nor was prosperity ever as widespread as the Moscow exhibit implied. The suburban lifestyle was beyond the reach of the working poor, Spanish-speaking immigrants, and most African Americans. And in the South, a civil rights revolution was in the making.

Economic Powerhouse

The United States enjoyed enormous economic advantages at the close of World War II. While the Europeans and Japanese were still picking though the rubble, America stood poised to enter a postwar boom. The American economy benefited from stable

The Kitchen Debate

At the Moscow Fair in 1959, the United States put on display some of the technological wonders of American home life. When Vice President Richard Nixon visited, he and Soviet Premier Nikita Khrushchev had an impromptu debate over the relative merits of their rival systems, with the up-to-date American kitchen as a case in point. This photograph shows the debate in progress. Khrushchev is the bald man pointing his finger at Nixon. On the other side of Nixon stands Leonid Brezhnev, who would become Khrushchev's successor. Getty Images.

For more help analyzing this image, see the Online Study Guide at **bedfordstmartins.com/henrettaconcise.**

internal markets, heavy investment in research and development, and rapid diffusion of new technology. For the first time, employers generally accepted collective bargaining, which for workers translated into rising wages, expanding benefits, and a growing rate of home ownership. At the heart of this postwar prosperity lay the involvement of the federal government. Public outlays for defense and domestic programs gave a huge boost to the economy. Not least, the federal government recognized that prosperity rested on global foundations. U.S. corporations and banking institutions soon so dominated the world economy that the postwar period has rightly been called the Pax Americana.

Engines of Economic Growth

American global supremacy rested partly on economic institutions created at a United Nations conference at Bretton Woods, New Hampshire, in July 1944. The World Bank provided loans for the reconstruction of war-torn Europe as well as for the development of Third World countries. A second institution, the International Monetary Fund (IMF), was set up to stabilize currencies and provide a predictable monetary environment for trade, with the U.S. dollar serving as the benchmark for other currencies. In 1947, multinational trade negotiations resulted in the first General Agreement on Tariffs and Trade (GATT), which established an international framework for overseeing trade rules and practices.

The World Bank, the IMF, and GATT were the cornerstones of the so-called Bretton Woods system that guided the world economy after the war. The Bretton Woods system encouraged stable prices, the reduction of tariffs, flexible domestic markets, and international trade based on fixed exchange rates. All this effectively served America's conception of the global economy, paralleling America's ambitious diplomatic aims in the Cold War.

A second linchpin of postwar prosperity was defense spending. The military-industrial complex that President Eisenhower identified in his 1961 Farewell Address had its roots in the business-government partnerships of two world wars. But after 1945, unlike 1918, the massive commitment of government dollars for defense continued. Even though the country was technically at peace, the economy and the government operated practically on a war footing, in a state of permanent mobilization.

Based at the sprawling Pentagon in Arlington, Virginia, the Defense Department evolved into a massive bureaucracy. In the name of national security, defense-related industries entered into long-term relationships with the Pentagon. Some companies did so much business with the government that they in effect became contractors for the Defense Department. Over 60 percent of the income of Boeing, General Dynamics, and Raytheon came from military contracts, and the percentages were even higher for Lockheed and Republic Aviation. All of these were giant enterprises, given an inside track because of the Pentagon's inclination to favor the largest firms.

As permanent mobilization took hold, science, industry, and the federal government became increasingly intertwined. According to the National Science Foundation, federal money underwrote 90 percent of the cost of research on aviation and space, 65 percent for electricity and electronics, 42 percent for scientific instruments, and even 24 percent for automobiles. With the government footing the bill, corporations lost little time in transforming new technology into useful products. Backed by the Pentagon, IBM pressed ahead with its research on integrated circuits, which were crucial to the computer revolution.

The defense buildup created jobs—lots of them. Taking into account the indirect benefits (the additional jobs created to serve and support defense workers), perhaps one worker in seven nationally owed his or her job to the military-industrial complex by the 1960s. But increased military spending also limited the resources for domestic social needs. Critics of military spending calculated the tradeoffs: The money spent for a nuclear aircraft carrier and support ships could have paid for a subway system for Washington, D.C.; the cost of one Huey helicopter could have built sixty-six units of low-income housing.

America's annual Gross Domestic Product (GDP) jumped from $213 billion in 1945 to more than $500 billion in 1960; by 1970, it exceeded $1 trillion. To working Americans, this sustained economic growth meant a 25 percent rise in real income between 1946 and 1959. The downside was that while in earlier peacetime years, military spending had constituted only 1 percent of GDP, now it represented 10 percent.

Postwar prosperity featured low inflation. After the burst of high prices in the immediate postwar period, inflation slowed to 2 to 3 percent annually, and it stayed

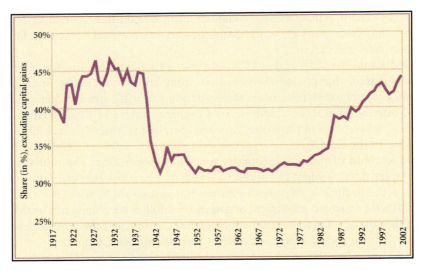

FIGURE 27.1 Income Inequality, 1917–2002

This graph shows the share of total income (minus capital gains) going to the richest 10 percent of Americans, a figure that economists regard as a good proxy for economic inequality more generally in the country. Most Americans living in the post–New Deal decades had good reason to feel a sense of economic well-being: In these four decades, they were sharing more equitably in the fruits of industrialism than they ever had before or would afterward.

low until the escalation of the Vietnam War in the mid-1960s. Low inflation meant stable and predictable prices. Feeling secure about the future, Americans were eager to spend and rightly felt that they were better off than ever before. In 1940, 43 percent of American families owned their homes; by 1960, 62 percent did. In that period, moreover, income inequality dropped sharply, the share of total income going to the top tenth down by nearly one-third from the 45 percent it had been in 1940 (Figure 27.1). The fastest rate of income growth, in fact, was at the sixtieth percentile. However, the picture was not as rosy at the bottom, where poverty stubbornly hung on. In *The Affluent Society* (1958), the economist John Kenneth Galbraith argued that the poor were only an "afterthought" in the minds of economists and politicians. Yet, as Galbraith noted, one in thirteen families at the time earned less than $1,000 a year.

The Corporate Order

For over half a century, the consolidation of economic power into big corporate firms had characterized American enterprise. That tendency continued—indeed, it accelerated. In 1970, the top four U.S. automakers produced 91 percent of all motor vehicles sold in the country; the top four firms in tires produced 72 percent, those in cigarettes 84 percent, and those in detergents 70 percent.

The classic, vertically integrated corporation of the early twentieth century, originally designed to service a national market (see Chapter 17), was now driven increasingly by research and new technology. CBS, for example, hired the Hungarian inventor Peter Goldmark, who perfected color television during the 1940s, long-playing records in the 1950s, and a video recording system in the 1960s. As the head of CBS Laboratories, Goldmark patented more than a hundred devices and created multiple new markets for his happy employer. Because big outfits such as CBS had the deepest pockets, they were the firms best able to diversify through investment in industrial research.

Deep pockets also financed sophisticated advertising that enabled large corporations to break into hitherto resistant markets. This was the case with beer, for example, where loyalty to local brews in their infinite variety was legendary. To erode that preference, Anheuser-Busch and other national producers sponsored televised sports, parlaying the aura of championship games into national acceptance of their standardized "lighter" beers. "Bud, the King of Beers" was just as good for the little guy as for the big-league star. By 1970, big multiplant brewers controlled 70 percent of the beer market.

More revolutionary was the sudden rise of the conglomerates, giant enterprises consisting of firms in unrelated industries. Conglomerate building resulted in the nation's third great merger wave. (The first two had taken place in the 1890s and the 1920s.) Because of their diverse holdings, conglomerates were shielded from instability in any single market. International Telephone and Telegraph transformed itself into a conglomerate by acquiring Continental Baking (famous for Wonder Bread), Sheraton Hotels, Avis Rent-a-Car, Levitt and Sons home builders, and Hartford Fire Insurance. Ling-Temco-Vought, another conglomerate, produced steel, built ships, developed real estate, and brought cattle to market.

Expansion into foreign markets also spurred corporate growth. At a time when "Made in Japan" still meant shoddy workmanship, U.S. products were considered the best in the world. Especially when domestic demand became saturated or recessions cut into sales, American firms looked overseas. During the 1950s, U.S. exports nearly doubled, giving the nation a trade surplus of close to $5 billion in 1960. By the 1970s, Gillette, IBM, Mobil, and Coca-Cola made more than half their profits abroad.

Directing such giant enterprises required managers to place more emphasis on planning. Companies recruited top executives who had business school training; the ability to manage information; and skills in corporate planning, marketing, and investment. A new generation of corporate chieftains emerged, operating in a complex environment that demanded long-range forecasting and close coordination with investment banks, law firms, and federal regulators.

To staff their bureaucracies, the postwar corporate giants required a huge supply of white-collar foot soldiers. Companies turned to the universities, which, fueled partly by the GI Bill, had grown explosively after 1945. Better educated than their elders, the members of the new managerial class advanced more quickly and at a younger age into responsible jobs. As one participant-observer remarked: "If you had a college diploma, a dark suit, and anything between the ears, it was like an escalator; you just stood there and moved up." (He was talking about men; few women gained entrance to the managerial ranks.)

Corporations offered lifetime employment, but they also expected lifetime loyalty. Atlas Van Lines, which was in the business of moving these people, estimated that corporate managers were transferred an average of fourteen times—once every two and a half years—during their careers. Perpetually mobile IBM managers joked that the company's initials stood for "I've Been Moved."

Climbing the corporate ladder rewarded men without hard edges—the "well adjusted." In *The Lonely Crowd* (1950), the sociologist David Reisman contrasted the independent businessmen and professionals of earlier years with the managerial class of the postwar world. He concluded that the new corporate men were "other-directed," more attuned to their associates than driven by their own goals. The sociologist William Whyte painted a somber picture of "organization men" who left the home "spiritually as well as physically to take the vows of organization life." A recurring theme of the 1950s, in fact, was that the conformity demanded of "the man in the gray flannel suit" (the title of Sloan Wilson's popular novel) was stifling creativity and blighting lives.

Labor-Management Accord

For the first time, collective bargaining became a major factor in the nation's economic life. In the past, thanks to the bitter resistance of antiunion employers, collective bargaining had been confined to a narrow band of craft trades and a few industries, primarily coal mining, railroading, and the metal trades. The power balance shifted during the Great Depression (see Chapter 23), and by the time the dust settled after World War II, labor unions overwhelmingly represented America's industrial workforce. The question then became: How would labor's power be used?

In late 1945, Walter Reuther of the United Auto Workers (UAW) challenged General Motors in a fundamental way. The youthful Reuther was thinking big, beyond a single company or even a single industry. He aimed at nothing less than a reshaped, high-employment economy. To jump-start it, he demanded a 30 percent wage hike with no price increase for GM cars, and when General Motors said no, it couldn't afford that, Reuther demanded that the company "open the books."

General Motors implacably resisted this "opening wedge" into the rights of management. The company took a 113-day strike, rebuffed the government's intervention, and soundly defeated the UAW. Having made its point, General Motors laid out the terms for a durable relationship. It would accept the UAW as its bargaining partner and guarantee GM workers an ever higher living standard. The price was that the UAW abandon its assault on the company's "right to manage." On signing the five-year GM contract of 1950 — the Treaty of Detroit, it was called — Reuther accepted the company's terms.

The Treaty of Detroit opened the way for a more broadly based "labor-management accord" — not industrial peace, because the country still experienced many strikes, but general acceptance of collective bargaining as the method for setting the terms of employment. For industrial workers, the result was rising real income, from $54.92 a week in 1949 to $71.81 (in 1947–1949 dollars) in 1959. The average worker with three dependents gained 18 percent in spendable real income in that period. In addition, collective bargaining delivered greater leisure (more paid holidays and longer vacations) and, in a startling departure, a social safety net.

In postwar Europe, America's allies were constructing welfare states. That was the preference of American unions as well. But having lost the bruising battle in Washington for national health care, the unions turned to the bargaining table. By the end of the 1950s, union contracts commonly provided defined-benefit pension plans (supplementing Social Security); company-paid health insurance; and, for two million workers, mainly in steel and automaking, a guaranteed annual wage (via supplementary unemployment benefits). Collective bargaining had become, in effect, the American alternative to the European welfare state.

The sum of these union gains was a new sociological phenomenon, the "affluent" worker—as evidenced by relocation to the suburbs, by homeownership, by increased ownership of cars and other durable goods, and, an infallible sign of rising expectations, by installment buying. For union workers, the contract became, as Reuther boasted, the passport into the middle class. Generally overlooked, however, were the many unorganized workers with no such passport—those consigned to casual labor or low-wage jobs in the service sector. In retrospect, economists came to recognize that America had developed a two-tiered, inequitable labor system.

The labor-management accord that generated the good life for so many workers seemed in the 1950s absolutely secure. The union rivalries of the 1930s abated. In 1955, the industrial-union and craft-union wings joined together in the AFL-CIO, representing 90 percent of the nation's 17.5 million union members. At its head stood George Meany, a cigar-chomping former New York plumber who, in his blunt way, conveyed the reassuring message that organized labor had matured and was management's fit partner.

The labor-management accord, impressive though it was, never was as durable as it seemed. Vulnerabilities lurked, even in the accord's heyday. For one thing, the sheltered markets, the essential condition for passing on the costs of collective bargaining, were in fact quite fragile. In certain industries, the lead firms were already losing market share—for example, in meatpacking and steel—and nowhere, not even in automaking, was their dominance truly secure. A second, more obvious vulnerability was the nonunion South, which the unions failed to organize, despite a strenuous postwar drive. The South's success at attracting companies pointed to a third, most basic vulnerability: the abiding antiunionism of American employers. At heart, they regarded the labor-management accord as a negotiated truce, not a permanent peace. It was only a matter of time and the onset of a more competitive environment before the scattered antiunion forays of the 1950s turned into a full-scale counteroffensive.

The postwar labor-management accord turned out to be a transitory event, not a permanent condition of American economic life. In a larger sense, that was also true of the postwar boom.

▶ In what ways can the prosperity of the 1950s be explained by the Cold War?

▶ Why is "the man in the gray flannel suit" the representative businessman of the 1950s?

▶ What do we mean by the "labor-management accord"?

The Affluent Society

Prosperity is more easily measured—how much an economy produces, how much people earn—than is the good life that prosperity actually buys. For the 1950s, however, the contours of the American good life emerged with exceptional distinctness: a preference for suburban living, a high valuation on consumption, and a devotion to family and domesticity. In this section, we ask: Why those particular choices? And with what—not necessarily happy—consequences?

The Suburban Explosion

Migration to the suburbs had been going on for a hundred years but never before on the scale that the country experienced after World War II. Within a decade or so, farmland on the outskirts of cities filled up with tract housing and shopping malls. Entire counties that had once been rural, such as San Mateo, south of San Francisco, went suburban. By 1960, more people lived in suburbs than in cities.

Home construction had ground to halt during the Great Depression, and returning veterans, dreaming of home and family, faced a critical housing shortage. After the war, construction surged to meet pent-up demand. One-fourth of the country's entire housing stock in 1960 had not even existed a decade earlier.

An innovative Long Island building contractor, William J. Levitt, revolutionized the suburban housing market by applying mass-production techniques and turning out new homes at a dizzying speed. Levitt's basic four-room house, complete with kitchen appliances, was priced at $7,990 in 1947. Levitt did not need to advertise; word of mouth brought buyers flocking to his developments in New York, Pennsylvania, and New Jersey (all called Levittown, naturally). Dozens of other developers, including California's shipping magnate Henry J. Kaiser, were soon snapping up cheap famland and building subdivisions around the country.

Even at $7,990, Levitt's homes would have been beyond the means of young families had the traditional home-financing standard—half down and ten years to pay off the balance—still prevailed. That is where the Federal Housing Administration (FHA) and the Veterans Administration (VA) came in. After the war, the FHA insured thirty-year mortages with as little as 5 percent down and interest at 2 or 3 percent. The VA was even more lenient, requiring only a token $1 down for qualified ex-GIs. FHA and VA mortages best explain why, after hovering around 45 percent for the previous half-century, home ownership jumped to 60 percent by 1960.

What purchasers of Levitt's houses got, in addition to a good deal, were homogeneous communities. The developments contained few old people or unmarried adults. Even the trees were young. There were regulations about maintaining lawns, and no laundry could be hung out on the weekends. Then there was the matter of race. Levitt's houses came with **restrictive covenants** prohibiting occupancy "by members of other than the Caucasian Race." (Restrictive covenants often applied to Jews and Catholics as well.)

Levitt, a marketing genius, knew his customers. The United Auto Workers learned the hard way. After the war, the CIO union launched an ambitious campaign for open-housing ordinances in the Detroit area. White auto workers rebelled, rebuking the union leadership by voting for racist politicans who promised to keep white neighborhoods white. A leading advocate of racial equality nationally, the UAW quietly shelved the fight at the local level. In *Shelley v. Kraemer* (1948), the Supreme Court outlawed restrictive covenants, but the practice persisted informally long afterward. What kept it going was the "red-lining" policy by the FHA and VA, which routinely refused mortgages to blacks seeking to buy in white neighborhoods.

Suburban living, although a nationwide phenomenon, was most at home in the Sun Belt, where taxes were low, the climate was mild, and open space allowed for sprawling subdivisions (Map 27.1). Fueled by World War II, the South and West began to boom. Florida added 3.5 million people, many of them retired, between 1940 and 1970. Texas profited from an expanding petrochemical industry. Most dramatic was California's growth, spurred especially by lots of work in the state's defense-related aircraft and electronics industries. California's climate and job opportunities acted as magnets pulling people from all parts of the country. By 1970, California contained one-tenth of the nation's population and surpassed New York as the most populous state.

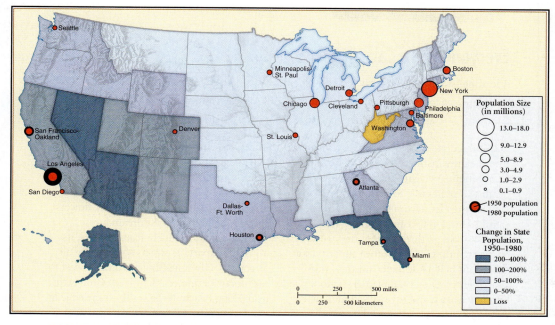

MAP 27.1 Shifting Population Patterns, 1950–1980

A metropolitan area is generally defined as a central city that in combination with its surrounding territory forms an integrated economic and social unit. The U.S. Census Bureau introduced the Standard Metropolitan Statistical Area (SMSA) in 1950, but later changes in the definition of SMSA have made it difficult to generalize from the 1950 figures. This map compares the population of central cities in 1950 with population figures for the more broadly defined metropolitan areas in 1980 to illustrate the extent and geographical distribution of metropolitan growth in the postwar period.

For more help analyzing this map, see the Online Study Guide at **bedfordstmartins.com/henrettaconcise**.

Boosters heralded the booming development of the Sun Belt. But growth came at a price. In the arid Southwest, increasing demands for water and energy made for environmental problems. As cities competed for scarce water resources, they depleted underground aquifers and dammed scenic rivers. The proliferation of coal-burning power plants increased air pollution, and so did traffic. The West's nuclear industry, while good for the economy, also brought nuclear waste, uranium mines, and atomic test sites. And growth had a way of consuming the easy, uncongested living that had attracted people to the Sun Belt in the first place. Still, for folks occupying those ranch-style houses with their nice lawns, barbecues, and air-conditioning, suburban living seemed at its best in sunny California or Arizona.

Without automobiles, suburban growth on such a massive scale would have been impossible. Planners laid out subdivisions on the assumption that everybody would drive. And they did—to get to work, to take the children to Little League, to shop. With gas plentiful at 15 cents a gallon, no one cared about the fuel efficiency of their V-8 engines or seemed to mind the elaborate tail fins and chrome that weighed down their cars. In 1945, Americans owned twenty-five million cars; by 1965, the number had tripled to seventy-five million (see Voices from Abroad, p. 804).

Everyone Has a Car   HANOCH BARTOV

A leading Israeli writer, Hanoch Bartov spent two years in the United States working as a newspaper correspondent. As a newcomer to Los Angeles in the early 1960s, he was both fascinated and appalled by Americans' love affair with the automobile.

Our immediate decision to buy a car sprang from healthy instincts. Only later did I learn from bitter experience that in California, death was preferable to living without one. Neither the views from the plane nor the weird excursion that first evening hinted at what I would go through that first week.

Very simple—the nearest supermarket was about half a kilometer south of our apartment, the regional primary school two kilometers east, and my son's kindergarten even farther away. A trip to the post office—an undertaking, to the bank—an ordeal, to work—an impossibility.

Truth be told: the Los Angeles municipality . . . does have public transportation.

Buses go once an hour along the city's boulevards and avenues, gathering all the wretched of the earth, the poor and the needy, the old ladies forbidden by their grandchildren to drive, and other eccentric types. But few people can depend on buses. . . . There are no tramways. No one thought of a subway. Railroads—not now and not in the future.

Why? Because everyone has a car. A man invited me to his house, saying, "We are neighbors, within ten minutes of each other." After walking for an hour and a half I realized what he meant—"ten minute drive within the speed limit." Simply put, he never thought I might interpret his remark to refer to the walking distance. . . .

At first perhaps people relished the freedom and independence a car provided. You get in, sit down, and grab the steering wheel, your mobility exceeding that of any other generation. No wonder people refuse to live downtown. . . . Instead, they get a piece of the desert, far from town, at half price, drag a water hose, grow grass, flowers, and trees, and build their dream house. . . .

The result? A widely scattered city, its houses far apart, its streets stretched in all directions. Olympic Boulevard from west to east, forty kilometers. Sepulveda Boulevard, from Long Beach in the south to the edge of the desert, forty kilometers. Altogether covering 1,200 square kilometers. As of now.

Why "as of now"? Because greater distances mean more commuting, and more commuting leads to more cars. More cars means problems that push people even farther away from the city, which chases after them.

The urban sprawl is only one side effect. Two, some say three, million cars require an array of services. . . . Why bother parking, getting out, getting in, getting up and sitting down, when you can simply "drive in"? . . . That is how dirty laundry is deposited, electricity and water bills paid. . . . That is how the anniversary wreath is laid on the graves of loved ones. There are drive-in movies. And, yes, we saw it with our own eyes: drive-in churches. Only in death is a man separated from his car and buried alone.

SOURCE: Oscar and Lilian Handlin, eds., *From the Outer World* (Cambridge, MA: Harvard University Press, 1997), 293–296.

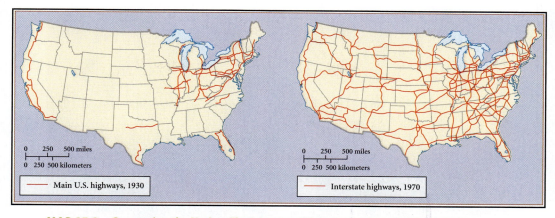

MAP 27.2   Connecting the Nation: The Interstate Highway System, 1930 and 1970
The 1956 Interstate Highway Act paved the way for an extensive network of federal highways throughout the nation. The act pleased American drivers and enhanced their love affair with the automobile. It also benefited the petroleum, construction, trucking, real estate, and tourist industries. The new highway system promoted the nation's economic integration, facilitated the growth of suburbs, and contributed to the erosion of distinct regional identities within the United States.

More cars required more highways, and the federal government obliged. In 1947, Congress authorized the construction of 37,000 miles of highways; major new legislation in 1956 increased this commitment by another 42,500 miles (Map 27.2). One of the largest civil-engineering projects in history, the new interstate system linked the entire country, with far-reaching effects on both the cities and the countryside. The interstate highways rerouted traffic away from small towns, bypassed well-traveled main roads such as the cross-country Route 66, and cut wide swaths through old neighborhoods in the cities.

Mass transit systems, such as those of Los Angeles and the San Francisco Bay Area, gave way to freeways. Federal highway funding specifically excluded mass transit, and the auto industry was no friend either. General Motors made a practice of buying up trolley lines and scrapping them. By 1960, two-thirds of Americans drove to work each day. In Sun Belt cities such as Los Angeles and Phoenix, the proportion came closer to 100 percent.

The Search for Security

There was a reason why Congress called the 1956 legislation creating America's modern freeway system the National Interstate and *Defense* Highways Act. The four-lane freeways, used every day by commuters, might some day, in a nuclear war, evacuate them to safety. That fact captured as well as anything the underside of postwar life, when suburban living abided side by side with the shadow of annihilation.

The Cold War, reaching as it did across the globe, was omnipresent at home as well. Most alarming was the nuclear standoff with the Soviet Union. Bomb shelters and civil defense drills provided a daily reminder of mushroom clouds. In the late 1950s, a small but growing number of citizens raised questions about radioactive fallout from above-ground bomb tests. By the late 1950s, nuclear testing had become a

Duck and Cover

The nation's Civil Defense Agency's efforts to alert Americans to the threat of a nuclear attack extended to children in schools, where repeated drills taught them to "duck and cover" as protection against the impact of an atomic blast. Variations of this 1954 scene at Franklin Township School in Quakertown, New Jersey, were repeated all over the nation. Paul F. Kutta/Courtesy, Reminiscences Magazine.

high-profile issue, and protest groups such as SANE (the National Committee for a Sane Nuclear Policy) and Physicians for Social Responsibility had emerged, calling for an international test ban. Federal investigators later documented illnesses, deaths, and birth defects among "downwinders"—people who lived near nuclear test sites and weapons. The most shocking revelations came in 1993, when the Department of Energy released previously classified documents on human radiation experiments conducted in the late 1940s and 1950s, experiments that had been undertaken with little concern for or understanding of the adverse effects on the subjects.

In an age of anxiety, Americans yearned for a reaffirmation of faith. Church membership jumped from 49 percent of the population in 1940 to 70 percent in 1960. People flocked to the Evangelical Protestant denominations, beneficiaries of a remarkable new crop of preachers. Most eloquent was the young Reverend Billy Graham, who made brilliant use of television, radio, and advertising to spread the gospel.

The religious reawakening meshed, in a time of Cold War, with Americans' view of themselves as a righteous people opposed to "godless Communism." In 1954, the phrase "under God" was inserted into the Pledge of Allegiance, and after 1956, U.S. coins carried the words "In God We Trust."

Despite its evangelical bent, the resurgence of religion had a distinctly moderate tone. An ecumenical movement bringing Catholics, Protestants, and Jews together flourished, and so did a concern for the here-and-now. In his popular television program, Catholic Bishop Fulton J. Sheen asked, "Is life worth living?" He and countless others answered that it was. None was more affirmative than Norman Vincent Peale, whose best-selling book *The Power of Positive Thinking* (1952) embodied the therapeutic use of religion as an antidote to the stresses of modern life.

Consumer Culture

In some respects, postwar consumerism seemed like the 1920s all over again: an abundance of new gadgets and appliances, the craze for automobiles, and new types of mass media. Yet there was a significant difference. In the 1950s, consumption became associated with citizenship. Buying things, once a sign of personal indulgence, now meant participating fully in American society and, moreover, fulfilling a social responsibility. By spending, Americans fueled a high-employment economy. What the suburban family consumed, asserted *Life* magazine in a photo essay featuring one such family, would help to ensure "full employment and improved living standards for the rest of the nation."

As in the past, product makers sought to stimulate consumer demand through aggressive advertising. More money was spent in 1951 on advertising ($6.5 billion) than on the public schools ($5 billion). The 1950s gave Americans the Marlboro Man; M&Ms that melt in your mouth, not in your hand; Wonder Bread to build strong bodies in twelve ways; and the "does she or doesn't she?" Clairol hair-coloring woman. Motivational research delved into the subconscious to find out how the messages should be pitched. Like other features of the consumer culture, this one got its share of muckraking in Vance Packer's best-selling *The Hidden Persuaders* (1957).

Advertising heavily promoted the appliances that began to fill the suburban kitchen. In 1946, automatic washing machines replaced the old machines with hand-cranked wringers, and clothes dryers also came on the market. Commercial laundries across the country struggled to stay in business. Another new item was the home freezer, which encouraged the dramatic growth of the frozen-food industry. Partly because of all the electrical appliances, consumer use of electricity doubled during the 1950s.

Television's arrival was swift and overpowering. There were only 7,000 TV sets in American homes in 1947, yet a year later, the CBS and NBC radio networks began offering regular programming, and by 1950, Americans owned 7.3 million sets. Ten years later, 87 percent of American homes had at least one television set.

Although licensed by the Federal Communications Commission (FCC), television stations, like radio, depended entirely on advertising for profits. Soon, television supplanted radio as the chief diffuser of popular culture. Movies, too, lost the cultural dominance they had once enjoyed. Movie attendance shrank throughout the postwar period, and movie studios increasingly relied on overseas distribution to earn a profit.

What Americans saw on television, besides the omnipresent commercials, was an overwhelmingly white, Anglo-Saxon world of nuclear families, suburban homes, and middle-class life. A typical show was *Father Knows Best*, starring Robert Young and

Jane Wyatt. Father left home each morning wearing a suit and carrying a briefcase. Mother was a full-time housewife, always tending to her three children but, as a stereotypical female, prone to bad driving and tears. The children were sometimes rebellious, but family conflicts were invariably resolved. *The Honeymooners*, starring Jackie Gleason as a Brooklyn bus driver, and *The Life of Riley*, a situation comedy featuring a California aircraft worker, were rare in their treatment of working-class lives. Black characters such as Rochester in Jack Benny's comedy show appeared mainly as sidekicks and servants.

The types of television programs that were developed in the 1950s built on older entertainment genres but also pioneered new ones. Taking its cue from the movies, television offered some thirty westerns by 1959, including *Gunsmoke*, *Wagon Train*, and *Bonanza*. Professional sports became big-time television, far exceeding the potential of radio. Programming geared toward children, such as *The Mickey Mouse Club*, *Howdy Doody*, and *Captain Kangaroo*, created the first generation of children glued to the tube.

Although the new medium did offer some serious programming, notably live theater and documentaries, FCC Commissioner Newton Minow concluded in 1963 that television was "a vast wasteland." But it did what it intended, which was to sell products and fill America's leisure hours with reassuring entertainment.

The Baby Boom

A popular 1945 song was called "Gotta Make Up for Lost Time," and Americans did just that. Two things were noteworthy about the families they formed after World War II. First, marriages were remarkably stable. Not until the mid-1960s did the divorce rate begin to rise sharply. Second, married couples were intent on having babies. Everyone expected to have several children — it was part of adulthood, almost a citizen's responsibility. After a century and a half of decline, the birthrate shot up: More babies were born between 1948 and 1953 than in the previous thirty years.

One of the reasons for this baby boom was that everyone was having children at the same time. A second was a drop in the marriage age — down to twenty-two for men, on the average, and twenty for women. Younger parents meant a bumper crop of children. Women who came of age in the 1930s averaged 2.4 children; their counterparts in the 1950s averaged 3.2 children. The baby boom peaked in 1957 and remained at a high level until the early 1960s.

To keep all those baby boom children healthy and happy, middle-class parents increasingly relied on the advice of experts. Dr. Benjamin Spock's best-selling *Baby and Child Care* sold one million copies a year after its publication in 1946. Spock urged mothers to abandon the rigid feeding and baby-care schedules of an earlier generation. New mothers found Spock's commonsense approach liberating without being wholly reassured. If mothers were too protective, Spock and others argued, they might hamper their children's preparation for adult life. Mothers who wanted to work outside the home felt guilty because Spock recommended that they be constantly available for their children.

Less subject to fashion were the advances in diet, public health, and medical practice that made for healthier children. Serious illnesses became merely routine after the introduction of such "miracle drugs" as penicillin (introduced in 1943), streptomycin (1945), and cortisone (1946). When Dr. Jonas Salk perfected a polio vaccine in 1954, he became a national hero. The free distribution of Salk's vaccine in the nation's schools, followed in 1961 by Dr. Albert Sabin's oral polio vaccine, demonstrated the potential of government-sponsored public health programs. The baby boom gave the nation's educational system a boost. The new middle class, America's first college-educated generation, placed a high value on education. Suburban parents approved 90 percent of proposed school bond issues during the 1950s. By 1970, school expenditures accounted for 7.2 percent of the gross national product, double the 1950 level. In the 1960s, the baby boom generation swelled college enrollments and, not coincidentally, the ranks of student protesters (see Chapter 28).

The passage of time revealed the ever-widening impact of the baby boom. When baby boomers competed for jobs during the 1970s, the labor market became tight. When career-oriented baby boomers belatedly began having children in the 1980s, the birthrate jumped. And in our own time, as baby boomers begin retiring, huge funding problems threaten to engulf Social Security and Medicare. Who would have thought that the intimate decisions of so many couples after World War II would be affecting American life well into the twenty-first century?

Contradictions in Women's Lives

"The suburban housewife was the dream image of the young American woman," the feminist Betty Friedan wrote of the 1950s. "She was healthy, beautiful, educated, concerned only about her husband, her children, and her home." Friedan gave up a psychology fellowship to marry, move to the suburbs, and raise three children. "Determined that I find the feminine fulfillment that eluded my mother . . . I lived the life of a suburban housewife that was everyone's dream at the time."

The idea that a woman's place was in the home was, of course, not new. What Betty Friedan called the "feminine mystique" of the 1950s—that "the highest value and the only commitment for women is the fulfillment of their own femininity"—bore a remarkable similarity to the nineteenth century's cult of true womanhood.

The updated version drew on new elements of twentieth-century science and culture. Psychologists equated motherhood with "normal" female identity and suggested that career-minded mothers needed therapy. Television and film depicted career women as social misfits, the heavies in movies such as *Mildred Pierce*. The postwar consumer culture also emphasized woman's domestic role as purchasing agent for home and family. "Love is said in many ways," ran an ad for toilet paper. Another asked, "Can a woman ever feel right cooking on a dirty range?"

Although the feminine mystique held cultural sway, it was by no means as all-encompassing as Friedan implied in her 1963 best-seller, *The Feminine Mystique*. Indeed, Friedan herself resisted the stereotype, doing freelance journalism while at home and, as a result of that work, stumbling onto the subject and writing the book that made her famous. Middle-class wives often found constructive outlets in the League of Women Voters, the PTA, and their churches. As in earlier periods, some women used the rhetoric of domesticity to justify political activism, enlisting in campaigns for community improvement, racial integration, and nuclear disarmament. As for working-class women, many of them doubtless would have loved to embrace domesticity if only they could. The economic needs of their families demanded otherwise.

The feminine mystique notwithstanding, more than one-third of American women in the 1950s held jobs outside the home. As the service sector expanded, so did the demand for workers in jobs traditionally filled by women.

Occupational segmentation still haunted women. Until 1964, the classified sections of newspapers separated employment ads into "Help Wanted Male" and "Help Wanted Female." More than 80 percent of all employed women did stereotypical "women's work" as salespeople, health-care technicians, waitresses, stewardesses, domestic servants, receptionists, telephone operators, and secretaries. In 1960, women represented only 3.5 percent of lawyers (many top law schools did not admit women at all) and 6.1 percent of physicians but 97 percent of nurses, 85 percent of librarians, and 57 percent of social workers. Along with women's jobs went women's pay, which averaged 60 percent of men's pay in 1963.

What was new was the range of women at work. At the turn of the century, the typical female worker had been young and unmarried. By midcentury, she was in her forties, married, and with children in school. In 1940, only 15 percent of wives had worked. By 1960, 30 percent did, and by 1970, it was 40 percent.

A Woman's Dilemma in Postwar America

This 1959 *Saturday Evening Post* cover depicts some of the difficult choices women faced in the postwar era. Women's consignment to low-paid, dead-end jobs in the service sector encouraged many to become full-time homemakers. Once back in their suburban homes, however, many middle-class women felt isolated and trapped in endless rounds of cooking, cleaning, and diaper changing. 1959 SEPS: Licensed by Curtis Publishing Company, Indianapolis, IN. All rights reserved. www.curtispublishing.com.

Married women worked to supplement family income. Even in the prosperous 1950s, the wages of many men could not pay for what middle-class life demanded: cars, houses, vacations, and college educations for the children. Poorer households needed more than one wage earner just to get by.

How could American society steadfastly uphold the domestic ideal when so many wives and mothers were out of the house and at work? In many ways, the contradiction was hidden by the women themselves. Fearing public disapproval, women usually justified their work in family-oriented terms: "Of course I believe a woman's place is at home, but I took this job to save for college for our children." Moreover, when women took jobs outside the home, they still bore full responsibility for child care and household management. As one overburdened woman noted, she now had "two full-time jobs instead of just one—underpaid clerical worker and unpaid housekeeper."

Youth Culture

In 1956, only partly in jest, the CBS radio commentator Eric Sevareid questioned "whether the teenagers will take over the United States lock, stock, living room, and garage." Sevareid was grumbling about American youth culture, a phenomenon that had first been noticed in the 1920s and had its roots in lengthening years of education, the role of peer groups, and the consumer tastes of teenagers. Like so much else in the 1950s, the youth culture came down to having money.

Market research revealed a distinct teen market to be exploited. *Newsweek* noted with awe in 1951 that the aggregate of the $3 weekly spending money of the average teenager was enough to buy 190 million candy bars, 130 million soft drinks, and 230 million sticks of gum. In 1956, advertisers projected an adolescent market of $9 billion for transistor radios (first introduced in 1952), 45-rpm records, clothing, and fads such as Silly Putty (1950) and Hula Hoops (1958). Increasingly, advertisers targeted the young, both to capture their spending money and to exploit their influence on family purchases. Note the changing slogans for Pepsi-Cola: "Twice as much for a nickel" (1935), "Be sociable—have a Pepsi" (1948), "Now it's Pepsi for those who think young" (1960), and finally "the Pepsi Generation" (1965).

Hollywood movies played a large role in fostering a teenage culture. At a time when Americans were being lured by television, young people made up the largest audience for motion pictures. Soon Hollywood studios catered to them with films such as *The Wild One* (1951), starring Marlon Brando, and *Rebel Without a Cause* (1955), starring James Dean. "What are you rebelling against?" a waitress asks Brando in *The Wild One*. "Whattaya got?" he replies.

What really defined this generation, however, was its music. Rejecting the romantic ballads of the 1940s, teenagers discovered rock 'n' roll, an amalgam of white country and western music and black-inspired rhythm and blues. The Cleveland disc jockey Alan Freed played a major role in introducing white America to the black-influenced sound by playing what were called race records. "If I could find a white man who had the Negro sound and the Negro feel, I could make a billion dollars," said the owner of a record company. The performer who fit that bill was Elvis Presley, who rocketed into instant celebrity in 1956 with his hit records "Hound Dog" and "Heartbreak Hotel."

Between 1953 and 1959, record sales increased from $213 million to $603 million, with rock 'n' roll as the driving force.

Many unhappy adults saw in rock 'n' roll music, teen movies, and magazines such as *Mad* (introduced in 1952) an invitation to race mixing, rebellion, and disorder. The media featured hundreds of stories on problem teens, and in 1955, a Senate subcommittee headed by Estes Kefauver conducted a high-profile investigation of juvenile delinquency and its origins in the popular media. Denunciations of course only bounced off the new youth culture or, if anything, increased its popularity.

Cultural Dissenters

Youth rebellion was only one aspect of a broader discontent with the conformist culture of the 1950s. Artists, jazz musicians, and writers expressed their alienation in a remarkable flowering of intensely personal, introspective art forms. In New York, Jackson Pollock and other painters developed an inventive style that became known as abstract expressionism. Swirling and splattering paint onto giant canvases, Pollock emphasized self-expression in the act of painting.

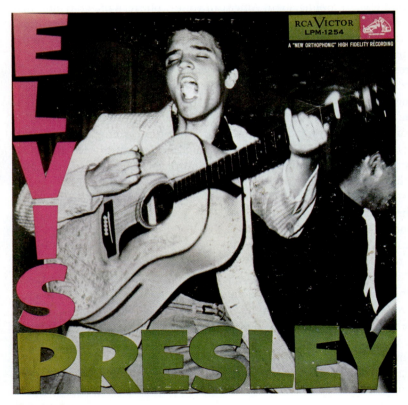

Elvis Presley
The young Elvis Presley, shown here on the cover of his first album in 1956, embodied cultural rebellion against the conservatism and triviality of adult life in the 1950s. © 1956 BGM Music.

A similar trend characterized jazz, where black musicians developed a hard-driving improvisational style known as bebop. Whether the "hot" bebop of saxophonist Charlie Parker or the more subdued "cool" West Coast sound of the trumpeter Miles Davis, postwar jazz was cerebral, intimate, and individualistic. As such, it stood in stark contrast to the commercialized, dance-oriented "swing" bands of the 1930s and 1940s.

Black jazz musicians found eager fans not only in the African American community but also among young white Beats, a group of writers and poets centered in New York and San Francisco who disdained middle-class conformity and suburban materialism. In his poem *Howl* (1956), which became a manifesto of the Beat generation, Allen Ginsberg lamented: "I saw the best minds of my generation destroyed by madness, starving hysterical naked, dragging themselves through the negro streets at dawn looking for an angry fix." In works such as Jack Kerouac's novel *On the Road* (1957), the Beats glorified spontaneity, sexual adventurism, drug use, and spirituality. Like other members of the postwar generation, the Beats were apolitical; their rebellion was strictly cultural. In the 1960s, however, the Beats would inspire a new generation of young rebels angry at both the political and cultural status quo.

▶ In what ways did the growth of the Sun Belt reflect key themes of the suburban explosion?

▶ What was the relationship between consumer culture and the emphasis on family life in the postwar era?

▶ Is it correct to say that the 1950s was exclusively a time of cultural conformity?

The Other America

While middle-class whites flocked to the suburbs, an opposite stream of poor and working-class migrants, many of them southern blacks, moved into the cities. What these urban newcomers inherited was a declining economy and a decaying environment. To those enjoying prosperity, "the Other America"—as the social critic Michael Harrington called it in 1962—remained largely invisible. Only in the South, where African Americans organized to combat segregation, did the stain of social injustice catch the nation's attention.

Immigrants and Migrants

Ever since the passage of the National Origins Act of 1924 (see Chapter 23), U.S. immigration policy had aimed mainly at keeping foreigners out. Anti-immigrant sentiment intensified during the Great Depression, hardly budging even to rescue Jews fleeing Nazi persecution. World War II caused the bar to be lowered slightly, enabling returning servicemen to bring home war brides and, under the Displaced Persons Act (1948), permitting the entry of approximately 415,000 Europeans, among them former Nazis such as Werner von Braun, the rocket scientist. The overt anti-Asian bias of America's immigration laws also became untenable. In a gesture to an important war ally, the Chinese Exclusion Act was repealed in 1943. More far-reaching was the 1952 McCarran-Walter Act, which (in addition to barring Communists and other radicals) ended the exclusion under the 1924 act of Japanese, Koreans, and Southeast Asians.

Although not many came until later, the impact on Asian immigrant communities was considerable. On the eve of World War II, Chinatowns were populated primarily by men. Although most of them were married, their wives remained in China. The repeal of the Chinese Exclusion Act and the granting of naturalization rights encouraged those men to bring their wives to America. The result was a more normal, family-oriented community, a development also seen in the Filipino American and Japanese American communities. Approximately 135,000 men and 100,000 women of Chinese origin were living in the United States in 1960, mostly in New York State and California.

After the national-origins quota system went into effect in 1924, Mexico replaced eastern and southern Europe as the nation's labor reservoir. During World War II, the federal government introduced the *bracero* (temporary worker) program to ease wartime labor shortages (see Chapter 25) and then revived the program in 1951, during the Korean War. At its peak in 1959, Mexicans on temporary permits accounted for one-quarter of the nation's seasonal workers.

The federal government's ability to control the flow, however, was strictly limited. Mexicans came illegally, and by the time the *bracero* program ended in 1964, many of that group—an estimated 350,000—had settled in the United States. When unemployment became a problem during the recession of 1953–1954, federal authorities responded by deporting many Mexicans in a program grimly named Operation Wetback (because Mexican migrants often waded across the Rio Grande), but the Mexican population in the United States continued to rise nonetheless.

Mostly, they settled in to Los Angeles, Long Beach, El Paso, and other southwestern cities, following the crops during the harvest season or working in the expanding service sector. But many also went north, augmenting well-established Mexican American communites in Chicago, Detroit, Kansas City, and Denver. Although still important for American agriculture, more Mexican Americans by 1960 were employed as industrial and service workers.

Another major group of Spanish-speaking migrants came from Puerto Rico. American citizens since 1917, Puerto Ricans enjoyed an unrestricted right to move to the mainland United States. Migration increased dramatically after World War II, when mechanization of the island's sugarcane agriculture pushed many Puerto Ricans off the land. Airlines began to offer cheap direct flights between San Juan and New York City. With the fare at about $50, two weeks' wages, Puerto Ricans became America's first immigrants with the luxury of arriving by air.

Most Puerto Ricans went to New York, where they settled first in East ("Spanish") Harlem and then scattered in neighborhoods across the city's five boroughs. This massive migration, which increased the Puerto Rican population to 613,000 by 1960, transformed the ethnic composition of the city. More Puerto Ricans now lived in New York City than in San Juan. They faced conditions common to all recent immigrants: crowded and deteriorating housing, segregation, menial jobs, poor schools, and the problems of a bilingual existence.

Cuban refugees constituted the third largest group of Spanish-speaking immigrants. In the six years after Fidel Castro's seizure of power in 1959 (see Chapter 28), an estimated 180,000 people fled Cuba for the United States. The Cuban refugee community grew so quickly that it turned Miami into a cosmopolitan, bilingual city almost overnight. Unlike other urban migrants, Miami's Cubans quickly prospered, in large part because they had arrived with money and middle-class skills.

In western cities, an influx of Native Americans also contributed to the rise in the nonwhite urban population. In 1953, Congress authorized a program terminating the autonomous status of the Indian tribes and encouraging voluntary migration from the reservations. The Bureau of Indian Affairs subsidized moving costs and established relocation centers in San Francisco, Denver, Chicago, and other cities. Despite the program's assimilationist goal, the 60,000 Native Americans who migrated to the cities mostly settled together in ghetto neighborhoods, with little prospect of adjusting successfully to an urban environment.

African Americans came in large number from the rural South, continuing the Great Migration that had begun during World War I (see Chapter 22). Black migration was hastened by the transformation of southern agriculture. Synthetic fabrics cut into the demand for cotton, reducing cotton acreage from 43 million acres in 1930 to less than 15 million acres in 1960. On top of that, mechanization reduced the need for farm labor. The mechanical cotton picker, introduced in 1944, effectively destroyed the sharecropper system. Although both whites and blacks fled the land, the exodus was greatest among blacks. By 1990, only 69,000 black farmers remained nationwide, a tiny fraction of the country's farmers.

Where did these displaced farmfolk go? White southerners from Appalachia moved north to "hillbilly" ghettos, such as Cincinnati's Over the Rhine neighborhood and Chicago's Uptown. As many as three million blacks headed to Chicago, New York, Washington, Detroit, Los Angeles, and other cities. Certain sections of Chicago seemed like the Mississippi Delta transplanted, so pervasive were the migrants. By 1960, about half the nation's black population was living outside the South, compared with only 23 percent before World War II.

The Urban Crisis

Migration to American cities, whether from Europe or rural America, had always been attended by hardship, by poverty, slum housing, and cultural dislocation. So severe had these problems seemed half a century earlier that they had helped to spark the reform wave of the Progressive era (see Chapter 20). But hardship then had been temporary, a way station on the path to a better life. That had been true initially of the post-1941 migration, when blacks found jobs in the defense industry and, in the postwar boom, in Detroit auto plants and Chicago meatpacking houses.

Later migrants were not as lucky. By the 1950s, the economy was changing. The manufacturing sector was contracting, and technological advances—what people then called "automation"—hit unskilled and semiskilled jobs especially hard. These were the "jobs in which Negroes are disproportionately concentrated," noted the civil rights activist Bayard Rustin. Black migrants, Rustin warned, were becoming economically superfluous, and in that respect their situation was far bleaker than anything faced by earlier immigrants.

A second difference involved race. Every immigrant wave—Irish, Italian, Slavic, Jewish—had been greeted by hostility, but none as virulent as that experienced by black migrants. In the 1950s, a more tolerant era, they were spared the race rioting that had afflicted their predecessors. But racism in its more covert forms held them back at every turn: by housing restrictions, by schools increasingly segregated, by an urban infrastructure that was underfunded and decaying because whites fled to the suburbs. In the 1950s, the nation's twelve largest cities lost 3.6 million whites while gaining 4.5 million nonwhites.

As if joblessness and discrimination were not enough, black ghettoes were hit during the 1950s by a frenzy of urban renewal. Seeking to revitalize city centers, urban planners, politicians, and real estate developers proposed razing blighted neighborhoods to make way for modern construction projects.

Local residents were rarely consulted about whether they wanted their neighborhoods "renewed." In Boston, almost one-third of the old city was demolished — including the historic West End, a long-established Italian neighborhood — to make way for a new highway, high-rise housing, and government and commercial buildings. In San Francisco, some 4,000 residents of the Western Addition, a predominantly black neighborhood, lost out to an urban renewal program that built luxury housing, a shopping center, and an express boulevard. Between 1949 and 1967, urban renewal demolished almost 400,000 buildings and displaced 1.4 million people.

The urban experts knew what to do with these people. They would be relocated to federally funded housing projects, an outgrowth of New Deal housing policy, now much expanded and combined with generous funding for slum clearance. However well intentioned, these grim projects had a distrastrous impact on black community life, destroying neighborhoods and relegating the inhabitants to social isolation. The notorious Robert Taylor Homes in Chicago, a huge complex of 28 sixteen-story buildings and 20,000 residents, almost all black, became a breeding ground for crime and hopelessness.

In 1962, the Swedish sociologist Gunnar Myrdal (author of *An American Dilemma*, a pioneering book about the country's race relations) wondered whether shrinking economic opportunity in the United States might not "trap an 'under-class' of unemployed and, gradually, unemployable and underemployed persons and families at the bottom of a society." Myrdal's term *underclass* — referring to a population permanently mired in poverty and dependency — would figure centrally in future American debates about social policy. It 1962, however, *underclass* was a newly coined word, describing a phenomenon that had not yet been noticed but was already well under way in the inner cities of 1950s America.

The Emerging Civil Rights Struggle

Segregation prevailed in the South. In most southern states, blacks could not eat in restaurants patronized by whites or use the same waiting rooms at bus stations. All forms of public transportation were rigidly segregated by custom or by law. Even drinking fountains were labeled "White" and "Colored."

Blacks understood that segregation would never be abolished without grassroots struggle. But that was not their only weapon. They also had the Bill of Rights and the great Reconstruction amendments to the Constitution. In this respect, fighting segregation was different from fighting poverty. Blacks had no constitutional right not to be poor, but they did have constitutional rights not to be discriminated against, if only these rights could be exercised. The Cold War, moreover, gave civil rights advocates added leverage because America's reputation in the world now counted to America's leaders. So the battle against racial injustice, as it took shape after World War II, proceeded on two tracks: on the ground, where blacks began to stand up for their rights, and in the courts and corridors of power, where words sometimes mattered more than action.

During World War II, the National Association for the Advancement of Colored People (NAACP) redoubled its efforts to combat discrimination in housing, transportation, and jobs. Black demands for justice continued into the postwar years, spurred by symbolic victories, as when Jackie Robinson broke through the color line in major league baseball by joining the Brooklyn Dodgers in 1947.

African American leaders also had hopes for President Truman. Although capable of racist language, Truman supported civil rights on moral grounds. Moreover, he understood the growing importance of the black vote in key northern states, a fact driven home by his surprise 1948 victory. Truman also worried about America's image abroad. It did not help that the Soviet Union compared the South's treatment of blacks with the Nazis' treatment of the Jews.

Lacking support in Congress, Truman turned to executive action. In 1946, he appointed a National Civil Rights Commission, whose 1947 report called for robust federal action on behalf of civil rights. In 1948, under pressure from A. Philip Randolph's Committee Against Jim Crow in Military Service, Truman signed an executive order desegregating the armed forces. Then, with his hand strengthened by the victory for civil rights at the 1948 Democratic convention, Truman went on the offensive, pushing legislation on a variety of fronts, including voting rights and equal employment opportunity. Invariably, his efforts were defeated by filibustering southern senators.

With Dwight Eisenhower as president, civil rights no longer had a champion in the White House. But in the meantime, NAACP lawyers Thurgood Marshall and William Hastie had been preparing the legal ground in a series of test cases challenging racial discrimination, and in 1954 they hit pay dirt.

The case involved Linda Brown, a black pupil in Topeka, Kansas, who had been forced to attend a distant segregated school rather than the nearby white elementary school. In *Brown v. Board of Education*, the NAACP's chief counsel, Thurgood Marshall, argued that such segregation was unconstitutional because it denied Linda Brown the "equal protection of the laws" guaranteed by the Fourteenth Amendment. In a unanimous decision on May 17, 1954, the Supreme Court agreed, overturning the "separate but equal" doctrine of *Plessy v. Ferguson* (see Chapter 19). Speaking for the Court, the new Chief Justice Earl Warren wrote:

> To separate Negro children . . . solely because of their race generates a feeling of inferiority as to their status in the community that may affect their hearts and minds in a way unlikely ever to be undone. . . . . We conclude that in the field of public education the doctrine of "separate but equal" has no place. Separate educational facilities are inherently unequal.

In an implementing 1955 decision known as *Brown II*, the Court declared simply that integration should proceed "with all deliberate speed."

In the South, however, the call went out for "massive resistance." A Southern Manifesto signed in 1956 by 101 members of Congress denounced the *Brown* decision as "a clear abuse of judicial power" and encouraged their constituents to defy it. That year, 500,000 southerners joined White Citizens' Councils dedicated to blocking school integration. Some whites revived the old tactics of violence and intimidation, swelling the ranks of the Ku Klux Klan to levels not seen since the 1920s.

President Eisenhower accepted the *Brown* decision as the law of the land, but he thought it a mistake. He was not happy about committing federal power to enforce it. A crisis in Little Rock, Arkansas, finally forced his hand. In September 1957, nine black students attempted to enroll at the all-white Central High School. Governor Orval Faubus called out the National Guard to bar them. Then the mob took over. Every day, the nine students had to run a gauntlet of angry whites chanting, "Go back to the jungle." As the vicious scenes played out on television night after night, Eisenhower acted. He sent 1,000 federal troops to Little Rock and nationalized the Arkansas National Guard, ordering them to protect the black students. Eisenhower thus became the first president since Reconstruction to use federal troops to enforce the rights of blacks.

The *Brown* decision validated the NAACP's legal strategy, but white resistance also revealed that winning in court was not enough. Prompted by one small act of defiance, southern black leaders unveiled a new tactic: nonviolent protest.

On December 1, 1955, Rosa Parks, a seamstress in Montgomery, Alabama, refused to give up her seat on a bus to a white man. She was arrested and charged with violating a local segregation ordinance. Parks's act was not the spur-of-the-moment decision that it seemed. A woman of sterling reputation and a long-time NAACP member, she had been chosen to play that part. Middle-aged and unassuming, Rosa Parks fit the bill perfectly for the NAACP's challenge against segregated buses.

Once the die was cast, the black community turned for leadership to the Reverend Martin Luther King Jr., the recently appointed pastor of Montgomery's Dexter Street Baptist Church. The son of a prominent Atlanta minister, King embraced the teachings of Mahatma Gandhi, whose campaigns of passive resistance had sparked India's independence from Britain in 1947. After Rosa Parks's arrest, King endorsed a plan by a local black women's organization to boycott Montgomery's bus system.

For the next 381 days, Montgomery blacks formed car pools or walked to work. The bus company neared bankruptcy, and downtown stores complained about the loss of business. But only after the Supreme Court ruled in November 1956 that bus segregation was unconstitutional did the city of Montgomery finally comply. "My feets is tired, but my soul is rested," said one satisfied woman boycotter.

The Montgomery bus boycott catapulted King to national prominence. In 1957, along with the Reverend Ralph Abernathy, he founded the Southern Christian Leadership Conference (SCLC), based in Atlanta. The black church, long the center of African American social and cultural life, now lent its moral and organizational strength to the civil rights movement. Black churchwomen were a tower of strength, transferring the skills honed by years of church work to the fight for civil rights justice. Soon the SCLC joined the NAACP as one of the main advocacy groups for racial justice.

The battle for civil rights entered a new phase in Greensboro, North Carolina, on February 1, 1960, when four black college students took seats at the whites-only lunch counter at the local Woolworth's. They were determined to "sit in" until they were served. Although they were arrested, the tactic worked—the Woolworth's lunch counter was desegregated—and sit-ins quickly spread to other southern cities (see American Voices, p. 819). A few months later, Ella Baker, an administrator with the SCLC, helped to

Desegregating Lunch Counters FRANKLIN MCCAIN

Franklin McCain was one of the four African American students at North Carolina A&T College in Greensboro, North Carolina, who sat down at the Woolworth's lunch counter on February 1, 1960, setting off by that simple act a wave of student sit-ins that rocked the South and initiated a national civil rights movement. In the following interview, McCain describes how he and his pals took that momentous step.

The planning process was on a Sunday night, I remember it quite well. I think it was Joseph who said, "It's time that we take some action now. We've been getting together, and we've been, up to this point, still like most people we've talked about for the past few weeks or so—that is, people who talk a lot but, in fact, take very little action." After selecting the technique, then we said, "Let's go down and just ask for service." It certainly wasn't titled a "sit-in" or "sit-down" at that time. "Let's just go down to Woolworth's tomorrow and ask for service, and the tactic is going to be simply this: we'll just stay there."

. . . Once getting there . . . we did make purchases of school supplies and took the patience and time to get receipts for our purchases, and Joseph and myself went over to the counter and asked to be served coffee and doughnuts. As anticipated, the reply was, "I'm sorry, we don't serve you here." And of course we said, "We just beg to disagree with you. We've in fact already been served."

. . . At that point there was a policeman who had walked in off the street, who was pacing the aisle . . . behind us, where we were seated, with his club in his hand, just sort of knocking it in his hand, and just looking mean and red and a little bit upset and a little bit disgusted. And you had the feeling that he didn't know what the hell to do. . . . Usually his defense is offense, and

we've provoked him, yes, but we haven't provoked outwardly enough for him to resort to violence. And I think this is just killing him; you can see it all over him.

If it's possible to know what it means to have your soul cleansed—I felt pretty clean at that time. I probably felt better on that day than I've ever felt in my life. Seems like a lot of feelings of guilt or what-have-you suddenly left me, and I felt as though I had gained my manhood. . . . Not Franklin McCain only as an individual, but I felt as though the manhood of a number of other black persons had been restored and had gotten some respect from just that one day.

The movement started out as a movement of nonviolence and a Christian movement. . . . We knew that probably the most powerful and potent weapon that people have literally no defense for is love, kindness. That is, whip the enemy with something that he doesn't understand. . . . The individual who had probably the most influence on us was Gandhi. . . . Yes, Martin Luther King's name was well-known when the sit-in movement was in effect, but . . . no, he was not the individual we had upmost in mind when we started the sit-in movement.

SOURCE: Clayborne Carson et al., eds., *The Eyes on the Prize Civil Rights Reader* (New York: Viking, 1991), 114–116.

The Greensboro Four

Pictured here are the four African American students who, entirely on their own, decided to demand service at the Woolworth's whites-only lunch counter in Greensboro, North Carolina, and started a sit-down movement across the South. Second from the left is Franklin McCain, whose interview appears in American Voices on p. 819. © Bettmann/Corbis.

▶ Who were the people who occupied "the Other America"? Why were they there rather than in mainstream America?

▶ What were the key components of the urban crisis?

▶ What is the significance of the *Brown v. Board of Education of Topeka* decision?

organize the Student Nonviolent Coordinating Committee (SNCC, known as "Snick") to facilitate student sit-ins. By the end of the year, about 50,000 people had participated in sit-ins or other demonstrations, and 3,600 of them had been jailed. But in 126 cities across the South, blacks were at last able to eat at Woolworth's lunch counters.

The victories so far had been limited, but the groundwork had been laid for a civil rights offensive that would transform the nation's race relations.

SUMMARY

We have explored how, at the very time that it became mired in the Cold War, the United States entered an unparalleled era of prosperity. Indeed, the Cold War was one of the engines of prosperity. The postwar economy was marked especially by the dominance of big corporations. Corporate dominance in turn helped to make possible the labor-management accord that spread the benefits of prosperity to workers beyond the dreams of earlier generations.

After years of depression and war-induced insecurity, Americans turned inward toward religion, home, and family. Postwar couples married young, had several children, and—if they were white and middle class—raised their children in a climate of suburban comfort and consumerism. The profamily orientation of the 1950s celebrated social conformity and traditional gender roles, even though millions of women entered the workforce in those years. Cultural conformity provoked resistance, however, both by the burgeoning youth culture and by a remarkably inventive generation of painters, musicians, and writers.

Not everyone, moreover, shared the postwar prosperity. Postwar cities increasingly became places of last resort for the nation's poor. Black migrants, unlike earlier immigrants, encountered an urban economy that had little use for them. Without opportunity and faced by pervasive racism, they were on their way to becoming, many of them, an American underclass. In the South, however, discrimination produced a civil rights uprising that white America could not ignore. Many of the smoldering contradictions of the postwar period—Cold War anxiety in the midst of suburban domesticity, tensions in women's lives, economic and racial inequality—helped to spur the protest movements of the 1960s.

Connections: Economy

In the 1950s, as we noted in the essay opening Part Six, "no country had an economy that was competitive with America's." The roots of that supremacy went back into the late nineteenth century when, as we discussed in Chapter 17, heavy industry, mass-production technology, and a corporate business structure emerged. In the 1920s (Chapter 23), this industrial economy was refined, and after the hiatus of the

TIMELINE

1944 ▸ Bretton Woods economic conference	**1955** ▸ Montgomery bus boycott ▸ begins
▸ World Bank and International Monetary Fund (IMF) founded	▸ AFL and CIO merge
1946 ▸ First edition of Dr. Spock's *Baby and Child Care*	**1956** ▸ National Interstate and Defense Highways Act
1947 ▸ First Levittown built	▸ Elvis Presley's breakthrough records
▸ Jackie Robinson joins the Brooklyn Dodgers	**1957** ▸ Peak of postwar baby boom
1948 ▸ Beginning of network television	▸ Eisenhower sends U.S. troops to enforce integration of Little Rock Central High School
1950 ▸ Treaty of Detroit initiates labor-management accord	▸ Southern Christian Leadership Conference (SCLC) founded
1953 ▸ Operation Wetback	**1960** ▸ Student sit-ins in Greensboro, North Carolina
1954 ▸ *Brown v. Board of Education of Topeka*	

Great Depression, it became the basis for the post–World War II economic boom. In Chapter 29, we describe the first stages in the decline of this manufacturing economy during the 1970s. The postwar consumer culture had roots that went back into the 1920s (Chapter 23), while the accompanying suburbanization went back even earlier, into the nineteenth century (Chapter 18). Similarly, we can trace back to earlier discussions the migratory patterns (see Chapters 17 and 22), the decay of the cities (see Chapter 18), and the rise of the civil rights movement (see Chapter 20) that characterized the 1950s. The civil rights movement of that decade was, of course, only a precursor of the great struggles of the 1960s (Chapter 28) and 1970s (Chapter 29).

FOR FURTHER EXPLORATION

Two engaging introductions to postwar society are Paul Boyer, *Promises to Keep* (1995), and David Halberstam, *The Fifties* (1993). Nelson Lichtenstein, *State of the Union: A Century of American Labor* (2002), offers a searching account of the labor-management accord. The best book on the consumer culture is Lizabeth Cohen, *A Consumers' Republic: The Politics of Mass Consumption in Postwar America* (2003). Elaine Tyler May, *Homeward Bound* (1988), is the classic introduction to postwar family life. For youth culture, see William Graebner, *Coming of Age in Buffalo* (1990), and a classic of the period, Paul Goodman, *Growing Up Absurd* (1960). On the urban crisis, see especially Nicholas Lemann, *The Promised Land: The Great Migration and How It Changed America* (1991), and Thomas J. Sugrue, *The Origins of the Urban Crisis: Race and Inequality in Postwar Detroit* (1996). Taylor Branch's biography of Martin Luther King Jr., *Parting the Waters: America in the King Years 1954–1963* (1988), while focusing on King's leadership, provides an engaging account of the early civil rights movement.

Literary Kicks: The Beat Generation, at **www.litkicks.com/BeatPages/msg.jsp ?what=BeatGen**, is an independent site created by New York writer Levi Asher devoted to the literature of the Beat generation. The *Arkansas Democrat-Gazette* has compiled materials from two Arkansas newspapers covering the Central High School crisis in Little Rock in 1957 at **www.ardemgaz.com/prev/central**.

TEST YOUR KNOWLEDGE

To assess your mastery of the material in this chapter and for Web sites, images, and documents related to this chapter, visit **bedfordstmartins.com/henrettaconcise**.

The Liberal Consensus: Flaming Out

1960–1968

In our excessive involvement in the affairs of other countries, we are not only . . . denying our own people the proper enjoyment of their resources; we are also denying the world the example of a free society enjoying its freedom to the fullest. This is regettable indeed for a nation that aspires to teach democracy to other nations.

— Senator J. William Fulbright, 1966

On Inauguration Day, 1961, standing bare-headed in the wintry January brightness, the freshly sworn-in president issued a ringing declaration: "Let the word go forth from this time and place, to friend and foe alike, that the torch has passed to a new generation of Americans, born in this century, tempered by war, disciplined by a hard and bitter peace, proud of our ancient heritage." John F. Kennedy challenged Americans everywhere: "Ask not what your country can do for you, ask what you can do for your country." And, more than anyone might have expected, Americans responded. "There's a moral wave building among today's youth," said a civil rights volunteer in 1964, "and I intend to catch it."

Kennedy's politics of expectation might initially have been mostly a matter of atmospherics, but over time it built into the greatest burst of liberal reform since the New Deal, producing landmark civil rights laws, Medicare, the War on Poverty, and much more. All this—the triumph of the liberal consensus—starts with the indelible image of the youthful Kennedy exhorting the country on that Inauguration Day in 1961.

Fast forward to August 1968, to the Democratic National Convention in Chicago. Kennedy is dead, assassinated in 1963. His civil rights mentor, Martin Luther King Jr., is dead, assassinated. His younger brother and heir apparent, Bobby, is dead, assassinated. And his successor in the White House, Lyndon B. Johnson, is so discredited that he has withdrawn his name from nomination for reelection.

On the streets of Chicago, police teargassed and clubbed demonstrators, who screamed (as the TV cameras rolled), "The whole world is watching!" Some of them had once been the idealistic young people of Kennedy's exhortation. Now they detested everything that Kennedy's liberalism stood for. Inside the convention hall, the proceedings were chaotic, the atmosphere poisonous, the delegates bitterly divided over Vietnam. As expected, Johnson's vice president, Hubert Humphrey, easily won the nomination, but he hadn't been done any favors. He later acknowledged going home feeling not triumphant but "heartbroken, battered, and defeated." The Chicago convention had been "a disaster."

In this chapter, we undertake to explain how Kennedy's stirring inauguration metamorphosed into the searing Democratic National Convention of 1968. Between those two events, indelible in America's memory, the liberal consensus flamed out.

John F. Kennedy and the Politics of Expectation

Starting in the days of FDR, Americans came increasingly to look to Washington for answers to the nation's problems. Few presidents were happier to oblige than John Kennedy. He came to Washington primed for action, promising that his "New Frontier" would get America moving again. The British journalist Henry Fairley called Kennedy's activism "the politics of expectation." Soon enough, expectation came up against unyielding reality, but Kennedy's can-do style nevertheless left a lasting imprint on American politics.

The New Politics

Charisma, style, and personality — these, more than platforms and issues, were hallmarks of a new brand of politics. With the power of the media in mind, a younger generation of politicians saw in television a new way of reaching the voters directly. Candidates drifted away from traditional party organizations, with their machinery for delivering the votes on election day. By using the media, campaigns could bypass the party structures and touch, if only with a thirty-second commercial, the ordinary citizen.

The new politics was John Kennedy's natural environment. Kennedy, a Harvard alumnus, World War II hero, and senator from Massachusetts, had inherited his love of politics from his grandfathers, both colorful Irish Catholic politicians in Boston. Ambitious, hard-driving, and deeply aware of style, the forty-three-year-old Kennedy made use of his many advantages to become, as novelist Norman Mailer put it, "our leading man." His one disadvantage — that he was Catholic in a country that had never elected a Catholic president — he masterfully neutralized. His family's wealth and energetic fundraising financed an exceptionally expensive campaign. And thanks to media advisors and his youthful, attractive personality, Kennedy projected a superb television image.

His Republican opponent, Eisenhower's vice president Richard M. Nixon, was a more seasoned politician but personally awkward and ill-endowed for combat in the new politics. The great innovation of the 1960 campaign was a series of four nationally televised debates. Nixon, less photogenic than Kennedy, looked sallow and unshaven under the intense studio lights. Polls showed that television did sway political

The Kennedy Magnetism

John Kennedy, the Democratic candidate for president in 1960, used his youth and personality to attract voters. Here, the Massachusetts senator draws an enthusiastic crowd at a campaign stop in Elgin, Illinois. Wide World Photos, Inc.

perceptions: Voters who heard the first debate on the radio concluded that Nixon had won, but those who viewed it on television favored Kennedy.

Despite the edge Kennedy enjoyed in the debates, he won only the narrowest of electoral victories, receiving 49.7 percent of the popular vote to Nixon's 49.5 percent. Kennedy attracted Catholics, blacks, and the labor vote; his vice presidential running mate, Lyndon Johnson from Texas, brought in southern Democrats. Yet only 120,000 votes separated the two candidates, and the shift of a few thousand votes in key states such as Illinois (where Chicago Mayor Richard Daley's machine miraculously generated the needed margin) would have reversed the outcome.

The Kennedy Administration

Kennedy's vigor attracted unusually able and ambitious people, including Robert McNamara, a renowned systems analyst and former head of Ford Motor Company, as secretary of defense, and C. Douglas Dillon, a highly admired Republican banker, as secretary of the treasury. A host of trusted advisors and academics—"the best and the brightest," journalist David Halberstam called them—flocked to Washington to join the New Frontier. Included on the team as attorney general was Kennedy's kid brother, Robert, a trusted advisor who had made a name as a hard-hitting investigator of organized crime. Not everyone was enchanted. Kennedy's people "might be every bit as intelligent as you say," House Speaker Sam Rayburn told his old friend Lyndon Johnson, "but I'd feel a whole lot better about them if just one of them had run for sheriff once." Sure enough, the new administration immediately got into hot water.

In January 1961, the Soviet Union announced that it intended to support "wars of national liberation" wherever in the world they occurred. Kennedy took Soviet Premier Nikita Khrushchev's words as a challenge, especially as they applied to Cuba, where in 1959 Fidel Castro had overthrown the dictator Fulgencio Batista and declared a revolution. Determined to keep Cuba out of the Soviet orbit, Kennedy took up plans by the Eisenhower administration to dispatch Cuban exiles from Nicaragua to foment an anti-Castro uprising.

Trained by the Central Intelligence Agency, the invaders were ill-prepared for their task and betrayed by the CIA's inept planning. On landing at Cuba's Bay of Pigs on April 17, 1961, the force of 1,400 was apprehended and crushed by Castro's troops. The anticipated popular uprising never happened. Kennedy had the good sense to reject CIA pleas for a U.S. air strike. And he was gracious in defeat. He went before the American people and took full responsibility for the fiasco.

Kennedy redeemed himself with a series of bold initiatives. One was the Peace Corps, which embodied the call to public service in his Inaugural Address. Thousands of men and women agreed to devote two or more years to programs teaching English to Filipino schoolchildren or helping African villagers obtain clean water. Exhibiting the idealism of the early 1960s, the Peace Corps was also a Cold War weapon intended to show the so-called Third World that there was a better way than Communism.

Also embodying this aim were ambitious programs of economic assistance. The State Department's Agency for International Development coordinated foreign aid for the Third World, and its Food for Peace program distributed surplus agricultural products. In 1961, the president proposed a "ten-year plan for the Americas" called the Alliance for Progress, a $20 billion partnership between the United States and Latin America that was intended to reverse the cycle of poverty and stimulate economic growth.

Kennedy was also keen on space exploration. Early in his administration, he proposed that the nation commit itself to landing a man on the moon within the decade. Two weeks later, on May 5, 1961, Alan Shepard became the first American in space (beaten there by the Soviet cosmonaut Yuri Gagarin's 108-hour flight). The following year, John Glenn manned the first space mission to orbit the earth. Capitalizing on America's fascination with space flight, Kennedy persuaded Congress to increase funding for the National Aeronautics and Space Administration (NASA), enabling the United States to pull ahead of the Soviet Union. (Kennedy's men on the moon arrived there in 1969.)

Kennedy's most striking domestic achievement—another of his bold moves—was the application of modern economic theory to government fiscal policy. The Keynesian approach of deliberate deficit spending to stimulate economic growth was already well established. Now, in addition to deficit spending, Kennedy's economic advisors proposed sharp tax cuts, which, they argued, would generate more consumer spending, more jobs, and ultimately higher tax revenues. Congress balked at this unorthodox proposal, but it made its way through in 1964, marking a milestone in the use of tax cuts to encourage economic growth, an approach later embraced by Republican fiscal conservatives (see Chapter 30).

Kennedy was less engaged by the more humdrum matters of social policy, notwithstanding the ambitious agenda of his presidential campaign. Having been only narrowly elected, Kennedy was stymied by the lack of a strong popular mandate. He was also a cautious politician, unwilling to expend capital when the odds were against him. Kennedy managed to push through legislation raising the minimum wage and expanding Social Security, but on other issues—federal aid to education, mass transportation, medical insurance for the elderly—he gave up in the face of conservative opposition in Congress.

The Civil Rights Movement Stirs

Kennedy was equally cautious about civil rights. Despite a campaign commitment, he failed to deliver on a civil rights bill. The opposition in Congress, where segregationist southern Democrats dominated key committees, just seemed too formidable. But civil rights was unlike other domestic issues. Its fate was going to be decided not in the halls of Congress but on the streets of southern cities.

Emboldened by the sit-in tactics of the Student Nonviolent Coordinating Committee (SNCC), the interracial Congress of Racial Equality (CORE) organized a series of "freedom rides" in 1961 on interstate bus lines throughout the South. The aim was to call attention to blatant violations of recent Supreme Court rulings against segregation in interstate commerce. The activists who signed on, mostly young, both black and white, knew that they were taking their lives in their hands. Club-wielding Klansmen attacked the buses with stones. Outside Anniston, Alabama, one bus was fire-bombed. The freedom riders escaped only moments before it exploded. Some of them were then brutally beaten. Freedom riders and news reporters were also viciously attacked by Klansmen in Birmingham and Montgomery. State authorities refused to intervene. "I cannot guarantee protection for this bunch of rabble rousers," declared Governor John Patterson.

That left it up to Washington. Although Kennedy discouraged the freedom rides, beatings shown on the nightly news forced Attorney General Robert Kennedy to dispatch federal marshals. Civil rights activists learned the value of nonviolent protest that provoked violent white resistance.

This lesson was confirmed when Martin Luther King Jr. called for demonstrations in "the most segregated city in the United States": Birmingham, Alabama. In April 1963, thousands of black marchers tried to picket Birmingham's department stores. They were met by police, who used snarling dogs, electric cattle prods, and high-pressure fire hoses to break up the crowds. Television cameras captured the scene for the evening news.

Outraged by the brutality, President Kennedy decided that it was time to step in. On June 11, 1963, after Alabama governor George Wallace barred two black students from the state university, Kennedy denounced racism on television and promised a new civil rights bill. Black leaders hailed Kennedy's "Second Emancipation Proclamation." That night, Medgar Evers, president of the Mississippi chapter of the NAACP, was shot in the back in his driveway in Jackson. The martyrdom of Evers became a spur to further action.

To marshal support for Kennedy's bill, civil rights leaders adopted a tactic that A. Philip Randolph had first advanced in 1941 (see Chapter 25): a massive demonstration in Washington. Although the planning was not primarily done by Martin Luther King Jr., he was the public face of the March on Washington on August 28, 1963. It was King's dramatic "I Have a Dream" speech, ending with the exclamation from an old Negro spiritual—"Free at last! Free at last! Thank God almighty, we are free at last!"—that captured the nation's imagination. The sight of 250,000 blacks and whites marching solemnly together marked the high point of the civil rights movement and confirmed King's position as the leading spokesperson for the black cause.

Although the March on Washington galvanized public opinion, it changed few congressional votes. Southern senators continued to block Kennedy's legislation. In September, a Baptist church in Birmingham was bombed, and four black Sunday

The March on Washington
The Reverend Martin Luther King Jr. (1929–1968) was one of the most eloquent advocates of the civil rights movement. For many, his "I have a dream" speech was the high point of the 1963 March on Washington, but the focus on the charismatic King has meant that the importance of other civil rights leaders is frequently overlooked. Bob Adelman / Magnum Photos, Inc.

school students were killed, shocking the nation and bringing the civil rights battle to a boiling point.

Kennedy, Cold Warrior

Foreign affairs gave greater scope for Kennedy's fertile mind. A resolute cold warrior, Kennedy took a hard line against Communism. In contrast to Eisenhower, whose cost-saving New Look program had emphasized the American nuclear arsenal, Kennedy proposed a new policy of "flexible response" that called for an increase in conventional forces so that the nation would be prepared "to deter all wars, general or limited, nuclear or conventional, large or small." Kennedy's defense budget soon reached the highest share of total federal expenditures since the advent of the Cold War.

Already strained by the Bay of Pigs, U.S.-Soviet relations deteriorated further in June 1961 when Soviet Premier Khrushchev isolated Communist-controlled East Berlin from the city's western sector. Kennedy responded by dispatching 40,000 more troops to Europe. In mid-August, to stop the exodus of East Germans, the Communist regime began constructing the Berlin Wall, policed by border guards with orders to shoot to kill. Until it came down in 1989, the Berlin Wall served as the supreme symbol of the Cold War.

The climactic confrontation came in October 1962. In a somber televised address, Kennedy revealed that reconnaissance planes had spotted Soviet-built bases for intermediate-range ballistic missiles in Cuba. Some of those weapons had already been installed, and more were on the way. Kennedy announced that the United States would impose a "quarantine on all offensive military equipment" intended for Cuba. But as the world held its breath, the ships carrying Soviet missiles turned back. After a week of tense negotiations, both Kennedy and Khrushchev made concessions: Kennedy pledged not to invade Cuba, and Khrushchev promised to dismantle the missile bases. Kennedy also secretly ordered U.S. missiles to be removed from Turkey at Khrushchev's insistence.

The risk of nuclear war, greater during the Cuban missile crisis than at any other time in the Cold War, prompted a slight thaw in U.S.-Soviet relations. As national security advisor McGeorge Bundy put it, both sides were chastened by "having come so close to the edge." Kennedy softened his Cold War rhetoric, and chastened Soviet leaders agreed to talk. In August 1963, the three principal nuclear powers—the United States, the Soviet Union, and Great Britain—announced a ban on the testing of nuclear weapons in the atmosphere. The two sides also agreed to establish a Washington-Moscow telecommunications "hotline" so that leaders could contact each other quickly in a crisis.

But no matter how much American officials talked about opening channels, relations with the Soviet Union remained tense, and containment remained the cornerstone of U.S. policy.

The Vietnam Puzzle

When Kennedy became president, he inherited Eisenhower's involvement in Vietnam. Kennedy saw Vietnam in much the same Cold War terms. But what really grabbed him was the chance to test the counterinsurgency doctrine associated with his flexible

Buddhist Protest, 1966
Buddhist nun Thich Nu Thanh Quang burns to death at the Dieu de Pagoda in Hue, South Vietnam, in a ritual act of suicide in protest against the Catholic regime on May 29, 1966. Its inability to win over the Buddhist population was a major source of weakness for the South Vietnamese government.
AP Images.

For more help analyzing this image, see the Online Study Guide at **bedfordstmartins .com/henrettaconcise.**

response military strategy. The army was training U.S. Special Forces, called Green Berets for their distinctive headgear, to engage in unconventional, small-group warfare. Kennedy and his advisors wanted to try out the Green Berets in the Vietnamese jungles.

Despite American aid, the corrupt and repressive Diem regime installed by Eisenhower in 1954 was losing ground. By 1961, Diem's opponents, with backing from North Vietnam, had formed a revolutionary movement known as the National Liberation Front (NLF). The NLF's guerrilla forces — the Vietcong — found a receptive audience among peasants alienated by Diem's "strategic hamlet" program, which uprooted whole villages and moved them into barbed-wire compounds. Buddhists charged Diem, a Catholic, with religious persecution. Starting in May 1963, militant Buddhists staged dramatic demonstrations, including several self-immolations that were recorded by American television crews. Losing patience with Diem, Kennedy let it be known in Saigon that the United States would support a military coup. On November 1, 1963, Diem was overthrown and assassinated, an eventuality that Kennedy had evidently not anticipated. At that point, there were about 16,000 American "advisors" (an elastic term that included helicopter crews and Special Forces) in Vietnam.

In a CBS interview, Kennedy had remarked that it was up to the South Vietnamese whether "their war" would be won or lost. Advisors close to the president later argued that, had he lived and run strongly in the 1964 election, he would have cut America's losses and left. But that argument downplays the geopolitical stakes in Vietnam. The United States was now engaged in a global war against Communism. Giving up in Vietnam would weaken America's "credibility." And under the prevailing "domino theory," other pro-American states would topple after Vietnam's loss. Kennedy subscribed to these Cold War tenets. Whether he might have surmounted them down the road is — like how Lincoln might have handled Reconstruction after the Civil War had he lived — an unanswerable historical question.

Assassination

On November 22, 1963, Kennedy went to Texas on a political trip. As he and his wife, Jacqueline, rode in an open car past the Texas School Book Depository in Dallas, he was shot through the head and neck by a sniper. Kennedy died within the hour. (The accused killer, Lee Harvey Oswald, a twenty-four-year-old loner, was himself killed while in custody a few days later.) Before Air Force One left Dallas to take the president's body back to Washington, a grim-faced Lyndon Johnson was sworn in as president. Kennedy's stunned widow, still wearing her bloodstained pink suit, looked on.

Kennedy's youthful image, the trauma of his assassination, and the nation's sense of loss contributed to a powerful Kennedy mystique. His canonization after death capped what had been an extraordinarily stage-managed presidency. An admiring country saw in Jack and Jackie Kennedy an ideal American marriage (he was, in fact, an obsessive womanizer); in Kennedy, the epitome of robust good health (although he was actually afflicted by Addison's disease and kept going by potent medications); and in the Kennedy White House, a glamorous world of high fashion and celebrity.

No presidency ever matched the Kennedy aura of "Camelot"—named after the mythical realm of King Arthur in the hit musical of that title—but every president after him embraced the idea, with greater or lesser success, that image mattered as much as reality, maybe more, in conducting a politically effective presidency. In Kennedy's case, the ultimate irony was that his image as martyred leader produced grander legislative results than anything he might have achieved as a live president in the White House.

▶ Why was Kennedy an effective politician?

▶ Why did civil rights become a big issue during the Kennedy years?

▶ What were the results of Kennedy's foreign policy?

Lyndon B. Johnson and the Great Society

Lyndon Johnson was a seasoned Texas politician, a longtime Senate leader who was most at home in the back rooms of power. Compared to Kennedy, Johnson was a rough-edged character who had scrambled his way up, without too many scruples, to wealth and political eminence. But unlike many other bootstrap successes, he never forgot his hill-country origins or lost his sympathy for the downtrodden. Johnson lacked the Kennedy aura, but he capitalized on Kennedy's assassination, applying his astonishing energy and negotiating skills to bring to fruition many of Kennedy's stalled programs and more of his own, in an ambitious program that he called the "Great Society."

The Momentum for Civil Rights

On assuming the presidency, Lyndon Johnson promptly pushed for civil rights legislation as a memorial to his slain predecessor. His motives were both political and personal. As a politician, he wanted the Democratic Party to benefit from the national groundswell for civil rights. Although he was aware of the price the party would pay in the South, it was more important to him, as a southerner, to reach across regional lines and show that he was president of all the people. Achieving historic civil rights legislation would, he hoped, place his mark on the presidency.

Overcoming a southern filibuster, Congress approved in June 1964 the most far-reaching civil rights law since Reconstruction. The keystone of the Civil Rights Act, Title VII, outlawed discrimination in employment on the basis of race, religion, national origin, or sex. Another section guaranteed equal access to public accommodations and schools. The law granted new enforcement powers to the U.S. attorney general and established the Equal Employment Opportunity Commission to implement the prohibition against job discrimination. It was a law with real teeth. But it left untouched the obstacles to black voting rights.

So protesters went back into the streets. In 1964, civil rights organizations mounted a major campaign in Mississippi. Known as "Freedom Summer," the effort drew several thousand volunteers from across the country, including many white college students. They established freedom schools for black children and conducted a major voter registration drive. So fierce was the reaction that only about 1,200 black voters were registered that summer, at a cost of 15 murdered civil rights workers.

The urgent need for federal action became even clearer in March 1965, when Martin Luther King Jr. called for a march from Selma, Alabama, to the state capital in Montgomery to protest the murder of a voting-rights activist. As soon as the marchers left Selma, mounted state troopers attacked with tear gas and clubs. The scene was shown on national television that night. Calling the episode "an American tragedy," President Johnson went back to Congress.

The Voting Rights Act, which passed on August 6, 1965, outlawed the literacy tests and other devices that prevented blacks from registering to vote and authorized the attorney general to send federal examiners to register voters in any county where registration was less than 50 percent. Together with the Twenty-fourth Amendment (1964), which outlawed the poll tax in federal elections, the Voting Rights Act enabled millions of blacks to vote for the first time since the post-Reconstruction era.

In the South, the results were stunning. In 1960, only 20 percent of blacks had been registered to vote; by 1971, registration reached 62 percent (Map 28.1). As Hartman Turnbow, a Mississippi farmer who risked his life to register in 1964, later declared, "It won't never go back where it was."

Enacting the Liberal Agenda

Johnson's success with the Voting Rights Act had stemmed in part from the 1964 election, when he had faced Republican Barry Goldwater of Arizona. An archconservative, Goldwater ran on an anti-Communist, antigovernment platform, offering "a choice, not an echo." There would be no Republican "Dime Store New Deal" this time around. The voters didn't buy it. Johnson and his running mate, Hubert H. Humphrey of Minnesota, won in a landslide. In the long run, Goldwater's candidacy marked the beginning of a grassroots conservative revolt that would eventually transform the Republican Party. In the short run, however, Johnson's sweeping victory opened the path to the legislative programs of the "Great Society."

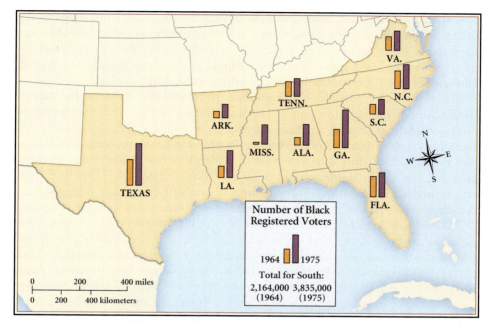

MAP 28.1 Black Voter Registration in the South, 1964 and 1975

After passage of the Voting Rights Act of 1965, black registration in the South increased dramatically. The bars on the map show the number of blacks registered in 1964, before the act was passed, and in 1975, after it had been in effect for ten years. States in the Deep South, such as Mississippi, Alabama, and Georgia, had the biggest rises.

Like most New Deal liberals, Johnson held an expansive view of the role of government. Now he had a popular mandate and, equally important, the filibuster-proof Senate majority he needed to push his programs forward.

One of Johnson's first successes was breaking the congressional deadlock on aid to education. Passed in April 1965, the Elementary and Secondary Education Act authorized $1 billion in federal funds, sidestepping the religious issue by dispensing aid to public and parochial schools alike on the basis of the number of needy children in attendance. Six months later, Johnson signed the Higher Education Act, providing federal scholarships for college students.

Johnson also had the votes he needed to achieve some form of national health insurance. Realizing that the game was up, the American Medical Association fell back to a demand that services be provided through the existing private system of doctors and hospitals. On that basis, two new programs came forth: Medicare, a health plan for the elderly funded by a surcharge on Social Security payroll taxes, and Medicaid, a health plan for the poor paid for by general tax revenues and administered by the states.

Also high on the Great Society's agenda was environmental reform. President Johnson pressed for an expanded national park system, improvement of the nation's air and water, protection for endangered species, and stronger land-use planning. At the insistence of his wife, Lady Bird Johnson, he promoted the Highway Beautification Act of 1965. While past conservation efforts had concentrated on preserving the nation's natural resources, Secretary of the Interior Stewart Udall emphasized quality of life, battling the problem "of vanishing beauty, of increasing ugliness, of shrinking open space, and of an overall environment that is diminished daily by pollution and noise and blight." In a similar vein, the National Endowments for the Arts and the Humanities (1965) supported the work of artists, writers, and scholars.

It even became possible, at this moment of reform zeal, to tackle the nation's discriminatory immigration policy. The Immigration Act of 1965 abandoned the quota system that favored northern Europeans, replacing it with numerical limits that did not discriminate among nations. To promote family reunification, the law also provided that close relatives of legal residents in the United States could be admitted outside the numerical limits, an exception that especially benefited Asian and Latin American immigrants. The ethnic diversity of our nation today—and of our campuses—goes back to that 1965 Immigration Act.

What drove Johnson hardest, however, was his determination to "end poverty in our time." The president called it a national disgrace that in the midst of plenty, one-fifth of all Americans—hidden from most other people's sight in Appalachia, in urban ghettos, in migrant labor camps, and on Indian reservations—lived in poverty. Many had fallen through the cracks and were not served by New Deal–era welfare programs.

One tactic was shoring up those programs. The Great Society broadened Social Security to include waiters and waitresses, domestic servants, farmworkers, and hospital employees. Social welfare expenditures increased rapidly, especially for Aid to Families with Dependent Children, as did public housing and rent subsidy programs. Food stamps, begun in 1964 mainly to stabilize farm prices, grew into a major source of assistance to low-income families.

The Economic Opportunity Act of 1964 was the Great Society's showcase in the War on Poverty. Head Start provided free nursery schools to prepare disadvantaged preschoolers for kindergarten. The Job Corps and Upward Bound provided young people with training and jobs. Volunteers in Service to America (VISTA), modeled on the Peace Corps, provided technical assistance to the urban and rural poor. An array of regional development programs aimed, like foreign aid, at spurring economic growth in impoverished areas.

The Community Action Program operated on the principle of "maximum feasible participation," encouraging its clients to demand a voice in the decisions that affected their lives. Allied to Community Action organizers were lawyers employed by the Legal Services Program to provide the poor with effective representation in the legal system.

Empowering the downtrodden, however, put strains on the diverse New Deal coalition—middle-class and poor; white and nonwhite; Protestant, Jewish, and Catholic; urban and rural—that Johnson rallied to the Great Society. Inevitably, the demands of certain groups—blacks' demands for civil rights, for example, or the urban poor's claims on political power—conflicted with the interests of other Democrats. Competition for federal largesse was keen, and the shortage of funds left many promises unfulfilled, especially when the Vietnam War began to siphon funding from domestic programs. In 1966, the government spent $22 billion on the Vietnam War and only $1.2 billion on the War on Poverty. Ultimately, Martin Luther King Jr. remarked, the Great Society was "shot down on the battlefields of Vietnam."

How much was achieved remains in dispute. The proportion of Americans living below the poverty line dropped from 20 percent to 13 percent between 1963 and 1968. African Americans did even better. In the 1960s, the black poverty rate fell by half as millions of blacks moved into the middle class. Conservatives, however, credited the decade's booming economy more than government programs. Moreover, distribution of wealth remained highly skewed. In relative terms, the bottom 20 percent remained as far behind as ever.

Partly perhaps because Johnson's lofty rhetoric had raised expectations, Democrats readily fell victim to disillusionment with the War on Poverty. In the end, as it began to fracture, the New Deal coalition was not strong enough to resist a growing challenge by conservatives to civil rights and social welfare benefits.

> ▶ Why, after years of resistance, did Congress pass the great civil rights acts of 1964 and 1965?
>
> ▶ What were the key components of the Great Society?
>
> ▶ What factors limited the success of the War on Poverty?

Into the Quagmire, 1963–1968

Just as Kennedy had inherited Vietnam from Eisenhower, so Lyndon Johnson inherited Vietnam from Kennedy. Johnson's inheritance was more burdensome, however, for by now, only massive American intervention could prevent the collapse of South Vietnam (Map 28.2). Johnson was a subscriber, like Kennedy, to the Cold War tenets of global containment. But whereas in Kennedy's case, second thoughts might have prevailed, that was an impossibility with Johnson. "I am not going to lose Vietnam," he vowed on taking office. "I am not going to be the President who saw Southeast Asia go the way China went."

Escalation

Johnson was unwilling to level with the American people. For one thing, he doubted that they had the stomach for the course he was contemplating. For another, he did not want to endanger his grand domestic agenda. He felt that he "had no choice but to keep my foreign policy in the wings" because "the day it exploded into a major debate on the war, that day would be the beginning of the end of the Great Society." So he ran in 1964 on the pledge that there be no escalation—no American boys fighting Vietnam's fight—although he intended to do exactly that.

During the summer of 1964, Johnson got reports that North Vietnamese torpedo boats had fired on the destroyer *Maddox*. In the first attack, on August 2, the damage inflicted was limited to a single bullet hole; a second, on August 4, later proved to be only misread radar sightings. It didn't matter. In a national emergency, real or imagined, the president's call to arms is hard to resist. In the entire Congress, only two senators voted against Johnson's request for authorization to "take all necessary measures to repel any armed attack against the forces of the United States and to prevent further aggression." The Gulf of Tonkin resolution handed Johnson a mandate to conduct operations in Vietnam as he saw fit.

MAP 28.2 The Vietnam War, 1968

The Vietnam War was a guerrilla war, fought in skirmishes and inconclusive encounters rather than decisive battles. Supporters of the National Liberation Front filtered into South Vietnam along the Ho Chi Minh Trail, which wound through Laos and Cambodia. In January 1968, Vietcong forces launched the Tet offensive, a surprise attack on many South Vietnamese cities and provincial centers. Despite American battlefield victories, vulnerability to these attacks served to undermine U.S. credibility and fueled opposition to the war. After a 1973 cease-fire was signed, the United States withdrew its troops, and in 1975, South Vietnam fell to the northern forces. The country was reunited under Communist rule in April of that year.

For more help analyzing this map, see the Online Study Guide at **bedfordstmartins.com/henrettaconcise**.

With the 1964 election safely behind him, Johnson began an American takeover of the war in Vietnam. The escalation, beginning in the early months of 1965, took two forms: deployment of American ground troops and the intensification of bombing against North Vietnam.

On March 8, 1965, the first Marines waded ashore at Da Nang, ostensibly to protect the huge American air base there. Soon they were skirmishing with the enemy. By 1966, more than 380,000 American soldiers were stationed in Vietnam; by 1967, 485,000; and by 1968, 536,000. The escalating demands of General William Westmoreland, the commander of U.S. forces, confirmed a fear Kennedy had expressed before his death that requesting troops was like taking a drink: "The effect wears off and you have to take another."

In the meantime, in an operation called Rolling Thunder, a bombing campaign escalated against North Vietnam. A special target was the Ho Chi Minh Trail, an elaborate network of trails, bridges, and shelters that stretched from North Vietnam through Cambodia and Laos into South Vietnam. By 1968, a million tons of bombs had fallen on North Vietnam—800 tons a day for three and a half years. Twice that tonnage was dropped on the jungles of South Vietnam as U.S. forces tried to flush out the Vietcong fighters.

To the surprise of American planners, the bombing had little effect on the Vietcong's ability to wage war. The North Vietnamese quickly rebuilt roads and bridges, moved munitions plants underground, and constructed a network of tunnels and shelters. Instead of destroying the morale of the North Vietnamese, Operation Rolling Thunder hardened their will to fight.

The massive commitment of troops and air power devastated Vietnam's countryside. After one harsh but not unusual engagement, a commanding officer reported, using the logic of the time, that "it became necessary to destroy the town in order to save it." Besides the bombing, a defoliation campaign began to deprive guerrillas of cover, destroying crops and undercutting the economic base of Vietnamese society. (In later years, defoliants such as Agent Orange were found to have highly toxic effects on humans, including the GIs serving in Vietnam.) In Saigon and other South Vietnamese cities, American soldiers and dollars distorted local economies, fostered corruption and prostitution, and triggered inflation and black-market activity.

Johnson's advisors debated about why American arms were failing to turn the tide of the war. Some argued that military action could accomplish little without reform in Saigon. Others complained that the United States never fully committed itself to a "total victory" (see American Voices, p. 838). Military strategy was inextricably tied to political considerations. For domestic reasons, policymakers often searched for an elusive middle ground between all-out invasion of North Vietnam (and the possibility of war with China) and disengagement. Hoping to win a **war of attrition**, the Johnson administration gambled that American superiority in personnel and weaponry would ultimately triumph.

Public Opinion on Vietnam

Johnson had reason to be confident of the American people. A broad, steady consensus had formed in earlier years favorable to Washington's conduct of the Cold War. Both Democrats and Republicans approved Johnson's escalation in Vietnam, and so did public opinion polls in 1965 and 1966. But then opinion began to shift.

Every night, Americans saw on their television screens the carnage of war and dead and wounded Americans. Journalists began to write about a "credibility gap." The Johnson administration, they charged, was concealing bad news about the war's progress. In February 1966, television coverage of hearings by the Senate Foreign

The Toll of War   DONALD L. WHITFIELD AND GAYLE SMITH

The Vietnam War produced a rich and graphic literature: novels, journalists' reports, personal letters, and interviews. The following documents are from interviews with two Americans who served in the war and then talked about it afterward.

Donald L. Whitfield, a draftee from Alabama: I'm gonna be honest with you. I had heard some about Vietnam in 1968, but I was a poor fellow and I didn't keep up with it. I was working at a Standard Oil station making eight dollars a day. . . . When I got my letter from the draft lady, I appealed it on the reason it was just me and my sister at home. We were a poor family and they needed me at home, but it did no good.

My company did a lot of patrolling. We got the roughest damn deal. Shit, I thought I was going to get killed every night. I was terrified the whole time.

We didn't have no trouble with the blacks. I saw movies that said we done the blacks wrong, but it wasn't like that where I was. Let's put it like this: they make pretty good soldiers, but they're not what we are. White Americans, can't nobody whip our ass. We're the baddest son of a bitches on the face of this earth. You can take a hundred Russians and twenty-five Americans, and we'll whip their ass. . . .

I feel cheated about Vietnam, I sure do. Political restrictions—we won every goddamned battle we was in, but didn't win the whole goddamn little country. . . . Before I die, the Democratic-controlled Congress of this country—and I blame it on 'em—they gonna goddamn apologize to the Vietnam veterans.

Gayle Smith, a combat nurse: I objected to the war and I got the idea into my head of going there to bring people back.

I started thinking about it in 1966 and knew that I would eventually go when I felt I was prepared enough. . . .

Boy, I remember how they came in all torn up. It was incredible. The first time a medevac came in, I got right into it. I didn't have a lot of feeling at that time. It was later on that I began to have a lot of feeling about it, after I'd seen it over and over and over again. . . . I turned that pain into anger and hatred and placed it onto the Vietnamese. . . . I did not consider the Vietnamese to be people. They were human, but they weren't people. They weren't like us, so it was okay to kill them. It was okay to hate them. . . . And for a long time I swore that if the Vietnamese ever came to this country I'd kill them.

It was in a Vietnam veterans group that I realized that all my hatred for the Vietnamese and my wanting to kill them was really a reflection of all the pain that I had felt for seeing all those young men die and hurt. . . . I would stand there and look at them and think to myself, "You've just lost your leg for no reason at all." Or "You're going to die and it's for nothing." For nothing. I would never, never say that to them, but they knew it.

SOURCES: James R. Wilson, *Landing Zones: Southern Veterans Remember Vietnam* (Durham, NC: Duke University Press, 1990), 203, 204, 207, 209, 210; Albert Santoli, ed., *Everything We Had* (New York: Random House, 1981), 141–148.

Relations Committee (chaired by J. William Fulbright, an outspoken critic of the war) raised further questions about the administration's policy.

Economic problems put Johnson even more on the defensive. The Vietnam War cost the taxpayers $27 billion in 1967, pushing the deficit from $9.8 billion to $23 billion. Military spending nudged the inflation rate upward. Only in the summer of 1967 did Johnson ask for a 10 percent surcharge on income taxes. By then, the inflationary spiral that would plague the U.S. economy throughout the 1970s was well under way.

Out of these troubling developments an antiwar movement began to crystallize. Its core, in addition to long-standing pacifist groups, was a new generation of peace activists such as SANE (the National Committee for a Sane Nuclear Policy), which in the 1950s had protested atmospheric nuclear testing. After the escalation in 1965, they were joined by student groups, clergy, civil rights advocates, even Dr. Spock, whose books on child care had helped raise many of the students.

The antiwar movement was soon capable of mounting mass demonstrations in Washington, bringing out 20,000 to 30,000 people at a time. Although they were a diverse lot, participants in these rallies shared a skepticism about U.S. policy in Vietnam. They charged variously that intervention was antithetical to American ideals; that an independent, anti-Communist South Vietnam was unattainable; and that no American objective justified the suffering that was being inflicted on the Vietnamese people (see Voices from Abroad, p. 840).

Student Activism

College students, many of them inspired by the black students of Greensboro, North Carolina, who had sparked the wave of sit-ins across in the South (see Chapter 27), became conspicuous in the antiwar movement. Often raised in a privileged environment and inculcated with faith in America, they began to question everything about a world they had not made.

In June 1962, forty students from Big Ten and Ivy League universities met in Port Huron, Michigan, to found Students for a Democratic Society (SDS). Tom Hayden wrote a manifesto, the Port Huron Statement, expressing their disillusionment with the consumer culture and the gulf between rich and poor. These students rejected Cold War foreign policy, including but not limited to the Vietnam conflict. The founders of SDS referred to their movement as the "New Left" to distinguish themselves from the "Old Left"—Communists and Socialists of the 1930s and 1940s.

The first demonstrations erupted in the fall of 1964 at the University of California at Berkeley after administrators banned political activity in Sproul Plaza, where student groups had traditionally distributed leaflets and recruited members. In protest, student organizations formed the Free Speech Movement and organized a sit-in at the administration building. Some students had just returned from Freedom Summer in Mississippi, radicalized by their experience. Mario Savio spoke for many when he compared the conflict in Berkeley to the civil rights struggle in the South: "The same rights are at stake in both places—the right to participate as citizens in a democratic society and to struggle against the same enemy." Emboldened by the Berkeley movement, students across the nation were soon protesting their universities' academic policies and then, more passionately, the Vietnam War.

Vietnam and the World Freedom Struggle   CHE GUEVARA

Che Guevara was a middle-class, medically trained Argentinian who enlisted in Castro's Cuban Revolution and became a world icon of guerrilla resistance. In 1965, he left Cuba to foment revolutionary struggle in Africa and Latin America. Two years later, he was captured in Bolivia and executed. Between his departure from Cuba and his death in Bolivia in 1967, he made only one public statement, which he titled "Vietnam and the World Freedom Struggle."

This is the painful reality: Vietnam, a nation representing the aspirations and the hopes for victory of the entire world of the disinherited, is tragically alone. . . .

And—what grandeur has been shown by this people! What stoicism and valor in this people! And what a lesson for the world their struggle holds!

It will be a long time before we know if President Johnson ever seriously thought of initiating some of the popular reforms necessary to soften the sharpness of the class contradictions that are appearing with explosive force and more and more frequently.

What is certain is that the improvements announced under the pompous label of the Great Society have gone down the drain in Vietnam.

The greatest of the imperialist powers feels in its own heart the drain caused by a poor, backward country; and its fabulous economy feels the effect of the war. . . .

And for us, the exploited of the world, what should our role be in this? . . .

Our part, the responsibility of the exploited and backward areas of the world, is to eliminate the bases sustaining imperialism—our oppressed peoples, from whom capital, raw materials, technicians and cheap labor are extracted, and to whom new capital, means of domination, arms and all kinds of goods are exported, submerging us in absolute dependence.

The fundamental element of this strategic goal will be, then, the real liberation of the peoples, a liberation that will be obtained through armed struggle in the majority of cases, and which, in the Americas, will have almost unfailingly the property of becoming converted into a socialist revolution.

In focusing on the destruction of imperialism, it is necessary to identify its head, which is none other than the United States of North America. . . .

The adversary must not be underestimated; the North American soldier has technical ability and is backed by means of such magnitude as to make him formidable. He lacks the essential ideological motivation which his most hated rivals of today have to the highest degree—the Vietnamese soldiers. . . .

Over there, the imperialist troops encounter the discomforts of those accustomed to the standard of living which the North American nation boasts. They have to confront a hostile land, the insecurity of those who cannot move without feeling that they are walking on enemy territory; death for those who go outside of fortified redoubts; the permanent hostility of the entire population.

All this continues to provoke repercussions inside the United States; it is going to arouse a factor that was attenuated in the days of the full vigor of imperialism—the class struggle inside its own territory.

SOURCE: Ernesto C. Guevara, *Che Guevara Speaks* (New York: Pathfinder Press, 1967), 144–159.

One spur to student protest was the military's Selective Service System, which in January 1966 abolished automatic student deferments. To avoid the draft, young men enlisted in the National Guard, declared themselves conscientious objectors, or became draft dodgers. Some left the country, most often for Canada or Sweden. In public demonstrations, opponents of the war burned their draft cards, picketed induction centers, and, on a few occasions, broke into Selective Service offices and destroyed records.

As antiwar protests multiplied, students began to link their universities to the war effort. In some cases, as much as 60 percent of a university's research budget came from government contracts. Protesters blocked recruiters from Dow Chemical Company, the producer of napalm and Agent Orange. Arguing that universities should not train students for war, they demanded that the Reserve Officer Training Corps (ROTC) be removed from college campuses.

Students were soon on the front line of the campaign against the war. In October 1967, more than 100,000 demonstrators marched on Washington, D.C., as part of "Stop the Draft Week." The event culminated in a "siege of the Pentagon," as protesters clashed with police and federal marshals. Hundreds of people were arrested. Lyndon Johnson, who had once dismissed antiwar protesters as "nervous Nellies," rebellious children, or Communist dupes, now faced formidable student opposition to his policies.

▶ What difficulties did the United States face in fighting a war against North Vietnam and the Vietcong in South Vietnam?

▶ Why did President Johnson suffer a "credibility gap" over Vietnam?

▶ What was the student role in the antiwar movement? How can we explain students' willingness to protest the war?

Coming Apart

In the student demonstrations, the SDS, and the Berkeley Free Speech Movement, more obviously was at stake than Vietnam. Indeed, antiwar protest was part of a variegated, broad-based attack on the status quo — "the Movement," to its participants — that not only challenged Cold War assumptions, but also blasted America's liberal consensus.

The roots of this assault went back to the 1950s, to when the Beats denigrated capitalism, teenagers defied their elders, and African American sit-ins protested racial injustice. By the mid-1960s, this angry disaffection had broadened into a many-sided attack on mainstream America.

The Counterculture

While the New Left plotted against the political and economic "system," many other young Americans embarked on a general revolt against authority and middle-class respectability. The "hippie"—attired in ragged blue jeans, tie-dyed T-shirts, beads, and army fatigues, with long, unkempt hair—symbolized the new counterculture.

Not surprisingly, given the importance of rock 'n' roll in the 1950s, popular music helped to define the counterculture. Folk singer Pete Seeger set the tone for the era's idealism with songs such as the antiwar ballad "Where Have All the Flowers Gone?" In

1963, the year of the Birmingham demonstrations and President Kennedy's assassination, Bob Dylan's "Blowin' in the Wind" reflected the impatience of people whose faith in America was wearing thin.

Other winds of change in popular music came from the Beatles, four working-class Brits who burst on the American scene early in 1964. The Beatles' music, by turns lyrical and driving, was awe-inspiring, spawning a commercial and cultural phenomenon known as Beatlemania. American youth's embrace of the Beatles deepened the generational divide between teenagers and their elders. The Beatles also helped to pave the way for the more rebellious, angrier music of other British groups, notably the Rolling Stones.

The recreational use of drugs — especially marijuana and the hallucinogen popularly known as LSD or "acid" — was celebrated in popular music. San Francisco bands such as the Grateful Dead and Jefferson Airplane and musicians such as Jimi Hendrix developed a musical style known as "acid rock," which was characterized by long, heavily amplified guitar solos accompanied by psychedelic lighting effects. In August 1969, 400,000 young people journeyed to Bethel, New York, to "get high" on music, drugs, and sex at the three-day Woodstock Music and Art Fair.

Jimi Hendrix at Woodstock
The three-day outdoor Woodstock concert in August 1969 was a defining moment in the counterculture as 400,000 young people journeyed to Bethel, New York, for a weekend of music, drugs, and sex. Jimi Hendrix closed the show early Sunday morning with an electrifying version of "The Star-Spangled Banner." More overtly political than most counterculture music, Hendrix's rendition featured sound effects that seemed to evoke the violence of the Vietnam War. Michael Wadleigh, who directed the documentary *Woodstock,* called Hendrix's performance "his challenge to American foreign policy." Allan Koss/Image Bank.

For a brief time, adherents of the counterculture believed that a new age was dawning. They experimented with communal living and glorified uninhibited sexuality. In 1967, the "world's first Human Be-In" drew 20,000 people to Golden Gate Park in San Francisco. The Beat poet Allen Ginsberg "purified" the site with a Buddhist ritual, and the LSD advocate Timothy Leary, a former Harvard psychology teacher, urged the gathering to "turn on to the scene, tune in to what is happening, and drop out."

That summer—dubbed the "Summer of Love"—San Francisco's Haight-Ashbury, New York's East Village, and Chicago's Uptown neighborhoods swelled with young dropouts, drifters, and teenage runaways whom the media dubbed "flower children." Their faith in instant love and peace quickly turned sour, however, as they suffered bad drug trips, sexually transmitted diseases, loneliness, and violence. Although many young people kept their distance, media coverage made it seem as though all of American youth was rejecting the nation's social and cultural norms.

Beyond Civil Rights

Among young blacks, knocking the mainstream meant something else. It meant rejecting the established civil rights leadership, with its faith in the courts and legislative change. It meant an eye for an eye, not Martin Luther King's nonviolence. It meant wondering why blacks wanted to be integrated with whites anyway. Above all, it expressed fury at the black poverty and white racism that were beyond the reach of civil rights laws.

Black rage had expressed itself historically in demands for racial separation, espoused in the late nineteenth century by the Back to Africa movement (see Chapter 19) and in the 1920s by Marcus Garvey (see Chapter 23). In the 1960s, the leading exponent of black separatism was the Nation of Islam, which fused a rejection of Christianity with a strong dose of self-improvement. Black Muslims, as they were known, adhered to a strict code of personal behavior, with the men recognizable by their dark suits and white shirts, the women by their long dresses and head coverings. Black Muslims preached an apocalyptic brand of Islam, anticipating the day when Allah would banish the white "devils" and give the black nation justice. Although its full converts numbered only about 10,000, the Nation of Islam had a wide popular following in urban ghettoes.

The most charismatic Black Muslim was Malcolm X (the X stood for his African family name, lost under slavery). A spellbinding speaker, Malcolm X preached a philosophy of militant separatism, although he advocated violence only for self-defense. Hostile to mainstream civil rights organizations, he caustically referred to the 1963 March on Washington as the "Farce on Washington." In 1964, after a power struggle with the founder, Elijah Muhammad, Malcolm X broke with the Nation of Islam. While he remained a black nationalist, his antiwhite views moderated, and he began to talk in terms of class struggle uniting poor whites and blacks. But he got no farther. On February 21, 1965, Malcolm X was assassinated while delivering a speech in Harlem. Three Black Muslims were later convicted of his murder.

A more secular brand of black nationalism emerged in 1966 when SNCC and CORE activists, following the lead of Stokely Carmichael, began to call for black self-reliance under the banner of "Black Power." Amid growing distrust of whites, SNCC declared itself a blacks-only organization and ejected white members. In the same year, Huey

Newton and Bobby Seale, two college students in Oakland, California, founded the Black Panthers, a militant self-defense organization dedicated to protecting blacks from police violence. The Panthers' organization quickly spread to other cities, where members undertook a wide range of community organizing projects. Their rhetoric, however, declared their affinity for Third World revolutionary movements and armed struggle.

Among the most significant legacies of Black Power was the assertion of racial pride. Rejecting white society, blacks wore African clothing and hairstyles and awakened an interest in black history, art, and literature.

The rage expressed by Black Power boiled over, in inchoate form, in a wave of riots that struck the nation's cities. The first "long hot summer" began in July 1964 in New York City when police shot a black criminal suspect in Harlem. Angry youths looted and rioted there for a week. Over the next four years, the volatile issue of police brutality set off riots in dozens of cities. In August 1965, the arrest of a young black motorist in the Watts section of Los Angeles sparked six days of rioting that left thirty-four people dead. The riots of 1967 were the most serious, engulfing twenty-two cities in July and August (Map 28.3). Forty-three people were

MAP 28.3 Racial Unrest in America's Cities, 1965–1968

American cities suffered through four "long hot summers" of rioting in the mid-1960s. In 1967, the worst year, riots broke out across the United States, including numerous locations in the South and West. The 1968 report of the National Advisory Commission on Civil Disorders targeted racism as the source of black rage: "What white Americans have never fully understood — but what the Negro can never forget — is that white society is deeply implicated in the ghetto. . . . White institutions created it, white institutions maintain it, and white society condones it." The riots' major impact on white America was to create a climate of fear that helped drain support from the larger civil rights movement.

killed in Detroit alone, nearly all of them black, and $50 million worth of property was destroyed.

Stirred by this turmoil, and by disappointment with his civil rights achievements, Martin Luther King Jr. began to confront the deep-seated problems of poverty and racism facing American blacks. He spoke out eloquently against the Vietnam War and planned a poor people's campaign to fight economic injustice. In support of that cause, he went to Memphis, Tennessee, to bolster a strike by predominantly black sanitation workers. There, on April 4, 1968, he was assassinated by escaped convict James Earl Ray. King's death set off a further round of urban rioting, with major violence breaking out in more than a hundred cities.

Although King died unfulfilled, he had set in motion permanent, indeed revolutionary, changes in American race relations. Thanks partly to his leadership, Jim Crow segregation ended, federal legislation ensured black Americans' most basic civil rights, and the white monopoly on political power in the South was broken. Not least, his example inspired other oppressed groups in America to enter the struggle for equal rights.

For Mexican Americans, the counterpart to Martin Luther King was César Chávez, although in Chávez's case, the conversion to economic struggle had come much earlier. He and Dolores Huerta had worked for the Community Service Organization, a California group founded in the 1950s to promote Mexican political participation and civil rights. Leaving that organization in 1962, Chávez concentrated on the agricultural region around Delano, California, and, with Huerta, organized the United Farm Workers (UFW), a union for migrant workers.

Huerta was a brilliant organizer, but it was the deeply spiritual and ascetic Chávez who embodied the moral force behind what was popularly called *La Causa*. A 1965 grape pickers' strike led the UFW to call a nationwide boycott of table grapes, bringing Chávez huge publicity and backing from the AFL-CIO. In a bid for attention to the struggle, Chávez staged a hunger strike in 1968, which ended dramatically after twenty-eight days with Senator Robert F. Kennedy at his side to break the fast. Victory came in 1970 when California grape growers signed contracts recognizing the UFW.

On a parallel track, Mexican Americans had been politically active since the 1930s (see Chapter 24), aiming to surmount the poverty and language barriers that obstructed political involvement. Those efforts paid off when the Mexican American Political Association (MAPA) mobilized support for John F. Kennedy. Over the next four years, MAPA and other organizations worked successfully to elect Mexican American candidates such as Edward Roybal of California and Henry González of Texas to Congress.

Younger Mexican Americans grew impatient with MAPA, however. The barrios of Los Angeles and other western cities produced the militant Brown Berets, modeled on the Black Panthers (who wore black berets). Rejecting the assimilationist approach of their elders, 1,500 Mexican American students met in Denver in 1969 to hammer out a new political and cultural agenda. They proclaimed a new term, *Chicano*, to replace *Mexican American*, and later organized a political party, La Raza Unida (The United Race), to promote Chicano interests. In California and other southwestern states, students staged demonstrations to press for bilingual education, the hiring of more Chicano teachers, and the creation of Chicano studies programs. By the 1970s, dozens of such programs were offered at universities throughout the region.

American Indians also found a model in black struggles. Numbering nearly 800,000 in the 1960s, they were exceedingly diverse, divided by language, tribal history, region, and degree of integration into American life. As a group, they shared a staggering unemployment rate (ten times the national average) and were the worst off in housing, disease rates, and access to education.

In the 1960s, the prevailing spirit of protest swept through Indian communities. Young militants, like their counterparts in the black civil rights movement, challenged the accommodationist approach of their elders in the National Congress of American Indians. Proposing a new name for themselves—Native Americans—they embraced the concept of "Red Power." Beginning in 1968 with the formation of a militant American Indian Movement (AIM), young Native Americans staged escalating protests, occupying the deserted federal penitentiary on Alcatraz Island in San Francisco Bay and sitting in at the headquarters of the hated Federal Bureau of Indian Affairs in Washington, D.C. In February 1973, a siege at Wounded Knee, South Dakota, the site of the infamous 1890 massacre of the Sioux, ended in a gun battle with the FBI. Although upsetting to many white onlookers, Native American protest did spur government action on tribal issues.

▶ What were the elements in the counterculture of the 1960s?

▶ How do you account for the Black Power movement?

▶ How do you explain the spillover of the black civil rights struggle into the Mexican American and Native American communities?

Wounded Knee Revisited

In 1973, members of the American Indian Movement staged a seventy-one-day protest at Wounded Knee, South Dakota, the site of the 1890 massacre of 200 Sioux by U.S. soldiers. The takeover of the site was sparked by the murder of a local Sioux by a group of whites but quickly expanded to include demands for basic reforms in federal Indian policy and tribal governance. © Bettmann/Corbis.

1968: A Year of Shocks

By 1968, a sense of crisis gripped the country. Riots in the cities, campus unrest, and a nose-thumbing counterculture seemed on the verge of tearing America apart. What crystallized the crisis was the fact that 1968 was an election year.

The Politics of Vietnam

President Johnson had gambled in 1965 on a quick victory in Vietnam, before the political cost of escalation came due. But there was no quick victory. North Vietnamese and Vietcong forces fought on, the South Vietnamese government lost ground, and American casualties mounted. By early 1968, the death rate had reached several hundred a week. Johnson and his generals kept insisting that there was "light at the end of the tunnel." Facts on the ground showed otherwise.

On January 30, 1968, the Vietcong unleashed a massive, well-coordinated assault in South Vietnam. Timed to coincide with Tet, the Vietnamese new year holiday, the offensive struck thirty-six provincial capitals and five of the six major cities, including Saigon, where the Vietcong nearly overran the supposedly impregnable U.S. embassy. In strictly military terms, the Tet offensive was a failure, with very heavy Vietcong losses. But psychologically, the effect was devastating. Television brought into American homes the shocking images: the American embassy under siege with a pistol-wielding staff member peering warily from a window; the Saigon police chief placing a pistol to the head of a Vietcong suspect and, live on TV, executing him.

The Tet offensive made a mockery of official pronouncements that the United States was winning the war. Just before Tet, a Gallup poll found that 56 percent of Americans considered themselves "hawks" (supporters of the war), while only 28 percent identified with the "doves" (war opponents). Three months later, doves outnumbered hawks 42 to 41 percent. Without embracing the peace movement, many Americans simply concluded that the war was unwinnable.

So did a growing faction within the Democratic Party. Even before Tet, Senator Eugene J. McCarthy of Minnesota had entered the Democratic primaries as an antiwar candidate. A core of student activists "went clean for Gene" by cutting their hair and putting away their jeans. President Johnson won the early New Hampshire primary, but McCarthy received a stunning 42.2 percent of the vote. To make matters worse for the president, McCarthy's showing propelled Senator Robert Kennedy, a far more formidable opponent, into the race.

At the end of an otherwise routine televised address on March 31, Johnson stunned the nation by announcing that he would not seek reelection. He also called for a partial halt to the bombing and vowed to devote his remaining months in office to the search for peace. On May 10, 1968, the United States and North Vietnam began preliminary peace talks in Paris.

But then, on June 5, 1968, just as he celebrated his victory in the California primary over Eugene McCarthy, Robert Kennedy was shot dead by a young Palestinian. Robert Kennedy's assassination was a calamity for the Democratic Party because only he had seemed able to surmount the party's fissures over Vietnam. In his brief but dramatic campaign, Kennedy had reached beyond the antiwar elements to traditional members of the New Deal coalition.

With Kennedy gone, the energy went out of the antiwar Democrats. McCarthy's campaign limped along, while Senator George S. McGovern of South Dakota entered the race in an effort to keep the Kennedy forces together. Meanwhile, Vice President Hubert H. Humphrey lined up pledges from traditional Democratic constituencies: unions, urban machines, and state political organizations. Democrats found themselves on the verge of nominating not an antiwar candidate but a public figure closely associated with Johnson's war policies.

At the August Democratic convention, the political divisions generated by the war consumed the party. Most of the drama occurred not in the convention hall but outside on the streets of Chicago. Thousands of protesters descended on the city. The most visible group, led by Jerry Rubin and Abbie Hoffman, a remarkable pair of troublemakers, claimed to represent the Youth International Party. To mock those inside the convention hall, these "Yippies" nominated a pig, Pigasus, for president. Their stunts, geared toward maximum media exposure, diverted attention from the more serious, far more numerous activists who had come to Chicago to protest the war.

Increasingly angry as protesters disrupted his convention, Democratic Mayor Richard J. Daley ordered the police to break up the demonstrations. Several nights of skirmishes between protesters and police culminated on the evening of the nominations. In what an official report later described as a "police riot," police officers attacked protesters with tear gas and clubs. As the nominating speeches proceeded, television networks broadcast films of the riot, cementing a popular impression of the Democrats as the party of disorder. Inside the hall, the Democrats dispiritedly nominated Hubert H. Humphrey, who chose Senator Edmund S. Muskie of Maine as his running mate. The delegates approved a middle-of-the-road platform that endorsed continued fighting in Vietnam while urging a diplomatic solution to the conflict.

Backlash

Political realignments are infrequent in American history. The last one had occurred in 1932, when many Republicans, despairing over the Great Depression, had switched sides and voted for FDR. The year 1968 was another such pivotal moment. Consider a forty-seven-year-old machinist's wife from Dayton, Ohio, described by the social scientists Ben J. Wattenberg and Richard Scammon in their book, *The Real Majority* (1970):

> That lady in Dayton is afraid to walk the streets alone at night . . . she has a mixed view about blacks and civil rights because she lived in neighborhood that became all black . . . her brother-in-law is a policeman [and] she is deeply distressed that her son is going to a community junior college where LSD was found on campus.

Growing up in the Great Depression, she was likely an admirer of FDR and perhaps even had his picture on her living room wall. Such working-class people were the heart and soul of the New Deal democracy. But now, in the sour aftermath of the Chicago convention, their votes were up for grabs. And as always, politicians with their noses to the wind were eager to oblige.

Governor George C. Wallace of Alabama, a third-party candidate, skillfully exploited working-class anxieties over student protests and urban riots. He called for "law and order" and denounced mothers on public assistance who, thanks to Johnson's Great Society, were "breeding children as a cash crop." Wallace skewered "overeducated, ivory-towered folks with pointed heads looking down their noses at us." Although no longer overtly a racist, Wallace traded on his fame as the segregationist governor who had stood up to the federal government during the Selma crisis of 1965. His hope was that by carrying the South, he could deny the major parties an electoral majority and force the 1968 election into the House of Representatives. That strategy failed, and Wallace's political star faded after a near-fatal shooting in 1972 left him paralyzed, but he had defined hot-button issues—liberal elitism, "welfare queens," and law and order—that worked wonders for the next generation of mainstream conservatives.

The Republican candidate, Richard Nixon, offered a more sophisticated version of Wallace's populism. After losing the presidential campaign in 1960 and after losing again in the California gubernatorial race in 1962, Nixon had seemed finished, but he engineered an amazing political comeback and in 1968 won the Republican presidential nomination. Nixon adopted what his advisors called the "southern strategy," which aimed at attracting southern voters still smarting over the civil rights gains by blacks. Nixon won over the key southerner, Senator Strom Thurmond of South Carolina, a Democrat-now-turned-Republican, and let it be known that while formally he had to support civil rights, his administration would go easy on enforcement. Nationally, Nixon appealed to people whom he called the "silent majority." Nixon pledged to represent the "quiet voice" of the "great majority of Americans, the forgotten Americans, the nonshouters, the nondemonstrators."

Despite the Democratic debacle in Chicago, the election actually proved to be close. In the last weeks of the campaign, Humphrey rallied by disassociating himself from Johnson's war policies. When on October 31 President Johnson announced a complete halt to the bombing of North Vietnam, Nixon countered by intimating that he had his own plan to end the war (in reality, no such plan existed). On election day, Nixon received 43.4 percent of the vote to Humphrey's 42.7 percent, defeating him by a scant 500,000 votes out of the seventy-three million that were cast. Wallace finished with 13.5 percent of the popular vote.

The close outcome masked the fact that 1968 really was a pivotal election. Humphrey received almost twelve million fewer votes than had Johnson in 1964. The South abandoned the Democratic Party, never to return. Nixon's "southern strategy" had worked. In the North, he and Wallace made significant inroads among traditionally Democratic voters. And while party divisions over Vietnam had been briefly patched up, the underlying ideological differences— signified by the rivalry of Hubert Humphrey

▶ What were the critical events of 1968 that have led historians to describe it as a "watershed year"?

▶ Why did the Democrats lose their grip as the majority party in the late 1960s?

▶ Why is the U.S. involvement in the Vietnam War so often called a "quagmire"?

and George McGovern — persisted, with a corrosive effect on the party's effectiveness. New Deal Democrats lost the unity of purpose that had served them for thirty years. Assaulted from both left and right, the liberal consensus was coming apart.

SUMMARY

In this chapter, we saw how the liberal consensus — agreement about a New Deal approach to the nation's social and economic ills — peaked in the mid-1960s and then, under the combined pressure of the Vietnam War and cultural conflict, flamed out. In the 1960 campaign, John F. Kennedy put forth the politics of expectation, only to see the ambitions of his New Frontier held in check by a deadlocked Congress and his own political caution. Following Kennedy's assassination in 1963, Lyndon Johnson advanced the most sweeping reform program since the New Deal, securing not only civil rights legislation, but also an array of programs in education, medical care, the environment, and, above all, his War on Poverty. But the Great Society fell short of its promise as Johnson escalated the American involvement in Vietnam.

The war bitterly divided Americans. Once expectations of victory dimmed, opposition to the war intensified, especially among young people horrified by the carnage and worried about the draft. The spirit of rebellion soon spilled beyond the antiwar movement. The New Left challenged the corporate dominance of society, while the more apolitical counterculture preached personal liberation through sex, drugs, music, and spirituality. Moving beyond civil rights, the Black Power movement encouraged racial pride and assertiveness, serving also as a model for Mexican Americans and Native Americans.

In 1968, the nation was rocked by the assassinations of Martin Luther King Jr. and Robert F. Kennedy. A wave of urban riots fueled a growing public desire for law and order. Adding to the national disquiet was a Democratic convention in August that was divided by the Vietnam war and under siege by rioting in the streets. A new wave of conservativism took hold of the country, contributing to the resurgence of the Republican Party under Richard Nixon.

Connections: Diplomacy and Politics

In the essay opening Part Six, we remarked that "[t]he interaction of the domestic and global — the links between liberalism and the Cold War — was especially clear [in the 1960s] because it was Vietnam that, more than anything, undermined the Great Society and the liberal consensus." In Chapter 26, we showed how that link between liberalism and the Cold War was forged during the Truman and Eisenhower administrations. In contrast to earlier periods, anti-Communism in its McCarthyite phase did not take aim at liberal reform. In the wake of Vietnam, this changed, and prosecution of the Cold War increasingly became an attack on the liberal consensus, a development that, as we shall see in Chapter 30, culminated under the leadership of Ronald Reagan in the 1980s.

TIMELINE

1960 ▸ John F. Kennedy elected president

1961 ▸ Peace Corps established

▸ Bay of Pigs invasion

▸ Berlin Wall erected

1962 ▸ Cuban missile crisis

▸ Students for a Democratic Society (SDS) founded

1963 ▸ Betty Friedan's *The Feminine Mystique*

▸ Civil rights protest in Birmingham, Alabama

▸ March on Washington

▸ Nuclear test ban treaty

▸ John F. Kennedy assassinated; Lyndon B. Johnson assumes presidency

1964 ▸ Freedom Summer

▸ Civil Rights Act

▸ Economic Opportunity Act inaugurates War on Poverty

▸ Free Speech Movement at Berkeley

▸ Gulf of Tonkin Resolution authorizes military action in Vietnam

1965 ▸ Immigration Act abolishes national quota system

▸ Voting Rights Act

▸ Medicare and Medicaid programs established

▸ Malcolm X assassinated

▸ Operation Rolling Thunder escalates bombing campaign

▸ First U.S. combat troops arrive in Vietnam

▸ Race riot in Watts district of Los Angeles

1966 ▸ Stokely Carmichael proclaims black power

1967 ▸ Hippie counterculture's "Summer of Love"

▸ 100,000 march in antiwar protest in Washington, D.C.

1968 ▸ Tet offensive dashes American hopes of victory

▸ Martin Luther King Jr. and Robert F. Kennedy assassinated

▸ Riot at Democratic National Convention in Chicago

▸ Richard Nixon elected president

▸ American Indian Movement (AIM) organized

FOR FURTHER EXPLORATION

Good starting points for understanding Kennedy's presidency are W. J. Rorabaugh, *Kennedy and the Promise of the Sixties* (2002), and David Halberstam, *The Best and the Brightest* (1972). For Lyndon Johnson, see Robert Dallek, *Flawed Giant* (1998). Harvard Sitkoff, *The Struggle for Black Equality* (1993), offers an engaging account of the civil rights movement. On Martin Luther King Jr., see Taylor Branch's three-part biography, *Parting the Waters: 1954–1963* (1988), *Pillar of Fire: 1963–1965* (1998), and *At Canaan's Edge: 1965–1968* (2005). On Vietnam, the basic history is George Herring, *America's Longest War: The United States and Vietnam* (1986). Secretary of Defense Robert McNamara offers an insider's view and a belated apologia in his *In Retrospect* (1995). Vivid accounts of dissent in the 1960s are Todd Gitlin, *The Sixties: Years of Hope, Days of Rage* (1987), and Maurice Isserman and Michael Kazin, *America*

Divided: The Civil War of the 1960s (1999). Ron Kovic's *Born on the Fourth of July* (1976) is one soldier's powerful account of Vietnam and its aftermath.

The John F. Kennedy Library and Museum's site at **www.jfklibrary.org** provides a large collection of records from Kennedy's presidency. A useful Vietnam site that includes official correspondence from 1941 to the fall of Saigon is at **www.mtholyoke .edu/acad/intrel/vietnam.htm**.

TEST YOUR KNOWLEDGE

To assess your mastery of the material in this chapter and for Web sites, images, and documents related to this chapter, visit **bedfordstmartins.com/henrettaconcise**.

Toward a Conservative America
The 1970s

The U.S., like the world around it, is in bad shape today. . . . In the expectation of perpetual plenty, Americans are desperate for answers. . . . It is not at all certain how graciously [they] will accept what is plainly today's economic reality: that there is no such thing as perpetual plenty and no party that does not eventually end.

—John Carsen-Parker, 1974

A headline of the 1970s read: "The United States Steel Corporation announced yesterday that it was closing 14 plants and mills in 8 states. About 13,000 production and white-collar workers will lose their jobs." A second headline read: "Weyerhaeuser Co. may trim about 1,000 salaried employees from its 11,000 member workforce over the next year." A third read: "Philadelphia: Food Fair Inc. plans to close 89 supermarkets in New York and Connecticut."

Imagine a citizen of the 1950s emerging from a time capsule. She is bewildered by these gloomy newspaper reports. What happened to America's vaunted economic supremacy? Equally bewildering is the sight of the all-powerful United States withdrawing from Vietnam, defeated by a third-tier country that this citizen has probably never heard of. And she is utterly stunned, as one whose notion of an American president is Dwight D. Eisenhower, to be told that the current president has been charged with obstruction of justice, has resigned in disgrace, and is leaving the White House.

Yet it's not all bad news. Who would have imagined Americans, in a time of joblessness and runaway inflation, mounting robust consumer and environmental movements? But that's what happened in the 1970s. Or the struggle for civil rights, far from pausing, intensifying and, in the case of women's and gay rights, breaking new ground? Or a potent conservative movement rising up in the millions in defense of traditional values?

If the historian is hard put to make sense of the 1970s, it's because these crosscurrents suggest a country in the throes of change. But with Ronald Reagan's election in 1980, Americans got a better sense of what was happening. They were leaving liberal America behind and entering an age of political conservatism.

The Nixon Years

Richard Nixon was a master of the black arts of politics. In the 1968 campaign, his appeal to the "silent majority" had done wonders at undermining the New Deal coalition. But Nixon was not prepared to offer a genuine alternative. And insofar as he tried, he came up against a Democrat-controlled Congress—itself a stubborn legacy of the liberal age. Like Kennedy, moreover, Nixon much preferred foreign affairs. But here, too, he was hobbled by his inheritance of the war in Vietnam.

So we have to mark Nixon down as a transitional figure—with one foot in the liberal past and the other in the conservative future—except in one respect: His departure was not transitional. He left with a big bang.

Nixon's Domestic Agenda

As a Republican candidate, Nixon necessarily ran on an antigovernment platform. Calling his approach the "New Federalism," he vowed to "reverse the flow of power and resources from the states and communities to Washington." Nixon proposed a revenue-sharing program that distributed a portion of federal tax revenues to the states as block grants, while scaling back the federal programs that had proliferated during Johnson's administration. He cut back War on Poverty programs, dismantled the Office of Economic Opportunity, and refused to spend billions of dollars appropriated by Congress for urban renewal, pollution control, and other environmental initiatives. In 1971, he vetoed a bill to establish a comprehensive national child-care system on the grounds that such "communal approaches to child rearing" endangered the American family.

Yet Nixon could be imaginative, even daring, when it came to social welfare. Strongly influenced by a key White House advisor, Daniel Moynihan, an independent-minded expert on urban affairs, Nixon proposed a Family Assistance Plan, which guaranteed a family of four $1,600 a year, plus $600 in food stamps. The appeal of this proposal lay in its simplicity: It would eliminate multiple layers of bureaucracy and pare down the nation's jerry-built welfare system. Attacked both by conservatives and liberals, however, Nixon's plan failed. Welfare reform was postponed for another day. So was national health insurance, another of Nixon's failed initiatives, in which he proposed a public/private system that would foster universal coverage.

No enemy of the major **entitlement programs**, Nixon expanded Medicare, Medicaid, and Social Security. And his administration introduced important new regulatory agencies—the Environmental Protection Agency (EPA) in 1970, the Occupational Safety and Health Administration (OSHA) in 1971, and the Consumer Products Safety Commission in 1972—that brought the federal government deep into areas hitherto only lightly regulated or not regulated at all.

Nixon's mixed record reflected the political crosscurrents of his time. His conservative base pushed in one direction; the Democratic Congress pushed in another. Consumer and environmental protections loomed large for the middle class. Social Security and Medicare mattered to the working-class voters he was appealing to. But Nixon was himself not a laissez-faire conservative, and — what especially distinguished him — he had a zest for experimenting with the mechanics of government.

Détente

Richard Nixon regarded himself as a "realist" in foreign affairs. That meant, above all, advancing the national interest. Everything else — commitments to allies, extending democracy abroad, championing human rights — came second, if that. Nixon's realism was seconded by his National Security Advisor, Henry Kissinger, although Kissinger had arrived at Nixon's view by a more scholarly route. As a Harvard professor, Kissinger had closely studied the nineteenth-century diplomat Metternich, who had crafted a balance-of-power system that stabilized Europe for an entire century.

Conducting foreign affairs Metternich's way, however, required a degree of secrecy that was antithetical to America's constitutional system. Nixon and Kissinger bypassed Congress, cut out the State Department (including the secretary of state, William Rogers), and established back channels to agencies whose expertise they needed. It was a dangerous game but one they played successfully for a time. Nixon and Kissinger were preparing to take advantage of international conditions that were ripe for change.

For one thing, all the major players were plagued by internal unrest. Street rioting almost brought down the French government in May 1968. German universities were hotbeds of dissent. On the Communist side, it had taken Russian tanks to crush a liberalizing challenge — the "Prague Spring" — in Czechoslovakia. But tanks suppressed only people; they couldn't destroy dissident ideas, which seeped even into the Soviet Union. And in China, Mao Zedong's Cultural Revolution had gotten out of hand, with young Red Guards turning on the regime. A shared sense of internal fragility made all the major powers receptive to an easing of international tensions.

Ultimately of greater importance, however, was an upheaval in the original arrangement of the Cold War. Once stalemate set in around 1950, neither superpower proved able to keep its side in line. In America's case, the most difficult partner was France, which, under the imperious Charles de Gaulle, thumbed its nose at the United States and walked away from NATO. That, however, was nothing compared to Soviet relations with China, which by 1969 had so deteriorated that the two countries were fighting a border war.

Nixon saw an opportunity. In 1971, he sent Kissinger secretly to Beijing (Peking) to explore an accommodation. Mao was thinking along the same lines, so an arrangement was not difficult to arrive at. The United States would back away from the Chinese Nationalists on Taiwan, permit China's admission to the United Nations (with a permanent seat on the Security Council), and eventually grant recognition (in 1978). In February 1972, President Nixon arrived in Beijing in a blaze of publicity to ratify the deal. This was the man who had clawed his way into prominence by railing against the Democrats for "losing" China and hounding Alger Hiss into prison. Nixon had impeccable anti-Communist credentials. That was why he felt free to come to Beijing, he remarked genially to Mao. "Those on the right can do what those on the left only talk about." Chairman Mao responded, "I like rightists."

Nixon then turned to the Soviet Union. He had already reached a secret understanding with Leonid Brezhnev, the Soviet premier, about Cuban issues left hanging after the missile crisis of 1962. In exchange for an American promise not to invade, the Soviets dismantled a submarine base and withheld offensive missiles from Castro. Three months after the Beijing summit, Nixon journeyed in another blaze of publicity to Moscow to sign the first Strategic Arms Limitations Treaty (SALT I) limiting the production and deployment of intercontinental ballistic missiles and antiballistic missile systems. SALT I, while technically modest, was intended as only a first step toward comprehensive arms limitation.

The summits in Beijing and Moscow inaugurated what came to be known as **détente** (in French: "relaxation of tensions"). Although the agreements themselves were quite limited and rocky times lay ahead, the fact was the Cold War had reached a turning point. Nixon had parlayed a strategic advantage—the dangerous rift in the Communist world—into a new tripartite balance of power. The world had become a less dangerous place. And Nixon hoped for a dividend over Vietnam.

Nixon's War

The concept of a bipolar world, already outmoded in Lyndon Johnson's time, was utterly refuted by Richard Nixon's embrace of détente. Yet when it came to Vietnam, Nixon picked up where Johnson had left off. Abandoning Vietnam, Nixon insisted, would damage America's "credibility" and make the country seem "a pitiful, helpless giant." And, like Johnson, Nixon had himself to consider. He was not going to be the first American president to lose a war. Nixon wanted peace, but only "peace with honor."

The North Vietnamese were not about to oblige him. The only outcome acceptable to them was a unified Vietnam under their control. What remained negotiable were the details—the terms of surrender—and that, plus the wiliness of the North Vietnamese negotiators, enabled the Paris talks begun by Johnson to continue, intermittently. But on the essentials, North Vietnam was immovable. So Nixon fashioned a two-pronged response.

To damp down criticism at home, he began delegating the ground fighting to the South Vietnamese. Under this new policy of "Vietnamization," American troop levels dropped from 543,000 in 1968 to 334,000 in 1971 to barely 24,000 by early 1973. American casualties—and the political liabilities they entailed—dropped correspondingly. But the killing in Vietnam continued. As the U.S. ambassador to Vietnam, Ellsworth Bunker, noted cynically, it was just a matter of changing "the color of the bodies."

In April 1972, as the fighting intensified, Nixon ordered B-52 bombing raids against North Vietnam. A month later, he approved the mining of North Vietnamese ports, something Johnson had never dared to do. Nixon had a freer hand because, in the spirit of détente, China no longer threatened to intervene. Nor was Brezhnev deterred from welcoming Nixon in May 1972 at the height of the B-52 bombing onslaught (which caused some Soviet casualties). The North Vietnamese might have felt more isolated, but supplies from China and the Soviet Union continued, and the Vietcong fought on.

At home, Nixon's war exacted a huge toll. Far from abating, the antiwar movement intensified. In November 1969, half a million demonstrators staged a huge protest in Washington. On April 30, 1970, as part of a secret bombing campaign against Vietminh supply lines operating in neutral Cambodia, American troops made an "incursion" to destroy enemy bases there. When news of the invasion of Cambodia came out, American campuses exploded in outrage, and for the first time, students died. On May 4, 1970, at Kent State University in Ohio, panicky National Guardsmen fired into an antiwar rally, killing four students and wounding eleven. At Jackson State College in Mississippi, Guardsmen stormed a dormitory, killing two black students. More than 450 colleges closed in protest. Across the country, the spring semester was essentially canceled.

The Vietnam poison infected even the military. In November 1969, the story of the My Lai Massacre broke, revealing the slaughter of 350 Vietnamese villagers by U.S. troops. The young lieutenant in command, William Calley, was court-martialed, and sentenced to life imprisonment. Released to his barracks at Nixon's order, Calley was eventually paroled. As the war dragged on, morale sank. Troops refused to go into combat; thousands of them turned to drugs. In the heat of battle, overbearing junior officers were sometimes "fragged"—killed by grenades of their own soldiers. At home, a group called Vietnam Veterans Against the War turned in their combat medals at demonstrations outside the U.S. Capitol.

Despite everything, Nixon persevered, hunkering down in the White House, castigating student protesters as "bums," and rallying a backlash against them. Hardhats became a patriotic symbol after New York construction workers beat demonstrators at a peace rally in May 1970. Slowly, Vietnamization eroded the antiwar opposition. With the army's manpower needs reduced, the draft was cut back (and ended entirely in 1973), deflating the ardor of many antiwar students. Militant groups such as the SDS splintered and became ineffective, while the SDS's violent offshoot, the Weathermen, were arrested or driven underground. In the end, Nixon outlasted his critics. What he couldn't outlast was North Vietnam.

With the 1972 election approaching, Nixon sent Henry Kissinger back to the Paris peace talks. In a key concession, Kissinger accepted the presence of North Vietnamese troops in South Vietnam. North Vietnam then agreed to an interim arrangement whereby the Saigon government would stay in power while a tripartite commission arranged a final settlement. With Kissinger's announcement that "peace is at hand," Nixon got the election lift he wanted, but the agreement was then sabotaged by General Nguyen Van Thieu, the South Vietnamese president. So Nixon, in one final spasm of bloodletting, unleashed the two-week "Christmas bombing," the most savage of the entire war. On January 27, 1973, the two sides signed the Paris Peace Accords, essentially restating the cease-fire agreement of the previous October.

Nixon hoped that with massive U.S. aid, the Thieu regime might survive. But Congress was in revolt. It refused appropriations for bombing Cambodia after August 15, 1973, and gradually cut back aid to South Vietnam. In March 1975, North Vietnamese forces launched a final offensive. On television, horrified American viewers watched as South Vietnamese officials and soldiers battled American embassy personnel to board the last helicopters out of Saigon. On April 29, 1975, Vietnam was reunited, and Saigon, the South Vietnamese capital, was renamed Ho Chi Minh City, after the founding father of the Communist regime.

Did this sad outcome matter? Yes, certainly, for America's Vietnamese friends, who lost jobs and property, spent years in "reeducation" camps, or fled the country. Yes, for next-door Cambodia, where the maniacal Khmer Rouge took over, murdered 1.7 million people, and drove the country nearly back to the Stone Age. For the United States, yes, for the wasted lives (58,000 dead, 300,000 wounded), the $150 billion spent, the slow-to-heal internal wounds, and the lost confidence in America's political leaders.

But in geopolitical terms? Not really. Defeat in South Vietnam did not mean, as successive American administrations had feared, victory for the Communist side because there no longer was a Communist "side." The Hanoi regime called itself Communist but never intended to be anybody's satellite, least of all China's, Vietnam's ancient enemy. (Within a few years, the two countries were fighting over disputed borders.) Today, after twenty years of embargo, America's relations with the People's Republic of Vietnam are normal, with diplomatic recognition having been granted in 1995. That event would hardly be worth mentioning but for the fact that it is a post-script to America's most disastrous military adventure of the twentieth century.

The 1972 Election

After the 1968 elections, the Democrats fell into disarray. Bent on sweeping away the old pros, George McGovern's followers took over the party, adopting new rules that granted women, blacks, and young people delegate seats "in reasonable relation to their presence in the population." With these reforms at their back, McGovern's army of antiwar activists blitzed the precinct-level caucuses. In the past, an alliance of urban machines, labor unions, and ethnic groups — the heart of the New Deal coalition — would almost certainly have rejected an upstart candidate such as McGovern. But at the 1972 convention, few of the party faithful qualified as delegates under the changed rules. The crowning insult came when the convention rejected the credentials of Chicago mayor Richard Daley and his delegation, seating instead an Illinois delegation led by Jesse Jackson, a firebrand young black minister and former aide to Martin Luther King Jr.

Capturing the party was one thing; beating the Republicans was quite another. McGovern was, in fact, a weak campaigner. He started badly at the convention, finally delivering his acceptance speech at 2:30 A.M. His running mate, Senator Thomas Eagleton of Missouri, turned out to have a history of mental illness and had to be replaced. And McGovern failed to mollify key party backers such as the AFL-CIO, which, for the first time in memory, refused to endorse the Democratic ticket.

McGovern was no match for Nixon, who pulled out all the stops. Using the advantages of incumbency, he gave the economy a well-timed lift and proclaimed (prematurely) a cease-fire in Vietnam. Nixon's appeal to the "silent majority"—people who "care about a strong United States, about patriotism, about moral and spiritual values"—was by now well honed, with added wrinkles about "forced" busing and law and order.

Nixon won in a landslide, receiving nearly 61 percent of the popular vote and carrying every state except Massachusetts and the District of Columbia. The returns revealed how fractured traditional Democratic voting blocs had become. McGovern received only 38 percent of the big-city Catholic vote and overall lost 42 percent of self-identified Democrats. The 1972 election marks a pivotal moment in the country's shift to the right. The full effect of that shift was delayed, however, by the president's soon-to-be-discovered self-inflicted wounds.

Watergate

On June 17, 1972, something strange happened at Washington's Watergate complex. Early that morning, five men carrying wiretapping equipment were apprehended breaking into the Democratic National Committee's (DNC) headquarters. Queried by the press, a White House spokesman dismissed the episode as "a third-rate burglary attempt." Wiretap equipment? At the DNC headquarters? Pressed further, Nixon himself denied any White House involvement in "this very bizarre incident."

In fact, the two masterminds of the break-in, G. Gordon Liddy and E. Howard Hunt, were former FBI and CIA agents currently working for Nixon's Committee to Re-elect the President (CREEP). Earlier, they had been on the White House payroll, hired in 1971 after the publication of the Pentagon Papers, a classified history of American involvement in Vietnam. Nixon was enraged at the leak of the documents by Daniel Ellsberg, a former Pentagon consultant and protégé of Kissinger's. In response, the president set up a clandestine squad, known as the "plumbers" because their job was to plug administration leaks and do other nasty jobs. Hunt and Liddy, two of the plumbers, burglarized Ellsberg's psychiatrist's office in an unsuccessful effort to discredit him. Now, as CREEP operatives, they were arranging illegal wiretaps at DNC headquarters, part of a campaign of "dirty tricks" against the Democrats.

The Watergate burglary was no isolated incident. It was part of a broad pattern of abuse of power by a White House obsessed with the antiwar movement. That siege mentality best explains why Nixon took a fatal misstep. He could have dissociated himself from the break-in by dismissing his guilty aides or even just by letting justice take its course. But it was election time, and Nixon hung tough. He arranged hush money for the burglars and instructed the CIA to stop an FBI investigation into the affair. This was obstruction of justice, a criminal offense.

Nixon kept the lid on until after the election, but then, as the wheels of justice turned, the lid came off. Found guilty in early 1973, one of the Watergate burglars, the security chief for CREEP, began to talk. In the meantime, two reporters at the *Washington Post*, Carl Bernstein and Bob Woodward, uncovered CREEP's illegal "slush fund" and its links to key White House aides. (Their informant, famously known as Deep Throat, was finally revealed in 2005 to be the second-in-command at the FBI, W. Mark Felt.) In May 1973, a Senate investigating committee began holding nationally televised hearings, at which Assistant Secretary of Commerce Jeb Magruder confessed his guilt and implicated former Attorney General John Mitchell, White House Counsel John Dean, and others. Dean, in turn, implicated Nixon. Just as startling, a former White House aide revealed that Nixon had installed a secret taping system in the Oval Office.

Under enormous pressure, Nixon eventually released some of the tapes, but there was a highly suspicious eighteen-minute gap. Finally, on June 23, 1974, the Supreme Court ordered Nixon to release the unexpurgated tapes. Lawyers found in them incontrovertible evidence that the president had ordered the cover-up. By then, the House Judiciary Committee was already considering articles of impeachment. Certain of being convicted by the Senate, Nixon became, on August 9, 1974, the first U.S. president to resign his office.

The next day, Vice President Gerald Ford was sworn in as president. Ford, the Republican minority leader in the House of Representatives, had replaced Vice President Spiro Agnew, who had himself resigned in 1973 for accepting kickbacks while governor of Maryland. The nation breathed a sigh of relief at the accession of this decent and honorable man to the White House. A month later, however, Ford stunned the nation by granting Nixon a "full, free, and absolute" pardon. Ford took that action, he said, to spare the country the agony of Nixon's criminal prosecution.

In Moscow, puzzled Kremlin leaders suspected a giant right-wing conspiracy against Nixon. They could not understand, recalled the Soviet ambassador to Washington at the time, "how a powerful president could be forced to resign . . . because of what they saw as a minor breach of conduct. Soviet history knew no parallel." That was one meaning of Watergate: that in America the rule of law prevailed (just barely—Nixon likely would have survived had he destroyed the tapes). A second meaning involved the constitutional separation of powers. As commander-in-chief, Nixon asserted unlimited authority, including wiretapping or worse, in the name of national security. Like the Kremlin leaders, he was perplexed at being brought down by a "pigmy-sized" incident like Watergate.

Congress pushed back, passing a raft of laws against the abuses of the Nixon administration: the War Powers Act (1973), reining in the president's ability to deploy U.S. forces without congressional approval; the Freedom of Information Act (1974), giving citizens access to federal records; the Fair Campaign Practices Act (1974), limiting contributions in presidential campaigns; and the Federal Intelligence Surveillance Act (1978), prohibiting domestic wiretapping without a warrant. Only in the short run, however, can it be said that these measures curbed America's tendency to embrace an imperial presidency.

▶ What do we mean when we say that Nixon was a "realist" in foreign affairs?

▶ Why did it take Nixon four years to reach a settlement with North Vietnam?

▶ How do you account for the Watergate scandal? What was its significance?

Battling for Civil Rights: The Second Stage

In the midst of Nixon's travail, the civil rights movement entered a second, more complicated stage. In the first stage, the landmark achievements—*Brown v. Board of Education* (1954), the Civil Rights Act of 1964, and the Voting Rights Act of 1965—had been bitterly resisted, but once those battles ended, the moral atmosphere shifted. In principle, at any rate, Americans no longer defended segregation, job discrimination, or the denial of voting rights. But now the time came for enforcing those rights—sometimes, it turned out, at the expense of other Americans, and that meant strife.

In the 1970s, moreover, the battle lines shifted as women and then gays mobilized and demanded equal rights. For many Americans, these demands were harder to handle because gender equality and sexual identity hit closer to home than did racial equality. The effect was galvanizing. In this second stage of the civil rights battle, a conservative movement burst forth, driven not by economic individualism but by moral values.

The Revival of Feminism

In the postwar years, feminism had languished, with few advocates and no burning issues. That changed dramatically during the 1960s, in response initially to the black civil rights movement and then to the decade's broader social upheaval. But the revival of feminism also sprang from the deeply felt needs of many women at this juncture in their lives.

Betty Friedan's indictment of suburban domesticity, *The Feminine Mystique*, appeared in 1963 (see Chapter 27). College-educated, middle-class women read Friedan's book and thought, "She's talking about me." *The Feminine Mystique*, after a slow start, became a run-away best seller. It persuaded women that self-realization was attainable through jobs, education, and escape from mind-deadening domesticity.

Paradoxically, *The Feminine Mystique* was a bit out of date. The domesticity that it described was already crumbling. More women were working outside the home, including married women (40 percent by 1970) and mothers with young children (30 percent by 1970). After the postwar baby boom, women were again having fewer children, aided now by the birth control pill, first marketed in 1960, and the intrauterine device. And more women were divorcing as the states liberalized divorce laws. Educational levels were also rising; by 1970, women made up 42 percent of the college population. All these changes undermined traditional gender roles and enabled women, as they read *The Feminine Mystique,* to embrace its liberating prescriptions.

Help also came from Washington. In 1961, Kennedy appointed a Presidential Commission on the Status of Women, which issued a 1963 report documenting job and educational discrimination. The result was some minor legislation but, more important, a network of activist women in public life that had formed in the course of the commission's work. A bigger breakthrough resulted from sheer inadvertence. Hoping to derail the pending Civil Rights Act of 1964, a key conservative, Representative Howard Smith of Virginia, mischievously added "sex" to the categories protected against discrimination under Title VII. The act passed anyway, and to everyone's surprise, women suddenly had a powerful tool for fighting sex discrimination — provided, of course, that the Equal Employment Opportunity Commission could be prodded into doing its job.

With that objective in mind, Friedan and others founded the National Organization for Women (NOW) in 1966. Modeled on the NAACP, NOW intended to be a civil rights organization for women with the aim of bringing "women into full participation in . . . American society now, exercising all the privileges and responsibilities thereof in truly equal partnership with men" — a classic statement of feminism. Under Friedan's leadership, membership grew to 15,000 by 1971, and NOW became, like the NAACP, a powerful voice for equal rights.

Women's Liberation
Arguing that beauty contests were degrading to women, members of the National Women's Liberation Party staged a protest against the Miss America pageant held in Atlantic City, New Jersey, in September 1968. Wide World Photos, Inc.

For more help analyzing this image, see the Online Study Guide at **bedfordstmartins.com/henrettaconcise.**

The 1960s spawned a new brand of feminism: women's liberation. These feminists were primarily younger, college-educated women fresh from the New Left and antiwar movements, whose male leaders, they discovered, were no better than the frat boys they had known in college. Women who tried to raise feminist issues in these movements were shouted off the platform with jeers like "Move on, little girl, we have more important issues to talk about here than women's liberation."

Fed up with this treatment, women radicals broke away and organized on their own. Unlike NOW, women's liberation was loosely structured, little more than an alliance of collectives in New York, San Francisco, and other big cities. "Women's lib," as it was dubbed by a skeptical media, went public in 1968 at the Miss America pageant. Most eye-catching was a "freedom trash can" into which women were invited to fling false eyelashes, hair curlers, brassieres, and girdles—all branded as symbols of female oppression. Women's liberation was a phenomenon of the 1960s, mirroring the identity politics of Black Power activists and the self-dramatization of the counterculture.

Before 1969, most women got involved by word of mouth. After that, the media brought women's issues to a wider audience. New terms such as *sexism* and *male chauvinism* became part of the national vocabulary. As converts flooded in, the two branches of the women's movement began to converge. Radical women realized that key feminist goals — child care, equal pay, and abortion rights — could best be achieved in the political arena. At the same time, more traditional activists developed a broader view of women's oppression. Although still largely white and middle class, feminists began to think of themselves as part of a broad social crusade. Only later did the movement grapple with the fact that as much divided women — race, class, age, sexual preference — as united them.

Women's opportunities expanded dramatically in higher education. Formerly all-male bastions, such as Yale, Princeton, and the U.S. Military Academy, admitted women undergraduates for the first time. Hundreds of colleges started women's studies programs, and the proportion of women attending graduate and professional schools rose markedly. With the adoption of Title IX in 1972, Congress broadened the 1964 Civil Rights Act to include educational institutions, prohibiting colleges and universities that received federal funds from discriminating on the basis of sex. By requiring comparable funding for sports programs, Title IX made women's athletics a real presence on college campuses.

Women also became increasingly visible in public life. Actively promoted by the National Women's Political Caucus, Bella Abzug, Elizabeth Holtzman, Shirley Chisholm, Patricia Schroeder, and Geraldine Ferraro went to Congress; Ella T. Grasso became Connecticut's governor in 1974; as did Dixie Lee Ray in Washington State in 1976. Congress authorized child-care tax deductions for working parents in 1972 and in 1974 passed the Equal Credit Opportunity Act, which enabled married women to get credit, including credit cards and mortgages, in their own names. In 1977, 20,000 women went to Houston for the first National Women's Conference. Their "National Plan of Action" represented a hard-won consensus on topics ranging from homemakers' rights to the needs of older women and, most controversially, abortion.

Buoyed by its successes, the women's movement renewed the fight for an Equal Rights Amendment (ERA) to the Constitution. First introduced in 1923, the ERA stated, in its entirety, "Equality of rights under the law shall not be denied or abridged by the United States or any State on the basis of sex." In the early days, the women's movement had split over the ERA because the amendment jeopardized protective legislation for women. That fear, while not wholly gone, no longer prevented feminists of all varieties from favoring the amendment. As much as anything, the ERA became a symbolic statement of women's equality. Congress enthusiastically adopted the amendment in 1972, and within two years, thirty-four states had ratified it. But then progress abruptly halted (Map 29.1).

For this, credit goes chiefly to a remarkable woman, Phyllis Schlafly, a lawyer who had long been active in conservative causes. Despite her own flourishing career, Schlafly advocated traditional roles for women. The ERA, she proclaimed, would create an unnatural "unisex society," with women drafted into the army and forced to use single-sex toilets and locker rooms. Grassroots networks mobilized, showing up at statehouses with home-baked bread and apple pies. As labels on baked goods at one anti-ERA rally expressed it: "My heart and hand went into this dough / For the sake of the family please vote no." It was a message that resonated widely, especially among those troubled by the rapid pace of social change (see American Voices, p. 865). The ERA never was ratified, despite a congressional extension of the deadline to June 30, 1982.

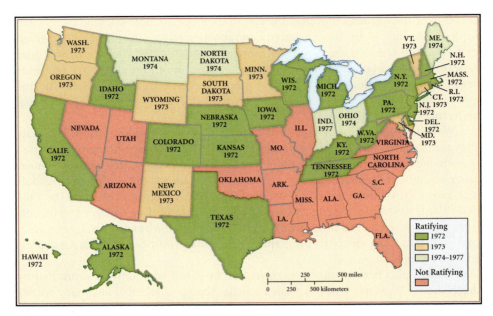

MAP 29.1 States Ratifying the Equal Rights Amendment, 1972–1977

The Equal Rights Amendment (ERA) quickly won support in 1972 and 1973 but then stalled. ERAmerica, a coalition of women's groups formed in 1976, lobbied extensively, particularly in Florida, North Carolina, and Illinois, but failed to sway the conservative legislatures in those states. After Indiana ratified in 1977, the amendment still lacked three votes toward the three-fourths majority needed to pass. Efforts to revive the ERA in the 1980s were unsuccessful, and it remains a dead issue.

Parallel to, and inspired by, the feminist movement, homosexual men and women launched their own protest movement. The crystallizing event was the "Stonewall riot" of 1969 in New York City, when patrons of a gay bar fought back against police harassment. In the assertion of pride that followed, activists began to call themselves *gay* rather than homosexual. Gay advocacy groups, newspapers, and political organizations proliferated, as did vibrant gay communities in New York's Greenwich Village, San Francisco's Castro district, and other urban enclaves. In 1973, the National Gay Task Force launched a campaign to make gay men and lesbians a protected group under laws covering employment and housing rights.

Like the ERA, gay rights came under attack from conservatives. When the Miami city council passed a measure banning discrimination against gay men and lesbians in 1977, the singer Anita Bryant led a campaign to repeal the law by popular referendum. Later that year, voters overturned the measure by a two-to-one majority, prompting similar antigay campaigns around the country. Once again, the country was witnessing the clash between equal rights for an oppressed minority and the moral values of a conservative majority.

Enforcing Civil Rights

The Equal Rights Amendment provoked a political struggle. Supporters and opponents mobilized and lobbied their legislators. The losing side, bitter though it might

Against the Equal Rights Amendment JERRY FALWELL AND SAM ERVIN

The Equal Rights Amendment, after languishing for many years, looked like it would ride the civil rights wave and finally be adopted. But after the amendment was approved by Congress in 1972, the conservative opposition became so intense that it failed to be ratified by three-quarters of the states. Here are the arguments of two prominent opponents: Jerry Falwell, a famous television evangelist and the founder of the Moral Majority, and Sam Ervin, senator from North Carolina from 1954 to 1974 and a key figure in the Watergate investigation.

The Reverend Falwell: The Equal Rights Amendment is a delusion. I believe that women deserve more than equal rights. And, in families and in nations where the Bible is believed, Christian women are honored above men. . . . Men and women have differing strengths. The Equal Rights Amendment can never do for women what needs to be done for them. Women need to know Jesus Christ as their Lord and Savior and be under His Lordship. They need a man who knows Jesus Christ as his Lord and Savior, and they need to be part of a home where their husband is a godly leader and where there is a Christian family. . . . A definite violation of Holy Scripture, ERA defies the mandate that "the husband is the head of the wife, even as Christ is the head of the church" (Ep. 5:23). In 1 Peter 3:7 we read that husbands are to give their wives honor as unto the weaker vessel, that they are both heirs together of the grace of life. Because a woman is weaker does not mean that she is less important.

Senator Ervin: Let us consider for a moment whether there be a rational basis for reasonable distinctions between men and women in any of the relationships or undertakings of life.

When He created them, God made physiological and functional differences between men and women. These differences confer upon men a greater capacity to perform arduous and hazardous physical tasks. Some wise people even profess the belief that there may be psychological differences between men and women. To justify their belief, they assert that women possess an intuitive power to distinguish between wisdom and folly, good and evil. . . .

The Congress and the legislatures of the various states have enacted certain laws based upon the conviction that the physiological and functional differences between men and women make it advisable to exempt or exclude women from certain arduous and hazardous activities in order to protect their health and safety. . . . Among federal laws of this nature are the Selective Service Act, which confines compulsory military service to men. . . . Among the state laws of this kind are laws which limit hours during which women can work, and bar them from engaging in occupations particularly arduous and hazardous such as mining.

If the Equal Rights Amendment should be interpreted by the Supreme Court to forbid any legal distinctions between men and women, all existing and future laws of this nature would be nullified.

SOURCES: Jerry Falwell, *Listen America* (New York: Doubleday, 1980), 150–115; The *Congressional Record,* 15 February 1972 (Washington, DC: Government Printing Office, 1972).

be, could not say its voice had been unheard. But the civil rights struggle largely bypassed this democratic process. For one thing, under the American constitutional system fundamental rights trumped majority rule—which was why, for example, *Brown v. Board of Education* had struck down state-mandated segregated schooling. If the issue had been left to the people, school segregation would not have ended. Moreover, *enforcing* civil rights was a judicial and/or executive responsibility. Courts and federal agencies did the heavy lifting. And that—the unaccountability of the key actors—fed the outrage of many Americans already feeling threatened by the gains of protected minorities.

When Congress banned job discrimination in the Civil Rights Act (1964), all that it required was that employers hire on a merit basis and without regard to race, religion, ethnicity, or sex. The wave of urban riots made the Johnson administration think again. The Kerner Commission (1968), after investigating the causes behind the rioting, strongly urged a massive federal effort at countering white racism that held blacks back and deprived them of hope.

One result was affirmative action—procedures designed to take into account the disadvantaged position of minorities after centuries of discrimination. First advanced by the Labor Department in 1968, affirmative action was refined by a series of court rulings that identified acceptable procedures, including hiring and enrollment goals, special recruitment and training programs, and set-asides (specially reserved slots).

Aided by affirmative action, African American enrollment in colleges and universities doubled between 1970 and 1977. Blacks moved into white-collar professions, found new opportunities in civil service, and got better access to union jobs. Latinos did as well as blacks, and white women did far better.

Affirmative action, however, did not sit well with many whites, who felt that the deck was being stacked against them. Much of the organized support came from conservative groups that had opposed civil rights reform all along. Now they shifted their ground to complaints about "reverse discrimination." The spark, however, was provided by an open letter in 1972 by Jewish organizations that had always supported civil rights but now, seared by the memory of quotas that had kept Jewish students out of elite colleges, came out against affirmative action. In 1978, Allan Bakke, a white man, sued the University of California Medical School at Davis for rejecting him in favor of less-qualified minority candidates. The Supreme Court rejected the medical school's quota system, which set aside 16 of 100 places for "disadvantaged" students. The Court ordered Bakke admitted but indicated that a more flexible approach, in which racial factors could be considered along with other factors, would still pass muster. *Bakke v. University of California* thus upheld affirmative action but, by rejecting straightforward implementation, also called it into question.

The other main civil rights objective—desegregating the schools—produced even more fireworks. For fifteen years, southern states, by a variety of stratagems, had fended off court directives that they move to integration "with all deliberate speed" (see Chapter 27). In 1968, hardly one-third of all black children in the South attended schools with whites. At that point, the federal courts got serious and, in a series of stiff decisions, ordered an end to "dual school systems." Where this did not happen, the courts intervened directly. In 1971, in a landmark decision, the Supreme Court imposed a county-wide busing plan on Charlotte-Mecklenburg, North Carolina. In

An Antibusing Confrontation in Boston

Tensions over court-ordered busing ran high in Boston in 1976. When a black lawyer tried to cross the city hall plaza during an antibusing demonstration, he became a victim of Boston's climate of racial hatred and violence. This Pulitzer Prize–winning photograph by Stanley Forman for the Boston *Herald American* shows a protester about to impale the man with a flagstaff. Stanley Forman.

this case, integration went smoothly, and the South as a whole essentially gave up the fight. By the mid-1970s, 86 percent of black children were attending school with whites.

But in the North, where segregated schooling was also a fact of life—arising, however, from residential patterns, not legally mandated separation—busing orders sparked intense opposition. In South Boston, a strongly Irish Catholic working-class neighborhood, mobs attacked African American students bused in from Roxbury. Armed police were required to keep South Boston High School open.

As a solution to segregation, busing came up against cherished attachments to neighborhood schooling. Busing also had the perverse effect of speeding up "white flight" to the suburbs, as, for example, in Detroit, where a black city was encircled by white suburbs. To integrate Detroit schools would have required merging city and suburban districts, which, in fact, was what a lower court ordered in 1971. But in *Milliken v. Bradley* (1974), the Supreme Court reversed the lower court. Thereafter, busing as a means of achieving racial balance fell out of favor.

But in the meantime, "forced busing," much touted by Nixon in the 1972 campaign, added to the grievances of conservatives, not least by reminding them of how much they hated what they perceived as the arrogance of unelected judges.

The decision that initiated the tumult over busing—*Brown v. Board of Education* (1954)—also triggered a larger judicial revolution. Traditionally, it was liberals, not conservatives, who favored *judicial restraint,* which roughly meant that courts should defer to legislatures. After many years of complaining that the courts were too active in overturning progressive legislation, the liberals finally triumphed in 1937, when the Supreme Court reversed itself and let stand key New Deal laws—to the shock and outrage of conservatives.

That history explains why many respected liberal jurists and legal scholars, while favoring racial equality, were uneasy about the *Brown* decision. They thought that it violated principles of judicial restraint they had spent lifetimes defending. What ultimately persuaded them was a shift in the big issues coming before the Court.

When property rights had been at stake, conservatives favored activist courts willing to curb antibusiness legislatures. Now that human rights came foremost, it was the turn of liberals to celebrate activist judges and, preeminently, the man whom President Eisenhower appointed chief justice of the Supreme Court in 1953: Earl Warren. A popular Republican governor of California, Warren surprised many, including Eisenhower, by his robust advocacy of civil rights and civil liberties. If conservatives found reason to bewail judicial activism, there was no one they blamed more than Chief Justice Warren.

Consider these landmark Warren Court decisions. On the treatment of criminals: that they had a constitutional right to counsel (1963, 1964) and to be informed by arresting officers of their right to remain silent (1966). On indecency: that pornography was protected by freedom of the press unless shown to be "utterly without redeeming social importance" (1964). On prayers and Bible reading in the schools: that religious ritual of any kind violated the constitutional separation of church and state (1962, 1963). On reproductive rights: In *Griswold v. Connecticut* (1965), the Supreme Court struck down an 1879 state law prohibiting the purchase and use of contraceptive devices by couples as a violation of their constitutional right of privacy.

Griswold opened the way for *Roe v. Wade* (1973), which declared the antiabortion laws of Texas and Georgia unconstitutional. Abortions performed during the first trimester were protected by the right of privacy (following *Griswold*). At the time and afterward, some legal authorities questioned whether the Constitution recognized any such privacy right. Moreover, individual states were already legalizing abortion. Nevertheless, the Supreme Court chose to move forward, translating a policy matter that was traditionally state-regulated into a national, constitutionally protected right.

► What were the sources of growth for the women's rights movement?

► Why did enforcing civil rights prove more controversial than passing civil rights legislation?

► Why did the conservative/liberal alignment on judicial restraint change after 1954?

For the women's movement and liberals generally, *Roe v. Wade* was a great, if unanticipated, victory. For evangelical Christians, Catholics, and conservatives generally, it was a bitter pill. Other rights-creating issues — "coddling" criminals, prohibiting school prayer, protecting pornography — had a polarizing effect. But *Roe v. Wade* was in a class by itself. In 1976, opponents convinced Congress to deny Medicaid funds for abortions, an opening round in a protracted campaign against *Roe v. Wade* that continues to this day.

Lean Years

On top of everything else, the economy went into a tailspin. Oil supplies suddenly fell short, disrupting industry and sending gas prices sky-high. At the same time, the United States found itself challenged by foreign competitors making better and cheaper products. All the economic indicators — inflation, employment, productivity, growth — turned negative. In such times, quality-of-life concerns normally get short shrift. Not in the 1970s, when, alongside economic distress, environmental and consumer movements began to flourish.

Energy Crisis

Modern economies run on oil. And if the oil stops, woe follows. Something like that happened to the United States in the 1970s. Once the world's leading producer, the United States was heavily dependent on imported oil, mostly from the Persian Gulf (Figure 29.1). American and European oil companies had discovered and developed the Middle Eastern fields, but control had been wrested away by the Muslim states as they threw off the remnants of European colonialism. Foreign companies still extracted and marketed the oil — only they had the expertise — but they did so under profit-sharing agreements with the Persian Gulf states. In 1960, these nations and other oil-rich developing countries formed the Organization of Petroleum Exporting Countries (OPEC). OPEC was a cartel, and had it been a domestic enterprise, it would

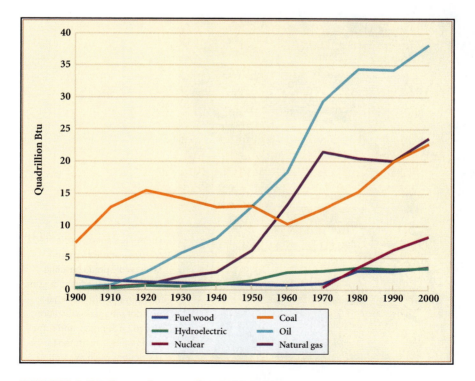

FIGURE 29.1 U.S. Energy Consumption, 1900–2000

Coal was the nation's primary source of energy until the 1950s, when oil and natural gas became the dominant fuels. The use of nuclear and hydroelectric power also rose substantially in the postwar era. During the 1980s, fuel-efficient automobiles and conservation measures reduced total energy use, but in the 1990s, energy consumption rose significantly. SOURCE: *World Almanac 2002.*

have been an unlawful conspiracy in restraint of trade. But nothing prevented independent countries from forming a cartel. During the 1960s, with the world awash in oil, OPEC was in fact ineffective.

That changed in 1973, when Egypt and Syria invaded Israel, initiating the Yom Kippur War. Israel prevailed but only after being resupplied by an emergency American airlift. Already resentful of Western support for Israel, the Arab states declared an oil embargo. The effect was devastating, forcing many Americans to spend hours in line at the pumps and pushing gas prices up by 40 percent. Oil had become a political weapon. And the West's vulnerability stood revealed. In 1979, after a second shortage caused by the Iranian revolution, oil prices peaked at $34 a barrel, ten times higher than the price in 1973.

The United States scrambled to meet its energy needs. A national speed limit of 55 miles an hour was imposed to conserve fuel. Americans began to buy smaller, more fuel-efficient cars but not from Detroit, which was tooled up to produce "gas guzzlers." Pretty soon VWs, Toyotas, and Datsuns (Nissans at a later date) dotted American highways while sales of American cars slumped. The effect on the economy

No Gas

During the energy crisis of 1973 to 1974, American motorists faced widespread gasoline shortages for the first time since World War II. Although gas was not rationed, gas stations closed on Sundays, and some communities instituted further restrictions, such as creating systems by which motorists with license plates ending in even numbers could purchase gas on certain days, alternate days being reserved for odd numbers. Star/Stockphoto.com.

was considerable because one of every six jobs in the country was generated directly or indirectly by the auto industry. Even worse was the raging inflation set off by the oil shortage. Worst of all perhaps was the psychic shock to Americans at the discovery that their well-being was hostage to forces beyond their control.

Environmentalism

The energy crisis—and the realization it drove home that the earth's resources were not limitless—gave a huge boost to the environmental movement. In some ways, environmentalism was an offshoot of the 1960s counterculture. Activists talked about the "rights of nature," just as they had about the rights of women or blacks. Antiwar activism translated readily into protest tactics against polluters and wilderness destroyers. More fundamentally, however, environmentalism was a feature of America's advanced consumer society. Now that they had the basic necessities and then some, Americans wanted a quality of life defined by a healthy environment and by access to unspoiled nature.

The modern movement began in 1962 when Rachel Carson published *Silent Spring*, a stunning analysis of the impact of the pesticide DDT on the food chain. There followed a succession of galvanizing issues: an environmentally destructive Alaskan oil pipeline, a proposed airport in the Florida Everglades, and a huge oil spill in January 1969 off the coast of Santa Barbara, California. Environmentalism became certifiably a mass movement on the first Earth Day, April 22, 1970, when twenty million citizens gathered in communities across the country to express their support for the endangered planet.

The mother of environmental wars in the 1970s was the controversy over nuclear power. Electricity from the atom—what could be better? That was how Americans had greeted the arrival of power-generating nuclear technology in the 1950s. By 1974, utility companies were operating forty-two nuclear power plants, with a hundred more planned. Given the oil crisis, nuclear energy might have seemed a godsend. Besides, unlike coal- or oil-driven plants, nuclear operations produced no air pollutants.

But environmentalists saw only the dangers. A meltdown would be catastrophic, and so, in slow motion, might be radioactive wastes. These fears seemed to be confirmed in March 1979, when the reactor core at a nuclear plant at Three Mile Island near Harrisburg, Pennsylvania, came close to meltdown. A prompt shutdown saved the plant, but the near-catastrophe enabled environmentalists to win the battle over nuclear energy. After the incident at Three Mile Island, the utility industry stopped building nuclear-powered plants.

Environmentalism helped to rekindle a consumer movement that had languished after the Progressive era (see Chapter 20). The key figure was Ralph Nader, a young Harvard-educated lawyer whose book *Unsafe at Any Speed* (1965) attacked General Motors for putting flashy styling ahead of safety in the rear-engine Chevrolet Corvair. Buoyed by his success, Nader in 1969 launched a Washington-based consumer protection organization that spawned a national network of activists fighting everything from consumer fraud to dangerous toys. Staffed largely by volunteers known as "Nader's Raiders," the organization pioneered the class-action suit, which enabled lawyers to represent an entire pool of grievants in a single litigation. In Nader's wake, dozens of groups emerged to combat the tobacco industry, unethical insurance and credit practices, and a host of other consumer problems.

Environmentalists proved remarkably adept at sparking governmental action. In 1969, Congress passed the National Environmental Policy Act, which required developers to file environmental impact statements assessing the effect of their projects on ecosystems. The next year, Nixon established the Environmental Protection Agency (EPA) and signed the Clean Air Act, which established standards for auto emissions that caused air pollution. Following the lead of several states, Congress banned the use of DDT in 1972 and, in 1980, created the Superfund to finance the cleanup of toxic waste sites. The Endangered Species Act (1973) expanded the scope of the Endangered Animals Act of 1964, protecting such species as snail darters and spotted owls. On the consumer front, a big victory was the establishment of the federal Consumer Products Safety Commission in 1972.

These environmental successes were not universally applauded, however. Fuel-economy standards for cars were said to hinder an auto industry that was struggling to keep up with foreign competitors. Corporations resented environmental regulations, but so did many of their workers, who believed that tightened standards threatened their jobs. "IF YOU'RE HUNGRY AND OUT OF WORK, EAT AN ENVIRONMENTALIST," read one labor union's bumper sticker. In a time of rising unemployment, activists clashed head-on with proponents of economic growth.

Economic Woes

In addition to the energy crisis, the economy was beset by a host of longer-term problems. Government spending for the Vietnam War and the Great Society made for a growing federal deficit and spiraling inflation. In the industrial sector, the country faced growing competition from Germany and Japan. America's share of world trade dropped from 32 percent in 1955 to 18 percent in 1970 and was headed downward. As a result, in 1971, the United States posted its first trade deficit in almost a century, and the value of the dollar fell to its lowest level since World War II.

Gross domestic product (GDP), which had been increasing at a sizzling 4.1 percent per year in the 1960s, dropped after 1970 to 2.9 percent. In a blow to national pride, nine western European countries surpassed the United States in per capita GDP by 1980. The economy was also hit by a devastating combination of unemployment and inflation—*stagflation,* so called—that contradicted a basic principle taught by economists: Prices were not supposed to rise in a stagnant economy. In the 1970s, they did.

For ordinary Americans, the reality of stagflation was a noticeable decline in the standard of living as discretionary income per worker dropped 18 percent between 1973 and the early 1980s. Many families were kept afloat only by the second income brought in by working women.

America's economic woes struck hardest at the industrial sector, which suddenly — shockingly—began to be dismantled. Worst hit was the steel industry, which for seventy-five years had been the economy's crown jewel. Its problems were, ironically, partly a product of good fortune. Only the American steel industry had been left unscathed by World War II. In the postwar years, that gave U.S. producers an open, hugely profitable field, but it also left them saddled with outdated plants and equipment. When the German and Japanese industries rebuilt—with the aid of American funding and technology—they incorporated the latest and best of everything. More-over, the American industry's natural advantages were eroding. With its abundant iron ore reserves exhausted, the industry competed for raw materials on global markets like everyone else. Meanwhile, advances in international shipping deprived it of the comparative advantage of location.

Distant from markets and lacking natural resources, Japan nevertheless built a powerhouse of an industry. When Japanese steel flooded in during the 1970s, the American industry was simply overwhelmed. A massive dismantling began, including the entire Pittsburgh region. By the time the smoke cleared in the mid-1980s, the American steel industry was competitive again, but it was a shadow of its former self.

The steel industry was the prime example of what became known as *deindustrialization*. The country was in the throes of an economic transformation that left it largely stripped of its industrial base. A swath of the Northeast and Midwest, the country's manufacturing heartland, became the nation's "Rust Belt" (Map 29.2), strewn with abandoned plants and dying communities.

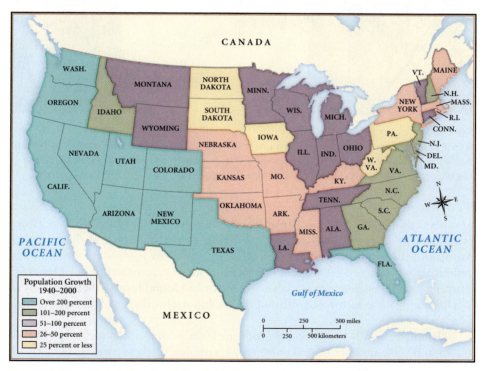

MAP 29.2 From Rust Belt to Sun Belt, 1940–2000

One of the most significant developments of the post–World War II era was the growth of the Sun Belt. Sparked by federal spending for military bases, the defense industry, and the space program, states of the South and Southwest experienced an economic boom in the 1950s. This growth was further enhanced in the 1970s as the heavily industrialized regions of the Northeast and Midwest declined and migrants from what was quickly dubbed the "Rust Belt" headed to the South and West in search of jobs. Rising political influence accompanied the economic and demographic growth of the Sun Belt, which has provided an important base for the Republican Party.

For more help analyzing this map, see the Online Study Guide at **bedfordstmartins.com/henrettaconcise**.

Symbol of the Rust Belt

A padlock on the gate of Youngstown, Ohio's United States Steel mill symbolizes the creation of the Rust Belt when economic hard times in the 1970s led to widespread plant closures in the industrial areas of the Midwest and Northeast and an exodus to the booming Sun Belt (see Map 29.2). © Bettmann/Corbis.

Many thousands of blue-collar workers lost well-paid union jobs. What they faced is revealed by the 4,100 steelworkers left jobless by the shutdown of the Campbell Works of the Youngstown Sheet & Tube Co. in 1977. Two years later, one-third had retired early at half pay. Ten percent had moved. Fifteen percent were still jobless, with unemployment benefits long gone. Forty percent had found local work but mostly in low-paying, service-sector jobs. Most of these Ohio steelworkers had fallen from their perch in the middle class.

Deindustrialization dealt harshly with the labor movement. In the early 1970s, as inflation hit, the number of strikes surged; 2.4 million workers participated in work stoppages in 1970 alone. Challenged by foreign competition, industry resisted union demands, and labor's bargaining power waned. In these hard years, the much-vaunted labor-management accord of the 1950s went bust. Instead of seeking higher wages, unions now mainly fought to save jobs. In the 1970s, union membership dropped sharply, with industrial unions—the Rust Belt unions—especially hard hit. By the end of the 1980s, only 16 percent of American workers were organized. The impact on liberal politics was huge. With labor's decline, a main buttress of the New Deal coalition was coming undone.

The economic crisis also hardened antitax sentiment, reversing a postwar spirit of generous public investment. The premier example was California. With stagflation, real estate values rocketed upward, and so did property taxes. Hardest hit were retirees and others on fixed incomes. Into this dire situation stepped Howard Jarvis, an anti–New Dealer cut from the same cloth as the ERA-hating Phyllis Schlafly and, like her, a genius at mobilizing a grassroots movement. Despite opposition by virtually the entire state establishment, Californians voted overwhelmingly for Proposition 13, which rolled back property taxes, capped future increases, and harnessed all tax measures—state or local—to a two-thirds voting requirement.

As a vehicle for hobbling public spending, Proposition 13 was extraordinarily effective. Per capita funding of California public schools plunged from the top tier to the bottom (next to Mississippi). Proposition 13 also pulled off the neat trick of hugely benefiting wealthy homeowners and businesses (commercial property got the same protection), under the shelter of California's elderly. More broadly, Proposition 13 inspired tax revolts across the country and gave conservatives an enduring issue: No New Taxes.

The cardinal marker of New Deal liberalism had been a remarkable decline in income inequality (see Figure 27.1 on p. 798). Now, in the 1970s, that trend reversed, and the wealthiest Americans began to pull ahead again until, in our own time, the income share of the top tenth—45 percent—is back where it was in the Roaring Twenties.

▶ Why did the United States enter an energy crisis in the 1970s?

▶ What were the major concerns of the environmentalist movement?

▶ What were the causes and effects of deindustrialization?

Politics in the Wake of Watergate

Nixon's resignation in 1974 left American politics in limbo. Popular disdain for politicians, already evident in declining voter turnout, deepened. "Don't vote," read one bumper sticker in 1976. "It only encourages them."

Watergate damaged short-term Republican prospects but also shifted the party's balance rightward. It was telling that Gerald Ford, in advance of his 1976 reelection bid, dumped his vice president, Nelson Rockefeller, a liberal Republican, for a conservative running mate, Senator Robert Dole of Kansas.

As for the Democrats, Watergate granted them a reprieve, a second chance at recapturing their eroding base. But that required leadership, not something the party's freewheeling rules for choosing a candidate could guarantee. Any governor with a nice head of hair, a winning manner, some money in the bank, and a semblance of organization had a shot at the party's nomination.

Jimmy Carter: The Outsider as President

"Jimmy Who?" was how journalists first responded when James E. Carter, governor of Georgia and self-styled peanut farmer, emerged from the pack and went on to win the Democratic nomination. Trading on Watergate, Carter pledged to restore morality to the White House. "I will never lie to you," he promised voters. Carter played up his credentials as a Washington outsider, although he made sure, in selecting Senator Walter F. Mondale of Minnesota, to have a running mate with ties to traditional Democratic voting blocs. Ford, still wounded by his pardon of Nixon, was a fairly easy mark. Carter won with 50 percent of the popular vote to Ford's 48 percent.

For a time, Carter got some mileage as an outsider, the common man who walked back to the White House after the Inauguration, delivered fireside chats in a cardigan sweater, and carried his own bags. The fact that he was a born-again Christian also played well. But Carter's inexperience began to tell. His outsider strategy made for chilly relations with congressional leaders. Disdainful of the Democratic establishment, Carter relied heavily on inexperienced advisors from Georgia. And he himself, a prodigious worker, was an inveterate micromanager, exhausting himself over details better left to underlings.

On the domestic front, Carter's big challenge was managing the economy. The problems that he faced defied easy solution. Most confounding was stagflation. If the government focused on inflation—forcing prices down by increasing taxes or raising interest rates—unemployment became worse. If the government tried to stimulate employment, inflation became worse. Seeking to cut through this conundrum, Nixon had imposed prices and wage controls in 1971—a brave try but one that created more problems than it solved.

Carter lacked Nixon's daring. At heart, in fact, he was an economic conservative. He toyed with the idea of an "industrial policy" to bail out the ailing manufacturing sector but moved instead in a free-market direction by lifting the New Deal–era regulation of the airline, trucking, and railroad industries. **Deregulation** stimulated competition and cut prices but also drove firms out of business and hurt unionized workers.

Taking office after a sharp mid-1970s downturn, Carter offered a stimulus package that was at cross-purposes with the Federal Reserve Board's efforts to contain inflation by raising interest rates. Then turmoil in the Middle East in 1979 curtailed oil supplies, and gas prices jumped again. In a major TV address, Carter lectured Americans about the nation's "crisis of the spirit." He called energy conservation "the moral equivalent of war"—or, in the media's shorthand, "MEOW," aptly capturing the nation's assessment of Carter's homily. By then, his approval rating had fallen below 30 percent. And it was no wonder: an inflation rate over 11 percent, failing industries, long lines at the pumps. It seemed the worst of all possible economic worlds (see Voices from Abroad, p. 877).

Carter and the World

In foreign affairs, President Carter had a firmer sense of what he was about. He was the anti-Nixon, a world leader who rejected Kissinger's "realism" in favor of human rights and peacemaking. Carter established the Office of Human Rights in the State Department and withdrew economic and military aid from repressive regimes in Argentina, Uruguay, and Ethiopia, although he still funded equally repressive U.S. allies like the Philippines, South Korea, and South Africa. In Latin America, Carter punctured an enduring symbol of Yankee imperialism by signing a treaty on September 7, 1977, turning control of the Panama Canal over to Panama (effective December 31, 1999). Despite a conservative outcry, the Senate narrowly approved the treaty.

America's Crisis of Faith FEI XIAOTONG

Fei Xiaotong, a Chinese sociologist whose often sympathetic treatment of America got him into trouble with the Communist regime, regained prominence after relations with America warmed in the 1970s. After participating in an official delegation to the United States in 1979, Fei wrote a series of essays entitled "Glimpses of America." In this passage, he responds to President Jimmy Carter's assertion in his famous "malaise" speech of 1979 that Americans faced a spiritual crisis.

I read in the newspaper that the energy crisis in the United States is getting worse and worse. I hear that after spending several days of quiet thought in his mountain retreat, President Carter decided that America's real problem is not the energy crisis but a "crisis of faith." The way it is told is that vast numbers of people have lost their faith in the present government and in the political system. . . . Even more serious, he believes that the masses have come to have doubts about traditional American values, and if this continues, in his opinion, the future of America is terrible to imagine. He made a sad and worried speech . . . but if he has truly realized that the present American social system has lost popular support, that should be considered a good thing because at least it shows that the old method of just treating the symptoms will no longer work.

In fact, loss of faith . . . did not begin with the energy crisis. The spectacular advances in science and technology in America in the last decade or two and the unceasing rise in the forces of production are good. But the social system remains unchanged. . . . The ruling class, to be sure, still has the power to keep on finding ways of dealing with the endless series of crises, but the masses of people are coming increasingly to feel that they have fallen unwittingly into a situation where their fate is controlled by others, like a moth in a spiderweb, unable to struggle free. Not only the blacks of Harlem—who are clearly able to earn their own living but still have to rely on welfare to support themselves without dignity—but even well-off families in gardenlike suburban residences worry all day that some accident may suddenly rob them of everything. . . . No wonder people complain that civilization was created by humans, but humans have been enslaved by it. Such a feeling is natural in a society like America's. Carter is right to call this feeling of helplessness a "crisis of faith," for it is a doubting of the present culture. Only he should realize that the present crisis has been long in the making and is already deep. . . .

But to end with the crisis of faith does violence to my original intention. History is a stream that flows on and cannot be stopped. Words must be cut off, but history goes bubbling on. It is inconceivable that America will come to a standstill at any crisis point. I have full faith in the great American people and hope that they will continue to make even greater contributions to the progress of mankind. . . .

SOURCE: R. David Arkush and Leo O. Lee, trans. and eds., *Land Without Ghosts: Chinese Impressions of America from the Mid-Nineteenth Century to the Present* (Berkeley: University of California Press, 1989).

A Framework for Peace
President Jimmy Carter's greatest foreign-policy achievement was the personal diplomacy he exerted to persuade President Anwar el-Sadat of Egypt (left) and Prime Minister Menachem Begin of Israel (right) to sign a peace treaty in 1978. The signing of the Camp David Accords marked an important first step in constructing a framework for peace in the Middle East. Jimmy Carter Presidential Library.

President Carter scored his greatest success by tackling the intractable Arab-Israeli conflict. In 1978, he invited Israel's prime minister Menachem Begin and Egyptian president Anwar el-Sadat to Camp David. For two weeks, Carter kept the discussions going and finally persuaded Sadat and Begin to adopt a "framework for peace," under which Egypt recognized Israel and received back the Sinai Peninsula, which Israel had occupied since 1967.

Though deploring "inordinate fear of Communism," Carter's efforts at improving relations with the Soviet Union foundered. He caused resentment by criticizing the Kremlin's record on human rights. Negotiations for arms reductions went slowly, and when the SALT II agreement limiting bombers and missiles was finally signed in 1979, Senate hawks objected. Hopes for Senate ratification collapsed when the Soviet Union invaded Afghanistan that December. Treating the invasion as a major crisis, Carter placed an embargo on wheat shipments to the Soviet Union, called for increased defense spending, and declared an American boycott of the 1980 summer Olympics in Moscow. In a fateful decision, Carter began providing covert assistance to anti-Soviet fighters in Afghanistan, some of whom metamorphosed into anti-American Islamic radicals in later years.

Carter's undoing came in Iran, however. The Shah, Muhammad Reza Pahlavi, was an American client, installed by the CIA in 1953 (see Chapter 26). Thereafter, the United States counted Iran as a faithful ally, a bulwark in the troubled Middle East, and a steady source of oil. Notwithstanding his fine words, Carter followed the same path as his Cold War predecessors, overlooking the crimes of Iran's CIA-trained secret police, SAVAK, and mounting popular enmity toward the United States. Early in 1979, the Shah was driven into exile by an Iranian revolution that brought the Shiite cleric Ayatollah Ruhollah Khomeini to power.

In October 1979, the United States admitted the deposed Shah, who was suffering from cancer, for medical treatment. In response, Iranian students seized the U.S. embassy in Tehran, taking sixty-six Americans hostage. The captors demanded that the Shah be returned to Iran for trial, but the United States refused. Instead, President Carter suspended arms sales to Iran and froze Iranian assets in American banks.

For the next fourteen months, the hostage crisis paralyzed Jimmy Carter's presidency. Night after night, humiliating pictures of blindfolded hostages appeared on television newscasts. An attempt to mount a military rescue in April 1980 had to be aborted because of equipment failures in the desert. During the withdrawal, one of the helicopters collided with a transport plane, setting off ammunition explosions and causing multiple American casualties. After this fiasco, the torturous negotiations, simplified by the Shah's death, finally succeeded. As a parting shot, the Iranians waited until the day Carter left office to deliver the hostages.

Every war president in the twentieth century — Wilson, FDR, Truman, Johnson — had been a Democrat. So Carter performed a remarkable feat: Single-handedly, he marked the Democrats indelibly as the party of wimps. All the elements were now in place for the triumph of the conservatives. All they needed was a leader.

▶ Why did Jimmy Carter have so much trouble managing the economy?

▶ What distinguished Carter's conduct of foreign policy from Nixon's?

▶ What were the major causes of the apparent weakening of the United States as a super-power during this period?

SUMMARY

As we have seen, the 1970s constitute a transitional period, with one foot in the liberal past and the other foot in the conservative future. This was evident in Richard Nixon's presidency, which tried to consolidate a new Republican majority yet also accepted, and in some ways expanded, an activist state. In foreign policy, similarly, Nixon moved in two directions, capitalizing on Communist divisions to move toward détente yet adhering to Cold War assumptions in Vietnam. The drift toward Republican supremacy was cut short by the Watergate scandal, which forced Nixon to resign in 1974.

For much of the 1970s, Americans struggled with economic problems, including inflation, energy shortages, stagnation of income, and deindustrialization. Despite diminishing expectations, Americans actively supported movements for environmental and consumer protection. The battle for civil rights entered a second stage, expanding to encompass women's and gay rights and, in the realm of racial justice, focusing more on problems of enforcement. One effect, however, was a new, more conservative social mood that began to challenge liberal values in politics and society more generally.

The presidencies of Gerald Ford and Jimmy Carter did little to restore Americans' faith in their political leaders. Carter failed to resolve the economic crisis besetting the nation; and his foreign policy, while high-minded, ran into comparable difficulties, topped off by the Iranian hostage crisis of 1979.

Connections: Society

In this chapter, we discussed the second stage of the civil rights revolution, which, like the first stage, prompted strong opposition. In the 1960s, however, the resistance was regional, limited to the South, whereas in the 1970s, the resistance became national and, in contrast to the defense of racial segregation, touched concerns that many Americans considered legitimate and important. In the case of women's rights, we can trace back to the battle over woman suffrage (see Chapter 19) how strongly felt the belief had historically been about the proper role of women. In the case of enforcement of civil rights, the roots of resistance cannot be located in a single chapter but are embedded in traditions of individual rights, going back to the Revolutionary era, that made Americans uncomfortable with arguments that favored affirmative action or court-mandated

TIMELINE

1966	► National Organization for Women (NOW) founded		► Arab oil embargo; gas shortages
1968	► Richard Nixon elected president	**1974**	► Nixon resigns over Watergate; Ford becomes president and pardons Nixon
1969	► Stonewall riot, start of gay liberation movement		► Busing controversy in Boston
	► Vietnam moratorium called in protest of war	**1975**	► Fall of Saigon
1970	► Earth Day first observed	**1976**	► Jimmy Carter elected president
	► Environmental Protection Agency established	**1978**	► Carter brokers Camp David accords between Egypt and Israel
	► Nixon orders invasion of Cambodia; renewed antiwar protests		► Proposition 13 reduces California taxes
	► Killings at Kent State and Jackson State		► *Bakke v. University of California* limits affirmative action
1971	► Pentagon Papers published		
1972	► Watergate break-in; Nixon reelected	**1979**	► Three Mile Island nuclear accident
	► Nixon visits People's Republic of China		► Hostages seized at American embassy in Tehran, Iran
	► SALT I Treaty with Soviet Union		► Soviet Union invades Afghanistan
1973	► *Roe v. Wade* legalizes abortion	**1980**	► "Superfund" created to clean up toxic land sites
	► Endangered Species Act		
	► Paris Peace Accords		
	► War Powers Act		

busing. Historically, the obligations of citizenship had not entailed parting with rights or privileges to advance the rights or privileges of others. As we will see in Chapter 30, the potency of these conservative views fueled a political revolution in the age of Ronald Reagan.

FOR FURTHER EXPLORATION

Peter N. Carroll, *It Seemed Like Nothing Happened* (1982), provides an overview of the period. Gary Wills, *Nixon Agonistes,* rev. ed. (1990), judges Nixon to be a product of his times. For Watergate, a starting point is the books by the *Washington Post* journalists who broke the scandal, Carl Bernstein and Bob Woodward: *All the President's Men* (1974) and *The Final Days* (1976). Stanley Kutler, *The Wars of Watergate* (1990), is the definitive history. Gary Sick, a Jimmy Carter White House advisor on Iran, offers an insider's account of the hostage crisis in *All Fall Down: America's Tragic Encounter with Iran* (1986). Thomas Byrne Edsall with Mary D. Edsall, *Chain Reaction: The Impact of Race, Rights, and Taxes on American Politics* (1991), examines some of the divisive social issues of the 1970s. J. Anthony Lukas, *Common Ground* (1985), tells the story of the Boston busing crisis through the biographies of three families. Barbara Ehrenreich examines the backlash against feminism in *Hearts of Men* (1984).

For the Watergate scandal, see **nixon.archives.gov/index.php**, which provides transcripts of the infamous tapes as well as other useful links to archival holdings concerning Richard Nixon's presidency. Documents from the Women's Liberation Movement, culled from the Duke University Special Collections Library, at **scriptorium.lib .duke.edu/wlm**, emphasize the women's movement of the late 1960s and early 1970s.

TEST YOUR KNOWLEDGE

To assess your mastery of the material in this chapter and for Web sites, images, and documents related to this chapter, visit **bedfordstmartins.com/henrettaconcise**.

PART SEVEN

A Divided Nation in a Disordered World

1980–2008

DIPLOMACY	GOVERNMENT	ECONOMY
Beyond the Cold War	**Conservative ascendancy**	**Uneven affluence and globalization**
1980 ▶ Ronald Reagan begins arms buildup ▶ INF Treaty (1988) ▶ Berlin Wall falls (1989)	▶ New Right and Evangelical Christians help to elect Ronald Reagan ▶ Reagan cuts taxes and federal regulatory system	▶ Reaganomics; budget and trade deficits soar ▶ Labor union membership declines
1990 ▶ First Persian Gulf War (1990) ▶ Soviet Union collapses; end of the Cold War ▶ U.S. peacekeeping forces in Bosnia	▶ Republican "Contract with America" (1994) ▶ Bill Clinton advances moderate Democratic policies; wins welfare reform and NAFTA ▶ Clinton impeached and acquitted (1998–1999)	▶ New technology prompts productivity rise ▶ Global competition cuts U.S. manufacturing; jobs outsourced
2000 ▶ Al Qaeda attacks on the World Trade Center and the Pentagon (2001) ▶ United States and allies fight Taliban in Afghanistan ▶ United States invades Iraq (2003); costly insurgency begins ▶ North Korea tests nuclear weapons; stalemate with Iran over nuclear program	▶ George W. Bush chosen as president in contested election (2000) ▶ Bush pushes faith-based initiatives and No Child Left Behind ▶ USA PATRIOT Act passed (2002) ▶ *Hamdan v. Rumsfeld* (2006) overturns detainee policies	▶ Bush tax cuts cause budget deficits to soar ▶ Income inequality increases ▶ Huge trade deficits with China ▶ Collapse of housing boom causes major financial crisis

SOCIETY	TECHNOLOGY AND SCIENCE
Demographic change and culture wars	**Media and the information revolution**
▸ Advent of "Yuppies" ▸ Rise in Hispanic and Asian immigration ▸ Crime and drug crises in the cities ▸ AIDS epidemic	▸ Cable News Network (CNN) founded (1980) ▸ Television industry deregulation ▸ Compact discs and cell phones invented
▸ Los Angeles race riots (1992) ▸ "Culture Wars" over affirmative action, feminism, abortion, and gay rights	▸ Dramatic growth of the Internet and World Wide Web ▸ America Online rises and declines ▸ Biotech revolution enhances medical treatment
▸ Many states ban gay marriages ▸ "Minutemen" patrol Mexican border; immigration changes proposed; stalemate results ▸ Baby boomers begin to retire; new federal drug benefits for elderly	▸ Broadband access grows ▸ "Blogging" and "YouTubing" increase ▸ "Creation Science" controversy ▸ Bush limits federal stem-cell research ▸ Environmental issues intensify as evidence of global warming becomes definitive

In 1992, former president Richard M. Nixon remarked, "History is never worth reading until it's fifty years old. It takes fifty years before you're able to come back and evaluate a man or a period of time." Nixon's comments remind us that writing recent history poses a particular challenge; not knowing the future, we cannot say which present-day trends will prove to be of lasting importance. Part Seven is therefore a work in progress; its perspective will change as events unfold. It has five broad themes: the ascendancy of the Republican Party and the New Right, the impact of economic globalization, social conflicts stemming from cultural diversity, the revolution in information technology, and the end of the Cold War and the rise of Muslim terrorism.

GOVERNMENT

With Ronald Reagan's election in 1980, "New Right" conservatism began its ascendancy. The conservatives sought to roll back the social welfare state created by the New Deal and the Great Society. Presidents Reagan and George H. W. Bush cut taxes, limited federal regulation, and appointed conservative-minded federal judges. Democrat Bill Clinton won passage of some welfare measures but pursued a centrist policy. Evangelical Christians and conservative lawmakers brought abortion, gay rights, and other cultural issues into the political arena, setting off controversies that revealed sharp divisions among the American people. George W. Bush capitalized on these divisions to win the presidency, but his record as an economic conservative was more ambiguous than Reagan's or his father's because, while he was a tax cutter and free-marketeer, he was also an undisciplined spender who plunged the federal budget into severe deficit. By the end of his presidency, it was no longer clear that New Right conservatism was in the ascendancy.

DIPLOMACY

Suddenly, in the late 1980s, the Soviet Union and its satellite Communist regimes in Eastern Europe collapsed, leaving the United States as the only military superpower. Expecting to lead in the creation of a "new world order," the United States actively countered civil wars, terrorist activities, and military aggression in many parts of the world. In 1991, it fought the Persian Gulf War in response to Iraq's invasion of Kuwait; in the late 1990s, it led military action in Serbia and Bosnia. In 2001, responding to terrorist assaults on New York and Washington by the radical Islamic group Al Qaeda, President George W. Bush attacked Al Qaeda's bases in Afghanistan. He then ordered an invasion of Iraq in 2003 that quickly toppled the dictator Saddam Hussein but triggered civil chaos and a violent insurgency that, as of 2008, had cost the United States $500 billion and 30,000 casualties.

ECONOMY

The American economy grew substantially between 1980 and 2007, thanks to the increased productivity of workers and robust spending by American consumers. Republican tax cuts spurred investment but also contributed to budget deficits and a widening gap between rich and poor citizens. The Federal Reserve kept interest rates low and made credit so cheap that a speculative housing boom developed. The end of the Cold War allowed the worldwide expansion of capitalism. American-run multinational corporations shifted manufacturing facilities to China and other low-wage countries at the expense of American workers. The resulting flood of cheap foreign-made goods benefited consumers but created a massive American trade deficit. Because of the trade imbalance, budget deficits, and the housing bubble, American prosperity rested on shaky foundations. In 2008, as the housing bubble burst and a financial crisis set in, the economy slid into recession.

SOCIETY

During these decades, American society grew ever more diverse in demographic composition and cultural values. Increased immigration from Latin America and Asia added to cultural tensions and produced a new nativist movement. Continuing battles over affirmative action, abortion, sexual standards, homosexuality, feminism, and religion in public life took on an increasingly passionate character, which hindered the achievement of politically negotiated compromises. Political paralysis was most striking in the cases of illegal immigration and Social Security, in which bitterly contested solutions ended in stalemate.

TECHNOLOGY AND SCIENCE

Scientific knowledge and technological advances likewise triggered cultural conflicts. Religious conservatives invoked a faith-based ideology that challenged the legitimacy of scientific evidence and led to battles over the teaching of evolution and funding for stem-cell research. The new electronic world likewise raised troubling issues. Would cable TV, with its multitude of choices, further erode a common American culture? Would the World Wide Web facilitate the outsourcing of American middle-class jobs? Would computer technology allow governments and private data-collecting businesses to track the lives and limit the freedom of American citizens?

A "new world order," a New Right ascendancy, a new global economy, massive immigration, and a technological revolution: We live in a time of rapid change and continuing challenges that will test the resilience of American society and the creativity of American leaders.

The Reagan Revolution and the End of the Cold War

1980–2001

> Whether or not he was a great president, Ronald Reagan was a great man, in the sense that he changed the way people thought.
>
> —Richard Reeves, 2004

"Mr. Gorbachev, tear down this wall!" demanded President Ronald Reagan in a Berlin speech in June 1987, addressing his remarks to Soviet leader Mikhail Gorbachev in Moscow. Two years later, in November 1989, millions of television viewers worldwide watched jubilant Germans themselves knock down the Berlin Wall. The cement and barbed wire barrier, which had divided the city since 1961, was a vivid symbol of Communist repression and the Cold War division of Europe. More than 400 East Germans had lost their lives trying to escape to West Berlin. Now East and West Berliners, young and old, danced on the remains of the forbidding wall. Then, in 1991, the Soviet Union itself dissolved, ending the Cold War. A new world order was in the making.

The end of the Cold War was partly the result of a dramatic change in American political life. The election of President Ronald Reagan began a conservative political ascendancy that has continued into the twenty-first century. Supported by the Republican Party's **New Right**, Reagan took an aggressive stance toward the Soviet Union and the liberal ideology that had informed American public policy since the New Deal of Franklin D. Roosevelt (1933–1945). However, the Republicans' domestic agenda was complicated by a split between religious conservatives, who demanded strong government action to implement their faith-based policies, and economic conservatives, who favored limited government and free markets. Moreover, the Democratic Party remained a potent—and flexible—political force. Acknowledging the rightward shift in the country's mood, Democrat Bill Clinton trod a centrist path that led him to the White House in 1992 and again in 1996. "The era of big government is over," Clinton declared. At home as well as abroad, a new order emerged during the last decades of the century.

The Wall Comes Down
As the Communist government of East Germany collapsed, West Berliners showed their contempt for the wall dividing the city by defacing it with graffiti. Then, in November 1989, East and West Berliners destroyed huge sections of the wall with sledgehammers, an act of psychic liberation that symbolized the end of the Cold War. Alexandra Avakian/Woodfin Camp & Associates.

The Rise of Conservatism

The Great Depression of the 1930s and World War II had discredited the traditional conservative program of limited government at home and political isolationism abroad. Although the conservatives' crusade against Communism revived their political fortunes during the Cold War, they failed to devise a set of domestic policies that won the allegiance of American voters. Then, in the late 1970s, conservative Republicans took advantage of serious blunders by liberal Democrats and built a formidable political coalition.

Reagan and the Emergence of the New Right

The personal odyssey of Ronald Reagan embodies the story of New Right Republican conservatism. Before World War II, Reagan was a well-known movie actor and a New Deal Democrat and admirer of Franklin Roosevelt. However, he turned away from the New Deal, partly from self-interest (he disliked paying high taxes) and partly on principle. As head of the Screen Actors Guild from 1947 to 1952, Reagan had to deal with its Communist members, who formed the extreme left wing of the liberal New Deal. Dismayed by their hard-line tactics and goals, he became a militant anti-Communist conservative and a well-known spokesperson for the General Electric Corporation. In the early 1960s, Reagan joined the Republican Party and threw himself into California politics, speaking for conservative causes and candidates.

Ronald Reagan came to national attention in 1964 with a televised speech at the Republican convention supporting archconservative Barry Goldwater for the presidency (see Chapter 28). Just as the "Cross of Gold" speech elevated William Jennings Bryan to fame in 1896, so Reagan's address, titled "A Time for Choosing," secured his political future. Backed financially by wealthy southern Californians, he won the state's governorship in 1968 and again in 1972. Reagan's impassioned rhetoric supporting limited government, low taxation, and law and order won broad support among citizens of the most populous state and made him a force in national politics. After narrowly losing a bid to become the Republican presidential nominee in 1976, Reagan counted on his growing popularity to make him the party's candidate in 1980.

In 1964, the conservative message preached by Ronald Reagan and Barry Goldwater had appealed to few American voters. Then came the series of events that undermined the liberal agenda of the Democratic Party: a stagnating economy, the failed war in Vietnam, African American riots, a judiciary that legalized abortion and enforced school busing, and an expanded federal regulatory state. By the mid-1970s, conservatism commanded greater popular support. In the South, long a Democratic stronghold, whites hostile to federal civil rights legislation voted Republican in increasing numbers. Simultaneously, middle-class suburbanites and migrants to the Sun Belt states endorsed the conservative agenda of combating crime, limiting social welfare spending, and increasing expenditures on military defense.

Strong New Right grassroots organizations spread the message. In 1964, nearly four million volunteers had campaigned for Barry Goldwater; now they swung their support to Ronald Reagan. Skilled conservative political operatives such as Richard Viguerie, a Louisiana-born Catholic and antiabortion activist, applied new computer technology to political campaigning. They used computerized mailing lists to solicit campaign funds, drum up support for conservative causes, and get out the vote on election day.

Other support for the New Right came from think tanks funded by wealthy conservatives. The Heritage Foundation, the American Enterprise Institute, and the

Cato Institute issued policy proposals and persistently attacked liberal legislation and the permissive culture that they claimed it had spawned. These organizations blended the traditional conservative themes of individualism and free markets with the hot-button "social issues" of affirmative action, the welfare state, and changing gender roles and sexual values. They also fostered the growth of a cadre of conservative intellectuals. For decades, William F. Buckley, the founder and editor of the *National Review*, and Milton Friedman, the Nobel Prize–winning laissez-faire economist at the University of Chicago, were virtually the only nationally prominent conservative intellectuals. Now they were joined on the public stage by the so-called neoconservatives—well-known intellectuals such as Jeane Kirkpatrick, Nathan Glazer, and Norman Podhoretz, editor of *Commentary* magazine. Many neoconservatives had once advocated radical and liberal causes. Vehemently recanting their former views, they now bolstered the intellectual respectability of the Republican Right. As liberal New York senator Daniel Moynihan remarked, suddenly "the GOP has become a party of ideas."

The most striking addition to the conservative coalition was the Religious Right, which had previously had a limited political presence. Drawing its membership from conservative Catholics and Protestant evangelicals, the Religious Right condemned divorce, abortion, premarital sex, and feminism. Charismatic television

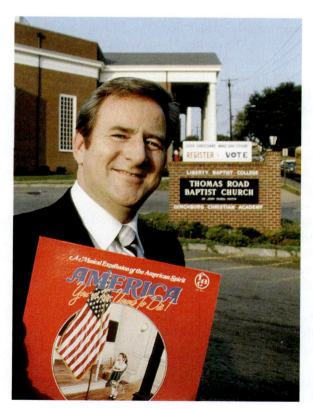

Jerry Falwell

The resurgence of evangelical religion in the 1970s was accompanied by a conservative movement in politics known as the New Right or the Christian Right. Founded in 1979 by televangelist Jerry Falwell, the Moral Majority was one of the earliest New Right groups, committed to promoting "family values" and (as the title to the record album suggests) patriotism in American society and politics.

Dennis Brack/Black Star.

For more help analyzing this image, see the Online Study Guide at **bedfordstmartins.com/henrettaconcise**.

evangelists such as Pat Robertson, the son of a U.S. senator, and Jerry Falwell, the founder of the Moral Majority, emerged as the champions of a faith-based political agenda. As these cultural conservatives attacked Democratic liberals for support-ing lenient treatment of criminals, permissive sexuality, and welfare payments to unmarried mothers with multiple children, economic conservatives called for cuts in taxes and government regulations. Ronald Reagan endorsed both conservative programs and, with the support of both groups, captured the Republican presi-dential nomination in 1980 (see American Voices, p. 891). To win the votes of moderate Republicans, Reagan chose former CIA director George H. W. Bush as his running mate.

The Election of 1980

President Jimmy Carter's sinking popularity virtually doomed his bid for reelection. When the Democrats renominated him over his liberal challenger, Edward (Ted) Kennedy of Massachusetts, Carter's approval rating was stunningly low: A mere 21 percent of Americans believed that he was an effective president. The reasons were clear: Economically, millions of citizens were feeling the pinch from stagnant wages, high inflation, crippling mortgage rates, and an unemployment rate of nearly 8 percent (see Chapter 29). In international affairs, the nation blamed Carter for his weak response to Soviet expansion and the Iranians' seizure of American diplomats.

The incumbent president found himself constantly on the defensive, while Rea-gan remained upbeat and decisive. "This is the greatest country in the world," Reagan reassured the nation in his warm baritone voice. "We have the talent, we have the drive. . . . All we need is the leadership." To emphasize his intention to be a formi-dable international leader, Reagan hinted that he would take strong action to win the hostages' return. To signal his rejection of liberal policies, the California gov-ernor declared his opposition to affirmative action and forced busing and promised to get "the government off our backs." Most important, Reagan effectively appealed to the many Americans who felt financially insecure. In a televised debate with Carter, Rea-gan emphasized the hardships facing working- and middle-class Americans in an era of "stagflation"—stagnant wages amidst rapidly rising prices—and asked them: "Are you better off today than you were four years ago?"

In November, the voters gave a clear answer. They repudiated Carter, giving him only 41 percent of the vote. Independent candidate John Anderson garnered 8 per-cent, and Reagan won easily, with 51 percent of the popular vote. Moreover, the Republicans elected thirty-three new members of the House of Representatives and twelve new senators, which gave them control of the U.S. Senate for the first time since 1954.

Superior financial resources contributed to the Republicans' success: Two-thirds of all corporate donations to political action committees went to conservative Republican candidates. While the Democratic Party saw its key constituency—organized labor—dwindle in size and influence, the GOP used its ample funds to reach voters through a sophisticated television campaign and direct-mail advertisements. "Madison Avenue" advertising techniques—long used to sell commercial products—now dominated

The Moral Majority and Its Critics
DONALD E. WILDMON AND A. BARTLETT GIAMATTI

Modern liberals favor the separation of church and state and are ethical pluralists—that is, they are skeptical of absolute moral principles. Conservative Christians challenge the legitimacy of pluralism and seek through political action and legislation to make their religion an integral part of public life. Donald Wildmon is a Christian minister and a grassroots religious activist. A. Bartlett Giamatti was the president of Yale University (1978–1986) and subsequently president of the National (Baseball) League.

DONALD E. WILDMON, "Network Television as a Moral Danger"

One night during the Christmas holidays of 1976, I decided to watch television with my family. . . . Not far into the program was a scene of adultery. . . . I asked one of the children to change channels. . . . In the second program, we were shocked with some crude profanity. . . .

As I sat in my den that night, I became angry. I had been disturbed by the deterioration of morals I had witnessed in the media and society during the previous twenty-five years. This was accompanied by a dramatic rise in crime, a proliferation of pornography, increasingly explicit sexual lyrics in music, increasing numbers of broken homes. . . .

Realizing that these changes were being brought into the sanctity of my home, I decided I could and would no longer remain silent . . . Out of that decision came the . . . Coalition for Better Television. . . . Network television is the greatest educator we have. . . . It is teaching that adultery is an acceptable and approved lifestyle. . . . It is teaching that hardly anyone goes to church, that very few people in our society are Christian or live by Christian principles. How? By simply censoring Christian characters, Christian values, and Christian culture from the programs.

If within the next five years we fail to turn the tide of this humanist value system which seeks to replace our Christian heritage, then we have . . . lost the battle.

A. BARTLETT GIAMATTI, "The Moral Majority as a Threat to Liberty"

A self-proclaimed "Moral Majority" . . . threaten the values [of pluralism and freedom]. . . .

From the maw of this "morality" come those who presume to know what justice for all is . . . who presume to know which books are fit to read, which television programs are fit to watch. . . . the tax-exempt Savonarolas who believe they, and they alone, possess the "truth." There is no debate, no discussion, no dissent. They know. There is only one set of overarching political and spiritual and social beliefs; whatever view does not conform . . . is by definition relativistic, negative, secular, immoral, against the family, anti-free enterprise, un-American.

What dangerous, malicious nonsense. . . .

We should be concerned that so much of our political and religious leadership acts intimidated for the moment and will not say with clarity that this most recent denial of the legitimacy of differentness is a radical assault on the very pluralism of peoples, political beliefs, values, forms of merit and systems of religion our country was founded to welcome and foster.

SOURCES: Donald E. Wildmon, *The Home Invaders* (Elgin, IL: Victor Books, 1985), 3–7; Yale University Archives.

political campaigning. Slickly produced ads trumpeted the virtues of a political candidate and smeared the record—and, increasingly, the reputation—of his or her opponent.

The Republicans' aggressive campaigning furthered the realignment of the American electorate that had begun during the 1970s. The core of the Republican Party remained the relatively affluent, white, Protestant voters who supported balanced budgets, opposed government activism, feared crime and communism, and believed in a strong national defense. Now two large groups of former Democrats had joined the Republican cause: southern whites who opposed civil rights legislation and so-called Reagan Democrats, Catholic blue-collar workers who took alarm at antiwar protestors, feminist demands, and welfare expenditures. Reagan Republicanism also attracted young voters and residents of rapidly growing suburban communities in Texas, Arizona, and California.

The Religious Right also contributed to the Republican victory. The Moral Majority claimed that it had registered two million new voters for the 1980 election, and the Republican Party's platform reflected its influence. The platform called for a constitutional ban on abortion, voluntary prayer in public schools, and a mandatory death penalty for certain crimes. The Republicans also demanded an end to court-mandated busing and, for the first time in forty years, opposed the Equal Rights Amendment. Within the Republican Party, conservatism had triumphed.

Reagan's victory led some observers to predict a long-lasting alteration in American voting patters. *U.S. News & World Report* proclaimed "A Massive Shift [to the] . . . Right." Other commentators noted that Reagan had won a bare majority of the popular vote and that many working-class voters—disillusioned Democrats—stayed home. Rather than an endorsement of conservatism, one analyst called the election a "landslide vote of no confidence in an incompetent administration." Nonetheless, Ronald Reagan's victory raised the possibility of a dramatic shift in government policies. The new president claimed that the American public had given him a mandate for sweeping change. His success or failure would determine the significance of the election and the New Right.

► Which were the key groups of the new Republican coalition? Were their goals complementary? Contradictory?

► What factors led to Ronald Reagan's election in 1980?

The Reagan Presidency, 1981–1989

At age sixty-nine, Ronald Reagan was the oldest man to assume the presidency. His appearance and demeanor belied his age. Concerned since his acting days with his physical fitness, Reagan conveyed a sense of vigor and purpose. His folksy humor endeared him to millions, who overlooked his indifference to details of public policy and embraced his optimistic message of national pride. Even when major scandals shook his administration, Reagan maintained his popularity. Critics dubbed him "the Teflon president," since nothing damaging seemed to stick. But sympathetic observers called

Reagan "the Great Communicator" and marveled at his success in advancing the conservatives' economic and cultural agenda.

Reaganomics

The Republican president kept his political message clear and simple. "Government is not the solution," he declared. "Government is the problem." In his first year in office, Reagan and his chief advisor, James A. Baker III, quickly set new government priorities. To roll back the expanded liberal state, they launched a three-pronged assault on federal taxes, social welfare spending, and the regulatory bureaucracy. To win the Cold War, they advocated a vast increase in defense spending. And to match the resurgent economies of Germany and Japan, whom the United States had defeated in World War II and then helped to rebuild, they set out to restore American leadership of the world's capitalist societies.

To achieve this economic goal, the new administration advanced a set of policies, quickly dubbed "Reaganomics," to increase the supply of goods. The theory underlying supply-side economics, as this approach was called, emphasized the importance of investment in productive enterprises. According to George Gilder, a major supply-side theorist, the best way to bolster investment was to reduce the taxes paid by business corporations and wealthy Americans, who could then use these funds to expand production. Supply-siders maintained that the resulting economic expansion would increase government revenues and offset the loss of tax dollars stemming from the original tax cuts.

Taking advantage of Republican control of the Senate and his personal popularity following a failed assassination attempt, Reagan won congressional approval of the Economic Recovery Tax Act (ERTA). The act reduced income tax rates paid by most Americans by 23 percent over three years. For the wealthiest Americans—those with millions to invest—the highest marginal tax rate dropped from 70 to 50 percent. The act also slashed estate taxes, the levies on inheritances instituted during the Progressive era to prevent the transmission of huge fortunes from one generation to the next. Finally, the new legislation trimmed the taxes paid by business corporations by $150 billion over a period of five years. As a result of ERTA, by 1986, the annual revenue of the federal government had been cut by $200 billion.

David Stockman, Reagan's budget director, hoped to match this reduction in tax revenue with a comparable cutback in federal expenditures. To meet this ambitious goal, he proposed substantial cuts in Social Security and Medicare. But Congress—and the president—rejected his proposals. They were not willing to antagonize middle-class and elderly voters who viewed these government entitlements as sacred. As neoconservative columnist George Will noted ironically, "Americans are conservative. What they want to conserve is the New Deal." This contradiction between Republican ideology and political reality would frustrate the GOP into the twenty-first century.

In a futile attempt to balance the budget, Stockman advocated spending cuts for programs for food stamps, unemployment compensation, and Aid to Families with Dependent Children (AFDC). In the administration's view, these programs represented the worst features of Lyndon Johnson's Great Society, being handouts to economic drones at the expense of hardworking taxpayers. Congress approved some cutbacks but preserved most of these welfare programs because of their importance; in 1980, some twenty-one million people received food stamps. Congress likewise continued to lavish huge subsidies and tariff protection on wealthy farmers and business corporations — "welfare for the rich," as critics labeled it. As the administration's spending cuts fell far short of its goal, the federal budget deficit increased dramatically.

Military spending accounted for most of the growing federal deficit, and President Reagan was its strongest supporter. "Defense is not a budget item," he declared, "you spend what you need." To "make America number one again," Reagan and Defense Secretary Caspar Weinberger pushed through Congress a five-year, $1.2 trillion military spending program. The administration revived the B-1 bomber, which President Carter had canceled because of its great expense and limited usefulness, and continued development of the MX, a new missile system that Carter had approved. Reagan's most ambitious weapons plan, proposed in 1983, was the controversial Strategic Defense Initiative (SDI). Popularly known as "Star Wars" because of its science-fiction-like character, SDI proposed a system of laser-equipped satellites that would detect and destroy incoming ballistic missiles carrying atomic weapons. Would it work? Most scientists were dubious. Secretary of State George Shultz thought it was "lunacy," and even Weinberger, who liked every weapons system he saw, dismissed the idea. Nonetheless, Congress approved initial funding for the enormously expensive project. During Reagan's presidency, military spending accounted for nearly one-fourth of all federal expenditures and produced a skyrocketing national debt. By the time Reagan left office, the federal deficit had tripled, rising from $930 billion in 1981 to $2.8 trillion in 1989. Every American citizen — from infant to senior citizen — now owed a hidden debt of $11,000.

Advocates of Reaganomics asserted that excessive regulation by federal agencies impeded economic growth. Some of these bureaucracies, such as the U.S. Department of Labor, had risen to prominence during the New Deal; others, such as the Environmental Protection Agency (EPA) and the Occupational Safety and Health Administration, had been created by Democratic Congresses during Johnson's Great Society and the Nixon administration (see Chapters 24, 28, and 29). Although these agencies provided many services to business corporations, they also increased their costs — by protecting the rights of workers, ordering safety improvements in factories, and requiring expensive equipment to limit the release of toxic chemicals into the environment. To reduce the reach of federal regulatory agencies, the Reagan administration cut their budgets — by an average of 12 percent. Invoking the "New Federalism" advocated by President Nixon, it transferred some regulatory responsibilities to state governments.

The Reagan administration also crippled the regulatory agencies by staffing them with leaders who were hostile to the agencies' missions. James Watt, an outspoken conservative who headed the Department of the Interior, attacked environmentalists as "a left-wing cult." Acting on his free-enterprise principles, Watt opened public lands for use by private businesses — oil and coal corporations, large-scale ranchers, and timber companies. Already under heavy criticism for these economic giveaways, Watt had to resign in 1983 when he dismissively characterized members of a public commission as "a black, a woman, two Jews, and a cripple." Anne Gorsuch Burford, whom Reagan appointed to head the EPA, likewise resigned when she was implicated in a money scandal and refused to provide Congress with documents on the Superfund program, which cleans up toxic waste sites. The Sierra Club and other environmental groups aroused enough public outrage about these appointees that the administration changed its position. During President Reagan's second term, he significantly increased the EPA's budget and added acreage to the National Wilderness Preservation System and animals and plants to the endangered species lists.

Ultimately, politics in a democracy is "the art of the possible," and savvy politicians know when to advance and when to retreat. Having attained two of his prime goals — a major tax cut and a dramatic increase in defense spending — Reagan did not seriously attempt to scale back big government and the welfare state. When Reagan left office in 1989, federal spending stood at 22.1 percent of the gross domestic product (GDP) and federal taxes at 19 percent of GDP, both virtually the same as in 1981. In the meantime, the federal deficit had tripled in size, and the number of civilian government workers had actually increased from 2.9 to 3.1 million. This outcome — so different from the president's lofty rhetoric about balancing budgets and downsizing government — elicited harsh criticism from conservative commentators. There was no "Reagan Revolution," as one noted bitterly.

Reagan's Second Term

On entering office in 1981, President Reagan had supported the tight money policy of the Federal Reserve Board headed by Paul Volcker. By raising interest rates to the extraordinarily high level of 18 percent, Volcker had quickly cut the high inflation of the Carter years. But this deflationary policy caused an economic recession that put some ten million Americans out of work. The president's approval rating plummeted, and in the elections of 1982, Democrats picked up twenty-six seats in the House of Representatives and seven state governorships.

The economy — and the president's popularity — quickly revived. During the 1984 election campaign, Reagan hailed his tax cuts as the reason for the economic resurgence. His campaign theme, "It's Morning in America," suggested that a new day of prosperity had dawned. The Democrats nominated former vice president Walter Mondale of Minnesota. With strong ties to labor unions, ethnic groups, and party leaders, Mondale epitomized the New Deal coalition. To appeal to women voters, Mondale selected Representative Geraldine Ferraro of New York as his running mate — the first woman to run on the presidential ticket of a major political party. Neither Ferraro's presence nor Mondale's credentials made a difference. The incumbent president won a landslide victory, losing only Minnesota and the District of Columbia. Still, Democrats retained their majority in the House and, in 1986, regained control of the Senate.

A major scandal marred Reagan's second term. Early in 1986, news leaked out that the administration had negotiated an arms-for-hostages deal with the revolutionary Islamic government of Iran. For years, the president had denounced Iran as an "outlaw state" and a supporter of terrorism. But in 1985, he wanted its help. To win Iran's assistance in freeing some American hostages held by Hezbollah, a pro-Iranian Shiite group in Lebanon, the administration covertly sold arms to the "outlaw state."

While this secret Iranian arms deal was diplomatically and politically controversial, the use of resulting profits in Nicaragua was patently illegal. In 1981, the Reagan administration had suspended aid to Nicaragua. Its goal was the ouster of the left-wing

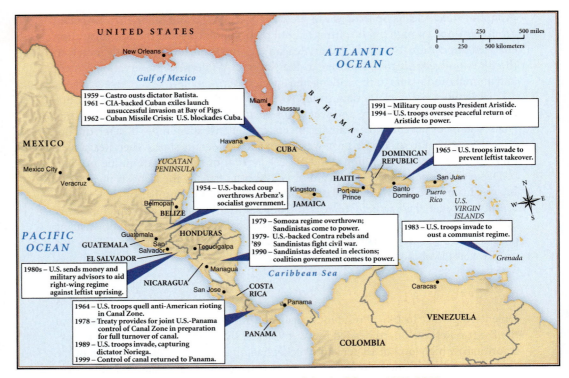

MAP 30.1 U.S. Involvement in Latin America and the Caribbean, 1954–2000

Ever since the Monroe Doctrine (1823), the United States has claimed a special interest in Latin America. During the Cold War, U.S. foreign policy focused on containing instability and the appeal of Communism in a region plagued by poverty and military dictatorships. The American government provided economic aid to address social needs and it intervened with military forces (or by supporting military coups) to remove unfriendly or socialist governments. The Reagan administration's support of the Contra rebels in Nicaragua, aspects of which were contrary to U.S. law, was one of those interventions.

Sandinista government. It claimed that the Sandinistas were pursuing socialist policies detrimental to American business interests, forming a military alliance with Fidel Castro in Cuba, and supporting a leftist rebellion in neighboring El Salvador (Map 30.1). To overthrow the elected Sandinista government, President Reagan ordered the Central Intelligence Agency (CIA) to aid an armed Nicaraguan opposition group called the Contras. Although Reagan praised the Contras as "freedom fighters," Congress worried that the president and other executive branch agencies were assuming war-making powers that the Constitution reserved to the legislature. In 1984, Congress banned the CIA and any other government agency from providing any military support to the Contras. Oliver North, a lieutenant colonel in the U.S. Marines and an aide to the National Security Council, consciously defied that ban. With the tacit or explicit consent of high-ranking administration officials, including the president, North used the profits from the Iranian arms deal to assist the Contras. When asked whether he knew of North's illegal actions, Reagan replied, "I don't remember." Still swayed by Reagan's charm, the public accepted this convenient loss of memory. Nonetheless, the Iran-Contra affair resulted in the prosecution of Colonel North and several other officials and jeopardized the president's historical reputation. Most Americans were shocked by Reagan's dealings with Iran and its allies. Weakened by the Iran-Contra scandal, Reagan proposed no bold domestic policy initiatives in his last two years.

However, the president continued to shape the judiciary. During his two terms, Reagan appointed 368 federal court judges, most of them with conservative credentials, and three Supreme Court justices: Sandra Day O'Connor, Antonin Scalia, and Anthony Kennedy. O'Connor, the first woman to serve on the court, coauthored an important decision supporting a woman's right to an abortion and, as a "swing" vote between liberals and conservatives, shaped the court's decision making. Kennedy was also a judicial moderate, leaving Scalia as Reagan's only genuinely conservative appointee. But Reagan also elevated Justice William Rehnquist, a conservative Nixon appointee, to the position of chief justice. Under Rehnquist's leadership (1986–2005), the court's conservatives took an extremely activist stance, limiting the reach of federal laws, ending court-ordered busing, and extending constitutional protection to certain kinds of property. However, on controversial issues such as individual liberties, abortion rights, affirmative action, and the rights of criminal defendants, O'Connor led the court toward a moderate position. Consequently, the justices watered down, but did not usually overturn, the liberal rulings of the Warren Court (1954–1967). Still, a more conservative federal judiciary stood as a significant institutional legacy of the Reagan presidency.

> ▶ What were the key elements of Reagan's domestic policy?
>
> ▶ What limits did Reagan face in promoting his policies? What were his successes and failures?

Defeating Communism and Creating a New World Order

Ronald Reagan entered office determined to confront the Soviet Union diplomatically and militarily. Backed by Republican hard-liners, Reagan unleashed some of the harshest Cold War rhetoric since the 1950s, labeling the Soviet Union an "evil empire" and vowing that it would end up "on the ash heap of history." By his second term, Reagan had decided that this goal would be best achieved by actively cooperating with Mikhail Gorbachev, the reform-minded Russian Communist leader. The downfall of the Soviet Union in 1991 ended the nearly fifty-year-long Cold War, but a new set of foreign challenges quickly appeared.

The End of the Cold War

The collapse of the Soviet Union was the result of external pressure from the United States and the internal weaknesses of the Communist economy. To defeat the Soviets, the administration pursued a two-pronged strategy. First, it abandoned the policy of détente and set about rearming America. This buildup in American military strength, reasoned hard-line Secretary of Defense Caspar Weinberger, would force the Soviets into an arms race that would strain their economy and cause domestic unrest. Second, the president supported the initiatives of CIA director William Casey. Casey sought to roll back Soviet influence in the Third World by funding guerrillas who were trying to overthrow pro-Communist governments in Angola, Mozambique, Afghanistan, and Central America.

These strategies placed new pressures on the Communist regime. The Soviet system of state socialism and central economic planning had transformed Russia from an agricultural to an industrial society. But it had done so very inefficiently. Lacking the discipline of a market economy, most enterprises hoarded raw materials, employed too many workers, and did not develop new products. Except in military weaponry and space technology, the Russian economy fell farther and farther behind those of capitalist societies, and most people in the Soviet bloc endured a low standard of living. Moreover, the Soviet invasion of Afghanistan, like the American war in Vietnam, turned out to be major blunder — an unwinnable war that cost vast amounts of money, destroyed military morale, and undermined popular support of the Communist government.

Mikhail Gorbachev, a younger Russian leader who became general secretary of the Communist Party in 1985, recognized the need for internal economic reform, technological progress, and an end to the war in Afghanistan. His policies of *glasnost* (openness) and *perestroika* (economic restructuring) spurred widespread criticism of the rigid institutions and authoritarian controls of the Communist regime. To lessen tensions with the United States, Gorbachev met with Reagan in 1985, and the two leaders established a warm personal rapport. By 1987, they had agreed to eliminate all intermediate-range nuclear missiles based in Europe. A year later, Gorbachev ordered Soviet troops out of Afghanistan, and Reagan replaced many of his hard-line advisors with policymakers who favored a renewal of détente.

As Gorbachev's reforms revealed the flaws of the Soviet system, the peoples of eastern and central Europe demanded the ouster of their Communist governments. In Poland, the Roman Catholic Church and its pope — Polish-born John Paul II — joined with Solidarity, the trade union movement led by Lech Walesa, to overthrow the pro-Soviet regime. In 1956 and 1964, Russian troops had quashed similar popular uprisings in Hungary and East Germany. Now they did not intervene, and a series of peaceful uprisings — "Velvet Revolutions" — created a new political order throughout the region. The destruction of the Berlin Wall in November 1989 symbolized the end of Communist rule in central Europe.

Two years later, the Soviet Union collapsed. Alarmed by Gorbachev's reforms, Soviet military leaders seized him in August 1991. But widespread popular opposition led by Boris Yeltsin, the president of the Russian Republic, thwarted their efforts to oust Gorbachev from office. This failure broke the dominance of the Communist Party. On December 25, 1991, the Union of Soviet Socialist Republics formally dissolved to make way for an eleven-member Commonwealth of Independent States (CIS). The Russian Republic assumed leadership of the CIS, but the Soviet Union was no more (Map 30.2).

In 1956, Nikita Khrushchev had told the United States, "We will bury you," but now the tombstone read, "The Soviet Union, 1917–1991." For more than forty years, the United States had fought a bitter economic and ideological battle against its Communist foe, a struggle that had exerted an enormous impact on American society. By linking the campaign for African American rights to the diplomatic competition

MAP 30.2 The Collapse of the Soviet Union and the Creation of Independent States, 1989–1991

The collapse of Soviet Communism dramatically altered the political landscape of central Europe and central Asia. The Warsaw Pact, the Soviet Union's answer to NATO, vanished. West Germany and East Germany reunited, and the nations that had been created by the Versailles Treaty of 1919 — Estonia, Latvia, Lithuania, Poland, Czechoslovakia, Hungary, and Yugoslavia — reasserted their independence or split into smaller ethnically defined nations. The Soviet republics bordering Russia, from Belarus in the west to Kyrgyzstan in the east, also became independent states while remaining loosely bound with Russia in the Commonwealth of Independent States (CIS).

For more help analyzing this map, see the Online Study Guide at **bedfordstmartins.com/henrettaconcise**.

with the Soviet Union for the allegiance of the peoples in the Third World, liberal politicians had advanced the cause of racial equality in the United States. However, by labeling social welfare legislation as "communistic," conservative politicians had limited its extent — as had the staggering cost of the Cold War. American taxpayers had spent some $4 trillion on nuclear weapons and trillions more on conventional arms. The physical and psychological costs were equally high: radiation from atomic weapons tests, anti-Communist witch hunts, and — most pervasive of all — a constant fear of nuclear annihilation. "Nobody — no country, no party, no person — 'won' the cold war," concluded George Kennan, the architect in 1947 of the American policy of containment, because its cost was so high and both sides benefited greatly from its end.

Of course, most Americans had no qualms about proclaiming victory, and advocates of free-market capitalism, particularly conservative Republicans, celebrated the outcome. The collapse of Communism in Eastern Europe and the disintegration of the Soviet Union itself, they argued, demonstrated that they had been right all along.

Ronald Reagan's role in facilitating the end of the Cold War was probably his most important achievement. Otherwise, his presidency left a mixed legacy. Despite his pledge to get the federal government "off our backs," he failed to reduce its size or scope. Social Security and other entitlement programs remained untouched, and enormous military spending outweighed cuts in other programs. Determined not to divide the country, Reagan did not actively push controversial policies espoused by the Religious Right. He called for tax credits for private religious schools, restrictions on abortions, and a constitutional amendment to permit prayer in public schools but did not expend his political capital to secure these measures.

While Reagan failed to roll back the social welfare and regulatory state of the New Deal–Great Society era, he changed the dynamic of American politics. The Reagan presidency restored popular belief that America—and individual Americans—could enjoy increasing prosperity. And his antigovernment rhetoric won many adherents, as did his bold and fiscally dangerous tax cuts. As one historian has summed up Reagan's domestic legacy: "For the next twenty years at least, American policies would focus on retrenchment and cost-savings, budget cuts and tax cuts, deregulation and policy redefinitions." Social welfare liberalism, ascendant since 1933, was now on the defensive.

The Presidency of George H. W. Bush

George H. W. Bush, Reagan's vice president and successor, was a man of intelligence, courage, and ambition. Born to wealth and high status, he served with distinction as a naval aviator hero during World War II and then graduated Phi Beta Kappa from Yale University. Bush prospered as a Texas oil developer and member of Congress and served as ambassador to the United Nations during the presidency of Richard Nixon and as head of the CIA in the Ford Administration. Although Bush lacked Reagan's extraordinary charisma and commanding presence, he had personal strengths that his predecessor lacked.

George Bush won the Republican nomination in 1988 and chose as the vice presidential candidate a young conservative Indiana senator, Dan Quayle. In the Democratic primaries, Governor Michael Dukakis of Massachusetts easily outpolled the charismatic civil rights leader Jesse Jackson, whose populist Rainbow Coalition brought together minority and liberal groups within the party. Dukakis chose Senator Lloyd Bentsen of Texas as his running mate.

The election campaign took on a harsh tone as brief television "attack ads" took precedence over a thoughtful discussion of policy issues. The Republicans' mantra was "Read My Lips: No New Taxes," a sound bite drawn from a Bush speech. The Bush campaign charged that Dukakis was "a card-carrying member" of the American Civil Liberties Union, a liberal free-speech organization, and that he was "soft on crime." Bush supporters repeatedly ran TV ads focused on Willie Horton, a convicted African American murderer who had raped a woman while on furlough from a prison in Governor Dukakis's state of Massachusetts. Placed on the defensive by these attacks, Dukakis failed to mount an effective campaign or to unify the liberal and moderate factions within Democratic Party. Bush carried thirty-eight states, winning the popular vote by 53.4 percent to 45.6 percent, but Democrats retained control of the House of Representatives and the Senate.

Faced with a Democratic Congress and personally interested in foreign affairs, George H. W. Bush proposed few distinctive domestic initiatives. Rather, congressional Democrats took the lead. They enacted legislation allowing workers to take leave for family and medical emergencies, a measure that Bush vetoed. Then, over the president's opposition, the Democrats secured legislation enlarging the rights of workers who claimed discrimination because of their race or gender. With the president's support, congressional liberals also won approval of the Americans with Disabilities Act, a major piece of legislation that significantly enhanced the legal rights of physically disabled people in employment, public transportation, and housing.

As Democratic politicians seized the initiative in Congress, conservative Republican judges made their presence known in the courts. In *Webster v. Reproductive Health Services* (1989), the Supreme Court upheld the authority of state governments to limit the use of public funds and facilities for abortions. The justices also allowed a regulation that prevented federally funded health clinics from discussing abortion with their clients. Then, in the important case of *Planned Parenthood of Southeastern Pennsylvania v. Casey* (1992), the court upheld a Pennsylvania law requiring a twenty-four-hour waiting period prior to an abortion. Surveying these and other decisions, a reporter suggested that 1989 was "The Year the Court Turned Right," with a conservative majority ready and willing to limit or invalidate liberal legislation and legal precedents.

This observation was only partly correct. The Court was not yet firmly conservative in character. Although the *Casey* decision, coauthored by Reagan appointees Sandra Day O'Connor and Anthony Kennedy, upheld certain restrictions on abortions, it affirmed the "essential holding" in *Roe v. Wade* that women had a constitutional right to control their bodies. Justice David Souter, appointed to the Court by Bush in 1990, voted with O'Connor and Kennedy to uphold *Roe* and, like O'Connor, emerged as an ideologically moderate justice on a range of issues.

Bush's other appointment to the Court was Clarence Thomas, an African American conservative with little judicial experience or legal expertise. Thomas's nomination proved controversial; he was opposed by the NAACP, the Urban League, and other black groups and was accused of sexual harassment by Anita Hill, an African American law professor. Hill told the all-male Senate Judiciary Committee that Thomas had sexually harassed her when they were colleagues at a federal agency. Despite these charges, Republicans in the Senate won Thomas's confirmation by a narrow margin. Once on the bench, Thomas took his cues from his conservative colleagues, Chief Justice William Rehnquist and Justice Antonin Scalia.

The controversy over Clarence Thomas hurt Bush at the polls. Democrats accused Republicans of ignoring sexual harassment, an issue of concern to many women, and vowed to mobilize female voters. In the election of 1992, the number of women, mostly Democrats, elected to the Senate increased from three to seven, and in the House it rose from thirty to forty-eight.

Bush's main political problems stemmed from the huge budget deficit bequeathed by Ronald Reagan. In 1985, Congress had enacted the Gramm-Rudman Act, which mandated automatic cuts in government programs in 1991 if the budget remained wildly out of balance. That moment had now come. Unless Congress and the president acted, there would be a shutdown of all nonessential government departments and the layoff of thousands of employees. To resolve the crisis, Congress enacted legislation that cut spending and significantly increased taxes. Abandoning his pledge of "No New Taxes," Bush signed the legislation, earning the enmity of conservative Republicans and diminishing his chances for reelection in 1992.

Bush also struggled with an economic recession that began in 1990 and stretched into the middle of 1991. As unemployment mounted, the president could do little because the funding for many federal programs—including housing, public works, and social services—had been shifted to state and local governments during the Reagan years. The states faced similar problems because the economic slowdown sharply eroded their tax revenues. Indeed, to balance their budgets, as required by their constitutions, states laid off workers and cut social spending. The combination of the tax increase, which alienated Republican conservatives, and a tepid federal response to the recession, which turned independent voters against the administration, became crucial factors in preventing George H. W. Bush's reelection in 1992.

Reagan, Bush, and the Middle East, 1980–1991

The end of the Cold War left the United States as the only military superpower and raised the prospect of a "new world order" dominated by the United States and its European and Asian allies. But American diplomats now confronted an array of regional, religious, and ethnic conflicts that defied easy solutions. Those in the Middle East—the oil-rich lands stretching from Iran to Algeria—remained the most pressing and the most threatening to American interests.

Like previous presidents, Ronald Reagan had little success in resolving the conflicts between the Jewish state of Israel and its Muslim Arab neighbors. In 1982, the Reagan administration initially supported Israel's invasion of Lebanon, a military operation intended to destroy the Palestine Liberation Organization (PLO), which had taken over part of that country. As the invasion turned into a violence-ridden occupation, the administration urged an Israeli withdrawal and in 1984 dispatched American Marines as "peacekeepers," a decision that it quickly regretted. Lebanese Muslim militants, angered by American support for Israel, targeted the Marines with a truck bomb, killing 241 soldiers; rather than confronting the bombers, Reagan withdrew the American forces. Three years later, Palestinians living in the Gaza Strip and along the West Bank of the Jordan River—territories occupied by Israel since 1967—mounted an *intifada*, a civilian uprising against Israeli authority. In response, American diplomats stepped up their efforts to persuade the PLO and Arab nations to accept the legitimacy of Israel and to convince the Israelis to allow the creation of a Palestinian state. Neither initiative met with much success.

American policymakers faced a second set of problems in the oil-rich nations of Iran and Iraq. In September 1980, the revolutionary Shiite Islamic nation of Iran, headed by Ayatollah Khomeini, came under attack from Iraq, a secular state headed by the ruthless dictator Saddam Hussein and his Sunni Muslim followers. The war stemmed from boundary disputes over deep water ports in the Persian Gulf, which were essential to shipping oil. The fighting was intense and long lasting—a war of attrition that claimed a million casualties. The Reagan administration ignored Hussein's brutal repression of his political opponents in Iraq and the murder (using poison gas) of thousands of Iraqi Kurds and provided Hussein with military intelligence and other aid. Its goals were to maintain supplies of Iraqi oil, undermine the Iranian "outlaw state," and preserve a balance of power in the Middle East. Finally, in 1988, an armistice ended the inconclusive war, both sides still claiming the territory that sparked the conflict.

Two years later, in August 1990, Saddam Hussein again went to war to expand Iraq's boundaries and oil supply (see Voices from Abroad, p. 904). His troops quickly conquered Kuwait, Iraq's small oil-rich neighbor, and threatened Saudi Arabia, the site of one-fifth of the world's known oil reserves and an informal ally of the United States. To preserve Western access to oil, President George H. W. Bush sponsored a series of resolutions in the United Nations Security Council condemning Iraq, calling for its withdrawal from Kuwait, and imposing an embargo and trade sanctions. When Hussein refused to withdraw, Bush successfully prodded the UN to authorize the use of force. Demonstrating great diplomatic finesse, the president organized a military coalition of thirty-four nations. Dividing mostly along party lines, the House of Representatives authorized American participation by a vote of 252 to 182, and the Senate agreed by the close margin of 52 to 47.

The coalition forces led by the United States quickly won the war for the "liberation of Kuwait." A month of American air strikes crushed the communication network of the Iraqi army, destroyed its air forces, and weakened the morale of its soldiers. A land offensive then swiftly forced the withdrawal of Iraqi forces from Kuwait. To avoid a protracted struggle and retain French and Russian support for the UN coalition, President G. H. W. Bush wisely decided against occupying Iraq and removing Saddam Hussein from power. Instead, he won passage of UN Resolution 687, which imposed economic sanctions against Iraq unless it allowed unfettered inspection of its weapons systems, destroyed all biological and chemical arms, and unconditionally pledged not to develop nuclear weapons.

Men — and Women — at War
Women played visible roles in the Persian Gulf War and made up about 10 percent of the American troops. In the last decades of the twentieth century, ever larger numbers of women chose military careers and, although prohibited from most fighting roles, were increasingly assigned to combat zones. Luc Delahaye/SIPA Press.

A Holy War Against the United States SADDAM HUSSEIN

After Iraq invaded Kuwait in August 1990, President Saddam Hussein of Iraq justified the action in the language of *jihad*, or Muslim holy war. Although Hussein was a secular ruler who kept religion and Muslim mullahs out of public life, he knew that many Iraqis were devout Muslims. He also recognized that Islamic fundamentalism had become part of the political discourse of the Arab world, particularly in relations with Western nations.

This great crisis started on the 2nd of August, between the faithful rulers and presidents of these nations—the unjust rulers who have abused everything that is noble and holy until they are now standing in a position which enables the devil to manipulate them. This is the great crisis of this age in this great part of the world where the material side of life has surpassed the spiritual one and the moral one. . . . This is the war of right against wrong and is a crisis between Allah's teachings and the devil.

Allah the Almighty has made his choice—the choice for the fighters and the strugglers who are in favor of principles, God has chosen the arena for this crisis to be the Arab World, and has put the Arabs in a progressive position in which the Iraqis are among the foremost. And to confirm once more the meaning that God taught us ever since the first light of faith and belief, which is that the arena of the Arab World is the arena of the first belief and Arabs have always been an example and a model for belief and faith in God Almighty and are the ones who are worthy of true happiness.

It is now your turn, Arabs, to save all humanity and not just save yourselves, and to show the principles and meanings of the message of Islam, of which you are all believers and of which you are all leaders.

It is now your turn to save humanity from the unjust powers who are corrupt and exploit us and are so proud of their positions, and these are led by the United States of America. . . .

For, as we know out of a story from the Holy Koran, the rulers, the corrupt rulers, have always been ousted by their people for it is a right on all of us to carry out the holy jihad, the holy war of Islam, to liberate the holy shrines of Islam. . . .

We call upon all Arabs, each according to his potentials and capabilities within the teachings of Allah and according to the Muslim holy war of jihad, to fight this U.S. presence of nonbelievers. . . . And we hail the people of Saudi Arabia who are being fooled by their rulers, as well as the people of dear Egypt, as well as all the people of the Arab nations who are not of the same position as their leaders, and they believe in their pride and their sovereignty over their land. We call on them to revolt against their traitors, their rulers, and to fight foreign presence in the holy lands. And we support them, and more important, that God is with them.

SOURCE: *New York Times*, September 6, 1990, A19.

The military victory, low incidence of American casualties, and quick withdrawal produced a euphoric reaction at home. "By God, we've kicked the Vietnam syndrome once and for all," Bush gloated, as his approval rating shot up precipitously. The president spoke too soon. Saddam Hussein remained a problem for American policymakers, who worried that he wanted to dominate the region. Hussein's ambitions were one factor that, in March 2003, would cause Bush's son, President George W. Bush, to initiate another war in Iraq, one that would be much more protracted, expensive, and bloody for Americans and Iraqis alike — indeed, a new Vietnam-like quagmire (see Chapter 32).

Thus, the end of the Cold War brought not peace but two very hot wars in the Middle East. For half a century, the United States and the Soviet Union had tried to divide the world into two rival economic and ideological blocs: communist and capitalist. The next half century promised a new set of struggles, one of them between a Western-led agenda of economic and cultural globalization and an anti-Western ideology of Muslim and Arab regionalism.

> ▶ What factors led to the end of the Cold War?
>
> ▶ Why did the United States intervene in the conflicts between Iraq and Iran and between Iraq and Kuwait? What were American goals in each case?

The Clinton Presidency, 1993–2001

The election of 1992 brought a Democrat, Arkansas governor Bill Clinton, to the White House. A profound admirer of John F. Kennedy, Clinton hoped to rekindle the idealistic vision of the slain president. Like Kennedy, Clinton was a political pragmatist. Distancing himself from liberals and special-interest groups, he styled himself a "New Democrat" who would bring "Reagan Democrats" and middle-class voters back to the party.

Clinton's Early Record

Raised first in Hope, Arkansas, by his grandparents and then in Hot Springs after his mother married an abusive alcoholic, Clinton left home to study at Georgetown University. He won a Rhodes scholarship to Oxford and earned a law degree at Yale, where he married a classmate, Hillary Rodham. Returning to Arkansas, he entered politics and won election to six two-year terms as governor. In 1991, at age forty-five, he was energetic, ambitious, and a policy "wonk," extraordinarily well informed about political issues.

Clinton became the Democratic candidate but only after surviving charges that he dodged the draft to avoid service in Vietnam, smoked marijuana, and cheated repeatedly on his wife. Although all those stories had an element of truth, Clinton adroitly talked his way into the presidential nomination: he had charisma and a way with words. For his running mate, he chose Al Gore, a second-term senator from Tennessee. Gore was about the same age as Clinton, making them the first baby boom national ticket as well as the first all-southern ticket.

President Bush easily won renomination over his lone opponent, the conservative columnist Pat Buchanan. But Bush allowed the Religious Right to dominate the Republican convention and write a conservative platform that alienated many political moderates. The Bush campaign suffered especially from the independent candidacy of Texas billionaire H. Ross Perot, whose condemnation of the rising federal deficit and the influence of corporate lobbyists on Congress attracted many middle-class voters.

The Democrats mounted an aggressive campaign that focused on Clinton's domestic agenda: He promised a tax cut for the middle classes, universal health insurance, and a reduction of the huge Republican budget deficit. Freed from the demands of the Cold War, Democrats hoped that an emphasis on domestic issues would sweep them to victory. They were right. On election day, Bush could not overcome voters' discontent over the weak economy and conservatives' disgust at his tax hikes. He received only 37 percent of the popular vote as millions of Republicans cast their ballots for Ross Perot, who won more votes (19 percent) than any independent candidate since Theodore Roosevelt in 1912. With 43 percent of the vote, Clinton easily won the election. Moreover, the Democratic Party retained control of both houses of Congress, ending twelve years of divided government. Still, there were dark clouds on the horizon. Bill Clinton entered the White House supported by only a minority of voters and opposed by political enemies who considered him "a pot-smoking, philandering, draft-dodger." He would need great skill and luck to fulfill his dream of going down in history as a great president.

Clinton's ambition exceeded his abilities. The first year of his administration was riddled by mistakes: failed nominations of two attorney generals, embarrassing patronage revelations, and an unsuccessful attempt to end a ban on homosexuals in the military. The president looked like a political amateur, out of his depth. Then came a major failure on the enormously difficult issue of health-care legislation.

Clinton's goal was to provide a system of health care that would cover all Americans. Although the United States spends a higher percentage of its gross national product (GNP) on medical care than any other nation, it is the only major industrialized country that does not provide government-guaranteed health insurance to all citizens.

A Forceful and Controversial First Lady and Senator
Drawing inspiration from Eleanor Roosevelt, Hillary Rodham Clinton hoped that the country was ready for a First Lady who actively shaped policy. It wasn't, or at least it wasn't ready for her health-care plan. Subsequently, Hillary Rodham Clinton assumed a less visible role in administration policymaking. In 2001, she won election to the U.S. Senate from New York and in 2008 nearly became the Democratic nominee for president. Robert Trippet/SIPA Press.

With medical costs and insurance premiums spiraling out of control, the president designated his wife, attorney Hillary Rodham Clinton, to head a task force to draft new legislation. This appointment was controversial because no First Lady had ever played a formal role in policymaking. But it suited the times: In many American families, both husbands and wives held decision-making positions in the workforce.

The recommendations of the task force were even more controversial. Recognizing the potency of Reagan's attack on "big government," the task force proposed a system of "managed competition," in which private insurance companies and market forces would reign in health-care expenditures. The cost of this system would fall heavily on employers, who had to pay 80 percent of their workers' health benefits; consequently, many smaller businesses campaigned strongly against it. By mid-1994, Democratic leaders in Congress declared that the Clintons' universal health-care proposal was dead. Forty million Americans, 15 percent of the population, remained without health coverage.

Addressing other concerns of social welfare Democrats, Clinton appointed two prochoice liberal jurists, Ruth Bader Ginsburg and Stephen Breyer, to the Supreme Court. He also placed women and members of racial minorities in cabinet positions. Janet Reno became attorney general, the first woman to head the Department of Justice; Donna E. Shalala headed the Department of Health and Human Services; and in Clinton's second term, Madeleine Albright served as the first female secretary of state. Clinton chose an African American, Ron Brown, as secretary of commerce and two Latinos, Henry Cisneros and Frederico Peña, to head the Department of Housing and Urban Development and the Department of Transportation, respectively.

The Clinton administration's policies toward families, abortion, and crime likewise appealed to liberal Democrats. In 1993, Clinton signed the Family and Medical Leave Act, which had twice been vetoed by President Bush, and the Clinic Entrance Act, which made it a federal crime to obstruct people entering hospitals or abortion clinics. Clinton's administration also won approval of two gun-control measures, on handguns and assault weapons, though neither law lowered gun sales or the murder rate. But Clinton "got tough on crime" (and muted criticism from conservatives) by securing funding for 100,000 new police officers in local communities across the nation.

The president had equal success with the centrist New Democrat elements of his political agenda. Shortly before leaving office, George H. W. Bush had signed the North American Free Trade Agreement (NAFTA), an arrangement among the United States, Canada, and Mexico to create a free-trade zone covering all of North America. The Clinton administration pushed the measure through Congress, where it was bitterly contested. American manufacturers looking for new markets or hoping to move their plants to Mexico, where workers' wages were much lower, strongly supported NAFTA. Labor unions—a traditional Democratic constituency—opposed the agreement because it would cut American jobs. Environmentalists likewise condemned the pact because antipollution laws were weak (and even more weakly enforced) south of the border. However, the Clinton administration was filled with free-trade advocates, including Treasury Secretary Lloyd Bentsen, Labor Secretary Robert Reich, and Robert Rubin, a Wall Street investment banker who headed the National Economic Council. With Clinton's support, they pushed NAFTA through Congress by assembling a coalition of free-trade Democrats and Republicans.

A Bipartisan Balanced Budget

Throughout his time in the White House, Bill Clinton worked to reduce federal deficits by increasing taxes and restraining spending. On August 5, 1997, a smiling President Clinton signed a balanced budget bill, surrounded by congressional leaders including Republican John Kasich of Ohio (front row, far right), Chair of the House Budget Committee, and Republican Newt Gingrich of Georgia (front row, second from right), the Speaker of the House. Also looking on with satisfaction was Vice President Al Gore, who already had hopes for the presidency in 2000. Ron Edmonds/Wide World Photos, Inc.

Significantly, Clinton took effective action to reduce the budget deficits of the Reagan-Bush presidencies. In 1993, Clinton secured a five-year budget package that would reduce the federal deficit by $500 billion. Republicans unanimously opposed the proposal because it raised taxes on corporations and wealthy individuals, and liberal Democrats complained because it limited social spending. Clinton also paid a price; he had to abandon his campaign promise to lower taxes for the middle class. But shared sacrifice led to shared rewards. By 1998, Clinton's fiscal policies had balanced the federal budget and had begun to pay down the federal debt—at a rate of $156 billion a year between 1999 and 2001. As fiscal sanity returned to Washington, the economy boomed, thanks in part to the low interest rates stemming from deficit reduction. Ready access to cheap oil between 1986 and 2001 also fueled the growing economy. During Clinton's two terms in office, unemployment fell from 6 percent to 4 percent, the GNP increased at an annual rate of 3 percent (twice that of Japan), the stock market more than doubled in value, and home ownership rose to an all-time high.

The Republican Resurgence

The failure of health reform and the passage of NAFTA discouraged liberal Democrats even as Clinton's policies on homosexuals, guns, and abortion energized conservative Republicans. "Clinton-haters"—those who denied his fitness to be president— hammered away at his involvement in an allegedly fraudulent Arkansas real estate deal known as "Whitewater." To address these allegations, the Clinton administration appointed an independent prosecutor to investigate the case.

In the meantime, the midterm election of 1994 became a referendum on the Clinton presidency, and its results transformed the political landscape. In a well-organized campaign strongly supported by the National Rifle Association and the Religious Right, Republicans gained fifty-two seats in the House of Representatives, giving them a majority for the first time since 1954. They also retook control of the Senate and captured eleven governorships.

Leading the Republican charge was Representative Newt Gingrich of Georgia, who became the new Speaker of the House. An intellectually adept and aggressive conservative, Gingrich masterminded the Republican campaign by advancing a "Contract with America." If given a majority, he vowed that Republicans would secure votes on a series of proposals in the first one hundred days of the new Congress. The contract included constitutional amendments to balance the budget and set term limits for members of Congress. It also promised significant tax cuts, reductions in welfare programs, anticrime initiatives, and cutbacks in federal regulations. These initiatives signaled the advance of the conservative-backed Reagan Revolution of 1980 and again put the Democrats on the defensive. In his State of the Union message of 1996, Clinton suggested that "the era of big government is over." For the rest of his presidency, he avoided expansive social welfare proposals and sought Republican support for a centrist, New Democrat program.

Although the Republicans controlled Congress, they, like Reagan before them, failed to make significant cuts in the federal budget. Most big-budget items were politically or economically untouchable. The Treasury had to pay interest on the national debt; the military budget had to be met; the Social Security system had to be funded. When Republicans passed a government funding act in 1995 that included tax cuts for the wealthy and reduced funding for Medicare, Clinton vetoed the legislation, thereby shutting down many government offices for three weeks. Depicted by Democrats and many independent observers as heartless opponents of aid for senior citizens, the Republicans admitted defeat and gave the president a bill that he would sign.

Republicans had greater success in reforming the welfare system, a measure that saved relatively little money but carried a big ideological message. The AFDC (Aid to Families with Dependent Children) program provided average annual payments (including food stamps) of $7,740 to needy families, an amount well below the established poverty line. Still, many taxpaying Americans believed, with some justification, that the AFDC program perpetuated poverty by encouraging women recipients to bear children and to remain on welfare rather than seeking employment. Both Democrat- and Republican-run state legislatures had already imposed work requirements on people receiving welfare. In August 1996, the federal government did the same when President Clinton signed the Personal Responsibility and Work Opportunity Act. This historic overhaul of federal entitlements ended the guarantee of cash assistance by abolishing AFDC, required most adult recipients to find work within two years, and gave states wide discretion in running their welfare programs.

The Republican takeover of Congress united the usually faction-ridden Democrats behind Clinton, who easily captured the party's nomination in 1996. The Republicans settled on Senate majority leader Bob Dole of Kansas as their presidential candidate. A veteran of World War II, in which he lost the use of an arm, Dole was a safe but uninspiring candidate, lacking both personal charisma and innovative policies. He called for both a 15 percent tax cut and a balanced budget, a fiscal combination that few Americans believed possible. On election day, Clinton took 49 percent of the popular vote to 41 percent for Dole. Ross Perot, who failed to build his inspiring reform movement of 1992 into a viable political party, received 8 percent. By dint of great effort—dozens of risky vetoes, centrist initiatives, and determined fund-raising—Clinton had staged a heroic comeback from the electoral disaster of 1994. Still, Republicans retained control of Congress and, angered by Clinton's reelection, conservatives returned to Washington eager to engage in partisan combat.

Clinton's Impeachment

Clinton's hopes for a distinguished place in history unraveled halfway through his second term when a sex scandal led to his impeachment. The impeachment charges stemmed from Clinton's sworn testimony in a lawsuit filed by Paula Jones, a former Arkansas state employee. In that testimony and on national television, Clinton denied having sexually harassed Jones during his governorship. Those denials might (or might not) have been truthful. But Clinton also denied having had a sexual affair with Monica Lewinsky, a former White House intern—a charge that proved to be true. Independent prosecutor Kenneth Starr, a conservative Republican, concluded that Clinton had lied under oath regarding Lewinsky and obstructed justice and that these actions were grounds for impeachment.

Viewed historically, Americans have usually defined "high crimes and misdemeanors"—the constitutional standard for impeachment—as involving a serious abuse of public trust that endangered the republic. In 1998, conservative Republicans favored a much lower standard because they did not accept "Slick Willy" Clinton's legitimacy as president. In reply to the question "Why do you hate Clinton so much?," one conservative declared, "I hate him because he's a womanizing, Elvis-loving, non-inhaling, truth-shading, war-protesting, draft-dodging, abortion-protecting, gay-promoting, gun-hating baby boomer. That's why." Seeing Clinton as an embodiment of the permissive social values of the 1960s, conservative Republicans vowed to oust him from office. On December 19, the House of Representatives narrowly approved two articles of impeachment: one for perjury for lying to a grand jury about his liaison with Lewinsky and a second for obstruction of justice by encouraging others to lie on his behalf. Only a minority of Americans supported the House's action; according to a CBS News poll, 38 percent supported impeachment while 58 percent opposed it.

Lacking public support, Republicans in the Senate fell well short of the two-thirds majority they needed to remove the president. But like Andrew Johnson, the only other president to be tried by the Senate (see Chapter 15), Bill Clinton and the Democratic Party paid a high price for his acquittal. Preoccupied with defending himself, the president was unable to fashion a moderate Democratic alternative to the Republicans' conservative domestic agenda. The American people also paid a high price because the Republicans' vendetta against Clinton kept his administration from addressing important problems of foreign policy.

Foreign Policy at the End of the Twentieth Century

Unlike George H. W. Bush, Clinton claimed no expertise in international affairs. "Foreign policy is not what I came here to do," he lamented amidst a series of minor international crises. Neither of his main advisors, Secretary of State Warren Christopher and Secretary of Defense Les Aspin, had a strategic vision of America's role in the post–Cold War world. Consequently, Clinton pursued a cautious diplomatic policy. Unless important American interests were directly threatened, he avoided a commitment of U.S. influence and troops.

Clinton's caution stemmed in part from a harrowing episode in the east African country of Somalia, where ethnic warfare had created political chaos and massive famine. President Bush had approved American participation in a UN peacekeeping force, and Clinton had added additional troops. When bloody fighting in October 1993 killed eighteen American soldiers and wounded eighty-four, Clinton gradually withdrew the troops. No vital U.S. interests were at stake in Somalia, and it was unlikely that the peacekeepers could quell the factional violence. For similar reasons, Clinton refused in 1994 to dispatch American forces to the central African nation of Rwanda, where ethnic conflict had escalated to genocide—the slaughter by ethnic Hutus of at least 800,000 people, mostly ethnic Tutsis.

Clinton gave closer attention to events in the Caribbean. In 1991, a military coup in Haiti had deposed Jean-Bertrand Aristide, the democratically elected president, and Clinton had criticized President Bush's refusal to grant asylum to refugees fleeing the new Haitian regime. Once in the White House, Clinton reversed his stance. He recognized that a massive influx of impoverished Haitian "boat people" would strain welfare services and increase racial tension. Consequently, the new president called for Aristide's return to power and, by threatening a U.S. invasion, forced Haiti's military rulers to step down. American troops maintained Aristide in power until March 1995, when the United Nations assumed peacemaking responsibilities.

Another set of internal conflicts—based on ethnicity, religion, and nationality—led in 1991 to the disintegration of the Communist nation of Yugoslavia. First, the Roman Catholic regions of Slovenia and Croatia declared independence from Yugoslavia, which was dominated by Russian Orthodox Serbians. Then, in 1992, the heavily Muslim province of Bosnia-Herzegovina declared its independence. However, the Serbian residents of Bosnia refused to live in a Muslim-run multiethnic state. Supported financially and militarily by Slobodan Milosevic, the Serbian nationalistic leader of Yugoslavia, the Bosnian Serbs launched their own breakaway state and began a ruthless campaign of "ethnic cleansing." To make Bosnia an all-Serbian society, they drove Muslims and Croats from their homes, executed tens of thousands of men, raped equally large numbers of women, and forced the survivors into crowded refugee camps.

Fearing a Vietnam-like quagmire, President Clinton and Western European leaders hesitated to take military action against the Serbs. Finally, in November 1995, Clinton organized a NATO-led bombing campaign and peacekeeping effort that ended the Serbs' vicious expansionist drive. Four years later, a similar Serb-led campaign of ethnic cleansing began in Kosovo, a province of Yugoslavia inhabited primarily by Albanian-speaking Muslims. Again led by the United States, NATO intervened with airstrikes and military forces to preserve Kosovo's autonomy (Map 30.3). Against its inclinations, the Clinton administration had gradually adopted a policy of active engagement in nations beset with internal conflict.

In the Middle East, Clinton was as unsuccessful as previous presidents in resolving the long-standing conflict between Jews and Arabs. In 1993, he arranged a meeting in Washington between Israeli prime minister Yitzhak Rabin and Yasser Arafat, chairman of the Palestine Liberation Organization. Urged on by Clinton, they negotiated an agreement that allowed some autonomy to Palestinians living in the Israeli-occupied

MAP 30.3 Ethnic Conflict in the Balkans: The Breakup of Yugoslavia, 1991–1992

The collapse of the Soviet Union spurred the disintegration of the independent Communist nation of Yugoslavia, a multiethnic and multireligious state held together after 1945 by the near-dictatorial authority of Josip Broz Tito (1892–1980). Torn by ethnic and religious hatreds, Yugoslavia splintered into warring states. Slovenia and Macedonia won their independence in 1991, but Russian Orthodox Serbia, headed by president Slobodan Milosevic, tried to rule the rest of the Balkan peoples. Roman Catholic Croatia freed itself from Serb rule in 1995, and, after ruthless Serbian aggression against Muslims in Bosnia and later in Kosovo, the United States and NATO intervened militarily to create the separate states of Bosnia-Herzegovina (1995) and Montenegro (2006) and the autonomous Muslim province of Kosovo (1999). In 2008, Kosovo declared itself an independent republic, a claim not recognized by Serbia and Russia.

territories of the Gaza Strip and the West Bank. The hope that this agreement would lead to a general peace settlement was short lived. In 1995, a Jewish religious terrorist assassinated Rabin; the new prime minister, Benjamin Netanyahu of the religious Likud Party, reverted to a hard-line policy against the Palestinians.

Hard-line religious and political groups sprang up in the Muslim world as well, dashing hopes for Middle Eastern peace and sparking new conflicts. During the 1990s, radical Islamic movements staged armed insurgencies in parts of Russia and China and threatened existing governments in the Muslim states of Algeria, Egypt, Pakistan, and Indonesia. These insurgent groups also mounted terrorist attacks against the United States, which they condemned as the main agent of economic globalization and cultural imperialism. In 1993, radical Muslim immigrants set off a bomb in the World Trade Center in New York City. Five years later, Muslim terrorists used truck bombs to blow up the American embassies in Kenya and Tanzania, and in 2000, they bombed an American warship, the USS *Cole*, in the port of Aden in Yemen. The Clinton administration knew that these attacks were the work of Al Qaeda, a network of terrorists organized by the wealthy Saudi exile Osama bin Laden, but no one—in the State Department, CIA, or Pentagon—knew how to counter these Islamic extremists (see Chapter 32).

"We have slain a large dragon," CIA director James Woolsey observed as the Soviet Union collapsed in 1991. But, he quickly added, "We live now in a jungle filled with a bewildering variety of poisonous snakes. And in many ways, the dragon was easier to keep track of." As the century ended, Woolsey's words rang true. The Balkan and African crises, the Middle Eastern morass, and radical Islamic terrorist groups served as potent reminders of a world in conflict and the limits of American power. If the world was not quite as dangerous as it had been during the Cold War era, it was no less problematic.

▶ How, if at all, did the "New Democrat" domestic policies of Bill Clinton differ from the policies of Ronald Reagan and George H. W. Bush?

▶ Which scandal was the more serious: the Iran-Contra affair or the Monica Lewinsky affair? How do you explain the different outcomes for Ronald Reagan and Bill Clinton?

▶ Compare and contrast the foreign policies of Bill Clinton, George H. W. Bush, and Ronald Reagan.

SUMMARY

The end of the twentieth century was a time of momentous change. Internationally, the collapse of the Soviet Union brought an end to the Cold War; concurrently, the growing importance of Middle Eastern oil and radical Islamic movements raised new diplomatic and military challenges.

Domestically, the rise of conservatism returned the Republican party to power. Rather than "getting the government off our backs," President Ronald Reagan simply used its power in different ways. "Reaganomics" shifted wealth into the hands of military contractors and affluent Americans, mostly at the expense of the poor. Middle-class

Americans—the majority of the population—generally prospered during the 1980s but divided sharply over cultural issues. Influenced by the Religious Right, the Republican Party vigorously attacked the welfare state and liberal cultural values.

These economic and cultural issues played out in the politics of the 1990s. Bill Clinton's centrist, "New Democrat," policies reflected the conservative mood of the electorate and brought him two terms in the White House. However, the Republican congressional landslide of 1994 limited Clinton's options, as did his sexual misconduct, which in 1998 led to his impeachment and loss of political effectiveness. As the century ended, American society was experiencing both cultural conflict and a technological revolution that promised to transform many aspects of life.

Connections: Government and Politics

Future historians will debate Ronald Reagan's impact on the two great events discussed in this chapter: the triumph of conservatism and the end of the Cold War. However, they will probably agree with our observation, in the essay opening Part Seven, that once the conservatives were in power, their agenda was "to roll back the social welfare state."

In previous chapters, we watched the slow emergence of the powerful federal government that conservatives attacked. Prefigured by the regulatory legislation of the Progressive era (Chapter 20), a strong national state emerged during the New Deal. As we saw in Chapter 24, the Roosevelt administration responded to the Great Depression by creating a federal bureaucracy and the Social Security system. But the rise of federal authority also stemmed from World War II and the Cold War. Those conflicts, as we saw in Chapters 25 and 26, brought massive increases in government spending, taxes, and employees—and a vast military-industrial complex of private corporations. In fact, after 1945, so many individuals, social groups, and business corporations became dependent on favorable legislation or government subsidies that, as we explained in this chapter, conservative politicians have not been able to reduce the size or scope of the federal government.

FOR FURTHER EXPLORATION

James T. Patterson, *Restless Giant: The United States from Watergate to Bush v. Gore* (2005), provides a solid analysis. For evangelical politics, see Frances FitzGerald, *Cities on a Hill* (1986); William Martin, *With God on Our Side* (1996); and Lisa McGerr, *Suburban Warriors* (2001). On the Reagan and George H. W. Bush presidencies, read Lou Cannon, *President Reagan: The Role of a Lifetime* (2000); Haynes Johnson, *Sleepwalking Through History* (1992); and John Greene, *The Presidency of George Bush* (2000).

Richard A. Melanson, *American Foreign Policy Since the Vietnam War* (1991), and Raymond Garthoff, *The Great Transition: Russian-American Politics and the End of the Cold War* (1994) cover those topics. Two fine Web sites on the Cold War are **www.gwu.edu/~nsarchiv** and **www.wilsoncenter.org/index.cfm?fuseaction=topics .home&topic_id=1409**. For the Gulf War, see Michael Gordon and Bernard Trainor, *The Generals' War* (1995), and **www.pbs.org/wgbh/pages/frontline/gulf**.

For the Clinton years, consult William Berman, *From the Center to the Edge* (2001), and Joe Klein, *The Natural: The Misunderstood Presidency of Bill Clinton* (2002). Richard A. Posner, *An Affair of State* (1999), probes the legal aspects of the Clinton impeachment; for online materials go to **jurist.law.pitt.edu/impeach.htm#Public**.

TIMELINE

1970s	▶	Rise of New Right	**1990–1991** ▶	Persian Gulf War
1981	▶	Ronald Reagan elected; Republicans control Senate	▶	Americans with Disabilities Act
	▶	Economic Recovery Tax Act (ERTA)	**1991** ▶	Dissolution of Soviet Union ends Cold War
	▶	Military expenditures increase; regulatory agencies downsized	▶	Clarence Thomas named to Supreme Court
	▶	Sandra Day O'Connor appointed to Supreme Court	**1992** ▶	Democratic moderate Bill Clinton elected
1981–1989	▶	National debt triples	▶	*Planned Parenthood v. Casey* upholds *Roe v. Wade*
	▶	New Right think tanks gain influence	**1993** ▶	Congress passes Family and Medical Leave Act
	▶	U.S. assists Iraq in war against Iran	▶	North American Free Trade Agreement (NAFTA)
1983	▶	Strategic Defense Initiative (Star Wars)	**1994** ▶	Clinton fails to win universal health insurance but reduces budget deficit and national debt
1985	▶	Gramm-Rudman Budget Act		
	▶	Mikhail Gorbachev takes power	▶	Republicans gain control of Congress
1986	▶	Iran-Contra scandal weakens Reagan	**1995** ▶	U.S. troops enforce peace in Bosnia
	▶	William Rehnquist named chief justice	**1996** ▶	Personal Responsibility and Work Opportunity Act
1987	▶	United States and Soviet Union limit missiles in Europe	**1998–1999** ▶	Clinton impeached and acquitted
1988	▶	George H. W. Bush elected	▶	American military intervention in Bosnia and Serbia
1989	▶	Destruction of Berlin Wall; "Velvet Revolutions" in Eastern Europe	▶	Rise of radical Islamic movements and Al Qaeda terrorists

Other interesting political studies include Steven Gillon, *"That's Not What We Meant to Do"* (2001); Fred Greenstein, *The Presidential Difference: Leadership Style from FDR to George W. Bush* (2000); and Ted Halstead and Michael Lind, *The Radical Center: The Future of American Politics* (2001).

TEST YOUR KNOWLEDGE

To assess your mastery of the material in this chapter and for Web sites, images, and documents related to this chapter, visit **bedfordstmartins.com/henrettaconcise**.

A Dynamic Economy, A Divided People
1980–2000

> What Christians have got to do is take back this country. I honestly believe that in my lifetime we will see a country once again governed by Christians and Christian values.
>
> — Ralph Reed, 1990

As 1999 came to a close, a technological disaster threatened millions of computers around the world. For decades, programmers had used a two-digit field to describe dates, recording 1950 as simply "50." What would happen when the clock flashed to 2000? Would millions of computers record it as 1900, magically shifting the world a century back in time? Would the computers crash and wipe out the data of millions of users? As it turned out, the great "Y2K" (shorthand for "year 2000") fear proved unfounded, as thousands of software programmers patched the world's computer systems and avoided a disaster.

The moment was nonetheless symbolic. As Y2K showed, the fates of the world's many peoples were directly tied to one another electronically and in many other ways. In centuries past, epidemical diseases — the Black Death, cholera, and influenza — had periodically swept across the world, bringing death to its peoples. Now millions of the world's citizens were linked together on a daily basis: working in export-oriented factories, watching movies and television programs made in other countries, flying quickly between continents, and — most amazing of all — having pictures of their towns snapped by satellite cameras and beamed instantly around the world. The globe was growing smaller.

But it was not necessarily becoming more harmonious. "Globalization," the movement of goods, money, ideas, and organizations across political boundaries, created many conflicts. Likewise, modern means of communication made Americans more conscious of their differences — racial, ethnic, religious, ideological — and sharpened cultural conflict. In particular, New Right Christian conservatives squared off against social welfare liberals in an intense series of "culture wars."

America in the Global Economy and Society

In the last decades of the twentieth century, bread-and-butter issues loomed large in the minds of many Americans. The abrupt rise in global oil prices in the 1970s ended the era of American affluence (1945–1973) and triggered a corrosive "stagflation" that heaped hardship on the poor, shrank middle-class expectations, and shook the confidence of policymakers and business executives. It would take ingenuity and a bit of luck to restore America's well-being and self-confidence.

The Economic Challenge

Until the 1970s, the United States had been the world's leading exporter of agricultural products, manufactured goods, and investment capital. Then American manufacturers lost market share, undercut by cheaper and better-designed products from Germany and Japan (see Chapter 29). By 1985, for the first time since 1915, the United States registered a negative balance of international payments. It now imported more goods than it exported, a trade deficit fueled by soaring imports of oil, which increased from two million to twelve million barrels per day between 1960 and 2000. Moreover, America's earnings from foreign investments did not offset the imbalance in trade. The United States became a debtor (rather than a creditor) nation; each year, it had to borrow money to maintain the standard of living many Americans had come to expect.

The rapid ascent of the Japanese economy to the world's second largest was a key factor in this historic reversal. More than one-third of the American annual trade deficit of $138 billion in the 1980s was from trade with Japan, whose corporations exported huge quantities of electronic goods (TVs, VCRs, microwave ovens) and made nearly one-quarter of all cars bought in the United States. Reflecting these trading profits, Japan's Nikkei stock index tripled in value between 1965 and 1975 and then tripled again by 1985. Japanese businesses bought up prime pieces of real estate, such as New York City's Rockefeller Center, and took over well-known American corporations. The purchase by Sony Corporation of two American icons, Columbia Pictures and CBS Records, was a telling signal of Japan's economic power.

Meanwhile, American businesses grappled with a worrisome decline in productivity. Between 1973 and 1992, American productivity (the amount of goods or services per hour of work) grew at the meager rate of 1 percent a year, a far cry from the post–World War II rate of 3 percent annually. Consequently, the wages of most employees stagnated, and because of foreign competition, the number of high-paying, union-protected manufacturing jobs shrank. Unemployed industrial workers took whatever jobs they could find, usually minimum-wage positions as "sales associates" (a glorified title for menial workers) in fast-food franchises or in massive retail stores, such as Wal-Mart or Home Depot. By 1985, more people in the United States worked for McDonald's slinging Big Macs than rolled out rails, girders, and sheet steel in the nation's steel industry. Middle-class Americans—baby boomers included—also found themselves with less economic security as corporations reduced the number, pay, and pensions of middle-level managers and back-office accountants.

The Turn to Prosperity

Between 1985 and 1990, American corporate executives and workers learned how to compete against their German and Japanese rivals. One key was the use of information processing, which had been pioneered by Microsoft, Cisco, Sun, and other American companies. As corporations outfitted their plants and offices with computers, robots, and other "smart" machines, the productivity of the workforce rose. Nucor, a steel-maker in North Carolina, used electric arc furnaces, which are cheaper and more efficient than conventional blast furnaces, to compete successfully against foreign firms. Other American manufacturers cut costs by adopting the Japanese system of rapid inventory resupply.

Reflecting these initiatives, Dow Jones stock price index of leading American corporations doubled from 1,000 to 2,000 during the 1980s and then soared to 8,000 by the end of the 1990s. Increased productivity and profits fueled only a part of this rise. The Securities and Exchange Commission encouraged the entrance of small-scale investors into the stock market by encouraging the creation of discount brokerage firms. The growing wealth of pension funds was even more important and reflected a more problematic development. Increasingly, American corporations switched from providing pensions to their workers to contributing to their 401(k) stock accounts, causing the percentage of American families who owned some stock to rise from 13 to 51 percent between 1980 and 2000. This gain came at a high price: Workers could no longer count on a defined-benefit pension for life; instead, they had to hope that their stock investments provided sufficient funds for their old age.

The rise in stock values unleashed a wave of corporate mergers as companies used stock to buy up competitors. As these deals multiplied, so did the number of traders who profited illegally from insider knowledge. The most notorious white-collar criminal was Ivan Boesky. "I think greed is healthy," Boesky told a business school graduating class. "You can be greedy and still feel good about yourself." At least until you are caught! Convicted of illegal trading, Boesky was sentenced to three and a half years in prison (he served two) and had to disgorge $50 million from his illicit profits and another $50 million in fines.

While sleazy financiers such as Boesky gave corporate millionaires a bad name, successful business executives basked in the Reagan administration's reverence for wealth. When the president christened self-made entrepreneurs "the heroes for the eighties," he probably had Lee Iacocca in mind. Born to Italian immigrants and trained as an engineer, Iacocca rose through the ranks to become president of the Ford Motor Corporation. In 1978, he took over the ailing Chrysler auto company and turned it into a profitable company, securing a crucial $1.5 billion loan from the U.S. government, pushing the development of new cars, and selling them on TV. His patriotic-tinged commercials echoed Reagan's rhetoric: "Let's make American mean something again."

Real estate entrepreneur Donald Trump had his own vision of what America meant. In 1983, the flamboyant Trump built the equally flamboyant Trump Towers in New York City. At the entrance of the $200 million apartment building stood two enormous bronze "T's," a display of self-promotion reinforced by the media. Calling him "The Donald," a nickname used by Trump's first wife, TV reporters and magazines commented relentlessly on his marriages, divorces, and glitzy lifestyle.

Trump personified the materialistic values of the Reagan era. Accustomed to the extravagance of Hollywood, Ronald and Nancy Reagan created an aura of affluence in the White House that contrasted sharply with the austerity of Jimmy and Rosalynn Carter. At President Carter's inauguration in 1977, his family dressed simply, walked to the ceremony, and led an evening of restrained merrymaking; four years later, Reagan and his wealthy Republican supporters racked up inauguration expenses of $16 million. Critics lambasted the extravagance of Trump and the Reagans, but many Americans joined with them in celebrating the return of American prosperity and promise.

The economic resurgence of the late 1980s did not restore America's once dominant position in the international economy, however. The nation's heavy industries — steel, autos, chemicals — continued to lose market share, owing to weak corporate leadership and the relatively high wages received by American workers. Still, during the 1990s, the economy of the United States grew at the impressive average rate of 3 percent per year. Moreover, its main international competitors were now struggling. In Germany and France, high taxes and high wages stifled economic growth, while in 1989 in Japan, there were spectacular busts in the real estate and stock markets, which had been driven to dizzying heights by speculators. Its banking system burdened by billions of yen in bad debts, Japan limped through the 1990s with a meager annual growth rate of 1.1 percent.

Meanwhile, boom times came to the United States. During Bill Clinton's two terms in the White House (1993–2001), the stock market value of American companies nearly tripled. This boom, which was fueled by the flow of funds into high-tech and e-commerce firms, enriched American citizens and their governments. Middle-income families who held 401(k) pension plans saw their retirement savings suddenly double, and the tax revenue from stock sales and profits provided a windfall for the state and federal governments. By 2000, the Clinton administration had paid off half of the enormous national debt created during the Reagan and Bush presidencies. Looking forward, the Congressional Budget Office projected an astonishing surplus of $4.6 trillion in federal revenue over the coming decade — a prospect that proved too good to be true.

The New Social Pyramid

The new prosperity was not equally shared. The top tenth of American taxpayers, the primary beneficiaries of President Reagan's tax cuts and economic policies, raised their share of the national income to the extreme levels of the 1920s. By 1998, the income of the 13,000 American families at the very top of the increasingly steep social pyramid was greater than that of the poorest *twenty million* families.

As the rich got richer, many middle-class Americans enjoyed a modest affluence. The well-educated baby boomers who entered the labor force in the early 1980s took high-paying jobs in the rapidly growing professional and technology sectors of the economy. These young urban professionals — the Yuppies, as they were called — were exemplars of materialistic values. Yuppies (and Buppies, their black counterparts) dined at gourmet restaurants, enjoyed vacations at elaborate resorts, and lived in large suburban houses filled with expensive consumer goods. The majority of Americans could not afford the new luxuries; but some experienced them vicariously by watching

Barbie Goes to Work

Since 1959, the shapely Barbie doll has symbolized the "feminine mystique," the female as sexual object, and has helped to diffuse this view of American womanhood around the nation and the globe. More than 500 million Barbies have been sold in 140 countries. Barbie moves with the times. In 1985, she got her first computer, and in 1999, this doll and CD set transformed Barbie into a working woman, earning her own bread in the corporate workplace and, perhaps, with something intelligent to say! BARBIE is a registered trademark used with permission by Mattel, Inc. © 2008 Mattel, Inc. All Rights Reserved.

Lifestyles of the Rich and Famous, a popular TV series that debuted in 1984. Every week, host Robin Leach took audiences into the mansions of people who enjoyed "champagne wishes and caviar dreams."

Wishes and dreams were all that most working-class Americans could enjoy, because the real wages of manufacturing and retail workers continued to stagnate. To bolster their families' income and exercise their talents, married women increasingly took paid employment. By 1994, 58 percent of adult women were in the labor force, up from 38 percent in 1962. Women's pay remained low, averaging about 70 percent of that of men, and many women did double duty. As one working mother with young children remarked, "You're on duty at work. You come home, and you're on duty" again.

Some women entered male-dominated fields, such as medicine, law, skilled trades, law enforcement, and the military, but the majority still labored in traditional fields, such as teaching, nursing, and sales work. In fact, one in five working women held a clerical or secretarial job, the same proportion as in 1950. Still, as women flooded the labor force, cultural expectations changed. Men learned to accept women as coworkers—and even as bosses—and took responsibility for more household tasks. In the 1950s, over 60 percent of American children grew up in the type of household depicted in the Hollywood movies and TV shows of that decade: employed father, homemaker wife, and young children. By the 1990s, only about 30 percent of children lived in such families.

During these boom decades, poor Americans—some thirty-one million people—just managed to hang on. Citizens entitled to Medicare, food stamps, and Aid to Families with Dependent Children received about the same level of government benefits in the 1990s as they had in 1980, but the number of homeless citizens doubled. A Community Services Society report explained why: "Something happens—a job is lost, unemployment benefits run out, creditors and banks move in to foreclose, eviction proceedings begin—and quite suddenly the respectable poor find themselves among the disreputable homeless."

The collapse of the boom hit the rich as well as the poor. A spectacular "bust" of the overinflated stock market in late 2000 resulted in a 40 percent fall in stock values. Their savings suddenly worth less, older Americans delayed their retirements; laid-off workers looked for new jobs. Faced with falling tax revenues, state governments cut services to balance their budgets, and the federal government once again spent billions more than it collected.

Globalization

As Americans sought economic security during the 1990s, they faced a new challenge: the globalization of economic life. Over the centuries, Americans had sold their tobacco, cotton, wheat, and industrial goods in foreign markets, and they had long received loans, manufactures, and millions of immigrants from other countries. But the intensity of international exchange varied over time, and it was again on the upswing. The end of the Cold War shattered the political barriers that had restrained international trade and impeded capitalist development of vast areas of the world. Moreover, new communication and transportation systems—container ships, communication satellites, fiber-optic cables, jet cargo planes—were shrinking the world at a rapid pace.

When the Cold War ended, the leading capitalist industrial nations had already formed the Group of Seven (or G-7) to discuss and manage global economic policy. The G-7 nations—the United States, Britain, Germany, Italy, Japan, Canada, and France—directed the activities of the major international financial organizations: the World Bank, the International Monetary Fund, and the General Agreement on Tariffs and Trade (GATT). During the 1990s, these organizations became more inclusive. Russia joined the G-7, which became the Group of Eight; and in 1995, GATT evolved into the World Trade Organization (WTO), with nearly 150 member nations.

Working through the WTO, the promoters of freer global trade achieved some of their goals. They won reductions in tariff rates and removal of some restrictions to the free international movement of capital investments and profits. The WTO also negotiated agreements that facilitated international telecommunications, the settlement of contractual disputes, and (with less success) the protection of intellectual property rights. Many agreements benefited the wealthier industrial nations; in return, they agreed to increase their imports of agricultural products, textiles, and raw materials from developing countries. Thanks to such measures, the value of American imports and exports rose from 17 percent of GNP in 1978 to 25 percent in 2000. By then, the worldwide volume of international exchange in goods and money had risen to about $1 trillion per day.

MAP 31.1 Growth of the European Community, 1951–2005

The European Community (EU) began in the 1950s as a loose organization of western European nations. Over the course of the following decades, it created stronger central institutions, such as a European Parliament in Strasbourg, the EU Commission and its powerful bureaucracy in Brussels, and a Court of Justice in Luxembourg. With the collapse of Communism, the EU has expanded to include the nations of eastern and central Europe. It now includes twenty-five nations and 450 million people.

For more help analyzing this map, see the Online Study Guide at **bedfordstmartins.com/henrettaconcise**.

As globalization—the worldwide flow of capital and goods—accelerated, so did the integration of regional economies. In 1991, the nations of western Europe created the European Union (EU) and moved toward the creation of a single federal state, somewhat like the United States. Beginning as a free-trade zone, the EU subsequently allowed the free movement of its peoples among member countries without passports. In 2002, the EU introduced a single currency, the euro, which soon rivaled the dollar and the Japanese yen as a major international currency (Map 31.1). To offset the economic clout of the European bloc, in 1993 the United States, Canada, and Mexico signed the North American Free Trade Agreement (NAFTA). This treaty, as ratified by the U.S. Congress, envisioned the eventual creation of a free-trade zone covering all of North America; in 2005, some of its provisions were extended to the Caribbean and South America. In East Asia, the capitalist nations of Japan, South Korea, Taiwan, and

"McWorld" and Globalization in Saudi Arabia

Many of the leading multinational corporations transforming the world's economy are purveyors of American-style consumer goods, such as Nike and Disney products. McDonald's was so successful in developing international markets, with more than 13,000 foreign outlets, that "McWorld" has become the shorthand term used by many observers to refer to the globalization of culture. AP/Wide World Photos.

For more help analyzing this image, see the Online Study Guide at **bedfordstmartins.com/henrettaconcise**.

Singapore consulted on economic policy; as China developed a quasi-capitalist economy and became a major exporter of manufactures, its Communist-led government joined their deliberations.

The proliferation of multinational business corporations revealed the extent of globalization. In 1970, there were 7,000 corporations with offices and factories in multiple countries; by 2000, the number had exploded to 63,000. Many of the most powerful multinationals are American based. Wal-Mart, the biggest retailer in the United States, is also the world's largest corporation, with 1,200 stores in other nations and $32 billion in foreign sales. The McDonald's restaurant chain had 1,000 outlets outside the United States in 1980; twenty years later, there were nearly 13,000, and "McWorld" had become a popular shorthand term for globalization. While retaining its emphasis on American-style fast food, the company adapted its menu to local markets. In Finland, customers could purchase a McRye; in Chile, a McNifica; and in India, Veg McCurry Pan.

The intensification of globalization dealt another blow to the already fragile position of organized labor in the United States. In the 1950s, 33 percent of non-farm workers belonged to unions; by 1980, the number had fallen to 20 percent, and President Reagan pushed it still lower. When federal workers represented by the Professional Air Traffic Controllers' Organization went on strike in 1981 for higher pay and benefits, the president declared the strike illegal, fired 11,000 controllers who did not return to work, and broke the union. Heartened by Reagan's militant antiunion stance, corporate managers resisted workers' demands at Eastern Airlines and Caterpillar Tractors. A few unions, such as the West Coast Longshoremen's Union and the Teamsters' Union, won important strikes, but their successes did not reverse the long decline of organized labor. Union members represented only 13.9 percent of the labor force by 1998 and only 12.5 percent by 2004.

Globalization played an important role in this decline. Seeking cheap labor, many American multinational corporations closed their factories in the United States and "outsourced" manufacturing jobs to plants in Mexico, eastern Europe, and especially Asia. The athletic sportswear firm Nike was a prime example. Ignoring ideological boundaries, the company established manufacturing plants for its shoes and apparel in Communist Vietnam and China as well as in capitalist Indonesia. By the mid-1990s, Nike had 150 factories in Asia that employed more than 450,000 workers, most of whom received low wages, endured harsh working conditions, and had no health or pension benefits. Highly skilled jobs were outsourced as well. American corporations — Chase Manhattan Bank, Dell Computer, General Electric,

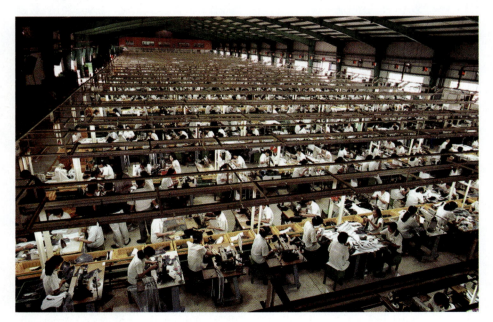

A Nike Factory in China
In 2005, Nike produced its shoes and sportswear at 124 plants in China; additional factories were located in other low-wage countries. Most of the Chinese plants are run by contractors, who house the workers — mostly women between the ages of sixteen and twenty-five — in crowded dormitories. The wages are low, about $3 a day, but more than the women could earn if they remained in their rural villages. AP Images.

and many others — hired English-speaking Indians to staff consumer call centers; and many American firms hired electrical engineers and computer technicians in Bangalore and other Indian high-tech centers.

From the standpoint of corporate profits, outsourcing made sense. In 2005, a graduate of the California Institute of Technology could expect a starting salary of $56,000, whereas a graduate of the Indian Institute of Technology commanded only one-third as much. Viewed from a national economic perspective, the outsourcing of skilled American jobs was more problematic. Unlike the "brain drain" that brought tens of thousands of foreign-born doctors, engineers, scientists, and technicians to the United States and enriched its society, outsourcing undermined the wages of American workers and professionals and threatened the long-term vitality of the nation's economy.

Outsourcing had a cultural as well as an economic impact. One of Nike's advertising campaigns, using American basketball superstar Michael Jordan, sold millions of pairs of shoes and made Jordan an international celebrity. It also spread American entrepreneurial values as Nike's ads urged people around the world to "Just Do It." Some of them took up the challenge. Yao Ming, a 7'6" basketball star in China, joined the Houston Rockets; more than a dozen other outstanding players from European and Asian countries also played in the National Basketball Association. In professional sports, as in multinational corporations, owners now drew their employees and profits from around the world.

Life and Death in a Global Society

The exponential growth in the movement of people and ideas was yet another marker of a shrinking world. Every day, an estimated two million travelers and immigrants crossed an international border. Ideas moved even faster. Communications satellites transmitted phone conversations, television programs, and business data through the air, while fiber-optic cables instantaneously connected e-mail users and World Wide Web servers on distant continents.

As the globe shrank in size, certain dangers increased in magnitude. In 1918 and 1919, soldiers inadvertently carried a killer virus from the United States to Europe and then to the rest of the world (see Chapter 22). That vicious bird flu pandemic killed fifty million people. The human immunodeficiency virus (HIV), an equally deadly (though slower-acting) disease, developed in Africa when a chimpanzee virus jumped to humans; immigrants carried it to Haiti and then to the United States during the 1970s. In 1981, American physicians identified HIV as a new virus, one that was causing the deaths of hundreds of gay men, who had become its main carriers. Within two decades, HIV, which causes AIDS (acquired immunodeficiency syndrome), had spread worldwide, infected over fifty million people of both sexes, and killed more than twenty million.

Within the United States, AIDS took thousands of lives — more than were lost in the Korean and Vietnam wars combined. Then, between 1995 and 1999, American deaths from HIV dropped 30 percent. This decline, the result of treatment strategies using a combination of new drugs, led to cautious optimism about controlling the disease, for which there is no cure. The high cost of these drugs limited their availability, particularly in poor nations. In sub-Saharan Africa, the HIV crisis has reached epi-demic proportions, with thirty million infections. China and South Asia also have millions of infected people—five million in India alone.

Other life-threatening diseases have the potential to spread around the world in days. In February 2003, a viral respiratory illness known as SARS (severe acute respiratory syndrome) appeared in China. Within a few months, the disease had infected over 8,000 people and killed almost 800 in two dozen countries in North and South America, Europe, and Asia. Public health officials fear that a new bird virus pandemic could soon cause millions of deaths.

The remorseless growth of the human population carries its own threats. In some countries, the combination of more people and rapid economic development has destroyed irreplaceable natural resources. During the last three decades in Brazil, land-hungry peasants, lumber companies, and agribusinesses have cut down roughly one-third of the region's ancient rain forests. In Taiwan and China, waste products from mines, factories, and power plants have polluted nearly every river, killing fish and rendering the water unsafe to drink.

Industrialized nations are also major polluters. As millions of cars and thousands of power plants in Europe, North America, and, increasingly, in China burned coal, oil, and other hydrocarbons, they raised the temperature of the atmosphere and the acidity of the oceans, with potentially momentous consequences. Similarly, the decades-long release into the atmosphere of chlorofluorocarbons (CFCs)—compounds used in industrial cleaning agents, refrigerators, and aerosol cans—significantly depleted the layer of ozone that protects humans from the sun's dangerous ultraviolet rays.

Such dangers prompted thousands of Americans to join environmental protec-tion organizations, such as the Sierra Club and the Nature Conservancy. These groups, and the Environmental Protection Agency, curtailed some pollution but failed to win political support for policies that would conserve natural resources. Take the auto industry. Ignoring warnings of global warming and tightening oil supplies, the Reagan and Bush administrations refused to support legislation requiring more fuel-efficient cars. General Motors and Ford continued to build, promote, and sell high-profit, gas-guzzling SUVs and small trucks. This strategy provided short-term profits, but as gasoline prices rose and Americans bought more fuel-efficient Japanese cars, GM and Ford suffered huge financial losses.

Still, the American government supported a few environmental initiatives. In 1987, the United States was one of thirty-four nations that signed the Montreal Protocol, which banned the production of ozone-damaging CFCs by 1999. And it joined sixty-three other countries in the Basel Convention of 1994, which ended the export of haz-ardous wastes to developing countries. But American corporations have resisted efforts to curb global warming. Although President Clinton signed the Kyoto Treaty of 1998, which committed industrialized countries to reducing greenhouse-gas emissions, the U.S. Senate refused to ratify the agreement. In 2001, the administration of George W. Bush rejected the Kyoto accord because it did not apply to China and other developing countries, which were some of the worst polluters, and because it would increase the costs to American corporations.

Governmental and corporate resistance to measures that would protect the envi-ronment gave rise to new political movements, such as Public Citizens' Global Watch.

Accusing multinational corporations of failing to protect their workers or the environment, Global Watch spearheaded a massive protest at the World Trade Organization meeting in Seattle in 1999. Thousands of activists, including union members, environmentalists, and students, disrupted the city and prevented the WTO from convening. As one protestor explained, people "can't go to the polls and talk to these big conglomerates. So they had to take to the streets and talk to them." Similar protests against globalization have occurred at meetings of the World Bank, International Monetary Fund, and the G-8 nations.

Indeed, on the occasion of a G-8 meeting in Scotland in 2005, critics mounted a worldwide protest against the financial impact of globalization on poor countries. "Live-8" assembled an international cast of music stars who gave free concerts at ten venues stretching from London to Tokyo and from Philadelphia to Johannesburg. Broadcast on television and the World Wide Web, the concerts helped to persuade the G-8 nations to forgive billions of dollars of debts owned by African nations. But the concerts did nothing to address the internal corruption that continues to inhibit African development. Still, by using the communication infrastructure of the global world, critics had forced a discussion of the impact of the global economy.

▶ What were the sources of the American economic recovery of the 1980s and 1990s? Who benefited from it and who did not, and why was that the case?

▶ Define *globalization*. Why did it occur? What has been its impact in different parts of the world?

The New Technology

The technological advances that enabled Live-8 had already changed the character of everyday life for millions of Americans. Computers, cell phones, the Internet and World Wide Web, the iPod, and other electronic devices altered work, leisure, and access to knowledge in stunning ways.

The Computer Revolution

Scientists devised the first computers—information-processing machines that stored and manipulated data—for military purposes during World War II. Subsequently, the federal government funded computer research to achieve military superiority during the Cold War. Using this research, private companies built large mainframe computers. In 1952, CBS News used UNIVAC (Universal Automatic Computer), the first commercial computer system, to predict the outcome of the presidential election.

UNIVAC and other first-generation computers were cumbersome machines. They used heat-emitting vacuum tubes for computation power and had to be placed in large air-conditioned rooms. In 1947, scientists at Bell Labs invented the transistor, a tiny silicon device that amplifies a signal or opens and closes a circuit many times each second. The transistor revolutionized the electronics industry and allowed technicians to build a second generation of computers that were smaller, more powerful, and much cheaper to manufacture. Then in 1959, scientists invented the integrated circuit—a silicon microchip composed of many interconnected transistors—and ushered in the third computer generation. Another great breakthrough came in 1971 with the development of the microprocessor, which placed the entire central processing unit of a computer on a single silicon chip about the size of the letter "O" on this page. By the mid-1970s, a few chips provided as much processing power as a World War II–era computer.

The day of the personal computer (PC) had arrived. In 1977, the Apple Corporation offered Apple II, a personal computer for $1,195 (about $4,000 today), a price middle-class Americans could afford. When Apple II became a runaway success, other companies scrambled to get into the market. International Business Machines (IBM) offered its first personal computer in 1981. In three decades, the computer had moved from a few military research centers to thousands of corporate offices and then to millions of peoples' homes. In the process, it created huge entrepreneurial opportunities and a host of overnight millionaires.

Making computers user-friendly was the major challenge of the PC revolution. In the early 1970s, two former high-school classmates, Bill Gates, age nineteen, and Paul Allen, age twenty-one, set a goal of putting "a personal computer on every desk and in every home." They perceived that the key was the software, the programs that told the electronic components (the hardware) what to do. In 1975, they founded the Microsoft

Triumph of the Geeks: Microsoft Employees, 1978
This group portrait shows eleven of Microsoft's thirteen employees as the company was about to relocate from Albuquerque, New Mexico, to Seattle, Washington. The oldest member was Paul Allen (front row, far right), age twenty-five; Bill Gates (front row, far left) was twenty-three. Three decades later, Allen was worth $20 billion, Gates had given nearly $30 billion (of his fortune of $100 billion) to his charitable foundation, and Microsoft had more than 50,000 employees. Courtesy, Bob Wallace.

Corporation, whose MS-DOS and Windows operating systems soon dominated the software industry. Microsoft's phenomenal success stemmed primarily from the company's ability to anticipate industry trends, develop products quickly, and market them relentlessly. By 2000, the company's products ran nine out of every ten personal computers in the United States and a majority of those around the world. Bill Gates and Paul Allen became billionaires, and Microsoft exploded into a huge company with 57,000 employees and annual revenue of $38 billion. Indeed, Microsoft's near-monopoly of basic computer operating systems prompted government regulators in the United States and the European Union to lodge antitrust suits against the company and force changes in its business practices.

During the 1990s, personal computers grew even more significant with the spread of the Internet and the World Wide Web. Like the computer itself, the Internet was the product of military-based research. During the 1970s, the Pentagon set up a system of hundreds of computers (or "servers") that were widely dispersed across the United States and connected to each other by copper wires (and later by fiber-optic cables). The Pentagon designed this decentralized Internet system to preserve military communications in a Soviet nuclear attack, but it was soon used by government scientists, academic specialists, and military contractors to exchange electronic text messages. By the 1980s, the e-mail system had spread to universities, businesses, and the general public.

The debut in 1991 of the graphics-based World Wide Web, a collection of servers that allowed access to millions of documents, pictures, and other materials, enhanced the popular appeal and commercial possibilities of the Internet. By 2006, nearly 70 percent of all Americans and more than one billion people worldwide used the Internet to send messages and to view material on the Web. The Web allowed companies, organizations, and individuals to create their own Web sites, incorporating visual, audio, and textual information. Businesses used the World Wide Web to sell their products and services; e-commerce transactions totaled $114 billion in 2003 and $172 billion in 2005. During his unsuccessful bid for the 2004 Democratic presidential nomination, Governor Howard Dean of Vermont demonstrated the political potential of the Internet, using it to raise money and mobilize grassroots support for his campaign, and other politicians and social activists followed his lead.

Thousands of businesses were already using networked computers, creating the modern electronic office. Small companies kept their records and did all their correspondence and billing on a few desktop machines; large corporations set up linked computers that shared a common database. Some employees no longer came physically to the office; some days they worked as "telecommuters," with their home computers and fax machines connected to the office network by telephone lines, fiber-optic cables, and wireless systems.

Computers, the Internet, and the Web transformed leisure as well as work. Millions of Americans used e-mail to stay in touch with families and friends and joined online chat rooms, dating services, and interactive games. Those with broadband connections watched streaming videos of news events and downloaded music videos and feature films. With the debut of MySpace, Facebook, and YouTube, countless numbers of people placed their life histories and personal videos on the Web for all to see. Interestingly — and importantly — millions of Web users tried to persuade others to see the world as they do by creating personal online diaries called "web-logs," a name that was soon shortened to "blogs." By 2004, there were eight million bloggers offering their perspectives on politics, current events, the environment, morals, and much more.

More profoundly, the Web empowered people by providing easy access to knowledge. For nearly two centuries, local public libraries had served that function; now, more and more material in libraries was instantly available in a home or office. Using powerful search engines such as Google and Yahoo!, people could easily locate information—some wonderfully accurate and some distressingly problematic—on nearly every subject under the sun. Millions of Americans regularly read newspapers online and acquired medical information about diet, drugs, and disease. Students and scholars mined the Web's digital archives and online journals; lawyers used Lexis-Nexis programs for immediate access to hundreds of cases on specific legal issues. Many things that libraries did well, the Web did wonderfully.

Advances in electronic technology resulted in the rapid creation of new leisure and business products. The 1980s saw the introduction of videocassette recorders (VCRs), compact disc (CD) players, cellular telephones, and inexpensive fax machines. Hand-held video camcorders joined film-based cameras as instruments for preserving family memories; parents videotaped their children's lives—sports achievements, graduations, and marriages—and played them on the home television screen. By 2000, cameras took digital pictures that could be stored and transmitted on computers, digital video discs (DVDs) became the newest technology for viewing movies, and TiVo (a direct video recording system) allowed people to view TV programs when they wished. Television itself was steadily transformed, as manufacturers devised higher-resolution pictures, flat LCD and plasma screens, and high-definition transmission systems.

Wireless telephones (cell phones), which became available in the 1980s, presaged a communications revolution. By 2003, two-thirds of American adults carried these portable devices, and people under age thirty used them in an increasing variety of ways: to take pictures, play games, and send text messages. The cell phone revolution, like the cultural revolution of the 1960s, was mostly the work of the young, who dragged their parents into the new age of instant communication.

Like all new technologies, the electronics revolution raised a host of social issues and legal conflicts. Many disputes involved the pirating of intellectual property though the illegal reproduction of a computer program or a content file. To protect their copyrighted products, which usually cost millions of dollars to develop, Microsoft and other software companies used a variety of technical stratagems. The recording industry turned to the legal system to shut down the Napster program, which allowed music buffs to share songs through the Web and burn their own CDs. Yet intellectual piracy continues because governments in China and elsewhere refuse to protect copyrights and because of the decentralized aspects of the new technology. Just as the American military set up hundreds of servers to work around a Soviet attack, so the existence of millions of PCs (and skilled operators) has thwarted efforts to police their use.

Computers empowered scientists as well as citizens. Researchers in many scientific disciplines used powerful supercomputers to analyze complex natural and human phenomena ranging from economic forecasting to nuclear fusion to human genetics. In 1990, officials at the National Science Foundation allocated $350 million for the Human Genome Project. The project's goal was to map the human genetic code and unravel the mysteries of DNA (deoxyribonucleic acid), the basic building block of all living things. In 1998, Celera Genomics, a private company backed by pharmaceutical corporations, launched a competing project in hopes of developing profitable drugs. Eventually, the two groups pooled their efforts and, by 2003, had built a map of every human gene and posted it, free of charge, on the Web.

As scientists devised this sophisticated genetic technology, they sparked new moral debates. Should individuals convicted of a felony be required to submit a DNA sample for a police database? Should employers or insurance companies be permitted to use genetic testing for purposes of hiring or health-care coverage? Should the stem cells from aborted (or in vitro produced) fetuses be used in the search for cures for Alzheimer's, AIDS, and other debilitating diseases? (See Chapter 32.)

As commentators debated these biomedical issues, other observers worried about the impact of the new computer-based technology. Would the use of recorded telephone menus, automated teller machines at banks, and scanners in retail stores gradually create a machine-driven world in which people had little contact with each other? Would the use of the Web by children and youths expose them to sexual abuse? Could personal and financial privacy be preserved in a digital world in which businesses and governments could easily create an electronic profile of people's lives and hack into their computers?

Political questions were equally challenging. What were the implications of the Patriot Act of 2001 (see Chapter 32), which permits the federal government to monitor citizens' telephone, e-mail, Web, and library usage electronically? Is the loss of civil privacy and liberty an acceptable price to pay for increased security from terrorists? Such questions, debated throughout the twentieth century, acquired increased urgency in the electronic age.

Technology and the Control of Popular Culture

Americans have reveled in mass-consumption culture ever since the 1920s, when automobiles, electric appliances, and radios enhanced the quality of everyday life and leisure. By exposing citizens to the same movies and radio programs, these new media laid the basis for a homogeneous national popular culture. During the 1950s, the spread of television—and its domination by three networks: ABC, CBS, and NBC—likewise promoted the emergence among middle-class Americans of a more uniform cultural outlook.

During the 1970s, new technological developments reshaped the television industry and the cultural landscape. The advent of cable and satellite broadcasting brought more specialized networks and programs into American living rooms. People could now get news around the clock from Ted Turner's CNN (Cable News Network), watch myriad sports events on the ESPN channels, and tune in to the Fox network for innovative entertainment and conservative political commentary. By the 1990s, millions of viewers had access to dozens, sometimes hundreds, of specialized channels. They could watch old or new movies, golf tournaments, and cooking classes; view religious or African American or Hispanic programming; and buy goods on home-shopping channels. By 1998, such specialized programming had captured 53 percent of the prime-time TV audience.

One of the most successful niche channels was MTV (Music Television), which debuted in 1981. Initially, its main offerings were slickly made videos featuring popular vocalists, who acted out the words of their songs. Essentially advertisements for albums (and, later, CDs), these videos were extremely popular among teenagers, who became devoted viewers. With its flashy colors, creative choreography, and exciting visual effects, MTV popularized singers such as Michael Jackson and Madonna and emphasized visual and aural stimulation.

Sexual stimulation likewise became a central motif, first in commercials and then in TV shows. As a TV executive explained, "In a cluttering environment where there are so many more media, you have to be more explicit and daring to stand out." In the 1980s, network stations featured steamy plots on daytime and evening soaps, such as *Dallas* and *Dynasty,* while in the 1990s, cable shows, such as Home Box Office's (HBO) *Sex in the City,* aired partial nudity and explicit discussion of sexual relations. Talk-show hosts ranging from the respectable Oprah Winfrey to the shocking Jerry Springer recruited ordinary Americans to share the secrets of their personal lives, which often involved sexuality, drug abuse, and domestic violence. As the American pop artist Andy Warhol had predicted, ordinary people embraced the opportunity to expose their lives and be "world-famous for 15 minutes."

As TV became ever more "stimulating," critics charged that it promoted violence. For evidence, they cited television dramas such as HBO's critically acclaimed series *The Sopranos,* which interwove the personal lives of a Mafia family with the amoral and relentless violence of their business deals. Did the impact of the dozens of such violence-focused dramas, combined with the widespread availability of guns, increase the already high American murder rate? Did it play a role in a series of shootings by students, such as the murder of twelve students and a teacher at Columbine High School in Colorado in 1999 and of thirty-two people at Virginia Tech University in 2007? Some lawmakers thought so. In a half-hearted effort to thwart youthful violence, Congress stipulated in the Telecommunication Reform Act of 1996 that manufacturers include a "V-chip" in new TV sets to allow parents to block specific programs.

As the controversy over TV violence indicated, technology never operates in a social and political vacuum. The expansion of specialized programming stemmed in part from policies set by the Federal Communications Commission (FCC) during the Reagan administration. Mark Fowler, the FCC chair at the time, shared the president's disdain for government regulation of business. "Television is just another appliance. . . . It's a toaster with pictures," Fowler suggested, as the FCC eliminated requirements that stations provide extensive news programming and subsidize debate on controversial political issues. Freed from such public service responsibilities, TV newscasts increasingly focused on lurid events, such as floods, fires, murders, and scandals connected to celebrities. The troubled marriage and divorce of Prince Charles of England and Lady Diana, for instance, and her subsequent death saturated the airwaves, and the distinction between news and entertainment became ever more blurred.

Fowler's FCC also minimized controls over children's programming. Soon cartoon programs such as *G.I. Joe* and *Care Bears* became extended advertisements for licensed replicas of their main characters. Even the characters of the Public Broadcasting Service's popular *Sesame Street* joined the parade of licensed replicas. Responding to complaints from parents and children's advocates, Congress enacted the Children's Television Act of 1990, which reinstated some restrictions on advertising, but the commercialization of childhood proceeded nonetheless.

Television stations were increasingly owned by a handful of large companies. In 1985, Congress raised the number of television stations a company could own from seven to twelve, and subsequent regulations allowed even more concentration in media ownership. In 2003, one company owned eight radio stations and three television stations in a single city, in addition to a newspaper and a TV cable system. On the national level, there was a similar trend toward monopolization. In 1990, Warner Communications merged with Time/Life to create an enormous entertainment corporation that included the Warner Brothers film studio, HBO, TNT, Six Flags, the Atlanta Braves, Atlantic Records, and the magazines of Time, Inc. (*Time, Fortune, Sports Illustrated,* and *People*). In 1995, the company brought in $21 billion in revenues. Subsequently, Warner Communications merged with America Online (renamed simply "AOL" in 2006), which was then the largest provider of Internet access. Although this merger turned out to be a poor business decision, it testified to the growing cultural influence of a few giant corporations.

Australian-born entrepreneur Rupert Murdoch stands as the exemplar of concentrated media ownership in the new global economy. As of 2004, Murdoch owned satellite TV companies in five countries and a worldwide total of 175 newspapers; in the United States, his holdings included Direct TV, the Fox TV network, the Twentieth Century Fox Studio, the *New York Post,* thirty-five television stations, and—as of 2007—the *Wall Street Journal.* A conservative ideologue as well as an entrepreneur, Murdoch has used his news empire to promote his political views. His career suggests not only the fact of globalization, but also the power of conservative individuals and multinational corporations at the beginning of the twenty-first century.

▶ What are the most important aspects of the computer and electronics revolutions? What are the social consequences of this changing technology?

▶ How did the television industry change in recent decades? Why does it matter?

Culture Wars

Times of economic affluence, such as the 1950s, often encourage social harmony by damping down class conflict. Such was not the case in the prosperous 1980s and 1990s, which were marked by unrelenting warfare over cultural issues. These "culture wars" generally pitted religious conservatives against secular liberals and were often instigated by political strategists to assist a candidate or a party. The main hot-button issues were racial and ethnic pluralism, "family values," and the status of women and of gay Americans.

An Increasingly Pluralistic Society

In 1992, Republican presidential hopeful Patrick Buchanan warned Americans that their country was "undergoing the greatest invasion in its history, a migration of millions of illegal aliens a year from Mexico." A sharp-tongued cultural warrior, Buchanan exaggerated—but not by much. According to the Census Bureau, the population of the United States grew from 203 million people in 1970 to 280 million in 2000. Of that increase of 77 million, immigrants accounted for 28 million, with legal entrants numbering 21 million and illegal aliens adding another 7 million (Figure 31.1). Relatively few—legal or illegal—came from Europe (2 million) and Africa (about 600,000), the historical homelands of most American citizens. The overwhelming majority, some 25 million, came either from East Asia (9 million) or Latin America (16 million).

These immigrants and their children profoundly altered the demography of many states and the entire nation. By 2000, 27 percent of California's population was foreign-born; Asians, Hispanics, and native-born blacks constituted a majority of the state's residents. Nationally, there were now more Hispanics (about 35 million) than

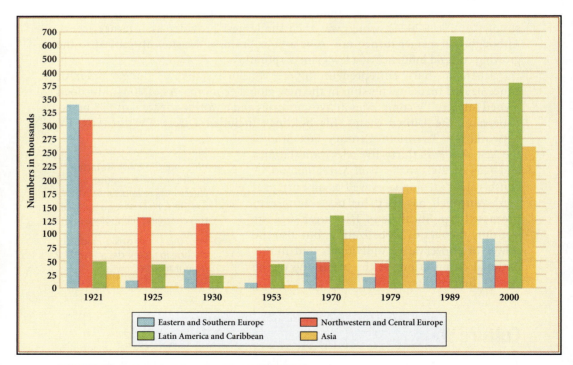

FIGURE 31.1 American Immigration, 1920–2000

Legislation inspired by nativism slowed the influx of immigrants after 1920, as did the Great Depression during the 1930s and World War II during the 1940s. Note the high rate of non-European immigration since the 1970s, the result of new eligibility rules in the Immigration Act of 1965 (see Chapters 27 and 28). The dramatic increase since 1980 in the number of migrants from Latin America and Asia reflects American economic prosperity, traditionally a magnet for migrants, and the rapid acceleration of illegal immigration.

African Americans (34 million), and Asians numbered over 12 million. On the basis of current rates of immigration and births, demographers predicted that by 2050, non-Hispanic whites would make up just 50 percent of the population, in contrast to 70 percent in 2000. As Buchanan claimed, a "great invasion" was indeed changing the character—and the color—of American society. Small wonder that ethnicity and immigration were prominent themes of the culture wars.

The massive inflow of legal immigrants was the unintended result of the Immigration Act of 1965, which allowed family members to join those already legally resident in the United States. Hispanics took advantage of this provision; millions of Mexicans came to the United States to join their families, and hundreds of thousands arrived from El Salvador, Guatemala, and the Dominican Republic. Historically, most Hispanics had lived in California, Texas, and New Mexico; now they settled in cities throughout the country and made up 16 percent of the population in Florida and New York (Map 31.2).

Most Hispanics were poor men and women seeking a better life. They willingly worked for low wages, cleaning homes, tending lawns, servicing hotel rooms, painting houses, and working construction. Many labored for cash, no questions asked. Cash workers did not usually pay income or Social Security taxes, but like those on regular payrolls, they sent funds to their families in Latin America and urged them to migrate—legally or illegally. Their hopes lay in the future, especially in their American-born children, who could claim the rights of U.S. citizens (see American Voices, p. 937).

Most Asian migrants came from China, the Philippines, South Korea, India, and Pakistan. In addition, 700,000 refugees came to the U.S. from Indochina (Vietnam, Laos, and Cambodia) after the Vietnam War. Some Asians were well educated or entrepreneurial and adapted quickly to life in America. But a majority lacked professional or vocational skills and initially took low-paying jobs.

As in the past, the immigrants congregated in ethnic enclaves. In Los Angeles, Koreans created a thriving community in "Koreatown"; in Brooklyn, New York, Russian Jews settled in "Little Odessa"; Hispanic migrants took over entire sections of Chicago, the District of Columbia, Dallas, and Houston. Ethnic entrepreneurs catered to their tastes, establishing restaurants, food stores, clothing shops, and native-language newspapers, while mainstream department stores, car dealers, and politicians vied for their dollars and votes. Although many immigrants worked and shopped outside their ethnic enclaves, they usually socialized, worshipped, and married within the community.

Many native-born Americans worried about the massive scale of the "new immigration." As with the Irish and German influx of the 1840s and the central and southern European Jewish and Catholic immigration of the 1890s, critics pointed out that immigrants assimilated slowly, depressed wages for all workers, and raised crime rates and gang activity in urban areas. They also sounded potent new themes reflecting modern concerns: that rapid population growth endangered the environment and saddled governments with millions of dollars in costs for schools, hospitals, police, and social services. Addressing these issues, Congress included provisions in the Welfare Reform Act of 1996 that curtailed the access of legal immigrants to food stamps and other welfare benefits.

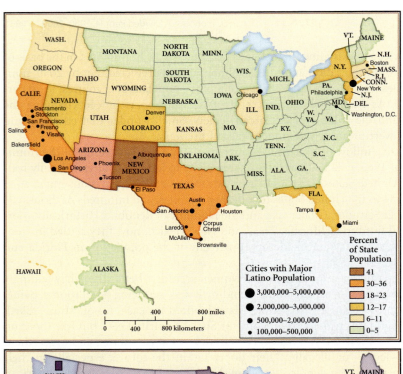

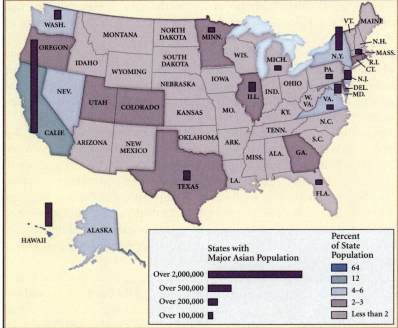

MAP 31.2 Hispanic and Asian Populations, 2000

In 2000, people of Hispanic descent made up more than 11 percent of the American population; they now outnumber African Americans as the largest minority group. Asian Americans accounted for an additional 4 percent of the population. Demographers predict that by the year 2050, only about half of the U.S. population will be composed of non-Hispanic whites. Note the high percentage of Hispanics and Asians in California and certain other states.

Cheap Labor: Immigration and Globalization GEORGE STITH AND PETRA MATA

Immigrants populated the United States, and immigrants continue to remake it. But for whose benefit? Under what conditions? And at whose expense? Those are three of the questions raised by the following testimonials. A native-born white American, George Stith testified in 1952 before a congressional committee that was considering whether to expand or restrict the Mexican "guest worker" (*braceros*) program. Petra Mata was an immigrant from Mexico "insourced" to work for low wages; subsequently her job was "outsourced," sent abroad to a low-wage country because of free trade and globalization.

George Stith: My address is Star Route Box 5, Gould, Ark. All my life I have worked on cotton plantations. When I was 4 years old my family moved to southern Illinois, near Cairo. We picked cotton in southeast Missouri, and west Tennessee nearly every year. We later moved across the river into Missouri and share-cropped. In 1930 we moved back to Arkansas. I don't know whether I am a migratory worker or not, but we certainly did a lot of migrating. . . .

For a long time I had heard about labor shortages in the West and how Mexican workers were being imported. I was sure that no people would be imported from Mexico to work on farms in Arkansas. There were too many people living in the little towns and cities who go out to chop and pick cotton. . . .

The importation of Mexican nationals into Arkansas did not begin until the fall of 1949. Cotton-picking wages in my section were good. We were getting $4 per 100 pounds for picking. As soon as the Mexicans were brought in the wages started falling. Wages were cut to $3.25 and $3 per 100 pounds. In many cases local farm workers could not get jobs at all. . . . The cotton plantation owners kept the Mexicans at work and would not employ Negro and white pickers.

Petra Mata: I was born in Mexico. . . . In 1969, my husband and I came to the U.S. believing we would find better opportunities for our children and ourselves. We first arrived without documents, then became legal, and finally became citizens. For years I moved from job to job until I was employed in 1976 by the most popular company in the market, Levi Strauss & Company. I earned $9.73 an hour and also had vacation and sick leave. Levi's provided me and my family with a stable situation, and in return I was a loyal employee and worked there for fourteen years.

On January 16, 1990, Levi's closed its plant in San Antonio, Texas, where I had been working, leaving 1,150 workers unemployed, a majority of whom were Mexican-American women. The company moved its factory to Costa Rica. . . .

As a result of being laid off, I personally lost my house, my method of transportation, and the tranquility of my home. . . . At that time, I had not the slightest idea what free trade was or meant. . . .

Our governments make agreements behind closed doors without participation from the working persons who are most affected by these decisions — decisions that to my knowledge only benefit large corporations and those in positions of power.

SOURCES: Migratory Labor, *Hearings Before Subcommittee on Labor and Labor-Management Relations*, 82nd Congress, 2nd session (Washington, D.C.: U.S. Government Printing Office, 1952), 89–90; Christine Ahn, ed., *Shafted: Free Trade and America's Working Poor* (Oakland, CA: Food First Books, 2003), 32–35.

Significantly, state governments have led the efforts to deal with illegal immigration. In 1986, California voters overwhelmingly supported Proposition 63, which established English as the state's "official language"; seventeen other states followed suit. Eight years later, Californians approved Proposition 187, a ballot initiative forthrightly named "Save Our State," which barred illegal aliens from public schools, nonemergency care at public health clinics, and all other state social services. The initiative also required law enforcement officers, school administrators, and social workers to report suspected illegal immigrants to the federal Immigration and Naturalization Service. When a federal judge ruled that Proposition 187 was unconstitutional, supporters of the measure demanded that Congress take action to curtail legal immigration and expel illegal aliens.

An unlikely coalition of politicians prevented the passage of such federal legislation. Various businesses (such as Marriott and other hotel corporations, meatpacking plants, construction firms, and large-scale farmers) wanted a plentiful supply of low-wage labor and lobbied probusiness Republicans to reject laws restricting immigration. Liberal Democrats also opposed such legislation because they supported ethnic pluralism and cultural diversity. Indeed, in 1986, Congress enacted (and President Reagan signed) a measure that granted amnesty to nearly two million illegal aliens and, in its lack of rigorous enforcement provisions, ensured that the flood of illegal immigrants would continue, as indeed it has. As of 2008, Congress had still proved stunningly unable to come to grips with a pressing national problem.

The dramatic increase in Asians and Hispanics brought benefits to some African Americans. As immigrant workers took the lowest paid jobs in the construction, manufacturing, and hotel service industries, many blacks used their experience and ability to speak English to move into supervisory positions. Some of these African Americans joined the ranks of the middle class and moved to better lives in the suburbs. Yet blacks who remained in the inner cities now earned less and paid more for housing because massive immigration cut wages and drove up rents. Many inner-city black children suffered as well, as overcrowded and underfunded schools diverted scarce resources to bilingual education for Spanish- and Chinese-speaking students.

Still, government policy continued to provide African Americans (and Hispanics and white women) with preferential treatment, such as hiring for public sector jobs, "set-aside" programs for minority-owned businesses, and university admissions and hiring. Conservatives argued that such governmental "social engineering" programs were deeply flawed because they promoted "reverse discrimination" against white men and resulted in the selection and promotion of less-qualified applicants. During the 1990s, they—along with many Americans who believed in equal opportunity—demanded an end to such legal privileges.

Once again, California stood at the center of the debate. In 1995, under pressure from Republican governor Pete Wilson, the regents of the University of California scrapped their twenty-year-old policy of affirmative action. A year later, California voters approved Proposition 209, which banished affirmative action privileges in state employment and public education. When the number of Hispanic and African Americans qualified for admission to the flagship Berkeley campus of the University of California plummeted (their places taken primarily by high-scoring Asian Americans), conservatives hailed the result as proving that affirmative action had lowered intellectual standards. Avoiding a direct reply to that charge, liberals maintained that state universities should educate potential leaders of all ethnic and racial groups.

Affirmative action remained controversial. In 2001, the California Regents devised a new admissions plan to assist certain minority applicants; two years later, the U.S. Supreme Court invalidated one affirmative action plan at the University of Michigan but allowed racial preference policies that promoted a "diverse" student body. In the face of growing public and judicial opposition, the future of such programs was uncertain.

While affirmative action programs assisted some African Americans to rise into the middle classes, they did not address the social problems of poorer blacks. Millions of young African Americans lived in households headed by wage-earning single mothers who had neither the time nor the energy to supervise their children's lives. Many of their daughters bore babies at an early age, while their sons ran with street gangs and dealt in illegal drugs. To address drug use and the crimes that it generated, the Reagan administration urged young people to "Just Say No." This campaign had some success in cutting drug use among middle-class black and white teenagers but did not staunch the dangerous flow of crack cocaine into poor African American neighborhoods. "The police are losing the war against crack," *Newsweek* noted grimly in 1986, "and the war is turning the ghettos of major cities into something like a domestic Vietnam." Indeed, the murderous rivalry among black drug dealers took the lives of thousands of young African American men, and police efforts to stop drug trafficking brought the arrest and imprisonment of tens of thousands more.

In April 1992, this seething underworld of urban crime and violence erupted in five days of race riots in Los Angeles. The worst civil disorder since the 1960s, the violence took sixty lives and caused $850 million in damage. The riot was triggered by the acquittal (on all but one charge) of four white Los Angeles police officers who had been accused of using excessive force in arresting a black motorist, Rodney King, who had led them on a wild car chase.

To Live and Die in L.A.
As rioters looted stores in South-Central Los Angeles and burned over 1,000 buildings, the devastation recalled that caused by the African American riots in Watts in 1965. But Los Angeles was now a much more diverse community. More than 40 percent of those arrested in 1992 were Hispanic, and the rioters attacked Koreans and other Asians as well as whites. Silvie Kreiss/Liason.

The riot exposed the acute rifts between urban blacks and their immigrant neighbors. Many Los Angeles blacks resented recent immigrants from Korea who had set up successful grocery stores and other retail businesses. When blacks tried to loot and burn these businesses during the riot, the Koreans fought them off with guns. Frustrated by high unemployment and crowded housing conditions, Hispanics joined in the rioting and accounted for more than half of those arrested and one-third of those killed. The riots expressed black rage at the outcome of the Rodney King case and also, in the looting of property, the class-based frustration of poor African Americans and immigrant Hispanics (see Voices from Abroad, p. 941).

In 1995, Los Angeles police worried about another black-led riot as the trial of O. J. Simpson neared its end. A renowned African American football player and well-paid representative for Hertz Rental Cars, Simpson was accused of the brutal murders of his ex-wife, Nicole Brown Simpson, a white woman, and her boyfriend. The prosecution produced damning evidence of Simpson's guilt, but black defense attorney Johnnie Cochran argued that a police detective had tampered with the evidence. More important, Cochran played the "race card," encouraging the predominately black jury to view Simpson as a victim of racial prejudice and to acquit him. Although a substantial majority of whites, in Los Angeles and the nation, believed that Simpson was guilty, they peacefully accepted the jury's verdict of "not guilty." In the 1990s, unlike the 1920s and 1940s, whites no longer resorted to rioting to take revenge against blacks. Now it was African Americans who took to the streets.

For most of the twentieth century, advocates for civil rights for African Americans and other minorities promoted their "integration" into the wider society and culture. Integration had been the dream of Dr. Martin Luther King Jr. and Hispanic farmworkers' organizer César Chávez (see Chapter 28). Beginning in the 1970s, however, some blacks and Hispanics rejected integration in favor of "black power" and "multiculturalism" and sought the creation of racially and ethnically defined institutions. Some liberals supported this multicultural agenda, but Arthur Schlesinger Jr. (a well-known historian and advisor to President Kennedy) and many other liberals opposed such separatist schemes. Conservative commentators, such as George F. Will, William Bennett, and Patrick Buchanan, uniformly condemned multiculturalism as a threat to core American values. Fearing the "balkanization," or fragmentation, of American culture, they opposed classroom instruction of immigrant children in their native languages and university curricula that deemphasized the importance of European culture.

This warfare over culture issues extended into Congress. Believing that the programs aired on public television stations and the grants awarded by the National Endowments for the Arts and the Humanities promoted multiculturalism, conservative lawmakers tried to cut off their funding. When that effort failed, they drastically reduced the organizations' budgets. Conservatives also took aim at the antiracist and antisexist regulations and speech codes that had been adopted by many colleges. Demanding the protection of the First Amendment right of free speech, conservatives (along with liberals in the American Civil Liberties Union) opposed attempts to regulate "hate" speech.

A U.S. Epidemic and Its Causes   JANET DALEY

Around 8:30 P.M. on April 19, 1989, gangs of youths began to beat up joggers and bicyclists in New York City's Central Park. About the same time, Trisha Meilli, an American investment banker of Italian descent, was brutally raped, beaten, and left for dead in the park. Five black and Hispanic young men from Harlem, arrested initially because of the gang attacks, confessed to assaulting Meilli and served prison terms of seven to eleven years. In 2002, long after Daley's article appeared in an English newspaper, *The Independent*, DNA tests pinned the attack on Matias Reyes, a convicted serial rapist and murderer who was born in Puerto Rico.

The trial in New York of the Central Park rapists has brought into focus two tacit assumptions that underpin conventional wisdom about America and the prognosis for our own [English] future.

The first is that everything wrong with American society is a result of its "system" (that is, its political and economic organisation). The second is that as our "system" becomes more like that of the United States (more free-market based), we shall inevitably suffer the same problems of a mindlessly violent underclass. . . .

Both of these contentions seem to me wrong. To begin with, the notion that a country's social mores and attitudes are brought about entirely by the form of its government and economy is a bit of Marxist theoretical baggage that ought to be thrown out. . . .

Many of the worst instances of anarchic violence in America — such as the attack on the Central Park jogger — do not arise from the underclass in the proper economic sense at all. These boys were not notably poor, or from families without aspirations. . . .

Those aspects of American life that are most repugnant — its lunatic viciousness and criminality — can be accounted for by purely historical circumstances. . . . The United States is an enormous continental landmass which was settled in an ad hoc, opportunist fashion by disparate groups of people with different motivations and lifestyles. . . .

Into this mix early this century came a great wave of Sicilians who brought with them their own family industry. The Mafia gained a hold in America at a time when law enforcement was nominal and social insecurity was universal. . . . [I]t now runs the gambling, prostitution and drug empires of America. . . .

This . . . influence of organised crime which arose through a historical coincidence — the arrival of a particular subculture in a loosely organised country which, for separate historical reasons, had committed itself constitutionally to the citizen's right to bear arms — is more central to the current problems of the U.S. than its capitalist economy or its political ideology.

To describe Britain as inevitably on the same road is simple historical ignorance. For a stable and deeply conservative society to come to grips with immigrant groups may present us with a challenge, but it can never lead to the conditions with which America is faced, and which are the result of attempting to build a society from scratch out of a diverse and discordant collection of peoples.

SOURCE: *The Independent* (London), August 29, 1990, 18.

Conflicting Values: Women's and Gay Rights

Conservatives were equally worried about the state of American families. They pointed to the 40 percent rate of divorce among whites and the 70 percent rate of out-of-wedlock pregnancies among blacks. The "abrasive experiments of two liberal decades," they charged, had eroded respect for marriage and family values. To members of the Religious Right, there was a wide range of culprits: legislators who enacted liberal divorce laws, funded child care, and allowed welfare payments to unmarried mothers, as well as judges who condoned abortion and banished religious instruction from public schools. In defending "traditional family values," religious conservatives were particularly intent on resisting the claims made by women and homosexuals.

In the 1980s, public opinion polls showed strong support for many feminist goals, including equal pay in the workplace, an equitable sharing of household and child-care responsibilities, and personal control of reproductive decisions. But in *Backlash: The Undeclared War on American Women* (1991), journalist Susan Faludi warned that conservative social groups had launched an all-out campaign against the feminist agenda of civic equality for women. In response, the predominately middle-class National Organization for Women (NOW) expanded its membership to include "Third Wave" feminists. These new feminists focused on the distinctive concerns of women of color, lesbians, and working women. Younger feminist women also felt more secure in their sexuality; many identified with the pop music star Madonna, whose outrageous sexualized style seemed to empower her rather than making her a sex object.

Abortion was central to the cultural warfare between feminists and religious conservatives and a defining issue between Democrats and Republicans. Feminists viewed the issue from the perspective of the pregnant woman; they argued that the right to a legal, safe abortion was crucial to her control over her life. Conversely, religious conservatives viewed abortion from the perspective of the unborn fetus and claimed that its rights trumped those of the living mother. Indeed, in cases of a difficult childbirth, some conservatives would sacrifice the life of the mother to save that of the fetus. To dramatize the larger issues at stake, the antiabortion movement christened itself as "pro-life," while proponents of abortion rights described themselves as "pro-choice." Both ideologies had roots in the American commitment to "life, liberty, and the pursuit of happiness." The question remained: Whose life? Whose liberty? Whose definition of happiness?

The male hierarchy of the Catholic Church offered its answer to such questions in 1971, when it sponsored the National Right to Life Committee. Church leaders launched a graphic media campaign to build popular support for the Church's anti-abortion stance, distributing films of late-term fetuses in utero and photographs of tiny fetal hands. By the 1980s, fundamentalist Protestants had assumed leadership of the antiabortion movement, which became increasingly confrontational and politically powerful.

Pressed by antiabortion groups, state legislatures passed laws that regulated the provision of abortion services. These laws required underage girls to obtain parental permission for abortions, denied public funding of abortions for poor women, and mandated waiting periods and elaborate counseling. In *Webster v. Reproductive Health Services* (1989) and *Planned Parenthood of Southeastern Pennsylvania v. Casey* (1992), the Supreme Court accepted the constitutionality of many of these restrictions but upheld the right of women to an abortion in the early state of pregnancy. Federal courts also continued to overturn state laws that prohibited late-term abortions when the life of the mother was in danger.

The debate over abortion stirred deep emotions. During the 1990s, evangelical Protestant activists mounted protests outside abortion clinics and harassed their staffs and clients. Pro-life extremists advocated killing the doctors and nurses who performed abortions, and a few carried out their threats. In 1994, an anti-abortion activist killed two workers at Massachusetts abortion clinics and wounded five others; other religiously motivated extremists murdered doctors in Florida and New York and posted "hit lists" on the Web naming doctors who performed abortions. Cultural warfare had turned deadly, resorting to terror to achieve its ends.

The issue of homosexuality stirred equally deep passions—on all sides. As more gay men and women "came out of the closet" in the years after Stonewall (see Chapter 29), they demanded a variety of protections and privileges. Defining themselves as an oppressed minority, gays sought legislation that would protect them from discrimination in housing, education, public accommodations, and employment. Public opinion initially opposed such initiatives, but by the 1990s, many cities and states banned discrimination on the basis of sexual orientation.

This legislation did not end the conflict. Gay groups asserted that civic equality included extensive legal rights for same-sex couples, such as eligibility for workplace health-care coverage on the same basis as married heterosexuals. Indeed, many homosexuals wanted their partnerships recognized as legal marriages and treated identically to opposite-sex unions.

The Religious Right had long condemned homosexuality as morally wrong. Pat Robertson, North Carolina senator Jesse Helms, and other conservatives campaigned vigorously against measures that would extend rights to gays. In 1992, conservatives in Colorado won a voter-approved amendment to the state constitution that prevented local governments from enacting ordinances protecting gays and lesbians, a measure that the Supreme Court subsequently overturned as unconstitutional. In 1998, Congress entered the fray by enacting the Defense of Marriage Act, which allowed states to refuse to recognize gay marriages or civil unions formed in other jurisdictions. However, in *Lawrence v. Texas* (2003), the Supreme Court limited the power of states to prohibit private homosexual activity between consenting adults. As the new century began, the debate over legal rights for gays and lesbians rivaled in fervor and importance those over immigration, abortion, and affirmative action. These cultural issues joined economic issues relating to globalization in shaping the dynamics of American politics.

▶ Who are the new immigrants? Why is their presence controversial?

▶ What were the main issues in the various cultural wars of the 1980s and 1990s? Why were those struggles so intense?

SUMMARY

The revival of the American economy after 1980 stemmed from the defense buildup, which poured in billions of dollars, and the resurgence of American corporations, which invested heavily in research and new technologies. As the Japanese and German economies faltered, the United States reasserted its leading role in the global economy. American and European multinational firms pushed forward the process of globalization; and people, goods, and investment capital moved easily across political boundaries. At home, economic growth increased social inequality, and poverty and crime continued to plague America's inner cities.

Technological innovations boosted the American economy and transformed daily life. The computer revolution changed the ways in which Americans shopped, worked, learned, and stayed in touch with family and friends. Cable and satellite technology altered television programming and provided Americans with a wider variety of entertainment choices.

As our account has suggested, globalization and technology accentuated cultural conflicts within the United States. Advances in biomedical science revived old moral debates, and the arrival of millions of Asians and Latin Americans sparked debates about illegal immigration and ethnic diversity. Conservatives spoke out strongly and effectively in discussions of "family values." Debates over women's rights, abortion, affirmative action, and the legal rights of homosexuals intensified. As the nation entered the twenty-first century, its people were divided by cultural values as well as by economic class and racial identity.

Connections: Society and Technology

Cultural conflict has been a significant feature of recent American life. As we noted in the essay that opened Part Seven:

> Increased immigration . . . produced a new nativist movement. Continuing battles over affirmative action, abortion, sexual standards, homosexuality, feminism, and religion in public life took on an increasingly passionate character.

Neither set of issues was new. During the 1920s (Chapter 23), nativist sentiment forced the passage of a National Origins Act that restricted immigration. That decade also witnessed Prohibition, a failed attempt to impose a moral code by force of law. Both immigration and moral issues came to the fore again in the 1960s. As we saw in Chapter 28, the Immigration Act of 1965 produced a larger and more diverse flow of immigrants, and young people led a cultural revolution that challenged traditional practices and values. The battle over social mores resumed in the 1980s, as we noted in Chapter 31, as moral and sexual conservatives attempted a cultural counterrevolution.

That struggle continues in a world shaped by the technology of cable TV, the computer chip, and the Web, which—like the automobile and the movies in the 1920s—have expanded people's knowledge and choices. In such ways does technology influence, but not determine, cultural outcomes.

TIMELINE

1980s
- ▶ Rise of "Yuppies" (young urban professionals)
- ▶ Japan emerges as major economic power
- ▶ Married women enter workforce in greater numbers
- ▶ Lee Iacocca revives Chrysler Corporation
- ▶ Bill Gates and Microsoft capture software market
- ▶ Immigration of Latinos and Asians grows
- ▶ Conservatives challenge affirmative action

1981
- ▶ Reagan crushes air traffic controllers' strike
- ▶ AIDS epidemic identified; soon spreads worldwide

1985
- ▶ United States becomes debtor nation

1987
- ▶ Montreal protocol cuts ozone loss

1990s
- ▶ Stock market boom continues
- ▶ Globalization intensifies; American jobs outsourced
- ▶ Wal-Mart becomes major economic force

- ▶ Decline of labor unions continues
- ▶ Personal computer and small electronics revolution
- ▶ Spread of World Wide Web (WWW)
- ▶ Human Genome Project unravels structure of DNA
- ▶ Deregulation of TV industry; concentration of media ownership
- ▶ Opposition to immigration and multiculturalism grows

1991
- ▶ European Union formed

1992
- ▶ Los Angeles race riots

1993
- ▶ North American Free Trade Agreement (NAFTA)

1995
- ▶ World Trade Organization (WTO) created

1998
- ▶ Battles over gay rights intensify; Congress passes Defense of Marriage Act

1999
- ▶ Protests against WTO policies

2001
- ▶ President George W. Bush rejects Kyoto environmental treaty

FOR FURTHER EXPLORATION

Alfred Eckes Jr. and Thomas Zeilin's *Globalization and the American Century* (2003) links American prosperity to globalization. On social class, read David Brooks, *Bobos in Paradise: The New Upper Class* (2000); Barbara Ehrenreich, *Fear of Falling: The Inner Life of the Middle Class* (1989); and Nelson Lichtenstein, *State of the Union: A Century of American Labor* (2002). See also Godfrey Hodgson, *More Equal Than Others* (2004), and John Skrentny, *The Minority Rights Revolution* (2002). Fine studies of family life are Stephanie Coontz, *The Way We Never Were* (1992), and Arlie Hochschild, *The Second Shift: Working Parents and the Revolution at Home* (2002).

Provocative studies of technology include Howard Segal, *Future Imperfect* (1994), and Edward Tenner, *Why Things Bite Back* (1996). For the impact of television, see Mary Ann Watson, *Defining Visions* (1998), and Leonard Downie Jr. and Robert G. Kaiser, *The News About the News* (2002). On environmental issues, consult Adam Rose, *The Bulldozer in the Countryside* (2001). For AIDS, go to **www.nytimes.com** and search for "AIDS at 25."

On the culture wars, see Gertrude Himmelfarb, *One Nation, Two Cultures* (1999), and James Hunter, *Culture Wars* (1991). Terry Anderson, *The Pursuit of Fairness* (2004), and Jennifer Hochschild, *Facing Up to the American Dream* (1996), cover race relations. Roger Daniels and Otis Graham, *Debating Immigration, 1882–Present* (2001), Nicolaus Mills, ed., *Arguing Immigration* (1994), and "The New Americans" at **www.pbs.org/independentlens/newamericans** cover that controversial topic.

TEST YOUR KNOWLEDGE

To assess your mastery of the material in this chapter and for Web sites, images, and documents related to this chapter, visit **bedfordstmartins.com/henrettaconcise**.

Stumbling into the Twenty-First Century

Even a government as powerful as America's seems inadequate to crucial challenges—from the physical threat of terrorism to the economic wrenching of globalization. The political world, to many, seems out of joint.

—Michael Oreskes, February 3, 2008

Few Americans alive at the time ever forgot the Japanese attack on Pearl Harbor on December 7, 1941. "You wake up on a Sunday morning," one person later reflected, "and the world as you know it ends." Sixty years later, on the bright morning of September 11, 2001, Americans felt exactly the same way as they watched the collapse of the two 110-story towers of New York City's World Trade Center. They knew that the nation had arrived at another defining moment.

The attack by Al Qaeda terrorists, like that of the Japanese on Hawaii, caught the nation by surprise—and for good reason. Only in retrospect did the Al Qaeda threat come sharply into focus. Yes, Osama bin Laden, the wealthy Saudi-born leader of Al Qaeda, had called in 1998 for a *jihad*, a holy war, against America. Al Qaeda operatives had bombed American embassies in Kenya and Tanzania in 1998 and the USS *Cole*, an American warship visiting Yemen, in 2000. But no one, not at the CIA or the Pentagon, not President Bill Clinton or George W. Bush, imagined suicidal terrorists ramming commercial jets full of captive passengers into the World Trade Center and the Pentagon. Al Qaeda's brutal audacity simply exceeded American experience.

Once a minor annoyance, this band of terrorists became defined—no doubt to Osama bin Laden's great satisfaction—as an existential threat, on a par with the Nazis of 1941 or the nuclear-armed Soviets of 1950. America's global mission became the War on Terror. The cost of that effort, which is not finished, has been high: wars in Afghanistan and Iraq, $500 billion expended (as of 2008), tens of thousands of dead and wounded American soldiers, hundreds of thousands of Iraqi casualties, a soiled image around the world. Gone are the high hopes inspired by the Cold War's end. Instead, the United States has entered the twenty-first century off its stride, somehow ill equipped, despite its military and economic preeminence, for the challenges it now faces.

The Advent of George W. Bush

Less than a year before 9/11, Americans lived through a different kind of trauma. So closely contested was the presidential election of November 2000 that only after the Supreme Court intervened, a full month later, did George W. Bush's victory become certain. Having lost the popular vote, the new president might have been expected to govern in a moderate, bipartisan fashion. Instead, he proceeded as if he had won a popular mandate, in the process redefining Republican conservatism and America's conduct as a global power.

The Contested Election of 2000

George Bush's adversary in the election was Al Gore, Clinton's vice president. Both candidates came from privileged backgrounds, but where Al Gore was a straight arrow—divinity student, journalist, elected to Congress at the age of twenty-eight—Bush had been at that age a bit of a hell-raiser, going through what he himself described as a "nomadic" period of "irresponsible youth." Still, Karl Rove, his future political guru, saw something in the happy-go-lucky Bush and became a steadfast ally. Bush became a Texas oil man, unsuccessfully, and ran for the House of Representatives in 1978, unsuccessfully. After his father George H. W. Bush became president, George W. finally made it in business as managing partner of the Texas Rangers baseball franchise. In 1994, with Rove at his side, he was elected governor of Texas and was on his way.

On the campaign trail, Bush presented himself as the genuine article, a regular guy. He ran as an outsider, deploring Washington partisanship and casting himself as a "uniter, not a divider." On domestic policy, he stood for "compassionate conservatism." Bush's campaign was orchestrated by Rove, a supremely gifted strategist and political in-fighter. One of Rove's maxims was to find the right message and stick to it. That was George W. Bush, always "on message."

Al Gore, by contrast, never settled on a message. Vacillating between Clinton's centrism and his own liberalism, he gave the unfortunate impression of a man without fixed principles. If Bush was the superior campaigner, Vice President Gore was the beneficiary of the prosperity of the Clinton years. Gore chose, however, to distance himself from the scandal-ridden Clinton—a decision that cost him votes. Gore's real nemesis was Ralph Nader, whose Green Party candidacy drew away votes that certainly would have carried Gore to victory. As it was, Gore won the popular vote, amassing 50.9 million votes to 50.4 million for Bush, only to fall short in the Electoral College, 267 to 271.

The Democrats challenged the tally in Florida and demanded hand recounts in several counties. A month of tumult followed, until the U.S. Supreme Court, voting strictly along conservative/liberal lines, ordered the recount stopped and let Bush's victory stand. Recounting ballots in only selected counties, the Court reasoned, violated the rights of other Floridians under the Fourteenth Amendment's equal protection clause. As if acknowledging the frailty of this argument, the Court declared *Bush v. Gore* a one-shot deal, not to be regarded as precedent. Many legal experts had been surprised that the Supreme Court had even accepted the case. The likeliest reason for why it did was that cutting short the controversy seemed preferable to having it thrust into a bitterly divided House of Representatives, with unforeseeable consequences. But by making a transparently political decision, Justice John Paul Stevens warned, the conservative majority undermined "the Nation's confidence in the judge as an impartial guardian of the rule of law." Still, the Court's ruling stuck. Gore had always played by the rules and did so now, conceding the election to his Republican opponent.

The Bush Agenda

Although George Bush had positioned himself as a moderate, countertendencies drove his administration from the start. Foremost was his vice president, Richard Cheney, an uncompromising, conservative Republican. Ordinarily, the politics of vice presidents don't matter much, but Cheney was not an ordinary vice president. A seasoned Washington player, he became, with Bush's consent, virtually a co-president. Into the administration also came Bush's campaign advisor, Karl Rove, whose advice made for an exceptionally politicized White House. In particular, Rove foreclosed the easygoing centrism of Bush the campaigner by arguing that a permanent Republican majority could be built on the party's conservative base.

On Capitol Hill, Rove's hard line was reinforced by Tom DeLay, the House majority leader. As Newt Gingrich's second-in-command in 1995, DeLay had declared "all-out war" on the Democrats, and he was as good as his word. He masterminded the K Street Project (named after the street where many of Washington's major lobbyists had their headquarters) that achieved a Republican lock on the big-money lobbying firms. Everything then fell into place. Lobbyists got access; House members got campaign funding; and, as paymaster, DeLay got a disciplined rank-and-file. Some of that money ended up underwriting a Republican takeover of the Texas legislature, which then gerrymandered five extra Republican congressional districts.

With that cushion, DeLay had a safe House majority and no need to deal with Democrats. The Senate, although more collegial, went through a similar hardening process. After 2002, with Republicans in control of both Congress and the White House, any pretense at bipartisan lawmaking ended. Out of these disparate elements — Bush's compassionate conservatism, Rove's political calculations, and exceptionally combative allies — emerged a hybrid brand of conservatism that defies easy classification.

After his wayward early years, George W. Bush had become — at the hands of the Reverend Billy Graham, he claimed — a born-again Christian, and he made his conversion a centerpiece of his administration. A prayer opened cabinet meetings, a Bible study class met at the White House, and a "faith-based initiative" funded church-related programs that emphasized abstinence and family values. Although the money involved was modest — a small fraction of total federal funding of social-service agencies — Bush's faith-based initiative offered concrete witness of his commitment to the Religious Right. Evangelical leaders had an ally in the White House, a true believer in their moral agenda.

Bush's campaign had been blessedly free of Republican race-baiting, such as his father's Willie Horton ad (featuring a black murderer) in the 1988 race against the

Colin Powell and Condoleezza Rice
Colin Powell, a distinguished army general, and Condoleezza Rice, a former Stanford professor, were leading figures in the Bush administration — Powell as secretary of state and Rice as national security advisor and, after Powell's retirement, as his successor — and powerful symbols of Bush's efforts at racial inclusiveness. Here, they are seated side by side, attending a state dinner at the Grand Palace in Bangkok, Thailand, October 19, 2003. Paul J. Richards/AFP/Getty Images.

hapless Michael Dukakis (see Chapter 30). By contrast, George W. was determinedly inclusive. Black speakers and entertainers featured prominently at the Republican convention; among those most prominently featured were General Colin Powell, a former chair of the Joint Chiefs of Staff, who became secretary of state, and Condoleezza Rice, a foreign-policy expert at Stanford, who became national security advisor and then, in Bush's second term, Powell's successor as secretary of state. Mexican Americans also figured prominently, and Bush, on easy terms with Texas's Latino community, was committed to finding a middle ground for resolving the increasingly contentious crisis over illegal immigrants.

On civil rights, the new administration was conservative, routinely opposing affirmative action in cases before the courts. But when it came to equal opportunity, Bush was a crusader. He spoke feelingly of "the soft prejudice of low expectations," and that arresting phrase launched him into the thickets of educational reform. The result was Bush's No Child Left Behind Act (2001), which increased federal funding for primary and secondary education and, to the satisfaction of conservatives who favored school choice, allowed students in underperforming schools to transfer to better institutions. But the main thrust of the law was hardly conservative. No Child Left Behind overrode time-honored local control, imposing federal standards for student performance as a means of disciplining a lagging educational system.

State officials and teachers complained that the program was underfunded, that the emphasis on testing distorted educational practice, and that a program emanating from Washington was bound to have unintended consequences (such as tempting school districts to encourage low-scoring students to drop out). So intense was the gathering opposition that Congressional reauthorization failed in 2007, and the program's future became increasingly problematic. Whatever its ultimate fate, however, there can be no denying the vaulting ambition of No Child Left Behind or the degree to which it departed from conservative canons of states' rights and federal restraint.

Equally confounding was Bush's response to the nation's festering health-care crisis. Despite hand-wringing by fiscal conservatives, the president looked on benignly as Medicare costs jumped from $433 billion to $627 billion during his first five years in office. What did grab Bush's attention was a gaping hole in Medicare benefits. Without drug coverage, desperate seniors were taking hazardous risks with Internet purchases or turning to Canada for cheaper medicines. Preempting the Democrats, the Bush administration in 2003 muscled through Congress a budget-busting drug-benefit bill.

The conservative side of this bill was in the particulars: First, there was to be no negotiating by Medicare for bulk purchases, although that was how Canada and America's own Veterans Administration had cut drug costs; second, provision would be not directly by Medicare but only via private insurers, which would compete for Medicare customers; third, copayments would be substantial, topping out at $3,600 for beneficiaries with big drug bills. In its solicitude for private business, Bush's drug program was soundly conservative but with the government picking up the tab.

The domestic issue that most engaged President Bush, as it had Ronald Reagan, was taxes. Bush's Economic Growth and Tax Relief Act of 2001 had something for everyone. It slashed income tax rates, extended the earned income credit for the poor, and phased out the estate tax by 2010 (when it would resume, unless Congress acted, at the original high rate). A second round of cuts in 2003 targeted dividend income and capital gains. His signature cuts—those favoring big estates and well-to-do owners of stocks and bonds—especially skewed the distribution of tax benefits upwards (Table 32.1).

Critics warned that such massive tax cuts would plunge the federal government into debt. Bush was unperturbed. He was not of the conservative school that favored tax cuts as a means of shrinking the government—"starving the beast," as Reaganites

TABLE 32.1 Impact of the Bush Tax Cuts, 2001–2003

Income in 2003	Number of Taxpayers	Average Gross Income	Total Tax Cut	Average % Change in Taxes Paid
Less than $50,000	92,093,452	$19,521	$435	−48 %
$50,000–100,000	26,915,091	70,096	1,656	−21
$100,000–200,000	8,878,643	131,797	3,625	−17
$200,000–500,000	1,999,061	288,296	7,088	−10
$500,000–1,000,000	356,140	677,294	22,479	−12
$1,000,000–10,000,000	175,157	2,146,100	84,666	−13
$10,000,000 or more	6,126	25,975,532	1,019,369	−15

SOURCE: *New York Times*, April 5, 2006.

had called it. In fact, as it turned out, he was himself a champion spender. By 2006, federal expenditures had jumped 33 percent, at a faster clip than under any president since Lyndon Johnson. Midway through Bush's second term the national debt stood at over $8 trillion, much of it owned by foreign investors, who also financed the nation's huge trade deficit. On top of that, staggering Social Security and Medicare obligations were coming due for retiring baby boomers. It seemed that these burdens — in per capita terms, the national debt currently stands at $28,000 for every man, woman, and child — would be passed on to future generations.

▶ Explain how, having lost the popular vote in 2000, Bush nevertheless became president.

▶ In what ways did Bush's policies depart from traditional conservatism?

How Bush's presidency might have fared in normal times is another of those unanswerable questions of history. As a candidate in 2000, George W. Bush had said little about foreign policy. He had assumed that his administration would rise or fall on his domestic program. With 9/11, an altogether different political scenario unfolded.

American Hegemony Challenged

The dictionary defines *hegemony* as "predominant influence exercised by one state over others." That was the United States in 2001, the hegemonic power in the world, unrivaled now that the Soviet Union was gone. It was therefore incumbent on the United States, George W. Bush often said, to be "humble" in its relations with other states. Bush's campaign words, however, masked his true bent, which was aggressively muscular. In this, Bush was heartily seconded by his vice president, a Cold Warrior of many years' standing. Cheney's key ally was the new secretary of defense, Donald Rumsfeld, who brought in a high-powered team of neoconservatives. The "neocons" championed "benevolent hegemony": the untrammeled use of America's power, military power if need be, to fashion a better, more democratic world.

In a striking display of unilateralism, the new administration walked away from an array of completed or pending diplomatic agreements. It repudiated the International Criminal Court and a UN convention banning biological weapons, and it cancelled nuclear test bans, weapons reduction, and antiballistic missile treaties. Most startling was its withdrawal from the Kyoto Protocol on global warming. When participating countries met in Bonn, Germany, in July 2001 to refine the protocol and satisfy America's objections, the U.S. representative was instructed not to participate. All too soon, the United States would be looking for the world's support.

September 11, 2001

On that sunny September morning, nineteen Al Qaeda terrorists hijacked four commercial jets and flew two of them into New York City's World Trade Center, destroying its twin towers and killing over 2,600 people. A third plane plowed into the Pentagon, near Washington, D.C. The fourth, presumably headed for the White House or possibly the U.S. Capitol, crashed in Pennsylvania when the passengers fought back and thwarted the hijackers.

September 11, 2001

Photographers on the scene after a plane crashed into the north tower of New York City's World Trade Center found themselves recording a defining moment in the nation's history. When a second airliner approached and then slammed into the building's south tower at 9:03 A.M., the nation knew that this was no accident. The United States was under attack. Of the 2,843 people killed on September 11, 2,617 died at the World Trade Center. Robert Clark/AURORA.

On September 14, as soon as he got his bearings, President Bush headed for "ground zero" at the World Trade Center, embraced rescue workers standing in the rubble, picked up a bullhorn, and stirred the nation. As an outburst of patriotism swept the United States, Bush proclaimed a "War on Terror" and vowed to carry the battle to Al Qaeda.

Operating out of Afghanistan, where they had been harbored by the fundamentalist Taliban regime, the elusive Al Qaeda briefly offered a clear target. The United States attacked, not with conventional forces but by deploying military advisors and supplies that bolstered anti-Taliban rebel forces. While Afghani allies carried the ground war, American planes rained destruction on the enemy. By early 2002, this lethal combination had ousted the Taliban regime, destroyed Al Qaeda's training camps, and killed or captured many of its operatives. The big prize, Al Qaeda leader Osama bin Laden, retreated to a mountain redoubt. Inexplicably, U.S. Special Operations forces failed to press the attack. Bin Laden evidently bought off the local war lords and escaped over the border into Pakistan.

The War on Terror: Iraq

At this point, the Bush administration could have declared victory and relegated the unfinished business — tracking down the Al Qaeda remnants, stabilizing Afghanistan, and shaking up the nation's security agencies — to a postvictory operational phase. President Bush had no such inclination. For him, the War on Terror was not a metaphor, but the real thing, an open-ended war that required putting aside business-as-usual.

On the domestic side, Bush declared the terrorist threat too big to be contained by ordinary law-enforcement means. He wanted the government's powers of domestic surveillance placed on a wartime footing. With little debate, Congress passed by virtual acclamation the USA PATRIOT Act (Uniting and Strengthening America by Providing Appropriate Tools Required to Intercept and Obstruct Terrorism). True to its title, the Patriot Act granted the administration sweeping authority to monitor citizens and apprehend suspected terrorists.

On the international front, the War on Terror called forth a policy of preventive war. Under international law, only an imminent threat justified a nation's right to strike first. Now, under the so-called Bush doctrine, the United States lowered the bar. It reserved for itself the right to act in "anticipatory self-defense." President Bush singled out Iran, North Korea, and Iraq—"an axis of evil"—as the targeted states.

Of the three, Iraq seemed the easiest mark, a pushover for Secretary Rumsfeld's lean, high-tech military. Neoconservatives in the Pentagon regarded Iraq as unfinished business, left over from the Gulf War of 1991 (see Chapter 30). More grandly, they regarded Iraq as America's chance to unveil its mission to democratize the world. Iraqis, they believed, would surely abandon the tyrant Saddam Hussein and embrace democracy if given half a chance. The democratizing effect would spread across the Middle East, toppling or reforming other unpopular Arab regimes and stabilizing the region. That in turn would secure the Middle East's oil supply, whose fragility Saddam's invasion of Kuwait had made all too clear. It was the oil, of course, that was of vital interest to the United States (Map 32.1).

None of these considerations, either singly or together, met Bush's declared threshold for preventive war. So Bush reluctantly acceded to the demand by America's anxious European allies that the United States go to the UN Security Council. The question was: Did Iraq have weapons of mass destruction (WMD) that threatened the United States? After the Gulf War, UN inspectors had rooted out chemical and biological stockpiles and an unexpectedly advanced nuclear program, but Saddam expelled the inspectors in 1998, and no one could be certain whether these programs had resumed. At Secretary of State Powell's behest, the Security Council approved Resolution 1441, which demanded that Saddam Hussein allow the return of the UN weapons inspectors. Unexpectedly, he agreed.

Most of the nations that supported Resolution 1441 saw it as means of defusing the crisis: The main thing was to keep talking. The Bush administration saw Resolution 1441 as a prelude to war: The main thing was to get on with the invasion. Naturally, the diplomatic parrying became rancorous. Most mysterious was Saddam, who actually had no WMDs but, by his obstructive efforts, acted as if he did. Since he did not, the UN inspectors came up empty-handed. Nevertheless, the Bush administration, gearing up for war, insisted that Iraq constituted a "grave and gathering danger" and, despite the failure to secure a second, legitimizing UN resolution, invaded in March 2003.

America's one major ally was Great Britain. A handful of other governments joined "the coalition of the willing," braving popular opposition at home to do so. Relations with France and Germany became poisonous. Even neighboring Mexico and Canada condemned the invasion, and Turkey, a key military ally, refused transit permission, ruining the army's plan for a northern thrust into Iraq. As for the Arab world, it exploded in anti-American demonstrations.

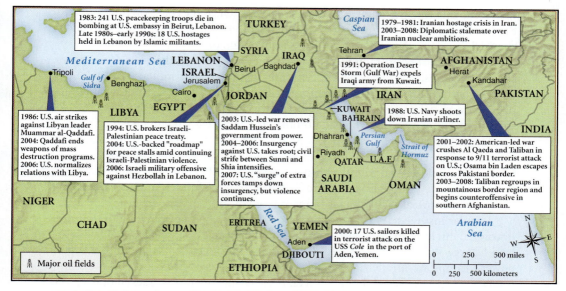

1983: 241 U.S. peacekeeping troops die in bombing at U.S. embassy in Beirut, Lebanon. Late 1980s–early 1990s: 18 U.S. hostages held in Lebanon by Islamic militants.

1979–1981: Iranian hostage crisis in Iran. 2003–2008: Diplomatic stalemate over Iranian nuclear ambitions.

1991: Operation Desert Storm (Gulf War) expels Iraqi army from Kuwait.

1986: U.S. air strikes against Libyan leader Muammar al-Qaddafi. 2004: Qaddafi ends weapons of mass destruction programs. 2006: U.S. normalizes relations with Libya.

1994: U.S. brokers Israeli-Palestinian peace treaty. 2004: U.S.-backed "roadmap" for peace stalls amid continuing Israeli-Palestinian violence. 2006: Israeli military offensive against Hezbollah in Lebanon.

2003: U.S.-led war removes Saddam Hussein's government from power. 2004–2006: Insurgency against U.S. takes root; civil strife between Sunni and Shia intensifies. 2007: U.S. "surge" of extra forces tamps down insurgency, but violence continues.

1988: U.S. Navy shoots down Iranian airliner.

2001–2002: American-led war crushes Al Qaeda and Taliban in response to 9/11 terrorist attack on U.S.; Osama bin Laden escapes across Pakistani border. 2003–2008: Taliban regroups in mountainous border region and begins counteroffensive in southern Afghanistan.

2000: 17 U.S. sailors killed in terrorist attack on the USS *Cole* in the port of Aden, Yemen.

Major oil fields

MAP 32.1 U.S. Involvement in the Middle East, 1979–2008

The United States has long played an active role in the Middle East, pursuing the twin goals of protecting Israel's security and ensuring a reliable supply of low-cost oil from the Persian Gulf. In 1991, with the blessing of the United Nations, President George H. W. Bush sent 540,000 American troops to liberate Kuwait from Iraq. In 2003, the United States again fought Iraq, this time driving Saddam Hussein from power and occupying the country. The Middle East has also been the site of terrorist activities targeting U.S. interests, most notably the suicide attack, presumably by Al Qaeda operatives, on the USS *Cole* as it was refueling in Yemen. Al Qaeda terrorism against sites in the United States on September 11, 2001, provoked a U.S.-led UN attack on Afghanistan that overthrew the Islamic fundamentalist Taliban government.

For more help analyzing this map, see the Online Study Guide at **bedfordstmartins.com/henrettaconcise**.

As in Afghanistan, the war began with massive air attacks that were intended to "shock and awe." *Time* magazine reported that targets around the capital city of Baghdad "got pulverized." Within three weeks, American troops had taken the Iraqi capital. The regime collapsed, and its leaders went into hiding (Saddam Hussein was captured nine months later). On May 1, President Bush flew onto the aircraft carrier *Abraham Lincoln* in a Navy jet dressed in fighter pilot's togs. Framed by a "Mission Accomplished" banner, Bush declared victory. In fact, the battle in Iraq had not ended; it was just beginning.

Despite meticulous military planning, the Pentagon had made no provision for postconflict operations. The president and his advisors had simply assumed an easy transition, with a quick draw-down of forces by September. Early in the assault, however, Saddam's paramilitary—the *fedayeen*—began mounting attacks behind the lines, particularly on U.S. supply convoys. Rumsfeld ordered the advance onward, refusing to acknowledge, as army commanders immediately recognized, an insurgency in the making. An opportunity to nip it in the bud was lost. The secretary of defense was similarly dismissive of the many well-respected, knowledgeable voices warning that occupying Iraq was going to be no picnic. So when, as the coalition forces arrived, the Iraqi police and civil authorities simply dissolved, the American military had no contingency plans and not enough troops to maintain order.

Thousands of poor Iraqis looted everything they could get their hands on: stores, shops, museums, industrial plants, government offices, and military arsenals. The looting shattered the infrastructure of Iraq's cities, leaving them without reliable supplies of electricity and water. In the midst of this turmoil, the insurgency got started, sparked by Sunni Muslims who had dominated Iraq under Saddam's Baathist regime. The Shiite majority, long oppressed by Saddam, at first welcomed the Americans, but extremist Shiite elements soon turned hostile, and U.S. forces found themselves under fire from both sides. And with the borders unguarded, Al Qaeda supporters flocked in from all over the Middle East, eager to do battle with the infidel Americans, bringing along a *jihadi* specialty: the suicide bomber (see Voices from Abroad, p. 957).

Popular insurgencies are a problem from hell for superpowers. Lyndon Johnson discovered this in Vietnam. Soviet premier Leonid Brezhnev discovered it in Afghanistan. And George W. Bush rediscovered it in Iraq. The intractable fact is that the superpower's troops are invaders. Although hard for Americans to believe, that was how Iraqis of all stripes viewed the U.S. forces. If the occupying forces cracked down hard, the civilian population suffered and turned hostile. If the occupying forces relented, insurgents became bolder and took control, as occurred, for example, at the Sunni strongholds of Ramadi and Fallujah. The one proven alternative, to pacify and hold insurgent areas, required far more soldiers than Secretary of Defense Rumsfeld was willing to commit to Iraq. Nor did planners reckon with the fact that in a war against insurgents, no occupation force comes out with clean hands. In Iraq, that painful truth burst forth graphically in photographs showing American guards at Baghdad's Abu Ghraib prison abusing and torturing suspected insurgents. The ghastly images shocked the world. For Muslims, they offered final proof of American treachery.

At that low point, in 2004, the United States had spent upward of $100 billion. A thousand American soldiers had died, and 10,000 more had been wounded, many maimed for life. But if the United States pulled out, Iraq would descend into chaos. So, as Bush took to saying, the United States had to "stay the course."

The Election of 2004

Once the fruitless scouring for Iraqi WMDs ended, the Bush administration came under relentless questioning. How had the United States gotten into this war? Was it a case of faulty intelligence? Or had the president misled the country? The administration dug itself into a deeper hole by trying to discredit critics. Bush did better by changing the terms of the debate. His real objective, he now argued, was rescuing the Iraqi people from Saddam's oppressive regime. Even so, the situation in Iraq ate away at the president's once-unbeatable ratings. As the bad news persisted, Bush's reelection in 2004 became a race against time.

For Democrats, the Iraq quandary was just as bad. How could they criticize the war without appearing unpatriotic? Moreover, many leading Democrats were themselves implicated. They had supported the 2002 resolution authorizing the president's use of force. So they had no choice but to embrace the war and find a way of turning

A Strategy for the Iraq Insurgency   ABU MUSAB AL-ZARQAWI

From 2004 to June 2006, when he was killed by American forces, Abu Musab al-Zarqawi led the Al Qaeda–linked insurgency in Iraq. In this effort, he was bent on expelling all Western influences from the Islamic world. But al-Zarqawi was also engaged in a struggle *inside* the Islamic world. He was Sunni, and he regarded the other branch of Islam, the Shia, as heretics and as vile as the hated West. Early in 2004, as he was taking up his struggle in Iraq, al-Zarqawi wrote the following letter, which outlined the deadly strategy of sectarian violence he proposed to follow.

God favored the [Islamic] nation with jihad on His behalf in the land of Mesopotamia [the ancient name for Iraq]. . . . The Americans . . . came to Iraq with all its people, pride, and haughtiness toward God and his Prophet. It thought that the matter would be somewhat easy. . . . But it collided with a completely different reality. The operations of the brother mujahidin [fighters] began from the first moment. . . . This forced the Americans to conclude a deal with the Shi'a, the most evil of mankind. . . .

[The Shi'a are] the insurmountable obstacle, the lurking snake, the crafty and malicious scorpion, the spying enemy, and the penetrating venom. . . . Shi'ism is the looming danger and the true challenge [and] is a religion that has nothing in common with Islam. . . .

America did not come to leave, and it will not leave no matter how numerous its wounds become and how much of its blood is spilled. It is looking to the near future, when it hopes to disappear into its bases secure and at ease and put the battlefields of Iraq into the hands of the foundling government with an army and police that will bring [the terror] of Saddam . . . back to the people. There is no doubt that the space in which we can move has begun to shrink and that the grip around the throats of the [Arab and Sunni] mujahidin has begun to tighten. With the deployment of soldiers and police, the future has become frightening. . . .

The Shi'a. . . . in our opinion are the key to change. I mean that targeting and hitting them in [their] religious, political, and military depth will provoke them to . . . bare the teeth of the hidden rancor working in their breasts. If we succeed in dragging them into the arena of sectarian war, it will become possible to awaken the inattentive Sunnis as they feel imminent danger and annihilating death at the hands of these [Shi'a]. . . .

I come back and again say that the only solution is for us to strike the religious, military, and other cadres among the Shi'a with blow after blow until they bend to the Sunnis. . . . God's religion is more precious than lives and souls. When the overwhelming majority stands in the ranks of truth, there has to be sacrifice for this religion. Let blood be spilled. . . .

SOURCE: Documents on Terrorist Abu Musab al-Zarqawi, 2004. www-personal.umich.edu/~jrcole/zarqawi/zarqawi.htm.

Abu Ghraib

This is an image obtained by the Associated Press showing a detainee bent over with his hands on the bars of a cell while being watched by a comfortably seated soldier at the Abu Ghraib prison in late 2003. Although displaying one of milder forms of torture documented at Abu Ghraib, this photograph captured all too vividly the humiliating treatment of detainees that outraged the Muslim world. AP Images.

it against the Republicans, which meant, first, driving home the administration's mistakes and, second, knocking the president off his pedestal.

The obvious man for that job was Senator John Kerry of Massachusetts. In the early primaries, Kerry had run poorly, and but for an infusion of family cash, he would have been forced out. But there was one thing in Kerry's favor: He was a real Vietnam hero, twice wounded and decorated for bravery—in contrast to the president (who had spent the Vietnam years safely perched in the Texas Air National Guard). As the primary season wound down, Kerry surged ahead and won the nomination.

The Democratic convention in August was a tableau of patriotism, filled with waving flags, retired generals, Kerry's Vietnam buddies, and the candidate himself arriving on stage with a snappy salute: "Reporting for duty." Only the Republicans could have done it better, and when their turn came, with the commander-in-chief as their nominee, in fact they did.

The campaign that followed was at once inspiring and dispiriting. Both parties worked hard at mobilizing voters. The Democrats excelled at Internet-driven efforts to raise money and reach activists, while the GOP outdid the Democrats at motivating its base, thanks especially to the church networks it had cultivated. For once, complaints about voter passivity did not apply. That was the inspiring part. The rest of it—the substance of the campaign—was a dispiriting exercise in attack ads and political choreography.

A sudden onslaught of slickly produced television ads by a group calling itself Swift Boat Veterans for Truth falsely charging that Kerry had lied to win his medals fatally undercut his advantage. Nor did it help that Kerry, as a three-term senator, had a lengthy record that was easily mined for hard-to-explain votes, as, for example, why had he voted against, before he voted for, an Iraqi funding bill? Republicans tagged him a "flip-flopper," and the accusation, endlessly repeated, stuck.

The strangest feature of the campaign was the distorting effect of the federal electoral system. In the forty or more states that were safely Democratic or Republican, people saw very little of the candidates, while voters in the few contested states were inundated by attack ads and door-ringing volunteers. These open states became the testing ground for Karl Rove's strategy of rallying the party's socially conservative base. Just in the nick of time, a gift fell into his lap: a ruling by the Supreme Court of Massachusetts that gay people had a constitutional right to marry. No issue—not even abortion—was better calculated to galvanize social conservatives. In the eleven states that rushed to adopt constitutional bans on gay marriage, every one succeeded. Bush joined in with a call for a federal constitutional ban.

Nearly 60 percent of eligible voters—the highest percentage since 1968—went to the polls. Bush beat Kerry by 286 electoral votes to 252. The crucial state was Ohio, where a gay marriage ban passed by 62 percent, probably giving the president his slim margin there. He also did well, despite Iraq, on national security. Voters told interviewers that Bush made them feel "safer." Bush was no longer a minority president. He had won a clear, if narrow, popular majority. In the flush of victory, the president spoke confidently of newly won "political capital" that he had big plans for spending.

> ▶ What was the connection between 9/11 and the war in Iraq?
>
> ▶ Why did the war in Iraq not go according to plan?
>
> ▶ Can you explain why President Bush was reelected in 2004?

Unfinished Business

When a presidential term ends, historians who follows its course are prone to think, "Well, that's done." And similarly with a political campaign: "We know who won, so that's finished." This sense of finality is an illusion, of course, conjured up by the natural form of historical narrative, which calls for beginnings and endings. The reality, in President Bush's case, was not of anything concluded but, on the contrary, as events continued to unfold, of a cascade of problems and uncertainties—what we might characterize as unfinished business. In this final section, we attempt a preliminary accounting of that post-2004 unfinished business.

A Wounded Presidency

George W. Bush outran the clock on Iraq in the 2004 campaign. But the problems kept coming. If the insurgency was bad news, civil war was worse. By 2006, Sunnis and Shiites were at each other's throats. Iraq became a race between insurgent efforts at fomenting civil war and American efforts at establishing a stable government.

With no end in sight, recriminations over the Iraqi tangle kept bubbling up. In April 2006, half a dozen retired generals broke the military code of silence and called for Secretary Rumsfeld's resignation. "The commitment of our forces in this fight," charged Marine Lieutenant General Gregory Newbold in one widely quoted article, "was done with a casualness and swagger that are the special province of those who have never had to execute these missions—or bury the results." By the time General Newbold penned those searing words, 2,300 troops had died in Iraq, $300 billion had been spent, and public opinion had shifted decisively: 57 percent of Americans thought the war a mistake.

Bush's vulnerability was revealed most graphically when he approved a contract for a Dubai-owned company to operate American seaports. So vociferous was congressional opposition that the president backed down and scrapped the deal. Increasingly, he came under attack from his own base: from Christian conservatives who felt betrayed by Bush's postelection silence on the gay marriage amendment and from right-wingers who, when serious debate began in mid-2006, preferred a punitive solution to the problem of illegal immigrants. Bush's biggest asset, his can-do aura, was punctured by his administration's slow response to Hurricane Katrina, which devastated New Orleans in August 2005.

Meanwhile, Tom DeLay's K Street Project imploded. The lobbying scandals that brought it down cast a shadow on DeLay. Already under indictment for money laundering in the Texas gerrymandering scheme, he resigned from the House. His crony, ace lobbyist Jack Abramoff, fingered other senior Republicans before heading off to jail, and to top things off, in October 2006, a sex scandal brought down Republican congressman Mark Foley, a champion of family values, raising damaging questions about negligent oversight by the party leadership. As Democratic charges of a "culture of corruption" sank in, approval ratings for the Republican-dominated Congress sank to record lows.

The bill came due in the midterm elections. The Democrats regained control of the House and, against all odds (they needed to take five out of six contested Republican seats), captured the Senate by a single seat. Gone was the heady talk, sparked by Bush's 2004 victory, of a permanent Republican majority. A dramatic shift in the independent vote—something like 25 percent of independents who had gone for Bush in 2004 voted Democratic in 2006—did the trick. Moreover, Republicans lost control of six governorships and ten state legislatures, putting at risk the gerrymandered advantage they had so assiduously built in those states.

No one knew whether 2006 presaged a new political realignment or just a temporary Republican setback. But the immediate impact was evident, even before the returns were in. The Democrats, cowed by Iraq in 2004, had taken heart and made the midterm elections a referendum on the war. Finally acknowledging the war's unpopularity, President Bush began to give ground. He officially retired the phrase "stay the course," lowered his sights from a democratic Iraq to a stable Iraq, and indicated that he was open to suggestions. The day after the election, Secretary of Defense Rumsfeld resigned. Bush was bowing to a new reality: The opposition party controlled Congress.

In the American political system, however, it is the president, not Congress, who bestrides the country. Presidents such as Franklin D. Roosevelt and Ronald Reagan

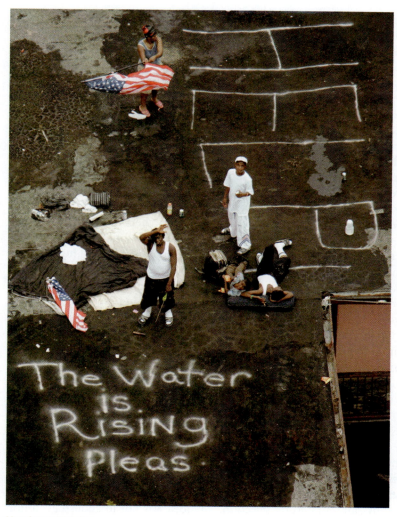

Hurricane Katrina

When Hurricane Katrina bore down on New Orleans on August 29, 2005, officials thought at first that the city had avoided the brunt of the storm, but the impact was great enough to breach the surrounding earthen dams and flood New Orleans, hitting hardest the lower-lying neighborhoods where poor blacks lived. Two days later, the people on the roof of this apartment house were still stranded and desperately awaiting rescue. Images like this one of suffering ghetto dwellers brought home a truth that many Americans had forgotten: A black underclass still exists in this country. © Smiley N. Pool/Dallas Morning News/Corbis.

For more help analyzing this image, see the Online Study Guide at **bedfordstmartins.com/henrettaconcise**.

make a huge difference, indelibly marking and perhaps even redefining the country. But even the least of incumbents, because of the power of the office, leave the historian with a lot to think about, including, most notably, what has been left unresolved. As his presidency wound down, that seemed likely to be a big part of George W. Bush's legacy: lots of unfinished business.

What Kind of America?

Terri Schiavo's tragedy could have happened in any family. She was a young woman who had fallen into a deep coma after a heart seizure in 1990. When her husband asked that her feeding tube be removed in 1998, her devoutly Catholic parents filed a lawsuit to stop him. On appeal, the Florida courts eventually ruled in the husband's favor. That normally would have concluded this family tragedy. Instead, conservative Republicans intervened, transforming Schiavo's plight into a right-to-life crusade. With much fanfare, Congress enacted emergency legislation on March 23, 2005, transferring the case to the federal courts — to no avail. The U.S. Supreme Court turned down a final appeal, and Terri Schiavo was allowed to die. An autopsy confirmed her irreversible vegetative state.

What was essentially symbolic in the Schiavo case became hugely consequential in the controversy over stem-cell research. Medical researchers discovered that stem cells, the embryonic cells that develop into specialized body-building cells, can be programmed to fight diseases and regenerate damaged organs, offering hope to millions of stricken Americans. But the stem cells have to be harvested from live embryos — albeit frozen specimens that were left unused at fertility clinics — and that provoked an outcry from right-to-life advocates. "There is no such thing as a spare embryo," intoned President Bush. He proposed that federal funding be continued, but only for projects utilizing the handful of existing stem-cell lines.

In making that compromise, the president acknowledged the painful choices posed by stem-cell research. It was difficult, in truth, to deny the benefits, not only medically, but also for America's scientific edge in the world (see American Voices, p. 963). Challenging Bush, California in 2002 passed a major bond issue for state-financed stem-cell research. Other states followed, and in July 2006, Congress defied the president and passed a bill funding stem-cell research, only to be defeated by Bush's veto.

On another front, the battle between science and faith raged over that old bugbear, Darwinism. In place of creationism, antievolutionists advanced a new theory, "intelligent design," which argued that some biological phenomena were too complex to be explained by random natural selection. The idea was not to abolish evolution but to offer intelligent design as an alternative and then to "teach the controversy." The courts, however, were having none of it. In a case involving the school district in Dover, Pennsylvania, a federal judge declared intelligent design just a screen for creationism and, like creationism, an unconstitutional intrusion of religion into the public schools.

In the nature of things, neither side completely prevails in such value-laden conflicts, although, in the case of stem-cell research, science may resolve the standoff by finding a way, as researchers reported in late 2007, of developing stem cells without using embryos. In the ebb and flow, it appeared that even with Bush behind them, faith-based conservatives had not gained the upper hand against science. An exception, probably temporary, was inside the federal government itself, where political appointees regularly stifled or ignored unwelcome scientific findings, such as those on the morning-after birth control pill and global warming. In the latter case, as the scientific consensus became overwhelming and the dire consequences for planet Earth

Uncommon Moms CANDI CUSHMAN

Embryonic stem-cell research ignited the same sense of moral outrage among Christian conservatives as did abortion. In the case of stem-cell research, however, the moral high ground was harder to maintain because of the hoped-for medical benefits. Although scientists were actively seeking alternative stem-cell sources, many Americans were impatient with the restrictions Bush had placed on federal funding of embryonic stem-cell research, and by 2004 opposition to the president's position, even by some Republicans, was increasing in Congress. In this article, we see the pro-life counterattack by Focus on the Family, the conservative organization. Since this article was published in 2004, there have been several breakthroughs in adult stem-cell research, that may resolve the controversy over embryonic stem-cell research.

Most credible scientists will admit that an embryo is a human being, with all of the DNA and chromosomes that a human being will ever need from birth to death. But some researchers and lawmakers don't want you to know that. Because they want you to think it should be legal to use federal funds to destroy this human being—so small that it is nothing more than a "dot," claimed one U.S. Senator—to help cure diseases like multiple sclerosis and Parkinson's. This sort of spin has convinced a majority of Americans to support embryonic stem cell research (ESCR)—in which a human embryo is destroyed while its stem cells are harvested. . . .

It might be easy for pro-life citizens . . . to feel discouraged. . . . They can take heart, however, because pro-life moms are walking the halls of Congress. And they're cutting through all that emotional hype by showing politicians the faces of the embryos they're proposing to kill.

One of those faces belongs to Mikayla Tesdall, a bouncy three-year-old girl with blond pigtails who loves to sing worship songs to whoever will listen. Mikayla is a Snowflake—the name given to six dozen adopted babies who began life as frozen embryos. Not too long ago, these crawling, talking toddlers were stored in the freezers of in-vitro fertilization clinics across the country. . . . until the Nightlight Christian Adoptions agency in California devised a way to rescue them by allowing infertile married couples to adopt them. Thus began an amazing process, in which Mikayla's adoptive mother, Sharon, had the little girl implanted in her womb as an embryo. . . .

And that personal experience has transformed Tesdall and other formerly apolitical moms into passionate pro-life warriors. They've been surprisingly effective, gaining access to places even some of the slickest lobbyists can't get into, like the White House. . . . They had a singular mission in mind: presenting Democrats and Republicans alike with undeniable proof that a human being is sacred and worth protecting at any stage—whether an embryo or a fully developed baby.

"What I had transferred inside me was a life," Tesdall said. "And it's because I love my child that I have to speak for those without voices—the other embryos. . . . God taught me through that process how to listen to Him . . . and I very clearly feel the presence of God and the Holy Spirit pointing me in this direction."

SOURCE: Candi Cushman, "Uncommon Moms," *Citizen Magazine*. Copyright © 2004 Focus on the Family. http://www.family.org/cforum/citizenmag/features/a0035021.cfm

incontrovertible — the glaciers really were melting! — the administration began to give way, at least rhetorically, with talk about joining a global treaty to reduce carbon emissions. And while Bush's appointees at the Environmental Protection Agency still threw up roadblocks, they were clearly engaged only in a holding action against inexorable pressures for tighter, more effective environmental regulation.

Where science cannot be invoked — as, for example, on gay marriage — social conservatives did better; and on abortion, their pre-eminent issue, the legal terrain shifted in their favor.

As a campaigner, Bush made no bones about his intentions: He meant to appoint conservative judges. In the first term, his lower court nominees provoked fierce, if ultimately futile, opposition from Senate Democrats. In 2005, with Justice Sandra Day O'Connor's retirement and Chief Justice William Rehnquist's death, two Supreme Court seats opened up. In finding replacements, President Bush was the beneficiary of a remarkable conservative project, dating back to the early 1980s, to prepare a future Supreme Court. Candidates were identified in law school, awarded prestigious clerkships, brought into the Reagan administration for seasoning, and then appointed to the federal bench. Bush's nominees, John G. Roberts and Samuel Alito, both appellate federal judges, were graduates of that conservative project. They were superbly qualified jurists and hence, despite their avowed conservatism, invulnerable to Democratic attack.

Although much else was at stake, the litmus test was abortion, as Bush discovered when, prior to Alito, he nominated his White House counsel, Harriet Myers, to the Court. Distrusting her pro-life bona fides, social conservatives erupted in fury and forced the president to withdraw her nomination. Even so, while well pleased with Roberts and Alito, pro-lifers could not expect miracles from them. Both appointees had said as much when, under close Senate questioning, they expressed respect for settled precedent, including *Roe v. Wade*. However, that did not stop them from reversing a seven-year-old decision that had upheld the legality of partial-birth (or late-stage) abortions, although they declined to join Justices Thomas and Scalia in a separate opinion rejecting *Roe v. Wade* itself.

If the battle over reproductive rights remained unsettled, the same could not be said for the American judiciary, which was moving unambiguously to the right. The spring 2007 term produced a notable range of decisions — on school integration, equal job opportunity, free speech, and corporate interests — that broke on the conservative side, all by 5 to 4. It appears that the conservative project, twenty years in the making, has been accomplished.

Among the challenges facing the new Court, none was likely to be more consequential than adjudicating the limits on presidential powers in post-9/11 America. After the terrorist attack, Attorney General John Ashcroft proclaimed a new "paradigm of prevention." A dragnet swept through Muslim communities, calling on 80,000 immigrants to register and be fingerprinted. About 5,000 foreign nationals were imprisoned, held in a kind of preventive detention on minor charges. On another front, applying the Patriot Act aggressively, the Justice Department launched a massive information-gathering effort that drew on the customer records of financial firms, Internet providers, and telecommunications companies. Despite growing disquiet, Congress reauthorized the Patriot Act in early 2006 with only cosmetic changes.

The administration was not satisfied, however, with the powers granted it by Congress. In December 2005, the *New York Times* published a bombshell: a secret National Security Agency (NSA) program that violated the Federal Information Surveillance Act by eavesdropping on telephone and e-mail traffic between domestic and foreign sites without court warrants. At congressional hearings, Ashcroft's successor, Attorney General Alberto Gonzales, was unrepentant. He refused to divulge any particulars about the NSA program on grounds of national security, and he invoked, as legal justification, the president's inherent powers as commander in chief. Presidents in every major war, Gonzales argued, had invoked the powers that Bush now claimed.

But they had not done so behind Congress's back. Bush's secret NSA order, in fact, rested on more than security concerns. It expressed a bold effort to regain executive powers that leading members of the administration—especially Vice President Cheney and Secretary of Defense Rumsfeld, both once Nixon appointees—believed had been lost after Watergate (see Chapter 29). They espoused a "unitary" presidency, that is, a presidency superior to Congress and the judiciary. Most telling was Bush's aggressive (if unpublicized) use of "signing statements" accompanying new laws, which declared his authority to ignore the portions of the laws of which he disapproved. The libertarian Cato Institute, a pillar of the conservative establishment, concluded, after surveying the record, that "far from defending the Constitution, President Bush has repeatedly sought to strip out the limits the document places on federal power."

What made this offensive possible, however, was national security, and that became the terrain of legal battle. The defining issue involved the treatment of Al Qaeda and Taliban detainees whom the administration had declared "unlawful combatants" and, as such, not entitled to the rights either of prisoners of war under the Geneva Conventions or of criminals under American law. Their treatment was strictly up to the executive branch, and, indeed, in devising a policy, it acted irregularly, bypassing its own normal channels and delegating the task to a few lawyers operating out of the vice president's office. The torture authorized by this policy—of which that at Abu Ghraib was only the most notorious—blackened America's reputation abroad, while at home the detainee program became entangled in ever-mounting legal challenges.

On June 29, 2006, *Hamdan v. Rumsfeld* struck down the military tribunals that had been set up to try the detainees being held at Guantanamo. The Supreme Court declared that the Geneva Conventions on prisoners of war applied to the detainees, that the tribunals fell short of "the judicial guarantees which are recognized as indispensable by all civilized peoples," and that, in any case, such tribunals required congressional authorization. By declaring that he had no "blank check," the Court challenged Bush's prosecution of the War on Terror at a fundamental level and forced him to turn to Congress.

In the hard bargaining that followed, Bush mostly prevailed. The Military Commissions Act of 2006 granted him the missing authorization, with only limited procedural constraints on the tribunals and considerable flexibility on interrogation methods. But court challenges kept coming—especially over the denial of habeas corpus to foreign detainees—and the constitutional issues remained far from resolved. The War on Terror differed from previous wars because, as President Bush was fond of saying, it had no discernible end. So this time, the country cannot wait for peace to restore constitutional protections. How Americans strike the balance between security and civil liberties remains an open question, with the danger, as one critic put it, of sacrificing for the sake of security "the very values we are fighting for."

On domestic policy, Bush's big idea, generated by right-wing think tanks, was an "ownership society." Ownership implied property, and in the American value system, property almost always trumped the public interest. Let the people do for themselves, an ownership society proclaimed, and get intrusive government out of the way. As a first installment, Bush added a provision to the 2003 drug-benefit bill encouraging people to buy low-cost (high-deductible) private insurance by offering tax-sheltered health savings accounts that would be drawn on for routine medical expenses. Then, after his 2004 triumph, he raised his sights. In the name of reforming Social Security, Bush proposed that a portion of the payroll tax be diverted into separate accounts that could be invested in the stock market. Unlike Social Security proper, with its guaranteed payout, the individual would own the account, free to seek higher returns but at a greater risk.

Despite a strenuous sales campaign, Bush's plan for privatizing Social Security fell flat. It seemed that, at least for their old age, Americans preferred a guaranteed monthly check. The hallmark of an ownership society was, of course, ever-lower taxes ("it's your money," Bush liked to say), but here too, the president was stymied. He could not budge the Democratic opposition into making his tax cuts of 2001 and 2003 permanent.

The stalemate, however, cut both ways. The veto is a potent weapon for any president, however weakened, and although Bush had not used the veto even once in his first term, now he wielded it freely, even on so politically charged an issue as children's health. Four million American children lacked any medical insurance, but when Democrats proposed bringing these children into an existing state-run program, Bush said no. It would cost too much, tempt families to drop private plans, and only advance "the Democrats' goal of a government-run health system." Bush vetoed the measure, and despite defections by nervous Republicans, his veto stuck.

The president was taking his stand for an ownership society. But whether Americans would follow, whether they were prepared to accept the accompanying hazards, no one knew. In certain ways, America really was becoming more of an ownership society, as pensions gave way to 401(k) plans—a private-sector counterpart, in effect, to Bush's plan for Social Security—and home ownership surged, thanks to low interest rates and lax lending standards. Rising stock and housing prices certainly underscored the advantages of ownership.

But the post-9/11 boom also contained manifold hazards. In the swift-moving economy, job security was becoming a memory. Employers shifted escalating health-care costs to employees, while forty-seven million Americans lacked medical insurance altogether. Despite a robust economy—gross domestic product grew by 18 percent after 2001—the number of Americans in poverty increased to 36.5 million, and the median real income of working-age families dropped, something that had never before happened in a time of economic expansion. They kept spending, but only by borrowing. Consumer debt doubled in six years, throwing the national savings rate into *negative* territory. In Bush's ownership society, it seemed, only the rich came out ahead—the top 5 percent whose income kept rising while everyone else's fell behind.

Then, in 2007, the red-hot housing market faltered. The subprime lending that had underwritten the boom turned sour as prices dropped, and overstretched home buyers defaulted on their mortgages. In a new financial wrinkle, these mortgages had been repackaged in complex ways as mortgage-based securities, whose value suddenly tanked. In July 2007, two Bear Stearns hedge funds operating in this market failed, signaling a crisis that soon forced even the nation's mightiest banks, such as Citigroup and Bank of America, to take write-downs on their mortgage-based holdings that mounted into the billions. As credit markets froze, the economy fell into recession, but it was different from the usual cyclical downturn because, like the boom-and-bust cycle that ushered in the Great Depression, this one exposed a failing financial system.

In the 1930s, the New Deal responded by regulating Wall Street. The subprime debacle of 2007 is likely to trigger a second regulatory era. In the back-and-forth between conservative and liberal, the question has always been: Should the government do more or less? In uncertain times, like 2008, the country's answer is generally for more government and that, by definition, means a loss of faith in Bush's ownership society.

What Kind of World?

Generals say that no military strategy survives the first battle of war. The same might be said of diplomacy, certainly of President Bush's diplomacy. At the outset, he operated on the presumption of America's world primacy. Iraq swiftly exposed one fallacy. As an instrument of foreign policy, America's military power proved sorely wanting; it was a better diplomatic weapon held in reserve than unleashed. More fundamentally, however, the administration overestimated its post–Cold War supremacy. Other nations did not submit gladly, and had they been so inclined, Bush's early unilateralism—his actions on global warming, arms reductions treaties, and Iraq—finished off that possibility.

By the time Bush realized his mistake, in mid-2003, the harm had been done. Thereafter, his administration scrambled to rebuild coalitions, enlist the United Nations, and manage diplomatically problems he had once thought resolvable by force or bluster. In the realm of foreign affairs, the nation's unfinished business was mainly about a chastened superpower struggling to catch up with events that had spun out of control.

Beyond anyone's expectations, the end of the Cold War altered the world's diplomatic landscape. The European Union (EU) expanded to the east, integrating the nations of central Europe into its ranks. Communist China turned toward capitalism, seized the opportunities of globalization, and challenged Japan for the leadership of East Asia. Oil-rich Muslim nations, stretching across the Middle East to Kazakhstan and south to Indonesia, grew increasingly conscious of their wealth, religious identity, and potential geopolitical power. The old categories of the Cold War—Free World, Communist World, Third World—broke down, and despite America's military supremacy, a new multipolar system was emerging.

The European Union now embraced twenty-five countries and 450 million people, the third largest population in the world, behind China and India, and accounted for a fifth of all global imports and exports. Its money—the euro—emerged as one of the world's preferred currencies for international exchange.

Thanks to its declining value on world currency markets, the American dollar was no longer supreme. The EU, however, was far from becoming a European version of the United States. Internal tensions ran deep, as became clear in the splintered response to Iraq, and resistance to a supranational EU authority in Brussels was, if anything, intensifying. European countries, moreover, preferred social programs to armies and posed no military challenge to the United States. Even so, the old commonality of interest was gone, and on a variety of issues, Europe was as much a rival as an ally of the United States.

In China's case, the tilt was emphatically toward rivalry. A vast nation of 1.3 billion people, China became the fastest-growing economy in the world. The Bush administration welcomed China's embrace of capitalism, and American consumers were beneficiaries of its cheap exports. But the economic tensions were many—over the enormous trade imbalance ($170 billion in 2004), over millions of American jobs lost, over rampant pirating of American intellectual property, over lead paint in children's toys. China remained a one-party state, and that produced tensions over human rights. And as China flexed its muscles, it threatened America's interests in East Asia and became an increasingly formidable rival worldwide.

As China's economy grew, so did its appetite for oil, and so, consequently, did world oil prices. While American consumers grumbled about paying $4.00 a gallon for gasoline, policymakers worried about the empowering of oil-producing countries. This was most evident in the case of Russia, which, after reeling economically in the 1990s, revived on a surge of oil revenues. In 2001, George Bush said that he had looked into President Vladimir Putin's soul and found that he was a good guy. That was when Russia was down. Putin turned out not to be such a good guy when Russia got back on its feet. He took authoritarian control at home, threatened neighboring former Soviet republics, and stood up to the United States in various ways. He was, with some success, reasserting Russia's place in the world. In a lesser way, oil money emboldened Iran and even a bloc of South American countries led by rabidly anti-Yankee Hugo Chavez of Venezuela. For the United States, higher oil prices meant less global leverage.

Where its weakened leverage registered most was in America's uphill struggle to contain the spread of atomic weapons. During the Cold War, only the Big Five—the United States, Britain, France, the Soviet Union, and China—plus Israel possessed nuclear arms. Most nations adhered to the Nuclear Non-Proliferation Treaty of 1968, which was policed by the International Atomic Energy Agency (IAEA).

Two of the nonsignatories, India and Pakistan, spurred by their bitter rivalry over Kashmir, secretly developed nuclear weapons during the 1990s. In a rogue operation, the Pakistani nuclear scientist Dr. A. Q. Khan sold two other Muslim states, Libya and Iran, nuclear designs and equipment. Pakistan also traded the technology to Communist North Korea in exchange for missiles targeted at India.

North Korea, a desperately poor Stalinist country, bet the house on nuclear weapons development, which it used variously as blackmail to extract aid and as insurance against real and imagined enemies. The Clinton administration had offered food, oil, and a nuclear power plant, but the agreement broke down in the late 1990s amid bitter recriminations and well-founded charges of North Korean cheating. The Bush administration wanted to crack down, but having failed to bring along China, Russia, and

South Korea, it had to settle for more talk. Evidently seeing the U.S. invasion of Iraq as an object lesson, North Korea rushed ahead with its nuclear program. In October 2006, it conducted an underground test of a nuclear device.

Iran played a more devious game. A signatory of the Non-Proliferation Treaty, Iran took the position that, while not wanting nuclear weapons, it had a right under the treaty to develop peaceful nuclear energy. Learning how to enrich plant-grade uranium, however, opens the path to weapons-grade uranium. In 2002, Iranian dissidents alerted the IAEA to secret nuclear sites, and while the Iran government adamantly denied it, everyone else concluded that they were bent on building atomic bombs. As with North Korea, the Bush administration took a tough line, including, until it became entangled in Iraq, a credible military threat. After that, the United States was reduced to a mix of diplomacy and economic sanctions, but as with North Korea, its efforts have been hobbled by Russia and China, both with economic stakes in Iran. Meanwhile, Iranian elections unexpectedly produced a hard-line Islamic president, Mahmoud Ahmadinejad, who regularly threatened destruction of Israel. In April 2006, Ahmadinejad triumphantly announced that Iran had mastered the enrichment process for plant-grade uranium.

Nuclear diplomacy, however, is a murky world, full of surprises. One such surprise was Libya, which suddenly abandoned a costly nuclear black-market program in 2003 and came in from the diplomatic cold. In late 2007, with its bomb stockpile a bigger bargaining chip, North Korea signaled a willingness to do likewise in exchange for hefty aid and normalized relations with the United States. To the dismay of hard-liners, Bush did not say no.

Even Iran became a question mark when the U.S. intelligence estimate of 2007 concluded that, contrary to earlier findings, Iran's work on nuclear weapons had halted in 2003. If the implications were unclear (uranium enrichment, which Iran still pursued, mattered far more for a nuclear arms program than did bomb design), not so the administration's determination to keep Iran in nuclear check. But in a multipolar world, that was a tall order, even against an apocalyptic country like Iran.

In Iran's case, at least, there was a state to hold responsible. Utterly beyond America's experience was Islamic extremism that had no address. After 9/11, the global manhunt largely dismantled the Al Qaeda network. Thereafter, Osama bin Laden served far more as a symbolic than as an operational figure. But as a symbolic figure, he inspired many in the Muslim world. Al Qaeda metastasized into amorphous cells, unknown in number, operating more or less independently but with equally murderous intent. Suicide bombings took a heavy toll in Madrid, London, Bali, and, increasingly, in Muslim countries. This violence was only the entering wedge of anti-Western rage that permeated the Muslim world, a fact brought shockingly home to Europeans in early 2006 by widespread rioting after mocking cartoons of the prophet Muhammad were printed in a Danish newspaper.

In the past, the United States had regarded Islamic extremism as an internal problem of its Middle Eastern allies, generally turning a blind eye to their repressive tactics. In his second inaugural address, President Bush signaled a major policy shift. The United States, he proclaimed, was committed to ending tyranny around the world. In so doing, Bush revived the Wilsonian strain in American foreign policy — the conviction that the country's democratic principles should govern its dealings with the world—but with a harder edge than President Wilson ever imagined when he championed the League of Nations after World War I (see Chapter 22).

Convinced that democracy was the answer to Islamic radicalism, Bush pressed for political reform in the Middle East. But when, as a result, Egypt's regime eased up in the 2005 elections, the militant Muslim Brotherhood gained strength, prompting another government crackdown. Early in 2006, Palestinians voted for the hard-line Hamas, which was on America's list of terrorist organizations. Hamas took office but refused to disband its fighters, who in June 2007 turned on the Palestinian Authority's military in Gaza and split it off from the West Bank. In Lebanon, the radical Shiite Hezbollah pursued a similar double-breasted strategy, participating in elections but maintaining armed control of its own region and, in July 2006, provoking a savage Israeli response that devastated much of Lebanon. Participating in elections, it seemed, was no antidote to Islamic extremism.

Pakistan epitomized America's dilemma but with far more at stake. Ever since gaining independence in 1947, Pakistan has swung into and out of military rule, always on the verge of genuine democracy but never quite achieving it. In 1999, another army coup brought General Pervez Musharraf to power. Islamic radicalism made headway under his regime, and so did the Taliban, as Pakistan's proxy in next-door Afghanistan. After 9/11, Musharraf turned abruptly against the Taliban and, to America's relief, became an ally in the War on Terror. But Musharraf did not, or could not, control the tribal border provinces, havens from which the Taliban returned in force to Afghanistan and from which Al Qaeda and allied Islamic extremists mounted ever bloodier attacks on the Pakistani heartland. As Musharraf's regime became increasingly unstable, the United States pressed for greater democracy, only to see its plans collapse with the assassination of former Prime Minister Benazir Bhutto on December 27, 2007. The nightmare scenario is for this Muslim nation of eighty million, armed with nuclear weapons, to fall into chaos and/or extremist domination.

In Pakistan, of course, the United States was mostly an anxious bystander. Iraq, however, was Bush's project. Under American prodding, Iraqis held two national elections, wrote a constitution, established a parliament, and, in May 2006, after much wrangling, installed a prime minister. Beneath the formalities, however, Iraqi politics ran strictly along ethnic and sectarian lines. The dominant Shiite parties answered to their respective clerics and, as with Hamas and Hezbollah, maintained their private militias even while participating in the new government. Insurgent attacks, capped by the bombing of a revered Samarra mosque in February 2006, finally pushed the Shiites over the edge. Their militias began in earnest to retaliate against Sunnis, utilizing death squads that were hardly distinguishable from the official police. As the carnage spread, a de facto partitioning began, with mass migrations from mixed Sunni-Shiite areas, and civil war became a real possibility (Map 32.2).

The Bush administration managed to drag the warring sides back from the abyss by a "surge" of 30,000 more troops, announced in January 2007. Simultaneously, evidently by coincidence, the insurgency began to fracture, with many of the Sunni tribes turning against the Al Qaeda–inspired extremists and allying with the Americans. After some of the bloodiest months of the war, violence declined markedly in the second half of 2007. But a fully operational Iraqi military remained years away.

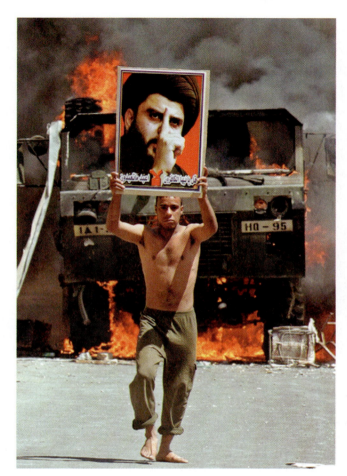

Chaos in Iraq

No figure was more adept at inciting chaos in Iraq than the young radical Shiite cleric Moqtada al-Sadr, who had a huge following among the Shiite poor, especially in the Baghdad slums. Here, he is pictured in the poster held aloft by a supporter celebrating the burning of a U.S. Army truck after an American action in the Shula neighborhood of Baghdad. Initially, al-Sadr aimed his ire at the invading Americans, but with the intensification of sectarian strife, he turned his death squads loose on the Sunnis while also becoming, in 2006, a powerful behind-the-scenes player in the new Iraqi government. Al-Sadr was emblematic of the subterranean complexities of Iraqi society that flummoxed the Bush administration when it undertook to bring democracy to Iraq.
© Ceerwan Aziz/Reuters/Corbis.

Shiite-Sunni reconciliation seemed equally remote as the two sides jockeyed over oil revenues and power-sharing, while the third major ethnic group, the Kurds in the north, seemed bent on quasi-independence. Congressional Democrats argued that the Shiite-dominated government would remain ineffective as long as the American crutch was there. But Bush, with his veto power intact, warded off their demands for early troop withdrawals.

In an unguarded moment, Bush had remarked that Iraq would be a problem for the next administration. His admission is an apt epitaph for the Iraq adventure. Six months and out—that was what the Pentagon hawks had expected. They never imagined that this sideshow—a quick victory on the way to bigger and better things—would bog down the Bush administration and become its defining event. They had misread the nature of global politics: Problems that force was meant to solve can turn around and bite you back.

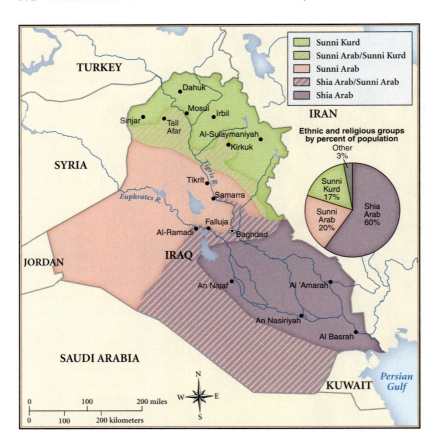

MAP 32.2 Ethnoreligious Groups in Iraq, 2008
Like other Middle Eastern countries, Iraq did not have a homogeneous population. It was divided along religious lines between Sunni and Shiite Muslims (plus some Christians and, until they fled to Israel after 1948, many Jews) and ethnically among Arabs, Kurds, and Turkomen. When Iraq had been created under a League of Nations mandate after World War I, the British, who were in charge, installed the minority Sunni as the dominant political element, an arrangement that persisted until the United States toppled Saddam Hussein in 2003. The bitter internal strife that ensued stems from long-standing ethnoreligious divisions in Iraq, and among the possible outcomes, one is a de facto division of the country into autonomous Shiite, Sunni, and Kurdish regions.

Even if the best happened, if against the odds Iraq held together, in global terms America would still have failed because, in Islamic eyes, the Iraqi involvement had fatally tainted Western-style democracy. It had undercut Bush's global strategy for turning the tide against Islamic militancy, tarnished America's leadership in the world, and complicated its battle against nuclear proliferation. And if, by chance, Iraq went badly, the entire Middle East could go up in flames. The awful realization dawned that beyond the cost in blood and treasure, Iraq had exacted a terrible toll on America's strategic interests in the world.

Departing presidents, although they wield full executive powers until the last day, tend to fade politically as they become, in the cruel lingo of the pundits, "lame ducks." No twentieth-century president faded so much, however, or became so lame a duck, as did George W. Bush. So toxic had he become—his disapproval rating ranged close to 80 percent—that he neither attended his own party's convention nor, despite his zest for it, did any campaigning for the ticket. How to craft a Republican campaign after eight years of a Bush presidency? That was the party's abiding problem in 2008.

If any candidate held the answer, it was the Republican nominee, Senator John McCain of Arizona. McCain was a veteran lawmaker, an authentic war hero, and famously independent. He had challenged Bush in the 2000 primaries, and thereafter, even during the President's glory days, he defied party discipline and opposed the administration on tax cuts for the rich, campaign finance reform, torture of prisoners, and prosecution of the Iraq war. But McCain realized that making a run for the White House meant first securing the Republican base. So he made peace with evangelical leaders he had earlier denounced as "agents of intolerance." He reversed himself on the Bush tax cuts and, step by step, moderated his Republican unorthodoxy. Most telling was his selection of Sarah Palin, a small-town mayor recently elected governor of Alaska, as his running mate. A Pentecostal Christian and avid right-to-lifer, the young and telegenic Palin became the darling of the Republican right, but not of the many moderates and independents who considered her unqualified for the vice-presidency. Palin's nomination encapsulated McCain's dilemma. Was he running as the great American "maverick" or as more of the same, just (as Democrats liked to say) for Bush's third term?

His Democratic opponent, Barack Obama, also faced daunting, if different, challenges. In a bruising primary campaign, he had overtaken the front-runner Hillary Rodham Clinton with a remarkable display of grass-roots organizing and soaring oratory. But her unexpected defeat, and with it the lost chance for America's first woman president, was a bitter pill for Senator Clinton's loyal supporters. Winning them over was Obama's first challenge. Second was to make the country comfortable with him personally. The product of a mixed marriage, a Kenyan father and Kansas-born mother, Obama had lived as a child in Indonesia and grown up under his grandmother's care in Hawaii. Were Americans ready for a black president, and one with so exotic a background to boot? Finally, there was the question of Obama's readiness. He was forty-seven years old, a first-term senator from Illinois, and before that a state senator, part-time law professor, and Chicago community organizer. Was he really prepared for the White House? Midway through the primary season, in answer to Clinton's jibes, Obama toned down the rhetoric about "change" and began more prosaically to address issues of national policy. And he took care, in choosing a running mate, to select a senator deeply experienced in foreign affairs, Joseph Biden of Delaware. Still, despite his natural advantage as the anti-incumbent candidate, Obama failed to gain traction against McCain. When the conventions adjourned, pollsters declared the contest a dead heat.

Then, in mid-September, the simmering mortgage-related economic crisis suddenly worsened. Forced to write down huge losses, financial giants began to run out of capital. The U.S. Treasury intervened massively, but in a major miscalculation, it let the investment bank Lehman Brothers go under. Panic erupted around the world and the financial system essentially froze. Not even the prospect of a $700 billion bailout got the system going again.

TIMELINE

2000 ► George W. Bush wins contested presidential election

2001 ► Al Qaeda terrorists attack World Trade Center and Pentagon on September 11

► Congress passes USA PATRIOT Act

2002 ► No Child Left Behind Act becomes law

► United States defeats Taliban in Afghanistan

2003 ► United States invades Iraq in March

2004 ► Torture at Abu Ghraib prison revealed

► Bush wins reelection

2005 ► Bush's attempt at privatizing Social Security fails

► Hurricane Katrina devastates Gulf Coast

► John G. Roberts appointed chief justice of Supreme Court

► Secret NSA domestic eavesdropping program revealed

2006 ► Samuel A. Alito appointed to Supreme Court, securing conservative majority

► Iran announces successful uranium enrichment program; North Korea tests nuclear device

► *Hamdan v. Rumsfeld* (2006) strikes down military tribunals for Guantanamo prisoners

► President Bush vetoes stem-cell research bill

► Democrats regain control of Congress

2007 ► "Surge" of 30,000 additional troops for Iraq; Sunni insurgency slows

► Onset of subprime mortgage crisis; economy slides into recession

2008 ► Barack Obama elected president; Bush era ends

This was a financial crisis beyond anything since the Great Depression. That was how economists assessed it. Ordinary Americans measured it by the wreckage of their lives. The 401(k) accounts on which they counted for retirement were decimated by the plunging stock market. One in five home owners—not counting the hundreds of thousands facing foreclosures—was "under water," with houses worth less than their mortgages. Small businesses found themselves cut off from long-established lines of bank credit. As the economy contracted, anxiety spread about looming job losses and lost health insurance.

In hard times, the party in power takes the blame, deserved or undeserved. This time the blame was deserved. It was something to behold when Alan Greenspan, Republican guru of free markets and revered former head of the Federal Reserve, took the chair at a congressional hearing and publicly confessed his error. The market, it turned out, wasn't as perfect or self-correcting as he had thought. For McCain's campaign, the financial crisis was devastating. For one thing, it blotted out his great advantage, that he was the stronger candidate on national security. That McCain might have been right about the "surge" in Iraq now seemed of little consequence. Moreover, economics was not his strong suit. He had said so himself. When the financial crisis struck, McCain responded erratically and unconvincingly. In the end, he fell back on the Republican mantra of cutting taxes. In his frustration, McCain lashed out at his opponent and the campaign turned uglier.

Obama, for his part, kept his cool. He proved, in fact, to be a man of exceptional composure and self-possession. His focus was on rescuing the middle class. He proposed a stimulus package, a 90-day moratorium on foreclosures, aid to cash-strapped states and cities, and extended unemployment benefits. For the longer term, he put forth a program of financial re-regulation, a more equitable tax structure, and expanded health insurance. Months of relentless exposure, plus a steady performance in three debates, quieted doubts about Obama's readiness. With his cool demeanor and evident mastery of complex issues, he gave the impression that he, if anyone, could handle the nation's problems.

On November 4, 2008, the people spoke. Barack Obama scored a ringing victory, taking 53 percent of the popular vote—the first Democratic president to win by an outright majority since Jimmy Carter in 1976—and a better than 2-to-1 margin in the Electoral College. The first thing that struck the country was that it had elected a black president. The race issue had in fact been muffled during the campaign, thanks to McCain's restraint, but now, in his concession speech, McCain spoke movingly of Obama's victory as a turning of the page on the nation's racist past. The ecstatic crowd greeting Obama in Chicago made it evident that many, many Americans shared McCain's feelings. Obama's victory also signaled generational change. As the first post-1960s president, he was unscarred by past culture wars and maybe capable, as he promised, of reconciling a divided country. Finally, Obama's victory revealed tectonic

Election Night, Chicago
Barack and Michelle Obama take in the cheers of a jubilant crowd at Grant Park after his victory speech.
© Shawn Thew/epa/Corbis.

shifts in the electorate. He had not only energized the black vote, but won over Hispanics, single women, and white-collar suburbanites, changing America's blue/red voting map and shifting such Republican strongholds as North Carolina, Virginia, Colorado, and Indiana into the Democratic column.

Now, with the White House and Congress in their hands, it was up to the Democrats. The problems they faced were daunting—draining wars in Iraq and Afghanistan, diplomatic challenges galore, energy shortages, health care crises, a failed financial system, and an economy beggared by years of excess. It was by no means clear that Barack Obama, despite his campaign promises, had the answers, any more than had President Roosevelt when he took office in the throes of the Great Depression. By creating the New Deal, FDR inaugurated a half-century of American liberalism. That era ended with Ronald Reagan's presidency. Was a new liberal era beginning? No one knew. Everything depends on what Barack Obama makes of the mandate the American people have given him.

FOR FURTHER EXPLORATION

A good starting point for learning about President Bush's background is Bill Minutaglia, *First Son: George W. Bush and the Bush Family Dynasty* (1999). Cass R. Sunstein and Richard A. Epstein, eds., *The Vote: Bush, Gore, and the Supreme Court* (2001), is an assessment by a range of legal scholars on *Bush v. Gore*. Two sympathetic accounts of President Bush's leadership are David Frum, *The Right Man: The Surprise Presidency of George W. Bush* (2003), and Fred Barnes, *Rebel-in-Chief: Inside the Bold and Controversial Presidency of George W. Bush* (2006). Bush's domestic record is treated less kindly by Bruce Bartlett, *Impostor: How George W. Bush Bankrupted America and Betrayed the Reagan Legacy* (2006); Douglas Brinkley, *The Great Deluge: Hurricane Katrina, New Orleans, and the Mississippi Gulf Coast* (2006); and the recently retired head of the Federal Reserve, Alan Greenspan, *The Age of Turbulence: Adventures in a New World* (2007).

On the aftermath of 9/11, see Richard A. Clarke, *Against All Enemies: Inside America's War on Terror* (2004); Seymour M. Hersh, *Chain of Command: The Road from 9/11 to Abu Ghraib* (2004); James Risen, *State of War: The Secret History of the CIA and Bush Administration* (2006); and Bob Woodward, *Plan of Attack* (2004). The architects of Bush's foreign policy are treated in Jacob Heilbrunn, *They Knew They Were Right: The Rise of the Neocons* (2007). Especially informative about the prosecution of the Iraq war is Michael R. Gordon and Bernard R. Trainor, *Cobra II: The Inside Story of the Invasion and Occupation of Iraq* (2006). Joseph Margulies, *Guantanamo and the Abuse of Presidential Power* (2006), is by a lawyer for one of the detainees. A scholarly treatment of the constitutional issues is Bruce Ackerman, *Before the Next Attack: Preserving Civil Liberties in an Age of Terrorism* (2006).

Two PBS Web sites—**www.pbs.org/frontline/insurgency** and **www.pbs.org/wgbh/pages/frontline/storm**—offer interviews, analysis, and links concerning the Iraqi insurgency and the aftermath of Hurricane Katrina, as well as access to the *Frontline* documentaries on both subjects.

TEST YOUR KNOWLEDGE

To assess your mastery of the material in this chapter and for Web sites, images, and documents related to this chapter, visit **bedfordstmartins.com/henrettaconcise**.

Documents

The Declaration of Independence

The Unanimous Declaration of the Thirteen United States of America

When in the Course of human events, it becomes necessary for one people to dissolve the political bands which have connected them with another, and to assume among the Powers of the earth, the separate and equal station to which the Laws of Nature and of Nature's God entitle them, a decent respect to the opinions of mankind requires that they should declare the causes which impel them to the separation.

We hold these truths to be self-evident, that all men are created equal, that they are endowed by their Creator with certain unalienable rights, that among these are Life, Liberty, and the pursuit of Happiness. That to secure these rights, Governments are instituted among Men, deriving their just powers from the consent of the governed. That whenever any Form of Government becomes destructive of these ends, it is the Right of the People to alter or to abolish it, and to institute new Government, laying its foundation on such principles and organizing its powers in such form, as to them shall seem most likely to effect their Safety and Happiness. Prudence, indeed, will dictate that Governments long established should not be changed for light and transient causes; and accordingly all experience hath shown, that mankind are more disposed to suffer, while evils are sufferable, than to right themselves by abolishing the forms to which they are accustomed. But when a long train of abuses and usurpations, pursuing invariably the same Object evinces a design to reduce them under absolute Despotism, it is their right, it is their duty, to throw off such Government, and to provide new Guards for their future security. — Such has been the patient sufferance of these Colonies; and such is now the necessity which constrains them to alter their former Systems of Government. The history of the present King of Great Britain is a history of repeated injuries and usurpations, all having in direct object the establishment of an absolute Tyranny over these States. To prove this, let Facts be submitted to a candid world.

He has refused his Assent to Laws, the most wholesome and necessary for the public good.

He has forbidden his Governors to pass Laws of immediate and pressing importance, unless suspended in their operation till his Assent should be obtained; and, when so suspended, he has utterly neglected to attend to them.

He has refused to pass other Laws for the accommodation of large districts of people, unless those people would relinquish the right of Representation in the Legislature, a right inestimable to them and formidable to tyrants only.

He has called together legislative bodies at places unusual, uncomfortable, and distant from the depository of their public Records, for the sole purpose of fatiguing them into compliance with his measures.

He has dissolved Representative Houses repeatedly, for opposing with manly firmness his invasions on the rights of the people.

He has refused for a long time, after such dissolutions, to cause others to be elected; whereby the Legislative powers, incapable of Annihilation, have returned to the People at large for their exercise; the State remaining in the mean time exposed to all the dangers of invasion from without and convulsions within.

He has endeavoured to prevent the population of these States; for that purpose obstructing the Laws of Naturalization of Foreigners; refusing to pass others to encourage their migrations hither, and raising the conditions of new Appropriations of Lands.

He has obstructed the Administration of Justice, by refusing his Assent to Laws for establishing Judiciary powers.

He has made Judges dependent on his Will alone, for the tenure of their offices, and the amount and payment of their salaries.

He has erected a multitude of New Offices, and sent hither swarms of Officers to harass our People, and eat out their substance.

He has kept among us, in times of peace, Standing Armies without the Consent of our legislature.

He has combined with others to subject us to a jurisdiction foreign to our constitution, and unacknowledged by our laws; giving his Assent to their Acts of pretended Legislation:

For quartering large bodies of armed troops among us:

For protecting them, by a mock Trial, from Punishment for any Murders which they should commit on the Inhabitants of these States:

For cutting off our Trade with all parts of the world:

For imposing taxes on us without our Consent:

For depriving us in many cases, of the benefits of Trial by jury:

For transporting us beyond Seas to be tried for pretended offences:

For abolishing the free System of English Laws in a neighbouring Province, establishing therein an Arbitrary government, and enlarging its Boundaries so as to render it at once an example and fit instrument for introducing the same absolute rule into these Colonies:

For taking away our Charters, abolishing our most valuable Laws, and altering fundamentally the Forms of our Governments:

For suspending our own Legislatures, and declaring themselves invested with Power to legislate for us in all cases whatsoever.

He has abdicated Government here, by declaring us out of his Protection and waging War against us.

He has plundered our seas, ravaged our Coasts, burnt our towns, and destroyed the lives of our people.

He is at this time transporting large armies of foreign mercenaries to compleat the works of death, desolation, and tyranny, already begun with circumstances of Cruelty & perfidy scarcely paralleled in the most barbarous ages, and totally unworthy the Head of a civilized nation.

He has constrained our fellow Citizens taken Captive on the high Seas to bear Arms against their Country, to become the executioners of their friends and Brethren, or to fall themselves by their Hands.

He has excited domestic insurrections amongst us, and has endeavoured to bring on the inhabitants of our frontiers, the merciless Indian Savages, whose known rule of warfare, is an undistinguished destruction of all ages, sexes, and conditions.

In every stage of these Oppressions We have Petitioned for Redress in the most humble terms: Our repeated petitions have been answered only by repeated injury. A Prince, whose character is thus marked by every act which may define a Tyrant, is unfit to be the ruler of a free people.

Nor have We been wanting in attention to our British brethren. We have warned them from time to time of attempts by their legislature to extend an unwarrantable jurisdiction over us. We have reminded them of the circumstances of our emigration and settlement here. We have appealed to their native justice and magnanimity, and we have conjured them by the ties of our common kindred to disavow these usurpations, which, would inevitably interrupt our connections and correspondence. They too have been deaf to the voice of justice and of consanguinity. We must, therefore, acquiesce in the necessity, which denounces our Separation, and hold them, as we hold the rest of mankind, Enemies in War, in Peace Friends.

We, therefore, the Representatives of the United States of America, in General Congress, Assembled, appealing to the Supreme Judge of the world for the rectitude of our intentions, do, in the Name, and by Authority of the good People of these Colonies, solemnly publish and declare, That these United Colonies are, and of Right ought to be FREE AND INDEPENDENT STATES; that they are Absolved from all Allegiance to the British Crown, and that all political connection between them and the State of Great Britain, is and ought to be totally dissolved; and that as Free and Independent States, they have full Power to levy War, conclude Peace, contract Alliances, establish Commerce, and to do all other Acts and Things which Independent States may of right do. And for the support of this Declaration, with a firm reliance on the Protection of Divine Providence, we mutually pledge to each other our Lives, our Fortunes, and our sacred Honor.

John Hancock

Button Gwinnett	George Wythe	James Wilson	Josiah Bartlett
Lyman Hall	Richard Henry Lee	Geo. Ross	Wm. Whipple
Geo. Walton	Th. Jefferson	Caesar Rodney	Saml. Adams
Wm. Hooper	Benja. Harrison	Geo. Read	John Adams
Joseph Hewes	Thos. Nelson, Jr.	Thos. M'Kean	Robt. Treat Paine
John Penn	Francis Lightfoot Lee	Wm. Floyd	Elbridge Gerry
Edward Rutledge	Carter Braxton	Phil. Livingston	Step. Hopkins
Thos. Heyward, Junr.	Robt. Morris	Frans. Lewis	William Ellery

Thomas Lynch, Junr.	Benjamin Rush	Lewis Morris	Roger Sherman
Arthur Middleton	Benja. Franklin	Richd. Stockton	Sam'el Huntington
Samuel Chase	John Morton	Jno. Witherspoon	Wm. Williams
Wm. Paca	Geo. Clymer	Fras. Hopkinson	Oliver Wolcott
Thos. Stone	Jas. Smith	John Hart	Matthew Thornton
Charles Carroll of Carrollton	Geo. Taylor	Abra. Clark	

The Articles of Confederation and Perpetual Union

Between the states of New Hampshire, Massachusetts Bay, Rhode Island and Providence Plantations, Connecticut, New York, New Jersey, Pennsylvania, Delaware, Maryland, Virginia, North Carolina, South Carolina, Georgia.*

Article 1

The stile of this confederacy shall be "The United States of America."

Article 2

Each State retains its sovereignty, freedom and independence, and every power, jurisdiction, and right, which is not by this confederation expressly delegated to the United States, in Congress assembled.

Article 3

The said states hereby severally enter into a firm league of friendship with each other for their common defence, the security of their liberties and their mutual and general welfare; binding themselves to assist each other against all force offered to, or attacks made upon them, or any of them, on account of religion, sovereignty, trade, or any other pretence whatever.

Article 4

The better to secure and perpetuate mutual friendship and intercourse among the people of the different states in this union, the free inhabitants of each of these states, paupers, vagabonds, and fugitives from justice excepted, shall be entitled to all privileges and immunities of free citizens in the several states; and the people of each State shall have free ingress and regress to and from any other State, and shall enjoy therein all the privileges of trade and commerce, subject to the same duties, impositions, and restrictions, as the inhabitants thereof respectively; provided, that such restrictions shall not extend so far as to prevent the removal of property, imported into any State, to any other State of which the owner is an inhabitant; provided also, that no imposition,

---

*This copy of the final draft of the Articles of Confederation is taken from the *Journals,* 9:907–25, November 15, 1777.

duties, or restriction, shall be laid by any State on the property of the United States, or either of them.

If any person guilty of, or charged with treason, felony, or other high misdemeanor in any State, shall flee from justice and be found in any of the United States, he shall, upon demand of the governor or executive power of the State from which he fled, be delivered up and removed to the State having jurisdiction of his offence.

Full faith and credit shall be given in each of these states to the records, acts, and judicial proceedings of the courts and magistrates of every other State.

Article 5

For the more convenient management of the general interests of the United States, delegates shall be annually appointed, in such manner as the legislature of each State shall direct, to meet in Congress, on the 1st Monday in November in every year, with a power reserved to each State to recall its delegates, or any of them, at any time within the year, and to send others in their stead for the remainder of the year.

No State shall be represented in Congress by less than two, nor by more than seven members; and no person shall be capable of being a delegate for more than three years in any term of six years; nor shall any person, being a delegate, be capable of holding any office under the United States, for which he, or any other for his benefit, receives any salary, fees, or emolument of any kind.

Each State shall maintain its own delegates in a meeting of the states, and while they act as members of the committee of the states.

In determining questions in the United States, in Congress assembled, each State shall have one vote.

Freedom of speech and debate in Congress shall not be impeached or questioned in any court or place out of Congress: and the members of Congress shall be protected in their persons from arrests and imprisonments, during the time of their going to and from, and attendance on Congress, except for treason, felony, or breach of the peace.

Article 6

No State, without the consent of the United States, in Congress assembled, shall send any embassy to, or receive any embassy from, or enter into any conference, agreement, alliance, or treaty with any king, prince, or state; nor shall any person, holding any office of profit or trust under the United States, or any of them, accept of any present, emolument, office or title, of any kind whatever, from any king, prince, or foreign state; nor shall the United States, in Congress assembled, or any of them, grant any title of nobility.

No two or more states shall enter into any treaty, confederation, or alliance, what-ever, between them, without the consent of the United States, in Congress assembled, specifying accurately the purposes for which the same is to be entered into, and how long it shall continue.

No state shall lay any imposts or duties which may interfere with any stipula-tions in treaties entered into by the United States, in Congress assembled, with any king, prince, or state, in pursuance of any treaties already proposed by Congress to the courts of France and Spain.

No vessels of war shall be kept up in time of peace by any State, except such number only as shall be deemed necessary by the United States, in Congress assembled, for the defence of such State or its trade; nor shall any body of forces be kept up by any State, in time of peace, except such number only as, in the judgment of the United States, in Congress assembled, shall be deemed requisite to garrison the forts necessary for the defence of such State; but every State shall always keep up a well regulated and disciplined militia, sufficiently armed and accoutred, and shall provide, and constantly have ready for use, in public stores, a due number of field pieces and tents, and a proper quantity of arms, ammunition and camp equipage.

No State shall engage in any war without the consent of the United States, in Congress assembled, unless such State be actually invaded by enemies, or shall have received certain advice of a resolution being formed by some nation of Indians to invade such State, and the danger is so imminent as not to admit of a delay till the United States, in Congress assembled, can be consulted; nor shall any State grant commissions to any ships or vessels of war, nor letters of marque or reprisal, except it be after a declaration of war by the United States, in Congress assembled, and then only against the kingdom or state, and the subjects thereof, against which war has been so declared, and under such regulations as shall be established by the United States, in Congress assembled, unless such State be infested by pirates, in which case vessels of war may be fitted out for that occasion, and kept so long as the danger shall continue, or until the United States, in Congress assembled, shall determine otherwise.

Article 7

When land forces are raised by any State for the common defence, all officers of or under the rank of colonel, shall be appointed by the legislature of each State respectively, by whom such forces shall be raised, or in such manner as such State shall direct; and all vacancies shall be filled up by the State which first made the appointment.

Article 8

All charges of war and all other expences, that shall be incurred for the common defence or general welfare, and allowed by the United States, in Congress assembled, shall be defrayed out of a common treasury, which shall be supplied by the several states, in proportion to the value of all land within each State, granted to or surveyed for any person, as such land and the buildings and improvements thereon shall be estimated according to such mode as the United States, in Congress assembled, shall, from time to time, direct and appoint.

The taxes for paying that proportion shall be laid and levied by the authority and direction of the legislatures of the several states, within the time agreed upon by the United States, in Congress assembled.

Article 9

The United States, in Congress assembled, shall have the sole and exclusive right and power of determining on peace and war, except in the cases mentioned in the 6th article; of sending and receiving ambassadors; entering into treaties and alliances, provided that no treaty of commerce shall be made, whereby the legislative power of the respective states shall be restrained from imposing such imposts and duties on foreigners as their own people are subjected to, or from prohibiting the exportation or importation of any species of goods or commodities whatsoever; of establishing rules for deciding, in all cases, what captures on land or water shall be legal, and in what manner prizes, taken by land or naval forces in the service of the United States, shall be divided or appropriated; or granting letters of marque and reprisal in times of peace; appointing courts for the trial of piracies and felonies committed on the high seas, and establishing courts for receiving and determining, finally, appeals in all cases of captures; provided, that no member of Congress shall be appointed a judge of any of the said courts.

The United States, in Congress assembled, shall also be the last resort on appeal in all disputes and differences now subsisting, or that hereafter may arise between two or more states concerning boundary, jurisdiction or any other cause whatever; which authority shall always be exercised in the manner following: whenever the legislative or executive authority, or lawful agent of any State, in controversy with another, shall present a petition to Congress, stating the matter in question, and praying for a hearing, notice thereof shall be given, by order of Congress, to the legislative or executive authority of the other State in controversy, and a day assigned for the appearance of the parties by their lawful agents, who shall then be directed to appoint, by joint consent, commissioners or judges to constitute a court for hearing and determining the matter in question; but, if they cannot agree, Congress shall name three persons out of each of the United States, and from the list of such persons each party shall alternately strike out one, the petitioners beginning, until the number shall be reduced to thirteen; and from that number not less than seven, nor more than nine names, as Congress shall direct, shall, in the presence of Congress, be drawn out by lot; and the persons whose names shall be so drawn, or any five of them, shall be commissioners or judges to hear and finally determine the controversy, so always as a major part of the judges who shall hear the cause shall agree in the determination; and if either party shall neglect to attend at the day appointed, without shewing reasons which Congress shall judge sufficient, or, being present, shall refuse to strike, the Congress shall proceed to nominate three persons out of each State, and the secretary of Congress shall strike in behalf of such party absent or refusing; and the judgment and sentence of the court to be appointed, in the manner before prescribed, shall be final and conclusive; and if any of the parties shall refuse to submit to the authority of such court, or to appear or defend their claim or cause, the court shall nevertheless proceed to pronounce sentence or judgment, which shall, in like manner, be final and decisive, the judgment or sentence and other proceedings begin, in either case, transmitted to Congress, and lodged among the acts of Congress for the security of the parties concerned: provided, that every commissioner, before he sits in judgment, shall take an oath, to be administered by one of the judges of the supreme or superior court of the State where the cause shall be tried, "well and truly to hear and determine the matter in question, according to the best of his judgment, without favour, affection, or hope of reward:" provided, also, that no State shall be deprived of territory for the benefit of the United States.

All controversies concerning the private right of soil, claimed under different grants of two or more states, whose jurisdictions, as they may respect such lands and the states which passed such grants, are adjusted, the said grants, or either of them, being at the same time claimed to have originated antecedent to such settlement of jurisdiction, shall, on the petition of either party to the Congress of the United States, be finally determined, as near as may be, in the same manner as is before prescribed for deciding disputes respecting territorial jurisdiction between different states.

The United States, in Congress assembled, shall also have the sole and exclusive right and power of regulating the alloy and value of coin struck by their own authority, or by that of the respective states; fixing the standard of weights and measures throughout the United States; regulating the trade and managing all affairs with the Indians not members of any of the states; provided that the legislative right of any State within its own limits be not infringed or violated; establishing and regulating post offices from one State to another throughout all the United States, and exacting such postage on the papers passing through the same as may be requisite to defray the expences of the said office; appointing all officers of the land forces in the service of the United States, excepting regimental officers; appointing all the officers of the naval forces, and commissioning all officers whatever in the service of the United States; making rules for the government and regulation of the said land and naval forces, and directing their operations.

The United States, in Congress assembled, shall have authority to appoint a committee to sit in the recess of Congress, to be denominated "a Committee of the States," and to consist of one delegate from each State, and to appoint such other committees and civil officers as may be necessary for managing the general affairs of the United States, under their direction; to appoint one of their number to preside; provided that no person be allowed to serve in the office of president more than one year in any term of three years; to ascertain the necessary sums of money to be raised for the service of the United States, and to appropriate and apply the same for defraying the public expences; to borrow money or emit bills on the credit of the United States, transmitting, every half year, to the respective states, an account of the sums of money so borrowed or emitted; to build and equip a navy; to agree upon the number of land forces, and to make requisitions from each State for in quota, in proportion to the number of white inhabitants in such State; which requisitions shall be binding; and thereupon, the legislature of each State shall appoint the regimental officers, raise the men, and cloathe, arm, and equip them in a soldier-like manner, at the expence of the United States; and the officers and men so cloathed, armed, and equipped, shall march to the place appointed and within the time agreed on by the United States, in Congress assembled; but if the United States, in Congress assembled, shall, on consideration of circumstances, judge proper that any State should not raise men, or should raise a smaller number than its quota, and that any other State should raise a greater number of men than the quota thereof, such extra number shall be raised, officered, cloathed, armed, and equipped in the same manner as the quota of such State, unless the legislature of such State shall judge that such extra number cannot be safely spared out of the same, in which case they shall raise, officer, cloathe, arm, and equip as many of such extra number as they judge can be safely spared. And the officers and men so cloathed, armed, and equipped, shall march to the place appointed and within the time agreed on by the United States, in Congress assembled.

The United States, in Congress assembled, shall never engage in a war, nor grant letters of marque and reprisal in time of peace, nor enter into any treaties or alliances, nor coin money, nor regulate the value thereof, nor ascertain the sums and expences necessary for the defence and welfare of the United States, or any of them: nor emit bills, nor borrow money on the credit of the United States, nor appropriate money, nor agree upon the number of vessels of war to be built or purchased, or the number of land or sea forces to be raised, nor appoint a commander in chief of the army or navy, unless nine states assent to the same; nor shall a question on any other point, except for adjourning from day to day, be determined, unless by the votes of a majority of the United States, in Congress assembled.

The Congress of the United States shall have power to adjourn to any time within the year, and to any place within the United States, so that no period of adjournment be for a longer duration than the space of six months, and shall publish the journal of their proceedings monthly, except such parts thereof, relating to treaties, alliances or military operations, as, in their judgment, require secrecy; and the yeas and nays of the delegates of each State on any question shall be entered on the journal, when it is desired by any delegate; and the delegates of a State, or any of them, at his, or their request, shall be furnished with a transcript of the said journal, except such parts as are above excepted, to lay before the legislatures of the several states.

Article 10

The committee of the states, or any nine of them, shall be authorized to execute, in the recess of Congress, such of the powers of Congress as the United States, in Congress assembled, by the consent of nine states, shall, from time to time, think expedient to vest them with; provided, that no power be delegated to the said committee, for the exercise of which, by the articles of confederation, the voice of nine states, in the Congress of the United States assembled, is requisite.

Article 11

Canada acceding to this confederation, and joining in the measures of the United States, shall be admitted into and entitled to all the advantages of this union; but no other colony shall be admitted into the same, unless such admission be agreed to by nine states.

Article 12

All bills of credit emitted, monies borrowed and debts contracted by, or under the authority of Congress before the assembling of the United States, in pursuance of the present confederation, shall be deemed and considered as a charge against the United States, for payment and satisfaction whereof the said United States and the public faith are hereby solemnly pledged.

Article 13

Every State shall abide by the determinations of the United States, in Congress assembled, on all questions which, by this confederation, are submitted to them. And the articles of this confederation shall be inviolably observed by every State, and the union shall be perpetual; nor shall any alteration at any time hereafter be made in any of them, unless such alteration be agreed to in a Congress of the United States, and be afterwards confirmed by the legislatures of every State.

These articles shall be proposed to the legislatures of all the United States, to be considered, and if approved of by them, they are advised to authorize their delegates to ratify the same in the Congress of the United States; which being done, the same shall become conclusive.

The Constitution of the United States

We the People of the United States, in Order to form a more perfect Union, establish Justice, insure domestic Tranquility, provide for the common defence, promote the general Welfare, and secure the Blessings of Liberty to ourselves and our Posterity, do ordain and establish this Constitution for the United States of America.

Article I

Section 1.   All legislative Powers herein granted shall be vested in a Congress of the United States, which shall consist of a Senate and a House of Representatives.

Section 2.   The House of Representatives shall be composed of Members chosen every second Year by the People of the several States, and the Electors in each State shall have the Qualifications requisite for Electors of the most numerous Branch of the State Legislature.

No Person shall be a Representative who shall not have attained to the Age of twenty-five Years, and been seven Years a Citizen of the United States, and who shall not, when elected, be an Inhabitant of that State in which he shall be chosen.

Representatives and direct Taxes shall be apportioned among the several States which may be included within this Union, according to their respective Numbers, *which shall be determined by adding to the whole Number of free Persons, including those bound to Service for a Term of Years, and excluding Indians not taxed, three fifths of all other Persons** The actual Enumeration shall be made within three Years after the first Meeting of the Congress of the United States, and within every subsequent Term of ten Years, in such Manner as they shall by Law direct. The Number of Representatives shall not exceed one for every thirty Thousand, but each State shall have at Least one Representative; and *until such enumeration shall be made, the State of New Hampshire shall be entitled to chuse three, Massachusetts eight, Rhode Island and Providence Plantations one, Connecticut five, New-York six, New Jersey four, Pennsylvania eight, Delaware one, Maryland six, Virginia ten, North Carolina five, South Carolina five, and Georgia three.*

When vacancies happen in the Representation from any State, the Executive Authority thereof shall issue Writs of Election to fill such Vacancies.

The House of Representatives shall chuse their Speaker and other Officers; and shall have the sole Power of Impeachment.

Note: The Constitution became effective March 4,1789. Provisions in italics have been changed by constitutional amendment.

*Changed by Section 2 of the Fourteenth Amendment.

Section 3.   The Senate of the United States shall be composed of two Senators from each State, *chosen by the Legislature thereof,** for six Years; and each Senator shall have one Vote.

Immediately after they shall be assembled in Consequence of the first Election, they shall be divided as equally as may be into three Classes. The Seats of the Senators of the first Class shall be vacated at the Expiration of the second Year, of the second Class at the Expiration of the fourth Year, and of the third Class at the Expiration of the sixth Year, so that one-third may be chosen every second Year; *and if Vacancies happen by Resignation, or otherwise, during the Recess of the Legislature of any State, the Executive thereof may make temporary Appointments until the next Meeting of the Legislature, which shall then fill such Vacancies.*†

No person shall be a Senator who shall not have attained to the Age of thirty Years, and been nine Years a Citizen of the United States, and who shall not, when elected, be an Inhabitant of that State for which he shall be chosen.

The Vice President of the United States shall be President of the Senate, but shall have no Vote, unless they be equally divided.

The Senate shall chuse their other Officers, and also a President pro tempore, in the absence of the Vice President, or when he shall exercise the Office of President of the United States.

The Senate shall have the sole Power to try all Impeachments. When sitting for that Purpose, they shall be on Oath or Affirmation. When the President of the United States is tried, the Chief Justice shall preside; And no Person shall be convicted without the Concurrence of two thirds of the Members present.

Judgment in Cases of Impeachment shall not extend further than to removal from Office, and disqualification to hold and enjoy any Office of honor, Trust or Profit under the United States: but the Party convicted shall nevertheless be liable and subject to Indictment, Trial, Judgment and Punishment, according to Law.

Section 4.   The Times, Places and Manner of holding Elections for Senators and Representatives, shall be prescribed in each State by the Legislature thereof, but the Congress may at any time by Law make or alter such Regulations, except as to the Places of Chusing Senators.

The Congress shall assemble at least once in every Year, and such Meeting *shall be on the first Monday in December, unless they shall by Law appoint a different Day.*‡

Section 5.   Each House shall be the Judge of the Elections, Returns and Qualifications of its own Members, and a Majority of each shall constitute a Quorum to do Business; but a smaller number may adjourn from day to day, and may be authorized to compel the Attendance of absent Members, in such Manner, and under such Penalties, as each House may provide.

Each House may determine the Rules of its Proceedings, punish its Members for disorderly Behavior, and, with the Concurrence of two thirds, expel a Member.

---

*Changed by Section 1 of the Seventeenth Amendment.
†Changed by Clause 2 of the Seventeenth Amendment.
‡Changed by Section 2 of the Twentieth Amendment.

Each House shall keep a Journal of its Proceedings, and from time to time publish the same, excepting such Parts as may in their Judgment require Secrecy; and the Yeas and Nays of the Members of either House on any question shall, at the Desire of one-fifth of those Present, be entered on the Journal.

Neither House, during the Session of Congress, shall, without the Consent of the other, adjourn for more than three days, nor to any other Place than that in which the two Houses shall be sitting.

Section 6.   The Senators and Representatives shall receive a Compensation for their Services, to be ascertained by Law, and paid out of the Treasury of the United States. They shall in all Cases, except Treason, Felony and Breach of the Peace, be privileged from Arrest during their Attendance at the Session of their respective Houses, and in going to and returning from the same; and for any Speech or Debate in either House, they shall not be questioned in any other Place.

No Senator or Representative shall, during the Time for which he was elected, be appointed to any civil Office under the Authority of the United States, which shall have been created, or the Emoluments whereof shall have been increased, during such time; and no Person holding any Office under the United States, shall be a Member of either House during his Continuance in Office.

Section 7.   All Bills for raising Revenue shall originate in the House of Representatives; but the Senate may propose or concur with Amendments as on other Bills.

Every Bill which shall have passed the House of Representatives and the Senate, shall, before it becomes a Law, be presented to the President of the United States; If he approve he shall sign it, but if not he shall return it, with his Objections to that House in which it shall have originated, who shall enter the Objections at large on their Journal, and proceed to reconsider it. If after such Reconsideration two thirds of that House shall agree to pass the Bill, it shall be sent, together with the Objections, to the other House, by which it shall likewise be reconsidered, and if approved by two thirds of that House, it shall become a Law. But in all such Cases the Votes of both Houses shall be determined by Yeas and Nays, and the Names of the Persons voting for and against the Bill shall be entered on the Journal of each House respectively. If any Bill shall not be returned by the President within ten Days (Sundays excepted) after it shall have been presented to him, the Same shall be a Law, in like Manner as if he had signed it, unless the Congress by their Adjournment prevent its Return, in which Case it shall not be a Law.

Every Order, Resolution, or Vote to which the Concurrence of the Senate and the House of Representatives may be necessary (except on a question of Adjournment) shall be presented to the President of the United States; and before the Same shall take Effect, shall be approved by him, or being disapproved by him, shall be repassed by two thirds of the Senate and House of Representatives, according to the Rules and Limitations prescribed in the Case of a Bill.

Section 8.   The Congress shall have Power To lay and collect Taxes, Duties, Imposts and Excises, to pay the Debts and provide for the common Defence and general Welfare of the United States; but all Duties, Imposts and Excises shall be uniform throughout the United States;

To borrow money on the credit of the United States;

To regulate Commerce with foreign Nations, and among the several States, and with the Indian Tribes;

To establish an uniform Rule of Naturalization, and uniform Laws on the subject of Bankruptcies throughout the United States;

To coin Money, regulate the Value thereof, and of foreign Coin, and fix the Standard of Weights and Measures;

To provide for the Punishment of counterfeiting the Securities and current Coin of the United States;

To establish Post Offices and post Roads;

To promote the Progress of Science and useful Arts, by securing for limited Times to Authors and Inventors the exclusive Right to their respective Writings and Discoveries;

To constitute Tribunals inferior to the supreme Court;

To define and punish Piracies and Felonies committed on the high Seas, and Offenses against the Law of Nations;

To declare War, grant Letters of Marque and Reprisal, and make Rules concerning Captures on Land and Water;

To raise and support Armies, but no Appropriation of Money to that Use shall be for a longer Term than two Years;

To provide and maintain a Navy;

To make Rules for the Government and Regulation of the land and naval Forces;

To provide for calling forth the Militia to execute the Laws of the Union, suppress Insurrections and repel Invasions;

To provide for organizing, arming, and disciplining the Militia, and for governing such Part of them as may be employed in the Service of the United States, reserving to the States respectively, the Appointment of the Officers, and the Authority of training the Militia according to the discipline prescribed by Congress;

To exercise exclusive Legislation in all Cases whatsoever, over such District (not exceeding ten Miles square) as may, by Cession of particular States, and the acceptance of Congress, become the Seat of Government of the United States, and to exercise like Authority over all Places purchased by the Consent of the Legislature of the State in which the Same shall be, for the Erection of Forts, Magazines, Arsenals, dock-Yards, and other needful Buildings;—And

To make all Laws which shall be necessary and proper for carrying into Execution the foregoing Powers, and all other Powers vested by this Constitution in the Government of the United States, or in any Department or Officer thereof.

Section 9. *The Migration or Importation of such Persons as any of the States now existing shall think proper to admit, shall not be prohibited by the Congress prior to the Year one thousand eight hundred and eight but a tax or duty may be imposed on such Importation, not exceeding ten dollars for each Person.*

The privilege of the Writ of Habeas Corpus shall not be suspended, unless when in Cases of Rebellion or Invasion the public Safety may require it.

No Bill of Attainder or ex post facto Law shall be passed.

No capitation, or other direct, Tax shall be laid, unless in Proportion to the Census or Enumeration herein before directed to be taken.*

No Tax or Duty shall be laid on Articles exported from any State.

No Preference shall be given by any Regulation of Commerce or Revenue to the Ports of one State over those of another: nor shall Vessels bound to, or from, one State, be obliged to enter, clear, or pay Duties in another.

No Money shall be drawn from the Treasury, but in Consequence of Appropriations made by law; and a regular Statement and Account of the Receipts and Expenditures of all public Money shall be published from time to time.

No Title of Nobility shall be granted by the United States: And no Person holding any Office of Profit or Trust under them, shall, without the Consent of the Congress, accept of any present, Emolument, Office, or Title, of any kind whatever, from any King, Prince, or foreign State.

Section 10. No State shall enter into any Treaty, Alliance, or Confederation; grant Letters of Marque and Reprisal; coin Money; emit Bills of Credit; make any Thing but gold and silver Coin a Tender in Payment of Debts; pass any Bill of Attainder, ex post facto Law, or Law impairing the Obligation of Contracts, or grant any Title of Nobility.

No State shall, without the Consent of the Congress, lay any Imposts or Duties on Imports or Exports, except what may be absolutely necessary for executing its inspection Laws: and the net Produce of all Duties and Imposts, laid by any State on Imports or Exports, shall be for the Use of the Treasury of the United States; and all such Laws shall be subject to the Revision and Control of the Congress.

No State shall, without the Consent of the Congress, lay any duty of Tonnage, keep Troops, or Ships of War in time of Peace, enter into any Agreement or Compact with another State, or with a foreign Power, or engage in War, unless actually invaded, or in such imminent Danger as will not admit of delay.

Article II

Section 1. The executive Power shall be vested in a President of the United States of America. He shall hold his Office during the Term of four Years, and, together with the Vice President, chosen for the same Term, be elected, as follows:

Each State shall appoint, in such Manner as the Legislature thereof may direct, a Number of Electors, equal to the whole Number of Senators and Representatives to which the State may be entitled in the Congress; but no Senator or Representative, or Person holding an Office of Trust or Profit under the United States, shall be appointed an Elector.

The Electors shall meet in their respective States, and vote by Ballot for two Persons, of whom one at least shall not be an Inhabitant of the same State with themselves. And they shall make a List of all the Persons voted for, and of the Number of Votes for each; which List they shall sign and certify, and transmit sealed to the Seat of the Government of the United States, directed to the President of the Senate. The President of the Senate shall,

---

*Changed by the Sixteenth Amendment

in the Presence of the Senate and House of Representatives, open all the Certificates, and the Votes shall then be counted. The Person having the greatest Number of Votes shall be the President, if such Number be a Majority of the whole Number of Electors appointed; and if there be more than one who have such Majority, and have an equal Number of Votes, then the House of Representatives shall immediately chuse by Ballot one of them for President; and if no Person have a Majority, then from the five highest on the List the said House shall in like Manner chuse the President. But in chusing the President, the Votes shall be taken by States, the Representation from each State having one Vote; a quorum for this Purpose shall consist of a Member or Members from two thirds of the States, and a Majority of all the States shall be necessary to a Choice. In every Case, after the Choice of the President, the Person having the greatest Number of Votes of the Electors shall be the Vice President. But if there should remain two or more who have equal Votes, the Senate shall chuse from them by Ballot the Vice President.*

The Congress may determine the Time of chusing the Electors, and the Day on which they shall give their Votes; which Day shall be the same throughout the United States.

No Person except a natural born Citizen, or a Citizen of the United States, at the time of the Adoption of this Constitution, shall be eligible to the Office of President; neither shall any Person be eligible to that Office who shall not have attained to the Age of thirty five Years, and been fourteen years a Resident within the United States.

In Case of the Removal of the President from Office, or of his Death, Resignation, or Inability to discharge the Powers and Duties of the said Office, the same shall devolve on the Vice President, *and the Congress may by Law provide for the Case of Removal, Death, Resignation, or Inability, both of the President and Vice President, declaring what Officer shall then act as President, and such Officer shall act accordingly, until the Disability be removed, or a President shall be elected.*†

The President shall, at stated Times, receive for his Services a Compensation, which shall neither be increased nor diminished during the Period for which he shall have been elected, and he shall not receive within that Period any other Emolument from the United States, or any of them.

Before he enter on the Execution of his Office, he shall take the following Oath or Affirmation:—"I do solemnly swear (or affirm) that I will faithfully execute the Office of President of the United States, and will to the best of my Ability, preserve, protect and defend the Constitution of the United States."

Section 2. The President shall be Commander in Chief of the Army and Navy of the United States, and of the Militia of the several States, when called into the actual Service of the United States; he may require the Opinion, in writing, of the principal Officer in each of the executive Departments, upon any Subject relating to the Duties of their respective Offices, and he shall have Power to Grant Reprieves and pardons for Offences against the United States, except in Cases of Impeachment.

He shall have Power, by and with the Advice and Consent of the Senate, to make Treaties, provided two thirds of the Senators present concur; and he shall nominate,

---

*Superseded by the Twelfth Amendment.
†Modified by the Twenty-fifth Amendment.

and by and with the Advice and Consent of the Senate, shall appoint Ambassadors, other public Ministers and Consuls, Judges of the supreme Court, and all other Officers of the United States, whose Appointments are not herein otherwise provided for, and which shall be established by Law: but the Congress may by Law vest the Appointment of such inferior Officers, as they think proper, in the President alone, in the Courts of Law, or in the Heads of Departments.

The President shall have Power to fill up all Vacancies that may happen during the Recess of the Senate, by granting Commissions which shall expire at the End of their next Session.

Section 3.   He shall from time to time give to the Congress Information of the State of the Union, and recommend to their Consideration such Measures as he shall judge necessary and expedient; he may, on extraordinary Occasions, convene both Houses, or either of them, and in Case of Disagreement between them, with Respect to the Time of Adjournment, he may adjourn them to such Time as he shall think proper; he shall receive Ambassadors and other public Ministers; he shall take care that the Laws be faithfully executed, and shall Commission all the Officers of the United States.

Section 4.   The President, Vice President and all civil Officers of the United States, shall be removed from Office on Impeachment for, and Conviction of, Treason, Bribery, or other high Crimes and Misdemeanors.

Article III
Section 1.   The judicial Power of the United States, shall be vested in one supreme Court, and in such inferior Courts as the Congress may from time to time ordain and establish. The Judges, both of the supreme and inferior courts, shall hold their Offices during good Behaviour, and shall, at stated Times, receive for their Services a Compensation, which shall not be diminished during their Continuance in Office.

Section 2.   The judicial Power shall extend to all Cases, in Law and Equity, arising under this Constitution, the Laws of the United States, and Treaties made, or which shall be made, under their Authority; — to all Cases affecting Ambassadors, other public Ministers and Consuls; — to all Cases of admiralty and maritime Jurisdiction; — to Controversies to which the United States shall be a Party; — to Controversies between two or more States; — *between a State and Citizens of another State,** — between Citizens of different States; — between Citizens of the same State claiming Lands under Grants of different States, and between a State, or the Citizens thereof, and foreign States, Citizens or Subjects.

In all Cases affecting Ambassadors, other public Ministers and Consuls, and those in which a State shall be Party, the supreme Court shall have original Jurisdiction. In all the other Cases before mentioned, the supreme Court shall have appellate Jurisdiction, both as to Law and Fact, with such Exceptions, and under such Regulations as the Congress shall make.

---

*Restricted by the Eleventh Amendment.

The trial of all Crimes, except in Cases of Impeachment, shall be by Jury; and such Trial shall be held in the State where said Crimes shall have been committed; but when not committed within any State, the Trial shall be at such Place or Places as the Congress may by Law have directed.

Section 3.　Treason against the United States, shall consist only in levying War against them, or in adhering to their Enemies, giving them Aid and Comfort. No Person shall be convicted of Treason unless on the Testimony of two Witnesses to the same overt Act, or on Confession in open Court.

The Congress shall have Power to declare the Punishment of Treason, but no Attainder of Treason shall work Corruption of Blood, or Forefeiture except during the Life of the Person attainted.

Article IV

Section 1.　Full Faith and Credit shall be given in each State to the public Acts, Records, and judicial Proceedings of every other State. And the Congress may by general Laws prescribe the Manner in which such Acts, Records, and Proceedings shall be proved, and the Effect thereof.

Section 2.　The Citizens of each State shall be entitled to all Privileges and Immunities of Citizens in the several States.

A Person charged in any State with Treason, Felony, or other Crime, who shall flee from Justice, and be found in another State, shall on demand of the executive Authority of the State from which he fled, be delivered up, to be removed to the State having Jurisdiction of the Crime.

No Person held to Service or Labour in one State, under the Laws thereof, escaping into another, shall, in Consequence of any Law or Regulation therein, be discharged from such Service or Labour, but shall be delivered up on Claim of the Party to whom such Service or Labour may be due. *

Section 3.　New States may be admitted by the Congress into this Union; but no new State shall be formed or erected within the Jurisdiction of any other State; nor any State be formed by the Junction of two or more States, or parts of States, without the Consent of the Legislatures of the States concerned as well as of the Congress.

The Congress shall have Power to dispose of and make all needful Rules and Regulations respecting the Territory or other Property belonging to the United States; and nothing in this Constitution shall be so construed as to Prejudice any Claims of the United States, or of any particular State.

Section 4.　The United States shall guarantee to every State in this Union a Republican Form of Government, and shall protect each of them against Invasion; and on Application of the Legislature, or of the Executive (when the Legislature cannot be convened) against domestic Violence.

———————————————

*Superseded by the Thirteenth Amendment.

Article V

The Congress, whenever two thirds of both Houses shall deem it necessary, shall propose Amendments to this Constitution, or, on the Application of the Legislatures of two thirds of the several States, shall call a Convention for proposing Amendments, which, in either Case, shall be valid to all Intents and Purposes, as Part of this Constitution, when ratified by the Legislatures of three fourths of the several States, or by Conventions in three fourths thereof, as the one or the other Mode of Ratification may be proposed by the Congress; Provided that no Amendment which may be made prior to the Year One thousand eight hundred and eight shall in any Manner affect the first and fourth Clauses in the Ninth Section of the first Article; and that no State, without its Consent, shall be deprived of its equal Suffrage in the Senate.

Article VI

All Debts contracted and Engagements entered into, before the Adoption of this Constitution, shall be as valid against the United States under this Constitution, as under the Confederation.

This Constitution, and the Laws of the United States which shall be made in Pursuance thereof; and all Treaties made, or which shall be made, under the Authority of the United States, shall be the supreme Law of the Land; and the Judges in every State shall be bound thereby, any Thing in the Constitution or Laws of any State to the Contrary notwithstanding.

The Senators and Representatives before mentioned, and the Members of the several State Legislatures, and all executive and judicial Officers, both of the United States and of the several States, shall be bound by Oath or Affirmation, to support this Constitution; but no religious Test shall ever be required as a Qualification to any Office or public Trust under the United States.

Article VII

The Ratification of the Conventions of nine States shall be sufficient for the Establishment of this Constitution between the States so ratifying the Same.

Done in Convention by the Unanimous Consent of the States present the Seventeenth Day of September in the Year of our Lord one thousand seven hundred and Eighty seven and of the Independence of the United States of America the Twelfth. In Witness whereof We have hereunto subscribed our Names.

Go. Washington
President and deputy from Virginia

New *Hampshire*	*New Jersey*	*Delaware*	*North Carolina*
John Langdon	Wil. Livingston	Geo. Read	Wm. Blount
Nicholas Gilman	David Brearley	Gunning Bedford jun	Richd. Dobbs Spaight
	Wm. Paterson	John Dickenson	Hu Williamson
	Jona. Dayton	Richard Bassett	
		Jaco. Broom	

Massachusetts	Pennsylvania	Maryland	South Carolina
Nathaniel Gorham	B. Franklin	James McHenry	J. Rutledge
Rufus King	Thomas Mifflin	Dan. of St. Thos. Jenifer	Charles Cotesworth
	Robt. Morris	Danl. Carroll	Pickney
Connecticut	Geo. Clymer		Pierce Butler
Wm. Saml. Johnson	Thos. FitzSimons	*Virginia*	
Roger Sherman	Jared Ingersoll	John Blair	*Georgia*
	James Wilson	James Madison, Jr.	William Few
New York	Gouv. Morris		Abr. Baldwin
Alexander Hamilton			

Amendments to the Constitution

Amendment I [1791]*

Congress shall make no law respecting an establishment of religion, or prohibiting the free exercise thereof; or abridging the freedom of speech, or of the press; or the right of the people peaceably to assemble, and to petition the Government for a redress of grievances.

Amendment II [1791]

A well regulated Militia, being necessary to the security of a free State, the right of the people to keep and bear Arms shall not be infringed.

Amendment III [1791]

No Soldier shall, in time of peace, be quartered in any house, without the consent of the Owner, nor in time of war, but in a manner to be prescribed by law.

Amendment IV [1791]

The right of the people to be secure in their persons, houses, papers, and effects, against unreasonable searches and seizures, shall not be violated, and no Warrants shall issue, but upon probable cause, supported by Oath or affirmation, and particularly describing the place to be searched, and the persons or things to be seized.

Amendment V [1791]

No person shall be held to answer for a capital or otherwise infamous crime, unless on a presentment or indictment of a Grand Jury, except in cases arising in the land or naval forces, or in the Militia, when in actual service in time of War or public danger; nor shall any person be subject for the same offence to be twice put in jeopardy of life or limb; nor shall be compelled in any criminal case to be a witness against himself, nor be deprived of life, liberty, or property, without due process of law; nor shall private property be taken for public use, without just compensation.

---

*The dates in brackets indicate when the amendments were ratified.

Amendment VI [1791]

In all criminal prosecutions, the accused shall enjoy the right to a speedy and public trial, by an impartial jury of the State and district wherein the crime shall have been committed, which district shall have been previously ascertained by law, and to be informed of the nature and cause of the accusation; to be confronted with the witnesses against him; to have compulsory process for obtaining witnesses in his favor, and to have the Assistance of Counsel for his defence.

Amendment VII [1791]

In suits at common law, where the value in controversy shall exceed twenty dollars, the right of trial by jury shall be preserved, and no fact tried by a jury, shall be otherwise reexamined in any Court of the United States, than according to the Rules of the common law.

Amendment VIII [1791]

Excessive bail shall not be required, nor excessive fines imposed, nor cruel and unusual punishments inflicted.

Amendment IX [1791]

The enumeration in the Constitution, of certain rights, shall not be construed to deny or disparage others retained by the people.

Amendment X [1791]

The powers not delegated to the United States by the Constitution, nor prohibited by it to the States, are reserved to the States respectively, or to the people.

Amendment XI [1798]

The Judicial power of the United States shall not be construed to extend to any suit in law or equity, commenced or prosecuted against one of the United States by Citizens of another State, or by Citizens or subjects of any foreign state.

Amendment XII [1804]

The Electors shall meet in their respective States and vote by ballot for President and Vice-President, one of whom, at least, shall not be an inhabitant of the same State with themselves; they shall name in their ballots the person voted for as President, and in distinct ballots the person voted for as Vice-President, and they shall make distinct lists of all persons voted for as President, and of all persons voted for as Vice-President, and of the number of votes for each, which lists they shall sign and certify, and transmit sealed to the seat of the government of the United States, directed to the President of the Senate;—the President of the Senate shall, in the presence of the Senate and House of Representatives, open all the certificates and the votes shall then be counted;—The person having the greatest number of votes for President, shall be the President, if such number be a majority of the whole number of Electors appointed;

and if no person have such majority, then from the persons having the highest numbers not exceeding three on the list of those voted for as President, the House of Representatives shall choose immediately, by ballot, the President. But in choosing the President, the votes shall be taken by States, the representation from each State having one vote; a quorum for this purpose shall consist of a member or members from two-thirds of the States, and a majority of all the States shall be necessary to a choice. And if the House of Representatives shall not choose a President whenever the right of choice shall devolve upon them, before *the fourth day of March* next following, then the Vice-President shall act as President, as in the case of the death or other constitutional disability of the President.* — The person having the greatest number of votes as Vice-President, shall be the Vice-President, if such number be a majority of the whole number of Electors appointed, and if no person have a majority, then from the two highest numbers on the list, the Senate shall choose the Vice-President; a quorum for the purpose shall consist of two-thirds of the whole number of Senators, and a majority of the whole number shall be necessary to a choice. But no person constitutionally ineligible to the office of President shall be eligible to that of Vice-President of the United States.

Amendment XIII [1865]

Section 1. Neither slavery nor involuntary servitude, except as a punishment for crime whereof the party shall have been duly convicted, shall exist within the United States, or any place subject to their jurisdiction.

Section 2. Congress shall have power to enforce this article by appropriate legislation.

Amendment XIV [1868]

Section 1. All persons born or naturalized in the United States, and subject to the jurisdiction thereof, are citizens of the United States and of the State wherein they reside. No State shall make or enforce any law which shall abridge the privileges or immunities of citizens of the United States; nor shall any State deprive any person of life, liberty, or property, without due process of law; nor deny to any person within its jurisdiction the equal protection of the laws.

Section 2. Representatives shall be apportioned among the several States according to their respective numbers, counting the whole number of persons in each State, excluding Indians not taxed. But when the right to vote at any election for the choice of electors for President and Vice-President of the United States, Representatives in Congress, the Executive and Judicial officers of a State, or the members of the Legislature thereof, is denied to any of the male inhabitants of such State, being twenty-one years of age, and citizens of the United States, or in any way abridged, except for participation in rebellion, or other crime, the basis of representation therein shall be reduced in the proportion which the number of such male citizens shall bear to the whole number of male citizens twenty-one years of age in such State.

---

*Superseded by Section 3 of the Twentieth Amendment.

Section 3. No person shall be a Senator or Representative in Congress, or elector of President and Vice-President, or hold any office, civil or military, under the United States, or under any State, who, having previously taken an oath, as a member of Congress, or as an officer of the United States, or as a member of any State legislature, or as an executive or judicial officer of any State, to support the Constitution of the United States, shall have engaged in insurrection or rebellion against the same, or given aid or comfort to the enemies thereof. Congress may by a vote of two-thirds of each house, remove such disability.

Section 4. The validity of the public debt of the United States, authorized by law, including debts incurred for payment of pensions and bounties for services in suppressing insurrection or rebellion, shall not be questioned. But neither the United States nor any State shall assume or pay any debt or obligation incurred in aid of insurrection or rebellion against the United States, or any claim for the loss or emancipation of any slave; but all such debts, obligations and claims shall be held illegal and void.

Section 5. The Congress shall have power to enforce, by appropriate legislation, the provisions of this article.

Amendment XV [1870]

Section 1. The right of citizens of the United States to vote shall not be denied or abridged by the United States or by any State on account of race, color, or previous condition of servitude—

Section 2. The Congress shall have power to enforce this article by appropriate legislation.

Amendment XVI [1913]

The Congress shall have power to lay and collect taxes on incomes, from whatever source derived, without apportionment among the several States, and without regard to any census or enumeration.

Amendment XVII [1913]

The Senate of the United States shall be composed of two Senators from each State, elected by the people thereof, for six years; and each Senator shall have one vote. The electors in each State shall have the qualifications requisite for electors of the most numerous branch of the State legislatures.

When vacancies happen in the representation of any State in the Senate, the executive authority of such State shall issue writs of election to fill such vacancies: *Provided,* That the legislature of any State may empower the executive thereof to make temporary appointments until the people fill the vacancies by election as the legislature may direct.

This amendment shall not be so construed as to affect the election or term of any Senator chosen before it becomes valid as part of the Constitution.

Amendment XVIII [1919]

Section 1.   After one year from the ratification of this article the manufacture, sale, or transportation of intoxicating liquors within, the importation thereof into, or the exportation thereof from the United States and all territory subject to the jurisdiction hereof for beverage purposes is hereby prohibited.

Section 2.   The Congress and the several States shall have concurrent power to enforce this article by appropriate legislation.

Section 3.   This article shall be inoperative unless it shall have been ratified as an amendment to the Constitution by the legislatures of the several States, as provided by the Constitution, within seven years from the date of submission hereof to the States by the Congress.*

Amendment XIX [1920]

The right of citizens of the United States to vote shall not be denied or abridged by the United States or by any State on account of sex.

Congress shall have power to enforce this article by appropriate legislation.

Amendment XX [1933]

Section 1.   The terms of the President and Vice-President shall end at noon on the 20th day of January, and the terms of Senators and Representatives at noon on the 3d day of January, of the years in which such terms would have ended if this article had not been ratified; and the terms of their successors shall then begin.

Section 2.   The Congress shall assemble at least once in every year, and such meeting shall begin at noon on the 3d day of January, unless they shall by law appoint a different day.

Section 3.   If, at the time fixed for the beginning of the term of the President, the President elect shall have died, the Vice-President elect shall become President. If a President shall not have been chosen before the time fixed for the beginning of his term, or if the President elect shall have failed to qualify, then the Vice-President elect shall act as President until a President shall have qualified; and the Congress may by law provide for the case wherein neither a President elect nor a Vice-President elect shall have qualified, declaring who shall then act as President, or the manner in which one who is to act shall be selected, and such person shall act accordingly until a President or Vice-President shall have qualified.

Section 4.   The Congress may by law provide for the case of the death of any of the persons from whom the House of Representatives may choose a President whenever the right of choice shall have devolved upon them, and for the case of the death of any of the persons from whom the Senate may choose a Vice-President whenever the right of choice shall have devolved upon them.

---

*Repealed by Section 1 of the Twenty-first Amendment.

Section 5 Sections 1 and 2 shall take effect on the 15th day of October following the ratification of this article.

Section 6. This article shall be inoperative unless it shall have been ratified as an amendment to the Constitution by the legislatures of three-fourths of the several States within seven years from the date of its submission.

Amendment XXI [1933]

Section 1. The eighteenth article of amendment to the Constitution of the United States is hereby repealed.

Section 2. The transportation or importation into any State, Territory, or possession of the United States for delivery or use therein of intoxicating liquors, in violation of the laws thereof, is hereby prohibited.

Section 3. This article shall be inoperative unless it shall have been ratified as an amendment to the Constitution by conventions in the several States, as provided in the Constitution, within seven years from the date of submission hereof to the States by the Congress.

Amendment XXII [1951]

Section 1. No person shall be elected to the office of President more than twice, and no person who has held the office of President, or acted as President, for more than two years of a term to which some other person was elected President shall be elected to the office of the President more than once. But this Article shall not apply to any person holding the office of President when this Article was proposed by the Congress, and shall not prevent any person who may be holding the office of President, or acting as President, during the term within which this Article becomes operative from holding the office of the President or acting as President during the remainder of such term.

Section 2. This article shall be inoperative unless it shall have been ratified as an amendment to the Constitution by the legislatures of three-fourths of the several States within seven years from the date of its submission to the States by the Congress.

Amendment XXIII [1961]

Section 1. The District constituting the seat of Government of the United States shall appoint in such manner as the Congress may direct:

A number of electors of President and Vice-President equal to the whole number of Senators and Representatives in Congress to which the District would be entitled if it were a State, but in no event more than the least populous State; they shall be in addition to those appointed by the States, but they shall be considered, for the purposes of the election of President and Vice-President, to be electors appointed by a State; and they shall meet in the District and perform such duties as provided by the twelfth article of amendment.

Section 2. The Congress shall have power to enforce this article by appropriate legislation.

Amendment XXIV [1964]

Section 1. The right of citizens of the United States to vote in any primary or other election for President or Vice-President, for electors for President or Vice-President, or for Senator or Representative in Congress, shall not be denied or abridged by the United States or any State by reason of failure to pay any poll tax or other tax.

Section 2. The Congress shall have power to enforce this article by appropriate legislation.

Amendment XXV [1967]

Section 1. In case of the removal of the President from office or of his death or resignation, the Vice-President shall become President.

Section 2. Whenever there is a vacancy in the office of the Vice-President, the President shall nominate a Vice-President who shall take office upon confirmation by a majority vote of both houses of Congress.

Section 3. Whenever the President transmits to the President pro tempore of the Senate and the Speaker of the House of Representatives his written declaration that he is unable to discharge the powers and duties of his office, and until he transmits to them a written declaration to the contrary, such powers and duties shall be discharged by the Vice-President as Acting President.

Section 4. Whenever the Vice-President and a majority of either the principal officers of the executive departments or of such other body as Congress may by law provide, transmit to the President pro tempore of the Senate and the Speaker of the House of Representatives their written declaration that the President is unable to discharge the powers and duties of his office, the Vice-President shall immediately assume the powers and duties of the office as Acting President.

Thereafter, when the President transmits to the President pro tempore of the Senate and the Speaker of the House of Representatives his written declaration that no inability exists, he shall resume the powers and duties of his office unless the Vice-President and a majority of either the principal officers of the executive department or of such other body as Congress may by law provide, transmit within four days to the President pro tempore of the Senate and the Speaker of the House of Representatives their written declaration that the President is unable to discharge the powers and duties of his office. Thereupon Congress shall decide the issue, assembling within forty-eight hours for that purpose if not in session. If the Congress, within twenty-one days after receipt of the latter written declaration, or, if Congress is not in session, within twenty-one days after Congress is required to assemble, determines by two-thirds vote of both Houses that the President is unable to discharge the powers and duties of his office, the Vice-President shall continue to discharge the same as Acting President; otherwise, the President shall resume the powers and duties of his office.

Amendment XXVI [1971]

Section 1.   The right of citizens of the United States, who are eighteen years of age or older, to vote shall not be denied or abridged by the United States or by any State on account of age.

Section 2.   The Congress shall have power to enforce this article by appropriate legislation.

Amendment XXVII [1992]

No law varying the compensation for services of the Senators and Representatives, shall take effect, until an election of Representatives shall have intervened.

Appendix

TABLE 1	Territorial Expansion		
Territory	**Date Acquired**	**Square Miles**	**How Acquired**
Original states and territories	1783	888,685	Treaty of Paris
Louisiana Purchase	1803	827,192	Purchased from France
Florida	1819	72,003	Adams-Onís Treaty
Texas	1845	390,143	Annexation of independent country
Oregon	1846	285,580	Oregon Boundary Treaty
Mexican cession	1848	529,017	Treaty of Guadalupe Hidalgo
Gadsden Purchase	1853	29,640	Purchased from Mexico
Midway Islands	1867	2	Annexation of uninhabited islands
Alaska	1867	589,757	Purchased from Russia
Hawaii	1898	6,450	Annexation of independent country
Wake Island	1898	3	Annexation of uninhabited island
Puerto Rico	1899	3,435	Treaty of Paris
Guam	1899	212	Treaty of Paris
The Philippines	1899–1946	115,600	Treaty of Paris; granted independence
American Samoa	1900	76	Treaty with Germany and Great Britain
Panama Canal Zone	1904–1978	553	Hay–Bunau-Varilla Treaty
U.S. Virgin Islands	1917	133	Purchased from Denmark
Trust Territory of the Pacific Islands*	1947	717	United Nations Trusteeship

*A number of these islands have since been granted independence: Federated States of Micronesia, 1990; Marshall Islands, 1991; Palau, 1994.

TABLE 2	The Labor Force (thousands of workers)						
Year	Agriculture	Mining	Manufacturing	Construction	Trade	Other	Total
1810	1,950	11	75	—	—	294	2,330
1840	3,570	32	500	290	350	918	5,660
1850	4,520	102	1,200	410	530	1,488	8,250
1860	5,880	176	1,530	520	890	2,114	11,110
1870	6,790	180	2,470	780	1,310	1,400	12,930
1880	8,920	280	3,290	900	1,930	2,070	17,390
1890	9,960	440	4,390	1,510	2,960	4,060	23,320
1900	11,680	637	5,895	1,665	3,970	5,223	29,070
1910	11,770	1,068	8,332	1,949	5,320	9,041	37,480
1920	10,790	1,180	11,190	1,233	5,845	11,372	41,610
1930	10,560	1,009	9,884	1,988	8,122	17,267	48,830
1940	9,575	925	11,309	1,876	9,328	23,277	56,290
1950	7,870	901	15,648	3,029	12,152	25,870	65,470
1960	5,970	709	17,145	3,640	14,051	32,545	74,060
1970	3,463	516	20,746	4,818	15,008	34,127	78,678
1980	3,364	979	21,942	6,215	20,191	46,612	99,303
1990	3,186	730	21,184	7,696	24,269	60,849	118,793
2000	2,464	475	19,644	9,931	15,763	88,260	136,537

SOURCES: U.S. Bureau of the Census, *Historical Statistics of the United States, Colonial Times to 1970* (1975), 139; *Statistical Abstract of the United States, 1998*, table 675; *Statistical Abstract of the United States, 2006.*

Percentage of labor force

Services

Manufacturing, mining, construction

Agriculture

1810 1840 1850 1860 1870 1880 1890 1900 1910 1920 1930 1940 1950 1960 1970 1980 1990 2000

Source: Historical Statistics of the United States, Colonial Times to 1970 (1975), 139; Statistical Abstract of the United States, 1998, table 675.

Changing Labor Patterns

TABLE 3	American Population				
Year	Population	Percent Increase	Year	Population	Percent Increase
1610	350	—	1810	7,239,881	36.4
1620	2,300	557.1	1820	9,638,453	33.1
1630	4,600	100.0	1830	12,866,020	33.5
1640	26,600	478.3	1840	17,069,453	32.7
1650	50,400	90.8	1850	23,191,876	35.9
1660	75,100	49.0	1860	31,443,321	35.6
1670	111,900	49.0	1870	39,818,449	26.6
1680	151,500	35.4	1880	50,155,783	26.0
1690	210,400	38.9	1890	62,947,714	25.5
1700	250,900	19.2	1900	75,994,575	20.7
1710	331,700	32.2	1910	91,972,266	21.0
1720	466,200	40.5	1920	105,710,620	14.9
1730	629,400	35.0	1930	122,775,046	16.1
1740	905,600	43.9	1940	131,669,275	7.2
1750	1,170,800	29.3	1950	150,697,361	14.5
1760	1,593,600	36.1	1960	179,323,175	19.0
1770	2,148,100	34.8	1970	203,235,298	13.3
1780	2,780,400	29.4	1980	226,545,805	11.5
1790	3,929,214	41.3	1990	248,709,873	9.8
1800	5,308,483	35.1	2000	281,421,906	13.2
			2007	301,621,157	7.0

Note: These figures largely ignore the Native American population. Census takers never made any effort to count the Native American population that lived outside their reserved political areas and compiled only casual and incomplete enumerations of those living within their jurisdictions until 1890. In that year, the federal government attempted a full count of the Indian population: The Census found 125,719 Indians in 1890, compared with only 12,543 in 1870 and 33,985 in 1880.

SOURCES: U.S. Bureau of the Census, *Historical Statistics of the United States, Colonial Times to 1970* (1975); *Statistical Abstract of the United States, 2001;* U.S. Bureau of the Census, Population Finder, http://factfinder.census.gov.

TABLE 4	Presidential Elections				

Year	Candidates	Parties	Percentage of Popular Vote	Electoral Vote	Percentage of Voter Participation
1789	**George Washington**	No party designations	*	69	
	John Adams[†]			34	
	Other candidates			35	
1792	**George Washington**	No party designations		132	
	John Adams			77	
	George Clinton			50	
	Other candidates			5	
1796	**John Adams**	Federalist		71	
	Thomas Jefferson	Democratic-Republican		68	
	Thomas Pinckney	Federalist		59	
	Aaron Burr	Democratic-Republican		30	
	Other candidates			48	
1800	**Thomas Jefferson**	Democratic-Republican		73	
	Aaron Burr	Democratic-Republican		73	
	John Adams	Federalist		65	
	Charles C. Pinckney	Federalist		64	
	John Jay	Federalist		1	
1804	**Thomas Jefferson**	Democratic-Republican		162	
	Charles C. Pinckney	Federalist		14	
1808	**James Madison**	Democratic-Republican		122	
	Charles C. Pinckney	Federalist		47	
	George Clinton	Democratic-Republican		6	
1812	**James Madison**	Democratic-Republican		128	
	De Witt Clinton	Federalist		89	
1816	**James Monroe**	Democratic-Republican		183	
	Rufus King	Federalist		34	
1820	**James Monroe**	Democratic-Republican		231	
	John Quincy Adams	Independent Republican		1	
1824	**John Quincy Adams**	Democratic-Republican	30.5	84	26.9
	Andrew Jackson	Democratic-Republican	43.1	99	
	Henry Clay	Democratic-Republican	13.2	37	
	William H. Crawford	Democratic-Republican	13.1	41	
1828	**Andrew Jackson**	Democratic	56.0	178	57.6
	John Quincy Adams	National Republican	44.0	83	
1832	**Andrew Jackson**	Democratic	54.5	219	55.4
	Henry Clay	National Republican	37.5	49	
	William Wirt	Anti-Masonic	8.0	7	
	John Floyd	Democratic	‡	11	
1836	**Martin Van Buren**	Democratic	50.9	170	57.8
	William H. Harrison	Whig		73	
	Hugh L. White	Whig		26	
	Daniel Webster	Whig	49.1	14	
	W. P. Mangum	Whig		11	

(continued on next page)

*Prior to 1824, most presidential electors were chosen by state legislators rather than by popular vote.

[†]Before the Twelfth Amendment was passed in 1804, the Electoral College voted for two presidential candidates; the runner-up became vice president.

[‡]Percentages below 2.0 have been omitted. Hence the percentage of popular vote might not total 100 percent.

Year	Candidates	Parties	Percentage of Popular Vote	Electoral Vote	Percentage of Voter Participation
1840	**William H. Harrison**	Whig	53.1	234	80.2
	Martin Van Buren	Democratic	46.9	60	
1844	**James K. Polk**	Democratic	49.6	170	78.9
	Henry Clay	Whig	48.1	105	
	James G. Birney	Liberty	2.3	0	
1848	**Zachary Taylor**	Whig	47.4	163	72.7
	Lewis Cass	Democratic	42.5	127	
	Martin Van Buren	Free Soil	10.1	0	
1852	**Franklin Pierce**	Democratic	50.9	254	69.6
	Winfield Scott	Whig	44.1	42	
	John P. Hale	Free Soil	5.0	0	
1856	**James Buchanan**	Democratic	45.3	174	78.9
	John C. Frémont	Republican	33.1	114	
	Millard Fillmore	American	21.6	8	
1860	**Abraham Lincoln**	Republican	39.8	180	81.2
	Stephen A. Douglas	Democratic	29.5	12	
	John C. Breckinridge	Democratic	18.1	72	
	John Bell	Constitutional Union	12.6	39	
1864	**Abraham Lincoln**	Republican	55.0	212	73.8
	George B. McClellan	Democratic	45.0	21	
1868	**Ulysses S. Grant**	Republican	52.7	214	78.1
	Horatio Seymour	Democratic	47.3	80	
1872	**Ulysses S. Grant**	Republican	55.6	286	71.3
	Horace Greeley	Democratic	43.9	0	
1876	**Rutherford B. Hayes**	Republican	48.0	185	81.8
	Samuel J. Tilden	Democratic	51.0	184	
1880	**James A. Garfield**	Republican	48.5	214	79.4
	Winfield S. Hancock	Democratic	48.1	155	
	James B. Weaver	Greenback-Labor	3.4	0	
1884	**Grover Cleveland**	Democratic	48.5	219	77.5
	James G. Blaine	Republican	48.2	182	
1888	**Benjamin Harrison**	Republican	47.9	233	79.3
	Grover Cleveland	Democratic	48.6	168	
1892	**Grover Cleveland**	Democratic	46.1	277	74.7
	Benjamin Harrison	Republican	43.0	145	
	James B. Weaver	People's	8.5	22	
1896	**William McKinley**	Republican	51.1	271	79.3
	William J. Bryan	Democratic	47.7	176	
1900	**William McKinley**	Republican	51.7	292	73.2
	William J. Bryan	Democratic; Populist	45.5	155	
1904	**Theodore Roosevelt**	Republican	57.4	336	65.2
	Alton B. Parker	Democratic	37.6	140	
	Eugene V. Debs	Socialist	3.0	0	
1908	**William H. Taft**	Republican	51.6	321	65.4
	William J. Bryan	Democratic	43.1	162	
	Eugene V. Debs	Socialist	2.8	0	

Year	Candidates	Parties	Percentage of Popular Vote	Electoral Vote	Percentage of Voter Participation
1912	**Woodrow Wilson**	Democratic	41.9	435	58.8
	Theodore Roosevelt	Progressive	27.4	88	
	William H. Taft	Republican	23.2	8	
1916	**Woodrow Wilson**	Democratic	49.4	277	61.6
	Charles E. Hughes	Republican	46.2	254	
	A. L. Benson	Socialist	3.2	0	
1920	**Warren G. Harding**	Republican	60.4	404	49.2
	James M. Cox	Democratic	34.2	127	
	Eugene V. Debs	Socialist	3.4	0	
1924	**Calvin Coolidge**	Republican	54.0	382	48.9
	John W. Davis	Democratic	28.8	136	
	Robert M. La Follette	Progressive	16.6	13	
1928	**Herbert C. Hoover**	Republican	58.2	444	56.9
	Alfred E. Smith	Democratic	40.9	87	
1932	**Franklin D. Roosevelt**	Democratic	57.4	472	56.9
	Herbert C. Hoover	Republican	39.7	59	
1936	**Franklin D. Roosevelt**	Democratic	60.8	523	61.0
	Alfred M. Landon	Republican	36.5	8	
1940	**Franklin D. Roosevelt**	Democratic	54.8	449	62.5
	Wendell L. Willkie	Republican	44.8	82	
1944	**Franklin D. Roosevelt**	Democratic	53.5	432	55.9
	Thomas E. Dewey	Republican	46.0	99	
1948	**Harry S Truman**	Democratic	49.6	303	53.0
	Thomas E. Dewey	Republican	45.1	189	
1952	**Dwight D. Eisenhower**	Republican	55.1	442	63.3
	Adlai E. Stevenson	Democratic	44.4	89	
1956	**Dwight D. Eisenhower**	Republican	57.6	457	60.6
	Adlai E. Stevenson	Democratic	42.1	73	
1960	**John F. Kennedy**	Democratic	49.7	303	64.0
	Richard M. Nixon	Republican	49.5	219	
1964	**Lyndon B. Johnson**	Democratic	61.1	486	61.7
	Barry M. Goldwater	Republican	38.5	52	
1968	**Richard M. Nixon**	Republican	43.4	301	60.6
	Hubert H. Humphrey	Democratic	42.7	191	
	George C. Wallace	American Independent	13.5	46	
1972	**Richard M. Nixon**	Republican	60.7	520	55.5
	George S. McGovern	Democratic	37.5	17	
1976	**Jimmy Carter**	Democratic	50.1	297	54.3
	Gerald R. Ford	Republican	48.0	240	
1980	**Ronald W. Reagan**	Republican	50.7	489	53.0
	Jimmy Carter	Democratic	41.0	49	
	John B. Anderson	Independent	6.6	0	
1984	**Ronald W. Reagan**	Republican	58.4	525	52.9
	Walter F. Mondale	Democratic	41.6	13	

(continued on next page)

Year	Candidates	Parties	Percentage of Popular Vote	Electoral Vote	Percentage of Voter Participation
1988	**George H. W. Bush**	Republican	53.4	426	50.3
	Michael Dukakis	Democratic	45.6	111*	
1992	**William J. Clinton**	Democratic	43.7	370	55.1
	George H. W. Bush	Republican	38.0	168	
	H. Ross Perot	Independent	19.0	0	
1996	**William J. Clinton**	Democratic	49	379	49.0
	Robert J. Dole	Republican	41	159	
	H. Ross Perot	Reform	8	0	
2000	**George W. Bush**	Republican	47.9	271	51.3
	Albert A. Gore	Democratic	48.4	266†	
	Ralph Nader	Green Party	2.7	0	
2004	**George W. Bush**	Republican	51.0	286	59.0
	John F. Kerry	Democratic	48.0	252	
2008	**Barack Obama**	Democratic	53.0	364	61.2
	John McCain	Republican	46.0	174	

*One Dukakis elector cast a vote for Lloyd Bentsen.
†One Gore elector abstained.

Glossary

A Note to Students This list of terms will help you with the vocabulary of history. Many of these terms refer to broad, enduring concepts that appear not only in your textbook but also in the historical literature more generally and in discussions of current events. The terms appear in bold print at their first use in each volume. The glossary notes the pages on which the terms appear in bold print. For definitions and discussions of other unfamiliar words and concepts, consult the book's index or a dictionary.

American Renaissance A burst of American literature during the 1840s, highlighted by the novels of Herman Melville and Nathaniel Hawthorne; the essays of Ralph Waldo Emerson, Henry David Thoreau, and Margaret Fuller; and the poetry of Walt Whitman. (p. 238)

American System The mercantilist system of national economic development advocated by Henry Clay and adopted by John Quincy Adams. It had three interrelated parts: a national bank to manage the nation's financial system; protective tariffs to encourage American industry and provide revenue; and a nationally funded network of roads, canals, and railroads. (p. 293)

anarchism The advocacy of a stateless society achieved by revolutionary means. Feared for their views, anarchists became the scapegoats for the 1886 Haymarket Square bombing. (p. 516)

Anglo-Saxonism A theory widely held in the late nineteenth century that the English-speaking peoples were racially superior and, for that reason, justified in colonizing and dominating the peoples of less-developed areas of the world. Combined with Social Darwinism, Anglo-Saxonism fueled American expansionism in the late nineteenth century. (p. 615)

armistice A temporary cessation of military hostilities. World War I ended when the armistice signed in November 1918 led to the Versailles Treaty of 1919. (p. 647)

artisan republicanism An ideology that celebrated small-scale producers, men and women who owned their own shops (or farms), and defined the ideal republican society as one constituted by, and dedicated to the welfare of, independent workers and citizens. (p. 268)

Benevolent Empire A broad-ranging campaign of moral and institutional reforms inspired by Evangelical Christian ideals and endorsed by upper-middle-class men and women in the 1820s. Ministers who promoted benevolent reform insisted that people who had experienced saving grace should provide moral guidance and charity to the less fortunate. (p. 281)

bills of exchange Credit slips that British manufacturers, West Indian planters, and American merchants used in the eighteenth century in place of currency to settle transactions. (p. 86)

Black Codes Laws passed by southern states after the Civil War denying ex-slaves the civil rights enjoyed by whites and intended to force blacks back to the plantations. (p. 439)

blacklist A list of people to be excluded from an activity or organization. Throughout the nineteenth century, employers blacklisted workers affiliated with unions. In the 1950s, governments and private businesses blacklisted alleged Communists, denying them positions in government, motion pictures, and many industries and unions. (pp. 312, 783)

business cycle The periodic rise and fall of business activity characteristic of market-driven, capitalist economies. To increase profits, producers increase output; as supply exceeds demand, there is a cutback in production and an economic recession. In the United States, major periods of expansion (1802–1818, 1824–1836, 1846–1856, 1865–1873, 1896–1914, and 1922–1928) were followed either by relatively short financial panics (1819–1822 and 1857–1860) or by extended economic depressions (1837–1843, 1873–1896, and 1929–1939). Since 1945, government intervention has moderated the business cycle. (pp. 227, 692)

capitalism A system of economic production based on the private ownership of property and the contractual exchange for profit of goods, labor, and money (capital). In the United States before 1820, a full-scale capitalist economy — and society — emerged during the Market Revolution (1820–1850) and reached its pinnacle during the final decades of the century. See *Market Revolution*. (p. 225)

carpetbaggers A derisive name given by Southerners to Northerners who moved to the South during Reconstruction. Former Confederates despised these Northerners as transient exploiters. Carpetbaggers actually were a varied group, including Union veterans who had served in the South, reformers eager to help the ex-slaves, and others looking for business opportunities. (p. 450)

caste system A form of social organization that divides a society along relatively rigid lines of status based primarily on birth. (p. 27)

chattel slavery A system of bondage in which a slave has the legal status of property and so can be bought and sold like property. (p. 49)

civic humanism The belief that individuals owe a service to their community and its government. During the Italian Renaissance, political theorists argued that selfless service was crucial in a republic, a form of government in which authority lies in the hands of some or all of the citizenry. (p. 17)

civil religion A term used by historians to refer to a religious-like reverence for various political institutions and ideologies. An example is the belief in "republicanism" after the American Revolution. (p. 188)

clan A group of families that share a real or legendary common ancestor. Most native peoples north of the Rio Grande consisted of a group of clans, which combined to form a distinct people based on language and culture. (p. 9)

classical liberalism An ideology based on the economic principles of private property and competitive markets propounded by Adam Smith and the political ideas of individual liberty and limited government advanced by John Locke. Also see *laissez-faire.* (p. 307)

closed shop A workplace in which a job seeker had to be a union member to gain employment. In the nineteenth century, the closed shop was favored by craft unions as a method of keeping out incompetent and lower-wage workers and of strengthening the unions' bargaining position with employers. (p. 514)

closed-shop agreement A labor contract in which an employer agrees to hire only union members. Many employers strongly opposed these agreements and went to court to try to have them declared illegal. (p. 312)

collective bargaining A process of negotiation between labor unions and employers, particularly favored by the American Federation of Labor (AFL). Led by Samuel Gompers, the AFL accepted the new industrial order but fought for a bigger share of the profits for the workers. (p. 513)

Columbian Exchange The transfer in the sixteenth century of agricultural products, people, and diseases from the Western Hemisphere to other continents and from those other continents to the Western Hemisphere. (p. 27)

common law The centuries-old body of English law based on custom and judicial interpretation, not legislation, and evolving case by case on the basis of precedent. The common law was transmitted to America along with English settlement and became the foundation of American law at the state and local levels. In the United States, even more than in Britain, the common law gave the courts supremacy over the legislatures in many areas of law. (pp. 49, 589)

companionate marriage A marriage based on equality and mutual respect—both republican values. Although husbands in these marriages retained significant legal power, they increasingly came to see their wives as partners rather than as inferiors or dependents. (p. 234)

conscience Whigs Whig politicians who opposed the Mexican War (1846–1848) on moral grounds. They maintained that the purpose of the war was to expand and perpetuate slavery. They feared that the addition of more slave states would ensure the South's control of the national government and undermine a society of yeomen farmers and "free labor" in the North. (p. 386)

conservation Advocacy for the protection of the natural environment for sustained use. As applied by Theodore Roosevelt, conservation accepted development of public lands, provided that this was in the public interest and not wastefully destructive. In contrast, preservationists valued wilderness in its natural state and were more broadly opposed to development. (p. 598)

craft worker An artisan or other worker who has a specific craft or skill. For example, a mason, a cabinetmaker, a printer, or a weaver. (p. 267)

cultural pluralism A term coined in 1924 that posits that multiple levels of identity, including religious and ethnic diversity, can be a source of strength in a democratic nation and that such cultural differences should be respected and valued. (p. 720)

deficit spending Government spending in excess of tax revenues based on the ideas of British economist John Maynard Keynes. During the Great Depression, Keynes argued that governments should go into debt to stimulate a stagnant economy. (p. 714)

deflation The sustained decline of prices, generally accompanying an economic depression, but in the United States after the Civil War, the result of rapidly rising productivity, market competition, and a tight money supply. (p. 574)

deist, deism The Enlightenment-influenced belief that the Christian God created the universe and then left it to run according to natural laws. (p. 110)

deregulation Process of removing or limiting federal regulatory mechanisms, justified on the basis of promoting competition and streamlining government bureaucracy. President Carter began deregulation in the 1970s, starting with the airline, trucking, and communications industries. The process continued under subsequent administrations. (p. 876)

détente From the French word for "a relaxation of tension," this term was used to signify the new foreign policy of President Nixon, which sought a reduction of hostility between the United States and the Soviet Union and China in the early 1970s. (p. 856)

direct primary The selection of party candidates by a popular vote rather than by the party convention, this progressive reform was especially pressed by Robert La Follette, who viewed it as an instrument for breaking the grip of machines on the political parties. In the South, where it was limited to whites, the primary was a means of disfranchising blacks. (p. 591)

division of labor A system of manufacture that assigns specific — and repetitive — tasks to each worker. The system was first implemented between 1800 and 1830 in the shoe industry and soon became general practice throughout the manufacturing sector of the U.S. economy. Although it improved productivity, it eroded workers' control and sense of achievement. (p. 261)

dollar diplomacy Policy adopted by President Taft that emphasized the connection between America's economic and political interests overseas. The benefits would flow in both directions: Business would gain from diplomatic efforts in its behalf, while the strengthened American economic presence overseas would give added leverage to American diplomacy. (p. 630)

domino theory An American Cold War concept associated with the containment policy that posited that the loss of one country to Communism would lead to the toppling of other non-Communist regimes. The term was first used by President Eisenhower, who warned of "falling dominos" in Southeast Asia if Vietnam became Communist. (p. 790)

dower, dower right A legal right originating in Europe and carried to America that provided a widow with the use of one-third of the family's land and goods during her lifetime. (p. 16)

enclosure acts Laws passed in sixteenth-century England that allowed landowners to fence in the open fields that surrounded many villages and to use them for grazing sheep. This enclosure of the fields left peasants without land to cultivate, forcing them to work as wage laborers or as wool spinners and weavers. (p. 32)

encomiendas Land grants in America given by the Spanish kings to privileged landholders (*encomenderos*) in the sixteenth century. *Encomiendas* gave the landholders legal control over native peoples who lived on or near their estates. (p. 27)

entitlement programs The kind of government program that provides individuals with personal benefits to which potential beneficiaries have a legal right whenever they meet eligibility conditions specified by the law authorizing the program. Examples include Social Security, Medicare, unemployment compensation, and agricultural price supports. (p. 854)

established church A church that is given privileged legal status by the government. Before 1776, most of the American colonies had established churches that were supported by public taxes; often, they were the only legally permitted religious institutions. By 1830, no state had a legally established church, though most states gave legal and financial privileges to religious institutions. (p. 245)

ethnocultural Refers to the distinctive social characteristics of immigrants and religious groups, especially in determining their party loyalties and stance on political issues touching personal behavior and public morality. (p. 559)

ethnocultural politics The argument by historians that people's political allegiance and voting in the nineteenth and twentieth centuries was determined less by party policy than by their membership in a specific ethnic or religious group. (p. 316)

factory A structure first built by manufacturers in the early nineteenth century to concentrate all aspects of production—and the machinery needed to increase output—in one location. (p. 261)

Federalists Supporters of the Constitution of 1787, which created a strong central government, called themselves Federalists; those who feared that a strong central government would corrupt the nation's newly won liberty came to be known as Antifederalists. (p. 187)

feminists Women who subscribed to the doctrine advanced in the early twentieth century by women activists that women should be equal to men in all areas of life. Earlier women activists and suffragists had accepted the notion of separate spheres for men and women, but feminists sought to overcome all barriers to equality and full personal development. (p. 586)

fiscal policy The range of decisions involving the finances of the federal government. These decisions include how much to tax, how much to spend, and what level of resulting deficit or surplus is acceptable. Such decisions—fiscal policy—have a big effect on a nation's allocation of economic resources, the distribution of income, and the level of economic activity. (p. 781)

Fourteen Points President Wilson proposed these principles as a basis for the peace negotiations at Versailles in 1919. They included open diplomacy, freedom of the seas, free trade, territorial integrity, arms reduction, national self-determination, and establishment of the League of Nations. (p. 660)

franchise The right to vote. During the 1820s and 1830s, most states revised their constitutions to extend the vote to all adult white males. In 1870, the Fifteenth Amendment gave the vote to black men; in 1920, the Nineteenth Amendment extended the franchise to women. (p. 291)

freehold, freeholder Property owned in its entirety, without feudal dues or landlord obligations. The first settlers of New England instituted this landholding system because they repudiated exploitative leaseholds and feudal obligations. Freeholders have the legal right to improve, transfer, or sell their property. (p. 50)

free market A system of economic exchange in which prices are determined by supply and demand and no producer or consumer dominates the market. The term also refers to markets that are not subject to government regulation. (p. 184)

free-soil movement A political movement of the 1840s that opposed the expansion of slavery. Motivating its members — mostly white yeomen farmers — was their belief that slavery benefited "aristocratic men," who exploited slave labor. Free-soilers wanted farm families to settle the western territories and install democratic republican values and institutions there. The short-lived Free-Soil Party (1848–1854) stood for "free soil, free labor, free men," which subsequently became the program of the Republican Party. (p. 388)

fundamentalism, fundamentalist Any movement that pursues a "pure" and rigid belief system. In the United States, it usually refers to Evangelical Protestants who interpret the Bible literally. In the 1920s, fundamentalists opposed modernist Protestants, who reconciled Christianity with Darwin's theory of evolution and other scientific discoveries. Fundamentalists' promotion of antievolution laws for public schools led to the famous Scopes trial of 1925; in recent decades, fundamentalists have strongly supported legislation to prohibit abortions, gay marriages, and stem-cell research. (p. 687)

gang-labor system A collective system of work discipline used on southern cotton plantations in the mid-nineteenth century to enforce work norms and achieve greater productivity. Planters assigned tasks to gangs of enslaved workers which were constantly supervised by white overseers or black drivers. (pp. 361, 443)

general strike A strike that draws in all the workers in a society, with the intention of shutting the entire system down. Radical groups such as the Industrial Workers of the World (IWW) in the early twentieth century saw the general strike as the means for initiating a social revolution. (p. 520)

gentility A refined style of living and elaborate manners that came to be highly prized among well-to-do English families after 1600. (p. 85)

gentry A class of English men and women who were substantial landholders but lacked the social privileges and titles of nobility. During the Price Revolution of the sixteenth century, the relative wealth and status of the gentry rose while those of the aristocracy fell. (p. 32)

gerrymander The political strategy (named after the early nineteenth-century politician Elbridge Gerry) of changing the boundaries of voting districts to give the dominant party an advantage. (p. 566)

ghetto Term describing an urban neighborhood composed of the poor, and occasionally used to describe any tight-knit community containing a single ethnic or class group. Ghettos came into being in the nineteenth century, in tandem with the enormous influx of immigrants to American cities. (p. 536)

Great American Desert The name given to the drought-stricken Great Plains by Euro-Americans in the early nineteenth century. Believing the region to be unfit for cultivation or agriculture, Congress designated the Great Plains as permanent Indian country in 1834. (p. 471)

greenbacks Paper money issued by the U.S. Treasury during the Civil War to finance the war effort. Greenbacks had the status of legal tender in all public and private transactions. Because greenbacks were issued in large amounts, their value fell during the war to forty cents (as compared to a gold or silver dollar), but they gradually recovered their full value as the Union government won the war and subsequently reduced its war-related debt. (p. 421)

guild An organization of skilled workers in medieval and early modern Europe that regulated a craft. Guilds did not develop in colonial America because artisans generally were in short supply. (p. 18)

habeas corpus Latin for "bring forth the body," a legal writ forcing government authorities to justify their arrest and detention of an individual. Rooted in English common law, habeas corpus was made a formal privilege in the U.S. Constitution (Article 1, Section 9), which also allows its suspension in cases of invasion or insurrection. During the Civil War, Lincoln suspended habeas corpus to deter anti-Union activities. The USA PATRIOT Act (2001) likewise suspends this privilege in cases of suspected terrorism, but the constitutional legitimacy of this and other provisions of the act have not been definitively decided by the courts. (p. 418)

heresy A religious doctrine that is inconsistent with the teachings of a church. Some of the Crusades between 1096 and 1291 targeted groups of Christians whose beliefs the leaders of the Roman Catholic Church judged to be heretical. (p. 17)

home rule A rallying cry used by southern Democrats who portrayed Reconstruction governments as illegitimate—imposed on the South—and themselves as the only party capable of restoring the South to "home rule." By 1876, northern Republicans were inclined to accept this claim. (p. 460)

homespun Cloth spun and woven "at home" by American women and traditionally worn by poorer colonists. During the boycotts of British goods, wearing homespun clothes became a political act, and even people who could afford better made cloth wore homespun fabrics. Making homespun cloth allowed women to contribute directly to the Patriot movement. (p. 144)

ideology A systematic philosophy or political theory that prescribes a set of values or beliefs and/or purports to explain the character of the social world. (pp. 17, 556)

impeachment First step in the constitutional process for removing the president from office, in which the House of Representatives passes charges of wrongdoing (articles of impeachment). The Senate then conducts a trial to determine whether the impeached president is guilty of the charges. (p. 448)

indenture A contract that required service for a specified period. In the seventeenth century, thousands of workers came to North America as indentured servants. In exchange for agreeing to work for four or five years without wages, the workers received passage across the Atlantic, room and board, and status as a free person at the end of the contract period. (pp. 33, 489)

indulgence A certificate granted by the Catholic Church that claimed to pardon a sinner from punishment in the afterlife. In his *Ninety-five Theses*, written in 1517, Martin Luther condemned the sale of indulgences, a common practice among Catholic clergy. (p. 28)

Industrial Revolution The fabrication of goods, usually in well-organized factories, by machines powered by waterwheels, steam engines, or electrical engines. The Industrial Revolution began in the English textile industry in the 1750s and spread to the United States around 1800. The new machine technology vastly increased the output of goods, and the spread of the factory system split industrial society into a class of wealthy capitalist owners and a mass of propertyless wage-earning workers. (p. 260)

industrial union All workers in a single industry (for example, automobile, railroad, or mining) organized into a single association, regardless of skill, rather than into separate craft-based associations. The American Railway Union, formed in the 1880s, was one of the first industrial unions in the nation. (p. 518)

injunction A court order that immediately requires or prohibits an activity, either temporarily or permanently. Between the 1830s and the 1930s, probusiness judges often issued injunctions to stop workers from picketing or striking. (p. 313)

isolationism, isolationist A foreign-policy stance that favored limited American involvement with other nations, especially with respect to political agreements or diplomatic alliances. The common view of post–World War I U.S. foreign policy is that it was isolationist, but in fact, the United States played an active role in world trade and finance. (p. 662)

Jim Crow A term first heard in antebellum minstrel shows to designate black behavior and used in the age of segregation to designate facilities restricted to blacks, such as Jim Crow railway cars. (p. 568)

jingoism This term came to refer to the superpatriotism that took hold in the mid-1890s during the American dispute with Spain over Cuba. Jingoes were enthusiastic about a military solution as a way of showing the nation's mettle, and when diplomacy failed, they got their wish with the Spanish-American War of 1898. (p. 616)

joint-stock corporation A financial organization devised by English merchants around 1550 that subsequently facilitated the colonization of North America. In these corporations, a number of investors pooled their capital and, in return, received shares of stock in the enterprise in proportion to their share of the total investment. (p. 53)

Keynesian economics The theory, developed by British economist John Maynard Keynes in the 1930s, that purposeful government intervention into the economy (through lowering or raising taxes, interest rates, and government spending) can affect the level of overall economic activity and thereby prevent both severe depressions and runaway inflation. (p. 714)

"King Cotton" A term that describes the importance of raw cotton in the nineteenth-century international economy. More specifically, the Confederate belief during the Civil War that their cotton was so important to the British and French economies that those governments would recognize the South as an independent nation and supply it with loans and arms. (p. 420)

labor theory of value The belief that human labor produces value. Adherents argued that the price of a product should be determined not by the market (supply and demand) but by the amount of work required to make it and that most of the price should be paid to the person who produced it. The idea was popularized by the National Trades' Union and other labor leaders in the mid-nineteenth century. (p. 268)

laissez-faire French for "let do" or "leave alone." The principle that the less government does, the better, particularly in reference to the economy. This was the dominant philosophy of American government in the late nineteenth century and the guiding light of conservative politics in the twentieth. (pp. 307, 554)

land bank An institution, established by a colonial legislature, that printed paper money and lent it to farmers, taking a lien on their land to ensure repayment. (p. 93)

leasehold, leaseholder A piece of property rented out by means of a formal contract for a period of time. The contract specified the obligations of the owner and the lessee. Some leaseholds ran for "three lives"—those of the lessee, his son or heir, and his grandson. (p. 96)

liberal, liberalism Terms that in the nineteenth century referred to support for limited government and individual responsibility but that evolved in the twentieth century to mean support for an activist state and social welfare. In the nineteenth century, Mugwumps were liberals. In the twentieth century, New Dealers were liberals. (p. 459)

liberal consensus Refers to widespread agreement among Americans in the decades after World War II that the progovernment policies of the New Deal were desirable and should be continued. In politics, the liberal consensus was reflected in the relatively small differences on economic and social policies between Republicans and Democrats until the advent of Ronald Reagan. (p. 788)

lien (crop lien) A legal device that enables a creditor to take possession of the property of a borrower, including the right to have it sold in payment of the debt. Furnishing merchants took such liens on cotton crops as collateral for supplies advanced to sharecroppers during the growing season. This system trapped farmers in a cycle of debt and made them vulnerable to exploitation by the furnishing merchant. (p. 455)

literacy tests The requirement that an ability to read be demonstrated as a qualification for the right to vote. It was a device easily used by registrars to prevent blacks from voting, whether they could read or not, and was widely adopted across the South beginning with Mississippi in 1890. (p. 562)

machine tools Cutting, boring, and drilling machines used to produce standardized metal parts, which were then assembled into products like sewing machines. The rapid development of machine tools by American inventors throughout the nineteenth century was a factor in the rapid spread of industrialization. (pp. 266, 511)

Manifest Destiny A term coined by John L. O'Sullivan in 1845 to describe the idea that American citizens should settle the North American continent from the Atlantic to the Pacific Ocean. Adding geographical and secular dimensions to the Second Great Awakening, Manifest Destiny implied that the spread of American republican institutions and Protestant churches across the continent was part of God's plan for the world. In the late nineteenth century, the concept was broadened to include overseas expansion. (p. 378)

manorial system A quasi-feudal system of landholding. In the Hudson River valley of New York, wealthy landlords leased out farms to tenants, who paid rent and a quarter of value of all improvements (houses, barns, etc.) if they sold the lease; tenants also owed the landlord a number of days of personal service each year. (p. 67)

manumission From the Latin *manumittere*, "to release from the hand," the legal act of relinquishing property rights in slaves. In 1782, the Virginia assembly passed an act allowing manumission; within a decade, planters had freed 10,000 slaves. Worried that a large free black population would threaten the institution of slavery, the assembly repealed the law in 1792. (p. 239)

Market Revolution The dramatic increase between 1820 and 1850 in the exchange of goods and services in market transactions. The Market Revolution was the result of the increased output of farms and factories, the entrepreneurial activities of traders and merchants, and the development of a transportation network of roads, canals, and railroads. (p. 260)

mass production A system of factory production that often combines sophisticated machinery, a disciplined labor force, and assembly lines to turn out vast quantities of identical goods at low cost. In the nineteenth century, the textile and meatpacking industries pioneered mass production, which eventually became the standard mode for making consumer goods from cigarettes to automobiles to telephones, radios, televisions, and computers. (pp. 261, 511)

matrilineal A system of family organization in which social identity and property descend through the female line. Children are raised in their mother's household, which is headed by her brother (their uncle), who assumes many of the responsibilities assigned to a biological father in a patrilineal society. (p. 11)

mechanic A nineteenth-century term for a skilled craftsman who built, repaired, and improved machinery and machine tools for industry. Mechanics developed a professional identity and established institutes to spread their skills and knowledge. (p. 262)

mercantilism A set of governmental policies designed to enhance national wealth by active intervention into the economy. In different forms, mercantilism was practiced by Elizabeth I in the 1570s, by Parliament in the Navigation Acts (1650–1773), by American state governments (1790–1840), and by the Japanese government after World War II. In colonial America, the policies encouraged the production of agricultural goods and raw materials for export to Britain, where they were sold to other European nations or made into finished goods. (p. 32)

mestizo A person of mixed racial ancestry; specifically, the child of a European and a Native American. (p. 27)

middle class A term first used in England around 1800 to describe traders and propertied townspeople. In the early-nineteenth-century United States, it referred both to an economic group (of prosperous farmers, artisans, and traders) and to a cultural outlook (of self-discipline, hard work, and social mobility). In the twentieth century, the term embraced white-collar (office) workers, college-educated people, and propertied consumers. (p. 231)

Middle Passage The brutal sea voyage from Africa to the Americas in the eighteenth and nineteenth centuries that took the lives of nearly a million enslaved Africans. (p. 78)

military-industrial complex A term first used by President Eisenhower in his farewell address in 1961, it refers to the interlinkage of the military and the defense industry that emerged with the arms buildup of the Cold War. Eisenhower particularly warned against the "unwarranted influence" that the military-industrial complex might exert on public policy. (p. 792)

Minutemen Colonial militiamen who stood ready to mobilize on short notice during the imperial crisis of the 1770s. These volunteers formed the core of the citizens' army that met British troops at Lexington and Concord in April 1775. (p. 153)

muckrakers Journalists in the early twentieth century whose stock-in-trade was exposure of the corruption of big business and government. Theodore Roosevelt gave them the name as a term of reproach. The term comes from a character in *Pilgrim's Progress*, a religious allegory by John Bunyan. (p. 583)

national debt The financial obligations of the U.S. government for money borrowed from its citizens and foreign investors. Alexander Hamilton wanted wealthy Americans to invest in the national debt so that they would support the new national government. In recent decades, that same logic has led the American government to encourage crucial foreign nations—Saudi Arabia and Japan, for example—to invest billions in the U.S. national debt. (p. 195)

nationalize, nationalization Government seizure and ownership of a business or natural resource. In the 1890s, the Populist Party demanded nationalization of American railroads; in the 1950s, the seizure by Cuba of sugar plantations and gambling casinos owned by American citizens sparked a long-lasting diplomatic conflict. (p. 573)

national self-determination This concept, derived from European history, holds that language groups have the right to form sovereign states. A central component of Woodrow Wilson's Fourteen Points, it challenged the multinational empires of pre-1914 Europe (Ottoman, Austro-Hungarian, German, and Russian) and the colonial empires of Germany, France, and Britain. The right of national self-determination continues to be invoked by ethnic groups without independent states, such as the Basques in Spain, the Kurds in Turkey and Iraq, and the Palestinians in the Middle East. (p. 660)

nativist, nativism Antiforeign sentiment in the United States that fueled drives against the immigration of Irish and Germans in the 1840s and 1850s, the Chinese and Japanese in the 1880s and 1890s, migrants from eastern and southern Europe in the 1910s and 1920s, and Mexicans in the 1990s and 2000s. Nativism prompted the Chinese Exclusion Act of 1882, the Immigration Restriction Act of 1924, and the internment of Japanese Americans during World War II. (p. 685)

New Right A conservative political movement that began in the 1960s, with the Republican presidential campaign of Barry Goldwater, and assisted the election of Ronald Reagan in 1980. New Right activists generally support unilateral action in foreign affairs and governmental policies to limit abortions, same-sex relationships, and affirmative action. (p. 886)

nullification The constitutional argument that a state could void a law passed by Congress. The concept had its origins in the Kentucky and Virginia resolutions of 1798, which were drafted by Thomas Jefferson and James Madison, and was fully developed in John C. Calhoun's *South Carolina Exposition and Protest* (1828) and in the Ordinance of Nullification (1832). (p. 300)

oligopoly In economics, the situation in which a small number of large-scale companies dominates and sets prices in a given industry (steel making, automobile manufacturing). (p. 500)

outwork A system of manufacturing, also known as *putting out*, that was used extensively in the English woolen industry in the sixteenth and seventeenth centuries. Merchants bought wool and then hired landless peasants who lived in small cottages to spin and weave it into cloth, which the merchants would sell in English and foreign markets. (p. 31)

pagan A person whose spiritual beliefs center on the natural world. Pagans do not worship a supernatural God; instead, they pay homage to spirits and spiritual forces that dwell in the natural world. (p. 16)

party caucus A meeting held by a political party to choose candidates, make policies, and enforce party discipline. (p. 292)

patronage The power of elected officials to grant government jobs and favors to their supporters; also the jobs and favors themselves. Beginning around 1820, politicians systematically used—and abused—patronage to create and maintain strong party loyalties. After 1870, political reformers gradually introduced merit-based civil service systems in state and federal governments to reduce patronage abuses, but they have continued to the present and now cost taxpayers billions of dollars. (pp. 292, 553)

peasant The traditional term for a farm worker in Europe. Some peasants owned land, but many leased or rented small plots from landlords. In some regions, peasants lived in communities with strong collective institutions. (p. 14)

peonage (debt peonage) As cotton prices declined during the 1870s, many sharecroppers fell into permanent debt. Merchants often conspired with landowners to make the debt a pretext for forced labor, or peonage. (p. 455)

personal-liberty laws Laws enacted in many northern states to protect free blacks and fugitive slaves from southern slave catchers. Early laws required a formal hearing before a local court. When the Supreme Court declared these kinds of provisions unconstitutional in *Prigg v. Pennsylvania* (1842), new laws prohibited state officials from helping slave catchers. (p. 394)

pocket veto Presidential way to kill a piece of legislation without issuing a formal veto. When congressional Republicans passed the Wade-Davis Bill in 1864, a harsher alternative to President Lincoln's restoration plan, Lincoln used this method to kill it by simply not signing the bill and letting it expire after Congress adjourned. (p. 438)

political machine A highly organized group, often led by a "boss," that controls the policies of a political party. Political reformers believed that the machines were antidemocratic, and Robert La Follette and other Progressive-era leaders made them a special target. These reformers denied the machines their traditional patronage by creating a merit-based civil service, and they limited party bosses' power to nominate candidates by the primary election system. (pp. 292, 540)

poll taxes Taxes paid for the privilege of voting, used in the South beginning during Reconstruction to disfranchise freedmen. Nationally, the northern states used poll taxes to keep immigrants and others deemed unworthy from voting. (p. 449)

polygamy The practice of marriage of a man to multiple wives. Polygamy was customary among many African peoples and was practiced by many Mormons in the United States, particularly between 1840 and 1890. (p. 38)

popular sovereignty The democratic republican principle that ultimate power resides in the hands of a broad electorate. Popular sovereignty dictates that voters directly or indirectly (through their elected representatives) approve the laws that govern them and ratify the constitutions of their state and national governments. During the 1850s, the U.S. Congress applied the principle to western lands by enacting legislation giving territorial residents the authority to determine the status of slavery. (p. 158)

pragmatism A philosophical doctrine developed primarily by William James that denied the existence of absolute truths and argued that ideas should be judged by their practical consequences. Problem solving, not ultimate ends, was the proper concern of philosophy, in James's view. Pragmatism provided a key intellectual foundation for progressivism. (p. 583)

praying town A Native American settlement in seventeenth-century New England supervised by a Puritan minister. Puritans used these settlements to encourage Indians to adopt English culture and Protestant Christianity. (p. 59)

predestination The idea that God chooses certain people for salvation even before they are born. Sixteenth-century theologian John Calvin was the main proponent of this doctrine, which was a fundamental tenet of Puritan theology. (p. 29)

preservation, preservationist Early-twentieth-century activists, such as John Muir, who fought to protect the natural environment from commercial exploitation, particularly in the American West. (p. 598)

Price Revolution The impact of the high rate of inflation in Europe in the mid-1500s. American gold and silver, brought to Europe by Spain, doubled the money supply at a time when the population also was increasing. The increase in prices caused profound social changes, reducing the political power of the aristocracy and leaving many peasant families on the brink of poverty, thus setting the stage for substantial migration to America. (p. 32)

primogeniture The practice of passing family land, by will or custom, to the eldest son. Republican-minded Americans of the Revolutionary era disapproved of this practice but did not prohibit it. But most states enacted laws specifying that if a father dies without a will, all his children must receive an equal portion of his estate. (p. 16)

probate inventory An accounting of a person's property at the time of death, as recorded by court-appointed officials. Probate inventories provide detailed lists of personal property, household items, and financial assets and debts and tell historians a good deal about people's lives. (p. 88)

proprietors Groups of settlers who received land grants from the General Courts of Massachusetts Bay and Connecticut, mostly between 1630 and 1720. The proprietors distributed the land among themselves, usually on the basis of social status and family need. This system encouraged widespread ownership of land in New England. (p. 57)

protective tariff A tax on imports levied to protect domestic products from foreign competition. Protective tariffs were particularly controversial in the 1830s and again between 1880 and 1914, when protectionist Whigs or Republicans opposed free-trade Democrats over this issue. Recently, battles over NAFTA (the North American Free Trade Agreement) and globalization have revived this controversy, with free-trade Republicans opposed by protectionist Democrats. (p. 196)

pueblos Multistory and multiroom stone or mud-brick buildings that were built as residences by native peoples in the southwestern United States. (p. 10)

pump priming Term first used during the Great Depression of the 1930s to describe the practice of using increased government spending to stimulate a broad economic recovery. (p. 694)

Radical Whigs An eighteenth-century faction in Parliament that protested corruption in government, the growing cost of the British empire, and the rise of a wealthy class of government-related financiers. (p. 89)

reconquista The campaign by Spanish Catholics to drive North African Moors (Muslim Arabs) from the Spanish lands. After a centuries-long effort, the Spaniards defeated the Moors at Granada in 1492 and secured control of all of Spain. (p. 22)

republic A state without a monarch that has a representative system of government. In European city-states, elected representatives came from an elite of aristocrats and merchants; in the American states, they represented "the people," defined initially as property-owning male citizens and gradually expanded to include most adult inhabitants. (p. 17)

republicanism A political ideology that repudiates rule by kings and princes and celebrates a representative system of government. Historically, most republics limited active political participation to men of property. After 1800, the United States became a democratic republic, with widespread participation by white adult men of all social classes and, after 1920, by adult women. (p. 174)

republican motherhood The idea that the primary political role of American women was to instill a sense of patriotic duty and republican virtue in their children and mold the children into exemplary republican citizens. (p. 236)

residual powers The Constitutional principle that powers not explicitly granted to the federal government belong to the states. (p. 557)

restrictive covenants Clauses in real estate transactions intended to prevent the sale or rental of properties to classes of the population considered "undesirable," such as African Americans, Jews, or Asians. The Supreme Court decision in *Shelley v. Kraemer* (1948) declared such clauses unenforceable, but they continued to be instituted informally in spite of the ruling. (p. 802)

revenue tariff A tax on imports levied to pay the expenses of the national government. See *protective tariff.* (p. 196)

revival, revivalism An outburst of religious enthusiasm, often prompted by the preaching of a charismatic Baptist or Methodist minister. The Great Awakening of the 1740s was significant, but it was the revival that swept across the United States between the 1790s and 1850s that imparted a deep religiosity to the culture. Subsequent revivals in the 1880s and 1890s and in the late twentieth century helped to maintain a strong Evangelical Protestant culture in America. (p. 110)

rotten boroughs Tiny electoral districts for Parliament whose voters were controlled by wealthy aristocrats or merchants. In the 1760s, Radical Whig John Wilkes called for the elimination of rotten boroughs to make Parliament more representative of the property-owning classes. (p. 135)

rural ideal Concept advanced by the landscape architect Andrew Jackson Downing urging the benefits of rural life, it was especially influential among middle-class Americans making their livings in cities but attracted to the suburbs. (p. 528)

salutary neglect A term often used to describe British colonial policy during the reigns of George I (r. 1714–1727) and George II (r. 1727–1760). By relaxing their supervision of internal colonial affairs, royal bureaucrats inadvertently assisted in the rise of self-government in North America. (p. 89)

scalawags Southern whites who joined the Republicans during Reconstruction and were ridiculed by ex-Confederates as worthless traitors. They included ex-Whigs and yeomen farmers who had not supported the Confederacy and who believed that an alliance with the Republicans was the best way to attract northern capital and rebuild the South. (p. 450)

scientific management A system of organizing work, developed by Frederick W. Taylor in the late nineteenth century, designed to get the maximum output from the individual worker and reduce the cost of production, using methods such as the time-and-motion study to determine how factory work should be organized. The system was never applied in its totality in any industry, but it contributed to the rise of the "efficiency expert" and the field of industrial psychology. (p. 512)

secondary labor boycott A technique used by unions during a strike in which pressure is applied on a second party to bring pressure on the primary target and force it to accept demands. A secondary labor boycott was used in the Great Pullman Boycott of 1894 and failed when the government intervened. (p. 517)

secret ballot Before 1890, most Americans voted in "public." That is, voters either announced their vote to a clerk or handed in a ballot that had been printed by—and so was recognizable as the work of—a political party. Voting in "private" or in "secret" was first used on a wide scale in Australia. When the practice was adopted in the United States around 1890, it was known as the "Australian ballot." (p. 364)

self-made man A nineteenth-century ideal; an ideology that celebrated men who rose to wealth or social prominence from humble origins through self-discipline, hard work, and temperate habits. (pp. 280, 696)

sentimentalism A late-eighteenth-century European cultural movement that emphasized emotions. Sentimentalism came to the United States around 1800 and influenced literature (romantic novels), theater (melodrama), and religion (revivalism). It also encouraged marriages based on love rather than on financial considerations. (p. 233)

separate spheres Term used by contemporaries and historians to describe the nineteenth-century view that men and women have different gender-defined characteristics and, consequently, that the sexes should inhabit different social worlds. Men should control the public sphere of politics and economics, while women should manage the private sphere of home and family. In mid-nineteenth-century America, this cultural understanding was both sharply defined and hotly contested. (pp. 345, 563)

separation of powers The constitutional arrangement that gives the three governmental branches—executive, legislative, and judicial—independent standing, thereby diffusing the federal government's overall power and reducing the chances that it might turn tyrannical and threaten the liberties of the people. (p. 438)

severalty Individual ownership of land. The term applied to the Dawes Severalty Act of 1890, which undertook to end tribal ownership and grant Indians deeds to individual holdings, i.e., severalty. (p. 480)

sharecropping The labor system by which freedmen agreed to exchange a portion of their harvested crops with the landowner for use of the land, a house, and tools. A compromise between freedmen and white landowners, this system developed in the cash-strapped South because the freedmen wanted to work their own land but lacked the money to buy it, while white landowners needed agricultural laborers but did not have money to pay wages. (p. 453)

Social Darwinism The application of Charles Darwin's biological theory of evolution by natural selection to the development of society, this late-nineteenth-century principle encouraged the notion that societies progress as a result of competition and the "survival of the fittest." Intervention by the state in this process was thought to be counterproductive because it impeded healthy progress. Social Darwinists justified the increasing inequality of late-nineteenth-century industrial American society as natural. (p. 557)

socialism A theory of social and economic organization based on the common ownership of goods. Utopian socialists of the early nineteenth century envisioned small planned communities; later socialists campaigned for state ownership of railroads and large industries. (p. 326)

Sons of Liberty Colonists—primarily middling merchants and artisans—who banded together to protest the Stamp Act and other imperial reforms of the 1760s. The Sons first appeared in Boston in 1765 and were soon imitated in other colonies. (p. 138)

specie Gold and silver coin, the most trusted currency in the preindustrial world. (p. 69)

spoils system The widespread award of public jobs to political supporters after an electoral victory. In 1829, Andrew Jackson instituted the system on the national level, arguing that the rotation of officeholders was preferable to a permanent group of bureaucrats. The spoils system became a central—and corrupting—element in American political life. (pp. 292, 553)

states' rights An interpretation of the Constitution that exalts the sovereignty of the states and circumscribes the authority of the national government. Expressed first by Antifederalists in the debate over the Constitution and then in the Virginia and Kentucky resolutions of 1798, the ideology of states' rights informed white southerners' resistance to the high tariffs in the 1820s and 1830s, to legislation limiting the spread of slavery, and to attempts by the national government in the mid-twentieth century to end Jim Crow practices and promote racial equality. (p. 201)

subtreasury system A scheme deriving from the Texas Exchange, a cooperative in the 1880s, through which cotton farmers received cheap loans and marketed their crops. When the Texas Exchange failed in 1891, Populists proposed that the federal government take over these functions on a national basis through a "subtreasury," which would have had the added benefit of increasing the stock of money in the country and thus pushing up prices. (p. 571)

suburbanization The movement of the upper and middle classes beyond city limits to less crowded areas with larger homes that are connected to city centers by streetcar or subway lines. By 1910, 25 percent of the population lived in these new communities. The 1990 census revealed that the majority of Americans lived in the suburbs. (p. 531)

suffrage The right to vote. Classical republican ideology limited suffrage to property owners, who had "a stake in society." Between 1810 and 1860, state constitutions extended the vote to virtually all adult white men and some free black men. Since then, suffrage has expanded toward universality as barriers of race, gender, and age have fallen. In the late nineteenth and early twentieth centuries, women activists on behalf of the vote were known as "suffragists." (pp. 231, 447)

syndicalism A revolutionary movement that, like socialism, believed in the Marxist principle of class struggle, but advocated the organization of society on the basis of industrial unionism. This approach was advocated by the Industrial Workers of the World (IWW) at the start of the twentieth century. (p. 520)

tariff A tax on imports, which has two purposes: raising revenue for the government and protecting domestic products from foreign competition. A hot political issue throughout much of American history, the tariff became particularly controversial in the late nineteenth century as protection-minded Republicans and pro-free-trade Democrats made it the centerpiece of their political campaigns. (p. 553)

temperance movement A long-term effort by various reform groups to encourage individuals and governments to limit the consumption of alcoholic beverages. Leading temperance groups include the American Temperance Society of the 1830s, the Washingtonian Association of the 1840s, the Women's Christian Temperance Union of the late nineteenth century, and Alcoholics Anonymous, which was founded in the 1930s. (p. 284)

Third World This term came into use in the post–World War II era to describe developing nations and former colonies that were not aligned with either the West or the Soviet Union. Geographically, it referred to Asia, Africa, Latin America, and the Middle East. (p. 789)

total war A form of warfare, new to the nineteenth and twentieth centuries, that mobilized all of a society's resources and subjected the lives and property of enemy civilians to attack. Governments now mobilized massive armies of conscripted civilians and destroyed enemy industries and their civilian workers. American examples include Sherman's march through Georgia in the Civil War and the massive American bombing of Dresden, Hamburg, and Tokyo during World War II and of North Vietnam during the Vietnam War. (p. 417)

town meeting A system of local government in New England in which all male heads of households met regularly to elect selectmen, levy local taxes, and regulate markets, roads, and schools. (p. 57)

trade slaves Africans held in bondage who were not considered members of the society and were sold from one African kingdom to another or to foreign merchants. For centuries, Arab merchants carried trade slaves from sub-Saharan Africa to the Mediterranean region; around 1440, Portuguese ship captains joined in this trade. (p. 21)

transcendentalism A nineteenth-century American intellectual movement, inspired by European Romanticism, that posited the existence of an ideal world of mystical knowledge and harmony beyond the world of the senses. As articulated by Ralph Waldo Emerson and Henry David Thoreau, transcendentalism called for the critical examination of society and emphasized individuality, self-reliance, and nonconformity. (p. 320)

trusts A term that was originally applied to a specific form of business organization that enabled participating firms to assign the operation of their properties to a board of trustees but which, by the early twentieth century, was applied more generally to corporate mergers and business combinations that exerted monopoly power over an industry. It was in this latter sense that progressives referred to firms such as United States Steel and Standard Oil as trusts. (p. 596)

union shop The requirement that, after gaining employment, a worker must join a union, as distinct from the closed shop, which requires union membership before gaining employment. (p. 780)

vaudeville A professional stage show composed of singing, dancing, and comedy routines that changed live entertainment from its seedier predecessors such as minstrel shows to family entertainment for the urban masses. Vaudeville became popular in the 1880s and 1890s, the years just before the introduction of movies. (p. 543)

vice-admiralty court A tribunal presided over by a judge, with no jury. The Sugar Act of 1764 required that offenders be tried in a vice-admiralty court rather than in a common-law tribunal, where a jury decides guilt or innocence. This provision of the act provoked protests from merchant-smugglers, who were accustomed to acquittal by sympathetic local juries. (p. 136)

virtual representation The claim made by British politicians that the colonists were virtually (and thus adequately) represented in Parliament by those members who were merchants connected with the American trade and who were absentee sugar planters with estates in the West Indies. (p. 137)

voluntarism The view that citizens should themselves improve their lives rather than rely on the efforts of the state. Especially favored by Samuel Gompers, voluntarism was a key idea within the labor movement but one that it gradually abandoned in the course of the twentieth century. (p. 589)

war of attrition A military strategy of small-scale attacks used, usually by the weaker side, to sap the resources and morale of the stronger army. Examples include the attacks carried out by Patriot militias in the South during the War of Independence and the guerrilla tactics of the Vietcong and North Vietnamese during the Vietnam War. (pp. 172, 837)

welfare capitalism A system of labor relations that stresses management's responsibility for employees' well-being. Originating in the 1920s, welfare capitalism offered such benefits as stock plans, health care, and old-age pensions. Its goal was to maintain a stable workforce and undercut the growth of trade unions. (p. 676)

welfare state A nation that provides for the basic needs of its citizens, such as old-age pensions, unemployment compensation, child-care facilities, education, and health care. Industrialized countries in Europe began to provide such programs around 1900; the New Deal of the 1930s brought them to the United States. In the twenty-first century, aging populations and the emergence of a global economy (the transfer of jobs to low-wage countries) threaten the economic foundation of the European and American welfare systems. (p. 711)

Whigs An English political party that demanded a constitutional (rather than an absolutist) monarchy. The English Whigs rose to power following the Glorious Revolution of 1688 and governed Britain until the eve of the American Revolution. In the 1830s, an American political party headed by Henry Clay and Daniel Webster took the name *Whig* to protest the "monarchical" actions of Andrew Jackson, whom they dubbed "King Andrew I." (p. 308)

white-collar Middle-class professionals who are salaried workers rather than business owners or wage laborers; they first appeared in large numbers during the industrial expansion in the late nineteenth century. Their ranks were composed of lawyers, engineers, and chemists as well as salesmen, accountants, and advertising managers. (p. 503)

yellow-dog contract An agreement by a worker, as a condition of employment, not to join a union. Employers in the late nineteenth century used this along with the blacklist and violent strikebreaking to fight unionization of their workforces. (p. 516)

yellow journalism Term that refers to newspapers that specialize in sensationalistic reporting. The name came from the ink used in Hearst's *New York Journal* to print the first comic strip to appear in color in 1895 and is generally associated with the inflammatory reporting leading up to the Spanish-American War of 1898. (p. 546)

yeoman In England between 1500 and 1800, a farmer who owned enough land to support his family in reasonable comfort. In America, Thomas Jefferson envisioned a nation of yeomen, that is, of politically and financially independent farmers. (p. 14)

Credits

Chapter 2

"Magisterial Justice in Maryland." From John Demos, ed., *Remarkable Providence: Readings in Early American History* (Boston: Northeastern University Press, Copyright © 1972), pp. 135–137. Reprinted with permission of the University Press of New England.

Chapter 3

Alexander Spotswood, "Confronting the House of Burgesses." From R. A. Brock, ed., *The Official Letters of Alexander Spotswood* (Richmond: Virginia Historical Society, 1885). Reprinted with permission of the Virginia Historical Society.

Chapter 7

William Cobbett, "Peter Porcupine Attacks Pro-French Americans." Reprinted from David A. Wilson, ed., *Peter Porcupine in America: Pamphlets on Republicanism and Revolution.* Copyright © 1994 by Cornell University. Reprinted with permission of Cornell University Press.

Chapter 8

Caroline Howard Gilman, "Female Submission in Marriage." From Anya Jabour, ed., *Major Problems in the History of American Families and Children.* Copyright © 2005 Houghton Mifflin Co. Reprinted with permission.

Chapter 9

Ernst Stille, "German Immigrants in the Midwest." From Walter D. Kamphoefner, Wolfgang Helbid, and Ulrike Sommer, eds., *News from the Land of Freedom: German Immigrants Write Home.* Copyright © 1988 by C. H. Beck'sche Verlagsbuchhandlung. English trans. by Susan Carter Vogel, copyright © 1991 Cornell University Press. Reprinted with permission of Cornell University Press.

Chapter 10

Alexis de Tocqueville, "Parties in the United States." From *Democracy in America,* by Alexis de Tocqueville, trans. Henry Reeve. Copyright © 1945 and renewed 1973 by Alfred A. Knopf, a division of Random House, Inc. Used with permission of Alfred A. Knopf, a division of Random House, Inc.

Chapter 11

"The Mystical World of the Shakers." From Noel Rae, ed., *Witnessing America.* Copyright © by Noel Rae and the Stonesong Press LLC. Used with permission of the publisher.

Chapter 12

Figure 12.1: "The Surge in Cotton Production, 1835–1860." Adapted from Figure 25 in *Time on the Cross: The Economics of American Negro Slavery* by Robert William Fogel and Stanley L. Engerman. Copyright © 1974 by Robert William Fogel and Stanley L. Engerman. Used with permission of W. W. Norton & Company, Inc.

Bernhard, Duke of Saxe-Weimar-Eisenach, "The Racial Complexities of Southern Society." From C. J. Jeronimus, ed., *Travels by His Highness Duke Bernhard of Saxe-Weimar-Eisenach Through North America in the Years 1825 and 1826*, trans. William Jeronimus. Copyright © 2001, University Press of America. Used with permission of the publisher.

Mollie Dawson, "Memories of Slavery." From *Bullwhip Days* by James Mellon. Copyright © 1998 by James Mellon. Used by permission of Grove/Atlantic, Inc.

Chapter 13

Axalla John Hoole, "'Bleeding Kansas': A Southern View." From William Stanley Hoole, ed., "A Southerner's View of the Kansas Situation, 1856–1857," from *Kansas Historical Quarterly 3* (1934). Used with permission of the Kansas State Historical Society.

Salomon de Rothschild, "A French Banker Analyzes the Election of 1860 and the Threat of Secession." From Sigmund Diamond, ed. and trans., *A Casual View of America, 1859–1861: The Home Letters of Salomon de Rothschild*. Copyright © 1961 by the Board of Trustees of the Leland Stanford Jr. University, renewed by author 1985. All rights reserved. Used with permission of Stanford University Press, www.sup.org.

Chapter 14

Ernest Duvergier de Hauranne, "German Immigrants and the Civil War Within Missouri." From *A Frenchman in Lincoln's America* by Ernest de Hauranne. Copyright © 1974 R. R. Donnelley & Sons. Reprinted with permission. Lakeside.classic@lakesideclassicbooks.com.

Chapter 15

David Macrae, "The Devastated South." From Allan Nevins, ed., *America Through British Eyes* (Gloucester, MA: Peter Smith Publisher, Inc., 1968). Used with permission of the publisher.

Jourdon Anderson, "Relishing Freedom." From *Looking for America*, Second Edition, Volume 1, by Stanley I. Kutler. Copyright © 1979, 1976 by Stanley I. Kutler. Used with permission of W. W. Norton & Company, Inc.

Chapter 16

Baron Joseph Alexander von Hübner, "A Western Boom Town." From Oscar Handlin, ed., *This Was America* (Cambridge, MA: Harvard University Press, 1949). Reprinted with permission of the author.

Chapter 17

Count Vay de Vaya und Luskod, "Pittsburgh Inferno." From Oscar Handlin, ed., *This Was America* (Cambridge, MA: Harvard University Press, 1949). Reprinted with permission of the author.

John Brophy, "A Miner's Son." From *American Labor: The Twentieth Century* by Jerold S. Auerbach (Bobbs-Merrill, 1966). Reprinted with permission of the author.

Chapter 18

José Martí, "Coney Island, 1881." From *The America of José Martí: Selected Writings,* trans. Juan de Onís. (New York: Noonday Press, 1954). Used with permission of Farrar, Straus & Giroux LLC.

Chapter 19

Ernst Below, "Beer and German American Politics." From Oscar Handlin, ed., *This Was America* (Cambridge, MA: Harvard University Press, 1949). Reprinted with permission of the author.

Chapter 20

James Bryce, "America in 1905: 'Business Is King.'" From Allan Nevins, ed., *America Through British Eyes* (Gloucester, MA: Peter Smith Publisher, Inc., 1968). Used with permission of the publisher.

Chapter 21

Jean Hess, Émile Zola, and Ruben Dario, "American Goliath." Dario excerpts from "To Roosevelt." From *Selected Poems of Ruben Dario* by Ruben Dario, trans. Lysander Kemp. Copyright © 1965, renewed 1993. Reprinted with permission of the University of Texas Press.

Chapter 22

"The Great Migration." Letters from *Journal of Negro History* 4 (1919). Reprinted with permission of the Association for the Study of African-American History & Life.

Chapter 23

Mary Agnes Hamilton, "Breadlines and Beggars." From Allan Nevins, ed., *America Through British Eyes* (Gloucester, MA: Peter Smith Publisher, Inc., 1968). Used with permission of the publisher.

Chapter 24

"Ordinary People Respond to the New Deal." Letters from *Down and Out in the Great Depression: Letters from the Forgotten Man* by Robert S. McElvaine. Copyright © 1983 by the University of North Carolina Press. Foreword copyright © 2008 by the University of North Carolina Press. Used by permission of the publisher, www.uncpress.unc.edu.

Odette Keun, "A Foreigner Looks at the Tennessee Valley Authority." From Oscar Handlin, ed., *This Was America* (Cambridge, MA: Harvard University Press, 1949). Reprinted with permission of the author.

Chapter 25

Peggy Terry and Fanny Christina Hill, "Wider Opportunity and Personal Tragedy." Terry excerpt from *The Good War: An Oral History of World War Two* by Studs Terkel. Copyright © 1984 by Studs Terkel. Used with permission of Donadio & Olson, Inc., as agents for the author. Hill excerpt from "Fanny Christina Hill" from *Rosie the Riveter Revisited* by Sherna Berger Gluck. Copyright © 1987 by Sherna B. Gluck. Used with permission of the author.

Anton Bilek, "Japanese Abuse of Prisoners of War." Excerpt from *The Good War: An Oral History of World War Two* by Studs Terkel. Copyright © 1984 by Studs Terkel. Used with permission of Donadio & Olson, Inc., as agents for the author.

Chapter 26

Mark Goodson, "Red Hunting on the Quiz Shows." From *Red Scare: Memories of the American History: An Oral History* by Griffin Fariello. Copyright © 1995 by Griffin Fariello. Used by permission of W. W. Norton & Company, Inc.

Jean Monnet, "Truman's Generous Proposal." From *Memoirs* by Jean Monnet. Introduction by George W. Ball, translated by Richard Mayne, translation copyright © 1978 by Doubleday, a division of Random House, Inc. Used with permission of Doubleday, a division of Random House, Inc.

Chapter 27

Franklin McCain, "Desegregating Lunch Counters." From *My Soul Is Rested: Movement Days in the Deep South Remembered* by Howell Raines. Copyright © by Howell Raines. Used with permission of the Reiter Agency Ltd. as agents for the author.

Hanoch Bartov, "Everyone Has a Car." From Oscar and Lilian Handlin, eds., *From the Outer World* (Cambridge, MA: Harvard University Press, 1997), pp. 293–296. Used with permission of the author.

Chapter 28

Donald L. Whitfield and Gayle Smith, "The Toll of War." Whitfield excerpt from *Landing Zones: Southern Veterans Remember Vietnam* by James R. Wilson. Copyright © 1990 Duke University Press. Used with permission of Duke University Press. Smith excerpt from *Everything We Had* by Albert Santoli. Copyright © 1981 by Albert Santoli and Vietnam Veterans of America. Used by permission of Random House, Inc.

Che Guevara, "Vietnam and the World Freedom Struggle." From *Che Guevara Speaks* by Ernesto Che Guevara. Copyright © 1967, 2000 by Pathfinder Press. Reprinted by permission of Pathfinder Press.

Chapter 29

Fei Xiaotong, "America's Crisis of Faith." From R. David Arkush and Leo O. Lee, trans. and eds., *Land Without Ghosts: Chinese Impressions of America from the Mid-Nineteenth Century to the Present.* Copyright © 1989 University of California Press. Used with permission of the publisher.

Chapter 30

Donald E. Wildmon, "The Moral Majority and Its Critics." From *The Home Invaders.* Copyright © 1985 Victor Books. Used with permission of the American Family Association.

Saddam Hussein, "A Holy War Against the United States." Excerpted from "Confrontation in the Gulf: Iraqi Statement Declaring War of 'Right against Wrong,'" from *The New York Times,* September 6, 1990, Section A, p. 19. Used with permission of *The New York Times.*

Chapter 31

George Stith and Petra Mata, "Cheap Labor: Immigration and Globalization." From Christine Ahn, ed., *Shafted: Free Trade and America's Working Poor.* Copyright © 2003 Food First Books/ Institute for Policy Development, a non-profit organization whose mission is to eliminate the injustices that cause hunger. Used with permission of the Institute for Policy Development.

Janet Daley, "A U.S. Epidemic and Its Causes." From *The Independent,* August 29, 1990, p. 18. Used with permission of Independent Newspapers, London.

Chapter 32

Table 32.1: "The Impact of the Bush Tax Cuts, 2001–2003." From *The New York Times,* April 5, 2006. Reprinted with permission of *The New York Times.*

Abu Musab al-Zarqawi, "Strategy for the Iraq Insurgency." From Documents on Terrorist Abu Musab al-Zarqawi, 2004, www-personal.umich.edu/~jrcole/zarqawi/zarqawi.htm. Used with permission of Juan Cole, University of Michigan.

Candi Cushman, "Uncommon Moms." Adapted from the article in the January 2005 *Focus on the Family Citizen* magazine. Copyright © 2005, Focus on the Family. All rights reserved. International copyright secured. Used by permission.

Index

A note about the index: Names of individuals appear in boldface; biographical dates are included for major historical figures. Letters in parentheses following pages refer to: (*f*) figures, including charts and graphs; (*i*) illustrations, including photographs and artifacts; (*m*) maps; and (*t*) tables.

Christian Right, 889(i)

Christopher, Warren, 911

Chrysler, 918

church and state, separation of, 54, 868, 891

churches. *See also* religion(s); specific churches and religions
African American, 24, 335, 452–453, 540, 818
established, 245
in First Great Awakening, 113
men and women in, 252
prohibition and, 657
women and, 809

Churchill, Winston, 733
Atlantic Charter and, 736, 749
at Tehran conference, 750
at Yalta, 756–757, 756(i)

Church of England. *See also* Anglicans
Pilgrims and, 53

Church of Jesus Christ of Latter-Day Saints. *See* Mormons

Church of Scotland, Knox and, 29

Churubusco, Mexico, battle at, 386

CIA. *See* Central Intelligence Agency

cigarette factories, women in, 505

Cincinnati, 277, 529
as "Porkopolis," 261, 262(i)

Cincinnati Red Stockings, 546

CIO. *See* Congress of Industrial Organizations

circuit courts, 194

Cisneros, Henry, 907

cities and towns, 523–530. *See also* urban areas; urbanization; specific locations
African Americans in, 540, 654–655, 939
cattle towns, 472
after Civil War, 440
culture in, 543–548
free blacks in, 371, 444
ghettos in, 536(i), 816
growth of, 276–278, 332, 523, 524(t)
immigrants in, 333, 535–540
industrialization and, 466
migrations to, 503, 814–815
mining camps and, 484
New England settlement patterns, 58(m)
in 1920s, 684

political machines in, 540–541
populations of, 86, 535–536
race riots in, 844–845, 844(m)
religions in, 541–543
social fragmentation in, 279
suburban growth and, 802
urban renewal in, 816
wealthy in, 278
western boom town, 485

Citigroup, 967

citizens and citizenship
for African Americans, 399, 441
for *Californios,* 487
for children of immigrants, 935
former Spanish territories and, 622
for Native Americans, 480
in Pennsylvania, 176
property as requirement for, 174
for resident aliens, 209
after Revolution, 176–177

"City Beautiful" movement, 528

city planners, rural ideal and, 528

city-states, Indian, 11–13

City upon a Hill, Massachusetts Bay as, 53

civic humanism, 17–18

Civil Defense Agency, 806(i)

civil defense drills, 805

civil disobedience, 324

Civilian Conservation Corps (CCC), 704, 712(m), 717, 719, 744

civilians, in Revolutionary War, 167

civilization(s). *See* specific civilizations

civil liberties, security and, 966

civil rights
black nationalism and, 843–844
Bush, George W., and, 950
Eisenhower and, 817, 818
for gays, 861
integration and, 941
job discrimination and, 866
Johnson, Lyndon, and, 831–832
Kennedy, John F., and, 827–829
for Mexican Americans, 845
for Native Americans, 846
school desegregation and, 866–867
Truman and, 781, 817
Warren and, 868
for women, 861–864

of former Confederates, 446

Displaced Person Act (1948), 813

dissenters

discrimination against, 245

in Middle Atlantic colonies, 104

Dissertation on the English Language
(Webster), 237–238

Distant Early Warning system, 788

district courts, 194. *See also* courts

District of Columbia, 208. *See also*
Washington, D.C.

abolition of slave trade in, 392

end of slavery in, 423

diversity

in Clinton cabinet, 907

of cowboys, 472–473, 472(*i*)

cultural, 285

in Middle Atlantic colonies, 69,
102–105

in New Netherland, 42

religious (1750), 106(*m*)

divine right of kings, 70

Charles I (England) and, 53

division of labor, 261

divorce, 808, 861, 942

Dix, Dorothea, 341, 419–420

Dixiecrats, 780

DNA (deoxyribonucleic acid), 931

documentary artists, in New Deal, 726

Doeg Indians, 51

Dole, Robert, 875, 910

dollar (U.S.), decline in value, 968

"dollar-a-year men," 738

dollar diplomacy, 630

domesticity, of middle class, 532–533,
532(*i*)

Domestic Manners of the Americans (Frances
Trollope), 248, 290

domestic servants, women as, 508

domestic slave trade, 351–356

Dominican Republic, 22, 935

as Santo Domingo, 610

U.S. intervention in, 627, 678

Dominion of New England, 70–71, 72, 89

domino theory, 790, 830

Donelson, Fort, battle at, 417

Doniphan, Alfred A., 387(*m*)

Dorr, Retha Childe, 563

Dos Passos, John, 689, 726

Doubleday, Abner, 545

"Double-V" campaign, 741

doughboys, 646

Douglas, Stephen A. (1813–1861), 377,
399, 411

Compromise of 1850 and, 391

debates with Lincoln, 401–402

election of 1852 and, 394

election of 1860 and, 402, 404

expansionism of, 388

Kansas-Nebraska Act and, 395

popular sovereignty and, 391, 401

Douglas, William O., 713

Douglass, Frederick (1818–1895), 337,
388–389, 394, 426

emancipation and, 423

free-soil movement and, 388, 389

on Fugitive Slave Act, 393

on minstrel shows, 334(*i*)

on voting rights, 449, 450

Dow Chemical Company, 841

dower, 16, 98

Dow Jones stock price index, 918

Downing, Andrew Jackson, 531

Doy, John, 396(*i*)

draft (military)

in Civil War, 418–419, 427, 432

for Vietnam War, 841, 857

in World War I, 646

in World War II, 740

Drake, Edwin L., 500

Drake, Mary, 350

Drayton, William Henry, 203

Dred Scott v. Sandford (1856), 218, 397–399,
401, 402

Dreiser, Theodore, 523, 529, 689

drug-benefit bill, 951, 966

drugs

for HIV, 925–926

in poor African American neighborhoods, 940

recreational use of, 842

in Vietnam War, 857

Dry Dock Bank, 312

dry farming, 476

Dual Alliance, 631

Du Bois, W. E. B., 594, 689

Jiang Jieshi (**Chiang Kai-shek**, China), 776
jihad (holy war), 904
   against America, 949
   suicide bombers and, 956
Jim Crow laws, 333, 593
   in Georgia, 569
   in World War II, 740
jingoism, 616, 617
Job Corps, 834
jobs. *See also* employment
   for African Americans, 540
   automation and, 815
   baby boom and, 809
   defense buildup and, 797
   for free blacks, 371
   for Hispanics, 488
   outsourcing of, 924–925
   white-collar, 503
   for women, 810, 920
job security, 966
Joffre, Joseph, 646
John Paul II (pope), 898
Johnson, Andrew (1808–1875), 437,
     438–439, 439(*i*)
   amnesty plan of, 443
   Congress vs., 445–446
   election of 1864 and, 430, 439
   Fourteenth Amendment and, 445
   impeachment of, 448, 911
   as president (1865–1869), 439–441,
     447–448
   Reconstruction plan of, 439, 441, 443
Johnson, Gabriel, 89
Johnson, Hiram, 587, 591, 662
Johnson, Lady Bird, 833
Johnson, Lyndon B. (1908–1973), 823, 826
   assumption of presidency, 831
   civil rights movement and, 832
   credibility gap of, 837
   election of 1960 and, 825
   election of 1964 and, 832, 836
   election of 1968 and, 823, 847
   Great Society of, 831–835
   legislation under, 708
   New Deal coalition and, 834, 835
   as president (1963–1969), 831–835, 841
   Vietnam policy of, 835–839, 849
Johnson, Samuel, 238

Johnson, William, 117
Johnston, Albert Sidney, 417
Johnston, Joseph E., 430
Johnston, Joshua, 373
joint-stock corporation, Massachusetts Bay
     Colony as, 53
Jones, Bobby, 684
Jones, Charles C., 367
Jones, Nathaniel, 161
Jones, Paula, 910
Jones Act (1916), 624
Jones and Laughlin Steel Company,
     505–506, 524
Jordan, Michael, 925
Joseph, Chief (Nez Percé Indian
     chief), 478
journalism
   crusading, 583
   yellow, 546
Judaism. *See* Jews and Judaism
judges. *See* courts; Supreme Court (U.S.);
     specific judges
judicial restraint, 867–868
judicial review, 201, 220
judicial supremacy, 558
judiciary. *See also* court(s); Supreme Court
     (U.S.)
   Jefferson and, 208–209
   power of, 208
   Reagan appointments to, 897
   Supreme Court and, 184
Judiciary Act
   of 1789, 194, 209
   of 1801, 208, 209
Julian, George W., 446
Jungle, The (Sinclair), 599
Justice Act (1774), 149
Justice Department
   antiradicalism division of, 665
   Roosevelt, Theodore, and, 598
   in World War I, 659
Just Say No antidrug campaign, 940
juvenile delinquency, Senate subcommittee
     on, 812

Kaiser, Henry J., 738, 739(*i*), 802
Kaiser Permanente Medical Care Program,
     738–739

manufactures, Hamilton's report
    on (1791), 195
manufacturing, 260, 612
    China trade and, 613
    colonial, 86
    decline in, 917
    in England, 120
    in Great Depression, 706
    increase in, 229, 495
    innovation in, 266–267
    in 1920s, 675
    in Revolutionary War, 165–166
    in seaport cities, 277
    tariff protection of, 295
manumission, 239, 240, 371
    documents for free blacks, 374
Mao Zedong (**Mao Tse-tung,** China), 776,
    855, 856
Marbury, William, 209
Marbury v. Madison (1803), 209, 218
March of Time, The (newsreels), 726
March on Washington (1963), 828, 828(*i*)
"March to the Sea." *See* Sherman, William
    Tecumseh
Marcy, William L., 298–299, 394
Mariana Islands, 619
marijuana use, 842
Marines
    bombing of barracks in Lebanon, 902
    in Mexican War, 386
    in Vietnam War, 836–837
Marion, Francis ("Swamp Fox"), 172
maritime economy, in North, 86–88
market(s)
    foreign, 612–613
    teen, 811
market control, large-scale enterprise and, 500
market economy, 229. *See also* economy
    Sioux-white trade and, 470
Market Revolution, 260, 269–277
Marquette, Jacques, 40
marriage. *See also* intermarriage
    age at, 234
    companionate, 234
    cousin, 368–369
    domestic slave trade and, 354–356
    female submission in, 235
    freedmen and, 444

of gays, 943, 959
    homesteaders and, 474
    land given for, 98
    in late 19th century, 533–534
    mixed-sex praying and, 252
    in New Orleans society, 359
    in 1950s, 808
    of planters, 358
    Quaker, 107
    republican system of, 232–234
    slave, 78, 82, 354, 356, 368–369, 372
married women. *See also* women
    credit for, 863
    in middle class, 532–533
    in 1930s, 718
    property rights of, 345
    rights of, 451
    in workforce, 506–508, 811
Married Women's Property Law (New York,
    1848), 345(*i*)
Marshall, George C., 771
Marshall, John, 208, 211
    Cherokee nation and, 303
    Constitution and, 218–219
    on contract rights, 220
    trade and, 273–274
Marshall, Thurgood, 817
Marshall Islands, 755(*m*)
Marshall Plan, 771, 772
Martí, José, 544, 616
Martin, Bradley, 530
Martin, Joseph J., 778
Martin, Josiah, 155
Martin, Thomas S., 645
Martineau, Harriet, 290
Martinique, British in, 118
Marx, Karl, 518
Marxist socialism, 518
Mary (England, r. 1688–1694), 71, 72
Maryland, 45–46
    Civil War and, 411–412
    German farmers in, 105(*i*)
    magisterial justice in, 47
    McCulloch v. Maryland and, 219
    secession and, 409, 411
    slavery in, 81, 431
    uprising in, 71–72
    western land claims of, 177, 178(*m*)

New England Emigrant Aid Society, 396
New Federalism (Nixon), 854, 894
Newfoundland
British acquisition of, 73
colony in, 43
New France, 40–41, 117
New Freedom of Wilson, Woodrow, 602
New Frontier of Kennedy, John F.,
824, 826
New Guinea, in World War II, 755(m)
New Hampshire, 86, 207
Massachusetts Bay and, 69
Scots-Irish in, 105
New Jersey, 67, 100. See also Middle
Atlantic region
in Dominion of New England, 70
Quakers and culture in, 104
in Revolution, 163, 164(m)
suffrage in, 231–232
women voters in, 175
New Jersey Plan, 183–184
New Left movement, 839, 841
New Light Presbyterians, 156
Princeton founded by, 113
in South, 114
New Lights, 112–113
New Look program (Eisenhower), 829
Newman, Nath, 372
New Mexico, 486
Anglos in, 487
European and Native American
cultures in, 487
mestizo population of, 487
Mexican War and, 385, 388
peoples of, 10
settlements in, 486
Spanish missionaries in, 38
New Nationalism, of Roosevelt,
Theodore, 601
"New Negro," 689
New Netherland, 31, 41–43
English in, 70
as New York, 67
New Orleans, 277
American access to, 210
Battle of, 217(m), 218
Civil War and, 417
establishment of, 40

Hurricane Katrina in, 960, 961
planter families in, 358
racial life in, 359
sale to U.S., 211
shipment to, 209
slave mart in, 353
in War of 1812, 216, 217(m)
water route to New York, 273
Newport, Rhode Island, 86
New Right, 889(i)
Christian conservatives in, 916
Reagan and, 886, 888–890
New Salem, Illinois, 400
New South, 503–505, 504(m)
race and politics in, 564–570
New Spain, 37–39, 486
boundary with, 220
colonies in present-day U.S., 37(m)
settlers to West from, 482
newspapers. See also specific
newspapers
African American, 335
antislavery, 389
circulation (1870–1909), 546(t)
for immigrants, 538, 539
urban, 546–547
Newton, Huey, 843–844
Newton, Isaac, 108
new woman, 534, 535
new world. See also America(s)
use of term, 22
New York, 42, 67, 100. See also Middle
Atlantic region
in Dominion of New England, 70
Erie Canal in, 271–273
frontier of, 73
Iroquois in, 40
land speculation in, 207–208
Leisler's rebellion in, 72
Loyalists in, 177
manumission in, 240
Married Women's Property Law (1848)
in, 345(i)
police power of, 307
rebellion in, 71
social legislation in, 674
voting rights in, 291
women's rights in, 345, 346

as president (1837–1841), 305, 313, 380
as secretary of state, 298
tariffs and, 296
ten-hour workday (1840), 313
as vice president, 302
Vance, Zebulon, 418
Vanderbilt, Cornelius, 498, 548
Vanderbilt, George W., 547–548
Vanderbilt family, 530
Van Dusen, Larry, 726
Vann, James, 303
Van Rensselaer family, 100, 121
Vanzetti, Bartolomeo, 665–666, 666(*i*)
vaqueros (cowboys), 487
vaudeville, 543
Vauxhall Motor Company, 676
Vay de Vaya und Luskod (Count), 507
V-chip, 932
Venezuela
crisis over (1895), 614
oil in, 676
Venona intercepts, 782
Veracruz (Mexico)
capture of, 386
U.S. invasion of, 631
Verdun, battle at, 643
Vergennes (Comte de), 169
Vermont, 207
Versailles Treaty (1783), 173
Versailles Treaty (1919), 660–663, 899(*m*)
Mussolini on, 733
vertical integration, 500, 503, 596, 798
Vespucci, Amerigo, 22–23
veterans
GI Bill for, 744
in Great Depression, 696
pensions for, 591
Veterans Administration (VA), 802
vetoes. *See also* specific presidents and laws
by Bush, George H. W., 900, 907
by Bush, George W., 966
by Clinton, 909
by Johnson, Andrew, 445, 447
by Nixon, 854
presidential power of, 184
vice, suppression of, 533
vice-admiralty courts, 136, 144
viceroys, 486

Vicksburg, siege of, 424, 428, 431
Victorian age, sexuality in, 533
videocassette recorders (VCRs), 930
Vietcong, 836(*m*), 847, 856
Vietminh, 790, 857
Vietnam. *See also* Vietnam War
Cold War and, 829–830
diplomatic recognition of, 858
Eisenhower and, 789–790
immigrants from, 935
partition of, 791
reunification of, 857
United States in, 790, 791
"Vietnam and the World Freedom Struggle"
(Guevara), 840
Vietnamization, 856, 857
Vietnam Veterans Against the War, 857
Vietnam War (1961–1975), 798, 836(*m*),
935. *See also* antiwar movement
Agent Orange and, 837, 841
bombing campaigns in, 836, 837, 856,
857, 858
Cambodia and, 857
casualties in, 847, 856
cease-fire in (1973), 836(*m*), 857
credibility gap in, 837
economy and, 839, 872
election of 1968 and, 849
fall of Saigon and, 857
guerrilla tactics in, 836(*m*)
Gulf of Tonkin resolution and, 835
Johnson administration and, 835–837
Kennedy administration and, 829–830
My Lai massacre and, 857
Nixon administration and, 856–858
Operation Rolling Thunder and, 837
Paris peace talks and, 857
Tet offensive and, 836(*m*), 847
troops in, 836–837, 838, 857
War on Poverty and, 834
women and, 838
Viguerie, Richard, 888
Villa, Pancho, 631, 632(*i*), 645
Vindication of the Rights of Woman, A
(Wollstonecraft), 236
violence
by antiabortion movement, 943
against Bonus Army, 696